A Flexible Organization for Instructors

D1412345

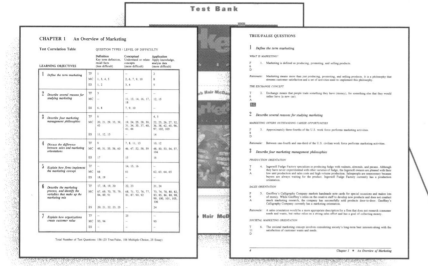

Test Bank Questions

are grouped by learning objective, so that you can thoroughly test all objectives —or emphasize the ones you feel are most important. Correlation tables at the beginning of each chapter make it easy to prepare tests that cover the objectives at the level of difficulty appropriate for your students.

WesTest

Text Learning Objectives

form the framework for organizing your lectures, selecting support materials, and customizing tests for your students.

Instructor's Resource CD-ROM

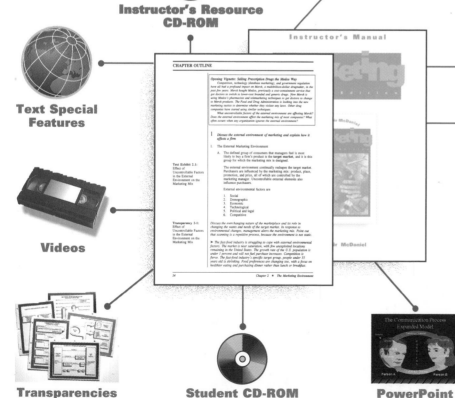

Text Special Features

Videos

Transparencies

Student CD-ROM

PowerPoint

Supplemental Articles

Class Activities

All Lecture Support Materials

come together under their appropriate objectives in the *Instructor's Manual Lecture Outlines*, for thorough coverage of all objectives. Annotations tell you the appropriate times to integrate transparencies, text special features, additional examples, supplemental articles and activities, and end-of-chapter pedagogy into your lectures—a smorgasbord of teaching aids from which to choose.

Marketing

Fourth Edition

Charles W. Lamb, Jr.

M. J. Neeley Professor of Marketing

M. J. Neeley School of Business

Texas Christian University

Joseph F. Hair, Jr.

Alvin C. Copeland Endowed Chair of Franchising

and Director, Entrepreneurship Institute

Louisiana State University

Carl McDaniel

Chairman, Department of Marketing

College of Business Administration

University of Texas at Arlington

SOUTH-WESTERN College Publishing

An International Thomson Publishing Company

Publishing Team Director: John Szilagyi
Acquisitions Editor: Dreis Van Landuyt
Developmental Editor: Susan Carson
Media Technology Editor: Sherie Skladany
Production Editor: Shelley Brewer
Production House: WordCrafters Editorial Services, Inc.
Internal Design: Ellen Pettengell Design
Internal and Cover Illustration: Victoria Kann
Opener and Spot Photography: Blink Studios
Cover Design: Joe Devine
Photo Research: Jennifer Mayhall
Marketing Manager: Steve Scoble
Manufacturing Coordinator: Sue Disselkamp

Library of Congress Cataloging-in-Publication Data
Lamb, Charles W.
    Marketing / Charles W. Lamb, Joseph H. Hair, Carl McDaniel. — 4th
  ed.
      p. cm.
    Includes bibliographical references and index.
    ISBN 0-538-87011-7
    1. Marketing. 2. Marketing—Management. I. Hair, Joseph F.
  II. McDaniel, Carl D. III. Title.
HF5415.L2624 1998
658.8—dc21   97-17422
                                                                  CIP

1 2 3 4 5 6 7 8 9 Ki 5 4 3 2 1 0 9 8 7

Printed in the United States of America

International Thomson Publishing
South-Western College Publishing is an ITP Company. The ITP trademark is used under
license.

Brief Contents

Contents

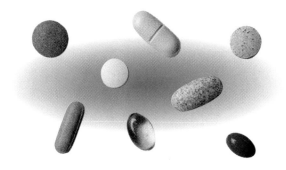

A Special Features Sampler for Students

Marketing students who have come before you have taught us a lot about what you want your textbook to be. You want cutting-edge technology. You want to use the Internet to learn. You want current topics that relate to the real world. You want interesting examples that are relevant to your life. You want an enjoyable writing style. You want videos. And you want study aids that will help you succeed on tests. This text will meet and exceed your expectations in all of these important areas – and many others. Here is just a sample of the features you will find as you explore with us the exciting world of marketing.

Internet Marketing

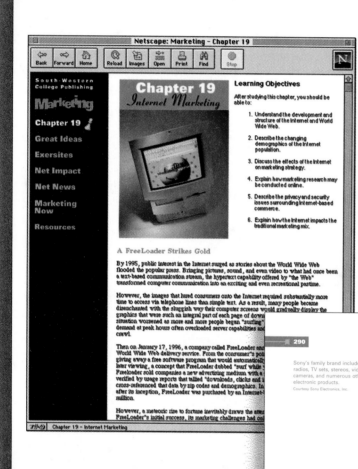

Netscape: Marketing - Chapter 19

South-Western College Publishing

Marketing

Chapter 19

Great Ideas

Exersites

Net Impact

Net News

Marketing Now

Resources

Chapter 19
Internet Marketing

Learning Objectives

After studying this chapter, you should be able to:

1. Understand the development and structure of the Internet and World Wide Web.

2. Describe the changing demographics of the Internet population.

3. Discuss the effects of the Internet on marketing strategy.

4. Explain how marketing research may be conducted online.

5. Describe the privacy and security issues surrounding Internet-based commerce.

6. Explain how the Internet impacts the traditional marketing mix.

A FreeLoader Strikes Gold

By 1995, public interest in the Internet surged as stories about the World Wide Web flooded the popular press. Bringing pictures, sound, and even video to what had once been a text-based communication stream, the hypertext capability offered by "the Web" transformed computer communication into an exciting and even recreational pastime.

However, the images that lured consumers onto the Internet required substantially more time to access via telephone lines than simple text. As a result, many people became disenchanted with the sluggish way their computer screens would gradually display the graphics that were such an integral part of each page of downloaded material. The situation worsened as more and more people began "surfing" the Internet and demand at peak hours often overloaded server capabilities and brought the net to a crawl.

Then on January 17, 1996, a company called FreeLoader announced a new World Wide Web delivery service. From the consumer's point of view, FreeLoader was giving away a free software program that would automatically download Web sites for later viewing, a concept that FreeLoader dubbed "surf while you sleep." FreeLoader sold companies a new advertising medium with a target audience verified by usage reports that tallied "downloads, clicks and impressions" and cross-referenced that data by zip codes and demographics. In just four months after its inception, FreeLoader was purchased by an Internet-based company for $38 million.

However, a meteoric rise to fortune inevitably draws the attention of others. Despite FreeLoader's initial success, its marketing challenges had only begun. [...]

Chapter 19 – Internet Marketing

---

1 Chapter 19, Internet Marketing

The Internet is the fastest growing marketing medium today. You'll experience the full impact of the Internet on marketing through this new chapter. You won't find this chapter in your text though. It's located on the Web at **http://www.swcollege.com/lamb.html**. Examples come to life as you link to company pages. This chapter will introduce you to the Internet as a marketing tool and will give you the tools you need to develop Internet marketing strategies.

---

2 Internet Examples, Activities and References

Internet examples and activities are integrated throughout each chapter. Examples within the chapters take you to Web pages and ask you to evaluate the marketing strategies you see. End-of-chapter activities challenge you to analyze current examples of Internet marketing and to develop your own strategies. You'll also discover valuable resources on the Web for marketers. Updates for all URLs are available to you at the **Marketing** Web site, **http://www.swcollege.com/lamb.html**.

Sony's family brand includes radios, TV sets, stereos, video cameras, and numerous other electronic products.
Courtesy Sony Electronics, Inc.

the same brand name for a pair of dress socks and a baseball bat. Procter & Gamble targets different segments of the laundry detergent market with Bold, Cheer, Dash, Dreft, Era, Gain, Ivory Snow, Oxydol, Solo, and Tide. Marriott International, Inc., also targets different market segments with Courtyard by Marriott, Residence Inn, and Fairfield Inn.

family brand
Marketing several different products under the same brand name.

On the other hand, a company that markets several different products under the same brand name is using a **family brand**. For example, Sony's family brand includes radios, television sets, stereos, and other electronic products. A brand name can only be stretched so far, however. Do you know the differences among Holiday Inn, Holiday Inn Express, Holiday Inn Select, Holiday Inn Sunspree Resort, Holiday Inn Garden Court, and Holiday Inn Hotel & Suites? Neither do most travelers.[24]

Breyers
McIlhenny Company
Frito-Lay
How does Breyers market individual brands, family brands, and cobrands via its Web site? Compare the McIlhenny Company site and the Frito-Lay site. Which is the most effective in establishing brand identity?

http://www.icecreamusa.com/
http://www.tabasco.com/
http://www.fritolay.com/

cobranding
Placing two or more brand names on a product or its package.

Cobranding

Cobranding entails placing two or more brand names on a product or its package. Cobranding is a useful strategy when a combination of brand names enhances the prestige or perceived value of a product or when it benefits brand owners and users. Cobranded Six Flags Theme Parks/Master Cards allow cardholders to earn points toward season passes, free admissions, and in-park spending vouchers at Six Flags theme parks throughout the United States.[25]

Cobranding may also be used to identify product ingredients or components. The brand name NutraSweet and its familiar brand mark appear on more than 3,000 food and beverage products. Intel, the microprocessor company, pays microcomputer manufacturers like IBM, Dell, and Compaq to include "Intel inside" in their advertising, on the computers, and on the boxes they are packed in.

Interactive Marketing, Multimedia and Video

3 Principles of Marketing CD-ROM
by Daniel L. Wardlow, San Francisco State University

This interactive masterpiece is fully integrated with **Marketing**. HotLinks in each chapter direct you to a dozen interactive simulations, games, and videos that demonstrate marketing concepts with full motion and sound. Text concepts literally come to life with this powerful multimedia tool.

Just how hard is it to win the Malcolm Baldrige award? Find out how award winner Milliken & Co. fulfilled the 11 core values and walked away with the award at **Hot Link—Baldrige Award.**

the Baldrige Award is whether the firm meets customer expectations. The customer must be number one. To qualify for the award, a company must also show continuous improvement. Company leaders and employees must participate actively, and they must respond quickly to data and analysis. Companies that have received the Baldrige Award include IBM, Federal Express, the Nuclear Fuel Division of Westinghouse, and Xerox Business Products and Systems.

3 Explain the techniques of quality improvement.

quality function deployment (QFD)
A technique that helps companies translate customer design requirements into product specifications.

Automobile companies continually redesign their products to better serve the market. Continuous improvement is also important in the service industries.
© Kevin Horan/Tony Stone Images

Essential Quality Techniques

Several techniques used in the TQM approach distinguish it from traditional ways of doing business. These techniques include quality function deployment, benchmarking, continuous improvement, reduced cycle time, and analysis of process problems.

Quality Function Deployment

Quality function deployment (QFD) is a technique that helps companies translate customer design requirements into product specifications. It is a way for companies to stay close to customers and build their expectations into products. This technique uses a quality chart that directly relates what customers want with how goods will be designed and produced to satisfy those wants. The QFD chart thus provides customer-based guidelines for developing the best design.

Benchmarking is the process of rating a company's products against the best products in the world, including those in other industries. "The best" includes both functional characteristics of products and customer satisfaction ratings. Benchmarking allows a firm to set performance targets and continuously reach toward those targets. For example, one type of benchmarking develops a competitive profile against an industry average. In the automobile industry, J. D. Powers, an independent research firm, gathers customer satisfaction data on numerous models of cars and sells this information to automobile firms. These firms can then compare their performance to an average derived from the aggregate industry data.

Continuous Improvement

Continuous improvement is a commitment to constantly seek ways of doing things better in order to maintain and improve quality. Companywide teams try to prevent problems and systematically improve key processes instead of troubleshooting problems as they occur. Continuous improvement also means looking for innovative production methods, shortening product-development time, and continually measuring performance using statistical methods.

Continuous improvement can be used in service companies as well as in manufacturing companies. Paine & Associates, a California public relations firm, implemented a continuous improvement approach to stimulate creative thinking for media campaigns. A series of minor changes, ranging

---

13. What locations does ProNet serve? Obtain information about at least one arts-and-entertainment venture for three different regions. How does ProNet handle language and translation issues?

http://www.pronett.com/

14. What services does the Netzmarkt cyber-mall offer American businesses interested in marketing to Germans?

http://www.netzmarkt.de/neu/hinweise.htm

Application for Small Business

John Arpin, a 20-something design engineer, sat down once too often in the cold snow to remove his boots from the heavy plastic bindings of his snowboard. As he loosened the plastic straps, it occurred to him that there had to be a better way to attach boots to a snowboard. The idea for a step-in snowboard binding was born. After two years of research and testing, the Arpin binding finally reached the marketplace. Snowboarding is the fastest growing winter sport in America, averaging about 30 percent per year. By the year 2000, industry sales should reach $2 billion. John's company achieved $12 million in sales by the end of 1997. Now John wants to go global.

Questions

1. What are John's options for "going global"?
2. What problems in the global external environment might the firm face?

Video Case

Starbucks Coffee Goes to Japan

Recently, Starbucks Coffee opened its first store in Japan. Starbucks' management believes that Japan's coffee market is on the verge of a revolution similar to what has occurred in the United States. Unlike other American food chains such as McDonald's or Kentucky Fried Chicken, Starbucks hasn't altered anything for the international market. Kentucky Fried Chicken, for example, sells noodle dishes as well as chicken in its stores. A Starbucks executive says, "Hopefully if you walk into a Starbucks in Los Angeles, San Francisco, or Tokyo, you wouldn't notice any difference." The only concession to global marketing by Starbucks is a joint venture with a Japanese company rather than going it alone.

Starbucks may not be any different in Japan, but the market is very different from the United States. Rent on the Tokyo store is $35,000 a month, which is three times more expensive than its most costly American location. Workers are paid about $10 an hour. To this, Starbucks must add shipping costs of bringing mugs and other merchandise over from the United States. To make money, the company says it needs 30 to 40 percent more transactions than in a typical American Starbucks store.

One of Starbucks' major competitors is Pronto. Its sales have skyrocketed from 500 million yen in 1989 to 8.4 billion yen in 1995. This growth was not dependent on coffee alone. The shops sell sandwiches and pasta during the day. At night, Pronto Coffee is turned into a restaurant and bar. Pronto says that, on average, customers spend $4 during the day and $18 at night. Pronto believes that, without the evening restaurant and alcohol sales, it would be impossible to cover its costs for rent and employees.

Starbucks feels that it can make it on coffee alone. It notes that, in 1995, Japan imported 380,000 tons of coffee beans. This is 40 percent more than only a decade ago, making Japan third in the world for coffee imports, behind only the United States and Germany. Starbucks plans to rely on its exotic lattes and cappuccinos to gain market share. Yet competitors respond that lattes and cappuccinos are more labor intensive than simply pouring a cup of coffee out of a machine. This will further drive up Starbucks' costs.

Questions

1. Do you think that Starbucks will be successful in Japan without altering its Americanized marketing mix?
2. If you were going to alter the marketing mix, what variable would you change first? Why?
3. Discuss how each of the uncontrollable variables in the external environment might affect Starbucks doing business in Japan.

---

4 Video Cases and Examples

Videos cases add an extra dimension to end-of-chapter case studies. Not only will you read about a company, but you will also see and hear about that company in the videos. Video examples for each chapter come from CNBC Business News and from the Blue Chip video series focusing on successful small businesses. These videos are current and professionally produced to bring the real world right into your classroom.

A Marketing Plan from Marketing Pros

Chapter 2

Strategic Planning: Developing and Implementing a Marketing Plan

he corporate jet business reached a low point in 1992, but business has been growing each year since. Cessna Aircraft Corporation and Gulfstream Aircraft, Inc., introduced new business jets during 1996. The Cessna Citation X and the Gulfstream V offer different product benefits that do not make them directly competitive with each other.

The Citation X, at 600 miles per hour, is the fastest civilian airplane (except for the Concorde). Cessna boasts that its plane can fly executives from New York to California for breakfast and then back to the East Coast in time for dinner. Compared with slower planes, a Citation X can save 190 hours of executive time in a typical year. The speed capability means more ground time without violating pilot-fatigue guidelines. The plane, which holds 12 passengers and two pilots, is priced at about $18 million.

The Gulfstream V is priced at about $35 million. The plane boasts the advantage of range: It can go 7,500 miles without refueling, making it the longest range business jet. Instead of a speed advantage, it offers more space and can hold up to 18 passengers. In addition, company spokespersons argue that by refueling less

often, there is less ground time, which makes travel time faster without faster airspeeds. Further, the Gulfstream V can cruise at 51,000 feet, which puts it above commercial airliners and above headwinds. That means the plane can set its course as the shortest distance between two points rather than flying around air traffic and weather patterns.

Into this growth market come the competitors: Canada's Bombardier, Inc., which makes Learjets, has the Global Express, with a range and size similar to the Gulfstream V, but for $5 million less. France and Israel also have $15 million midsize jets, but not as fast as the Citation X.[1] The most unusual competitor is the Carter-Copter, a hybrid airplane helicopter that can fly nonstop from New York to Los Angeles at 400 miles per hour (a 6½-hour flight). Traditional helicopters can't go faster than 250 miles per hour. The CarterCopter is powered by an inexpensive V-6 race-car engine and carries five people.[2]

How do manufacturers of new products plan to bring their offerings to the marketplace? How can the Citation X, Gulfstream V, and Carter-Copter be marketed successfully, given the competition?

5 Chapter 2, Strategic Planning: Developing and Implementing a Marketing Plan

The marketing plan is introduced in a new chapter on strategic planning. You'll develop tools and techniques for effective strategic planning, and learn how to structure, implement, evaluate, and control your plan. This chapter will provide you with the practical tools you need to succeed in today's competitive environment.

Part One

Marketing Planning Activities

THE WORLD OF MARKETING

In the world of marketing, there are many different types of products and services offered to many different markets. Throughout this text, you will construct a marketing plan for your chosen company. Writing a marketing plan will give you a full depth of understanding for your company, its customers, and its marketing mix elements. The company you choose should be one that interests you, such as the manufacturer of your favorite product, a local business where you would like to work, or even a business you would like to start yourself to satisfy an unmet need or want. Also refer to Exhibit 2.8 for additional marketing plan subjects.

1. Describe your chosen company. How long has it been in business, or when will it start business? Who are the key players? Is the company small or large? Does it offers a good or service? What are the strengths and weaknesses of this company? What is the orientation and organizational culture?

MarketingBuilder Exercise:
- **Top 20 Questions** template

2. Define the business mission statement for your chosen company (or evaluate and modify an existing mission statement).

3. Set marketing objectives for your chosen company. Make sure the objectives fit the criteria for good objectives.

4. Scan the marketing environment. Identify opportunities and threats to your chosen company in areas such as technology, the economy, the political and legal environment, and competition. Is your competition foreign, domestic, or both? Also identify opportunities and threats based on possible market targets, including social factors, demographic factors, and multicultural issues.

MarketingBuilder Exercises:
- **Industry Analysis** portion of the **Market Analysis** template
- **Competitive Analysis Matrix** spreadsheet
- **Competition** portion of the **Market Analysis** template
- **Competitive Roundup** portion of the **Market Analysis** template
- **Strengths, Weaknesses, Opportunities,** and **Threats** sections of the **Market Analysis** template

5. Does your chosen business have a differential or competitive ad-

vantage? If there is not one, there is no point in marketing the product. Can you create a sustainable advantage with skills, resources, or elements of the marketing mix?

6. Assume your company is or will be marketing globally. How should your company enter the global marketplace? How will international issues affect your firm?

7. Identify any ethical issues that could impact your chosen firm. What steps should be taken to handle these issues?

8. Is there a key factor or assumption that you are using when performing your SWOT analysis? What would happen if this key factor or assumption did not exist?

MarketingBuilder Exercises:
- **Business Risk** portion of the **Market Analysis** template
- **Environmental Risk** portion of the **Market Analysis** template
- **Elements of Risk** table in the **Market Analysis** template

147

6 End-of-Part Activities Feature
MarketingBuilder *Express*

New end-of-part activities guide you through the development of a comprehensive marketing plan. You can complete these activities by using the model in the text or by using a new *Express* Version of top-selling **MarketingBuilder** software by JIAN. The original Academic Version of **MarketingBuilder** can also be used to complete these activities. You'll learn to develop a successful plan using the same tools chosen by today's marketing professionals.

The Most Current Topics

7 Global Marketing

The world is getting smaller. Improved communications and distribution systems are creating opportunities in third-world countries. Marketers have new formidable competitors as well as market opportunities. This text will help you think globally by integrating global examples and issues throughout each chapter. Watch for the global icon shown here and for the "Global Perspectives" boxes in each chapter.

Global Perspectives

Pepsi Retools for More Intensive Global Competition

Foreign markets are becoming ever more crucial to U.S. soft-drink makers, but Pepsi's message has been losing something in the translation. While overseas sales of both Coca-Cola and Pepsi are growing between 7% and 10% a year, Coca-Cola outsells Pepsi abroad nearly 3 to 1. And Coca-Cola already earns more than 80% of its profits abroad, compared with Pepsi's 30%.

Overseas, some Pepsi billboards are more than 20 years old—and its image is all over the map: A grocery store in Hamburg uses red stripes, a bodega in Guatemala uses '70s-era lettering and a Shanghai restaurant displays a mainly white Pepsi sign. A hodgepodge of commercials features a variety of spokespeople, ranging from cartoons and babies to doddering butlers. Worse yet, consumers say the cola tastes different in different countries.

So PepsiCo Inc. is unveiling a radical, if risky, comeback plan. Code-named "Project Blue," it's expected to cost $500 million. It calls for revamping manufacturing and distribution to get a consistent [...] e globe,

as well as an overhaul of marketing and advertising.

Pepsi is even scrapping its signature red-white-and-blue colors in favor of electric blue. Started in 1996 in more than 20 countries, the new blue is being plastered on all its trucks, coolers, cans and bottles. The switch is expected to reach the U.S. by the year 2000. Project Blue also includes new freshness standards and quality controls. The company is even training a team of tasters to sample drinks from around the world.

Yet Project Blue carries big risks—especially in light of Coca-Cola's ill-fated attempt a few years ago to reformulate classic Coke. Pepsi hasn't made such a drastic logo change in more than 40 years. And with the project's high costs come high expectations: Pepsi is counting on nothing less than a long-term sales turnaround.

Pepsi's bottlers are also ner-

vous. Many of the independent companies that make and sell Pepsi overseas will have to scrap or redo all of their red-white-and-blue signs and vending machines, plus over 30,000 trucks and more than 10 billion cans and bottles. Though Pepsi will pick up some of the costs, its U.K. bottler, for instance, has had to boost marketing spending by 30% to 40% to support Project Blue.

Another concern is whether repackaging will increase Pepsi's overseas identity crisis. Coca-Cola's red has become the world standard for soft drinks, and many marketing experts say Pepsi will have a tough time bucking that tradition with blue.

Pepsi is taking strong measures to become more competitive globally. What are some additional things Pepsi can do to help ensure the success of Project Blue? Do you think Pepsi should have started Project Blue in the United States before going global?

Ethics in Marketing

"Alcopops": An Ethical Dilemma for U.S. Brewers

Have British schoolchildren heard about Hooper's Hooch, a new lemony alcoholic beverage from British brewer Bass PLC? You bet they have.

Mention the drink, which packs more alcohol than some beers, and a group of 13- and 14-year-olds in London begins chanting, "Hooch! Hooch! Hooch!" and reciting its slogan, "One taste and you're Hooched."

Alcoholic lemonades, colas, and orange drinks, known as "alcopops," are creating a huge stir in the alcoholic-beverage industry. Over a dozen different brands have been launched in Britain.

And now they are beginning to cross the Atlantic. Bass recently began test-marketing Hooper's Hooch in Miami and San Diego, and major U.S. brewers are said to be watching with interest. Britain's Thornlodge Ltd. says it's negotiating with an undisclosed American brewer for U.S. distribution of Mrs. Pucker's, a fruit-flavored alcoholic soda developed by a former Anheuser-Busch executive.

The trend alarms regulators and antialcohol groups, who say the sweet drinks, containing 4 percent to 5.5 percent alcohol, blatantly appeal to teenagers. Britain's Advertising Standards Authority has banned a series of ads for Hooper's Hooch featuring a mischievous cartoon lemon, in a flap reminiscent of protests in the U.S. over the Joe Camel icon used in Camel cigarette advertising.

"These drinks are there to help people who don't have a taste for alcohol develop one," says Mark Bennett of the British advocacy group, Alcohol Concern. In Britain, where drinking laws are somewhat looser than in the U.S., youngsters under 18 can't purchase alcohol, but legally can drink it in certain restaurants and in their homes.

At a time when sales of most types of alcoholic beverages are stagnant, industry analysts say alcopops have the potential to become a major new category bridging the gap between beer and hard liquor. "There is a soft-drink generation that grew up drinking Pepsi and Coke and Orangina," says a London marketing consultant who monitors the beverage industry. "For them to move to drinking hard

spirits, it's a big leap. Alcoholic soft drinks fit right in the middle."

Brewers and spirits companies contend the drinks are no more appealing to young people than other adult alcoholic beverages, and they stress that they are clearly labeled as to their alcohol content. Many explicitly use "alcoholic" in their brand names. Mrs. Pucker's label even states that the drink may taste like orangeade, but "it is deceptively strong in alcohol." Fermented fruit juice is the main ingredient of many of the brands, including Hooper's Hooch. Others get their kick from grain alcohol.

To suggest that the new drinks induce underage drinking is "totally false logic," says Jane Sabini, a spokeswoman for Bass' brewing unit. "If brands like Hooper's Hooch had not become available," she adds, "most underage drinkers would be drinking other alcoholic drinks just as they did before."

Is it ethical for brewers to market so-called alcopops? Critics claim these products are aimed at teenagers. Brewers contend the drinks are no more appealing to young people than other adult alcoholic beverages. What do you think? Should these products be barred in the U.S.?

From feudalism to crowded medieval marketplaces to the Home Shopping Club, learn how marketers have sold their products throughout the ages at **Hot Link—A Brief History of Marketing**

the toy industry, you should now understand that the [...] all firms and their marketing mixes. The opening [...] tition, technology, and ever-changing consumer tastes [...] uncontrollable factors also have a profound effect on [...] Kenner. Evolving demographics (fewer children in key [...] g product safety, and changing economic conditions all [...] business. Also, environmental factors can affect each [...] the legal environment for toy manufacturers (e.g., dis- [...] ica's two largest toy manufacturers) can lead to more [...] try that ignores the external environment is doomed to

needs are addressed. As Ford Motor Company Chairman, Alex Trotman, stated, "The customer, not Ford, determines how many vehicles we sell."[5] Key issues in developing competitive advantage today include creating customer value, maintaining customer satisfaction, and building long-term relationships.

Customer Value

Customer value is the ratio of benefits to the sacrifice necessary to obtain those benefits. The customer determines the value of both the benefits and the sacrifices. Creating customer value is a core business strategy of many successful firms. As American Airlines Chairman Robert L. Crandall has stated, "With

customer value
The ratio of benefits to the sacrifice necessary to obtain those benefits.

8 Ethics in Marketing

How should alcohol and tobacco be advertised? Is it ethical for brewers to market drinks with an appeal to teenagers? Ethical issues are seldom black-and-white. Where will you draw the line? Put yourself into the situations described in the text's "Ethics in Marketing" boxed features and cases. How would you answer the questions raised there?

The Most Current Topics

Sample page 352

WHAT IS CUSTOMER VALUE?

1 Define customer value.

Companies today are facing accelerating change in many areas, including better educated and more demanding consumers, new technology, and the globalization of markets. As a result, competition is the toughest it has ever been. More and more, the key to building and sustaining a long-range competitive advantage is the commitment to delivering superior customer value, as the examples in the opening story illustrate.

In Chapter 1, customer value was defined as the customer's perception of the ratio of benefits to the sacrifice necessary to obtain those benefits. Customers receive benefits in the form of functionality, performance, durability, design, ease of use, and serviceability. To receive those benefits, they give up money, time, and effort.

Customer value is not simply a matter of high quality. A high-quality product that is available only at a high price will not be perceived as a value. Nor will bare-bones service or low-quality goods selling for a low price. Instead, customers value goods and services of the quality they expect that are sold at prices they are willing to pay. Value marketing can be used to sell a $44,000 Nissan Infiniti Q45 as well as a $3 Tyson frozen chicken dinner.

Marketers interested in customer value

- **Offer products that perform:** This is the bare minimum. Consumers have lost patience with shoddy merchandise.
- **Give consumers more than they expect:** Soon after Toyota launched Lexus, the company had to order a recall. The weekend before the recall, dealers phoned all the Lexus owners in the United States, personally making arrangements to pick up their cars and offering replacement vehicles.
- **Avoid unrealistic pricing:** Consumers couldn't understand why Kellogg's cereals commanded a premium over other brands, so Kellogg's market share fell 5 percent in the late 1980s.
- **Give the buyer facts:** Today's sophisticated consumer wants informative advertising and knowledgeable salespeople.
- **Offer organizationwide commitment in service and after-sales support.** Take the example of Southwest Airlines...

This Wal-Mart ad emphasizes two key components of its customer value—friendly service and low prices.
Courtesy Wal-Mart

Friendly Service Comes From The Heart ...

...And The Caring People At Wal-Mart

WAL★MART *Always*

Friendly Service and Low Prices...

The current emphasis on... "total quality" programs that... These programs mainly tried... improving production process... ments usually got much less a... Associates, a maker of scientific... principles in a number of area... systems increased on-time deli...

Chapter 9

9 Customer Value and Relationship Marketing

Companies have found that, to stay competitive, all operations—from marketing to billing—must focus on adding value for customers. Being truly customer-driven means building relationships with customers. These key topics are discussed in detail in Chapter 13, Customer Value and Quality, and are integrated throughout the text. Watch for the icon shown here.

Sample page 96

year) is China. A population of 1.2 billion is producing a gross domestic product of over $1.2 trillion a year. This new industrial giant will be the world's largest manufacturing zone, the largest market for such key industries as telecommunications and aerospace, and one of the largest users of capital.

Industrializing societies such as China and India offer opportunities for entrepreneurs with skill and imagination. The following "Marketing and Small Business" box is but one example.

fully industrialized society The fifth stage of economic development, a society that is an exporter of manufactured products, many of which are based on advanced technology.

The Fully Industrialized Society

The **fully industrialized society**, the fifth stage of economic development, is an exporter of manufactured products, many of which are based on advanced technology. Examples include automobiles, computers, airplanes, oil exploration equipment, and

Marketing and Small Business

The Video Van Distribution Channel Works in India

About 70 percent of India's 900 million people live in rural areas. More than half of all Indian villagers are illiterate, and only one-third live in a household with a television set. Conventional American marketing practices simply won't work. Enter J. K. Jain, a New Delhi doctor, who invented the video van. The video van is just that—a van with a large video screen in the rear door. Dr. Jain used his vans originally to spread political propaganda for an opposition party that was denied air time on state-run television.

Between elections, the vans were idle, so Dr. Jain approached consumer-goods companies in 1989. Since then his fleet has swelled from 28 to 125, advertising products as disparate as detergent, pharmaceuticals, and fans. Each van typically visits three villages a day. Consumer companies generally deploy vans year-round, except for three months during the monsoon season. Dr. Jain charges 88,000 rupees ($2,520) a month for a van, which comes outfitted with video gear and a generator.

Colgate-Palmolive, the giant U.S. consumer products company, is a believer in video vans. Many consumers in rural India are not fa-

miliar with toothpaste. But they find out once Dr. Jain's video van bumps into town. In Andarsul, a dusty village of 10,000 in Maharashtra state, a van decked out with oversize "dummy" Colgate toothpaste tubes arrives on market day. It's the first time the van has called on Andarsul, which draws farmers and field workers from nearby hamlets to its weekly market.

Over the blare of a popular movie melody, a marketer invites shoppers to the vehicle. He also throws open the rear door, revealing a video screen. Before long, about 100 men and children have jostled for a viewing spot. (Women generally don't go to market in the Indian countryside.)

In one scene of the 27-minute infomercial, villagers Kamla and Vijay are about to spend their wedding night together. As a passionate Vijay bends over to kiss his bride, she pulls away in disgust. He asks what's wrong. She's embarrassed to say. The attentive audi-

ence is puzzled until it realizes the problem is Vijay's breath.

As the story unfolds through dialogue, song, and dance, the newlyweds consult a dentist and then reconcile. The subtext is clear: Colgate is good for your breath, teeth, and love life. Village harmony is served, too. After the dentist explains that traditional oral-hygiene methods, such as charcoal powder, are ineffective and even harmful, the video ends with Kamla, Vijay, and their neighbors happily brushing their teeth.

The audience applauds enthusiastically and then rushes to get free samples at a stall beside the van. A Colgate marketer demonstrates how to use the toothpaste and a toothbrush. To encourage parents to buy a tube, he offers free Colgate brushes to a few children, only to leave many little hands grabbing for more.

Do you think Dr. Jain's concept would work in the United States? Why or why not?

Source: From "In Rural India, Video Vans Sell Toothpaste and Shampoo" by Miriam Jordan, Wall Street Journal, January 10, 1996. Reprinted by permission of Wall Street Journal. © 1996 Dow Jones & Company, Inc. All Rights Reserved.

Chapter 10

10 Small Business Issues

Chances are good that you'll work for a small business (or start your own) sometime in your career. With this in mind, we've integrated examples from small enterprises throughout the book. In addition, "Marketing and Small Business" boxes examine specific issues from a small-business point of view. An "Application for Small Business" at the end of every chapter gives you a chance to apply what you've learned to a small-business setting.

Real Insights from the Real World

11 Signature Series Cases and Videos

When seeking advice regarding new challenges, we instinctively turn to people in the know for insight and guidance. **Marketing** makes that simple. Signature Series Cases present the inside story from a wide variety of marketing experts. You'll learn about marketing from the first-hand accounts of specialists at well known companies such as Ford Motor Company and Tandy. And you'll learn from Shaquille O'Neal what makes famous athletes such good product spokespeople.

Signature Series Video Case

Mary P. Klupp

Fabulous Technology Offers Many New Features for Tomorrow's Automobiles— But Will the Consumer Buy It?

by Mary Klupp
Futures Research Manager,
Ford Motor Company

Technology has created dramatic changes in automobiles during the past few decades. Today's Ford is certainly not like your grandfather's. From fuel-efficient engines to numerous safety features, today's vehicles are a better value for the money because of technology. For example, many vehicles now offer a remote keyless entry system that enables you to open or lock your vehicle from outside with a push of a button.

Ford's engineers continue to be leaders in creating and designing new features for tomorrow's trucks, minivans, utility sports vehicles, and cars. A recent marketing research study conducted by Ford took a look at some of the new ideas generated by their engineers to determine: (a) if target customers were interested in a particular feature, and (b) if the concept has appeal, will consumers pay the suggested retail price. The research took place in both the [...]h the King-

[...]hnology
[...] com-
[...]al in-
[...]puters.
[...]grated
[...]itative
[...]evalua-
[...]ducted
[...] ten in
[...]fy cus-
[...]pecific

[...]hnology
[...]ollows:

Cargo Retention Device

Floor Mounted Cargo Net (US $50/UK £30)

Retractable Cargo Net (US $150/UK £100)

Liftgate Cargo Net (US $50/UK £30)

The *Cargo Retention Device* prevents objects in the cargo area of the vehicle from sliding forward in the event of a sudden stop. Three versions of the *Cargo Retention Device* are available: the Floor Mounted Cargo Net (secured with attachments at the ceiling and the load floor); the Retractable Cargo Net (similar to the Floor Mounted Cargo Net, but can be retracted into a roller shade on the back of the seat); and the Liftgate Cargo Net (automatically covers the cargo when liftgate is closed).

Cooled/Heated Seats (US $450, UK £160)

The Cooled and Heated Seat system controls the temperature of the driver's seat by pumping liquid through tubes inside the seat. This system is turned on by a switch on the dash board and can be adjusted to cool or heat. The System works on both cloth and leather seats.

Fingerprint Passive Entry (US $700, reg. power locks— $250/UK £360, central locks—£200)

Finger Print Passive Entry allows the driver to gain access to vehicles equipped with power locks, without the use of a key. The driver's own finger print is used as a unique identification to lock and unlock the vehicle. The vehicle recognizes the driver's finger print through the use of a touch pad. To lock the driver's door or all the vehicle's doors, simply touch the pad for half a second. (UK VERSION) Finger Print Passive Entry is also available for easy trunk or liftgate access. The vehicle can still be locked or unlocked with a key.

Fold Out Storage Container (US $150/UK £70)

The Fold Out Storage Container provides access to items stored in the forward part of the cargo area which is not easily accessible by shorter individuals. Items such as loose toys, or a stroller can be easily and conveniently stored.

Front Impact Warning

Indicator Light and Tone (US $300, UK £150)

Indicator Light and Voice (US $300/UK £150)

Indicator Light and Brake Tap (US $350/UK £180)

The Front Impact Warning System alerts drivers when approaching another vehicle or object. Sensors located in the bumper detect obstacles in front of the vehicle. The Front Impact Warning System combines an

---

Part One

Critical Thinking Case

HOOTERS, INC.

Everyone seems to be taking sides when it comes to Hooters. The many fans of the fast-growing restaurant chain like its affordable food and drink, served up by friendly waitresses in a cheery atmosphere. Typical Hooters outlets feature rustic pine floors and tables, spicy chicken wings, and beer by the pitcher. TV monitors run nonstop sports videos, and the background music is golden oldies from the 1960s.

Critics claim the chain's appeal is blatantly sexist, from its name (slang for breasts) to the showcasing of its

waitresses, called "Hooter Girls," dressed in skimpy, revealing uniforms. Critics accuse the chain of fostering a climate in which sexual harassment can thrive. "The name should be changed because of the derogatory references to human

anatomy," says the leader of a Fairfax, Virginia, group founded to protest the opening of a Hooters outlet.

Big profits can still be made from sexism, even in the 1990s. From its birth in 1983 in Clearwater, Florida, Hooters expansion is running at full speed, with restaurants operating in 37 states and Puerto Rico and plans for the entire United States and international markets. Typical Hooters restaurants serve an average of 500 customers a day, with waiting lines at lunch and dinner.

Hooters uses every opportunity to flaunt its naughty name. The chain annually sells about $5 million worth

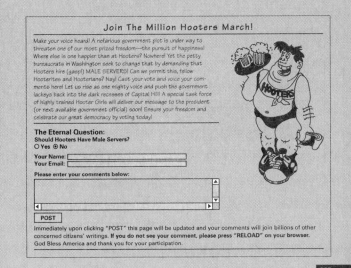

Join The Million Hooters March!

Make your voice heard! A nefarious government plot is under way to threaten one of our most prized freedom—the pursuit of happiness! Where else is one happier than at Hooters? Nowhere! Yet the petty bureaucrats in Washington seek to change that by demanding that Hooters hire (gasp!) MALE SERVERS! Can we permit this, fellow Hooterites and Hooterians? Nay! Cast your vote and voice your comments here! Let us rise as one mighty voice and push the government lackeys back into the dark recesses of Capital Hill! A special task force of highly trained Hooter Girls will deliver our message to the president (or next available government official) soon! Ensure your freedom and celebrate our great democracy by voting today!

The Eternal Question:
Should Hooters Have Male Servers?
○ Yes ◉ No

Your Name: [   ]
Your Email: [   ]

Please enter your comments below:
[   ]

[POST]

Immediately upon clicking "POST" this page will be updated and your comments will join billions of other concerned citizens' writings. **If you do not see your comment, please press "RELOAD" on your browser.** God Bless America and thank you for your participation.

145

---

12 Critical Thinking Cases

End-of-part Critical Thinking Cases give you the chance to apply what you've learned to a real company situation. You'll examine a variety of well-known companies, including Hooter's, Walgreens, and Long John Silver's. Do you agree with what these companies have done? What concepts from the text support your point of view? These cases will challenge you to evaluate marketing strategies and to develop your marketing skill.

Chapter 14

Channels and Physical Distribution

Getting the attention of college students today is not easy. Just ask the large product manufacturers like Kellogg's and Calvin Klein who have attempted to introduce their products and services on campuses throughout the United States. These manufacturers have found that college students are not very receptive to marketing ploys. In fact, most college students maintain a general attitude of distrust toward marketing activities. In addition, most college students are very cautious about advertising and do not appreciate hard selling techniques.

In an effort to get the attention of college students and overcome their reluctance to marketing activities, manufacturers have contracted with marketing organizations who specialize in the college student market. Examples of such organizations include MarketSource, Collegiate Marketing Co., and American Collegiate Marketing who provide services such as distribution of college magazines and newspapers like *U* and *Link*, sponsorship of campus events like concerts and movies, local promotion of products by posters and flyers, and the distribution of sample products.

These specialty organizations have also experienced difficulty marketing to the college student market. Faulty distribution has plagued many of their efforts to distribute free samples

and to promote products and services through campus activities. Some distribution problems for free samples include putting samples in areas students do not frequent, such as low-traffic areas of bookstores; making students show identification and sign in to receive samples; and losing samples to visitors, such as high school students or other noncollege students. In addition, there is often a lack of control over how many samples are taken by each person when the samples are distributed. For other promotional activities, such as magazine and newspaper advertisements, the placement of the advertisements may be untimely, with ads running the day after the activity, and posters may never be displayed.

To overcome these problems, organizations such as MarketSource have identified ways to distribute products and services to the college market with the least waste. First, they prefer not to use direct mail or bulk distribution. Oftentimes, the mail never leaves the large boxes in which it is delivered. If the bulk mail is removed from the box, it may never be placed into individual mail boxes. Instead, it is often placed

in stacks for passersby. Second, bookstores are being monitored to ensure timely and efficient distribution of samples and promotional materials. Samples or flyers which are distributed through bookstores are coded so they can be tracked to determine which bookstores are following appropriate distribution procedures. For posters, companies are employing resident students to aid in distribution. Student employees are screened thoroughly and paid well to distribute posters and flyers on campuses. In order to monitor student employees, companies provide students with disposable cameras and ask that the students photograph their work. The students are then paid when the film is processed. All of these changes have managed to reduce, but not eliminate, waste in the channel from the product manu-

---

Each chapter begins with a high-interest, real-life situation designed to introduce you to chapter concepts. Each situation concludes with a series of questions that anticipate key issues in the chapter. How is McDonald's targeting adults? How does Coca-Cola utilize its unique shape to stimulate customer awareness and purchasing? You'll discover the answers to these questions and more as you cover each chapter.

---

14 **Looking Back at the Opening Examples**

You have finished reading the chapter... so what have you learned? Can you now answer the questions posed in the opening example? Test yourself. Then read the "Looking Back" section at the end of the chapter where we answer the questions for you. If you got the right answers, then you are ready to go on to the chapter cases!

408

Part Four   Distribution Decisions

need to acquire and, depending on the type of product they are importing, the tariffs, quotas, and other regulations that apply in each country. Another important factor to consider is the transportation infrastructure in a country. For example, the Commonwealth of Independent States (the former Soviet Union) has little transportation infrastructure outside the major cities, such as roads that can withstand heavy freight trucks, and few reliable transportation companies of any type. Pilferage and hijackings of freight are also common. Distributors have had similar experiences in China, as the "Global Perspectives" box relates.

LOOKING BACK

As you complete this chapter, you should be able to see how marketing channels operate and how physical distribution is necessary to move goods from the manufacturer to the final consumer. The structure of marketing channels often varies given the consumer target market. For example, as the opening story discussed, many product manufacturers are facing difficulty reaching the college student market. Since college students are cautious about marketers, many companies have employed fellow students to distribute their products on college campuses. In the future, these companies expect to utilize the Internet as a distribution channel for information about and purchase orders for their products and services.

KEY TERMS

automatic identification *399*

automatic storage and retrieval systems (AS/RS) *399*

containerization *399*

contract logistics *406*

discrepancy of assortment *383*

discrepancy of quantity *382*

direct channel *386*

dual distribution (multiple distribution) *388*

electronic data interchange (EDI) *402*

electronic distribution *405*

exclusive distribution *392*

intensive distribution *391*

inventory control system *400*

just-in-time (JIT) inventory management *400*

logistics *394*

marketing channel (channel of distribution) *382*

SUMMARY

1 *Explain what a marketing channel is and why intermediaries are needed.* Marketing channels are composed of members that perform negotiating functions. Some intermediaries buy and resell products; other intermediaries aid the exchange of ownership between buyers and sellers without taking title. Nonmember channel participants do not engage in negotiating activities and function as an auxiliary part of the marketing channel structure.

Intermediaries are often included in marketing channels for three important reasons. First, the specialized expertise of intermediaries may improve the overall efficiency of marketing channels. Second, intermediaries may help overcome discrepancies by making products available in quantities and assortments desired by consumers and business buyers and at locations convenient to them. Third, intermediaries reduce the number of transactions required to distribute goods from producers to consumers and end users.

2 *Describe the functions and activities of marketing channel members.* Marketing channel members perform three basic types of functions. Transactional functions include contacting and promoting, negotiating, and risk taking. Logistical functions performed by channel members include physical distribution and sorting functions. Finally, channel members may perform facilitating functions, such as researching and financing.

3 *Discuss the differences among marketing channels for consumer and industrial products.* Marketing channels for consumer and business products vary in degree of complexity. The simplest consumer product channel involves direct selling from producers to consumers. Businesses may sell directly to business or government buyers. Marketing channels grow more complex as intermediaries become involved. Consumer product channel intermediaries include agents, brokers, wholesalers, and retailers. Business product channel intermediaries include agents, brokers, and industrial distributors.

Preface

*T*oday's marketers face a marketplace that is becoming simultaneously more competitive, specialized, global, and Internet-reliant. To succeed in today's changing environment, successful marketing requires – now more than ever – a balance of creativity and knowledge. Knowledge is, indeed, bliss. With its steadily growing market share, *Marketing*, Fourth Edition has demonstrated that it is the premier source for new and essential marketing knowledge. Students can learn it all with this comprehensive, current text. Instructors can have it all with a complete, high-tech supplement package.

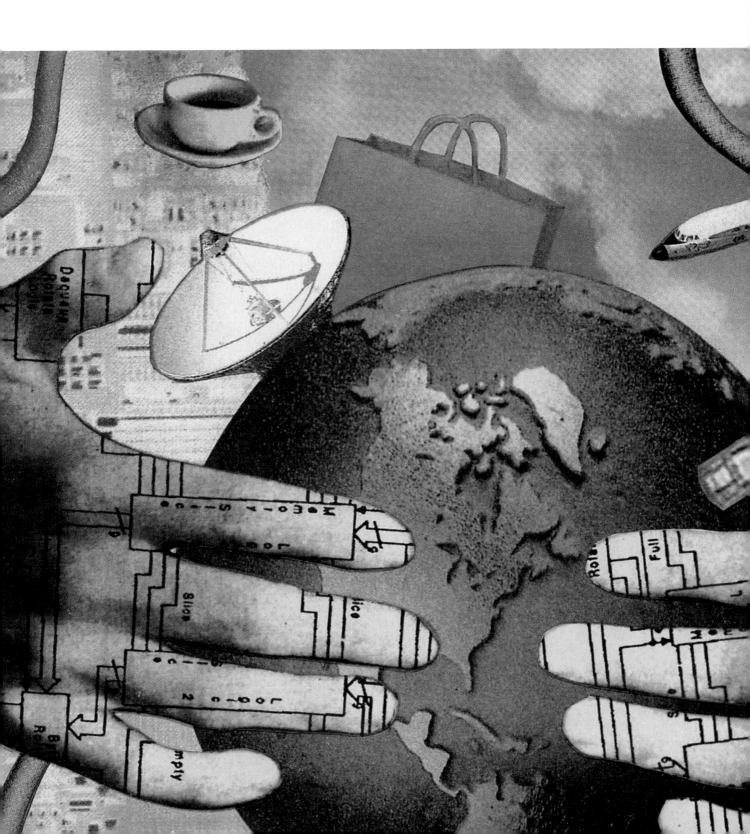

CUSTOMER-DRIVEN INNOVATIONS FOR THE 4TH EDITION

The guiding principle of this and past editions of *Marketing* is that of building relationships. Relationship marketing is discussed in Chapter 1, and we believe in it completely. We seek to build long-term relationships with our customers (both professors and students) that result in trust and confidence in our product. Our success is proven as the number of "new relationships" dramatically increases with each edition.

We feel a strong sense of responsibility to provide you and your students with the most exciting and up-to-date text and useful supplement package possible. To accomplish this, we have listened to your desires and comments and incorporated your feedback into *Marketing*, Fourth Edition.

Shorter and Sweeter

You have expressed to us with each edition that "the text is easy to read and full of timely student-oriented examples." We have maintained this in the current edition with hundreds of new examples. We have done extensive research for the Fourth Edition to continue to offer a comprehensive introduction to the field of marketing. Simultaneously, we have reduced the length of the text by over a hundred pages! You now have a comprehensive and enjoyable book to read that can easily be covered in one term.

A New Table of Contents Based on Instructor Feedback

Employers and instructors have told us that strategic planning has reemerged as a critical success factor in global business. The strategic plan forms the foundation for a marketing plan which generates revenue (or enables a nonprofit organization to reach its goal) and enables a firm to survive and prosper. With this in mind, we have created a new Chapter 2 that discusses strategic planning and building a marketing plan.

"Ethics and Social Responsibility" has been moved to Chapter 5 from Chapter 21, signifying its pervasive importance in all marketing decision making. Indeed, society demands that all businesspeople recognize their social responsibilities and set the highest possible ethical standards.

Chapter 13, "Customer Value, Quality, and Satisfaction," has been moved to the end of Part 3, " Product Decisions," where you told us it most logically fits. We also took your suggestions and combined coverage of marketing channels and physical distribution into a single chapter, Chapter 14. Retailing and wholesaling were reduced from two chapters to one. Multicultural marketing is no longer a stand-alone chapter, but has been fully integrated throughout the text. In addition, you will find expanded coverage of multicultural marketing in Chapter 3, "The Marketing Environment." A final important change to the table of contents is a new chapter (Chapter 19) on Internet marketing. It is introduced in the text, but the chapter itself is found on the World Wide Web, **http://www.swcollege.com/lamb.html**

New Internet Coverage

The Fourth Edition features a hot, new Internet chapter that focuses on the Internet's impact on marketing strategy and the marketing mix. The pros and cons of conducting marketing research on the Net are also explained. The chapter concludes with a discussion of privacy and issues of doing business via the Internet. Additionally, Internet coverage is integrated throughout the text and identified for you by a special icon.

New Internet Activities and Real-Time Examples

Each chapter contains several Internet activities tied to organizations mentioned in the text. For example, as students read about how McDonald's segments and targets markets, they're directed to real-time examples on McDonald's Web page. In addition, we conclude each chapter with additional Internet activities that relate to chapter content. Students find valuable on-line resources and learn to analyze current Internet marketing strategies.

New End-of-Part Activities Help Students Build a Marketing Plan

Chapter 2 discusses the purpose and components of a marketing plan. As chapter topics such as market segmentation and consumer behavior are discussed, the corresponding end-of-part exercises direct students to create related portions of their marketing plan. By the end of the semester, your class will have developed a complete marketing plan.

New MarketingBuilder Express

An "express" version of JIAN's popular Marketing*Builder* software, this tool contains everything students need to develop a marketing plan. Students can complete the new end-of-part marketing plan activities using the shorter Marketing*Builder* Express software templates or using the original Academic Version of Marketing*Builder*.

New Integration of Wardlow's Marketing CD-ROM

Twelve specially selected modules from the new *Principles of Marketing* CD-ROM by Daniel Wardlow, San Francisco State University, are integrated throughout the text. "Hot Links" in the margin direct students to exciting simulations, videos, and examples that relate to the text material being covered. Students interested in knowing more about retailing can go to "Hot Link" Retailing Today. Other sample "Hot Links" are entitled *A Brief History of Marketing*, *Influences on Marketing Strategy*, and *The Product Life Cycle*.

A New Internet Site Connects You to Our Marketing Virtual Community: http://www.swcollege.com/lamb.html

A new Internet site supports the text, featuring updates to URLs in the text, additional real-time marketing cases, new Chapter 19 on "Internet Marketing," updates and articles, links to companies discussed in the text, plus a variety of materials to supplement your course.

CLASSIC VALUE-BASED FEATURES HAVE BEEN UPDATED AND ENHANCED

Signature Case Series by Successful Businesspeople

To help bring the text to life for students, we have asked some of America's most successful businesspeople to prepare short written cases – most with videos – about specific marketing concepts. We call this our "Signature Series" because we have asked these authors to sign their cases, signifying that they personally prepared the case for *Marketing*.

The Fourth Edition features several new signature cases. Mary Klupp, research manager of Customer Information, "Futures" and Strategy Group of Ford Motor Company, demonstrates how Ford takes new technology features, such as a night vision system, and assesses consumer demand for the items. Ronald LaBorde, president and CEO of Piccadilly Cafeterias, Inc., discusses the selection of promotional approaches based on market research and customer preferences. Short biographical sketches of each Signature Series author appear on p. xxxvii of the Preface.

Video Cases and Examples for Each Chapter

You can bring marketing concepts to life with our video cases and examples. For each chapter, we have chosen one video case and three current CNBC or Blue Chip video clips. These videos highlight the issues discussed in each chapter and present the very latest developments in marketing. Some segments provide current profiles of companies discussed in the chapter. Others demonstrate text concepts with visual examples from the real world. Blue Chip video examples highlight successful small businesses. A detailed Video Instructor's Manual previews each clip and keys it to the chapter content for easy integration.

Small Business and Entrepreneurship Are Emphasized in Every Chapter

Many students will either work for a small business or strike out on their own to form an organization. For this reason, each chapter contains a feature box entitled "Marketing and Small Business" and an "Application for Small Business" appears at the end of each chapter. The "Marketing and Small Business" boxes apply general marketing concepts to the world of small business. The "Applications" are minicases designed to illustrate how small businesses can create strategies and tactics using the material in the chapter. Anyone with an entrepreneurial flair will enjoy these features.

Customer Value and Quality Are Emphasized in Every Chapter

Delivering superior customer value is now key to success in an increasingly competitive marketplace. Chapter 13 addresses issues of value and quality in detail and in the appropriate context of product decisions. Additionally, examples are integrated and identified by icons throughout the text.

Careers in Marketing

The Appendix presents information on a variety of marketing careers, with job descriptions and career paths, to familiarize students with employment opportunities in marketing. This appendix also indicates what people in various marketing positions typically earn and how students should go about marketing themselves to prospective employers. A series of custom-produced video vignettes features recent graduates who explain how principles from the text apply to the real world of marketing.

GLOBAL MARKETING CONCEPTS THROUGHOUT THE TEXT

 Today most businesses compete not only locally and nationally, but globally as well. Companies that have never given a thought to exporting now face competition from abroad. "Thinking globally" should be a part of every manager's tactical and strategic planning. Accordingly, we address this topic in detail early in Chapter 4. We have also integrated numerous global examples within the body of the text and identified them with the icon shown in the margin.

Global marketing is fully integrated throughout the book, cases, and videos as well. Our "Global Perspectives" boxes, which appear in most chapters, provide expanded global examples and concepts. Each box concludes with thought-provoking questions carefully prepared to stimulate class discussion. For example, the box in Chapter 7 describes the emergence of a middle class in Poland and asks students to decide if a Polish middle class would be a promising target market for American companies.

FOCUS ON ETHICS

 In this edition we continue our emphasis on ethics. "Ethics and Social Responsibility" has been moved from Chapter 21 to Chapter 5 to demonstrate its importance in management decision making. The "Ethics in Marketing" boxes, complete with questions focusing on ethical decision making, have been revised and added to every chapter. Questions and cases designed to highlight ethical issues, such as the Hooter's case appearing at the end of Part One, give students a sense of the complexity of ethics issues as the cases lead them to look at the issues from all sides.

VALUE-DRIVEN PEDAGOGY PUTS YOU IN THE KNOW

Our pedagogy has been developed in response to what you told us delivers value to you and your students. You told us that current examples are important to you, so we have included all-new opening vignettes, new examples throughout the text, and new CNBC and Blue Chip video examples correlated to every chapter. You told us that cases that students find relevant are important to you, so we have added new Signature Series Cases and replaced most of the video cases with new, current videos. You said that many of your students planned a career in small business, so we have numerous new small business examples, "Marketing and Small Business" boxes, and all-new small business exercises at the end of each chapter.

Finally, you told us that the Integrated Learning System helped you organize your lectures and helped your students study more effectively, so we have retained that important feature.

Fully Integrated Learning System

3

The text and all major supplements are organized around the learning objectives that appear at the beginning of each chapter to provide you and your students with an easy-to-use Integrated Learning System. A numbered icon like the one shown in the margin identifies each objective in each chapter and appears next to its related material throughout the text, Instructor's Manual, Test Bank, and Study Guide. In other words, every learning objective links the text, Study Guide, Test Bank, and all components of the Instructor's Manual. The system is illustrated on the inside front cover of the text.

Chapter learning objectives are the linchpin of the Integrated Learning System. They provide a structure for your lesson plans – everything you need to assure complete coverage of each objective icon. Do you want to stress more on learning objective 4, Chapter 8, "Describe bases commonly used to segment consumer markets"? No problem. Go to the Instructor's Manual, objective 4, Chapter 8, and you'll find supplemental material. Do you want to emphasize the same objective on an exam? Go to the correlation table at the beginning of every chapter in the Test Bank. Here you will find under Chapter 8, learning objective 4, a matrix that lists question types (Definitions, Conceptual, or Applications) and level of difficulty. Now you can test on objective 4 by type of question and degree of difficulty. This value-driven system for you, the instructor, delivers what it promises – full integration.

The integrated system also delivers value for students as they prepare for exams. The learning objective icons identify all the material in the text and Study Guide that relate to each specific learning objective. Students can easily check their grasp of each objective by reading the text sections, reviewing the corresponding summary section, answering the Study Guide questions for that objective, and returning to the appropriate text sections for further review when they have difficulty with any of the questions. Students can quickly identify all material relating to an objective by simply looking for the learning objective icon.

Text Pedagogy That Adds Value, Excites Students, and Reinforces Learning

Pedagogical features are meant to reinforce learning, but they need not be boring. We have created teaching tools within the text that will excite student interest as well as teach.

- **Opening Vignettes, Revisited at Chapter Conclusions:** Each chapter begins with a new, current, real-world story about a marketing decision or situation facing a company. A special section before the chapter summary called "Looking Back" answers the teaser questions posed in the opening vignette and helps illustrate how the chapter material relates to the real world of marketing.

- **Key Terms:** Key terms appear in boldface in the text, with definitions in the margins, making it easy for students to check their understanding of key definitions. A complete alphabetical list of key terms appears at the end of each chapter as a study checklist, with page citations for easy reference.

- **Chapter Summaries:** Each chapter ends with a summary that distills the main points of the chapter. Chapter summaries are organized around the learning objectives so that students can use them as a quick check on their achievement of learning goals.

- **Discussion and Writing Questions:** To help students improve their writing skills, we have included writing exercises with the discussion questions at the end of each chapter. These exercises are marked with the icon shown here. The writing questions are designed to be brief so that students can accomplish writing assignments in a short time and grading time is minimized.

- **New Team Activities:** The ability to work collaboratively is key to success in today's business world. New end-of-chapter team activities, identified by the icon shown here, give students opportunities to learn to work together.

- **Application for Small Business:** These short scenarios prompt students to apply marketing concepts to small business settings. Each scenario ends with provocative questions to aid student analysis.

- **Critical Thinking Part Cases:** Our society has an enormous capacity for generating data, but our ability to use the data to make good decisions has lagged behind. In the hope of better preparing the next generation of business leaders, many educators are beginning to place greater emphasis on developing critical thinking skills.

    Marketing, Fourth Edition, contributes to this effort with a more challenging, comprehensive case at the end of each of the seven major parts – five of them new for this edition. Critical Thinking Cases feature nationally known companies like Ben and Jerry's, Long John Silver's, and Walgreen's. Additional Critical Thinking Cases are available in the *Cases*, *Marketing Activities*, and *Team Projects* supplement.

- **Video Cases:** A video case appears at the end of every chapter to add a visual dimension to case analysis. Most of the cases are new for this edition. Companies featured in the video cases include Ford Motor Company, New England Culinary Institute, and Community Coffee.

- **Signature Series Cases:** Several chapters also conclude with cases from the Signature Series, most of which have accompanying videos. These cases are discussed in more detail on p. xxxvii of this preface.

INNOVATIVE STUDENT SUPPLEMENTS

Marketing, Fourth Edition, provides an excellent vehicle for students to learn the fundamentals. However, to truly understand the subject, students need to apply the principles to real-life situations. We have provided a variety of supplements that give students the opportunity to apply concepts through hands-on activities.

- ***Principles of Marketing CD-ROM by Daniel Wardlow*** (ISBN 0-538-88116-X)*:* Students are directed to this interactive CD-ROM throughout the text. This special Lamb, Hair, McDaniel version of the CD-ROM contains 12 powerful modules featuring multimedia simulations that demonstrate marketing concepts with full motion and sound.

- ***Comprehensive GradeMaker Study Guide*** (ISBN 0-538-87012-5)*:* All questions in the Study Guide are keyed to the learning objectives by numbered icons. In addition to true/false, multiple choice, and essay questions, every chapter includes application questions, many in the form of short scenarios. Study Guide questions were designed to be similar in type and difficulty level to the Test Bank questions, so that review using the Study Guide will help students improve their test scores. The guide also includes chapter outlines with definitions of key terms, a synopsis of key points under the learning objectives, and vocabulary practice.

- *MarketingBuilder Express Software* (ISBN 0-538-87574-7)*:* We are pleased to make available to users of *Marketing,* Fourth Edition, software by JIAN, specifically designed for creating a marketing plan.
- *PowerNotes* (ISBN 0-538-87838-X)*:* This lecture guide for students provides all PowerPoint images with space for note taking.
- *Fancy Footwork* (ISBN 0-538-82642-8) *and Export to Win! Computer Simulations* (ISBN 0-538-81725-9)*:* These computer simulations enable students to make real-world product decisions. *Fancy Footwork* guides students through the development of strategies for the four Ps in marketing a new line of athletic footwear. *Export to Win!* helps students understand exporting and international marketing.

INNOVATIVE INSTRUCTOR'S SUPPLEMENTS

All components of our comprehensive support package have been developed to help you prepare lectures and tests as quickly and easily as possible. We provide a wealth of information and activities beyond the text to supplement your lectures, as well as teaching aids in a variety of formats to fit your own teaching style.

Instructor Resource CD-ROM

Managing your classroom resources is now easier than ever. The new Instructor Resource CD-ROM (ISBN 0-538-87024-9) contains all key instructor supplements – Instructor's Manual, Test Bank, and PowerPoint.

Marketing: An Interactive Approach, Version 1.0, by Daniel L. Wardlow, San Francisco State University

This CD-ROM contains all 32 interactive modules, each designed to bring marketing to life. Use multimedia simulations, video, and examples to drive classroom discussion and add impact to your lectures. It is available in PC version (ISBN 0-538-86975-5) and Mac version (ISBN 0-538-87542-9).

A Value-Based Instructor's Manual, the Core of Our Integrated Learning System

Now available in print (ISBN 0-538-87015-X) or on disk (ISBN 0-538-87016-8). Each chapter of the Instructor's Manual begins with the learning objectives and a brief summary of the key points covered by each objective. The Integrated Learning System then comes together in the detailed outlines of each chapter. Each outline, integrated with the textbook and with other supplements through the learning objectives, refers you to the support materials at the appropriate points in the lecture: transparencies with discussion suggestions, additional examples not included in the text, exhibits, supplemental articles, additional activities, boxed material, and discussion questions. These outlines assist you in organizing lectures, choosing support materials, bringing in outside examples not mentioned in the book, and taking full advantage of text discussion.

In addition to complete solutions to text questions and cases, the manual supplies ethical scenarios, summaries of current articles, and class activities. Our manual is truly "one-stop shopping" for everything you need for your complete teaching system.

Comprehensive Test Bank and Windows Testing Software

To complete the integrated system, our enhanced Test Bank (ISBN 0-538-87017-6), like the other supplements, is organized around the learning objectives. It is available in print and new Windows software formats (Westest) (ISBN 0-538-87801-0).

A correlation table at the beginning of each test bank chapter classifies each question according to type, complexity, and learning objective covered. Using this table, you can create exams with the appropriate mix of question types and level of difficulty for your class. You can choose to prepare tests that cover all learning objectives or emphasize those you feel are most important. The Test Bank is one of the most comprehensive on the market, with over 3,300 true/false, multiple-choice, and essay questions.

Complete Video Package and Instructor's Manual

This video package (ISBN's 0-538-87025-7, 0-538-87026-5, 0-538-87027-3, 0-538-87028-1, 0-538-87029-X, 0-538-84973-8) adds visual impact and current, real-world examples to your lecture presentation. The package includes 21 Video Cases, over 60 CNBC and Blue Chip Video Examples, and 7 Career Videos. A detailed Video Instructor's Manual (ISBN 0-538-87800-2) describes each video and provides suggestions for using the videos in your course.

Other Outstanding Supplements

- *Cases, Marketing Activities, and Team Projects* (ISBN 0-538-87013-3): Use this supplement to challenge students with additional cases, marketing experiential exercises, and short applied marketing tasks for every chapter. In addition, the supplement contains team projects and a comprehensive class exercise for developing interpersonal skills.

- *PowerPoint Slides* (ISBN 0-538-87023-0): More than 225 full-color images are provided with *Marketing*, Fourth Edition. Most are creatively prepared visuals that do not repeat the text. Only images that highlight concepts central to the chapter are from the textbook. All you need is Windows to run the PowerPoint viewer and an LCD panel for classroom display.

- *Transparency Acetates* (ISBN 0-538-87019-2): All images prepared in PowerPoint are also available as acetate transparencies. Images are tied to the Integrated Learning System through the Instructor's Manual lecture outlines. Transparencies and their discussion prompts appear within the learning objective content where they apply.

- *New Instructor's Handbook* (ISBN 0-538-83017-4): This helpful booklet was specifically designed for instructors preparing to teach their first course in principles of marketing. It provides helpful hints on developing a course outline, lecturing, testing, giving feedback, and assigning projects.

- *New Edition of Great Ideas for Teaching Marketing* (ISBN 0-538-87021-4): Edited by the authors of the textbook, *Great Ideas for Teaching Marketing*, Fourth Edition, is a collection of suggestions for improving marketing education by enhancing teaching excellence. The publication includes teaching tips and ideas submitted by over 200 marketing educators from the United States and Canada.

ACKNOWLEDGMENTS

A textbook and supplements package like this never just "happens." Without the innovative thinking and support of many people, this book and package would not exist. Our good fortune has enabled us to work with a team of true professionals in both the academic and publishing environments.

The most pleasant task we have is expressing our gratitude to this "value-building" team. We appreciate the support and encouragement we have received from our colleagues and deans at Texas Christian University, Louisiana State University, and the University of Texas at Arlington. We could not have done without the advice and help of Susan Carson who has made the Fourth Edition a reality. A special thanks goes to Dreis Van Landuyt, our editor, for his suggestions and support. We also owe our deepest gratitude to the ITP sales force which has built an increasing number of "new customer relationships" with each successive edition. We look forward to the many new relationships you are creating now and in the future.

Our secretaries and administrative assistants, Fran Eller at TCU, RoseAnn Reddick at UTA, and Susan Sartwell at LSU, typed and retyped thousands of pages of manuscript, provided important quality control, and helped keep the project (and us) on schedule. Their dedication, hard work, and support were exemplary.

We would also like to acknowledge several other colleagues who played important roles in the development of this book. Julie Baker, University of Texas at Arlington, and Amelie Storment provided valuable assistance in the development of several chapters for this edition. Erika Matulich, Texas Christian University, contributed to the development of Chapter 2. And J. D. Mosley-Matchett, University of Texas at Arlington, contributed to the development of Chapter 19 as well as the Internet activities throughout the text.

Finally, we are particularly indebted to our reviewers:

Wayne Alexander
Moorhead State University

Linda Anglin
Mankato State University

Thomas S. Bennett
Gaston College

James C. Boespflug
Arapahoe Community College

Victoria Bush
University of Mississippi

Joseph E. Cantrell
DeAnza College

G. L. Carr
University of Alaska Anchorage

Deborah Chiviges Calhoun
College of Notre Dame of Maryland

John Alan Davis
Mohave Community College

William M. Diamond
SUNY – Albany

Jacqueline K. Eastman
Valdosta State University

Kevin M. Elliott
Mankato State University

Karen A. Evans
Herkimer County Community College

Randall S. Hansen
Stetson University

Hari S. Hariharan
University of Wisconsin – Madison

Dorothy R. Harpool
Wichita State University

Timothy S. Hatten
Black Hills State University

James E. Hazeltine
Northeastern Illinois University

Patricia M. Hopkins
California State Polytechnic

Kenneth R. Laird
Southern Connecticut State University

Kenneth D. Lawrence
New Jersey Institute of Technology

J. Gordon Long
Georgia College

Karl Mann
Tennessee Tech University

Cathy L. Martin
Northeast Louisiana University

Irving Mason
Herkimer County Community College

Anil M. Pandya
Northeastern Illinois University

Michael M. Pearson
Loyola University, New Orleans

Constantine G. Petrides
Borough of Manhattan Community College

Peter A. Schneider
Seton Hall University

Donald R. Self
Auburn University at Montgomery

Mark T. Spence
Southern Connecticut State College

James E. Stoddard
University of New Hampshire

Albert J. Taylor
Austin Peay State University

Janice E. Taylor
Miami University of Ohio

Ronald D. Taylor
Mississippi State University

Sandra T. Vernon
Fayetteville Technical Community College

Charles R. Vitaska
Metro State College, Denver

James F. Wenthe
Georgia College

Linda Berns Wright
Mississippi State University

William R. Wynd
Eastern Washington University

MEET THE SIGNATURE SERIES AUTHORS

Mary P. Klupp *Research Manager, Ford Motor Company Marketing and Sales*
Mary P. Klupp has been a research manager for Ford Motor Company's Marketing and Sales since June 1991. Her most recent assignment as strategic and "futures" research manager began in June 1993. Her previous assignments included customer satisfaction, advertising, and concept research. Ms. Klupp holds a bachelor of science degree in mathematics from Gannon University, Erie, Pennsylvania. Her master's degree in mathematics is from the University of Detroit.

Ronald A. LaBorde *President and CEO, Piccadilly Cafeterias, Inc.*
Ronald A. LaBorde is president and CEO of Piccadilly Cafeterias, Inc. Mr. LaBorde joined Piccadilly in 1982 as assistant controller and also held the additional positions of controller and corporate secretary. In 1992 he assumed the position of chief financial officer and was elected as a member of the board of directors. He was named president and CEO in June 1995. Piccadilly owns and operates 128 cafeterias in 16 states and 7 Ralph & Kacoo's seafood restaurants in three states and has annual sales in excess of $300 million.

Teri G. Fontenot *President and CEO, Woman's Health Foundation*
Teri G. Fontenot has been the president and CEO of Woman's Health Foundation since April 1996. Ms. Fontenot began her health-care career at St. Francis Medical Center as chief financial officer. She served as vice president/CFO at Southwest Florida Regional Medical Center, as senior vice president/COO of Woman's Hospital, and as executive vice president of Woman's Health Foundation before assuming her current position. Ms. Fontenot graduated with honors from the University of Mississippi with a degree in accounting. She received her master's degree in business administration from Northeast Louisiana University.

Shaquille O'Neal *Center, Los Angeles Lakers*
Shaquille O'Neal, the number-one pick in the 1992 NBA draft, was the most anticipated player in the history of basketball. In his second season, he led the Orlando Magic to its first-ever playoff appearance, was in the top five of the NBA in scoring and field goal percentage, and was voted as a starter in the NBA All-Star game for the second time. In the 1994 World Games, Shaq was awarded the Most Valuable Player for the Games. Now playing for the Los Angeles Lakers, Shaq's basketball talents continue to shine. As one of the most popular celebrities in sports today, Shaq has been featured in global, cutting-edge commercials endorsing Reebok and Pepsi. His name and likeness are featured on Spalding basketballs, SkyBox trading cards, video games, and Kenner toys. He's also appeared in several feature-length movies.

John V. Roach *Chairman and CEO, Tandy Corporation*
John V. Roach began his career at Tandy Corporation in 1967 as general manager of Tandy Computer Services. In 1982, he was named chairman of the board and chief executive officer. He also serves as a member of the board of directors of Justin Industries, City Club, Van Cliburn Foundation, and Electrical Industries Association. He is chairman of the board of his alma mater, Texas Christian University, where he earned a B.A. in physics and math and an MBA.

   Mr. Roach has received many leadership awards, including Financial World's Chief Executive Officer of the Year in 1981, Forbes Magazine's Business Speaker of the Year in 1988, and Financial World's CEO of the Decade in Specialty Retailing in 1989. He has been recognized by Texas Christian University as a Distinguished Alumnus and by the University of Texas at Arlington College of Business as a Distinguished Business Leader. He was inducted into the Texas Business Hall of Fame in 1994.

Gian M. Fulgoni *Chairman and CEO, Information Resources, Inc.*
Mr. Fulgoni is chairman and chief executive officer of Information Resources, Inc. IRI offers a complete line of scanner-based information services for the consumer packaged goods industry and decision support software for use across a wide variety of industries and governmental agencies worldwide. Since its founding in 1979, IRI has grown rapidly to become the second largest market research company in the world and the fortieth largest independent software vendor. In both 1984 and 1985, the company was listed by *Inc.* magazine in the "Inc. 100" list of fastest growing public companies. In the words of *The Wall Street Journal* and *The New York Times*, IRI has become known as "the pioneer/trail blazer in the field of marketing research using UPC scanners."

   In recognition of his efforts in guiding the development of InfoScan, Mr. Fulgoni was honored in 1990 by Peat Marwick as one of four Illinois High Tech Entrepreneurs of the Year.

   In 1991, Mr. Fulgoni was awarded the "bronze award" by The Wall Street Transcript, one of three awards recognizing the extent to which a company's CEO has taken proper steps to enhance overall value of the company for the benefit of its shareholders.

   Educated in England, Mr. Fulgoni holds an honors degree in physics from the University of Manchester and a master's degree in marketing from the University of Lancaster.

MEET THE AUTHORS

Charles W. Lamb, Jr. – Texas Christian University

Charles Lamb is the M. J. Neeley Professor of Marketing, M. J. Neeley School of Business, Texas Christian University. He served as chair of the TCU marketing department from 1982 to 1988.

Lamb has authored or co-authored more than a dozen books and anthologies on marketing topics and over 100 articles that have appeared in academic journals and conference proceedings.

He is vice president for publications for the Academy of Marketing Science, a member of the American Marketing Association Education Council, a member of the board of directors of the American Association for Advances in Health Care Research, and a past president of the Southwestern Marketing Association.

Lamb earned an associate degree in business administration from Sinclair Community College, a bachelor's degree from Miami University, an MBA from Wright State University, and a doctorate from Kent State University. He previously served as assistant and associate professor of marketing at Texas A&M University.

Joseph F. Hair, Jr. – Louisiana State University

Joseph Hair is Alvin C. Copeland Endowed Chair of Franchising and Director, Entrepreneurship Institute Louisiana State University. Previously, Hair held the Phil B. Hardin Chair of Marketing at the University of Mississippi. He has taught graduate and undergraduate marketing and marketing research courses.

Hair has authored 27 books, monographs, and cases and over 60 articles in scholarly journals. He also has participated on many university committees and has chaired numerous departmental task forces. He serves on the editorial review boards of several journals.

He is a member of the American Marketing Association, Academy of Marketing Science, Southern Marketing Association, and Southwestern Marketing Association.

Hair holds a bachelor's degree in economics, a master's degree in marketing, and a doctorate in marketing, all from the University of Florida. He also serves as a marketing consultant to businesses in a variety of industries, ranging from food and retailing to financial services, health care, electronics, and the U.S. Departments of Agriculture and Interior.

Carl McDaniel – University of Texas – Arlington

Carl McDaniel is a professor of marketing at the University of Texas – Arlington, where he has been chairman of the marketing department since 1976. He has been an instructor for more than 20 years and is the recipient of several awards for outstanding teaching. McDaniel has also been a district sales manager for Southwestern Bell Telephone Company. Currently, he serves as a board member of the North Texas Higher Education Authority.

In addition to Marketing, McDaniel also has co-authored numerous textbooks in marketing and business. McDaniel's research has appeared in such publications as the *Journal of Marketing Research*, *Journal of the Academy of Marketing Science*, and *California Management Review*.

McDaniel is a member of the American Marketing Association, Academy of Marketing Science, Southern Marketing Association, Southwestern Marketing Association, and Western Marketing Association.

Besides his academic experience, McDaniel has business experience as the co-owner of a marketing research firm. During the winter and spring of 1995, McDaniel served as Senior Consultant to the International Trade Centre (ITC), Geneva, Switzerland. The ITC's mission is to help developing nations increase their exports. He has a bachelor's degree from the University of Arkansas and his master's degree and doctorate from Arizona State University.

The World of Marketing

1 Define the term *marketing*.

2 Describe four marketing management philosophies.

3 Discuss the differences between sales and marketing orientations.

4 Explain how firms implement the marketing concept.

5 Describe the marketing process.

6 Describe several reasons for studying marketing.

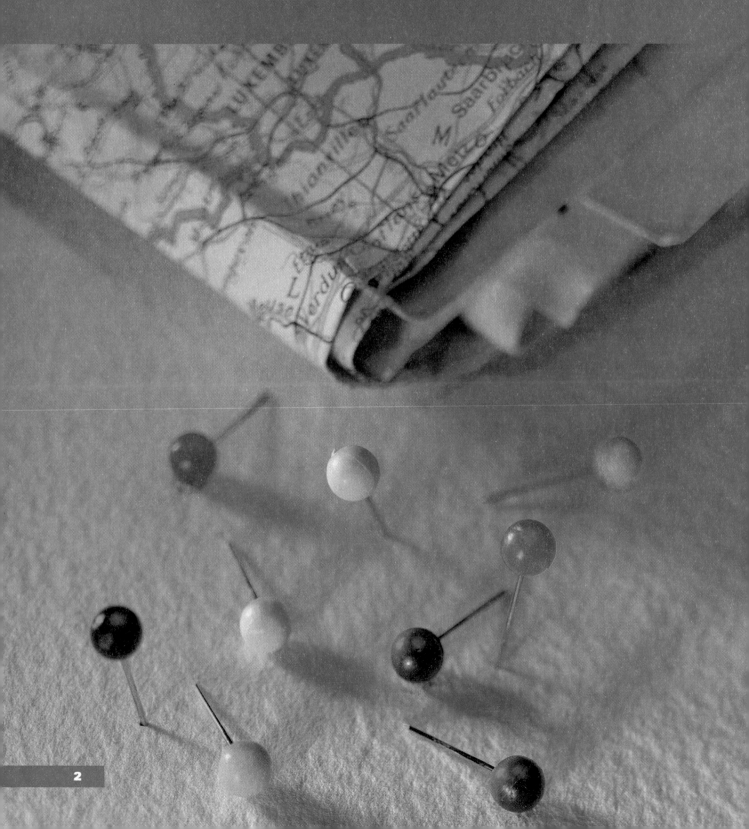

Chapter 1

An Overview of Marketing

Robert Sallada walked into a Staples store in Charlottesville, Virginia, looking for some map pins but not much in the way of service. He expected, he says dismissively, the kind of shopping experience that "Kmart is the epitome of." Staples, after all, is an office-supplies discount store. Turned out the store didn't have the unusual variety of map pins Sallada was after, but the sales associate helping him was quickly on the phone to the manufacturer of a similar pin. After Sallada returned to his 15-employee furniture business, the Staples worker faxed him information on the pins. All this, Sallada marvels, for an order of no more than $20. Says he, still sounding incredulous: "I walked in a few months later, and the clerk remembered my name. It really impressed me." Sallada is now a regular Staples shopper and plans to spend a couple of thousand dollars annually at the store.

What Sallada and many others now realize is that Staples cares deeply, very deeply, about pleasing customers. Such pampering, combined with great prices, has helped transform Staples into America's hottest retailer.

But that kind of success doesn't mean Staples can rest easy. Competition is heating up in the rapidly growing, $8 billion office superstore business. Tough competitors like Office Depot and OfficeMax are also cutting costs and boosting service. Says CEO and founder Tom Stemberg, "We clearly need to become more intimate with our customers. We're way better at service than we were two years ago, but I don't think we're nearly as good as we need to be."

While Staples still intends to offer great prices on its paper, pens, fax machines, and other office supplies, its main strategy is to grow by providing customers with the best solutions to their problems.

To get to know its customers, Staples has been compiling lots of information about buying habits and storing that information in a massive database. To get the information, Staples uses a membership card, which gives customers a discount on certain items every time they produce the card at the register. Each time a customer uses the card, Staples collects information about his (or her) buying habits. The company, for instance, does well with lawyers and dentists but not with school principals. Staples uses this knowledge to locate new stores where they will be convenient for their customers—such as in neighborhoods with lots of law offices.

Another advantage of knowing who your customers are: You can work on building long-term relationships. Staples wants to do everything it can to get its best customers coming back to its stores. Since the database knows who those folks are, Staples can try to win their loyalty by offering them special discounts. In its Cincinnati stores, for instance, Staples is experimenting with a new rebate card that offers discounts to small-business customers who spend at least $100 a month. The database also alerts Staples to once-loyal customers who have left the flock. When a salesperson sees that someone who, say, bought six cases of copier paper for six months has stopped cold, he (or she) can call to find out why, and to ask if Staples can do anything to win the customer back.[1]

Describe Staples's apparent management philosophy. How has the company implemented this philosophy? These issues are explored in Chapter 1.

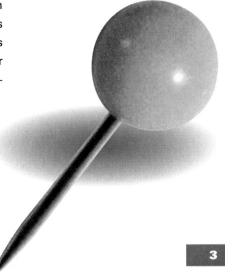

Staples Virtual Office Superstore How does Staples' WWW site reflect its commitment to service?
http://www.staples.com/

WHAT IS MARKETING?

1 Define the term *marketing.*

American Marketing Association
How does AMA Online target its resources to managers? to students?

http://www.ama.org/

marketing
The process of planning and executing the conception, pricing, promotion, and distribution of ideas, goods, and services to create exchanges that satisfy individual and organizational goals.

concept of exchange
Idea that people give up something to receive something they would rather have.

What does the term *marketing* mean to you? Many people think it means the same as personal selling. Others think marketing is the same as personal selling and advertising. Still others believe marketing has something to do with making products available in stores, arranging displays, and maintaining inventories of products for future sales. Actually, marketing includes all of these activities and more.

Marketing has two facets. First, it is a philosophy, an attitude, a perspective, or a management orientation that stresses customer satisfaction. Second, marketing is a set of activities used to implement this philosophy. The American Marketing Association's definition encompasses both perspectives: "**Marketing** is the process of planning and executing the conception, pricing, promotion, and distribution of ideas, goods, and services to create exchanges that satisfy individual and organizational goals."[2]

THE CONCEPT OF EXCHANGE

Exchange is the key term in the definition of marketing. The **concept of exchange** is quite simple. It means that people give up something to receive something they would rather have. Normally we think of money as the medium of exchange. We "give up" money to "get" the goods and services we want. Exchange does not require money, however. Two persons may barter or trade such items as baseball cards or oil paintings.

Five conditions must be satisfied for any kind of exchange to take place:

- There must be at least two parties.
- Each party must have something the other party values.
- Each party must be able to communicate with the other party and deliver the goods or services sought by the other trading party.
- Each party must be free to accept or reject the other's offer.
- Each party must want to deal with the other party.[3]

Exchange will not necessarily take place even if all these conditions exist. They are, however, necessary for exchange to be possible. For example, you may place an advertisement in your local newspaper stating that your used automobile is for sale at a certain price. Several people may call you to ask about the car, some may test-drive it, and one or more may even make you an offer. All five conditions are necessary for an exchange to exist. But unless you reach an agreement with a buyer and actually sell the car, an exchange will not take place. Notice that marketing can occur even if an exchange does not occur. In the example just discussed, you would have engaged in marketing even if no one bought your used automobile.

MARKETING MANAGEMENT PHILOSOPHIES

2 Describe four marketing management philosophies.

Four competing philosophies strongly influence an organization's marketing activities. These philosophies are commonly referred to as production, sales, marketing, and societal marketing orientations.

Production Orientation

A **production orientation** is a philosophy that focuses on the internal capabilities of the firm rather than on the desires and needs of the marketplace. A production orientation means that management assesses its resources and asks these questions: "What can we do best?" "What can our engineers design?" "What is easy to produce, given our equipment?" In the case of a service organization, managers ask, "What services are most convenient for the firm to offer?" and "Where do our talents lie?" Some have referred to this orientation as a "Field-of-Dreams" marketing strategy, referring to the movie line, "If we build it, they'll come."

There is nothing wrong with assessing a firm's capabilities; in fact, such assessments are major considerations in strategic marketing planning (see Chapter 2). A production orientation falls short because it does not consider whether the goods and services that the firm produces most efficiently also meet the needs of the marketplace. PPG Industries provides an interesting example. Throughout the 1980s researchers at PPG spent considerable time, effort, and money developing a bluish windshield that would let in filtered sunlight but block out the heat. Scientists were convinced that this new product would be significantly better than existing windshields. However, when the new windshield was introduced in 1991, the automobile manufacturers refused to buy it. They didn't like the color or the price. "We developed a great mousetrap, but there were no mice," reported Gary Weber, vice president for science and technology.[4]

A production orientation does not necessarily doom a company to failure, particularly not in the short run. Sometimes what a firm can best produce is exactly what the market wants. In other situations, as when competition is weak or demand exceeds supply, a production-oriented firm can survive and even prosper. More often, however, firms that succeed in competitive markets have a clear understanding that they must first determine what customers want and then produce it, rather than focus on what company management thinks should be produced.

production orientation
A philosophy that focuses on the internal capabilities of the firm rather than on the desires and needs of the marketplace.

Sales Orientation

A **sales orientation** is based on the ideas that people will buy more goods and services if aggressive sales techniques are used and that high sales result in high profits. Not only are sales to the final buyer emphasized, but intermediaries are also encouraged to push manufacturers' products more aggressively. To sales-oriented firms, marketing means selling things and collecting money.

sales orientation
Idea that people will buy more goods and services if aggressive sales techniques are used and that high sales result in high profits.

The fundamental problem with a sales orientation, as with a production orientation, is a lack of understanding of the needs and wants of the marketplace. Sales-oriented companies often find that, despite the quality of their sales force, they cannot convince people to buy goods or services that are neither wanted nor needed.

Marketing Orientation

marketing orientation
Philosophy that assumes that a sale does not depend on an aggressive sales force but rather on a customer's decision to purchase a product.

marketing concept
Idea that the social and economic justification for an organization's existence is the satisfaction of customer wants and needs while meeting organizational objectives.

A **marketing orientation,** which is the foundation of contemporary marketing philosophy, is based on an understanding that a sale depends not on an aggressive sales force, but rather on a customer's decision to purchase a product. What a business thinks it produces is not of primary importance to its success. Instead, what a customer thinks he or she is buying—the perceived value—defines a business. Perceived value also determines a business' products and its potential to prosper. To marketing-oriented firms, marketing means building relationships with customers.

This philosophy, called the **marketing concept,** is simple and intuitively appealing. It states that the social and economic justification for an organization's existence is the satisfaction of customer wants and needs while meeting organizational objectives. The marketing concept includes the following:

- Focusing on customer wants so the organization can distinguish its product(s) from competitors' offerings;

- Integrating all the organization's activities, including production, to satisfy these wants;

- Achieving long-term goals for the organization by satisfying customer wants and needs legally and responsibly.

Today, companies of all types are applying the marketing concept. For example, Wal-Mart Stores has become the leading discount retailer in the United States by focusing on what its customers want: everyday low prices, items always in stock, and cashiers always available. While Wal-Mart was growing

Wal-Mart has become the leading U.S. discount retailer by focusing on what customers want. The company's campaign to keep up its momentum includes building Supercenters that combine food and general merchandise.
Gary Krambeck/The Chicago Tribune

rapidly throughout the 1980s and 1990s, Sears Roebuck and Company was losing business to newer specialty stores, superstores, and discounters. What happened? Sears lost out to competitors that were doing a better job of satisfying customers' wants and needs. "We didn't know who we wanted to serve," concedes CEO Arthur C. Martinez. "That was a huge hole in our strategy. It was also not clear what basis we thought we could win against the competition."[5]

Wal-Mart Online
How does Wal-Mart Online reflect the company's commitment to its customers?
http://www.wal-mart.com/

Societal Marketing Orientation

One reason a marketing-oriented organization may choose not to deliver the benefits sought by customers is that these benefits may not be good for individuals or society. This important refinement of the marketing concept, called the **societal marketing concept,** states that an organization exists not only to satisfy customer wants and needs and to meet organizational objectives but also to preserve or enhance individuals' and society's long-term best interests. Marketing "environmentally friendly" products and containers, discussed in Chapter 20, is consistent with a societal marketing orientation. The "Ethics in Marketing" story in this section illustrates another aspect of the societal marketing concept.

societal marketing concept The idea that an organization exists not only to satisfy customer wants and needs and to meet organizational objectives but also to preserve or enhance individuals' and society's long-term best interests.

THE DIFFERENCES BETWEEN SALES AND MARKETING ORIENTATIONS

As noted at the beginning of this chapter, many people confuse the terms *sales* and *marketing*. These orientations are substantially different, however. Exhibit 1.1 compares the two orientations in terms of five characteristics: the organization's focus, the firm's business, those to whom the product is directed, the firm's primary goal, and tools the organization uses to achieve its goals.

3 Discuss the differences between sales and marketing orientations.

The Organization's Focus

Personnel in sales-oriented firms tend to be "inward looking," focusing on selling what the organization makes rather than making what the market wants. Many of the historic sources of competitive advantage—technology, innovation, economies of scale—allowed companies to focus their efforts internally and prosper.[6] Today, most successful firms have shifted to an external, customer-oriented focus. This focus acknowledges that no amount of technical superiority will bring success unless customer

Exhibit 1.1 *Differences between Sales and Marketing Orientations*

	What is the organization's focus?	What business are you in?	To whom is the product directed?	What is your primary goal?	How do you seek to achieve your goal?
Sales orientation	Inward, upon the organization's needs	Selling goods and services	Everybody	Profit through maximum sales volume	Primarily through intensive promotion
Marketing orientation	Outward, upon the wants and preferences of customers	Satisfying consumer wants and needs	Specific groups of people	Profit through customer satisfaction	Through coordinated marketing activities

Ethics in Marketing

"Alcopops": An Ethical Dilemma for U.S. Brewers

Have British schoolchildren heard about Hooper's Hooch, a new lemony alcoholic beverage from British brewer Bass PLC? You bet they have.

Mention the drink, which packs more alcohol than some beers, and a group of 13- and 14-year-olds in London begins chanting, "Hooch! Hooch! Hooch!" and reciting its slogan, "One taste and you're Hooched."

Alcoholic lemonades, colas, and orange drinks, known as "alcopops," are creating a huge stir in the alcoholic-beverage industry. Over a dozen different brands have been launched in Britain.

And now they are beginning to cross the Atlantic. Bass recently began test-marketing Hooper's Hooch in Miami and San Diego, and major U.S. brewers are said to be watching with interest. Britain's Thornlodge Ltd. says it's negotiating with an undisclosed American brewer for U.S. distribution of Mrs. Pucker's, a fruit-flavored alcoholic soda developed by a former Anheuser-Busch executive.

The trend alarms regulators and antialcohol groups, who say the sweet drinks, containing 4 percent to 5.5 percent alcohol, blatantly appeal to teenagers. Britain's Ad-vertising Standards Authority has banned a series of ads for Hooper's Hooch featuring a mischievous cartoon lemon, in a flap reminiscent of protests in the U.S. over the Joe Camel icon used in Camel cigarette advertising.

"These drinks are there to help people who don't have a taste for alcohol develop one," says Mark Bennett of the British advocacy group, Alcohol Concern. In Britain, where drinking laws are somewhat looser than in the U.S., youngsters under 18 can't purchase alcohol, but legally can drink it in certain restaurants and in their homes.

At a time when sales of most types of alcoholic beverages are stagnant, industry analysts say alcopops have the potential to become a major new category bridging the gap between beer and hard liquor. "There is a soft-drink generation that grew up drinking Pepsi and Coke and Orangina," says a London marketing consultant who monitors the beverage industry. "For them to move to drinking hard spirits, it's a big leap. Alcoholic soft drinks fit right in the middle."

Brewers and spirits companies contend the drinks are no more appealing to young people than other adult alcoholic beverages, and they stress that they are clearly labeled as to their alcohol content. Many explicitly use "alcoholic" in their brand names. Mrs. Pucker's label even states that the drink may taste like orangeade, but "it is deceptively strong in alcohol." Fermented fruit juice is the main ingredient of many of the brands, including Hooper's Hooch. Others get their kick from grain alcohol.

To suggest that the new drinks induce underage drinking is "totally false logic," says Jane Sabini, a spokeswoman for Bass' brewing unit. "If brands like Hooper's Hooch had not become available," she adds, "most underage drinkers would be drinking other alcoholic drinks just as they did before."[7]

Is it ethical for brewers to market so-called alcopops? Critics claim these products are aimed at teenagers. Brewers contend the drinks are no more appealing to young people than other adult alcoholic beverages. What do you think? Should these products be barred in the U.S.?

From feudalism to crowded medieval market-places to the Home Shopping Club, learn how marketers have sold their products throughout the ages at **Hot Link—A Brief History of Marketing**

customer value
The ratio of benefits to the sacrifice necessary to obtain those benefits.

needs are addressed. As Ford Motor Company Chairman, Alex Trotman, stated, "The customer, not Ford, determines how many vehicles we sell."[8] Key issues in developing competitive advantage today include creating customer value, maintaining customer satisfaction, and building long-term relationships.

Customer Value

Customer value is the ratio of benefits to the sacrifice necessary to obtain those benefits. The customer determines the value of both the benefits and the sacrifices. Creating customer value is a core business strategy of many successful firms. As American Airlines Chairman Robert L. Crandall has stated, "With business around the world becoming ever-more global, airlines, like other companies, must find ways to provide superior value."[9]

The automobile industry also illustrates the importance of creating customer value. To penetrate the fiercely competitive luxury automobile market, Lexus adopted a customer-driven approach, with particular emphasis on service. Lexus stresses product quality with a standard of zero defects in manufacturing. The service quality goal is to treat each customer as one would treat a guest in one's home, to pursue the perfect person-to-person relationship, and to strive to improve continually. This pursuit has enabled Lexus to establish a clear quality image and capture a significant share of the luxury car market. Customer value is explored in more detail in Chapter 13.

Customer Satisfaction

Customer satisfaction is the feeling that a product has met or exceeded the customer's expectations. Staples, the office supply retailer described at the beginning of this chapter, intends to offer great prices on its paper, pens, fax machines, and other office supplies, but its main strategy is to grow by providing customers with the best solutions to their problems. The idea is to emulate customer-intimate companies like Home Depot and Airborne Express. These companies do not pursue one-time transactions: They cultivate relationships.[10] Customer satisfaction is examined in more detail in Chapter 13.

Building Relationships

Relationship marketing is the name of a strategy that entails forging long-term partnerships with customers. Companies build relationships with customers by offering value and providing customer satisfaction. Companies benefit from repeat sales and referrals that lead to increases in sales, market share, and profits. Costs fall because it is less expensive to serve existing customers than to attract new ones. Keeping a customer costs about one-fourth of what it costs to attract a new customer, and the probability of retaining a customer is over 60 percent, while the probability of landing a new customer is less than 30 percent.[11]

Customers also benefit from stable relationships with suppliers. Business buyers have found that partnerships with their suppliers are essential to producing high-quality products while cutting costs.[12] Customers remain loyal to firms that provide them greater value and satisfaction than they expect from competing firms.[13] This value and satisfaction can come in a variety of forms ranging from financial benefits to a sense of well-being or confidence in a supplier to structural bonds.[14]

Frequent-flyer programs are an example of financial incentives to customers in exchange for their continuing patronage. After flying a certain number of miles or flying a specified number of times, the frequent-flyer program participant earns a free flight or some other award such as free lodging. Frequent-flyer programs en-

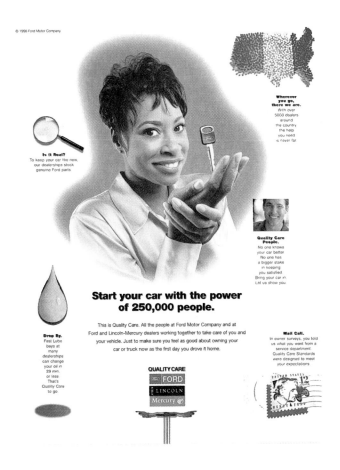

Start your car with the power of 250,000 people.

This is Quality Care. All the people at Ford Motor Company and at Ford and Lincoln-Mercury dealers working together to take care of you and your vehicle. Just to make sure you feel as good about owning your car or truck now as the first day you drove it home.

QUALITY CARE
FORD
LINCOLN
Mercury

Ford Motor Company, through its "Quality Care" advertising, focuses on customer needs. Technical superiority cannot guarantee success unless customers are satisfied.
Courtesy Ford Motor Company

Frequent flyer programs encourage customers to become loyal to specific airlines and rewards them for their continuing patronage.
© Terry Vine/Tiny Stone Images

courage customers to become loyal to specific airlines and reward them for this behavior.

A sense of well-being occurs when one establishes an ongoing relationship with a provider such as a physician, bank, hairdresser, or accountant. The social bonding that takes place between provider and customer involves personalization and customization of the relationship. Firms can enhance these bonds by referring to customers by name and providing continuity of service through the same representative.[15]

Federal Express' Powership program, which installs computer terminals in the offices of high-volume customers, is an example of structural bonding. Powership comprises a series of automated shipping and invoicing systems that save customers time and money while solidifying their loyalty to Federal Express. The systems are scaled to customers' usage. Customers receive a free electronic weighing scale, microcomputer terminal with modem, bar-code scanner, and laser printer. Powership rates packages with the correct charges, combines package weights by destination to provide volume discounts, and prints address labels from the customer's own database. Users can automatically prepare their own invoices, analyze their shipping expenses, and trace their packages through Federal Express' tracking system.[16]

Customer-Oriented Personnel

For an organization to be focused on customers, employees' attitudes and actions must be customer oriented. An employee may be the only contact a particular customer has with the firm. In that customer's eyes, the employee is the firm. Any person, department, or division that is not customer oriented weakens the positive image of the entire organization. For example, a potential customer who is greeted discourteously may well assume that the employee's attitude represents the whole firm.

According to J. W. "Bill" Marriott, Jr., CEO of Marriott International, "Our basic philosophy is to make sure our associates (employees) are very happy and that they work to go the extra mile—take care of customers and have fun doing it."[17] Every employee is cross-trained to handle all major guest services. Many other successful companies are making sure their employees focus on customers' needs.

The Role of Training

Leading marketers recognize the role of employee training in customer service. For example, all new employees at Disneyland and Walt Disney World must attend Disney University, a special training program for Disney employees. They must first pass Traditions 1, a daylong course focusing on the Disney philosophy and operational procedures. Then they go on to specialized training. Similarly, McDonald's has Hamburger University. At American Express' Quality University, line employees and managers learn how to treat customers. There is an extra payoff for companies such as Disney and McDonald's that train their employees to be customer oriented. When employees make their customers happy, the employees are more likely to derive satisfaction from their jobs. Having contented workers who are committed to their jobs leads to better customer service and greater employee retention.

American Express
How does American Express market its services to small business via the WWW?

http://www.americanexpress.com/

Empowerment

In addition to training, many marketing-oriented firms are giving employees more authority to solve customer problems on the spot. The term used to describe this delegation of authority is **empowerment.** Federal Express' customer service representatives are trained and empowered to resolve customer problems. Although the average Federal Express transaction costs only $16, the customer service representatives are empowered to spend up to $100 to resolve a customer problem.[18]

Employees of Satisfaction Guaranteed Eateries, Inc., a highly successful restaurant chain whose motto is synonymous with its name, have wide authority to please customers. Founder and CEO Timothy Firnstal states: "I instituted the idea that employees could and should do *anything* to keep the customer happy. In the event of an error or delay, any employee, right down to the busboy, could provide complimentary wine or desserts, or pick up the entire tab, if necessary."[19] Empowerment gives customers the feeling that their concerns are being addressed and gives employees the feeling that their expertise matters. The result is greater satisfaction for both customers and employees.

empowerment
Delegation of authority to solve customers' problems quickly—usually by the first person that the customer notifies regarding a problem.

Teamwork

Many organizations, such as Southwest Airlines and Walt Disney World, that are frequently noted for delivering superior customer value and providing high levels of customer satisfaction assign employees to teams and teach them team-building skills. **Teamwork** entails collaborative efforts of people to accomplish common objectives. Job performance, company performance, product value, and customer satisfaction all improve when people in the same department or work group begin supporting and assisting each other, and emphasize cooperation instead of competition.[20] Performance is also enhanced when people in different areas of responsibility such as production and sales or sales and service practice teamwork, with the ultimate goal of delivering superior customer value and satisfaction.

teamwork
Collaborative efforts of people to accomplish common objectives.

The Firm's Business

As Exhibit 1.1 illustrates, a sales-oriented firm defines its business (or mission) in terms of goods and services. A marketing-oriented firm defines its business in terms of the benefits its customers seek. People who spend their money, time, and energy expect to receive benefits, not just goods and services. This distinction has enormous implications.

Teamwork—the collaborative efforts of people in different areas of responsibility—enhances job performance.
© David Joel/Tony Stone Images

Because of the limited way it defines its business, a sales-oriented firm often misses opportunities to serve customers whose wants can be met through only a wide range of product offerings instead of specific products. For example, in 1990 Encyclopedia Britannica earned more than $40 million after taxes. Just four years later, after three consecutive years of losses, the sales force had collapsed. How did this respected company sink so low? Britannica managers saw that competitors were beginning to use CD-ROM to store huge masses of information but chose to ignore the new computer technology.[21] It's not hard to see why parents would rather give their children an encyclopedia on a compact disc instead of a printed one. The CD versions are either given away or sold by other publishers for under $400. A full set of the Encyclopedia Britannica costs a minimum of $1,500, weighs 118 pounds, and takes four and a half feet of shelf space.[22] If Britannica had defined its business as providing information instead of publishing books, it might not have suffered such a precipitous fall.

Answering the question "What is this firm's business?" in terms of the benefits customers seek, instead of goods and services, has at least three important advantages:

- It ensures that the firm keeps focusing on customers and avoids becoming preoccupied with goods, services, or the organization's internal needs.
- It encourages innovation and creativity by reminding people that there are many ways to satisfy customer wants.
- It stimulates an awareness of changes in customer desires and preferences so that product offerings are more likely to remain relevant.

The marketing concept and the idea of focusing on customer wants do not mean that customers will always receive everything they want. It is not possible, for example, to profitably manufacture and market for $25 automobile tires that will last for 100,000 miles. Furthermore, customers' preferences must be mediated by sound professional judgment as to how to deliver the benefits they seek. As one adage suggests, "People don't know what they want—they only want what they know." Consumers have a limited set of experiences. They are unlikely to request anything beyond those experiences because they are not aware of benefits they may gain from other potential offerings. For example, before the automobile, people knew they wanted quicker, more convenient transportation, but could not express their need for a car.

Those to Whom the Product Is Directed

A sales-oriented organization targets its products at "everybody" or "the average customer." A marketing-oriented organization aims at specific groups of people (see Exhibit 1.1). The fallacy of developing products directed at the average user is that relatively few average users actually exist. Typically, populations are characterized by diversity. An average is simply a midpoint in some set of characteristics. Because most potential customers are not "average," they are not likely to be attracted to an average product marketed to the average customer.

Consider the market for shampoo as one simple example. There are shampoos for oily hair, dry hair, and dandruff. Some shampoos remove the gray or color hair. Special shampoos are marketed for infants and elderly people. There is even shampoo for people with average or normal hair (whatever that is), but this is a fairly small portion of the total market for shampoo. A marketing-oriented organization recognizes that different customer groups and their wants vary. It may therefore need to develop different goods, services, and promotional appeals. A marketing-oriented organization carefully analyzes the market and divides it into groups of people who are fairly similar in terms of selected characteristics. Then the organization develops marketing programs that will bring about mutually satisfying exchanges with one or more of those groups. Consider this example:

Paying attention to the customer isn't exactly a new concept. Back in the 1920s, General Motors Corporation helped write the book on customer satisfaction by designing cars for every lifestyle and pocketbook. This was a breakthrough for an industry that had been largely driven by production needs ever since Henry Ford promised any color as long as it was black. Chapter 8 thoroughly explores the topic of analyzing markets and selecting those that appear to be most promising to the firm.

The Firm's Primary Goal

As Exhibit 1.1 illustrates, a sales-oriented organization seeks to achieve profitability through sales volume and tries to convince potential customers to buy, even if the seller knows that the customer and product are mismatched. Sales-oriented organizations place a higher premium on making a sale than on developing a long-term relationship with a customer. In contrast, the ultimate goal of most marketing-oriented organizations is to make a profit by creating customer value, providing customer satisfaction, and building long-term relationships with customers.

Tools the Organization Uses to Achieve Its Goals

Sales-oriented organizations seek to generate sales volume through intensive promotional activities, mainly personal selling and advertising. In contrast, marketing-oriented organizations recognize that promotion decisions are only one of four basic marketing-tools decisions that have to be made: product decisions, place (or distribution) decisions, promotion decisions, and pricing decisions. Chapters 10 through 19 focus on these topics. A marketing-oriented organization recognizes each of these four components as important. On the other hand, sales-oriented organizations view promotion as the primary means of achieving their goals.

A Word of Caution

This comparison of sales and marketing orientations is not meant to belittle the role of promotion, especially personal selling, in the marketing mix. Promotion is the means by which organizations communicate with present and prospective customers about the merits and characteristics of their organization and products. Effective promotion is an essential part of effective marketing. Salespeople who work for marketing-oriented organizations are generally perceived by their customers to be problem solvers and important links to supply sources and new products. Chapter 18 examines the nature of personal selling in more detail.

IMPLEMENTATION OF THE MARKETING CONCEPT

In an established organization, changing to a customer-driven corporate culture must occur gradually. Furthermore, middle managers alone cannot effect a change in corporate culture; they must have the total support of the CEO and other top executives. According to Thomas J. Pritzker, president of Hyatt Hotels, the notion that a customer orientation can just be turned on is a fallacy: "Management has to set a tone and then constantly push, push, push."[23]

4 Explain how firms implement the marketing concept.

The success of Nordstrom, the Seattle-based retailer, illustrates the results of strong management support for customer-oriented service. Employees can do almost anything to satisfy shoppers. One story, which the company doesn't deny, tells of a customer who got his money back on a tire, even though Nordstrom doesn't sell tires. In 1993, Nordstrom received the highest overall customer satisfaction rating from 2,000 shoppers who participated in a study ranking 70 U.S. retail and department store chains on attributes such as price, convenience, and quality of offerings.[24]

Changes in Authority and Responsibility

Changing from a production or sales orientation to a marketing orientation often requires major revisions in relationships within the firm. Nonmarketing people who have been making marketing decisions, such as production managers, may suddenly lose their authority. Personnel in such areas as marketing research may find that they have gained considerable authority. One way of winning acceptance for the marketing concept is to get everyone who will be affected by the change to participate in the planning process. It is important to remember, however, that during a period of change, some human relations problems are inevitable. Implementing the marketing concept slowly rather than in a revolutionary fashion normally smooths the transition.

When a person or a company has been doing something a certain way for many years, change often comes very hard. For example, the top management of Xerox Corporation spent much of the 1970s building huge layers of bureaucracy and wasting millions of dollars developing products that never reached the marketplace. It took Xerox ten years to realize that its old strategy of throwing people at problems and raising prices as costs went up just wouldn't work. It wasn't until 1980 that Xerox finally realized how capable its Japanese counterparts were and how little Xerox knew about customer wants.[25] At that point, the company started making the changes that eventually pulled it out of the doldrums.

Front-Line Experience for Management

Detroit Diesel Corporation requires all managers and distributors to call or visit four customers a day. At Xerox, executives spend one day a month taking complaints from customers about machines, bills, and service. At Hyatt Hotels, senior executives, including the president, put in time as bellhops.[26] Marriott International's CEO logs an average of 200,000 travel miles each year visiting the company's hotels, inspecting them, and talking to employees at all levels in the organization. According to Bill Marriott, "CEOs don't listen enough. The people who work for them know more about their particular areas than the chief executive."[27] Walt Disney World's managers also join the "front line" each year to participate in a program called *cross utilization*. For a week, the bosses sell tickets or popcorn, dish out ice cream or hot dogs, load and unload rides, park cars, drive the monorail or trains, or take on any of the 100 "onstage" jobs that make the park come alive for guests.

Southwest Airlines CEO Herb Kelleher spends at least one day every quarter doing another job.
© Nation's Business/T. Michael Keza

THE MARKETING PROCESS

Marketing managers are responsible for a variety of activities that together represent the marketing process. These include:

5 Describe the marketing process.

- Understanding the organization's mission and the role marketing plays in fulfilling that mission.
- Setting marketing objectives.
- Gathering, analyzing, and interpreting information about the organization's situation, including its strengths and weaknesses, as well as opportunities and threats in the environment. The "Global Perspectives" box in this chapter illustrates the importance of analyzing situations.
- Developing a marketing strategy by deciding exactly which wants, and whose wants, the organization will try to satisfy (target market strategy), and by developing appropriate marketing activities (the marketing mix) to satisfy the desires of selected target markets. The marketing mix combines product, distribution, promotion, and pricing strategies in a way that creates exchanges that satisfy individual and organizational goals.
- Implementing the marketing strategy.
- Designing performance measures.
- Periodically evaluating marketing efforts, and making changes if needed.

These activities and their relationships form the foundation on which the rest of the book is based. The table of contents at the beginning shows the order in which the activities are described. Exhibit 2.1 in Chapter 2 illustrates their interrelationships.

Global Perspectives

China: A $300 Billion Consumer Market

China is catching up to the hyperbole it excited, prematurely, years ago: a place that can make or break multinationals. Until recently, makers of cosmetics, beverages, shampoo, soap, and other daily goods considered China a frontier outpost, a place to test the waters with small joint ventures and limited distribution. Now, P&G, S. C. Johnson & Sons, Inc., and Johnson & Johnson of the U.S., along with Unilever Group of Britain and the Netherlands, Henkel KGAA and Wella AG of Germany, Kao Corp. of Japan, and Nestle SA of Switzerland, all invest lavishly and deem anything less than nationwide sales a failure.

And that's probably only the beginning. Consumer goods spending, at $300 billion per year in 1994, is rising much faster in China than in any developed country. P&G's sales have surged 50 percent a year. Here is how John Pepper, P&G's chief executive and a principal architect of its China strategy, figures it: If the average Chinese doubles spending on laundry detergent by the year 2000, as P&G expects, the company's sales in

that category alone will rise to $500 million—even assuming that P&G doesn't raise its current 20 percent market share. "The potential is enormous for us in China," Mr. Pepper says. "One out of five people in the world lives there, and we have the kinds of products people use day in and day out."[28]

Why have European and U.S. firms been so slow in aggressively marketing in China? What other consumer products companies should consider the market opportunity in China? Why do you think China's government is allowing Western companies such easy access to consumer markets?

WHY STUDY MARKETING?

6 Describe several reasons for studying marketing.

Now that you understand the meaning of the term *marketing*, why it is important to adopt a marketing orientation, and how organizations implement this philosophy, you may be asking, "What's in it for me?" or "Why should I study marketing?" These are important questions, whether you are majoring in a business field other than marketing (such as accounting, finance, or management information systems) or a non-business field (such as journalism, economics, or agriculture). There are several important reasons to study marketing: Marketing plays an important role in society, marketing is important to businesses, marketing offers outstanding career opportunities, and marketing affects your life every day.

Marketing Plays an Important Role in Society

U.S. Census Bureau
How might you use the Census Bureau's WWW site to analyze a specific market segment?

http://www.census.gov/

The U.S. Bureau of the Census predicts that the total population of the United States will reach 268 million by the end of the 1990s. Think about how many transactions are needed each day to feed, clothe, and shelter a population of this size. The number is huge. And yet it all works quite well, partly because the well-developed U.S. economic system efficiently distributes the output of farms and factories. A typical U.S. family, for example, consumes 2.5 tons of food a year. Marketing makes food available when we want it, in desired quantities, at accessible locations, and in sanitary and convenient packages and forms (such as instant and frozen foods).

Marketing Is Important to Businesses

Marketing makes food available when we want it, in desired quantities, at accessible locations, and in sanitary and convenient packages and forms.
© 1994 Ted Horowitz/The Stock Market

The fundamental objectives of most businesses are survival, profits, and growth. Marketing contributes directly to achieving these objectives. Marketing includes the following activities, which are vital to business organizations: assessing the wants and satisfactions of present and potential customers, designing and managing product offerings, determining prices and pricing policies, developing distribution strategies, and communicating with present and potential customers.

All businesspeople, regardless of specialization or area of responsibility, need to be familiar with the terminology and fundamentals of accounting, finance, management, and marketing. People in all business areas need to be able to communicate with specialists in other areas. Furthermore, marketing is not just a job done by people in a marketing department. Marketing is a part of the job of everyone in the organization. As David Packard of Hewlett Packard put it: "Marketing is too important to be left to the marketing department."[29] Therefore, a basic understanding of marketing is important to all businesspeople.

Marketing Offers Outstanding Career Opportunities

Between a fourth and a third of the entire civilian workforce in the United States performs marketing activities. Marketing offers great career opportunities in such ar-

Marketing and Small Business

Choosing a Franchisor

Have you ever thought about owning and operating your own business? If so, have you considered becoming part of a franchise organization such as McDonald's, Pizza Hut, Weight Watchers, Century 21, or H&R Block?

Franchising, discussed in more detail in Chapter 15, is a huge and rapidly growing industry that includes more than 3,000 franchisors and over 550,000 franchisees. *Business Week* offers the following tips for choosing a franchisor:

- Select a company with a well-accepted trademark.
- Talk to current franchisees and those who have recently left the system. Franchisors are required by law to provide such names.
- Ask franchisors about any litigation against the company and research it further.
- Evaluate the franchisor's busi-

ness and marketing plans. Make sure ad dollars will get pumped back into your franchise market.
- Keep a record of conversations, including date, persons talked to, and promises made. Some issues to consider are How close by can the franchisor place a competing unit? and Are franchisees subject to mandatory arbitration?
- Include any promises made by the franchisor in the final written agreement. Otherwise, they probably won't be binding.
- Work with an experienced franchise attorney and a financial consultant who understands the franchising business.[30]

For more information about franchising, contact one or more of the following associations:

American Association of
   Franchisees and Dealers
P. O. Box 81887
San Diego, California 92138-1887
Telephone: (619) 235-2556
Franchisee Infoline: 1 (800)
   733-9585

American Franchisee Association
53 W. Jackson Blvd., Suite 205
Chicago, Illinois 60604
Telephone: 1 (800) 334-4232

International Franchise Assn.
1350 New York Ave., 9th Floor
Washington, D. C. 20005-4709
Telephone: (202) 628-8000

 http://www.franchise-conxions.com/franchise_org.html
(Franchise ConXions list of franchise associations)

"Compared to the fast food franchise we had before, Mail Boxes Etc.® is a piece of cake."

Laura and Cecil Triplet,
Owners, Mail Boxes Etc. #2315
Elk Grove, California

"Sure, we work hard now, too. It takes patience and energy to make a go of any business. Before we decided on MBE, we did our homework. We read what the experts had to say. We saw opportunity with MBE.

Two years ago we opened our MBE Center in Elk Grove, California. Ours is one of over 3,000 Centers worldwide. The advantages of being part of a large national network like this are many — like the training, national advertising, and local and national support."

If you have an appetite for opportunity, look into Mail Boxes Etc. today. Call 1-800-456-0414 for more information on franchising opportunities in the U.S. and internationally. In Canada call 1-800-661-MBEC.

#1 Business Services Franchise in the world.

MBE MAIL BOXES ETC.

IT'S NOT WHAT WE DO. IT'S HOW WE DO IT.™

Mail Boxes Etc.® Franchised Centers are independently owned and operated ©1996 Mail Boxes Etc *Entrepreneur Magazine, 1993, 1994 1995, and 1996

Mail Boxes Etc. is one of thousands of franchises in a huge and growing industry.
© Courtesy Mail Boxes Etc., USA, Inc.

eas as professional selling, marketing research, advertising, retail buying, distribution management, product management, product development, and wholesaling. Marketing career opportunities also exist in a variety of nonbusiness organizations, including hospitals, museums, universities, the armed forces, and various government and social service agencies. (See Chapter 12.)

As the world marketplace becomes more challenging, U.S. companies of all sizes are going to have to become better marketers. The "Marketing and Small Business" box in this chapter offers several tips for those who might be interested in owning and operating their own business franchise. The American Marketing Association also publishes a book, *Careers in Marketing and the Employment Kit*, that provides extensive information about career opportunities in marketing.

Marketing Affects Your Life Every Day

Marketing plays a major role in your everyday life. You participate in the marketing process as a consumer of goods and services. About half of every dollar you spend pays for marketing costs, such as marketing research, product development, packaging, transportation, storage, advertising, and sales expenses. By developing a better understanding of marketing, you will become a better-informed consumer. You will better understand the buying process and be able to negotiate more effectively with sellers. Moreover, you will be better prepared to demand satisfaction when the goods and services you buy do not meet the standards promised by the manufacturer or the marketer.

LOOKING AHEAD

This book is divided into 21 chapters organized into six major parts. The chapters are written from the marketing manager's perspective. Each chapter begins with a brief list of learning objectives followed by a short story about a marketing situation faced by a firm or industry. At the end of each of these opening vignettes, thought-provoking questions link the story to the subject addressed in the chapter. Your instructor may wish to begin chapter discussions by asking members of your class to share their views about the questions.

The examples of global marketing highlighted in most chapters will help you understand that marketing takes place all over the world, between buyers and sellers in different countries. These and other global marketing examples throughout the book, marked with the icon shown in the margin, are intended to help you develop a global perspective on marketing.

Examples of efforts to enhance customer value and quality are provided throughout the book and marked with the icon shown in the margin.

Marketing ethics is another important topic selected for special treatment throughout the book. Chapters include highlighted stories about firms or industries that have faced ethical dilemmas or have engaged in practices that some consider unethical. Questions are posed to focus your thinking on the key ethical issues raised in each story.

Entrepreneurship and small-business applications are also highlighted with icons and special boxes. Every chapter also includes an application case related to small business. This material illustrates how entrepreneurs and small businesses can use the principles and concepts discussed in the book.

End-of-chapter materials include a final comment on the chapter-opening vignette ("Looking Back"), a summary of the major topics examined, a listing of the key terms introduced in the chapter, and discussion and writing questions (writing questions are identified with the icon in the margin). Specific Internet and Team activities appear in the writing and discussion questions. These are identified by appropriate icons. Video cases with discussion questions conclude each chapter. All these features are intended to help you develop a more thorough understanding of marketing and enjoy the learning process.

The remaining chapters in Part 1 introduce you to the activities involved in developing a marketing plan, the dynamic environment in which marketing decisions must be made, and global marketing. Part 2 covers consumer decision making and buyer behavior; business-to-business marketing; the concepts of positioning, market segmentation, and targeting; and the nature and uses of marketing research and decision support systems. Parts 3 through 6 examine the elements of the marketing mix—product, distribution, promotion, and pricing. An appendix describing a variety of careers in marketing concludes the book.

LOOKING BACK

Look back at the story at the beginning of this chapter about Staples office supply firm. You should now find the questions at the end of the story to be simple and straightforward. All evidence indicates that Staples is a customer-oriented firm with a commitment to delivering customer satisfaction and value. Staples is also committed to establishing long-term relationships with customers. This is a good illustration of the marketing concept in action.

In September 1996, Staples merged with its largest competitor, Office Depot, Inc. The merger created a new company, Staples/Office Depot, with more than 1,000 stores and revenues of $10 billion. The merged stores, now called "Staples, The Office Depot," control about 10 percent of the U.S. retail office supply business, about three times the market share of their largest competitor, Office Max, Inc. The former competitors pursued similar operating philosophies: discount prices and excellent customer service.

SUMMARY

1 *Define the term marketing.* The ultimate goal of all marketing activity is to facilitate mutually satisfying exchanges between parties. The activities of marketing include the conception, pricing, promotion, and distribution of ideas, goods, and services.

2 *Describe four marketing management philosophies.* The role of marketing and the character of marketing activities within an organization are strongly influenced by its philosophy and orientation. A production-oriented organization focuses on the internal capabilities of the firm rather than on the desires and needs of the marketplace. A sales orientation is based on the beliefs that people will buy more products if aggressive sales techniques are used and that high sales volumes produce high profits. A marketing-oriented organization focuses on satisfying customer wants and needs while meeting organizational objectives. A societal marketing orientation goes beyond a marketing orientation to include the preservation or enhancement of individuals' and society's long-term best interests.

3 *Discuss the differences between sales and marketing orientations.* First, sales-oriented firms focus on their own needs; marketing-oriented firms focus on customers' needs and preferences. Second, sales-oriented companies consider themselves to be deliverers of goods and services, whereas marketing-oriented companies view themselves as satisfiers of customers. Third, sales-oriented firms direct their products to everyone; marketing-oriented firms aim at specific segments of the population. Fourth, although the primary goal of both types of firms is profit, sales-oriented businesses pursue maximum sales volume through intensive promotion, whereas marketing-oriented businesses pursue customer satisfaction through coordinated marketing activities.

KEY TERMS

concept of exchange *4*

customer satisfaction *10*

customer value *8*

empowerment *11*

marketing *4*

marketing concept *6*

marketing orientation *6*

production orientation *5*

relationship marketing *10*

sales orientation *5*

societal marketing concept *7*

teamwork *11*

4 *Explain how firms implement the marketing concept.* To implement the marketing concept successfully, management must enthusiastically embrace and endorse the concept and encourage its spread throughout the organization. Changing from a production or sales orientation to a marketing orientation often requires changes in authority and responsibility and front-line experience for management.

5 *Describe the marketing process.* The marketing process includes understanding the organization's mission and the role marketing plays in fulfilling that mission, setting marketing objectives, scanning the environment, developing a marketing strategy by selecting a target market strategy, developing and implementing a marketing mix, implementing the strategy, designing performance measures, evaluating marketing efforts and making changes if needed. The marketing mix combines product, distribution (place), promotion, and pricing strategies in a way that creates exchanges satisfying to individual and organizational objectives.

6 *Describe several reasons for studying marketing.* First, marketing affects the allocation of goods and services that influence a nation's economy and standard of living. Second, an understanding of marketing is crucial to understanding most businesses. Third, career opportunities in marketing are diverse, profitable, and expected to increase significantly during the 1990s. Fourth, understanding marketing makes consumers more informed.

Discussion and Writing Questions

1. Your company president has decided to restructure the firm and become more market oriented. She is going to announce the changes at an upcoming meeting. She has asked you to prepare a short speech outlining the general reasons for the new company orientation.

2. Donald E. Petersen, chairman of the board of Ford Motor Company, remarked, "If we aren't customer driven, our cars won't be either." Explain how this statement reflects the marketing concept.

3. A friend of yours agrees with the adage "People don't know what they want—they only want what they know." Write your friend a letter expressing the extent to which you think marketers shape consumer wants.

4. Your local supermarket's slogan is "It's your store." However, when you asked one of the stock people to help you find a bag of chips, he told you it was not his job and that you should look a little harder. On your way out, you noticed a sign with an address for complaints. Draft a letter explaining why the supermarket's slogan will never be credible unless their employees carry it out.

5. Give an example of a company that might be successfully following a production orientation. Why might a firm in this industry be successful following such an orientation?

6. Form a small group of three or four members. Suppose you and your colleagues all work for an up-and-coming gourmet coffee company that has several stores, mostly in large cities across the United States. Your team has been assigned the task of assessing whether or not the company should begin marketing on the Internet.

   Each member has been assigned to visit three or four Internet sites for ideas. Some possibilities are:

   Toys R Us at
   http://www.toysrus.com

   Walmart at
   http://www.wal-mart.com

   Godiva chocolates at
   http://www.godiva.com

   Levi Strauss at
   http://www.levi.com

   Use your imagination and look up others. As you can see, many companies are easy to find, as long as you can spell their names. Typically, you would use the following:

   http://www.companyname.com

   Has Internet marketing helped the companies whose sites you visited? If so, how? What factors should your company consider before committing to Internet activity? Prepare a 3–5 minute presentation to give to your class.

7. What is the AMA? What does it do? How do its services benefit marketers?

   http://www.ama.org/

8. What is an ExciteSeeing Tour? What kind of business tours does this site offer?

   http://tours.excite.com/

Application for Small Business

Christine Louise graduated from college in June 1995 and decided to open a women's footwear store called Sisi's Shoes. Since high school, she had always wanted to run her own business. On the very first day the store was open, a customer asked Christine if she guaranteed the products she sold. Christine proudly replied, "Every shoe that is purchased from Sisi's Shoes has a lifetime guarantee. If at any time you are not satisfied with your shoes, you can return them to the store for a full refund of your purchase price."

Questions

1. What marketing management philosophy is Christine expressing? Why have you reached this conclusion?

2. Do you think a lifetime guarantee for this kind of product is too generous? Why or why not?

3. Do you think this policy will contribute to success or to bankruptcy?

4. Suggest other customer-service policies that might be appropriate for Sisi's Shoes.

Lanier Worldwide

Lanier Worldwide, a subsidiary of Harris Corp., markets office products in every county and parish in the United States and in over 80 other countries. Lanier serves over one million small, medium-size, and large business customers in the U.S. alone. Product offerings include copying systems, facsimile systems, information management systems, dictation systems, and presentation systems. From fiscal 1995 to 1996, sales increased 9 percent and net income grew by 27 percent. Sales were strong in both domestic and international markets.

Lanier's stated mission is "to be recognized worldwide as the preferred provider of office solutions, dedicated to total customer satisfaction." Every one of Lanier's more than 7,500 employees, including the president and CEO, knows his or her responsibilities in achieving the corporate mission.

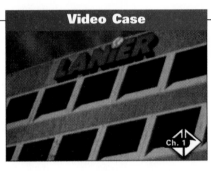

Video Case

Ch. 1

The philosophy unifying all Lanier employees, regardless of job title or responsibility, is called Customer Vision. Simply stated, Customer Vision means seeing Lanier's business through its customers' eyes and responding to their needs as a team, at or above expectations. It is a philosophy adhered to by Lanier and its dealer operations. It encompasses all products. Most importantly, Customer Vision differentiates Lanier from its competition.

According to industry analysts, Lanier backs its wide array of office solutions with the most comprehensive performance and service guarantee in the market. If a customer is dissatisfied with a new Lanier system, he or she need only request a replacement with similar features.

Depending on the product, Lanier's Performance Promise also guarantees 98 to 100 percent uptime; reimbursement for downtime; free loaners; toll-free after-hours technical assistance every day of the year; and the availability of parts and supplies for no less than 10 years.

Questions

1. Describe Lanier's marketing management philosophy. Cite information from the case and video to support your answer.

2. Why does Lanier's mission statement refer to office solutions rather than office products?

3. Explain how Lanier has implemented its marketing management philosophy.

4. What is an internal customer? How does a company like Lanier market to internal customers?

LEARNING OBJECTIVES *After studying this chapter, you should be able to:*

1 Understand the importance of strategic marketing and writing the marketing plan.

2 Define an appropriate business mission statement.

3 Know the criteria for stating good marketing objectives.

4 Explain the components of a situation analysis.

5 Identify strategic alternatives and describe tools used to help select alternatives.

6 Discuss target market strategies.

7 Describe elements of the marketing mix.

8 Understand why implementation, evaluation, and control of the marketing plan is necessary.

9 Know how to structure a basic marketing plan.

10 Identify several techniques that help make strategic planning effective.

Strategic Planning: Developing and Implementing a Marketing Plan

The corporate jet business reached a low point in 1992, but business has been growing each year since. Cessna Aircraft Corporation and Gulfstream Aircraft, Inc., introduced new business jets during 1996. The Cessna Citation X and the Gulfstream V offer different product benefits that do not make them directly competitive with each other.

The Citation X, at 600 miles per hour, is the fastest civilian airplane (except for the Concorde). Cessna boasts that its plane can fly executives from New York to California for breakfast and then back to the East Coast in time for dinner. Compared with slower planes, a Citation X can save 190 hours of executive time in a typical year. The speed capability means more ground time without violating pilot-fatigue guidelines. The plane, which holds 12 passengers and two pilots, is priced at about $18 million.

The Gulfstream V is priced at about $35 million. The plane boasts the advantage of range: It can go 7,500 miles without refueling, making it the longest range business jet. Instead of a speed advantage, it offers more space and can hold up to 18 passengers. In addition, company spokespersons argue that by refueling less

often, there is less ground time, which makes travel time faster without faster airspeeds. Further, the Gulfstream V can cruise at 51,000 feet, which puts it above commercial airliners and above headwinds. That means the plane can set its course as the shortest distance between two points rather than flying around air traffic and weather patterns.

Into this growth market come the competitors: Canada's Bombardier, Inc., which makes Learjets, has the Global Express, with a range and size similar to the Gulfstream V, but for $5 million less. France and Israel also have $15 million midsize jets, but not as fast as the Citation X.[1] The most unusual competitor is the Carter-Copter, a hybrid airplane helicopter that can fly nonstop from New York to Los

Angeles at 400 miles per hour (a 6½-hour flight). Traditional helicopters can't go faster than 250 miles per hour. The CarterCopter is powered by an inexpensive V-6 race-car engine and carries five people.[2]

How do manufacturers of new products plan to bring their offerings to the marketplace? How can the Citation X, Gulfstream V, and Carter-Copter be marketed successfully, given the competition?

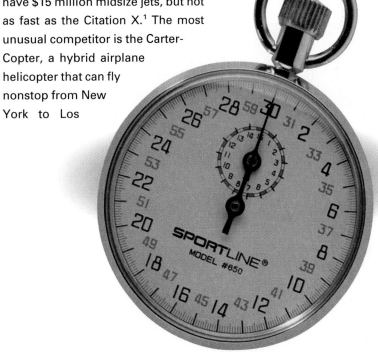

THE NATURE OF STRATEGIC PLANNING

1 Understand the importance of strategic marketing and writing the marketing plan.

strategic planning
The managerial process of creating and maintaining a fit between the organization's objectives and resources and evolving market opportunities.

planning
The process of anticipating future events and determining strategies to achieve organizational objectives in the future.

marketing planning
Designing activities relating to marketing objectives and the changing marketing environment.

This ad reflects Compaq's decision to switch its target market to consumers who buy personal computers. This strategy is proving very successful.
Courtesy Compaq Computer Corporation

Strategic planning is the managerial process of creating and maintaining a fit between the organization's objectives and resources and evolving market opportunities. The goal of strategic planning is long-run profitability and growth. Thus, strategic decisions require long-term commitments of resources.

A strategic error can threaten the firm's survival. On the other hand, a good strategic plan can help protect a firm's resources against competitive onslaughts.[3] For instance, if the March of Dimes had decided to focus on fighting polio, the organization would no longer exist. Most of us view polio as a conquered disease. The March of Dimes survived by making the strategic decision to switch to fighting birth defects.

Strategic marketing management addresses two questions: What is the organization's main activity at a particular time? How will it reach its goals? Here are some examples of strategic decisions:

- Black & Decker's decision to buy General Electric's small consumer appliance division (a strategic success)
- Sears and IBM's joint effort to create the Prodigy on-line computer service, a billion-dollar investment (a strategic failure)
- Procter & Gamble's decision to move to everyday low pricing (a strategic success)
- Compaq Computer Corporation's decision to broaden its product line from leading-edge, high-performance PC products to include the entire range of quality, value-priced desktop, portable and PC servers for all customers. (a strategic success)

All these decisions have affected or will affect each organization's long-run course, its allocation of resources, and ultimately its financial success. In contrast, an operating decision, such as changing the package design for Post's cornflakes or altering the sweetness of a Seven Seas salad dressing, probably won't have a big impact on the long-run profitability of the company.

How do companies go about strategic marketing planning? How do employees know how to implement the long-term goals of the firm? The answer is a marketing plan.

WHAT IS A MARKETING PLAN?

Planning is the process of anticipating events and determining strategies to achieve organizational objectives in the future. **Marketing planning** involves designing activities relating to marketing objectives and the changing marketing environment. Marketing planning is the basis for all marketing strategies and decisions. Issues such as product lines, distribution channels, marketing communications, and pricing are all delineated in the **marketing plan**. The marketing plan is a written document that acts as a guidebook of marketing activities for the marketing manager. In this chapter, you will learn the importance of writing a marketing plan and the types of information contained in a marketing plan.

Why Write a Marketing Plan?

By specifying objectives and defining the actions required to attain them, a marketing plan provides the basis by which actual and expected performance can be compared. Marketing can be one of the most expensive and complicated business components, but is one of the most important business activities. The written marketing plan provides clearly stated activities that help employees understand and work toward common goals.

Writing a marketing plan allows you to examine the marketing environment in conjunction with the inner workings of the business. Once the marketing plan is written, it serves as a reference point for the success of future activities. Finally, the marketing plan allows the marketing manager to enter the marketplace with an awareness of possibilities and problems.

marketing plan
A written document that acts as a guidebook of marketing activities for the marketing manager.

Marketing Plan Elements

Marketing plans can be presented in many different ways. Most businesses need a written marketing plan because the scope of a marketing plan is large and can be complex. Details about tasks and activity assignments may be lost if communicated verbally. Regardless of the way a marketing plan is presented, there are elements common to all marketing plans. These include defining the business mission and objectives, performing a situation analysis, delineating a target market, and establishing components of the marketing mix. Other elements that may be included in a plan are budgets, implementation timetables, required marketing research efforts, or elements of advanced strategic planning. Exhibit 2.1 shows these elements, which are also described subsequently. An example of a thumbnail marketing plan sketch in contained in Exhibit 2.2.

Exhibit 2.1
The Marketing Process

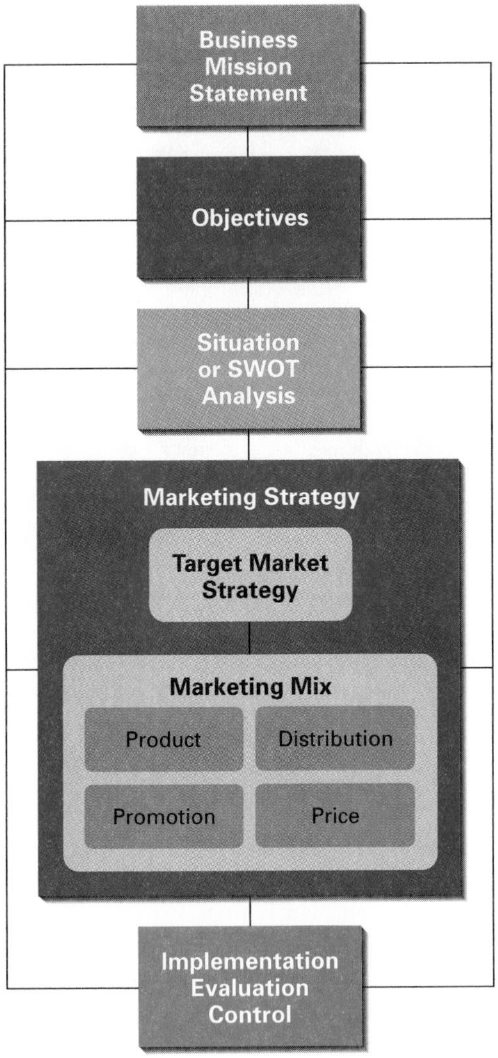

Exhibit 2.2
Sample Summary Marketing Plan

Business Mission:	Ultracel is in the business of providing advanced communications technology and communications convenience to mobile telephone users.
Marketing Objective:	To achieve 20 percent, in dollar volume, of the personal communications service (PCS) cellular telephone market by year's end, 1998.
Situation Analysis:	
Strengths:	Well-funded organization, highly skilled workforce with low turnover, excellent relationships with suppliers, product differential, and sustainable competitive advantage of patented color screen.
Weaknesses:	Company name not well known, small firm with no manufacturing cost advantages, no long-term contracts with distributors, inexperience in the cellular telephone market.
Opportunities:	Explosive growth of cellular phone users, worldwide acceptance of cellular technology, newly available digital networks.
Threats:	Heavy competition from Motorola, Sony, and Nokia; technology is incompatible with current analog systems, not everyone can afford the systems, potential governmental regulation.
Target Market Selection:	Young, mobile executives in North America and Europe with incomes over $200,000 per year, frequent travelers, computer dependent.
Marketing Mix:	
Product:	PCS cellular telephone. Brand name: Ultracel-2000. Features: simultaneous voice/data communication, Internet access, operation within buildings, linkups to data subscription and e-mail services, computer data storage, color screen, lightweight, 48-hour battery, three-year unlimited warranty on parts and labor, 24-hour technical support, leather or titanium carrying case.
Place:	Available through cellular telephone retailers, upscale computer retailers, or via mail-order company direct. Products transported via airplane and temperature-controlled motor carrier.
Promotion:	50 manufacturer's representatives for sales force, with 25% commissions. Advertising in print media, cable television, and outdoor billboards. Sales promotion in the form of introductory product rebates, technology trade shows. Public relations efforts to news media and sponsorship of world-championship sporting events.
Price:	Retail price of $1,250 (compared to Nokia at $2,000, Motorola at $1,500, and Sony at $500). Assuming mild price sensitivity and future price wars.
Implementation:	First Quarter: Complete marketing research on price, design promotional campaign, sign contracts with manufacturer's reps. Second quarter: Public relations campaign, product introduction at trade shows, rollout of advertising. Third quarter: Test international markets.

DEFINE THE BUSINESS MISSION

2 Define an appropriate business mission statement.

The foundation of any marketing plan is first answering the question, "What business are we in and where are we going?" The answer is the firm's **mission statement.** Business mission definition profoundly affects long-run resource allocation, profitability, and survival. The mission statement is based on a careful analysis of benefits sought by present and potential customers and an analysis of existing and antic-

Exhibit 2.3
*Coca-Cola's Mission
Statement*

"We exist to create value for our share owners on a long-term basis by building a business that enhances The Coca-Cola Company's trademarks. This also is our ultimate commitment.

As the world's largest beverage company, we refresh the world. We do this by developing superior soft drinks, both carbonated and non-carbonated, and profitable non-alcoholic beverage systems that create value for our Company, our bottling partners and our customers.

In creating value, we succeed or fail based on our ability to perform as stewards of several key assets:

• Coca-Cola, the world's most powerful trademark, and other highly valuable trademarks.
• The world's most effective and pervasive distribution system.
• Satisfied customers, who make a good profit selling our products.
• Our people, who are ultimately responsible for building this enterprise.
• Our abundant resources, which must be intelligently allocated.
• Our strong global leadership in the beverage industry in particular and in the business world in general."

ipated environmental conditions. The firm's long-term vision, embodied in the mission statement, establishes boundaries for all subsequent decisions, objectives, and strategies. Coca-Cola's mission statement is shown in Exhibit 2.3.

A mission statement should focus on the market or markets the organization is attempting to serve rather than on the good or service offered. Otherwise, a new technology may quickly make the good or service obsolete and the mission statement irrelevant to company functions. Business mission statements that are stated too narrowly suffer from marketing myopia. **Marketing myopia** means that the business is defined in terms of goods and services rather than in terms of the benefits that customers seek.[4] In this context, myopia means narrow, short-term thinking. For example, Frito-Lay defines its mission as being in the snack-food business rather than in the corn chip business. The mission of sports teams is not just to play games, but to serve the interests of the fans. AT&T does not sell telephones or long distance services; it markets communications technology.

Alternatively, business missions may be stated too broadly. "To be a leading consumer goods manufacturer and marketer" is probably too broad a mission statement for any firm except Procter & Gamble. Care must be taken when stat-

mission statement
The firm's long-term vision based on a careful analysis of benefits sought by present and potential customers and analysis of existing and anticipated environmental conditions.

marketing myopia
Business defined in terms of goods and services rather than in terms of the benefits that customers seek.

The mission of a sports team is not just to play games, but to serve the interests of its fans.
© Corbis-Bettmann

ing what business a firm is in. The mission of Saturn Corporation, a subsidiary of General Motors, is "to design, manufacture, and market vehicles to compete on a global scale, as well as re-establish American technology as the standard for automotive quality."[5] By correctly stating the business mission, in terms of the benefits that customers seek, the foundation for the marketing plan is set. Many companies are focusing on designing more appropriate mission statements because these statements are frequently displayed on the World Wide Web.

The organization may need to define a mission statement and objectives for a **strategic business unit (SBU),** which is a subgroup of a single business or collection of related businesses within the larger organization. A properly defined SBU should have a distinct mission and specific target market, control over its resources, its own competitors, and plans independent of the other SBUs in the organization. Thus, a large firm such as Kraft General Foods may have marketing plans for each of its SBUs, which include breakfast foods, desserts, pet foods, and beverages.

strategic business unit (SBU)
A subgroup of a single business or collection of related businesses within the larger organization.

SET MARKETING PLAN OBJECTIVES

3 Know the criteria for stating good marketing objectives.

Before the details of a marketing plan can be developed, goals and objectives for the plan must be stated. Without objectives, there is no basis for measuring the success of marketing plan activities. For example, in mid-1996, Microsoft had about a 10 percent market share in the Web-browser software business. Is this good or bad? Without previously stated objectives, there is no way to know. Actually, Microsoft had a goal of having a 30 percent market share, so its objectives were not met.[6]

A **marketing objective** is a statement of what is to be accomplished through marketing activities. To be useful, stated objectives should meet several criteria. First, objectives should be realistic, measurable, and time specific. It is tempting to state that the objective is *to be the best marketer of ferret food.* However, what is "best" for one firm might be sales of one million pounds of ferret food per year, and to another firm, "best" might mean dominant market share. It may also be unrealistic for start-up firms or new products to command a dominant market share, given other competitors in the marketplace. Finally, by what time should the goal be met? A more realistic objective would be *to achieve 10 percent dollar market share in the specialty pet food market within 12 months of product introduction.*

Second, objectives must also be consistent and indicate the priorities of the organization. Specifically, objectives flow from the business mission statement to the rest of the marketing plan. Exhibit 2.4 shows some well-stated and poorly stated objectives. Notice how well they do or do not meet the preceding criteria.

marketing objective
A statement of what is to be accomplished through marketing activities.

Exhibit 2.4
Examples of Marketing Objectives

Poorly Stated Objectives	**Well-Stated Objectives**
Our objective is to be a leader in the industry in terms of new product development.	Our objective is to spend 12% of sales revenue between 1997 and 1998 on research and development in an effort to introduce at least five new products in 1999.
Our objective is to maximize profits.	Our objective is to achieve a 10% return on investment during 1997, with a payback on new investments of no longer than four years.
Our objective is to serve customers better.	Our objective is to obtain customer satisfaction ratings of at least 90% on the 1997 annual customer satisfaction survey and to retain at least 85% of our 1997 customers as repeat purchasers in 1998.
Our objective is to be the best that we can be.	Our objective is to increase market share from 30% to 40% in 1998 by increasing promotional expenditures by 14%.

Carefully specified objectives serve several functions. First, they communicate marketing management philosophies and provide direction for lower level marketing managers so marketing efforts are integrated and pointed in a consistent direction. Objectives also serve as motivators by creating something for employees to strive for. When objectives are attainable and challenging, they motivate those charged with achieving them. Additionally, the process of writing specific objectives forces executives to clarify their thinking. Finally, objectives form a basis for control: The effectiveness of a plan can be gauged in light of the stated goals.

CONDUCT A SITUATION ANALYSIS

Before specific marketing activities can be defined, marketers must understand the current and potential environment that the product or service will be marketed in. A situation analysis is sometimes referred to as a **SWOT analysis**; that is, the firm should identify its internal strengths (S) and weaknesses (W) and also examine external opportunities (O) and threats (T).

When examining internal strengths and weaknesses, the marketing manager should focus on organizational resources such as production costs, marketing skills, financial

SWOT analysis
Identifying internal strengths (S) and weaknesses (W) and also examining external opportunities (O) and threats (T).

4 Explain the components of a situation analysis.

Global Perspectives
A Traffic Jam of Auto Makers

India will be the next major car market for the 21st century, with car purchase growth rates at 25 percent annually. The market potential is huge: Demand for cars in India could reach 2 million annually. Currently, car ownership in India is 3.6 automobiles per 1,000 people, which is among the world's lowest rate. (The United States boasts 560 cars per 1,000.) There clearly exists a lot of room for growth, especially because the industry was deregulated in 1991. These numbers are attracting a number of carmakers, including General Motors, Ford, Fiat, Daewoo Motor, Mercedez-Benz, Hyundai, Peugot, Mitsubishi, and Suzuki.

However, before jumping into an international market, care must be taken to thoroughly understand the marketing environment. Lured by India's huge potential for growth, some car manufacturers have hit a bumpy road. Fierce competition, marketing errors, labor trouble, a lack of suitable partnerships, high taxes, and infrastructure problems are just some of the hazards.

Although 70 percent of Indian car sales are in the mass market, GM, Mercedes, and Fiat elected to enter the premium market. Unfortunately, the premium prices of these cars cost Indian consumers 16 to 34 months' income (as opposed to 6 months' of income in America), so the cars are too pricey for most Indian consumers. Other factors affecting cost and price are import duties for parts (a prohibitive 110 percent), high taxes (almost 50 percent of the car's retail price), and one of the world's most expensive markets for fuel.

Alternatively, the mass market is already dominated by a single player. The $7,000 Maruti 800 (made by Suzuki) accounts for 65 percent of all car sales. Competition will be fierce to make headway into this market, with Volkswagen,

BMW, and Toyota planning to jump in as well.

One of India's great attractions is cheap and abundant labor. However, the labor force is a major problem. Labor troubles have led to crippling strikes, apathetic managers and workers, and dismal productivity. Indian workers make an average of 5 cars per worker per year, compared to the global standard of over 40 cars per worker per year.

Streets in India are a crumbling infrastructure; only 20 percent of the 1.5 million miles of road are car-worthy. Finding local suppliers for parts is tricky if one wants to maintain quality standards, and importing parts means a waiting time of a month for a single screw. Language and cultural barriers have also challenged global competitors.[7]

Who will survive in this potentially lucrative, but highly problematic market? What environment factors will be key in defining marketing plans for India?

environmental scanning
Collection and interpretation of information about forces, events, and relationships in the external environment that may affect the future of the organization or the implementation of the marketing plan.

H&R Block, Inc.
What market opportunities does H&R Block address using its Web site? What key advantages does the firm offer to users?

http://www.handrblock.com/

resources, company or brand image, employee capabilities, and available technology. For example, a potential weakness for Valujet airlines is the age of its airplane fleet, which could indicate an image of danger or low quality. A potential strength is the low operating costs of the airline. Another issue to consider in this section of the marketing plan is the historical background of the firm, such as its sales and profit history.

When examining external opportunities and threats, marketing managers must analyze aspects of the marketing environment. This process is called environmental scanning. **Environmental scanning** is the collection and interpretation of information about forces, events, and relationships in the external environment that may affect the future of the organization or the implementation of the marketing plan. Environmental scanning helps identify market opportunities and threats and provides guidelines for the design of marketing strategy. The six most often studied macroenvironmental forces are social, demographic, economic, technological, political and legal, and competitive forces. These forces are examined in detail in Chapter 3. For example, H&R Block, a tax preparation service, benefits from complex changes in tax codes that motivate citizens to have taxes prepared by a professional. Alternatively, tax-simplification or flat-tax plans would allow people to easily prepare their own returns.

Corporate culture is the pattern of basic assumptions an organization has accepted to cope with the firm's internal environment and the changing external environment. Internally, corporate culture is concerned with such issues as worker loyalty, centralization or decentralization of decision making, promotion criteria, and problem-solving techniques. Corporate culture regarding the external environment is revealed by the way the firm reacts to problems and opportunities. Organizational response to the external environment can be categorized into four types:

Patron's of Shirley D's café in Manchester, NH, can read about the proposed flat tax, which would simplify income tax preparation.
© Mark Peterson/SABA

- *Prospector:* focuses on identifying and capitalizing on emerging market opportunities, thus emphasizing research and communication with the market. Because of its strong external orientation, the prospector tends to build and maintain an excellent information system and product development program. A prospector prefers strategic alternatives that tap new markets or that develop new goods and services. Both Ralston Purina and Philip Morris have a prospector culture. They are both leaders in bringing new consumer goods to market. U.S. Surgical is also a prospector. The fastest selling surgical instruments today are those that use laparoscopes to do procedures through tiny incisions. U.S. Surgical has almost an 85 percent market share of the $3 billion laparoscopic instrument market. About half of U.S. Surgical's sales come from instruments introduced within the past five years.

- *Reactor:* the opposite of the prospector. Instead of looking for opportunities, it responds to environmental pressures when forced to do so. The reactor is a follower, not a leader, and lacks a strategic focus. Emphasis is on maintaining the status quo despite environmental change. A reactor will avoid any strategic alternative that takes it out of its niche or that calls for bold, risk-taking action. Reactors include Woolworth's, Wrigley's, and Revco Drug.

- *Defender:* has a specific market domain and does not search outside that domain for new opportunities.

Instead, it tries to "defend its turf." A defender looks favorably on any strategic alternative that helps reduce operating costs. The risk, however, is that market changes might go unnoticed. Even if the defender detects such changes, it typically is unable to adjust its business practices in response. American Home Products, a defender, has probably undermined its future. Its corporate culture has emphasized strict cost controls for years. Until recently, managers had to get central management's approval for any expenditure over $500. New-product development suffered as a result.

Ralston Purina
Review the corporate information and annual report for Ralston Purina. What evidence do you find of this company's prospector culture?

http://www.ralston.com/

- *Analyzer:* tends to be both conservative and aggressive. It usually operates in at least one stable market and tries to defend its position in that market. An analyzer also tries to identify emerging opportunities in other markets. Unlike the prospector, the analyzer is not an aggressive risk taker. Usually "second in" to new product markets, the analyzer does have the advantage of observing and learning from other firms' new-product problems. Delta Airlines, Bethlehem Steel, Aetna Insurance, and Alberto-Culver can be categorized as analyzers.

Strategic Windows

One technique for identifying opportunities is to seek strategic windows. A **strategic window** is the limited period during which the "fit" between the key requirements of a market and the particular competencies of a firm are at an optimum. For example, in 1994, Netscape recognized the need for user-friendly and organized Web-browser software to take advantage of the exploding popularity of the Internet and the World Wide Web. By 1996, Netscape had about 90 percent of this market, mostly because it was able to introduce its product before Microsoft, Inc.[8] Another time-based opportunity is the opening of Mexico's long-distance telephone market in 1997, allowing firms such as MCI and GTE an opportunity in this fast-growth service market.[9]

The concept of strategic windows is not limited to huge corporations: small businesses must also know when to take advantage of their strategic windows. The "Marketing and Small Business" example provides an example of taking care of an opportunity.

strategic window
The limited period during which the "fit" between the key requirements of a market and the particular competencies of a firm are at an optimum.

Netscape found its strategic window in 1994. Today, the company has 90% of the market because it entered the market before Microsoft.
© 1995 Ed Kashi

Marketing and Small Business

Pickle Queen Jumps Through a Strategic Window

Shirley Stimpert had little success selling pickled vegetables to retailers near her farm in western Kansas, where home-canned produce is nothing special. But when she sent a sample to Bloomingdale's in New York, an order came back—a $20,000 order. "Barry had to peel me off the ceiling," she says, referring to her husband.

Four years later, Mrs. Stimpert's pickles can be found in gourmet food stores across the country selling for as much as $25 a jar (64 ounces). And her 160-acre farm—which for years had failed to produce sufficient income to support a family—now supports 22 employees. "This thing just grew feet and started running away without us," says Mrs. Stimpert, who was born on the farm 47 years ago.

Growing crops has been a tough profession for years, but opportunities abound for farmers willing to package and promote their own products. Gourmet food retailers such as Dean & DeLuca in Wash-

ington, D.C., and New York and Whole Foods Market Inc., with branches in Southern California and Texas, need new products to fill their shelves. Branches of a new retail operation—Old Farmer's Almanac General Stores—are selling overalls, garden tools, Mrs. Stimpert's pickles, and more.

It seems that urbanites are willing to pay a premium for items that originate in—or at least evoke—rural America. After opening stores in Chicago, Dallas, and Minneapolis in November, Old Farmer's Almanac quickly sold its entire supply of $3.95 jars of apple butter, peach butter, and pumpkin butter made by a farm family in Rogers, Arkansas. "Products associated with American country living are very hot," says Barry Parker, chief

executive of apparel retailer County Seat, Inc., which launched Old Farmer's in a venture with the almanac publisher.

Few are better marketers than Mrs. Stimpert. Although she attributes her success in part to her recipe, it never won any county-fair ribbons; and even her biggest fans say that what sets her product apart is salesmanship rather than taste. Her pickles—sold under the Pickle Cottage label—come in Mason jars, affixed to which is a tag that says, "from our cottage to yours."

Demand has now exceeded supply for Mrs. Stimpert's pickles. Now they must buy some of the cucumbers and other vegetables they pickle from other farmers. Still, the Pickle Cottage retains a mom-and-pop quality. The Stimperts have no computer, and the word "protein" is regularly misspelled on their labels.[10]

Strategic Alternatives

5 Identify strategic alternatives and describe tools used to help select alternatives.

To discover a marketing opportunity or strategic window, management must know how to identify the alternatives. One method for developing alternatives is the strategic opportunity matrix (see Exhibit 2.5), which matches products with markets. Firms can explore these four options:

- *Market penetration:* A firm using the **market penetration** alternative would try to increase market share among existing customers. If Kraft General Foods started a major campaign for Maxwell House coffee, with aggressive advertising and cents-off coupons to existing customers, it would be following a penetration strategy. Customer databases, discussed in Chapter 9, help managers implement this strategy.

Dean & DeLuca
A wide array of new product offerings are advertised at this site. What new strategic opportunities do you see for a small business?

http://www.dean-deluca.com/

- *Market development:* **Market development** means attracting new customers to existing products. Ideally, new uses for old products stimulate additional sales among existing customers while also bringing in new buyers. McDonald's, for example, has opened restaurants in Russia, China, and Italy and is eagerly ex-

	Present product	New product
Present market	**Market penetration:** Kraft General Foods creates a major promotion campaign with an increased budget for Maxwell House coffee.	**Product development:** ConAgra creates Healthy Choice frozen dinners.
New market	**Market development:** McDonald's opens restaurants in Moscow.	**Diversification:** LTV develops the monorail for the Dallas-Fort Worth airport.

Exhibit 2.5
Strategic Opportunity Matrix

panding into Eastern European countries. In the nonprofit area, the growing emphasis on continuing education and executive development by colleges and universities is a market development strategy.

- *Product development:* A product development strategy entails the creation of new products for present markets. The beer industry, for example, is creating "craft brews" which seem like specialty beers brewed in microbreweries. Often, however, such is not the case. Maui Beer Company's Aloha Lager sells its Hawaiian image with a picture of a hula dancer on the label. But it is brewed in Portland, Oregon, by giant G. Heileman Brewing Company. Faux-antique labels on Pete's Wicked Ale, one of the nation's hottest craft beers, brag that the beer is brewed "one batch at a time. Carefully." That may be, but the batches are 400 barrels each, and the brewing is done by giant Stroh Brewery Company, maker of Old Milwaukee beer. Icehouse and Red Dog labels identify the maker as Plank Road Brewery. The real brewer: No. 2 beer heavyweight Miller, a unit of Philip Morris Companies, which is using the Plank Road name to get a piece of the craft-brew market.[11]

    Managers following this strategy can rely on their extensive knowledge of the target audience. They usually have a good feel for what customers like and dislike about current products and what existing needs are not being met. In addition, managers can rely on the established distribution channels.

- *Diversification:* **Diversification** is a strategy of increasing sales by introducing new products into new markets. For example, LTV Corporation, a steel producer, diversified into the monorail business. Sony practiced a diversification strategy when it acquired Columbia Pictures; although motion pictures are not a new product in the marketplace, they were a new product for Sony. Coca-Cola manufactures and markets water-treatment and water-conditioning equipment, which has been a very challenging task for the traditional soft-drink company. A diversification strategy can be quite risky when a firm is entering unfamiliar markets. On the other hand, it can be very profitable when a firm is entering markets with little or no competition.

market penetration
A marketing strategy that tries to increase market share among existing customers.

market development
Attracting new customers to existing products.

diversification
A strategy of increasing sales by introducing new products into new markets.

McDonald's has attracted new buyers for its well-known products in China, Russia, and Italy. It is continuing its market development in Eastern Europe.
© Jeff Greenberg

Selecting a Strategic Alternative

Selecting which alternative to pursue depends on the overall company philosophy and culture. The choice also depends on the tool used to make the decision. Companies generally have one of two philosophies about when they expect profits: They either pursue profits right away or first seek to increase market share and then pursue profits. In the long run, market share and profitability are compatible goals. Many companies have long followed this credo: Build market share, and profits will surely follow. Michelin, the tire producer, consistently sacrifices short-term profits to achieve market share. But attitudes may be changing. Lou Gerstner, CEO of IBM, has stressed profitability over market share, quality, and customer service since taking over the company. As you can see, the same strategic alternative may be viewed entirely differently by firms with different corporate cultures.[12] A highly desirable alternative for one organization may be completely unattractive to another firm.

A number of tools exist that can help managers select a strategic alternative. The most common of these tools are in matrix form. Two of these matrix tools are described in more detail below.

Portfolio Matrix

Recall that large organizations engaged in strategic planning may create strategic business units. Each SBU has its own rate of return on investment, growth potential, and associated risk. Management must find a balance among the SBUs that yields the overall organization's desired growth and profits with an acceptable level of risk. Some SBUs generate large amounts of cash over and above what is required for operating expenses or for more marketing, production, or inventory. Other SBUs need cash to foster growth. The challenge is to balance the organization's "portfolio" of SBUs for the best long-term performance.

To determine the future cash contributions and cash requirements that can be expected for each SBU, managers can use the Boston Consulting Group's portfolio matrix. A matrix is a self-contained framework within which something originates and develops. The **portfolio matrix** classifies each SBU by its present or forecasted growth and market share. The underlying assumption is that market share and profitability are strongly linked. The measure of market share used in the portfolio approach is *relative market share*, the ratio between the company's share and the share of the largest competitor. For example, if firm *A* has a 50 percent share and the competitor has 5 percent, the ratio is 10 to 1. If firm *A* has a 10 percent market share and the largest competitor has 20 percent, the ratio is 0.5 to 1.

Exhibit 2.6 is a hypothetical portfolio matrix for a large computer manufacturer. The size of the circle in each cell of the matrix represents dollar sales of the SBU relative to dollar sales of the company's other SBUs. These are the categories used in the matrix:

- *Stars:* A **star** is a market leader that is growing fast. For example, computer manufacturers have identified the notebook model as a star. Star SBUs usually have large profits, but need a lot of cash to finance rapid growth. The best marketing tactic for them is to protect their existing market share by reinvesting earnings in product improvement, better distribution, more promotion, and production efficiency. Management must strive to capture most of the new users as they enter the market.

- *Cash cows:* A **cash cow** is an SBU that usually generates more cash than it needs to maintain its market share. It is in a low-growth market, but the product has a dominant market share. Personal computers are categorized as cash cows in Exhibit 2.6. The basic strategy for a cash cow is to maintain market dominance by being the price leader and making technological improvements in the product. Managers should resist pressure to extend the basic line unless they can dramatically increase demand. Instead, they should allocate excess cash to the product categories for which growth prospects are the greatest. For instance, Clorox Corporation owns Kingsford Charcoal, Match Charcoal Lighter, Prime Choice steak sauce, Cooking Ease spray lubricant for frying foods, and a restaurant chain. Its cash cow is Clorox bleach, with a 60 percent market share in a low-growth market. Clorox Corporation was highly successful in stretching the Clorox line to include a liquid formula in

---

portfolio matrix
Tool for allocating resources among products or strategic business units on the basis of relative market share and market growth rate.

star
In the portfolio matrix, a business unit that is a fast-growing market leader.

cash cow
In the portfolio matrix, a business unit that usually generates more cash than it needs to maintain its market share.

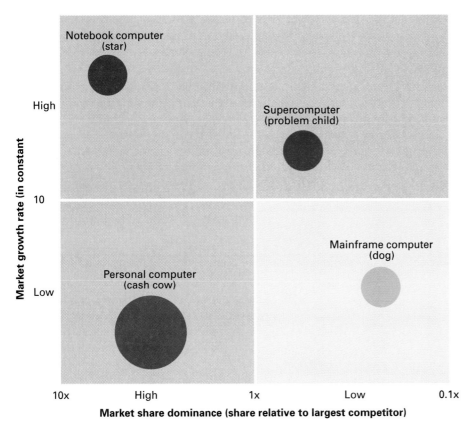

Exhibit 2.6
Portfolio Matrix for a Large Computer Manufacturer

Note: The size of the circle represents the dollar sales relative to sales of other SBUs on the matrix—for example, 10× means that sales are 10 times greater than those of the next largest competitor.

addition to the original dry bleach. Another example is Heinz, which has two cash cows: catsup and Weight Watchers frozen dinners.

- *Problem children:* A **problem child,** also called a **question mark,** shows rapid growth but poor profit margins. It has a low market share in a high-growth industry. Problem children need a great deal of cash. Without cash support, they eventually become dogs. The strategy options are to invest heavily to gain better market share, acquire competitors to get the necessary market share, or drop the SBU. Sometimes a firm can reposition the products of the problem child SBU to move it into the star category.

- *Dogs:* A **dog** has low growth potential and a small market share. Most dogs eventually leave the marketplace. In the computer manufacturer example, the mainframe computer has become a dog. Other examples include Jack-in-the-Box shrimp dinners, Warner-Lambert's Reef mouthwash, and Campbell's Red Kettle soups. Frito-Lay has produced several dogs, including Stuffers cheese-filled snacks, Rumbles granola nuggets, and Toppels cheese-topped crackers—a trio irreverently known as Stumbles, Tumbles, and Twofers. The strategy options for dogs are to harvest or divest.

After classifying the company's SBUs in the matrix, the next step is to allocate future resources for each. The four basic strategies are to:

- *Build:* If an organization has an SBU that it believes has the potential to be a star (probably a problem child at present), building would be an appropriate goal. The organization may decide to give up short-term profits and use its financial resources to achieve this goal. Procter & Gamble built Pringles from a money loser to a record profit maker in the mid-1990s.

problem child (question mark)
In the portfolio matrix, a business unit that shows rapid growth but poor profit margins.

dog
In the portfolio matrix, a business unit that has low growth potential and a small market share.

- *Hold:* If an SBU is a very successful cash cow, a key goal would surely be to hold or preserve market share so the organization can take advantage of the very positive cash flow. Bisquick has been a prosperous cash cow for General Mills for over two decades.

- *Harvest:* This strategy is appropriate for all SBUs except those classified as stars. The basic goal is to increase the short-term cash return without too much concern for the long-run impact. It is especially worthwhile when more cash is needed from a cash cow with long-run prospects that are unfavorable because of a low market growth rate. For instance, Lever Brothers has been harvesting Lifebuoy soap for a number of years with little promotional backing.

- *Divest:* Getting rid of SBUs with low shares of low-growth markets is often appropriate. Problem children and dogs are most suitable for this strategy. Procter & Gamble dropped Cincaprin, a coated aspirin, because of its low growth potential.

Market Attractiveness/Company Strength Matrix

market attractiveness/ company strength matrix Tool for allocating resources among strategic business units on the basis of how attractive a market is and how well the firm is positioned to take advantage of opportunities in that market.

A second model for selecting strategic alternatives, originally developed by General Electric, is known as the **market attractiveness/company strength matrix.** The dimensions used in this matrix—market attractiveness and company strength—are richer and more complete than those used in the portfolio matrix, but are much harder to quantify.

Exhibit 2.7 presents a market attractiveness/company strength matrix. The horizontal axis, business position, refers to how well positioned the organization is to take advantage of market opportunities. Does the firm have the technology it needs to ef-

Exhibit 2.7
Market Attractiveness/ Company Strength Matrix

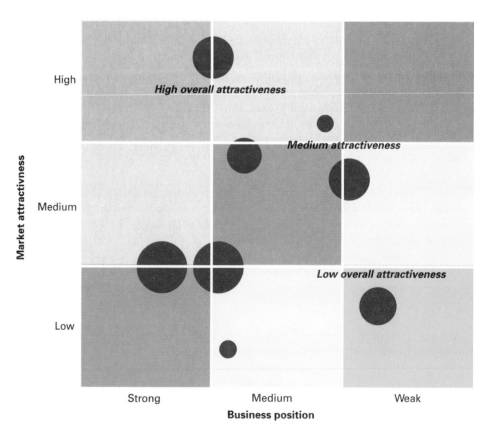

Note: Circle size represents dollar sales volume relative to sales of other SBUs on the matrix.

fectively penetrate the market? Are its financial resources adequate? Can manufacturing costs be held below those of the competition? Will the firm have bargaining power over suppliers? Can the firm cope with change? The vertical axis measures the attractiveness of a market, which is expressed both quantitatively and qualitatively. Some attributes of an attractive market are high profitability, rapid growth, a lack of government regulation, consumer insensitivity to a price increase, a lack of competition, and availability of technology. The grid is divided into three overall attractiveness zones for each dimension: high, medium, and low.

Those SBUs (or markets) that have low overall attractiveness should be avoided if the organization is not already serving them. If the firm is in these markets, it should either harvest or divest the SBUs. The organization should selectively maintain markets with medium attractiveness. If attractiveness begins to slip, then the organization should withdraw from the market.

Conditions that are highly attractive—an attractive market plus a strong business position—are the best candidates for investment. For instance, Black & Decker used marketing research to uncover a market for the "serious do-it-yourselfer." These people were willing to pay a premium price for quality home tools. For example, research found that this group of consumers wanted a cordless drill that didn't run out of power before the job was complete. Black & Decker responded with a new line called Quantum.

Differential Advantage

To have a successful marketing plan, one must seek a differential advantage over the competition when examining internal strengths and external marketplace opportunities. A **differential advantage** is one or more unique aspects of an organization that cause target consumers to patronize that firm rather than competitors. A differential advantage may exist solely in the firm's image. For example, IBM has differential advantages in its reputation and its ability to provide entire systems solutions. Differential advantages may also occur in any element of the marketing mix. Superior product quality gives a firm such as Hewlett-Packard a competitive advantage over other laser-printer makers by offering customer value. Wal-Mart has an advantage over Kmart by having a very low-cost and efficient distribution system, but Kmart

differential advantage
One or more unique aspects of an organization that cause target consumers to patronize that firm rather than competitors.

Intel's image is a differential advantage. Its superior advertising has made the Intel Pentium computer chip a household term.
Courtesy Intel Corporation

Guess who makes the Pentium processor even more fun?

has better store locations. Intel has produced superior advertisements that have made the Intel Pentium computer chip a household term. Suave hair-care products compete on the basis of low price.

The two basic sources of differential advantage are superior skills and superior resources. *Superior skills* are the managers' and workers' unique capabilities, which distinguish them from employees of competing firms. For example, Microsoft benefits from the vision and technical expertise of CEO Bill Gates. DuPont technicians created a new production process that gives the company a 20 percent cost savings. The superior customer service skills of Nordstrom give that department store chain a superior skill differential advantage.

Superior resources are a more tangible form of differential advantage. For example, popular brand names such as Coke, Nike, or Texaco have immeasurable value. Sony has large, high-tech manufacturing facilities that cannot be easily copied. Fort Howard Paper's differential advantage lies in its cost-saving manufacturing process. Chapparal Steel is so efficient in its steel production and casting process that it is the only U.S. steel producer that ships to Japan.

sustainable competitive advantage
A differential advantage that cannot be copied by the competition.

The key to having a differential advantage is the ability to sustain that advantage. A **sustainable competitive advantage** is a competitive advantage that cannot be copied by the competition. Top-Flite recently introduced the new Strata golf ball. At $3 each, these balls cost three times as much as regular golf balls, but they are flying off the shelf. The Strata has a patented, three-layer construction that improves handling and increases distance. The patent offers a sustainable competitive advantage over Titleist, the number-one competitor.[13] Datril was introduced into the pain-reliever market and was touted as being exactly like Tylenol, only cheaper. Tylenol responded by lowering its price, thus destroying Datril's differential advantage and ability to remain on the market. In this case, low price was not a sustainable competitive advantage. Without a differential advantage, target customers don't perceive any reason to patronize an organization instead of its competitors.

Top-Flite
What new products are advertised at Top-Flite's home page? Do these new products offer competitive advantages? What advantages do you see?

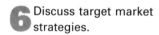

DESCRIBE THE MARKETING STRATEGY

marketing strategy
The activity of selecting and describing one or more target markets, and developing and maintaining a marketing mix that will produce mutually satisfying exchanges with target markets.

Marketing strategy involves the activities of selecting and describing one or more target markets and developing and maintaining a marketing mix that will produce mutually satisfying exchanges with target markets.

Target Market Strategy

6 Discuss target market strategies.

market opportunity analysis
The description and estimation of the size and sales potential of market segments that are of interest to the firm and the assessment of key competitors in these market segments.

A market segment is a group of individuals or organizations that share one or more characteristics. They therefore have relatively similar product needs. For example, parents of newborn babies need products such as formula, diapers, and special foods. The target market strategy identifies which market segment or segments to focus on. This process begins with a market opportunity analysis, or MOA. **Market opportunity analysis** is the description and estimation of the size and sales potential of market segments that are of interest to the firm and the assessment of key competitors in these market segments. After the market segments are described, one or more may be targeted by the firm. There are three general strategies for selecting target markets: appealing to the entire market with one marketing mix, concentrating on one segment, and appealing to multiple market segments using multiple marketing mixes. The characteristics, advantages, and disadvantages of each strategic option are examined in Chapter 8. Target markets could be smokers who are concerned about white teeth (the target of Topol toothpaste), people concerned about sugar and calories in their soft drinks (Diet Coke), or college students needing inexpensive about-town transportation (Yamaha Razz scooter).

Any market segment that is targeted must be fully described. Demographics, psychographics, and buyer behavior should be assessed. Buyer behavior is covered in Chapters 6 and 7. If segments are differentiated by ethnicity, multicultural aspects of the marketing mix should be examined. If the target market is international, it is especially important to describe differences in culture, economic and technological development, and political structure that may affect the marketing plan. Global marketing is covered in more detail in Chapter 4.

Military strategy is a proven tool in the hands of warriors, but can it be used in the consumer war between Colgate-Palmolive and Procter & Gamble? See how marketers make the most of military strategy at **Hot Links—Military Strategy as an Inspiration for Marketing Strategy.**

The Marketing Mix

The term **marketing mix** refers to a unique blend of product, distribution, promotion, and pricing strategies designed to produce mutually satisfying exchanges with a target market. Distribution is sometimes referred to as place, thus giving us the **"four Ps"** of the marketing mix: product, place, promotion, and price. The marketing manager can control each component of the marketing mix, but the strategies for all four components must be blended to achieve optimal results. Any marketing mix is only as good as its weakest component. For example, the first pump toothpastes were distributed over cosmetic counters and failed. Not until pump toothpastes were distributed the same way as tube toothpastes did the products succeed. The best promotion and the lowest price cannot save a poor product. Similarly, an excellent product with poor distribution, pricing, or promotion will likely fail.

Successful marketing mixes have been carefully designed to satisfy target markets. At first glance, McDonald's and Wendy's may appear to have roughly identical marketing mixes, because they are both in the fast-food hamburger business. However, McDonald's has been most successful with targeting parents with young children for lunchtime meals, while Wendy's targets the adult crowd for lunches and dinner. McDonald's has playgrounds, Ronald McDonald the clown, and special children's Happy Meals. Wendy's has salad bars, carpeted restaurants, and no playgrounds.

7 Describe elements of the marketing mix.

marketing mix
A unique blend of product, distribution, promotion, and pricing strategies designed to produce mutually satisfying exchanges with a target market.

four Ps
Product, place, promotion, and price, which together make up the marketing mix.

Rumi Miyamoto, one of Japan's few car saleswomen, tells a prospective buyer about the benefits of owning a Ford. The buyer is seeking a car with German reliability, Japanese high tech, and American atmosphere. Will the Mustang fit the bill?
© Tom Wagner/SABA

WOULD YOU LIKE SOME CARATS WITH YOUR CHOCOLATE?

Bedazzle your beloved by winning one of these breathtaking diamond rings. But beware, for these brilliant beauties can be
found only in special boxes of Godiva Valentine's Day chocolates. For the Godiva boutique nearest you, call 1-800-9-GODIVA.
Or visit us on the Internet at www.godiva.com. Or AOL [keyword: GODIVA].

New York   Paris   **GODIVA**   Tokyo   Brussels
Chocolatier

A Godiva chocolate has many
product elements: the chocolate itself, a fancy gold wrap-
per, a customer satisfaction
guarantee, and a prestigious
brand name.

Variations in marketing mixes do not occur by chance. Astute marketing managers devise marketing strategies to gain advantages over competitors and best serve the needs and wants of a particular target market segment. By manipulating elements of the marketing mix, marketing managers can fine-tune the customer offering and achieve competitive success.

Product Strategies

Typically, the marketing mix starts with the product "P." The heart of the marketing mix, the starting point, is the product offering and product strategy. It is hard to design a distribution strategy, decide on a promotion campaign, or set a price without knowing the product to be marketed.

The product includes not only the physical unit, but also its package, warranty, after-sale service, brand name, company image, value, and many other factors. A Godiva chocolate has many product elements: the chocolate itself, a trademark gold gift box or "ballotin," a customer satisfaction guarantee, and the prestige of the Godiva brand name. We buy things not only for what they do (benefits), but also for what they mean to us (status, quality, or reputation).

Products can be tangible goods such as computers, ideas like those offered by a consultant, or services such as medical care. Products should also offer customer value. Product decisions are covered in Chapters 10 and 11. Services marketing is detailed in Chapter 12, and Chapter 13 discusses aspects of customer value and quality.

Distribution (Place) Strategies

Distribution strategies are concerned with making products available when and where customers want them. Would you rather buy a kiwi fruit at the 24-hour grocery store in walking distance, or have to fly to Australia to pick your own? A part of this place "P" is physical distribution, which involves all the business activities concerned with storing and transporting raw materials or finished products. The goal of distribution is to make sure products arrive in usable condition at designated places when needed. Distribution strategies are covered in Chapters 14 and 15.

Promotion Strategies

Promotion includes personal selling, advertising, sales promotion, and public relations. Promotion's role in the marketing mix is to bring about mutually satisfying exchanges with target markets by informing, educating, persuading, and reminding them about the benefits of an organization or a product. A good promotion strategy, like that used for Microsoft's Windows 95 software, can dramatically increase sales. Each element of the promotion "P" is coordinated and managed with the others to create a promotional blend or mix. These integrated marketing communications activities are described in Chapters 16, 17, and 18.

Pricing Strategies

Price is what a buyer must give up to obtain a product. It is often the most flexible of the four marketing mix elements—the quickest element to change. Marketers can raise or lower prices more frequently and easily than they can change other marketing mix variables. Price is an important competitive weapon and is very important to the organization overall, because price multiplied by the number of units sold equals total revenue for the firm. Pricing decisions are covered in Chapters 20 and 21.

IMPLEMENTATION, EVALUATION, AND CONTROL OF THE MARKETING PLAN

Implementation is the process that turns marketing plans into action assignments and ensures that these assignments are executed in a way that accomplishes the plans' objectives. Implementation activities may involve detailed job assignments, activity descriptions, time lines, budgets, and lots of communication. Although implementation is essentially "doing what you said you were going to do," many organizations repeatedly experience failures in strategy implementation. Brilliant marketing plans are doomed to fail if they are not properly implemented. These detailed communications may or may not be part of the written marketing plan. If they are not part of the plan, they should be specified elsewhere, as soon as the plan has been communicated.

After a marketing plan is implemented, it should be evaluated. **Evaluation** entails gauging the extent to which marketing objectives have been achieved during the specified period. Four common reasons for failing to achieve a marketing objective are unrealistic marketing objectives, inappropriate marketing strategies in the plan, poor implementation, and changes in the environment after the objective was specified and the strategy was implemented.

Once a plan is chosen and implemented, its effectiveness must be monitored. **Control** provides the mechanisms for evaluating marketing results in light of the plan's goals and for correcting actions that do not help the organization reach those goals within budget guidelines. Firms need to establish formal and informal control programs to make the entire operation more efficient.

Perhaps the broadest control device available to marketing managers is the marketing audit. A **marketing audit** is a thorough, systematic, periodic evaluation of the goals, strategies, structure, and performance of the marketing organization. A marketing audit helps management allocate marketing resources efficiently. The marketing audit has four characteristics. It is:

- *Comprehensive:* The marketing audit covers all the major marketing issues facing an organization and not just trouble spots.
- *Systematic:* The marketing audit takes place in an orderly sequence and covers the organization's marketing environment, internal marketing system, and specific marketing activities. The diagnosis is followed by an action plan with both short-run and long-run proposals for improving overall marketing effectiveness.
- *Independent:* The marketing audit is normally conducted by an inside or outside party that is independent enough to have top management's confidence and to be objective.
- *Periodic:* The marketing audit should be carried out on a regular schedule instead of only in a crisis. Whether it seems successful or is in deep trouble, any organization can benefit greatly from such an audit.

Although the main purpose of the marketing audit is to develop a full profile of the organization's marketing effort and to provide a basis for developing and revising the marketing plan, it is also an excellent way to improve communication and raise the level of marketing consciousness within the organization. That is, it is a useful vehicle for selling the philosophy and techniques of strategic marketing to other members of the organization.

---

8 Understand why implementation, evaluation, and control of the marketing plan is necessary.

implementation
The process that turns marketing plans into action assignments and ensures that these assignments are executed in a way that accomplishes the plans' objectives.

evaluation
Gauging the extent to which marketing objectives have been achieved during the specified time period.

control
Provides the mechanisms for evaluating marketing results in light of the plan's goals and for correcting actions that do not help the organization reach those goals within budget guidelines.

marketing audit
A thorough, systematic, periodic evaluation of the goals, strategies, structure, and performance of the marketing organization.

WRITING THE MARKETING PLAN

9 Know how to structure a basic marketing plan.

The creation and implementation of a complete marketing plan will allow the organization to achieve marketing objectives and succeed. However, the marketing plan is only as good as the information it contains and the effort, creativity, and thought that went into its creation. The importance of having a good marketing information system (covered in Chapter 9) is critical to a thorough and accurate situation analysis. The role of managerial intuition is also important in the creation and selection of marketing strategies. Managers must weigh the accuracy of any information they obtain against their own judgment when making a marketing decision.

Note that the overall structure of the marketing plan (Exhibit 2.1) should not be viewed as a series of sequential planning steps. Many of the marketing plan elements are decided upon simultaneously and in conjunction with one another. Similarly, the sample summary marketing plan (Exhibit 2.2) does not begin to cover the intricacies and detail of a full marketing plan. Further, the content of every marketing plan is different, depending on the organization and its mission, objectives, targets, and marketing mix components. Visualize how the marketing plan in Exhibit 2.2 would differ if only cellular communication connectivity services (and not the physical products) were being offered. How would the plan differ if the target market consisted of Fortune 500 firms with large sales forces instead of executives?

The outline in Exhibit 2.8 is an expanded set of questions that can guide the formulation of a marketing plan. However, this outline should not be regarded as the only correct format for a marketing plan. Many organizations have their own distinctive format or terminology used for creating such a plan. Every marketing plan should be unique to the firm for which it was created. Remember that although the format and order of presentation should be flexible, the same types of questions and topic areas should be covered in any marketing plan.

As you can see by the extent of the marketing plan outline in Exhibit 2.8, creating a complete marketing plan is not a simple or quick effort. However, it can be instructive to create summary marketing plans such as the sample summary plan shown in Exhibit 2.2 to get a quick idea of what a firm's marketing strategy is all about.

EFFECTIVE STRATEGIC PLANNING

10 Identify several techniques that help make strategic planning effective.

Effective strategic planning requires continual attention and creativity, as well as a commitment from management:

- Strategic planning is not an annual exercise, in which managers go through the motions and forget about it until the next year. Rather, strategic planning should be an ongoing process, because the environment is continually changing and the firm's resources and capabilities are continually evolving.

- Sound planning is based on creativity. Managers should challenge assumptions about the firm and the environment and establish new strategies. For example, major oil companies developed the concept of the gasoline service station in an age when cars needed frequent and rather elaborate servicing. They held on to the full-service approach, but independents were quick to respond to new realities and moved to lower cost self-service and convenience-store operations. The majors took several decades to catch up.

- Perhaps the most critical element in successful strategic planning is top management's support and participation. For example, Compaq Computer posted its first quarterly loss ever in fall 1991. It immediately ousted its founder and promoted Echard Pfeiffer to CEO. Compaq's Mr. Pfeiffer, 53 years old, says he exhorted people "to compete for market share across the entire spec-

Exhibit 2.8 *Marketing Plan Outline*

I. Business Mission
- What is the mission of the firm? What business is it in? How well is its mission understood throughout the organization? Five years from now, what business does it wish to be in?
- Does the firm define its business in terms of benefits its customers want rather than in terms of goods and services?

II. Objectives
- Is the firm's mission statement able to be translated into operational terms regarding the firm's objectives?
- What are the stated objectives of the organization? Are they formally written down? Do they lead logically to clearly stated marketing objectives? Are objectives based on sales, profits, or customers?
- Are the organization's marketing objectives stated in hierarchical order? Are they specific, so that progress toward achievement can be measured? Are the objectives reasonable in light of the organization's resources? Are the objectives ambiguous? Do the objectives specify a time frame?
- Is the firm's main goal to maximize customer satisfaction or to get as many customers as possible?

III. Situation Analysis (SWOT Analysis)
- Is there a strategic window that must be taken into account?
- Have one or more differential advantages been identified in the SWOT analysis?
- Are these advantages sustainable against the competition?

A. Internal Strengths and Weaknesses
- What is the history of the firm, including sales, profits, and organizational philosophies?
- What is the nature of the firm and its current situation?
- What resources does the firm have (financial, human, time, experience, asset, skill).
- What policies inhibit the achievement of the firm's objectives with respect to organization, resource allocation, operations, hiring, training, and so on?

B. External Opportunities and Threats
- Social: What major social and lifestyle trends will have an impact on the firm? What action has the firm been taking in response to these trends?
- Demographics: What impact will forecasted trends in the size, age, profile, and distribution of population have on the firm? How will the changing nature of the family, the increase in the proportion of women in the workforce, and changes in the ethnic composition of the population affect the firm? What action has the firm taken in response to these developments and trends? Has the firm reevaluated its traditional products and expanded the range of specialized offerings to respond to these changes?
- Economic: What major trends in taxation and income sources will have an impact on the firm? What action has the firm taken in response to these trends?

- Political, Legal, and Financial: What laws are now being proposed at international, federal, state, and local levels that could affect marketing strategy and tactics? What recent changes in regulations and court decisions affect the firm? What political changes at each government level are taking place? What action has the firm taken in response to these legal and political changes?
- Competition: Which organizations are competing with the firm directly by offering a similar product? Which organizations are competing with the firm indirectly by securing its prime prospects' time, money, energy, or commitment? What new competitive trends seem likely to emerge? How effective is the competition? What benefits do competitors offer that the firm does not? Is it appropriate for the firm to compete?
- Technological: What major technological changes are occurring that affect the firm?
- Ecological: What is the outlook for the cost and availability of natural resources and energy needed by the firm? Are the firm's products, services, and operations environmentally friendly?

IV. Marketing Strategy
A. Target Market Strategy
- Are the members of each market homogeneous or heterogeneous with respect to geographic, sociodemographic, and behavioral characteristics?
- What are the size, growth rate, and national and regional trends in each of the organization's market segments?
- Is the size of each market segment sufficiently large or important to warrant a unique marketing mix?
- Are market segments measurable and accessible to distribution and communication efforts?
- Which are the high- or low-opportunity segments?
- What are the evolving needs and satisfactions being sought by target markets?
- What benefits does the organization offer to each segment? How do these benefits compare with benefits offered by competitors?
- Is the firm positioning itself with a unique product? Is the product needed?
- How much of the firm's business is repeat versus new business? What percentage of the public can be classified as nonusers, light users, and heavy users?
- How do current target markets rate the firm and its competitors with respect to reputation, quality, and price? What is the firm's image with the specific market segments it seeks to serve?
- Does the firm try to direct its products only to specific groups of people or to everybody?
- Who buys the firm's products? How does a potential customer find out about the organization? When and how does a person become a customer?
- What are the major objections given by potential customers as to why they do not buy the firm's products?

continued

Exhibit 2.8 *Marketing Plan Outline (continued)*

- How do customers find out about and decide what to purchase? When and where?
- Should the firm seek to expand, contract, or change the emphasis of its selected target markets? If so, in which target markets and how vigorously?
- Could the firm more usefully withdraw from some areas in which there are alternative suppliers and use its resources to serve new, unserved customer groups?
- What publics other than target markets (financial, media, government, citizen, local, general, and internal) represent opportunities or problems for the firm?

B. Marketing Mix
- Does the firm seek to achieve its goal chiefly through the coordinated use of marketing activities (product, distribution, promotion, and pricing) or only through intensive promotion?
- Are the objectives and roles of each element of the marketing mix clearly specified?

1. Product
   - What are the major product/service offerings of the firm? Do they complement each other, or is there unnecessary duplication?
   - What are the features and benefits of each product offering?
   - Where is the firm and each major product in its life cycle?
   - What are the pressures among various target markets to increase or decrease the range and quality of products?
   - What are the major weaknesses in each product area? What are the major complaints? What goes wrong most often?
   - Is the product name easy to pronounce? Spell? Recall? Is it descriptive, and does it communicate the benefits the product offers? Does the name distinguish the firm or product from all others?
   - What warranties are offered with the product? Are there other ways to guarantee customer satisfaction?
   - Does the product offer good customer value?
   - How is customer service handled? How is the quality of service assessed?

2. Place/Distribution
   - Should the firm try to deliver its offerings directly to customers, or can it better deliver selected offerings by involving other organizations? What channel(s) should be used in distributing product offerings?
   - What physical distribution facilities should be used? Where should they be located? What should be their major characteristics?
   - Are members of the target market willing and able to travel some distance to buy the product?
   - How good is access to facilities? Can access be improved? Which facilities need priority attention in these areas?
   - How are facility locations chosen? Is the site accessible to the target markets? Is it visible to the target markets?
   - What are the location and atmosphere of retail establishments? Do these retailers satisfy customers?
   - When are products made available to users (season of year, day of week, time of day)? Are these times most appropriate?

3. Promotion
   - How does a typical customer find out about the firm's products?
   - Does the message the firm delivers gain the attention of the intended target audience? Does it address the wants and needs of the target market, and does it suggest benefits or a means for satisfying these wants? Is the message appropriately positioned?
   - Does the promotion effort effectively inform, persuade, educate, and remind customers about the firm's products?
   - Does the firm establish budgets and measure the effectiveness of promotional efforts?

   a. Advertising
      - Which media are currently being used? Has the firm chosen the type of media that will best reach its target markets?
      - Are the types of media used the most cost effective, and do they contribute positively to the firm's image?
      - Are the dates and times the ads will appear the most appropriate? Has the firm prepared several versions of its advertisements?
      - Does the organization use an outside advertising agency? What functions does the ad agency perform for the organization?
      - What system is used to handle consumer inquiries resulting from advertising and promotions? What follow-up is done?

   b. Public Relations
      - Is there a well-conceived public relations and publicity program? Can the program respond to bad publicity?
      - How is public relations normally handled by the firm? By whom? Have those responsible nurtured working relationships with media outlets?
      - Is the firm using all available public relations avenues? Is an effort being made to understand each of the publicity outlets' needs and to provide each with story types that will appeal to its audience in readily usable forms?
      - What do the annual reports say about the firm and its products? Who is being effectively reached by this vehicle? Does the benefit of publication justify the cost?

   c. Personal Selling
      - How much of a typical salesperson's time is spent soliciting new customers, compared to serving existing customers?
      - How is it determined which prospect will be

Exhibit 2.8 *Marketing Plan Outline (continued)*

called on and by whom? How is the frequency of contacts determined?
- How is the sales force compensated? Are there incentives for encouraging more business?
- How is the sales force organized and managed?
- Has the sales force prepared an approach tailored to each prospect?
- Does the firm match sales personnel with the target market characteristics?
- Is there appropriate follow-up to the initial personal selling effort? Are customers made to feel appreciated?
- Can database or direct marketing be used to replace or supplement the sales force?

  d. Sales Promotion
- What is the specific purpose of each sales promotion activity? Why is it offered? What does it try to achieve?
- What categories of sales promotion are being used? Are sales promotions directed to the trade, the final consumer, or both?
- Is the effort directed at all the firm's key publics or restricted to only potential customers?

4. Price
- What levels of pricing and specific prices should be used?
- What mechanisms does the firm have to ensure that the prices charged are acceptable to customers?
- How price sensitive are customers?
- If a price change is put into effect, how will the number of customers change? Will total revenue increase or decrease?
- Which method is used for establishing a price:

the going rate, demand-oriented prices, or cost-based prices?
- What discounts are offered and with what rationale?
- Has the firm considered the psychological dimensions of price?
- Have price increases kept pace with cost increases, inflation, and competitive levels?
- How are price promotions used?
- Do interested prospects have opportunities to sample products at an introductory price?
- What methods of payment are accepted? Is it in the firm's best interest to use these various methods?

V. Implementation, Evaluation, and Control
- Is the marketing organization structured appropriately to implement the marketing plan?
- What specific activities must take place? Who is responsible for these activities?
- What is the implementation timetable?
- What other marketing research is necessary?
- What will the financial impact of this plan be on a one-year projected income statement? How does projected income compare with expected revenue if the plan is not implemented?
- What are the performance standards?
- What monitoring procedures (audits) will take place and when?
- Does it seem as though the firm is trying to do too much or not enough?
- Are the core marketing strategies for achieving objectives sound? Are the objectives being met, and are the objectives appropriate?
- Are enough resources (or too many resources) budgeted to accomplish the marketing objectives?

trum" of the PC market instead of focusing on high-priced products. "That was a simple change," he recalls. But such a strategic shift is so radical that "you have to communicate it a hundred times or more. It doesn't sink in the first few times."[14]

During the first year after he assumed Compaq's No. 1 job, Mr. Pfeiffer unveiled a new line of bargain-priced machines and also mounted an assault on the small-business and home-PC markets. In addition, he overhauled the manufacturing process and expanded abroad.

LOOKING BACK

Look back at the competitive market of corporate jets. Each market entrant has sought a differential advantage, such as the speed of the Citation X, the range of the Gulfstream V, or the low cost of the CarterCopter. Each competitor is using a marketing plan that includes a business mission, objectives, a situation analysis, a target market definition, and a description of the marketing mix elements (product, place, promotion, and price). The story makes clear the differences in product and price of-

ferings; promotion and distribution differences are assumed as well. Although all these forms of corporate transportation are targeting the corporate travel market, other segments in the transportation market seek different benefits and have differing abilities to afford transportation. A good marketing plan will help each firm to become and remain successful.

KEY TERMS

cash cow *34*

control *41*

differential advantage *37*

diversification *33*

dog *35*

environmental scanning *30*

evaluation *41*

four Ps *39*

implementation *41*

market attractiveness/company strength matrix *36*

market development *33*

marketing audit *41*

marketing mix *39*

marketing myopia *27*

marketing objective *28*

marketing plan *25*

marketing planning *24*

marketing strategy *38*

market opportunity analysis *38*

market penetration *33*

mission statement *27*

planning *24*

portfolio matrix *34*

problem child (question mark) *35*

star *34*

strategic business unit (SBU) *28*

strategic planning *24*

strategic window *31*

sustainable competitive advantage *38*

SWOT analysis *29*

SUMMARY

1 *Understand the importance of strategic marketing and writing the marketing plan.* Strategic marketing planning is the basis for all marketing strategies and decisions. The marketing plan is a written document that acts as a guidebook of marketing activities for the marketing manager. By specifying objectives and defining the actions required to attain them, a marketing plan provides the basis on which actual and expected performance can be compared.

2 *Define an appropriate business mission statement.* The mission statement is based on a careful analysis of benefits sought by present and potential customers and an analysis of existing and anticipated environmental conditions. The firm's long-term vision, embodied in the mission statement, establishes boundaries for all subsequent decisions, objectives, and strategies. A mission statement should focus on the market or markets the organization is attempting to serve, rather than on the good or service offered.

3 *Know the criteria for stating good marketing objectives.* Objectives should be realistic, measurable, and time specific. Objectives must also be consistent and indicate the priorities of the organization.

4 *Explain the components of a situation analysis.* In the situation (or SWOT) analysis, the firm should identify its internal strengths (S) and weaknesses (W) and also examine external opportunities (O) and threats (T). When examining external opportunities and threats, marketing managers must analyze aspects of the marketing environment in a process called environmental scanning. The six most often studied macroenvironmental forces are social, demographic, economic, technological, political and legal, and competitive forces. During the situation analysis, the marketer should try to identify any strategic windows. Additionally, it is crucial that a differential advantage be identified and that it be established that this is a sustainable competitive advantage.

5 *Identify strategic alternatives and describe tools used to help select alternatives.* The strategic opportunity matrix can be used to help management develop strategic alternatives. The four options are market penetration, product development, market development, and diversification. The portfolio matrix is a method of determining the profit potential and investment requirements of a firm's SBUs by classifying them as stars, cash cows, problem children, or dogs and then determining appropriate resource allocations for each. A more detailed alternative to the portfolio matrix is the market attractiveness/company strength matrix, which measures company and market viability.

6 *Discuss target market strategies.* The target market strategy identifies which market segment or segments to focus on. The process begins with a market opportunity analysis, or MOA, which describes and estimates the size and sales potential of market segments that are of interest to the firm. In addition, an assessment of key competitors in these market segments is performed. After the market segments are described, one or more may be targeted by the firm. The three strategies for selecting target markets are appealing to the entire market with one marketing mix, concentrating on one segment, and appealing to multiple market segments using multiple marketing mixes.

7 *Describe elements of the marketing mix.* The marketing mix (or "four Ps") is a blend of product, distribution (place), promotion, and pricing strategies designed to produce mutually satisfying exchanges with a target market. The starting point of the marketing mix is the product offering. Products can be tangible goods, ideas, or services. Distribution strategies are concerned with making products available when and where customers want them. Promotion includes personal selling, advertising, sales promotion, and public relations. Price is what a buyer must give up to obtain a product and is often the easiest to change of the four marketing mix elements.

8 *Understand why implementation, evaluation, and control of the marketing plan is necessary.* Before a marketing plan can work, it must be implemented; that is, people must perform the actions in the plan. The plan should also be evaluated to see if it has achieved its objectives. Poor implementation can be a major factor in a plan's failure. Control provides the mechanisms for evaluating marketing results in light of the plan's goals and for correcting actions that do not help the organization reach those goals within budget guidelines.

9 *Know how to structure a basic marketing plan.* Although there is no set formula for a marketing plan, or a single correct outline, basic factors that should be covered include stating the business mission, setting objectives, performing a situation analysis of internal and external environmental forces, selecting one or more target markets, delineating a marketing mix (product, place, promotion, and price), and establishing ways to implement, evaluate, and control the plan.

10 *Identify several techniques that help make strategic planning effective.* First, management must realize that strategic planning is an ongoing process and not a once-a-year exercise. Second, good strategic planning involves a high level of creativity. Finally, top management's support and cooperation are required.

Discussion and Writing Questions

1. Your cousins want to start their own business, and they are in a hurry. They have decided not to write a marketing plan, because they have already gotten funding from your uncle and do not need a formal proposal, and writing such a document would take too long. Explain why it is important for them to write a plan anyway.

2. How can a new company best define its business mission statement? Can you find examples of good and bad mission statements on the Internet?

How could you improve these mission statements?

3. The new marketing manager has stated that the marketing objective of the firm is to do the best job of satisfying the needs and wants of the customer. Explain that although this objective is admirable, it does not meet the criteria for a good objective. What are these criteria? What is a specific example of a better objective?

4. Break into small groups and discuss examples (at least two per person) of the last few products you have purchased. What were the specific strategies used to achieve a differential advantage? Is that differential advantage sustainable against the competition?

5. Perform a mini-situation analysis by stating one strength, one weakness, one opportunity, and one threat to the CarterCopter described in the opening vignette to this chapter. What are the strategic growth options available for CarterCopter, based on your evaluation? Where does Carter-Copter fit on the two strategic matrices discussed in the text?

6. You are tasked with deciding the

marketing strategy for a transportation service. How do the elements of the marketing mix change when the target market is (a) corporate international business travelers, (b) low-income workers without personal transportation, or (c) companies with urgent documents or perishable materials to get to customers?

7. Create a marketing plan to increase enrollment in your school. Write down each step, and describe the controls on the plan's implementation.

8. How has Sony fit its environmental action plan into its marketing plan?

http://www.sony.co.jp/CorporateCruise/

9. How do the following Web sites compare? How do these sites seem to fit into each company's marketing plan?

http://www.mcdonalds.com/

http://www.wendys.com/

Application for Small Business

Child-related businesses aren't just kid stuff anymore. Companies catering to the little ones are big news. Societal trends are making their mark on child-related businesses. Parents are concerned about their children's mental fitness. Shrinking school budgets and decaying school systems have left a wide-open niche for entrepreneurs to fill. Companies that provide all types of extracurricular educational programs, from music lessons to science classes, are sizzling. Because many children don't get enough access to computers in the classroom, and because computer know-how is essential to any child's future, successful programs that train kids in computer use are especially popular.

To respond to this need, the CyberPlay Computer Exploration Center was started in 1995 in Florida. Upon graduation, you would like to buy the franchise rights to open your own CyberPlay center in your hometown. Franchise rights cost between $340,000 and $940,000.[15] A partner has agreed to supply $500,000 of start-up capital.

Questions

1. What is an appropriate mission statement for your new business?
2. What is a specific objective you would like to achieve?
3. What are the strengths, weaknesses, opportunities, and threats in this situation?
4. What strategic growth options can CyberPlay pursue?
5. Where does CyberPlay fit on strategic matrix tools?
6. Is your target market schools, parents, or children? Why?
7. What are the elements of your marketing mix? Describe a brief strategy for each of the four Ps.

VIDEO CASE

New England Culinary Institute

The New England Culinary Institute is based in Montpelier, Vermont, and is now one of the finest small schools for culinary training. When the school first started 15 years ago, there was no faculty, no money, no facilities, no curriculum, no accreditation, and many other competitors (over 600 other schools nationwide).

The mission of the New England Culinary Institute is to be the best small culinary school in the nation. Managers decided that the first priority was to attract top faculty, so they hired the executive chef of Yale University before the Culinary Institute opened. A board of advisors was formed, including top chefs, managers, and owners of leading restaurants. The curriculum was modeled after medical schools and the European model of learning, which includes internships and hands-on apprenticeships for students.

A strategic decision was also made to continue to invest in people, not facilities. Instead of building school facilities, students started classes in a local hotel kitchen. Now students learn and work in four restaurants, two cafeterias, a bake shop, a college food service, and banquet and catering operations. Currently, one-third of the revenue of the New England Culinary Institute comes from these food services. (The rest is from tuition.)

The school is not only attracting star chefs, but students from every state in the country and around the world. Students receive personal attention in very small classes (no more than seven students assigned to one chef) and a maximum amount of hands-on training. Graduates are receiving top jobs after completing their bachelor of arts at the New England Culinary Institute.

Questions

1. Write a business mission statement for the New England Culinary Institute.
2. Translate the goals of the New England Culinary Institute into

specific and measurable objectives.

3. Conduct a brief SWOT analysis for the New England Culinary Institute.

4. How would you classify the organizational culture of the New England Culinary Institute in terms of its response to the environment?

5. What strategic growth alternative is the New England Culinary Institute currently pursuing?

6. Where would you place the New England Culinary Institute in a portfolio matrix?

7. Briefly outline the four marketing mix elements for the New England Culinary Institute.

8. How should the New England Culinary Institute follow up and control its strategic marketing plan?

LEARNING OBJECTIVES *After studying this chapter, you should be able to:*

1 Discuss the external environment of marketing and explain how it affects a firm.

2 Describe the social factors that affect marketing.

3 Explain the importance to marketing managers of current demographic trends.

4 Explain the importance to marketing managers of multiculturalism and growing ethnic markets.

5 Identify consumer and marketer reactions to the state of the economy.

6 Identify the impact of technology on a firm.

7 Discuss the political and legal environment of marketing.

8 Explain the basics of foreign and domestic competition.

The Marketing Environment

What's hot in toys today? Hasbro's featured attraction is a line of Star Wars action figures—derived from a movie series that began nearly 20 years ago. There's Pro-Doh, a knock-off of Play-Doh, which had its premiere in 1956; and Orbix Cube, which began as Rubik's Cube in 1981. As for Mattel, the No. 1 toy maker, it devotes much of its energy to repackaging Barbie, now a well-preserved doll of 37 years. Of the 15 top-selling toys and games on the market today, only three are toy-company inventions that originated since 1995.

Adds Frank Reysen, the editor of *Playthings,* an industry magazine: "One wonders if toy makers are running out of ideas."

Toy makers deny that. "I think there is a great premium on creativity by toy companies," says Alfred Verrecchia, chief operating officer of Hasbro, who notes that the company turns over 25 percent of its product line each year. He says Hasbro is as creative as ever, albeit with an emphasis on lengthening the value of a toy by planning for it to have an extended life.

Still, Hasbro spends only about a third as much on toy research and development (R&D) as it does on marketing. Mattel spends more than five times as much on marketing as on product development and design. Part of the reason is that toy makers get some of their ideas from free-lance toy inventors, not just their own R&D. Nonetheless, "marketing is the name of the game in the toy industry," says a Mattel spokesman, Glenn Bozarth.

Bozarth says Mattel's strategy is partly an outcome of watching too many highfliers flame out. The industry was rocked by the demise in the 1980s of hot-product shops like Coleco Industries, Inc., which launched Cabbage Patch Kids, and Worlds of Wonder, Inc., producer of Teddy Ruxpin and Laser Tag. "Mattel's point of view is that a toy maker must be a brand builder to survive," he says.

But if building brands comes at the expense of invention, the toy companies are running a different type of risk—that of missing out on blockbuster categories. That's what happened with video games. Having given up after some early forays into video games, major U.S. toy companies have watched Japanese companies like Sega Enterprises, Inc., and Nintendo Co. take that business from zero to $6 billion in annual sales. Sales of traditional toys, meanwhile, are sluggish—hampered by a lack of blockbusters.

Robert Steiner has seen both the old and the new. The son of Kenner's, Inc., (makers of the Easy Bake oven and the Spirograf draw-

ing toy) founder, he says that "the toy industry used to be a 'better mousetrap' business." Until the 1970s, products were made to appeal to parents, and manufacturers had the luxury of designing sophisticated toys because they could count on the department stores, where most were sold, to demonstrate new products for consumers.

But when discounters like Kmart and Wal-Mart took over toy retailing in the late 1970s and 1980s, Mr. Steiner says, they didn't employ salespeople with the time to demonstrate or explain toys. Instead, the discounters placed the responsibility of product promotion on manufacturers—whose recourse then became television. Toy advertising on

TV—about $9 million a year in the early 1960s—reached over $1 billion a year by the mid-1990s. The first movie-toy blockbuster was a Star Wars line in 1977.

Today, the most valued people in a toy company's development department "aren't idea guys, but people who can draw," says Bruce Whitehill, a game inventor who has worked for Mattel, Hasbro's Milton Bradley unit, and others. The illustrators' value, he explains, lies in sketching new prototypes for old characters such as Barbie or Batman. The day he reported to work at Milton Bradley, Whitehill says, he was told two things: Invent games with the head buyer at Toys R Us in mind, not the consumer; and don't create games that can't be explained in a 30-second commercial on TV. In other words, the real target customer is the toy buyer for major chains—not the child or the parent.[1]

Changing consumer tastes and values, domestic and international competition, and the employment of new and different technologies (e.g., promoting toys via television) had a strong impact on the toy industry. Technology, competition, and consumer tastes are uncontrollable factors in the marketing environment. Does the external environment affect the marketing mix of most companies? What other uncontrollable factors in the external environment might affect the toy industry? What might happen to any company that ignores the external environment?

Hasbro, Inc.
Mattel, Inc.
How does Hasbro utilize its WWW site to build brand identity? Compare Mattel's site with Hasbro's. Which builds brand identity most effectively? Why?
http://www.hasbro.com/

---

1 Discuss the external environment of marketing and explain how it affects a firm.

target market
A defined group most likely to buy a firm's product.

THE EXTERNAL MARKETING ENVIRONMENT

As you learned in Chapters 1 and 2, managers create a marketing mix by uniquely combining product, distribution, promotion, and price strategies. The marketing mix is, of course, under the firm's control and is designed to appeal to a specific group of potential buyers. A **target market** is a defined group that managers feel is most likely to buy a firm's product.

Over time, managers must alter the marketing mix because of changes in the environment in which consumers live, work, and make purchasing decisions. For example, up until the 1970s toys were primarily designed to appeal to parents. Now they are designed to appeal to buyers at huge discount specialty chains like Toys R Us. This means that toy distribution has largely shifted from "mom and pop" toy stores to the chain discounters. Also, as markets mature, some new consumers become part of the target market; others drop out. Those who remain may have different tastes, needs, incomes, lifestyles, and buying habits than the original target consumers.

Although managers can control the marketing mix, they cannot control elements in the external environment that continually mold and reshape the target market. Exhibit 3.1 shows the controllable and uncontrollable variables that affect the target market, whether it consists of consumers or business purchasers. The uncontrollable elements in the center of the diagram continually evolve and create changes in the target market. In contrast, managers can shape and reshape the marketing mix, depicted on the left side of the exhibit, to influence the target market.

UNDERSTANDING THE EXTERNAL ENVIRONMENT

Unless marketing managers understand the external environment, the firm cannot intelligently plan for the future. Thus, many organizations assemble a team of specialists to continually collect and evaluate environmental information, a process called environmental scanning. The goal in gathering the environmental data is to identify future market opportunities and threats.

For example, as technology continues to blur the line between personal computers and compact disc players, a company like Sony may find itself competing against a company like Compaq. Research shows that children would like to find more games

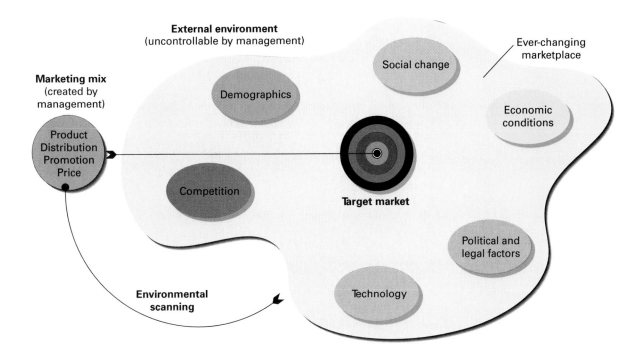

External environment
(uncontrollable by management)

Social change

Ever-changing
marketplace

Demographics

Economic
conditions

Marketing mix
(created by
management)

Product
Distribution
Promotion
Price

Competition

Target market

Political and
legal factors

Environmental
scanning

Technology

bundled with computer software, while adults are more likely to mention desiring various word-processing and business-related software.[2] Is this information an opportunity or a threat to Compaq marketing managers?

Note how two companies have responded to other environmental trends:

- The average age of the traditional target market for some models of Cadillac is approaching 70. An aging target market means big problems for the company. Cadillac's share of the roughly 1.2 million-unit luxury market is now 15 percent, down from 24 percent in 1989. To offset this trend, Cadillac created the Catera. Its target market is entry-level luxury car buyers, i.e., buyers of the BMW 3-series or the Lexus ES300. The Catera has drawn praise from automotive magazines, but they are lukewarm about its styling.[3]

- Changing social trends towards casualness have finally reached the office. Many firms now have a "dress-down" day on Fridays, when coats and ties aren't required. When Schwab, the discount stockbroker, considered offering a "dress-down" day it called its San Francisco neighbor, Levi Strauss and Company, the blue jeans and casual wear manufacturer, for a little fashion advice. What it got was a lot more than advice: The world's largest branded-apparel maker sent over brochures showing how dress could be casual without being sloppy. It provided lists of other companies that had successfully shed traditional attire and studies that showed how the apparel shift had improved workers' productivity and morale. And Levi's dispatched a video that it produced on the subject of casual business wear, which Schwab played in its cafeteria and at meetings. "People asked whether we were pushing Levi's merchandise," recalls Julius James, a human-resource director.[4] The campaign, which has cost Levi's only $5 million so far, has

Exhibit 3.1
Effect of Uncontrollable Factors in the External Environment on the Marketing Mix

Cadillac created the Catera to appeal to entry-level luxury car buyers. The company hopes to offset the problems of an aging target market with a model that appeals to younger buyers.
© Michael L. Abramson

ranged from putting on fashion shows featuring the company's clothing, to staffing a toll-free number for employers who have questions about casual business wear, to holding seminars for human-resource directors. Levi's is responding to changing dress codes (social/cultural trends) by changing its promotional and product strategy.

Evolving lifestyles, changing attitudes, and emerging technology—all outside the direct control of the companies—led Mattel to develop different kinds of toys, Levi's to alter its promotional plans, and Cadillac to produce a new car for a younger target market. Sometimes the changing environment can pose a threat. When it does, the challenge to marketing managers is to convert the threat into an opportunity. Consider the following example:

> What do you do when you're in the suntan business and America decides to end its love affair with the sun? As the sale of sunblocks climbed, Coppertone was frustrated in its attempt to get its share of the emerging market. "Coppertone is for tanning, not for blocking," consumers seemed to be saying.
>
>   So the company went back to its origins—a cute little girl with a dog nipping at her bathing suit and the slogan "Tan, Don't Burn." Whom do you want to protect most from the sun? Children. What's the most important quality a children's sunblock should have? Waterproofing.

Coppertone called its new sunblock Water Babies and featured the name on the package along with the little girl and the dog. The Coppertone logo was visible but smaller. Water Babies has been an enormous success. Not only is the product profitable, but it's also helping Coppertone keep pace with a trend toward sensible skin care.[5]

Environmental Management

No one business is large or powerful enough to create major change in the external environment. Thus, marketing managers are basically adapters rather than agents of change. For example, despite the huge size of General Motors, Ford, and Chrysler, these companies have only recently been able to stem the competitive push by the Japanese for an ever-growing share of the U.S. automobile market. Competition is basically an uncontrollable element in the external environment.

However, a firm is not always completely at the mercy of the external environment. Sometimes a firm can influence external events. For example, extensive lobbying by Federal Express enabled it to recently acquire virtually all of the Japanese routes which it has sought. Japan had originally opposed new cargo routes for Federal Express. The favorable decision was based upon months of lobbying by Federal Express at the White House, at several agencies, and in Congress for help in overcoming Japanese resistance.[6] When a company implements strategies that attempt to shape the external environment within which it operates, it is engaging in **environmental management.**

The factors within the external environment that are important to marketing managers can be classified as social, demographic, economic, technological, political and legal, and competitive.

environmental management
When a company implements strategies that attempt to shape the external environment within which it operates.

SOCIAL FACTORS

2 Describe the social factors that affect marketing.

Social change is perhaps the most difficult external variable for marketing managers to forecast, influence, or integrate into marketing plans. Social factors include our attitudes, values, and lifestyles. Social factors influence the products people buy, the prices paid for products, the effectiveness of specific promotions, and how, where, and when people expect to purchase products.

Marketing-Oriented Values of the 1990s

Today's consumers are demanding, inquisitive, and discriminating. No longer willing to tolerate products that break down, they are insisting on high-quality goods that save time, energy, and often calories. U.S. consumers rank the characteristics of product quality as (1) reliability, (2) durability, (3) easy maintenance, (4) ease of use, (5) a trusted brand name, and (6) a low price. Shoppers are also concerned about nutrition and want to know what's in their food. In the late 1980s, barely a third of grocery shoppers read labels on the foods they bought; today half of them do.[7]

Today's shoppers are also environmentalists. Eight in 10 U.S. consumers regard themselves as environmentalists, and half of those say they are strong ones.[8] Four out of five shoppers are willing to pay 5 percent more for products packaged with recyclable or biodegradable materials. Many marketers predict that by the year 2000 it will be very hard to sell a product that isn't environmentally friendly.

In the 1990s, fewer consumers say that expensive cars, designer clothes, pleasure trips, and "gold" credit cards are necessary components of a happy life. Instead, they put value on nonmaterial accomplishments, such as having control of their lives and being able to take a day off when they want.[9] Dual-career families have a **poverty of time,** with few hours to do anything but work and commute to work, handle family situations, do housework, shop, sleep, and eat. Of the people who say they don't have enough time, only 33 percent said that they were very happy with their lives.[10]

There's a sense that the daily slack of earlier eras—the weekday golf foursome, the bridge games and vegetable gardens, the three-martini lunches, chats across the fence, and pure, uncontrollable laughter—is fast disappearing. Work consumes a huge portion of Americans' days. Their productivity pressure is exacerbated by the explosion in two-income households: No chief operating officer manages the family—even though, with aging parents and growing children, it is an increasingly complex unit. Also, in the age of the "virtual office" (working at home with a computer and modem), it has become increasingly difficult for many professionals to separate or measure the time they spend on work or leisure.

poverty of time
Lack of time to do anything but work, commute to work, handle family situations, do housework, shop, sleep, and eat.

The Growth of Component Lifestyles

People in the United States today are piecing together **component lifestyles.** A lifestyle is a mode of living; it is the way people decide to live their lives. In other words, they are choosing products and services that meet diverse needs and interests rather than conforming to traditional stereotypes.

In the past, a person's profession—for instance, banker—defined his or her lifestyle. Today a person can be a banker and also a gourmet, fitness enthusiast, dedicated single parent, and conservationist. Each of these lifestyles is associated with different goods and services and represents a target audience. For example, for the gourmet, marketers offer cooking utensils, wines, and exotic foods through magazines like *Bon Appetit* and *Gourmet.* The fitness enthusiast buys Adidas equipment and special jogging outfits and reads *Runner* magazine. Component lifestyles increase the complexity of consumers' buying habits. The banker may own a BMW but change the oil himself or herself. He or she may buy fast food for lunch but French wine for dinner, own sophisticated photographic equipment and a low-priced home stereo, and shop for socks at Kmart or Wal-Mart and suits or dresses at Brooks Brothers.

component lifestyles
Practice of choosing goods and services that meet one's diverse needs and interests rather than conforming to a single, traditional lifestyle.

The Changing Role of Families and Working Women

Component lifestyles have evolved because consumers can choose from a growing number of goods and services, and most have the money to exercise more options. Rising purchasing power has resulted from the growth of dual-income families. Approximately 58 percent of all females between 16 and 65 years old are now in the

Saturn's advertising is designed to attract women not only as buyers but also as employees in its sales force. Women comprise 16% of Saturn's sales staff and 64% of its cars are purchased by women.

© 1996 Saturn Corporation, used with permission. Copyright 1996 GM Corp. Used with permission GM Media Archives.

Titleist
How does Titleist utilize its Web site to appeal to women?

http://www.titleist.com/

workforce, and female participation in the labor force is expected to grow to 63 percent by 2005.[11] By the mid-1990s, more than 7.7 million women-owned businesses in the United States generated $1.4 trillion in revenues.[12] The phenomenon of working women has probably had a greater effect on marketing than any other social change has.

As women's earnings grow, so do their levels of expertise, experience, and authority. Working-age women are not the same group businesses targeted 30 years ago. They expect different things in life—from their jobs, from their spouses, and from the products and services they buy.

The automotive industry has finally begun to realize the power of women in vehicle purchase decisions. Women are the principal buyers for 45 percent of all cars and trucks sold in the United States.[13] Saturn's advertising aims to attract women as customers, but also to woo them into the business. In an industry with a woefully small representation of women in sales, 16 percent of Saturn's sales staff are women, compared with 7 percent industrywide. This has had a visible impact on sales to women. Even though about half of all automotive purchases are made by women, Saturn claims that women buy 64 percent of its cars.[14]

Women are also purchasing more "typically male" products. *Cigar Aficionado* magazine published an article on women and cigars recently. The cover of another issue featured supermodel Linda Evangelista with a cigar. Cigar maker Consolidated Cigar Corporation of Fort Lauderdale plans to introduce two special shapes designed for women, to be sold under the Don Diego brand. The new cigars will be large enough to provide full flavor, but tapered at the ends to make them easier to light and more comfortable for the smaller female hand.

Women account for about 20 percent of the $15 billion spent annually on golf equipment, merchandise, and playing fees. "The largest growth areas today are juniors—girls under age 18—and business women aged 25 to 39," says Paul Oppedisano, manager of marketing services for the LPGA. "Half of female golfers are under age 40."[15]

Manufacturers are paying attention. "Although Izod is the biggest player in the clothing industry for both men and women," says Oppedisano, "Liz Claiborne has developed an entire line of golf apparel." And last year, Titleist introduced Pinnacle for Women golf balls in conjunction with the Susan G. Komen Breast Cancer Foundation. The balls are imprinted with the foundation's universally recognized symbol for breast cancer awareness.

Many companies are catering to women because their affluence is growing. Others do so because women pay more. The issue is discussed in the following "Ethics in Marketing" box.

The growth in the number of working women has meant an increase in dual-career families. Although dual-career families typically have greater household incomes, they have less time for family activities (poverty of time). Their purchasing roles (which define the items traditionally bought by the man or the woman) are changing, as are their purchasing patterns. Consequently, new opportu-

Ethics in Marketing

Why Do Women Pay More?

It's well known that women often earn less than men in similar jobs, even when they have similar education and experience. It's also true that they pay more for products and services ranging from haircuts to cars.

Why do women's haircuts cost more than men's? The "traditional" response is that it takes longer to cut more hair. But two in three haircutters surveyed by the New York City Department of Consumer Affairs charge women 25 percent more than men for a basic shampoo, cut, and blow dry, averaging $20 versus $16 for men. Does it really take 25 percent longer to cut women's hair, regardless of its length, texture, and amount of styling?

For years, dry cleaners have cited the same reasons for pricing women's services higher. It is harder to press a woman's shirt with equipment designed for men's shirts. Clothing merchants usually have different staff altering men's and women's clothing, so it is harder to make true comparisons based on difficulty of the job. However, the fact remains that many stores still offer most alterations free to men, but not to women.

Women pay more for gender-specific items, too. Although it's impossible to make a direct comparison between bras and T-shirts or pantyhose and socks, it's clear that women pay more for their underclothes than men do. In fact, American women spend twice as much as men on clothing. Some of this difference is discretionary; no law says that women have to have three dozen pairs of shoes or that they need a new winter coat every year. On the other hand, American society exerts enormous pressure on women to look good and stay in fashion.

Do you think price differences between men and women's purchases can be economically justified? It is well documented that women will pay more for the same new car than a man. How can this be justified? What, in general, can be done about the male/female price discrimination problem?

Source: From "Why Women Pay More" by Gerry Myers. *American Demographics* magazine, April 1996. © 1996. Reprinted with permission.

---

nities are being created. For example, small businesses are opening daily that cater to dual-career households by offering specialized goods and services. Ice cream and yogurt parlors, cafes, and sports footwear shops have proliferated. With more women than ever working full time, there is a special demand for new household services. San Francisco Grocery Express, a warehouse operation, uses computers to take customers' telephone orders. Customers refer to a catalog listing grocery items and prices. Later, vans deliver the food to the purchasers' front doors.

Working women are now able to telephone in grocery orders and have them delivered to their front doors.
© John Abbott

Is It a New Social Trend or a Fad?

Distinguishing between a new social trend or a fad at an early stage can create numerous opportunities or prevent investing monies on the wrong product. Being first to act on a new trend can create a powerful advantage over the competition. It happened to Starbucks coffee, which capitalized on a new consumer desire for higher quality and greater variety in coffee. It's working for Snackwell's cookies and crackers, which do the best job of combining good taste with reduced fat. And when Taco Bell first recognized the power of value pricing, it gained a powerful competitive advantage.

On the other hand, companies that miss a trend will spend their time playing catch-up to the competition. The American auto industry has spent decades paying the cost of ignoring early signs that consumers wanted cars to be smaller, higher in quality, and more fuel efficient.

Correctly identifying a fad has its own benefits. Aggressive marketers can make a lot of money by reaping the short-term rewards of a fad and abandoning it just as it begins to lose its impact. More conservative companies can safely ignore a short-lived fad and concentrate on opportunities with more long-term potential. Exhibit 3.2 provides a short checklist to help marketers determine if something is a trend or a fad.

DEMOGRAPHIC FACTORS

Demographic factors—another uncontrollable variable in the external environment—are also extremely important to marketing managers. **Demography** is the study of people's vital statistics, such as their age, race and ethnicity, and location. Demographics are significant because the basis for any market is people. Demographic characteristics are strongly related to consumer buyer behavior in the marketplace and are good predictors of how the target market will respond to a specific marketing mix. This section describes some marketing trends related to age and location. We will begin by taking a closer look at key age groups.

Today's Preteens: Born to Shop

By some measures, preteens have greater **discretionary income** (money beyond necessities and taxes) than college students do. Parents give preteens as much as $14.4 billion a year to spend as they wish, and children influence household purchases amounting to more than $132 billion a year.[16] Almost without thinking about it, parents are creating the next generation of spenders.

How does spending behavior begin? When do children start making consumer choices and influencing those of their parents? There is a five-stage process for becoming a shopper:

- Stage 1, *observing*, consists of children's initial interactions with the marketplace. The first thing children learn is that the satisfying objects they usually get from their parents have commercial sources. In this stage, children make sensory contact with the marketplace and construct their first mental images of marketplace objects and symbols, such as Ronald McDonald.

---

demography
The study of people's vital statistics, such as their age, race and ethnicity, and location.

discretionary income
Money beyond necessities and taxes.

3 Explain the importance to marketing managers of current demographic trends.

Ronald McDonald is one of the first mental images of the marketplace that children develop.
© REUTERS/Carl Ho/Archive Photos

Exhibit 3.2 *Is It a Trend or a Fad?*

1. Does it fit with basic lifestyle changes?

Increased divorce rates, delayed child-bearing, more working women, and worker mobility have all had major implications for goods and services. A critical question is the degree to which a new development is consistent with these important lifestyle and value changes. Which ones support the change? Which ones conflict with it? If a new development complements other important changes, it is much more likely to be a trend. If it conflicts with these basic lifestyle changes, it is almost certain to be a fad.

When a new style or product is introduced, ask yourself whether it goes with the flow of these trends. For example, we might notice fashion models sporting a new hairstyle that is attractive but requires a lot of time and effort to care for. It is unlikely that a woman who is physically active—say, a frequent jogger—would adopt this new hairstyle.

2. What are the benefits?

What benefits do consumers receive from the new product or service? How many benefits does it have, and how strong are they? Do consumers feel good about the new product, or were they reluctantly forced to change? There has been a long-term increase in the consumption of fish and poultry, despite our long-standing love affair with beef. Compared with beef, they are healthier, lower in fat and calories, and more socially acceptable. Serving these foods is also a way to show concern for one's family. Tofu is relatively inexpensive and has fewer calories than some parts of chicken. But it still tastes like library paste to most Americans.

3. Can it be personalized?

The desire for greater individuality and different ways of self-expression has been one of our most important value changes in recent years, especially among baby boomers. The more adaptable it is, the greater chance it has of becoming a trend. For example, the overarching consumer desire to promote health and well-being can be expressed by different people in different ways—through dietary changes, exercise, not smoking, and stress reduction, to name a few. That's one important reason why healthy living is a trend.

4. Is it a trend or a side effect?

We should distinguish between a basic trend and the specific expressions of that trend. The expressions will emerge and be replaced by other expressions of the basic theme, while the trend continues to grow. One example is exercise. Different kinds of exercise, such as jogging, tennis, handball, walking, in-line skating, and low-impact aerobics, can all be described as different ways to express a desire for increased physical fitness. The specific activities may be fads that can rise and fall in popularity, while the basic health/wellness trend continues unabated.

5. What other changes have occurred?

Is the new development supported by developments in other areas? If it stands alone, it is more likely to be a fad. When the miniskirt was adopted in the 1960s, it caused an immediate and major change in the hosiery market. Pantyhose and tights grew from 10 percent of the women's hosiery market to more than 80 percent of the market in less than two years. Unfortunately, sales are declining. The movement to less formal dress, including "dress-down Fridays" and growth in at-home working, is driving down pantyhose sales.

6. Who has adopted the change?

It is always important to determine which consumers have changed their behavior. Two questions are particularly valuable in determining whether a new development will become a trend: support from unexpected sources and the degree of support from key groups. When the number of working women started to increase in the 1950s, most of the new workers were mothers whose children were school-aged or older. The women typically worked to buy extras or to finance a college education. There was little to suggest that these women had a permanent commitment to work. But it was a very different matter when mothers of young children started to work. This development reflected basic changes in social values and support from an unexpected source.

Two consumer groups are particularly important to the long-term potential of a new development. They are working women, especially mothers who hold professional-level jobs, and the older half of the baby-boom generation. If the new development is rejected by these two groups, it has virtually no chance of becoming a major trend.

Source: From "How to Tell Fads From Trends" by Martin G. Letcher. *American Demographics* magazine, December 1994. © 1994. Reprinted with permission.

- Stage 2, *making requests*, occurs while babies are still totally dependent on their parents. Through pointing, gesturing, and vocalizing, very young children convey to parents that they see something they want.

- Shopping actually begins at stage 3—*making selections*. Choosing something is the first physical act taken by an independent consumer, and it occurs as children learn to walk. As children make requests and parents fulfill them, children begin to develop a memory of the store location of certain products. Children also express their desire for independence by locating and retrieving satisfying products themselves. With permission, children leave their parents and move on their own through the store maze.

- Stage 4, *making assisted purchases,* begins when children give money in exchange for goods while the parent supervises. Instead of obtaining desired objects from their parents, children in this stage are asking for and receiving permission to obtain objects from others. Children become primary consumers who spend their own money on their own needs and wants. On average, children reach this stage at the age of $5\frac{1}{2}$.[17]

- The final stage is stage 5, *making independent purchases.* Some children make purchases without parents as early as 4 years old, but the average age is 8. The interval between stage 4 and stage 5 is the longest period of time between stages. It reflects the difficulty of learning a complex exchange system and the reluctance of many parents to let children go to stores on their own.

Many marketers recognize the importance of reaching the children's market early. Kodak not only donates cameras and film to schools as part of its Using Cameras in the Curriculum program (for kids in kindergarten through grade six), but also lines up photofinishers who will donate ther time developing the film. The company weaves environmental themes into its program. Kodak hopes to draw the 6-to-11-year-old crowd with the school program, as it did with its single-use camera decorated with characters from the hit movie *Aladdin.* For kids "too old" for such things, Kodak launched the Photo fX 35mm camera for $39.95, a "real" camera that "looks like Mom and Dad's."[18]

Teenagers: Lots of Money and Strong Opinions

Teenagers spend about $100 billion per year. Around $63 billion is their own money and the rest is family money. In total, teens spend an amount equal to half of the U.S. defense budget. Today, teenagers may be the only family members with time to stand in line at the grocery store. More than half of teenage girls and more than one-third of teenage boys do some food shopping each week for their family.

Teenagers influence household spending in four familiar ways. First, when teenagers or children accompany their parents to the store, their parents often let them add some "gimmes" to the cart. Second, teenagers influence their parents even when they are not with them, by encouraging them to buy preferred brands. Either the teen specifically requests a brand, or parents know that if they don't buy exactly what the teen wants, the purchase might go to waste. Third, teens influence adult purchases when parents actively seek their counsel. Teens often know more about certain products than their parents do; think of computers, stereos, or the latest brand of designer jeans. Fourth, teens influence parent purchasing when they ask for gifts. Teens are rarely shy about letting their parents know what they want for a birthday or other special holiday.[19]

The quality of "cool" is of paramount importance to teens when they evaluate brands. Quality in and of itself may not sell a product to teens, but it is the fundamental criterion of a cool brand. The brands teens consider to be the coolest—Nike, Guess, Levi's, Gap, and Sega—are all perceived by teens to be of high quality. After quality, the most common cool qualifier is that it is "for people my age." Teens seem to prefer things that are specifically for them, whether it's language, fashion, advertising, or brands.

Generation X: Savvy and Cynical

generation X
People who are currently between the ages of 18 and 29 years of age.

In 1997, approximately 47 million consumers were between the ages of 18 and 29. This group has been labeled **generation X.** It is the first generation of latchkey children—products of dual-career households or, in roughly half of cases, of divorced or separated parents. Generation X began entering the workforce in the era of down-sizing and downturn, so its members are likelier than the previous generation to be unemployed, underemployed, and living at home with Mom and Dad. On the other hand, 10 million are full-time college students, and 15 million are married and not living at home.[20] Yet, as a generation that's been bombarded by multiple media since their cradle days, they're savvy and cynical consumers.

The members of generation X don't mind indulging themselves. Among the young women of generation X, 38 percent go to the movies in a given month, compared with 19 percent of the women who are now in their 30s and 40s. The members of generation X devote a larger-than-average share of their spending dollars to restaurant meals, alcoholic beverages, clothing, and electronic items such as televisions and stereos.[21] One survey found that the members of generation X aspire to having a home of their own (87 percent), a lot of money (42 percent), a swimming pool (42 percent), and a vacation home (41 percent).[22] They are more materialistic than past generations, but have less hope of achieving their goals.

Perhaps it is this combination of high aspirations and low expectations that makes generation X such a challenge for marketers. "This is a generation that hates to be marketed to," says Scott Kauffman, vice president of broadcast and news media at *Entertainment Weekly*. "You have the youth of America reading novels in which chapters are titled, 'I am not a target market.'"[23]

For decades, Ford has marketed its light-duty pickups by showing roughness and toughness. Advertisements featured trucks climbing rugged mountains or four-wheeling through mud. But Ford quickly realized that this was not going to work with generation Xers.

Ford chose to lead with a new product. The company created a new version of its popular Ranger pickup, giving it flares on the fenders, jazzy graphics, and a youthful new name: Splash. The promotion campaign attempted to infuse the vehicle with personality by combining adventuresome sports with the truck. For example, one ad features a young surfer shooting the curl in the bed of a Splash parked in the middle of a wheat field. There is minimal copy—just one line listing five features and a new logo.[24]

Generation Xers are savvy and cynical consumers. They are more materialistic than earlier generations, but have less hope of achieving their goals. This makes them a challenge for marketers.

© PhotoDisc, Inc.

Baby Boomers: America's Mass Market

Almost 78 million babies were born in the United States between 1946 and 1964, which created a huge market.[25] The oldest **baby boomers** are now over 50, but they cling to their youth. One study found that baby boomers see themselves as continuing to be very active after they turn 50. They won't even think of themselves as being senior citizens until after they turn 60 (39 percent) or 70 (42 percent).[26]

This group cherishes convenience, which has resulted in a growing demand for home delivery of items like large appliances, furniture, and groceries. In addition, the spreading culture of convenience explains the tremendous appeal of prepared take-out foods and the necessity of VCRs and portable telephones.

Baby boomers' parents raised their children to think for and of themselves. Studies of child-rearing practices show that parents of the 1950s and 1960s consistently ranked "to think for themselves" as the number-one trait they wanted to nurture in their children.[27] Postwar affluence also allowed parents to indulge their children as never before. They invested in their children's skills by sending them to college. They encouraged their children to succeed in a job market that rewarded competitive drive more than cooperative spirit and individual skills more than teamwork.

In turn, the sheer size of the generation encouraged businesses to promote to the emerging individuality of baby boomers. Even before the oldest baby boomers started earning their own living more than two decades ago, astute businesspeople saw the profits that come from giving millions of young people what they want. Businesses offered individualistic baby boomers a growing array of customized products and services—houses, cars, furniture, appliances, clothes, vacations, jobs, leisure time, and even beliefs. One product that baby boomers have adopted to express their interests and individuality is decorative flags. The trend began in Richmond, Virginia, as explained in the following "Marketing and Small Business" story.

Marketing and Small Business

Mrs. Jones "Runs It Up the Flagpole"

For a city obsessed with tradition, where the first Thai restaurant was named after Confederate Lt. Gen. P.G.T. Beauregard, modern fads are about as welcome as the flu in Richmond.

Except when it comes to flags. Not Old Glory or the Stars and Bars, but decorative flags—those relentlessly cheerful banners depicting everything from reindeer and roses to pumpkins and poodles.

Blame it all on Millie Jones. Several years ago, Mrs. Jones sewed together decorative Scandinavian patches and hung the finished banner from her window in Richmond's historic Fan District. Puzzled neighbors wondered in hushed conversation if it was a Viet Cong flag. A local reporter called, asking why she had hung a "pillowcase" outside her home. Then, to announce the birth of her son, Mrs. Jones stitched an image of a train with puffs of smoke proclaiming "It's a boy" and ran the banner up her flagpole. Soon, she was receiving requests for coats of arms and other flags. Orders from outside Richmond fluttered in.

By 1990, Mrs. Jones was being called the new Betsy Ross—a moniker she gladly accepts. Letters addressed simply to "The Flag Lady, Richmond, Va.," arrived at her door. Actors James Garner and Jack Lemmon became customers. Today, flag aficionados from all parts make the pilgrimage to Richmond for a tailor-made Millie Jones flag. Mrs. Jones's Festival Flags Unlimited, Inc., expects to produce 10,000 banners annually. Fully one-third of the flags, which typically cost at least $75 each, will be sold in Richmond. Other producers now are also selling hundreds of thousands of decorative flags across the country. Maybe it's more than a simple fad.[28]

Are Mrs. Jones' flags a fad today? Or do these flags represent a trend? Review Exhibit 3.2 and defend your answer.

The importance of individualism among baby boomers led to a **personalized economy.** A personalized economy delivers goods and services at a good value on demand. Successful businesses in a personalized economy give customers what they want when they want it. To do this, they must know their customers extremely well. In fact, the intimacy between producer and consumer is exactly what makes an economy personalized.

 In the personalized economy, successful products share three characteristics:

- *Customization:* Products are custom designed and marketed to ever-smaller target markets. Today, for example, there are hundreds of cable TV channels from which to choose. In 1950, the average grocery store carried about 4,000 items; today, that number is closer to 16,000, as manufacturers target increasingly specific needs.[29]

- *Immediacy:* Successful businesses deliver products and services at the convenience of the consumer rather than the producer. Banc One, with locations in the eastern and southern states, for example, opens some of its branches on Saturdays and Sundays. Its 24-hour hot line, staffed by real people, solves problems at the customer's convenience. The immediacy of the personalized economy explains the booming business in 1-hour film processing, walk-in medical clinics, and 30-minute pizzas.

- *Value:* Businesses must price competitively or create innovative products that can command premium prices. Even the most innovative products quickly become commodities in the fast-paced personalized economy, however. Apple fell prey to this danger: Its once-innovative Macintosh computers must now compete against less expensive machines that offer similar functions.

As the age of today's average consumer moves toward 40, average consumption patterns are also changing. People in their early 40s tend to focus on their families and finances. As this group grows in number, its members will buy more furniture from manufacturers like Lazy Boy, American Martindale, Baker, and Drexel-Heritage to replace the furniture they bought early in their marriages. The demand for family counselors and wellness programs should also increase. Additionally, discount investment brokers like Charles Schwab and mutual funds like Fidelity and Dreyfus should profit. However, baby boomers are more likely than any other age group to have negative opinions about financial services such as banking and stockbrokers.[30] This may reflect the boomers' mistrust of authority. Because middle-aged consumers buy more reading materials than any other age group, the market for books and magazines should remain strong throughout the 1990s. People who buy magazines on the newsstand tend to be younger, so newsstand sales may falter while subscription sales take off.

Right now, baby boomers are concerned with their children and their jobs. These worries will fade as the kids move out of the house and boomers retire. But some things will never change. Baby boomers may always be a little selfish about their leisure time. They may always be a little careless about the way they spend their money. They will probably remain suspicious of the status quo. And they will always love rock and roll.

Older Consumers: Not Just Grandparents

As mentioned above, the oldest baby boomers have already crossed the 50 year-plus threshold that many demographers use to define the "mature market." Yet, today's mature consumers are wealthier, healthier, and better educated than those of earlier generations.[31] Although they make up only 26 percent of the population, 50-plus consumers buy half of all domestic cars, half of all silverware, and nearly half of all home remodeling.[32] Smart marketers are already targeting this growing segment. By 2020, over a third of the population will be 50 years old or older.

Many marketers have yet to tap the full potential of the huge and lucrative senior market because of enduring misconceptions about mature adults, all based on stereotypes. Here are a few:

- *Stereotype:* Older consumers are sick or ailing. *Fact:* A full 85 percent of mature citizens report themselves to be in good or excellent health. Over two-thirds of the elderly have no chronic health problems.[33] People like Mick Jagger are approaching 55.[34] These people are fit and healthy.
- *Stereotype:* Older consumers are sedentary. *Fact:* Of all travel dollars spent in the United States, 80 percent are spent by people over 50 years old.
- *Stereotype:* Older consumers have a poor retention rate. *Fact:* Senior citizens are readers and much less influenced by TV than are younger consumers.[35] Not only do they retain what they read, but they are willing to read far more copy than younger people are.
- *Stereotype:* Older consumers are interested only in price and are intolerant of change. *Fact:* Although senior citizens are as interested in price as anyone else, they are more interested in value. And a generation that has survived the better part of a century characterized by more technological change than any other in history can hardly be considered resistant to change.[36]

Acceptance of change, however, doesn't mean a lack of brand loyalty. For example, the most critical factor in determining car-owner loyalty is age. The oldest consumers (ages 65 and up) are twice as loyal to the make of car as the youngest customers are.[37] The cars most popular with older Americans are Lincoln, Cadillac, and Buick.

Marketers who want to actively pursue the mature market must understand it. Aging consumers create some obvious opportunities. JCPenney's Easy Dressing clothes feature Velcro-fastened clothing for women with arthritis or other ailments who may have difficulty with zippers or buttons. Sales from the first Easy Dressing catalog were three times higher than expected.[38] Chicago-based Cadaco offers a line of games with easy-to-read big print and larger game pieces. The series focuses on nostalgia by including Michigan rummy, hearts, poker, and bingo. Trivia buffs more familiar with Mitch Miller than Guns 'n' Roses can play Parker Brothers' "The Vintage Years" edition of Trivial Pursuit. The game, aimed at the age 50+ crowd, poses questions covering the era from Charles Lindbergh to Dwight D. Eisenhower. Consider these other examples, as well, of savvy marketers targeting the mature market:

- To counter sliding grip strength associated with advancing age, Procter & Gamble offers its Tide laundry detergent with snap-on lids rather than the usual perforated flap.
- Wheaton Medical Technologies markets a pill bottle that has a tiny battery-operated clock which registers the time the container was last opened to take out a pill.
- Knowing that grandparents purchase 25 percent of all toys (about $819 per year spent on their grandkids), F.A.O. Schwartz has added a Grandma's Shop to its two largest stores, complete with older adult salespeople.

Marketers must overcome stereotypes about mature adults in order to attract them as consumers. Mature adults are fit and healthy, retain what they read, and are interested in value.
© 1996 PhotoDisc, Inc.

- Mattel, Inc., invited readers of *Modern Maturity* to join its Grandparents Club. For a $10 fee, readers could receive a book of discount coupons; meanwhile, Mattel acquired an invaluable mailing list of potential customers.[39]

As people move through life, they inevitably change their habits. A prime example is in the area of health lifestyles. Exhibit 3.3 shows that younger people aren't so worried about getting their vitamins. Older consumers pay more attention to their

Exhibit 3.3 *Health Lifestyles of the Young, Older, and Boomer Consumers*

YOUTH: 18- to 34-YEAR-OLDS

- 42% use vitamins or supplements or try to eat mostly organic foods.
- 59% almost always read labels to find out about content of food.
- 47% have a stressful job or frequently feel a great deal of stress.
- 36% restrict the amount of red meat they eat.
- 71% have checked blood pressure and cholesterol in the past year.
- 70% could easily run or jog a mile.
- 78% have a family doctor.
- 15% drink three or more cups of coffee a day.
- 24% regularly do yoga, meditation or other stress-reducing exercises.
- 9% drink an alcoholic beverage almost every day.
- 17% smoke more than a half a pack of cigarettes a day.
- 8% have a chronic disease or condition requiring regular care.

BOOMERS: 35- to 54-YEAR-OLDS

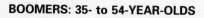

- 21% smoke more than a half a pack of cigarettes a day.
- 20% have a chronic disease or condition requiring regular care.
- 51% use vitamins or supplements or try to eat mostly organic foods.
- 63% almost always read labels to find out about content of food.
- 57% have a stressful job or frequently feel a great deal of stress.
- 49% restrict the amount of red meat they eat.
- 78% have checked blood pressure and cholesterol in past year.
- 46% could easily run or jog a mile.
- 87% have a family doctor.
- 32% drink three or more cups of coffee a day.
- 25% regularly do yoga, meditation, or other stress-reducing exercises.
- 11% drink an alcoholic beverage almost every day.

(continued)

Exhibit 3.3 *Health Lifestyles of the Young, Older, and Boomer Consumers (continued)*

SENIORS: 55 YEARS AND OVER

- 14% smoke more than a half a pack of cigarettes a day.
- 49% have a chronic disease or condition requiring regular care.
- 60% use vitamins or supplements or try to eat mostly organic foods.
- 64% almost always read labels to find out about content of food.
- 20% have a stressful job or frequently feel a great deal of stress.
- 51% restrict the amount of red meat they eat.
- 94% have checked blood pressure and cholesterol in past year.
- 22% could easily run or jog a mile.
- 91% have a family doctor.
- 30% drink three or more cups of coffee a day.
- 20% regularly do yoga, meditation or other stress-reducing exercises.
- 14% drink an alcoholic beverage almost every day.

Source: "Lifestyles of the Young, Old and In-Between," *Wall Street Journal,* 28 June 1996, p. R4.

cholesterol levels and blood pressure. Those in the middle ages feel the stress of hard work, which may contribute to why they are the biggest smokers. As lifestyles change, so does the demand for specific goods and services.

Americans on the Move

The average U.S. citizen moves every six years.[40] This trend has implications for marketers. A large influx of new people into an area creates many new marketing opportunities for all types of businesses. Remember, the primary basis of all consumer marketing is people. Conversely, significant out-migration from a city or town may force many of its businesses to move or close down. The cities with the greatest projected population growth from 1995–2005 are Houston, Washington, D.C., Atlanta, San Diego, Phoenix, Orlando, and Dallas.[41]

The United States experiences both immigration from other countries and migration within U.S. borders. In the past decade, the six states with the highest levels of immigration from abroad were California, New York, New Jersey, Illinois, Texas, and Massachusetts. The six states with the greatest population increases due to interstate migration were Florida, Georgia, North Carolina, Virginia, Washington, and Arizona.[42]

GROWING ETHNIC MARKETS

4 Explain the importance to marketing managers of multiculturalism and growing ethnic markets.

The United States is undergoing a new demographic transition: It is becoming a multicultural society. The 1990 census found that 8 in 10 people in the United States are white, down from 9 in 10 in 1960. During the remainder of the 1990s, the United States will shift further from a society dominated by whites and rooted in Western culture to a society characterized by three large racial and ethnic minorities: African-

Americans, U.S. Hispanics, and Asian-Americans. All three minorities will grow in size and in share of the population, while the white majority declines as a percentage of the total. Native Americans and people with roots in Australia, the Middle East, the former Soviet Union, and other parts of the world will further enrich the fabric of U.S. society.

The labor force of the past was dominated by white men who are now retiring. Today's senior workers are equal parts women and men, and still overwhelmingly white. But down in the entry-level jobs of 1998, a multicultural labor force is emerging. The proportion of workers who are non-Hispanic whites should decrease from 77 percent in 1997 to 74 percent in 2005.

Because so many white men are retiring, the non-Hispanic white labor force will grow only 8 percent between 1994 and 2005. The number of Hispanic workers should grow 36 percent, due to the continued immigration of young adults, higher birth rates, and relatively few retirees. These forces will also boost the number of Asian workers by 39 percent. The number of black workers will increase by 15 percent, a rate slightly slower than the rate of growth of black adults in general (16.5 percent).[43]

Ethnic and Cultural Diversity

Multiculturalism occurs when all major ethnic groups in an area—such as a city, county, or census tract—are roughly equally represented. Because of its current demographic transition, the trend in the United States is toward greater multiculturalism.

Exhibit 3.4 depicts levels of multiculturalism by county. Four of New York City's five boroughs are among the 10 most ethnically diverse counties in the country.[44] San

multiculturalism
When all major ethnic groups in an area—such as a city, county, or census tract—are roughly equally represented.

Exhibit 3.4
Levels of Ethnic Diversity in the United States, by County

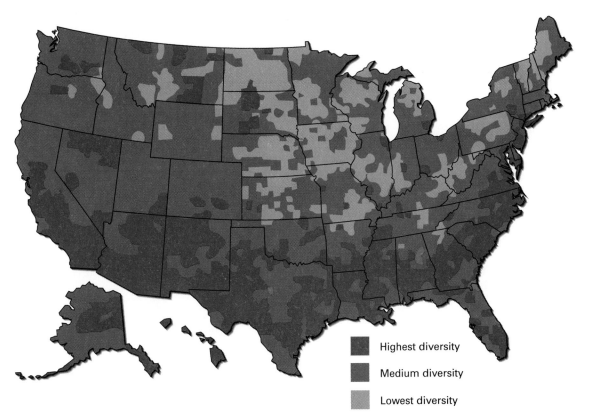

Highest diversity

Medium diversity

Lowest diversity

Source: James Allen and Eugene Turner, "Where Diversity Reigns," *American Demographics,* August 1990, p. 37. Copyright © *American Demographics.* For subscription information, please call (800) 828-1133.

Francisco County is the most diverse in the nation. The proportions of major ethnic groups are closer to being equal there than anywhere else. People of many ancestries have long been attracted to the area. The least multicultural region is a broad swath stretching from northern New England through the Midwest and into Montana. These counties have few people other than whites. The counties with the very lowest level of diversity are found in the agricultural heartland: Nebraska and Iowa.

Marketing Implications of Multiculturalism

The demographic shift and growing multiculturalism create new challenges and opportunities for marketers. The U.S. population grew from 226 million in 1980 to 260 million in 1998, much of that growth taking place in minority markets. Asians are the nation's fastest growing minority group, increasing 108 percent in the 1980s, to 7.3 million. The Hispanic population grew 53 percent, to 22.3 million; with 7.7 million new members, it had the biggest numerical gain of any minority group. African-Americans, who remain the largest minority, saw their numbers increase during the past decade by 13 percent, to 30 million. In contrast, the number of non-Hispanic whites grew by 4.4 percent. In 1994, about a quarter of the U.S. population were members of minority groups. The last census identified 110 different ethnic groups in the United States.[45]

Demographic shifts will be even more pronounced in the future. Exhibit 3.5 compares the 1997 population mix and the forecasted population mix for 2023. Note that Hispanics will be the fastest growing segment of the population. The diversity of the U.S. population is projected to stabilize around 2023, as the birthrate among minorities levels off.

The marketer's task in a diverse society is more challenging because of differences in educational level and demand for goods and services. What's more, ethnic markets are not homogeneous. There is not an African-American market or a Hispanic market, any more than there is a white market. Instead, there are many niches within ethnic markets that require micromarketing strategies. For example, African Eye, which offers women's designer fashions from Africa, attracted

Exhibit 3.5

Multicultural Makeup of the United States

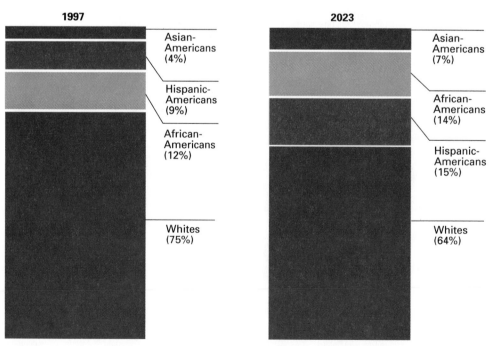

Source: U. S. Department of Labor, Bureau of the Census projections.

a thousand women to a fashion show at Prince Georges Plaza near Washington, D.C. The show featured the latest creations by Alfadi, a high-fashion Nigerian designer, who also hosted the show. African Eye's dresses and outfits blend African and Western influences and are priced at $50 to $600. Says Mozella Perry Ademiluyi, the president and cofounder of African Eye: "Our customer is professional, 30 to 65, has an income level of $30,000-plus and often is well-traveled. They don't just want to wear something that is African. They want something that is well-tailored, unique, and creative as well."[46]

An alternative to the niche strategy is to maintain a brand's core identity while straddling different languages, cultures, ages, and incomes with different promotional campaigns. Levi Strauss, for example, publishes *501 Button-Fly Report* for 14- to 24-year-olds, with Spike Lee interviewing spelunkers, roadies, cemetery tour guides, and others on what they do in their jeans. For men ages 25 and up, Levi's runs separate ads on sports programs and in magazines, showing adults in pursuits like touch football and outings with the kids. A Hispanic campaign, in TV and outdoor advertising, follows two men through their day, from working to teaching a boy to play softball. "*Levi's siempre quedan bien*"—"Levi's always fit well"—is the theme.[47]

A third strategy for multicultural marketing is to seek common interests, motivations, or needs across ethnic groups. This strategy is sometimes called **stitching niches**, which means combining ethnic, age, income, and lifestyle markets, on some common basis, to form a large market. The result may be a cross-cultural product, such as a frozen pizza-flavored egg roll. Or it may be a product that serves several ethnic markets simultaneously. Ringling Brothers and Barnum and Bailey Circus showcases acts that appeal to many ethnic groups. It broadened its appeal to Asian-Americans by adding the "Mysterious Oriental Art of Hair Hanging." Marguerite Michelle, known as the "ravishing Rapunzel," is suspended in the air on a wire attached to her waist-length hair. When the circus comes to town, the Mexican-born Michelle also goes on Spanish-language radio shows to build recognition for Ringling in the Hispanic market. The circus is promoted as "*El Espectáculo Más Grande del Mundo.*"[48]

stitching niches
Strategy for multicultural marketing which combines ethnic, age, income, and lifestyle markets, on some common basis, to form a large market.

ECONOMIC FACTORS

In addition to social and demographic factors, marketing managers must understand and react to the economic environment. The three economic areas of greatest concern to most marketers are the distribution of consumer income, inflation, and recession.

5 Identify consumer and marketer reactions to the state of the economy.

Rising Incomes

As disposable (or after-tax) incomes rise, more families and individuals can afford the "good life." Fortunately, U.S. incomes have continued to rise. After adjustment for inflation, median incomes in the United States rose 4 percent between 1980 and 1996.

Today about two-thirds of all U.S. households earn a "middle-class" income. The rough boundaries for a middle-class income are $18,000, comfortably above poverty, to about $75,000, just short of wealth. In 1997, almost half the households were in the upper end of the $18,000 to $75,000 range, as opposed to only a quarter in 1980. The percentage of households earning above $75,000 is now over 8 percent.[49] As a result, Americans are buying more goods and services than ever before. For example, in raising a child to age 17, a middle-class family will spend about $124,000 in 1997 dollars. This new level of affluence is not limited to professionals or even individuals within specific age or education brackets. Rather, it cuts across all household types, well beyond what businesses traditionally consider to be markets for high-priced goods and services. This rising affluence stems primarily from the increasing number of dual-income families.

During the remainder of the 1990s, many marketing managers will focus on families with incomes over $35,000, because this group will have the most discretionary income. The average American household has over $12,000 in discretionary income each year. Some marketers will concentrate their efforts on higher quality, higher priced goods and services. The Lexus automobile and American Airlines' "international class" service for business-class seats on transcontinental flights are examples of this trend.

Inflation

inflation
A general rise in prices without a corresponding increase in wages, which results in decreased purchasing power.

Inflation is a general rise in prices without a corresponding increase in wages, which results in decreased purchasing power. Fortunately, the United States has had a low rate of inflation for over a decade. The mid-1990s have been marked by an inflation rate under 4 percent. These economic conditions benefit marketers, because real wages, and hence purchasing power, go up when inflation stays down. A significant increase in inflation almost always depresses real wages and the ability to buy more goods and services.

In times of low inflation, businesses seeking to increase their profit margins can do so only by increasing their efficiency. If they significantly increase prices, no one will purchase their goods or services.

In more inflationary times, marketers use a number of pricing strategies to cope. (See Chapter 21 for more on these strategies.) But in general, marketers must be aware that inflation causes consumers to either build up or diminish their brand loyalty. In one research session, a consumer panelist noted, "I used to use just Betty Crocker mixes, but now I think of either Betty Crocker or Duncan Hines, depending on which is on sale." Another participant said, "Pennies count now, and so I look at the whole shelf, and I read the ingredients. I don't really understand, but I can tell if it's exactly the same. So now I use this cheaper brand, and honestly, it works just as well." Inflation pressures consumers to make more economical purchases. However, most consumers try hard to maintain their standard of living.

In creating marketing strategies to cope with inflation, managers must realize that, despite what happens to the seller's cost, the buyer is not going to pay more for a product than the subjective value he or she places on it. No matter how compelling the justification might be for a 10 percent price increase, marketers must always examine its impact on demand. Many marketers try to hold prices level as long as is practical.

Recession

recession
A period of economic activity when income, production, and employment tend to fall—all of which reduce demand for goods and services.

A **recession** is a period of economic activity when income, production, and employment tend to fall—all of which reduce demand for goods and services. The problems of inflation and recession go hand in hand, yet recession requires different marketing strategies:

- *Improve existing products and introduce new ones:* The goal is to reduce production hours, waste, and the cost of materials. Recessions increase the demand for goods and services that are economical and efficient, offer value, help organizations streamline practices and procedures, and improve customer service.

- *Maintain and expand customer services:* In a recession, many organizations postpone the purchase of new equipment and materials. Sales of replacement parts and other services may become an important source of income.

- *Emphasize top-of-the-line products and promote product value:* Customers with less to spend will seek demonstrated quality, durability, satisfaction, and capacity to save time and money. High-priced, high-value items consistently fare well during recessions.

TECHNOLOGICAL AND RESOURCE FACTORS

Sometimes new technology is an effective weapon against inflation and recession. New machines that reduce production costs can be one of a firm's most valuable assets. The power of a personal-computer microchip doubles about every 18 months.[50] Our ability, as a nation, to maintain and build wealth depends in large part on the speed and effectiveness with which we invent and adopt machines that lift productivity. For example, coal mining is typically thought of as unskilled, backbreaking labor. But visit Cyprus Amax Mineral Company's Twenty-mile Mine near Oak Creek, Colorado, and you will find workers with push-button controls who walk along massive machines that shear 30-inch slices from an 850-foot coal wall. Laptop computers help miners track equipment breakdowns and water quality.

U.S. companies often have difficulty translating the results of R&D into goods and services. The Japanese are masters at making this transformation. For example, VCRs, flat-panel displays, and compact disc players are based on U.S. research that wasn't exploited at home. The United States excels at **basic research** (or pure research), which attempts to expand the frontiers of knowledge but is not aimed at a specific, pragmatic problem. Basic research aims to confirm an existing theory or to learn more about a concept or phenomenon. For example, basic research might focus on high-energy physics. **Applied research,** in contrast, attempts to develop new or improved products. It is where the United States sometimes falls short, although many U.S. companies do conduct applied research. For example, Motorola is using applied research to create Iridium, a constellation of 66 satellites that will offer telephone service anywhere on the globe.[51] Commercial service is scheduled for 1998.

The U.S. government spends about $76 billion a year on R&D; private industry spends another $85 billion. In the 1990s, the United States has thus far spent 16 percent more on R&D than Japan, Germany, France, and the United Kingdom combined. Yet these four countries together spend 12 percent more than the United States on R&D not related to defense.[52]

R&D expenditures are only a rough measure of where the United States stands in terms of innovation. A look at management of the R&D process can be even more revealing. U.S. managers tend to be obsessed with short-term profits (one to three years) and minimal risk taking. The result is an infatuation with slight variations of existing products, which are often very profitable, instead of true innovations. Developing new products like Honey Nut Cheerios and Diet Cherry Coke is probably not the path to world economic leadership.

To regain its world leadership, the United States must promote innovation. One way is to reduce the tax on capital gains, which slashes the reward for successful innovation. The capital-gains tax is higher in the United States than in any other developed country. In the United States, a start-up company that had doubled in value over the past decade would have provided its investors with a return, after inflation and the capital-gains tax, of just over 1 percent annually. Under those rules, many managers ask, "Why bother?"

Companies must also learn how to innovate, and large R&D budgets aren't the sole answer. One of the biggest R&D spenders in the United States is General Motors, which by most standards is not a leading innovator. On the other hand, Corning has relatively low R&D budgets, but is arguably one of the five most innovative companies in the world. The difference is in management and corporate culture.

Again, we might take a cue from the Japanese. In Japan, a team composed of engineers, scientists, marketers, and manufacturers works simultaneously at three levels of innovation. At the lowest level, they seek small improvements in an existing product. At the second, they try for a significant jump, such as Sony's move from the microcassette tape recorder to the Walkman. The third is true innovation, an entirely new product. The idea is to produce three new products

6 Identify the impact of technology on a firm.

basic research
Pure research which aims to confirm an existing theory or to learn more about a concept or phenomenon.

applied research
Attempts to develop new or improved products.

to replace each current product, with the same investment of time and money. One of the three may then become the new market leader and produce the innovator's profit.

Companies must also learn to foster and encourage innovation. Rubbermaid teaches its people to let ideas flow from its so-called core competencies, the things it does best. Bud Hellman, who used to run a Rubbermaid subsidiary, was touring one of the company's picnic-cooler plants in the late 1980s when he suddenly realized he could use its plastic blow-molding technique to make a durable, lightweight, inexpensive line of office furniture. The result was the Work Manager System, which accounts for 60 percent of sales at Rubbermaid's furniture division. Toro, a Minnesota maker of mowers and other lawn equipment, fosters innovation by letting all employees know they won't be penalized for taking a risk on new ideas that fail. Bell Atlantic started what it calls its Champion program. Any employee with a good idea gets to leave his or her job for a while, at full pay and benefits, and receive training in such skills as writing a business plan and organizing a development schedule. The innovator also gets money to invest in the idea. The employee becomes the idea's champion, with a strong incentive to develop it successfully. The innovator can invest 10 percent of his or her salary in the project and give up bonuses in return for 5 percent of the revenues if the product gets to market. Since the company started the program in 1989, Champion has generated 2 patents, with 11 more pending.

Despite some problems, innovation is alive and well. Many scientists believe the world will see more innovations between 1995 and 2005 than we have seen in the previous hundred years. Computer technology will begin to play an even bigger role in the innovation process. For example, a new software program called Invention Machine Lab helps inspire and speed invention. The software forces product developers to confront the contradiction between objectives that's at the heart of every design problem. To help resolve such contradictions, it draws on 95 "inventive principles" derived from nearly 2.5 million patents—such as "color changes" or "segmentation." It also steers inventors toward effects drawn from physics, chemistry, and geometry that may be useful, and it suggests how the invention could evolve.

In designing a better vacuum cleaner, a product developer used the "Principles" module of the software to pose a contradiction between "intensity" and "use of energy." The software suggested using "pulsation." The designer used this cue to create a cycling of the suction on and off rapidly so the vacuum could be pushed during the lulls. The brainstorming "Effect" module suggested various ways to get rid of something—in this case, dust. One method, using ultrasound, seemed useful for making dust vibrate off of carpets.

POLITICAL AND LEGAL FACTORS

7 Discuss the political and legal environment of marketing.

Business needs government regulation to protect innovators of new technology, the interests of society in general, one business from another, and consumers. In turn, government needs business, because the marketplace generates taxes that support public efforts to educate our youth, protect our shores, and so on. The private sector also serves as a counterweight to government. The decentralization of power inherent in a private-enterprise system supplies the limitation on government essential for the survival of a democracy.

Every aspect of the marketing mix is subject to laws and restrictions. It is the duty of marketing managers or their legal assistants to understand these laws and conform to them, because failure to comply with regulations can have major consequences for a firm. Sometimes just sensing trends and taking corrective action before a government agency acts can help avoid regulation.

However, the challenge is not simply to keep the marketing department out of trouble, but to help it implement creative new programs to accomplish marketing objectives. It is all too easy for a marketing manager or sometimes a lawyer to say no to a marketing innovation that actually entails little risk. For example, an overly cautious lawyer could hold up sales of a desirable new product by warning that the package design could prompt a copyright infringement suit. Thus, it is important to understand thoroughly the laws established by the federal government, state governments, and regulatory agencies to control marketing-related issues.

Federal Legislation

Federal laws that affect marketing fall into several categories. First, the Sherman Act, the Clayton Act, the Federal Trade Commission Act, the Celler-Kefauver Antimerger Act, and the Hart-Scott-Rodino Act were passed to regulate the competitive environment. Second, the Robinson-Patman Act was designed to regulate pricing practices. Third, the Wheeler-Lea Act was created to control false advertising. These key pieces of legislation are summarized in Exhibit 3.6.

State Laws

State legislation that affects marketing varies. Oregon, for example, limits utility advertising to 0.5 percent of the company's net income. California has forced industry to improve consumer products and has also enacted legislation to lower the energy consumption of refrigerators, freezers, and air conditioners. Several states, including

Legislation	Impact on marketing
Sherman Act of 1890	Makes trusts and conspiracies in restraint of trade illegal; makes monopolies and attempts to monopolize a misdemeanor
Clayton Act of 1914	Outlaws discrimination in prices to different buyers; prohibits tying contracts (which require the buyer of one product to also buy another item in the line); makes illegal the combining of two or more competing corporations by pooling ownership of stock.
Federal Trade Commission Act of 1914	Creates the Federal Trade Commission to deal with antitrust matters; outlaws unfair methods of competition.
Robinson-Patman Act of 1936	Prohibits charging different prices to different buyers of merchandise of like grade and quantity; requires sellers to make any supplementary services or allowances available to all purchasers on a proportionately equal basis.
Wheeler-Lea Amendments to the FTC Act of 1938	Broadens the Federal Trade Commission's power to prohibit practices that might injure the public without affecting competition; outlaws false and deceptive advertising.
Lanham Act of 1946	Establishes protection for trademarks.
Celler-Kefauver Antimerger Act of 1950	Strengthens the Clayton Act to prevent corporate acquisitions that reduce competition.
Hart-Scott-Rodino Act of 1976	Requires large companies to notify the government of their intent to merge.

Exhibit 3.6
Primary U.S. Laws That Affect Marketing

New Mexico and Kansas, are considering levying a tax on all in-state commercial advertising.

Regulatory Agencies

Although some state regulatory bodies more actively pursue violations of their marketing statutes, federal regulators generally have the greatest clout. The Consumer Product Safety Commission, the Federal Trade Commission, and the Food and Drug Administration are the three federal agencies most directly and actively involved in marketing affairs. These agencies, plus others, are discussed throughout the book, but a brief introduction is in order at this point.

The sole purpose of the **Consumer Product Safety Commission (CPSC)** is to protect the health and safety of consumers in and around their homes. The CPSC has the power to set mandatory safety standards for almost all products that consumers use (about 15,000 items). The CPSC consists of a 5-member committee and about 1,100 staff members, including technicians, lawyers, and administrative help. The commission can fine offending firms up to $500,000 and sentence their officers to up to a year in prison. It can also ban dangerous products from the marketplace.

The **Federal Trade Commission (FTC)** also consists of five members, each holding office for seven years. The Federal Trade Commission is empowered to prevent persons or corporations from using unfair methods of competition in commerce. It is authorized to investigate the practices of business combinations and to conduct hearings on antitrust matters and deceptive advertising. The FTC has a vast array of regulatory powers. (See Exhibit 3.7.) Nevertheless, it is not invincible. For example, the FTC had proposed to ban all advertising to children under age 8, to ban all advertising of the sugared products that are most likely to cause tooth decay to children under age 12, and to require dental health and nutritional advertisements to be paid for by industry. Business reacted by lobbying to reduce the FTC's power. The

Food and Drug Administration (FDA) Federal agency charged with enforcing regulations against selling and distributing adulterated, misbranded, or hazardous food and drug products.

Consumer Product Safety Commission (CPSC) Federal agency established to protect the health and safety of consumers in and around their homes.

Federal Trade Commission (FTC) Federal agency empowered to prevent enforcing persons or corporations from using unfair methods of competition in commerce.

Exhibit 3.7

Powers of the Federal Trade Commission

Remedy	Procedure
Cease-and-desist order	A final order is issued to cease an illegal practice—and is often challenged in the courts.
Consent decree	A business consents to stop the questionable practice without admitting its illegality.
Affirmative disclosure	An advertiser is required to provide additional information about products in advertisements.
Corrective advertising	An advertiser is required to correct the past effects of misleading advertising. (For example, 25% of a firm's media budget must be spent on FTC-approved advertisements or FTC-specified advertising.)
Restitution	Refunds are required to be given to consumers misled by deceptive advertising. According to a 1975 court-of-appeals decision, this remedy cannot be used except for practices carried out after the issuance of a cease-and-desist order (still on appeal).
Counteradvertising	The FTC proposed that the Federal Communications Commission permit advertisements in broadcast media to counteract advertising claims (also that free time be provided under certain conditions).

two-year lobbying effort resulted in passage of the FTC Improvement Act of 1980. The major provisions of the act are as follows:

- It bans the use of unfairness as a standard for industrywide rules against advertising. All the proposals concerning children's advertising were therefore suspended, because they were based almost entirely on the unfairness standard.
- It requires oversight hearings on the FTC every six months. This congressional review is designed to keep the commission accountable. Moreover, it keeps Congress aware of one of the many regulatory agencies it has created and is responsible for monitoring.

Businesses rarely band together to create change in the legal environment as they did to pass the FTC Improvement Act. Generally, marketing managers only react to legislation, regulation, and edicts. It is usually less costly to stay attuned to the regulatory environment than to fight the government. If marketers had toned down their hard-hitting advertisements to children, they might have avoided an FTC inquiry altogether. The **Food and Drug Administration (FDA),** another powerful agency, is charged with enforcing regulations against selling and distributing adulterated, misbranded, or hazardous food and drug products. It has recently taken a very aggressive stance against tobacco products.

Federal Trade Commission
As a marketing manager, how would you use the FTC Web site in designing a new marketing campaign?

http://www.ftc.gov/index.html

Food and Drug Administration
What topics are currently receiving attention in FDA News? What effect has the attention had on marketers?

http://www.fda.gov/hometext.html

COMPETITIVE FACTORS

The competitive environment encompasses the number of competitors a firm must face, the relative size of the competitors, and the degree of interdependence within the industry. Management has little control over the competitive environment con-

8 Explain the basics of foreign and domestic competition.

The FDA is taking an aggressive stance against tobacco products. Here the heads of the largest U.S. tobacco companies are sworn in before a congressional committee meeting.

© John Duricka/AP Wide World Photos

fronting a firm. Yet the marketing mix, particularly pricing, depends on the type and amount of competition.

The Economics of Competition

Economists recognize four basic models of competition, based mainly on the number of competitors and the nature of the products produced. Exhibit 3.8 summarizes the characteristics of the four basic models and the key task of the marketing manager within each competitive situation. The type of competition has a great effect on pricing strategies and the ability of a firm to set a target price. Pricing is discussed in further detail in Chapters 20 and 21.

How does the latest Stephen King novel compete with two tickets to the new Arnold Schwarzenegger movie? Why would anyone prefer watching the video of "Terminator 2" to going out to a movie theatre? For tips on the relationships between competitors, go to **Hot Link—The Nature of Competition.**

At one extreme of economic competition is the **monopoly,** in which one firm controls the output and price of a product for which there are no close substitutes. In other words, the firm is the industry; there are no direct competitors. Utility companies are the most common form of monopoly in the United States. In addition, a patent can give a company monopoly power for a time. Xerox, for example, held the patent on the dry-paper copying process. Not until the patent expired and competitors entered the marketplace did dry-paper copiers fall significantly in price.

At the other extreme of the competitive spectrum is pure competition. A **purely competitive market** is characterized by a large number of sellers marketing a standardized product to a group of buyers who are well informed about the marketplace. New competitors can easily enter the marketplace and sell their entire output at the prevailing market price. In a purely competitive market, it would not make sense for one firm to raise the price of a product, a buyer would simply go elsewhere and get the same merchandise at the prevailing market price. Similarly, there would be no reason to advertise, because the pure competitor can sell its entire output at the prevailing market price without advertising. A purely competitive market doesn't exist in the real world. However, some industries closely mirror the model—most notably, such agricultural markets as wheat, cotton, soybeans, and corn.

monopoly
When one firm controls the output and price of a product for which there are no close substitutes.

purely competitive market
A large number of sellers marketing a standardized product to a group of buyers who are well informed about the marketplace.

Exhibit 3.8 *Types of Economic Competition*

Type of Competition	Number of Firms	Type of Product	Ease of Market Entry	Price Control	Importance of Promotion	Key Marketing Task
Monopoly	One	Unique (no substitute)	Blocked	Complete	Little or none	Maintain blocked entry through public relations, huge advertising expenditures, or other means
Monopolistic Competition	Numerous	Similar	Few barriers	Some	Very important	Maintain differentiated product
Oligopoly	Few	Similar	Major barriers	Some, with care	Important	Understand competition and react quickly; strive for non-price advantage
Pure Competition	Numerous	Homogeneous	No barriers	None	None	Attempt to lower product and distribution costs

When a relatively small number of firms dominate the market for a good or service, the industry is an **oligopoly.** Automobile, aircraft, supercomputer, and tire and rubber producers all compete in oligopolistic markets. Oligopolies can also exist at a lower competitive level. If a town in the Arizona desert had only four or five service stations, they would be competing as an oligopoly. Because they have few competitors, the actions of one firm have a direct impact on the others. This interdependence characterizes an oligopoly. The close relationship among firms often leads to collusion and price fixing, which are illegal under federal and state laws. Rather than fix prices, some industries simply follow a price leader. The leader is typically the dominant firm in terms of assets, market share, or geographic coverage. Marketing managers do not have a lot of pricing flexibility in an oligopoly. They must be alert to price changes and quickly match price decreases or lose a significant amount of market share. To further secure a position in the marketplace, marketing managers should stress service, product quality, and other nonprice forms of competition.

Monopolistic competition refers to a situation in which a relatively large number of suppliers offer similar, but not identical, products. Examples include laundries, hair stylists, aspirin producers, gasoline producers, lawyers, and airlines in major markets. Each firm has a comparatively small percentage of the total market, so each has limited control over market price. Firms attempt to distinguish their offerings through brand names, trademarks, packaging, advertisements, and services. With monopolistic competition, consumers tend to prefer the products of specific firms and, within limits, will pay a higher price. In other words, they tend to think, "I like Prell shampoo because it's a little different. But if the price goes up too much, I know Prell is not that different, so I'll switch to something else." Thus, the seller has some control over price, but only within a limited range. If the marketing manager raises prices too high, the company could lose its entire market.

oligopoly
An industry where a relatively small number of firms dominate the market for a good or service.

monopolistic competition
A situation in which a relatively large number of suppliers offer similar but not identical products.

Competition for Market Share

As U.S. population growth slows, costs rise, and available resources tighten, firms find that they must work harder to maintain their profits and market share regardless of the form of the competitive market. Take, for example, the salty snacks market. Recently, Anheuser-Bush announced that it was selling its Eagle snacks business because it couldn't compete against Frito-Lay. One consultant noted, "Frito's is a fortress—I would tell anyone trying to get into the salty snack business not to impinge on Frito's territory or you'll get crushed."[53] Eagle is only the latest example. Borden, Inc., sold off many of its regional snack companies in 1994 as part of a huge restructuring. Industry executives say dozens of regional companies have collapsed in the past year or two under Frito-Lay's weight.

Frito-Lay is feeding much of its growth with new products. The company's approach has been two-pronged—expanding its core line of Fritos, Doritos, Rold Gold Pretzels, and Lays potato chips, while branching out into new "better for you" products like Baked Lays, Baked Tostitos, and Rold Gold Fat Free Pretzels. Its cheesier Doritos have turned the previously sleepy chip into a billion-dollar brand, and spicier flavors have made Lays the No. 1 potato chip.

Frito-Lay also kills the competition with its distribution. Over its 35-year history, the company has built a network of 42 plants, 12,800 delivery people, and more than 900 tractor trailers into a retail delivery powerhouse. The company was one of the first to give its drivers handheld computers to transmit sales back to headquarters. Frito-Lay is working on another overhaul of its distribution operation to better serve its expanding range of retail customers—everything from drugstores and discount giants to grocery stores and convenience marts.

 Smaller firms can often survive in highly competitive markets by generating products of exceptional quality or by offering goods and services that fulfill unique needs. For example, Steiger Tractor Company has be-

Coca-Cola uses distribution to gain competitive advantage in U.S. and international markets.
© Paul Chesley/Tony Stone Images

come a viable competitor in an old and stable market. The company produces a big articulated tractor, which bends in the middle to make turning easier. Using all four wheels for traction enables it to pull bigger loads. An articulated tractor can cut a farmer's labor costs by as much as 33 percent per acre.

The Steiger tractor example illustrates that, with a good marketing mix, small firms can still compete effectively against the giants. Regardless of company size, the marketing mix of product, distribution, promotion, and price represents management's tools of competition. Steiger developed a unique product in order to compete. Lexus, AT&T, and Compaq computers have used product quality to gain and hold market share. Coca-Cola and 7-Eleven stores use distribution to gain competitive advantage. Firms like Wal-Mart, Toys R Us, and Thrifty Car Rental use price as a primary means of competition. Some companies, like Kraft General Foods and Procter & Gamble, are superior competitors in every aspect of their marketing mix. They have an excellent research staff that enables them to bring out the right products, an efficient distribution system involving thousands of stores and institutions, aggressive pricing, and a very large promotion budget. For example, Kraft General Foods spends over $100 million a year advertising Maxwell House coffee, and Procter & Gamble does the same for Folgers.

Global Competition

Both Kraft General Foods and Procter & Gamble are savvy international competitors as well. They each conduct business in over a hundred different nations. Many foreign competitors also consider the United States to be a ripe target market. Thus, a U.S. marketing manager can no longer worry about only domestic competitors. In automobiles, textiles, watches, televisions, steel, and many other areas, foreign competition has been strong. Global competition is discussed in much more detail in Chapter 4.

In the past, foreign firms penetrated U.S. markets by concentrating on price, but today the emphasis has switched to product quality. Nestlé, Sony, Rolls Royce, and Sandoz Pharmaceuticals are noted for quality, not cheap prices.

With the expansion of global marketing, U.S. companies often battle each other in international markets just as intensively as in the domestic market. Consider the case of Pepsi Cola in the following "Global Perspectives" box.

Global Perspectives

Pepsi Retools for More Intensive Global Competition

Foreign markets are becoming ever more crucial to U.S. soft-drink makers, but Pepsi's message has been losing something in the translation. While overseas sales of both Coca-Cola and Pepsi are growing between 7% and 10% a year, Coca-Cola outsells Pepsi abroad nearly 3 to 1. And Coca-Cola already earns more than 80% of its profits abroad, compared with Pepsi's 30%.

Overseas, some Pepsi billboards are more than 20 years old—and its image is all over the map: A grocery store in Hamburg uses red stripes, a bodega in Guatemala uses '70s-era lettering and a Shanghai restaurant displays a mainly white Pepsi sign. A hodgepodge of commercials features a variety of spokespeople, ranging from cartoons and babies to doddering butlers. Worse yet, consumers say the cola tastes different in different countries.

So PepsiCo Inc. is unveiling a radical, if risky, comeback plan. Code-named "Project Blue," it's expected to cost $500 million. It calls for revamping manufacturing and distribution to get a consistent-tasting drink throughout the globe,

as well as an overhaul of marketing and advertising.

Pepsi is even scrapping its signature red-white-and-blue colors in favor of electric blue. Started in 1996 in more than 20 countries, the new blue is being plastered on all its trucks, coolers, cans and bottles. The switch is expected to reach the U.S. by the year 2000. Project Blue also includes new freshness standards and quality controls. The company is even training a team of tasters to sample drinks from around the world.

Yet Project Blue carries big risks—especially in light of Coca-Cola's ill-fated attempt a few years ago to reformulate classic Coke. Pepsi hasn't made such a drastic logo change in more than 40 years. And with the project's high costs come high expectations: Pepsi is counting on nothing less than a long-term sales turnaround.

Pepsi's bottlers are also nervous. Many of the independent companies that make and sell Pepsi overseas will have to scrap or redo all of their red-white-and-blue signs and vending machines, plus over 30,000 trucks and more than 10 billion cans and bottles. Though Pepsi will pick up some of the costs, its U.K. bottler, for instance, has had to boost marketing spending by 30% to 40% to support Project Blue.

Another concern is whether repackaging will increase Pepsi's overseas identity crisis. Coca-Cola's red has become the world standard for soft drinks, and many marketing experts say Pepsi will have a tough time bucking that tradition with blue.

Pepsi is taking strong measures to become more competitive globally. What are some additional things Pepsi can do to help ensure the success of Project Blue? Do you think Pepsi should have started Project Blue in the United States before going global?

Source: From "Seeing Red Abroad, Pepsi Rolls Out a New Blue Can," *Wall Street Journal*, April 2, 1996. Reprinted by permission of *Wall Street Journal*. © 1996 Dow Jones & Company, Inc. All Rights Reserved Worldwide.

LOOKING BACK

Looking back at the story on the toy industry, you should now understand that the external environment affects all firms and their marketing mixes. The opening vignette illustrated how competition, technology, and ever-changing consumer tastes affect the toy industry. Other uncontrollable factors also have a profound effect on firms like Hasbro, Mattel, and Kenner. Evolving demographics (fewer children in key target markets), laws regarding product safety, and changing economic conditions all alter the way toy companies do business. Also, environmental factors can affect each other. For example, changes in the legal environment for toy manufacturers (e.g., disallowing the merger of America's two largest toy manufacturers) can lead to more intense competition. Any industry that ignores the external environment is doomed to failure in the long run.

KEY TERMS

applied research *71*

baby boomer *62*

basic research *71*

component lifestyle *55*

Consumer Product Safety
Commission (CPSC) *74*

demography *58*

discretionary income *58*

environmental manage-
ment *54*

Federal Trade Commission
(FTC) *74*

Food and Drug
Administration (FDA) *74*

generation X *60*

inflation *70*

monopolistic competi-
tion *77*

monopoly *76*

multiculturalism *67*

oligopoly *77*

personalized economy *63*

poverty of time *55*

purely competitive
market *76*

recession *70*

stitching niches *69*

target market *52*

SUMMARY

1 *Discuss the external environment of marketing and explain how it affects a firm.* The external marketing environment consists of social, demographic, economic, technological, political and legal, and competitive variables. Marketers generally cannot control the elements of the external environment. Instead, they must understand how the external environment is changing and the impact of change on the target market. Then marketing managers can create a marketing mix to effectively meet the needs of target customers.

2 *Describe the social factors that affect marketing.* Within the external environment, social factors are perhaps the most difficult for marketers to anticipate. Several major social trends are currently shaping marketing strategies. First, people of all ages have a broader range of interests, defying traditional consumer profiles. Second, changing gender roles are bringing more women into the workforce and increasing the number of men who shop. Third, a greater number of dual-career families has led to a poverty of time, creating a demand for timesaving goods and services.

3 *Explain the importance to marketing managers of current demographic trends.* Today, several basic demographic patterns are influencing marketing mixes. Because the U.S. population is growing at a slower rate, marketers can no longer rely on profits from generally expanding markets. Marketers are also faced with increasingly experienced consumers among the younger generations, many of whom are "turned off" by traditional marketing mixes. And because the population is also growing older, marketers are offering more products that appeal to middle-aged and elderly markets.

4 *Explain the importance to marketing managers of multiculturalism and growing ethnic markets.* Multiculturalism occurs when all major ethnic groups in an area are roughly equally represented. Growing multiculturalism makes the marketer's task more challenging. Niches within ethnic markets may require micromarketing strategies. An alternative to a niche strategy is maintaining a core brand identity while straddling different languages, cultures, ages, and incomes with different promotional campaigns. A third strategy is to seek common interests, motivations, or needs across ethnic groups.

5 *Identify consumer and marketer reactions to the state of the economy.* Marketers are currently targeting the increasing number of consumers with higher discretionary income by offering higher quality, higher priced goods and services. During a time of inflation, marketers generally attempt to maintain level pricing in order to avoid losing customer brand loyalty. During times of recession, many marketers maintain or reduce prices to counter the effects of decreased demand; they also concentrate on increasing production efficiency and improving customer service.

6 *Identify the impact of technology on a firm.* Monitoring new technology is essential to keeping up with competitors in today's marketing environment. For example, in the technologically advanced United States, many companies are losing business to Japanese competitors, who are prospering by concentrating their efforts on developing marketable applications for the latest technological innovations. In the United States, many R&D expenditures go into developing refinements of existing products. U.S. companies must learn to foster and encourage innovation. Without innovation, U.S. companies can't compete in global markets.

7 *Discuss the political and legal environment of marketing.* All marketing activities are subject to state and federal laws and the rulings of regulatory agencies. Marketers are responsible for remaining aware of and abiding by such regulations. Some key federal laws that affect marketing are the Sherman Act, Clayton Act, Federal Trade Commission Act, Robinson-Patman Act, Wheeler-Lea Amendment to the FTC Act, Lanham Act, Celler-Kefauver Antimerger Act, and Hart-Scott-Rodino Act. The Consumer Product Safety Commission, the Federal Trade Commission, and the Food and Drug Administration are the three federal agencies most involved in regulating marketing activities.

8 *Explain the basics of foreign and domestic competition.* The four economic models of competition are monopoly, pure competition, oligopoly, and monopolistic competition. Declining population growth, rising costs, and shortages of resources have heightened domestic competition. Yet with an effective marketing mix, small firms continue to be able to compete with the giants. Meanwhile, dwindling international barriers are bringing in more foreign competitors and offering expanding opportunities for U.S. companies abroad.

Discussion and Writing Questions

1. What is the purpose of environmental scanning? Give an example.

2. Every country has a set of core values and beliefs. These values may vary somewhat from region to region of the nation. Identify five core values for your area of the country. Clip magazine advertisements that reflect these values and bring them to class.

3. Baby boomers in America are aging. Describe how this might affect the marketing mix for the following:
   a. Bally's Health Clubs
   b. McDonald's
   c. Whirlpool Corporation
   d. the State of Florida
   e. JCPenney

4. You have been asked to address a local chamber of commerce on the subject of the growing singles market. Prepare an outline for your talk.

5. Identify two products that represent a trend and two that are fads. Use the criteria discussed in the chapter to explain why each is a trend or a fad.

6. Periods of inflation require firms to alter their marketing mix. A recent economic forecast expects inflation to be almost 10 percent during the next 18 months. Your company manufactures hand tools for the home gardener. Write a memo to the company president explaining how the firm may have to alter its marketing mix.

7. Give three examples in which technology has benefited marketers. Also, give several examples in which firms have been hurt by not keeping up with technological change.

8. Form six teams. Each team is responsible for one of the uncontrollable elements in the marketing environment. Your boss, the company president, has asked each team to provide a one-year and a five-year forecast of what major trends the firm will face. The firm is in the telecommunications equipment industry. It has no plans to become a telecommunications service provider, for example, like MCI and AT&T. Each team should use the library, the Internet, and other data sources to make its forecasts. Each team member should examine a minimum of one data source. The team should then pool its data and prepare its recommendation. A spokesperson for each team should present the findings to the class.

9. How does litigation affect the marketing environment for Phillip Morris? Select two lawsuit reports from the following Web site that illustrate your answer.

   http://www.businesswire.com/cnn/mo.htm

10. Why would electronic cash be considered a necessary element for Internet business transactions?

    http://www.digicash.com/

Application for Small Business

In 1992, Bo Peabody and Brett Hershey founded Tripod. The company's main product is an Internet site, http://www.tripod. com/, that offers 18-to-34-year-olds a complete resume and job-hunting service, as well as the tools to create and maintain a free place to house their own individual home pages. There are also travel and purchasing discounts, contests, e-mailed reminders of important dates and deadlines, and information from financial-service providers interested in forming relationships with young people. Working with a network of Tripod representatives recruited on more than a hundred college campuses, the company has already registered more than 50,000 members and has even more users.

Questions

1. Refer back to Exhibit 3.1 and explain how the external environment could affect Tripod.
2. How could each uncontrollable variable influence Tripod's venture?

Video Case

Life Fitness Company

In 1977, Augie Neato had an idea for combining an exercise bike and a computer. For nine months, Neato hit the road in his motor home trying to sell his idea. During that time, he sold 11 bikes instead of the thousands that he had imagined. Neato decided that the only way to make sales was to get people to try the product first. So he began putting the bikes in health clubs and letting people rent them by the half hour. Once the health club owners saw that customers liked the bike, sales of Neato's company, Life Fitness, began to escalate rapidly.

In 1984 Neato sold the company to Bally Manufacturing, a producer of gaming devices. Bally didn't just provide capital for a growing business; it already owned a chain of 350 health clubs. Those clubs were a captive market for Life Fitness products and a place to test new ideas. Over the next seven years, Life Fitness products were sold to thousands of health clubs around the nation. Bally then restructured and decided that Life Fitness no longer fit its strategic plan. With the help of an investment

banking group, Neato jumped at the opportunity to reacquire his idea and products.

Neato noted two basic changes in consumers' fitness behavior in the early 1990s: Membership in health clubs was slowing down, and people were beginning to exercise at home. Baby boomers, the primary target market for health clubs, were experiencing an ever-increasing poverty of time. Neato knew that if he could provide the same quality exercise experience in the home as in the club, he would have a winner.

In 1993, Neato decided to tackle the consumer market. His decision posed a critical challenge for Life Fitness Company: How could it expand into the consumer market without losing market share in the pro-

fessional market? Neato knew that he could capitalize on the well-known Life Fitness name. One immediate problem, however, was balancing the quality level of the professional Life Fitness equipment with the price that individual consumers were willing to pay.

Life Fitness' new direction is paying off. Consumer products accounted for 33 percent of company sales in 1996. Life Fitness expects that consumer products will make up 66 percent of total sales by 1999.

http://www.hotnew.com/ fitness/

Questions

1. Explain how Life Fitness could capitalize on a poverty of time.
2. What other external variables might affect Life Fitness Company?
3. Describe the target market for Life Fitness consumer products.
4. How might the marketing mixes for Life Fitness consumer products and professional products differ?

1 Discuss the importance of global marketing.

2 Discuss the impact of multinational firms on the world economy.

3 Describe the external environment facing global marketers.

4 Identify the various ways of entering the global marketplace.

5 List the basic elements involved in developing a global marketing mix.

Chapter 4

Developing a Global Vision

When America's new-age beverage, Snapple, hit Japan's shores in 1994, thousands of stores stocked peach-flavored iced tea, pink lemonade, and other Snapple variations. Ads declared that "The Snapple Phenomenon Has Landed." But the phenomenon has quietly retreated, leaving in its wake a lesson on how not to market consumer food products in an increasingly import-hungry Japan.

Snapple sales have fallen to 120,000 bottles a month from a monthly 2.4 million bottles in 1994. Soon sales will stop altogether: Quaker Oats Co., which acquired Snapple Beverages Corp. in 1994, stopped shipping Snapple drinks to Japan in January 1997.

What went wrong? It became clear in 1997 that Japanese consumers loathe some of the very traits that made Snapple popular—at least for a time—in the U.S.: the cloudy appearance of the teas, the sweet fruit-juice flavorings—and all that *stuff* floating in the bottles. Yet Quaker wouldn't change its drinks to suit local tastes, says Hisao Takeda, a Tokyo marketing consultant who represented Snapple in Japan. Making matters worse, he says, Quaker skimped on marketing. "The way they handled Snapple's launch fit right into the stereotypical image of the shortsighted American firm totally preoccupied with immediate results," he says.

Quaker acknowledged Snapple's poor showing in Japan, but wasn't inclined to take all the blame. Ronald Bottrell, a Quaker spokesman, said the company believed the "disappointing launch" of Snapple's drinks in Japan was due partly to Quaker's "inability to secure sufficient distribution" and partly to the company's shift of focus away from international expansion and toward restoring Snapple to profitability in the U.S. Attempts to restore U.S. market share came to an end in March 1997 when Quaker sold Snapple to TRIARC for $300 million. Quaker had paid $1.7 billion for the Snapple line 1994.

When the U.S. complains of Japan's supposedly closed markets, Japanese trade officials often launch into a familiar—and often specious—refrain: American products just don't suit the Japanese consumer. Sometimes they're right. On the other hand, Japan is buying more U.S. food products than ever. Processed-food imports from the U.S. totaled $4.4 billion last year, up 96 percent in five years. Some of these imports are the same as what is sold to Americans. Unaltered Snickers bars and M&M's sell well in Japan, for example.

Yet there's no accounting for taste buds, as some American exporters have discovered. Frito-Lay, Inc., for example, has watched several snacks get crushed. It stopped selling Ruffles potato chips in Japan last year after just a year on the market (too salty for Japan, Frito-Lay says), and its Cheetos sales have plummeted since last September (too cheesy; and Japanese don't like their fingers turning orange).

"For all the talk about the Americanization of lifestyles here, Japanese taste buds remain traditional," preferring subtle flavors and textures, says Tamao Yanauchi, a marketing consultant.

Is it possible to market products the same all over the world? If not, when should domestic and global marketing mixes be significantly different? Are international markets becoming increasingly important to U.S. companies like Quaker Oats? Is globalization the wave of the future in international marketing?

Source: From "Snapple in Japan: How a Splash Dried Up" by Norihiko Shirouza. *Wall Street Journal,* April 15 1996. Reprinted by permission of *Wall Street Journal.* © 1996 Dow Jones & Company, Inc. All Rights Reserved Worldwide.

Snapple Beverages Corporation
Does the Snapple Web site position itself well for global markets? Why or why not?

http://www.snapple.com/

THE REWARDS OF GLOBAL MARKETING

1 Discuss the importance of global marketing.

global marketing
Marketing to target markets throughout the world.

global vision
Recognizing and reacting to international marketing opportunities, being aware of threats from foreign competitors in all markets, and effectively using international distribution networks.

Today, global revolutions are under way in many areas of our lives: management, politics, communications, technology. The word *global* has assumed a new meaning, referring to a boundless mobility and competition in social, business, and intellectual arenas. No longer just an option, **global marketing** (marketing to target markets throughout the world) has become an imperative for business.

U.S. managers must develop a global vision not only to recognize and react to international marketing opportunities but also to remain competitive at home. Often a U.S. firm's toughest domestic competition comes from foreign companies. Moreover, a global vision enables a manager to understand that customer and distribution networks operate worldwide, blurring geographic and political barriers and making them increasingly irrelevant to business decisions. In summary, having **global vision** means recognizing and reacting to international marketing opportunities, being aware of threats from foreign competitors in all markets, and effectively using international distribution networks.

Over the past two decades, world trade has climbed from $200 billion a year to $7 trillion. Countries and companies that were never considered major players in global marketing are now important, some of them showing great skill.

Today, marketers face many challenges to their customary practices. Product development costs are rising, the life of products is getting shorter, and new technology is spreading around the world faster than ever. But marketing winners relish the pace of change instead of fearing it.

An excellent example of a company with global vision is Whirlpool Corporation,

Whirlpool Corporation
What evidence of a global vision do you find at Whirlpool's site? How does Whirlpool describe itself as a company?

http://www.whirlpool.com/

headquartered in Benton Harbor, Michigan. Whirlpool recently purchased the remaining interest in a joint venture it had formed with the Major Appliance Division of Philips, which is headquartered in Eindhoven, Holland. The administrative offices of Whirlpool Europe are in Comerio, Italy. On the 12-person management committee sit managers from Sweden, Holland, Italy, the United States, India, South Africa, and Belgium. Managers from different cultures help companies refine their global vision. Whirlpool now makes appliances in 12 countries and sells them in 140; 38 percent of revenues come from abroad.[1]

Adopting a global vision can be very lucrative for a company. Gillette, for example, gets about two-thirds of its revenue from its international division. About 70 percent of General Motors' profits come from operations outside the United States. While Cheetos and Ruffles haven't done very well in Japan, the potato chip has been quite successful. PepsiCo's (owner of Frito-Lay) overseas snack business brings in more than $3.25 billion annually.[2]

Global marketing is not a one-way street, whereby only U.S. companies sell their wares and services throughout the world. Foreign competition in the domestic market used to be relatively rare but now is found in almost every industry. In fact, in many industries the United States has lost significant market share to imported products. In the last 10 years, the percentage of machine tools imported from other countries grew from 23 percent to 46 percent.[3] In electronics, cameras, automobiles, fine china, tractors, leather goods, and a host of other consumer and industrial products, U.S. companies have struggled at home to maintain their market shares against foreign competitors.

For the past two decades, U.S. companies often appear to not be competitive with foreign rivals. Today, however, America has embarked on a new productivity boom. In the 1990s, nonfarm productivity has been rising at a 2.2 percent rate annually, more than twice the rate of the previous two decades.[4] The U.S. has the highest productivity among all industrialized countries. The U.S., for example, has 63 personal computers per 100 employed workers, to Japan's 17.[5] The U.S. is the low-cost producer among industrialized nations, with unit labor costs rising more slowly than in either Japan or Germany. American manufacturers are 10 to 20 percent more productive than German or Japanese manufacturers, and the U.S. service sector is 30 to 50 percent more productive. American business is fully prepared to compete in the global marketplace.

The Importance of Global Marketing to the United States

Many countries depend more on international commerce than the United States does. For example, France, Great Britain, and Germany all derive more than 19 percent of their gross domestic product from world trade, compared to about 12 percent for the United States.[6] Nevertheless, the impact of international business on the U.S. economy is still impressive:

- The United States exports about a fifth of its industrial production and a third of its farm products.[7]
- One of every 16 jobs in the United States is directly or indirectly supported by exports.
- U.S. businesses export over $500 billion in goods to foreign countries every year, and almost a third of U.S. corporate profits is derived from our international trade and foreign investment.[8]
- In 1996, exports accounted for 20 percent of America's growth in economic activity.[9]
- The United States is the world's leading exporter of grain, selling more than $12 billion of this product a year to foreign countries, or about one-third of all agricultural exports.[10]
- Chemicals, office machinery and computers, automobiles, aircraft, and electrical and industrial machinery make up almost half of all nonagricultural exports.

These statistics might seem to imply that practically every business in the United States is selling its wares throughout the world, but nothing could be further from the truth. About 85 percent of all U.S. exports of manufactured goods are shipped by 250 companies; less than 10 percent of all manufacturing businesses, or around

U.S. businesses export over $500 billion in goods to international markets every year. Chemicals, office machinery and computers, cars, aircraft, and electronic and industrial machinery make up almost half of all nonagricultural exports.

© 1996 PhotoDisc, Inc.

25,000 companies, export their goods on a regular basis.[11] Most small and medium-size firms are essentially nonparticipants in global trade and marketing. Only the very large multinational companies have seriously attempted to compete worldwide. Fortunately, more of the smaller companies are now aggressively pursuing international markets.

MULTINATIONAL FIRMS

2 Discuss the impact of multinational firms on the world economy.

multinational corporation
A company that is heavily engaged in international trade, beyond exporting and importing.

The United States has a number of large companies that are global marketers. Many of them have been very successful. A company that is heavily engaged in international trade, beyond exporting and importing, is called a **multinational corporation.** Multinational corporations move resources, goods, services, and skills across national boundaries without regard to the country in which the headquarters is located. The leading multinational firms in the world are listed in Exhibit 4.1.

A multinational corporation is more than a business entity, as the following paragraph explains:

> The multinational corporation is, among other things, a private "government," often richer in assets and more populous in stockholders and employees than are some of the nation-states in which it carries on business. It is simultaneously a "citizen" of several nation-states, owing obedience to their laws and paying them taxes, yet having its own objectives and being responsive to a management located in a foreign nation. Small won-

Exhibit 4.1
The World's Largest Multinational Firms

Rank*	Company	Country	Revenues ($ millions)	Assets ($ millions)
1	Mitsubishi	Japan	184,365.2	91,920.6
2	Mitsui	Japan	181,518.7	68,770.9
3	Itochu	Japan	169,164.6	65,708.9
4	General Motors	U.S.	168,828.6	217,123.4
5	Sumitomo	Japan	167,530.7	50,268.9
6	Marubeni	Japan	161,057.4	71,439.3
7	Ford Motor	U.S.	137,137.0	243,283.0
8	Toyota Motor	Japan	111,052.0	106,004.2
9	Exxon	U.S.	110,009.0	91,296.0
10	Royal Dutch/Shell Group	Brit./Neth.	109,833.7	118,011.6
11	Nissho Iwai	Japan	97,886.4	46,753.8
12	Wal-Mart Stores	U.S.	93,627.0	37,871.0
13	Hitachi	Japan	84,167.1	91,620.9
14	Nippon Life Insurance	Japan	83,206.7	364,762.5
15	Nippon Telegraph & Telephone	Japan	81,937.2	127,077.3
16	AT&T	U.S.	79,609.0	88,884.0
17	Daimler-Benz	Germany	72,256.1	63,813.2
18	Intl. Business Machines	U.S.	71,940.0	80,292.0
19	Matsushita Electric Industrial	Japan	70,398.4	74,876.9
20	General Electric	U.S.	70,028.0	228,035.0
21	Tomen	Japan	67,755.8	22,365.6
22	Mobil	U.S.	66,724.0	42,138.0
23	Nissan Motor	Japan	62,568.5	66,276.6
24	Volkswagen	Germany	61,489.1	58,610.7
25	Siemens	Germany	60,673.6	57,346.6

*Ranked by 1995 sales volume.
Source: "The Fortune Global 500," *Fortune*, 5 August 1996, p. F1.

der that some critics see in it an irresponsible instrument of private economic power or of economic "imperialism" by its home country. Others view it as an international carrier of advanced management science and technology, an agent for the global transmission of cultures bringing closer the day when a common set of ideals will unite mankind.[12]

Many multinational corporations are enormous. For example, the sales of both Exxon and General Motors are larger than the gross domestic product of all but 22 nations in the world. A multinational company may have several worldwide headquarters, depending on where certain markets or technologies are. Britain's APV, a maker of food-processing equipment, has a different headquarters for each of its worldwide businesses. Hewlett-Packard moved the headquarters of its personal computer business from the United States to Grenoble, France. ABB Asea Brown Boveri, the European electrical engineering giant based in Zurich, Switzerland, groups its thousands of products and services into 50 or so business areas. Each is run by a leadership team that crafts global business strategy, sets product development priorities, and decides where to make its products. None of the teams work out of Zurich headquarters; they are scattered around the world. Leadership for power transformers is based in Germany, electric drives in Finland, and process automation in the United States.[13]

The Multinational Advantage

Large multinationals have several advantages over other companies. For instance, multinationals can often overcome trade problems. Taiwan and South Korea have long had an embargo against Japanese cars for political reasons and to help domestic carmakers. Yet Honda USA, a Japanese-owned company based in the United States, sends Accords to Taiwan and Korea. Another example is Germany's BASF, a major chemical and drug manufacturer. Its biotechnology research at home is challenged by the environmentally conscious Green movement. So BASF moved its cancer and immune-system research to Cambridge, Massachusetts.

Another advantage for multinationals is their ability to sidestep regulatory problems. U.S. drugmaker SmithKline and Britain's Beecham decided to merge in part so they could avoid licensing and regulatory hassles in their largest markets. The merged company can say it's an insider in both Europe and the United States. "When we go to Brussels, we're a member state [of the European Union]," one executive explains. "And when we go to Washington, we're an American company."[14]

Multinationals can also shift production from one plant to another as market conditions change. When European demand for a certain solvent declined, Dow Chemical instructed its German plant to switch to manufacturing a chemical that had been imported from Louisiana and Texas. Computer models help Dow make decisions like these so it can run its plants more efficiently and keep costs down.

Multinationals can also tap new technology from around the world. Xerox has introduced some 80 different office copiers in the United States that were designed and built by Fuji Xerox, its joint venture with a Japanese company. Versions of the superconcentrated detergent that Procter & Gamble first formulated in Japan in response to a rival's product are now being sold under the Ariel brand name in Europe and being tested under the Cheer and Tide labels in the United States. Also, consider Otis Elevator's development of the Elevonic 411, an elevator that is programmed to send more cars to floors where demand is high. It was developed by six research centers in five countries. Otis's group in Farmington, Connecticut, handled the systems integration, a Japanese group designed the special motor drives that make the elevators ride smoothly, a French group perfected the door systems, a German group handled the electronics, and a Spanish group took care of the small-geared components. Otis says the international effort saved more than $10 million in design costs and cut the process from four years to two.

Ethics in Marketing

Governments Don't Always "Play Fair" in Global Trade

A German electronics giant pays bribes to win export sales. France demands 20 percent of Vietnam's telecommunications market in exchange for aid. A European aerospace company threatens to block European Union membership for Turkey and Malta unless their national airlines purchase its planes. It's all part of a nasty, multibillion-dollar war being waged over global markets.

Consider these questionable practices:[15]

1. **Bribes:** A German high-tech company, identified by sources as Siemens, allegedly offered bribes in connection with bids on 11 contracts from 1987 to 1994. It won 7 of the deals. Siemens won't comment.

2. **Pulled Loans:** France warned an African government that it would withdraw government guarantees on outstanding loans if Alcatel didn't win a $20 million telecom switching contract. Alcatel declined comment. Government officials couldn't be reached.

3. **Debt Forgiveness:** To help a Japanese company win a $30 million super-computer order from Brazil, the Bank of Japan said it would credit the purchase against Brazil's debt to Tokyo. Bank of Japan says it knows nothing of the incident, but NEC did win such a contract.

Is it alright for governments to help their multinational firms win contracts in the global marketplace? If so, what kind of help is OK and what is unethical? If a multinational simply does nothing when its government takes an unethical position in favor of the company, is the firm also guilty of unethical behavior?

Communications and technology have made the world smaller so that everyone wants many of the things they have heard about, seen, or experienced. Thus, global markets have emerged for standardized consumer products on a large scale.

© Jeff Greenberg

Finally, multinationals can often save a lot in labor costs, even in highly unionized countries. For example, Xerox started moving copier-rebuilding work to Mexico, where wages are much lower. Its union in Rochester, New York, objected because it saw that members' jobs were at risk. Eventually the union agreed to change work styles and to improve productivity to keep the jobs at home.

Competing in the global marketplace often gets "rough and tumble" for even giant multinationals. Sometimes even governments become involved to help "tilt the playing field" in favor of a domestic company. The "Ethics in Marketing" box offers a few examples from a classified U.S. government report.

Global Marketing Standardization

Traditionally, marketing-oriented multinational corporations have operated somewhat differently in each country. They use a strategy of providing different product features, packaging, advertising, and so on. However, Ted Levitt, a Harvard professor, described a trend toward what he referred to as "global marketing," with a slightly different meaning.[16] He contended that communication and technology have made the world smaller, so that almost everyone everywhere wants all the things they have heard about, seen, or experienced. Thus, he saw the emergence of global markets for standardized consumer products on a huge scale, as opposed to segmented foreign markets with different products. In this book, global marketing is defined as individuals and organizations using a global vision to effectively market goods and services across national boundaries. To make the distinction, we can refer to Levitt's notion as **global marketing standardization.**

Global marketing standardization presumes that the markets throughout the world are becoming more alike. Firms practicing global marketing standardization produce "globally standardized products" to be sold the same way all over the world. Uniform production should enable companies to lower production and marketing costs and increase profits. However, research indicates that superior sales and profits do not necessarily follow from global standardization.[17]

global marketing standardization
Production of uniform products that can be sold the same way all over the world.

Levitt cited Coca-Cola, Colgate-Palmolive, and McDonald's as successful global marketers. However, Levitt's critics point out that the success of these three companies is really based on variation, not on offering the same product everywhere. McDonald's, for example, changes its salad dressings for French tastes and sells beer and mineral water in its restaurants there. It also offers different products to suit tastes in Germany (where it offers beer) as well as in Japan (where it offers sake). Further, the fact that Coca-Cola and Colgate-Palmolive sell some of their products in more than 160 countries does not signify that they have adopted a high degree of standardization for all their products globally. Only three Coca-Cola brands are standardized, and one of them, Sprite, has a different formulation in Japan. Some Colgate-Palmolive products are marketed in just a few countries. Axion paste dishwashing detergent, for example, was formulated for developing countries, and La Croix Plus detergent was custom made for the French market. Colgate toothpaste is marketed the same way globally, although its advanced Gum Protection Formula is used in only 27 nations.

Coca-Cola Company
How does Coca-Cola's mission statement reflect its commitment to global markets? Does the site, as a whole, reflect this commitment?

http://www.cocacola.com/

Colgate-Palmolive
Compare the Colgate-Palmolive site with the Coca-Cola site. Which more strongly conveys a global image?

http://www.colgate.com/

Nevertheless, some multinational corporations are moving toward a degree of global marketing standardization. Nike, for example, designed a standardized global marketing plan for its Air 180 shoes. Its advanced air cushioning system is visible through the shoe's clear midsole. For greater adaptability, the television commercials for the shoes are not narrated. Instead, the commercials use title cards, translated into various languages, to identify Nike and promote the worldwide availability of the Air 180 model. Ads use the company's "Just do it" theme. Similarly, Eastman Kodak has launched a world brand of blank tapes for videocassette recorders. Procter & Gamble (P&G) calls its new philosophy "global planning." The idea is to determine which product modifications are necessary from country to country while trying to minimize those modifications. P&G has at least four products that are marketed similarly in most parts of the world: Camay soap, Crest toothpaste, Head and Shoulders shampoo, and Pampers diapers. However, the smell of Camay, the flavor of Crest, and the formula of Head and Shoulders, as well as the advertising, vary from country to country.

Procter and Gamble
Visit P&G's World Telescope to learn more about the company's global community. What countries do you find there?

http://www.pg.com/

THE EXTERNAL ENVIRONMENT FACING GLOBAL MARKETERS

A global marketer or a firm considering global marketing faces problems, often due to the external environment, as many of the same environmental factors that operate in the domestic market also exist internationally. These factors include culture, economic and technological development, political structure, demographic makeup, and natural resources.

3 Describe the external environment facing global marketers.

Culture

Central to any society is the common set of values shared by its citizens that determine what is socially acceptable. Culture underlies the family, the educational system, religion, and the social class system. The network of social organizations generates overlapping roles and status positions. These values and roles have a tremendous effect on people's preferences and thus on marketers' options. Inca Kola, a fruity, greenish-yellow carbonated drink, is the largest selling soft drink in Peru. Despite being compared to "liquid bubble gum," the drink has become a symbol of national pride and heritage. The drink was invented in Peru and contains only fruit indigenous to the country. A local consumer of about a six-pack per day says, "I drink Inca Kola because it makes me feel like a Peruvian." He tells his young daughter, "This is our drink, not something invented overseas. It is named for your ancestors, the great Inca warriors."[18]

Language is another important aspect of culture. Marketers must take care in translating product names, slogans, and promotional messages so as not to convey the wrong meaning. For example, Mitsubishi Motors had to rename its Pajero model in Spanish-speaking countries because the term describes a sexual activity. Toyota Motors' MR2 model dropped the number 2 in France because the combination sounds like a French swearword.[19] The literal translation of Coca-Cola in Chinese characters means "bite the wax tadpole." Marketers must be careful in translating promotions, product instructions, and other materials from one language to another. Consider the sign posted in guest rooms at the Jiazhou Hotel in Leshan in Western China, shown in Exhibit 4.2. (Typos are theirs.)

Each country has its own customs and traditions that determine business practices and influence negotiations with foreign customers. In many countries, personal relationships are more important than financial considerations. For instance, skipping social engagements in Mexico may lead to lost sales. Negotiations in Japan often include long evenings of dining, drinking, and entertaining, and only after a close

Exhibit 4.2

Jiazhou Hotel–Leshan, China Notice to Guests

According to the "Fire Control Regulations of P.R.C.," "Fire Control Management Regulations of High Buildings," "Hotels Public Security Measurements' and Public Security's request, all guests should obey the following rules:

1. Wild drinking, disturbance, gambling, drug-taking, lecherous acts, prostitution, obscene and superstitious painting, calligraphy and videotape recordings disseminating and projecting are strictly forbidden.
2. Guns, bullets, explosives, poisonous and radiative items (including inflammable chemical items) are not allowed inside the hotel.
3. Quite is always required in the hotel.
4. You are not allowed to keep unregistered guests in room overnight or sublet the room/bed to another person.
5. The use of electric stoves, irons, ovens and other electric equipment is not allowed. Copymachines, telex and other office facilities can not be installed without approval.
6. Burning substance, setting off firecrackers, piling up inflammable items and the washing of items with inflammable liquid are prohibited in the buildings. Smokers must be aware of fire control and not smoke in bed.
7. Raising birds, poultry and livestock is forbidden within the room.

We can only provide a pleasant and quiet environment with your help. The hotel management has the authority to impose a fire or refuse to accomadate any person violating the above rules. Action could be taken by the Government Public Security Department on any person who violates the above rules and causes serious damage.
Thank you for your co-operation!

personal relationship has been formed do business negotiations begin. The Japanese go through a very elaborate ritual when exchanging business cards. An American businesswoman had no idea about this important cultural tradition. She came into a meeting and tossed some of her business cards across the table at a group of stunned Japanese executives. One of them turned his back on her and walked out. The deal never went through.[20]

In the United States, we prefer written contracts. If a party violates the terms of the contract, legal actions are frequently taken. However, in China, where trust is important to business dealings, oral agreements mean more. The written contract represents the beginning of a negotiation process, and many changes are to be expected.

Even if English is spoken during negotiations, communication problems still occur. For instance, the Japanese may say yes or maybe when they really mean no, to avoid making their foreign counterparts lose face and feel embarrassed. When the Taiwanese shake their heads back and forth, they mean yes, not no.

Exhibit 4.3 summarizes some important cultural considerations; several additional examples are discussed in this chapter's section on marketing mix.

Successful multinational marketers understand that employees must learn to appreciate these differences among cultures. Motorola, for example, has opened a special center for cultural training at its headquarters in Schaumburg, Illinois. Many firms are hiring "cultural consultants," such as Bob Waisfisz of The Hague, Netherlands, to speak to their employees. Waisfisz often uses humor in his presentations. He notes, for example, that "in Germany, everything is forbidden unless it's allowed. In Britain, everything is allowed unless it's forbidden. And in France, everything is allowed even if it's forbidden."[21]

Fortunately, some habits and customs seem to be the same throughout much of the world. A recent study of 37,743 consumers from 40 different countries found that 95 percent brushed their teeth daily.[22] Other activities that majorities worldwide engage in include reading a newspaper, listening to the radio, taking a shower, and washing their hair.

Differences in these cultural factors ...	... Affect values and habits relating to:
Assumptions and attitudes	Time One's proper purpose in life The future This life versus the hereafter Duty and responsibility
Personal beliefs and aspirations	Right and wrong Sources of pride Sources of fear and concern Extent of one's hopes Individual versus society
Interpersonal relationships	Source of authority Care or empathy for others Importance of family obligations Objects of loyalty Tolerance for personal differences
Social structure	Interclass mobility Class or caste systems Urban–village–farm origins Determinants of states

Exhibit 4.3

Important Cultural Considerations in International Marketing

Economic and Technological Development

A second major factor in the external environment facing the global marketer is the level of economic development in the countries where it operates. In general, complex and sophisticated industries are found in developed countries, and more basic industries are found in less developed nations. Higher average family incomes are common in the more developed countries compared to the least developed markets. Larger incomes mean greater purchasing power and demand not only for consumer goods and services but also for the machinery and workers required to produce consumer goods. A glimpse of what families earn throughout the world in shown in Exhibit 4.4.

To appreciate marketing opportunities (or lack of them), it is helpful to examine the five stages of economic growth and technological development: traditional society, preindustrial society, takeoff economy, industrializing society, and fully industrialized society.

The Traditional Society

traditional society
A society in the earliest stages of economic development, largely agricultural, with a social structure and value system that provide little opportunity for upward mobility.

Countries in the traditional stage are in the earliest phase of development. A **traditional society** is largely agricultural, with a social structure and value system that provide little opportunity for upward mobility. The culture may be highly stable, and economic growth may not get started without a powerful disruptive force. Therefore, to introduce single units of technology into such a country is probably wasted effort. In Ghana, for instance, a tollway 16 miles long and six lanes wide, intended to modernize distribution, does not connect to any city or village or other road.

Exhibit 4.4
What the World Earns

High consumption levels are concentrated in a small share of households worldwide.

(percent distribution of households by annual consumption level, 1993)

Note: Consumption is in U.S. dollars on a purchase-power-parity basis. Percentage may add to more than 100 percent due to rounding.

Source: World Bank and Global Business Opportunities

The Preindustrial Society

The second stage of economic development, the **preindustrial society,** involves economic and social change and the emergence of a middle class with an entrepreneurial spirit. Nationalism may begin to rise, along with restrictions on multinational organizations. Countries like Madagascar and Uganda are in this stage. Effective marketing in these countries is very difficult because they lack the modern distribution and communication systems that U.S. marketers often take for granted. Peru, for example, did not establish a television network until 1975.

preindustrial society
A society in the second stage of economic development, involving economic and social change and the emergence of a middle class with an entrepreneurial spirit.

The Takeoff Economy

The **takeoff economy** is the period of transition from a developing to a developed nation. New industries arise, and a generally healthy social and political climate emerges. Thailand, Malaysia, and Vietnam have entered the takeoff stage. For example, in recent years Thailand has had one of the fastest rates of economic growth in the world. Investors from Japan, Taiwan, and the United States are bringing capital and new technology to Thailand. In an effort to develop its economy, Vietnam now offers large tax breaks to foreign investors who promise jobs. Gold Medal Footware, headquartered in Taiwan, now employs 500 young workers in Danang and hopes to increase the number to 2,500.[23]

takeoff economy
The third stage of economic development involves a period of transition from a developing to a developed nation.

The Industrializing Society

The fourth phase of economic development is the **industrializing society.** During this era, technology spreads from sectors of the economy that powered the takeoff to the rest of the nation. Mexico, China, India, and Brazil are among the nations in this phase of development.

Countries in the industrializing stage begin to produce capital goods and consumer durable products. These industries also foster economic growth. As a result, a large middle class begins to emerge, and the demand for luxuries and services grows.

One of the fastest growing economies in the world today (about 10 percent per

industrializing society
The fourth stage of economic development when technology spreads from sectors of the economy that powered the takeoff to the rest of the nation.

Malaysia has entered the takeoff stage of development. It is in a period of transition from developing to developed nation.

© Jeff Greenberg

year) is China. A population of 1.2 billion is producing a gross domestic product of over $1.2 trillion a year. This new industrial giant will be the world's largest manufacturing zone, the largest market for such key industries as telecommunications and aerospace, and one of the largest users of capital.

Industrializing societies such as China and India offer opportunities for entrepreneurs with skill and imagination. The following "Marketing and Small Business" box is but one example.

fully industrialized society
The fifth stage of economic development, a society that is an exporter of manufactured products, many of which are based on advanced technology.

The Fully Industrialized Society

The **fully industrialized society,** the fifth stage of economic development, is an exporter of manufactured products, many of which are based on advanced technology. Examples include automobiles, computers, airplanes, oil exploration equipment, and

---

Marketing and Small Business

The Video Van Distribution Channel Works in India

About 70 percent of India's 900 million people live in rural areas. More than half of all Indian villagers are illiterate, and only one-third live in a household with a television set. Conventional American marketing practices simply won't work. Enter J. K. Jain, a New Delhi doctor, who invented the video van. The video van is just that—a van with a large video screen in the rear door. Dr. Jain used his vans originally to spread political propaganda for an opposition party that was denied air time on state-run television.

Between elections, the vans were idle, so Dr. Jain approached consumer-goods companies in 1989. Since then his fleet has swelled from 28 to 125, advertising products as disparate as detergent, pharmaceuticals, and fans. Each van typically visits three villages a day. Consumer companies generally deploy vans year-round, except for three months during the monsoon season. Dr. Jain charges 88,000 rupees ($2,520) a month for a van, which comes outfitted with video gear and a generator.

Colgate-Palmolive, the giant U.S. consumer products company, is a believer in video vans. Many consumers in rural India are not fa-

miliar with toothpaste. But they find out once Dr. Jain's video van bumps into town. In Andarsul, a dusty village of 10,000 in Maharashtra state, a van decked out with oversize "dummy" Colgate toothpaste tubes arrives on market day. It's the first time the van has called on Andarsul, which draws farmers and field workers from nearby hamlets to its weekly market.

Over the blare of a popular movie melody, a marketer invites shoppers to the vehicle. He also throws open the rear door, revealing a video screen. Before long, about 100 men and children have jostled for a viewing spot. (Women generally don't go to market in the Indian countryside.)

In one scene of the 27-minute infomercial, villagers Kamla and Vijay are about to spend their wedding night together. As a passionate Vijay bends over to kiss his bride, she pulls away in disgust. He asks what's wrong. She's embarrassed to say. The attentive audi-

ence is puzzled until it realizes the problem is Vijay's breath.

As the story unfolds through dialogue, song, and dance, the newlyweds consult a dentist and then reconcile. The subtext is clear: Colgate is good for your breath, teeth, and love life. Village harmony is served, too. After the dentist explains that traditional oral-hygiene methods, such as charcoal powder, are ineffective and even harmful, the video ends with Kamla, Vijay, and their neighbors happily brushing their teeth.

The audience applauds enthusiastically and then rushes to get free samples at a stall beside the van. A Colgate marketer demonstrates how to use the toothpaste and a toothbrush. To encourage parents to buy a tube, he offers free Colgate brushes to a few children, only to leave many little hands grabbing for more.

Do you think Dr. Jain's concept would work in the United States? Why or why not?

Source: From "In Rural India, Video Vans Sell Toothpaste and Shampoo" by Miriam Jordan, *Wall Street Journal*, January 10, 1996. Reprinted by permission of *Wall Street Journal*. © 1996 Dow Jones & Company, Inc. All Rights Reserved.

telecommunications gear. Great Britain, Japan, Germany, France, Canada, and the United States fall into this category.

The wealth of the industrialized nations creates tremendous market potential. Therefore, industrialized countries trade extensively. Also, industrialized nations usually ship manufactured goods to developing countries in exchange for raw materials like petroleum, precious metals, and bauxite.

Political Structure

Political structure is a third important variable facing global marketers. Government policies run the gamut from no private ownership and minimal individual freedom to little central government and maximum personal freedom. As rights of private property increase, government-owned industries and centralized planning tend to decrease. But rarely will a political environment be at one extreme or the other. India, for instance, is a republic with elements of socialism, monopoly capitalism, and competitive capitalism in its political ideology.

Many countries are changing from a centrally planned economy to a market-oriented one. East Germany has made the fastest transformation because its dominant western half was already there. Eastern European nations like Hungary and Poland have also been moving quickly with market reforms. Many of the reforms have increased foreign trade and investment. For example, in Poland, foreigners are now allowed to invest in all areas of industry, including agriculture, manufacturing, and trade. Poland even gives companies that invest in certain sectors some tax advantages.

Russia is progressing more slowly than many Eastern European countries, but it is still headed in the direction of a market-oriented economy. Over 5,000 Russian managers are studying abroad, and many more are studying market-oriented principles within Russia. Today, over 25,000 foreign companies have invested in Russia. However, many changes in the Russian economy are still desperately needed. About 90 percent of all Russians are living below the poverty level.[24]

Changes leading to market-oriented economies are not restricted to Eastern Europe and Russia. Many countries within Latin America are also attempting market reforms. Countries like Brazil, Argentina, and Mexico are reducing government

Russia, which is headed toward a market-oriented economy, is progressing more slowly than many other Eastern European countries.
© Jeff Greenberg

control over many sectors of the economy. They are also selling state-owned companies to foreign and domestic investors and removing trade barriers that have protected their markets against foreign competition. Brazil has now overtaken Italy and Mexico to become the tenth largest automobile manufacturer in the world.[25] India has recently opened up its market of 900 million consumers. While India's per capita average income is quite low ($330), an estimated 100-million-plus Indians have enough income to be considered middle class.[26]

Another trend in the political environment is the growth of nationalist sentiments among citizens who have strong loyalties and devotion to their country. Failure to appreciate emerging nationalist feelings can create major problems for multinational firms. In 1995, Hindus in India smashed Pepsi bottles and burned Pepsi posters. And the country's first Kentucky Fried Chicken, in Bangalore, was targeted by protesters claiming to defend Indian culture against Western encroachment.

Another potential cloud on the horizon for some types of companies doing business abroad is the threat of nationalization. Some countries have nationalized (taken ownership of) certain industries or companies, such as airlines in Italy and Volvo in Sweden, to infuse more capital into their development. Industries are also nationalized to allow domestic corporations to sell vital goods below cost. For example, for many years France has been supplying coal to users at a loss.

Legal Considerations

Closely related to and often intertwined with the political environment are legal considerations. Nationalistic sentiments of the French led to a 1996 law that requires pop music stations to play at least 40 percent of their songs in French. (French teenagers love American and English rock and roll.)[27] Christian Bellanger, president of a popular Paris station called "Skyrock," said the law was "totalitarian and useless. The major (French) recording companies do not produce enough good French music to fill the schedule."[28] The measure is being policed by the government's watchdog audio visual committee, the Conseil Superieur de l'Audovisuel. With the help of computers, the official ear will be tuned to about 1,300 radio stations, which risk losing their broadcast licenses if they break the law.

Legal structures are designed to either encourage or limit trade. Some examples follow:

- *Tariff:* tax levied on the goods entering a country. For example, trucks imported into the United States face a 25 percent tariff. Since the 1930s, tariffs have tended to decrease as a barrier to trade. But they have often been replaced by nontariff barriers, such as quotas, boycotts, and other restrictions.

- *Quota:* limit on the amount of a specific product that can enter a country. The United States has strict quotas for imported textiles, sugar, and many dairy products. Several U.S. companies have sought quotas as a means of protection from foreign competition. For example, Harley-Davidson convinced the U.S. government to place quotas on large motorcycles imported into the United States. These quotas gave the company the opportunity to improve its quality and compete with Japanese motorcycles.

- *Boycott:* exclusion of all products from certain countries or companies. Governments use boycotts to exclude companies from countries with whom they have a political dispute. Several Arab nations boycotted Coca-Cola because it maintained distributors in Israel.

- *Exchange control:* law compelling a company earning foreign exchange from its exports to sell it to a control agency, usually a central bank. A company wishing to buy goods abroad must first obtain foreign exchange from the control agency. Generally, exchange controls limit the importation of luxuries. For instance, Avon Products drastically cut back new production lines and products in the Philippines because exchange controls prevented the conversion of pesos to dollars to ship back to the home office. The pesos had to be used in the Philippines. China restricts the amount of foreign currency each Chinese company is allowed to keep from its exports. Therefore, Chinese companies must usually get the government's approval to release funds before they can buy products from foreign companies.

- *Market grouping:* also known as a common trade alliance; occurs when several countries agree to work together to form a common trade area that enhances trade opportunities. The best-known market grouping is the European Community (EC), whose members are Belgium, France, Germany, Italy, Luxembourg, the Netherlands, Denmark, Ireland, Spain, the United Kingdom, Portugal, and Greece. The EC has been evolving for nearly four decades, yet until recently, many trade barriers existed among member nations.

- *Trade agreement:* agreement to stimulate international trade. Not all government efforts are meant to stifle imports or investment by foreign corporations. The **Uruguay Round** of trade negotiations, which created the World Trade Organization, is an agreement to dramatically lower trade barriers worldwide. Adopted in 1994, the agreement was signed by 117 nations in Marrakesh, Morocco. It is the most ambitious global trade agreement ever negotiated. The Agreement reduces tariffs by one-third worldwide. This, in turn, should raise global income by $235 billion annually by 2005. Perhaps most notable is the recognition of the new global realities. For the first time there is an agreement covering services, intellectual property rights, and trade-related investment measures such as exchange controls.

  The Uruguay Round makes several major changes in world trading practices:

  - *Entertainment, pharmaceuticals, integrated circuits, and software:* New rules will protect patents, copyrights, and trademarks for 20 years. Computer programs receive 50 years' protection and semiconductor chips receive 10 years.' But many developing nations will have a decade to phase in patent protection for drugs. France, which limits the number of U.S. movies and T.V. shows that can be shown, refused to liberalize market access for the U.S. entertainment industry.

  - *Financial, legal, and accounting services:* Services come under international trading rules for the first time, potentially creating a vast opportunity for these competitive U.S. industries. Now it will be easier to admit managers and key personnel into a country. Licensing standards for professionals, such as doctors, cannot discriminate against foreign applicants. That is, foreign applicants cannot be held to higher standards than domestic practitioners.

  - *Agriculture:* Europe will gradually reduce farm subsidies, opening new opportunities for such U.S. farm exports as wheat and corn. Japan and Korea will begin to import rice. But growers of U.S. sugar, citrus fruit, and peanuts will have their subsidies trimmed.

  - *Textiles and apparel:* Strict quotas limiting imports from developing countries will be phased out over 10 years, causing further job loss in the U.S. clothing trade. But retailers and consumers will be the big winners, because quotas now add $15 billion a year to clothing prices.

  - *A new trade organization:* The new **World Trade Organization (WTO)** replaces the old **General Agreement on Tariffs and Trade (GATT)**, which was created in 1948. The old GATT agreements provided extensive loopholes that enabled countries to avoid the trade-barrier reduction agreements. It was like obeying the law if you wanted to! Today, all WTO members must fully comply with all agreements under the Uruguay Round. The WTO also has an effective dispute settlement procedure with strict time limits to resolve disputes.

    The new service agreement under the Uruguay Round requires member countries to create adequate penalties against counterfeiting and piracy. China, which wants to join the WTO, has done little to control its rampant piracy problem. U.S. producers of records, books, motion pictures, and software lose

Uruguay Round
An agreement to dramatically lower trade barriers worldwide.

World Trade Organization (WTO)
A new trade organization that replaces the old General Agreement on Trade and Tariffs (GATT).

General Agreement on Tariffs and Trade (GATT)
Provided loopholes that enabled countries to avoid trade-barrier reduction agreements.

about $2.5 billion a year to Chinese piracy.[29] Chinese authorities have destroyed 800,000 pirated audio and videocassettes and more than 40,000 software programs. Some $3 million worth of fines have been levied in connection with 9,000 cases of trademark violation. Yet, the government has failed to close 29 known plants pirating music and computer CDs. These production facilities have politically connected backers.[30]

The trend toward globalization has brought to the fore several specific examples of the influence of political structures and legal considerations: Japanese keiretsu, the North American Free Trade Agreement, and the European Union.

Japanese Keiretsu

Japanese nationalism produced the **keiretsu,** or societies of business, which take two main forms. Bank-centered keiretsu are massive industrial combines of 20 to 45 core companies centered on a bank (see Exhibit 4.5).

keiretsu

Japanese society of business, which takes one of two main forms: a bank-centered keiretsu, or a massive industrial combine centered around a bank; and a supply keiretsu, or a group of companies dominated by the major manufacturer they provide with supplies.

Exhibit 4.5

A Japanese Keiretsu

The Sumitomo Group

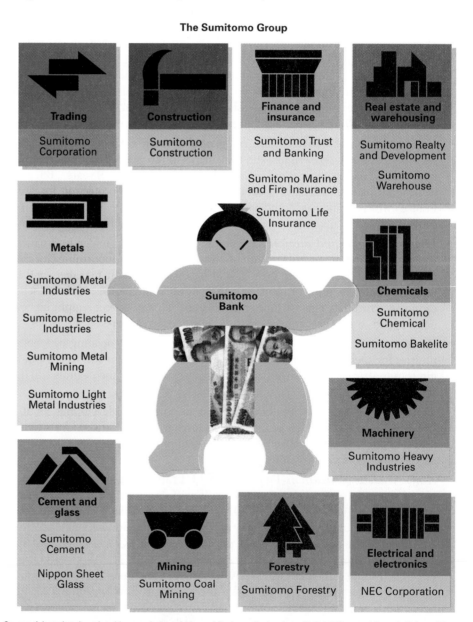

They enable companies to share business risk and provide a way to allocate investment to strategic industries. Supply keiretsu are groups of companies dominated by the major manufacturer they provide with supplies. Keiretsu exist with the blessing of the Japanese government. After World War II, Japan wanted to help reestablish industry by encouraging cooperation. The Japanese government was also hoping the strong networks would help keep out foreign companies.[31]

Keiretsu have indeed blocked U.S. companies, and others, from the Japanese market. Consider the Matsushita keiretsu. Matsushita, one of the worlds' top 20 manufacturers, makes Panasonic, National, Technics, and Quasar brands. Matsushita also controls a chain of about 25,000 National retail stores in Japan, which together generate more than half of Matsushita's domestic sales. From batteries to refrigerators, these shops agree to sell no other brands or just a few others. And the dealers agree to sell at manufacturers' recommended prices. In return, Matsushita essentially guarantees the livelihoods of the stores' owners. The Japan Fair Trade Commission has estimated that almost 90 percent of all domestic business transactions are "among parties involved in a long-standing relationship of some sort."[32]

Trade talks between Japan and the United States in 1992 centered on keiretsu, with little success. The U.S. government demanded that the keiretsu be opened to U.S. companies. But Japanese officials were reluctant to acknowledge the need to reform the keiretsu, arguing that they make the Japanese economy more efficient.[33]

The North American Free Trade Agreement

The **North American Free Trade Agreement (NAFTA)** created the world's largest free-trade zone. The agreement was ratified by the U.S. Congress in 1993. It includes Canada, the United States, and Mexico, with a combined population of 360 million and economy of $6 trillion.[34]

Canada, the largest U.S. trading partner, entered a free-trade agreement with the United States in 1988. Most of the new long-run opportunities for U.S. business under NAFTA are thus in Mexico, America's third largest trading partner. Tariffs on Mexican exports to the U.S. averaged just 4 percent before the treaty was signed, and most goods entered the U.S. duty-free. Therefore, NAFTA opened the Mexican market primarily to U.S. companies. When the treaty went into effect, tariffs on about half the items traded across the Rio Grande disappeared. The pact removed a web of

North American Free Trade Agreement (NAFTA)
An agreement between Canada, the United States, and Mexico that created the world's largest free-trade zone.

NAFTA removed a web of Mexican licensing requirements, quotas, and tariffs that limited transactions in U.S. goods and services. However, Mexico has been in a recession which has reduced U.S. opportunities there.
© Jeff Greenberg

Mexican licensing requirements, quotas, and tariffs that limited transactions in U.S. goods and services. For instance, the pact allows U.S. and Canadian financial-services companies to own subsidiaries in Mexico for the first time in 50 years. However, a nagging deep recession in Mexico has, to date, limited American opportunities in the country. In a recent survey, 70 percent of U.S. corporations said that NAFTA had no effect on their businesses, while 24 percent reported positive results, and 6 percent described negative results.[35]

The real test of NAFTA will be whether it delivers rising prosperity on both sides of the Rio Grande. For Mexicans, NAFTA must provide rising wages, better benefits, and an expanding middle class with enough purchasing power to keep buying goods from the United States and Canada. That scenario is plausible in the long run, but not guaranteed. As for the United States, its gross domestic product will grow about $30 billion a year once NAFTA is fully implemented.[36] But for Americans, the trade agreement will need to prove that it can produce more well-paying jobs than it destroys. Although estimates of the employment effects of NAFTA vary widely, almost every study agrees that there will be gains. Through mid-1996, however, the U.S. jobs created by NAFTA have been disappointing. About 55,000 U.S. workers lost their jobs by January 1996 and 84,000 jobs have been created, for a net gain of 29,000 American jobs.[37]

The intent of U.S. politicians is to ultimately expand NAFTA to South American and, indeed, all Latin American countries. Chile was to be the first new entrant into the organization. Wrangling within the U.S. Congress has blocked NAFTA expansion so far. The lack of American prosperity and job growth attributable to NAFTA has stalled congressional expansion of the agreement. As a result, countries south of the U.S. border have been forming their own trade agreements. Latin and South American nations are creating a maze of trading arrangements.

Mercosur
The largest new trade agreement which includes Brazil, Argentina, Uruguay, and Paraguay.

The largest new trade agreement is **Mercosur,** which includes Brazil, Argentina, Uruguay, and Paraguay. The elimination of most tariffs among the trading partners has resulted in trade revenues currently over $16 billion annually.[38] The economic boom created by Mercosur will undoubtedly cause other nations to seek trade agreements on their own or enter Mercosur. The European Union, discussed next, hopes to have a free-trade pact with Mercosur by 2005.

The European Union

Maastricht Treaty
Agreement among twelve countries of the European Community to pursue economic, monetary, and political union.

In 1993, all 12 member countries of the European Community ratified the **Maastricht Treaty.** The treaty, named after the Dutch town where it was developed, proposes to take the EC further toward economic, monetary, and political union. Officially called the Treaty on European Union, the document outlines plans for tightening bonds among the member states and creating a single market. The European Commission, which drafted the treaty, predicts that Maastricht will create 1.8 million new jobs by 1999. Also, retail prices in the European Union are expected to fall by a minimum of 6 percent.[39]

Although the heart of the treaty deals with developing a unified European market, Maastricht is also intended to increase integration among the European Union members in areas much closer to the core of national sovereignty. The treaty calls for economic and monetary coordination, including a common currency and an independent central bank by 1999. At present, it seems that this goal will probably not be met. Common foreign, security, and defense policies are also goals, as well as European citizenship—whereby any European Union citizen can live, work, vote, and run for office anywhere in the member countries. The treaty standardizes trade rules and coordinates health and safety standards. Duties, customs procedures, and taxes are also standardized. A driver hauling cargo from Amsterdam to Lisbon can now clear four border crossings by showing a single piece of paper. Before the Maastricht Treaty, the same driver would have carried two pounds of paper to cross the same borders. The overall goal is to end the need for a special product for each country—for example, a different Braun electric razor for Italy, Germany, France, and so forth. Goods marked GEC (goods for EC) can be traded freely, without being retested at each border.

Some economists have called the European Union the "United States of Europe." It is an attractive market, with 320 million consumers and purchasing power almost equal to that of the United States. But the European Union will probably never be a United States of Europe. For one thing, even in a united Europe, marketers will not be able to produce a single Europroduct for a generic Euroconsumer. With nine different languages and individual national customs, Europe will always be far more diverse than the United States. Thus, product differences will continue. It will be a long time, for instance, before the French begin drinking the instant coffee that Britons enjoy. Preferences for washing machines also differ: British homemakers want front-loaders, and the French want top-loaders; Germans like lots of settings and high spin speeds; Italians like lower speeds. Even European companies that think they understand Euroconsumers often have difficulties producing "the right product":

> Atag Holdings NV, a diversified Dutch company whose main business is kitchen appliances, reckoned it was well-placed to expand abroad. Its plant is a mile from the Dutch/German border and near Europe's geographic and population center. And Lidwien Jacobs, a product manager, says she was confident Atag could cater to both the "potato" and "spaghetti" belts—marketers' terms for consumer preferences in northern and southern Europe. But, as Atag quickly discovered, preferences vary much more than that. "To sell in America, you need one or two types of ceramic stove top," Ms. Jacobs says. "In Europe, you need 11."
>
> Belgians, who cook in huge pots, require extra-large burners. Germans like oval pots, and burners to fit. Italians boil large pots of water quickly, for pasta. The French need small burners and very low temperatures for simmering sauces and broths. Such quirks affect every detail. Germans like oven knobs on the front, the French on top. Even clock placement differs. And Atag has had to test market 28 colors. While Continentals prefer black and white, the British demand a vast range, including peach, pigeon blue and mint green.
>
> "Whatever the product, the British are always different," Ms. Jacobs says with a sigh. Another snag: "Domestic," the name of Atag's basic oven, turns off buyers in Britain, where "domestic" is a synonym for "servant."
>
> Atag's kitchenware unit has lifted foreign sales to 25 percent of its total from 4 percent in the mid-1980s. But it now believes that its range of designs and speed in delivering them, rather than the magic bullet of a Euro-product, will keep it competitive. "People would fight another war, I think, to keep their own cooking habits," Ms. Jacobs jokes.[40]

An entirely different type of problem facing global marketers is the possibility of a protectionist movement by the European Union against outsiders. For example, European automakers have proposed holding Japanese imports at roughly their current 10 percent market share. The Irish, Danes, and Dutch don't make cars and have unrestricted home markets; they would be unhappy about limited imports of Toyotas and Datsuns. But France has a strict quota on Japanese cars to protect Renault and Peugeot. These local carmakers could be hurt if the quota is raised at all.

Interestingly, a number of big U.S. companies are already considered more "European" than many European companies. Coke and Kellogg's are considered classic European brand names. Ford and General Motors compete for the largest share of auto sales on the continent. IBM and Digital Equipment dominate their markets. General Electric, AT&T, and Westinghouse are already strong all over Europe and have invested heavily in new manufacturing facilities throughout the continent.

Although many U.S. firms are well prepared to contend with European competition, the rivalry is perhaps more intense there than anywhere else in the world. In the long run, it is questionable whether Europe has room for eight mass-market automakers, including Ford and GM, when the United States sustains just three. Similarly, an integrated Europe probably doesn't need 12 national airlines.

Demographic Makeup

The three most densely populated nations in the world are China, India, and Indonesia. But that fact alone is not particularly useful to marketers. They also need to know whether the population is mostly urban or rural, because marketers may not have easy access to rural consumers. In Belgium about 90 percent of the population lives in an urban setting, whereas in Kenya almost 80 percent of the population lives in a rural setting. Belgium is thus the more attractive market.

Just as important as population is personal income within a country. The wealthiest countries in the world include Japan, the United States, Switzerland, Sweden, Canada, Germany, and several of the Arab oil-producing nations. At the other extreme are countries like Mali and Bangladesh, with a fraction of the per capita purchasing power of the United States. However, a low per capita income is not in itself enough reason to avoid a country. In countries with low per capita incomes, wealth is not evenly distributed. There are pockets of upper- and middle-class consumers in just about every country of the world. In some cases, such as India, the number of consumers is surprisingly large.

The most significant global economic news of the past decade is the rise of a global middle class. From Shekou, China, to Mexico City and countless cities in between, there are traffic jams, bustling bulldozers, and people hawking tickets to various events. These are all symptoms of a growing middle class. In China, per capita incomes are rising 8.5 percent annually; they are growing at a 6.5 percent annual rate in East Asia.[41] Developing countries, excluding Eastern Europe and the former Soviet Union, should grow about 5 percent annually over the next decade.

Growing economies demand professionals. In Asia, accountants, stock analysts, bankers, and even middle managers are in short supply. Rising affluence also creates demand for consumer durables such as refrigerators, VCRs, and automobiles. As Central Europe's middle class grows, Whirlpool expects its sales to grow over 6 percent annually.[42] Companies like Procter & Gamble and Gillette offer an array of products at different price points to attract and keep customers as they move up the income scale. The percentage of the world's population that lives in industrialized nations has been declining since 1960, because industrialized nations have grown slowly and developing nations have grown rapidly. In this decade, more than 90 percent of the world's population growth will occur in developing countries and only 10 percent in the industrialized nations. The United Nations reports that by the year 2000, 79 percent of the world's population will reside in developing countries—for example, Guinea, Bolivia, and Pakistan.

Natural Resources

A final factor in the external environment that has become more evident in the past decade is the shortage of natural resources. For example, petroleum shortages have created huge amounts of wealth for oil-producing countries such as Norway, Saudi Arabia, and the United Arab Emirates. Both consumer and industrial markets have blossomed in these countries. Other countries—such as Indonesia, Mexico, and Venezuela—were able to borrow heavily against oil reserves in order to develop more rapidly. On the other hand, industrial countries like Japan, the United States, and much of Western Europe experienced rampant inflation in the 1970s and an enormous transfer of wealth to the petroleum-rich nations. But during much of the 1980s and 1990s, when the price of oil fell, the petroleum-rich nations suffered. Many were not able to service their foreign debts when their oil revenues were sharply reduced. However, Iraq's invasion of Kuwait in 1990 led to a rapid increase in the price of oil and focused attention on the dependence of industrialized countries on oil imports. The price of oil once again declined following the defeat of Iraq, but the U.S. dependence on foreign oil will likely remain high in the remainder of the 1990s.

Petroleum is not the only natural resource that affects international marketing. Warm climate and lack of water mean that many of Africa's countries will remain importers of foodstuffs. The United States, on the other hand, must rely on Africa for many precious metals. Japan depends heavily on the United States for timber and logs. A Minnesota company manufactures and sells a million pairs of disposable chopsticks to Japan each year. The list could go on, but the point is clear. Vast differences in natural resources create international dependencies, huge shifts of wealth, inflation and recession, export opportunities for countries with abundant resources, and even a stimulus for military intervention.

GLOBAL MARKETING BY THE INDIVIDUAL FIRM

A company should consider entering the global marketplace only after its management has a solid grasp of the global environment. Some relevant questions are "What are our options in selling abroad?" "How difficult is global marketing?" and "What are the potential risks and returns?" Concrete answers to these questions would probably encourage the many U.S. firms not selling overseas to venture into the international arena. Foreign sales could be an important source of profits.

4 Identify the various ways of entering the global marketplace.

Companies decide to "go global" for a number of reasons. Perhaps the most stimulating reason is to earn additional profits. Managers may feel that international sales will result in higher profit margins or more added-on profits. A second stimulus is that a firm may have a unique product or technological advantage not available to other international competitors. Such advantages should result in major business successes abroad. In other situations, management may have exclusive market information about foreign customers, marketplaces, or market situations not known to others. While exclusivity can provide an initial motivation for international marketing, managers must realize that competitors can be expected to catch up with the information advantage of the firm. Finally, saturated domestic markets, excess capacity, and potential for economies of scale can also be motivators to "go global." Economies of scale mean that average per-unit production costs fall as output is increased.

Many firms form multinational partnerships—called strategic alliances—to assist them in penetrating global markets; strategic alliances are examined in Chapter 7. Five other methods of entering the global marketplace are, in order of risk, export, licensing, contract manufacturing, the joint venture, and direct investment. (See Exhibit 4.6.)

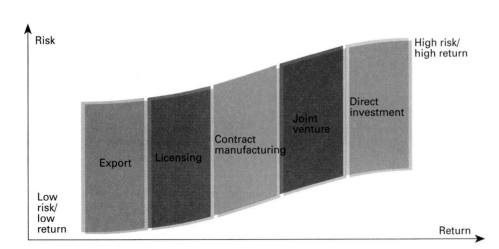

Exhibit 4.6

Risk Levels for Five Methods of Entering the Global Marketplace

Exporting is not limited to huge corporations. In fact, small companies account for 96% of all U.S. exporters, but only 30% of export volume.
© Ken Touchton

Export

 When a company decides to enter the global market, exporting is usually the least complicated and least risky alternative. **Exporting** is selling domestically produced products to buyers in another country. A company, for example, can sell directly to foreign importers or buyers. Exporting is not limited to huge corporations such as General Motors or Westinghouse. Indeed, small companies account for 96 percent of all U.S. exporters, but only 30 percent of the export volume.[43] Many small businesses claim that they lack the money, time, or knowledge of foreign markets that exporting requires. The U.S. Department of Commerce is trying to make it increasingly easy for small businesses to enter exporting. The department has created a pilot program in which it has hired a private company to represent up to 50 small businesses at specific international trade fairs. For example, FTS, Incorporated, was hired to represent small firms at a trade show in Italy in late 1996. The company handed out company brochures and other sales information to interested prospective Italian clients. Also, after the show was over, FTS gave each participating American company a list of potential Italian distributors for their products. Each American firm paid only $2,500 to be represented at the trade fair. For companies interested in exporting, the U.S. government stands ready to help in a variety of ways. Some of the federal resources available to companies wanting to enter exporting are shown in Exhibit 4.7.

Instead of selling directly to foreign buyers, a company may decide to sell to intermediaries located in its domestic market. The most common intermediary is the export merchant, also known as a **buyer for export,** who is usually treated like a domestic customer by the domestic manufacturer. The buyer for export assumes all risks and sells internationally for its own account. The domestic firm is involved only to the extent that its products are bought in foreign markets.

A second type of intermediary is the **export broker,** who plays the traditional broker's role by bringing buyer and seller together. The manufacturer still retains title and assumes all the risks. Export brokers operate primarily in agriculture and raw materials.

Export agents, a third type of intermediary, are foreign sales agents–distributors who live in the foreign country and perform the same functions as domestic manu-

exporting
Selling domestically produced products to buyers in another country.

buyer for export
Intermediary in the global market that assumes all ownership risks and sells globally for its own account.

export broker
Intermediary who plays the traditional broker's role by bringing buyer and seller together.

export agent
Intermediary that acts like a manufacturer's agent for the exporter. The export agent lives in the foreign market.

Exhibit 4.7 *Resources to Aid Companies Interested in Exporting*

General Trade Information

The U.S. Department of Commerce (DOC) operates a multitude of programs and services designed for people and companies with interest in conducting business abroad:

- **The Trade Information Center Fax Retrieval Hotline** is a 24-hour fax information service. Dial (800) USA-TRADE from your Touch-Tone™ phone, follow the instructions, and the information you request will be automatically faxed to you.
- **Flash Facts** is another 24-hour DOC fax retrieval service for information on specific countries. Here are some of the main numbers to call:

Eastern Europe Business Information Center:
(202) 482-5749
Offices of the Americas (Mexico, Canada, Latin America and the Caribbean):
(800) 872-8723
Asia Business Center (Southeast Asia, Korea, Vietnam, China, Taiwan, Hong Kong, Australia and New Zealand):
(202) 482-3875
Business Information Service for the Newly Independent (former USSR) States:
(202) 482-3145
Uruguay Round of the General Agreement on Tariffs and Trade (GATT):
(800) USA-TRADE
Business Information Center for Northern Ireland:
(202) 501-7488

- **The National Trade Data Bank (NTDB)** is a "one-stop" source for export promotion and international trade data, collected by 17 U.S. government agencies.
    The NTDB is available on CD-ROM and by subscription via fax-on-demand and the Internet as part of STAT-USA (http://www.stat-usa.gov). For information on all of NTDB's services and costs, call (202) 482-1986.

Trade & Project Financing

- **The Export–Import Bank of the United States (Eximbank)** facilitates the export of U.S. goods and services by providing loans, guarantees, and insurance coverage. Call (800) 565-3946.
- **The Overseas Private Investment Corporation (OPIC)** provides investment services, financing, and political risk insurance in more than 130 developing countries. Call (202) 336-8799.
- **The Export Credit Guarantee** program of the Foreign Agriculture Service of the Department of Agriculture offers risk protection for U.S. exporters against nonpayment by foreign banks. Call (202) 720-3224.
- **The U.S. Small Business Administration** offers a 24-hour electronic bulletin board with professional marketing services, and information on trade shows and other promotions overseas. Call (800) 827-5722.
- **The World Trade Centers Association,** with a total membership of 400,000 companies worldwide, provides international trade information, including freight forwarders, customs brokers, and international companies. Call (212) 432-2626.

- **The United States Council for International Business** is the official U.S. affiliate of the International Chamber of Commerce. Call (212) 354-4480.

Trade Fairs & Exhibitions

- **Certified Trade Fairs,** endorsed by the U.S. Department of Commerce, provide good opportunities to promote exports. For information, call Trade Fair Certification, (202) 482-1609.
- **Matchmaker Trade Delegations** are DOC-recruited and -planned missions designed to introduce businesses to representatives and distributors overseas. For further information, call (202) 482-3119.
- **The Certified Trade Missions Program,** sponsored by the International Trade Administration (ITA), provides a flexible format in which to conduct country-specific business overseas. Call (202) 482-4908.

Government Publications

- **The Export Yellow Pages** is a free directory of U.S. manufacturers, banks, service organizations, and export trading companies seeking to do business abroad. Contact your local DOC district office.
- **Eastern Europe Looks for Partners,** published bimonthly by the Central and Eastern Europe Business Information Center, highlights new markets and business opportunities for U.S. firms. Call (202) 482-2645.
- **Destination Japan: A Business Guide for the 90's,** published by the Japan Export Information Center, is a basic guide to doing business with Japan. Call (703) 487-4650 and ask for stock no. PB94164787.
- **Commercial News USA,** published by the ITA, is a 10-time-yearly catalog–magazine to promote U.S. products and services to overseas markets. It is disseminated to 125,000 business readers via U.S. embassies and consulates in 155 countries. For paid listings and advertising rates, call (202) 482-4918.
- **Business America,** published by the ITA, is a monthly compendium of U.S. trade policies and features a calendar of trade shows, exhibitions, fairs, and seminars. Call (202) 512-1800.

Internet Opportunities

Use your browser or on-line service with Internet access to connect to the World Wide Web portion of the Internet. Then, try one of the search engines such as Yahoo (http://www.Yahoo.com) to find relevant international business information.

    Here are some of the resources currently listed in Yahoo's "International Economy" directory:
US Council for International Business:
http://www.uscib.org
Russian and East European Studies Business and Economic Resources:
http://www.pitt.edu/~cjp/rsecon.html
Berkeley Roundtable on International Economy:
http://server.berkeley.edu/BRIE
Pacific Region Forum on Business and Management Communication:
gopher://hoshi.cic.sfu.ca/11/dlam/business/forum

Source: U.S. Department of Commerce.

facturers' agents, helping with international financing, shipping, and so on. The U.S. Department of Commerce has an agent–distributor service that helps about 5,000 U.S. companies a year find an agent or distributor in virtually any country of the world. A second category of agents resides in the manufacturer's country but represents foreign buyers. This type of agent acts as a hired purchasing agent for foreign customers operating in the exporter's home market.

Licensing

licensing
The legal process whereby a licensor agrees to let another firm use its manufacturing process, trademarks, patents, trade secrets, or other proprietary knowledge.

Another effective way for a firm to move into the global arena with relatively little risk is to sell a license to manufacture its product to someone in a foreign country. **Licensing** is the legal process whereby a licensor allows another firm to use its manufacturing process, trademarks, patents, trade secrets, or other proprietary knowledge. The licensee, in turn, pays the licensor a royalty or fee agreed on by both parties.

Because it has many advantages, U.S. companies have eagerly embraced the licensing concept. For instance, Philip Morris licensed Labatt Brewing Company to produce Miller High Life in Canada. The Spalding Company receives more than $2 million annually from licensing agreements on its sporting goods. Fruit-of-the-Loom manufactures nothing itself abroad but lends its name through licensing to 45 consumer items in Japan alone, for at least 1 percent of the licensee's gross sales.

A licensor must make sure it can exercise the control over the licensee's activities needed to ensure proper quality, pricing, distribution, and so on. Licensing may also create a new competitor in the long run, if the licensee decides to void the license agreement. International law is often ineffective in stopping such actions. Two common ways of maintaining effective control over licensees are shipping one or more critical components from the United States or locally registering patents and trademarks to the U.S. firm, not to the licensee.

U.S. franchisers operate more than 32,000 outlets in foreign countries. Over half are for fast-food or business services.
© Jeff Greenberg

Franchising is one form of licensing that has grown rapidly in recent years. More than 350 U.S. franchisors operate more than 32,000 outlets in foreign countries, bringing in sales of $6 billion. Over half the international franchises are for fast-food restaurants and business services. As with other forms of licensing, maintaining control over the franchisees is important. For instance, McDonald's was forced to take legal action to buy back its Paris outlets, because the franchisee failed to maintain quality standards. McDonald's claimed the Paris franchise was dirty and provided poor service and food. Investigators found dog droppings inside one outlet, and the franchise charged extra for catsup and hid the straws from customers. Because of the damage to McDonald's reputation, the chain was able to develop only 67 outlets in all of France, compared to 270 in Great Britain and 270 in Germany. To reestablish itself, McDonald's decided to project French style and class. The first outlet to appear after McDonald's repurchased its franchise was in a handsome turn-of-the-century building on one of Paris's grand boulevards.

Contract Manufacturing

Firms that do not want to become involved in licensing or to become heavily involved in global marketing may engage in **contract manufacturing,** which is private-label manufacturing by a foreign company. The foreign company produces a certain volume of products to specification, with the domestic firm's brand name on the goods. The domestic company usually handles the marketing. Thus, the domestic firm can broaden its global marketing base without investing in overseas plant and equipment. After establishing a solid base, the domestic firm may switch to a joint venture or direct investment.

contract manufacturing
Private label manufacturing by a foreign company.

Joint Venture

Joint ventures are quite similar to licensing agreements. In a **joint venture,** the domestic firm buys part of a foreign company or joins with a foreign company to create a new entity. A joint venture is a quick and relatively inexpensive way to "go global." It also can be very risky. Many joint ventures fail. Others fall victim to a takeover, in which one partner buys out the other. In a survey of 150 companies involved in joint ventures that ended, three-quarters were found to have been taken over by Japanese partners. Gary Hamel, a professor at the London Business School, regards joint ventures as "a race to learn": The partner that learns fastest comes to dominate the relationship and can then rewrite its terms.[44] Thus, a joint venture becomes a new form of competition.

joint venture
When a domestic firm buys part of a foreign company or joins with a foreign company to create a new entity.

One American company that strongly believes in joint ventures is Whirlpool. In Asia, the company has six joint ventures ranging from producing "Snowflake" refrigerators in Beijing to manufacturing "Narcissus" washers in Shanghai. Whirlpool's ultimate goal is to export air conditioners it makes in China to other parts of Asia. But like dozens of other brands made in China, the Raybo units produced by Whirlpool's joint venture—in Shenzhen, China—tend to be copies of Japanese designs. The problem is that they aren't as well made as the Japanese originals.

For future model years, this means that improving the durability of the compressor—the heart of an air conditioner—is a must. So is an overhaul of the unit itself. "Until we have a product that we feel represents a modern, upscale product, we're not going to put the Whirlpool name on it," says William Marohn, Whirlpool's president and chief operating officer.[45]

The goals for the current model year have been more immediate. Whirlpool first had to ensure adequate supplies of parts as the factory in Shenzhen revved up to its goal of producing as many as 1,200 units a day. Also, China's plan, announced in late 1996, to put an end to duty-free imports of factory machinery complicates matters. Whirlpool officials must figure out what to take in before the new rules take effect.

In a successful joint venture, both parties gain valuable skills from the alliance. In the General Motors–Suzuki joint venture in Canada, for example, both parties have contributed and gained. The alliance, CAMI Automotive, was formed to manufacture low-end cars for the U.S. market. The plant, run by Suzuki management, produces the Geo Metro/Suzuki Swift—the smallest, highest-gas-mileage GM car sold in North America—as well as the Geo Tracker/Suzuki Sidekick sport utility vehicle. Through CAMI, Suzuki has gained access to GM's dealer network and an expanded market for parts and components. GM avoided the cost of developing low-end cars and obtained models it needed to revitalize the lower end of its product line and its average fuel-economy rating. The CAMI factory may be one of the most productive plants in North America. There GM has learned how Japanese carmakers use work teams, run flexible assembly lines, and manage quality control.[46]

Direct Investment

Active ownership of a foreign company or of overseas manufacturing or marketing facilities is **direct foreign investment.** Worldwide foreign direct investment was about $350 billion in 1996.[47] Direct investors have either a controlling interest or a large minority interest in the firm. Thus, they have the greatest potential reward and the greatest potential risk. Federal Express lost $1.2 billion in its attempt to build a hub in Europe.[48] It created a huge infrastructure but couldn't generate the package volume to support it. To control losses, the company fired 6,600 international employees and closed offices in over 100 European cities. On the other hand, direct in-

direct foreign investment
Active ownership of a foreign company or of overseas manufacturing or marketing facilities.

vestment can often lead to rapid success. MTV has been in the European market only since 1988, yet since 1994 it has had more viewers in Europe than in the United States.[49]

Sometimes firms make direct investments because they can find no suitable local partners. Also, direct investments avoid the communication problems and conflicts of interest that can arise with joint ventures. Other firms simply don't want to share their technology, which they fear may be stolen or ultimately used against them by creating a new competitor. Texas Instruments (TI) has historically been one of the latter companies. "TI was a technology company that hated to share anything," said Akira Ishikawa, senior vice president of TI's semiconductor group. "It wasn't in the culture to share or teach the most advanced semiconductor technologies. It was taboo. If you talked about that, you might be fired immediately."[50] Now TI has changed its attitude and entered into five Asian joint ventures. The reason was primarily to spread its financial risk.

A firm may make a direct foreign investment by acquiring an interest in an existing company or by building new facilities. It might do so because it has trouble transferring some resource to a foreign operation or getting that resource locally. One important resource is personnel, especially managers. If the local labor market is tight, the firm may buy an entire foreign firm and retain all its employees instead of paying higher salaries than competitors.

The United States is a popular place for direct investment by foreign companies. In 1996, the value of foreign-owned businesses in the United States was over $450 billion.

THE GLOBAL MARKETING MIX

5 List the basic elements involved in developing a global marketing mix.

To succeed, firms seeking to enter into foreign trade must still adhere to the principles of the marketing mix. Information gathered on foreign markets through research is the basis for the four Ps of global marketing strategy: product, place (distribution), promotion, and price. Marketing managers who understand the advantages and disadvantages of different ways to enter the global market and the effect of the external environment on the firm's marketing mix have a better chance of reaching their goals.

The first step in creating a marketing mix is developing a thorough understanding of the global target market. Often this knowledge can be obtained through the same types of marketing research used in the domestic market (see Chapter 9). However, global marketing research is conducted in vastly different environments. Conducting a survey can be difficult in developing countries, where telephone ownership is rare and mail delivery slow or sporadic. Drawing samples based on known population parameters is often difficult because of the lack of data. In some cities in South America, Mexico, and Asia, street maps are unavailable, streets are unidentified, and houses are unnumbered. Moreover, the questions a marketer can ask may differ in other cultures. In some cultures, people tend to be more private than in the United States and do not like to respond to personal questions on surveys. For instance, in France, questions about one's age and income are considered especially rude.

Product and Promotion

With the proper information, a good marketing mix can be developed. One important decision is whether to alter the product or the promotion for the global marketplace. One study suggests that a standardized global marketing strategy may be the best approach, at least for marketing efforts in Western nations.[51] Other options are to radically change the product or to adjust either the promotional message or the product to suit local conditions.

One Product, One Message

The strategy of global marketing standardization, which was discussed earlier, means developing a single product for all markets and promoting it the same way all over the world. For instance, Procter & Gamble uses the same product and promotional themes for Head and Shoulders in China as it does in the U.S. The advertising draws attention to a person's dandruff problem, which stands out in a nation of black-haired people. Head and Shoulders is now the best-selling shampoo in China despite costing over 300 percent more than local brands.[52] Buoyed by its success with Head and Shoulders, Procter & Gamble is using the same product and same promotion strategy with Tide detergent in China. In 1996, it used another common promotion tactic that it has found to be successful in the U.S. The company spent half-a-million dollars to reach agreements with local washing machine manufacturers, which now include a free box of Tide with every new washer.

Using the same products and promotion themes as the U.S. market, Motorola has about 14 percent of Japan's recently deregulated and growing cellular phone market. Compaq is achieving a growing share of Japan's PC market, following the same strategy but pricing their products 20 to 40 percent below those of key rival, NEC Corporation.[53]

Global media—especially satellite and cable TV networks like Cable News Network International, MTV Networks, and British Sky Broadcasting—make it possible to beam advertising to audiences unreachable a few years ago. "Eighteen-year-olds in Paris have more in common with eighteen-year-olds in New York than with their own parents," says William Roedy, director of MTV Europe. Almost all of MTV's advertisers run unified, English-language campaigns in the 28 nations the firm reaches. The audiences "buy the same products, go to the same movies, listen to the same music, sip the same colas. Global advertising merely works on that premise."[54] Although teens throughout the world prefer movies above all other forms of television programming, they are closely followed by music videos, stand-up comedy, and then sports.[55]

When Ford unveiled its Mondeo global car in Europe, it decided on a direct-mail campaign in 15 nations. The advertising theme was "Beauty with inner strength," which plays well with the primarily male, young-to-middle-aged target market. Both

Using a strategy of global marketing standardization, Procter & Gamble uses the same product and promotional themes for Head and Shoulders in China as it does in the U.S.

© 1993 Mary Beth Camp/Matrix

Ford and non-Ford owners were targeted, using dealer-generated mailing lists and lists purchased from brokers. Each direct-mail packet contained the name and address of the local Ford dealer. The campaign mailed 850,000 packets, which resulted in a stunning 160,000 showroom visits. Perhaps one reason for the success of the campaign is that most Europeans rarely receive direct-mail promotions. The average Belgian gets 78 pieces of direct mail a year, a German 61 pieces, a French consumer 55, and an English citizen 42. In Spain it's 24, and in Ireland the average person gets just 11—less than one direct-mail letter or catalog every month.[56]

Both Nike and Reebok spend over $100 million a year in promotion outside the United States. Each company practices global marketing standardization to keep its messages clear and its products desirable. Both companies have exploited basketball's surging popularity around the world. Nike sends Charles Barkley of the Houston Rockets to Europe and Asia touting its products. Reebok counters by sending basketball superstar Shaquille O'Neal overseas as its ambassador. One of the main appeals of sneakers is their American style; therefore, the more American an advertising commercial, the better it is. The tag lines—whether in Italy, Germany, Japan, or France—all read the same way in English: "Just do it" and "Planet Reebok." NBA All Star Patrick Ewing has created his own global marketing standardization program. He owns Ewing Athletic, which manufactures his signature footware. His commercials, now shown in 70 overseas markets, feature the "Ew the Man" tag line.[57]

Even a one-product, one-message strategy may call for some changes to suit local needs, such as variations in the product's measurement units, package sizes, and labeling. Pillsbury, for example, changed the measurement unit for its cake mixes because adding "cups of" has no meaning in many developing countries. Also, in developing countries, packages are often smaller so that consumers with limited incomes can buy them. For instance, cigarettes, chewing gum, and razor blades may be sold individually instead of in packages.

Unchanged products may fail simply because of cultural factors. The game *Trivial Pursuit* failed in Japan. It seems that getting the answers wrong can be seen as a loss of face. Any type of war game tends to do very poorly in Germany, despite the fact that Germany is by far the world's biggest game-playing nation. A successful game in Germany has plenty of details and thick rulebooks. Monopoly remains the world's favorite board game; it seems to overcome all cultural barriers. The game is available in 25 languages, including Russian, Croatian, and Hebrew.[58]

Product Invention

In the context of global marketing, product invention can be taken to mean either creating a new product for a market or drastically changing an existing product. For the Japanese market, Nabisco had to remove the cream filling from its Oreo cookies because Japanese children thought they were too sweet. Ford thinks it can save billions on its product development costs by developing a single small-car chassis and then altering its styling to suit different countries.[59] Campbell Soup invented a watercress and duck-gizzard soup that is now selling well in China. It is also considering a cream of snake soup.[60] Frito Lay's most popular potato chip in Thailand is shrimp flavored. Dormont Manufacturing Company makes a simple gas hose that hooks up to deep-fat fryers and similar appliances. Sounds like something that could be sold globally, right? Wrong—in Europe differing national standards means that a different hose is required for each country.[61] Minutiae such as the color of the plastic coating or how the end pieces should be attached to the rest of the hose and the couplings themselves create a myriad of design problems for Dormont Manufacturing.

Consumers in different countries use products differently. For example, in many countries, clothing is worn much longer between washings than in the United States, so a more durable fabric must be produced and marketed. For Peru, Goodyear developed a tire that contains a higher percentage of natural rubber and has better treads than tires manufactured elsewhere in order to handle the tough Peruvian driving conditions. Rubbermaid has sold millions of open-top wastebaskets in America; Europeans, picky about garbage peeking out of bins, wanted bins with tight lids that snap into place.[62]

Message Adaptation

Another global marketing strategy is to maintain the same basic product but alter the promotional strategy. Bicycles are mainly pleasure vehicles in the United States. In many parts of the world, however, they are a family's main mode of transportation. Thus, promotion in these countries should stress durability and efficiency. In contrast, U.S. advertising may emphasize escaping and having fun.

Harley-Davidson decided that its American promotion theme, "One steady constant in an increasingly screwed-up world," wouldn't appeal to the Japanese market. The Japanese ads combine American images with traditional Japanese ones: American riders passing a geisha in a rickshaw, Japanese ponies nibbling at a Harley motorcycle. Waiting lists for Harleys in Japan are now six months long.[63]

Unlike Harley-Davidson, Ocean Spray Cranberries failed in Japan. The company shortened the name to Cranby to make it easier to say and served up a bland version for the Japanese palate. But sales were disappointing, and the company pulled out quickly, though it has recently reintroduced several cranberry drinks. "We're introducing an unknown fruit in an unknown brand in a foreign market that's unknown to us," says Ocean Spray's president and chief executive, John S. Llewellyn, Jr. "It's not like selling apples or oranges."[64] The company is trying again in Australia. In one self-effacing commercial, two New England farmers land on an Australian beach during a surfing contest. The spectators are wearing bathing suits, but the Americans, dressed in baseball caps and winter jackets, haven't figured out that it's almost summer in the Southern Hemisphere. After a short discourse on Ocean Spray and cranberries, one of the visitors concedes that the drinks have "an unusual taste," but he also maintains that "they'll grow on you."

Global marketers find that promotion is a daunting task in some countries. For example, commercial television time is readily available in Canada but severely restricted in Germany. Until recently, marketers in Indonesia had only one subscription TV channel with few viewers (120,000 out of a nation of 180 million people). Because of this limited television audience, several marketers, such as the country's main Toyota dealer, had to develop direct-mail campaigns to reach their target markets.

Some cultures view a product as having less value if it has to be advertised. In other nations, claims that seem exaggerated by U.S. standards are commonplace. On the other hand, Germany does not permit advertisers to state that their products are "best" or "better" than those of competitors, a description commonly used in U.S. advertising. The hard-sell tactics and sexual themes so common in U.S. advertising are taboo in many countries. Procter & Gamble's advertisements for Cheer detergents were voted least popular in Japan because they used hard-sell testimonials. The negative reaction forced P&G to withdraw Cheer from the Japanese market. In the Middle East, pictures of women in print advertisements have been covered with censor's ink.

Language barriers, translation problems, and cultural differences have generated numerous headaches for international marketing managers. Consider these examples:

- A toothpaste claiming to give users white teeth was especially inappropriate in many areas of Southeast Asia, where the well-to-do chew betel nuts and black teeth are a sign of higher social status.

- Procter & Gamble's Japanese advertising for Camay soap nearly devastated the product. In one commercial, a man meeting a woman for the first time immediately compared her skin to that of a fine porcelain doll. Although the ad had worked in other Asian countries, the man came across as rude and disrespectful in Japan.

- Coca-Cola took out full-page ads in Greek newspapers apologizing for an earlier ad that showed the Parthenon's white marble columns tapered like a Coke bottle. Greeks have great respect for their ancient temples and were highly indignant. The general secretary of the Greek Culture Ministry said, "Whoever insults the Parthenon insults Greece."[65]

Product Adaptation

Another alternative for global marketers is to slightly alter a basic product to meet local conditions. Additional pizza toppings offered by Domino's in Japan include corn, curry, squid, and spinach. When Lewis Woolf Griptight, a British manufacturer of infant accessories such as pacifiers came to the U.S., it found subtle differences between United Kingdom and American parents. Elizabeth Lee, marketing manager, noted, "There are subtle differences, but many problems are the same. Whether a cup spills in America or in Madagascar or in the U.K., moms aren't going to like it," she said. "We didn't need to redo all the research to find out that people didn't want cups that spill, but we still had to do research on things like color and packaging."[66] The brand name "Kiddiwinks" is a British word for children. In the U.S., the name was changed to "Binky" because of positive parental reactions in marketing research tests.

Meeting ISO 9000 Standards

Regardless of whether a company adapts an existing product, sells a product that is identical to one in the United States, or invents something entirely new, it may need to meet global quality standards like ISO 9000. **ISO 9000** (pronounced "ice-o nine thousand") is a standard of quality management, hugely popular in Europe, that is rapidly taking hold in the United States and around the globe.

The ISO 9000 series was created in the late 1980s by the International Organization for Standardization. The set of five technical standards, known collectively as ISO 9000, was designed to offer a uniform way of determining whether manufacturing plants and service organizations have sound quality procedures. To register, a company must undergo a third-party audit of its manufacturing and customer-service processes, covering everything from how it designs, produces, and installs its goods to how it inspects, packages, and markets them. Worldwide, more than 30,000 certificates have been issued to document compliance with the standards. Says Richard Thompson, vice president and general manager of Caterpillar's engine division, whose Mossville, Illinois, plant was among the first U.S. diesel engine factories to win the certificate: "Today, having ISO 9000 is a competitive advantage. Tomorrow, it will be the ante to the global poker game."[67]

DuPont, General Electric, Eastman Kodak, British Telecom, and Philips Electronics are among the big-name companies that are urging—or even coercing—suppliers to adopt ISO 9000. GE's plastics business, for instance, commanded 340 vendors to meet the standard. Declares John Yates, general manager of global sourcing for the company: "There is absolutely no negotiation. If you want to work with us, you have to get it."[68]

ISO 9000
A standard of quality management, hugely popular in Europe, that is rapidly taking hold in the United States and around the globe.

Pricing

Once marketing managers have determined a global product and promotion strategy, they can select the remainder of the marketing mix. Pricing presents some unique problems in the global sphere. Exporters must not only cover their production costs but also consider transportation costs, insurance, taxes, and tariffs. When deciding on a final price, marketers must also determine what customers are willing to spend on a particular product. Marketers also need to ensure that their foreign buyers will pay them. Because developing nations lack mass purchasing power, selling to them often poses special pricing problems. Sometimes a product can be simplified in order to lower the price. However, the firm must not assume that low-income countries are willing to accept lower quality. Although the nomads of the Sahara are very poor, they still buy expensive fabrics to make their clothing. Their survival in harsh conditions and extreme temperatures requires this expense. Additionally, certain expensive luxury items can be sold almost anywhere.

Companies must also be careful not to be so enthusiastic about entering a market, that they extend credit haphazardly. Compaq Computers' sales have been growing very rapidly in China, but partially because it has been giving away computers against its will. Recently a Chinese distributor failed to repay $32 million for computers that Compaq had extended on credit. Analysts say Compaq is now owed over $100 million by delinquent dealers and distributors in China.[69]

Dumping

Dumping is generally considered to be the sale of an exported product at a price lower than that charged for the same or a like product in the "home" market of the exporter. This practice is thought of as a form of price discrimination that can potentially harm the importing nation's competing industries. Dumping may occur as a result of exporter business strategies that include (1) trying to increase an overseas market share, (2) temporarily distributing products in overseas markets to offset slack demand in the home market, (3) lowering unit costs by exploiting large-scale production, and (4) attempting to maintain stable prices during periods of exchange rate fluctuations.

Historically, the dumping of goods has presented serious problems in international trade. As a result, dumping has led to significant disagreements among countries and diverse views about its harmfulness. Some trade economists view dumping as harmful only when it involves the use of "predatory" practices that intentionally try to eliminate competition and gain monopoly power in a market. They believe that predatory dumping rarely occurs and that antidumping enforcement is a protectionist tool whose cost to consumers and import-using industries exceeds the benefits to the industries receiving protection.

The Uruguay Round rewrites the international law on dumping. The agreement states:

1. Dumping disputes will be resolved by the World Trade Organization.
2. Dumping terms are specifically defined. For example, the "dumped price" must be at least five percent below the home market price before it is considered dumping.
3. At least 25 percent of the members of an industry must support its government filing a dumping complaint with the World Trade Organization. In other words, a government can't file a complaint if only one or two firms complain (unless they make up 25 percent of the industry).

Countertrade

Global trade does not always involve cash. Countertrade is a fast-growing way to conduct global business. In **countertrade,** all or part of the payment for goods or services is in the form of other goods or services. Countertrade is thus a form of barter (swapping goods for goods), an age-old practice whose origins have been traced back to cave dwellers. The U.S. Commerce Department says that roughly 30 percent of

dumping
The sale of an exported product at a price lower than that charged for the same or a like product in the "home" market of the exporter.

countertrade
Form of trade in which all or part of the payment for goods or services is in the form of other goods or services.

all global trade is countertrade.[70] In fact, both India and China have made billion-dollar government purchasing lists, with most of the goods to be paid for by countertrade.

One common type of countertrade is straight barter. For example, PepsiCo sends Pepsi syrup to Russian bottling plants and in payment gets Stolichnaya vodka, which is then marketed in the West. Another form of countertrade is the compensation agreement. Typically, a company provides technology and equipment for a plant in a developing nation and agrees to take full or partial payment in goods produced by that plant. For example, General Tire Company supplied equipment and know-how for a Romanian truck tire plant. In turn, General Tire sold the tires it received from the plant in the United States under the Victoria brand name. Pierre Cardin gives technical advice to China in exchange for silk and cashmere. In these cases, both sides benefit even though they don't use cash.

Distribution

Solving promotional, price, and product problems does not guarantee global marketing success. The product still has to get adequate distribution. For example, Europeans don't play sports as much as Americans do, so they don't visit sporting-goods stores as often. Realizing this, Reebok started selling its shoes in about 800 traditional shoe stores in France. In one year, the company doubled its French sales. Harley-Davidson had to open two company-owned stores in Japan to get distribution for its Harley clothing and clothing accessories.

The Japanese distribution system is considered the most complicated in the world. Imported goods wind their way through layers of agents, wholesalers, and retailers. For example, a bottle of 96 aspirins costs about $20 because the bottle passes through at least six wholesalers, each of whom increases the selling price. The result is that the Japanese consumer pays the world's most exorbitant prices. These distribution channels seem to be based on historical and traditional patterns of socially arranged trade-offs, which Japanese officials claim are very hard for the government to change. Today, however, the system seems to be changing because of pressure from the Japanese consumer. Japanese shoppers are now placing low prices ahead of quality in their purchasing decisions.[71] The retailer who can cut distribution costs and therefore the retail price gets the sale. For example, Kojima, a Japanese electronics superstore chain like the U.S. chains, Circuit City or Best Buy, had to bypass GE's Japanese distribution partner Toshiba to import its merchandise at a good price. Toshiba's distribution system required refrigerators to pass through too many hands before it reached the retailer. Kojima went directly to GE headquarters in the U.S. and persuaded the company to sell it refrigerators, which were then shipped directly to Kojima. It is now selling GE refrigerators for about $800, which is half the price of a typical Japanese model.[72]

Retail institutions in other countries also may differ from what a company is used to in its domestic market. The terms *department store* and *supermarket* may refer to types of retail outlets that are very different from those found in the United States. Japanese supermarkets, for example, are large multistory buildings that sell not only food but also clothing, furniture, and home appliances. Department stores are even larger outlets, but unlike their U.S. counterparts, they emphasize foodstuffs and operate a restaurant on the premises. For a variety of reasons, U.S.-type retail outlets do not exist or are impractical in developing countries. For instance, con-

Because of a traditional multi-layered distribution system, Japanese consumers pay the world's highest prices. Japanese consumers are now placing low prices ahead of quality in their purchasing decisions.

© Robert Wallis/SABA

sumers may not have the storage space to keep food for several days. Refrigerators, when available, are usually small and do not allow for bulk storage. Attempting to build new retail outlets can be a frustrating battle. In Germany's Ruhr Valley, the discounter All Kauf SB-Warenhaus GmbH has struggled to build a store for 15 years on land that it owns. Local authorities are blocking construction, however, because they are afraid the store will hurt local retailers.[73]

Channels of distribution and the physical infrastructure are also inadequate in many developing nations. In China, for example, most goods are carried on poles or human backs, in wheelbarrows and handcarts, or, increasingly (and this is an important advance), on bicycles. Procter & Gamble has resorted to taking traffic maps of the 228 Chinese cities with at least 200,000 citizens and marking them up with locations of small mom-and-pop shops and the big department stores. Divisions of its "ground troops," often wearing white sports shirts with "Winning Team" written on the back, "blitz" each locale and sell and distribute P&G products. Even street-stall owners get a personal pitch.

Compaq and IBM have found getting computers into Chinese stores a major puzzle. Delivery trucks aren't allowed into Beijing in daylight, forcing companies into midnight deliveries and long delays. And shipping by rail "is different from other parts of the world, where everything gets shipped in containers," says Lamson Ip, an IBM PC manager. "Here, I've seen [cargo handlers] virtually throw our cartons into trains."[74]

Such conditions can endanger reputations as well as products. When Chinese customers complained to IBM that it was palming off year-old machines as new, IBM officials were puzzled. Finally, they identified the culprit: Dust had seeped inside each carton despite two layers of plastic sheeting. Another layer ended the complaints. "That wasn't IBM—that was China," says James Vance, IBM's assistant factory manager in Shenzhen.[75]

LOOKING BACK

Look back at the story about Snapple not selling in Japan. Where it can be applied, the global marketing standardization of product lines offers significant economic benefits. However, different cultures, languages, levels of economic development, and distribution channels in global markets usually require either new products or modified products. Pricing, promotion, and distribution strategies must often be altered as well.

There is no doubt that international markets will become even more important to large U.S. companies like Quaker Oats. These markets will also become more important to medium-size and smaller companies. Globalization is the wave of the future in international marketing.

SUMMARY

1 *Discuss the importance of global marketing.* Businesspeople who adopt a global vision are better able to identify global marketing opportunities, understand the nature of global networks, and engage foreign competition in domestic markets.

2 *Discuss the impact of multinationals on the world economy.* Multinational corporations are international traders that regularly operate across national borders. Because of their vast size and financial, technological, and material resources, multinational corporations have a great influence on the world economy. They have the ability to overcome trade problems, save on labor costs, and tap new technology.

KEY TERMS

buyer for export *106*

contract manufacturing *109*

countertrade *115*

direct foreign investment *109*

dumping *115*

export agent *106*

export broker *106*

exporting *106*

fully industrialized society *96*

General Agreement on Tariffs and Trade (GATT) *99*

global marketing *86*

global marketing standardization *91*

global vision *86*

industrializing society *95*

3 *Describe the external environment facing global marketers.* Global marketers face the same environmental factors as they do domestically: culture, economic and technological development, political structures, demography, and natural resources. Cultural considerations include societal values, attitudes and beliefs, language, and customary business practices. A country's economic and technological status depends on its stage of industrial development: traditional society, preindustrial society, takeoff economy, industrializing society, or fully industrialized society. The political structure is shaped by political ideology and such policies as tariffs, quotas, boycotts, exchange controls, trade agreements, and market groupings. Demographic variables include population, income distribution, and growth rate.

4 *Identify the various ways of entering the global marketplace.* Firms use the following strategies to enter global markets, in descending order of risk and profit: direct investment, joint venture, contract manufacturing, licensing, and export.

5 *List the basic elements involved in developing a global marketing mix.* A firm's major consideration is how much it will adjust the four P's—product, promotion, place (distribution), and price—within each country. One strategy is to use one product and one promotion message worldwide. A second strategy is to create new products for global markets. A third strategy is to keep the product basically the same but alter the promotional message. A fourth strategy is to slightly alter the product to meet local conditions.

Discussion and Writing Questions

1. Many marketers now believe that teenagers in the developed countries are becoming "global consumers." That is, they all want and buy the same goods and services. Do you think this is true? If so, what has caused the phenomenon?

2. The sale of cigarettes in many developed countries either has peaked out or is declining. However, the developing markets represent major growth markets. Should U.S. tobacco companies capitalize on this opportunity?

3. Renault and Peugeot dominate the French market but have no presence in the U.S. market. Why do you think that this is true?

4. Candartel, an upscale manufacturer of lamps and lampshades in America, has decided to "go global." Top management is having trouble deciding how to develop the market. What are some market entry options for the firm?

5. Rubbermaid, the U.S. manufacturer of kitchen products and other household items, is considering moving to global marketing standardization. What are the pros and cons of this strategy?

6. Suppose you are marketing manager for a consumer products firm that is about to undertake its first expansion abroad. Write a memo for your staff reminding them of the role culture will play in the new venture. Give examples.

7. What is meant by "having a global vision"? Why is it important?

8. Suppose your state senator has asked you to contribute a brief article to her constituents' newsletter that answers the question, "Will there ever be a 'United States of Europe'?" Write a draft of your article, and include reasons why or why not.

9. Divide into six teams. Each team will be responsible for one of the following industries: entertainment; pharmaceuticals; computers and software; financial, legal, or accounting services; agriculture; and textiles and apparel. Interview one or more executives in each of these industries to determine how the Uruguay Round and NAFTA have affected and will affect their organizations. If a local firm cannot be contacted in your industry, use the library and the Internet to prepare your report.

10. What are the major barriers to international trade? Explain how government policies may be used to either restrict or stimulate global marketing.

11. Explain the impact of the Uruguay Round.

12. How does the Web site called "The Paris Pages" handle language and translation issues?

http://www.paris.org/

13. What locations does ProNet serve? Obtain information about at least one arts-and-entertainment venture for three different regions. How does ProNet handle language and translation issues?

http://www.pronett.com/

14. What services does the Netzmarkt cyber-mall offer American businesses interested in marketing to Germans?

http://www.netzmarkt.de/neu/hinweise.htm

Application for Small Business

John Arpin, a 20-something design engineer, sat down once too often in the cold snow to remove his boots from the heavy plastic bindings of his snowboard. As he loosened the plastic straps, it occurred to him that there had to be a better way to attach boots to a snowboard. The idea for a step-in snowboard binding was born. After two years of research and testing, the Arpin binding finally reached the marketplace. Snowboarding is the fastest growing winter sport in America, averaging about 30 percent per year. By the year 2000, industry sales should reach $2 billion. John's company achieved $12 million in sales by the end of 1997. Now John wants to go global.

Questions

1. What are John's options for "going global"?
2. What problems in the global external environment might the firm face?

Video Case

Starbucks Coffee Goes to Japan

Recently, Starbucks Coffee opened its first store in Japan. Starbucks' management believes that Japan's coffee market is on the verge of a revolution similar to what has occurred in the United States. Unlike other American food chains such as McDonald's or Kentucky Fried Chicken, Starbucks hasn't altered anything for the international market. Kentucky Fried Chicken, for example, sells noodle dishes as well as chicken in its stores. A Starbucks executive says, "Hopefully if you walk into a Starbucks in Los Angeles, San Francisco, or Tokyo, you wouldn't notice any difference." The only concession to global marketing by Starbucks is a joint venture with a Japanese company rather than going it alone.

Starbucks may not be any different in Japan, but the market is very different from the United States. Rent on the Tokyo store is $35,000 a month, which is three times more expensive than its most costly American location. Workers are paid about $10 an hour. To this, Starbucks must add shipping costs of bringing mugs and other merchandise over from the United States. To make money, the company says it needs 30 to 40 percent more transactions than in a typical American Starbucks store.

One of Starbucks' major competitors is Pronto. Its sales have skyrocketed from 500 million yen in 1989 to 8.4 billion yen in 1995. This growth was not dependent on coffee alone. The shops sell sandwiches and pasta during the day. At night, Pronto Coffee is turned into a restaurant and bar. Pronto says that, on average, customers spend $4 during the day and $18 at night. Pronto believes that, without the evening restaurant and alcohol sales, it would be impossible to cover its costs for rent and employees.

Starbucks feels that it can make it on coffee alone. It notes that, in 1995, Japan imported 380,000 tons of coffee beans. This is 40 percent more than only a decade ago, making Japan third in the world for coffee imports, behind only the United States and Germany. Starbucks plans to rely on its exotic lattes and cappuccinos to gain market share. Yet competitors respond that lattes and cappuccinos are more labor intensive than simply pouring a cup of coffee out of a machine. This will further drive up Starbucks' costs.

Questions

1. Do you think that Starbucks will be successful in Japan without altering its Americanized marketing mix?
2. If you were going to alter the marketing mix, what variable would you change first? Why?
3. Discuss how each of the uncontrollable variables in the external environment might affect Starbucks doing business in Japan.

1 Explain the meaning of business ethics.

2 Describe the nature of ethical decision making.

3 Discuss several current ethical dilemmas.

4 Analyze ethical issues related to global marketing.

5 Discuss corporate social responsibility.

6 Suggest ways organizations should respond to ethical issues.

Chapter 5

Ethics and Social Responsibility

Handguns of all types are literally filling the streets of America. For years it was the cheap "Saturday Night Specials" carried by criminals, particularly inner-city youths. More recently, the industry's hottest sellers are powerful, high-quality "ultra-compact" pocket pistols small enough to fit easily into a woman's evening purse or a man's pocket. Gun control advocates and politicians thought they had passed legislation to restrict handgun sales. But the gun industry adapted by creating a new, deadlier generation of pocket pistols and marketing them to first-time gun buyers, many of them women, who want maximum protection and have the money to pay top dollar. Ranging typically from $200 to $700, the new ultracompacts cost more than three times as much as the under-$50 Saturday Night Specials. Made only in .38-caliber size and higher—compared to .22 or .25 for Saturday Night Specials—the ultracompacts use premium bullets with maximum stopping power. Demand for these guns has been fueled by the 31 states that have passed conceal-and-carry laws in recent years. These laws give law-abiding citizens the right to carry concealed weapons, with few restrictions except a background check, a short waiting period, and, in some instances, a required training course on gun usage.

Two of the industry's biggest competitors are marketing their guns to different segments. Glock is targeting the upper end of the market with its baby Glocks that come in 9-millimeter and .40-caliber versions and retail for about $500. In contrast, Smith & Wesson's Sigma .380 sells for as little as $199 in some stores, and the company will soon launch a lower priced 9-millimeter as well.

This new generation of handguns adds to the potential for violence in the streets. Every year, some 400,000 Davis, Jennings, and Raven Saturday Night Specials are churned out by three offshoot companies of the Jennings family. Selling for as little as $25, these are the starter guns for the low-income fearful, the criminal, and, increasingly, the very young. To a startling degree, they also figure disproportionately in robberies and murders, piling up an alarming toll of casualties and an unending litany of violence.

Like any other business, the Jennings clan targets its market. The Davis, Jennings, and Raven pistols sell in all sorts of neighborhoods throughout the United States, but too often the buyers are inner-city youths. Some

neighborhoods have become virtual free-fire zones. For example, a Raven gun was used by a 15-year-old to rob and murder three cocaine dealers in Brooklyn. A 14-year-old in California was suspended from school after a Jennings .22 was found in his locker. And a 5-year-old in the Bronx was found carrying a loaded Raven to kindergarten in his pocket. The Jennings family denies that their guns figure predominantly in the inner city. Their customers, they say, "are just regular, everyday people who don't have the finances to buy higher-priced guns."

Gun manufacturers are not under any legal obligation to evaluate the markets they sell to, nor are they required to comply with any safety standards. But some companies have made changes out of a sense of social responsibility. For example, Wal-Mart stopped selling handguns in

its stores, although it still sells them by catalog. Indeed, to reinforce its stance against handguns, Wal-Mart recently refused to sell a new CD released by Grammy winner Sheryl Crow because she suggested in one line of the lyrics that children are killing each other with guns bought from Wal-Mart. Similarly, Toys R Us has stopped selling certain realistic toy guns as a result of an increase in shootings that involve children and teenagers. In several instances, teenagers have pointed toys guns at police, and police have shot at the teens, causing death or injury.

Not everyone sees handguns as a problem. The National Rifle Associa-

tion (NRA) ran an ad campaign in women's magazines that played on women's concern about being the victim of armed criminals. An NRA spokesperson said the purpose of the ads was not to promote gun ownership but to offer an 800 number that women could call with questions about self-defense. The NRA added callers' names to its mailing lists for direct-mail campaigns.[1]

Should companies like Glock and Smith & Wesson be allowed to play on consumers' fears of violence by marketing these powerful new handguns that are so easy to conceal? Should the Jennings companies feel some responsibility to control the vi-

olence their guns are involved in? Was Wal-Mart's refusal to sell Sheryl Crow's new CD a form of censorship? Should Toys R Us feel compelled to stop selling popular toy guns because of a few incidents involving police and children? Are these companies exercising social responsibility, or are they taking away consumers' buying-decision power?

Smith & Wesson Corp. Does Smith & Wesson address ethical concerns regarding handguns via its Web site? If so, how?

http://www.smith-wesson.com/

ETHICAL BEHAVIOR IN BUSINESS

1 Explain the meaning of business ethics.

ethics
The moral principles or values that generally govern the conduct of an individual or a group.

Ethics refers to the moral principles or values that generally govern the conduct of an individual or a group. Ethics also can be viewed as the standard of behavior by which conduct is judged. Standards that are legal may not always be ethical, and vice versa. Laws are the values and standards enforceable by the courts. Ethics consists of personal moral principles and values rather than societal prescriptions.

Defining the boundaries of ethicality and legality can be difficult. Often, judgment is needed to determine whether an action that may be legal is indeed ethical. For example, advertising liquor, tobacco, and X-rated movies in college newspapers is not illegal in many states. But is it ethical? In the following situations, judgment plays a major role in defining ethical and legal boundaries. After you read each piece, try to determine whether it can be placed neatly into one of the following categories: ethical and legal, ethical and illegal, unethical and legal, unethical and illegal.

- Manufacturers of many types of fruit drinks use packaging and bottles that look like Bartles and Jaynes wine coolers. It is not lost on these manufacturers that there's a lot of buying power out there in MTV-land that they can tap into, and this packaging can motivate kids to drink tons of the brew and spend millions to do so. Critics say they are marketing an innocent fruit drink to kids in a bottle that's as close to the shape of a liquor bottle or wine cooler as they can make it, and kids will love it because it has the look and feel of a pint bottle of liquor or wine. Moreover, they say kids drink a lot of the stuff because they can pretend they are drinking booze, and even worse, it prompts kids to imitate the behaviors of alcohol-drinking adults. Fruit drink marketers say this is ridiculous.[2]

- Merck & Co. recently introduced a new drug to fight AIDS called Crixivan. Instead of following traditional pharmaceutical distribution channels, the company decided to offer the drug through a single mail-order distributor. The product is being sold at a 37 percent markup, angering both AIDS patients and pharmacies. AIDS organizations are protesting the limited distribution and high price of the new potentially lifesaving drug. Pharmacies are distraught over losing their loyal customers. Merck & Co., however, believes it is acting in a socially responsible manner by spending millions to develop a superior product and offering the drug at a lower cost than other competing products.[3]

- Buyers for retail stores have accepted gifts from suppliers' and manufacturers' representatives for many years. These gifts may include free meals, samples of products, tickets to theater or sporting events, golf games, and fishing or hunting trips. Many in the industry see these gifts as added perks of the job and find the practice acceptable. However, other companies do not share this ready acceptance. Companies like Wal-Mart feel that preferential treatment such as inside information on bids given to gift-giving suppliers and manufacturers costs customers millions by resulting in higher prices. In contrast, proponents of gift giving state that customers maintain the freedom to shop around, thereby releasing retailers from responsibility.[4]

- Saturday morning television is filled with commercials promoting fat-filled foods to children. For example, Pizza Hut, Little Caesar's, McDonald's, Burger King, and Wendy's promote only their high-fat foods to children on Saturday morning television, even though these restaurants have healthier items available. Commercials for high-fat foods have increased despite federal recommendations that children follow a low-fat diet. Almost three times as many foods featured in children's ads get a third or more of their calories from fat, compared to three years ago.[5]

- The U.S. Department of Health unveiled a series of radio and television advertisements urging sexually active young people to use latex condoms. These ads were meant to help slow the spread of HIV, the virus that causes AIDS. In one ad, a woman and a man are kissing and giggling and talking about whether he brought a condom. Because he did not, she flicks on the light and puts an end to their lovemaking. Then male and female announcers explain that the use of a latex condom can prevent HIV infection. Religious groups believe these ads result in sexual arousal and promote promiscuity instead of abstinence.[6]

- Members of morning walking clubs, which often walk in the local mall, have to pass food courts. Most members of the walking clubs are the elderly, seeking a healthier lifestyle in a climate-controlled environment. Some of the restaurants in the food courts have begun opening as early as 6 A.M. to serve mall walkers after their morning stroll. Many of the shops offer low-priced breakfast specials and two-for-one specials. Most of the breakfast items they sell, however, are fat-filled treats, such as biscuits, chocolate cookies, muffins, and doughnuts. Some senior-citizen advocates feel that purchasing these fat-filled foods defeats the whole purpose of exercising and that the mall management is taking advantage of senior adults.[7]

In spite of federal recommendations that children follow a low-fat diet, Saturday morning TV is filled with commercials promoting fat-filled foods.
© Stephanie Rausser 1996/FPG

- Big U.S. baby formula companies give free sample packs of formula to new mothers leaving hospitals with their infants. Formula companies have also given money to the American Academy of Pediatrics; in turn, members of the Academy recommend those formulas and give samples to mothers. A change in formula can make a baby sick; therefore, a mother is reluctant to change formula after her baby becomes accustomed to it. Abbott Laboratories, which holds 51 percent of the baby formula market, has used these tactics to promote its Similac formula. Critics note that the price of a 13-ounce can of Similac has more than tripled in the last 12 years.[8]

- Barney is a large purple dinosaur who appears in his own television show on PBS, "Barney and Friends." Parents are upset because pledge drives interrupt the show. These pitches offer Barney tapes and toys to those who contribute to public television. The Federal Communications Commission is investigating whether the campaigns violate rules on advertising to children during children's shows. PBS representatives feel that soliciting during children's shows is acceptable because the local station and the shows are both supported by individuals' contributions.[9]

As you probably noticed, few of these situations fit neatly into one category. Some are clearly legal but could be viewed as ethical by some consumers and unethical by others. Although others were ruled illegal, a case could be made for their legality and ethicality.

How do people develop an understanding of which types of behavior are ethical? **Morals** are the rules people develop as a result of cultural values and norms. Culture is a socializing force that dictates what is right and wrong. Moral standards may also reflect the laws and regulations that affect social and economic behavior. Thus, morals can be considered a foundation of ethical behavior.

Morals are usually characterized as good or bad. "Good" and "bad" have different connotations, including "effective" and "ineffective." A good salesperson makes or exceeds the assigned quota. If the salesperson sells a new stereo or television set to a disadvantaged consumer knowing full well that the person can't keep up the monthly payments, is the salesperson still a good one? What if the sale enables the salesperson to exceed his or her quota?

Another set of connotations for "good" and "bad" are "conforming" and "deviant" behaviors. A doctor who runs large ads for discounts on open-heart surgery would be considered bad or unprofessional, in the sense of not conforming to the norms of the medical profession. "Bad" and "good" are also used to express the distinction between criminal and law-abiding behavior. And finally, the terms "good" and "bad" as defined by different religions, differ markedly. A Moslem who eats pork would be considered bad, as would a fundamentalist Christian who drinks whiskey.

Morality and Business Ethics

Today's business ethics actually consists of a subset of major life values learned since birth. The values businesspeople use to make decisions have been acquired through family, educational, and religious institutions.

Ethical values are situation specific and time oriented. Nevertheless, everyone must have an ethical base that applies to conduct in the business world and in personal life. One approach to developing a personal set of ethics is to examine the consequences of a particular act. Who is helped or hurt? How long lasting are the consequences? What actions produce the greatest good for the greatest number of people? A second approach stresses the importance of rules. Rules come in the form of customs, laws, professional standards, and common sense. Consider these examples of rules:

- Always treat others as you would like to be treated.
- Copying copyrighted computer software is against the law.
- It is wrong to lie, bribe, or exploit.

The last approach emphasizes the development of moral character within individuals. Ethical development can be thought of as having three levels:[10]

- *Preconventional morality,* the most basic level, is childlike. It is calculating, self-centered, and even selfish, based on what will be immediately punished or re-

---

morals

The rules people develop as a result of cultural values and norms.

warded. Fortunately, most businesspeople have progressed beyond the self-centered and manipulative actions of preconventional morality.

- *Conventional morality* moves from an egocentric viewpoint toward the expectations of society. Loyalty and obedience to the organization (or society) become paramount. At the level of conventional morality, an ethical marketing decision would be concerned only with whether or not it is legal and how it will be viewed by others. This type of morality could be likened to the adage "When in Rome, do as the Romans do."

- *Postconventional morality* represents the morality of the mature adult. At this level, people are less concerned about how others might see them and more concerned about how they see and judge themselves over the long run. A marketing decision maker who has attained a postconventional level of morality might ask, "Even though it is legal and will increase company profits, is it right in the long run? Might it do more harm than good in the end?"

Ethics and Marketing Management

Many consumers perceive marketing activities, particularly advertising and sales, as unethical and manipulative by nature. For instance, consumers often equate marketing with misleading advertisements, pushy salespeople, and high prices for poor-quality products. Indeed, some areas of marketing are particularly vulnerable to unethical behavior: product management, retailing, advertising, distribution, pricing, and personal selling. Consider the following statistics, which seem to show that people in the United States, in general, distrust businesspeople and marketers:

- A *Business Week*/Harris poll indicated that white-collar crime is thought to be very common (by 49 percent of respondents) or somewhat common (41 percent), and 46 percent of respondents believe that the ethical standards of business executives are only fair.

- A *Time* magazine study suggested that 76 percent of the populace see a lack of business ethics in business managers as contributing to the decline of U.S. moral standards.

- A Touche Ross survey reported the general feeling, even among businesspeople, that business ethics problems portrayed in the media have not been overblown or exaggerated.

- A Gallup study found that of all the various occupations, selling and advertising were judged to be near the bottom of the scale for honesty and ethical standards, with only attorneys being worse. Marketing managers must often weigh the needs of the organization against the needs of others (for instance, customers, suppliers, or society as a whole). Objective marketing considerations can conflict with ethical standards. For example, salespeople find themselves facing conflicting wants from the customer: high-quality products and low prices. They can feel tremendous pressure to compromise their own personal ethics for the apparent good of the business, the customer, or themselves. Rigid sales or production quotas, risk of losing the sale, increased competition, lack of ethical guidelines, and greed often lead to unethical behavior in marketing.

Some of the major ethical problems confronting marketing managers are listed in Exhibit 5.1.

Many people believe that white-collar crime is common and that business executives' ethics are only fair.

© 1988 Brownie Harris/The Stock Market

Exhibit 5.1
*Unethical Practices
Marketing Managers
May Have to Deal With*

- Entertainment and gift giving
- False or misleading advertising
- Misrepresentation of goods, services, and company capabilities
- Lies told customers in order to get the sale
- Manipulation of data (falsifying or misusing statistics or information)
- Misleading product or service warranties
- Unfair manipulation of customers
- Exploitation of children and/or disadvantaged groups

- Invasion of customer privacy
- Sex-oriented advertising appeals
- Product or service deception
- Unsafe products or services
- Price deception
- Price discrimination
- Unfair remarks and inaccurate statements about competitors
- Smaller amounts of product in the same-size packages
- Stereotypical portrayals of women, minority groups, and senior citizens

ETHICAL DECISION MAKING

2 Describe the nature of ethical decision making.

How do businesspeople make ethical decisions? There is no cut-and-dried answer. Studies show that the following factors tend to influence ethical decision making and judgments:[11]

- *Extent of ethical problems within the organization:* Marketing professionals who perceive fewer ethical problems in their organizations tend to disapprove more strongly of "unethical" or questionable practices than those who perceive more ethical problems. Apparently, the healthier the ethical environment, the greater is the likelihood that marketers will take a strong stand against questionable practices.

- *Top-management actions on ethics:* Top managers can influence the behavior of marketing professionals by encouraging ethical behavior and discouraging unethical behavior.

- *Potential magnitude of the consequences:* The greater the harm done to victims, the more likely it is that marketing professionals will recognize a problem as unethical.

- *Social consensus:* The greater the degree of agreement among managerial peers that an action is harmful, the more likely it is that marketers will recognize a problem as ethical.

- *Probability of a harmful outcome:* The greater the likelihood that an action will result in a harmful outcome, the more likely it is that marketers will recognize a problem as unethical.

- *Length of time between the decision and the onset of consequences:* The shorter the length of time between the action and the onset of negative consequences, the more likely it is that marketers will perceive a problem as unethical.

- *Number of people to be affected:* The greater the number of persons affected by a negative outcome, the more likely it is that marketers will recognize a problem as unethical.

The framework presented in Exhibit 5.2 is helpful in understanding ethical decision making in business. The diagram indicates that individual and corporate culture factors interact with ethical issue intensity (the perceived relevance or importance of an ethical issue to the individual or work group) to determine ethical evaluations and intentions, and, ultimately, ethical behavior.

Exhibit 5.2
Framework for Understanding Ethical Decision Making in Business

Source: Adapted from O. C. Ferrell and John Fraedrich, *Business Ethics* (Boston: Houghton Mifflin, 1997), p. 94.

Ethical Guidelines

Many organizations have become more interested in ethical issues. One sign of this interest is the increase in the number of large companies that appoint ethics officers–from virtually none five years ago to almost 25 percent of large corporations now. In addition, many companies of various sizes have developed a **code of ethics** as a guideline to help marketing managers and other employees make better decisions. In fact, in a recent national study, it was found that 60 percent of the companies maintained a code of ethics, 33 percent offered ethics training, and 33 percent employed an ethics officer.[12] Some of the most highly praised codes of ethics are those of Boeing, GTE, Hewlett-Packard, Johnson & Johnson, and Norton Company.

Creating ethics guidelines has several advantages:

- It helps employees identify what their firm recognizes as acceptable business practices.

- A code of ethics can be an effective internal control on behavior, which is more desirable than external controls like government regulation.

- A written code helps employees avoid confusion when determining whether their decisions are ethical.

- The process of formulating the code of ethics facilitates discussion among employees about what is right and wrong and ultimately creates better decisions.

The Golden Rule: words to live by or only when they don't impact sales? Learn the factors that impact ethical decisions and try your hand at dealing with ethical situations. Test your ethical decision making at **Hot Link—Marketing Ethics.**

University of British Columbia
Centre for Applied Ethics
Research corporate codes of ethics through the Applied Ethics Resources. Compare the codes of three companies. What common themes do you find?

http://www.ethics.ubc.ca/

code of ethics
A guideline to help marketing managers and other employees make better decisions.

Businesses, however, must be careful not to make their code of ethics too vague or too detailed. Codes that are too vague give little or no guidance to employees in their day-to-day activities. Codes that are too detailed encourage employees to substitute rules for judgment. For instance, if employees are involved in questionable behavior, they may use the absence of a written rule as a reason to continue behaving that way, even though their conscience may be saying no. The checklist in Exhibit 5.3 is an example of a simple but helpful set of ethical guidelines. Following the checklist will not guarantee the "rightness" of a decision, but it will improve the chances of the decision's being ethical.

Although many companies have issued policies on ethical behavior, marketing managers must still put the policies into effect. They must address the classic "matter of degree" issue. For example, marketing researchers must often resort to deception to

Hewlett-Packard's code of
ethics for employees at all levels has been highly praised.
Courtesy of Hewlett-Packard Company

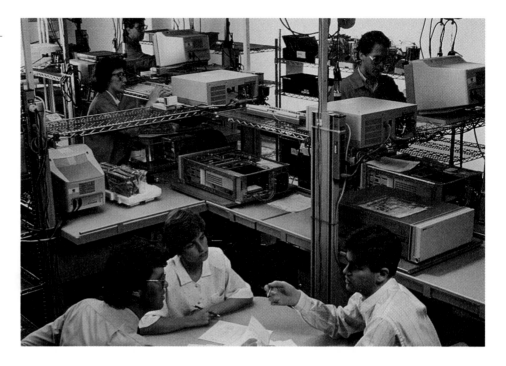

obtain unbiased answers to their research questions. Asking for a few minutes of a respondent's time is dishonest if the researcher knows the interview will last 45 minutes. Should researchers conducting focus groups inform the respondents that there are observers behind a one-way mirror? When respondents know they're being watched, they sometimes are less likely to talk and interact freely. Does a client have an ethical right to obtain questionnaires with the names and addresses of respondents from a market research firm? Many of these concerns have been addressed by the Professional Standards Committee of the American Marketing Association. The American Marketing Association's code of ethics is included on its Web site at www.ama.com.

Even the best ethics programs don't always work. Dow Corning was among the first corporations to set up a formal ethics program. Through a committee made up of company executives, Dow Corning's program sought to create a corporate culture with high ethical standards. The company audited compliance with its standards, communicated with employees about ethics, included ethics in training programs, and

Exhibit 5.3
Ethics Checklist

- Does the decision benefit one person or group but hurt or not benefit other individuals or groups? In other words, is my decision fair to all concerned?
- Would individuals or groups, particularly customers, be upset if they knew about my decision?
- Has important information been overlooked because my decision was made without input from other knowledgeable individuals or groups?
- Does my decision presume that my company is an exception to a common practice in this industry and that I therefore have the authority to break a rule?
- Would my decision offend or upset qualified job applicants?
- Will my decision create conflict between individuals or groups within the company?
- Will I have to pull rank or use coercion to implement my decision?
- Would I prefer to avoid the consequences of my decision?
- Did I avoid truthfully answering any of the above questions by telling myself that the risks of getting caught are low or that I could get away with the potentially unethical behavior?

surveyed employees about their ethics practices twice a year. Yet the system seemingly failed: Dow Corning was accused of covering up safety problems with the silicone breast implants the company produced. Internal documents suggest that Dow Corning was aware of the safety problems for years and tried to keep the public from learning of them.

CURRENT ETHICAL DILEMMAS

Today, marketing managers face several ethical issues. Three of the major ones are tobacco and alcohol promotion, consumer privacy, and so-called green marketing. Limited space prevents us from exploring many other ethical dilemmas, such as marketing to young children, marketing that promotes sex-role stereotyping, misleading advertising and product labeling, and marketing to the disadvantaged.

3 Discuss several current ethical dilemmas.

Tobacco and Alcohol Promotion

Never have the tobacco and alcohol industries experienced such strong attacks as they have in the 1990s. One example is the criticism of the R. J. Reynolds Tobacco Company's promotion of its Camel brand cigarettes with a cartoon mascot, Joe Camel. Some of the Camel ads have targeted women. For instance, full-color ads show female camels smoking cigarettes at a "watering hole" while male camels keep a close eye on them. Critics feel that these ads may encourage young women to smoke.[13]

Critics also claim that the Joe Camel campaign targets children and teenagers in an attempt to turn them into smokers. Several studies show that this claim may have some basis. For instance, studies published in the *Journal of the American Medical Association* found that Camel ads are highly effective in reaching children. In one study, many members of a small group of six-year-olds were nearly as familiar with Joe Camel as they were with the Disney Channel's Mickey Mouse logo. Another study found that, when consumers were asked to judge the age of models in cigarette ads, 17 percent of the models were perceived to be under the age of 25, an apparent violation of the tobacco industry's voluntary advertising code. Additionally, cigarette ads featuring young people were found to appear more often in magazines with younger audiences. Finally, a recent study found that teenagers' smoking habits were linked to the brands of cigarettes most aggressively advertised. The Centers for Disease Control found that the most heavily advertised cigarette brands—Marlboro, Newport, and Camel—were also the most preferred brands among smokers aged 12 to 18. In fact, 86 percent of the teenagers surveyed regularly bought one of the three brands, compared with only 35 percent of other adult smokers.[14]

Studies like these have prompted the U.S. surgeon general to call for a ban of all tobacco advertising in magazines and in retail stores. (Tobacco advertising is already banned from the airwaves.) Other branches of the federal government are also seeking to control tobacco advertising. The U.S. Supreme Court has ruled that smokers may sue cigarette makers for hiding or distorting the health dangers of tobacco, which gives tobacco companies a substantial incentive for being truthful and including disclaimers on packages and in ads. Congress is also considering some antismoking laws, including ones that would allow individual states to regulate tobacco advertising, prohibit tobacco ads that can be seen by minors, limit outdoor advertising, and end tax deductibility for tobacco products. The Federal Trade Commission is under pressure to prohibit advertising of any kind for low-tar cigarettes, which are

Critics claim that R. J. Reynolds' Joe Camel campaign targets children and teenagers. One study found that six-year-olds were almost as familiar with Joe Camel as they were with Mickey Mouse.
© Peter A. Harris/AP Wide World Photos

thought to lull smokers into a false sense of security. Efforts like these have spilled over to the states as well. One California bill would ban the use of cartoons in advertising for dangerous products, especially cigarettes.[15]

Proponents of a tobacco advertising ban were encouraged by a Florida ruling in late 1996 that granted a substantial award to an individual who sued Brown and Williamson Tobacco Company. The decision is being appealed, but if it stands, it will be the first time a tobacco company has paid any money to a plaintiff.

Although tobacco advertising is now banned from TV and radio, activists claim that the ads are sneaking onto the airwaves when television cameras focus on a stadium scoreboard or zoom in on an outfielder. In response to public sentiment, a number of big sports stadiums have eliminated tobacco ads, and some are prohibiting smoking even though they are outdoor stadiums.

Antismoking activists are not just trying to ban tobacco advertising; they are also using modern marketing techniques to "sell" their point of view. In California, for example, sophisticated ads funded by the state's cigarette tax attempted to persuade the state's 7 million smokers to kick the habit. The campaign targeted young women, teenagers, and immigrants. It was estimated to have cost the tobacco industry some $1.1 billion in lost sales in California.[16]

In response to public sentiment against smoking, the R. J. Reynolds Tobacco Co. has developed a new cigarette, Eclipse, which claims to reduce secondhand smoke by almost 90 percent and produce significantly less ash and odor. Eclipse, however, does not eliminate the substantial amount of carbon monoxide and nicotine that are linked to higher risks of cardiovascular disease and smoking-related deaths. Thus, a new concern of public health officials is how this "considerate cigarette" will be marketed. Officials fear that advertising and promotion may lead uninformed consumers to believe that the new cigarette is safer. The FDA has yet to determine whether the new product will be classified as a cigarette or a drug. The outcome of that decision will determine the degree of regulation governing the promotion of the product.[17]

The alcoholic beverage industry has not fared much better. Beer commercials are limited to one minute per hour during college basketball championship games. The U.S. surgeon general has also attacked alcohol advertising, asserting that its reliance on sex and sports imagery encourages underage drinkers. Low-alcohol, brightly labeled alcoholic drinks have come under fire because critics feel that this packaging will lure teenagers and increase alcohol abuse among them. Congress requires health warnings in all alcoholic beverage ads. Unfortunately, warning labels on tobacco and alcohol ads appear to be more effective in raising societal awareness of the dangers than in altering individual behavior.[18]

The Bureau of Alcohol, Tobacco, and Firearms has spoken out against many alcohol products that it feels are aimed at inner-city dwellers. Examples include PowerMaster, a potent malt liquor whose name had to be changed because of its connotation of strong alcoholic content, and St. Ides Premium Malt Liquor, whose commercials use rappers like Ice Cube and the Getto Boys to lure young drinkers. Colt 45, a high-alcohol-content malt liquor, targets young inner-city youth by its use in ads of a first-generation college graduate role model. Use of this role model is part of Colt 45's effort to have a hipper image, a change from its mid-1980s appeal to older black men.[19]

The controversy over alcohol advertisements heated up in late 1996. The broadcast industry had voluntarily banned hard liquor advertising for decades, but Seagrams America broke that agreement when it began advertising its Crown Royal Canadian whiskey on television stations. Initially, only about 25 stations agreed to run the ads, but industry observers said that a congressional backlash over liquor ads could result in a federal ban on all alcohol advertising.

Many tobacco and alcohol companies are submitting to activists' pressures with new campaigns telling kids not to smoke and drink. The big tobacco companies and their trade group, the Tobacco Institute, have launched youth antismoking campaigns focusing on the peer pressure associated with smoking. Anheuser-Busch spends millions annually on its "Know When to Say When" campaign. Likewise, Miller Brewing has tripled spending on its responsible-drinking program, which it emphasizes during holidays and spring break.

Critics question the sincerity of tobacco and alcohol companies' antismoking and antidrinking ads. Many feel the ads challenge children to smoke and drink. Others believe that the industry's efforts to discourage teen drinking and smoking have been drowned out by the overabundance of upbeat ads. Still others feel the ads are the industry's last effort to fend off possible regulation. In fact, beer companies are not just trying to discourage regulation but are trying to keep beer ads from being banned altogether.

Because the banning of alcohol and tobacco advertising could have a very big economic impact, others are also concerned. The Leadership Council on Advertising Issues estimates that if tobacco advertising were banned, 7,904 newspaper jobs would disappear and 165 magazines would go out of business. If beer and wine advertising on television were canceled, another 4,232 jobs would be lost, plus an enormous chunk of network sports programming. Without ads for hard liquor, another 84 magazines would fold, including many for African-Americans.[20]

Tobacco and alcoholic beverage companies can't necessarily escape the pressure by shifting into overseas markets. Tobacco companies, in particular, are facing tougher laws and regulations all over the world. The executive body of the European Union has recommended a ban on tobacco ads throughout the trade bloc. It would eliminate tobacco ads from magazines and other publications, billboards, and movie theaters and prohibit tobacco company logos on T-shirts and on the sides of racing cars. Ads would be allowed only inside tobacco shops. The European Union's ban on TV tobacco advertising took effect in 1991. Other countries—among them, Taiwan, Australia, China, and Thailand—are also seeking to curb tobacco advertising or to stiffen regulations. Canada has some of the world's toughest antismoking regulations. Tobacco display advertising is banned from retail stores. Cigarette packages must be printed with large health warnings and must include inserts detailing the hazards of smoking. Canadian law also bans tobacco advertising in newspapers and magazines and on billboards.

In contrast, Hungary may loosen its regulation of tobacco advertising. Cigarette ads were banned in 1978, but the country is considering a bill allowing cigarette ads in those counties where antismoking programs are set up.

Consumer Privacy

Today's computer technology can collect and analyze mountains of data. Thus, it is easy for companies to compile alarmingly detailed profiles of millions of their customers, with everything from salaries and home values to ages and weights of family members.

Sometimes the companies that collect the information sell it to direct marketers. Many consumers resent this use of information provided in business transactions. In one study, almost 8 in 10 U.S. citizens agreed that if the Declaration of Independence were to be written today, they would probably add privacy to the list of fundamental rights—along with life, liberty, and the pursuit of happiness. The majority also believed that they had lost all control over the use of personal information.[21]

The number of marketers being accused of abusing consumer privacy issues is mounting. American Express has acknowledged that information about its cardholders' lifestyles and spending habits was offered for joint marketing efforts with merchants. After the news created controversy, Blockbuster Entertainment scrapped plans to sell information to direct marketers about its customers' video-renting habits. Equifax, the giant credit-reporting agency, with over 120 million names in its files, also gave up the practice of providing mailing lists to direct marketers after the New York State attorney general threatened a lawsuit.

Even physicians and pharmacists routinely open their patients' records to data collectors, who peddle the records to pharmaceutical companies wanting to know exactly how well their products are selling. Critics of this practice say the custodians of medical records have no right to share such information with an unregulated business without patients' knowledge or consent. The practice especially alarms patients with AIDS, mental illness, and other conditions in which a breach of privacy can have far-reaching consequences.

Many companies are using the privacy issue as a marketing weapon. AT&T aired television ads attacking MCI's Friends and Family program, which offers 20 percent off some calls in exchange for customer referrals. In one AT&T ad, a woman becomes outraged when a telemarketer asks for the phone numbers of people close to her. In another ad, a man returns home to be bombarded by nasty messages on his answering machine from friends whose names and numbers he gave to MCI.

Technological advances enable computers to build models of customer behavior based on previous transactions. For instance, when people call 800 or 900 numbers, caller ID services can be used to record their phone number, and then the company can find their names and addresses and put them on a mailing list. New legislation is being considered that would require callers' consent before their personal information is reused or sold.

But even by sending in a coupon, filling out a warranty card, or entering a sweepstakes, consumers are volunteering information to marketers. That information can be combined with information from publically available sources, such as Census information or Internet usage patterns, to identify, as targets for marketing efforts, clusters of consumers who have similar interests and income. Retailers can compile similar lists with information from checkout scanners. Critics feel these practices are an invasion of consumers' privacy. Consumers are unknowingly arming marketers with information that will help the marketers sell them more goods and services.[22]

Retail marketers can compile lists of potential customers who have similar interests and income using information from checkout scanners.
© David Young-Wolff/Tony Stone Images

Green Marketing

Green marketing refers to the marketing of products and packages that are less toxic than normal, are more durable, contain reusable materials, or are made of recyclable materials. In short, these are products considered environmentally friendly, and their marketers are "environmentally responsible."

Many Americans are worried about the environment. Studies show that environmentally conscious consumers cannot be singled out by distinguishing demographic characteristics such as age or income, but instead are consumers representing various market segments which share the belief that their actions can help solve environmental problems. Most Americans tend to blame businesses for the environmental problems they see. Typical beliefs include the following:

- Industrial pollution is the main reason for our environmental problems.
- Products that businesses use in manufacturing harm the environment most.
- Businesses are guilty of not developing environmentally sound consumer products.
- The usage of disposable packaging by fast-food businesses and consumer product manufacturers should be restricted.[23]

Consumers blame themselves, too. Seventy percent say consumers are more interested in convenience than in environmentally sound products. Over half admit they are not willing to pay more for environmentally safer products. Companies like Bic, which specializes in disposable products, found that consumers are happy to pay for convenience. They don't seem to mind that the 4 billion pens, 3 million razors, and 800,000 plastic lighters that Bic produces annually end up in landfills. In fact, the company's two refillable pens account for less than 5 percent of sales, a figure that has been steadily declining.[24]

Still, many companies are becoming environmentally sensitive. Some companies have found that implementing "green-marketing strategies" may be a competitive advantage.[25] For example, the Duracell and Eveready battery companies have reduced the levels of mercury in their batteries and will eventually market mercury-free products. Sanyo sells its rechargeable batteries in a plastic tube that can be mailed back. The company then recycles both the tubes and the cadmium batteries. Turtle Wax car-wash products and detergents are biodegradable and can be "digested" by waste-treatment plants. The company's plastic containers are made of recyclable plastic, and its spray products do not use propellants that damage the ozone layer in the earth's upper atmosphere.[26] Similarly, L'eggs redesigned its trademark plastic egg package and replaced it with a more environmentally friendly cardboard package.

Critics contend that green-marketing campaigns are nothing more than an attempt to capitalize on people's concerns about the environment. One research group studied 35 U.S. corporations and found that many of them are using "green marketing" as a smokescreen while they continue to pollute the environment.[27]

Many companies have also been charged with making false or misleading environmental claims in their packaging or advertising. In response, many states and the Federal Trade Commission have issued guidelines for green marketers. For instance, California's truth-in-environmental-advertising law makes it harder for companies to use the words "recycled" and "recyclable" for packaging. The FTC's guidelines strongly encourage manufacturers and marketers to back up environmental claims with competent and reliable scientific evidence and to avoid overstating a product's environmental benefits.

 U.S. consumers are not the only ones becoming environmentally sensitive. Around the world, consumers and marketers alike are taking steps to preserve the earth and its atmosphere. Germany is one of the most envi-

green marketing
The marketing of products and packages that are less toxic than normal, are more durable, contain reusable materials, or are made of recyclable materials.

Marketing and Small Business

Will Being a Green Marketer Help Your Business Succeed?

Enviro Care is a "green" store owned by a California couple. The birth of their son on Earth Day gave them the idea to start a retail business selling organic clothing and other environmentally friendly items. Enviro Care had its first profit two years after it began operation. Enviro Care is no different from more than 200 other environment-minded small businesses in the United States. Kevin Connelly, publisher of *Natural Connection,* a trade journal for small retailers of environmental products, has seen the owners of these businesses learn too slowly that success requires more than a concern for ecology: "A lot of these people got into this on principle but had no business or retail background."

Many environmentally conscious entrepreneurs thought consumers would be eager to buy their products. They underestimated the challenge of fundamental business tasks, like marketing new products. Organizations such as the Green Business Conference and the National Green Retailing Association have been formed to help entrepreneurs who own environment-friendly stores. These groups have conferences featuring seminars and workshops designed to provide education for consumers and professionals on topics ranging from "Staying Afloat In Today's Turbulent Marketplace" to "The Greening of The Internet: Surfing The Green Wave."

Earth-friendly retailers and green businesses will need help to succeed in a tough market. Indeed, one of the sessions at the 1996 Green Business Conference in Los Angeles focused on the question of whether the environmental marketing and merchandising movement has peaked, or whether there might be room for smart operators to carve out new opportunities? The conclusion of the panel discussion was that there are still opportunities, but competition in the future, particularly strategies based predominantly on green marketing, will be very challenging.[28]

Would you frequent a store or purchase goods and services on the basis that they are environmentally friendly? What other programs could the National Green Retailing Association offer that would appeal to ecologically friendly entrepreneurs? What different challenges does a small "green" retailer face who has a concern for the environment, but not a business background?

ronmentally advanced countries. One German law calls for 60 percent of packaging to be recycled within five years of the law's passage. German carmakers are now installing plants to recycle car parts. In Canada, a federal program called Environmental Choice sets environmental standards for products claiming to be environmentally friendly. Guidelines have been introduced for 34 product types, and more than 600 products have been certified through the program. The following "Global Perspectives" box identifies some of the major ethical issues faced by international marketers.

CULTURAL DIFFERENCES IN ETHICS

4 Analyze ethical issues related to global marketing.

Studies suggest that ethical beliefs vary only little from culture to culture. Certain practices, however, such as the use of illegal payments and bribes, are far more acceptable in some places than in others. Some countries have a dual standard concerning illegal payments. For example, German businesspeople typically treat bribes as tax-deductible business expenses. In Russia, bribes and connections in the government are essential for doing business. For bureaucratic tasks, such as registering a business, bribing a public official is the fastest method. It usually costs about 100,000 rubles ($500). What we call bribery is a natural way of doing business in some other cultures. Do these widespread practices suggest that global marketers should adopt a "When in Rome, do as the Romans do" mentality?

Global Perspectives

As the number of multinational firms increases, companies and nations inevitably become more interdependent, and they must learn to cooperate for mutual benefit. However, because of cultural differences, increased interdependence also heightens the potential for conflicts, many of which involve marketing ethics. In fact, developing nations may have trouble imposing their marketing, environmental, and human rights regulations on large multinational firms. Some of the major ethical issues faced by international marketers are:[29]

- *Traditional small-scale bribery:* payment of a small sum of money (for example, a "grease payment" or kickback), typically to a foreign official, in exchange for his or her violation of some official duty or responsibility in an effort to speed routine government actions
- *Large-scale bribery:* relatively large payment (for example, a political contribution) intended to allow a violation of the law or to influence policy directly or indirectly
- *Gifts, favors, and entertainment:* lavish gifts, opportunities for personal travel at the company's expense, gifts received after the completion of a transaction, expensive entertainment
- *Pricing:* unfair differential pricing, questionable invoicing (when the buyer requests a written invoice showing a price other than the actual price paid), pricing to force out local competition, dumping products at prices well below those in the home country, pricing practices that are illegal in the home country but legal in the host country (for example, price-fixing agreements)
- *Products and technology:* products and technology that are banned for use in the home country but permitted in the host country (such as products containing asbestos or DDT), or products that appear unsuitable or inappropriate for use by the people in the host country
- *Tax evasion:* practices used specifically to evade taxes, such as transfer pricing (adjusting prices paid between affiliates and the parent company so as to affect the allocation of profits), "tax havens" (shifting profits to a low-tax jurisdiction), adjusted interest payments on intrafirm loans, and questionable management and service fees charged between affiliates and the parent company
- *Illegal or immoral activities in the host country:* practices such as polluting the environment; maintaining unsafe working conditions; copying products or technology where protection of patents, trade names, or trademarks has not been enforced; and short-weighting overseas shipments so as to charge a phantom weight
- *Questionable commissions to channel members:* unreasonably large commissions or fees paid to channel members, such as sales agents, middlemen, consultants, dealers, and importers
- *Cultural differences:* differences between cultures involving potential misunderstandings related to the traditional requirements of the exchange process (for example, transactions regarded as bribes by one culture but acceptable in another)—including gifts, monetary payments, favors, entertainment, and political contributions that are not considered part of normal business practices in one's own culture
- *Involvement in political affairs:* marketing activities related to politics, including the exertion of political influence by multinationals, marketing activities when either the home or the host country is at war, and illegal technology transfer.

Rank the preceding practices from those that would be least difficult to avoid to those that would be most difficult to avoid. Should international marketers who cannot avoid these practices simply be forbidden to sell products in a particular country?

Yet another example of cultural differences is the Japanese reluctance to enforce their antitrust laws. Everyday business practices, from retail pricing to business structuring, ignore antitrust regulations against restraint of trade, monopolies, and price discrimination. Not surprisingly, the Japanese are tolerant of scandals involving antitrust violations, favoritism, price fixing, bribery, and other activities considered unethical in the United States.

China has promised to crack down on retailers of counterfeit CDs. In one year, officials confiscated and destroyed 2 million fake CDs.
© AP/Wide World Photos

Foreign Corrupt Practices Act
Prohibits U.S. corporations from making illegal payments to public officials of foreign governments to obtain business rights or to enhance their business dealings in that country.

Concern about U.S. corporations' use of illegal payments and bribes in international business dealings led to passage of the **Foreign Corrupt Practices Act.** This act prohibits U.S. corporations from making illegal payments to public officials of foreign governments to obtain business rights or to enhance their business dealings in those countries. The act has been criticized for putting U.S. businesses at a competitive disadvantage. Many contend that bribery is an unpleasant but necessary part of international business.

EXPLOITATION OF DEVELOPING COUNTRIES

For companies, the benefits of seeking international growth are several. A company that cannot grow further in its domestic market may reap increased sales and economies of scale not only by exporting its product but also by producing it abroad. A company may also wish to diversify its political and economic risk by spreading its operations across several nations.

Expanding into developing countries offers multinational companies the benefits of low-cost labor and natural resources. But many multinational firms have been criticized for exploiting developing countries. Although the firms' business practices may be legal, many business ethicists argue that they are unethical. The problem is compounded by the intense competition among developing countries for industrial development. Ethical standards are often overlooked by governments hungry for jobs or tax revenues.

Take the tobacco industry, for instance. With tobacco sales decreasing and regulations stiffening in the United States and Western Europe, tobacco companies have come to believe that their future lies elsewhere: in China, Asia, Africa, Eastern Europe, and Russia. Despite the known health risks of their product, the large tobacco companies are pushing their way into markets that typically have few marketing or health-labeling controls. In Hungary, Marlboro cigarettes are sometimes handed out to young fans at pop concerts. In the last 10 years, cigarette advertising on Japanese television has soared from 40th to 2nd place in air time and value; it appears even during children's shows.

Interestingly, at a time when smoking is being discouraged in the United States, U.S. trade representatives are talking to developing countries like China and Thailand about lowering their tariffs on foreign cigarettes. Japan, Taiwan, and South Korea have already given in to the threats. Entering these developing countries, the tobacco companies and trade representatives insist, will help U.S. tobacco manufacturers make up for losses in their home market.

Environmental issues are another example. As U.S. environmental laws and regulations gain strength, many companies are moving their operations to developing countries, where it is often less expensive to operate. These countries generally enforce minimal or no clean-air and waste-disposal regulations. For example, an increasing number of U.S. companies have located manufacturing plants called *maquiladoras* in Mexico, along the U.S.–Mexican border. Mexico has few pollution laws, and so *maquiladoras* have been allowed to pollute the air and water and dump hazardous wastes along the border. Many blame the *maquiladoras* for "not putting back into the border area what they have been taking out," referring to the region's inadequate sewers and water-treatment plants.

Because Mexico has been eager to attract foreign employers, *maquiladoras* pay little in taxes, which would normally go toward improving the country's infrastructure.

Ciudad Juárez, a populous and polluted *maquiladora* city bordering El Paso, Texas, generates millions of gallons of sewage a day and has no sewage system at all. Many fear that the North American Free Trade Agreement (NAFTA) will result in further environmental problems in Mexico, as well as in Canada and the United States, because of the environmental compromises required to ensure passage of the bill.

CORPORATE SOCIAL RESPONSIBILITY

Ethics and social responsibility are closely intertwined. Besides questioning tobacco companies' ethics, one might ask whether they are acting in a socially responsible manner when they promote tobacco. Are companies that produce low-cost handguns socially responsible in light of the fact that these guns are used in the majority of inner-city crimes? **Corporate social responsibility** is business's concern for society's welfare. This concern is demonstrated by managers who consider both the long-range best interests of the company and the company's relationship to the society within which it operates.

One theorist suggests that total corporate social responsibility has four components: economic, legal, ethical, and philanthropic.[30] The **pyramid of corporate social responsibility,** shown in Exhibit 5.4, portrays economic performance as the foundation for the other three responsibilities. At the same time that it pursues profits (economic responsibility), however, business is expected to obey the law (legal responsibility); to do what is right, just, and fair (ethical responsibility); and to be a good corporate citizen (philanthropic responsibility). These four components are distinct but together constitute the whole. Still, if the company doesn't make a profit, then the other three responsibilities are moot.

5 Discuss corporate social responsibility.

corporate social responsibility
Business's concern for society's welfare.

pyramid of corporate social responsibility
Model that suggests corporate social responsibility is composed of economic, legal, ethical, and philanthropic responsibilities and that the firm's economic performance supports the entire structure.

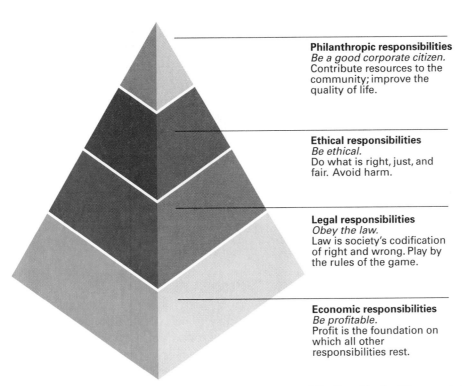

Exhibit 5.4
Pyramid of Corporate Social Responsibility

Philanthropic responsibilities
Be a good corporate citizen.
Contribute resources to the community; improve the quality of life.

Ethical responsibilities
Be ethical.
Do what is right, just, and fair. Avoid harm.

Legal responsibilities
Obey the law.
Law is society's codification of right and wrong. Play by the rules of the game.

Economic responsibilities
Be profitable.
Profit is the foundation on which all other responsibilities rest.

Source: Adapted from Archie B. Carroll, "The Pyramid of Corporate Social Responsibility: Toward the Moral Management of Organizational Stakeholders," *Business Horizons,* July–August 1991, pp. 39–48.

Many companies are already working to make the world a better place to live. Consider these examples:

- Colby Care Nurses, Inc., a home health care service located in Los Angeles County, is offering much-needed health care to predominantly black and Hispanic communities that are not often covered by other providers. The company prides itself on giving back to the community by employing its residents and providing role models for its young people.[31]

Metropolitan Life Insurance Company
Apple Computer, Inc.
Ben & Jerry's
How are these companies publicizing their community involvement via the Web?
Describe the community activities of each. Does the marketing of community involvement enhance the images of the companies?

http://www.metlife.com/
http:/www.apple.com/
http://www.benjerry.com/

- Metropolitan Life donates over $1 million a year and Levi Strauss over $500,000 to AIDS education and support services.[32]
- Ben & Jerry's, the premium ice cream maker, sent seven workers to live with Cree Indians in Canada to see how they've been displaced by a new hydroelectric power complex.[33]
- Jantzen, the world's leading swimsuit manufacturer, makes direct grants through its clean water campaign to organizations that preserve and clean up beaches and waterways.[34]
- Apple Computer donates almost $10 million in computer equipment and advice to U.S. schools annually.
- G.D. Searle began a program in which its representatives regularly call hypertension (high blood pressure) patients, reminding them to take their medicine.[35]

- Ricoh, a Japanese office equipment maker, has developed a reverse copier that strips away the toner and allows the copy paper to be used again.[36]

Multinational companies also have important social responsibilities. In many cases a corporation can be a dynamic force for social change in host countries. For example, multinational corporations played a major role in breaking down apartheid (separation of the races) in South Africa, through their economic pressure on the South African government. Over 300 apartheid laws were compiled over the years, based purely on the pigmentation of people's skin. Among other things, these laws forced blacks to live in the most arid regions of South Africa, banned mixed marriages, and segregated the schools. To protest apartheid, many multinational corporations closed their South African operations altogether. Other companies refused to trade with South Africa. These actions seriously impeded South Africa's economy, and by the early 1990s the government began making major social reforms. Once apartheid officially ended in the early 1990s, many of the companies that had participated in the boycott resumed their operations in South Africa.

RESPONDING TO ETHICS PROBLEMS

6 Suggest ways organizations should respond to ethical issues.

As managers and employees face increasingly complex ethical issues, effectively responding to those issues becomes more important. Nearly one-third of employees surveyed nationally by the Ethics Resource Center felt pressure to engage in misconduct to achieve business objectives. Moreover, nearly one-third report seeing misconduct, but less than half are reporting it.[37] When the opportunity to engage in unethical conduct is as prevalent as this survey indicates, companies are vulnerable not only to ethical problems, but also to legal violations if employees do not know how

Exhibit 5.5
Minimum Requirements for Ethical Compliance Programs

1. Standards and procedures that are reasonably capable of detecting and preventing misconduct.
2. High-level personnel responsible for ethics compliance programs.
3. No substantial authority given to individuals with a propensity for misconduct.
4. Effective communication of standards and procedures via ethics training programs.
5. Establishment of systems to monitor, audit, and report misconduct.
6. Consistent enforcement of standards, codes, and punishment.
7. Continuous improvement of the ethical compliance program.

Adapted from: O. C. Ferrell and John Fraedrich, *Business Ethics,* 3d. ed. (Boston: Houghton Mifflin, 1997), pp. 172–173.

to make the correct decision. To respond to this situation, organizations should develop ethical compliance programs.[38]

An ethical compliance program for an organization should help reduce the possibility of ethics violations and encourage the organization to be more socially responsible by raising awareness levels. Moreover, such programs would help employees to better understand the values of business and to comply with policies and codes of conduct that create the organization's ethical climate. The minimum suggested requirements for ethical compliance programs are shown in Exhibit 5.5.

LOOKING BACK

In light of what you have learned in this chapter, think back now to the opening story on the marketing of handguns. You will probably agree that gunmakers should be more socially responsible in marketing their products. You may also agree that gunmakers should be more concerned with product safety instead of producing and selling as many guns as possible. Finally, hopefully, you will agree that ethical approaches are important in business.

Although quite a few companies in the United States lack a sense of social responsibility, many others try hard to be socially responsible. For example, Wal-Mart,

One of Marriott's human resources programs involves training and employing people with disabilities.
© 1991 Dennis Brack/Black Star

Shoney's, Office Depot, McDonald's, and many others have programs to employ the physically disadvantaged. Also, many companies have programs that have registered thousands of voters during elections.

KEY TERMS

code of ethics   *127*

corporate social responsibility   *137*

ethics   *122*

Foreign Corrupt Practices Act   *136*

green marketing   *133*

morals   *124*

pyramid of corporate social responsibility   *137*

SUMMARY

1 *Explain the meaning of business ethics.* Ethics refers to moral principles governing the conduct of an individual or group. Judgment is often needed to determine what is ethical versus what is legal. Morals are rules or habits that people develop as a result of cultural values and norms. Morals can be considered the foundation of ethical behavior.

2 *Describe the nature of ethical decision making.* Business ethics may be viewed as a subset of the values of society as a whole. The ethical conduct of businesspeople is shaped by societal elements, including family, education, religion, social movements, and so on. As members of society, businesspeople are morally obligated to consider the ethical implications of their decisions.

Ethical decision making is approached in three basic ways. The first approach examines the consequences of decisions. The second approach relies on rules and laws to guide decision making. The third approach is based on a theory of moral development that places individuals or groups in one of three developmental stages: preconventional morality, conventional morality, or postconventional morality.

Consumers often perceive marketing activities as unethical and manipulative. Marketers may find themselves in situations in which the needs of the business and the needs of customers, suppliers, or society as a whole are at odds. Three major factors have been found to influence the ethical behavior of marketing professionals: the extent of ethical problems within an organization, top management's actions regarding ethics, and the individual's role within an organization. Many companies develop a code of ethics to help their employees make ethical decisions. A code of ethics can help employees identify acceptable business practices, can be an effective internal control on behavior, can help employees avoid confusion when determining the ethicality of decisions, and can facilitate discussion about what is right and wrong.

3 *Discuss several current ethical dilemmas.* The major ethical dilemmas for marketing managers explored in this chapter include tobacco and alcohol promotion, consumer privacy, and green marketing. Other issues that were not discussed are marketing to young children, marketing that promotes sexual harassment, misleading advertising and product labels, and marketing to the disadvantaged.

4 *Analyze ethical issues related to global marketing.* Marketing managers selling their goods or services globally should also be aware of what is considered ethical behavior in other countries. For example, bribery is often a standard business practice in other countries, although it is considered illegal and unethical in the United States. Multinational marketers must also be careful not to exploit developing countries that have unsophisticated marketing and environmental regulations.

5 *Discuss corporate social responsibility.* Responsibility in business refers to a firm's concern for the way its decisions affect society. There are several arguments in support of social responsibility. First, many consumers feel business should take responsibility for the social costs of economic growth. A second argument contends that firms act in their own best interest when they help improve the environment within which they operate. Third, firms can avoid restrictive government regulation by responding willingly to societal concerns.

Finally, some people argue that because firms have the resources to solve social problems, they are morally obligated to do so. In contrast, there are critics who argue against corporate social responsibility. According to one argument, the free-enterprise system has no way to decide which social programs should have priority. A second argument contends that firms involved in social programs do not generate the profits needed to support the business's activities and earn a fair return for stockholders.

In spite of the arguments against corporate social responsibility, most business-people believe they should do more than pursue only profits. Although a company must consider its economic needs first, it must also operate within the law, do what is ethical and fair, and be a good corporate citizen.

6 *Suggest ways organizations should respond to ethical issues.* Organizations should implement ethical compliance programs. These programs should include established and widely displayed standards and procedures to identify and deal with unethical conduct. Systems also should be in place to monitor conduct and ensure continuous updating and improvement in compliance programs.

Discussion and Writing Questions

1. Cite examples of preconventional, conventional, and post-conventional moral conduct in marketing.

2. Write a paragraph discussing the ethical dilemma in the following situation and identifying possible solutions: An insurance agent forgets to get the required signature from one of her clients who is buying an automobile insurance policy. The client acknowledges the purchase by giving the agent a signed personal check for the full amount. To avoid embarrassment and inconvenience, the agent forges the client's signature on the insurance application and sends it to the insurance company for processing.

3. Write a paragraph discussing the ethical dilemma in the following situation and identifying possible solutions: Jill works for a company that requires random drug testing. She and several of her friends at the company occasionally smoke a joint or two of marijuana on weekends. She overheard her boss discussing the next time the random drug tests would be required and who would be tested. Jill and two of her friends were on the list, but the drug test was not scheduled until the traces would be out of her system, if she stopped immediately.

4. Describe an ethical dilemma in contemporary marketing not covered in this chapter. How could the dilemma be solved?

5. What is green marketing? Why is it controversial?

6. Suppose you have been asked to develop a set of arguments in favor of a random drug testing policy in your company. Identify a set of reasons that may justify such a policy.

7. Select three other team members. Review the proposed minimum requirements for an ethical compliance program presented in this chapter. Do you think these are adequate for organizations? Why or why not? What other requirements do you think should be included? Finally, select two team members to present the argument that the minimum requirements are adequate and two to present the argument that other requirements should be included.

8. What's the latest news at the following Web site? How can marketers benefit from such information?

http://www.ipo.org/

9. What social responsibility concerns could be raised about the following Web site? For which issues does the Web site seem to exhibit social responsibility?

http://www.netcasino.com/

Application for Small Business

The Ice House is a seafood restaurant located near the campus of the local university. It has been open about a year and a half, but the owner is struggling because it is a new business and competition is fierce from established restaurants and new entries in the market. The owner employs many students as waiters and waitresses, bartenders, and cashiers. Wendy has been employed there for about six months and has observed other students undercharging friends and giving them free food items and drinks. She feels a better control system would improve the owner's profits and would get rid of some dishonest employees.

Questions

1. Should Wendy report the other students who are giving away food and drinks to their friends?

2. Since Wendy is an accounting major, would it be better for her to suggest some financial controls the owner could use to eliminate the opportunity for undercharging customers, instead of reporting the other students?

Alcohol and Tobacco Advertising: How Should It Be Treated?

A substantial proportion of advertising for consumer products is aimed at young adults. In marketing, we refer to this as targeted advertising toward specific market segments. Cars, soap, toothpaste, beer, cereal, soft drinks, apparel, cologne—all of these heavily advertised products have strategies with young adults as their target audiences. The same is true of alcohol and tobacco. Of course, alcohol and tobacco advertisements portray these products as being preferred by the young, thin, and beautiful, the carefree and active, the rich and glamorous. But so do many other products and services.

Consider the following examples. When was the last time you saw a minivan advertisement with an obese housewife driving, five or six kids screaming at each other, and a dirty, barking dog hanging out the window? Or a TV ad for a sports car with a balding, old man behind the wheel? Or a toothpaste ad by an ugly person with crooked teeth grinning at you? Can't think of one, can you? What about beer? A typical scene is a bunch of guys sitting around a TV watching a football or basketball game. All are good looking, well dressed, and have flat stomachs and perfect teeth. Even the teenagers in the acne commercials have only one or two pimples. This is not reality. But it sure helps to make advertising strategies successful.

Consider the problem faced by the alcohol and tobacco makers. If suc-

Video Case

cessful advertising depends on targeting young adults, then why shouldn't alcohol and tobacco companies be allowed to do it too? Moreover, isn't this a violation of the First Amendment of free speech?

The controversy over alcohol and tobacco advertising aimed at young adults and children has heated up recently. For example, the beer industry insists that it does not target kids. But its commercials are often seen by underage viewers. Molson beer advertises on 10:00 P.M. episodes of "Beavis & Butt-Head," and Nielsen Media Research ratings show that 60 to 70 percent of all the show's viewers are under age 21. When a Schlitz Malt Liquor ad appeared on MTV during "My So-Called Life," a show about teenage girls, beer maker Stroh called the airing an aberration due to a last-minute programming switch. But Stroh regularly advertises Schlitz Malt Liquor during MTV's prime-time music video show at 8:30 P.M., when over 50 percent of the audience is under 21.

Some of the recent controversy is linked to the alcohol industry's decision to end its voluntary policy against radio and television advertising. No flood of liquor commercials

materialized, however, in part because the major broadcast networks refused to accept the ads and cable thus was the only television alternative. But the development rattled regulators and politicians so much that it led to a reexamination of all alcohol advertising. This in conjunction with the recent requirement for anyone age 27 or younger to provide proof of age to purchase cigarettes has brought alcohol and tobacco advertising to the forefront.

Questions

1. Should alcohol and tobacco companies be restricted in their advertising?

2. If yes, how can you do this? Could technology solve this problem with a "chip" in the equipment, or should this be primarily a parental responsibility?

3. Why should makers of other products, some of which may be harmful as well, be allowed to use targeted advertisements with no restrictions while tobacco and alcohol are regulated?

References

"Carload of Cablers Accepts Invitation for Spot of Booze," *Variety*, November 18, 1996, p. 27.

"Trickle of Television Liquor Ads Releases Torrent of Regulatory Uncertainty," *The New York Times*, January 12, 1997, p. 10.

"Underage Viewers Awash in Beer Ads, TV Survey Finds," *The Palm Beach Post*, January 7, 1997, p. 1-A.

Critical Thinking Case

BEN & JERRY'S ICE CREAM TACKLES THE RUSSIAN MARKET

Three years after it began a joint venture to make ice cream for the Russian market, Ben & Jerry's Homemade, Inc., only recently started to sell its product outside Karelia, the remote region where its factory is located.

But Ben & Jerry's is convinced that slow, methodical expansion is the recipe for long-term success here. The heart of that effort is to improve distribution, a key hurdle in emerging markets.

Russia still lacks a developed wholesale-distribution system that will deliver products to stores on time, consistently, and in good condition. To ensure quality, Ben & Jerry's and other companies are themselves creating a soup-to-nuts distribution system by buying trucks and training staff at stores that sell their products. It's expensive, but Ben & Jerry's hopes that by keeping quality high, they can win and keep the often-fickle Russian consumers.

"It would certainly be easier to expand if we dropped our standards," says Bram Kleppner, Ben & Jerry's manager of Russian operations. "But Russians know perfectly well what's junk and what's good, and they don't want to buy junk."

Ben & Jerry's started its joint venture, Iceverks, mainly as a goodwill gesture, in a bid to prove that high-quality ice cream can be made by Russian employees from mostly local ingredients. The company has since invested $500,000 in the venture, which includes a small plant in Petrozavodsk, the capital of Karelia, a sparsely populated province 700 miles north of Moscow. Iceverks, which is 70 percent owned by Ben & Jerry's, also operates three "scoop shops" in the region, replete with cow logos and whimsical flavors

such as "Chunky Monkey" and "Cherry Garcia."

The venture's ice cream became a local hit, and by 1994 Iceverks was in the black. Because Ben & Jerry's manufactures locally, its ice cream is relatively affordable. In Moscow, a cup of Baskin Robbins goes for about 4,200 rubles, or roughly one dollar, while a cone of Ben & Jerry's is 3,500 rubles. Russian ice cream costs about 3,000 rubles for a similar amount.

When Ben & Jerry's hired a new chief executive with an interest in international expansion, the company gave Iceverks the green light to move beyond Karelia. But Ben & Jerry's ran into problems getting its products to markets. Distribution in Russia is often controlled by a monopoly, usually with links to organized crime, which means that transport is expensive and arbitrary. Equipment such as refrigerated trucks and warehouses are in short supply, substandard, and expensive.

The first step for Ben & Jerry's was to find reliable Russian partners to navigate local distribution networks or set up new ones. Last fall, Iceverks chose its Moscow distributor, a tiny firm called Vessco, based on the fact that an Iceverks manager went to school with Vessco's director. Iceverks also found recent franchisees through personal connections, which assume increased importance in a country without a mechanism for arbitrating business disputes.

The venture looks for people who

already run a business in a particular city, because they are likely to know how to deal with the legitimate and not-so-legitimate authorities there. Vessco originally worked in the wholesale computer trade. The company has already brought Ben & Jerry's to 10 stores in Moscow and plans to expand to 5 others soon. Iceverks has signed up franchisees who have opened scoop shops in Yaroslavl, 180 miles north of Moscow, and in the Black Sea resort town of Sochi. A shop in St. Petersburg opened in late 1996.

Ben & Jerry's has invested in equipment down the line to get its product to market. It has brought in its own Western refrigerated trucks. And when it found that local stores didn't have freezers cold enough to store pints of ice cream, it leased, sold, and in some cases just gave them the equipment.

Sergei Metchulayev, Vessco's director, ensures that retailers maintain Ben & Jerry's image once the ice cream is in the stores. He teaches salespeople to keep the freezer clean, to be polite and explain flavors to customers, and to scoop the ice cream properly. Then he and his staff visit the stores to check up on them.

Teaching Western-style customer service is a challenge, Mr. Metchulayev finds. Stores call him only after flavors have completely run out. They fill Ben & Jerry's freezers with other companies' ice cream. Salespeople complain that the hard-frozen ice cream is hard to scoop.

But some Russian entrepreneurs are getting the message. At the Ben & Jerry's counter near the Lenin Komsomol Auto Plant in Moscow, two young salespeople immediately approach the shiny freezer whenever a potential customer comes by. They patiently explain the flavors, and they observe simple rules still rare in Russian retail, such as saying "thank you."

"We can't afford to have sales-people who are dirty and nasty," says Igor Kunin, whose firm runs the counter. "It's a bad advertisement for the brand."

Questions

1. Many food products have cultural implications. What kind of cultural problems might Ben & Jerry's face in Russia?
2. Ben & Jerry's is noted in the U.S. for being very socially conscious. Do you think entering into a joint venture in Russia as a "goodwill gesture" was a wise decision?
3. The case describes the company's problems as those relating primarily to distribution. What problems might they face with the other elements of the marketing mix?
4. Ben & Jerry's chose to enter the Russian market through a joint venture. What other avenue would you suggest as a means of entering this market? Defend your selection.
5. Judging from Ben & Jerry's success, what other American products do you think could be marketed in Russia? Evaluate the possible threats and opportunities they will encounter.
6. Compare the American consumer with a typical Russian consumer. What are some critical differences that a marketing manager must consider in creating a marketing mix for the Russian market?

Suggested Readings

Amy Miller, "Sundae School," *INC*, December 1995, pp. 17–18.

Hanna Rosin, "The Evil Empire," *New Republic*, 11 September 1995, pp. 22–25.

"Ben & Jerry Tell On Themselves," *Business Week*, 26 June 1995, p. 8.

Source: From "Ben & Jerry's Is Trying to Smooth Out Distribution in Russia As It Expands" by Neela Banerjee, *Wall Street Journal*, September 19, 1995. Reprinted by permission of *Wall Street Journal*, © 1995 Dow Jones & Company, Inc. All Rights Reserved Worldwide.

Critical Thinking Case

HOOTERS, INC.

Everyone seems to be taking sides when it comes to Hooters. The many fans of the fast-growing restaurant chain like its affordable food and drink, served up by friendly waitresses in a cheery atmosphere. Typical Hooters outlets feature rustic pine floors and tables, spicy chicken wings, and beer by the pitcher. TV monitors run nonstop sports videos, and the background music is golden oldies from the 1960s.

Critics claim the chain's appeal is blatantly sexist, from its name (slang for breasts) to the showcasing of its

waitresses, called "Hooter Girls," dressed in skimpy, revealing uniforms. Critics accuse the chain of fostering a climate in which sexual harassment can thrive. "The name should be changed because of the derogatory references to human

anatomy," says the leader of a Fairfax, Virginia, group founded to protest the opening of a Hooters outlet.

Big profits can still be made from sexism, even in the 1990s. From its birth in 1983 in Clearwater, Florida, Hooters expansion is running at full speed, with restaurants operating in 37 states and Puerto Rico and plans for the entire United States and international markets. Typical Hooters restaurants serve an average of 500 customers a day, with waiting lines at lunch and dinner.

Hooters uses every opportunity to flaunt its naughty name. The chain annually sells about $5 million worth

Join The Million Hooters March!

Make your voice heard! A nefarious government plot is under way to threaten one of our most prized freedom—the pursuit of happiness! Where else is one happier than at Hooters? Nowhere! Yet the petty bureaucrats in Washington seek to change that by demanding that Hooters hire (gasp!) MALE SERVERS! Can we permit this, fellow Hooterites and Hooterians? Nay! Cast your vote and voice your comments here! Let us rise as one mighty voice and push the government lackeys back into the dark recesses of Capital Hill! A special task force of highly trained Hooter Girls will deliver our message to the president (or next available government official) soon! Ensure your freedom and celebrate our great democracy by voting today!

The Eternal Question:
Should Hooters Have Male Servers?
○ Yes ⊙ No

Your Name: [_____]
Your Email: [_____]

Please enter your comments below:

[   ]

POST

Immediately upon clicking "POST" this page will be updated and your comments will join billions of other concerned citizens' writings. **If you do not see your comment, please press "RELOAD" on your browser.** God Bless America and thank you for your participation.

of Hooters T-shirts, hats, calendars, and other items. The controversial Hooter Girl uniform consists of running shoes, bright orange running shorts, and a cutoff T-shirt with the company's logo—an owl with two very large, saucer-shaped eyes—and the motto "More than a mouthful." (A company executive insists that the motto refers to Hooters' hamburgers.) Company officials say the chain's approach to sex is no different from that of *Sports Illustrated* magazine, which publishes an annual "swimsuit" issue. The magazine's readers "aren't checking out those girls' SAT scores," says the company's marketing vice president, adding that Hooters "doesn't cross the line of what the majority of people think is acceptable." Patrons claim the Hooter Girl uniform is no different from what you might see on someone in the mall or at the park.

All the same, at a time when national concern over men's sexual behavior has reached fever pitch, the chain's "Boys will be boys" attitude outrages feminists. The executive vice president of the National Organization for Women says Hooters "contributes to an atmosphere of sexual harassment." She further contends that Hooters resembles a nightclub or strip joint more than a neighborhood cafe. Protests focusing on Hooters' image have picked up as the chain has begun aggressive expansion beyond its Sunbelt base. In Fairfax, Virginia, a group that included the mayor and city council members collected 200 signatures on an anti-Hooters petition. In addition to requesting that the restaurant change its name, the group said employees should be allowed to wear uniforms "reflective of a basic family atmosphere." As it turned out, the outcry and attendant publicity helped attract a standing-room-only crowd to the restaurant's opening.

In one interesting twist of this controversial restaurant concept, one man filed a class-action lawsuit against the restaurant chain, alleging that Hooters acted in a discriminatory fashion when it declined to hire him as a waiter. Attorneys representing Hooters said the so-called Hooters girl is an essential component of the marketing goals of the restaurants and that there is nothing illegal about passing over a man for the job of Hooters girl because only women can meet the "bona fide occupational qualifications for the job." In an effort to get feedback and generate publicity, Hooters posted a survey on its Web site entitled "Join the Million Hooters March!" to obtain feedback on male servers. The survey, shown on p. 145, asked surfers to vote on the question of "whether Hooters should have male servers?" The response was overwhelmingly against male "Hooters Girls." The man's suit was dismissed in May, 1996, and Hooters was freed of job bias by the EEOC.

Recent trends in advertising seem to reveal a backlash against sensitivity regarding sexism. Hooters advertisements have blatantly promoted their sexist image. This "politically incorrect" approach appears to be working quite well, but the question remains: Can the restaurant survive and continue to grow without a change in the hostile environment? In one effort to soften its blatant approach, Hooters established HOO.C.E.F.—"The Hooters Community Endowment Fund"—to help communities raise monies for local and national charities. As a result, millions of dollars have been donated to many of the needy.

Questions

1. Hooters seems to be doing quite well despite charges that it promotes sexual harassment. Why do you think this is so?
2. Should Hooters have been required to hire male waiters as "Hooters Girls"?
3. Do you feel Hooters should be more socially responsible in its marketing techniques? Why or why not?
4. If you were the marketing vice president of Hooters, how would you address criticism of your marketing approach?

References

"Hooters Chain Is Freed of Job Bias Inquiry," *The New York Times*, 2 May 1996, p. B10.

"The EEOC Averts Its Eyes," *Business Week*, 13 May 1996, p. 54.

"Winners and Losers," *Time*, 27 November 1995, p. 32.

"There's a Hidden Menu in the Hooters Lawsuit," Knight-Ridder/Tribune News Service, 22 November 1995, p. 1122.

Eugene Carlson, "Restaurant Chain Tries to Cater to Two Types of Taste," *Wall Street Journal*, 20 March 1992, p. B2.

Joshua Levine, "In Your Face," *Forbes*, 22 November 1993, pp. 164–167.

Other information is available from the Hooters Web site, located @ www.hooters.com.

Marketing Planning Activities

THE WORLD OF MARKETING

*I*n the world of marketing, there are many different types of products and services offered to many different markets. Throughout this text, you will construct a marketing plan for your chosen company. Writing a marketing plan will give you a full depth of understanding for your company, its customers, and its marketing mix elements. The company you choose should be one that interests you, such as the manufacturer of your favorite product, a local business where you would like to work, or even a business you would like to start yourself to satisfy an unmet need or want. Also refer to Exhibit 2.8 for additional marketing plan subjects.

1. Describe your chosen company. How long has it been in business, or when will it start business? Who are the key players? Is the company small or large? Does it offers a good or service? What are the strengths and weaknesses of this company? What is the orientation and organizational culture?

Marketing*Builder* Exercise:

- **Top 20 Questions** template

2. Define the business mission statement for your chosen company (or evaluate and modify an existing mission statement).

3. Set marketing objectives for your chosen company. Make sure the objectives fit the criteria for good objectives.

4. Scan the marketing environment. Identify opportunities and threats to your chosen company in areas such as technology, the economy, the political and legal environment, and competition. Is your competition foreign, domestic, or both? Also identify opportunities and threats based on possible market targets, including social factors, demographic factors, and multicultural issues.

Marketing*Builder* Exercises:

- **Industry Analysis** portion of the **Market Analysis** template
- **Competitive Analysis Matrix** spreadsheet
- **Competition** portion of the **Market Analysis** template
- **Competitive Roundup** portion of the **Market Analysis** template
- **Strengths, Weaknesses, Opportunities**, and **Threats** sections of the **Market Analysis** template

5. Does your chosen business have a differential or competitive advantage? If there is not one, there is no point in marketing the product. Can you create a sustainable advantage with skills, resources, or elements of the marketing mix?

6. Assume your company is or will be marketing globally. How should your company enter the global marketplace? How will international issues affect your firm?

7. Identify any ethical issues that could impact your chosen firm. What steps should be taken to handle these issues?

8. Is there a key factor or assumption that you are using when performing your SWOT analysis? What would happen if this key factor or assumption did not exist?

Marketing*Builder* Exercises:

- **Business Risk** portion of the **Market Analysis** template
- **Environmental Risk** portion of the **Market Analysis** template
- **Elements of Risk** table in the **Market Analysis** template

Analyzing Marketing Opportunities

LEARNING OBJECTIVES *After studying this chapter, you should be able to:*

1 Explain why marketing managers should understand consumer behavior.

2 Analyze the components of the consumer decision-making process.

3 Explain the consumer's post-purchase evaluation process.

4 Identify the types of consumer buying decisions and discuss the significance of consumer involvement.

5 Identify and understand the individual factors that affect consumer buying decisions.

6 Identify and understand the social factors that affect consumer buying decisions.

Consumer Decision Making

Picture the scene: A young male tourist wanders into a dusty store in a faraway country. Behind the counter are a beautiful Asian woman and her stern, watchful father. The tourist, unable to speak their language, tries to describe what he wants by creating the shape of an hourglass with his hands. The father is not amused.

Without the product name being mentioned or even visible, most consumers know immediately what the poor tourist is trying to describe through his charades—a bottle of Coca-Cola.

Coca-Cola these days is capitalizing heavily on a marketing resource that none of its competitors has: a proprietary package that over the decades has become a bona fide cultural icon, an obvious symbol of differentiation. The company continues to boost worldwide sales by selling the same product in a distinctive package. From the classic Spencerian script, to the solid red disk that often frames its logo, to its unmistakably curvy bottle, the 110-year-old product is rich with tradition. And since millions of consumers have had a long, comfortable relationship with Coca-Cola, the company can use its history to great benefit in the marketplace.

Consumer perceptions have worked quite favorably for the soft drink giant. The global rollout in 1995 of Coke's signature plastic contour bottle to mimic the shape of its original 1915 curved glass bottle design helped the company gulp down a 50 percent market share of the cola market. According to Coke's consumer studies, people around the world prefer the contour bottle over competitors' straight-sided bottles by a five-to-one margin. Customers perceive five different levels of aesthetic consideration regarding the bottle: its appeal and "beautiful form"; its association with the "ultimate enjoyment" of Coca-Cola; the sensual look and feel; its role as a symbol of "specialness"; and the bottle's reputation as "social glue"—a universal symbol of unity. These attributes were especially true among teenagers around the world, most of whom had never seen the original glass contour bottle. Indeed, Coke's contour bottle is so much of a cultural icon, one which most consumers can identify immediately, that the Coca-Cola Company was first in line to benefit from the new United Kingdom patent law that seeks to protect colors, smells, sounds, and shapes.

Packages are sometimes called "silent salesmen," but what they really do is stimulate and seduce consumers. Packages are stimuli that transform ordinary things—like a bottle of cola, for instance—into objects of desire. They influence consumers' perceptions and make them hungry for things they may not even need or may not even want. In the eight seconds or so that it takes to choose a brand of soft drink, the bottle or package must scream or whine or purr its message of good taste or thirst-quenching ability loud and clear enough to grab a buyer's interest. The identity of a product often grows out of its external covering, its shell. What draws consumers to one brand over another is the message it is wrapped in. Coke's distinctive contour bottle, along with its red logo, is a powerful tool, says Coke's director of worldwide brand marketing, since "it's really shorthand for a promise of what's inside." As Harvard Business School professor Theodore Levitt's theory goes, "People use appearances to make judgements about reality."[1]

What other products can you think of that use a particular shape or color to stimulate consumers' awareness of and desire for their brand? What other factors besides perception influence consumers' purchasing patterns? Questions like these will be answered as you read about the consumer decision-making process.

THE IMPORTANCE OF UNDERSTANDING CONSUMER BEHAVIOR

1 Explain why marketing managers should understand consumer behavior.

consumer behavior
How consumers make purchase decisions and how they use and dispose of the purchased goods or services.

Consumers' product and service preferences are constantly changing. In order to address this constant state of flux and to create a proper marketing mix for a well-defined market, marketing managers must have a thorough knowledge of consumer behavior. **Consumer behavior** describes how consumers make purchase decisions and how they use and dispose of the purchased goods or services. The study of consumer behavior also includes the analysis of factors that influence purchase decisions and product use.

Understanding how consumers make purchase decisions can help marketing managers in several ways. For example, if a manager for an automobile company knows through research that gas mileage is the most important attribute for a certain target market, the manufacturer can redesign the product to meet that criterion. If the firm cannot change the design in the short run, it can use promotion in an effort to change consumers' decision-making criteria. For example, the manufacturer can advertise the car's maintenance-free features and sporty European style while downplaying gas mileage.

THE CONSUMER DECISION-MAKING PROCESS

2 Analyze the components of the consumer decision-making process.

consumer decision-making process
Step by step process used by consumers when buying goods or services.

When buying products, consumers generally follow the **consumer decision-making process** shown in Exhibit 6.1: (1) problem recognition, (2) information search, (3) evaluation of alternatives, (4) purchase, and (5) postpurchase behavior. These five steps represent a general process which moves the consumer from recognition of a product or service need to the evaluation of a purchase. This process is a guideline for studying how consumers make decisions. It is important to note that this guideline does not assume that consumers' decisions will proceed in order through all of the steps of the process. In fact, the consumer may end the process at any time. The consumer may not even make a purchase. Explanations as to why a consumer's progression through these steps may vary are offered at the end of the chapter in the section on the types of consumer buying decisions. Before addressing this issue, each step in the process will be described in greater detail.

Exhibit 6.1
Consumer Decision-Making Process

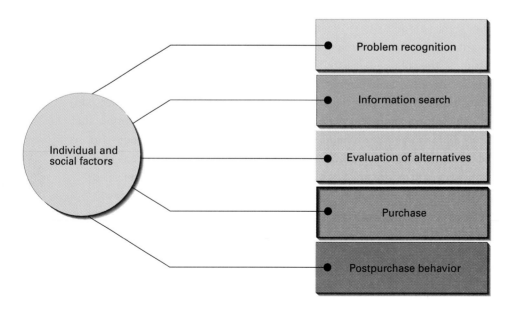

Problem Recognition

The first stage in the consumer decision-making process is problem recognition. **Problem recognition** occurs when consumers are faced with an imbalance between actual and desired states. For example, do you often feel thirsty after strenuous exercise? Has a television commercial for a new sports car ever made you wish you could buy it? Problem recognition is triggered when a consumer is exposed to either an internal or an external **stimulus.** Hunger and thirst are *internal stimuli;* the color of an automobile, the design of a package, a brand name mentioned by a friend, an advertisement on television, or cologne worn by a stranger are considered *external stimuli.*

A marketing manager's objective is to get consumers to recognize an imbalance between their present status and their preferred state. For example, marketers are now attempting to create consumer demand for added automobile features. Car manufacturers are developing car seats with built-in stereo speakers, under-seat storage space, electronically controlled temperature, and more comfortable seat belts.[2] Marketers want consumers to feel that they have to have these features in their new automobiles.

Marketing managers can create wants on the part of the consumer. A **want** exists when someone has an unfulfilled need and has determined that a particular good or service will satisfy it. Young children might want toys, video games, and baseball equipment. Teenagers may want compact discs, fashionable sneakers, and pizza. A want can be for a specific product or it can be for a certain attribute or feature of a product. For instance, older consumers want goods and services that offer convenience, comfort, and security. Remote-control appliances, home deliveries, speakerphones, and motorized carts are all designed for comfort and convenience. Likewise, a transmitter that can signal an ambulance or the police if the person wearing it has an emergency offers security for older consumers.

Consumers recognize unfulfilled wants in various ways. The two most common occur when a current product isn't performing properly and when the consumer is about to run out of something that is generally kept on hand. Consumers may also recognize unfulfilled wants if they hear about or see a product whose features make it seem superior to the one currently used. Such wants are usually created by advertising and other promotional activities. For example, a young teenager may develop a strong desire for a new Sega video game set after seeing it on display in a store.

Marketers selling their products in global markets must carefully observe the needs and wants of consumers in various regions. General Motors Corporation recently researched Japan's new car buyer market to determine what it would take to sell Japanese consumers on their Cavalier sedan. What they discovered was that, to the Japanese car buyer, how a car looks—inside and out—is more important than how it drives. Since Japan's typical small home can't accommodate many material goods, many Japanese treat their cars as their primary status symbol. Even for low-end models, standards are incredibly high. The exterior must be flawless, with narrow, perfectly uniform sheet-metal seams and mirrorlike paint jobs. Cloth interiors rival those of the finest of living room furniture. Plush pile carpeting is a requirement, as is a fifth floor mat to conceal the rear-floor hump. Due to narrow streets, the Japanese also prefer fold-

Can you figure out the buying roles of Mom and Dad when the detergent runs out? See how a routine response to a household problem works at **Hot Link—Buying Roles and Decision Making.**

problem recognition
Result of an imbalance between actual and desired states.

stimulus
Any unit of input affecting the five senses.

want
When someone has an unfulfilled need and has determined that a particular good or service will satisfy it.

A want can be for a specific product or it can be for a certain attribute or feature of a product. For teenagers, a particular brand of sneakers satisfies a want that is determined by fashion or the status designated to it by a peer group.

© John Abbott

up side-view mirrors. In addition, self-regulating air conditioning systems, computerized compasses, and top-notch stereos are often a must.[3]

Information Search

After recognizing a problem, consumers search for information about the various alternatives available to satisfy their wants. An information search can occur internally, externally, or both. **Internal information search** is the process of recalling information stored in the memory. This stored information stems largely from previous experience with a product. For instance, perhaps while shopping you encounter a brand of cake mix that you tried some time ago. By searching your memory, you can probably remember whether it tasted good, pleased guests, and was easy to prepare.

In contrast, an **external information search** seeks information in the outside environment. There are two basic types of external information sources: non-marketing-controlled and marketing-controlled. A **non-marketing-controlled information source** is not associated with marketers promoting a product. A friend, for example, might recommend an IBM personal computer because he or she bought one and likes it. Non-marketing-controlled information sources include personal experience (trying or observing a new product), personal sources (family, friends, acquaintances, and coworkers), and public sources such as Underwriters Laboratories, Consumer Reports, and other rating organizations.

A **marketing-controlled information source,** on the other hand, is biased toward a specific product because it originates with marketers promoting that product. Marketing-controlled information sources include mass-media advertising (radio, newspaper, television, and magazine advertising), sales promotion (contests, displays, premiums, and so forth), salespeople, and product labels and packaging. Many consumers are wary about the information they receive from marketing-controlled sources, arguing that most marketing campaigns stress the attributes of the product and don't mention the faults. These sentiments tend to be stronger among better-educated and higher-income consumers.

The extent to which an individual conducts an external search depends on his or her perceived risk, knowledge, prior experience, and level of interest in the good or service. Generally, as the perceived risk of the purchase increases, the consumer enlarges the search and considers more alternative brands. For instance, assume you want to buy a new car. The decision is a relatively risky one, mainly because of cost, so you are motivated to search for information about models, options, gas mileage, durability, passenger capacity, and so forth. You may also decide to gather information about more models because the trouble and time expended in finding the data are minimal compared to the cost of buying the wrong car. In contrast, you are less likely to expend great effort in searching for the right kind of bath soap. If you make the wrong selection, the cost is minimal and you will have the opportunity to make another selection in a short period of time. A study on the effect of consumers' level of perceived risk on the search for information on computer mail-order shopping found that those who perceiver higher risk with a purchase expend more effort in an external information search and consult a greater number of different types of information sources than do those who perceive lower levels of risk.[4]

A consumer's knowledge about the product or service will also affect the extent of an external information search. If the consumer is knowledgeable and informed about a potential purchase, he or she is less likely to need to search for additional information. In addition, the more knowledgeable the consumer is, the more efficiently he or she will conduct the search process, thereby requiring less time to search. Another closely related factor that affects the extent of a consumer's external search is confidence in one's decision-making ability. A confident consumer not only has plenty of stored information about the product but also feels self-assured about making the right decision. People lacking this confidence will continue an information

---

internal information search
The process of recalling information stored in the memory.

external information search
Seeking information in the outside environment.

non-marketing-controlled information source
Product information source that is not associated with advertising or promotion.

marketing-controlled information source
Product information source that originates with marketers promoting the product.

search even when they know a great deal about the product. Consumers with prior experience in buying a certain product will have less perceived risk than inexperienced consumers. Therefore, they will spend less time searching and limit the number of products that they consider.

A third factor influencing the external information search is product experience. Consumers who have had a positive prior experience with a product are more likely to limit their search to only those items related to the positive experience. For example, many consumers are loyal to Honda automobiles, which enjoy low repair rates and high customer satisfaction, and own more than one. Finally, the extent of the search undertaken is positively related to the amount of interest a consumer has in a product. That is, a consumer who is more interested in a product will spend more time searching for information and alternatives. For example, suppose you are a dedicated runner who reads jogging and fitness magazines and catalogs. In searching for a new pair of running shoes, you may enjoy reading about the new brands available and spend more time and effort than other buyers in deciding on the right shoe.

The consumer's information search should yield a group of brands, sometimes called the buyer's **evoked set** (or consideration set), which are the consumer's most preferred alternatives. From this set, the buyer will further evaluate the alternatives and make a choice. Consumers do not consider all the brands available in a product category, but they do rather seriously consider a much smaller set. For example, there are more than 30 brands of shampoos and more than 160 types of automobiles available in the United States, yet most consumers seriously contemplate only about four shampoos and no more than five automobiles when faced with a purchase decision.

evoked set (consideration set)
Group of brands, resulting from an information search, from which a buyer can choose.

Evaluation of Alternatives and Purchase

After getting information and constructing an evoked set of alternative products, the consumer is ready to make a decision. A consumer will use the information stored in memory and obtained from outside sources to develop a set of criteria. These standards help the consumer evaluate and compare alternatives. One way to begin narrowing the number of choices in the evoked set is to pick a product attribute and then exclude all products in the set that don't have that attribute. For instance, assume that John is thinking about buying a new compact disc player. He is interested in a remote control and the ability to hold several discs at one time (product attributes), so he excludes all compact disc players without these features.

Another way to narrow the number of choices is to use *cutoffs*, minimum or maximum levels of an attribute that an alternative must pass to be considered further. Suppose John still must choose from a wide array of remote-control, multidisc players. He then names another product attribute: price. Given the amount of money he has saved, John decides he cannot spend more than $200. Therefore, he can exclude all compact disc players priced above $200. A final way to narrow the choices is to rank the attributes under consideration in order of importance and evaluate the products based on how well they perform on the most important attributes. To reach a final decision, John would pick the most important attributes, such as a remote control or ability to hold several discs at a time, weigh the merits of each, and then evaluate alternative players on those criteria.

If new brands are added to an evoked set, the consumer's evaluation of the existing brands in that set changes. As a result, certain brands in the original set may become more desirable. For example, suppose John sees two compact disc players priced at $100 and $150. At the time, he may judge the $150 player as too expensive and choose not to purchase it. However, if he then adds to his list of alternatives another compact disc player that is priced at $250, he may come to judge the $150 one as less expensive and decide to purchase it.

The goal of the marketing manager is to determine which attributes are most important in influencing a consumer's choice. Several factors may collectively affect a consumer's evaluation of products. A single attribute, such as price, may not adequately explain how consumers form their evoked set.[5] Moreover, attributes thought to be important to the marketer may not be very important to the consumer. For example, one study found that automobile warranty coverage was the least important factor in a consumer's purchase of a car.[6]

Following the evaluation of alternatives, the consumer decides which product to buy or decides not to buy a product at all. If he or she decides to make a purchase, the next step in the process is an evaluation of the product after the purchase.

POSTPURCHASE BEHAVIOR

3 Explain the consumer's postpurchase evaluation process.

cognitive dissonance
Inner tension that a consumer experiences after recognizing an inconsistency between behavior and values or opinions.

In addition to displaying their product's superior quality, this Sharp ad assures purchasers of its copiers that they have made the right decision.
Courtesy Sharp Electronics Corporation

When buying products, consumers expect certain outcomes from the purchase. How well these expectations are met determines whether the consumer is satisfied or dissatisfied with the purchase. Consider this example: A person buys a used car with somewhat low expectations for the car's actual performance. Surprisingly, the car turns out to be one of the best cars she has ever owned. Thus, the buyer's satisfaction is high because her fairly low expectations were exceeded. On the other hand, a consumer who buys a brand-new car would expect it to perform especially well. But if the car turns out to be a lemon, she will be very dissatisfied because her high expectations have not been met. Price often creates high expectations. One study found that higher monthly cable TV bills were associated with greater expectations for cable service. Over time, cable subscribers tended to drop the premium-priced cable channels because their high expectations were not met.[7]

For the marketing manager, one important element of any postpurchase evaluation is reducing any lingering doubts that the decision was sound. When people recognize inconsistency between their values or opinions and their behavior, they tend to feel an inner tension called **cognitive dissonance.** For example, suppose a consumer spends half his monthly salary on a new high-tech stereo system. If he stops to think how much he has spent, he will probably feel dissonance. Dissonance occurs because the person knows the purchased product has some disadvantages as well as some advantages. In the case of the stereo, the disadvantage of cost battles the advantage of technological superiority.

Consumers try to reduce dissonance by justifying their decision. They might seek new information that reinforces positive ideas about the purchase, avoid information that contradicts their decision, or revoke the original decision by returning the product. People who have just bought a new car often read more advertisements for the car they have just bought than for other cars in order to reduce dissonance. In some instances, people deliberately seek contrary information in order to refute it and reduce dissonance. Dissatisfied customers sometimes rely on word of mouth to reduce cognitive dissonance by letting friends and family know they are displeased.

Marketing managers can help reduce dissonance through effective communication with purchasers. For example, a customer-service manager may slip a note inside the package congratulating the buyer on making a wise decision. Postpurchase letters sent by manufacturers and dissonance-reducing statements in instruction booklets may help customers feel at ease with their purchase. Advertising that displays

the product's superiority over competing brands or guarantees can also help relieve the possible dissonance of someone who has already bought the product. Infiniti car dealers, for example, recently offered refunds to new car buyers within three days of their purchase if they decided they were unsatisfied. Dealers also offered a price protection plan: if prices go down on a new Infiniti, anyone who paid more than the lower price in the previous 30 days was entitled to a refund of the difference.[8]

TYPES OF CONSUMER BUYING DECISIONS AND CONSUMER INVOLVEMENT

All consumer buying decisions generally fall along a continuum of three broad categories: routine response behavior, limited decision making, and extensive decision making (see Exhibit 6.2). Goods and services in these three categories can best be described in terms of five factors: level of consumer involvement, length of time to make a decision, cost of the good or service, degree of information search, and the number of alternatives considered. The level of consumer involvement is perhaps the most significant determinant in classifying buying decisions. **Involvement** is the amount of time and effort a buyer invests in the search, evaluation, and decision processes of consumer behavior.

Frequently purchased, low-cost goods and services are generally associated with **routine response behavior.** These goods and services can also be called low-involvement products because consumers spend little time on search and decision before making the purchase. Usually, buyers are familiar with several different brands in the product category but stick with one brand. Consumers engaged in routine response behavior normally don't experience problem recognition until they are exposed to advertising or see the product displayed on a store shelf. Consumers buy first and evaluate later, whereas the reverse is true for extensive decision making. A parent, for example, will not stand at the cereal shelf in the grocery store for 20 minutes thinking about which brand of cereal to buy for the children. Instead, he or she will walk by the shelf, find the family's usual brand, and put it into the cart.

Goods and services that are purchased regularly and that are not considered expensive are generally associated with **limited decision making.** These are also associated with low levels of involvement (although higher than routine decisions) because consumers do expend moderate effort in searching for information or in considering various alternatives. Suppose the children's usual brand of cereal, Kellogg's Corn Flakes, is unavailable in the grocery store. Completely out of cereal at home, the parent now must select another brand. Before making a final selection, he or she may pull from the shelf several brands similar to Kellogg's Corn Flakes,

---

4 Identify the types of consumer buying decisions and discuss the significance of consumer involvement.

involvement
The amount of time and effort a buyer invests in the search, evaluation, and decision processes of consumer behavior.

routine response behavior
Type of decision making exhibited by consumers buying frequently purchased, low-cost goods and services; requires little search and decision time.

limited decision making
Type of decision making exhibited by consumers buying regularly purchased, inexpensive goods and services; requires moderate search and decision time.

	ROUTINE	LIMITED	EXTENSIVE
INVOLVEMENT	low	low to moderate	high
TIME	short	short to moderate	long
COST	low	low to moderate	high
INFORMATION SEARCH	internal only	mostly internal	internal & external
NUMBER OF ALTERNATIVES	one	few	many

Exhibit 6.2
Continuum of Consumer Buying Decisions

Kellogg Company
General Mills, You Rule School
How does Kellogg's seek to differentiate its cereal via its Web site? How does Kellogg's approach compare to that of General Mills? Which site targets adults as decision makers? Which site targets kids?

http://www.kelloggs.com/
http://www.youruleschool.com/

extensive decision making
Most complex type of decision making exhibited by consumers buying unfamiliar, expensive or infrequently bought items; requires use of several criteria for evaluating options and much time for seeking information.

such as Corn Chex and Cheerios, to compare their nutritional value and calories and to decide whether the children will like the new cereal.

Consumers practice **extensive decision making** when buying an unfamiliar, expensive product or an infrequently bought item. This process is the most complex type of consumer buying decision and is associated with high involvement on the part of the consumer. This process resembles the model outlined in Exhibit 6.1. These consumers want to make the right decision, so they want to know as much as they can about the product category and available brands. People usually experience cognitive dissonance only when buying high-involvement products. Buyers use several criteria for evaluating their options and spend much time seeking information. Buying a home or a car, for example, requires extensive decision making.

The type of decision making that consumers use to purchase a product does not necessarily remain constant. For instance, if a routinely purchased product no longer satisfies, consumers may practice limited or extensive decision making to switch to another brand. And people who first use extensive decision making may then use limited or routine decision making for future purchases. For example, a new mother may first extensively evaluate several brands of disposable diapers before selecting one. Subsequent purchases of diapers will then become routine.

Factors Determining the Level of Consumer Involvement

The level of involvement in the purchase depends on five factors: previous experience, interest, perceived risk, situation, and social visibility.

- *Previous experience:* When consumers have had previous experience with a good or service, the level of involvement typically decreases. After repeated product trials, consumers learn to make quick choices. Because consumers are familiar with the product and know whether it will satisfy their needs, they become less involved in the purchase. For example, consumers with pollen allergies typically buy the sinus medicine that has relieved their symptoms in the past.

- *Interest:* Involvement is directly related to consumer interests, as in cars, music, movies, bicycling, or electronics. Naturally, these areas of interest vary from one individual to another. Although some people have little interest in nursing homes, a person with elderly parents in poor health may be highly interested.

- *Perceived risk of negative consequences:* As the perceived risk in purchasing a product increases, so does a consumer's level of involvement. The types of risks that concern consumers include financial risk, social risk, and psychological risk. First, financial risk is exposure to loss of wealth or purchasing power. Because high risk is associated with high-priced purchases, consumers tend to become extremely involved. Therefore, price and involvement are usually directly related: As price increases, so does the level of involvement. For example, someone who is thinking of buying a home will normally spend much time and effort to find the right one. Second, consumers take social risks when they buy products that can affect people's social opinions of them (for example, driving an old, beat-up car or wearing unstylish clothes). Third, buyers undergo psychological risk if they feel that making the wrong decision might cause some concern or anxiety. For example, should a working parent hire a babysitter or enroll the child in a day-care center?

- *Situation:* The circumstances of a purchase may temporarily transform a low-involvement decision into a high-involvement one. High involvement comes into play when the consumer perceives risk in a specific situation. For example, an individual might routinely buy low-priced brands of liquor and wine. However, when the boss visits, the consumer might make a high-involvement decision and buy more prestigious brands.

• *Social visibility:* Involvement also increases as the social visibility of a product increases. Products often on social display include clothing (especially designer labels), jewelry, cars, and furniture. All these items make a statement about the purchaser and, therefore, carry a social risk.

For more information on how various factors influence consumer involvement, refer to a recent assessment of antecedents and consequences of consumer involvement.[9]

Marketing Implications of Involvement

Marketing strategy varies depending on the level of involvement associated with the product. For high-involvement product purchases, marketing managers have several responsibilities. First, promotion to the target market should be extensive and informative. A good ad gives consumers the information they need for making the purchase decision as well as specifying the benefits and unique advantages of owning the product. For example, Jaguar runs lengthy ads that detail technical information about its luxury cars.

For low-involvement product purchases, consumers may not recognize their wants until they are in the store. Therefore, in-store promotion is an important tool when promoting low-involvement products. Marketing managers have to focus on package design so the product will be eye-catching and easily recognized on the shelf. Examples of products that take this approach are Campbell's soups, Tide detergent, Velveeta cheese, and Heinz catsup. In-store displays also stimulate sales of low-involvement products. A good display can explain the product's purpose and prompt recognition of a want. Displays of health and beauty-aid items in supermarkets have been known to increase sales many times above normal. Coupons, cents-off deals, and two-for-one offers also effectively promote low-involvement items.

Linking a product to a higher-involvement issue is another tactic that marketing managers can use to increase the sales of a low-involvement product. For example, many food products are no longer just nutritious but are also low in fat or cholesterol. Although packaged food may normally be a low-involvement product, reference to health issues raises the involvement level. Special K cereal has been around for several decades. To take advantage of today's interest in health and low-fat foods, it now advertises that its cereal contains no fat. Likewise, Rice Krispies promotes that fact that its formula is low in sugar, and Cheerios advertises that it is also an excellent source of oat bran.

INDIVIDUAL FACTORS INFLUENCING CONSUMER BUYING DECISIONS

The consumer decision-making process does not occur in a vacuum. On the contrary, several individual and social factors strongly influence the decision process. Exhibit 6.3 summarizes these influences. They have an effect from the time a consumer perceives a stimulus through postpurchase behavior. The individual factors that affect consumer behavior are unique to each person. These factors include perception; motivation; learning; values, beliefs, and attitudes; and personality, self-concept, and lifestyle.

Put your kids in Lands' End sleepwear, and you'll sleep better, too.

It's cozy and warm as a lullaby – but our Sleepwear is *practical*, too.

For unlike some fleece that "pills" in washing, Polartec 100 stubbornly resists pilling. So, our PJ's, Blanket Sleeper and Robes won't turn threadbare before your little one outgrows them.

The fit's generous – we cut our patterns on real boys and girls, not the usual stiff mannequins.

And while your youngster sleeps, you can leisurely shop the rest of our Lands' End Kids' catalog.

That is, if you're not grabbing a little nap yourself.

Soft, cozy Polartec 100 – holds in heat, yet breathes

Rib-knit cuff keeps its shape

Generous, "comfy" fit

Clean finished seams, no rough edges

Cotton feet (not sweaty plastic), with long-wearing rubber treads

LANDS' END
DIRECT MERCHANTS
Guaranteed. Period.

For our free catalog of clothing for kids – from tots to teens- call anytime
1-800-990-5421
(Please mention ad 20V)

This Lands' End ad tells consumers the benefits and advantages of its product, children's sleepwear, to help consumers make the purchase decision.
Courtesy Lands' End Inc.

5 Identify and understand the individual factors that affect consumer buying decisions.

Exhibit 6.3
Individual and Social Factors That Affect the Consumer Decision-Making Process

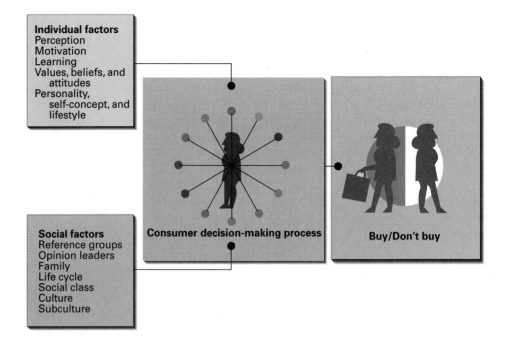

Individual factors
Perception
Motivation
Learning
Values, beliefs, and attitudes
Personality, self-concept, and lifestyle

Social factors
Reference groups
Opinion leaders
Family
Life cycle
Social class
Culture
Subculture

Consumer decision-making process

Buy/Don't buy

Perception

The world is full of stimuli. A stimulus is any unit of input affecting the five senses: sight, smell, taste, touch, hearing. The process by which we select, organize, and interpret these stimuli into a meaningful and coherent picture is called **perception.** In essence, perception is how we see the world around us and how we recognize that we have a consumption problem.

People cannot perceive every stimulus in their environment. Therefore, they use **selective exposure** to decide which stimuli to notice and which to ignore. A typical consumer is exposed to over 150 advertising messages a day but notices only between 11 and 20.

The familiarity of an object, contrast, movement, intensity (such as increased volume), and smell are cues that influence perception. Consumers use these cues to identify and define products and brands. The shape of a product's packaging, such as Coca-Cola's signature contour bottle discussed in the opening of the chapter, for instance, can influence perception. Color is another cue, and it plays a key role in consumers' perceptions. One study gave college students three different "flavors" of chocolate pudding that were, in reality, vanilla pudding with food coloring added to varying degrees. Students rated the dark brown pudding as having the best chocolate flavor and the two lighter puddings as being creamier. Not one of the students indicated he or she was tasting a flavor of pudding other than chocolate. Thus, color proved to be a critical cue for judging chocolate pudding. In fact, one might conclude that the color of the pudding was more important than its taste.[10]

What is perceived by consumers may also depend on the stimuli's vividness or shock value. Graphic warnings of the hazards associated with a product's use are perceived more readily and remembered more accurately than less vivid warnings or warnings that are written in text. "Sexier" ads excel at attracting the attention of younger consumers. Companies like Calvin Klein and Guess use sensuous ads to "cut through the clutter" of competing ads and other stimuli to capture the attention of the target audience. Similarly, Benetton ads use shock

perception
The process by which we select, organize, and interpret stimuli into a meaningful and coherent picture.

selective exposure
Process whereby a consumer notices certain stimuli and ignores other stimuli.

Guess? Inc.
Does the Guess? WWW site reflect the company's use of "sexier" ads? How does Guess? encourage membership in its VIP Lounge?

http://www.guess.com/

value to cut through the clutter by portraying taboo social issues, from racism to homosexuality.

Two other concepts closely related to selective exposure are selective distortion and selective retention. **Selective distortion** occurs when consumers change or distort information that conflicts with their feelings or beliefs. For example, suppose a consumer buys a Chrysler. After the purchase, if the consumer receives new information about a close alternative brand, such as a Ford, he or she may distort the information to make it more consistent with the prior view that the Chrysler is better than the Ford. Business travelers who fly often may distort or discount information about airline crashes because they must use air travel constantly in their jobs. People who smoke and have no plans to quit may distort information from medical reports and the Surgeon General about the link between cigarettes and lung cancer.

Selective retention is remembering only information that supports personal feelings or beliefs. The consumer forgets all information that may be inconsistent. After reading a pamphlet that contradicts one's political beliefs, for instance, a person may forget many of the points outlined in it.

Which stimuli will be perceived often depends on the individual. People can be exposed to the same stimuli under identical conditions but perceive them very differently. For example, two people viewing a TV commercial may have different interpretations of the advertising message. One person may be thoroughly engrossed by the message and become highly motivated to buy the product. Thirty seconds after the ad ends, the second person may not be able to recall the content of the message or even the product advertised.

selective distortion
Occurs when consumers change or distort information that conflicts with their feelings or beliefs.

selective retention
Remembering only information that supports personal feelings or beliefs.

Marketing Implications of Perception

Marketers must recognize the importance of cues, or signals, in consumers' perception of products. Marketing managers first identify the important attributes, such as price or quality, that the targeted consumers want in a product and then design signals to communicate these attributes. For example, consumers will pay more for candy wrapped in expensive-looking foil packages. But shiny labels on wine bottles signify less expensive wines; dull labels indicate more expensive wines. Anheuser-Busch raised the price on many of its less expensive beers to make its premier brand, Budweiser, more attractive to consumers.[11] Marketers also often use product warranties as a signal to consumers that the product is of higher quality than competing products. Consumers who perceive these warranties as highly credible generally perceive the product to be of higher quality.[12]

Of course, brand names send signals to consumers. The brand names of Close-Up toothpaste, DieHard batteries, and Frigidaire appliances, for example, identify important product qualities. Brand names that incorporate numbers or letters, such as Mazda RX-7 or WD-40, invoke images of masculine, high-tech, futuristic products.[13] Consumer also perceive quality and reliability with certain brand names. Companies watch their brand identity closely, in large part because a strong link has been established between perceived brand value and consumer loyalty. The ten brand names with the highest perceived value are Kodak Photographic Film, Disney World, National Geographic, The Discovery Channel, Mercedes-Benz, Disneyland, Hallmark, Waterford Crystal, Craftsman Power Tools, and Fisher-Price.[14]

Naming a product after a place can also add perceived value by association. The names Santa Fe and Dakota convey a

Fisher-Price is one of ten brand names with the highest perceived value.
Courtesy Fisher-Price, Inc.

Fisher-Price knows the only thing better than giving your kids the world. is letting them create their own.

Fisher-Price

A World Of Toys For Girls And Boys
Dream Doll House • Great Adventures Pirate Ship and Castle • Dream Palace

sense of openness, freedom, and youth, but products named after New Jersey or Detroit might conjure images of pollution and crime. Brand names that use the word Texas, for instance, evoke feelings of independence, opportunity, and fun because of the state's dramatic history and the fact that many consumers still think of Texas as embodying the American West.[15]

Marketing managers are also interested in the threshold level of perception: the minimum difference in a stimulus that the consumer will notice. This concept is sometimes referred to as the *just-noticeable difference.* For example, how much would Sony have to drop the price of a VCR before consumers recognized it as a bargain—$25? $50? or more? One study found that the just-noticeable difference in a stimulus is about a 20 percent change. For example, consumers will likely notice a 20 percent price decrease more quickly than a 15 percent decrease. This marketing principle can be applied to other marketing variables as well, such as package size or loudness of a broadcast advertisement.[16] Another study showed that the bargain-price threshold for a name brand is lower than that for a store brand. In other words, consumers perceive a bargain more readily when stores offer a small discount on a name-brand item than when they offer the same discount on a store brand; a larger discount is needed to achieve a similar effect for a store brand.[17]

Besides changing such stimuli as price, package size, and volume, marketers can change the product. For example, how many sporty features will General Motors have to add to a basic two-door sedan before consumers begin to perceive the model as a sports car? How many new services will a discount store like Kmart need to add before consumers perceive it as a full-service department store?

Marketing managers who intend to do business in global markets should be aware of how foreign consumers perceive their products. For instance, in Japan, product labels are often written in English or French even though they may not translate into anything meaningful. But many Japanese associate foreign words on product labels with the exotic, the expensive, and high quality. Likewise, many Europeans perceive U.S.-made goods as being higher in quality than locally produced goods. Marketers using down-home American imagery in advertising and marketing have experienced huge successes in Europe. For example, Jeep, calling itself "The American Legend" in Europe, saw sales surge to 25,000 in 1993 from 18,000 in 1991. Print advertising in the United Kingdom features a Jeep with English license plates in front of a log cabin flying a U.S. flag.[18]

Motivation

By studying motivation, marketers can analyze the major forces influencing consumers to buy or not buy products. When you buy a product, you usually do so to fulfill some kind of need. These needs become motives when aroused sufficiently. For instance, suppose this morning you were so hungry before class that you needed to eat something. In response to that need, you stopped at McDonald's for an Egg McMuffin. In other words, you were motivated by hunger to stop at McDonald's. **Motives** are the driving forces that cause a person to take action to satisfy specific needs.

Why are people driven by particular needs at particular times? One popular theory is **Maslow's hierarchy of needs,** shown in Exhibit 6.4, which arranges needs in ascending order of importance: physiological, safety, social, esteem, and self-actualization. As a person fulfills one need, a higher-level need becomes more important.

The most basic human needs are *physiological*—that is, needs for food, water, and shelter. Because they are essential to survival, these needs must be satisfied first. Ads showing a juicy hamburger or a runner gulping down Gatorade after a marathon exemplify the use of appeals to satisfy physiological needs.

Safety needs include security and freedom from pain and discomfort. Marketers often exploit consumers' fears and anxieties about safety to sell their products. For

motive
The driving force that causes a person to take action to satisfy specific needs.

Maslow's hierarchy of needs
Popular theory which arranges needs in ascending order of importance: physiological, safety, social, esteem, and self-actualization.

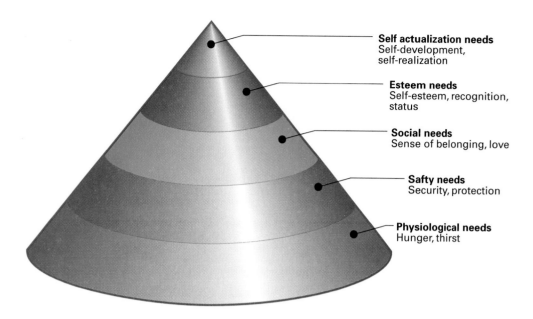

Self actualization needs
Self-development,
self-realization

Esteem needs
Self-esteem, recognition,
status

Social needs
Sense of belonging, love

Safty needs
Security, protection

Physiological needs
Hunger, thirst

example, Volvo ad campaigns have featured testimonials from real people who believe they survived terrible car crashes because they were driving a Volvo. Consumer
demand for products containing vitamin E have been soaring following several scientific studies that suggest the vitamin inhibits agents that attack cells and cause deterioration. Marketers have promoted other studies that conclude vitamin E may also
help ward off degenerative ailments such as heart disease and cancer and some symptoms of aging.[19] The "Ethics in Marketing" box on page 164 discusses how marketers
often play on consumers' fears to sell their products.

After physiological and safety needs have been fulfilled, *social* needs—especially
love and a sense of belonging—become the focus. Love includes acceptance by one's
peers as well as sex and romantic love. Marketing managers probably appeal more to
this need than to any other. Ads for clothes, cosmetics, and vacation packages suggest that buying the product can bring love. The need to belong is also a favorite of
marketers. Nike promotes its Air Jordan athletic shoes, for instance, as not just plain,
old sneakers; they're part fashion statement, part athletic statement. Lace them up,
and the wearer looks cool and plays cool—just like Michael Jordan, the shoe's
spokesperson and namesake.[20]

Love is acceptance without regard to one's contribution. Esteem is acceptance
based on one's contribution to the group. *Self-esteem* needs include self-respect and
a sense of accomplishment. Esteem needs also include prestige, fame, and recognition of one's accomplishments. Mont Blanc pens, Mercedes-Benz automobiles, and
Neiman Marcus stores all appeal to esteem needs.

The highest human need is *self-actualization*. It refers to finding self-fulfillment and
self-expression, reaching the point in life at which "people are what they feel they
should be." Maslow felt that very few people ever attain this level. Even so, advertisements may focus on this type of need. For example, American Express ads convey the
message that acquiring its card is one of the highest attainments in life. Likewise, the
U.S. Armed Forces' slogan urges young people to "Be all that you can be."

Learning

Almost all consumer behavior results from **learning,** which is the process that creates changes in behavior through experience and practice. It is not possible to ob-

Exhibit 6.4
*Maslow's Hierarchy of
Needs*

learning
The process that creates
changes in behavior
through experience and
practice.

Ethics in Marketing

Fear as a Marketing Tool: Does It Sell?

One in five American men will get prostate cancer. One in eight American women will get breast cancer. At least two million Americans are manic-depressive, and more than two million are schizophrenic. At least 60 million Americans have high blood pressure, 12 million have asthma, and four million have Alzheimer's disease. One in three Americans is obese.

With numbers like these, it is amazing there is anyone still here—let alone people living happy, healthy lives.

Projections of the incidence of disease are rampant these days, as a growing number of health-advocacy groups and marketers compete for people's limited attention and money. Most of the numbers are extrapolations or estimates, at best. Yet as the media report them and marketers exploit them, often uncritically and without context,

these conjectures assume the mantle of quantifiable fact.

Short of a simultaneous examination of every person in America (all on truth serum), it is impossible to count exactly how many people suffer from most diseases or health conditions. The government keeps a few statistics—on birth, death, cancer, and infectious diseases—but most conditions for which people consult a doctor wouldn't be recorded in a national database.

Yet government, business, and the media, each for its own reasons, want at least ballpark figures. Statisticians from advocacy groups oblige, offering data on everything

from destructive teeth grinding (as many as 20 percent of Americans) to lactose intolerance (20 percent of whites and 75 percent of blacks). Since big numbers get more attention than small ones, the estimates are often alarmingly high.

"Any group that's lobbying for money is going to try to maximize the number of deaths from their particular malady," says John Allen Paulos, a mathematics professor and author of *A Mathematician Reads the Newspaper*. "Then the numbers are often stated baldly, without context, definition or how they're arrived at."[21]

What current marketing or advertising examples can you think of that use alarming statistics to sell their products? Do you believe the estimates offered by the marketer? Would the use of such data cause you to distrust a marketer?

serve learning directly, but we can infer when it has occurred by a person's actions. For example, suppose you see an advertisement for a new and improved cold medicine. If you go to the store that day and buy that remedy, we infer that you have learned something about the cold medicine.

There are two types of learning: experiential and conceptual. *Experiential learning* occurs when an experience changes your behavior. For example, if you try the new cold medicine when you get home and it does not relieve your symptoms, you may not buy that brand again. *Conceptual learning* is not learned through direct experience. Assume, for example, that you are standing at a soft-drink machine and notice a new diet flavor with an artificial sweetener. But someone has told you that diet beverages leave an aftertaste, so you choose a different drink. You have learned that you would not like this new diet drink without ever trying it.

Reinforcement and repetition boost learning. Reinforcement can be positive or negative. If you see a vendor selling frozen yogurt (stimulus), buy it (response), and find the yogurt to be quite refreshing (reward), your behavior has been positively reinforced. On the other hand, if you buy a new flavor of yogurt and it does not taste good (negative reinforcement), you will not buy that flavor of yogurt again. Without positive or negative reinforcement, a person will not be motivated to repeat the behavior pattern or to avoid it. Thus, if a new brand evokes neutral feelings, some marketing activity, such as a price change or an increase in promotion, may be required to induce further consumption. Learning theory is helpful in reminding marketers that concrete and timely actions are what reinforce desired consumer behavior.

Repetition is a key strategy in promotional campaigns because it can lead to increased learning. Delta Airlines uses repetitious advertising so consumers will learn that "At Delta, we love to fly, and it shows." Generally, to heighten learning, advertising messages should be spread over time rather than clustered at one time.

A related learning concept useful to marketing managers is stimulus generalization. In theory, **stimulus generalization** occurs when one response is extended to a second stimulus similar to the first. Marketers often use a successful, well-known brand name for a family of products because it gives consumers familiarity with and knowledge about each product in the family. Such brand-name families spur the introduction of new products and facilitate the sale of existing items. Jell-O frozen pudding pops rely on the familiarity of Jell-O gelatin; Clorox laundry detergent relies on familiarity with Clorox bleach; and Ivory shampoo relies on familiarity with Ivory soap. General Mills recently introduced Betty Crocker-brand cereals, a brand name traditionally associated with dessert and side-dish mixes. In bringing the Betty Crocker name to the cereal aisle, General Mills hopes to stimulate cereal sales with a familiar face.[22] Branding is examined in more detail in Chapter 10.

Another form of stimulus generalization occurs when retailers or wholesalers design their packages to resemble well-known manufacturers' brands. Such imitation often confuses consumers, who buy the imitator thinking it's the original. U.S. manufacturers in foreign markets have sometimes found little, if any, brand protection. For example, in South Korea, Procter & Gamble's Ivory soap competes head-on with the Korean brand Bory, which has an almost identical logo on the package. Consumers dissatisfied with Bory may attribute their dissatisfaction to Ivory, never realizing that Bory is an imitator. Counterfeit products are also produced to look exactly like the original. For example, counterfeit Levi's jeans made in China are hot items in Europe, where Levi Strauss has had trouble keeping up with demand. The knockoffs look so much like the real thing that unsuspecting consumers don't know the difference—until after a few washes, when the belt loops fall off and the rivets begin to rust. Passage of the General Agreement on Tariffs and Trade, which was discussed in Chapter 4, should help to reduce counterfeiting.

The opposite of stimulus generalization is **stimulus discrimination,** which means learning to differentiate among similar products. Consumers usually prefer one product as more rewarding or stimulating. For example, some consumers prefer Coca-Cola and others prefer Pepsi; many insist they can taste a difference between the two brands.

stimulus generalization
A learning process that occurs when one response is extended to a second stimulus similar to the first.

stimulus discrimination
Learning to differentiate among similar products.

Imitation or counterfeit products are designed to confuse consumers, who buy the items thinking they are originals. This problem in common in foreign markets where there is often little brand protection.
© Mark Richards/CONTACT Press Images

With some types of products—such as aspirin, gasoline, bleach, and paper towels—marketers rely on promotion to point out brand differences that consumers would otherwise not recognize. This process, called *product differentiation*, is discussed in more detail in Chapter 10. Usually, product differentiation is based on superficial differences. For example, Bayer tells consumers that it's the aspirin "doctors recommend most."

Values, Beliefs, and Attitudes

value
An enduring belief that a specific mode of conduct is personally or socially preferable to another mode of conduct.

Learning helps people shape their value systems. In turn, values help determine self-concept, personality, and even lifestyle. A **value** is an enduring belief that a specific mode of conduct is personally or socially preferable to another mode of conduct. People's value systems have a great effect on their consumer behavior. Consumers with similar value systems tend to react alike to prices and other marketing-related inducements. Values also correspond to consumption patterns. People who want to protect the environment try to buy only products that don't harm it. Values can also influence consumers' TV viewing habits or the magazines they read. For instance, people who strongly object to violence avoid crime shows. Likewise, people who oppose pornography do not buy *Playboy*.

Value systems can vary quite a bit across cultures and subcultures. For example, leisure time is valued in the United States. Consumers spend a considerable amount of time and money on sporting events, movies, restaurants, vacations, and amusement parks. U.S. workers traditionally expect eight-hour days, five-day workweeks, and vacation time. Japanese workers, on the other hand, typically work 12-hour days and often work on Saturdays as well. Only half of Japanese workers use all their vacation time. One reason most Japanese don't take more time off is that they don't want to burden their colleagues by leaving early or taking a holiday. Traditional Japanese workers also feel that their work will suffer if they put effort into other things.

The personal values of target consumers often have important implications for marketing managers. For example, the personal value systems of baby boomers and generation Xers are quite different. Baby boomers have a strong sense of individualism. They succeeded in a job market that rewarded competitive drive more than cooperative spirit and that valued individual skills more than teamwork. Coming of age at a time when the economy seemed secure, baby boomers are very optimistic economically and have a basic feeling of financial security.[23] In contrast, the members of generation X are less confident than their predecessors about the stability of jobs, earnings, and relationships. Born into an increasingly diverse world, members of generation X also are more likely than their elders to accept differences in race, ethnicity, national origin, family structure, and lifestyle. Members of generation X are more likely to seek work that is personally fulfilling and to pursue a balance of work and leisure activities. And while they are not anti-advertising, they are repulsed by insincerity—and they are experts at spotting it.[24]

belief
An organized pattern of knowledge that an individual holds as true about his or her world.

Beliefs and attitudes are closely linked to values. A **belief** is an organized pattern of knowledge that an individual holds as true about his or her world. A consumer may believe that Sony's camcorder makes the best home videos, tolerates hard use, and is reasonably priced. These beliefs may be based on knowledge, faith, or hearsay. Consumers tend to develop a set of beliefs about a product's attributes and then, through these beliefs, form a *brand image*—a set of beliefs about a particular brand. In turn, the brand image shapes consumers' attitudes toward the product.

attitude
A learned tendency to respond consistently toward a given object, such as a brand.

Attitudes tend to be more enduring and complex than beliefs because they consist of clusters of interrelated beliefs. An **attitude** is a learned tendency to respond consistently toward a given object, such as a brand. Attitudes also encompass an individual's value system, which represents personal standards of good and bad, right and wrong, and so forth.

For an example of the nature of attitudes, consider the differing attitudes of consumers around the world toward the habit of purchasing on credit. Americans have long been enthusiastic about charging goods and services and are willing to pay high interest rates for the privilege of postponing payment. But to many European consumers, doing what amounts to taking out a loan— even a small one—to pay for anything seems absurd. Germans especially are reluctant to buy on credit. Italy has a sophisticated credit and banking system well suited to handling credit cards, but Italians prefer to carry cash, often huge wads of it. Most Japanese consumers have credit cards, but card purchases amount to less than 1 percent of all consumer transactions. The Japanese have long looked down on credit purchases but acquire cards to use while traveling abroad.[25]

If a good or service is meeting its profit goals, positive attitudes toward the product merely need to be reinforced. However, if the brand is not succeeding, the marketing manager must strive to change target consumers' attitudes toward it. This change can be accomplished in three ways: changing beliefs about the brand's attributes, changing the relative importance of these beliefs, and adding new beliefs.

Consumers around the world have very different attitudes about using credit cards. Americans are enthusiastic users whereas many Europeans are reluctant to buy anything on credit.
© 1996 PhotoDisc, Inc.

Changing Beliefs about Attributes

The first technique is to turn neutral or negative beliefs about product attributes into positive ones. For example, pork was losing sales to chicken because consumers thought pork was fatty and unhealthy. To counter this belief, pork producers launched the "Pork: The Other White Meat" campaign to reposition their product in the minds of consumers. The campaign tells consumers that pork is leaner, lower in calories, and lower in saturated fat than they think. Likewise, BMW is continuing its efforts to reposition itself as a safe, affordable vehicle for the entire family and to steer away from its image as a yuppie statement. Its new commercials concentrate on safety features, such as traction control; its print ads show children for the first time. BMW also hopes the campaign will convince consumers that the cars are not as expensive as they might think.[26] Newforge Foods is having difficulty convincing consumers that Spam, a canned-pork product, is made of quality ingredients. Research has shown that consumers believe that Spam is made of the "left-over" parts and is, therefore, an inferior product. Spam's advertising agency hopes to change this image by promoting the quality of the ingredients used to make Spam.[27]

Changing beliefs about a service can be more difficult because service attributes are intangible. Convincing consumers to switch hairstylists or lawyers or to go to a mall dental clinic can be much more difficult than getting them to change brands of razor blades. Image, which is also largely intangible, significantly determines service patronage. What is a "better doctor"? How do consumers become convinced that they will get better dental care in a mall than through a family dentist? Services marketing is explored in detail in Chapter 12.

Changing the Importance of Beliefs

The second approach to modifying attitudes is to change the relative importance of beliefs about an attribute. For years, consumers have known that bran cereals are high in natural fiber. The primary belief associated with this attribute is that the fiber tends to act as a mild, natural laxative. Today, however, cereal marketers promote the high fiber content of bran cereals as a possible factor in preventing certain types of cancer, vastly increasing the importance of this attribute in the minds of consumers.

General Electric has tried to change Japanese consumers' beliefs about the attributes that are most important to them in a refrigerator. Japanese manufacturers believe that Japanese consumers prefer the highly stylized and feature-studded appliances that domestic makers sell in small sizes. A typical Japanese-made refrigerator is a 9-cubic-foot $1,300 model with three doors and a compartment for raw fish. Larger Japanese models have six doors and list for around $3,200. GE discovered, however, that many Japanese would gladly trade these characteristics for larger, simpler, and cheaper models. Since more Japanese women are working after marriage and can't shop for food daily as their mothers did, big, inexpensive, two-door refrigerators suddenly make sense. As a result, GE quickly captured about 3 percent of the Japanese market with its modest $800 model.[28]

Adding New Beliefs

The third approach to transforming attitudes is to add new beliefs. Although changes in consumption patterns often come slowly, cereal marketers are betting that consumers will eventually warm up to the idea of cereal as a snack. A print ad for Ralston Purina's Cookie-Crisp cereal features a boy popping the sugary nuggets into his mouth while he does his homework. Boxes of Kellogg's Cracklin' Oat Bran boast that the cereal tastes like oatmeal cookies and makes "a great snack . . . anytime." Similarly, commercials for Quaker Oats 100% Natural cereal promote eating it straight from the box. Chewing gum makers are also attempting to add new beliefs about the uses of their product. Advertisements tout chewing gum as an alternative to smoking or as a way to remove food residue from one's teeth. For example, Trident sugarless gum advertises that it "actually helps fight cavities when you chew it after meals."[29] Likewise, Chrysler Corporation is now attempting to convince consumers that minivans should have four doors, instead of three. Since the debut of the four-door model, Chrysler has significantly outsold its competitors two to one.[30]

Adding new beliefs is not easy. For example, when Anheuser-Busch first introduced Bud Dry beer, consumers were confused because the word *dry* is commonly used to describe wines. Nevertheless, many consumers have since added the new belief that beer, too, can be described as dry. Volvo faced a similar problem in introducing its sporty 850 model. For over a quarter of a century, Volvo has successfully crafted an image as the safest car on the road. However, Volvo did such a good job driving home its safety message that consumers had a hard time imagining a Volvo as anything other than a boxy, steel-reinforced tank.

U.S. companies attempting to market their goods overseas may need to help consumers add new beliefs about a product in general. Many hygiene practices common in the United States, for example, are unheard of in foreign countries. In rural India, most Indians have never handled such products as a toothbrush or a tube of toothpaste. For generations, they have used charcoal powder and indigenous plants to cleanse their mouths. To educate Indians on the benefits of toothpaste, Colgate-Palmolive sends marketers to rural villages on market day equipped with a half-hour infomercial featuring Colgate toothpaste. A story of a couple on their wedding night sends Colgate's message: Colgate is good for your breath, teeth, and love life. The infomercial wraps up with a dentist explaining that the traditional oral-hygiene methods, such as charcoal powder, are ineffective. Free samples are passed out while a Colgate marketer demonstrates how to use the Colgate toothpaste and toothbrush.[31]

personality
Ways of organizing and grouping the consistencies of an individual's reactions to situations.

Personality, Self-Concept, and Lifestyle

Each consumer has a unique personality. **Personality** is a broad concept that can be thought of as a way of organizing and grouping the consistencies of an individual's reactions to situations. Thus, personality combines psychological makeup and envi-

Exhibit 6.5
Some Common Personality Traits

ronmental forces. It includes people's underlying dispositions, especially their most dominant characteristics. Some marketers believe that personality influences the types and brands of products purchased. For instance, the type of car, clothes, or jewelry a consumer buys may reflect one or more personality traits. Personality traits like those listed in Exhibit 6.5 may be used to describe a consumer's personality.

Self-concept, or self-perception, is how consumers perceive themselves. Self-concept includes attitudes, perceptions, beliefs, and self-evaluations. Although self-concept may change, the change is often gradual. Through self-concept, people define their identity, which in turn provides for consistent and coherent behavior.

Self-concept combines the **ideal self-image** (the way an individual would like to be) and the **real self-image** (how an individual actually perceives himself or herself). Generally, we try to raise our real self-image toward our ideal (or at least narrow the gap). Consumers seldom buy products that jeopardize their self-image. For example, someone who sees herself as a trendsetter wouldn't buy clothing that doesn't project a contemporary image.

Human behavior depends largely on self-concept. Because consumers want to protect their identity as individuals, the products they buy, the stores they patronize, and the credit cards they carry support their self-image. Men's and women's fragrances, for example, tend to reflect the self-images of their wearers. Chanel's Egoïste is for the man who has everything and knows it. Likewise, Elizabeth Taylor's White Diamonds perfume is "the fragrance dreams are made of," for all those women who strive for legendary beauty.[32]

By influencing the degree to which consumers perceive a good or service to be self-relevant, marketers can affect consumers' motivation to learn about, shop for, and buy a certain brand. Marketers also consider self-concept important because it helps explain the relationship between individuals' perceptions of themselves and their consumer behavior.

An important component of self-concept is *body image*, the perception of the attractiveness of one's own physical features. For example, individuals who have plastic surgery often experience significant improvements in their overall body image and self-concept. Moreover, a person's perception of body image can be a stronger reason for weight loss than either good health or other social factors.[33] Sales of at-home hair color to aging baby boomers have substantially increased as more middle-aged men and women color their hair in order to "age gracefully."[34] Johnson and Johnson is launching a skin cream, Renova, which fights the "appearance of wrinkles" to be targeted at the baby boomer generation.[35] GNC is capitalizing on consumers' desire for quick fixes by marketing pills which should produce "quick energy" for the consumer.[36] Likewise, health clubs, exercise equipment manufacturers, and diet plans target consumers who want to improve their self-concept by exercising and losing weight.

Personality and self-concept are reflected in lifestyle. A **lifestyle** is a mode of living, as identified by a person's activities, interests, and opinions. *Psychographics* is the analytical technique used to examine consumer lifestyles and to categorize consumers. Unlike personality characteristics, which are hard to describe and measure, lifestyle characteristics are useful in segmenting and targeting consumers. Many industries

self-concept
How consumers perceive themselves; self-perception.

ideal self-image
The way an individual would like to be.

real self-image
How an individual actually perceives himself or herself.

lifestyle
A mode of living, identified by a person's activities, interests, and opinions.

now use psychographics to better understand their market segments. For example, the auto industry has a psychographic segmentation scheme for classifying car buyers into one of six groups according to their attitudes toward cars and the driving experience. At the two extremes are "gearheads," true car enthusiasts who enjoy driving and working on their cars themselves, and "negatives," who view cars as a necessary evil that they would just as soon do without. Mobil Corporation has used psychographics to classify gasoline buyers into five groups: road warriors, true blues, generation F3, homebodies, and price shoppers.[37] These groups vary on their brand loyalty, amount purchased, method of payment, location preference, and usage of convenience stores. Psychographics and lifestyle segmentation schemes are discussed in more detail in Chapter 8.

SOCIAL FACTORS INFLUENCING CONSUMER BUYING DECISIONS

6 Identify and understand the social factors that affect consumer buying decisions.

The second major group of factors that influence consumer decision making are social factors, which include all effects on buyer behavior that result from interactions between a consumer and the external environment. Social factors include culture and subcultures, reference groups, opinion leaders, family, life cycle, and social class (refer back to Exhibit 6.3).

Culture

culture

The set of values, norms, attitudes, and other meaningful symbols that shape human behavior, as well as the artifacts, or products, of that behavior as they are transmitted from one generation to the next.

Culture is the set of values, norms, attitudes, and other meaningful symbols that shape human behavior, as well as the artifacts, or products, of that behavior as they are transmitted from one generation to the next. Culture is environmentally oriented. The nomads of Finland have developed a culture for Arctic survival. Similarly, people who live in the Brazilian jungle have created a culture suitable for tropical living.

Human interaction creates values and prescribes acceptable behavior for each culture. By establishing common expectations, culture gives order to society. Sometimes these expectations are coded into laws. For example, drivers in our culture must stop at a red light.

As long as a value or belief meets the society's needs, it remains part of the culture. If it is no longer functional, it fades away. Large families, for example, were valued in the 19th and early 20th centuries, when the U.S. economy was more agrarian. Children were considered an asset because they could help with the farmwork. Today, in an industrial economy, large families are not necessary.

Culture is dynamic. It adapts to changing needs and an evolving environment. The rapid growth of technology in this century has accelerated the rate of cultural change. TV has changed entertainment patterns and family communication and has heightened public awareness of political and other news events. Automation has increased the amount of leisure time we have and, in some ways, has changed the traditional work ethic. Cultural norms will continue to evolve because of our need for social patterns that solve problems.

Without understanding a culture, a firm has little chance of selling products in it. Colors, for example, may have different meanings in global markets than they do at home. In China, white is the color of mourning, and brides wear red; in the United States, black is for mourning, and brides wear white. Pepsi had a dominant market share in Southeast Asia until it changed the color of its coolers and vending equipment from deep regal blue to light ice blue. In that part of the world, light blue is associated with death and mourning.

Language is another important aspect of culture that global marketers must deal with. They must take care in translating product names, slogans, and promotional messages into foreign languages so as not to convey the wrong message. Consider the following examples of blunders made by marketers when delivering their message to Spanish-speaking consumers: General Motors discovered too late that Nova (the name of an economical car) literally means "doesn't go" in Spanish; Coors encouraged its English-speaking customers to "Turn it loose," but the phrase in Spanish means "Suffer from diarrhea"; and when Frank Perdue said, "It takes a tough man to make a tender chicken," Spanish speakers heard, "It takes a sexually stimulated man to make a chicken affectionate."

As more companies expand their operations globally, the need to understand the cultures of foreign countries becomes more important. Marketers should become familiar with the culture and adapt to it. What's all the rage in Boston could be a bust in Bombay if marketers are not sensitive to the nuances of the local culture. Read about the experiences several U.S. companies have had in adapting their products to foreign cultures in the "Global Perspectives" box.

Companies that wish to enter foreign markets, such as Russia, must become familiar with the culture and adapt to it.
© Jeff Greenberg

Global Perspectives

Marketing Across Cultures

Major U.S. companies are finding it's indeed a small world after all when it comes to finding new markets and consumers for their products, but they're also discovering that there are still big differences in consumers across cultures. For Pepsico's Frito-Lay unit, that means that the Cheetos being sold in China don't taste like the ones being served to Americans. Focus groups revealed that the cheesy taste of American Cheetos didn't tempt the taste buds of the Chinese. Instead, popular Chinese flavors of Cheetos include Savory American Cream and Zesty Japanese Steak. Frito-Lay's research to create the most appealing flavor of Cheetos for the Chinese market has paid off: In 1995, the company sold 100 million bags of Cheetos in a single Chinese province.

Although Coca-Cola generally does not tailor its flagship brand's taste to different markets, it does tailor its promotional activities to

different cultures. Coca-Cola recently launched its first global TV commercial pegged to the Lunar New Year in Hong Kong, China, Taiwan, Thailand, and Vietnam. The ad features a gigantic dragon festooned with 6,200 Coca-Cola cans. The commercial also shows the Chinese symbol for good luck in a holiday parade along with fireworks and drums. Coke's strategy seems to have paid off: In a recent survey of Chinese consumers, Coca-Cola was the second most highly recognized brand name.

Over the years, Rubbermaid has learned many major lessons in tailoring it products to foreign markets, especially Europe's various cultures. While most Americans like housewares in neutral blues or

almond colors, for instance, southern Europeans prefer red containers and customers in Holland want white. And while Rubbermaid sold millions of open-top waste baskets in America, Europeans, picky about garbage peeking out of bins, wanted bins with tight lids that snap into place. Rubbermaid now designs and introduces dozens of new products aimed specifically at Europe. Its multilingual catalogs feature products that address color and size preferences among various European countries. As a result, Rubbermaid is now the number two brand in European housewares.[38]

What are some possible reasons why marketers often ignore cultural differences when selling their products abroad? What steps could a marketer take to discern cultural differences before risking a product introduction in a foreign market?

Subculture

A culture can be divided into subcultures on the basis of demographic characteristics, geographic regions, political beliefs, religious beliefs, national and ethnic background, and the like. A **subculture** is a homogeneous group of people who share elements of the overall culture as well as cultural elements unique to their own group. Within subcultures, people's attitudes, values, and purchase decisions are even more similar than they are within the broader culture. Subcultural differences may result in considerable variation within a culture in what, how, when, and where people buy goods and services.

In the United States alone, countless subcultures can be identified. Many are concentrated geographically. People belonging to the Mormon religion, for example, are clustered mainly in Utah; Cajuns are located in the bayou regions of southern Louisiana. Hispanics are more predominant in those states that border Mexico; the majority of Chinese, Japanese, and Koreans are found in the Pacific region of the United States.

Other subcultures are geographically dispersed. For example, a recent study has identified Harley-Davidson bikers as a distinct subculture.[39] In addition, computer hackers, military families, and university professors may be found throughout the country. Yet they have identifiable attitudes and values that distinguish them from the larger culture.

Harley-Davidson MotorClothes
How does Harley-Davidson describe its particular subculture? What type of people would wear Harley-Davidson clothes?

http://www.harleydavidson.com/

If marketers can identify subcultures, they can then design special marketing programs to serve their needs. Kraft recently launched a brand of fast-melting white cheese and rich cream called Valle Lindo, Spanish for "beautiful valley," especially for Hispanic consumers. Ads for the products are in Spanish and air on Spanish-language television and radio stations. Kraft is also expanding its Spanish-language advertising for existing brand products popular among Hispanic consumers.[40] Similarly, Simon & Schuster, Inc., is launching a line of Spanish-language books, including translations of popular American titles.[41] Finally, Anheuser-Busch recently launched a specialty beer, called ZiegenBock, just for Texans and for sale only in the state. By tapping into Lone Star pride, the nation's largest brewer hopes to secure a niche in the state's budding specialty beer market.[42]

Reference Groups

All the formal and informal groups that influence the buying behavior of an individual are that person's **reference groups.** Consumers may use products or brands to identify with or become a member of a group. They learn from observing how members of their reference groups consume, and they use the same criteria to make their own consumer decisions.

Reference groups can be categorized very broadly as either direct or indirect (see Exhibit 6.6). Direct reference groups are face-to-face membership groups that touch people's lives directly. They can be either primary or secondary. **Primary membership groups** include all groups with which people interact regularly in an informal, face-to-face manner, such as family, friends, and coworkers. In contrast, people associate with **secondary membership groups** less consistently and more formally. These groups might include clubs, professional groups, and religious groups.

Consumers also are influenced by many indirect, nonmembership reference groups that they do not belong to. **Aspirational reference groups** are those that a person would like to join. To join an aspirational group, a person must at least conform to the norms of that group. (**Norms** are the values and attitudes deemed acceptable by

In primary membership groups, such as families, members interact with each other almost daily in an informal, face-to-face manner.
© Lawrence Migdale/Tony Stone Images

the group.) Thus, a person who wants to be elected to public office may begin to dress more conservatively, as other politicians do. He or she may go to many of the restaurants and social engagements that city and business leaders attend and try to play a role that is acceptable to voters and other influential people. A teenager, on the other hand, may dye his hair, experiment with body-piercing and tatoos, and listen to alternative music to fit in with the "in" group.

Nonaspirational reference groups, or dissociative groups, influence our behavior when we try to maintain distance from them. A consumer may avoid buying some types of clothing or cars, going to certain restaurants or stores, or even buying a home in a certain neighborhood in order to avoid being associated with a particular group.

The activities, values, and goals of reference groups directly influence consumer behavior. For marketers, reference groups have three important implications: They

norms
The values and attitudes deemed acceptable by the group.

nonaspirational reference groups
Groups that influence our behavior when we try to maintain distance from them. Also known as dissociative groups.

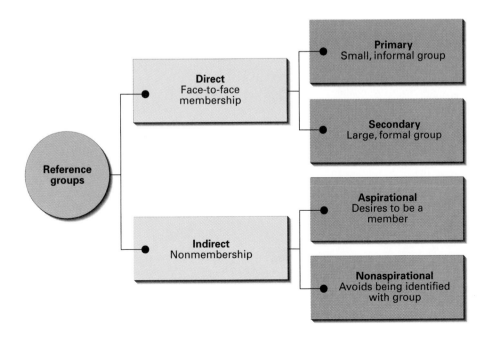

Exhibit 6.6
Types of Reference Groups

serve as information sources and influence perceptions; they affect an individual's aspiration levels; and their norms either constrain or stimulate consumer behavior. For example, over 40 percent of Americans seek the advice of family and friends when shopping for doctors, lawyers, or auto mechanics. Individuals also are likely to seek others' advice in selecting a restaurant for a special occasion or deciding which movie to see.[43]

Opinion Leaders

opinion leaders
Group leaders who influence others.

Reference groups frequently include individuals known as group leaders or **opinion leaders,** those who influence others. Obviously, it is important for marketing managers to persuade such people to purchase their goods or services. Many products and services that are integral parts of Americans' lives today got their initial boost from these influential opinion leaders. For example, VCRs were embraced by opinion leaders well ahead of the general public. Opinion leaders were also among the first to turn sport-utility vehicles and light trucks into the "family vehicle" of the 1990s.[44]

Opinion leaders are often the first to try new products and services out of pure curiosity. They are typically activists in their communities, on the job, and in the marketplace. Furthermore, opinion leaders tend to be self-indulgent which makes them more likely to explore unproven but intriguing products and services. This combination of curiosity, activism, and self-indulgence makes opinion leaders trendsetters in the consumer marketplace.[45] Exhibit 6.7 lists some products and services about which individuals often seek the advice of an opinion leader before purchasing.

Opinion leadership is a casual, face-to-face phenomenon and is usually very inconspicuous, so locating opinion leaders can be a challenge. Thus, marketers often try to create opinion leaders. They may use high school cheerleaders to model new fall fashions or civic leaders to promote insurance, new cars, and other merchandise.

Exhibit 6.7
Words of Wisdom: Opinion Leaders' Consumer Clout Extends Far Beyond Their Own Purchases

(average number of people to whom opinion leaders recommended products* in the past year, and millions of recommendations made, 1995)		
	Average Number of Recommendations	**Millions of Recommendations Made**
Restaurant	5.0	70
Vacation destination	5.1	44
TV show	4.9	45
Car	4.1	29
Retail store	4.7	29
Clothing	4.5	24
Consumer electronics	4.5	16
Office equipment	5.8	12
Stock, mutual fund, CD, etc.	3.4	12

*Among those who recommended the product at all.
Source: Roper Starch Worldwide, Inc., New York, NY. Adapted from "Maximizing the Market with Influentials, *American Demographics,* July 1995, p. 42.

On a national level, companies sometimes use movie stars, sports figures, and other celebrities to promote products, hoping they are appropriate opinion leaders. Popular celebrity endorsers include Candice Bergen, Michael Jordan, Bill Cosby, Shaquille O'Neal, Elizabeth Taylor, Joe Montana, and Cindy Crawford.[46]

The effectiveness of celebrity endorsements depends largely on how credible and attractive the spokesperson is and how familiar people are with him or her. Endorsements are most likely to succeed if an association between the spokesperson and the product can be established. For example, comedian Bill Cosby failed as an endorser for financial products but succeeded with such products as Kodak cameras and Jell-O gelatin. Consumers could not mentally link Bill Cosby with serious investment decisions but could associate him with leisure activities and everyday consumption. Additionally, in the selection of a celebrity endorser, marketers must consider the broader meanings associated with the endorser. Although the endorser may have certain attributes that are desirable for endorsing the product, he or she may also have other attributes that are inappropriate.

A marketing manager can also try to use opinion leaders through group sanctioning or referrals. For example, some companies sell products endorsed by the American Heart Association or the American Cancer Society. McNeil Consumer Products, for instance, joined forces with the Arthritis Foundation to launch the Arthritis Foundation line of pain relievers which quickly jumped to the number one selling pain reliever in the over-the-counter arthritis segment. McNeil and the Arthritis Foundation both saw a unique opportunity to reach the millions of Americans living with the disease.[47] Marketers also seek endorsements from schools, churches, cities, the military, and fraternal organizations as a form of group opinion leadership. Salespeople often ask to use opinion leaders' names as a means of achieving greater personal influence in a sales presentation.

Family

The family is the most important social institution for many consumers, strongly influencing values, attitudes, self-concept—and buying behavior. For example, a family that strongly values good health will have a grocery list distinctly different from that of a family that views every dinner as a gourmet event. Moreover, the family is responsible for the **socialization process,** the passing down of cultural values and norms to children. Children learn by observing their parents' consumption patterns, and so they will tend to shop in a similar pattern.

socialization process
Passing down cultural values and norms to children.

Decision-making roles among family members tend to vary significantly, depending on the type of item purchased. Family members assume a variety of roles in the purchase process. *Initiators* are the ones who suggest, initiate, or plant the seed for the purchase process. The initiator can be any member of the family. For example, Sister might initiate the product search by asking for a new bicycle as a birthday present. *Influencers* are those members of the family whose opinions are valued. In our example, Mom might function as a price-range watchdog, an influencer whose main role is to veto or approve price ranges. Brother may give his opinion on certain makes of bicycles. The *decision maker* is the member of the family who actually makes the decision to buy or not to buy. For example, Dad may choose the final brand and model of bicycle to buy after seeking further information from Sister about cosmetic features such as color and imposing additional criteria of his own, such as durability and safety. The *purchaser* (probably Dad or Mom) is the one who actually exchanges money for the product. Finally, the *consumer* is the actual user—Sister, in the case of the bicycle.

Marketers should consider family purchase situations along with the distribution of consumer and decision-maker roles among family members. Ordinary marketing views the individual as both decision maker and consumer. Family marketing adds

Exhibit 6.8

*Relationships Among
Purchasers and
Consumers in the Family*

		Purchase decision maker		
		One member	Some members	All members
Consumer	One member	1	2 Tennis racquet	3
	Some members	4 Sugar pops	5	6
	All members	7	8	9 Refrigerator

Source: Robert Boutilier, "Pulling the Family's Strings," *American Demographics,* August 1993, p. 46. Source: American Demographics magazine © 1993. Reprinted with permission.

three other possibilities: Sometimes more than one decision maker is involved; sometimes more than one consumer is involved; and sometimes the decision maker and the consumer are different people. Exhibit 6.8 represents the nine patterns of family purchasing relationships that are possible.[48]

Children today can have great influence over the purchase decisions of their parents. In many families, with both parents working and short on time, children may be encouraged to participate. In addition, children in single-parent households become more involved in family decision making at an earlier age than children in two-parent households. Children are especially influential in decisions about food. Children often help decide where the family goes for fast food, and many kids influence the choice of a full-service restaurant. Kids have input into the kinds of food the family eats at home as well, and many even influence the specific brands their parents buy. Finally, children influence purchase decisions for toys, clothes, vacations, recreation, and automobiles, even though they are usually not the actual purchasers of such items.

Family Life Cycle

The life-cycle stage of a family can also have a significant impact on consumer behavior. As Chapter 8 explains in more detail, the family life cycle is an orderly series of stages through which consumers' attitudes and behavioral tendencies evolve, through maturity, experience, and changing income and status.

Marketers often define their target markets in terms of family life cycle. For instance, young singles spend more than average on alcoholic beverages, education, and entertainment. New parents typically increase their spending on health care, clothing, housing, and food, while they decrease their spending on alcohol, education, and transportation. Households with older children spend more on food, entertainment, personal care products, and education, as well as cars and gasoline. After their children leave home, spending by older couples on vehicles, women's clothing, health care, and long-distance calls typically increases. Marketers should also be aware of the many nontraditional life-cycle paths that are common today, which provide insights into the needs and wants of such consumers as divorced parents, lifelong singles, and childless couples.

Social Class

The United States, like other societies, does have a social class system. A **social class** is a group of people who are considered nearly equal in status or community esteem, who regularly socialize among themselves both formally and informally, and who share behavioral norms.

social class
A group of people who are considered nearly equal in status or community esteem, who regularly socialize among themselves both formally and informally, and who share behavioral norms.

Exhibit 6.9
U.S. Social Classes

Upper classes Capitalist class	1%	People whose investment decisions shape the national economy; income mostly from assets, earned or inherited; university connections
Upper middle class	14%	Upper-level managers, professionals, owners of medium-sized businesses; college educated; family income nearly twice national average
Middle classes Middle class	33%	Middle-level white-collar, top-level blue-collar; education past high school typical; income somewhat above national average
Working class	32%	Middle-level blue-collar, lower-level white-collar; income slightly below national average
Lower classes Working poor	11–12%	Low-paid service workers and operatives; some high school education; below mainstream in living standard but above poverty line
Underclass	8–9%	People who are not regularly employed and who depend primarily on the welfare system for sustenance; little schooling; living standard below poverty line

Source: Adapted from Richard P. Coleman, "The Continuing Significance of Social Class to Marketing," *Journal of Consumer Research,* December 1983, p. 267; Dennis Gilbert and Joseph A. Kahl, *The American Class Structure: A Synthesis* (Homewood, IL: Dorsey Press, 1982), Ch. 11.

A number of techniques have been used to measure social class, and a number of criteria have been used to define it. One view of contemporary U.S. status structure is shown in Exhibit 6.9. Here are some additional observations about members of these classes:

- *Upper classes:* The upper classes consist of the very rich and the well-to-do. Upper-class individuals seem to think of themselves as nice-looking people and are concerned with personal appearance. They are more confident, outgoing, and culturally oriented than people of other social classes. They also seem a bit more permissive and are willing to tolerate alternative views. The upper social classes are more likely than other classes to try to contribute something to society—for example, by government service, volunteer work for charitable organizations, or active participation in civic affairs. In terms of consumer buying patterns, the affluent are more likely to own their own home and purchase new cars and trucks and are less likely to smoke. The very rich flex their financial muscles by spending more on owned vacation homes, vacations and cruises, and housekeeping and gardening services.[49]

- *Middle classes:* Middle-class consumers have a much different perspective on life. Attaining goals and achieving status and prestige are important. Compared with the lower classes, members of the middle classes have a stronger orientation outward, toward society in general and toward peers in particular. Apparently, the middle-class lifestyle is more dynamic than the relatively static lifestyle of the lower classes. Educational attainment seems to have the biggest impact on a person's social and economic status, with those people with some college experience but no degree falling closest to traditional concepts of the middle class. People falling into the middle class live in the gap between the haves and have-nots. They aspire to the lifestyle of the more affluent, but are constrained by the economic realities and cautious attitudes they share with the working class.[50]

The working class is a distinct subclass of the middle class. The working-class person depends heavily on relatives and community for economic and emotional support. Members of this social subclass rely on relatives for tips on job opportunities, for advice on purchases, and for help in times of trouble. The emphasis on family ties is one sign of this group's intensely local view of the world. For instance, working-class people like the local news far more than do middle-class audiences, who show more enthusiasm for national and world coverage. Working-class people also vacation closer to home and are more likely to visit relatives when they go on vacation.

- *Lower classes:* Lower-class members typically fall at or below the poverty level. This social class has the highest unemployment rate, and many individuals or families are subsidized through the welfare system. Many are illiterate, with little formal education. Lower-class members also have poorer physical and mental health and a shorter life span than members of other classes. Compared to more affluent consumers, lower-class consumers have poorer diets and typically purchase much different types of foods when they shop.

Lifestyle distinctions between the social classes are greater than the distinctions within a given class. The most significant separation between the classes is the one between the middle and lower classes. It is here that the major shift in lifestyles appears.

Marketers are interested in social class for two main reasons. First, social class often indicates which medium to use for advertising. Suppose an insurance company seeks to sell its policies to middle-class families. It might advertise during the local evening news because middle-class families tend to watch more television than other classes do. If the company wants to sell more policies to upscale individuals, it might place a print ad in a business publication like *The Wall Street Journal,* which is read by more educated and affluent people.

Second, social class may also tell marketers where certain types of consumers shop. Wealthy, upper-class shoppers tend to frequent expensive stores, places where members of the other classes might feel uncomfortable. Marketers also know that middle-class consumers regularly visit shopping malls. Therefore, marketers with products to sell to the middle class may decide to distribute their merchandise through malls.

Broad social class categories are becoming less useful to marketers as indicators of purchase behavior. One of the reasons seems to be the fragmentation of U.S. society into scores of distinct subgroups, each with unique tastes and yearnings. Recent economic trends have also added to the disintegration of broad class structures. Many thousands of the jobs that provided for a comfortable middle-class lifestyle, as well as long-term income security, have simply vanished. As a result, subgroups have formed within the vast middle class, each defined by different opportunities, expectations, and outlooks.[51]

While social class is becoming less of an indicator of purchase behavior in U.S. markets, in many overseas markets, social class has become a key determinant. Russia's transition to a market economy, for instance, has created a distinct class structure with upper-, middle-, and lower-class markets. While the super-rich who capitalized on the emerging market's opportunities appeared almost instantly, lately there are a surprising number of Russians who, despite high inflation and a weak currency, are working harder, earning more, and living better. These middle-class Russians are buying consumer goods ranging from television sets to automatic bread makers and are bolstering Russia's political and economic stability. At the core of Russia's new middle class are its young professionals and small business owners in the big cities. Russia's middle class has become the prime target for consumer goods marketers, such as Sony Corporation of Japan, which expects Russia to soon become its largest European market for color television sets.[52]

Marketing and Small Business

Selling to Multicultural Markets

While a lot has been said about understanding unique cultures and subcultures and tailoring marketing efforts to these particular groups, many small businesses cannot afford multiple marketing and advertising campaigns if their target market crosses cultural and subcultural lines. Unlike large national marketers with unlimited dollars to throw at their target markets, small businesses are particularly known for tight marketing and advertising budgets. Therefore, separate targeted marketing approaches specifically geared to each diverse group are generally out of the question for the small business owner.

Understanding what people have in common, therefore, may be as vital to small businesses as understanding their differences. A person's national origin or ethnic self-identification are important, but they may not necessarily bind that person to a group as much as the attitudes and lifestyles that arise from those backgrounds. Social values, methods of communication, and common interests can cross cultural boundaries. When marketing across cultures and subcultures, it helps if small businesses understand the common ground that racial and ethnic groups share without losing sight of their differences. In this way, instead of pursuing different approaches for each subculture being targeted, a small marketer can promote to a broad group of consumers with a singular approach.

Understanding their customers' cultural values is the first step small business owners can take to bridge the cultural gaps in their marketing. Conducting good research or getting access to recent marketing studies or statistics can help small marketers address the common aspects and differences in a target audience. For example, research reveals that Hispanic, African-American, and Asian-American communities value extended families, with grandparents especially revered. Religion and church-going are also an essential part of African-American and Hispanic subcultures. Marketing across these different subcultural groups could be tied together into one effort by using family or religious themes.

The second step is for the small business owner to understand its multicultural market's media behavior. Small businesses marketing to diverse groups should also consider multiple media channels as well as promotion that impacts multiple senses. Because some groups respond better to mass media and others respond to specialized media, using both can reach the widest possible audience. Additionally, some cultures have strong oral traditions, while others are more comfortable with written messages. Multicultural advertising should use a mix of pictures, sounds, and words to make its point. This usually means a blend of broadcast and print media.

It is also important to choose the right message and deliver it the right way when marketing across multicultural groups. Storytelling, for example, is a universal format of communication that transcends all cultures. Stories serve as a shorthand way to reference universal myths by bringing familiar stories to modern, everyday life. Small businesses can use storytellers who are local entertainers or dignitaries to convey a positive image across a broad group of consumers. When a small business wants to communicate with both specific and broad audiences at the same time, it might consider a layered message approach of using a local celebrity who is identified with a particular culture but who can also relate to all cultures. For example, a public-service announcement wanted to target black women at high risk of breast cancer without implying that the problem is limited to this group. The solution was to recruit a popular black recording artist who told a personal story about her family's experience with cancer.[53]

What could small businesses do to generate "word-of-mouth" promotion of their business to customers? What are some other ways that small businesses can effectively compete to sell to multicultural markets?

KEY TERMS

LOOKING BACK

Returning to the discussion that opened the chapter, you should now be able to see how individual and social factors affect the consumer decision-making process. In the vignette, you saw how Coca-Cola is capitalizing on the perceptions that consumers have worldwide about its packaging, in particular with its signature contour-shaped bottle. Specifically, through savvy marketing and advertising the company is attempting to increase sales of Coke around the world based on perceptions consumers hold about Coke's bottle that transcend to the benefits of the product inside. Consumer decision making is a fascinating and often intricate process. An appreciation of consumer behavior and the factors that influence it will help you identify target markets and design effective marketing mixes.

SUMMARY

1 *Explain why marketing managers should understand consumer behavior.* Consumer behavior describes how consumers make purchase decisions and how they use and dispose of the products they buy. An understanding of consumer behavior reduces marketing managers' uncertainty when they are defining a target market and designing a marketing mix.

2 *Analyze the components of the consumer decision-making process.* The consumer decision-making process begins with problem recognition, when stimuli trigger awareness of an unfulfilled want. If additional information is required to make a purchase decision, the consumer may engage in an internal or external information search. The consumer then evaluates the additional information and establishes purchase guidelines. Finally, a purchase decision is made.

3 *Explain the consumer's postpurchase evaluation process.* Consumer postpurchase evaluation is influenced by prepurchase expectations, the prepurchase information search, and the consumer's general level of self-confidence. Cognitive dissonance is the inner tension that a consumer experiences after recognizing a purchased product's disadvantages. When a purchase creates cognitive dissonance, consumers tend to react by seeking positive reinforcement for the purchase decision, avoiding negative information about the purchase decision, or revoking the purchase decision by returning the product.

4 *Identify the types of consumer buying decisions and discuss the significance of consumer involvement.* Consumer decision making falls into three broad categories. First, consumers exhibit routine response behavior for frequently purchased, low-cost items that require very little decision effort; routine response behavior is typically characterized by brand loyalty. Second, consumers engage in limited decision making for occasional purchases or for unfamiliar brands in familiar product categories. Third, consumers practice extensive decision making when making unfamiliar, expensive, or infrequent purchases. High-involvement decisions usually include an extensive information search and a thorough evaluation of alternatives. In contrast, low-involvement decisions are characterized by brand loyalty and a lack of personal identification with the product. The main factors affecting the level of consumer involvement are price, interest, perceived risk of negative consequences, situation, and social visibility.

5 *Identify and understand the individual factors that affect consumer buying decisions.* Individual factors include perception; motivation; learning; values, beliefs, and attitudes; and personality, self-concept, and lifestyle. Perception allows consumers to recognize their consumption problems. Motivation is what drives consumers to take action to satisfy specific consumption needs. Almost all consumer behavior results from learning, which is the process that creates changes in behavior through experience. Consumers with similar values, beliefs, and attitudes tend to react alike to marketing-related inducements. Finally, certain products and brands reflect consumers' personality, self-concept, and lifestyle.

6 *Identify and understand the social factors that affect consumer buying decisions.* Social factors include such external influences as reference groups, opinion leaders, family, family life cycle, social class, culture, and subculture. Consumers may use products or brands to identify with or become a member of a reference group. Opinion leaders are members of reference groups who influence others' purchase decisions. Family members also influence purchase decisions; children tend to shop in patterns similar to their parents'. Marketers often define their target markets in terms of consumers' life cycle stage, social class, culture, and subculture; consumers with similar characteristics generally have similar consumption patterns. Because all consumer behavior is shaped by individual and social factors, the main goal of marketing strategy is to understand and influence them.

Discussion and Writing Questions

1. Describe the three categories of consumer decision-making behavior. Name typical products for which each type of consumer behavior is used.

2. The type of decision making a consumer uses for a product does not necessarily remain constant. Why? Support your answer with an example from your own experience.

3. How do beliefs and attitudes influence consumer behavior? How can negative attitudes toward a product be changed? How can marketers alter beliefs about a product? Give some examples of how marketers have changed negative attitudes about a product or added or altered beliefs about a product.

4. Recall an occasion when you experienced cognitive dissonance about a purchase. In a letter to a friend, describe the event and explain what you did about it.

5. Family members play many different roles in the buying process: initiator, influencer, decision maker, purchaser, and consumer.

In your family, name who might play each of these roles in the purchase of a personal computer system, Froot Loops breakfast cereal, Calvin Klein Obsession cologne for men, and dinner at McDonald's.

6. You are a new marketing manager for a firm that produces a line of athletic shoes to be targeted to the college-student subculture. For your boss, write a memo listing some product attributes that might appeal to this subculture and recommend some marketing strategies.

7. With three other team members chosen from your class, identify a product that you want to research. Brainstorm with your group and first identify two or three competitive brands for your product. Then agree on how buyers decide to buy one of the competitive brands instead of the others. That is, what is the decision process for deciding to purchase one brand over the others. Then select several stores that sell one or more of the brands and interview the managers to get their input on what they think the decision process is

for your product/brands. Prepare a report that describes the decision process for the product/brands, including relevant individual and social factors, and present it to the class.

8. Discuss Toyota's online magazines. How is Toyota using these publications to increase customer involvement?

http://www.toyota.com/

9. How does the following Web site use "Personal Notification" to simplify the process of purchasing books?

http://www.amazon.com/

 Application for Small Business

Jamie's World Class Bicycles is located about three blocks from the university campus. There are several other bicycle shops within a 5-mile radius of the university, but Jamie's is the closest. About 40 percent of his business comes from students at the university and the remainder comes from the surrounding community residents. His major competitor is about seven blocks from campus but attracts more students to his store.

The brands of mountain bikes Jamie carries include Gary Fisher, Cannondale, and Kona. His competitor carries the same brands of mountain bikes plus two others: Raleigh and Marin. His competitor also carries three lines of road bikes. Jamie's strategy is a limited number of high-quality mountain bikes, knowledgeable salespeople, and quick repairs. His competitor has more brands and types of bikes and has been in business five years longer.

Questions

1. What factors do students consider when deciding which store to purchase a bicycle from? What factors do they consider when deciding on a particular brand of bicycle to purchase?

2. What can Jamie do to attract more students to his bike shop?

Video Case

Community Coffee
Ch. 6

Community Coffee Pursues the Gourmet Coffee Market

Community Coffee Company was founded by Henry Norman "Cap" Saurage in a little country store in Baton Rouge, Louisiana, in 1919. As a neighborhood grocer, Cap was very particular about the quality of his goods. To make sure that he provided only the tastiest coffee, he bought freshly roasted beans from New Orleans, blended them using his own secret recipe, ground and packaged the coffee by hand, and had it delivered to customers by horse-drawn wagon. Cap's friends and coffee customers in the local "community" liked his coffee so much that he named it Community® coffee in their honor.

Soon, Cap's coffee was so popular that he could no longer personally grind and package enough to meet the demand. In 1924, he closed his store, converted an old barn into a packaging plant and constructed the Baton Rouge Coffee Mill (right in his own backyard), and devoted himself to making Community coffee truly part of the local flavor.

From its humble beginnings, Community has grown to be the largest family-owned retail coffee brand in America. Today it offers many choices in ground coffee roasts and blends, as well as whole-bean gourmet coffees and teas. Community's market area spans a six-state region from Texas to western Florida. The company's share of the coffee market in south Louisiana exceeds 70 percent and, as a premium-positioned brand, the secret formulation behind its coffees has earned it a reputation throughout Louisiana as the "State Coffee of Louisiana." From coffee plantations around the globe, coffee beans are still chosen personally and hand-inspected when they arrive in the United States. In the tradition of Cap Saurage, highly knowledgeable experts taste every batch of coffee before Community will allow a single package to be delivered to retailers.

An important recent trend in the coffee category is the retail gourmet coffee market. Gourmet coffees are drawing new consumers and dollars and are the only growth segment in the coffee category. Indeed, the retail gourmet coffee market is big and growing rapidly, from about $1.5 billion in 1996 to an estimated $3.0 billion by the year 2000.

To better understand the gourmet coffee market, Community Coffee used input and research from consumers, grocery customers, and independent market research service companies. The specific objectives of the research were to identify any perceived problems associated with the current retail method of selling gourmet coffees and to develop a profile of potential customers. The research identified three problems to overcome. The first was freshness. Consumers perceived that gourmet coffee purchased in supermarkets was not as fresh as they would like it to be. A second problem was contamination. The current method of selling gourmet coffee in supermarkets involved grinding all coffees in the same grinder, thus resulting in a contamination problem by mixing trace amounts of different coffee flavors in each bag. The third problem was education. Consumers generally knew very little about the quality and flavor varieties of gourmet coffees.

The profile of potential gourmet coffee users is shown in Exhibit 6.10. The research also determined that the "whole experience," from purchase to preparation to consumption, is what motivates potential customers to purchase gourmet coffee.

To solve these problems and take advantage of this rapidly expanding market opportunity, Community Coffee developed the Fresh-O-Lator,™ a gourmet coffee dispensing system, for its Private Reserve® gourmet line of coffees. The Fresh-O-Lator gourmet coffee dispensing system is the first of its kind *ever* in grocery stores, with patent pending vacuum sealing

Exhibit 6.10

Who Is the Gourmet Coffee User?

- Age 25–44 years, primarily female
- College educated
- Employed full time
- High discretionary incomes
- Light TV watchers → heavy readers
- Consume specialty and gourmet products

technology to deliver the freshest, tastiest coffee beans possible, and a state-of-the art interactive computer and grinding machines for both flavored and nonflavored coffees. Flavored and unflavored coffees each have a separate in-store grinder which reduces flavor contamination possibilities and enhances the quality and value of all Private Reserve coffees.

The Fresh-O-Lator system ensures that the coffees are vacuum sealed and tamper-proof. The Fresh-O-Lator Gourmet Coffee Dispensing System is the only in-store coffee system that's completely tamper-proof, thus rendering the present whole-bean merchandising environment of potentially unsanitary, unsafe, and unsavory conditions obsolete. As Pat Pettijohn, president and CEO says, "This revolutionary system *guarantees* that our tantalizing, freshly roasted gourmet coffee beans stay in an airtight environment. This means better-tasting coffee. The 'Whooshing' sound the customer hears when turning the Fresh-O-Lator dispensing system's knob is the vacuum seal breaking to allow fresh beans to pour out. Each individually vacuumed cylinder instantly reseals after the customer releases the fully turned knob."

A consumer friendly audio-visual terminal built into the Fresh-O-Lator whole bean merchandiser allows customers to "shop the world" for just the "right" coffee. Recommendations are made by flavor, occasion, caffeinated or decaffeinated, country of origin, and so on, with a brief descriptive message that explains the special attributes of the selected beans.

As a premium coffee roaster with

Exhibit 6.11
Benefits of the Fresh-O-Lator Dispenser

- Largest selection of highest quality, 100% Arabica blended varietals, unblended varietals, flavored, and decaffeinated coffees
- Bulk whole beans (flavored, unflavored, decafs)
- Packaged whole beans (flavored, unflavored, decafs)
- Packaged ground roast flavored coffees
- Trial-size flavored coffees

over 77 years of supply relationships with top coffee producers throughout the world, Community Coffee offers superior product quality and selections via its Private Reserve Gourmet Coffee Collection of whole bean and ground coffees from over 17 countries of origin. Specific benefits of the Fresh-O-Lator in-store dispenser are shown in Exhibit 6.11.

To promote acceptance by supermarket chains, Community Coffee offered the following marketing support:

- *Co-op Marketing Funds*—Designed to generate consumer trial and involvement at the point of sale.
  - Funds generated by pound volume sold from each unit.
  - Marketing spending activity mutually agreed to by chain customers and Community Coffee Co. (account-specific marketing)
  - Focus of activities is on "direct involvement" with the end consumer.
- *Comprehensive Public Relations Program*—Targeted at creating consumer awareness of the Fresh-O-Lator's competitive points of difference (vacuum sealed/tamper-proof/computer-interactive/product quality/product selection)

- Tailored to each major marketing area where sufficient "mass" has been achieved.
- Uses all available media sources (print publications/radio/television).
- *Aggressive and Comprehensive Wet Sampling*—Conducted by Community-trained personnel who are knowledgeable about both the product they are serving and the operation and benefits of the Fresh-O-Lator system.
- Extensive use of coupons to stimulate consumer purchase after the sampling event.

Initial reactions by potential customers to the campaign were quite favorable.

Questions

1. Is gourmet coffee a high-involvement or low-involvement purchase process?
2. How might individual factors affect the decision to purchase gourmet coffee?
3. Which social factors would affect the purchase of gourmet coffee and why?
4. Is Community Coffee's Fresh-O-Lator in-store dispenser an effective way to penetrate this market?

1 Describe business-to-business marketing.

2 Discuss the role of relationship marketing and strategic alliances in business-to-business marketing.

3 Identify the four major categories of business-market customers.

4 Explain the standard industrial classification system.

5 Explain the major differences between business-to-business and consumer markets.

6 Describe the seven types of business-to-business goods and services.

7 Discuss the unique aspects of business-to-business buying behavior.

Chapter 7

Business-to-Business Marketing

erramarine Bioresearch, Inc., a small (less than 25 employees) high-tech biochemical firm located in San Diego County, California, was founded by a number of biochemists who wanted to find commercial applications for their biochemical expertise. Management decided to concentrate its efforts on producing diagnostic reagent chemicals that would be sold to manufacturers of blood-testing instruments. The idea was that Terramarine could become a subcontractor to the large instrument manufacturers. But success was slow in coming. After five years, the company had but two customers, both of whom had called on Terramarine thinking the company was a possible customer only to find it to be a supplier. Purchases by these two customers kept the firm in existence but little more. Then management learned of the Standard Industrial Classification (SIC) system.

After recognizing that the SIC could contribute to future marketing activities, Terramarine used Dun & Bradstreet's *Million Dollar Directory* and Standard and Poor's *Poor's Register* to find which SIC number was assigned to its two customers.

Both were listed under SIC 3821. Then, using the *Census of Manufactures and U.S. Industrial Outlook,* it was discovered that 346 firms in the United States were classified by this code. From those same sources and Sales & Marketing Management's *Survey of Industrial and Commercial Buying Power,* the company was also able to determine where these firms were located.

Through the *Million Dollar Directory,* the *Poor's Registry,* and industrial directories in states where concentrations of potential customers were located, Terramarine found company addresses, telephone numbers, and names of key executives. Using this list, the company passed on the information to its salespeople in the field. It also sent direct-mail

pieces to each prospect and called the larger prospects to arrange for possible sales calls. The end result of this very economical program was that the company discovered prospects previously unknown and built its marketing programs to attract these same prospects. Thus, use of the SIC system facilitated the development of a more focused and cost-effective marketing plan.[1]

 Dun & Bradstreet, Inc.
Standard & Poor's Equity Investor Services
What information can you access here that would be helpful in making marketing decisions? What can you learn about existing businesses?
http://www.dnb.com/
http://www.stockinfo.standardpoor. com/

WHAT IS BUSINESS-TO-BUSINESS MARKETING?

1 Describe business-to-business marketing.

business-to-business marketing
The marketing of goods and services to individuals and organizations for purposes other than personal consumption.

Business-to-business marketing is the marketing of goods and services to individuals and organizations for purposes other than personal consumption. The sale of an overhead projector to your college or university is an example of business-to-business marketing. Business-to-business products include those that are used to manufacture other products, that become part of another product, that aid the normal operations of an organization, or that are acquired for resale without any substantial change in form. The key characteristic distinguishing business-to-business products from consumer products is intended use, not physical characteristics. A product that is purchased for personal or family consumption or as a gift is a consumer good. If that same product, such as a microcomputer or a cellular telephone, is bought for use in a business, it is a business-to-business product.

RELATIONSHIP MARKETING AND STRATEGIC ALLIANCES

2 Discuss the role of relationship marketing and strategic alliances in business-to-business marketing.

As Chapter 1 explained, relationship marketing is the strategy that entails seeking and establishing ongoing partnerships with customers. Relationship marketing is redefining the fundamental roles of business buyers and sellers. Suppliers are making major adjustments in their thinking, management styles, and methods of responding to purchaser's standards and operational requirements. A satisfied customer is among the best sources of new business. That's because the customer knows that the supplier can meet expectations and deliver on what it promises, creating trust. And, trust is the foundation of most successful relationship marketing efforts.[2] Relationship marketing is not a faddish trend but rather is driven by strong business forces: the competitive need for quality, speed, and cost-effectiveness, as well as new design techniques.[3]

strategic alliance (strategic partnership)
A cooperative agreement between business firms.

A **strategic alliance,** sometimes called a strategic partnership, is a cooperative agreement between business firms. Strategic alliances can take the form of licensing or distribution agreements, joint ventures, research and development consortia, and

Dell's computers are marketed to businesses to aid in their normal day-to-day operation. The computers are not for personal use or resale.

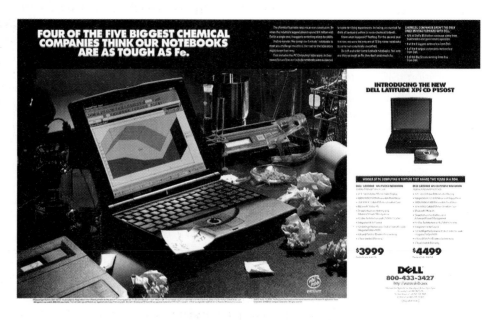

partnerships. They may be between manufacturers, between manufacturers and customers, between manufacturers and suppliers, and between manufacturers and channel intermediaries.

The trend toward forming strategic alliances is accelerating rapidly, particularly among high-tech firms. These companies have realized that strategic partnerships are more than just important—they are critical. Xerox management, for example, has decided that in order to maintain its leadership position in the reprographics industry, the company must "include suppliers as part of the Xerox family."[4] This strategy often means reducing the number of suppliers, treating those that remain as allies, sharing strategic information freely, and drawing on supplier expertise in developing new products that can meet the quality, cost, and delivery standards of the marketplace.

Business-to-business marketers form strategic alliances to achieve a variety of short- and long-term goals. Exhibit 7.1 identifies eight strategic reasons for companies to enter into strategic alliances.

Some strategic alliances are extremely successful and some are dismal failures. Four factors that clearly contribute to successful alliances are:[5]

Now Avis Offers Triple Miles

The employees of Avis introduce a future with more frequent flyer miles. When you fly any of these 10 major airlines, you can multiply the frequent flyer rental miles you would normally receive from Avis. You'll get **TRIPLE MILES** when you rent for a week and **DOUBLE MILES** with weekend rentals.* An advance reservation is required, and other restrictions apply. For more information and reservations, call Avis at **1-800-831-8000**, or call your travel consultant today. You can also visit us at the Avis Galaxy Web site, **http://www.avis.com**.

AVIS We try harder.®

As shown in this ad, Avis has a strategic alliance with several airlines; customers even earn frequent flyer miles when they rent Avis cars.

Courtesy Avis, Inc.

- *Choosing the right partner.* The right partner usually has some unique capability to contribute to the alliance, such as access to information, technology, or markets.

- *Creating a cooperative process.* A variety of sources, particularly those actually involved in managing strategic alliances, identify cooperation between partners as a key element of successful alliances.

- *Creating an accountability structure.* Someone within each organization must be responsible for making sure the alliance thrives and problems are resolved in an equitable and timely manner.

- *Observing and controlling bargaining positions.* Fully understanding one's own company's bargaining position is one of the strongest control mechanisms in developing and maintaining strategic alliances. Bargaining positions are based on knowing the other party's interests, long-term strategy, and possible options.

---

1. Reducing risks and costs of entering new markets.
2. Filling gaps in current market and technological bases.
3. Turning excess manufacturing capacity into profits.
4. Accelerating new product introductions.
5. Overcoming legal and trade barriers.
6. Extending the scope of existing operations.
7. Cutting costs when divesting operations.
8. Production economies of scale.

Exhibit 7.1
Frequently Cited Strategic Alliance Goals

Source: From "Strategic Alliances: Partnering for Success" by Julie Cohen Mason. Reprinted by permission of the publisher from *Management Review*, May 1993. Copyright © 1993, American Management Association, New York. All rights reserved.

Many strategic alliances fail to produce the benefits expected by the partners. Three general problems have been identified:

- Partners are often organized quite differently, complicating marketing and design decisions and creating problems in coordinating actions and establishing trust.

- Partners that work together well in one country may be poorly equipped to support each other in other countries, leading to problems in global alliances.

- Because of the quick pace of technological change, the most attractive partner today may not be the most attractive partner tomorrow, leading to problems in maintaining alliances over time.[6]

IBM
How does IBM market solutions to businesses? Compare solutions for larger industries with small and medium-sized enterprises. How do they differ?

http://www.ibm.com/

Strategic alliances often involve multinational partnerships. In Japan, IBM has a strategic alliance with Ricoh to distribute low-end computers and with Fuji Bank to market financial systems. IBM has similar links with other Japanese firms. Ford and Mazda have collaborated on at least 10 models. According to *Business Week*, at least a quarter of the Fords and Mazdas sold in the United States have benefited in some way from this successful strategic alliance.[7] The Global Perspectives box provides an example of strategic alliances between a U.S. manufacturer and six Asian producers of home appliances.

Global Perspectives

Whirlpool Ventures into a New Frontier

Between 1994 and 1996, Whirlpool Corp. spent $265 million to buy controlling interest in four competitors in China and two in India. Eventually, Whirlpool hopes to become one of Asia's top suppliers of washers, dryers, dishwashers, refrigerators, and household air conditioners.

According to *The Wall Street Journal*, Whirlpool management believes that the combination of Asia's fast growth and low proportion of households with modern appliances provides very promising market opportunities. For example, China has a population of over one billion people, but less than 10 percent of all households in China have air conditioners, microwave ovens, and clothes washers.

Whirlpool also hopes to export appliances manufactured in China to other Asian countries. In order to successfully implement this strategy, Whirlpool must substantially upgrade the quality of its joint venture partners' products. According to Whirlpool executives, the Chinese brands are not as reliable and durable as available Japanese brands. Typical air conditioners manufactured by Chinese partner firms last only five to eight years, which is half the life expectancy of a Whirlpool unit made in the United States. Whirlpool president

and CEO William Marohn was quoted in *The Wall Street Journal* as saying, "Until we have a product that we can feel represents a modern, upscale product, we're not going to put the Whirlpool name on it."

Why would Whirlpool invest $265 million just to buy partial ownership in Chinese companies that produce inferior products? Why not just export products made in the United States to Asia or build Whirlpool manufacturing facilities in China and elsewhere? Assess the Whirlpool joint ventures in terms of the general strategic alliance goals, factors that contribute to successful alliances, and the three general problems that commonly plague strategic alliances.[8]

MAJOR CATEGORIES OF BUSINESS-TO-BUSINESS CUSTOMERS

The business-to-business market consists of four major categories of customers: producers, resellers, governments, and institutions.

3 Identify the four major categories of business-market customers.

Producers

The producer segment of the business-to-business market includes profit-oriented individuals and organizations that use purchased goods and services to produce other products, to incorporate into other products, or to facilitate the daily operations of the organization. Examples of producers include construction, manufacturing, transportation, finance, real estate, and food service firms. In the United States there are over 13 million firms in the producer segment of the business-to-business market. Some of these firms are quite small and others are among the world's largest businesses.

Individual producers often buy large quantities of goods and services. Companies like General Motors spend more than $50 billion annually—more than the gross domestic product of Ireland, Portugal, Turkey, or Greece—on such business products as steel, metal components, and tires. Companies like AT&T and IBM spend over $50 million daily for business goods and services, such as computer chips and parts.[9]

Resellers

The reseller market includes retail and wholesale businesses that buy finished goods and resell them for a profit. A retailer sells mainly to final consumers; wholesalers sell mostly to retailers and other organizational customers. There are approximately 1.5 million retailers and 500,000 wholesalers operating in the United States. Consumer product firms like Procter & Gamble, Kraft General Foods, and Coca-Cola sell directly to large retailers and retail chains and through wholesalers to smaller retail units. Retailing and wholesaling are explored in detail in Chapter 15.

Retail and wholesale clothing stores are part of the reseller market because they buy finished goods and sell them to consumers.
© 1996 PhotoDisc, Inc.

Business product distributors are wholesalers that buy business products and resell them to business customers. They often carry thousands of items in stock and employ sales forces to call on business customers. Businesses that wish to buy a gross of pencils or 100 pounds of fertilizer typically purchase these items from local distributors rather than directly from manufacturers such as Empire Pencil or Dow Chemical.

Governments

A third major segment of the business-to-business market is government. Government organizations include thousands of federal, state, and local buying units. They make up what may be the largest single market for goods and services in the world.

Contracts for government purchases are often put out for bid. Interested vendors submit bids (usually sealed) to provide specified products during a particular time. Sometimes the lowest bidder is awarded the contract. When the lowest bidder is not awarded the contract, strong evidence must be presented to justify the decision. Grounds for rejecting the lowest bid include lack of experience, inadequate financing, or poor past performance. Bidding allows all potential suppliers a fair chance at winning government contracts and helps ensure that public funds are spent wisely. For more information about bidding, see the "Marketing and Small Business" box and the section on bid pricing in Chapter 21.

Marketing and Small Business

Bidding for Government Contracts

Government organizations are an excellent target market for small businesses. Many small companies have been very successful in this market, and governments offer some distinct advantages over other markets. For one thing, there's no doubt that the government will pay its bills, although it may take its time. Also, as a government contractor, a new small business gains credibility that can help in selling to private customers. In addition, governments buy nearly everything—from food to spark plugs to exotic scientific and technical equipment—and don't usually subject suppliers to the abrupt cancellations that, in industry, are a feature of recessions. By making progress payments as the steps of a project are completed, the government acts as a financing source for small businesses. Progress payments help small businesses buy the inventory needed to complete the contract. And in the view of some small-business owners, the government is a more objective buyer than many companies are.

Much government procurement is done on a bid basis, with the government advertising for bids, stating product specifications, and accepting the lowest bid that meets these specifications. Such a procedure sometimes results in the rejection of the lowest bids. For example, the Board of New York City's Metropolitan Transportation Authority must provide toilet paper in the more than one thousand restrooms included in the services of the system. When deciding whether or not to accept a toilet paper purchase in the amount of $168,840, which was higher than three other bids, the Authority Board asked the following question of management:

"Why did you reject the lower bids?" The president responded that the Authority had rejected one supplier because there was insufficient tissue on the roll, while two other suppliers were ruled out because their tissues were somewhat like sandpaper and obviously not soft enough. In light of this explanation, the board approved accepting the higher bid.[10]

Even though learning how to bid for government orders takes time and effort, many small business owners and managers conclude that the hassles of learning the bidding process are more than outweighed by the potential of landing government contracts.

As a member of the Board of New York's Metropolitan Transportation Authority, would you be willing to accept the president's rationale for rejecting the lower-priced bids? What additional information or evidence would you need?

Federal Government

Name just about any good or service and chances are that someone in the federal government uses it. The U.S. federal government is the world's largest customer.

Although much of the federal government's buying is centralized, no single federal agency contracts for all the government's requirements, and no single buyer in any agency purchases all that the agency needs. One can view the federal government as a combination of several large companies with overlapping responsibilities and thousands of small independent units.

U.S. General Services Administration
How might a marketer of telecommuncations services benefit from this government Web site?

http://www.gsa.gov/

One popular source of information about government procurement is *Commerce Business Daily*. Until recently, businesses hoping to sell to the federal government found the document unorganized and it often arrived too late to be useful. The new online version (http://www.govcon.com/) is more timely and lets contractors find leads using key word searches.[11]

State, County, and City Government

Selling to states, counties, and cities can be less frustrating for both small and large vendors than selling to the federal government. Paperwork is typically simpler and more manageable than it is at the federal level. On the other hand, vendors must decide which of the over 82,000 government units are likely to buy their wares. State and local buying agencies include school districts, highway departments, government-operated hospitals, and housing agencies.

Institutions

The fourth major segment of the business-to-business market is institutions that seek to achieve goals other than such ordinary business goals as profit, market share, and return on investment. This segment includes schools, hospitals, colleges and universities, churches, labor unions, fraternal organizations, civic clubs, foundations, and other so-called nonbusiness organizations.

Schools, whose goal is to educate children rather than to make a profit, are part of the institutional segment of the business-to-business market.
© 1996 PhotoDisc, inc.

THE STANDARD INDUSTRIAL CLASSIFICATION (SIC) SYSTEM

4 Explain the standard industrial classification system.

standard industrial classification system (SIC)
A detailed numbering system developed by the U.S. government to classify business and government organizations by their main economic activity.

The **standard industrial classification system (SIC)** is a detailed numbering system developed by the U.S. government to classify business and government organizations by their main economic activity. The SIC system divides the economy into 11 major divisions and assigns two-digit numbers to major industry groups within each division. For each two-digit code, the U.S. Census Bureau publishes data on total industry sales and employment. This information is further broken down by geographic region and is available for each county in the United States.

Two-digit SIC industry categories are then further divided into three, four, five, six, and seven-digit categories, which represent subindustries within the broader two-digit categories. Exhibit 7.2 shows an example of two-, three-, four-, and five-digit codes.

Exhibit 7.3 shows several SIC data sources that can be found in the reference sections of public and university libraries. The story about Terramarine Bioresearch, Inc., at the beginning of this chapter illustrated how several of these sources can be used by business-to-business marketers.

Although SIC data are helpful for analyzing, segmenting, and targeting markets, they have important limitations. For example, the federal government assigns only one code to each organization. Therefore, the system does not accurately describe firms that engage in many different activities or that provide various types of products. Another limitation is that some industries are not assigned codes. Examples include direct-response advertising agencies, telemarketing service bureaus, and list suppliers. Thus, for some business-to-business marketers, it may be impossible to determine a four-digit SIC code that describes present or prospective customers.[13] Still another limitation of the SIC system is that the *SIC Manual* is not revised frequently. The most recent revision was 1987. This manual replaced the 1972 manual and its 1977 amendments. Obviously, many new industries are omitted.

Exhibit 7.2

Breakdown of the Standard Industrial Classification System. Example: Manufacturers of Fabricated Metal Products.

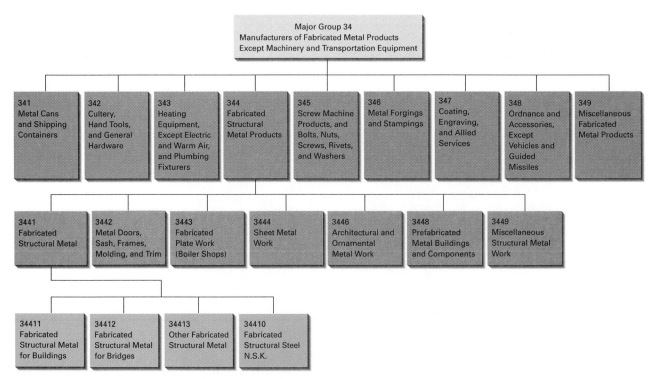

Exhibit 7.3 *Sources of Data on Domestic Business Markets Based on SIC*

Source	How Often Published	Number of Digits of SIC Information	Type of Data Contained
U.S. Census of Manufacturers, Mineral Industries, Wholesale Trade, Retail Trade, Selected Services, Construction	Every 5 years: 1967, 1972, 1977, 1982, 1987, 1992, etc.	2-, 3-, 4-, 5-, and 7-digit data	Detailed industry information by time periods, area, product classes
U.S. Survey of Manufacturers	Years other than when census is published	2-, 3-, 4-, and 5-digit data	Data similar to that in census of manufacturers but less detailed
U.S. Industrial Outlook	Annually	3-, 4-, and 5-digit data	Number of companies, where concentrated, past industry trends, projected trends
County Business Patterns	Annually	2-, 3-, and 4-digit data	Number of employees, taxable payrolls, total reporting units by state and county
Dun & Bradstreet's Annual Business Statistics Reports	Not published—computerized data bank	4-digit data	Number of establishments, number of large establishments, value of goods produced or distributed, or services rendered for total U.S. and by state and county
Private industrial directories (e.g., Standard and Poor's Register, Dun & Bradstreet's Million Dollar Directory, Ward's Business Directory of U.S. Private and Public Companies)	Annually	4-digit data	Company names, addresses, primary and secondary SICs, products produced, sales volumes, names of key executives
State/county/municipality directories (e.g., MacRae's State Industrial Directories, Harris Publishing	Varies—some annually, some every 2 years	4-digit data	Company names, addresses, primary and secondary SICs, products produced, sales volumes, names of key executives
Predicasts's "Basebook" and "Forecasts"	Quarterly, also in computerized data banks	7-digit data	Short- and long-term forecasts by SIC, article abstracts, market size measurements, time series data, annual growth rates, and data sources
Dun's Census of American Business	Annually	4-digit data	Number of companies, by employee size, by sales volume, by state and county
Databases (e.g., Dun & Bradstreet's "Market Identifiers," Trinet, Inc., Electronic Yellow Pages, Market Statistics, Thomas Marketing Information Center, National Trade Data Bank, American Business Directories	Not published—computerized data bank	4- and 5-digit data	Company names, addresses, SICs, sales volumes, products produced, number of employees, names of key executives, market share, estimated consumption of product/services, more detailed company data on request
Mailing list companies (e.g., National Business Lists R. L. Polk, Thomas, Ed Burnett, American Business Lists, Inc.)	Not published—computerized data bank	4- and 5-digit data	Labels, printouts, diskettes, tapes—company names and addresses, more detailed company data on request

Source: From *Business Marketing 6e* by Robert W. Haas. Copyright © 1995 South-Western College Publishing. Reprinted by permission.

Despite these limitations, the SIC has been, and will continue to be, an extremely valuable tool for business-to-business marketers. A new online SIC index makes current information more accessible (http://www.wave.net/upg/immigration/sic_index.html).

BUSINESS-TO-BUSINESS VERSUS CONSUMER MARKETS

5 Explain the major differences between business-to-business and consumer markets.

The basic philosophy and practice of marketing is the same whether the customer is a business organization or a consumer. Business markets do, however, have characteristics different from consumer markets. Exhibit 7.4 summarizes the main differences between business-to-business and consumer markets.

Demand

Consumer demand for products (discussed at length in Chapter 20) is quite different from demand in the business-to-business market. Unlike consumer demand, business-to-business demand is derived, inelastic, joint, and fluctuating.

Derived Demand

derived demand
The demand for business-to-business products.

The demand for business-to-business products is called **derived demand** because organizations buy products to be used in producing consumer products. In other words, the demand for business-to-business products is derived from the demand for consumer products. For example, car and truck manufacturers account for a major share of U.S. steel, rubber, and aluminum consumption.

Because demand is derived, business-to-business marketers must carefully monitor demand patterns and changing preferences in final consumer markets, even though their customers are not in those markets. Moreover, business-to-business marketers must carefully monitor their customers' forecasts, because derived demand is based on expectations of future demand for those customers' products.

Some business-to-business marketers not only monitor final consumer demand and customer forecasts but also try to influence final consumer demand. For example, the American Iron and Steel Institute (AISI) advertises "the benefits of canned food" on television and in magazines. The target of these ads is beverage purchasers and consumers. According to AISI's Bob Fatzinger, "We don't want the same thing happening to the food market as happened to the beverage industry."[14]

Exhibit 7.4
Major Characteristics of Business-to-Business Markets Compared to Consumer Markets

Characteristic	Business-to-business market	Consumer market
Demand	Organizational	Individual
Purchase volume	Larger	Smaller
Number of customers	Fewer	Many
Location of buyers	Geographically concentrated	Dispersed
Distribution structure	More direct	More indirect
Nature of buying	More professional	More personal
Nature of buying influence	Multiple	Single
Type of negotiations	More complex	Simpler
Use of reciprocity	Yes	No
Use of leasing	Greater	Lesser
Primary promotional method	Personal selling	Advertising

Inelastic Demand

The demand for many business-to-business products is inelastic with regard to price. *Inelastic demand* means that an increase or decrease in the price of the product will not significantly affect demand for the product.

The price of a product used in the production of, or as part of, a final product is often a minor part of the final product's total price. Therefore, demand for the final consumer product is not affected. If the price of automobile paint or spark plugs rose significantly, say 200 percent in one year, do you think the number of new automobiles sold that year would be affected? Probably not.

Joint Demand

Joint demand occurs when two or more items are used together in a final product. For example, a decline in the availability of memory chips will slow production of microcomputers, which will in turn reduce the demand for disk drives. Many business products, such as hammer heads and hammer handles, also exemplify joint demand.

Fluctuating Demand

The demand for business-to-business products—particularly new plants and equipment—tends to be more unstable than the demand for consumer products. A small increase or decrease in consumer demand can produce a much larger change in demand for the facilities and equipment needed to make the consumer product. Economists refer to this phenomenon as the **multiplier effect** (or accelerator principle).

Cummins Engine Company, a producer of heavy-duty diesel engines, uses sophisticated surface grinders to make parts. Suppose Cummins is using 20 surface grinders. Each machine lasts about 10 years. Purchases have been timed so two machines will wear out and be replaced annually. If the demand for engine parts does not change, two grinders will be bought this year. If the demand for parts declines slightly, only 18 grinders may be needed and Cummins won't replace the worn ones. However, suppose in the next year demand returns to previous levels plus a little more. To meet the new level of demand, Cummins will need to replace the two machines that wore out in the first year, the two that wore out in the second year, plus one or more additional machines. The multiplier effect works this way in many industries, producing highly fluctuating demand for business-to-business products.

Purchase Volume

Business-to-business customers buy in much larger quantities than consumers. Just think how large an order Kellogg typically places for the wheat bran and raisins used to manufacture Raisin Bran. Imagine the number of tires that Ford buys at one time.

Number of Customers

Business-to-business marketers usually have far fewer customers than consumer marketers. The advantage is that it is a lot easier to identify prospective buyers, monitor current customers' needs and levels of satisfaction, and personally attend to existing customers. The main disadvantage is that each customer becomes crucial—especially for those business-to-business manufacturers that have only one customer. In many cases, this customer is the U.S. government.

The American Iron and Steel Institute targets consumers of canned foods and beverages in its advertising. It keeps track of consumer demand and attempts to influence consumers to buy canned products.
© SuperStock, Inc.

joint demand
The demand for two or more items used together in a final product.

multiplier effect (accelerator principle)
Phenomenon in which a small increase or decrease in consumer demand can produce a much larger change in demand for the facilities and equipment needed to make the consumer product.

Location of Buyers

Business-to-business customers tend to be much more geographically concentrated than consumers. For instance, more than half the nation's business buyers are located in New York, California, Pennsylvania, Illinois, Ohio, Michigan, and New Jersey. The aircraft and microelectronics industries are concentrated on the West Coast, and many of the firms that supply the automobile manufacturing industry are located in and around Detroit.

Distribution Structure

Many consumer products pass through a distribution system that includes the producer, one or more wholesalers, and a retailer. However, because of many of the characteristics already mentioned, channels of distribution are typically shorter in business-to-business marketing. Direct channels, where manufacturers market directly to users, are much more common.

Many businesses that market directly to users are discovering that new media, such as CD-ROMs and the World Wide Web, offer great potential for reaching new and existing customers domestically and around the world, while reducing costs to both buyers and sellers.[15]

Nature of Buying

Unlike consumers, business buyers usually approach purchasing rather formally. Businesses use professionally trained purchasing agents or buyers who spend their entire career purchasing a limited number of items. They get to know the items and the sellers quite well. Some professional purchasers earn the designation of Certified Purchasing Manager (CPM) after participating in a rigorous certification program.

Nature of Buying Influence

Typically, more people are involved in a single business purchase decision than in a consumer purchase. Experts from fields as varied as quality control, marketing, and finance, as well as professional buyers and users, may be grouped in a buying center (discussed later in this chapter).

Type of Negotiations

Consumers are used to negotiating price on automobiles and real estate. But in most cases, American consumers expect sellers to set the price and other conditions of sale, such as time of delivery and credit terms. On the other hand, negotiating is common in business-to-business marketing. Buyers and sellers negotiate product specifications, delivery dates, payment terms, and other pricing matters. Sometimes these negotiations occur during many meetings over several months. Final contracts are often very long and detailed.

Use of Reciprocity

reciprocity
A practice where business purchasers choose to buy from their own customers.

Business purchasers often choose to buy from their own customers, a practice known as **reciprocity.** For example, General Motors buys engines for use in its automobiles and trucks from Borg Warner, which, in turn, buys many of the automobiles and trucks it needs from GM. This practice is neither unethical nor illegal unless one party coerces the other and the result is unfair competition. Reciprocity is generally considered a reasonable business practice. If all possible suppliers sell about the same product for about the same price, doesn't it make sense to buy from those firms that buy from you?

Use of Leasing

Consumers normally buy products rather than lease them. But businesses commonly lease expensive equipment such as computers, construction equipment and vehicles, and auto-mobiles. Leasing allows firms to reduce capital outflow, acquire a seller's latest products, receive better services, and gain tax advantages.

The lessor, the firm providing the product, may be either the manufacturer or an independent firm. The benefits to the lessor include greater total revenue from leasing compared to selling and a chance to do business with customers who cannot afford to buy.

Primary Promotional Method

Business-to-business marketers tend to emphasize personal selling in their promotion efforts, especially for expensive items, custom-designed products, large-volume purchases, and situations requiring negotiations. The sale of many business-to-business products requires a great deal of personal contact. Personal selling is discussed in more detail in Chapter 18.

TYPES OF BUSINESS-TO-BUSINESS PRODUCTS

Business-to-business products generally fall into one of the following seven categories, depending on their use: major equipment, accessory equipment, raw materials, component parts, processed materials, supplies, and business services.

Major Equipment

Major equipment includes such capital goods as large or expensive machines, mainframe computers, blast furnaces, generators, airplanes, and buildings. (These items are also commonly called **installations**.) Major equipment is depreciated over time rather than charged as an expense in the year it is purchased. In addition, major equipment is often custom-designed for each customer.

Personal selling is an important part of the marketing strategy for major equipment because distribution channels are almost always direct from the producer to the business user.

Accessory Equipment

Accessory equipment is generally less expensive and shorter-lived than major equipment. Examples include portable drills, power tools, microcomputers, and fax machines. Accessory equipment is often charged as an expense in the year it is bought rather than depreciated over its useful life. In contrast to major equipment, accessories are more often standardized and are usually bought by more customers. These customers tend to be widely dispersed. For example, all types of businesses buy microcomputers.

Local industrial distributors (wholesalers) play an important role in the marketing of accessory equipment because business buyers often purchase accessories from them. Regardless of where accessories are bought, advertising is a more vital promotional tool for accessory equipment than for major equipment.

Businesses commonly lease expensive equipment such as automobiles because it reduces capital outflow, allows them to acquire the latest models, gives them better services, and gains them tax advantages.
Copyright 1996 GM Corp. Used with permission GM Media Archives.

6 Describe the seven types of business-to-business goods and services.

major equipment (installations)
Capital goods such as large or expensive machines, mainframe computers, blast furnaces, generators, airplanes, and buildings.

accessory equipment
Goods, such as portable tools and office equipment, that are less expensive and shorter-lived than major equipment.

Raw materials, such as logs, become part of finished products and are generally purchased in huge quantities.
© 1996 PhotoDisc, Inc.

Raw Materials

raw materials
Unprocessed extractive or agricultural products, such as mineral ore, lumber, wheat, corn, fruits, vegetables, and fish.

Raw materials are unprocessed extractive or agricultural products—for example, mineral ore, lumber, wheat, corn, fruits, vegetables, and fish. Raw materials become part of finished products. Extensive users, such as steel or lumber mills and food canners, generally buy huge quantities of raw materials. Because there is often a large number of relatively small sellers of raw materials, none can greatly influence price or supply. Thus, the market tends to set the price of raw materials, and individual producers have little pricing flexibility.

Promotion is almost always via personal selling, and distribution channels are usually direct from producer to business user.

Component Parts

component parts
Either finished items ready for assembly or products that need very little processing before becoming part of some other product.

Component parts are either finished items ready for assembly or products that need very little processing before becoming part of some other product. Examples include spark plugs, tires, and electric motors for automobiles. A special feature of component parts is that they often retain their identity after becoming part of the final product. For example, automobile tires are clearly recognizable as part of a car. Moreover, because component parts often wear out, they may need to be replaced several times during the life of the final product. Thus, there are two important markets for many component parts: the original equipment manufacturer (OEM) market and the replacement market.

Many of the business-to-business features listed before in Exhibit 7.4 characterize the OEM market. The difference between unit costs and selling prices in the OEM market is often small, but profits can be quite substantial because of volume buying.

The replacement market is composed of organizations and individuals buying component parts to replace worn-out parts. Because components often retain their identity in final products, users may choose to replace a component part with the same brand used by the manufacturer—for example, the same brand of automobile tires or battery. The replacement market operates differently from the OEM market, however. Whether replacement buyers are organizations or individuals, they tend to demonstrate the characteristics of consumer markets that were shown in Exhibit 7.4.

Consider, for example, an automobile replacement part. Purchase volume is usually small, and there are many customers, geographically dispersed, who typically buy from car dealers or parts stores. Negotiations do not occur, and neither reciprocity nor leasing is usually an issue.

Manufacturers of component parts often direct their advertising toward replacement buyers. Cooper Tire & Rubber, for example, makes and markets component parts—automobile and truck tires—for the replacement market only. Ford and other car makers compete with independent firms in the market for replacement automobile parts.

Processed Materials

Processed materials are used directly in manufacturing other products. Unlike raw materials, they have had some processing. Examples include sheet metal, chemicals, specialty steel, lumber, corn syrup, and plastics. Unlike component parts, processed materials do not retain their identity in final products.

Most processed materials are marketed to OEMs or to distributors servicing the OEM market. Processed materials are generally bought according to customer specifications or to some industry standard, as is the case with steel and lumber. Price and service are important factors in choosing a vendor.

processed materials
Products used directly in manufacturing other products.

Supplies

Supplies are consumable items that do not become part of the final product—for example, lubricants, detergents, paper towels, pencils, and paper. Supplies are normally standardized items that purchasing agents routinely buy. Supplies typically have relatively short lives and are inexpensive compared to other business goods. Because supplies generally fall into one of three categories—maintenance, repair, or operating supplies—this category is often referred to as MRO items.

Competition in the MRO market is intense. Bic and Paper Mate, for example, battle for business purchases of inexpensive ballpoint pens.

supplies
Consumable items that do not become part of the final product.

Business Services

Business services are expense items that do not become part of a final product. Businesses often retain outside providers to perform janitorial, advertising, legal, management consulting, marketing research, maintenance, and other tasks. Hiring an outside provider makes sense when it costs less than hiring or assigning an employee to perform the task and when an outside provider is needed for particular expertise.

business services
Expense items that do not become part of a final product.

BUSINESS-TO-BUSINESS BUYING BEHAVIOR

As you probably have already concluded, business buyers behave differently from consumers. Understanding how purchase decisions are made in organizations is a first step in developing a business-to-business selling strategy. Five important aspects of business-to-business buying behavior are buying centers, evaluative criteria, buying situations, the purchase process, and customer service.

7 Discuss the unique aspects of business-to-business buying behavior.

Buying Centers

A **buying center** includes all those persons in an organization who become involved in the purchase decision. Membership and influence vary from company to company. For instance, in engineering-dominated firms like Bell Helicopter, the buying center may consist almost entirely of engineers. In marketing-oriented firms like Toyota and

buying center
All those persons who become involved in the purchase decision.

IBM, marketing and engineering have almost equal authority. In consumer goods firms like Procter & Gamble, product managers and other marketing decision makers may dominate the buying center. In a small manufacturing company, almost everyone may be a member.

The number of people involved in a buying center varies with the complexity and importance of a purchase decision. The composition of the buying group will usually change from one purchase to another and sometimes even during various stages of the buying process. To make matters more complicated, buying centers do not appear on formal organization charts.

For example, even though a formal committee may have been set up to choose a new plant site, it is only part of the buying center. Other people, like the company president, often play informal yet powerful roles. In a lengthy decision-making process, such as finding a new plant location, some members may drop out of the buying center when they can no longer play a useful role. Others whose talents are needed then become part of the center. No formal announcement of "who is in" and "who is out" is ever made.

Roles in the Buying Center

As in family purchasing decisions, several people may play a role in the business purchase process:

- *Initiator:* the person who first suggests making a purchase.
- *Influencers/evaluators:* people who influence the buying decision. They often help define specifications and provide information for evaluating options. Technical personnel are especially important as influencers.
- *Gatekeepers:* group members who regulate the flow of information. Frequently, the purchasing agent views the gatekeeping role as a source of his or her power. A secretary may also act as a gatekeeper by determining which vendors get an appointment with a buyer.
- *Decider:* the person who has the formal or informal power to choose or approve the selection of the supplier or brand. In complex situations, it is often difficult to determine who makes the final decision.
- *Purchaser:* the person who actually negotiates the purchase. It could be anyone from the president of the company to the purchasing agent, depending on the importance of the decision.
- *Users:* members of the organization who will actually use the product. Users often initiate the buying process and help define product specifications.

An example illustrating these basic roles is shown in Exhibit 7.5.

Implications of Buying Centers for the Marketing Manager

Successful vendors realize the importance of identifying who is in the decision-making unit, each member's relative influence in the buying decision, and each member's evaluative criteria. Successful selling strategies often focus on determining the most important buying influences and tailoring sales presentations to the evaluative criteria most important to these buying-center members. For example, Loctite Corporation, the manufacturer of Super-Glue and industrial adhesives and sealants, found that engineers were the most important influencers and deciders in adhesive and sealant purchase decisions. As a result, Loctite focused its marketing efforts on production and maintenance engineers.

Role	Illustration
Initiator	Division general manager proposes to replace company's computer network.
Influencers/evaluators	Corporate controller's office and vice president of data processing have an important say about which system and vendor the company will deal with.
Gatekeepers	Corporate departments for purchasing and data processing analyze company's needs and recommend likely matches with potential vendors.
Decider	Vice president of administration, with advice from others, selects vendor the company will deal with and system it will buy.
Purchaser	Purchasing agent negotiates terms of sale.
Users	All division employees use the computers.

Exhibit 7.5
Buying Center Roles for Computer Purchases

Evaluative Criteria

Business buyers evaluate products and suppliers against three important criteria: quality, service, and price—in that order.

- *Quality:* In this case, quality refers to technical suitability. A superior tool can do a better job in the production process, and superior packaging can increase dealer and consumer acceptance of a brand. Evaluation of quality also applies to the salesperson and the salesperson's firm. Business buyers want to deal with reputable salespeople and companies that are financially responsible. Quality improvement should be part of every organization's marketing strategy— and not just because it is a fad or "the thing to do" in the 1990s.

- *Service:* Almost as much as they want satisfactory products, business buyers want satisfactory service. A purchase offers several opportunities for service. Suppose a vendor is selling heavy equipment. Prepurchase service could include a survey of the buyer's needs. After thorough analysis of the survey findings, the vendor could prepare a report and recommendations in the form of a purchasing proposal. If a purchase results, postpurchase service might consist of installing the equipment and training those who will be using it. Postsale services may also include maintenance and repairs. Another service that business buyers seek is dependability of supply. They must be able to count on delivery of exactly what was ordered when it is scheduled to be delivered. Buyers also welcome services that help them sell their finished products. Services of this sort are especially appropriate when the seller's product is an identifiable part of the buyer's end product.

- *Price:* Business buyers want to buy at low prices—at the lowest prices, under most circumstances. However, a buyer who pressures a supplier to cut prices to a point where the supplier loses money on the sale almost forces shortcuts on quality. The buyer also may, in effect, force the supplier to quit selling to him or her. Then a new source of supply will have to be found.

Many international business buyers use similar evaluative criteria. One study of South African buyers of high-tech laboratory instruments found that they use the following evaluative criteria, in descending order: technical service, perceived product reliability, after-sales support, supplier's reputation, ease of maintenance, ease of operation, price, confidence in the sales representative, and product flexibility.[16]

Buying Situations

Often business firms, especially manufacturers, must decide whether to make something or buy it from an outside supplier. The decision is essentially one of economics. Can an item of similar quality be bought at a lower price elsewhere? If not, is manufacturing it in-house the best use of limited company resources? For example, Briggs & Stratton, a major manufacturer of four-cycle engines, might be able to save $150,000 annually on outside purchases by spending $500,000 on the equipment needed to produce gas throttles internally. Yet Briggs & Stratton could also use that $500,000 to upgrade its carburetor assembly line, which would save $225,000 annually.

If a firm does decide to buy a product instead of making it, the purchase will be a new buy, a modified rebuy, or a straight rebuy.

New Buy

new buy
A situation requiring the purchase of a product for the first time.

A **new buy** is a situation requiring the purchase of a product for the first time. For example, suppose a law firm decides to replace word-processing machinery with microcomputers. This situation represents the greatest opportunity for new vendors. No long-term relationship has been established (at least for this product), specifications may be somewhat fluid, and buyers are generally more open to new vendors.

If the new item is a raw material or a critical component part, the buyer cannot afford to run out of supply. The seller must be able to convince the buyer that the seller's firm can consistently deliver a high-quality product on time.

value engineering (value analysis)
The systematic search for less expensive substitutes.

New-buy situations often result from value engineering. **Value engineering** (also called value analysis) is the systematic search for less expensive substitutes. The goal is to identify goods and services that perform a given function at a lower total cost than those currently used. There is a growing tendency for buyers and potential suppliers to do value engineering studies. The vendor who can show the results of such studies will benefit during the negotiation process.

Modified Rebuy

modified rebuy
Situation where the purchaser wants some change in the original good or service.

A **modified rebuy** is normally less critical and less time-consuming than a new buy. In a modified-rebuy situation, the purchaser wants some change in the original good or service. It may be a new color, greater tensile strength in a component part, more respondents in a marketing research study, or additional services in a janitorial contract.

Because the two parties are familiar with each other and credibility has been established, buyer and seller can concentrate on the specifics of the modification. But in some cases, modified rebuys are open to outside bidders. The purchaser uses this strategy to ensure that the new terms are competitive. An example would be a law firm deciding to buy more powerful microcomputers. The firm may open the bidding to examine the price/quality offerings of several suppliers.

Straight Rebuy

straight rebuy
Buying situation in which the purchaser reorders the same goods or services without looking for new information or investigating other suppliers.

A **straight rebuy** is a situation vendors relish. The purchaser is not looking for new information or other suppliers. An order is placed, and the product is provided as in previous orders. Usually a straight rebuy is routine because the terms of the purchase have been hammered out in earlier negotiations. An example would be the law firm previously cited purchasing printer cartridges from the same supplier on a regular basis.

One common technique used in straight-rebuy situations is the purchasing contract. Purchasing contracts are used with products that are bought often and in high volume. In essence, the purchasing contract makes the buyer's decision making routine and promises the salesperson a sure sale. The advantage to the buyer is a quick, confident decision and, to the salesperson, reduced or eliminated competition. Voluntary Hospitals of America, Inc., an alliance of nearly 900 not-for-profit hospitals, has a contract to buy sutures, staples, and endoscopic surgical instruments exclusively from Johnson & Johnson. The contract generates about $250 million per year for Johnson & Johnson.[17]

Suppliers must remember not to take straight-rebuy relationships for granted. Retaining existing customers is much easier than attracting new ones.

The Purchase Process

The business-to-business purchase process is traced in Exhibit 7.6. It begins with recognition of a need. For example, a firm may realize that it must replace old machinery or expand its facilities.

The next step in the purchase sequence is a tentative decision on the type of product needed. Sometimes the buying firm then drafts product specifications. More of-

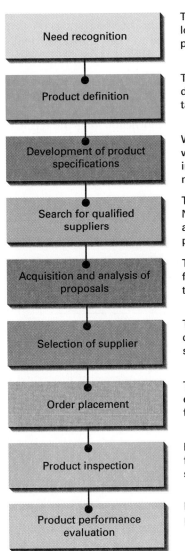

Need recognition — The user realizes that the current product either no longer can do the job or cannot do it as well as newer products.

Product definition — The user, having extensive knowledge of the task to be done, defines the type of product needed to complete the task.

Development of product specifications — When the product must be customized, the influencer works with the salesperson to develop specifications. The influencer is often an engineer who knows how to adapt machinery.

Search for qualified suppliers — The purchasing agent searches for qualified suppliers. Names of suppliers may be provided by influencers, such as quality control people, who have come in contact with potential suppliers at trade shows or exhibits.

Acquisition and analysis of proposals — The purchasing agent takes product proposals or "bids" from suppliers and, with the decision makers, analyzes the proposals.

Selection of supplier — The purchasing agent and other members of the buying center analyze alternative bids and vendors and select a supplier.

Order placement — The purchasing agent (usually) places the order and establishes the delivery and order routines, as well as the financial terms.

Product inspection — Receiving, inspection, or quality control employees check for shortages, damaged merchandise, or incorrect shipments.

Product performance evaluation — Purchasing agents and others monitor the supplier's performance. Users monitor the product's performance.

Exhibit 7.6
Business-to-Business Purchase Process

ten, though, members of the buying center select several potential sources of supply and begin negotiations. Purchasing agents may even keep lists of approved suppliers for various types of products. Negotiations begin with a discussion of the product needed, the time frame within which it is needed, and the terms of delivery. Negotiations often end when each of the potential suppliers submits a proposal with a bid, or price to be charged for the product. The buyer then analyzes the proposals and either selects the best one or asks suppliers for clarification.

Vendor Analysis

vendor analysis
Vendor rating systems used to compare suppliers on attributes the buying center views as important.

Buying centers, particularly in new-buy situations, use vendor rating systems, called **vendor analysis,** to compare suppliers on attributes the buying center views as important. Exhibit 7.7 illustrates the use of vendor analysis to compare microcomputer suppliers. The buying center has identified the six attributes in the left column as most important. Each vendor is then rated on each attribute. A potential vendor's score is determined by adding all the ratings and dividing by the total number of attributes. In the example, the vendor is strong except on the attributes of affordability and product-line depth. The purchasing agent has to decide how important these two attributes are.

A more sophisticated approach, which builds in assessments of each attribute's importance, first weights the attributes (for example, 1 for somewhat important, 2 for moderately important, and 3 for very important). These importance ratings are then multiplied by the vendor rating scores, which are totaled to yield an overall vendor score.

Completion of the Transaction

After analyzing vendors, selecting a source of supply, and negotiating the terms of the purchase, the buying firm issues a purchase order, making the transaction official. Purchase orders often include such details as product identification code or description, quantity and quality to be delivered, method and frequency of delivery, and payment terms.

Exhibit 7.7

Example of Vendor Analysis in a Microcomputer-Buying Situation

	Rating scale				
Attributes	Unacceptable (0)	Poor (1)	Fair (2)	Good (3)	Excellent (4)
Compatibility					X
Affordability			X		
Reliability					X
Product line depth			X		
Service/ support					X
Flexibility				X	

Total score: 4 + 2 + 4 + 2 + 4 + 3 = 19
Average score: 19 ÷ 6 = 3.17

When products are received, they are inspected for correctness, quantity, and quality and then checked into inventory. When the seller's invoice has been checked and found in order, payment is authorized. Once payment has been made, the transaction is complete. Although the transaction is complete at this point, the buyer will take note of the product and the supplier's performance through periodic evaluations. These evaluations will help the buyer determine whether to make future purchases from this supplier.

The Salesperson's Role

The salesperson plays a very important role throughout the purchase process. Salespeople often are the first to recognize that buyers need their product. Because they are the ones recognizing the need, they are in a position to influence the product's definition and specifications.

Salespeople who emphasize the need to the buyer are usually guaranteed that their company will be one of the suppliers considered. Good salespeople, knowing that at this point they have an "in" with this particular buyer, should ask questions to determine the buyer's potential budget for this purchase. With this type of information, the salesperson can prepare a bid within the buyer's price range. The salesperson's company will have a competitive edge.

If the sale is made, the salesperson should verify that the product is packaged and ready to be delivered on time and is received in good working condition, with all parts included. Finally, throughout their follow-up service, salespeople should ensure that the customer is fully satisfied with the product and that the seller has fulfilled all presale promises.

Purchasing Ethics

The ethics of business-to-business buyer and seller relationships are often scrutinized and sometimes criticized by superiors, associates, other prospective suppliers, the general public, and the news media. The National Association of Purchasing Management, mindful of the key problems often faced by professional buyers, developed the 11-point code of ethics shown in the "Ethics in Marketing" box.

Salespeople for Frito-Lay's Baked Lays chips anticipated consumers' desire for low-fat foods and played a role in getting grocery stores to stock and sell them.
© Ray Hand

Ethics in Marketing

The NAPM Code of Ethics

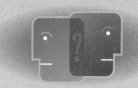

The National Association of Purchasing Management's code of ethics includes the following 11 items:

1. Interests of the firm are foremost in all dealings. This concept implicitly indicates that personal gain from business suppliers in the form of "commissions" (for example, gifts) cloud the objectivity necessary in making the best decision for the buying firm.
2. Buy without preference or prejudice. This calls for objectivity in vendor selection and avoiding conflict of interest when the buyer might have a financial interest in one particular vendor.
3. Seek maximum value in purchases. This statement reinforces the objective of receiving the maximum value at the lowest overall price to the buying firm.
4. Maintain a sound policy with regard to gifts. The cost of any gift is a marketing expense to the vendor that must be recaptured through higher prices.
5. Strive for knowledge about materials, processes, and practical methods. This is a reminder that the buyer should not merely process requisitions and purchase orders.
6. Be receptive to competent counsel from colleagues. This is a reminder to be open to new ideas and anything that might improve performance and further the goals of the employer.
7. Counsel and assist other buyers. This means seeking improvements, aiding others, and so forth.
8. Avoid "sharp practice." This includes misrepresentations in order to gain an unfair advantage over a vendor.
9. Subscribe to honesty and truth in dealings. This is similar to the sharp-practice point and emphasizes that honesty and truth will benefit the buyer in the future with like action from vendors.
10. Respect obligations. Obligations can range from contractual obligations to verbal understandings.
11. Provide prompt and courteous reception to vendors. A seller's time is as valuable as the buyer's, so a prompt reception of salespeople is encouraged.[18]

Do relatively inexpensive gifts at Christmas or other special occasions tend to "cloud the objectivity necessary" for professional buyers to make "the best decision for the buying firm"? When does a token of appreciation become a bribe? Propose a formal gift policy for the people responsible for purchasing in your firm.

Reprinted with permission from the publisher, the National Association of Purchasing Management, "Principles and Standards of Purchasing Practice," adopted January 1992.

Customer Service

Business-to-business marketers are increasingly recognizing the benefits of developing a formal system to monitor customer opinions and perceptions of the quality of customer service.[19] Companies like McDonald's, L. L. Bean, and Lexus build their strategies not only around products but also around a few highly developed service skills. Many firms are finding new ways to enhance customer service through technology. Business-to-business marketers are leading the way in adoption of new media technologies such as online services, CD-ROMs, and the World Wide Web on the Internet.[20] Federal Express Corp., for example, began a service on the World Wide Web in November 1994 that gave customers a direct window into FedEx's package-tracking database. FedEx is now saving about $2 million per year and improving customer service by replacing humans with a Web site.[21] Customer service is explored in more detail in Chapters 12 and 13.

Federal Express
How does Federal Express help companies achieve more profitable inventory management and just-in-time distribution?

http://www.fedex.com/

LOOKING BACK

Look back at the story about Terramarine Bioresearch, Inc., that appeared at the beginning of this chapter. Many business firms use reference materials that organize a wealth of marketing information based on the SIC system. As more and more of these government and private sources of information come on line, businesses will find incredible amounts of data available at the click of a mouse.

SUMMARY

1 *Describe business-to-business marketing.* Business-to-business marketing provides goods and services that are bought for use in business rather than for personal consumption. Intended use, not physical characteristics, distinguishes a business-to-business product from a consumer product.

2 *Discuss the role of relationship marketing and strategic alliances in business-to-business marketing.* Relationship marketing entails seeking and establishing long-term alliances or partnerships with customers. Companies form strategic alliances for a variety of reasons. Some fail miserably. The keys to success appear to be choosing a partner carefully and creating conditions where both parties benefit.

3 *Identify the four major categories of business-market customers.* Producer markets consist of for-profit organizations and individuals that buy products to use in producing other products, to use as components of other products, or to use in facilitating business operations. Reseller markets consist of wholesalers and retailers that buy finished products to resell for profit. Government markets include federal, state, county, and city governments that buy goods and services to support their own operations and serve the needs of citizens. Institutional markets consist of very diverse nonbusiness institutions whose main goals do not include profit.

4 *Explain the standard industrial classification system.* The standard industrial classification (SIC) system provides a way to identify, analyze, segment, and target business-to-business and government markets. Organizations can be identified and compared by a numeric code indicating type of economic activity (at the broadest level), industry, geographic region, subindustry, and product classification. Unfortunately, SIC codes are inadequate for identifying organizations that engage in many different activities or that provide a variety of products.

5 *Explain the major differences between business-to-business and consumer markets.* In business-to-business markets, demand is derived, price-inelastic, joint, and fluctuating. Purchase volume is much larger than in consumer markets. Customers are fewer in number and more geographically concentrated. Distribution channels are more direct. Buying is approached more formally using professional purchasing agents. More people are involved in the buying process, and negotiation is more complex. Reciprocity and leasing are more common. And finally, selling strategy in business-to-business markets normally focuses on personal contact rather than on advertising.

6 *Describe the seven types of business-to-business goods and services.* Major equipment includes capital goods, such as heavy machinery. Accessory equipment is typically less expensive and shorter-lived than major equipment. Raw materials are extractive or agricultural products that have not been processed. Component parts are finished or near-finished items to be used as parts of other products. Processed materials are used to manufacture other products. Supplies are consumable and not

KEY TERMS

accessory equipment *197*

business services *199*

business-to-business marketing *186*

buying center *199*

component parts *198*

derived demand *194*

joint demand *195*

major equipment *197*

modified rebuy *202*

multiplier effect *195*

new buy *202*

processed materials *199*

raw material *198*

reciprocity *196*

standard industrial classification system (SIC) *192*

straight rebuy *202*

strategic alliance *186*

supplies *199*

value engineering *202*

vendor analysis *204*

used as part of a final product. Business services are intangible products that many companies use in their operations.

7 *Discuss the unique aspects of business-to-business buying behavior.* Business-to-business buying behavior is distinguished by five fundamental characteristics. First, buying is normally undertaken by a buying center consisting of many people who range widely in authority level. Second, business buyers typically evaluate alternative products and suppliers based on quality, service, and price—in that order. Third, business-to-business buying falls into three general categories: new buys, modified rebuys, and straight rebuys. Fourth, business-to-business purchasing is a process that involves several steps, including developing product specifications, choosing a supplier, and evaluating supplier performance. Fifth, customer service before, during, and after the sale plays a big role in business-to-business purchase decisions.

Discussion and Writing Questions

1. How might derived demand affect the manufacturing of an automobile?

2. Why is relationship or personal selling the best way to promote in business-to-business marketing?

3. A colleague of yours has sent you an e-mail seeking your advice as he attempts to sell a new voice-mail system to a local business. Send him a return e-mail describing the various people who might influence the customer's buying decision. Be sure to include suggestions for dealing with the needs of each.

4. Intel Corporation supplies microprocessors to Compaq for use in their computers. Describe the buying situation in this relationship, keeping in mind the rapid advancement of technology in this industry.

5. In small groups, brainstorm examples of companies that feature the products in the different business-to-business categories. (Avoid examples already listed in the chapter.) Compile a list of 10 specific business-to-business products including at least one in each category. Then match up with

another group. Have each group take turns naming a product and have the other group identify its appropriate category. Try to resolve all discrepancies by discussion. It is certainly possible that some identified products might appropriately fit into more than one category.

6. The First American Group Purchasing Association (http://www.first.gpa.com) publishes a monthly list of the top 10 Web sites it considers most useful to small businesses. Visit one or more of these sites and then write a memo to a colleague who is considering starting a new business. Describe why he or she should visit this Web site.

7. What business publications, search facilities, sources, and services does the following Web site offer?

http://www.demographics.com/

8. How could you use the following site to help plan a business trip to Toronto? Name three articles featured in the latest issue of *Business To Business Magazine.*

http://www.business2business.on.ca/

Application for Small Business

Dan White is an independent video producer whose biggest client is the State of Illinois Agricultural Department. Although this account is big enough to support the entire business, Dan has developed other lines of business to eliminate the risks involved with having only one customer. Dan has also landed a sizeable account through a high school friend who is the vice president of Good Hands Insurance. This also happens to be the company that underwrites Dan's life insurance. Additionally, Dan is hired to work on various projects for large production companies. Dan generated this business through long-term relationships built by working on projects for the State of Illinois.

As Dan prepares his business plan for the upcoming year, he is contemplating several strategic changes. Due to the increasing speed in which the video industry is evolving, Dan has observed two important trends. First, he is finding it increasingly difficult to own the latest video equipment that his customers are demanding. Second, Dan's clients are not able to keep up with the recent developments in the industry and would be willing to pay more for his expertise. Dan is looking into a lease for new equipment and he is contemplating an increase in price.

Questions

1. What general classification (first two digits) would you assign to Dan's business in the Standard Industrial Code (SIC)? (Suggest a range.)

2. Is Dan's choice to use Good Hands insurance ethical? Why or why not?

3. How can Dan use the inelasticity of demand to his advantage?

4. Would you advise Dan to lease or buy the new equipment? Why?

Video Case

Amtech Corporation

When David Cook's father told him that scientists in Los Alamos, New Mexico, had created an interesting technology to track livestock in the fields, Cook investigated. In 1983, his company, Amtech Corporation, bought the patent rights to develop commercial applications. Today, the Dallas firm uses the technology to make electronic identification tags for cargo containers, railroad cars, and tollway vehicles. Amtech has become the leader in developing technology to serve the transportation industry around the world.

The original plans for Amtech included applications in everything from inventory control to ski lifts. The company scrapped applications such as warehouse tracking systems because its system offered no advantage over bar coding. Instead, it focused on transportation, where speedy data reading would be an asset. Amtech's technology identifies objects using radio signals to send and receive information, but its advantage is that it can electronically read tags at a good distance, at great speeds, and regardless of whether dirt, snow, or other debris covers the tag.

The most visible application among typical consumers are such tollways as the Lincoln Tunnel in New York City, the Dallas North Tollway, Oklahoma's PikePass, and 14 other tollways worldwide. Amtech's system uses a small, credit-card-sized device, called a *tolltag*, that is placed on the inside of a car's windshield. Transceivers, installed at the toll plazas, bounce radio beams off each tolltag to identify the motorist and debit his or her account. The system boasts a 99.9 percent accuracy rate in toll collection and has helped decrease traffic congestion and pollution. It has also reduced the operating costs of 350 toll plazas worldwide. Motorists like the convenience of the tolltags, which save time and fuel.

The railroad industry accounts for 67 percent of Amtech's sales. The company has no competition, thanks to an Association of American Railroads mandate that requires all U.S. railroads to employ Amtech's system to track boxcars. The system has also been endorsed by European railroads, including France's TGV bullet train, which can be tracked at speeds of 240 miles per hour. Amtech has enabled the rail industry to monitor performance, improve safety, and lower its costs.

Amtech's system was also selected as the industry standard for identification tags in the intermodal container industry. It is the only system that can track containers at a distance of 40 feet when they are being moved from one type of transportation vehicle to another—for example, from ship to train or from train to truck. The system has thus helped save time and money for the intermodal industry.

In addition, Amtech's technology is used by trucking companies and airlines to track freight and improve service. The company is currently exploring the possibilities of sending data to automobiles for on-board navigation.

Amtech Corporation executes the design, manufacturing, testing, installation, and service of its products. The company's innovation and excellence have allowed Amtech to remain the leader in providing the transportation industry with identification systems.

Questions

1. Select one target market for Amtech products. Go to the library and look up its SIC number in the *SIC Manual.* Prepare a brief analysis of this target market from information in *U.S. Industrial Outlook* and the *Census of Manufacturers.* You may use other sources as well.

2. Use the example of Amtech identification tags to illustrate how business-to-business markets are different from consumer markets.

3. Write a memo to David Cook proposing a new application for Amtech tags. Justify your recommendation.

References

Mitchell Schnurman, "Innovator's Firm Is Ready to Forge New Industry with Electronic Tags," *Fort Worth (Texas) Star-Telegram,* 6 August 1989, pp. 4-1, 4-7, 4-8.

R. Lee Sullivan, "Fast Lane," *Forbes,* 4 July 1994, pp. 112, 114.

LEARNING OBJECTIVES *After studying this chapter, you should be able to:*

1 Describe the characteristics of markets and market segments.

2 Explain the importance of market segmentation.

3 Discuss criteria for successful market segmentation.

4 Describe bases commonly used to segment consumer markets.

5 Describe the bases for segmenting business markets.

6 List the steps involved in segmenting markets.

7 Discuss alternative strategies for selecting target markets.

8 Explain how and why firms implement positioning strategies and how product differentiation plays a role.

9 Discuss global market segmentation and targeting issues.

Segmenting and Targeting Markets

Asked where they want to eat, many children pick McDonald's. Unfortunately for McDonald's, their parents often don't.

Now the home of the Happy Meal hopes to bring adults around to their youngsters' point of view. The nation's number one fast-food chain has introduced a line of sandwiches aimed at grown-ups and has backed it with an unprecedented marketing push. The first to make its debut was a hamburger called Arch Deluxe. The line represents "the biggest new-product introduction since the Big Mac more than 25 years ago," a McDonald's executive says.

The restaurant chain sees an opportunity in adult customers at a time when overall U.S. fast-food sales are sluggish. McDonald's admitted that while its research shows that 72 percent of consumers surveyed think McDonald's has the best burgers for kids, only 18 percent say it serves the best adult burger.

The Arch Deluxe, which comes in a potato-flour bun, consists of a quarter-pound of seasoned beef dressed with lettuce, tomato, cheese, onion, and a sauce of Dijon and stone-ground mustards and mayonnaise. Peppered bacon will be optional. The sandwich, pitched as "the burger with the grown-up taste," gives McDonald's a chance to play catch-up in this part of the market. Until now, the company had locked itself out of the $5 billion-a-year bacon-lettuce-and-tomato hamburger niche. Bacon is among the most popular dressings on burgers today, yet until now McDonald's has featured bacon only on promotional sandwiches which appear on menus intermittently.

Tomato has also been missing from most McDonald's burgers. While the ill-fated reduced-fat McLean Deluxe had a slice, the last regular hamburger with tomato was the McDLT, which came in a container that kept the meat hot and the veggies cold. McDonald's also introduced a Deluxe Chicken sandwich and larger Filet-O-Fish sandwich.

Whether all this marketing can give McDonald's a more mature image isn't clear. After years of putting small toys in its kids' meals and using a clown as its mascot, the chain may find it's tough to pull in more grown-ups.[1]

Based on this vignette, how would you define market segmentation and targeting? How is McDonald's targeting adults? Do you think the company will be successful in its new efforts?

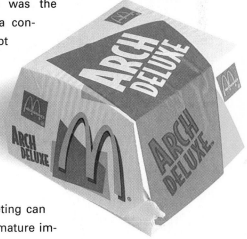

McDonald's Corporation
How does McDonald's Web site segment and target adult and children's markets?

http://www.mcdonalds.com/

MARKET SEGMENTATION

1 Describe the characteristics of markets and market segments.

market
People or organizations with needs or wants and the ability and willingness to buy.

market segment
A subgroup of people or organizations sharing one or more characteristics that cause them to have similar product needs.

market segmentation
The process of dividing a market into meaningful, relatively similar, and identifiable segments or groups.

Exhibit 8.1
Concept of Market Segmentation

The term *market* means different things to different people. We are all familiar with terms like *supermarket, stock market, labor market, fish market,* and *flea market.* All these types of markets share several characteristics. First, they are composed of people (consumer markets) or organizations (business markets). Second, these people or organizations have wants and needs that can be satisfied by particular product categories. Third, they have the ability to buy the products they seek. Fourth, they are willing to exchange their resources, usually money or credit, for desired products. In sum, a **market** is (1) people or organizations with (2) needs or wants and with (3) the ability and (4) the willingness to buy. A group of people that lacks any one of these characteristics is not a market.

Within a market, a **market segment** is a subgroup of people or organizations sharing one or more characteristics that cause them to have similar product needs. At one extreme, we can define every person and every organization in the world as a market segment because each is unique. At the other extreme, we can define the entire consumer market as one large market segment and the business-to-business market as another large segment. All people have some similar characteristics and needs, as do all organizations.

From a marketing perspective, it normally makes sense to describe market segments somewhere between the two extremes. The process of dividing a market into meaningful, relatively similar, and identifiable segments or groups is called **market segmentation.** The purpose of market segmentation is to enable the marketer to tailor marketing mixes to meet the needs of one or more specific segments.

Exhibit 8.1 illustrates the concept of market segmentation. Each box represents a market consisting of seven persons. This market might vary as follows: one homoge-

No market segmentation

Fully segmented market

Market segmentation by gender: M,F

Market segmentation by age group: 1,2,3

Market segmentation by gender and age group

neous market of seven people, a market consisting of seven individual segments, a market composed of two segments based on gender, a market composed of three age segments, or a market composed of five age and gender market segments. Age and gender and many other bases for segmenting markets are examined later in this chapter.

THE IMPORTANCE OF MARKET SEGMENTATION

Until the 1960s, few firms practiced market segmentation. When they did, it was more likely a haphazard effort than a formal marketing strategy. Before 1960, for example, the Coca-Cola Company produced only one beverage and aimed it at the entire soft-drink market. Today, Coca-Cola offers over a dozen different products to market segments based on diverse consumer preferences for flavors and calorie and caffeine content. Coca-Cola offers traditional soft drinks, "energy drinks" (such as Power Ade), flavored teas, and fruit drinks (Fruitopia).[2]

2 Explain the importance of market segmentation.

Market segmentation plays a key role in the marketing strategy of almost all successful organizations. Market segmentation is a powerful marketing tool for several reasons. Most important, nearly all markets include groups of people or organizations with different product needs and preferences. Market segmentation helps marketers define customer needs and wants more precisely. Because market segments differ in size and potential, segmentation helps decision makers more accurately define marketing objectives and better allocate resources. In turn, performance can be better evaluated when objectives are more precise.

The high-fashion furniture chain Domain offers an interesting example of how market segmentation can boost sales. Domain learned that its baby boomer clientele was as concerned about self-improvement as it was about decorating. To reach this segment, the store offered a series of in-store seminars that addressed topics such as women's issues and interior design. Repeat business of this group has increased 35 percent since the programs began. Another target segment was retired World War II and postwar clients, for whom the store offered narrower sofas with more back support that makes getting out of them easier. This segmentation approach allowed Domain to replace newspaper advertising with direct mail, bringing ad spending down 3 percent. Sales increased nearly 40 percent, to over $40 million.[3]

Judy George, owner of the Domain furniture chain, uses a segmentation approach to target baby boomers and retirees as purchasers of its high-fashion furniture.
© Steven L. Lewis

CRITERIA FOR SUCCESSFUL SEGMENTATION

Marketers segment markets for three important reasons. First, segmentation enables marketers to identify groups of customers with similar needs and to analyze the characteristics and buying behavior of these groups. Second, segmentation provides marketers with information to help them design marketing mixes specifically matched with the characteristics and desires of one or more segments. Third, segmentation is consistent with the marketing concept: satisfying customer wants and needs while meeting the organization's objectives.

To be useful, a segmentation scheme must produce segments that meet four basic criteria:

- *Substantiality:* A segment must be large enough to warrant developing and maintaining a special marketing mix. This criterion does not necessarily mean that a segment must have many potential customers. Marketers of custom-designed homes and business buildings, commercial airplanes, and large computer systems typically develop marketing programs

3 Discuss criteria for successful market segmentation.

tailored to each potential customer's needs. In most cases, however, a market segment needs many potential customers to make commercial sense. IBM and 15 of the largest U.S. banks started a company called Integrion Financial Network that will offer a number of online banking services to its customers. However, only 1 percent of all banking transactions are conducted online, making this segment risky in terms of substantiality.[4] Undoubtedly, Integrion hopes that this segment will grow in the future.

- *Identifiability and measurability:* Segments must be identifiable and their size measurable. Data about the population within geographic boundaries, the number of people in various age categories, and other social and demographic characteristics are often easy to get, and they provide fairly concrete measures of segment size. Say that a social service agency wants to identify segments by their readiness to participate in a drug and alcohol program or in prenatal care. Unless the agency can measure how many people are willing, indifferent, or unwilling to participate, it will have trouble gauging whether there are enough people to justify setting up the service.

- *Accessibility:* The firm must be able to reach members of targeted segments with customized marketing mixes. Some market segments are hard to reach—for example, senior citizens (especially those with reading or hearing disabilities), those who don't speak English, and the illiterate.

- *Responsiveness:* As Exhibit 8.1 illustrates, markets can be segmented using any criteria that seem logical. However, unless one market segment responds to a marketing mix differently from other segments, that segment need not be treated separately. For instance, if all customers are equally price-conscious about a product, there is no need to offer high-, medium-, and low-priced versions to different segments.

segmentation bases (variables)
Characteristics of individuals, groups, or organizations.

This *Modern Maturity* ad uses a multi-variable segment in targeting female baby boomers who are beginning to turn 50.
Courtesy Modern Maturity

Whose lips wear 1/3* of the lipstick?

It's on the lips of women 50+. They buy one in every three lipsticks.
And they buy the foundation and moisturizer to go with it.
If you're suffering from share shock, talk lipstick to 50+. Call up Steve Alexander at Modern Maturity, 212-599-1880, and up your share!

**Modern Maturity.
A new face.
A new voice.
A new market.**

BASES FOR SEGMENTING CONSUMER MARKETS

Marketers use **segmentation bases** or **variables**—characteristics of individuals, groups, or organizations—to divide a total market into segments. The choice of segmentation bases is crucial because an inappropriate segmentation strategy may lead to lost sales and missed profit opportunities. The key is to identify bases that will produce substantial, measurable, and accessible segments that exhibit different response patterns to marketing mixes.

Markets can be segmented using a single variable, such as age group, or several variables, such as age group, gender, and education. Although it is less precise, single-variable segmentation has the advantage of being simpler and easier to use than multiple-variable segmentation. The disadvantages of multiple-variable segmentation are that it is often harder to use than single-variable segmentation; usable secondary data are less likely to be available; and as the number of segmentation bases increases, the size of individual segments decreases. Nevertheless, the current trend is toward using more rather than fewer variables to segment most markets. Multiple-variable segmentation is clearly more precise than single-variable segmentation.

Consumer goods marketers commonly use one or more of the following characteristics to segment markets: geography, demographics, psychographics, benefits sought, and usage rate. A more detailed description of these characteristics follows.

4 Describe bases commonly used to segment consumer markets.

Geographic Segmentation

Geographic segmentation refers to segmenting markets by region of the country or world, market size, market density, or climate. *Market density* means the number of people within a unit of land, such as a census tract. Climate is commonly used for geographic segmentation because of its dramatic impact on residents' needs and purchasing behavior. Snowblowers, water and snow skis, clothing, and air-conditioning and heating systems are products with varying appeal, depending on climate.

Consumer goods companies take a regional approach to marketing for four reasons. First, many firms need to find new ways to generate sales because of sluggish and intensely competitive markets. Second, computerized checkout stations with scanners enable retailers to assess accurately which brands sell best in their region. Third, many packaged goods manufacturers are introducing new regional brands intended to appeal to local preferences. Fourth, a more regional approach allows consumer goods companies to react more quickly to competition. Coca-Cola USA, for example, developed a special marketing campaign for Texas. The campaign included a geographic theme, "Coca-Cola Texas—home of the real thing," and participation in the state's "Don't Mess with Texas" antilitter effort. The Global Perspectives box provides another example of geographic market segmentation.

geographic segmentation
Segmenting markets by region of the country or world, market size, market density, or climate.

Demographic Segmentation

Marketers often segment markets on the basis of demographic information because it is widely available and often related to consumers' buying and consuming behavior. Some common bases of **demographic segmentation** are age, gender, income, ethnic background, and family life cycle. The discussion here provides some important information about the main demographic segments.

demographic segmentation
Segmenting markets by age, gender, income, ethnic background, and family life cycle.

Age Segmentation

Children 4 to 12 years old influence a great deal of family consumption, spending about $4.6 billion annually on toys; $5.8 billion on food and beverages; about $1.5 billion on movies and spectator sports; $2.5 billion on clothes; and $1 billion at the video arcade. Furthermore, children directly influence about $170 million in family spending.[5] These age segments are therefore very attractive for a variety of product categories.

Other age segments are also appealing targets for marketers. There are 47 million consumers born between 1966 and 1976, termed "generation X," and they have $125 billion in spending power. Lowe's, the giant home-improvement chain, is trying to attract generation Xers by signing up as a sponsor for NASCAR, an autoracing organization that has a large following of this segment.[6] The computer literate generation Xers also are a large and viable market for the Internet.

Lowe's Companies, Inc.
How does Lowe's promote NASCAR sponsorship via this Web site? Does this promotion successfully target generation Xers?

http://www.lowes.com/

People between 35 and 44 are likely to have school-age children at home and to outspend all other age groups on food at home, housing, clothing, and alcohol. Those between 45 and 54 spend more than any other group on food away from home, transportation, entertainment, education, personal insurance, and pensions.[7] Research has shown that, contrary to popular opinion, 71 percent of those in the 50-plus age group are willing to

Global Perspectives

Poland Starting to See the Emergence of "Puppies"

In the last two years, Piotr and Danuta Jentes, Polish 30-some-things, have bought a second car and splurged on a $3,000 wind-surfer. Owners of a small business, they go to a private doctor, send their youngest child to a private day-care center, and spend a lot of money fixing up their home. And in rapidly Westernizing Poland, they are no longer a rarity.

For the first time, after the false hopes and smashed expectations that followed the collapse of communism in 1989, market research-ers and economists say they are seeing the emergence of a Polish middle class. Sometimes dubbed "puppies," these Polish yuppies are buying consumer goods like cars and refrigerators that Ameri-cans take for granted but that not so long ago were the preserve of the Communist apparatchiks. And they are showing a sophistication about their new-found buying power that economists say bodes well for the country—and for the Western companies that have made Poland a key base of investment in the former Communist bloc.

In a population of nearly 40 mil-lion, by far the largest in Central Europe, the size of the new Polish middle class is a matter of debate. But numerous indicators, experts say, verify its vitality:

- Car sales were up 40 percent in the first three months of 1996. More significantly, imported four-door Opels and Renaults, instead of two-door Polish-made Fiat putt-putts, made the big gains.
- In 1995, the volume of car loans also grew by 40 percent, albeit from almost nothing. But it is the change in the mind-set of Poles, who are accustomed to paying for everything in cash, that the growing financial services sector finds reassuring. GE Capital and Ford Credit, two big American pro-viders of financing for cars, opened operations in Poland last year.
- Deposits at savings banks grew by 14 percent in 1995, according to McKinsey & Company, the American management-consult-ing firm. This suggests that Poles, who are notorious for stashing savings under the mattress, have acquired more faith in their banks.

"The middle class has arrived and it's growing," said Kozinski, the marketing manager in Poland for General Motors, which plans to open a factory in southern Poland in 1998 that will eventually have the capacity to assemble 100,000 cars a year.

Its most visible members are small-business owners, employees of Western-owned companies and, increasingly, professionals in Polish companies. They are all starting out on the road to fulfilling dreams that many Western Europeans first began having in the 1950s: owning their own homes or apartments, buying a better or second car, en-suring a good education for their children, and taking annual vaca-tions abroad.[8]

Is the Polish middle class a promising target market for U.S. companies? What products could most effectively be marketed to this segment?

try new brands. Additionally, the over-50 group controls 77 percent of total finan-cial assets in this country and are healthier than most think.[9] The "Marketing and Small Business" box illustrates how age can influence financial service preferences.

Gender Segmentation

Marketers of products such as clothing, cosmetics, personal care items, mag-azines, jewelry, and footwear commonly segment markets by gender. For [I] example, 95 percent of users of Sports Zone, a World Wide Web site that offers a constant flow of sports news generated by ESPN (http://espnet.sportszone.com/), are men.[10] However, brands that have traditionally been marketed to men—such as Ford Mustang, Cadillac, and Midas Mufflers—are increasing their efforts to attract women. "Women's" products—such as cosmetics, household products, and furniture—are also being marketed to men.[11]

Marketing and Small Business

Lifestyle Matrix Marketing

Many Depression-era consumers are severely risk-averse when it comes to financial services products. They prefer secure investments like Treasury bonds and CDs, even though returns are low. They also prefer not to go into debt.

Lifestyle Matrix Marketing, a small company in Lafayette, California, has recently designed an insurance policy targeted at two generations that experienced the Depression—the World War II and

Depression cohorts. Policyholders give the issuing company, Lifetime Security Plan, the right to inherit their homes when they die. Until then, the policyholders, mostly retirees, live in their homes and receive a monthly stipend. Because people are living longer, this re-

lieves them of many financial worries. Lifetime even provides basic upkeep of the homes.

In contrast, members of the baby boom generation do not mind going into debt. Therefore, when they reach 70, they may be more interested in other insurance products. For example, a reverse mortgage—a loan against the equity of property—may appeal to this generation because they do not fear debt.[12]

Income Segmentation

Income is a popular demographic variable for segmenting markets because income level influences consumers' wants and determines their buying power. Many markets are segmented by income, including the markets for housing, clothing, automobiles, and food. For example, Toyota Motor Corporation is targeting a new, smaller sport-utility vehicle called RAV4 to those in lower-income groups. This vehicle sells for $10,000 less than Toyota's traditional four-wheel-drive 4Runner.[13] Wal-Mart, on the other hand, is moving away from its traditional rural and middle-income markets by targeting higher-income consumers in upscale areas. The retailer is spending more money on its stores, introducing more high-end merchandise, and upgrading apparel lines.[14]

Ethnic Segmentation

Many companies are segmenting their markets by ethnicity. The three largest ethnic markets are the African-American market, the Hispanic market, and the Asian-American market. African-Americans, numbering 32 million in 1996, are the largest minority group in the United States. The proportion of the population that is African-American will continue to grow well into the next century because the birth rate for African-Americans is 22.1 births per 1,000 persons, versus 14.8 for whites. Also, the death rate among African-Americans is lower than among the general population because of their lower average age. Total expenditures by this group top $270 billion a year. Increasingly, marketers are finding this market segment very rewarding.[15]

Researchers have found some differences in consumption patterns between African-Americans and other groups. For example, blacks and whites often have different preferences

Using ethnic market segmentation, Avon features Black History Month to entice African-American women to buy its products.
Courtesy Avon Products Inc.

CELEBRATING OUR BEAUTIFUL HERITAGE—EVERY DAY

This month, many of us look to explore our roots and discover the beauty of our ancestry. Avon celebrates **Black History Month** in February—and every day—through the pages of the **Avon Boutique.** This unique catalogue offers a full range of beauty products that meet the special needs of African-Americans. Plus a selection of unique gifts that celebrate the roots of **African-American culture** and can help keep the spirit of Black History Month alive—all year long. Available exclusively through an Avon Sales Representative. For the name of your Avon Representative, or to sell Avon, call 1-800-FOR-AVON.

AVON

in taste. Although blacks drink less coffee than average, they are much more likely than other Americans to lace their coffee with large amounts of sugar, cream, or nondairy creamer. Recognizing this trend, Coffee-Mate began marketing its product to blacks. It advertised in national magazines like *Ebony* and *Essence*, broadcast its message on local black radio stations, and used outdoor advertising in black neighborhoods.

The difference between blacks and whites also shows up in packaging choices. African-Americans have a strong preference for larger sizes of nonalcoholic beverages, for example. After the Coca-Cola Company discovered this phenomenon in the early 1970s, it began featuring and promoting 16-ounce bottles instead of the standard 12-ounce size when advertising to the black community.[16]

At least half of all Fortune 500 companies have launched some ethnic marketing activities.[17] Effectively penetrating the market, however, often requires a unique and distinctive marketing mix. Following are examples of how companies are targeting African-Americans:

- Coors uses event or sports marketing to attract African-American consumers. The company sponsors the Coors Lite Orlando Florida Football Classic because it has found that this sporting event attracts black males 21 to 34 years old.[18]

- Spiegel, the large catalog retailer, joined with the publisher of *Ebony* to develop a fashion line and catalog aimed at African-American women. Spiegel maintains that this group spends 6.5 percent of family income on apparel, compared with an average of 5 percent for all women. This catalog, to be called *E Style*, features clothes designed especially for African-American women. Its first issue was mailed to 1.5 million African-American women, including *Ebony* subscribers and current Spiegel customers.[19]

- African-Americans account for 15 percent of McDonald's business, so the group gets 15 percent of the marketing and advertising effort. Marketing professionals praise one McDonald's Breakfast Club campaign, which features "buppies" (black urban professionals) talking like African-Americans instead of whites.

By the end of 1995, the Hispanic population will approach 26 million people, and the year 2010 should see a Hispanic population of nearly 39 million.[20] Hispanics are one of the fastest-growing minority groups in the United States. The total purchasing power of the Hispanic market is over $170 billion annually.[21]

The concept of diversity is nowhere more evident than in the Hispanic culture. Mexican-Americans make up 60 percent of U.S. Hispanics and are highly concentrated in the Southwest. Puerto Rican-Americans are the second-largest Hispanic subgroup, at just 12 percent, but they dominate the Hispanic population of New York City. Cuban-Americans are the majority of Hispanics in South Florida, although they are just 5 percent of all U.S. Hispanics. The remaining 23 percent of Hispanics trace their lineage to Spain, South America, or Central America.[22]

Today, marketing managers are carefully targeting major segments of the Hispanic market. One series of

The Hispanic market has a total annual purchasing power of $170 billion. However, the diversity of this population and language differences present many challenges to those trying to target this market.
Courtesy First USA Bank

Now you can celebrate your heritage every time you use your Visa® Card.

Introducing the Hispanic Magazine Visa Card. Get a low **5.9%** APR introductory rate, no annual fee, balance transfer options. And its distinctive graphics tell the world you're proud of who you are.

1·800·FIRST US

Campbell Soup ads, for instance, features a woman cooking, but the individual ads differ in such details as the character's age, the setting, and the music. In the version for Cuban-Americans, a grandmother cooks in a plant-filled kitchen to the sounds of salsa and merengue music. In contrast, the Mexican-American ad shows a young wife preparing food in a brightly colored Southwestern-style kitchen with pop music playing in the background.

The diversity of the Hispanic population and the language differences create many challenges for those trying to target this market. Following are examples of companies targeting Hispanics:

- Many Hispanics are loyal to the brands found in their homeland. If these are not available, Hispanics will choose brands that reflect their native values and culture.[23] PepsiCo, which bought a controlling interest in Gamesa, one of Mexico's biggest cookie makers, has begun selling Gamesa products to U.S. Hispanics.

- The number of Spanish-language media outlets in the United States has increased steadily during the past decade. There are now 42 major Spanish-language magazines, 31 English or bilingual Hispanic-oriented magazines, and 103 Hispanic newspapers.[24] TV and radio outlets have expanded as well. Four national Hispanic radio networks air Spanish-language programming over 600 stations. An estimated 80 percent of Hispanics listen to radio.[25]

- Shopping malls are trying to attract Hispanic customers. The Tucson Mall in Arizona advertises on three Spanish-language radio stations and hires a mariachi music group to help it celebrate the Mexican holiday Cinco de Mayo. Half the mall's staff is bilingual. A Florida mall that attracts about 50,000 shoppers from Miami and Dade County appeals largely to Hispanics.[26]

During the past decade, the Asian-American population growth rate was twice that of Hispanics, 6 times that of African-Americans, and 20 times that of whites.[27] Like Hispanic-Americans, Asian-Americans are a diverse group with 13 submarkets. The five largest are Chinese (1.6 million), Filipino (1.4 million), Japanese (848,000), Asian Indians (815,000), and Koreans (799,000). Asian-American households are better educated and more affluent than those of any other racial or ethnic group, including whites. Their median household income was about $42,000 in 1996; 32 percent of Asian-American households have incomes of $50,000 or more, compared with only 29 percent of white households.[28]

Because Asian-Americans are better educated and have higher incomes than average, they are sometimes called a "marketer's dream." Some examples of companies targeting Asian-Americans include:

- Cadillac sponsored the Ameritech Senior Open Golf Tournament and ran Korean-language advertisements on a California television station.[29]

- Most Asian-Americans drink plenty of soda. Koreans are the exception, and only 52.1 percent of this group reported drinking soda in the previous three months. At the same time, Koreans drink more 7-Up than any other soda, a big difference from Asian-Americans in general, whose top soda preferences are Coke (55 percent) and Pepsi (18 percent).[30]

- Some entrepreneurs are building large enclosed malls that cater to Asian consumers. At the Aberdeen Centre near Vancouver, British Columbia, nearly 80 percent of the merchants are Chinese-Canadians, as are 80 percent of the customers. The mall offers fashions made in Hong Kong, a shop for traditional Chinese medicines, and a theater showing Chinese movies. Kung fu martial arts demonstrations and Chinese folk dances are held in the mall on weekends.

family life cycle (FLC)
A series of stages determined by a combination of age, marital status, and the presence or absence of children.

Exhibit 8.2
Family Life Cycle

Family Life-Cycle Segmentation

The demographic factors of gender, age, and income often do not sufficiently explain why consumer buying behavior varies. Frequently, differences in consumption patterns among people of the same age and gender result from their being in different stages of the family life cycle. The **family life cycle (FLC)** is a series of stages determined by a combination of age, marital status, and the presence or absence of children. As Chapter 6 explained, it is a valuable basis for segmenting markets.

Exhibit 8.2 illustrates both traditional and contemporary FLC patterns and shows how families' needs, incomes, resources, and expenditures differ at each stage. The horizontal flow shows the traditional family life cycle. The lower part of the exhibit

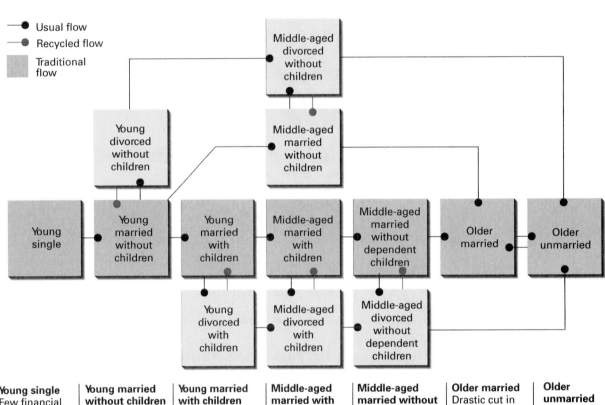

Young single	Young married without children	Young married with children	Middle-aged married with children	Middle-aged married without children	Older married	Older unmarried
Few financial burdens	Better off financially than they will be in near future	Home purchasing at peak	Financial position still better	Home ownership at peak	Drastic cut in income	Drastic cut in income
Fashion opinion leaders	Highest purchase rate and highest average purchase of durables	Liquid assets low	More wives work	Most satisfied with financial position and money saved	Keep home	Special need for attention, affection, and security
Recreation-oriented	Buy: cars, refrigerators, stoves, sensible and durable furniture, vacations	Dissatisfied with financial position and amount of money saved	Some children get jobs	Interested in travel, recreation, self-education	Buy: medical appliances, medical care, products that aid health, sleep, and digestion	Buy: same medical and product needs as other retired group
Buy: basic kitchen equipment, basic furniture, cars, equipment for mating game, vacations		Interested in new products	Hard to influence with advertising	Make gifts and contributions		
		Like advertised products	High average purchase of durables	Not interested in new products		
		Buy: washers, dryers, televisions, baby food, chest rubs, cough medicine, vitamins, dolls, wagons, sleds, skates	Buy: new and more tasteful furniture, auto travel, unnecessary appliances, boats, dental services, magazines	Buy: vacations, luxuries, home improvements		

gives some of the characteristics and purchase patterns of families in each stage of the traditional life cycle. The exhibit also acknowledges that about half of all first marriages end in divorce. When young marrieds move into the young divorced stage, their consumption patterns often revert back to those of the young single stage of the cycle. About four of five divorced persons remarry by middle age and reenter the traditional life cycle, as indicated by the "recycled flow" in the exhibit.

Psychographic Segmentation

Age, gender, income, ethnicity, family life-cycle stage, and other demographic variables are usually helpful in developing segmentation strategies, but often they don't paint the entire picture. Demographics provides the skeleton, but psychographics adds meat to the bones. **Psychographic segmentation** is market segmentation on the basis of the following variables:

- *Personality:* Personality reflects a person's traits, attitudes, and habits. Porsche Cars North America understood well the demographics of the Porsche owner: a 40-something male college graduate earning over $200,000 per year. However, research discovered that there were five personality types within this general demographic category that more effectively segmented Porsche buyers. Exhibit 8.3 describes the five segments. Porsche refined its marketing as a result of the study and, after a previous seven-year slump, the company's U.S. sales rose 48 percent.[31]

- *Motives:* Marketers of baby products and life insurance appeal to consumers' emotional motives, namely, to care for their loved ones. Using appeals to economy, reliability, and dependability, carmakers like Subaru and Suzuki target customers with rational motives. Carmakers like Mercedes-Benz, Jaguar, and Cadillac appeal to status-related motives.

- *Lifestyles:* Lifestyle segmentation divides people into groups according to the way they spend their time, the importance of the things around them, their beliefs, and socioeconomic characteristics such as income and education. For example, NPD Market Research identified the following five "eating lifestyles": meat-and-potato eaters; families with kids whose diets feature soda pop and sweetened cereal; dieters; natural-food eaters; and sophisticates—high-income urban families whose diets feature alcohol, Swiss cheese, and rye and pumpernickel breads.

psychographic segmentation
Market segmentation on the basis of personality, motives, lifestyles, and geodemographics.

Type	% of All Owners	Description
Top Guns	27%	Driven, ambitious types. Power and control matter. They expect to be noticed.
Elitists	24%	Old-money blue bloods. A car is just a car, no matter how expensive. It is not an extension of personality.
Proud Patrons	23%	Ownership is an end in itself. Their car is a trophy earned for hard work, and who cares if anyone sees them in it?
Bon Vivants	17%	Worldly jet setters and thrill seekers. Their car heightens the excitement in their already passionate lives.
Fantasists	9%	Walter Mitty types. Their car is an escape. Not only are they uninterested in impressing others with it, they also feel a little guilty about owning one.

Exhibit 8.3
Taxonomy of Porsche Buyers

Motive is one of the variables of psychographic segmentation. For example, marketers of baby products appeal to consumers' desires to care for their loved ones.
© 1996 PhotoDisc, Inc.

- *Geodemographics:* **Geodemographic segmentation** clusters potential customers into neighborhood lifestyle categories. It combines geographic, demographic, and lifestyle segmentations. Geodemographic segmentation helps marketers practice **micromarketing,** which is the development of marketing programs tailored to prospective buyers who live in small geographic regions, such as neighborhoods, or who have very specific lifestyle and demographic characteristics. Working with the idea that people in the same neighborhood tend to buy the same things, Target has tailored its merchandise in each store to the preferences of its patrons. For example, the Target store on Phoenix's eastern edge sells prayer candles but no child-toting bicycle trailers. The Target 15 minutes away in affluent Scottsdale, sells the trailers but no portable heaters; those can be found 20 minutes south, in Mesa.[32]

Target
Based on the contents of Target's Web site, how is Target targeting generation Xers? Baby boomers? Can you identify other target markets?

http://www.targetstores.com/

geodemographic segmentation
Segmenting potential customers into neighborhood lifestyle categories.

micromarketing
The development of marketing programs tailored to prospective buyers who live in small geographic regions, such as neighborhoods, or who have very specific lifestyle and demographic characteristics.

Psychographic variables can be used individually to segment markets or can be combined with other variables to provide more detailed descriptions of market segments. One well-known combination approach, offered by SRI International, is called VALS™ 2 (version 2 of SRI's Values and Lifestyles program). VALS 2 categorizes U.S. consumers by their values, beliefs, and lifestyles rather than by traditional demographic segmentation variables. Many advertising agencies have used VALS segmentation to create effective promotion campaigns.

As Exhibit 8.4 shows, the segments in VALS 2 are classified on two dimensions: vertically by their resources and horizontally by their self-orientation. Resources include education, income, self-confidence, health, eagerness to buy, intelligence, and energy level. The resources dimension is a continuum ranging from minimal to abundant. Resources generally increase from adolescence through middle age and decrease with extreme age, depression, financial reverses, and physical or psychological impairment. In contrast, the *self-orientation* dimension classifies three different ways of buying:

- Beliefs or principles—rather than feelings, events, or desire for approval—guide *principle-oriented* consumers in their choices.
- Other people's actions, approval, and opinions strongly influence *status-oriented* consumers.

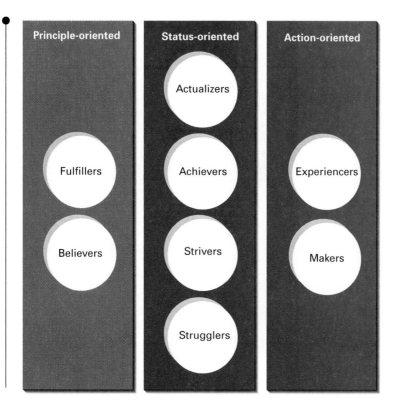

Exhibit 8.4
VALS™ 2 Dimensions

- *Action-oriented* consumers are prompted by a desire for social or physical activity, variety, and risk.

Exhibit 8.5 describes the eight VALS 2 psychographic segments. Using only the two key dimensions, resources and self-orientation, VALS 2 defines groups of adult consumers who have distinctive attitudes, behavior patterns, and decision-making styles.

Benefit Segmentation

Benefit segmentation is the process of grouping customers into market segments according to the benefits they seek from the product. Most types of market segmentation are based on the assumption that this variable and customers' needs are related. Benefit segmentation is different because it groups potential customers on the basis of their needs or wants rather than some other characteristic, such as age or gender. The snack-food market, for example, can be divided into six benefit segments, as shown in Exhibit 8.6.

Customer profiles can be developed by examining demographic information associated with people seeking certain benefits. This information can be used to match marketing strategies with selected target markets. For example, American Greetings' Create a Card kiosks located in airports offer benefits to time-pressed businesspeople, who can produce personalized greeting cards during free time spent waiting for a flight.[33]

benefit segmentation
The process of grouping customers into market segments according to the benefits they seek from the product.

Usage-Rate Segmentation

Usage-rate segmentation divides a market by the amount of product bought or consumed. Categories vary with the product, but they are likely to include some combination of the following: former users, potential users, first-time users, light or irreg-

usage-rate segmentation
Dividing a market by the amount of product bought or consumed.

Exhibit 8.5

VALS™ 2 Psychographic Segments

Actualizers are successful, sophisticated, active, "take-charge" people with high self-esteem and abundant resources. They are interested in growth and seek to develop, explore, and express themselves in a variety of ways. Their possessions and recreation choices reflect a cultivated taste for the finer things in life.

Fulfillers are mature, satisfied, comfortable, reflective people who value order, knowledge, and responsibility. Most are well educated, well informed about world events, and professionally employed. Fulfillers are conservative, practical consumers; they are concerned about value and durability in the products they buy.

Believers are conservative, conventional people with concrete beliefs and strong attachments to traditional institutions—family, church, community, and nation. As consumers they are conservative and predictable, favoring U.S. products and established brands.

Achievers are successful career- and work-oriented people who like to, and generally do, feel in control of their lives. Achievers live conventional lives, are politically conservative, and respect authority and the status quo. As consumers they favor established goods and services that demonstrate success to peers.

Strivers seek motivation, self-definition, and approval from the world around them. They are easily bored and impulsive. Money defines success for strivers, who lack enough of it. They emulate those who own more impressive possessions, but what they wish to obtain is generally beyond their reach.

Experiencers are young, vital, enthusiastic, and impulsive. They seek variety and excitement and combine an abstract disdain for conformity and authority with an outsider's awe of others' wealth, prestige, and power. Experiencers are avid consumers and spend much of their income on clothing, fast food, music, movies, and video.

Makers are practical people who value self-sufficiency. They live within a traditional context of family, practical work, and physical recreation and have little interest in what lies outside that context. They are unimpressed by material possessions other than those with a practical or functional purpose (for example, tools, pickup trucks, or fishing equipment).

Strugglers have lives that are constricted—chronically poor, ill educated, and low skilled. They lack strong social bonds; they are focused on meeting the urgent needs of the present moment. Aging strugglers are concerned about their health. Strugglers are cautious consumers who represent a very modest demand for most goods and services but are loyal to favorite brands.

80/20 principle
Principle that holds that 20 percent of all customers generate 80 percent of the demand.

ular users, medium users, and heavy users. Segmenting by usage rate enables marketers to focus their efforts on heavy users or to develop multiple marketing mixes aimed at different segments. Because heavy users often account for a sizeable portion of all product sales, some marketers focus on the heavy-user segment. For example, women buy 90 percent of all greeting cards.[34] Therefore, they are an attractive target market.

The **80/20 principle** holds that 20 percent of all customers generate 80 percent of the demand. Although the percentages are not usually exact, the general idea often holds true.

In a variant of usage-rate segmentation, some companies try to attract nonusers. Using a public database, Menly and James identified arthritis sufferers who did not use their pain reliever, Ecotrin. Three different direct-mail packages were sent to these nonusers: the first included a free sample with a 50¢ coupon, the second enclosed a $1 rebate coupon, and the third package had an invitation to send for a free sample. All three pro-

Toothpaste—from baking soda bubbles to flavor sparkles for kids, this market has fractured into many different segments. Learn how the fight against tooth decay has adjusted to meet the different needs of customers at **Hot Link—Market Segmentation.**

Exhibit 8.6 *Lifestyle Segmentation of the Snack-Food Market*

	Nutritional snackers	**Weight watchers**	**Guilty snackers**	**Party snackers**	**Indiscriminate snackers**	**Economical snackers**
% of snackers	22%	14%	9%	15%	15%	18%
Lifestyle characteristics	Self-assured, controlled	Outdoorsy, influential, venturesome	Highly anxious, isolated	Sociable	Hedonistic	Self-assured, price-oriented
Benefits sought	Nutritious, without artificial ingredients, natural	Low in calories, quick energy	Low in calories, good tasting	Good to serve guests, served with pride, go well with beverages	Good tasting, satisfies hunger	Low in price, best value
Consumption level of snacks	Light	Light	Heavy	Average	Heavy	Average
Type of snacks usually eaten	Fruits, vegetables, cheese	Yogurt, vegetables	Yogurt, cookies, crackers, candy	Nuts, potato chips, crackers, pretzels	Candy, ice cream, cookies, potato chips, pretzels, popcorn	No specific products
Demographics	Better educated, have younger children	Younger, single	Younger or older, female, lower socioeconomic status	Middle-aged, nonurban	Teenager	Have large family, better educated

motional offers resulted in at least a 50 percent redemption rate (compared to the usual nontargeted direct-mail response rate of 1 or 2 percent).[35]

BASES FOR SEGMENTING BUSINESS MARKETS

The business market consists of four broad segments: producers, resellers, institutions, and government. (For a detailed discussion of the characteristics of these segments, see Chapter 7.) Whether marketers focus on only one or on all four of these segments, they are likely to find diversity among potential customers. Thus, further market segmentation offers just as many benefits to business marketers as it does to consumer product marketers. Business market segmentation variables can be classified into two major categories: macrosegmentation variables and microsegmentation variables.

5 Describe the bases for segmenting business markets.

Macrosegmentation

Macrosegmentation variables are used to divide business markets into segments according to the following general characteristics:

- *Geographic location:* The demand for some business products varies considerably from one region to another. For instance, many computer hardware and software companies are located in the Silicon Valley region of California. Some markets tend to be regional because buyers prefer to purchase from local suppliers, and distant suppliers often have difficulty competing in terms of price and service. Therefore, firms that sell to geographically concentrated industries benefit by locating operations close to the market.

macrosegmentation
Method of dividing business markets into segments based on general characteristics such as geographic location, customer type, customer size, and product use.

IBM is changing its global marketing force from a geographic orientation to one based on customer type. The photo shows computers being delivered in Hanoi, Vietnam.
© REUTERS/Claro Cortes IV/Archive Photo

- *Customer type:* Segmenting by customer type allows business marketers to tailor their marketing mixes to the unique needs of particular types of organizations or industries. Many companies are finding this form of segmentation to be most responsive to conditions in the marketplace. For example, IBM is reorganizing its global marketing force from a geographic orientation to one based on customer type. The company plans to have 14 industry segments, including communications, finance, health, and manufacturing.[36]

- *Customer size:* Volume of purchase (heavy, moderate, and light) is a commonly used business-to-business segmentation basis. Another is the buying organization's size, which may affect its purchasing procedures, the types and quantities of products it needs, and its responses to different marketing mixes. Thus, banks, for instance, frequently offer different services, lines of credit, and overall attention to commercial customers based on their size.

- *Product use:* Many products, especially raw materials like steel, wood, and petroleum, have diverse applications. How customers use a product may influence the amount they buy, their buying criteria, and their selection of vendors. For example, a producer of springs may have customers that use the product in making machine tools, bicycles, surgical devices, office equipment, telephones, and missile systems.

Microsegmentation

Macrosegmentation often produces market segments that are too diverse for targeted marketing strategies. Thus, marketers often find it useful to divide macrosegments based on such variables as customer size or product use into smaller microsegments. **Microsegmentation** is the process of dividing business markets into segments based on the characteristics of decision-making units within a macrosegment. Microsegmentation enables the marketer to more clearly define market segments and more precisely define target markets. These are the typical microsegmentation variables:[37]

microsegmentation
The process of dividing business markets into segments based on the characteristics of decision-making units within a macrosegment.

- *Key purchasing criteria:* Marketers can segment some business markets by ranking purchasing criteria, such as product quality, prompt and reliable delivery, supplier reputation, technical support, and price. For example, Atlas Corporation developed a commanding position in the industrial door market by providing customized products in just 4 weeks, much faster than the industry average of 12 to 15 weeks. Atlas's primary market is companies with an immediate need for customized doors.

- *Purchasing strategies:* The purchasing strategies of buying organizations can shape microsegments. Two purchasing profiles that have been identified are satisficers and optimizers. **Satisficers** contact familiar suppliers and place the order with the first to satisfy product and delivery requirements. **Optimizers** consider numerous suppliers (both familiar and unfamiliar), solicit bids, and study all proposals carefully before selecting one. Recognizing satisficers and optimizers is quite easy. A few key questions during a sales call, such as "Why do you buy product X from vendor A?", usually produce answers that identify purchaser profiles.

- *Importance of purchase:* Classifying business customers according to the significance they attach to the purchase of a product is especially appropriate when customers use the product differently. This approach is also appropriate when the purchase is considered routine by some customers but very important by others. For instance, a small entrepreneur would consider a laser printer a major capital purchase, but a large office would find it a normal expense.

- *Personal characteristics:* The personal characteristics of purchase decision makers (their demographic characteristics, decision style, tolerance for risk, confidence level, job responsibilities, and so on) influence their buying behavior and thus offer a viable basis for segmenting some business markets. IBM computer buyers, for example, are sometimes characterized as being more risk averse than buyers of less expensive "clones" that perform essentially the same functions. In advertising, therefore, IBM stresses its reputation for high quality and reliability.

satisficers
Type of business customer that places an order with the first familiar supplier to satisfy product and delivery requirements.

optimizers
Type of business customer that considers numerous suppliers, both familiar and unfamiliar, solicits bids, and studies all proposals carefully before selecting one.

STEPS IN SEGMENTING A MARKET

The purpose of market segmentation, in both consumer and business markets, is to identify marketing opportunities. Exhibit 8.7 traces the steps in segmenting a market. Note that steps 5 and 6 are actually marketing activities that follow market segmentation (steps 1 through 4).

6 List the steps involved in segmenting markets.

1. *Select a market or product category for study:* Define the overall market or product category to be studied—one in which the firm already competes, a new but related market or product category, or a totally new one. For instance, Anheuser-Busch closely examined the beer market before introducing Michelob Light and Bud Light. Anheuser-Busch also carefully studied the market for salty snacks before introducing the Eagle brand.

2. *Choose a basis or bases for segmenting the market:* This step requires managerial insight, creativity, and market knowledge. There are no scientific procedures for selecting segmentation variables. However, a successful segmentation scheme must produce segments that meet the four basic criteria discussed earlier in this chapter.

Exhibit 8.7
Steps in Segmenting a Market and Subsequent Activities

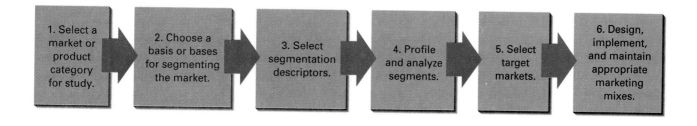

1. Select a market or product category for study.
2. Choose a basis or bases for segmenting the market.
3. Select segmentation descriptors.
4. Profile and analyze segments.
5. Select target markets.
6. Design, implement, and maintain appropriate marketing mixes.

3. *Select segmentation descriptors:* After choosing one or more bases, the marketer must select the segmentation descriptors. Descriptors identify the specific segmentation variables to use. For example, if a company selects demographics as a basis of segmentation, it may use age, occupation, and income as descriptors.

4. *Profile and analyze segments:* The profile should include the segments' size, expected growth, purchase frequency, current brand usage, brand loyalty, and long-term sales and profit potential. This information can then be used to rank potential market segments by profit opportunity, risk, consistency with organizational mission and objectives, and other factors important to the firm.

5. *Select target markets:* Selecting target markets is not a part of, but a natural outcome of, the segmentation process. It is a major decision that influences and often directly determines the firm's marketing mix. This topic is examined in greater detail later in this chapter.

6. *Design, implement, and maintain appropriate marketing mixes:* The marketing mix has been described as product, distribution, promotion, and pricing strategies intended to bring about mutually satisfying exchange relationships with target markets. Chapters 10 through 21 explore these topics in detail.

STRATEGIES FOR SELECTING TARGET MARKETS

So far this chapter has focused on the market segmentation process, which is only the first step in deciding who to approach about buying a product. The next task is to choose one or more target markets. A **target market** is a group of people or organizations for which an organization designs, implements, and maintains a marketing mix intended to meet the needs of that group, resulting in mutually satisfying exchanges. The three general strategies for selecting target markets—undifferentiated, concentrated, and multisegment targeting—are illustrated in Exhibit 8.8. Exhibit 8.9 illustrates the advantages and disadvantages of each targeting strategy.

Undifferentiated Targeting

A firm using an **undifferentiated targeting strategy** essentially adopts a mass-market philosophy, viewing the market as one big market with no individual segments.

---

target market
A group of people or organizations for which an organization designs, implements, and maintains a marketing mix intended to meet the needs of that group, resulting in mutually satisfying exchanges.

7 Discuss alternative strategies for selecting target markets.

undifferentiated targeting strategy
Marketing approach that views the market as one big market with no individual segments and thus requires a single marketing mix.

Exhibit 8.8
Three Strategies for Selecting Target Markets

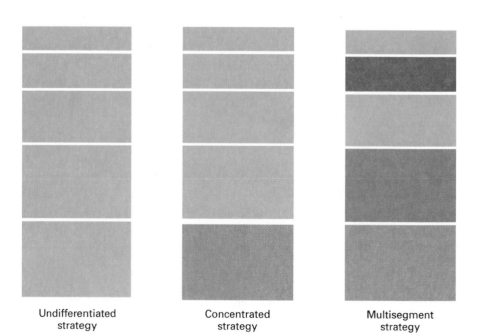

Undifferentiated strategy   Concentrated strategy   Multisegment strategy

Targeting Strategy	Advantages	Disadvantages
Undifferentiated targeting	• Potential savings on production/marketing costs	• Unimaginative product offerings • Company more susceptible to competition
Concentrated targeting	• Concentration of resources • Can better meet the needs of a narrowly defined segment • Allows some small firms to better compete with larger firms • Strong positioning	• Segments too small, or changing • Large competitors may more effectively market to niche segment
Multisegment targeting	• Greater financial success • Economies of scale in production/marketing	• High costs • Cannibalization

Exhibit 8.9

Advantages and Disadvantages of Target Marketing Strategies

The firm uses one marketing mix for the entire market. A firm that adopts an undifferentiated targeting strategy assumes that individual customers have similar needs that can be met with a common marketing mix.

The first firm in an industry sometimes uses an undifferentiated targeting strategy. With no competition, the firm may not need to tailor marketing mixes to the preferences of market segments. Henry Ford's famous quote about the Model T is a classic example of an undifferentiated targeting strategy: "They can have their car in any color they want, as long as it's black." At one time, Coca-Cola used this strategy with a single product and a single size of its familiar green bottle. Marketers of commodity products, such as flower and sugar, are also likely to use an undifferentiated targeting strategy.

One advantage of undifferentiated marketing is the potential for saving a lot on production and marketing. Because only one item is produced, the firm should be able to achieve economies of mass production. Also, marketing costs may be lower when there is only one product to promote and a single channel of distribution.

Too often, however, an undifferentiated strategy emerges by default rather than by design, reflecting a failure to consider the advantages of a segmented approach. The result is often sterile, unimaginative product offerings that have little appeal to anyone.

Another problem associated with undifferentiated targeting is that it makes the company more susceptible to competitive inroads. Hershey lost a big share of the candy market to Mars and other candy companies before it changed to a multisegment targeting strategy. Coca-Cola forfeited its position as the leading seller of cola drinks in supermarkets to Pepsi-Cola in the late 1950s, when Pepsi began offering several sizes of containers.

You might think a firm producing an unexciting product like toilet tissue would adopt an undifferentiated strategy. However, this market has industrial segments and consumer segments. Industrial buyers want an economical, single-ply product sold in boxes of a hundred

Domino uses an undifferentiated targeting strategy to market its sugar. Aside from grocery store brands, there is no real competition for its products.

Courtesy Domino Sugar Corporation

rolls. The consumer market demands a more versatile product in smaller quantities. Within the consumer market, the product is differentiated as colored or white, designer print or no print, cushioned or noncushioned, and economy priced or luxury priced. Fort Howard Corporation, the market share leader in industrial toilet paper, does not even sell to the consumer market.

Concentrated Targeting

concentrated targeting strategy
A strategy used to select one segment of a market for targeting marketing efforts.

niche
One segment of a market.

OshKosh B'Gosh, Inc., was so successful with its children's wear that it could not sell to anyone else. Faced with a concentrated market, the company is expanding into children's shoes, eyewear, and plush toys.
Courtesy OshKosh B'Gosh, Inc.

With a **concentrated targeting strategy,** a firm selects a market **niche** (one segment of a market) for targeting its marketing efforts. Because the firm is appealing to a single segment, it can concentrate on understanding the needs, motives, and satisfactions of that segment's members and on developing and maintaining a highly specialized marketing mix. Some firms find that concentrating resources and doing a better job of meeting the needs of a narrowly defined market segment is more profitable than spreading resources over several different segments.

For example, shopping center marketers have developed niche malls specifically to attract such groups as working women and African-Americans. The malls include a customized retail mix, easy parking, phone-in shopping, and targeted promotions.[38] Another example is Nucor Steel, which is small compared to the largest U.S. steel firms, but it concentrates its efforts on the steel joist segment of the steel market, and there it leads the industry.

 Small firms often adopt a concentrated targeting strategy to compete effectively with much larger firms. For example, game specialty stores are a growing group of niche retailers. These small, independent operators count on personal service and product selection, rather than price, to differentiate themselves from large discounters such as Toys R Us. Many of these game stores target the adult market, carrying classic games such as Monopoly as well as exotic chess and backgammon sets and gambling supplies.[39]

Some firms, on the other hand, use a concentrated strategy to establish a strong position in a desirable market segment. Porsche, for instance, targets a very upscale automobile market—"class appeal, not mass appeal."

Concentrated targeting violates the old adage, "Don't put all your eggs in one basket." If the chosen segment is too small or if it shrinks because of environmental changes, the firm may suffer negative consequences. For instance, OshKosh B'Gosh, Inc., was highly successful selling children's wear in the 1980s. It was so successful, however, that the children's line came to so define OshKosh's image that the company could not sell clothes to anyone else. Attempts at marketing older children's clothing, women's casual clothes, and maternity wear were all abandoned. Now, recognizing it is in the children's-wear business, the company is expanding into products such as kid's shoes, children's eyewear, and plush toys.[40]

A concentrated strategy can also be disastrous for a firm that is not successful in its narrowly defined target market. Before Procter & Gamble introduced Head and Shoulders shampoo several years ago, several small firms were already selling antidandruff shampoos. Head and Shoulders was introduced with a large promotional campaign, and the new brand captured over half the market immediately. Within a year, several of the firms that had been concentrating on this market segment went out of business.

Rembrandt Displays The Style That Makes Him Such A Renaissance Boy.

Rembrandt Ari Duran, age 8, New York, New York.

Strong lines and bold strokes combine to make the OshKosh B'Gosh holiday collection a body of art anyone can appreciate. For the store nearest you, call 1-800-282-4674.

The Biggest Name In Kids' Clothes.

Multisegment Targeting

A firm that chooses to serve two or more well-defined market segments and develops a distinct marketing mix for each has a **multisegment targeting strategy.** Stouffer's, for example, offers gourmet entrees for one segment of the frozen dinner market and Lean Cuisine for another. Hershey offers premium candies like Golden Almond chocolate bars, packaged in gold foil, that are marketed to an adult audience. Another chocolate bar, called RSVP, is targeted toward consumers who crave the taste of Godiva chocolates at the price of a Hershey bar. Cosmetics companies seek to increase sales and market share by targeting multiple age and ethnic groups. Maybelline and Cover Girl, for example, market different lines to teenage women, young adult women, older women, and African-American women.

Cover Girl Home Page
How does Cover Girl's WWW site target its products to different types of women?

http://www.covergirl.com/

multisegment targeting strategy
A strategy that chooses two or more well-defined market segments and develops a distinct marketing mix for each.

Sometimes organizations use different promotional appeals, rather than completely different marketing mixes, as the basis for a multisegment strategy. For example, different target markets are likely to be attracted to physical fitness programs called Keep Fit, Conditioning, Fitness Training, Slimnastics, Aerobics, Aerobic Dance, Health Club, Figure Control, Jazzercise, or Revitalize. Although the basic program content may be similar, the names are designed to meet different wants.

Multisegment targeting offers many potential benefits to firms, including greater sales volume, higher profits, larger market share, and economies of scale in manufacturing and marketing. Yet it also involves costs. Before deciding to use this strategy, firms should compare the benefits and costs of multisegment targeting to those of undifferentiated and concentrated targeting. The following list details the costs:

- *Product design costs:* A multisegment targeting strategy sometimes results in different products for different market segments. It may involve nothing more than a package or labeling change, or it may require a complete redesign of the product itself. An example of a slight modification is packaging Coca-Cola in various sizes and types of containers, such as 12-ounce cans and 2-liter bottles. In contrast, Compaq Computer incurred major costs in developing both desktop and laptop computers. Creating different products with unique features sought by different segments of the market can be very expensive.

- *Production costs:* Total production costs mount as a firm develops and markets different products for different market segments. Each manufacturing run may require a retooling of production equipment, during which time production lines are idle. The result is higher costs for the manufacturer.

- *Promotion costs:* Whether or not a firm produces a different product for each market segment, it normally must develop separate promotional strategies. Significant expenditures of human and financial resources are required. A firm normally must create different advertisements for each segment, and different media may be necessary for the ads.

- *Inventory costs:* The more market segments a firm tries to serve, the higher the inventory costs are likely to be. With inventory costs averaging between 20 and 30 percent of inventory sales value, a multisegment targeting strategy can be very expensive.

- *Marketing research costs:* An effective market segmentation strategy relies on accurate, detailed market information about consumer demographics; consumer reaction to various product designs or promotional appeals; consumer interests, attitudes, and opinions; and so on. Gathering this information can be a time-consuming and expensive process. For example, the Kroger supermarket chain conducts more than 250,000 consumer interviews each year to determine changing consumer wants.

- *Management costs:* A multisegment targeting strategy requires extra management time. As the number of segments increases, so does the number of decisions. The firm must coordinate the marketing mix for each targeted market segment.

- *Cannibalization:* **Cannibalization** occurs when sales of a new product cut into sales of a firm's existing products. For example, pharmaceutical firms have been introducing new over-the-counter antacids that block the production of stomach acids (like Tagamet HB or Pepcid AC), rather than treat heartburn with traditional antacids that work by neutralizing stomach acid (like Tums or Mylanta). However, these firms are aware that the new heartburn drugs are likely to cannibalize their traditional antacid products. In advertising Tagamet HB, for instance, SmithKline has to avoid comparing it to Tums, the firm's antacid moneymaker.[41]

Another potential cost to companies of multisegment targeting is loss of consumer goodwill that can result from the company's need for information, as is discussed in the "Ethics in Marketing" box.

POSITIONING

The term **positioning** refers to developing a specific marketing mix to influence potential customers' overall perception of a brand, product line, or organization in general. (**Position** is the place a product, brand, or group of products occupies in consumers' minds relative to competing offerings.) Consumer goods marketers are particularly concerned with positioning. Procter & Gamble, for example, markets 11 different laundry detergents, each with a unique position, as illustrated in Exhibit 8.10.

cannibalization
Situation that occurs when sales of a new product cut into sales of a firm's existing products.

positioning
Developing a specific marketing mix to influence potential customers' overall perception of a brand, product line, or organization in general.

position
The place a product, brand, or group of products occupies in consumers' minds relative to competing offerings.

8 Explain how and why firms implement positioning strategies and how product differentiation plays a role.

Ethics in Marketing

Less Privacy Seen as Trade-Off for Better Target Marketing

More efficient targeting has benefits for marketers, but it also has a disadvantage for consumers: less privacy. A recent consumer poll said 79% of those surveyed were concerned about privacy. Consumers were more concerned with the release of medical and financial information and less concerned about demographic information. Further research showed that there are seven areas where privacy becomes an issue: collection (too much information collected), internal unauthorized secondary use (running contests just to get databases), external unauthorized secondary use (selling to third parties), errors (especially on credit reports), improper access (who can look at the data), reduced judgment (consumers diminished to numbers), and combining data (companies forming cobranding deals).

The conflict over access to and control over information deals with striking a fair balance between individuals' privacy and the financial interests of business. Many consumers feel that companies commit a violation of trust by selling demographic information to third parties. Companies are using a variety of methods to gather demographic information. It has been estimated that 56 percent of the largest companies currently develop private databases and 10 percent plan to do so. The percentage is expected to reach 85 percent by 2000.[42]

Should consumers be concerned over demographic information being collected by companies? Can companies effectively do target marketing without demographic information? What would be a fair balance between consumers' right to privacy and companys' need for information?

Brand	Positioning	Market Share
Tide	Tough, powerful cleaning	31.1%
Cheer	Tough cleaning and color protection	8.2%
Bold	Detergent plus fabric softener	2.9%
Gain	Sunshine scent and odor-removing formula	2.6%
Era	Stain treatment and stain removal	2.2%
Dash	Value brand	1.8%
Oxydol	Bleach-boosted formula, whitening	1.4%
Solo	Detergent and fabric softener in liquid form	1.2%
Dreft	Outstanding cleaning for baby clothes, safe for tender skin	1.0%
Ivory Snow	Fabric and skin safety on baby clothes and fine washables	0.7%
Ariel	Tough cleaner, aimed at Hispanics	0.1%

Exhibit 8.10
Positioning of Procter & Gamble Detergents

Source: Adapted from, "Don't Look for P&G to Pare Detergents" by Jennifer Lawrence. Reprinted by permission from the May 3, 1993, issue of *Advertising Age.* Copyright © 1993 Crain Communications Inc.

Positioning assumes that consumers compare products on the basis of important features. Marketing efforts that emphasize irrelevant features are therefore likely to misfire. For example, Crystal Pepsi and a clear version of Coca-Cola's Tab failed because consumers perceived the "clear" positioning as more of a marketing gimmick than a benefit.[43]

Effective positioning requires assessing the positions occupied by competing products, determining the important dimensions underlying these positions, and choosing a position in the market where the organization's marketing efforts will have the greatest impact. If everyone else is making large, five-passenger automobiles that appeal to luxury, why not build small economy cars? If major competitors are all stressing low price, why not introduce a prestige brand? If your major competitors are colas, perhaps stress that your product is an "uncola."

Product Differentiation

Product differentiation is a positioning strategy that some firms use to distinguish their products from those of competitors. The distinctions can be either real or perceived. Tandem Computer designed machines with two central processing units and two memories for computer systems that can never afford to be down or lose their database (for example, an airline reservation system). In this case, Tandem used product differentiation to create a product with very real advantages for the target market.

Bleaches, aspirin, unleaded regular gasoline, and some soaps are differentiated by such trivial means as brand names, packaging, color, smell, or "secret" additives. The marketer attempts to convince consumers that a particular brand is distinctive and that they should demand it over competing brands.

Product differentiation can be difficult for some products. For instance, consumers do not see much difference in the gambling facilities of riverboat casinos, a growing industry in the United States. The Empress River Casino

product differentiation
A positioning strategy that some firms use to distinguish their products from those of competitors.

in the Chicago suburb of Joliet stresses customer service, maintaining that differences do exist in the people behind the tables and the setting in which they are located.[44]

Perceptual Mapping

perceptual mapping
A means of displaying or graphing, in two or more dimensions, the location of products, brands, or groups of products in customers' minds.

Perceptual mapping is a means of displaying or graphing, in two or more dimensions, the location of products, brands, or groups of products in customers' minds. For example, the perceptual map in Exhibit 8.11A is the result of a 1982 study by General Motors of consumers' perceptions of the five GM automobile divisions: Buick, Cadillac, Chevrolet, Oldsmobile, and Pontiac. Consumer perceptions are plotted on two axes. The horizontal axis ranges from conservative and family oriented at one extreme to expressive and personal at the other. The vertical axis is used to rate price perceptions, and it ranges from high to low. Note that in 1982 the various GM divisions were not perceived as especially distinctive. Consumers didn't clearly distinguish one brand from another, especially on the conservative/family versus expressive/personal dimension.

In 1984, General Motors was reorganized to reduce overlap and duplication among divisions and to produce fewer, more distinctive models. The perceptual map in Exhibit 8.11B shows GM's plans for **repositioning,** or changing consumers' percep-

Exhibit 8.11
Perceptual Maps and Positioning Strategies for General Motors Passenger Cars

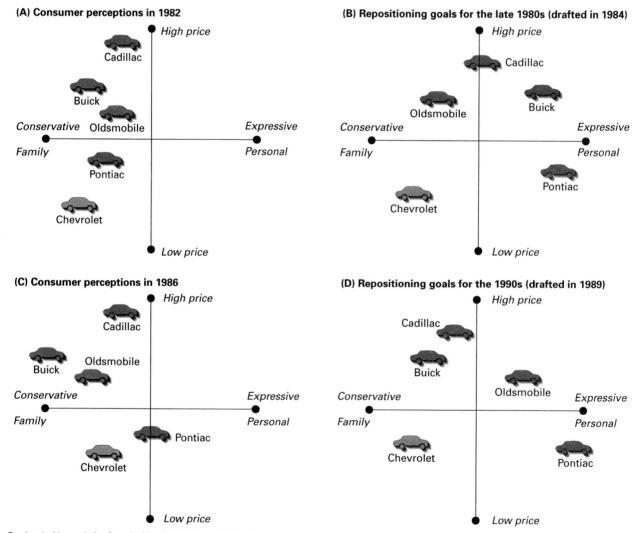

(A) Consumer perceptions in 1982

(B) Repositioning goals for the late 1980s (drafted in 1984)

(C) Consumer perceptions in 1986

(D) Repositioning goals for the 1990s (drafted in 1989)

Reprinted with permission from the May 3, 1993, issue of *Advertising Age.* Copyright © 1993, Crain Communications Inc.

tions of the various models, by the late 1980s. As Exhibit 8.11C shows, however, consumer perceptions changed very little between 1982 and 1986.

Positioning Bases

Firms use a variety of bases for positioning, including the following:[45]

- *Attribute:* A product is associated with an attribute, product feature, or customer benefit. For example, Rockport shoes are positioned as an always comfortable brand that is available in a range of styles from working shoes to dress shoes.[46]

- *Price and quality:* This positioning base may stress high price as a signal of quality or emphasize low price as an indication of value. Neiman Marcus uses the high-priced strategy; Kmart has successfully followed the price and value strategy. Cunard's, a London-based cruise-liner company that had fallen on hard times, was able to launch a turnaround by repositioning the brand to compete in the affluent consumer market. Changes included a new corporate identity, a series of elegant ad campaigns, and improved customer service.[47]

- *Use or application:* During the past few years, AT&T telephone service advertising has emphasized communicating with loved ones using the "Reach Out and Touch Someone" campaign. Stressing uses or applications can be an effective means of positioning a product with buyers. The advertising slogan, "Orange juice isn't just for breakfast anymore," is an effort to reposition the product, in terms of time and place of use, as an all-occasion beverage.

- *Product user:* This positioning base focuses on a personality or type of user. For instance, Zale Corporation has several jewelry store concepts, each positioned to a different user. The Zale stores cater to middle-of-the-road consumers with traditional styles. Their Gordon's stores appeal to a slightly older clientele with a contemporary look. Guild is positioned for the more affluent 50-plus consumer.[48]

- *Product class:* The objective here is to position the product as being associated with a particular category of products. An example is to position a margarine brand with respect to butter.

- *Competitor:* Positioning against competitors is part of any positioning strategy. The Avis rental car positioning as number two exemplifies positioning against specific competitors.

It is not unusual for a marketer to use more than one of these bases. The AT&T "Reach Out and Touch Someone" campaign that stressed use also emphasized the relatively low cost of long-distance calling. The Milk-Made Company is positioning its Cool Cow, a cholesterol-free milk product, to the youth market as a healthful yet hip alternative to soft drinks.[49]

AT&T
Which message does AT&T's Web site more strongly reinforce: the "Reach Out and Touch Someone" campaign or the economics of long-distance calling?

http://www.att.com/

GLOBAL ISSUES IN MARKET SEGMENTATION AND TARGETING

 Chapter 4 discussed the trend toward global market standardization, which enables firms like Coca-Cola, Colgate-Palmolive, McDonald's, and Nike to market similar products using similar marketing strategies in many different

9 Discuss global market segmentation and targeting issues.

Firms may be able to use a global market standardization approach to targeting "Asian yuppies" whose spending power and consumption rival those of their U.S. counter- parts.

© Caroline Parsons/Gamma Liaison

countries. This chapter has also discussed the trend toward targeting smaller, more precisely defined markets.

The tasks involved in segmenting markets, selecting target markets, and design- ing, implementing, and maintaining appropriate marketing mixes (described in Exhibit 8.7) are the same whether the marketer has a local perspective or a global vi- sion. The main difference is the segmentation variables commonly used. Countries of the world are commonly grouped using such variables as per capita gross domes- tic product, geography, religion, culture, or political system.

Some firms have tried to group countries of the world or customer segments around the world using lifestyle or psychographic variables. So-called "Asian yuppies"—in places like Singapore, Hong Kong, Japan, and South Korea—have substantial spend- ing power and exhibit purchase and consumption behavior similar to that of their better-known counterparts in the United States. In this case, firms may be able to use a global market standardization approach.

LOOKING BACK

In the vignette at the beginning of this chapter, market segmentation refers to the process of dividing a market into meaningful, relatively similar, and identifiable seg- ments or groups. Targeting is selecting one or more market segments for which an organization designs, implements, and maintains distinctive marketing mixes.

McDonald's is targeting adults with the Arch Deluxe, a burger that is advertised as "the burger with the grown-up taste." The company also offers a Deluxe Chicken sandwich and a larger Filet-O-Fish sandwich. While it may be difficult to predict McDonald's success with its new targeting strategy, the statistics quoted in the vi- gnette indicate the viability of the adult segment. Many adults feel that McDonald's has the best burgers for kids, so they probably already go to the restaurant for that reason. Once they are there, they are likely to try the new meal items. Providing the quality and taste of the sandwiches aimed at adults are good, the strategy has a good chance of success.

SUMMARY

1 *Describe the characteristics of markets and market segments.* A market is composed of individuals or organizations with the ability and willingness to make purchases to fulfill their needs or wants. A market segment is a group of individuals or organizations with similar product needs as a result of one or more common characteristics.

2 *Explain the importance of market segmentation.* Before the 1960s, few businesses targeted specific market segments. Today, segmentation is a crucial marketing strategy for nearly all successful organizations. Market segmentation enables marketers to tailor marketing mixes to meet the needs of particular population segments. Segmentation helps marketers identify consumer needs and preferences, areas of declining demand, and new marketing opportunities.

3 *Discuss criteria for successful market segmentation.* Successful market segmentation depends on four basic criteria. First, a market segment must be substantial; it must have enough potential customers to be viable. Second, a market segment must be identifiable and measurable. Third, members of a market segment must be accessible to marketing efforts. Fourth, a market segment must respond to particular marketing efforts in a way that distinguishes it from other segments.

4 *Describe bases commonly used to segment consumer markets.* There are five commonly used bases for segmenting consumer markets. Geographic segmentation is based on region, size, density, and climate characteristics. Demographic segmentation consists of age, gender, income level, ethnicity, and family life-cycle characteristics. Psychographic segmentation includes personality, motives, and lifestyle characteristics. Benefits sought is a type of segmentation that identifies customers according to the benefits they seek in a product. Finally, usage segmentation divides a market by the amount of product purchased or consumed.

5 *Describe the bases for segmenting business markets.* Business markets can be segmented on two bases. First, macrosegmentation divides markets according to general characteristics, such as location and customer type. Second, microsegmentation focuses on the decision-making units within macrosegments.

6 *List the steps involved in segmenting markets.* Six steps are involved when segmenting markets: (1) Select a market or product category for study, (2) choose a basis or bases for segmenting the market, (3) select segmentation descriptors, (4) profile and analyze segments, (5) select target markets, and (6) design, implement, and maintain appropriate marketing mixes.

7 *Discuss alternative strategies for selecting target markets.* Marketers select target markets using three different strategies: undifferentiated targeting, concentrated targeting, and multisegment targeting. An undifferentiated targeting strategy assumes that all members of a market have similar needs that can be met with a single marketing mix. A concentrated targeting strategy focuses all marketing efforts on a single market segment. Multisegment targeting is a strategy that uses two or more marketing mixes to target two or more market segments.

8 *Explain how and why firms implement positioning strategies and how product differentiation plays a role.* Positioning is used to influence consumer perceptions of a particular brand, product line, or organization in relation to competitors. The term *position* refers to the place that the offering occupies in consumers' minds.

KEY TERMS

benefit segmentation *223*

cannibalization *232*

concentrated targeting strategy *230*

demographic segmentation *215*

80/20 principle *224*

family life cycle (FLC) *220*

geodemographic segmentation *222*

geographic segmentation *215*

macrosegmentation *225*

market *212*

market segment *212*

market segmentation *212*

micromarketing *222*

microsegmentation *226*

multisegment targeting strategy *231*

niche *230*

optimizer *227*

perceptual mapping *234*

position *232*

positioning *232*

product differentiation *233*

psychographic segmentation *221*

repositioning *235*

satisficer *227*

segmentation base (variable) *214*

target market *228*

undifferentiated targeting strategy *228*

usage-rate segmentation *223*

To establish a unique position, firms use product differentiation—emphasizing the real or perceived differences between competing offerings. Products may be differentiated on the basis of attribute, price and quality, use or application, product user, product class, or competitor.

9 *Discuss global market segmentation and targeting issues.* The key tasks in market segmentation, targeting, and positioning, are the same regardless of whether the target market is local, regional, national, or multinational. The main differences are the variables used by marketers in analyzing markets and assessing opportunities and the resources needed to implement strategies.

Discussion and Writing Questions

1. Describe market segmentation in terms of the historical evolution of marketing.
2. Choose magazine ads for five different products. For each ad, write a description of the demographic and psychographic characteristics of the targeted market.
3. Using the descriptions of VALS psychographic segments in Exhibit 8.5, develop three different advertising messages to market a car to actualizers, fulfillers, and believers. Write a memo to the advertising director of the automobile company describing your three message strategies.
4. Form a team with two other students. Select a product category and brand that are familiar to your team. Using Exhibit 8.9, prepare a market segmentation report and describe a targeting plan.
5. Explain multisegment targeting. Describe a company not mentioned in the chapter that uses a multisegment targeting strategy.
6. Form a team with two or three other students. Create an idea for a new product. Describe the segment (or segments) you are going to target with the product and develop a positioning strategy for the product.
7. Distinguish three positioning strategies and identify firms that use them.
8. Select a group of people in your community with an unmet consumer need. Do you consider this a viable market segment? Why or why not?
9. Compare and contrast domestic market segmentation and international market segmentation.
10. Investigate how Delta Airlines uses its Web site to cater to its market segments.

   http://www.delta-air.com/

11. How are visitors to the following Web site segmented when seeking relevant job openings? Try this search engine and report your results.

   http://www.careermag.com/

12. Which VALS™2 type are you? What kinds of magazines are popular among people of your type?

   http://future.sri.com/vals/diamonds.html

Application for Small Business

Judy Brown has always loved working with animals. She has experience in pet grooming, boarding, and in-home pet sitting. Judy wants to open a full-service business utilizing her skills that is uniquely positioned in relation to the traditional pet grooming/boarding businesses that operate in the town where she lives. Customers that use these current pet services deliver their pets to the firms and later pick them up. Most are open between 9 A.M. and 6 P.M. from Monday through Friday.

Judy lives in a midsize city that is close to a major airport. Many hi-tech industries are located in or near her city, so there are a large number of men and women in managerial and information technology positions, and travel is a frequent part of their jobs. A lot of families have pets, so Judy thinks there is a market for pet-related services, despite the current competition.

Questions

1. How should Judy segment the market for pet services?
2. What targeting strategy should Judy use to start her business? Should this strategy change as her business prospers and grows?
3. How should Judy position her pet services business against her competition?

Video Case

Russell's Service Center

Ernest Russell and his wife, Alice, co-owners of Russell's Service Center, Inc., in Pass Christian, Mississippi, were convinced they could maintain an old-style gasoline station/auto repair business in the face of pressure to go to self-service pumps, probably linked to a convenience store.

Could they prove it? Could they successfully continue providing jobs for family members and full service to customers in a Gulf Coast community containing many older people, where even having a flat tire repaired would be difficult if their business vanished?

Prove it the Russells have. They left a location on a federal highway where they had a two-bay service garage and two pump islands with full- and self-service available. Now they are at a downtown intersection with five repair bays and fewer pumps. Sales have risen 11 percent in the past three years—but that doesn't really tell the story.

"Our profit dollars are in the repair part of the business, not gasoline sales," says Ernest Russell, whose management is hands-on. He not only tells employees what to do, but helps do it, while Alice keeps books, does public relations through civic and charity activities, and keeps an eye on daily operations. Ernest explains: "We are now a repair business offering gasoline as a convenience to the customers, rather than a gasoline service doing some repairs. Bottom line is what counts."

As a family business, he adds, "our sons, son-in-law, and nephews all . . . do their part in attracting customers and keeping them, with their courteous, helpful attitudes toward each person coming in." Local firemen are employed as part-timers. "This," says Ernest, "provides them with additional income—firemen in a small town don't make big salaries—and provides us with competent, dedicated employees."

The Russells had run their original service station for 11 years when they made their big move. Their first landlord, the old Gulf Oil—later bought by BP and Chevron—had planned to radically raise their rent but sold the property to a smaller outfit. The new landlord kept the rent constant; however, because taxes had risen, that was bound to change.

There was discussion about converting to a convenience store operation to bring in more revenue.

Then a gas station downtown closed. The Russells asked their bank to finance a purchase, but the bank didn't think a town of 7,000 could support their type of business. However, the Russells worked with other banks and their distributor, Munro Petroleum. Also, one of the property's owners was on their side. A Russell customer who saw a need for their type of business, he carried a second mortgage so they could buy the property.

Today, Russell's Service Center thrives in Pass Christian, providing a range of services including pickup and delivery and road assistance. Says Ernest Russell: "In a time when the full-service station is almost obsolete, we are still here." The community, he says, is "most appreciative."

Questions

1. What bases for market segmentation are addressed in the video? Describe how these bases apply to Russell's Service Center.
2. What segment bases or variables are most appropriate for the Russells to use in marketing their goods and services?
3. Define Russell's Service Center's target market.

LEARNING OBJECTIVES *After studying this chapter, you should be able to:*

1 Explain the concept and purpose of a marketing decision support system.

2 Discuss the nature of database marketing and micromarketing.

3 Define marketing research and explain its importance to marketing decision making.

4 Describe the steps involved in conducting a marketing research project.

5 Discuss the growing importance of scanner-based research.

6 Explain when marketing research should and should not be conducted.

Decision Support Systems and Marketing Research

*E*d Rzasa, vice president of marketing research for Boston Market, Golden, Colorado, believes that marketing research is the key to the chain's future growth. He believes that rapid, just-in-time research provides Boston Market managers the ability to quickly decide on something and then take immediate action. Marketing research has played a key role in the company's rapid growth.

Recently, the company changed from a product (Boston Rotisserie Chicken) to a place (Boston Market Home Style Meals). Rzasa said the company made the decision based on marketing research. The company introduced three new entrees: ham,

meatloaf, and turkey. Rzasa said that research showed that customers wanted more variety, and the name change had to show that the restaurants didn't serve only chicken.

Boston Market also launched a new product, Boston Market Hearth Honey Boneless Glazed Ham, in grocery stores and entered the lunchtime market with Boston Carver Sandwiches, all based on marketing research. It also tested several new ideas: triple-sauced barbecued chicken and dollar-oriented menus with $4 individual meals, $2 kids' meals, and $1 side items.[1]

Boston Market uses marketing research extensively. What are the

various techniques for conducting marketing research? Should managers always do marketing research before they make a decision? How does marketing research relate to decision support systems?

MARKETING DECISION SUPPORT SYSTEMS

1 Explain the concept and purpose of a marketing decision support system.

marketing intelligence
Everyday information about developments in the marketing environment that managers use to prepare and adjust marketing plans.

decision support system (DSS)
An interactive, flexible computerized information system that enables managers to obtain and manipulate information as they are making decisions.

Accurate and timely information is the lifeblood of marketing decision making. Good information can help maximize an organization's sales and efficiently use scarce company resources. To prepare and adjust marketing plans, managers need a system for gathering everyday information about developments in the marketing environment—that is, for gathering **marketing intelligence.** The system most commonly used these days for gathering marketing intelligence is called a *marketing decision support system.*

A marketing **decision support system (DSS)** is an interactive, flexible computerized information system that enables managers to obtain and manipulate information as they are making decisions. A DSS bypasses the information-processing specialist and gives managers access to useful data from their own desks.

These are the characteristics of a true DSS system:

- *Interactive:* Managers give simple instructions and see immediate results. The process is under their direct control; no computer programmer is needed. Managers don't have to wait for scheduled reports.
- *Flexible:* A DSS can sort, regroup, total, average, and manipulate the data in various ways. It will shift gears as the user changes topics, matching information to the problem at hand. For example, the CEO can see highly aggregated figures, and the marketing analyst can view very detailed breakouts.
- *Discovery-oriented:* Managers can probe for trends, isolate problems, and ask "what if" questions.
- *Accessible:* DSS is easy to learn and use by managers who aren't skilled with computers. Novice users should be able to choose a standard, or "default," method of using the system. They can bypass optional features so they can work with the basic system right away while gradually learning to apply its advanced features.

Quaker Oatmeal
Gatorade
How do these Quaker companies use e-mail to build their databases?

http://www.quakeroatmeal.com
http://gatorade.com

Quaker Oats' DSS, for example, contains about 2 billion facts about products, national trends, and the competition. Management credits the DSS with helping the company achieve a number one market share in several product categories, covering Quaker Oats cereals, Gatorade, Van de Camp pork and beans, Rice-a-Roni, and Aunt Jemima pancakes. More than 400 marketing professionals at Quaker Oats use the DSS daily. They use it for three major tasks: reporting, tracking, and running the standard reports; marketing planning, which automates the brand planning and budgeting process by adding "what if" analysis and marketing capabilities; and eliciting people's immediate answers to spontaneous marketing questions.

A hypothetical example showing how DSS can be used is provided by Renee Smith, vice president and manager of new products for Central Corporation. To evaluate sales of a recently introduced product, Renee can "call up" sales by the week, then by the month, breaking them out at her option by, say, customer segments. As she works at her desktop computer, her inquiries can go in several directions, depending on the decision at hand. If her train of thought raises questions about monthly sales last quarter compared to forecasts, she can use her DSS to analyze problems immediately. Renee might see that her new product's sales were significantly below forecast. Were her forecasts too optimistic? She compares other products' sales to her forecasts and finds that the targets were very accurate. Was something wrong with the product? Is her sales department getting insufficient leads, or is it not putting leads to good use? Thinking a minute about how to examine that question, she checks ratios of leads converted to sales product by product. The results disturb her. Only

5 percent of the new product's leads generated orders, compared to the company's 12 percent all-product average. Why? Renee guesses that the sales force is not supporting the new product vigorously enough. Quantitative information from the DSS perhaps could provide more evidence to back that suspicion. But already having enough quantitative knowledge to satisfy herself, the VP acts on her intuition and experience and decides to have a chat with her sales manager.

DATABASE MARKETING AND MICROMARKETING

Perhaps the fastest-growing use of DSS is for **database marketing,** which is the creation of a large computerized file of customers' and potential customers' profiles and purchase patterns. It is usually the key tool for successful micromarketing, which relies on very specific information about a market (see Chapter 8).

Specifically, database marketing can:

- Identify the most profitable and least profitable customers.
- Identify the most profitable market segments or individuals and target efforts with greater efficiency and effectiveness.
- Aim marketing efforts to those goods, services, and market segments that require the most support.
- Increase revenue through repackaging and repricing products for various market segments.
- Evaluate opportunities for offering new products and services.
- Identify products and services that are best-sellers and most profitable.

Beginning in the 1950s, network television enabled advertisers to "get the same message to everyone simultaneously." Database marketing can get a customized, individual message to everyone simultaneously through direct mail. This is why database marketing is sometimes called *micromarketing.* Database marketing can create a computerized form of the old-fashioned relationship that people used to have with the corner grocer, butcher, or baker. "A database is sort of a collective memory," says Richard G. Barlow, president of Frequency Marketing, Inc., a Cincinnati-based consulting firm. "It deals with you in the same personalized way as a mom-and-pop grocery store, where they knew customers by name and stocked what they wanted."[2] Donnelley Marketing Incorporated recently found that 56 percent of manufacturers and retailers were building databases, an additional 10 percent planned to do so, and 85 percent believed that they would need database marketing to be competitive beyond the year 2000.[3]

The size of many databases is astounding: Ford Motor Company, 50 million names; Kraft General Foods, 25 million; Citicorp, 30 million; and Kimberly Clark (maker of Huggies diapers), 10 million new parents' names. GM now has a database of 12 million GM credit card holders, giving the company access to a great deal of data on their buying habits. GM also surveys these customers to get information on driving habits and needs.

2 Discuss the nature of database marketing and micromarketing.

database marketing
The creation of a large computerized file of customers' and potential customers' profiles and purchase patterns.

Database marketing is usually the key to successful micromarketing, which relies on specific information about a market.
Courtesy Market Statistics, A Division of Bill Communications

Ford Motor Company
Citicorp
How does Ford use the Web to increase its database? Compare Citicorp's site to Ford's. Which company uses the Web more effectively to gain market information?

http://www.ford.com/us
http://www.citicorp.com/

Direct marketing and database marketing are not synonymous, although direct marketers have long led the way in using databases. With better targeting of prospects for products and promotions, greater ability to customize marketing messages and programs, and so on, database marketing clearly contributes to greater marketing efficiency. When practiced properly, it yields double-digit response rates, compared to 2 to 4 percent for "junk mail."[4] For example, Hilton Hotels offers targeted promotions to senior citizens through its Senior Honors program, prompting almost half of the members to take previously unplanned trips that included stays at a Hilton hotel or resort.

A technique of growing popularity for building a database is the creation of "customer clubs." Kraft, for example, has been inviting kids to join the Cheese & Macaroni Club. For three proofs-of-purchase, $2.95, and a completed membership form with the child's (and, of course, Mom's) address, Kraft will send a painter's cap, bracelet, shoelaces, a book of stickers, and other goodies. By requiring customers who respond to offers of free shirts, sleeping bags, or other merchandise to fill out detailed questionnaires, Philip Morris has built a database of about 26 million smokers.

Using its huge database, American Express has initiated what it calls "relationship billing," or customized monthly billing, that includes offers triggered by specific purchases such as flights and special store sales. Relationship billing has been rolled out in Europe, Canada, and Mexico, and AMEX claims an increase of 15 to 20 percent in year-over-year cardmember spending in Europe.[5]

Relationship billing allows AMEX to move closer to *mass customization*, the tailoring of communications/offers to individual customers. For example, rather than using broad demographics, AMEX might now define a market segment as "female business travelers who bought jewelry abroad on their last trip." Some of the company's offers have gone out to as few as 20 people but received very high response rates.

Database marketing provides tremendous opportunities for cross-selling related products. For example, Canon Computer Systems maintains a database of its 1.3 million customers. The company obtained a 50 percent response rate in a direct-mail solicitation asking printer owners if they wanted information on a new color scanner; buyers of scanners received four free ink cartridges for their printers.

Vons Company, Southern California's largest supermarket chain and ninth largest in America, has upgraded its check-approval card into a VonsClub card. The card was a foundation for creating a database that gave automatic discounts on items selected for promotion. Vons's objective was to build a comprehensive database of exactly what's in shoppers' baskets each time they leave the store. Using that data, Vons can better understand consumer behavior and send a monthly mailing of individually laser-printed discount coupons to each VonsClub member. Even food processors and manufacturers benefit from Vons's database. Beech-Nut, a maker of baby foods, has used the VonsClub mailer to identify every household that has purchased a baby product for the first time in the preceding eight weeks. Says Susan Widham, vice president of marketing at Beech-Nut, "This program enables me to target an offer specifically to a consumer based on the type and quantity of a product they buy, the frequency [with which] they buy it, and whether they buy my product or my competitor's."[6] Under consideration, she says, is a 50-cents-off coupon—to hold onto Beech-Nut customers—and a $1-off coupon for Gerber Products Co. customers, to get them to switch brands.

Database marketing concerns many Americans because of the potential for invasion of privacy. A recent study found that 45 percent strongly favor legislation that would regulate the use of consumer information, up from 23 percent in 1990.[7] The issue is discussed further in the "Ethics in Marketing" box.

Ethics in Marketing

Databases Can Probe into Your Life

Some companies rent their internal databases to obtain extra revenue. At times, this practice can raise important ethical questions. At one time Blockbuster planned to rent lists of customer rentals at its video stores. The plan was quickly dropped, however, when management found that federal law forbids video stores from disclosing information on movies that customers rent. Burger King doesn't rent its database. A spokesperson for the company noted, "We were concerned that if people knew their names would be sold, it would hamper participation in our Kid's Club."

One way information technology may invade privacy is through computer matching. This typically occurs when a manager accesses several large databases and matches data about an individual in one database with information about him or her in other databases. Usually, the match is made on the Social Security number because it is included on most documents and records pertaining to individuals. By combining databases through matching, a more extensive profile of individuals is obtained and, in this way, the man-

ager learns a great deal about an individual's shopping habits and personal characteristics—so that, ostensibly, better decisions can be made.

Database marketers can provide information on temptingly specific markets. For example, marketers can rent the names, addresses, and phone numbers of 16,000 Jewish singles with incomes of $50,000-plus compiled by Jewish Introductions International. Or perhaps they want to target National Credit Database's 6.2 million bank and retail credit accounts that had fallen behind 60 days or target 80,000 purchasers of Omega Artificial Intelligence Software's "Eliza" psychotherapy software.

Under pressure from New York State authorities, American Express disclosed it was telling merchants more about its cardholders' spending habits than it had previously acknowledged. The company revealed that information about cardholders' lifestyles and

spending habits was used to create joint marketing efforts with merchants. Previously, the company told cardholders that it merely provided merchants with a mailing list for marketing or promotions based on information in the initial application for the card.

As a result of an agreement with the New York Attorney General's office, American Express had to notify more than 20 million cardholders nationwide that it compiles profiles of spending behavior and that it uses the information for "target marketing" purposes. The cardholders would then have the option of having their information excluded from any future marketing efforts.

Should marketers be allowed to rent out their databases? What if they first offer consumers in the database the right to "opt out" by telling the businesses not to use their names for other purposes? Do you feel that legislation is needed to regulate the use of consumer information?

Sources: Jim Castelli, "How to Handle Personal Information," *American Demographics,* March 1996, pp. 50–58; Judith Waldrop, "The Business of Privacy," *American Demographics,* October 1994, pp. 46–55; and Diane Bowers, "Privacy Concerns and the Research Industry," *Marketing Research,* Spring 1994, pp. 48–49.

THE ROLE OF MARKETING RESEARCH

Marketing research is the process of planning, collecting, and analyzing data relevant to a marketing decision. The results of this analysis are then communicated to management. Marketing research plays a key role in the marketing system. It provides decision makers with data on the effectiveness of the current marketing mix and also insights for necessary changes. Furthermore, marketing research is a main data source for both management information systems and DSS.

Marketing research has three roles: descriptive, diagnostic, and predictive. Its *descriptive* role includes gathering and presenting factual statements. For example, what is the historic sales trend in the industry? What are consumers' attitudes toward a product and its advertising? Its *diagnostic* role includes explaining data. For instance, what was the impact on sales of a change in the design of the package? Its *predictive*

3 Define marketing research and explain its importance to marketing decision making.

marketing research
The process of planning, collecting, and analyzing data relevant to a marketing decision.

The U.S. Army used marketing research to develop a profile of the young person most likely to be positively influenced by its recruiting ads.
© Peter Beck/The Stock Market

function is to address "what if" questions. For example, how can the researcher use the descriptive and diagnostic research to predict the results of a planned marketing decision?

Differences Between Marketing Research and DSS

Because marketing research is problem oriented, managers use it when they need guidance to solve a specific problem. Marketing research, for example, has been used to find out what features consumers want in a new personal computer. It has also aided product development managers in deciding how much milk to add in a new cream sauce for frozen peas. The U.S. Army has used marketing research to develop a profile of the young person most likely to be positively influenced by recruiting ads.

In contrast, DSS continually channels information about environmental changes into the organization. This information is gathered from a variety of sources, both inside and outside the firm. One important information source is marketing research. For example, Mastic Corporation, a leading supplier of vinyl siding, asks its nationwide network of distributors and their dealers questions about product quality, Mastic's service to the distributor, the amount of vinyl the distributor sells, and the percentage used for new construction. This information then becomes part of Mastic's DSS. Other data in the system include new housing starts, national unemployment figures, age of housing, and changes in housing styles. Its marketing research is therefore a component or input source for its DSS.

Management Uses of Marketing Research

Marketing research can help managers in several ways. It improves the quality of decision making and helps managers trace problems. Most important, sound marketing research helps managers better understand the marketplace and alerts them to marketplace trends. Finally, marketing research helps managers gauge the perceived value of their goods and services as well as the level of customer satisfaction. A discussion of these benefits follows.

Improving the Quality of Decision Making

Managers can sharpen their decision making by using marketing research to explore the desirability of various marketing alternatives. For example, some years ago General Mills decided to expand into full-service restaurants. Marketing research indicated that the most popular ethnic food category in the United States was Italian and that interest in pasta and preference for Italian food would continue to increase. The company conducted many taste tests to find appropriate spice levels and to create a menu sure to please target customers. These marketing research studies led to the creation of The Olive Garden Italian restaurants, the fastest-growing and most popular full-service Italian restaurant chain in the nation.

Tracing Problems

Another way managers use marketing research is to find out why a plan backfires. Was the initial decision incorrect? Did an unforeseen change in the external environment cause the plan to fail? How can the same mistake be avoided in the future?

Keebler introduced Sweet Spots, a shortbread cookie with a huge chocolate drop on it, in 1992. It has had decent sales and is still on the market, but only after using marketing research to overcome several problems. Soon after introduction, Keebler increased the box size from 10 ounces at $2.29 to 15 ounces at $3.19. Demand immediately fell. Market research showed that Sweet Spots were now considered more of a luxury than an everyday item. Keebler lowered the price and went back to the 10-ounce box. Even though Sweet Spots originally was aimed at upscale adult females, the company also tried to appeal to kids. In subsequent research, Keebler found that the package graphics appealed to mothers but not to children.[8]

Understanding the Marketplace

 Managers also use marketing research to understand the dynamics of the marketplace. Assume that you have recently gone to work for a new company that will design, produce, and market a line of casual clothing for college students, called Movin' Up. Perhaps one of your first concerns would be brand loyalty. That is, are college students loyal to the same brands as their parents, or will they consider new brands? You might also ask whether college students are loyal to the same brands they used in high school. The graphs in Exhibit 9.1 show responses

Exhibit 9.1

A Survey of the College Market

A. Brand loyalty

Are you loyal to the same brands your parents purchase?

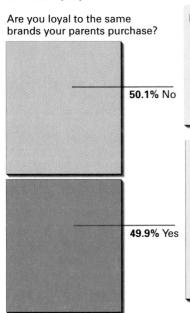

50.1% No

49.9% Yes

Are you loyal to the same brands that you used in high school?

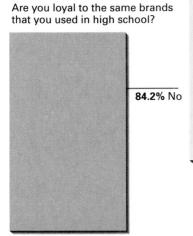

84.2% No

15.8% Yes

B. Media use

Medium	Average hours per day	Is that more or less time than spent in high school?		
		More	Less	Same
1. Radio	2.21	55.0%	32.5%	7.9%
2. Network TV	1.57	67.2	26.1	1.8
3. Cable TV	0.98	52.7	31.4	4.4
4. Newspapers	0.81	36.4	48.4	6.7
5. Magazines	0.67	48.5	36.2	6.2

C. Top 10 favorite magazines (in order)

Magazine	Points
1. *Cosmopolitan*	424
2. *Sport Illustrated*	399
3. *Time*	325
4. *Rolling Stone*	317
5. *Glamour*	315
6. *Vogue*	261
7. *Newsweek*	199
8. *People Weekly*	190
9. *Mademoiselle*	174
10. *Elle*	168

D. Top 10 cable networks (in order)

Network	Points
1. MTV	614
2. ESPN	350
3. HBO	343
4. CNN	240
5. Showtime	78
6. Nick at Nite	74
7. Cinemax	58
8. Dicovery	46
9. VH-1	45
10. TBS	42

E. Response to direct mail

Mailing	Responses
1. J. Crew	10.4%
2. Citibank Visa	10.0
3. American Express	7.1
4. L.L. Bean	6.3
5. Credit cards (nonspecific)	5.6
6. Magazine subscriptions (nonspecific)	4.8
7. Lands' End	3.7
8. MasterCard	3.3
9. Catalogs (nonspecific)	2.2
10. Publisher's Clearing House	2.2

F. Favorite print ads

Spot	Responses
1. Absolut Vodka	12.9%
2. Calvin Klein's Obsession	10.1
3. Nike	5.5
4. Calvin Klein's Eternity	2.2
5. Budweiser	2.0
6. Calvin Klein Jeans	1.8
7. Guess Jeans	1.8
8. Maxell Tapes	1.7
9. J&B Scotch	1.7
10. Benetton	1.5

G. Top 5 spring break locations

Locations	Responses
1. Home	33.3%
2. Florida	10.7
3. None	9.4
4. California	5.0
5. Colorado	4.7

***P**erhaps now, certain luxury cars will start referring to themselves as the Continental Airlines of automobiles.*

J.D. Power and Associates, a name synonymous with automotive excellence, has just awarded Continental the 1996 Frequent Flyer/J.D. Power and Associates Award for customer satisfaction as best airline for flights 500 miles and more.

Quite an achievement, considering that only last year we ranked at the bottom. But we're not resting on our laurels. In the coming year, we will continue to do the things that we believe helped us reach the top. Like being among the best in the business at getting you and your baggage to your destination on time to all of our 180 worldwide destinations. Providing an award-winning frequent flyer program, OnePass. And improving our in-flight service to include such quality brands as Pete's Wicked® Winter Brew and Brothers' Foglifter® Gourmet Coffee. All of which we believe should be standard features on any great airline. For reservations just call your travel agent or 1-800-523-FARE.

Continental
More airline for your money.®

Don't forget to ask for an E-Ticket. • Visit our web site at http://www.flycontinental.com

Continental Airlines was the highest ranked airline for flights 500 miles and more in the Frequent Flyer/J.D. Power and Associates 1996 Domestic Airline Frequent Flyer Satisfaction Study.℠ Study conducted among frequent airline travelers who completed 7086 individual flight evaluations. © 1996 Continental Airlines, Inc.

Companies like Continental Airlines recognize the importance of customer satisfaction.
Courtesy Continental Airlines, Inc.

General Motors, like all large businesses, determines how well it is doing in delivering value by measuring customer satisfaction.
Copyright 1996 GM Corp. Used with permission GM Media Archives.

GM drivers are **ALIKE.**

Or are they?

They're as different as the fifty states they live in. And they drive a lot of different kinds of cars and trucks for a lot of different reasons. But when J.D. Power and Associates asked new vehicle drivers about the quality, sales experience, and delivery of their vehicle, the GM owners were remarkably alike in their point of view. Together, they formed the very picture of satisfaction. And, in turn, consecutive top-ranked performance has earned General Motors a J.D. Power and Associates Chairman's Award.

General Motors is rated highest in satisfaction right from the start.

Based on performance among corporations selling more than 500,000 vehicles annually, including General Motors Corporation, American Honda Motor Company Inc., Chrysler Corporation, Ford Motor Company, Nissan Motor Corporation USA, and Toyota Motor Sales USA Inc., in J.D. Power and Associates 1992-1996 New Vehicle Sales Satisfaction Studies℠ measuring owner satisfaction with the sales experience, delivery and initial condition after the first 90 days of ownership.

- J.D. Power and Associates 1996 Chairman's Award

GM General Motors.

http://www.gm.com

to these questions that you might obtain through marketing research. (The data in Exhibit 9.1 are based on an actual marketing research study of 884 undergraduates at 15 universities across the country.)

Now suppose the company is tentatively planning to promote Movin' Up clothing through direct mail, magazines, and cable television. Management wants to know how much time college students spend each day with various media (see Exhibit 9.1). The advertising director, Sandra Jarboe, is also interested in the magazines college students read, the cable networks they watch, and the direct-mail pieces to which they respond, as shown in Exhibit 9.1. She is also curious about which print ads college students find most appealing. Sandra believes that this information might help her design the Movin' Up advertising campaign. In addition, the promotion manager, John Gates, is considering doing a fashion show of Movin' Up clothing at various popular spring break locations. Therefore, he needs to find out where college students go for spring break. As you can see, marketing research helps managers develop the marketing mix by providing insights into the lifestyles, preferences, and purchasing habits of target consumers.

Fostering Customer Value and Quality

The environment in which business operates is far more competitive and mercurial than it ever has been before. Consumers are less tolerant of poor quality and service, less forgiving, and less loyal to specific brands. Consumer expectations are moving to the highest level. A good product and a fair price are not enough; service must be excellent as well. High product quality, good service, and a fair price mean value—which is, as you will discover in Chapter 13, the cornerstone of customer satisfaction. Satisfied customers are more likely to establish long-term relationships with a company, which help create long-term profitability for the firm.

In such an environment, perceived customer satisfaction is the scorecard that tells a company how well it is doing in delivering value. Marketing research is the vehicle for measuring perceived satisfaction. Today, virtually all large businesses, ranging from IDS Financial Services to General Motors, measure customer satisfaction.

Pizza Hut launched its customer satisfaction tracking survey in January 1995; now it conducts about 50,000 surveys per week. Store managers' bonuses are tied to the research results; therefore, the questionnaire only deals with issues a manager can control. The survey deals with service, food, delivery, and/or dining-in experiences. Pizza Hut found a very strong relationship between satisfaction and frequency of dining in or ordering for delivery. The research also showed a weak relationship between short-term sales growth and customer loyalty. For example, customers rushed to buy the new Stuffed Crust Pizza, but there was no subsequent rise in loyalty. Because of service problems, new customers were not making return trips. The survey helped Pizza Hut identify the problems, and it now has a better understanding of how to handle the next major product launch.[9]

STEPS IN A MARKETING RESEARCH PROJECT

Virtually all firms that have adopted the marketing concept engage in some marketing research because it offers decision makers many benefits. Some companies spend millions on marketing research; others, particularly smaller firms, conduct informal, limited-scale research studies. For example, when Eurasia restaurant, serving Eurasian cuisine, first opened along Chicago's ritzy Michigan Avenue, it drew novelty seekers. But it turned off the important business lunch crowd, and sales began to decline. The owner surveyed several hundred businesspeople working within a mile of the restaurant. He found that they were confused by Eurasia's concept and wanted more traditional Asian fare at lower prices. In response, the restaurant altered its concept; it hired a Thai chef, revamped the menu, and cut prices. The dining room was soon full again.

Whether a research project costs $200 or $2 million, the same general process should be followed. The marketing research process is a scientific approach to decision making that maximizes the chance of getting accurate and meaningful results. Exhibit 9.2 traces the steps: (1) defining the marketing problem, (2) planning the research design and gathering primary data, (3) specifying the sampling procedures, (4) collecting the data, (5) analyzing the data, (6) preparing and presenting the report, and (7) following up.

4 Describe the steps involved in conducting a marketing research project.

Defining the Marketing Problem

The first step in the marketing research process must be to develop either a problem statement or a statement of research objectives on which the decision maker and the researcher can both agree. This step is not as easy as it sounds. But it is important because this statement directs the rest of the study. Some situations require only a simple problem statement; others lend themselves to a detailed statement of research objectives.

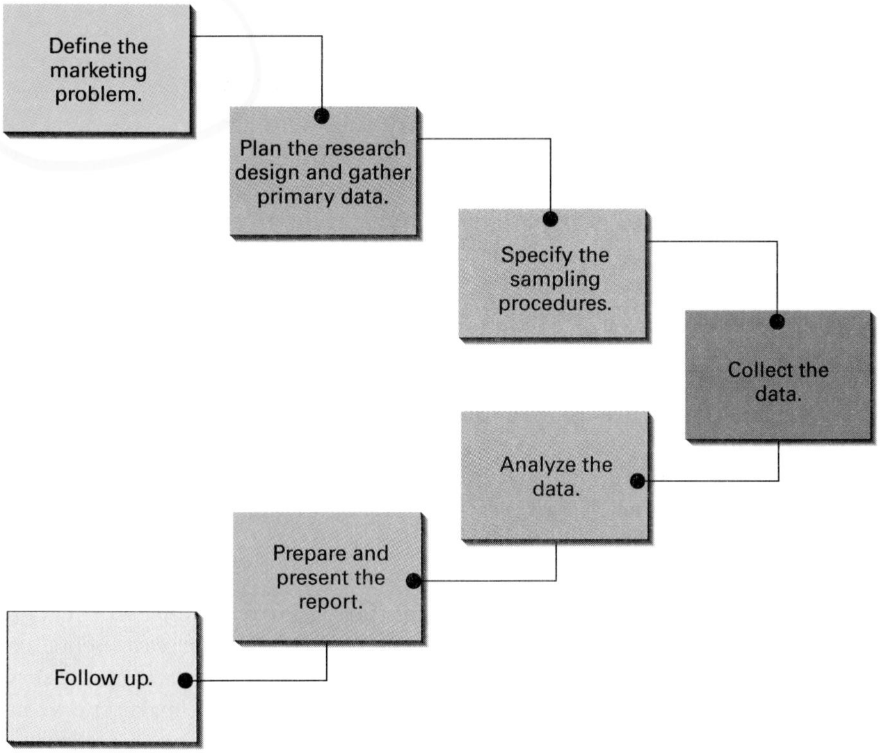

Exhibit 9.2
The Marketing Research Process

- Define the marketing problem.
- Plan the research design and gather primary data.
- Specify the sampling procedures.
- Collect the data.
- Analyze the data.
- Prepare and present the report.
- Follow up.

Situation Analysis

situation analysis
Extensive background investigation into a particular marketing problem.

In some cases, identifying and structuring the problem may itself become the objective of a major background investigation called a **situation analysis.** A situation analysis is especially important to the outside consultant or to any researcher dealing with a particular type of problem for the first time. Situation analysis permits the researcher to become immersed in the problem—to learn about the company, its products, its markets, its marketing history, the competition, and so forth. After gathering this background information, the researcher may need to backtrack and revise the problem statement and research objectives.

After completing a situation analysis, the researcher compiles a list of all the data required to meet the research objectives and then determines the types of data required for decision making. Often the researcher will begin with secondary data in order to further refine the problem statement or the statement of research objectives.

Secondary Data

secondary data
Data previously collected for any purpose other than the one at hand.

Secondary data are data previously collected for any purpose other than the one at hand. People both inside and outside the organization may have gathered secondary data to meet their needs. Exhibit 9.3 describes major sources of secondary data. Most research efforts rely at least partly on secondary data, which can usually be obtained quickly and inexpensively. The problem is locating relevant secondary data.

Secondary data save time and money if they help solve the researcher's problem. Even if the problem is not solved, secondary data have other advantages. They can aid in formulating the problem statement and suggest research methods and other types of data needed for solving the problem. In addition, secondary data can pinpoint the kinds of people to approach and their locations and serve as a basis of comparison for other data. The disadvantages of secondary data stem mainly from a mismatch between the researcher's unique problem and the purpose for which the secondary data were originally gathered, which are typically different. For example, a major consumer products manufacturer wanted to determine the market potential for a fireplace log made of coal rather than compressed wood byproducts. The researcher found plenty of secondary data about total wood consumed as fuel, quantities consumed in each state, and types of wood burned. Secondary data were also available about consumer attitudes and purchase patterns of wood byproduct fireplace logs. The wealth of secondary data provided the researcher with many insights into the artificial log market. Yet nowhere was there any information that would tell the firm whether consumers would buy artificial logs made of coal.

Online computerized databases have made gathering secondary data much easier.
Courtesy American Business Information, Inc.

The quality of secondary data may also pose a problem. Often secondary data sources do not give detailed information that would enable a researcher to assess their quality or relevance. Whenever possible, a researcher needs to address these important questions: Who gathered the data? Why were the data obtained? What methodology was used? How were classifications (such as heavy users versus light users) developed and defined? When was the information gathered?

Online Databases. Gathering traditional secondary data is often an arduous task. Researchers write requests for government, trade association, or other reports and then wait several weeks for a reply. Frequently, they make one or more trips to the library only to find that the needed reports are

Exhibit 9.3
*Major Sources of
Secondary Data*

Source	Description
Internal information	Internal company information may be helpful in solving a particular marketing problem. Examples include sales invoices, other accounting records, data from previous marketing research studies, and historical sales data.
Market research firms	Companies such as A. C. Nielsen, Arbitron, and IMS International are major sources of secondary data regarding market share for consumer products and the characteristics of media audiences.
Trade associations	Many trade associations, such as the National Industrial Conference Board and the National Retail Merchants Association, collect data of interest to members.
University research bureaus, professional associations, foundations	A variety of nonprofit organizations collect and disseminate data of interest to marketing researchers.
Commercial publications	*Advertising Age, Sales Management, Product Marketing, Merchandising Week,* and many other commercial publications provide useful research data.
Government data	The federal government is a treasure trove of secondary data. Among its reports are *Census of Housing, Census of Retail Trade, Census of Services Industries, Census of Manufacturers, Statistical Abstract of the US., Economic Indicators,* and *U.S. Industrial Outlook.* An increasing amount of government data can be accessed via the Internet. A tremendous number of census reports such as the *Current Population Survey, County Business Patterns,* and the *County and City Data* book can be reached through http://www.census.gov. Census data is also available on CD-ROM.
Online databases	Two excellent online databases are Profound's RESEARCHLINE or Dialog's MARKETFULL. Another good database is Hoover's BUSINESS RESOURCES. The latter offers detailed profiles of 1,500 businesses plus smaller profiles on 6,200 others. The key word on AOL is "Hoover" and on CompuServe the Go word is "Hoover."
CD-ROM database packages	Claritas has CD-ROM packages available to analyze market segments and to do demographic studies. Find/SVP offers hundreds of marketing research reports on CD-ROM.

Exhibit 9.3
*Major Sources of
Secondary Data*

checked out or missing. Today, however, online computerized databases have reduced the drudgery associated with gathering secondary data. An **online database** is a collection of public information accessible by anyone with the proper computer facilities. With over 10,000 online databases available, practically any topic of interest to a marketing researcher is contained in some database.

Hourly fees for consulting databases can range from nominal ($20) to expensive ($200 or more). The network through which users call the databases usually charges by the hour, too, and the charge is roughly equivalent to what you might spend if you had to call the database computer by long-distance telephone. Some databases also charge for the actual information users retrieve. A bibliographic citation might be free, but the full text of an article might cost a few dollars, and a corporate financial report might run $100 or more. Users must know what costs they're facing

online database
A collection of public information accessible to anyone with the proper computer facilities.

before they request a lot of information. Some vendors charge an annual flat fee that allows unlimited searches.

For a look at how an online database can affect decision making, consider the experience of Superior, Inc. (not its actual name), a large East Coast consumer goods firm. One morning its president woke up to some unpleasant news. A competitor was rumored to be marshaling its troops for an attack on the market for one of Superior's personal-care products, worth $30 million in annual sales. Later that day, concerned executives at Superior were already preparing to take a drastic step: slashing the price to defuse the competitive challenge.

Before taking that step, however, Superior's executives decided to do a little research. Their online database told them that the competitor had been bought several years earlier by a conglomerate. Next, a check of local business newspaper databases turned up evidence of an ad agency hiring new personnel to back up the rumored campaign. Further online searches revealed that the parent company had once tried to sell the unprofitable subsidiary. Another story indicated that the parent company's bonds were being downgraded and mentioned a lawsuit from a bond holder. And a business news database revealed that a senior executive of the parent company had recently retired, with no successor named. Other stories noted that two other executives had left and hinted at turmoil at the board level.

Superior's executives decided that what at first appeared to be an aggressive threat was actually no more than a gesture by a paralyzed firm unable to take new initiatives. "If there is any gold outside," beamed one Superior executive, "it looks like they just don't have a shovel to pick it up with." Result: Superior's president decided to maintain prices and thereby preserve company profits.

online database vendor
An intermediary that acquires databases from database creators.

Online Database Vendors. An **online database vendor** is an intermediary that acquires databases from database creators. Such vendors offer electronic mail, news, finance, sports, weather, airline schedules, software, encyclopedias, bibliographies, directories, full-text information, and numeric databases. Thus, a user can go to a single online vendor and gain access to a variety of databases. Billing is simplified because a single invoice is used for all the databases on the vendor's system. Because all of a vendor's databases have a standardized search procedure, this function is simplified. Online vendors also provide an index to help researchers determine which databases will most likely meet their needs.

Several of the most popular online vendors are CompuServe, America Online, Prodigy, Dow Jones News/Retrieval Service, and DIALOG. CompuServe is a subsidiary of H&R Block. DIALOG, a subsidiary of Knight-Ridder, offers more than 400 different databases containing more than 150 million items of information. Selected databases offered by several major online vendors are shown in Exhibit 9.4. The depth of the number and types of databases available are extraordinary. For example, CompuServe offers five U.S. demographics databases. A summary of each is detailed in Exhibit 9.5.

Exhibit 9.4
Selected Offerings of the Popular Online Vendors

Dow Jones	Dialog	CompuServe
Disclosure II (business database)	Disclosure II	Standard & Poor's General Information File
Dow Jones News	Management Contents	Washington Post
Current Quotes	Standard & Poor's Corporate Description	World Book Encyclopedia
Wall Street Journal	Books in Print	Microquote (stock information)
Academic American Encyclopedia	Electronic Yellow Pages	Business Information Wire
Cineman Movie Reviews	Magazine Index	AP News
AP News	AP News	Comp*U*Store
Comp*U*Store	OAG	OAG
OAG		

Exhibit 9.5

U.S. Demographic Databases Offered by CompuServe

- *Business Demographics* reports from market statistics are based on U.S. census information and are designed for business market analysis. Two types of reports are offered. The Business to Business Report includes information on all broad Standard Industrial Classification (SIC) categories, providing the total number of employees in each category for a designated geographical area. The Advertisers' Service Report offers data on businesses that constitute the SIC categories for Retail Trade. Each $10 report breaks down the total number of businesses for each specified geographical area in relation to company size. Both reports can be requested by zip code, county, state, metropolitan area, Arbitron TV markets, Nielsen TV markets, or the entire United States.
- *Cendata* offers U.S. census information directly from the U.S. Census Bureau, allowing you to spot patterns, trends, and correlations that make for informed decisions. This menu-based system offers several hundred thousand records culled from the censuses and surveys conducted by the Census Bureau for the entire United States, as well as specific states and counties, on such topics as agriculture, business, construction and housing, foreign trade, governments, manufacturing, population, and genealogy. Economic time-series data from the U.S. government are published on Cendata within an hour of its release to the media, offering users instant access to timely information on current economic developments. In addition to census reports, Cendata features explanatory articles that help make sense of the numerical data.
- *Neighborhood Demographic Reports* from CACI, Inc., provide basic demographic information by U.S. zip code. Four neighborhood reports are available: Demographics, Civic/Public Activity, Gift Idea, and Sports/Leisure Activity. Each report costs $10.
- *Superside* from CACI, Inc. allows you to narrow your search to specific and compact geographical areas. The reports are offered for the entire United States and every state, county, metropolitan area, Arbitron TV market, Nielsen TV market, place, census tract, minor civil division, and zip code in the country. Demographic reports are provided, covering general demographics, income, housing, education, employment, and current and projected-year forecasts. You can focus your search on one specific geographic area or enter more than one for a consolidated market report. Included are Demographic Reports based on the 1990 Census Profile, Update and Forecast Data, and Purchase Potential Reports, as well as ACORN Target Marketing, which analyzes and profiles consumers based on the type of residential area in which they live. Prices for reports range from $25 to $45.
- *US-State-County Reports* from CACI, Inc., offer demographic information for the entire United States or any state or county and include such data as total population, number of households, average age, average household income, type of households, occupations, race, and more. Each report costs $10.

Source: Reprinted courtesy of CompuServe.

How to Search. Online databases have two layers: individual records that make up the database and search software that picks out the records you want from the thousands or millions in the database. Think of search software as a robot that works at the speed of light. If you type in a word or phrase, the software will find every occurrence of that word or phrase in the database, exactly as you typed it and regardless of context. The system will respond with the number of records in the database that match your search.

Say you are interested in mentions of the president's home. A search of the phrase *white house* might retrieve 45 records—14 that pertain to 1600 Pennsylvania Avenue, four on the coffee brand, one on Marin County (an area known for the predominantly white color of its houses), and 26 from the White House Publishing Company in New Delhi, India.

Online database vendors provide several important advantages. First, the researcher can rapidly obtain a much greater variety of information than ever before. Second, by efficiently using online search procedures, the researcher can quickly pinpoint relevant data. Third, the large in-house staff formerly required to research and maintain files can be eliminated, reducing labor costs and increasing productivity. Finally, small firms can study the same secondary data as large organizations and do it just as efficiently.

Online database vendors have one potential disadvantage. A person unskilled at searching a database may be overwhelmed with data. Researchers must carefully choose the words used to locate the right citations, abstracts, and full-text stories. Thus, they must often familiarize themselves with new terminology to narrow the search. Boolean logic, which deals with inclusivity or exclusivity of sets, is a crucial element of successful online searches. The basic notions of AND, OR, and NOT are used to broaden or narrow the scope of a request.

CD-ROM Database Packages. A number of companies are now offering database packages on disk for personal computers. For example, Claritas has created two packages for market segmentation and demographic studies and for perceptual mapping: Compass/Agency for advertising agencies and Compass/Newspapers for newspapers. For Compass/Agency, Claritas recently added Arbitron radio ratings and data on product usage from Simmons Marketing Research Bureau and Mediamark. The Compass/Newspaper system contains more than 200 reports and maps. Users can also obtain data on subscribers, readership, and advertisers and display them as reports and maps or transfer the data to other standard software packages, such as spreadsheet, word-processing, and graphics applications.

The U.S. Department of Commerce has also made census data available for use on personal computers, including 1,300 categories of data on population, education, marital status, number of children in the home, home value or monthly rent, and income. The U.S. Census Bureau offers TIGER files, which map the location of all U.S. streets, highways, railroads, pipelines, power lines, airports, counties, municipalities, census tracts, census block groups, congressional districts, voter precincts, rivers, and lakes.

Planning the Research Design and Gathering Primary Data

Good secondary data can help researchers conduct a thorough situation analysis. With that information, researchers can list their unanswered questions and rank them. Researchers must then decide the exact information required to answer the questions. The **research design** specifies which research questions must be answered, how and when the data will be gathered, and how the data will be analyzed. Typically, the project budget is finalized after the research design has been approved.

Sometimes research questions can be answered by gathering more secondary data; otherwise, primary data may be needed. **Primary data,** or information collected for the first time, can be used for solving the particular problem under investigation. The main advantage of primary data is that they will answer a specific research question that secondary data cannot answer. For example, suppose Pillsbury has two new recipes for refrigerated dough for sugar cookies. Which one will consumers like better? Secondary data will not help answer this question. Instead, targeted consumers must try each recipe and evaluate the tastes, textures, and appearances of each cookie. Moreover, primary data are current and researchers know the source. Sometimes researchers gather the data themselves rather than assign projects to outside companies. Researchers also specify the methodology of the research. Secrecy can be maintained because the information is proprietary. In contrast, secondary data are available to all interested parties for relatively small fees.

Gathering primary data is expensive; costs can range from a few thousand dollars for a limited survey to several million for a nationwide study. For instance, a nationwide, 15-minute telephone interview with 1,000 adult males can cost $50,000 for everything, including a data analysis and report. Because primary data gathering is so expensive, firms commonly cut back on the number of interviews to save money. Larger companies that conduct many research projects use another cost-saving technique. They piggyback studies, or gather data on two different projects using one questionnaire. The drawback is that answering questions about, say, dog food and

research design
Specifies which research questions must be answered, how and when the data will be gathered, and how the data will be analyzed.

primary data
Information collected for the first time. Can be used for solving the particular problem under investigation.

gourmet coffee may be confusing to respondents. Piggybacking also requires a longer interview (sometimes a half hour or longer), which tires respondents. The quality of the answers typically declines, with people giving curt replies and thinking, "When will this end!" A lengthy interview also makes people less likely to participate in other research surveys.[10]

However, the disadvantages of primary data gathering are usually offset by the advantages. It is often the only way of solving a research problem. And with a variety of techniques available for research—including surveys, observations, and experiments—primary research can address almost any marketing question.

Survey Research

The most popular technique for gathering primary data is **survey research,** in which a researcher interacts with people to obtain facts, opinions, and attitudes. Exhibit 9.6 summarizes the characteristics of the most popular forms of survey research.

survey research
The most popular technique for gathering primary data in which a researcher interacts with people to obtain facts, opinions, and attitudes.

In-Home Interviews. Although in-home, personal interviews often provide high-quality information, they tend to be very expensive because of the interviewers' travel time and mileage costs. Therefore, market researchers tend to conduct fewer in-home personal interviews today than in the past.

Nevertheless, this form of survey research has some important advantages. The respondent is interviewed at home, in a natural setting where many consumption decisions are actually made. Also, the interviewer can show the respondent items (for example, package designs) or invite the respondent to taste or use a test product. An interviewer can also probe when necessary—a technique used to clarify a person's response. For example, an interviewer might ask, "What did you like best about the

Exhibit 9.6 *Characteristics of Various Types of Survey Research*

Characteristic	In-home personal interviews	Mall intercept interviews	Telephone interviews from interviewer's home	Central-location telephone interviews	Focus groups	Self-administered and one-time mail surveys	Mail panel surveys	E-mail interviews	Computer disk by mail
Cost	High	Moderate	Moderate to low	Moderate	Low	Low	Moderate	Moderate to low	Moderate
Time span	Moderate	Moderate	Fast	Fast	Fast	Slow	Relatively slow	Moderate	Relatively slow
Use of interviewer probes	Yes	Yes	Yes	Yes	Yes	No	Yes	Yes, if interactive	No
Ability to show concepts to respondent	Yes (also taste tests)	Yes (also taste tests)	No	No	Yes	Yes	Yes	Yes	Yes
Management control over interviewer	Low	Moderate	Low	High	High	n/a	n/a	High, if interviewer used	n/a
General data quality	High	Moderate	Moderate to low	High to moderate	Moderate	Moderate to low	Moderate	High to moderate	High to moderate
Ability to collect large amounts of data	High	Moderate	Moderate to low	Moderate to low	Moderate	Low to moderate	Moderate	High	High
Ability to handle complex questionnaires.	High	Moderate	Moderate	High if computer-aided	Low	Low	Low	High	High

salad dressing you just tried?" The respondent might reply, "Taste." This answer doesn't provide a lot of information, so the interviewer could probe by saying, "Can you tell me a little bit more about taste?" The respondent then elaborates: "Yes, it's not too sweet, it has the right amount of pepper, and I love that hint of garlic."

mall intercept interview
Survey research method that involves interviewing people in the common areas of shopping malls.

Mall Intercept Interviews. The **mall intercept interview** is conducted in the common areas of shopping malls. It is the economy version of the door-to-door interview personal contact between interviewer and respondent, minus the interviewer's travel time and mileage costs. To conduct this type of interview, the research firm rents office space in the mall or pays a significant daily fee. One drawback is that it is hard to get a representative sample of the population.

computer-assisted personal interviewing
Interviewing method in which the interviewer reads the questions from a computer screen and enters the respondent's data directly into the computer.

Mall intercept interviews must be brief. Only the shortest ones are conducted while respondents are standing. Usually researchers invite respondents to their office for interviews, which are still rarely over 15 minutes long. The researchers often show respondents concepts for new products or a test commercial or have them taste a new food product. The overall quality of mall intercept interviews is about the same as telephone interviews.

computer-assisted self-interviewing
Interviewing method in which a mall interviewer intercepts and directs willing respondents to nearby computer where the respondent reads questions off a computer screen and directly keys his or her answers into a computer.

Marketing researchers are applying new technology in mall interviewing. The first technique is **computer-assisted personal interviewing**. The researcher conducts in-person interviews, reads questions to the respondent off a computer screen, and directly keys the respondent's answers into the computer. A second approach is **computer-assisted self-interviewing**. A mall interviewer intercepts and directs willing respondents to nearby computers. Each respondent reads questions off a computer screen and directly keys his or her answers into a computer. The third use of technology is fully automated self-interviewing. Respondents are guided by interviewers or independently approach a centrally located computer station or kiosk, read questions off a screen, and directly key their answers into the station's computer.[11]

central-location telephone (CLT) facility
A specially designed phone room used to conduct telephone interviewing.

With computer-assisted interviewing, the interviewer reads questions off the screen and enters the respondents' data directly into the computer.
© 1996 PhotoDisc, Inc.

Telephone Interviews. Compared to the personal interview, the telephone interview costs less and may provide the best sample of any survey procedure. Although it is often criticized for providing poorer-quality data than the in-home personal interview, studies have shown that this criticism may not be deserved.[12]

Most telephone interviewing is conducted from a specially designed phone room called a **central-location telephone (CLT) facility.** A phone room has many phone lines, individual interviewing stations, sometimes monitoring equipment, and headsets. The use of Wide Area Telephone Service (WATS) lines permits the research firm to interview people nationwide from a single location.

Many CLT facilities offer computer-assisted interviewing. The interviewer reads the questions from a computer screen and enters the respondent's data directly into the computer. The researcher can stop the survey at any point and immediately print out the survey results. Thus, a researcher can get a sense of the project as it unfolds and fine-tune the research design as necessary. An on-line interviewing system can also save time and money because data entry occurs as the response is recorded rather than as a separate process after the interview. Hallmark Cards found that an interviewer administered a printed questionnaire for its Shoebox Greeting cards in 28 minutes. The same questionnaire administered with computer assistance took only 18 minutes.[13]

A new trend in telephone interviewing is **in-bound telephone surveys**. M/A/R/C, one of America's largest marketing research firms, has developed what it calls Brand Quality Monitoring. The process is simple: M/A/R/C sends a consumer an information packet with coupons for free samples of a client's product and a competitor's product, such as peanut butter, instant soup or microwave popcorn. The consumer is asked to use both products, one after the other. After using each sample, the survey respondent is asked to call a toll-free number that uses an interactive voice-mail system that operates 7 days a week, 24 hours a day. The system takes the consumer through a scripted menu of options. By pushing phone buttons, the consumer records his or her opinion about each product. M/A/R/C tabulates the results weekly and delivers them to clients in monthly, quarterly, or annual formats. By using database information, only consumers who use a particular product, such as cereal, are sent cereal coupons.[14]

Trish Shukers, Director of Survey Center Operations for Maritz Marketing Research, envisions in the near future a system she calls **integrated interviewing.** She describes it as follows:

> A potential respondent sees our survey ad on the Internet and uses a modem to dial our 800 number and reach our telephone center. A telephone interviewer receives the inbound call, screens to determine if the respondent is qualified, clicks an icon on the computer screen to send a fax about the survey to the respondent, and then transfers the respondent into an automated survey. If, at any time, the respondent has a question, he or she may return to the "live" interviewer.
>
> Imagine the possibilities of interviewing a respondent on-line and being able to display advertising copy or packaging prototypes (which we generally believe we have to do in person), and then administering a lengthy telephone interview (either live or automated) and e-mailing verbatim responses to the client at the end of the interview.[15]

E-mail Interviews. Telephone surveys have been the backbone of much consumer research during the past several decades because they are a fast, relatively cheap, and easy way to gather data. Yet answering machines, negative consumer attitudes toward phone surveys (due to misuse and telephone sales calls), and the growing number of unlisted phones have led marketing researchers to look for other media for gathering data. In 1996, nearly 40 percent of the U.S. population had a home computer and over 10 million people are online via the Internet and service providers such as CompuServe and America Online. E-mail is one of the applications most commonly used by persons online. It is estimated that a minimum of 15 million households will have modem-equipped PCs by the year 2000.[16]

Researchers typically use batch-type electronic mail to send **e-mail surveys** to potential respondents who use e-mail. Respondents key in their answers and send an e-mail reply. The big advantage of e-mail surveys is the rapid response rate. One recent survey had a 23.6 percent response rate after two days. This is shorter than the time usually required to distribute traditional mail surveys nationwide. After 14 days, the overall response rate was 48.8 percent, which is quite high compared to most mail or telephone surveys.[17] Also, because e-mail is a semi-interactive medium, respondents can inquire about the meaning of specific questions or pose other questions they might have.

E-mail surveys still face the problem of a limited number of subscribers being online. Also, the online population is skewed toward younger, more affluent males.[18] Other problems encountered include a large number of invalid e-mail addresses and the fact that e-mail questionnaires are easy to ignore and/or delete.

Mail Surveys. Mail surveys have several benefits: relatively low cost, elimination of interviewers and field supervisors, centralized control, and actual or promised anonymity for respondents (which may draw more candid responses). Some researchers feel that mail questionnaires give the respondent a chance to reply more thoughtfully and to check records, talk to family members, and so forth. Yet mail questionnaires usually produce low response rates.

Low response rates pose a problem because certain elements of the population tend to respond more than others. The resulting sample may therefore not represent the surveyed population. For example, the sample may have too many retired people and too few working people. In this instance, answers to a question about attitudes toward Social Security might indicate a much more favorable overall view of the sys-

in-bound telephone surveys
A new trend in telephone interviewing in which an information packet is sent to consumers, who are then asked to call a toll-free, interactive voice-mail system, and answer questions.

integrated interviewing
A new interviewing method in which a respondent is interviewed on the Internet.

e-mail surveys
Interviewing technique in which researchers use batch-type electronic mail to send surveys and respondents send reply via e-mail.

tem than is actually the case. Another serious problem with mail surveys is that no one probes respondents to clarify or elaborate on their answers.

Mail panels like those operated by Market Facts, National Family Opinion Research, and NPD Research offer an alternative to the one-shot mail survey. A mail panel consists of a sample of households recruited to participate by mail for a given period. Panel members often receive gifts in return for their participation. Essentially, the panel is a sample used several times. In contrast to one-time mail surveys, the response rates from mail panels are high. Rates of 70 percent (of those who agree to participate) are not uncommon.

Computer Disk by Mail. The **computer disk by mail survey** medium basically has all the advantages and disadvantages of a typical mail survey. An additional advantage is that a disk survey can incorporate skip patters into the survey. For example, a question might ask "Do you own a cat?" If the answer is "no" then you would skip all questions related to cat ownership. A disk survey will perform this function automatically. A disk survey can also use respondent-generated words in questions throughout the survey. Also, a disk survey can easily display a variety of graphics and directly relate them to questions. Finally, a disk survey eliminates the need to encode data from paper surveys. The primary disadvantage is that the respondent must have access and be willing to use a computer.

Focus Groups. A **focus group** is a type of personal interviewing. Often recruited by random telephone screening, 7 to 10 people with certain desired characteristics form a focus group. These qualified consumers are usually offered an incentive (typically $30 to $50) to participate in a group discussion. The meeting place (sometimes resembling a living room, sometimes featuring a conference table) has audiotaping and perhaps videotaping equipment. It also likely has a viewing room with a one-way mirror so that clients (manufacturers or retailers) may watch the session. During the session, a moderator, hired by the research company, leads the group discussion.

Focus groups are much more than question-and-answer interviews. The distinction is made between "group dynamics" and "group interviewing." The interaction provided in **group dynamics** is essential to the success of focus-group research; this interaction is the reason for conducting group rather than individual research. One of the essential postulates of group-session usage is the idea that a response from one person may become a stimulus for another, thereby generating an interplay of responses that may yield more than if the same number of people had contributed independently.

Focus groups are occasionally used to brainstorm new product ideas or to screen concepts for new products. Ford Motor Company, for example, asked consumers to drive several automobile prototypes. These "test drivers" were then brought together in focus groups. During the discussions, consumers complained that they were scuffing their shoes because the rear seats lacked foot room. In response, Ford sloped the floor underneath the front seats, widened the space between the seat adjustment tracks, and made the tracks in the Taurus and Sable models out of smooth plastic instead of metal.

A new system by Focus Vision Network allows client companies and advertising agencies to view live focus groups in Chicago, Dallas, Boston, and 15 other major cities. For example, the private satellite network lets a General Motors researcher observing a San Diego focus group control two cameras in the viewing room. The researcher can get a full-group view or a

computer disk by mail survey
Like a typical mail survey only the respondents receive and answer questions on a disk.

focus group
Seven to ten people who participate in a group discussion led by a moderator.

group dynamics
Interaction essential to the success of focus group research.

Ford Motor Company asks consumers to drive new automobiles and then brings them into a focus group to get their feedback.
Courtesy Ford Motor Company.

BEFORE OUR DESIGNERS CREATE A CAR THEY TALK TO OUTSIDE *EXPERTS.*

QUALITY IS JOB 1.

close-up, zoom, or pan the participants. The researcher can also communicate directly with the moderator using an ear receiver. Ogilvy and Mather (a large New York advertising agency) whose clients include StarKist Sea Foods, Seagrams, Mastercard, and Burger King) has installed the system.[19]

Companies are also beginning to conduct online focus groups. Nickelodeon, the cable television network for kids, had many questions about its programming. For example, do kids understand if Nickelodeon shows a sequence of program titles and air times? Karen Flischel, Nickelodeon's vice president of research, hit upon the idea of using CompuServe for online focus groups. Nickelodeon chose viewers who were CompuServe users.[20] The kids, ages 8 to 12, represent households with incomes ranging from $30,000 to $100,000. Half are minorities. All have personal computers and VCRs in their homes. Three times a week they log on for scheduled meetings during which Nickelodeon researchers lead discussions on a variety of topics. About a third of the sessions center on specific network programs. Armed with their keyboards, kids provide Nickelodeon with instant feedback. In one instance, they told researchers they were confused by the various locations shown in a segment of *The Tomorrow People*, a five-part series with events occurring around the world. Realizing that the sight of a double-decker bus wasn't enough for a kid to identify London, the producers wrote the name of the city on the screen.

Nick-at-Nite
How does Nickelodeon encourage site visitors to participate in market research?

http://nick-at-nite.com/

The media used to conduct marketing research, from telephone interviews to focus groups, are the same around the world. However, there are some important differences when conducting marketing research in other countries. These differences are discussed by Chris Van Derveer, president of an international marketing research firm, in the "Global Perspectives" box.

Global Perspectives

The Challenges of Global Marketing Research

The first debate in managing international research centers around technique. In our experience, telephone surveys have been effective regardless of where they are administered. Many research providers, in their bids, suggest in-person interviews for both the South American and Asian markets. Since business contacts in South America are much more social in nature, conventional wisdom says that the research method you use should be too. The in-person interview is viewed as more social than an impersonal telephone call. For the Asian markets, in-person interviews are often suggested because they allow the researcher to show proper respect for respondents.

In designing a questionnaire for a foreign market, the introduction and purpose of the survey should be described more fully than in the United States. Foreign respondents are generally more inquisitive and require a higher degree of formality than do Americans. You will find that a survey that requires 15 minutes here may take up to 40 minutes in Germany because German respondents like to talk more and the language is less concise than English. This longer response time adds to the cost of the research.

The major stumbling block of most international research is translation. Keep in mind that if you are researching five different markets/languages, the questionnaire must state exactly the same question in the same place for each of those five markets. Otherwise, you could tabulate two different sets of responses, offering nothing in the way of useful information.[21]

Can you think of some other problems that might be encountered in international marketing research? Do you think that it is as important to conduct marketing research in other countries as in the United States?

Questionnaire Design

open-ended question
Interview question that encourages an answer
phrased in the respon-
dent's own words.

closed-ended question
Interview question that
asks the respondent to
make a selection from a
limited list of responses.

scaled-response question
A closed-ended question
designed to measure the
intensity of a respondent's
answer.

All forms of survey research require a questionnaire. Questionnaires ensure that all respondents will be asked the same series of questions. Questionnaires include three basic types of questions: open-ended, closed-ended, and scaled-response (see Exhibit 9.7). An **open-ended question** encourages an answer phrased in the respondent's own words. Researchers get a rich array of information based on the respondent's frame of reference. In contrast, a **closed-ended question** asks the respondent to make a selection from a limited list of responses. Traditionally, marketing researchers separate the two-choice question (called *dichotomous*) from the many-item type (often called *multiple choice*). A **scaled-response question** is a closed-ended question designed to measure the intensity of a respondent's answer.

Closed-ended and scaled-response questions are easier to tabulate than open-ended questions because response choices are fixed. On the other hand, if the researcher is not careful in designing the closed-ended question, an important choice might be omitted. For example, suppose this question were asked on a food study: "What do you normally add to a taco, besides meat, that you have prepared at home?"

Exhibit 9.7 *Types of Questions Found on Questionnaires for National Market Research Surveys*

Open-Ended Questions

1. What advantages, if any, do you think ordering from a mail-order catalog offers compared to shopping at a local retail outlet? (*Probe:* What else?)

2. Why do you have one or more of your rugs or carpets professionally cleaned rather than having you or someone else in the household clean them?

3. What is there about the color of the eye shadow that makes you like it the best?

Closed-Ended Questions

Dichotomous

1. Did you heat the Danish product before serving it?

   Yes .1
   No .2

2. The federal government doesn't care what people like me think.

   Agree 1
   Disagree 2

Multiple choice

1. I'd like you to think back to the last footwear of any kind that you bought. I'll read you a list of descriptions and would like for you to tell me which category they fall into. (*Read list and check proper category.*)

   Dress and/or formal 1
   Casual 2
   Canvas/trainer/gym shoes 3
   Specialized athletic shoes 4
   Boots 5

2. In the last three months, have you used Noxzema skin cream. . . . (*Check all that apply.*)

   As a facial wash 1
   For moisturizing the skin 2
   For treating blemishes 3
   For cleansing the skin 4
   For treating dry skin 5
   For softening skin 6
   For sunburn 7
   For making the facial skin
       smooth 8

Scaled-Response Question

Now that you have used the rug cleaner, would you say that you. . . . (*Check one*)

____Would definitely buy it

____Would probably buy it

____Might or might not buy it

____Probably would not buy it

____Definitely would not buy it

Avocado	1
Cheese (Monterey Jack/cheddar)	2
Guacamole	3
Lettuce	4
Mexican hot sauce	5
Olives (black/green)	6
Onions (red/white)	7
Peppers (red/green)	8
Pimento	9
Sour cream	0

The list seems complete, doesn't it? However, consider the following responses: "I usually add a green, avocado-tasting hot sauce"; "I cut up a mixture of lettuce and spinach"; "I'm a vegetarian; I don't use meat at all. My taco is filled only with guacamole." How would you code these replies? As you can see, the question needs an "other" category.

A good question must also be asked clearly and concisely, and ambiguous language must be avoided. Take, for example, the question "Do you live within 10 minutes of here?" The answer depends on the mode of transportation (maybe the person walks), driving speed, perceived time, and other factors. Instead, respondents should see a map with certain areas highlighted and be asked whether they live within one of the areas.

Clarity also implies using reasonable terminology. A questionnaire is not a vocabulary test. Jargon should be avoided, and language should be geared to the target audience. A question such as, "What is the level of efficacy of your preponderant dishwasher powder?" would probably be greeted by a lot of blank stares. It would be much simpler to say "Are you (1) very satisfied, (2) somewhat satisfied, or (3) not satisfied with your current brand of dishwasher powder?"

Stating the survey's purpose at the beginning of the interview also improves clarity. The respondents should understand the study's intentions and the interviewer's expectations. Sometimes, of course, to get an unbiased response, the interviewer must disguise the true purpose of the study. If an interviewer says, "We're conducting an image study for American National Bank" and then proceeds to ask a series of questions about the bank, chances are the responses will be biased. Many times respondents will try to provide answers that they believe are "correct" or that the interviewer wants to hear.

Finally, to ensure clarity, the interviewer should avoid asking two questions in one; for example, "How did you like the taste and texture of the Pepperidge Farm coffee cake?" This should be divided into two questions, one concerning taste and the other texture.

A question should not only be clear but also unbiased. A question such as, "Have you purchased any quality Black & Decker tools in the past six months?" biases respondents to think of the topic in a certain way (in this case, to link quality and Black & Decker tools). Questions can also be leading: "Weren't you pleased with the good service you received last night at the Holiday Inn?" (The respondent is all but instructed to say yes.) These examples are quite obvious; unfortunately, bias is usually more subtle. Even an interviewer's clothing or gestures can create bias.

Observation Research

In contrast to survey research, **observation research** does not rely on direct interaction with people. The three types of observation research are people watching peo-

observation research
Research method that relies on three types of observation: people watching people, people watching activity, and machines watching people.

ple, people watching activity, and machines watching people. There are two types of *people watching people* research:

- *Mystery shoppers:* Researchers posing as customers observe the quality of service offered by retailers. The largest mystery shopper company is Shop 'N Chek, an Atlanta company that employs over 16,000 anonymous shoppers nationwide. The firm evaluates salespeople's courtesy for General Motors, flight service for United Airlines, and the efficiency of hamburger ordering for Wendy's, among other clients. Texaco recently introduced a program entitled "Building Tomorrow Together" that uses mystery shoppers to evaluate each of its 14,000 U.S. locations. All station managers, truck-stop owner-operators, and employees are eligible to earn recognition awards based heavily on the evaluations of mystery shoppers.[22]

- *One-way mirror observations:* At the Fisher-Price Play Laboratory, children are invited to spend 12 sessions playing with toys. Toy designers watch through one-way mirrors to see how children react to Fisher-Price's and other makers' toys. Fisher-Price, for example, had difficulty designing a toy lawn mower that children would play with. A designer, observing behind the mirror, noticed the children's fascination with soap bubbles. He then created a lawn mower that spewed soap bubbles. It sold over a million units in the first year.

audit
Form of observation research that features people examining and verifying the sale of a product.

One form of observation research that features people watching activity is known as an **audit,** the examination and verification of the sale of a product. Audits generally fall into two categories: retail audits, which measure sales to final consumers, and wholesale audits, which determine the amount of product moved from warehouses to retailers. Wholesalers and retailers allow auditors into their stores and stockrooms to examine the company's sales and order records in order to verify product flows. In turn, the retailers and wholesalers receive cash compensation and basic reports about their operations from the audit firms.

For *machines watching people,* the three types are:

- *Traffic counters:* The most common and most popular form of machine-based observation research relies on machines that measure the flow of vehicles over a stretch of roadway. Outdoor advertisers rely on traffic counts to determine the number of exposures per day to a billboard. Retailers use the information to de-

Outdoor advertisers rely on traffic counts to determine the number of exposures per day to a billboard.
© 1996 PhotoDisc, Inc.

cide where to place a store. Convenience stores, for example, require a moderately high traffic volume to be profitable.

- *VideOCart:* This machine uses infrared sensors in store ceilings to track shopping carts. The new system has spotted a lot of "dippers." These shoppers park their carts at the ends of aisles and then walk down, filling their arms with items from the shelves as they go. Retailers figure such shoppers probably buy less because they are limited by what they can carry.[23]

- *Passive people meter:* Soon a cameralike device will be available to measure the size of television audiences. The passive system, packaged to resemble a VCR and placed on top of the TV, will be programmed to recognize faces and record electronically when specific members of a family watch TV. It will note when viewers leave the room and even when they avert their eyes from the screen. Strangers would be listed simply as visitors. Passive people meters are eagerly anticipated because advertisers are demanding more proof of viewership and the networks are under pressure to show that advertising is reaching its intended targets. (Ratings are used to help set prices for commercial time.) An A.C. Nielsen executive has said that a passive system should yield "even higher quality, more accurate data because the respondents don't have to do anything" other than "be themselves." Already, however, the networks and advertisers are criticizing the passive people meter. One executive noted, "Who would want or allow one of those things in their bedroom?"[24] Others claim that the system requires bright light to operate properly. Also, the box has limited peripheral vision, so it might not sense all the people in a given room. Will the passive people meter work better than the present diary system? As of late 1996, the passive people meter had not been perfected. The four major networks are now working together to develop another mechanical device for measuring the size of television audiences.[25]

A.C. Nielsen Company, Inc.
How does A.C. Nielsen's 40,000-household Consumer Panel provide insights into consumer purchase behavior? What Internet resources are available through this site?

http://www.acnielsen.com/

All observation techniques offer at least two advantages over survey research. First, bias from the interviewing process is eliminated. Second, observation doesn't rely on the respondent's willingness to provide data.

Conversely, observation techniques also have two important disadvantages. First, subjective information is limited because motivations, attitudes, and feelings are not measured. Second, data collection costs may run high unless the observed behavior patterns occur frequently, briefly, or somewhat predictably.

Experiments

An **experiment** is another method a researcher can use to gather primary data. The researcher alters one or more variables—price, package design, shelf space, advertising theme, advertising expenditures—while observing the effects of those alterations on another variable (usually sales). The best experiments are those in which all factors are held constant except the ones being manipulated. The researcher can then observe that changes in sales, for example, result from changes in the amount of money spent on advertising.

Holding all other factors constant in the external environment is a monumental and costly, if not impossible, task. Such factors as competitors' actions, weather, and economic conditions are beyond the researcher's control. Yet market researchers have ways to account for the ever-changing external environment. Mars, the candy company, was losing sales to other candy companies. Traditional surveys showed that the

experiment
Method a researcher uses to gather primary data.

shrinking candy bar was not perceived as a good value. Mars wondered whether a bigger bar sold at the same price would increase sales enough to offset the higher ingredient costs. The company designed an experiment in which the marketing mix stayed the same in different markets but the size of the candy bar varied. The substantial increase in sales of the bigger bar quickly proved that the additional costs would be more than covered by the additional revenue. Mars increased the bar size—and its market share and profits.

Specifying the Sampling Procedures

Once the researchers decide how they will collect primary data, their next step is to select the sampling procedures they will use. A firm can seldom take a census of all possible users of a new product, nor can they all be interviewed. Therefore, a firm must select a sample of the group to be interviewed. A **sample** is a subset from a larger population.

Several questions must be answered before a sampling plan is chosen. First, the population or **universe** of interest must be defined. This is the group from which the sample will be drawn. It should include all the people whose opinions, behavior, preferences, attitudes, and so on are of interest to the marketer. For example, in a study whose purpose is to determine the market for a new canned dog food, the universe might be defined to include all current buyers of canned dog food.

After the universe has been defined, the next question is whether the sample must be representative of the population. If the answer is yes, a probability sample is needed. Otherwise, a nonprobability sample might be considered.

Probability Samples

A **probability sample** is one in which every element in the population has a known statistical likelihood of being selected. Its most desirable feature is that scientific rules can be used to ensure that the sample represents the population.

One type of probability sample is a random sample. A **random sample** must be arranged in such a way that every element of the population has an equal chance of being selected as part of the sample. For example, suppose a university is interested in getting a cross-section of student opinions on a proposed sports complex to be built using student activity fees. If the university can acquire an up-to-date list of all the enrolled students, it can draw a random sample by using random numbers from a table (found in most statistics books) to select students from the list. Common forms of probability and nonprobability samples are shown in Exhibit 9.8.

Nonprobability Samples

Any sample in which little or no attempt is made to get a representative cross-section of the population can be considered a **nonprobability sample.** A common form of a nonprobability sample is the **convenience sample,** based on using respondents who are convenient or readily accessible to the researcher—for instance, employees, friends, or relatives.

Nonprobability samples are acceptable as long as the researcher understands their nonrepresentative nature. Because of their lower cost, nonprobability samples are the basis of much marketing research.

Types of Errors

Whenever a sample is used in marketing research, two major types of error occur: measurement error and sampling error. **Measurement error** occurs when there is a difference between the information desired by the researcher and the information

---

sample
A subset of a population.

universe
The population from which a sample will be drawn.

probability sample
A sample in which every element in the population has a known statistical likelihood of being selected.

random sample
Sample arranged in such a way that every element of the population has an equal chance of being selected as part of the sample.

nonprobability sample
Any sample in which little or no attempt is made to get a representative cross section of the population.

convenience sample
A form of nonprobability sample using respondents who are convenient or readily accessible to the researcher, for example, employees, friends, or relatives.

measurement error
Error that occurs when there is a difference between the information desired by the researcher and the information provided by the measurement process.

Exhibit 9.8
Types of Samples

Probability Samples	
Simple random sample	Every member of the population has a known and equal chance of selection.
Stratified sample	Population is divided into mutually exclusive groups (such as gender or age), then random samples are drawn from *each* group.
Cluster sample	Population is divided into mutually exclusive groups (such as geographic areas), then a random sample of clusters is selected. The researcher then collects data from all the elements in the selected clusters or from a probability sample of elements within each selected cluster.
Systematic sample	A list of the population is obtained, i.e., all persons with a checking account at XYZ Bank, and a *skip interval* is obtained. The skip interval is obtained by dividing the sample size by the population size. If the sample size is 100 and the bank has 1,000 customers, then the skip interval is 10. The beginning number is randomly chosen within the skip interval. If the beginning number is 8, then the skip pattern would be 8, 18, 28, . . .
Nonprobability Samples	
Convenience sample	The researcher selects the easiest population members from which to obtain information.
Judgment sample	The researcher's selection criteria are based on personal judgment that the elements (persons) chosen will likely give accurate information.
Quota sample	The researcher finds a prescribed number of people in several categories, i.e., owners of large dogs versus owners of small dogs. Respondents are not selected on probability sampling criteria.
Snowball sample	The selection of additional respondents is made on the basis of referrals from the initial respondents. This is used when a desired type of respondent is hard to find, i.e., persons who have taken round-the-world cruises in the last three years. This technique employs the old adage, "birds of a feather flock together."

provided by the measurement process. For example, people may tell an interviewer that they purchase Coors beer when they do not. Measurement error generally tends to be larger than sampling error.

Sampling error occurs when a sample somehow does not represent the target population. Sampling error can be one of several types. Nonresponse error occurs when the sample actually interviewed differs from the sample drawn. This error happens because the original people selected to be interviewed either refused to cooperate or were inaccessible. For example, people who feel embarrassed about their drinking habits may refuse to talk about them.

Frame error, another type of sampling error, arises if the sample drawn from a population differs from the target population. For instance, suppose a telephone survey is conducted to find out Chicago beer drinkers' attitudes toward Coors. If a Chicago telephone directory is used as the *frame* (the device or list from which the respondents are selected), the survey will contain a frame error. Not all Chicago beer drinkers have a phone, and many phone numbers are unlisted. An ideal sample (for

sampling error
Error that occurs when a sample somehow does not represent the target population.

frame error
Error that occurs when a sample drawn from a population differs from the target population.

example, a sample with no frame error) matches all important characteristics of the target population to be surveyed. Could you find a perfect frame for Chicago beer drinkers?

Random error occurs because the selected sample is an imperfect representation of the overall population. Random error represents how accurately the chosen sample's true average (mean) value reflects the population's true average (mean) value. For example, we might take a random sample of beer drinkers in Chicago and find that 16 percent regularly drink Coors beer. The next day we might repeat the same sampling procedure and discover that 14 percent regularly drink Coors beer. The difference is due to random error.

Collecting the Data

Marketing research field service firms collect most primary data. A **field service firm** specializes in interviewing respondents on a subcontracted basis. Many have offices throughout the country. A typical marketing research study involves data collection in several cities, requiring the marketer to work with a comparable number of field service firms. To ensure uniformity among all subcontractors, detailed field instructions should be developed for every job. Nothing should be open to chance; no interpretations of procedures should be left to subcontractors.

Besides conducting interviews, field service firms provide focus group facilities, mall intercept locations, test product storage, and kitchen facilities to prepare test food products. They also conduct retail audits (counting the amount of a product sold off retail shelves). After an in-home interview is completed, field service supervisors validate the survey by recontacting about 15 percent of the respondents. The supervisors verify that certain responses were recorded properly and that the people were actually interviewed.

Analyzing the Data

After collecting the data, the marketing researcher proceeds to the next step in the research process: data analysis. The purpose of this analysis is to interpret and draw conclusions from the mass of collected data. The marketing researcher tries to organize and analyze those data by using one or more techniques common to marketing research: one-way frequency counts, cross-tabulations, and more sophisticated statistical analysis. Of these three techniques, one-way frequency counts are the simplest. One-way frequency tables record the responses to a question. For example, the answers to the question "What brand of microwave popcorn do you buy most often?" would provide a one-way frequency distribution. One-way frequency tables are always done in data analysis, at least as a first step, because they provide the researcher with a general picture of the study's results.

A **cross-tabulation,** or "cross-tab," lets the analyst look at the responses to one question in relation to the responses to one or more other questions. For example, what is the association between gender and the brand of microwave popcorn bought most frequently? Hypothetical answers to this question are shown in Exhibit 9.9. Although the Orville Reddenbacher brand was popular with both males and females, it was more popular with females. Compared with women, men strongly preferred Pop Rite, whereas women were more likely than men to buy Weight Watchers popcorn.

Researchers can use many other more powerful and sophisticated statistical techniques, such as hypothesis testing, measures of association, and regression analysis. A description of these tech-

random error
Error that occurs because the selected sample is an imperfect representation of the overall population.

field service firm
Firm that specializes in interviewing respondents on a subcontracted basis.

cross-tabulation
A method of analyzing data that lets the analyst look at the responses to one question in relation to the responses to one or more other questions.

After the data is collected, the next step is to analyze it to come up with interpretations and draw conclusions that marketers can use.
© 1996 PhotoDisc, Inc.

Brand	Purchase by Gender	
	Male	**Female**
Orville Reddenbacher	31%	48%
T.V. Time	12	6
Pop Rite	38	4
Act Two	7	23
Weight Watchers	4	18
Other	8	0

Exhibit 9.9
Hypothetical Cross-Tabulation Between Gender and Brand of Microwave Popcorn Purchased Most Frequently

niques goes beyond the scope of this book but can be found in any good marketing research textbook. The use of sophisticated statistical techniques depends on the researchers' objectives and the nature of the data gathered.

Preparing and Presenting the Report

After data analysis has been completed, the researcher must prepare the report and communicate the conclusions and recommendations to management. This is a key step in the process. If the marketing researcher wants managers to carry out the recommendations, he or she must convince them that the results are credible and justified by the data collected.

Researchers are usually required to present both written and oral reports on the project. These reports should be tailored to the audience. They should begin with a clear, concise statement of the research objectives, followed by a complete, but brief and simple, explanation of the research design or methodology employed. A summary of major findings should come next. The conclusion of the report should also present recommendations to management.

Most people who enter marketing will become research users rather than research suppliers. Thus, they must know what to notice in a report. As with many other items we purchase, quality is not always readily apparent. Nor does a high price guarantee superior quality. The basis for measuring the quality of a marketing research report is the research proposal. Did the report meet the objectives established in the proposal? Was the methodology outlined in the proposal followed? Are the conclusions based on logical deductions from the data analysis? Do the recommendations seem prudent, given the conclusions?

Another criterion is the quality of the writing. Is the style crisp and lucid? It has been said that if readers are offered the slightest opportunity to misunderstand, they probably will. The report should also be as concise as possible.

Following Up

The final step in the marketing research process is to follow up. The researcher should determine why management did or did not carry out the recommendations in the report. Was sufficient decision-making information included? What could have been done to make the report more useful to management? A good rapport between the product manager, or whoever authorized the project, and the market researcher is essential. Often they must work together on many studies throughout the year.

Many small companies don't have the time or money to engage in sophisticated, formal marketing research studies. Yet, that should not preclude them from doing

Marketing and Small Business

Marketing Research for Small Companies

Because most small businesses have limited financial resources and expertise, they often conclude that doing marketing research and creating an information system isn't worth the cost. Instead, managers of small businesses may rely on hunches or intuition when designing their marketing mix. In the absence of feedback from their customers, they sometimes institute practices that customers object to. Over time, the customer base begins to erode.

Many small-business owners who feel they are doing an outstanding job are unaware of the serious problems confronting them in the area of customer relations. For example, the owner-manager of a car dealership in a small community had this policy: "To present a high-volume, low-price dealership that has a reputation for good service." However, a random survey of customers who had used his service department showed they were dissatisfied and would no longer do business with him. If the dealer had asked some friends to pose as "mystery shoppers," the problem might not have ever occurred.

Marketing research could help small businesses avoid similar misapprehensions. However, "turn-key" marketing research projects, in which a research firm conducts the entire study and makes recommendations, tend to be expensive. A much less expensive alternative is

for the small business to do everything but the interviewing, which can be assigned to a market research field service. Perhaps the owner and employees can do the interviewing. Or perhaps an inexpensive mail survey would be better than personal interviews. Another money-saving idea is to create a simple database from customer information cards gathered by offering a drawing for a free lunch or prize. Finally, the Internet offers a wealth of information that can help the small businessperson better understand the competitive environment. For example, the Census County and City Data Book has demographic information of all types broken down by cities and even smaller units. It can be found at http://www.census.gov:80/stat_ abstract.

---

less complicated forms of research. The "Marketing and Small Business" box explains why it is important to conduct marketing research.

SCANNER-BASED RESEARCH

5 Discuss the growing importance of scanner-based research.

scanner-based research
A system for gathering information from a single group of respondents by continuously monitoring the advertising, promotion, and pricing they are exposed to and the things they buy.

BehaviorScan
Scanner-based research program that tracks the purchases of 3,000 households through store scanners.

Scanner-based research is a system for gathering information from a single group of respondents by continuously monitoring the advertising, promotion, and pricing they are exposed to and the things they buy. The variables measured are advertising campaigns, coupons, displays, and product prices. The result is a huge database of marketing efforts and consumer behavior. Scanner-based research is bringing ever closer the Holy Grail of marketing research: an accurate, objective picture of the direct causal relationship between different kinds of marketing efforts and actual sales.

The two major scanner-based suppliers are Information Resources Incorporated (IRI) and the A.C. Nielsen Company. Each has about half the market. However, IRI is the founder of scanner-based research.

IRI's first product is called **BehaviorScan.** A household panel (a group of 3,000 long-term participants in the research project) has been recruited and maintained in each BehaviorScan town. Panel members shop with an ID card, which is presented at the checkout in scanner-equipped grocery stores and drugstores, allowing IRI to track electronically each household's purchases, item by item, over time. It uses microcomputers to measure TV viewing in each panel household and can send special commercials to panel member television sets. With such a measure of household purchasing, it is possible to manipulate marketing variables, such as TV advertising or consumer promotions, or to introduce a new product and analyze real changes in consumer buying behavior.

IRI's most successful product, with sales of over $130 million per year and 740 U.S. clients, is InfoScan. **InfoScan** is a scanner-based sales-tracking service for the consumer packaged-goods industry. Retail sales, detailed consumer purchasing information (including measurement of store loyalty and total grocery basket expenditures), and promotional activity by manufacturers and retailers are monitored and evaluated for all bar-coded products.

WHEN SHOULD MARKETING RESEARCH BE CONDUCTED?

When managers have several possible solutions to a problem, they should not instinctively call for marketing research. In fact, the first decision to make is whether to conduct marketing research at all.

Some companies have been conducting research in certain markets for many years. Such firms understand the characteristics of target customers and their likes and dislikes about existing products. Under these circumstances, further research would be repetitive and waste money. Procter & Gamble, for example, has extensive knowledge of the coffee market. After it conducted initial taste tests with Folgers Instant Coffee, P&G went into national distribution without further research. Consolidated Foods Kitchen of Sara Lee followed the same strategy with its frozen croissants, as did Quaker Oats with Chewy Granola Bars. This tactic, however, does not always work. P&G marketers thought they understood the pain reliever market thoroughly, so they bypassed market research for Encaprin aspirin in capsules. Because it lacked a distinct competitive advantage over existing products, however, the product failed and was withdrawn from the market.

Managers rarely have such great trust in their judgment that they would refuse more information if it were available and free. But they might have enough confidence that they would be unwilling to pay very much for the information or to wait a long time to receive it. The willingness to acquire additional decision-making information depends on managers' perceptions of its quality, price, and timing. Of course, if perfect information were available—that is, the data conclusively showed which alternative to choose—decision makers would be willing to pay more for it than for information that still left uncertainty. In summary, research should only be undertaken when the expected value of the information is greater than the cost of obtaining it.

Retailer Urban Outfitters sends its marketing researchers to the streets to scout teen and young adult fashion trends.
© Guy Aroch

InfoScan
A scanner-based sales-tracking service for the consumer packaged-goods industry.

6 Explain when marketing research should and should not be conducted.

LOOKING BACK

Look back at the story about Boston Market that appeared at the beginning of this chapter. The company could have used experiments, observation, or survey research to conduct marketing research. If it chose to conduct survey research, the firm could use a number of media such as telephone, mail, or online research.

Unless a company has extensive knowledge of the problem at hand, which is based upon research, it should probably conduct marketing research. Yet, managers should also be reasonably sure that the cost of gathering the information will be less than the value of the data gathered.

Key marketing data often come from a company's own decision support system, which continually gathers data from a variety of sources and funnels it to decision

KEY TERMS

makers. They then manipulate the data to make better decisions. DSS data are often supplemented by marketing research information.

SUMMARY

1 *Explain the concept and purpose of a marketing decision support system.* Decision support systems make data instantly available to marketing managers and allow them to manipulate the data themselves to make marketing decisions. Four characteristics of decision support systems make them especially useful to marketing managers: They are interactive, flexible, discovery-oriented, and accessible. Decision support systems give managers access to information immediately and without outside assistance. They allow users to manipulate data in a variety of ways and to answer "what if" questions. And, finally, they are accessible to novice computer users.

2 *Discuss the nature of database marketing and micromarketing.* A marketing database is part of a decision support system composed of present and potential customers' profiles and purchasing patterns. Micromarketing is the creation of a large database of customers' and potential customers' profiles and purchasing patterns used to target households or even individuals. Micromarketing has several important functions. It identifies the potential profitability of specific customers and market segments. It helps determine effective packaging and pricing strategies for specific market segments. Furthermore, it provides insights into market opportunities for new products and services.

3 *Define marketing research and explain its importance to marketing decision making.* Marketing research is a process of collecting and analyzing data for the purpose of solving specific marketing problems. Marketers use marketing research to explore the profitability of marketing strategies. They can examine why particular strategies failed and analyze characteristics of specific market segments. Moreover, marketing research allows management to behave proactively rather than reactively by identifying newly emerging patterns in society and the economy.

4 *Describe the steps involved in conducting a marketing research project.* The marketing research process involves several basic steps. First, the researcher and the decision maker must agree on a problem statement or set of research objectives. Sometimes this step requires a background investigation referred to as a situation analysis, usually drawn partly from secondary sources. The researcher then creates an overall research design to specify how primary data will be gathered and analyzed. Before collecting data, the researcher decides whether the group to be interviewed will be a probability or nonprobability sample. Field service firms are often hired to carry out data collection. Once data have been collected, the researcher analyzes them using statistical analysis. The researcher then prepares and presents oral and written reports, with conclusions and recommendations, to management. As a final step, the researcher determines whether the recommendations were implemented and what could have been done to make the project more successful.

5 *Discuss the growing importance of scanner-based research.* A scanner-based research system enables marketers to monitor a market panel's exposure and reaction to such variables as advertising, coupons, store displays, packaging, and price. By analyzing these variables in relation to the panel's subsequent buying behavior, marketers gain useful insight into sales and marketing strategies.

6 *Explain when marketing research should and should not be conducted.* Marketing research helps managers by providing data to make better marketing decisions. However, firms must consider whether the expected benefits of marketing research outweigh its costs. Before approving a research budget, management also should make sure adequate decision-making information doesn't already exist.

Discussion and Writing Questions

1. The task of marketing is to create exchanges. What role might marketing research play in the facilitation of the exchange process?

2. Marketing research has traditionally been associated with manufacturers of consumer goods. Today, we are experiencing an increasing number of organizations, both profit and nonprofit, using marketing research. Why do you think this trend exists? Give some examples.

3. Write a reply to the following statement: "I own a restaurant in the downtown area. I see customers every day whom I know on a first-name basis. I understand their likes and dislikes. If I put something on the menu and it doesn't sell, I know that they didn't like it. I also read the magazine *Modern Restaurants*, so I know what the trends are in the industry. This is all of the marketing research I need to do."

4. Give an example of (a) the descriptive role of marketing research, (b) the diagnostic role, and (c) the predictive function of marketing research.

5. Critique the following methodologies and suggest more appropriate alternatives:
   a. A supermarket was interested in determining its image. It dropped a short questionnaire into the grocery bag of each customer before putting in the groceries.
   b. To assess the extent of its trade area, a shopping mall

stationed interviewers in the parking lot every Monday and Friday evening. Interviewers walked up to persons after they had parked their cars and asked them for their zip codes.
   c. To assess the popularity of a new movie, a major studio invited people to call a 900 number and vote yes, they would see it again, or no, they would not. Each caller was billed a two-dollar charge.

6. You have been charged with determining how to attract more business majors to your school. Write an outline of the steps you would take, including the sampling procedures, to accomplish the task.

7. Why is secondary data sometimes preferred to primary data?

8. In the absence of company problems, is there any reason to develop a marketing decision support system?

9. Discuss when focus groups should and should not be used.

10. Divide the class into teams of eight persons. Each group will conduct a focus group on the quality and number of services that your college is providing to its students. One person from each group should be chosen to act as moderator. Remember, it is the moderator's job to facilitate discussion, not to lead the discussion. These groups should last approximately 45 minutes. If possible, the groups should be videotaped or recorded. Upon completion, each group should write a brief report of its results. Consider offering to meet with the dean of

students to share the results of your research.

11. Find a city listed on the following Web site and describe the categories of marketing research information that this firm offers for it.

   http://www.usadata.com/ usadata/market/bymar.htm

12. What services are offered to market researchers at the following Internet site?

   http://www.anywhereonline. com/home2.htm

13. Try the "Software Walk-Through" for the marketing decision-support tool offered at the following Web site. How might this program aid marketers?

   http://www.allen.com/ marketview/

Application for Small Business

America's mail-order culture has created a product that you probably never think about—the foam peanut. It's a packaging utopia—sort of—it's lightweight, inexpensive, conforms in bulk to any shape, protects superbly, resists shifting in transit, and leaves no dusty residue. Also, it is indestructible, and that's the problem. Introduced around 1970, every styrofoam peanut ever made is still with us. Most are in landfills and will last about 500 years.

A young Phoenix company, Biofoam, thinks its all-natural peanut (also called Biofoam) makes more sense—for shippers, consumers, and the environment. Biofoam is made from grain sorghum. Stripped of its nutritional value, pressed into pellets, and conveyed through a giant popper, the stuff comes out looking like thousands of tan cheese doodles. The question is, "Will anybody buy the stuff?"

Questions

1. Do you think a small business like Biofoam really needs to conduct formal marketing research? Explain your answer.

2. If Biofoam decides to do marketing research, what are some of the topics that should be covered in the questionnaire?
3. Who should be interviewed?
4. What survey methods should be considered?

Category Management Using Information Resources, Inc. Scanner-Based Information

by Gian M. Fulgoni
Chairman and Chief Executive Officer
Information Resources, Inc.

Historically, marketing research had been viewed as a report card: How did the firm do last month? What was our market share? Which brands sold best in the Chicago territory? However, that began to change with the advent of weekly scanner-based data in the late 1980s.

Today, research information is being used by leading edge companies to guide their marketing efforts and increase their sales and profits in many different ways. One of the best examples of how information is being used is the emergence of fact-based selling strategies, in general, category management tactics, in particular. Category management is the sales and inventory management of a group of related products.

Fact-based selling, though simple in concept, requires a significant commitment to information and technology because management must first have the facts and understand them thoroughly before managers can use them effectively.

Category management, in turn, uses scanner-generated facts and also demands a willingness to move away from a narrow focus on one's own dealer brands (Brand "A" Iced Tea, for example) toward a broader view of the entire product category (ready-to-drink tea). The appeal of the cat-

egory management approach, which is being adopted by an increasing number of firms today, is that it will create true win/win scenarios for both the retailer and the manufacturer.

Category management techniques can impact sales in a number of ways: (1) by uncovering distribution opportunities; (2) by better utilization of shelf space; (3) by optimal pricing strategies; and (4) by more efficient promotional spending.

Some work Information Resources did with a ready-to-drink tea client illustrates the impact that one of these techniques, in this case a distribution analysis, can have. Following an examination of IRI sales data, the packaged goods manufacturer learned that one retail supermarket chain in a midwestern market was not carrying a number of its items, products that were selling quite well in the other

stores in the market. The data also showed that if the retailer added these items to his product mix and dropped some of the slower-selling items, overall sales of the ready-to-drink category in the grocery chain would increase. And, of course, the manufacturer's sales would increase as well, resulting in a win/win situation.

By analyzing sales results in those stores that carry the items, the manufacturer was able to bring the grocery chain a list of all ready-to-drink tea items that were not being stocked in its stores and the projected sales if the chain were to carry them. Shown below are the five largest sellers from that list and the projected sales of each of those items.

Item	Projected Annual Sales
Brand A tropical iced tea 15.5 oz.	$ 65,600
Brand A regular iced tea 15.5 oz.	59,400
Brand B raspberry iced tea 16 oz.	53,500
Brand A peach iced tea 64 oz.	44,500
Private label lemon iced 16 oz.	43,400
TOTAL PROJECTED SALES	$266,400

(Note the presence of a competitive item, Brand B's raspberry product, on the recommended list.)

A similar list of the items actually carried produced the five slowest selling items, whose total sales were only $31,300, and these were targeted for removal. (Although none of Brand A's products was among these slow moving products, fact-based selling would dictate that the manufacturer present the information to the retailer and, without any mitigating factors, recommend dropping even its own items.)

In this example, the retailer accepted the suggestions and looked forward to a sales increase in the ready-to-drink tea category of $235,100:

New sales from new items	$266,400
Lost sales from discontinued items	− 31,300
Net impact on retailer's sales	$235,100

Of course IRI's client, Manufacturer A, also anticipated additional sales from his three items that were being added of $169,500 ($65,600 + $59,400 + $44,500).

The tremendous value of a scanner data fact-based approach to selling becomes clear when it is realized that this is the potential impact of one type of category management analysis on one category in one retail account. IRI's manufacturer clients can use this type of analysis for virtually any category with retailers across the country. And if a particular distribution opportunity doesn't exist at another retailer, the manufacturer could examine its shelf space allocation, consider pricing adjustments or review promotional programs—each one a category of management oriented approach based on scanner-data facts.

Those companies who can gather, analyze, and apply information most efficiently will be the market leaders of tomorrow. Marketing research, no longer a simple report on the past, provides the facts to guide the way into that future.

Questions

1. How does scanner-based data provide insights into the future?
2. Why would a manufacturer recommend a competitor's product using category management?
3. What other ways can scanner-based data be used by managers?

Bon-Ton Department Stores

Bon-Ton Department Stores, a Pennsylvania-based chain, decided that it needed a better understanding of the marketplace. A nationally known marketing research firm was hired to determine what customers think of Bon-Ton, how well they like shopping at Bon-Ton, how high the general level of customer satisfaction is, and what attitudes are toward competing department stores. Bon-Ton shoppers were perceived as 25 to 40 years old, female, and professional.

Focus groups were convened in four Bon-Ton markets in Pennsylvania: Greensburg, Harrisburg, York, and Wilkes-Barre. To "loosen up" respondents and begin the conversation, they were asked, "Why do you go shopping?" Among the reasons offered by respondents were these: They saw advertisements announcing a sale, they were seeking a bargain, they were bored, they get a feeling of control from buying something, they shop to keep up with the latest styles, and they shop to reward

Video Case

themselves after going through a bad experience (such as going to the dentist). One woman said she lives alone and doesn't always want to go home after work, so she goes shopping instead. Another said, "If I'm uptight after work, I'll go shopping to relax." Asking respondents why they go shopping helped to get them thinking about the shopping experience.

Bon-Ton itself was viewed as friendly, well decorated, and stocked with quality, name-brand merchandise for all age groups. The chain was also characterized as computerized, a little homey, but also classy. On the negative side, one person said a gift box from Bon-Ton was "nothing special." Another said that the merchandising wasn't consistent; what was available one week might not be there the next. Yet another said goods were often too crowded together and seemed shopworn. In general, however, the image was positive.

The focus group sessions were followed by a telephone survey of a representative sample of Bon-Ton shoppers.

Questions

1. Poll fellow students on why they like to shop. What additional reasons for shopping can you uncover?
2. The focus groups revealed a generally positive image for Bon-Ton. Why would the company want to follow up with a telephone survey?
3. What courses of action are suggested by the data from the telephone survey?
4. Was the sample for the telephone survey drawn from the right population? Why or why not?

Critical Thinking Case

LONG JOHN SILVER'S REACHES OUT TO DRIVE-THROUGH CUSTOMERS

Conventional wisdom says that most consumers don't want to be bothered to participate in a research study. Well, that notion is being challenged by an increasingly popular technique in which the respondents are the ones who call the researcher. In this case, the "researcher" happens to be a machine, a sophisticated software program that lets respondents use their touch-tone telephones to take an "inbound" survey. Their impersonal nature, and the fact that the respondent controls when the interview is conducted, may be part of the reason inbound surveys earn better than average response rates for some users.

One firm that has successfully used in-bound surveys is Long John Silver's Restaurants, a quick-service seafood chain based in Lexington, Kentucky, with nearly 1,500 locations in 38 states, Canada, Singapore and Saudi Arabia. Long John Silver's uses Show N Tel, an in-bound survey program made by Interactive Communications Inc., Dallas, that runs on an interactive voice-response system.

As part of its regular research, the company uses the in-bound surveys to reach an elusive customer segment—drive-through and carry-out patrons. "A big part of our business is drive-through and carry-out customers," says Larry Noble, marketing research manager, Long John Silver's Restaurants. "While it's easy enough to talk to our dine-in customers, it can be difficult to get drive-through and carry-out customers. [The in-bound survey] has worked the best for us in reaching these people. Up until we did the surveys, we didn't have a lot of information on those customers. We've tried mail-in surveys but the return rate is historically low."

Cards were distributed to Long John Silver's carry-out and drive-through customers inviting them to call a toll-free number by midnight to participate in a short survey. In exchange they would be given a code at the end of the interview which validated the card as a coupon they could redeem for a free meal and beverage of their choice. When the respondents called in, they were greeted by the system: "Hello and thank you for calling the Long John Silver's Survey Line. We're interested in your opinions regarding your recent visit to our restaurant." Once it was established that the caller was using a touch-tone phone, he or she was told how long the survey would take and how to receive their incentive.

Long John Silver's customers were asked about the food items they purchased and given a rating scale to register their satisfaction on a number of attributes. Respondents also provided standard demographic information.

Mark Mulch, national project director, Interactive Communications, says that three types of question work well in an interactive survey: rating questions, in which respondents press a key corresponding to the correct number on the scale; data-entry questions, such as "How many minutes did it take for your order to be filled?"; and open-ended questions, where respondents explain why they weren't satisfied.

Respondents to the open-ended questions aren't told how much time they have to respond but Mulch reports that 45 seconds is typically enough time. Once they are through they press a key on the phone.

Clients receive the open-ended responses in transcribed form or on a cassette tape. The system also allows clients to call in and listen to the verbatim responses. So, for example, a store manager or an area manager can call up and get a quick read on customer satisfaction.

The system includes safeguards to prevent duplicate responses, Mulch says. "We can put a control device into the survey—for example, having respondents enter their phone number. If someone with that number has already called in, the computer would say 'I'm sorry we've already received a response from your household. Thanks for calling,' and give them the validation code anyway."

The system also can keep track of responses by store, allowing for limits on the number of responses from patrons of one location. "When the respondent calls in, they enter the store number and that raises the counter on that store so once they hit the target number the database cuts it off and says 'We're sorry, we've completed the interviews for this store.' Even though they've reached their quota, the respondent still gets the validation number to get their free meal, to reward them for going to the trouble of calling."

Questions

1. You are a regional manager for Long John Silver's. What are the five key things that you want to know from drive-through customers? Take-out customers?
2. What advantages do you see arising from a call-in survey? What are the disadvantages?

3. What other marketing research techniques could have been used to gather the data? Why weren't they used?

4. What method would you recommend to interview dine-in customers?

5. Does it make sense to interview nonpatrons of Long John Silver's? If so, what would you ask them?

6. Explain how database marketing might benefit Long John Silver's

Source: From, "Don't Call Us We'll Call You" by Joseph Rydholm, *Quirk's Marketing Research Review*, October 1995. Reprinted by permission.

Marketing Planning Activities

ANALYZING MARKETING OPPORTUNITIES

*T*he next step in preparing a marketing plan for the company you have already chosen is to get a thorough understanding of the marketing opportunities in terms of marketing to customers. The following activities will help you better understand the marketplace, which will increase your chances of success in developing an appropriate marketing mix. Also refer to Exhibit 2.8 for additional marketing plan subjects.

1. Identify the SIC code for your chosen company's industry. Perform a brief industry analysis (from U.S. *Industrial Outlook,* for example) of your firm's industry, based on the SIC code.

2. To whom does your company market (consumer, industrial, government, not-for-profit, or a combination of targets)? Within each market, are there specific segments or niches that your company can concentrate on? If so, which one(s) would you focus on and why? What are the factors used to create these segments?

Marketing*Builder* Exercise

- **Market Segment** portion of the **Market Analysis** template

3. Describe your company's target market segment(s). Use demographics, pyschographics, geographics, economic factors, size, growth rates, trends, SIC codes, and any other appropriate descriptors.

Marketing*Builder* Exercise

- **Customer Profile** portion of the **Market Analysis** template

4. Describe the decision-making process that customers go through when purchasing your company's product or service. What are the critical factors that influence this purchase-behavior process?

5. Choose four characteristics of your firm's product offering. Using these factors for axes, draw two positioning grids and fill in the quadrants with competitor's offerings as well as your own. Are there any "holes" of needs and wants that are not being filled?

Marketing*Builder* Exercises

- **Positioning** portion of the **Marketing Communications** template

6. Are there critical issues that must be explored with primary marketing research before you can implement your marketing plan? These might include items such as customer demand, purchase intentions, customer perceptions of product quality, price perceptions, reaction to critical promotion, and so on.

Marketing*Builder* Exercises

- **Product Launch Chart** spreadsheet
- **Operating Budget** spreadsheet
- **Sales Forecast and Analysis** spreadsheet

Product Decisions

1 Define the term "product."

2 Classify consumer products.

3 Define the terms "product item," "product line," and "product mix."

4 Describe marketing uses of branding.

5 Describe marketing uses of packaging and labeling.

6 Discuss global issues in branding and packaging.

7 Describe how and why product warranties are important marketing tools.

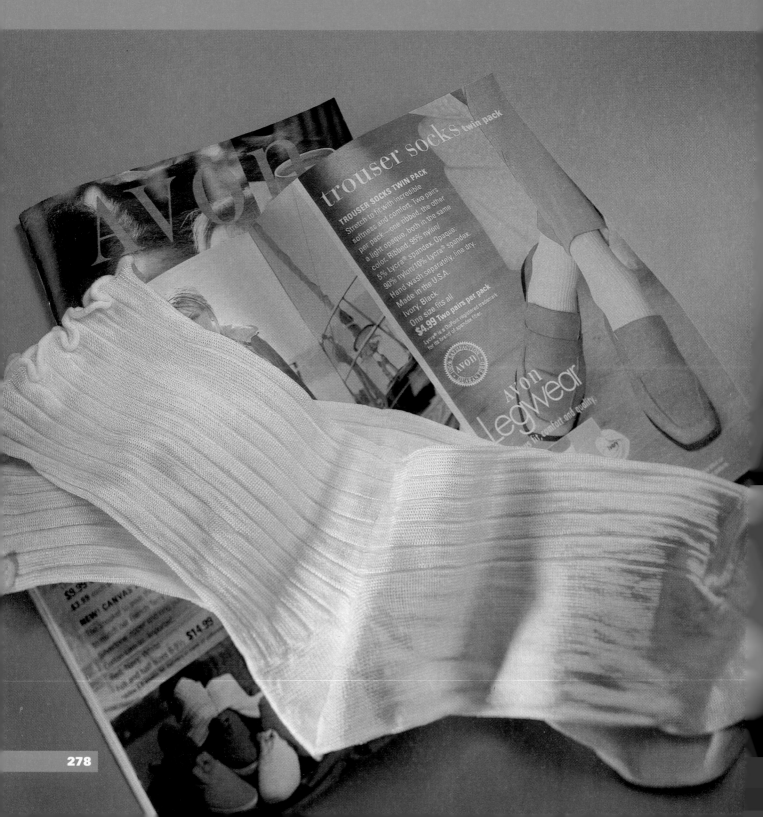

Chapter 10

Product Concepts

In mid-1994, Avon Products introduced Avon Style, a line of apparel that includes lingerie, hosiery, and casual sportswear. Consumers purchased $120 million worth of Avon Style merchandise during the first 10 months the new product line was on the market.

The success of Avon Style has encouraged company executives to add a new product line of home furnishings, including sheets, towels, and casual dishes. According to *Brandweek,* the move into home furnishings is a way for Avon to offset continuing weakness in its gift business, which has been flat or declining for several years.[1] Interestingly, Avon sold its health care division several years ago so that the company could focus more on its main business—beauty care products.

Avon also plans to launch a new line of hair care products and a new mail-order catalog called Avon Beauty, a Fashion by Mail. On-line sales opportunities are being explored along with several other new product line possibilities.[2]

Why would a cosmetics company like Avon begin offering apparel and home furnishings? Will Avon's reputation be helpful in marketing these new product lines? Do you think Avon's strategy is sound?

Avon Products, Inc.
What on-line sales opportunities are currently available at Avon's site? What evidence of new product lines do you find?
http://www.avon.com/

WHAT IS A PRODUCT?

1 Define the term "product."

The product offering, the heart of an organization's marketing program, is usually the starting point in creating a marketing mix. A marketing manager cannot determine a price, design a promotion strategy, or create a distribution channel until the firm has a product to sell. Moreover, an excellent distribution channel, a persuasive promotion campaign, and a fair price have no value with a poor or inadequate product offering.

product
Everything, both favorable and unfavorable, that a person receives in an exchange.

A **product** may be defined as everything, both favorable and unfavorable, that a person receives in an exchange. A product may be a tangible good like a pair of shoes, a service like a haircut, an idea like "don't litter," or any combination of these three. Packaging, style, color, options, and size are some typical product features. Just as important are intangibles such as service, the seller's image, the manufacturer's reputation, and the way consumers believe others will view the product.

To most people, the term "product" means a tangible good. However, services and ideas are also products. (Chapter 12 focuses specifically on the unique aspects of marketing services.) The marketing process identified in Chapter 1 is the same whether the product marketed is a good, a service, an idea, or some combination of these.

TYPES OF CONSUMER PRODUCTS

2 Classify consumer products.

Products can be classified as either business (industrial) or consumer products, depending on the buyer's intentions. The key distinction between the two types of products is their intended use. If the intended use is a business purpose, the product is classified as a business or industrial product. As explained in Chapter 7, a **business product** is used to manufacture other goods or services, to facilitate an organization's operations, or to resell to other customers. A **consumer product** is bought to satisfy an individual's personal wants. Sometimes the same item can be classified as either a business or a consumer product, depending on its intended use. Examples include lightbulbs, pencils and paper, and microcomputers.

business product (industrial product)
Products used to manufacture other goods or services, to facilitate an organization's operations, or to resell to other customers.

We need to know about product classifications because business and consumer products are marketed differently. They are marketed to different target markets and tend to use different distribution, promotion, and pricing strategies.

consumer product
Product bought to satisfy an individual's personal wants.

Exhibit 10.1
Classification of Consumer Products

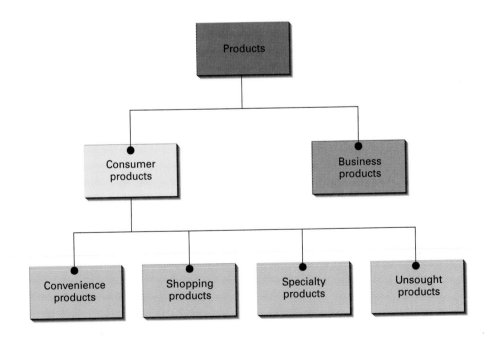

Chapter 7 examined seven categories of business products: major equipment, accessory equipment, component parts, processed materials, raw materials, supplies, and services. The current chapter examines an effective way of categorizing consumer products. Although there are several ways to classify them, the most popular approach includes these four types: convenience products, shopping products, specialty products, and unsought products. (See Exhibit 10.1.) This approach classifies products according to how much effort is normally used to shop for them.

Convenience Products

A **convenience product** is a relatively inexpensive item that merits little shopping effort. That is, a consumer is unwilling to shop extensively for such an item. Candy, soft drinks, combs, aspirin, small hardware items, dry cleaning, and car washes fall into the convenience product category.

Consumers buy convenience products regularly, usually without much planning. Nevertheless, consumers do know the brand names of popular convenience products, such as Coca-Cola, Bayer aspirin, and Right Guard deodorant. Convenience products normally require wide distribution in order to sell sufficient quantities to meet profit goals.

convenience product
A relatively inexpensive item that merits little shopping effort.

Shopping Products

A **shopping product** is usually more expensive than a convenience product and is found in fewer stores. Consumers usually buy a shopping product only after comparing several brands or stores on style, practicality, price, and lifestyle compatibility. They are willing to invest some effort into this process to get the desired benefits.

There are two types of shopping products: homogeneous and heterogeneous. Consumers perceive *homogeneous* shopping products as basically similar—for example, washers, dryers, refrigerators, and televisions. With homogeneous shopping products, consumers typically look for the lowest priced brand that has the desired features.

In contrast, consumers perceive *heterogeneous* shopping products as essentially different—for example, furniture, clothing, housing, and universities. Consumers often have trouble comparing heterogeneous shopping products because the prices, qual-

shopping product
Product that requires comparison shopping, because it is usually more expensive than a convenience product and found in fewer stores.

With homogeneous products such as televisions, consumers typically buy the lowest priced brand that has the desired features.
© Jeff Greenberg

ity, and features vary so much. The benefit of comparing heterogeneous shopping products is "finding the best product or brand for me"; this decision is often highly individual.

Specialty Products

specialty product
A particular item that consumers search extensively for and are very reluctant to accept substitutes.

When consumers search extensively for a particular item and are very reluctant to accept substitutes, that item is a **specialty product.** Fine watches, Rolls Royce automobiles, expensive stereo equipment, gourmet restaurants, and highly specialized forms of medical care are generally considered specialty products.

Marketers of specialty products often use selective, status-conscious advertising to maintain their product's exclusive image. Distribution is often limited to one or a very few outlets in a geographic area. Brand names and quality of service are often very important.

Unsought Products

unsought product
A product unknown to the potential buyer or a known product that the buyer does not actively seek.

A product unknown to the potential buyer or a known product that the buyer does not actively seek is referred to as an **unsought product.** New products fall into this category until advertising and distribution increase consumer awareness of them.

Some goods are always marketed as unsought items, especially needed products we do not like to think about or care to spend money on. Insurance, burial plots, encyclopedias, and similar items require aggressive personal selling and highly persuasive advertising. Salespeople actively seek leads to potential buyers. Because consumers usually do not seek out this type of product, the company must go directly to them through a salesperson, direct mail, or direct-response advertising.

PRODUCT ITEMS, LINES, AND MIXES

3 Define the terms "product item," "product line," and "product mix."

product item
A specific version of a product that can be designated as a distinct offering among an organization's products.

product line
A group of closely related product items.

product mix
All products an organization sells.

Rarely does a company sell a single product. More often, it sells a variety of things. A **product item** is a specific version of a product that can be designated as a distinct offering among an organization's products. Gillette's Trac II razor is an example of a product item. (See Exhibit 10.2.)

A group of closely related product items is a **product line.** For example, the column in Exhibit 10.2 titled "Blades and razors" represents one of Gillette's product lines. Different container sizes and shapes also distinguish items in a product line. Diet Coke, for example, is available in cans and various plastic containers. Each size and each container are a separate product item.

An organization's **product mix** includes all the products it sells. All Gillette's products—blades and razors, toiletries, writing instruments, and lighters—constitute its product mix. Each product item in the product mix may require a separate marketing strategy. In some cases, however, product lines and even entire product mixes share some marketing strategy components. The Pontiac division of General Motors, for example, promotes all Pontiac items and lines with its theme "We build excitement—Pontiac."

Organizations derive several benefits from organizing related items into product lines, including the following:

- *Advertising economies:* Product lines provide economies of scale in advertising. Several products can be advertised under the umbrella of the line. Campbell Soup, for example, can talk about its soup being "m-m-good" and promote the entire line.
- *Package uniformity:* A product line can benefit from package uniformity. All packages in the line may have a common look and still keep their individual identities. Campbell Soup is a good example.

Exhibit 10.2
*Gillette's Product Lines
and Product Mix*

Depth of the product lines	Width of the product mix			
	Blades and razors	**Toiletries**	**Writing instruments**	**Lighters**
	Sensor	Series	Paper Mate	Cricket
	Trac II	Adorn	Flair	S. T. Dupont
	Atra	Toni		
	Swivel	Right Guard		
	Double-Edge	Silkience		
	Super Adjustment	Soft and Dri		
	Lady Gillette	Foamy		
	Super Speed	Dry Look		
	Twin Injector	Dry Idea		
	Techmatic	Brush Plus		
	Three-Piece			
	Knack			
	Blades			

- *Standardized components:* Product lines allow firms to standardize components, thus reducing manufacturing and inventory costs. For example, many of the components Samsonite uses in its folding tables and chairs are also used in its patio furniture. General Motors uses the same parts on many automobile makes and models.

- *Efficient sales and distribution:* A product line enables sales personnel for companies like Procter & Gamble to provide a full range of choices to customers. Distributors and retailers are often more inclined to stock the company's products if it offers a full line. Transportation and warehousing costs are likely to be lower for a product line than for a collection of individual items.

Campbell Soup Company
How does Campbell promote its product line via this Web site?

http://www.campbellsoup.com/

- *Equivalent quality:* Purchasers usually expect and believe that all products in a line are about equal in quality. Consumers expect, for example, that all Campbell soups and all Mary Kay cosmetics will be of similar quality.

Product mix width (or breadth) refers to the number of product lines an organization offers. In Exhibit 10.2, for example, the width of Gillette's product mix is four product lines. **Product line depth** is the number of product items in a product line. As shown in Exhibit 10.2, the blades and razors product line consists of 12 product items; the toiletries product line includes 10 product items.

Firms increase the *width* of their product mix to diversify risk. To generate sales and boost profits, firms spread risk across many product lines rather than depending on only one or two. Firms also widen their product mix to capitalize on established reputations. For example, by introducing new product lines, Kodak capitalized on its image as a leader in photographic products. Kodak's product lines now include film, processing, still cameras, movie cameras, paper, and chemicals. The story at the beginning of this chapter describes Avon Product's recent efforts to widen the company's product mix by adding apparel, home furnishings, and other new product lines.

Firms increase the *depth* of product lines to attract buyers with different preferences, to increase sales and profits by further segmenting the market, to capitalize on economies of scale in production and marketing, and to even out seasonal sales patterns. Between 1970 and 1993, for example, Timex increased the depth of its wristwatch line from 300 items to 1,500 items.[3]

product mix width
The number of product lines an organization offers.

product line depth
The number of product items in a product line.

Adjustments to Product Items, Lines, and Mixes

Over time, firms change product items, lines, and mixes to take advantage of new technical or product developments or to respond to changes in the environment. They may adjust by modifying products, repositioning products, or extending or contracting product lines.

Product Modifications

product modification
Changing one or more of a product's characteristics.

Marketing managers must decide if and when to modify existing products. **Product modification** changes one or more of a product's characteristics:

- *Quality modification:* change in a product's dependability or durability. Reducing a product's quality may let the manufacturer lower the price and appeal to target markets unable to afford the original product. On the other hand, increasing quality can help the firm compete with rival firms. Increasing quality can also result in increased brand loyalty, greater ability to raise prices, or new opportunities for market segmentation. Automobile safety features such as antilock brakes and air bags are examples of this type of quality modification.

- *Functional modification:* change in a product's versatility, effectiveness, convenience, or safety. In response to widespread consumer perceptions that aerosol propellants are harmful to the environment, Dow Chemical began offering its bathroom cleaner in a trigger-spray version. The Procter & Gamble deodorant brands Right Guard, Old Spice, and Sure Pro are also available in nonaerosol trigger-spray or pump versions.[4]

- *Style modification:* aesthetic product change, rather than a quality or functional change. Clothing manufacturers commonly use style modifications to motivate customers to replace products before they are worn out. **Planned obsolescence** is a term commonly used to describe the practice of modifying products so those that have already been sold become obsolete before they actually need replacement. Some argue that planned obsolescence is wasteful; some claim it is unethical. Marketers respond that consumers favor style modifications because they like changes in the appearance of goods like clothing and cars. Marketers also contend that consumers, not manufacturers and marketers, decide when styles are obsolete.

planned obsolescence
The practice of modifying products so those that have already been sold become obsolete before they actually need replacement.

Is planned obsolescence wasteful or unethical? Marketers maintain that the consumer decides when clothing styles are obsolete.
©1996 PhotoDisc, Inc.

Repositioning

Repositioning, as Chapter 8 explained, is changing consumers' perceptions of a brand. For example, Kentucky Fried Chicken is trying to reposition itself to attract more health-conscious customers. The strategy includes gradually changing the restaurant's name to KFC, reducing dependence on the word "fried," and adding grilled, broiled, and baked poultry items to the menu. The Colonel's Rotisserie Gold, a marinated, slow-roasted chicken product, is what the company calls "its repositioning linchpin."[5]

Changing demographics, declining sales, or changes in the social environment often motivate firms to reposition established brands. For example, the changing demographics of snackers and eroding market share led Frito-Lay to reposition its top-selling brand, Fritos, after 58 years of successfully targeting all ages. The repositioning effort includes making major changes in the Fritos logo and packaging, focusing on those between the ages of 9 and 18, and launching a major new radio and TV advertising campaign. Playboy, one of the world's most well-known brands, is being repositioned to better reflect contemporary values and lifestyles. "Our core customers have always been men, but we're trying now to extend the brand attributes to couples," said Christie Hefner.[6] "Playboy is a classic American brand, a brand that is sexy, romantic, fun, and sophisticated. It should have a broader audience."[7]

Product Line Extensions

Product line extension occurs when a company's management decides to add products to an existing product line in order to compete more broadly in the industry. For instance, Mercedes-Benz AG plans to add 11 cars to its line of passenger vehicles between 1997 and 2000, including two "mini" city cars and a sports utility vehicle.[8] Miller Brewing Co.'s $70 million launch of its new flagship brand, Miller, in 1996 is another recent example of product line extension.[9]

product line extension
Adding additional products to an existing product line in order to compete more broadly in the industry.

Product Line Contraction

Does the world really need 31 varieties of Head & Shoulders shampoo? Or 52 versions of Crest? Procter & Gamble Co. has decided the answer is no.[10] Procter & Gamble (P&G) is contracting product lines by eliminating unpopular sizes, flavors, and other variations to make it easier for customers to find what they are looking for. After decades of introducing new-and-improved this, lemon-flavored that, and extra-jumbo-size the other thing, P&G has decided that its product lines are overextended.[11] Symptoms of product line overextension include the following:

- Some products in the line do not contribute to profits because of low sales or cannibalize sales of other items in the line.
- Manufacturing or marketing resources are disproportionately allocated to slow-moving products.
- Some items in the line are obsolete because of new product entries in the line or new products offered by competitors.

In mid-1996, Apple Computer announced plans to reduce the number of Macintosh models by 50 percent. According to Gilbert F. Amelio, chairman and CEO, the strategy is intended to "reduce Apple's costs and give it a chance to find new profit sources."[12]

Three major benefits are likely when a firm contracts overextended product lines. First, resources become concentrated on the most important products. Second, managers no longer waste resources trying to improve the sales and profits of poorly performing products. Third, new product items have a greater chance of being successful because more financial and human resources are available to manage them.

4 Describe marketing uses of branding.

brand
A name, term, symbol, design, or combination thereof that identifies a seller's products and differentiates them from competitors' products.

BRANDING

The success of any business or consumer product depends in part on the target market's ability to distinguish one product from another. Branding is the main tool marketers use to distinguish their products from the competition's.

A **brand** is a name, term, symbol, design, or combination thereof that identifies a seller's products and differentiates them from competitors' products. A **brand name** is that part of a brand that can be spoken, including letters (GM, YMCA), words

brand name
That part of a brand that can be spoken, including letters, words, and numbers.

Exhibit 10.3
Most Respected Brand Names in the United States

1. Kodak Photographic Film	6. Mercedes-Benz Automobiles
2. Disney World	7. Hallmark Greeting Cards
3. National Geographic	8. Waterford Crystal
4. The Discovery Channel	9. Craftsman Power Tools
5. Disneyland	10. Fisher-Price Toys

Source: Sean Mehegan, "A Picture of Quality," *Brandweek,* 8 April 1996, pp. 38–40.

brand mark
The elements of a brand that cannot be spoken.

(Chevrolet), and numbers (WD-40, 7-Eleven). The elements of a brand that cannot be spoken are called the **brand mark**—for example, the well-known Mercedes-Benz and Delta Airlines symbols.

Benefits of Branding

Branding has three main purposes: product identification, repeat sales, and new-product sales. The most important purpose is *product identification.* Branding allows marketers to distinguish their products from all others. Many brand names are familiar to consumers and indicate quality. Exhibit 10.3 lists, in order, the 10 brand names that U.S. consumers believe signify the highest quality products. The coolest brands, according to U.S. teenagers, are Nike, Levi's, Guess?, Gap, Coke, Pepsi, and Sega.[13]

brand equity
The value of company and brand names.

The term **brand equity** refers to the value of company and brand names. A brand that has high awareness, perceived quality, and brand loyalty among customers has high brand equity. A brand with strong brand equity is a valuable asset. According to one estimate, the brand equity of Coca-Cola is $36 billion, Marlboro $33 billion, and Kodak $10 billion.[14] Companies like Procter & Gamble spend over $5 million per day to reinforce the brand equity of their products.[15]

master brand
A brand so dominant in consumers' minds that they think of it immediately when a product category, use situation, product attribute, or customer benefit is mentioned.

The term **master brand** has been used to refer to a brand so dominant in consumers' minds that they think of it immediately when a product category, use, attribute, or customer benefit is mentioned.[16] Exhibit 10.4 lists the master brands in

Exhibit 10.4
Master Brands in Selected Product Categories

Product category	Master brand
Baking soda	Arm & Hammer
Adhesive bandages	Band-Aid
Rum	Bacardi
Antacids	Alka-Seltzer
Gelatin	Jell-O
Soup	Campbell's
Salt	Morton
Toy trains	Lionel
Cream cheese	Philadelphia
Crayons	Crayola
Petroleum jelly	Vaseline

Source: Peter H. Farquhar, et al., "Strategies for Leveraging Master Brands," *Marketing Research,* September 1992, pp. 32–43. Courtesy American Marketing Association.

several product categories. How many other brands can you name in these 11 categories? Can you name any other product categories in which the master brands listed in Exhibit 10.4 compete? Probably not many. Campbell's means soup to consumers; it doesn't mean high-quality food products.

What constitutes a good brand name? Most effective brand names have several of the following features:

- Easy to pronounce (by both domestic and foreign buyers)
- Easy to recognize
- Easy to remember
- Short
- Distinctive, unique
- Describes the product
- Describes product use
- Describes product benefits
- Has a positive connotation
- Reinforces the desired product image
- Is legally protectable in home and foreign markets of interest

Obviously no brand exhibits all of these characteristics. The most important issue is that the brand can be protected for exclusive use by its owner.

 U.S. brands command substantial premiums in many places around the world. Procter & Gamble's Whisper sanitary napkins sell for 10 times the price of local brands in China. Johnson & Johnson brands like Johnson's baby shampoo and Band-Aids command a 500 percent premium in China.[17] Gillette disposable razors sell for twice the price of local brands in India.

The best generator of *repeat sales* is satisfied customers.[18] Branding helps consumers identify products they wish to buy again and avoid those they do not. **Brand loyalty,** a consistent preference for one brand over all others, is quite high in some product categories. Over half the users in product categories such as cigarettes, mayonnaise, toothpaste, coffee, headache remedies, photographic film, bath soap, and catsup are loyal to one brand. The annual Monitor poll conducted by Yankelovich Partners reports that 74 percent of respondents "find a brand they like, then resist efforts to get them to change." Once consumers are convinced of the quality and value of a particular brand, it takes a lot of money and effort to change their minds.[19] Brand identity is essential to developing brand loyalty.

brand loyalty
A consistent preference for one brand over all others.

The third main purpose of branding is to facilitate *new-product sales*. Company and brand names like those listed in Exhibit 10.3 and Exhibit 10.4 are extremely useful when introducing new products.

The Internet provides firms a new alternative for generating brand awareness, promoting a desired brand image, stimulating new and repeat brand sales, and enhancing brand loyalty and building brand equity. However, as the following "Ethics in Marketing" box indicates, some groups feel that marketing on the Internet has gone too far. They have accused a number of firms, including Kellogg's Co. and Frito-Lay, of exploitative marketing on the Internet.

Branding Strategies

Firms face complex branding decisions. As Exhibit 10.5 illustrates, the first decision is whether to brand at all. Some firms actually use the lack of a brand name as a selling point. These unbranded products are called generic products. Firms that decide to brand their products may choose to follow a policy of using manufacturers' brands, private (distributor) brands, or both. In either case, they must then decide among a policy of individual branding (different brands for different products), family branding (common names for different products), or a combination of individual branding and family branding.

Ethics in Marketing

Exploitative Marketing to Children on the Internet

The Center for Media Education (CME), a nonprofit research group that advocates more education on television and in other media, has petitioned the Federal Trade Commission (FTC) to investigate what it considers exploitative marketing on the Internet and to set guidelines to protect children. CME contends that a number of well-known national brands have Web sites that are advertisements in disguise that unfairly target children. According to CME, the Web sites are designed "to capture the loyalty and spending power" of children, and many would violate children's advertising safeguards in traditional media,

including television. For example, CME reported that some Web sites invade children's privacy by offering prizes and rewards in exchange for personal information. Others exploit children by weaving advertisements and opportunities to buy with on-line activities such as sending e-mail or playing games.

Spokespersons for Kellogg's and Frito-Lay insist that their sites do not exploit children. "It is not a

soft sell," said Tod MacKenzie, spokesperson for Frito-Lay. "It is almost no sell."

The FTC does not regulate advertising for children over the Internet. However, the agency's jurisdiction over deceptive market practices does extend to the Internet.[20]

Do you think information on company or brand Web sites should be regulated by the FTC? Should television advertising guidelines apply to Web sites? Can you recall visiting any Web sites that you considered exploitative of children?

Generic Products versus Branded Products

generic product
A no-frills, no-brand-name, low-cost product that is simply identified by its product category.

A **generic product** is typically a no-frills, no-brand-name, low-cost product that is simply identified by its product category. (Note that a generic product and a brand name that becomes generic, such as cellophane, are not the same thing.) Generic products have captured significant market shares in some product categories, such as canned fruits, canned vegetables, and paper products. These unbranded products are frequently identified only by black stenciled lettering on white packages.

The main appeal of generics is their low price. Generic grocery products are usually 30 to 40 percent less expensive than manufacturers' brands in the same product category and 20 to 25 percent less expensive than retailer-owned brands.

Pharmaceuticals make up another product category where generics have made inroads. When patents on successful pharmaceutical products expire, low-cost generics rapidly appear on the market. For example, when the patent on Merck's popular antiarthritis drug Clinoril expired, sales declined by 50 percent almost immediately.

Exhibit 10.5
Major Branding Decisions

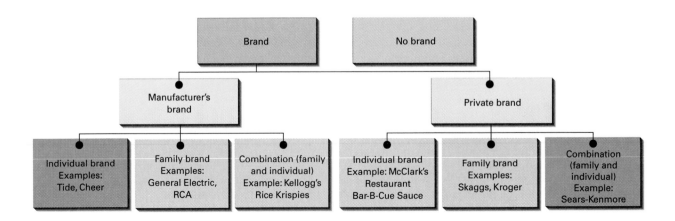

Manufacturers' Brands versus Private Brands

The brand name of a manufacturer—such as Kodak, Lazy Boy, and Fruit of the Loom—is called a **manufacturer's brand.** Sometimes the term *national brand* is used as a synonym for "manufacturer's brand." This term is not always accurate, however, because many manufacturers serve only regional markets. The term *manufacturer's brand* more precisely defines the brand's owner.

A **private brand** is a brand name owned by a wholesaler or a retailer. Hunt Club (a JCPenney brand), Sam's American Choice (Wal-Mart), and IGA (Independent Grocers' Association) are all private brands. A Gallup survey, conducted for the Private Label Manufacturers Association, revealed that 83 percent of consumers say they regularly buy less expensive retailer brands.[21] Private brands account for about 20 percent of supermarket sales, 8.6 percent of drugstore sales, and over 9 percent of mass merchandiser sales.[22]

Who buys private brands? According to one expert, "the young, discerning, educated shopper is the private label buyer." These individuals are willing to purchase private brands because they have confidence in their ability to assess quality and value.[23] Exhibit 10.6 illustrates key issues that wholesalers and retailers should consider in deciding whether to sell manufacturers' brands or private brands. Many firms, such as JCPenney, Kmart, and Safeway offer a combination of both.

Individual Brands versus Family Brands

Many companies use different brand names for different products; this practice is referred to as **individual branding.** Companies use individual brands when their products vary greatly in use or performance. For instance, it would not make sense to use

manufacturers' brand
The brand name of a manufacturer.

private brand
A brand name owned by a wholesaler or a retailer.

individual branding
Using different brand names for different products.

Key Advantages of Carrying Manufacturers' Brands	Key Advantages of Carrying Private Brands
• Heavy advertising to the consumer by manufacturers like Procter & Gamble helps develop strong consumer loyalties.	• A wholesaler or retailer can usually earn higher profits on its own brand. In addition, because the private brand is exclusive, there is less pressure to mark the price down to meet competition.
• Well-known manufacturers' brands, such as Kodak and Fisher-Price, can attract new customers and enhance the dealer's (wholesaler's or retailer's) prestige.	• A manufacturer can decide to drop a brand or a reseller at any time or even to become a direct competitor to its dealers.
• Many manufacturers offer rapid delivery, enabling the dealer to carry less inventory.	• A private brand ties the customer to the wholesaler or retailer. A person who wants a Die-Hard battery must go to Sears.
• If a dealer happens to sell a manufacturer's brand of poor quality, the customer may simply switch brands but remain loyal to the dealer.	• Wholesalers and retailers have no control over the intensity of distribution of manufacturers' brands. Wal-Mart store managers don't have to worry about competing with other sellers of Sam's American Choice products or Ol' Roy dog food. They know that these brands are sold only in Wal-Mart and Sam's Wholesale Club stores.

Exhibit 10.6

Comparing Manufacturers' and Private Brands from the Reseller's Perspective

Sony's family brand includes radios, TV sets, stereos, video cameras, and numerous other electronic products.
Courtesy Sony Electronics, Inc.

the same brand name for a pair of dress socks and a baseball bat. Procter & Gamble targets different segments of the laundry detergent market with Bold, Cheer, Dash, Dreft, Era, Gain, Ivory Snow, Oxydol, Solo, and Tide. Marriott International, Inc., also targets different market segments with Courtyard by Marriott, Residence Inn, and Fairfield Inn.

family brand
Marketing several different products under the same brand name.

On the other hand, a company that markets several different products under the same brand name is using a **family brand.** For example, Sony's family brand includes radios, television sets, stereos, and other electronic products. A brand name can only be stretched so far, however. Do you know the differences among Holiday Inn, Holiday Inn Express, Holiday Inn Select, Holiday Inn Sunspree Resort, Holiday Inn Garden Court, and Holiday Inn Hotel & Suites? Neither do most travelers.[24]

Breyers
McIlhenny Company
Frito-Lay
How does Breyers market individual brands, family brands, and cobrands via its Web site? Compare the McIlhenny Company site and the Frito-Lay site. Which is the most effective in establishing brand identity?

http://www.icecreamusa.com/
http://www.tabasco.com/
http://www.fritolay.com/

Cobranding

Cobranding entails placing two or more brand names on a product or its package. Cobranding is a useful strategy when a combination of brand names enhances the prestige or perceived value of a product or when it benefits brand owners and users. Cobranded Six Flags Theme Parks/Master Cards allow cardholders to earn points toward season passes, free admissions, and in-park spending vouchers at Six Flags theme parks throughout the United States.[25]

cobranding
Placing two or more brand names on a product or its package.

Cobranding may also be used to identify product ingredients or components. The brand name NutraSweet and its familiar brand mark appear on more than 3,000 food and beverage products. Intel, the microprocessor company, pays microcomputer manufacturers like IBM, Dell, and Compaq to include "Intel inside" in their advertising, on the computers, and on the boxes they are packed in.

Cobranding may also be used when two or more organizations wish to collaborate to offer a product. For example, Frito-Lay and McIllhenny's have joined together to market The Original Tabasco Chips.[26] Breyers cobrands ice cream with Reese's, Maxwell House, Sara Lee, and Hershey's.[27]

European firms have been slower to adopt cobranding than U.S. firms have. One reason is that European customers seem to be more skeptical than U.S. customers in trying new brands. European retailers also typically have less shelf space than their U.S. counterparts and are less willing to give new brands a try.[28]

Trademarks

A **trademark** is the exclusive right to use a brand or part of a brand. Others are prohibited from using the brand without permission. A **service mark** performs the same function for services, such as H&R Block and Weight Watchers. Parts of a brand or other product identification may qualify for trademark protection—for example:

- Shapes, such as the Jeep front grill and the Coca-Cola bottle, or even buildings, like Pizza Hut
- Ornamental color or design, such as the decoration on Nike tennis shoes, the black-and-copper color combination of a Duracell battery, Levi's small tag on the left side of the rear pocket of its jeans, or the cutoff black cone on the top of Cross pens
- Catchy phrases, such as Prudential's "Own a piece of the rock," Merrill Lynch's "We're bullish on America," and Budweiser's "This Bud's for you"
- Abbreviations, such as Bud, Coke, or The Met

The Harley-Davidson Motor Company has even applied to the U.S. Patent and Trademark Office to register the distinctive exhaust sound of its motorcycle engines as a trademark. The company cites several precedents for the Patent Office awarding a trademark registration for a sound, including the roar of the MGM lion and the ringing of the NBC chimes. Nine companies—among them four Japanese motorcycle manufacturers—have filed opposition to the application.[29]

trademark
The exclusive right to use a brand or part of a brand.

service mark
Trademark for a service.

Nike's very familiar swoosh is trademarked because it is part of the company's product identification.
© Linda Kaye/AP Wide World Photos

The Trademark Revision Act of 1988 allows organizations to register trademarks based on a bona fide intention to use them (normally, within six months following the issuance of the trademark) for 10 years. To renew the trademark, the company must prove it is using it. Rights to a trademark last as long as the mark is used. Normally, if the firm does not use it for two years, the trademark is considered abandoned, and a new user can claim exclusive ownership of the mark. Businesses planning to introduce new brands, trademarks, or packages should consider the following suggestions:[30]

- Check carefully before adopting a trademark or packaging style to make sure you're not infringing on someone else's.
- After a thorough search, consider registering your trademark.
- Make your packaging as distinctive as possible.
- Police your trademark.

generic product name
Identifies a product by class or type and cannot be trademarked.

Companies that fail to protect their trademarks face the problem of their product names becoming generic. A **generic product name** identifies a product by class or type and cannot be trademarked. Former brand names that were not sufficiently protected by their owners and were subsequently declared to be generic product names in U.S. courts include aspirin, cellophane, linoleum, thermos, kerosene, monopoly, cola, and shredded wheat.

Companies like Rolls Royce, Cross, Xerox, Levi's, Frigidaire, and McDonald's aggressively enforce their trademarks. Rolls Royce, Coca-Cola, and Xerox even run newspaper and magazine ads stating that their names are trademarks and should not be used as descriptive or generic terms. Some ads threaten lawsuits against competitors that violate trademarks.

Despite severe penalties for trademark violations, trademark infringement lawsuits are not uncommon. One of the major battles is over brand names that closely resemble another brand name. Coors Brewing, for example, sued Robert Corr, who produces a line of soft drinks under the name Corr's Beverages. Hyatt Hotels has blocked Hyatt Legal Services from featuring the term Hyatt in its advertising.

Companies must also contend with fake or unauthorized brands, such as fake Levi's jeans, Microsoft software, Rolex watches, Reebok and Nike footwear, and Louis Vuitton handbags. Levi Strauss has spent over $2 million on more than 600 investigations of counterfeit Levi's jeans. Other companies, including IBM and Coca-Cola, are very aggressive in trying to identify and eliminate counterfeiters.[31]

In Europe, you can sue counterfeiters only if your brand, logo, or trademark is formally registered. Until recently, formal registration was required in each country in which a company sought protection. A company can now register its trademark in all European Union (EU) member countries with one application.[32] The following "Global Perspectives" box describes the problem of counterfeit products in China.

PACKAGING

5 Describe marketing uses of packaging and labeling.

Packages have always served a practical function. That is, they hold contents together and protect goods as they move through the distribution channel. Today, however, packaging is also a container for promoting the product and making it easier and safer to use.

Packaging Functions

The three most important functions of packaging are to contain and protect products, promote products, and facilitate the storage, use, and convenience of products. A fourth function of packaging that is becoming increasingly important is to facilitate recycling and reduce environmental damage.

Global Perspectives

China Fails to Protect Foreign Companies' Trademarks and Other Property Rights

According to *Fortune* magazine, "China is in trouble. Its political system is unstable and plagued by corruption, [and] its booming economy is perilously brittle. The people in charge show little respect for human rights or copyrights."[33]

American businesses have long complained about Chinese firms copying U.S. trademarks, software, and other intellectual property. In grocery stores, you're likely to see a familiar red-and-white toothpaste box that looks very much like Colgate, canned foods with "Del Monte green" labels, and cereal boxes featuring a rooster that looks identical to Kellogg's. Closer inspection, however, reveals that the toothpaste is Cologate, the vegetable canner is Jia Long, and the cereal is Kongalu Corn Strips.[34]

Bootleg software is also common in China. In one factory raid,

5,700 disks with pirated Microsoft software were seized.[35]

The U.S. and China reached an accord in February 1995 under which Beijing committed to take actions to protect U.S. property. Little, if any, action has been taken to enforce the accord. In an effort to pressure China's leaders to implement the terms of the agreement more aggressively, the U.S. Trade Representative's office has listed China alone in its "Priority Foreign Country" category, meaning that China could be subject to sanctions.[36]

Most people believe that it is unethical to intentionally deceive cus-

tomers about the brands of products they are buying. But where should you draw the line between similarity in package design and violation of trademarks and copyrights? Should Colgate have a monopoly on toothpaste boxes in red and white? Does Del Monte's use of green labels mean other vegetable canners must pick another color? And is the barnyard rooster exclusively Kellogg's? What actions might be available to U.S. companies like Kellogg's that believe their copyrights and trademarks have been violated? What actions, if any, do you think the U.S. government should take to enforce prohibitions against trademark infringements when they occur in other countries?

Containing and Protecting Products

The most obvious function of packaging is to contain products that are liquid, granular, or otherwise divisible. Packaging also enables manufacturers, wholesalers, and retailers to market products in specific quantities, such as ounces.

Physical protection is another obvious function of packaging. Most products are handled several times between the time they are manufactured, harvested, or otherwise produced and the time they are consumed or used. Many products are shipped, stored, and inspected several times between production and consumption. Some, like milk, need to be refrigerated. Others, like beer, are sensitive to light. Still others, like medicines and bandages, need to be kept sterile. Packages protect products from breakage, evaporation, spillage, spoilage, light, heat, cold, infestation, and many other conditions.

Promoting Products

Packaging does more than identify the brand, list the ingredients, specify features, and give directions. A package differentiates a product from competing products and may associate a new product with a family of other products from the same manufacturer. A new Campbell soup, with the familiar red label, benefits from its obvious association with other Campbell soups.

Packages use designs, colors, shapes, and materials to try to influence consumers' perceptions and buying behavior. For example, Kimberly-Clark Corp. and Procter & Gamble Co. recently introduced a wide array of more appealing boxes for Kleenex and Puffs tissues. The idea is that if boxes are more attractive, people won't mind

In addition to its practical function of holding and protecting goods, packaging also serves to promote products and make them easier and safer to use.
© Brooks Walker/National Geographic Image Collections

sticking them in every room of the house. So far, the strategy appears to be working. Almost 25 percent of the money spent on this $1.5 billion market goes for premium varieties.[37]

Packaging has a measurable effect on sales. Quaker Oats revised the package for Rice-a-Roni without making any other changes in marketing strategy and experienced a 44 percent increase in sales in one year.

Facilitating Storage, Use, and Convenience

Wholesalers and retailers prefer packages that are easy to ship, store, and stock on shelves. They also like packages that protect products, prevent spoilage or breakage, and extend the product's shelf life.

Consumers' requirements for convenience cover many dimensions. Consumers are constantly seeking items that are easy to handle, open, and reclose, although some consumers want packages that are tamperproof or childproof. Consumers also want reusable and disposable packages. Surveys conducted by *Sales & Marketing Management* magazine revealed that consumers dislike—and avoid buying—leaky ice cream boxes, overly heavy or fat vinegar bottles, immovable pry-up lids on glass bottles, key-opener sardine cans, and hard-to-pour cereal boxes. Such packaging innovations as zipper tear strips, hinged lids, tab slots, screw-on tops, and pour spouts were introduced to solve these and other problems. Johnson & Johnson has introduced Tylenol FastCap, a new patented package that will open with a flick of the wrist.[38]

Some firms use packaging to segment markets. For example, the Tylenol FastCap is targeted to adults over 50 who suffer from arthritis and to households without young children.[39] Different-size packages appeal to heavy, moderate, and light users. Salt is sold in package sizes ranging from single serving to picnic size to giant economy size. Campbell soup is packaged in single-serving cans aimed at the elderly and singles market segments. Beer and soft drinks are similarly marketed in various package sizes and types. Packaging convenience can increase a product's utility and, therefore, its market share and profits.

Facilitating Recycling and Reducing Environmental Damage

One of the most important packaging issues in the 1990s is compatibility with the environment. According to one study, 90 percent of surveyed consumers say no more packaging material should be used than is necessary. The ability to recycle is also important.[40]

Some firms use their packaging to target environmentally concerned market segments. Brocato International, for example, markets shampoo and hair conditioner in bottles that are biodegradable in landfills. Procter & Gamble markets Sure Pro and Old Spice in "eco-friendly" pump-spray packages that do not rely on aerosol propellants. Other firms that have introduced pump sprays include S.C. Johnson (Pledge furniture polish), Reckitt & Coleman Household Products (Woolite rug cleaner), Rollout L.P. (Take 5 cleanser), and Richardson-Vicks (Vidal Sassoon hair spray).[41]

Labeling

persuasive labeling
Focuses on a promotional theme or logo and consumer information is secondary.

An integral part of any package is its label. Labeling generally takes one of two forms: persuasive or informational. **Persuasive labeling** focuses on a promotional theme or logo, and consumer information is secondary. Price Pfister developed a new persuasive label—featuring a picture of a faucet, the brand name, and the logo—with the goal of strengthening brand identity and becoming known as a brand instead of as a manufacturer.[42] Note that the standard promotional claims—such as "new," "improved," and "super"—are no longer very persuasive. Consumers have been saturated with "newness" and thus discount these claims.

 Informational labeling, in contrast, is designed to help consumers make proper product selections and lower their cognitive dissonance after the purchase. Sears attaches a "label of confidence" to all its floor coverings. This label gives such product information as durability, color, features, cleanability, care instructions, and construction standards. Most major furniture manufacturers affix labels to their wares that explain the products' construction features, such as type of frame, number of coils, and fabric characteristics. The Nutritional Labeling and Education Act of 1990 mandated detailed nutritional information on most food packages and standards for health claims on food packaging. An important outcome of this legislation is guidelines from the Food and Drug Administration for using terms like *low fat, light, reduced cholesterol, low sodium, low calorie, and fresh.*[43] Celentano, a New Jersey maker of Italian frozen foods, has capitalized on the new rules. Its label notes that, "as always," Celentano products don't contain additives, chemicals, preservatives, or artificial ingredients.[44]

Computerized optical scanners read the UPCs or bar codes and match them with brand names, package sizes, and prices.
© 1996 PhotoDisc, Inc.

informational labeling
Designed to help consumers make proper product selections and lower their cognitive dissonance after the purchase.

universal product codes (UPCs)
Series of thick and thin vertical lines (bar codes), readable by computerized optical scanners, that represent numbers used to track products.

Universal Product Codes

The **universal product codes (UPCs)** that appear on many items in supermarkets and other high-volume outlets were first introduced in 1974. Because the numerical codes appear as a series of thick and thin vertical lines, they are often called bar codes. The lines are read by computerized optical scanners that match codes with brand names, package sizes, and prices. They also print information on cash register tapes and help retailers rapidly and accurately prepare records of customer purchases, control inventories, and track sales. The UPC system and scanners are also used in single-source research. (See Chapter 9.)

GLOBAL ISSUES IN BRANDING AND PACKAGING

As the "Global Perspectives" box in this chapter indicates, brand imitations are widely available in some countries. Counterfeiting is also a major problem for some international marketers of prestigious brands, including the makers of Levi's jeans, Rolex and Seiko watches, and Gucci and Louis Vuitton handbags. International marketers must also address some other concerns regarding branding and packaging.

6 Discuss global issues in branding and packaging.

Branding

 When planning to enter a foreign market with an existing product, a firm has three options for handling the brand name:

- *One brand name everywhere:* This strategy is useful when the company markets mainly one product and the brand name does not have negative connotations in any local market. The Coca-Cola Company uses a one-brand-name strategy in 195 countries around the world. The advantages of a one-brand-name strategy are greater identification of the product from market to market and ease of coordinating promotion from market to market.

- *Adaptations and modifications:* A one-brand-name strategy is not possible when the name cannot be pronounced in the local language, when the brand name is owned by someone else, or when the brand name has a negative or vulgar connotation in the local language. The Mexican bread Bimbo might encounter some "correctness" problems in the U.S., and the Japanese coffee creamer Cheap might not be well received in the U.S. or Canada.[45]

- *Different brand names in different markets:* Local brand names are often used when translation or pronunciation problems occur, when the marketer wants the brand to appear to be a local brand, or when regulations require localization. Gillette's Silkience hair conditioner is called Soyance in France and Sientel in Italy. The adaptations were deemed to be more appealing in the local markets. Coca-Cola's Sprite brand had to be renamed Kin in Korea to satisfy a government prohibition on the unnecessary use of foreign words. Snuggle fabric softener is called FaFa in Japan, Cajoline in France, and other cuddly names elsewhere in the world.[46]

Packaging

Three aspects of packaging that are especially important in international marketing are labeling, aesthetics, and climate considerations. The major *labeling* concern is properly translating ingredient, promotional, and instructional information on labels. In Eastern Europe, packages of Ariel detergent are printed in 14 languages, from Latvian to Lithuanian.[47] Care must also be employed in meeting all local labeling requirements. Several years ago, an Italian judge ordered that all bottles of Coca-Cola be removed from retail shelves because the ingredients were not properly labeled. Labeling is also harder in countries like Belgium and Finland, which require it to be bilingual.

Package *aesthetics* may also require some attention. The key is to stay attuned to cultural traits in host countries. For example, colors may have different connotations. Red is associated with witchcraft in some countries, green may be a sign of danger, and white may be symbolic of death. Aesthetics also influence package size. Soft drinks are not sold in six-packs in countries that lack refrigeration. In some countries, products like detergent may be bought only in small quantities because of a lack of storage space. Other products, like cigarettes, may be bought in small quantities, and even single units, because of the low purchasing power of buyers.

Extreme *climates* and long-distance shipping necessitate sturdier and more durable packages for goods sold overseas. Spillage, spoilage, and breakage are all more important concerns when products are shipped long distances or frequently handled during shipping and storage. Packages may also have to ensure a longer product life if the time between production and consumption lengthens significantly.

PRODUCT WARRANTIES

Just as a package is designed to protect the product, a warranty protects the buyer and gives essential information about the product. A **warranty** confirms the quality or performance of a good or service. An **express warranty** is a written guarantee. Express warranties range from simple statements—such as "100 percent cotton" (a guarantee of quality) and "complete satisfaction guaranteed" (a statement of performance)—to extensive documents written in technical language. In contrast, an **implied warranty** is an unwritten guarantee that the good or service is fit for the purpose for which it was sold. All sales have an implied warranty under the Uniform Commercial Code.

Congress passed the Magnuson-Moss Warranty–Federal Trade Commission Improvement Act in 1975 to help consumers understand warranties and get action from manufacturers and dealers. A manufacturer that promises a full warranty must meet certain minimum standards, including repair "within a reasonable time and without charge" of any defects and replacement of the merchandise or a full refund if the product does not work "after a reasonable number of attempts" at repair. Any warranty that does not live up to this tough prescription must be "conspicuously" promoted as a limited warranty.

7 Describe how and why product warranties are important marketing tools.

warranty
Confirms the quality or performance of a good or service.

express warranty
A written guarantee.

implied warranty
An unwritten guarantee that the good or service is fit for the purpose for which it was sold.

LOOKING BACK

Look back at the story about Avon Products adding new product lines of apparel and home furnishings. Avon's strategy of increasing the width of its product mix is intended to capitalize on the established reputation of Avon. The company hopes to boost overall sales and products by adding these lines that are fairly inconsistent with its core product line. The Avon name has apparently been helpful in introducing the apparel line. It is not clear whether it can be successfully extended to home furnishings. It was not particularly helpful when Avon entered the health care business several years ago. The decision to expand into home furnishings may be partly due to recent successes of other apparel firms such as Calvin Klein, Guess?, and Liz Claiborne extending into the furnishings product category.

SUMMARY

1 *Define the term "product."* A product is anything, desired or not, that a person or organization receives in an exchange. The basic goal of purchasing decisions is to receive the tangible and intangible benefits associated with a product. Tangible aspects include packaging, style, color, size, and features. Intangible qualities include service, the retailer's image, the manufacturer's reputation, and the social status associated with a product. An organization's product offering is the crucial element in any marketing mix.

2 *Classify consumer products.* Consumer products are classified into four categories: convenience products, shopping products, specialty products, and unsought products. Convenience products are relatively inexpensive and require limited shopping effort. Shopping products are of two types: homogeneous and heteroge-

KEY TERMS

brand *285*

brand equity *286*

brand loyalty *287*

brand mark *286*

brand name *285*

business product (industrial product) *280*

cobranding *290*

consumer product *280*

convenience product *281*

neous. Because of the similarity of homogeneous products, they are differentiated mainly by price and features. In contrast, heterogeneous products appeal to consumers because of their distinct characteristics. Specialty products possess unique benefits that are highly desirable to certain customers. Finally, unsought products are either new products or products that require aggressive selling because they are generally avoided or overlooked by consumers.

3 *Define the terms "product item," "product line," and "product mix."* A product item is a specific version of a product that can be designated as a distinct offering among an organization's products. A product line is a group of closely related products offered by an organization. An organization's product mix includes all the products it sells. "Product mix width" refers to the number of product lines an organization offers. Product line depth is the number of product items in a product line. Firms modify existing products by changing their quality, functional characteristics, or style. Product line extension occurs when firms add new products to existing product lines.

4 *Describe marketing uses of branding.* A brand is a name, term, or symbol that identifies and differentiates a firm's products. Established brands encourage customer loyalty and help new products succeed. Branding strategies require decisions about individual, family, manufacturers', and private brands.

5 *Describe marketing uses of packaging and labeling.* Packaging has four functions: containing and protecting products; promoting products; facilitating product storage, use, and convenience; and facilitating recycling and reducing environmental damage. As a tool for promotion, packaging identifies the brand and its features. It also serves the critical function of differentiating a product from competing products and linking it with related products from the same manufacturer. The label is an integral part of the package, with persuasive and informational functions. In essence, the package is the marketer's last chance to influence buyers before they make a purchase decision.

6 *Discuss global issues in branding and packaging.* In addition to brand piracy, international marketers must address a variety of concerns regarding branding and packaging, including choosing a brand name policy, translating labels and meeting host-country labeling requirements, making packages aesthetically compatible with host-country cultures, and offering the sizes of packages preferred in host countries.

7 *Describe how and why product warranties are important marketing tools.* Product warranties are important tools because they offer consumers protection and help them gauge product quality.

Discussion and Writing Questions

1. A local civic organization has asked you to give a luncheon presentation about planned obsolescence. Rather than pursuing a negative approach by talking about how businesses exploit customers through planned obsolescence, you have decided to talk about the benefits of producing products that do not last forever. Prepare a one-page outline of your presentation.

2. A local retailer would like to introduce her own brand of shoes to sell alongside her current inventory. She has hired you to generate a report outlining the advantages and disadvantages of doing so. Write the report.

3. Identify five outstanding brand names, and explain why each is included in your list.

4. Break into small groups, and discuss the packaging of a product familiar to all of your group members. Make a brief presentation to your class describing the pros and cons of this package.

5. How have several snack food companies modified their prod-

uct to serve the emerging needs of their customers?

6. Your new boss has asked you to prepare a brief memo about the future of on-line supermarket shopping and its likely impact on packaging. Prepare an outline of your memo.

7. What is the product mix offered at the following Web site?

http://www.disney.com/

8. List the countries to which Levi Strauss & Co. markets through the following Web site. How do the product offerings differ between the United States and European selections?

http://www.levi.com/

Application for Small Business

The Green family owns one of the largest hog farms in northern Arkansas, known for raising the leanest hogs in the area. After graduating from college with a degree in marketing, E. Burton Green returned to the farm with a mind full of new ways to cash in on the farm's reputation. At the time, the family allowed the butcher at the local supermarket to use the Green name on those pork products that contained meat from the farm. In northern Arkansas, eating Green pork was a sign of status. E. Burton, eager to put his degree to work, convinced his family that they could make money off their name by selling their pork products already packaged to supermarkets. After hearing the idea, the family quickly met to formulate a plan to begin selling Green pork.

Questions

1. What type of product is the Green family selling? List your reasons.
2. What type of branding is the Green family using? List your reasons.
3. How should Green pork be packaged?
4. Assuming that the Green family wishes to reposition their pork products, what would be an optimal strategy?

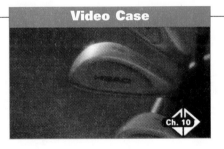

Video Case

Head Golf

Based in Boulder, Colorado, Head Golf was started in 1991 as a subsidiary of Head Sports. Building on its established brand name in the sporting equipment industry, Head wanted to expand its product portfolio, which primarily included ski and tennis equipment. The subsidiary complements Head Sports' portfolio by reducing the seasonality of ski equipment sales. The company also hoped to generate revenue that had been lost in the declining tennis industry. By providing high-quality golf clubs, shoes, and accessories, Head's vision was to compete as a full-service company against competitors such as Callaway, Cobra, Ping, and Lynx.

In the game of golf, new product developments are aimed at helping all levels of players improve their scores. Golfers, in general, are receptive to new products or concepts that can enhance their golfing performance. Thus, Head Golf offers a wide variety of products, including Premise clubs, Big Head woods and irons, putters, shoes, and accessories. The Premise metal woods and irons were the first line of clubs offered by Head. Premise clubs are built around a patented technology and are available in steel or graphite for both men and women.

The Big Head woods were introduced to compete against the oversized woods like Callaway's Big Bertha and Wilson's Killer Whale, which offer more power and precision to players. With an 11-percent bigger club face than the other oversized woods, the Big Head woods claim to be the most forgiving clubs in golf.

Encouraged by the success of its oversized metal woods, Head opted to extend its product line and develop oversized irons. The Big Head irons have a 33 percent larger effective hitting area, which makes them far more forgiving than conventional irons. In essence, with a 2-inch hitting area, Big Head irons enable golfers to "double their sweet spot." A shot that finds the club face will easily find the fairway.

One method that Head Golf uses to promote the Big Head irons is a demonstration known as the "two-ball test." Golfers try hitting two balls at the same time with the Big Head iron. Head advertises a toll-free telephone number that interested persons can call to learn about locations where they can try the two-ball test.

Questions

1. According to Exhibit 10.1, what type of product is the Big Head iron?
2. When your boss returned from a marketing seminar titled "Managing Marketing over the Product Life Cycle," she asked you to prepare a one-page report explaining the life cycle stage of golf clubs and the implications for Big Head clubs and making specific suggestions for marketing the Big Head line.
3. Evaluate the brand name Big Head. What are its advantages and disadvantages for marketing the new line of golf clubs?

LEARNING OBJECTIVES *After studying this chapter, you should be able to:*

1 Describe the six categories of new products and explain the importance of developing new products.

2 Explain the steps in the new-product development process.

3 Explain why some products succeed and others fail.

4 Discuss global issues in new-product development.

5 Describe the organizational groups or structures used to facilitate new-product development.

6 Explain the concept of product life cycles.

7 Explain the diffusion process through which new products are adopted.

Developing and Managing Products

Frito-Lay recently began marketing six familiar brands of potato and tortilla chips—Lay's in regular and mesquite barbeque flavors, Ruffles potato chips, Doritos, in ranch cheese and cool ranch, and Tostitos tortilla chips—made with Procter & Gamble's olestra, a fat substitute approved by the Federal Drug Administration (FDA) in 1996 for use in salty snacks. The new "Max" chips have no fat, have relatively few calories, and are said to taste like the real thing.

In one TV ad, a fisherman is shown walking on water after eating Lay's Max chips. The presumed "miracle" is equaled only by the discovery that the fat-free chips taste just like regular Lay's. The tag line notes, "One taste and you'll be a believer."[1]

Olestra is the first new nutrient to enter the food supply since aspartame was approved more than 20 years ago.[2] Procter & Gamble hopes olestra will become as popular in snack food as artificial sweetener has been in soft drinks. The task may not be as easy as it initially appears. Products made with the substance must carry a label informing consumers that they may suffer ill effects such as diarrhea and that olestra might deplete their bodies of some vitamins and certain nutrients. Packages must also carry a toll-free number for comments, and complaints must be forwarded to the FDA.[3]

Are the Max lines of Lay's, Ruffles, Doritos, and Tostitos new products? Is olestra a new product? Explain your answers.

CATEGORIES OF NEW PRODUCTS

1 Describe the six categories of new products and explain the importance of developing new products.

new product
Product new to the world, the market, the producer, the seller, or some combination of these.

The term **new product** is somewhat confusing, because its meaning varies widely. Actually, there are several "correct" definitions of the term. A product can be new to the world, to the market, to the producer or seller, or to some combination of these. There are six categories of new products:[4]

* *New-to-the-world products (also called discontinuous innovations):* These products create an entirely new market. The telephone, television, computer, and facsimile machine are commonly cited examples of new-to-the-world products.

* *New product lines:* These products, which the firm has not previously offered, allow it to enter an established market. Recall from Chapter 10 that Avon Products recently entered the apparel and home furnishings businesses. The rationale is to capitalize on Avon's strong image.

* *Additions to existing product lines:* This category includes new products that supplement a firm's established line. Hallmark recently announced the addition of 117 new greeting cards—for pets. According to Hallmark research, 75 percent of pet owners give Christmas presents to their pets, and 40 percent celebrate their pets' birthdays.[5] More than three-fourths of all new products introduced each year are line extensions—new varieties, formulations, sizes, and packaging of existing brands.[6]

* *Improvements or revisions of existing products:* The "new and improved" product may be significantly or slightly changed. Revlon's Color Stay Lipcolor has become the number-one-selling lipstick in drugstores and other mass merchandisers on the basis of a promise to last all day without smearing.[7] The "Ethics in Marketing" box in this section describes a new product strategy that entails modifying a product that is currently "under fire" by the Food and Drug Administration, the American Lung Association, the American Cancer Society, the American Heart Association, and others.

* *Repositioned products:* These are existing products targeted at new markets or market segments. Kraft Foods is currently trying to reposition Tang as a "hip" breakfast drink alternative to Kool-Aid and orange juice for kids 9 to 14 years of age.[8]

Procter & Gamble hopes that olestra, the first new nutrient to enter the food supply in 20 years, will become popular in snack foods.
© Brian Smale

- *Lower priced products:* This category refers to products that provide performance similar to competing brands at a lower price. Hewlett-Packard Co. introduced CopyJet, a combination color printer and color copier at about one-tenth the price of most conventional color copiers.[9]

THE NEW-PRODUCT DEVELOPMENT PROCESS

The management and technology consulting firm Booz, Allen and Hamilton has studied the new-product development process for over 30 years. Analyzing five major studies undertaken during this period, the firm has concluded that the companies most likely to succeed in developing and introducing new products are those that take the following actions:

- Make the long-term commitment needed to support innovation and new product development.

- Use a company-specific approach, driven by corporate objectives and strategies, with a well-defined new-product strategy at its core.

- Capitalize on experience to achieve and maintain competitive advantage.

- Establish an environment—a management style, organizational structure, and degree of top-management support—conducive to achieving company-specific new-product and corporate objectives.[10]

Most companies follow a formal new-product development process, usually starting with a new-product strategy. Exhibit 11.1 traces the seven-step process, which is discussed in detail below. The exhibit is funnel shaped to highlight the fact that each stage acts as a screen. The purpose is to filter out unworkable ideas.

+ Introducing
Televisions
for the next
generation.

Is this a new-to-the-world product or an improvement of an existing product?
Courtesy Zenith Electronics Corporation

2 Explain the steps in the new-product development process.

New-Product Strategy

A **new-product strategy** links the new-product development process with the objectives of the marketing department, the business unit, and the corporation. A new-product strategy must be compatible with these objectives, and in turn, all three objectives must be consistent with one another.

New-product strategy is part of the organization's overall marketing strategy. It sharpens the focus and provides general guidelines for generating, screening, and evaluating new-product ideas. The new-product strategy specifies the roles that new products must play in the organization's overall plan and describes the characteristics of products the organization wants to offer and the markets it wants to serve.[11]

new-product strategy
Linking the new-product development process with the objectives of the marketing department, the business unit, and the corporation.

Idea Generation

New-product ideas come from many sources, such as customers, employees, distributors, competitors, research and development, and consultants.

Ethics in Marketing

Marketing Smokeless Cigarettes

Barbara, a chatty, thirtyish suburbanite, stars in a promotional video R. J. Reynolds Tobacco Co. has distributed to thousands of smokers to sell Eclipse, its "smokeless" cigarette.

As she plumps the pillows of her living room couch and tends to her garden, Barbara sings the praises of a cigarette that won't stain her curtains and doesn't leave burn holes on her coffee table. "Now, Bill says I smell like my perfume," she says, then turns to dump a pile of finished Eclipses, which don't create ashes, into the trash can. "Instant clean, my favorite kind."

Eclipse cuts down on smoke largely by heating rather than burning tobacco. It has a carbon tip containing a small amount of to-

bacco that smokers light up. The tobacco burns for the first few puffs. Then the carbon tip heats up tobacco treated with glycerin, which makes up the rest of the cigarette.

Although Reynolds, a unit of RJR Nabisco Holding Corp., vigorously disputes the notion, public health officials and antismoking activists say the No. 2-rated tobacco firm is using Barbara's image to hawk Eclipse because the low-smoke cigarette is likely to appeal to women.

Reynolds denies targeting women smokers. The company says Eclipse's appeal is broad and that many people are attracted to the brand for many different reasons.[12]

Is Eclipse a new product? Explain your answer. What difference does it make whether Eclipse is targeted toward women or a broad market, which presumably means both women and men? How is Eclipse different from cigarettes targeted toward women such as Virginia Slims? Should Eclipse be subject to the same regulations as conventional cigarettes?

Source: From "Critics Say `Smokeless' Cigarettes Are Aimed at Women" by Suein Hwang, *Wall Street Journal*, May 31, 1996. Reprinted by permission of *Wall Street Journal*. © 1996 Dow Jones & Company, Inc. All Rights Reserved Worldwide.

Exhibit 11.1
New-Product Development Process

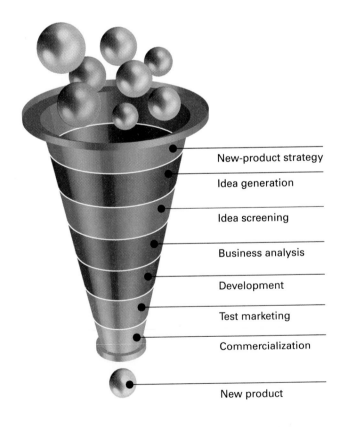

- New-product strategy
- Idea generation
- Idea screening
- Business analysis
- Development
- Test marketing
- Commercialization

New product

- 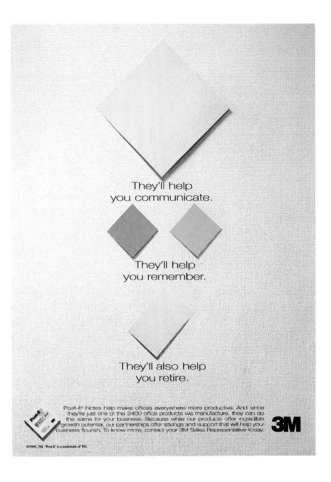 *Customers:* The marketing concept suggests that customers' wants and needs should be the springboard for developing new products. Thermos, the vacuum bottle manufacturer, provides an interesting example of how companies tap customers for ideas.[13] The company's first step in developing an innovative home barbecue grill was to send 10 members of its interdisciplinary new-product team into the field for about a month. Their assignment was to learn all about people's cookout needs and to invent a product to meet them. In cities that include Boston, Los Angeles, and Columbus, Ohio, the team conducted focus groups, visited people's homes, and even videotaped barbecues.

- *Employees:* Marketing personnel—advertising and marketing research employees, as well as salespeople—often create new-product ideas, because they analyze and are involved in the marketplace. Firms should encourage their employees to submit new-product ideas and reward them if their ideas are adopted. The very successful introduction of Post-it® Notes started with an employee's idea. In 1974, the research and development department of 3M's commercial tape division developed and patented the adhesive component of Post-it® Notes. However, it was a year before an employee of the commercial tape division, who sang in a church choir, identified a use for the adhesive. He had been using paper clips and slips of paper to mark places in hymn books. But the paper clips damaged his books, and the slips of paper fell out. The solution, as we now all know, was to apply the adhesive to small pieces of paper and sell them in packages.

An employee of 3M's commercial tape division came up with the idea of Post-it® Notes. Firms should encourage employees to submit new-product ideas and reward them if they are adopted.
Courtesy 3M

- *Distributors:* A well-trained sales force routinely asks distributors about needs that are not being met. Because they are closer to end users, distributors are often more aware of customer needs than manufacturers are. The inspiration for Rubbermaid's litter-free lunch box, named Sidekick, came from a distributor. The distributor suggested that Rubbermaid place some of its plastic containers inside a lunch box and sell the box as an alternative to plastic wrap and paper bags.

- *Competitors:* No firms rely solely on internally generated ideas for new products. A big part of any organization's marketing intelligence system should be monitoring the performance of competitors' products. One purpose of competitive monitoring is to determine which, if any, of the competitors' products should be copied. Competitive monitoring may include tracking products sold by a company's own customers.

There is plenty of information about competitors on the World Wide Web.[14] For example, Alta Vista (http://www.altavista.digital. com) is a powerful index tool that can be used to locate information about products and companies. Fuld & Co.'s competitive intelligence guide provides links to a variety of market intelligence sites. Information about competitor products can also be obtained by attending foreign food fairs, wine festivals, fashion shows, auto shows, and even carnivals. All yield inspiration, concepts, and contacts for possible foreign partnerships.[15]

Fuld & Company
What sources can you find at this site for competitive intelligence? Research competitive information for the health care industry. How might you, as a marketer, use this information?

http://www.fuld.com/

- *Research and development (R&D):* R&D is carried out in four distinct ways. *Basic research* is scientific research aimed at discovering new technologies. *Applied research* takes these new technologies and tries to find useful applications for them. **Product development** goes one step further by converting applications into marketable products. *Product modification* makes cosmetic or functional changes in existing products. Many new-product breakthroughs come from R&D activities. Pert Plus, Procter & Gamble's combination shampoo and conditioner, was invented in the laboratory.

- *Consultants:* Outside consultants are always available to examine a business and recommend product ideas. Examples include the Weston Group; Booz, Allen and Hamilton; and Management Decisions. Traditionally, consultants determine whether a company has a balanced portfolio of products and, if not, what new-product ideas are needed to offset the imbalance. For instance, an outside consultant conceived Airwick's highly successful Carpet Fresh carpet cleaner.

Creativity is the wellspring of new-product ideas, regardless of who comes up with them. A variety of approaches and techniques have been developed to stimulate creative thinking. The two considered most useful for generating new-product ideas are brainstorming and focus group exercises. The goal of **brainstorming** is to get a group to think of unlimited ways to vary a product or solve a problem. Group members avoid criticism of an idea, no matter how ridiculous it may seem. Objective evaluation is postponed. The sheer quantity of ideas is what matters. As noted in Chapter 9, an objective of focus group interviews is to stimulate insightful comments through group interaction. Focus groups usually comprise 7 to 10 people. Sometimes consumer focus groups generate excellent new-product ideas—for example, Cycle dog food, Stick-Up room deodorizers, Dustbuster vacuum cleaners, and Wendy's salad bar. In the industrial market, machine tools, keyboard designs, aircraft interiors, and backhoe accessories have evolved from focus groups.

Idea Screening

After new ideas have been generated, they pass through the first filter in the product development process. This stage, called **screening,** eliminates ideas that are inconsistent with the organization's new-product strategy or are obviously inappropriate for some other reason. The new-product committee, the new-product department, or some other formally appointed group performs the screening review. Most new-product ideas are rejected at the screening stage.

Concept tests are often used at the screening stage to rate concept (or product) alternatives. A **concept test** evaluates a new-product idea, usually before any prototype has been created. Typically, researchers get consumer reactions to descriptions and visual representations of a proposed product.

Concept tests are considered fairly good predictors of success for line extensions. They have also been relatively precise predictors of success for new products that are not copycat items, are not easily classified into existing product categories, and do not require major changes in consumer behavior—such as Betty Crocker Tuna Helper, Cycle dog food, and Libby Fruit Float. However, concept tests are usually inaccurate in predicting the success of new products that create new consumption patterns and require major changes in consumer behavior—such as microwave ovens, videocassette recorders, computers, and word processors.

Business Analysis

New-product ideas that survive the initial screening process move to the **business analysis** stage, where preliminary figures for demand, cost, sales, and profitability are calculated. For the first time, costs and revenues are estimated and compared.

---

product development
Marketing strategy that entails the creation of new products for present markets; process of converting applications for new technologies into marketable products.

brainstorming
Getting a group to think of unlimited ways to vary a product or solve a problem.

screening
The first filter in the product development process which eliminates ideas that are inconsistent with the organization's new-product strategy or are obviously inappropriate for some other reason.

concept test
Test to evaluate a new-product idea, usually before any prototype has been created.

business analysis
The second stage of the screening process where preliminary figures for demand, cost, sales, and profitability are calculated.

Depending on the nature of the product and the company, this process may be simple or complex.

The newness of the product, the size of the market, and the nature of competition all affect the accuracy of revenue projections.[16] In an established market like soft drinks, industry estimates of total market size are available. Forecasting market share for a new entry is a bigger challenge.

Analyzing overall economic trends and their impact on estimated sales is especially important in product categories that are sensitive to fluctuations in the business cycle. If consumers view the economy as uncertain and risky, they will put off buying durable goods like major home appliances, automobiles, and homes. Likewise, business buyers postpone major equipment purchases if they expect a recession.

These questions are commonly asked during the business analysis stage:

- What is the likely demand for the product?
- What impact would the new product probably have on total sales, profits, market share, and return on investment?
- How would the introduction of the product affect existing products? Would the new product cannibalize existing products?
- Would current customers benefit from the product?
- Would the product enhance the image of the company's overall product mix?
- Would the new product affect current employees in any way? Would it lead to hiring more people or reducing the size of the workforce?
- What new facilities, if any, would be needed?
- How might competitors respond?
- What is the risk of failure? Is the company willing to take the risk?

Answering these and related questions may require studies of markets, competition, costs, and technical capabilities. But at the end of this stage, management should have a good understanding of the product's market potential. This full understanding is important, because costs increase dramatically once a product idea enters the development stage.

The following "Marketing and Small Business" box provides a checklist that small businesses might use for evaluating new-product ideas.

Development

In the early stage of **development,** the R&D department or engineering department may develop a prototype of the product. During this stage, the firm should start sketching a marketing strategy. The marketing department should decide on the product's packaging, branding, labeling, and so forth. In addition, it should map out preliminary promotion, price, and distribution strategies. The technical feasibility of manufacturing the product at an acceptable cost should also be thoroughly examined.

development
Stage in the product development process in which a prototype is developed and a marketing strategy is outlined.

The development stage can last a long time and thus be very expensive. Crest toothpaste was in the development stage for 10 years. It took 18 years to develop Minute Rice, 15 years to develop the Polaroid Colorpack camera, 15 years to develop the Xerox copy machine, and 55 years to develop television. The redesign of the Ford Taurus, first introduced in 1986 and relaunched in 1996, took five years and $2.8 billion.[17]

The development process works best when all the involved areas (R&D, marketing, engineering, production, and even suppliers) work together rather than sequentially, a process called simultaneous product development. (See p. 315.) The Internet is a useful tool for improving communications between marketing personnel, advertising agencies, graphic designers, and others involved in developing products. On

Marketing and Small Business

Checklist for Evaluating New-Product Concepts

If a small business is lucky enough to have stable or increasing sales, new-product additions can boost profits and market share. Small-business managers must be careful, however, not to expand beyond the firm's financial capacities. A new product requires shelf space, investment in inventory, perhaps spare parts, and maybe even a new salesperson—all of which require an extra financial commitment.

A new small business usually has only one chance to "do it right." A failure in introducing a new product means bankruptcy and perhaps the loss of a person's life savings. Conversely, for the owner of an established small business who suddenly finds that his or her source of livelihood has evaporated, the right new product can help offset declining demand.

The product development process is generally the same for both large and small firms. However,

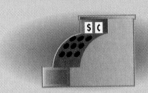

many entrepreneurs must do most steps in the process themselves rather than rely on specialists or outside consultants.

Here's a simple checklist for evaluating new-product concepts for a small business. By adding up the points, a small-business owner can more accurately estimate success.

1. Contribution to before-tax return on investment:

   More than 35 percent   +2
   25–35 percent   +1
   20–25 percent   −1
   Less than 20 percent   −2

2. Estimated annual sales:

   More than $10 million   +2
   $2 million–$10 million   +1
   $1 million–$1.99 million   −1
   Less than $1 million   −2

3. Estimated growth phase of product life cycle:

   More than three years   +2
   Two or three years   +1
   One or two years   −1
   Less than one year   2

4. Capital investment payback:

   Less than a year   +2
   One to two years   +1
   Two to three years   −1
   More than three years   −2

5. Premium-price potential:

   Weak or no competition, making entry easy   +2
   Mildly competitive entry conditions   +1
   Strongly competitive entry conditions   −1
   Entrenched competition that makes entry difficult   −2

This checklist is by no means complete. But a neutral or negative total score should give an entrepreneur reason to consider dropping the product concept.

The Product Development and Management Association's site. What innovations are happening today in new-product development? Which companies are the key innovators?

http://www.pdma.org

the net, multiple parties from a number of different companies can meet regularly with new ideas and information at their fingertips, an inexpensive way to help get products to the shelf faster.[18]

Laboratory tests are often conducted on prototype models during the development stage. User safety is an important aspect of laboratory testing, which actually subjects products to much more severe treatment than is expected by end users. The Consumer Product Safety Act of 1972 requires manufacturers to conduct a "reasonable testing program" to ensure that their products conform to established safety standards.

Many products that test well in the laboratory are also tried out in homes or businesses. Examples of product categories well suited for such use tests include human and pet food products, household cleaning products, and industrial chemicals and supplies. These products are all relatively inexpensive, and their performance characteristics are apparent to users.

Most products require some refinement based on the results of laboratory and use tests. A second stage of development often takes place before test marketing.

Scuba Barbie has to swim and kick for 15 hours to satisfy Mattel that she'll last for at least a year.

© 1994 José Azel/AURORA

Test Marketing

After products and marketing programs have been developed, they are usually tested in the marketplace. **Test marketing** is the limited introduction of a product and a marketing program to determine the reactions of potential customers in a market situation. Test marketing allows management to evaluate alternative strategies and to assess how well the various aspects of the marketing mix fit together. Febreze, Procter & Gamble Co.'s new spray that permanently removes odors from garments, such as cigarette smoke or pet odors, was test marketed in Phoenix, Salt Lake City, and Boise, Idaho in 1996.[19]

The cities chosen as test sites should reflect market conditions in the new product's projected market area. Yet no "magic city" exists that can universally represent market conditions, and a product's success in one city doesn't guarantee that it will be a nationwide hit. When selecting test market cities, researchers should therefore find locations where the demographics and purchasing habits mirror the overall market. The company should also have good distribution in test cities. Moreover, test locations should be isolated from the media. If the TV stations in a particular market reach a very large area outside that market, the advertising used for the test product may pull in many consumers from outside the market. The product may then appear more successful than it really is. Exhibit 11.2 provides a useful checklist of criteria for selecting test markets. Exhibit 11.3 lists the U.S. cities that are the most popular test markets.

test marketing
The limited introduction of a product and a marketing program to determine the reactions of potential customers in a market situation.

The High Costs of Test Marketing

Test marketing normally covers 1 to 3 percent of the United States, takes about 12 to 18 months, and costs between $1 million and $3 million.[20] Some products remain in test markets even longer. McDonald's spent 12 years developing and testing salads before introducing them. Despite the cost, many firms believe it is a lot better to fail in a test market than in a national introduction.

Because test marketing is so expensive, some companies do not test line extensions of well-known brands. For example, because the Folger's brand is well known, Procter

Exhibit 11.2
Checklist for Selecting Test Markets

In choosing a test market, many criteria need to be considered, especially the following:

Similarity to planned distribution outlets

Relative isolation from other cities

Availability of advertising media that will cooperate

Diversified cross section of ages, religions, cultural–societal preferences, etc.

No atypical purchasing habits

Representative population size

Typical per capita income

Good record as a test city, but not overly used

Not easily "jammed" by competitors

Stability of year-round sales

No dominant television station; multiple newspapers, magazines, and radio stations

Availability of retailers that will cooperate

Availability of research and audit services

Freedom from unusual influences, such as one industry's dominance or heavy tourism

Exhibit 11.3
Best U.S. Test Markets

Rank	Metropolitan area	1990 population
1	Detroit, MI	4,382,000
2	St. Louis, MO–IL	2,444,000
3	Charlotte–Gastonia–Rock Hill, NC–SC	1,162,000
4	Fort Worth–Arlington, TX	1,332,000
5	Kansas City, MO–KS	1,566,000
6	Indianapolis, IN	1,250,000
7	Philadelphia, PA–NJ	4,857,000
8	Wilmington, NC	120,000
9	Cincinnati, OH–KY–IN	1,453,000
10	Nashville, TN	985,000
11	Dayton–Springfield, OH	951,000
12	Jacksonville, FL	907,000
13	Toledo, OH	614,000
14	Greensboro–Winston-Salem–High Point, NC	942,000
15	Columbus, OH	1,377,000
16	Charlottesville, VA	131,000
17	Panama City, FL	127,000
18	Pensacola, FL	344,000
19	Milwaukee, WI	1,432,000
20	Cleveland, OH	1,831,000

Source: From "All American Markets" by Judith Waldrop, *American Demographics* magazine, January 1992. © 1992. Reprinted with permission.

& Gamble faced little risk in distributing its instant decaffeinated version nationally. Consolidated Foods Kitchen of Sara Lee followed the same approach with its frozen croissants. Other products introduced without being test marketed include General Foods' International Coffees, Quaker Oats' Chewy Granola Bars and Granola Dipps, and Pillsbury's Milk Break Bars.

Products that are frequently revised typically are not test marketed. For example, personal computer manufacturers did not test market machines with pentium processors before introducing the faster processing equipment. WordPerfect did not test market version 6.0 of its popular word-processing software. These upgrades or new and improved products are simply introduced without any test marketing. Marketing experience with earlier versions provides the information that would be gathered in test markets.

The high cost of test marketing is not purely financial. One unavoidable problem is that test marketing exposes the new product and its marketing mix to competitors before its introduction. Thus, the element of surprise is lost. Several years ago, for example, Procter & Gamble began testing a ready-to-spread Duncan Hines frosting. General Mills took note and rushed to market with its own Betty Crocker brand, which now is the best-selling brand of ready-to-spread frosting.[21]

Competitors can also sabotage or "jam" a testing program by introducing their own sales promotion, pricing, or advertising campaign. The purpose is to hide or distort the normal conditions that the testing firm might expect in the market. When PepsiCo tested its Mountain Dew sports drink in Minneapolis in 1990, Quaker Oats counterattacked furiously with coupons and ads for Gatorade.[22]

Alternatives to Test Marketing

Many firms are looking for cheaper, faster, safer alternatives to traditional test marketing. In the early 1980s, Information Resources Incorporated pioneered one alternative: single-source research using supermarket scanner data (discussed in Chapter 9). A typical supermarket scanner test costs about $300,000.

Another alternative to traditional test marketing is **simulated (laboratory) market testing.** Advertising and other promotional materials for several products, including the test product, are shown to members of the product's target market. These people are then taken to shop at a mock or real store, where their purchases are recorded. Shopper behavior, including repeat purchasing, is monitored to assess the product's likely performance under true market conditions. Research firms offer simulated market tests for $25,000 to $100,000, compared to $1 million or more for full-scale test marketing.

Despite these alternatives, most firms still consider test marketing essential for most new products. The high price of failure simply prohibits the widespread introduction of most new products without testing. Sometimes, however, when risks of failure are estimated to be low, it is better to skip test marketing and move directly from development to commercialization.

Commercialization

The final stage in the new-product development process is **commercialization,** the decision to market a product. The decision to commercialize the product sets several tasks in motion: ordering production materials and

simulated (laboratory) market testing
Presentation of advertising and other promotion materials for several products, including a test product, to members of the product's target market.

commercialization
The decision to market a product.

In the 1980s, Information Resources Incorporated pioneered research using supermarket scanner data. A typical supermarket scanner test costs about $300,000.
© Chuck Keeler/Tony Stone Images

equipment, starting production, building inventories, shipping the product to field distribution points, training the sales force, announcing the new product to the trade, and advertising to potential customers.

The time from the initial commercialization decision to the product's actual introduction varies. It can range from a few weeks for simple products that use existing equipment to several years for technical products that require custom manufacturing equipment.

The total cost of development and initial introduction can be staggering. U.S. companies spend over $125 billion each year on research and development, manufacturing, and marketing to introduce around 4,250 new brands.[23] Gillette alone spent over $200 million to develop and start manufacturing the Sensor razor and another $110 million for first-year advertising.

For some products, a well-planned Internet campaign can provide new-product information for people who are looking for the solutions that a particular new product offers. Attempting to reach customers at the point in time when they need a product is much more cost-effective and efficient than communicating with a target market that may eventually have a need for the product.[24]

WHY SOME NEW PRODUCTS SUCCEED AND OTHERS FAIL

3 Explain why some products succeed and others fail.

Associations, trade publications, consultants, and statistical bureaus estimate that the new-product failure rate is in the range of 80 to 90 percent and costs over $100 billion each year.[25] Many products fail simply because their manufacturers lack a well-developed marketing strategy. Moreover, they do not realize the importance of creating a product to meet the consumer's need rather than producing "what we know best."

Failure can be a matter of degree. Absolute failure occurs when a company cannot recoup its development, marketing, and production costs. The product actually loses money for the company. A relative product failure results when the product returns a profit but does not meet its profit or market share objectives. Relative failures can sometimes be repositioned or improved to become a viable part of a product line. For instance, Tony's Pizza failed until a home economist developed a crust that didn't taste like cardboard. Similarly, Pepperidge Farm's Deli's floundered until the quality of the ingredients was improved.

Despite the high cost and other risks of developing and testing new products, many companies—such as Rubbermaid, Campbell Soup, and Procter & Gamble—continue to develop and introduce new products. Some new products succeed and some fail. The most important factor in successful new-product introduction is a good match between the product and market needs—as the marketing concept would predict. The most important factor in product failures is a poor match between product characteristics and customer desires. New products that fail to offer unique, superior value are often ignored in the market. Other reasons why products fail include overestimation of market size, incorrect positioning, a price that is too high or too low, inadequate distribution, poor promotion, or simply an inferior product compared to those of competitors. Successful new products deliver a meaningful and perceivable benefit to a sizable number of people or organizations and are different in some meaningful way from their intended substitutes.[26] Firms that routinely experience success in new-product introductions tend to share the following characteristics:

- A history of carefully listening to customers
- An obsession with producing the best product possible
- A vision of what the market will be like in the future

- Strong leadership
- A commitment to new-product development
- A team approach to new-product development[27]

GLOBAL ISSUES IN NEW-PRODUCT DEVELOPMENT

Increasing globalization of markets and of competition provides a reason for multinational firms to consider new-product development from a worldwide perspective. A firm that starts with a global strategy is better able to develop products that are marketable worldwide. In many multinational corporations, every product is developed for potential worldwide distribution, and unique market requirements are built in whenever possible. For example, Procter & Gamble introduced Pampers Phases into global markets within one month of introducing the product in the United States. P&G's goal was to have the product on the shelf in 90 countries within one year. The objective was to establish brand loyalty among dealers and consumers before foreign competitors could react.

Some global marketers design their products to meet regulations and other key requirements in their major markets and then, if necessary, meet smaller markets' requirements country by country. For example, Nissan develops lead-country car models that can, with minor changes, be sold in most markets. For the remaining markets, Nissan provides other models that can readily be adapted. With this approach, Nissan has been able to reduce the number of its basic models from 48 to 18. There are, however, exceptions to this approach. The following "Global Perspectives" box describes Chrysler Corp.'s plans for developing a new car specifically for the Asian market.

4 Discuss global issues in new-product development.

#28

ORGANIZATION FOR NEW-PRODUCT DEVELOPMENT

To purposefully cultivate a steady stream of new products, an organized structure is essential. Yet in many firms, top managers tend to receive new-product ideas passively rather than actively soliciting them. Moreover, managers often poorly process

5 Describe the organizational groups or structures used to facilitate new-product development.

Global Perspectives

American Cars for Asian Markets

Chrysler Corp. is considering building a small, affordable car specifically for Asian markets such as India and Vietnam. The car would cost between $3,500 and $6,000 and would be produced with a local partner. The company said it has set no time frame for making a decision. The disclosure comes at a time when auto makers are trying to figure out how to build vehicles for developing markets that are at once safe and inexpensive.

Chrysler currently builds vehicles in several markets outside the U.S., including Western Europe, Latin America, and parts of Asia. "In most of these cases, it's existing North American vehicles. What's unique about the Asia possibility is the car would be specifi-

cally tailored for that market," a Chrysler spokesman said.[28]

Why do you think Chrysler is not planning to follow the pattern of building and marketing North American cars for the Asian market? Will the new vehicles be "new products"? If so, what category of new product best describes them?

The Technology and Innovation Management division of the Academy of Management, hosted by Chris Bart and his crew at McMaster University. What is innovation management? What journals and professional organizations might be of benefit to a marketer interested in new-product development?

http://irc.mcmaster.ca/irc/irc.htm

 # 29

new-product committee
An ad hoc group whose members manage the new-product development process.

new-product department
Performs the same functions as a new-product committee but on a full-time basis.

venture team
A market-oriented group staffed by a small number of representatives from different disciplines.

the ideas they do receive, and chance determines whether or not these ideas are fully considered.

One of the main requirements for generating new-product ideas and successfully introducing new products is support from top management. In addition, several kinds of groups or structures within an organization can facilitate the development of new products. These include new-product committees and departments, venture teams and intrepreneurs, and parallel engineering.

New-Product Committees and Departments

A **new-product committee** is an ad hoc group whose members manage the new-product development process. The members usually represent functional interests, such as manufacturing, research and development, finance, and marketing. Many organizations use new-product committees to screen ideas.

One alternative to a new-product committee is a **new-product department,** which performs the same functions as a new-product committee, but on a full-time basis. New-product departments typically recommend new-product objectives and programs, plan exploratory studies, evaluate concepts and ideas for new products, coordinate testing, and direct interdepartmental teams. Ideally, people in the product development department communicate regularly with their peers in the operating departments.

Setting up a formal department helps ensure that authority and responsibilities are well defined and delegated to specific individuals. A separate department with the authority to develop new products can be free from the undue influence of production, marketing, and other groups. A separate department also has the authority to accomplish its tasks. Thus, the new-product development manager can rely less on people outside his or her sphere of influence.

Venture Teams and Intrepreneurs

A **venture team** is a market-oriented group staffed by a small number of representatives from different disciplines. Team members from marketing, research and development, finance, and other areas focus on a single objective: planning their company's profitable entry into a new business. Venture groups are most often used to handle important business and product tasks that do not fit neatly into the existing organization, that demand more financial resources and longer times to mature than other organizational units can provide, and that require creativity neither sheltered nor inhibited by the larger organization. Unlike new-product committees, venture teams require a full-time commitment. In contrast to new-product departments, venture teams form and disband as needed instead of being stable departments within the overall organizational structure.

The term *intrapreneur* refers to an entrepreneur working inside a large organization. Many companies eager to foster innovation among employees have intrapreneurship programs. Bell Atlantic Corp. has an internal entrepreneurship program called Champion. It provides seed money, guidance, and training to potential entrepreneurs from any level of the company who propose new-product ideas. They can invest a portion of their wages in the project in exchange for a stake in the product when it is marketed.[29] Top management support for intrapreneurship, and a company culture that accepts the proposition that many good ideas never make it to market, are necessary for the success of the program.

Bell Atlantic's Champion program provides seed money, guidance, and training to intrapreneurs who propose new product ideas.
© Dave Hoffman

Simultaneous Product Development

The earlier a product is brought to market, the greater is the chance that profits will be strong. Delays lead to lost sales. Xerox learned that lesson the hard way: Its executives were stunned to discover that Japanese competitors were developing new copier models twice as fast as Xerox and at half the cost. Many U.S. firms, including the Big Three carmakers (General Motors, Ford, and Chrysler) are trying to find new ways to shorten their development cycles and be the first to market new products.

A new team-oriented approach to new-product development is called **simultaneous product development.** This approach enables firms to shorten the development process and reduce its cost. With simultaneous product development, all relevant functional areas and outside suppliers participate in all stages of the development process. Group members, whom General Electric Co. calls "one coffee pot" product development teams, perform development tasks together—thereby avoiding, for example, the need for designers to make changes when engineers or manufacturers are unable to meet design specifications.[30] Involving key suppliers early in the process enables them to design and develop critical component parts.

simultaneous product development
A new team-oriented approach to new-product development.

PRODUCT LIFE CYCLES

The product life cycle concept provides a way to trace the stages of a product's acceptance, from its introduction (birth) to its decline (death). As Exhibit 11.4 shows, a product progresses through four major stages: introduction, growth, maturity, and decline. Note that the product life cycle illustrated does not refer to any one brand; rather, it refers to the life cycle for a product category or product class. A **product category** includes all brands that satisfy a particular type of need. Product categories include, for example, passenger cars, cigarettes, soft drinks, and coffee.

The time a product spends in any one stage of the life cycle may vary dramatically. Some products, such as fad items, move through the entire cycle in weeks. Others, such as electric clothes washers and dryers, stay in the maturity stage for

6 Explain the concept of product life cycles.

product category
All brands that satisfy a particular type of need.

Exhibit 11.4
*Four Stages of the
Product Life Cycle*

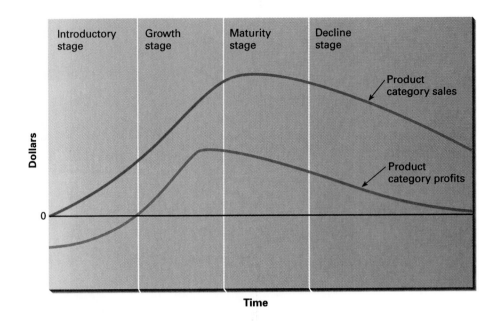

decades. Exhibit 11.4 illustrates the typical life cycle for a consumer durable good, such as a washer or dryer. In contrast, Exhibit 11.5 illustrates typical life cycles for styles (such as formal, business, or casual clothing), fashions (such as miniskirts or stirrup pants), and fads (such as leopard-print clothing). Changes in a product, its uses, its image, or its positioning can extend that product's life cycle.

The product life cycle concept does not tell managers the length of a product's life cycle or its duration in any stage. It does not dictate marketing strategy. It is simply a tool to help marketers forecast future events and suggest appropriate strategies.

Introductory Stage

introductory stage
The full-scale launch of a new product into the marketplace.

The **introductory stage** of the product life cycle represents the full-scale launch of a new product into the marketplace. Computer databases for personal use, room-deodorizing air-conditioning filters, and wind-powered home electric generators are all product categories that have recently entered the product life cycle.

Marketing costs in the introductory stage are normally high for several reasons. High dealer margins are often needed to obtain adequate distribution, and incentives are needed to get consumers to try the new product. Advertising expenses are high because of the need to educate consumers about the new product's benefits. Production costs are also often high in this stage, as product and manufacturing flaws

Exhibit 11.5
*Product Life Cycles for
Styles, Fashions, and
Fads*

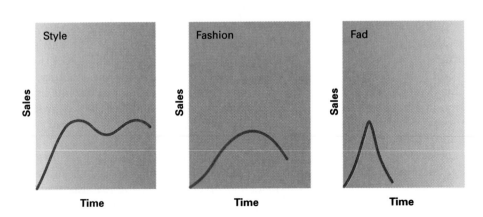

are identified and corrected and efforts are undertaken to develop mass-production economies.

As Exhibit 11.4 illustrates, sales normally increase slowly during the introductory stage. Moreover, profits are usually negative because of research and development costs, factory tooling, and high introduction costs. The length of the introductory phase is largely determined by product characteristics, such as the product's advantages over substitute products, the educational effort required to make the product known, and management's commitment of resources to the new item.

Growth Stage

If a product category survives the introductory stage, it advances to the **growth stage** of the life cycle. In this stage, sales typically grow at an increasing rate, many competitors enter the market, large companies may start to acquire small pioneering firms, and profits are healthy. Emphasis switches from primary demand promotion (for example, promoting compact disc players) to aggressive brand advertising and communication of the differences between brands (for example, promoting Sony versus Panasonic and RCA).

Maturity Stage

A period during which sales increase at a decreasing rate signals the beginning of the **maturity stage** of the life cycle. New users cannot be added indefinitely, and sooner or later the market approaches saturation. Normally, this is the longest stage of the product life cycle. Many major household appliances are in the maturity stage of their life cycles. For example, over half of

growth stage
The second stage of the product life cycle when sales typically grow at an increasing rate, many competitors enter the market, large companies may start acquiring small pioneering firms, and profits are healthy.

maturity stage
A period during which sales increase at a decreasing rate.

Is the Wiggly Wall Walker a boom, fad, or bust? Can you figure out what its product life cycle looks like? What in the world is it? For these answers and more, check out **Hot Link—The Product Life Cycle.**

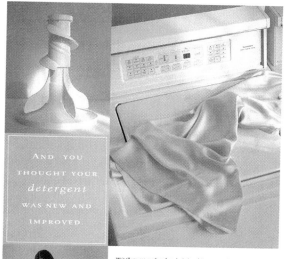

Many major household appliances are in the maturity stage of their life cycles. Far more washing machines are replaced than are sold to new users.

Courtesy Sears, Roebuck and Co.

all washer, dryer, and refrigerator purchases are replacements for worn-out products rather than purchases by new users. Powdered drink mixes and coffee are examples of other products in the maturity stage.

Decline Stage

decline stage
A long-run drop in sales.

A long-run drop in sales signals the beginning of the **decline stage.** The rate of decline is governed by how rapidly consumer tastes change or substitute products are adopted. Many convenience products and fad items lose their market overnight, leaving large inventories of unsold items, such as designer jeans. Others die more slowly, like citizen band (CB) radios, black-and-white console television sets, and nonelectronic wristwatches.

Implications for Marketing Management

The product life cycle concept encourages marketing managers to plan so they can take the initiative instead of reacting to past events. The product life cycle is especially useful as a predicting or forecasting tool. Because products pass through distinctive stages, it is often possible to estimate a product's location on the curve using historical data. Profits, like sales, tend to follow a predictable path over a product's life cycle.

It is important to realize, however, that products and brands in the maturity stage of the product life cycle do not necessarily slip directly into decline and then elimination. Several strategies are available to marketing managers to sustain, and even expand, sales of product categories or brands in the maturity stage:

- *Promoting more frequent use of the product by current customers:* The Florida Orange Growers Association successfully used this strategy in its "Orange Juice Is Not Just for Breakfast" campaign. Overall juice consumption rose following TV ads reminding people that orange juice is a healthy, refreshing beverage suitable for any time of the day.

- *Finding new target markets for the product:* Johnson's baby shampoo was remarkably successful in adding mothers, sisters, and later, fathers and brothers to the original target market of infants. The new theme, "It's mild enough to use every day," was the only change in the product's marketing strategy, yet it was enough to expand the target market's size several hundred percent.

- *Finding new uses for the product:* After decades of level sales, Arm & Hammer baking soda was promoted as a refrigerator freshener, plumbing system cleaner, litter box freshener, and even a toothpaste. Sales surged when each new suggested use appeared in print and television advertisements.

- *Pricing the brand below the market:* Bic pens and Timex watches revolutionized their industries. Their competitors had not successfully introduced brands of acceptable quality at low prices. The introduction of these two brands substantially changed the shape of the product life cycle for ballpoint pens and wristwatches.

- *Developing new distribution channels:* For years, Woolite fabric cleaner was sold only in department stores. Then American Home Products introduced the brand in supermarkets and grocery stores without changing the product, the price, or the promotional appeal. Sales tripled in the first year.

- *Adding new ingredients or eliminating old ingredients:* The laundry detergent industry has relied on this strategy to extend the life cycles of brands, adding whiteners, brighteners, bleaches, scents, and various other ingredients and attributes to products. Frito-Lay's new "Max" line of fat-free snacks containing Procter & Gamble's olestra fat replacement is an example of an effort to expand sales by changing or removing ingredients.[31]

Exhibit 11.6 *Typical Marketing Strategies during the Product Life Cycle*

Marketing mix strategy	Product life cycle stage			
	Introduction	**Growth**	**Maturity**	**Decline**
Product strategy	Limited number of models; frequent product modifications	Expanded number of models; frequent product modifications	Large number of models	Elimination of unprofitable models and brands
Distribution strategy	Distribution usually limited, depending on product; intensive efforts and high margins often needed to attract wholesalers and retailers	Expanded number of dealers; intensive efforts to establish long-term relationships with wholesalers and retailers	Extensive number of dealers; margins declining; intensive efforts to retain distributors and shelf space	Unprofitable outlets phased out
Promotion strategy	Develop product awareness; stimulate primary demand; use intensive personal selling to distributors; use sampling and couponing for consumers	Stimulate selective demand; advertise brand aggressively	Stimulate selective demand; advertise brand aggressively; promote heavily to retain dealers and customers	Phase out all promotion
Pricing strategy	Prices are usually high to recover development costs (see Chapter 20)	Prices begin to fall toward end of growth stage as result of competitive pressure	Prices continue to fall	Prices stabilize at relatively low level; small price rises are possible if competition is negligible

- *Making a dramatic new guarantee:* Spray'n Wash shifted from declining sales to rapidly growing sales almost immediately after offering this guarantee: "If Spray'n Wash doesn't remove a stain from a shirt—any shirt—we'll buy you a new shirt."

Exhibit 11.6 briefly summarizes some typical marketing strategies during each stage of the product life cycle.

THE SPREAD OF NEW PRODUCTS

Marketing and product managers have a better chance of successfully guiding a product through its life cycle if they understand how consumers learn about and adopt products. The product life cycle and the adoption process go hand in hand. A person who buys a new product never before tried may ultimately become an **adopter**, a consumer who was happy enough with his or her trial experience with a product to use it again.

7 Explain the diffusion process through which new products are adopted.

adopter
A consumer who was happy enough with his or her trial experience with a product to use it again.

Diffusion of Innovation

An **innovation** is a product perceived as new by a potential adopter. It really doesn't matter whether the product is "new to the world" or simply new to the individual. **Diffusion** is the process by which the adoption of an innovation spreads.

Five categories of adopters participate in the diffusion process:

- *Innovators:* the first $2\frac{1}{2}$ percent of all those who adopt the product. Innovators are eager to try new ideas and products, almost as an obsession. In addition to having higher incomes, they are more worldly and more active outside their community than noninnovators. They rely less on group norms and are more self-confident. Because they are well educated, they are more likely to get their information from scientific sources and experts. Innovators are characterized as being venturesome.

innovation
A product perceived as new by a potential adopter.

diffusion
The process by which the adoption of an innovation spreads.

- *Early adopters:* the next $13\frac{1}{2}$ percent to adopt the product. Although early adopters are not the very first, they do adopt early in the product's life cycle. Compared to innovators, they rely much more on group norms and values. They are also more oriented to the local community, in contrast to the innovator's worldly outlook. Early adopters are more likely than innovators to be opinion leaders because of their closer affiliation with groups. The respect of others is a dominant characteristic of early adopters.

- *Early majority:* the next 34 percent to adopt. The early majority weigh the pros and cons before adopting a new product. They are likely to collect more information and evaluate more brands than early adopters, therefore extending the adoption process. They rely on the group for information but are unlikely to be opinion leaders themselves. Instead, they tend to be opinion leaders' friends and neighbors. The early majority are an important link in the process of diffusing new ideas, because they are positioned between earlier and later adopters. A dominant characteristic of the early majority is deliberateness.

- *Late majority:* the next 34 percent to adopt. The late majority adopt a new product because most of their friends have already adopted it. Because they also rely on group norms, their adoption stems from pressure to conform. This group tends to be older and below average in income and education. They depend mainly on word-of-mouth communication rather than the mass media. The dominant characteristic of the late majority is skepticism.

- *Laggards:* the final 16 percent to adopt. Like innovators, laggards do not rely on group norms. Their independence is rooted in their ties to tradition. Thus, the past heavily influences their decisions. By the time laggards adopt an innovation, it has probably been outmoded and replaced by something else. For example, they may have bought their first black-and-white TV set after color television was already widely diffused. Laggards have the longest adoption time and the lowest socioeconomic status. They tend to be suspicious of new products and alienated from a rapidly advancing society. The dominant value of laggards is tradition. Marketers typically ignore laggards, who do not seem to be motivated by advertising or personal selling.

Exhibit 11.7 shows the relationship between the adopter categories and stages of the product life cycle. Note that the various categories of adopters first buy products

Exhibit 11.7

Relationship between the Diffusion Process and the Product Life Cycle

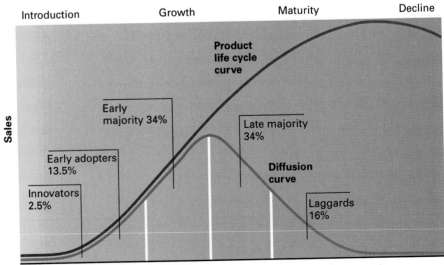

Diffusion curve: Percentage of total adoptions by category
Product life cycle curve: Time

in different stages of the product life cycle. Almost all sales in the maturity and de-cline stages represent repeat purchasing.

Product Characteristics and the Rate of Adoption

Five product characteristics can be used to predict and explain the rate of acceptance and diffusion of a new product:

- *Complexity:* the degree of difficulty involved in understanding and using a new product. The more complex the product, the slower is its diffusion. For instance, before many of their functions were automated, 35mm cameras were used pri-marily by hobbyists and professionals. They were just too complex for most peo-ple to learn to operate.
- *Compatibility:* the degree to which the new product is consistent with existing val-ues and product knowledge, past experiences, and current needs. Incompatible products diffuse more slowly than compatible products. For example, the intro-duction of contraceptives is incompatible in countries where religious beliefs dis-courage the use of birth control techniques.
- *Relative advantage:* the degree to which a product is perceived as superior to ex-isting substitutes. For example, because it reduces cooking time, the microwave oven has a clear relative advantage over a conventional oven.
- *Observability:* the degree to which the benefits or other results of using the prod-uct can be observed by others and communicated to target customers. For instance, fashion items and automobiles are highly visible and more observable than per-sonal care items.
- *"Trialability":* the degree to which a product can be tried on a limited basis. It is much easier to try a new toothpaste or breakfast cereal than a new automobile or microcomputer. Demonstrations in showrooms and test drives are different from in-home trial use. To stimulate trials, marketers use free-sampling programs, tast-ing displays, and small package sizes.

Marketing Implications of the Adoption Process

Two types of communication aid the diffusion process: word-of-mouth communica-tion among consumers and communication from marketers to consumers. *Word-of-mouth communication* within and across groups speeds diffusion. Opinion leaders dis-cuss new products with their followers and with other opinion leaders. Marketers must therefore ensure that opinion leaders have the types of information desired in the media that they use. Suppliers of some products, such as professional and health care services, rely almost solely on word-of-mouth communication for new business.

The second type of communication aiding the diffusion process is *communication directly from the marketer to potential adopters.* Messages directed toward early adopters should normally use different appeals than messages directed toward the early ma-jority, the late majority, or the laggards. Early adopters are more important than in-novators because they make up a larger group, are more socially active, and are usu-ally opinion leaders.

As the focus of a promotional campaign shifts from early adopters to the early ma-jority and the late majority, marketers should study the dominant characteristics, buy-ing behavior, and media characteristics of these target markets. Then they should re-vise messages and media strategy to fit. The diffusion model helps guide marketers in developing and implementing promotion strategy.

A pharmaceutical sales rep discusses new products with a doctor. Suppliers of health care products and services rely almost exclusively on word-of-mouth communication for new business.
© David J. Sams/Tony Stone Images

LOOKING BACK

Look back at the story at the beginning of this chapter about Frito-Lay's new Max chips. Both the Max line and the new ingredient, olestra, are new products. The Max chips fit into several categories of new products. They are clearly improvements or revisions of existing products. The Max line may also be described as additions to existing product lines or new product lines. Categorizing olestra is more difficult. Some might argue that it is "new to the world" based on the statement that it is the first new nutrient to enter the food supply in 20 years. Others will argue that it is simply a substitute ingredient and just an improvement or revision of an existing product. The answer to these questions is much less important than the discussion regarding the various positions. Ultimately, most classifications are subjective.

KEY TERMS

SUMMARY

1 *Describe the six categories of new products and explain the importance of developing new products.* New products can be classified as new-to-the-world products (discontinuous innovations), new product lines, additions to existing product lines, improvements or revisions of existing products, repositioned products, or lower cost products. To sustain or increase profits, a firm must introduce at least one new successful product before a previous product advances to the maturity stage and profit levels begin to drop. Several factors make it more important than ever for firms to consistently introduce new products: shortened product life cycles, rapidly changing technology and consumer priorities, the high rate of new-product failures, and the length of time needed to implement new-product ideas.

2 *Explain the steps in the new product-development process.* First, a firm forms a new-product strategy by outlining the characteristics and roles of future products. Then new-product ideas are generated by customers, employees, distributors, competitors, and internal research and development personnel. Once a product idea has survived initial screening by an appointed screening group, it undergoes business analysis to determine its potential profitability. If a product concept seems viable, it progresses into the development phase, in which the technical and economic feasibility of the manufacturing process is evaluated. The development phase also includes laboratory and use testing of a product for performance and safety. Following initial testing and refinement, most products are introduced in a test market to evaluate consumer response and marketing strategies. Finally, test market successes are propelled into full commercialization. The commercialization process means starting up production, building inventories, shipping to distributors, training a sales force, announcing the product to the trade, and advertising to consumers.

3 *Explain why some products succeed and others fail.* The most important factor in determining the success of a new product is the extent to which the product matches the needs of the market. Good matches are frequently successful. Poor matches are not.

4 *Discuss global issues in new-product development.* A marketer with global vision seeks to develop products that can easily be adapted to suit local needs. The goal is not simply to develop a standard product that can be sold worldwide.

5 *Describe the organizational groups or structures used to facilitate new-product development.* Firms facilitate the development of new products with new-product committees and departments and venture teams. New-product committees are composed of representatives of various branches of an organization and play mainly an advisory role. A new-product department may be a separate department, a high-level staff function, a part of marketing, or a part of research and development. Venture team members are recruited from within an organization to work full time on specific projects and are encouraged to take an "intrapreneurial" approach to new-product development. Some U.S. firms use an organizational structure popular in Japan, called simultaneous product development, in which all departments work together to develop new products.

6 *Explain the concept of product life cycles.* All product categories undergo a life cycle with four stages: introduction, growth, maturity, and decline. The rate at which products move through these stages varies dramatically. Marketing managers use the product life cycle concept as an analytical tool to forecast a product's future and devise effective marketing strategies.

7 *Explain the diffusion process through which new products are adopted.* The diffusion process is the spread of a new product from its producer to ultimate adopters. Adopters in the diffusion process belong to five categories: innovators, early adopters, the early majority, the late majority, and laggards. Product characteristics that affect the rate of adoption include product complexity, compatibility with existing social values, relative advantage over existing substitutes, visibility, and "trialability." The diffusion process is facilitated by word-of-mouth communication and communication from marketers to consumers.

Discussion and Writing Questions

1. What is the difference between new-product committees and venture teams?

2. List the advantages of simultaneous product development.

3. In small groups, brainstorm ideas for a new wet-weather clothing line. What type of product would potential customers want and need? Prepare and deliver a brief presentation to your class.

4. You are a marketing manager for Nike. Your department has come up with the

idea of manufacturing a baseball bat for use in colleges around the nation. Assuming you are in the business analysis stage, write a brief analysis based on the questions in the "Business Analysis" section of the chapter.

5. What are the major disadvantages to test marketing and how might they be avoided?

6. Describe some products whose adoption rates have been affected by complexity, compatibility, relative advantage, observability, and/or "trialability."

7. What type of adopter behavior do you typically follow? Explain.

8. Place the personal computer on the product life cycle curve, and give reasons for placing it where you did.

9. How could information from customer orders at the following site help the company's marketers plan new-product developments?

http://www.pizzahut.com

10. How is customer input affecting the development of Baked Lay's potato chips?

http://www.fritolay.com

Application for Small Business

Joyce Strand went to the oven to remove the newest batch of beef jerky that she would later sell to the Frontenac Central Store. To her surprise, she had turned the oven up too high, and the beef jerky had dried to a crisp. Although the texture was much different, the jerky still had its unmistakable taste. Joyce decided to take it to the Central Store anyway and let the customers decide. The new snack became a huge success in the snack food section of the store. Because of her recent success, Joyce began experimenting with different tastes and textures of snack foods that she sells at the Central Store. Realizing that innovation can be very profitable, Joyce now actively looks for new ways to please her customers.

Questions

1. How might Joyce ensure that proper attention is paid to developing new products?

2. What factors should she be aware of that might lead to product failure?

3. Prepare a list of criteria similar to those in the "Marketing and Small Business" box in this chapter that might be used to evaluate Joyce's new-product ideas.

Video Case

3M

The Minnesota Mining and Manufacturing Company, 3M, began with a mistake. When five Minnesotans bought land on the shores of Lake Superior in 1902, they planned to mine corundum. But the mine contained a low-grade ore that was useless. The company had two choices: Come up with something else or go out of business. 3M introduced a successful abrasive cloth for metal finishing, and today 3M is still know as the master of new-product innovation.

Innovation has always been encouraged at 3M; failure has never been discouraged. In 1922, Francis G. Okie came up with a new product, sandpaper, that would replace razor blades. Of course, the product failed, but Okie continued his work and eventually developed Wetordry sandpaper, a waterproof sandpaper that resulted in better finish on cars.

Wetordry became 3M's first huge success.

Today, 3M markets more than 60,000 products, including the ever-popular Post-It Notes, Scotch tape, Scotchgard stain repellant, and even heart–lung machines. In 1990, the firm earned $1.3 billion on sales of $13 billion, a 10 percent profit that is matched by few companies the size of 3M. During a period of falling stock prices, 3M stock continued to grow; it has tripled during the 1990s.

One secret of 3M's success is that the firm continues to extend its existing product lines by searching for innovations. For instance, Post-It Notes inventor Art Fry continues to look for line extensions, such as the new pop-ups that work like a box of tissues. At the same time, 3M developed dry-silver color technology which enabled Honeywell to introduce a computer printer that produces photographic-quality color pages.

At 3M, employees are encouraged to develop new products. Scientists are allowed to spend 15 percent of their time on personal projects of their choosing. Divisions in the firm are kept small, and each of the more than 40 divisions is seen as a separate company. This system helps employees realize that what they do really does count. Each division is required to generate 25 percent of its sales from products introduced in the last five years, a method that encourages new-product introduction.

3M has been called by some the most innovative company in the world. Perhaps no single factor makes innovation work at 3M. Maybe it is the fact that from the beginning the company had to innovate to survive, or because scientists have been allowed to fail, only to eventually achieve success. Whatever the reason, 3M continues to explore new-product innovations in hopes of making a better product than competitors' offerings.

Questions

1. Why are new products so important at 3M?
2. Describe the organizational groups or structures used to facilitate new-product development at 3M.
3. How does 3M generate ideas for new products?
4. Explain why you would or would not like to work at a company such as 3M.

LEARNING OBJECTIVES *After studying this chapter, you should be able to:*

1 Discuss the importance of services to the economy.

2 Discuss the differences between services and goods.

3 Explain why services marketing is important to manufacturers.

4 Develop marketing mixes for services.

5 Discuss relationship marketing in services.

6 Explain internal marketing in services.

7 Discuss global issues in services marketing.

8 Describe nonprofit organization marketing.

9 Explain the unique aspects of nonprofit organization marketing.

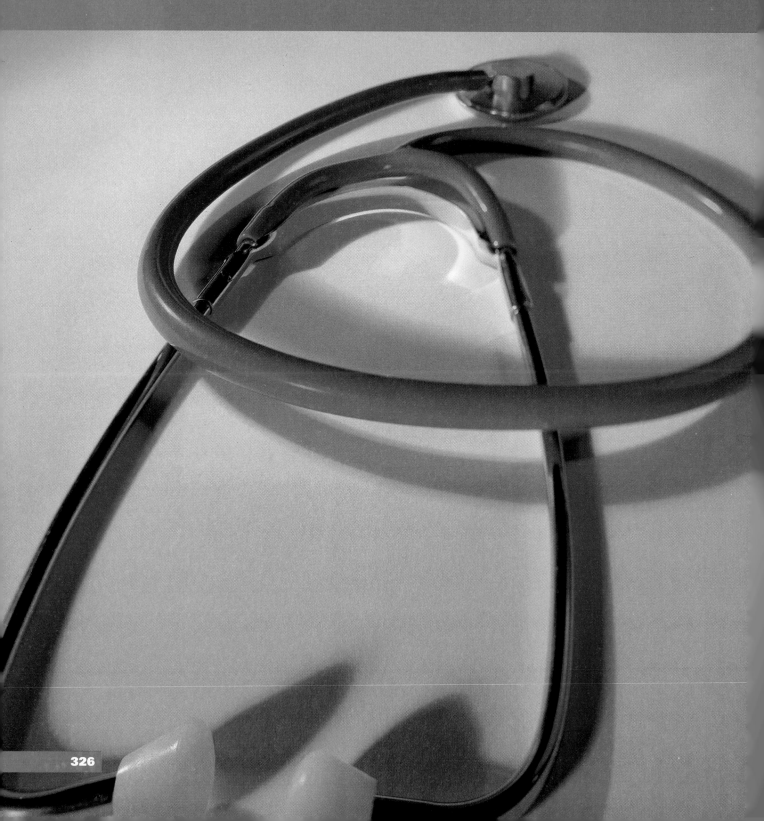

Services and Nonprofit Organization Marketing

Oxford Health Plans, Inc., a 12-year-old managed-care company, has doubled in size each year since 1991, capturing more than 1 million members and clobbering much bigger rivals in the New York market to do so. Profits jumped 71 percent in 1995, to $15.6 million, on sales of $1.77 billion, up 132 percent.

Oxford won legitimacy almost overnight by marketing a well-positioned service. Now, though, it must pursue the more difficult path of actually managing people's health care. Its new strategy is intensely systems driven and education oriented. If it succeeds, Oxford will have the capacity to determine who is likely to become sick, to show those people how to stay out of doctors' offices by taking care of themselves, and to give doctors both the medical and financial responsibility to decide what care is appropriate. Its marketing expertise gives Oxford a unique fix on members' demands and their medical status. Its doctors are given autonomy to decide on their patients' care—but increasingly, those decisions will be shaped by data that will tell Oxford what is necessary and what really works. The result, in theory, will be higher quality medicine at lower cost. It is, in the end, a compelling design—and it could represent the future of medicine.

Oxford organizes self-selecting groups of 40 to 100 physicians into "partnerships." Doctors are paid a percentage of patients' premiums, from a budget that fixes amounts for physician care, hospitalization, and prescription drugs. If one doctor sends a patient for an electrocardiogram, for example, the charge comes out of her group's budget. Oxford prepares quarterly reports, based on claims data, that detail the activity of each doctor in a group. Was a gallbladder patient sent to an expensive hospital? Was his stay unusually long?

The system is designed to play on individual ego, peer pressure, and financial self-interest. If doctors exceed their budget, they lose money; yet withholding care will bring higher costs over time. Oxford expects to cut more costs through a series of initiatives known as demand management. One of these initiatives involves identifying patients with chronic conditions and then creating courses of care to prevent the need for expensive treatment later. For example, Oxford spots asthma sufferers from claims data and patient surveys. It mails reams of self-care educational materials and a $10 peak-flow meter asthma patients can use to assess their condition. Then it sends field-workers to homes to instruct members on the use of the meter.

While broad academic studies of such efforts aren't yet conclusive, Oxford's results are positive. In two years, hospitalization of Medicaid asthma patients has dropped by about a third, producing a savings of some $300,000 a year to Oxford. Education programs for expectant mothers, who get incentives for scheduling preventive checkups, have reduced underweight babies by about a third. "That's smart," says Michael Schechter, an obstetrician in Greenwich, Connecticut. "That shows me they care more than the next company. And they're going to pick up savings down the road."[1]

How does a service, like health care, differ from goods (for example, cars, clothing, food items)? What kinds of service does Oxford's managed care offer its customers? How is Oxford building relationships with its customers?

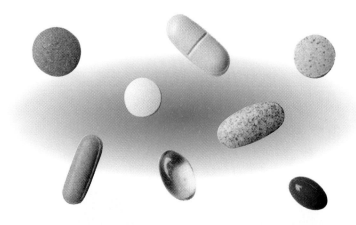

THE IMPORTANCE OF SERVICES

1 Discuss the importance of services to the economy.

service
The result of applying human or mechanical efforts to people or objects.

A **service** is the result of applying human or mechanical efforts to people or objects. Services involve a deed, a performance, or an effort that cannot be physically possessed. Today, the service sector substantially influences the U.S. economy. More than 8 in 10 workers currently labor to produce services, such as transportation, retail trade, and finance.[2] The service sector accounts for 74 percent of the U.S. gross domestic product, and services produced a balance-of-trade surplus that reached $55.7 billion in 1993 (compared to a $132.4 billion deficit for goods), which significantly reduced this country's overall trade deficit.[3]

U.S. Bureau of Labor Statistics
What data can you find at this site that would help predict market trends?

http://stats.bls.gov/

The demand for services is expected to continue. According to the Bureau of Labor Statistics, service occupations will be responsible for all net job growth through the year 2005, as can be seen in Exhibit 12.1. Much of this demand results from demographics. An aging population will need nurses, home health care, physical therapists, and social workers; two-earner families need child care, housecleaning, and lawn care services. Also increasing will be the demand for information managers, such as computer engineers, systems analysts, and paralegals.[4]

Services are also important to the world economy. In Great Britain, 73 percent of jobs are in services; 57 percent of German workers and 62 percent of Japanese workers are in services.[5]

The marketing process described in Chapter 1 is the same for all types of products, whether they be goods or services. Many ideas and strategies discussed throughout this book have been illustrated with service examples. In many ways, marketing is marketing, regardless of the product's characteristics. However, services have some unique characteristics that distinguish them from goods, and marketing strategies need to be adjusted for these characteristics.

2 Discuss the differences between services and goods.

Exhibit 12.1
Service-Producing Industries Will Continue to Account for Virtually All Job Growth

HOW SERVICES DIFFER FROM GOODS

Services have four unique characteristics that distinguish them from goods: intangibility, inseparability, heterogeneity, and perishability.

Nonfarm wage and salary employment (in millions)

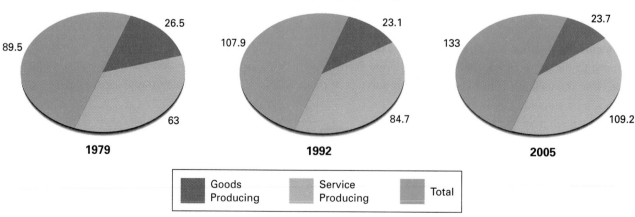

1979	89.5 26.5 63
1992	107.9 23.1 84.7
2005	133 23.7 109.2

Goods Producing   Service Producing   Total

Source: *Arlington Star Telegram*, September 2, 1996, p. B9.

Intangibility

The basic difference between services and goods is that services are intangible. Because of their **intangibility**, they cannot be touched, seen, tasted, heard, or felt in the same manner in which goods can be sensed. Services cannot be stored and are often easy to duplicate. Moreover, services are seldom based on any hidden technology, and no patent protection exists for services.

Evaluating the quality of services before or even after making a purchase is harder than evaluating the quality of goods because, compared to goods, services tend to exhibit fewer search qualities. A **search quality** is a characteristic that can be easily assessed before purchase—for instance, the color of an appliance or automobile. At the same time, services tend to exhibit more experience and credence qualities. An **experience quality** is a characteristic that can be assessed only after use, such as the quality of a meal in a restaurant or the actual experience of a vacation. A **credence quality** is a characteristic that consumers may have difficulty assessing even after purchase because they do not have the necessary knowledge or experience. Medical and consulting services are examples of services that exhibit credence qualities.

Unlike goods, services such as medical care are intangible—they can't be touched, seen, tasted, or felt.
© Roger Tully/Tony Stone Images

intangibility
Services that cannot be touched, seen, tasted, heard, or felt in the same manner in which goods can be sensed.

search quality
A characteristic that can be easily assessed before purchase.

experience quality
A characteristic that can be assessed only after use.

These characteristics also make it harder for marketers to communicate the benefits of an intangible service than to communicate the benefits of tangible goods. Thus, marketers often rely on tangible cues to communicate a service's nature and quality. For example, Allstate Insurance Company's use of the "good hands" symbol helps make tangible the benefit of protection that insurance provides.

The facilities that customers visit, or from which services are delivered, is a critical tangible part of the total service offering. For example, Barnes & Noble, the nation's top bookseller, was founded on the knowledge that for many consumers shopping is a form of entertainment. The stores were designed to provide a unique shopping experience, using a woody, traditional, soft-colored library atmosphere to please book lovers. Additionally, sophisticated modern architecture and graphics and stylish displays were used to satisfy customers. The company's superstores have cafes and big, heavy chairs and tables that people can use while browsing through piles of books. Management makes sure the stores' rest rooms are clean.[6]

Messages about the organization are communicated to customers through such elements as the decor, the clutter or neatness of service areas, and the staff's manners and dress. The Walt Disney organization is one of the best at managing tangible cues. Disneyland and Walt Disney World focus on the set (facility), the cast (personnel), and the audience. Hosts and hostesses (not employees) serve guests (not customers) at attractions and shops (not rides and stores). When cast members are hired, they are given written information about what training they will receive, when and where to report, and what to wear. They spend the first day on the job at "Disney University" learning about the Disney philosophy, management style, and history. The cast members also discover how all parts of the organization work together to provide the highest possible level of guest satisfaction. In the Magic Kingdom, the cast is just as important as the set.

Disney Home Page
Visit Disneyland via the Web. How does Disney reflect its commitment to guest services on its Web site? What services do you find?

http://www.disney.com/

credence quality
A characteristic that consumers may have difficulty assessing even after purchase because they do not have the necessary knowledge or experience.

inseparability
Characteristic of services that allows them to be produced and consumed simultaneously.

Inseparability

Goods are produced, sold, and then consumed. In contrast, services are often sold, produced, and consumed at the same time. In other words, their production and consumption are inseparable activities. **Inseparability** means that, because consumers must be present during the production of services like haircuts or surgery, they are actually involved in the production of the services they buy. That type of consumer involvement is rare in goods manufacturing. For example, in many fast-food restaurants, touch-activated video screens that display words and/or pictures where customers order their own meals can speed up the ordering process.[7]

Inseparability also means that services cannot normally be produced in a centralized location and consumed in decentralized locations, as goods typically are. Services are also inseparable from the perspective of the service provider. Thus, the quality of service that firms are able to deliver depends on the quality of their employees.

heterogeneity
Characteristic of services that makes them less standardized and uniform than goods.

perishability
Characteristic of services that prevents them from being stored, warehoused, or inventoried.

A Big Mac is the same everywhere, from Fort Worth to Moscow. Services, however, tend to be heterogeneous; that is, they are less standardized and uniform than goods.
© REUTERS/Stringer/Archive Photos

Heterogeneity

One great strength of McDonald's is consistency. Whether customers order a Big Mac and french fries in Fort Worth, Tokyo, or Moscow, they know exactly what they are going to get. This is not the case with many service providers. **Heterogeneity** means that services tend to be less standardized and uniform than goods. For example, physicians in a group practice or barbers in a barber shop differ within each group in their technical and interpersonal skills. A given physician's or barber's performance may even vary depending on time of day, physical health, or some other factor. Because services tend to be labor intensive and production and consumption are inseparable, consistency and quality control can be hard to achieve.

Standardization and training help increase consistency and reliability. Limited-menu restaurants like Pizza Hut and KFC offer customers high consistency from one visit to the next because of standardized preparation procedures. Another way to increase consistency is to mechanize the process. For example, banks have reduced the inconsistency of teller services by providing automated teller machines. Airport X-ray surveillance equipment has replaced manual searching of baggage. Automatic coin receptacles on toll roads have replaced human collectors. Automatic car washes have replaced the uneven quality of hand washing, waxing, and drying.

Perishability

Perishability means that services cannot be stored, warehoused, or inventoried. An empty hotel room or airplane seat produces no revenue that day. The revenue is lost. Yet service organizations are often forced to turn away full-price customers during peak periods.

One of the most important challenges in many service industries is finding ways to synchronize supply and demand. The philosophy that some revenue is better than none has prompted many hotels to offer deep discounts on weekends and during the off-season and has prompted airlines to adopt similar pricing strategies during off-peak hours. Car rental agencies, movie theaters, and restaurants also use discounts to encourage demand during nonpeak periods. UPS plans to carry passengers on planes normally occupied by freight to make use of its idle planes during weekends.[8]

SERVICES MARKETING IN MANUFACTURING

A comparison of goods and services marketing is beneficial, but in reality it is hard to distinguish clearly between manufacturing and service firms. Indeed, many manufacturing firms can point to service as a major factor in their success. For example, maintenance and repair services are important to buyers of copy machines.

One reason that goods manufacturers stress service is that it might give them a strong competitive advantage, especially in industries in which products are perceived as similar. In the automobile industry, for example, few quality differences between car brands are perceived by consumers. Knowing that, General Motors has developed new guidelines for sales techniques and quality customer service and will link dealer incentive payments to how well the guidelines are followed. Radio Shack expanded its product offerings from just consumer electronics (goods) to include delivery of merchandise and repair of consumer electronics (services).[9] A number of computer manufacturers are implementing remote support programs that enable service technicians to dial in, search around, and make changes so the computer owner is up and running right away.[10]

3 Explain why services marketing is important to manufacturers.

MARKETING MIXES FOR SERVICES

Services' unique characteristics—intangibility, inseparability, heterogeneity, and perishability—make marketing more challenging. Elements of the marketing mix (product, distribution, promotion, and pricing) need to be adjusted to meet the special needs created by these characteristics.

4 Develop marketing mixes for services.

Product (Service) Strategy

The development of "product" strategy in services marketing requires planning focused on the service process.[11] Three types of processing occur:

- *People processing* takes place when the service is directed at a customer. Examples are transportation services, hairstyling, health clubs, and dental and health care.
- *Possession processing* occurs when the service is directed at something a customer owns. Examples are lawn care, car repair, dry cleaning, and veterinary services.
- *Information processing* involves the use of technology (for example, computers) or brainpower. Examples are accounting, education, and legal and financial services.

Because customers' experiences and involvement differ for each of these types of services, marketing strategies may also differ. For example, people-processing services require more customer participation than do possession-processing services, which means marketing strategies for the former will need to focus more on inseparability and heterogeneity issues.

Core and Supplementary Services

The service offering can be viewed as a bundle of activities that includes the **core service,** which is the most basic benefit the customer is buying, and a group of **supplementary services** that support or enhance the core service. Exhibit 12.2 illustrates these concepts for Federal Express. The core service is overnight transportation and delivery of packages, which involves possession processing. The supplementary services, some of which involve information processing, include problem solving, advice and information, billing statements, and order taking.

core service
The most basic benefit the consumer is buying.

supplementary services
A group of services that support or enhance the core service.

Exhibit 12.2
Core and Supplementary Services for Federal Express

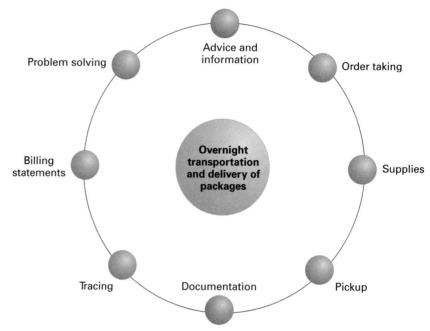

Source: From *Services Marketing*, 3E by Christopher H. Lovelock, © 1996. Adapted by permission of Prentice-Hall, Inc., Upper Saddle River, N.J.

In many service industries, the core service becomes a commodity as competition increases. Thus, firms usually emphasize supplementary services to create a competitive advantage. Hospitals like Richardson Medical Center in Texas are marketing AT&T's video telephones as a part of their maternity services. This supplementary service allows the family to see and hear the new baby. New parents pay the cost of a long-distance call; distant relatives rent a videophone at an AT&T Phone Center or take a videophone home for 24 hours.[12] On the other hand, some firms are positioning themselves in the marketplace by greatly reducing supplementary services. For example, Microtel Inn is an amenity-free hotel concept known as "fast lodging." These low-cost hotels have one- and two-bedroom accommodations and a swimming pool, but no meeting rooms or other services.[13]

Mass Customization

An important issue in developing the service offering is whether to customize or standardize it. Customized services are more flexible and respond to individual customers' needs. They also usually command a higher price. The traditional law firm, which treats each case differently according to the client's situation, offers customized services. Standardized services are more efficient and cost less. Unlike the traditional law firm, for example, Hyatt Legal Services offers low-cost, standardized service "packages" for those with uncomplicated legal needs, such as drawing up a will or mediating an uncontested divorce.

Instead of choosing to either standardize or customize a service, a firm may incorporate elements of both by adopting an emerging strategy called **mass customization.** Mass customization uses technology to deliver customized services on a mass basis. This results in giving each customer whatever she or he asks for. For example, Northwest Airlines developed interactive passenger entertainment centers where first- and business-class passengers can choose from a variety of services such as on-screen entertainment, shopping, and travel services and information.[14] Oxford Health Plans, described in the opening vignette, gives members individualized services with technology that identifies patients with chronic conditions. These patients

mass customization
A strategy that uses technology to deliver customized services on a mass basis.

are contacted by Oxford nurses or field-workers and given information that is designed to help them prevent the need for expensive future treatment.[15]

The Service Mix

Most service organizations market more than one service. For example, ChemLawn offers lawn care, shrub care, carpet cleaning, and industrial lawn services. Each organization's service mix represents a set of opportunities, risks, and challenges. Each part of the service mix should make a different contribution in achieving the firm's goals. To succeed, each service may also need a different level of financial support.

Designing a service strategy therefore means deciding what new services to introduce to which target market, what existing services to maintain, and what services to eliminate. For example, American Express Co. has added a new business called American Express Financial Direct that gives customers access to mutual funds, money market accounts, and discount brokerage services.[16]

Distribution Strategy

Distribution strategies for service organizations must focus on such issues as convenience, number of outlets, direct versus indirect distribution, location, and scheduling. A key factor influencing the selection of a service provider is convenience. Therefore, service firms must offer convenience. American Airlines, for example, invested millions of dollars developing the SABRE reservation system to make the reservation process more convenient for independent travel agents. This system is the most widely used reservation system in the industry.

An important distribution objective for many service firms is the *number of outlets* to use or the number of outlets to open during a certain time. Generally, the intensity of distribution should meet, but not exceed, the target market's needs and preferences. Having too few outlets may inconvenience customers; having too many outlets may boost costs unnecessarily. Intensity of distribution may also depend on the image desired, having only a few outlets may make the service seem more exclusive or selective.

The next service distribution decision is whether to distribute services to end users *directly or indirectly* through other firms. Because of the intangible nature of services, many service firms have to use direct distribution or franchising. Examples include legal, medical, accounting, and personal care services. The newest form of direct distribution is the Internet. For example, most of the major airlines are now using on-line services to sell tickets directly to consumers. This results in lower distribution costs for the airlines companies.[17] Other firms with standardized service packages—such as stock funds, airlines, and insurance companies—have developed indirect channels using independent intermediaries. For instance, Blockbuster Video is test marketing locating videocassette rental services in Wal-Mart stores.[18]

American Express has added a new business called Financial Direct as part of its service strategy. The service gives its customers access to mutual funds, money market accounts, and discount brokerage services.

Courtesy American Express Corporation. This permission shall be governed by the laws of the State of New York.

Delta Air Lines
Visit the SkyLinks Reservation Desk for an example of on-line reservations service. What other services does Delta offer on-line?

http://www.delta-air.com/index.htm/

NOW YOU CAN BUY TICKETS WITHOUT LEAVING YOUR PAD.

The airline that's always ahead of its time is online. Visit our Home Gate on the Internet's World Wide Web. With the click of a button you'll find everything from flight schedules to fare information to photos of our favorite planes. You can even purchase Ticketless Travel Online. So visit our Home Gate, and fly Southwest without leaving the ground. Find us at www.iflyswa.com

SOUTHWEST AIRLINES
A SYMBOL OF FREEDOM™

Southwest Airlines' customers can check flight schedules and fares and even purchase tickets through the company's Web site.

Courtesy Southwest Airlines

The *location* of a service most clearly reveals the relationship between its target market strategy and distribution strategy. Reportedly, Conrad Hilton claimed that the three most important factors in determining a hotel's success are "location, location, and location." Taco Bell, a subsidiary of PepsiCo, has changed from a regional quick-service restaurant chain with 1,500 outlets into a multinational food delivery company with more than 15,000 "points of access" (POAs). A POA is any place where people eat—airports, supermarkets, school cafeterias, or street corners.[19]

For time-dependent service providers like airlines, physicians, and dentists, *scheduling* is often a more important factor. For example, sometimes scheduling is the most important factor in a customer's choice of airline.

Promotion Strategy

Consumers and business users have more trouble evaluating services than goods, because services are less tangible. In turn, marketers have more trouble promoting intangible services than tangible goods. Here are four promotion strategies they can try:

- *Stressing tangible cues:* A tangible cue is a concrete symbol of the service offering. To make their intangible services more tangible, hotels turn down the bedcovers and put mints on the pillows. Insurance companies use symbols like rocks, blankets, umbrellas, and hands to help make their intangible services appear tangible. Merrill Lynch uses a bull to help give its services substance.

- *Using personal information sources:* A personal information source is someone consumers are familiar with (such as a celebrity) or someone they know or can relate to personally. Celebrity endorsements are sometimes used to reduce customers' perceived risk in choosing a service. Service firms may also seek to simulate positive word-of-mouth communication among present and prospective customers by using real customers in their ads. The House of Good Samaritan Hospital ran TV spots using testimonials of real patients who came to the hospital for treatment. This strategy was credited with substantially improving bottom-line profitability for Good Samaritan.[20]

- *Creating a strong organizational image:* One way to create an image is to manage the evidence, including the physical environment of the service facility, the appearance of the service employees, and the tangible items associated with a service (like stationery, bills, and business cards). For example, McDonald's has created a strong organizational image with its Golden Arches, relatively standardized interiors, and employee uniforms. Another way to create an image is through branding. MCI Communications has grown by creating and promoting brands in the commodity business of common-carrier long-distance service. Examples of MCI brands are Friends and Family and 1-800-COLLECT.[21]

- *Engaging in postpurchase communication:* Postpurchase communication refers to the follow-up activities that a service firm might engage in after a customer transaction. Postcard surveys, telephone calls, brochures, and various other types of follow-up show customers that their feedback matters and their patronage is appreciated.

Price Strategy

Considerations in pricing a service are similar to the pricing considerations to be discussed in Chapters 20 and 21. However, the unique characteristics of services present some special pricing challenges:[22]

- *Defining the unit of service consumption:* In order to price a service, it is important to define the unit of service consumption. For example, should pricing be based on completing a specific service task (cutting a customer's hair), or should it be time based (how long it takes to cut a customer's hair)? Some services include the consumption of goods, such as food and beverages. Restaurants charge customers for food and drink rather than the use of a table and chairs. Some transportation firms charge by distance; others charge a flat rate.

- *Pricing services composed of multiple elements:* For services that are composed of multiple elements, the issue is whether pricing should be based on a "bundle" of elements or whether each element should be priced separately. A bundled price may be preferable when consumers dislike having to pay "extra" for every part of the service (for example, paying extra for baggage or food on an airplane), and it is simpler for the firm to administer. For instance, MCI offers a basic communications package that costs $4.95 a month. The package includes 30 minutes of telephone time, five hours of Internet access, a personal number that can route calls to several locations, and a calling card.[23] Alternatively, customers may not want to pay for service elements they do not use. Many furniture stores now have "unbundled" delivery charges from the price of the furniture. Customers who wish to can pick up the furniture at the store, saving on the delivery fee.

- *Coping with deregulation:* Many service industries that have experienced deregulation in recent years have changed their pricing strategies. For example, when the airline industry was regulated, all airlines were required to charge the same price for tickets. But today airline passengers face a bewildering array of options when pricing a flight from one city to another. In fact, the lowest available fare may even differ from one ticketing agent to another. Similarly, deregulated financial service institutions must now carefully consider the amount to charge for loans, check-writing privileges, insurance policies, brokerage services, and other services.

Marketers should set performance objectives when pricing each service. Three categories of pricing objectives have been suggested:

- *Revenue-oriented pricing* focuses on maximizing the surplus of income over costs. A limitation of this approach is that determining costs can be difficult for many services.

- *Operations-oriented pricing* seeks to match supply and demand by varying prices. For example, matching hotel demand to the number of available rooms can be achieved by raising prices at peak times and decreasing them during slow times.

- *Patronage-oriented pricing* tries to maximize the number of customers using the service. Thus, prices vary with different market segments' ability to pay, and methods of payment (such as credit) are offered that increase the likelihood of a purchase.

A firm may need to use more than one type of pricing objective. In fact, all three objectives probably need to be included to some degree in pricing strategy, although the importance of each type may vary depending on the type of service provided, the prices that competitors are charging, the differing ability of various customer segments to pay, or the opportunity to negotiate price. For customized services (for example, legal services and construction services), customers may also have the ability to negotiate a price.

RELATIONSHIP MARKETING IN SERVICES

Discuss relationship marketing in services.

Many services involve ongoing interaction between the service organization and the customer. Thus, they can benefit from relationship marketing, the strategy described in Chapter 1 as a means of attracting, developing, and retaining customer relationships. The idea is to develop strong loyalty by creating satisfied customers who will buy additional services from the firm and are unlikely to switch to a competitor. Satisfied customers are also likely to engage in positive word-of-mouth communication, thereby helping to bring in new customers.

Many businesses have found that it is more cost effective to hang onto the customers they have than only to try to attract new ones. A bank executive, for example, found that increasing customer retention by 2 percent can have the same effect on profits as reducing costs by 10 percent.

It has been suggested that relationship marketing can be practiced at three levels (see Exhibit 12.3):[24]

- *Level 1:* The firm uses pricing incentives to encourage customers to continue doing business with it. Examples include the frequent-flyer programs offered by many airlines and the free or discounted travel services given to frequent hotel guests. This level of relationship marketing is the least effective in the long term because its price-based advantage is easily imitated by other firms.

- *Level 2:* This level of relationship marketing also uses pricing incentives but seeks to build social bonds with customers. The firm stays in touch with customers, learns about their needs, and designs services to meet those needs. Manhattan East Suite Hotels, for example, has compiled a database on the guests who have stayed at its nine luxurious New York City properties. Doormen greet arriving guests by name, and reservation agents know whether a guest prefers a room facing a certain direction or a nonsmoking room.[25] Level 2 relationship marketing has a higher potential for keeping the firm ahead of the competition than does level 1 relationship marketing.

- *Level 3:* At this level, the firm again uses financial and social bonds but adds structural bonds to the formula. Structural bonds are developed by offering value-added services that are not readily available from other firms. Hertz's #1 Club Gold program allows members to call and reserve a car, board a courtesy bus at the airport, tell the driver their name, and get dropped off in front of their car. Hertz also

Exhibit 12.3
Three Levels of Relationship Marketing

Level	Type of bond	Degree of service customization	Main element of marketing mix	Potential for long-term advantage over competitors
1	Financial	Low	Price	Low
2	Financial, social	Medium	Personal communication	Medium
3	Financial, social, structural	Medium to high	Service delivery	High

Source: Reprinted with permission of The Free Press, a division of Simon & Schuster from *MARKETING SERVICES: Competing Through Quality* by Leonard L. Berry and A. Parasuraman. Copyright © 1991 by The Free Press.

starts up the car and turns on the air conditioning or heat, depending on the temperature.[26] Marketing programs like this one have the strongest potential for sustaining long-term relationships with customers.

Hertz Corporation
What other marketing programs and special offers does Hertz feature at its Web site?

http://www.hertz.com/

INTERNAL MARKETING IN SERVICE FIRMS

Services are performances, so the quality of a firm's employees is an important part of building long-term relationships with customers. Employees who like their jobs and are satisfied with the firm they work for are more likely to deliver superior service to customers. In other words, a firm that makes its employees happy has a better chance of keeping its customers coming back. Thus, it is critical that service firms practice **internal marketing,** which means treating employees as customers and developing systems and benefits that satisfy their needs. These are the activities involved in internal marketing: competing for talent, offering a vision, training employees, stressing teamwork, giving employees more freedom to make decisions, measuring and rewarding good service performance, and knowing employees' needs.[27]

Companies have instituted a wide variety of programs designed to satisfy employees. A number of companies, including AT&T, Citicorp, and Aetna Life and Casualty, are investing millions of dollars in an effort to improve child and elder care for their employees.[28] United Airlines introduced a program allowing pilots and flight attendants more flexibility to swap job assignments with colleagues that reduced sick time by 17 percent in its first year.[29] These examples illustrate how service firms can invest in their most important resource—their employees.

6 Explain internal marketing in services.

internal marketing
Treating employees as customers and developing systems and benefits that satisfy their needs.

This ad shows Southwest Airlines' commitment to internal marketing. The company offers many benefits to its employees to keep them—and customers—happy.
Courtesy Southwest Airlines

GLOBAL ISSUES IN SERVICES MARKETING

7 Discuss global issues in services marketing.

The international marketing of services is a major part of global business, and the United States has become the world's largest exporter of services. Competition in international services is increasing rapidly, however.

To be successful in the global marketplace, service firms must first determine the nature of their core product. Then the marketing mix elements (additional services, pricing, promotion, distribution) should be designed to take into account each country's cultural, technological, and political environment.

Because of their competitive advantages, many U.S. service industries have been able to enter the global marketplace. U.S. banks, for example, have advantages in customer service and collections management. The field of construction and engineering services offers great global potential; U.S. companies have vast experience in this industry, so economies of scale are possible for machinery and materials, human resource management, and project management. The U.S. insurance industry has substantial knowledge about underwriting, risk evaluation, and insurance operations that it can export to other countries. Delivery services also have great potential for globalization, as the "Global Perspectives" box illustrates.

NONPROFIT ORGANIZATION MARKETING

8 Describe nonprofit organization marketing.

A **nonprofit organization** is an organization that exists to achieve some goal other than the usual business goals of profit, market share, or return on investment. Nonprofit organizations share important characteristics with private-sector service firms: Both market intangible products. Both often require the customer to be present during the production process. Both for-profit and nonprofit services vary greatly from producer to producer and from day to day, even from the same producer. Neither

Because of its competitive advantage, Sprint has been able to enter the global marketplace.

Courtesy Sprint Communications Company.

Global Perspectives
One World, One UPS

United Parcel Services (UPS) took its branding efforts to global proportions for the first time in 1996. UPS, the largest private courier in the world with 1994 revenues of $19.6 billion (FedEx had $8.5 billion, Airborne $1.9 billion), completed its global network in 1993, affiliating with local couriers to serve 200 countries.

The company sponsored the world's biggest sporting event, the 1996 Olympics. Its overall $70–100 million campaign outlay, including the rights fee, was the biggest push in its 88-year history. But it's an outlay that UPS marketing Vice President Peter Fredo saw as ideal in timing and scope for UPS not only to showcase its newly assembled worldwide network, but also to create, in effect, a one-world feeling uniting both the old and new among its 300,000 employees. "There is a link between the Olympic athletes image and the image UPS is seeking: a worldwide competitor," Fredo said. "UPS has

been pursuing worldwide service for the last decade, and it has now reached critical mass. The Olympics provide the perfect platform."

UPS wanted to energize its workforce with such programs as the Athlete Assistance Training Program, offering training and financial assistance to any employee vying for a slot on an Olympic team. Nine employees attempted to qualify for teams.

A consumer campaign used TV, print, and outdoor advertising to position UPS as a global competitor with the tag line "Moving at the speed of business." Ammirati & Puris/Lintas, N.Y., handled the campaign in the U.S., and McCann Worldwide, London, was recruited to handle advertising overseas, tailoring campaigns to several mar-

kets abroad, including Germany, England, France, Canada, Australia, and parts of Asia. New spots breaking during NBC's Olympic coverage compared UPS's speed, precision, and training to an Olympic athlete's. A sweepstakes awarded frequent customers and heavy-volume users trips to the Games and other prizes.

"We want to fulfill two branding goals through the timing and audience of the Games: greater global recognition, and internal branding unification," said Susan Rosenberg, UPS manager of marketing. "Many of our employees are from different foreign teams and will be participating in events we sponsor."[30]

Evaluate UPS's use of the Olympics to build a global marketing strategy. How is their global brand image "tangibilized"? What other marketing activities could UPS have used to develop using the Olympics theme?

for-profit nor nonprofit services can be stored in the way that tangible goods can be produced, saved, and sold at a later date.

Few people realize that nonprofit organizations account for over 20 percent of the economic activity in the United States. The cost of government, the predominant form of nonprofit organization, has become the biggest single item in the American family budget—more than housing, food, or health care. Together, federal, state, and local governments collect revenues that amount to more than a third of the U.S. gross domestic product. Moreover, they employ nearly one of every five nonagricultural civilian workers. In addition to government entities, nonprofit organizations include hundreds of thousands of private museums, theaters, schools, and churches.

What Is Nonprofit Organization Marketing?

Nonprofit organization marketing is the effort by nonprofit organizations to bring about mutually satisfying exchanges with target markets. Although these organizations vary substantially in size and purpose and operate in different environments, most perform the following marketing activities:

nonprofit organization
An organization that exists to achieve some goal other than the usual business goals of profit, market share, or return on investment.

nonprofit organization marketing
The effort by nonprofit organizations to bring about mutually satisfying exchanges with target markets.

Nonprofit organizations such as the Shedd Aquarium account for over 20 percent of the economic activity in the United States.
Courtesy Shedd Aquarium

(actual size)

Just imagine how impressive the entire exhibit is.

frogs!   Catch the world's largest collection now.
Because when leap year's over, so is the show.
Sponsored by Morton International, Inc.

Shedd AQUARIUM
Water Your Imagination

- Identify the customers they wish to serve or attract (although they usually use another term, such as *clients, patients, members,* or *sponsors*)
- Explicitly or implicitly specify objectives
- Develop, manage, and eliminate programs and services
- Decide on prices to charge (although they use other terms, such as *fees, donations, tuition, fares, fines,* or *rates*)
- Schedule events or programs, and determine where they will be held or where services will be offered
- Communicate their availability through brochures, signs, public service announcements, or advertisements

Often, the nonprofit organizations that carry out these functions do not realize they are engaged in marketing. Some nonprofit organizations have perhaps gone too far in adopting marketing techniques, as the accompanying "Ethics in Marketing" box explains.

Unique Aspects of Nonprofit Organization Marketing Strategies

9 Explain the unique aspects of nonprofit organization marketing.

Like their counterparts in business organizations, nonprofit managers develop marketing strategies to bring about mutually satisfying exchanges with target markets. However, marketing in nonprofit organizations is unique in many ways—including the setting of marketing objectives, the selection of target markets, and the development of appropriate marketing mixes.

Ethics in Marketing

How a Tiny Charity Transformed Itself into a Used-Car Giant

Tucked away in a crowded row of stucco homes, the Beth Aharon Day School is barely noticeable. Its wooden schoolhouse, badly in need of a paint job, has only six classrooms. Space is so tight that the principal works out of a shack near the playground. But behind the 84-student elementary school's low profile is an astonishingly large business. During the past few years, the charity that runs Beth Aharon has become one of the biggest used-car dealers in the country; it would rank among the top 50 for-profit used-car chains nationwide. By soliciting cars as donations and then auctioning them, the Jewish Educational Center (JEC) of San Francisco went from desperate financial straits in 1993 to a projected $7.3 million in car sales in 1996.

The JEC, established by Rabbi Bentziyon Pil and his wife Mattie to help Russian Jewish immigrants, has attracted thousands of car donors since 1991 with ads promising them hefty tax deductions. As it turns out, though, the state of California suspended its tax-ex-empt status from the early 1990s until just last year, according to the state attorney general's office. The JEC also isn't registered as a charitable organization—meaning it isn't permitted to solicit donations—in New Jersey or in New York, where it now advertises heavily with radio spots asking, "So why not donate that extra car?"

What's more, some car donors say they were misled into thinking that their cars would be given away to the needy, not sold. Nor have the immigrants the JEC was set up to help seen much of the money it has raised so far. The charity's primary program, the tiny Beth Aharon school, remains in poor repair. Another of its programs, called Kids Overcoming Katastrophe, has devoted the past year to hosting 12 youths from Chernobyl—but the JEC acknowledges that some aspects of the program, including lodging and medical care, are being provided either free or at a reduced rate by others.

One needy family, however, is surely doing better: The Pils themselves. A year ago, the family was crammed into a tiny house where six of their seven children shared a single bedroom. Now they rent a comfortable three-story home that Mrs. Pil's 24-year-old brother bought last summer for $472,000. Mr. Pil drives one of the most valuable cars ever donated to the JEC, a 1990 Cadillac. These days, he accessorizes the traditional black hat he wears as a Hasidic Jew with a digital pager on his waist. The Pils, while admitting they have made some mistakes due to inexperience, say that their intentions are good and they never misled donors.[31]

Do you think it is ethical for charities to engage in large-scale businesses like selling used cars? How can nonprofit organizations manage their images with the public that supports them? If the Pil's intentions are good, what can they do to regain trust?

Objectives

In the private sector, the profit motive is both an objective for guiding decisions and a criterion for evaluating results. Nonprofit organizations do not seek to make a profit for redistribution to owners or shareholders. Rather, their focus is often on generating enough funds to cover expenses. For example, the Methodist Church does not gauge its success by the amount of money left in offering plates. The Museum of Science and Industry does not base its performance evaluations on the dollar value of tokens put into the turnstile.

Most nonprofit organizations are expected to provide equitable, effective, and efficient services that respond to the wants and preferences of multiple constituencies. These include users, payers, donors, politicians, appointed officials, the media, and the general public. Nonprofit organizations cannot measure their success or failure in strictly financial terms.

The lack of a financial "bottom line" and the existence of multiple, diverse, intangible, and sometimes vague or conflicting objectives makes prioritizing objectives,

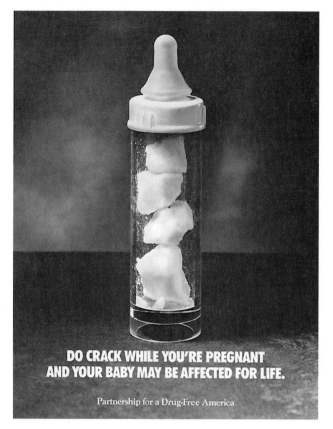

making decisions, and evaluating performance hard for nonprofit managers. They must often use approaches different from the ones commonly used in the private sector. For example, Planned Parenthood has devised a system for basing salary increases on how employees perform in relation to the objectives they set each year.

Target Markets

Three issues relating to target markets are unique to nonprofit organizations:

- *Apathetic or strongly opposed targets:* Private-sector organizations usually give priority to developing those market segments that are most likely to respond to particular offerings. In contrast, nonprofit organizations must often target those who are apathetic about or strongly opposed to receiving their services such as vaccinations, family-planning guidance, help for problems of drug or alcohol abuse, and psychological counseling.

- *Pressure to adopt undifferentiated segmentation strategies:* Nonprofit organizations often adopt undifferentiated strategies (see Chapter 8) by default. Sometimes they fail to recognize the advantages of targeting, or an undifferentiated approach may appear to offer economies of scale and low per-capita costs.In other instances, nonprofit organizations are pressured or required to serve the maximum number of people by targeting the average user. The problem with developing services targeted at the average user is that there are few "average" users. Therefore, such strategies typically fail to fully satisfy any market segment.

- *Complementary positioning:* The main role of many nonprofit organizations is to provide services, with available resources, to those who are not adequately served by private-sector organizations. As a result, the nonprofit organization must often complement rather than compete with the efforts of others. The positioning task is to identify underserved market segments and to develop marketing programs that match their needs rather than to target the niches that may be most profitable. For example, a university library may see itself as complementing the services of the public library, rather than as competing with it.

Product Decisions

There are three product-related distinctions between business and nonprofit organizations:

- *Benefit complexity:* Rather than simple product concepts, like "Fly the friendly skies" or "We earn money the old-fashioned way," nonprofit organizations often market complex behaviors or ideas. Examples include the need to exercise or eat right, not to drink and drive, and not to smoke tobacco. The benefits that a person receives are complex, long term, and intangible and therefore are more difficult to communicate to consumers.

- *Benefit strength:* The benefit strength of many nonprofit offerings is quite weak or indirect. What are the direct, personal benefits to you of driving 55 miles per hour, donating blood, or asking your neighbors to contribute money to a charity? In contrast, most private-sector service organizations can offer customers direct, personal benefits in an exchange relationship.

- *Involvement:* Many nonprofit organizations market products that elicit very low involvement ("Prevent forest fires" or "Don't litter") or very high involvement ("Join the military" or "Stop smoking"). The typical range for private-sector goods is much narrower. Traditional promotional tools may be inadequate to motivate adoption of either low- or high-involvement products.

Distribution Decisions

A nonprofit organization's capacity for distributing its service offerings to potential customer groups when and where they want them is typically a key variable in determining the success of those service offerings. For example, most state land-grant universities offer extension programs throughout their state to reach the general public. Many large universities have one or more satellite campus locations to provide easier access for students in other areas. Some educational institutions also offer classes to students at off-campus locations via interactive video technology.

The extent to which a service depends on fixed facilities has important implications for distribution decisions. Obviously, services like rail transit and lake fishing can be delivered only at specific points. Many nonprofit services, however, do not depend on special facilities. Counseling, for example, need not take place in agency offices; it may occur wherever counselors and clients can meet. Probation services, outreach youth programs, and educational courses taught on commuter trains are other examples of deliverable services.

Like for-profit firms, a number of nonprofit organizations are using the World Wide Web to distribute their services. For example, Relief Rock is an on-line site that was designed to raise money for relief efforts in Rwanda and now seeks donations for charities around the world. Relief Rock, targeted to generation X donors, lets users choose from several musical venues that provide free 30-second samplings of songs. At the end of each selection, a graphic of outstretched hands prompt users to make a pledge to any of 21 charities.[32]

Relief Rock
How does Relief Rock encourage contributions via the Web?

http://www.reliefnet.org/reliefrock/rock.htm

Fund-raising also requires good channels of distribution. The Salvation Army places its kettles in areas with heavy foot traffic during the Christmas season. The donations then flow mostly to local units, with a small amount going to the national office. Perhaps the most sophisticated fund-raising channel is the annual Jerry Lewis Muscular Dystrophy Telethon. Thousands of local telephone numbers are used to collect pledges at the grassroots level. Totals are then aggregated by the state or region, which provides the local talent and personalities for its portion of the annual program. Finally, the total gifts are reported nationally in Las Vegas, where Jerry Lewis and his staff coordinate the superstar entertainment portion of the program.

Promotion Decisions

Many nonprofit organizations are explicitly or implicitly prohibited from advertising, thus limiting their promotion options. Most federal agencies fall into this category. Other nonprofit organizations simply do not have the resources to retain advertising agencies, promotion consultants, or marketing staff. However, nonprofit organizations have a few special promotion resources to call on:

- *Professional volunteers:* Nonprofit organizations often seek out marketing, sales, and advertising professionals to help them develop and implement promotion strategies. In some instances, an advertising agency donates its services in exchange for potential long-term benefits. For example, one advertising agency donated its services to a major symphony because the symphony had a blue-ribbon board of directors. Donated services create goodwill, personal contacts, and general awareness of the donor's organization, reputation, and competency.

- *Sales promotion activities:* Sales promotion activities that make use of existing services or other resources are increasingly being used to draw attention to the offerings of nonprofit organizations. For example, the Edgewood Symphony Orchestra near Pittsburgh, Pennsylvania, gave free tickets to those who participated in a phone survey about the orchestra and who had not attended a concert but wanted to.[33]

- *Public service advertising:* A **public service advertisement (PSA)** is an announcement that promotes a program of a federal, state, or local government or of a nonprofit organization. Unlike a commercial advertiser, the sponsor of the PSA does not pay for the time or space. Instead, it is donated by the medium. The Advertising Council has developed PSAs that are some of the most memorable advertisements of all time. For example, Smokey the Bear reminded everyone to be careful not to start forest fires.

- *Licensing:* Some nonprofit organizations have found that licensing their names and/or images is an effective way to communicate to a large audience. For example, the Vatican is trying to raise money and spread the word about the Catholic church through a licensing program. This program will put images from the Vatican library's art collection, architecture, frescoes, and manuscripts on T-shirts, glassware, candles, and ornaments.[34]

public service advertisement (PSA) Announcement that promotes a program of a federal, state, or local government or of a nonprofit organization.

Pricing Decisions

Five key characteristics distinguish the pricing decisions of nonprofit organizations from those of the profit sector:

- *Pricing objectives:* Revenue is the main pricing objective in the profit sector or, more specifically, profit maximization, sales maximization, or target return on sales or investment. Many nonprofit organizations must also be concerned about revenue. However, nonprofit organizations often seek to either partially or fully defray costs rather than achieve a profit for distribution to stockholders. Nonprofit organizations also seek to redistribute income—for instance, through taxation and sliding-scale fees. Moreover, they strive to allocate resources fairly among individuals or households or across geographic or political boundaries.

- *Nonfinancial prices:* In many nonprofit situations, consumers are not charged a monetary price but instead must absorb nonmonetary costs. The importance of those costs is illustrated by the large number of eligible citizens who do not take advantage of so-called free services for the poverty stricken. In many public assistance programs, about half the people who are eligible don't participate. Nonmonetary costs consist of the opportunity cost of time, embarrassment costs, and effort costs.

- *Indirect payment:* Indirect payment through taxes is common to marketers of "free" services, such as libraries, fire protection, and police protection. Indirect payment is not a common practice in the profit sector.

- *Separation between payers and users:* By design, the services of many charitable organizations are provided for those who are relatively poor and largely paid for by those who have better finances. Although examples of separation between payers and users can be found in the profit sector (such as insurance claims), the practice is much less prevalent.

- *Below-cost pricing:* An example of below-cost pricing is university tuition. Virtually all private and public colleges and universities price their services below full cost. Another example is a community-based organization called Playing to Win. Located in East Harlem, Playing to Win serves low-income families, each of which pays $35 for six months of computer access. Because this organization is partially subsidized by a variety of public and private funding, it can offer below-cost access to the Internet.[35] This practice also exists in the profit sector, although it is generally an undesirable, temporary situation.

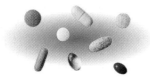

LOOKING BACK

Look back at the story about Oxford Health Plans that appeared at the beginning of this chapter. After reading the chapter, you should know the answers to the questions posed at the end of the story. Oxford's service differs from competing managed-care services because of its ability to customize services to meet individual customers' needs. In addition, Oxford is more oriented toward education and prevention of diseases than most managed-care organizations are.

Oxford is practicing the marketing concept because it can individualize its services, providing higher levels of customer satisfaction. This leads to greater customer loyalty and retention, which help the company to build long-term relationships with its customers.

KEY TERMS

core service *331*

credence quality *330*

experience quality *329*

heterogeneity *330*

inseparability *330*

intangibility *329*

internal marketing *337*

mass customization *332*

nonprofit organization *339*

nonprofit organization marketing *339*

perishability *330*

public service advertisement (PSA) *345*

search quality *329*

service *328*

supplementary service *331*

SUMMARY

1 *Discuss the importance of services to the economy.* The service sector plays a crucial role in the U.S. economy, employing about three-quarters of the workforce and accounting for more than 60 percent of the gross domestic product.

2 *Discuss the differences between services and goods.* Services are distinguished by four characteristics: intangibility, inseparability, heterogeneity, and perishability. Services are intangible in that they lack clearly identifiable physical characteristics, making it difficult for marketers to communicate their specific benefits to potential customers. The production and consumption of services are typically inseparable. Services are heterogeneous because their quality depends on such variables as the service provider, individual consumer, location, and so on. Finally, services are perishable in the sense that they cannot be stored or saved. As a result, synchronizing supply with demand is particularly challenging in the service industry.

3 *Explain why services marketing is important to manufacturers.* Although manufacturers are marketing mainly goods, the related services they provide often give them a competitive advantage—especially when competing goods are quite similar.

4 *Develop marketing mixes for services.* "Product" (service) strategy issues include what is being processed (people, possessions, information), core and supplementary services, customization versus standardization, and the service mix or portfolio. Distribution decisions involve convenience, number of outlets, direct versus indirect distribution, and scheduling. Stressing tangible cues, using personal sources of information, creating strong organizational images, and engaging in postpurchase communication are effective promotion strategies. Pricing objectives for services can be revenue oriented, operations oriented, patronage oriented, or any combination of the three.

5 *Discuss relationship marketing in services.* Relationship marketing in services involves attracting, developing, and retaining customer relationships. There are three levels of relationship marketing: Level 1 focuses on pricing incentives; level 2 uses pricing incentives and social bonds with customers; and level 3 uses pricing, social bonds, and structural bonds to build long-term relationships.

6 *Explain internal marketing in services.* Internal marketing means treating employees as customers and developing systems and benefits that satisfy their needs. Employees who like their jobs and are happy with the firm they work for are more likely to deliver good service. Internal marketing activities include competing for talent, offering a vision, training employees, stressing teamwork, giving employees freedom to make decisions, measuring and rewarding good service performance, and knowing employees' needs.

7 *Discuss global issues in services marketing.* The United States has become the world's largest exporter of services. Although competition is keen, the United States has a competitive advantage because of its vast experience in many service industries. To be successful globally, service firms must adjust their marketing mix for the environment of each target country.

8 *Describe nonprofit organization marketing.* Nonprofit organizations pursue goals other than profit, market share, and return on investment. Nonprofit organization marketing facilitates mutually satisfying exchanges between nonprofit organizations and their target markets.

9 *Explain the unique aspects of nonprofit organization marketing.* Several unique characteristics distinguish nonbusiness marketing strategy, including a concern with services and social behaviors rather than manufactured goods and profit; a difficult, undifferentiated, and in some ways marginal target market; a complex product that may have only indirect benefits and elicit very low involvement; a short, direct, immediate distribution channel; a relative lack of resources for promotion; and prices only indirectly related to the exchange between the producer and the consumer of services.

Discussion and Writing Questions

1. Explain what the search, experience, and credence qualities are for a university or college.

2. Assume that you are a manager of a financial services firm. Write a list of implications of intangibility for your firm.

3. You are applying for a job as a marketing manager for a service firm and have been asked how you would handle a mismatch between supply and demand. Write your answer as a memo to the vice president of marketing.

4. Form a team with at least two other classmates, and come up with an idea for a new service. Develop a marketing mix strategy for the new service.

5. For the service developed in Question 4, have the members of the team discuss how they would implement internal marketing.

6. Write a list of some of the issues you would have to consider in taking your new service (from Question 4) global. How would you change your marketing mix to address those issues?

7. Form a team with two or three classmates. Using the four promotion strategies discussed in the chapter, design a promotion strategy for your college or university.

8. Your local, nonprofit symphony is having problems attracting new patrons. Most of its current patrons are 50 years old and older. What other target markets might be viable? For each target market you choose, write down what promotion activities you would use to attract it.

9. What services does the following Web site of-

fer? How do visitors use the Special Offer List?

http://www.travelweb. com/

10. How can marketers benefit from the service offered at the following Web site? Select a subcategory under "Business" that has more than one entry, and describe the mailing lists you find.

http://www.liszt.com/

Application for Small Business

Carrie Jones is a well-known gourmet chef who is tired of working in restaurants and wants to go out on her own. She has decided to start a catering business, but wants to offer more than just the typical party catering service. She has been able to generate solid financial backing for her venture because of her outstanding reputation in the community, so upfront resources are not a large prob-

lem. Carrie has three people working for her currently.

Questions

1. What consumer or business segments should Carrie target?
2. What types of services should she offer that would differentiate her from a typical party catering service?
3. How could Carrie "tangibilize" the services she develops in Question 2 in her advertising?

Video Case

1-800-FLOWERS

Venture capitalists were losing $400,000 each month on their Dallas-based 1-800-FLOWERS business when Jim McCann, owner of New York-based floral retail chain Flora Plenty, took over the telephone rights and moved 1-800-FLOWERS to Westbury, New York. In an attempt to revive the business, McCann used his established network of 2,500 florists and his experience in the industry to provide excellent customer service. Today, the company enjoys annual sales of over $100 million, and McCann attributes this success to its impossible-to-forget name and its repeat customers.

In a time when consumers want convenience and expect good service, 1-800-FLOWERS has prospered. With its toll-free phone number and 24-hour service, the company has made ordering flowers as simple as making a phone call from home. The company receives orders from all over the globe in its three telemarketing centers and then transmits the customer requests via computer to a florist near the intended recipient. Customers like the guarantee, which promises a refund if customers are not satisfied for any reason. The

company also guarantees that fresh-cut floral arrangements will stay fresh for one week.

 In trying to build its business, 1-800-FLOWERS' advertisements have targeted the largest flower-buying group: white-collar men between 25 and 45 years old. This target market tends to be computer savvy, so the company also uses interactive computer media to market its products. Currently, 5 percent of 1-800-FLOWERS' sales come from the interactive market, but the company hopes to increase this number. 1-800-FLOWERS has begun offering on-line and interactive service with full-color images and descriptions on the Internet, America Online, CompuServe, eWorld, 2Market, and e Shop Plaza (http://www. 1800flowers.com).

New entrants in the flower-delivery business, such as 1-800-FLOW-

ERS, Calyx & Carolla Flower Catalog, and other on-line computer services, are threatening FTD, Inc., a company that dominated the floral business for years. In response to these new competitors, FTD has introduced its own toll-free telephone ordering service, called 1-800-SEND-FTD. FTD also offers a replacement or money-back guarantee and has formed a partnership with American Airlines to enable AAdvantage members to receive mileage for flower purchases.

Consumers now prefer the convenience of ordering directly from their homes and the timely delivery that the new companies provide. In response to the success of its flower service, 1-800-FLOWERS has launched other 800 numbers specifically for gift baskets, candy, and other goodies.

Questions

1. Earlier in this chapter, four unique characteristics of services were discussed. How is 1-800-FLOWERS effectively dealing with these characteristics in their marketing efforts?
2. How could 1-800-FLOWERS

incorporate the concept of mass customization?

3. Describe ways that 1-800-FLOWERS could use to develop long-term relationships with its customers.

References

James F. McCann, "Be Perfect or Die," *Success*, June 1993, p. 14.

Patrick M. Reilly, "Competitive Floral Delivery Networks Claim a Rose Isn't a Rose Isn't a Rose," *The Wall Street Journal*, 14 February 1994, pp. B1, B3.

"Fall & Winter Collections," 1-800-FLOWERS catalog, 1995–1996.

LEARNING OBJECTIVES *After studying this chapter, you should be able to:*

1 Define customer value.

2 Describe the customer value triad.

3 Explain the techniques of quality improvement.

4 Describe the roles of management, employees, and suppliers in quality improvement programs.

5 Distinguish between the three categories of services.

6 Describe the components of service quality.

7 Explain the gap model of service quality.

8 Discuss the components of value-based pricing.

9 Explain the two major determinants of customer satisfaction.

10 Name the economic effects of customer loyalty.

Customer Value, Quality, and Satisfaction

The ways in which consumers view products, define choices, and make purchases are changing. Consumers are becoming more discriminating overall, while at the same time showing a willingness to try new products that fill emerging needs.

For example, consumers increasingly are finding value in simplicity of choice and are less willing to trade their time for long lines, undifferentiated products, and a confusing array of merchandise. Unless some changes are made, shoppers may ultimately increase their spending in nontraditional outlets at the expense of supermarkets and mass-market stores. Mom-and-pop outlets will continue to see a resurgence because they offer selected inventory, personal service, and no lines.

Furthermore, as computer literacy increases, shopping will evolve from in-store to in-house. Television and Internet shopping will skyrocket. More products will be delivered to the home, possibly through a refrigerator or pantry that has both inside and outside access.

Solid, recognizable national, international, and private label brands will be very important to consumers. Consistent visual and sensory signals for a brand's logo and package will be critical to both catch the eye of the time-pressed shopper and reinforce the emotional link of consumers to their brands of choice. Additionally, labels will need to be easy to read and offer freshness dating.

In the food marketplace, an increasing percentage of meals will be eaten in the car, and travel food that is healthful, convenient, and not messy will increase in popularity. On the other hand, consumers will also be looking for an emotional satisfaction in their food consumption. An example might be a flavorful, complete, "home-made" main meal that will be purchased ready to eat, with china,

utensils, and other accessories included. These mobile meals, prepared in a bakerylike environment, will provide a sensory experience and the comfort signals consumers crave.[1]

What do the trends described above offer consumers in terms of greater value? Would these trends offer value to you? Can you think of any companies that are currently providing these kinds of value to consumers?

WHAT IS CUSTOMER VALUE?

1 Define customer value.

Companies today are facing accelerating change in many areas, including better educated and more demanding consumers, new technology, and the globalization of markets. As a result, competition is the toughest it has ever been. More and more, the key to building and sustaining a long-range competitive advantage is the commitment to delivering superior customer value, as the examples in the opening story illustrate.

In Chapter 1, customer value was defined as the customer's perception of the ratio of benefits to the sacrifice necessary to obtain those benefits. Customers receive benefits in the form of functionality, performance, durability, design, ease of use, and serviceability. To receive those benefits, they give up money, time, and effort.

Customer value is not simply a matter of high quality. A high-quality product that is available only at a high price will not be perceived as a value. Nor will bare-bones service or low-quality goods selling for a low price. Instead, customers value goods and services of the quality they expect that are sold at prices they are willing to pay. Value marketing can be used to sell a $44,000 Nissan Infiniti Q45 as well as a $3 Tyson frozen chicken dinner.

Marketers interested in customer value

- *Offer products that perform:* This is the bare minimum. Consumers have lost patience with shoddy merchandise.

- *Give consumers more than they expect:* Soon after Toyota launched Lexus, the company had to order a recall. The weekend before the recall, dealers phoned all the Lexus owners in the United States, personally making arrangements to pick up their cars and offering replacement vehicles.

- *Avoid unrealistic pricing:* Consumers couldn't understand why Kellogg's cereals commanded a premium over other brands, so Kellogg's market share fell 5 percent in the late 1980s.

- *Give the buyer facts:* Today's sophisticated consumer wants informative advertising and knowledgeable salespeople.

- *Offer organizationwide commitment in service and after-sales support.* Take the example of Southwest Airlines. People fly Southwest because the airline offers superior value. Although passengers do not get assigned seats or meals (just peanuts or crackers) when they use the airline, its service is reliable and friendly, and costs less than most major airlines. All Southwest employees are involved in the effort to satisfy customers. Pilots tend to the boarding gate when their help is needed, and ticket agents help move luggage. One reservation agent flew from Dallas to Tulsa with a frail, elderly woman whose son was afraid she couldn't handle the change of planes by herself on her way to St. Louis.[2]

The current emphasis on customer value evolved from the "total quality" programs that were popular in the 1980s. These programs mainly tried to improve product quality by improving production processes. Other customer requirements usually got much less attention. For example, Varian Associates, a maker of scientific equipment, adopted quality principles in a number of areas. Its unit that makes vacuum systems increased on-time delivery of its products from 42 to

This Wal-Mart ad emphasizes two key components of its customer value—friendly service and low prices.
Courtesy Wal-Mart

92 percent. But while Varian was obsessed with meeting production schedules, the staff in the vacuum-equipment unit did not return customers' phone calls, and the operation ended up losing market share. Similarly, Varian's radiation-equipment service department ranked first in its industry for prompt customer visits. However, the radiation-repair people were so rushed to meet deadlines that they left before explaining their work to customers. The imbalance in approach had a direct effect on the company's bottom line. After a $32 million profit in 1989, Varian's sales grew by only 3 percent in 1990, and the company posted a $4.1 million loss.[3]

Today, the most competitive companies are the ones that look beyond the quality of the goods they produce. Better product designs and faster manufacturing are always desirable, but the new perspective goes beyond the narrow quality standards of the past.

After its initially disappointing experiences with narrow total quality programs, Varian started looking for other ways to please customers and boost quality. When customers complained about the long time needed to set up Varian's radiology equipment at hospitals, the company painstakingly investigated several hundred possible solutions. In the end, Varian decided to change some of its procedures—for example, shipping cables in plastic bags rather than using "popcorn" filler as it had done in the past. This one change saved customers 30 minutes of cleanup time. The company also redesigned key parts to make them fit together more easily. Varian's delighted hospital customers saved an average of 95 hours in setup time, worth $50,000 per order. Varian also saved $1.8 million a year for itself.

Varian Associates, Inc.
How does Varian communicate its commitment to customers through its Web page? How is the company described? What customer services are offered?

http://www.varian.com/

A CUSTOMER VALUE FRAMEWORK

To maximize customer value, a firm must know whether it is meeting customers' expectations. Real customer value is defined by the customer, not the organization, and can therefore be ambiguous. A useful framework for understanding what customers want is the **customer value triad**.[4] As Exhibit 13.1 shows, the three legs of the triad are (perceived) goods quality, (perceived) service quality, and value-based prices. Goods quality and service quality are at the base of the triangle, indicating that they support value-based prices.

2 Describe the customer value triad.

customer value triad
Goods quality, service quality, and value-based prices—the components of customer value.

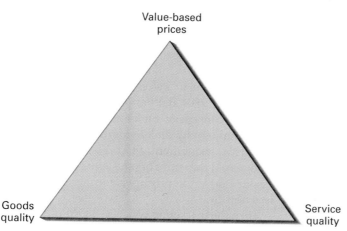

Exhibit 13.1
Customer Value Triad

Source: From *Creating Customer Value* by Earl Naumann. Copyright © 1995 South-Western College Publishing. Reprinted by permission.

Customer value is created when customer expectations in each of the three areas are met or exceeded. A company that fails to meet customer expectations in any one of the three areas is not delivering good customer value. Consider the recent problems at Compaq Computer, which had initially created a niche in portable personal computers. The quality of both Compaq's goods and services was fine, justifying premium prices 30 to 35 percent higher than the competition's. Compaq's customers believed that they were getting good value. But then Compaq became less responsive to change than its competitors. IBM personal computers, and IBM clones at even lower prices, closed the technological gap. Customers could no longer justify the price premium charged by Compaq, because competitive products conveyed better value. The quality of Compaq's goods did not deteriorate; the firm still made good computers. Compaq's service did not deteriorate; it still was viewed as very reliable. But the third leg of the value triad, price, was out of line with the other two. As a result, Compaq's sales and profits plummeted.

Although goods quality and service quality are presented as separate parts of the customer value triad, the differences between goods and services are not always clear from a customer's viewpoint. Almost every tangible good has some service associated with it. U.S. auto companies, for example, have typically produced stylish cars. However, customers perceive quality also in terms of the level of service they get from dealerships, and the lackadaisical service that once plagued U.S. nameplates made them vulnerable to Japanese carmakers.

It is also hard to think of a service that doesn't include tangible goods. A restaurant is a service firm, but does anyone doubt that the quality of associated goods (the food) is important? The same can be said for health care, hospitality and tourism, insurance, and other services. Many service businesses have a product as well as related services.

Customers tend to bundle goods-and-services features, quality perceptions, and fairness of price throughout the product's life and attach some value to the bundle. The bundle is then compared to competitive alternatives, and the best value is selected. Firms that focus on only one or two dimensions of the customer value triad and neglect the third may thus experience the same difficulties as Compaq. Dell Computer, for example, was able to undercut Compaq and other PC makers in price while providing high-quality products and services by selling to customers directly and creating a low-cost company culture.[5]

Value is as important in the international marketplace as it is in the United States, as the following "Global Perspectives" box illustrates.

GOODS QUALITY

Of the three elements of the customer value triad, goods quality has received the most attention over the past decade. The quality movement was easily the most important strategic issue of the 1980s and has probably been the most important business concept of the past 20 or 30 years. The organizational philosophy underlying the quality movement is **total quality management (TQM).** TQM is the coordination, throughout the entire organization, of efforts to provide high-quality goods and processes in order to ensure customer satisfaction.

Like the marketing concept, TQM programs are based on the need to understand customer requirements. Thus, marketing plays an important role in TQM, and traditional marketing techniques are often used to support the quality focus.

Dell Computer undercut its competitors' prices by selling directly to customers and creating a low-cost company culture.
© Ed Kashi

Global Perspectives

American Firms Find Niche in Japanese Market

Unlike some American industries that have trouble breaking into Japan's market, the mail-order catalog industry has been quite successful. Japanese shoppers are buying everything from LL Bean sportswear to Saks Fifth Avenue women's fashions.

These retailers are succeeding while other American businesses are still struggling because the merchants have found a market where Japanese companies are not fulfilling customer needs. Many middle- and upper-class consumers, especially the younger generation and city dwellers, have avoided Japanese catalogs for decades because of their hodgepodge mix of everything from cheap dresses and necklaces to diapers and dog food.

By contrast, American catalogs offer high-quality merchandise carefully aimed at specific groups. And they often contain two other items unusual in Japan: a lifetime, no-questions-asked guarantee and pictures of top models. Clothing with recognized U.S. labels also sells for much less in the catalogs than well-known Japanese fashions do in Japan's expensive department stores. In addition, more and more of the catalogs are being translated into Japanese to make it easier to use them.

Miko Takariji, an upper-middle-class working woman who has been hooked on such foreign catalogs for a few years, is representative of the new wave of Japanese consumers. She often looks through them at her home in Tokyo and orders clothing for herself and her husband. "'In Japan, it's almost impossible to find anything good quality at a reasonable price,' Takariji said. 'What I find in Japanese catalogs is cheap, but it looks cheap, too.'"[6]

Describe how American mail-order catalogs are offering Japanese customers superior value. What do Japanese mail-order companies need to do to compete? How can Japanese retail stores compete with American catalogs?

The key idea in TQM is that quality is important at every step of the production process. In contrast, earlier efforts at quality control relied on inspection of the finished goods. TQM strives to eliminate defects from the beginning. A good is inspected at the design stage, and the manufacturing process is engineered to be stable and reliable. Thoughtful, calculated design and a carefully controlled process result in a high-quality product.

Until recently, many managers were convinced that higher quality costs more. However, companies have come to realize that it costs more to do things poorly and then pay to fix problems than it does to do things right the first time. Additionally, greater productivity can result from quality improvements. In a firm that relies on inspection for quality control, more than half of all workers may be involved in finding and reworking defective goods. The total investment in this process may account for 20 to 50 percent of production costs.[7] Cabot Corporation, for example, saved $1 million a year and freed up new production capacity by reducing defects at one of its carbon-black plants by 90 percent over a two-year period.[8]

The Malcolm Baldrige National Quality Award, named for a former secretary of commerce, was established by the U.S. Congress in 1987 to recognize U.S. companies that offer world-class quality in their goods and services. The award also promotes awareness of quality and transfers information about quality to others in the business community.

The Baldrige Award is administered by the U.S. Department of Commerce's National Institute of Standards and Technology. The Baldrige Award examination board is made up of professionals from business and industry, universities, health care organizations, and government agencies. The most important criterion of

total quality management (TQM)
Coordination, throughout the entire organization, of efforts to provide high-quality goods, processes, and services in order to ensure customer satisfaction.

GTE Directories
GTE is a winner of the Malcolm Baldridge National Quality Award. Why did they win the award? How has a commitment to quality affected GTE?

http://directories.gte.net

Just how hard is it to win the Malcolm Baldrige award? Find out how award winner Milliken & Co. fulfilled the 11 core values and walked away with the award at **Hot Link—Baldrige Award.**

the Baldrige Award is whether the firm meets customer expectations. The customer must be number one. To qualify for the award, a company must also show continuous improvement. Company leaders and employees must participate actively, and they must respond quickly to data and analysis. Companies that have received the Baldrige Award include IBM, Federal Express, the Nuclear Fuel Division of Westinghouse, and Xerox Business Products and Systems.

Essential Quality Techniques

3 Explain the techniques of quality improvement.

Several techniques used in the TQM approach distinguish it from traditional ways of doing business. These techniques include quality function deployment, benchmarking, continuous improvement, reduced cycle time, and analysis of process problems.

quality function deployment (QFD)
A technique that helps companies translate customer design requirements into product specifications.

Automobile companies continually redesign their products to better serve the market. Continuous improvement is also important in the service industries.
© Kevin Horan/Tony Stone Images

Quality Function Deployment

Quality function deployment (QFD) is a technique that helps companies translate customer design requirements into product specifications. It is a way for companies to stay close to customers and build their expectations into products. This technique uses a quality chart that directly relates what customers want with how goods will be designed and produced to satisfy those wants. The QFD chart thus provides customer-based guidelines for developing the best design.

Benchmarking is the process of rating a company's products against the best products in the world, including those in other industries. "The best" includes both functional characteristics of products and customer satisfaction ratings. Benchmarking allows a firm to set performance targets and continuously reach toward those targets. For example, one type of benchmarking develops a competitive profile against an industry average. In the automobile industry, J. D. Powers, an independent research firm, gathers customer satisfaction data on numerous models of cars and sells this information to automobile firms. These firms can then compare their performance to an average derived from the aggregate industry data.

Continuous Improvement

Continuous improvement is a commitment to constantly seek ways of doing things better in order to maintain and improve quality. Companywide teams try to prevent problems and systematically improve key processes instead of troubleshooting problems as they occur. Continuous improvement also means looking for innovative production methods, shortening product-development time, and continually measuring performance using statistical methods.

Continuous improvement can be used in service companies as well as in manufacturing companies. Paine & Associates, a California public relations firm, implemented a continuous improvement approach to stimulate creative thinking for media campaigns. A series of minor changes, ranging from inviting more people to brainstorming sessions to using creativity tools such as flash cards resulted in such improvement, that in 1994 the agency was rated as one of the top 10 most creative agencies in the country.[9]

Reduced Cycle Time

One of the most effective ways to improve the quality of both goods and services is to reduce **cycle time,** which is the time from when production begins until the good or service is received by the customer. Companies with faster cycle times than their competitors can earn profits more quickly and dramatically increase their growth.

DuPont's Kalrez, a rubbery plastic, had a 90 percent market share in 1988, but Japanese competitors gained market share by offering better customer service. DuPont retaliated by shortening the time that it took to make Kalrez from 70 days to 16, cutting its order-filling lead times from 40 days to 16, and increasing on-time deliveries from 70 percent to 100 percent. Within three years, DuPont's Kalrez sales had gone up 22 percent.[10]

Analysis of Process Problems

Firms that want to engage in continuous improvement need methods for identifying the causes of problems. Statistical quality control is one tool used for identifying causes of problems. **Statistical quality control (SQC)** is a method of analyzing deviations in manufactured materials, parts, and goods. It was pioneered by Dr. W. Edwards Deming, a leader in the TQM movement in Japan, who believed that a statistical understanding of systems allows accurate diagnosis and solution of problems. Data such as output per hour, percentages of defects, and the time each operation takes are gathered and analyzed so improvements can be made. SQC enables engineers to determine which errors are avoidable and which are not and to find the causes of the controllable problems.

Pareto analysis is a method for identifying a company's biggest problems. The chief tool of Pareto analysis is a bar chart that ranks problems in descending order, usually based on their frequency of occurrence. Most companies find that the worst problems occur again and again. Thus, the most frequent problems can have the most negative impact on quality. The Pareto principle states that 80 percent of the problems are due to 20 percent of the causes. Pareto analysis directs management to concentrate on the biggest problems first. Then the next-most-frequent problems can be addressed, and so on, in a continuous attempt to improve quality. Exhibit 13.2 is an example of a Pareto chart for a package delivery company.

PARTICIPANTS IN THE QUALITY EFFORT

Top and middle management, employees, and suppliers all play an important role in making quality improvements.

Management

The vision and strategy underlying quality are built by top management, whose commitment must be more than just lip service. Top management is responsible for putting systems into place to implement quality efforts. One way for management to gain companywide support for TQM is to provide compensation or benefits tied to quality goals. For example, a number of health-maintenance organizations are beginning to survey their members every year to see how members like their physicians. Incentive pay for physicians is then tied in part to their scores on these patient questionnaires.

---

benchmarking
The process of rating a company's products against the best products in the world, including those in other industries.

continuous improvement
A commitment to constantly seek ways of doing things better in order to maintain and improve quality.

cycle time
Time from when production begins until the good is received by the customer.

statistical quality control (SQC)
A method of analyzing deviations in manufactured materials, parts, and goods.

Pareto analysis
A method for identifying a company's biggest problems using a bar chart that ranks problems in descending order, usually based on the events' frequency of occurrence.

4 Describe the roles of management, employees, and suppliers in quality improvement programs.

Exhibit 13.2

Pareto Chart Showing Elements That Affect Customer Satisfaction for a Package Delivery Company

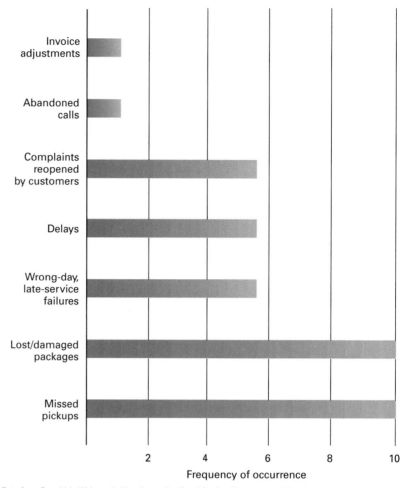

Source: Data from Donald L. Weintraub, "Implementing Total Quality Management." Reprinted by permission from the first quarter 1991 issue of *Prism,* the journal for senior management, published by Arthur D. Little, Inc.

Top management's commitment to TQM should filter down to supervisory levels of management. Middle managers become the conduit between top management and the employees who have the most contact with customers. Middle managers also become involved in designing and implementing quality programs for employees.

Employees

Employee participation in quality programs has three key ingredients:

- *Empowerment:* Empowering the workforce—delegating decision-making authority to employees, as described in Chapter 1—encourages more positive attitudes toward the job, helps to reduce cycle time, and frees management to spend more time formulating strategy. Examples abound of the positive effects of empowerment. AT&T Universal Card Services (UCS) became the second largest universal card (a combination general-purpose credit and long-distance calling card) in the industry in just 30 months. UCS management feels that empowered employees play a key role in "delighting the customer." For instance, customer-contact employees can grant credit line increases and adjust customers' bills without management approval. The company reports that over 98 percent of its customers rate overall service as better than the competition.[11]

- *Teamwork:* Teamwork is achieved when people work together to reach a common goal, and it means sharing both responsibility and decision making. Instead of competing with one another, as is common in many companies, employees work together. Employee teams facilitated and enhanced the operation of Arvin North American Automotive's quality system. Arvin North American is a leading manufacturer of automotive exhaust systems. These teams held weekly brainstorming sessions on how to implement quality concepts taught during training. The teams also submitted 521 improvement proposals in one year—all but 7 were approved by management. Such proposals have dramatically reduced waste throughout the organization, boosting the bottom line.[12]

Arvin Industries
What is Arvin's Quality Policy? How do they express their commitment to total customer satisfaction?

http://www.arvin.com/

- *Training:* Training employees in quality techniques is a central part of TQM. Training helps employees understand the corporate mission, their jobs, and TQM principles and measurement tools. Marlow Industries, a Dallas firm that makes custom thermoelectric coolers, was the 1991 small-business winner of the Baldrige Award for quality. The average Marlow employee spent almost 50 hours in training in 1991. Thomas Interior Systems, a small Chicago-area firm that designs and resells office furnishings, spends an amount equal to 2.5 percent of its total annual payroll costs on education and training. Each Thomas employee is required to spend 40 hours per year in training. This training takes place during employees' normal work schedules, and employees are paid their normal wage or salary for participating.[13]

Suppliers

Companies that adopt quality programs tend to encourage suppliers to start quality programs of their own. When one company is trying to produce defect-free output, it cannot tolerate defects in the materials and parts it buys from suppliers. Many firms are moving toward long-term contracts with fewer suppliers but are requiring better quality.

The examples of suppliers' involvement in quality are plentiful. Maremont Exhaust Products, a manufacturer of replacement exhaust products, has developed a comprehensive data tracking and Quality Problem Report (QPR) system to give its suppliers the information they need to improve their performance.[14] Motorola's Paging Products Group has won 60 percent global market share due partly to cooperation with suppliers that has brought significant advances in quality and technology amidst reductions in cost and cycle time. Supply costs have fallen 8 to 10 percent per year for many years.[15] Wilson Oxygen, a regional company in Austin, Texas, sells industrial products like welding supplies, beverage-dispensing systems, and industrial gases. Wilson has a quality evaluation team that works with suppliers to reduce costs by eliminating errors and improving service.[16]

The concept of just-in-time (JIT) inventory management, which will be discussed in detail in Chapter 14, is another example of how TQM has motivated closer cooperation between manufacturers and their suppliers. Quality is critical for suppliers of companies that use JIT, because poor-quality parts and supplies may not be detected if they are delivered at the last minute.

SERVICE QUALITY

Most products have some services associated with them. For example, a car purchase involves many additional services; all maintenance and warranty work is a form of service. There are also businesses in which service is the major output, such as restaurants, hotels, health care, and overnight delivery services. Whether one is talking about services that support a product, or service-focused industries, service quality is an important component of customer value, and it affects customer satisfaction ratings. Indeed, business executives rank the improvement of service quality as one of the most critical challenges facing them today. Thus, organizations are looking for creative ways to increase service quality:

- Many airline companies are enhancing their international premium-class services. For example, American Airlines is giving first- and business-class passengers more leg room and better food. British Airways' first-class passengers will sit in a semiprivate pear-wood berth featuring a seat that converts into a bed.[17]

- A tourist boom in Australia has resulted in a number of hotels turning to customer service–oriented courses to help them gain a competitive advantage. One nonprofit organization called AussieHost offers a training program for contact-level employees to improve the quality of customer service by instilling pride and professionalism in participants.[18]

- In the health care industry, a number of managed care companies are improving the quality of care by investing in preventive service programs for chronic ailments such as asthma and diabetes.[19]

Categories of Service

5 Distinguish between the three categories of services.

Service can be subdivided into three categories.[20] Managers who are concerned about improving service quality need to pay attention to all three of the following categories:

- *Presale service* furnishes the customer with information and assistance in the decision-making process. An example of an industry in which presale services are undergoing a revolution is the automobile industry. The dreaded auto showroom with its fast-talking salesmen and high-pressure tactics is becoming an endangered species. Car shoppers are using Internet buying services to examine car specifications and check prices. They are calling auto brokers who will handle the work of negotiating for them. Consumers are also visiting giant used-auto malls like CarMax where they can browse through the offerings from easy-to-use com-

Shoppers at Sam's Club in Atlanta can buy a Mercedes to go with their motor oil. Car buyers are referred to dealers who sell for a fixed price.
© Ann States/SABA

puter kiosks that print information on any car selected, and, best of all, they do not have to haggle about prices.[21]

Presale service may also be as simple as responding to a potential customer's questions in a timely fashion. Texas Instruments (TI) gets about 200,000 inquiries from potential customers each year. Over 95 percent of those inquiries get an answer within 2 hours, and virtually all inquiries get an answer within 24 hours. TI has developed an internal tracking system to ensure that no customer inquiries fall through the cracks. Such a swift response creates a positive image for all of TI's products. Presale service is not limited to manufacturing companies: Some insurance companies, for example, do a thorough needs analysis for potential customers to help them choose the best types of insurance.

- *Transaction service* is directly associated with the exchange transaction between a firm and its customers. One common type of transaction service is providing a fax number so customers can order by fax; some companies go a step further and give customers a computer and modem loaded with ordering software to speed order cycle times. Still others are beginning to take orders over the Internet.

  Transaction service could also include prompt dissemination of information about inventory surpluses or shortages, changes in lot sizes, or order fill rates. It could include commitment to firm delivery dates, as well as financing and credit terms. At a hotel or an airline, transaction service might include efficient check-in procedures.

- *Postsale service* occurs after the transaction. This is the support service that firms have traditionally stressed. For example, if an order is delayed, then the postsale service of providing information about the status of the order, back orders, or shipping delays becomes important. Customer service and complaint resolution processes also become important in such situations.

SERVICE QUALITY COMPONENTS

Customers evaluate service quality by the following five components:[22]

- *Reliability:* the ability to perform the service dependably, accurately, and consistently. Reliability is performing the service right the first time. This component has been found to be the one most important to consumers.

- *Responsiveness:* the ability to provide prompt service. Examples of responsiveness include calling the customer back quickly, serving lunch fast to someone who is in a hurry, or mailing a transaction slip immediately.

- *Assurance:* the knowledge and courtesy of employees and their ability to convey trust. Skilled employees who treat customers with respect and make customers feel that they can trust the firm exemplify assurance.

- *Empathy:* caring, individualized attention to customers. Firms whose employees recognize customers, call them by name, and learn their customers' specific requirements are providing empathy. A customer satisfaction survey of senior executives showed that MCI Communications was the top choice in long-distance carriers because it pays close attention to subscribers by routinely checking in on them.[23]

- *Tangibles:* the physical evidence of the service. The tangible parts of a service include the physical facilities, tools, and equipment used to provide the service, such as a doctor's office or an ATM, and the appearance of personnel.

6 Describe the components of service quality.

Overall service quality is measured by combining customers' evaluations for all five components. As shown in the "Marketing and Small Business" box, small companies

Marketing and Small Business

AT&T and MCI Take Aim at Internet Access Market

Recently, AT&T and MCI made their intentions of going after the growing Internet access market loud and clear. AT&T is offering all residential long-distance customers who sign up for its World-Net Service in 1996 five free hours of Internet access per month for an entire year. And MCI is touting similar competitive plans for its long-distance customers.

What does this mean for the approximately 3,000 existing Internet service providers (ISPs), many of which are small entrepreneurial companies? "To the entrepreneur, AT&T and MCI present a formidable challenge," says Don Heath, president and CEO of the Internet Society, which seeks global co-operation and coordination for the Internet. "They've got the resources and the capabilities to offer services entrepreneurs can't."

 Still, while AT&T and MCI are liable to snag a siz-able share of the market, a number of small companies providing Internet access don't feel too threatened. For instance, Jennifer Kraljevich, president of Tezcatlipoca, Inc., a Chicago-based Internet service provider with about 1,500 customers, believes that her clients—primarily businesses and "more serious customers than just the casual Web browser"—are different from potential AT&T and MCI recruits. "They'll tend to get people who are less interested in being on the cutting edge and more interested in just access," says Kraljevich.

Industry insiders believe that entrepreneurs have several advantages over the big guys. "Entre-preneurs can provide value that typically the long-distance companies can't," says Heath. "To remain competitive, entrepreneurs must provide the greater services PC owners are looking for." Some of the incentives entrepreneurs can offer include exclusive content and even building Web sites for their customers, says Heath.

Most in the industry agree that one of the best ways entrepreneurs can compete is through customer service. Firms that deliver ongoing technical support and customer service with a personal touch (and no busy signals) are likely to be a big draw.[24]

What components of service quality do small service providers in the Internet industry offer to their customers? Do they have a competitive advantage over larger companies, like AT&T and MCI? What could AT&T do to compete with the Internet entrepreneurs?

can compete effectively with large companies by paying close attention to the components of service quality.

THE GAP MODEL OF SERVICE QUALITY

7 Explain the gap model of service quality.

gap model
A model of service quality that identifies five gaps that can cause problems in service delivery and influence customer evaluations of service quality.

A model of service quality called the **gap model** identifies five gaps that can cause problems in service delivery and influence customer evaluations of service quality.[25] These gaps are illustrated in Exhibit 13.3:

- *Gap 1:* the gap between what customers want and what management thinks customers want. This gap results from a lack of understanding or a misinterpretation of the customers' needs, wants, or desires. A firm that does little or no customer satisfaction research is likely to experience this gap. An important step in closing gap 1 is to keep in touch with what customers want by doing research on customer needs and customer satisfaction.

- *Gap 2:* the gap between what management thinks customers want and the quality specifications that management develops to provide the service. Essentially, this gap is the result of management's inability to translate customers' needs into delivery systems within the firm. For example, Kentucky Fried Chicken once rated its managers' success according to "chicken efficiency," or how much chicken they threw away at the end of the night. Consumers who came in late at night would

Customer

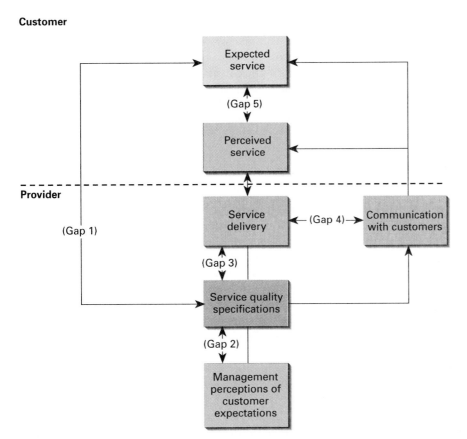

Exhibit 13.3
Gap Model of Service Quality

Source: Adopted with the permission of The Free Press, a division of Simon & Schuster, from *Delivering Quality Service: Balancing Customer Perceptions and Expectations* by Valarie A. Zeithaml, A. Parasuraman, and Leonard L. Berry. Copyright © 1990 by The Press.

either have to wait for chicken to be cooked or settle for chicken several hours old. The "chicken efficiency" measurement did not take customers into account, and financial performance suffered.[26]

- *Gap 3:* the gap between the service quality specifications and the service that is actually provided. If both gaps 1 and 2 have been closed, then gap 3 is due to the inability of management and employees to do what should be done. Poorly trained or poorly motivated workers can cause this gap. Management needs to ensure that employees have the skills and the proper tools to perform their jobs. Other techniques that help to close gap 3 are training employees so they know what management expects and encouraging teamwork.

- *Gap 4:* the gap between what the company provides and what the customer is told it provides. This is clearly a communication gap. It may include misleading or deceptive advertising campaigns promising more than the firm can deliver or doing "whatever it takes" to get the business. To close this gap, companies need to create realistic customer expectations through honest, accurate communication about what the firms can provide.

- *Gap 5:* the gap between the service that customers receive and the service they want. This gap can be positive or negative. For example, if a patient expects to wait 20 minutes in the physician's office before seeing the physician but waits only 10 minutes, the patient's evaluation of service quality will be high. However, a 40-minute wait would result in a lower evaluation.

When any one or more of these gaps are large, service quality is perceived as low. As the gaps shrink, service quality improves. Taco Bell, for example, had problems with gap 3, the gap between management's specifications for service quality and actual service delivery. Management's mistake was using the traditional methods to keep workers "under control." The result was high turnover and low morale—and, consequently, poor service to customers. Once management recognized the source of the problem, it started a program that transferred more control to the workers. By narrowing gap 3 and actually delivering the level of service that management knew was necessary in a competitive market, the company started to become more successful.[27]

VALUE-BASED PRICING

8 Discuss the components of value-based pricing.

value-based pricing
A pricing strategy that has grown out of the quality movement.

Value-based pricing is a pricing strategy that has grown out of the quality movement. Instead of figuring prices based on costs or competitors' prices, it starts with the customer, considers the competition, and then determines the appropriate price.[28] The basic assumption is that the firm is customer driven, seeking to understand the attributes customers want in the goods and services they buy and the value of that bundle of attributes to customers. Because very few firms operate in a pure monopoly, however, a marketer using value-based pricing must also determine the value to customers of competitive offerings. Customers evaluate the value of a product (not just its price) relative to the value of alternatives. In value-based pricing, therefore, the price of the product is set at a level that seems to the customer to be a good price compared with the prices of other options.

Procter & Gamble developed a new value-based pricing program after recognizing that pricing problems were behind lagging sales of such products as Tide detergent, Crest toothpaste, Vicks cough syrup, and Pampers diapers. Consumer demand for these products had fallen because their prices were higher than prices for competing brands. To restore sales, P&G shifted from a strategy of maintaining high list prices but offering frequent and irregular discounts to a value-pricing strategy based on everyday low prices (a strategy discussed in Chapter 21).[29]

In the automobile industry, value-based pricing is taking the form of one-price selling—that is, selling cars with a fixed set of popular options (such as air-conditioning, power windows and door locks, and a rear-window defroster) at a low, usually nonnegotiable package price. The base-level automobile plus these options would normally cost more. General Motors pioneered this pricing strategy in 1990 with the introduction of its Saturn line of cars.[30]

transaction cost
The immediate financial outlay or commitment that a customer must make, the purchase price.

life cycle cost
The expected additional cost that a customer will incur over the life of the product.

risk
The uncertainty about long-term costs.

nonmonetary sacrifice
The time and effort customers invest when making a purchase or receiving postsale services.

An important point about value-based pricing is that it does not simply reduce prices; it takes into account customers' perceptions of value. Earlier in the chapter, customer value was defined as the ratio of benefits to the sacrifice necessary to obtain those benefits. Customer sacrifice usually consists of transaction costs, life cycle costs, and some amount of risk. The **transaction cost** is the immediate financial outlay or commitment that a customer must make—in other words, the purchase price. The **life cycle cost** is the expected additional cost that a customer will incur over the life of the product. Because the life cycle cost is inherently based on expectations, there also is some degree of **risk** involved, which is the uncertainty about long-term costs. Another component of cost is **nonmonetary sacrifice**, which is the time and effort customers invest when making a purchase or receiving postsale services.

Transaction Costs

For a simple product with a short period of expected use, the transaction cost dominates the customer's decision process. There are very few life cycle costs associated with a can of vegetables, a soft drink, or a bottle of wine. Some small element of risk may be involved, such as choosing a wine that tastes bad, but the perceived risk is minor for many products.

Transaction costs represent a major decision criterion for undifferentiated products—those that differ very little from competing offerings. Because the customer can't make a choice on the basis of the product's attributes, the transaction cost, or price, becomes more important. For example, most consumers view gasoline as a generic, undifferentiated product and are sensitive to a price change of only a few cents per gallon. Texaco is attempting to overcome that perception by presenting a high-quality image for its System 3 gasoline. If Texaco succeeds in differentiating its gasoline somewhat, it will be able to charge a slightly higher price and still convey good value to customers.

Life Cycle Costs

The longer the expected life of the product, the more important life cycle cost becomes. One of the reasons that Caterpillar has been so successful is that, although transaction costs for its heavy equipment are higher than the competition's, life cycle costs are much lower. Thus, the total financial sacrifice is lower. Similarly, Hewlett-Packard has a dominant position in the laser printer market because its high transaction costs are offset by lower life cycle costs.

Life cycle costs are a factor in one of the problems facing the auto industry. The high transaction costs of new cars lead customers to keep their older cars longer. Car buyers see better value in keeping the old car, even with its higher life cycle costs of maintenance and repair.

Marketers of durable goods—such as automobiles, clothes washers and dryers, and televisions—must be aware that customers always form perceptions of expected life cycle costs. In the absence of information on which to base judgments, customer perceptions become subjective and often depend on brand image. The implication is that managers must understand the relative importance of life cycle costs in customers' decision processes. When life cycle costs are important, marketers should convey specific information that helps customers accurately formulate their expectations.

When buying such durable goods as televisions, consumers often form perceptions of expected life cycle costs based on brand image.
© Terry Vine/Tony Stone Images

Risk

The longer the expected life of the product, the more important risk becomes. With a long-lived product, the customer has trouble accurately evaluating how long it will last, and so financial sacrifice is harder to determine.

Let's assume that you need a new set of tires for your car. Your expected benefits might consist of 40,000 miles of tire life, certain performance and handling characteristics, and a road hazard warranty. Your sacrifice would be the transaction cost—say, $80 per tire—and the life cycle costs of rotating the tires each year and repairing flat tires. But if the tires last for only 25,000 or 30,000 or 35,000 miles instead of the 40,000 you expect, what happens to your perception of value? Unfortunately, you can never know for sure exactly how long tires will last, so some element of risk always enters the equation.

To overcome consumers' concerns about risk, marketers often offer warranties. In the auto industry, late-model used cars are often sold with an additional "maintenance policy." These policies, which typically cost $500 to $1,000, are an opportunity for the car buyer to reduce the higher risk of buying a used car. As the transaction costs of used cars and their expected life have increased, the perceived risk of buying them also has increased, creating an opportunity to sell a new service.

Nonmonetary Sacrifice

Along with the money customers give up to purchase a good or service, they also give up their time and they expend effort. The term "nonmonetary sacrifice" is used to represent the time and effort dimension of "price." Many customers, in certain situations, are willing to trade off monetary and nonmonetary sacrifice. For example, while small convenience stores like 7-Eleven may charge more for some items, customers who do not want to spend time in a large supermarket to hunt down one loaf of bread or a gallon of milk are willing to pay more because they can save time.

Companies that want to create a competitive advantage in today's value-conscious marketplace need to pay attention to ways they can increase customer convenience. A number of firms have successfully addressed issues of nonmonetary sacrifice. For example, United Airlines and Hilton Hotels and Resorts are testing a service that allows first- and business-class passengers to receive their room assignments and keys on board the airplane. Hyatt Hotels is testing automatic check-in kiosks and room-key dispensers.[31] Harris Methodist Hospital in Fort Worth, Texas, redesigned the service areas and systems in their emergency room to sharply reduce waiting times. As a result of their efforts, patient satisfaction scores are up, and Harris received one of five Quality Cup awards presented by the Rochester Institute of Technology and *USA Today*.[32]

CUSTOMER SATISFACTION

When maximizing customer value is the organization's goal, it needs to know how well it is meeting customer expectations. Customer satisfaction is the feeling that a product has met or exceeded the customer's expectations. An organization cannot always rely on customers to make their feelings known, however, and so it may deliberately set out to measure customer satisfaction levels.

Measurement of Customer Satisfaction

A program to measure customer satisfaction should be a permanent, ongoing process that translates what customers want into usable data. It should define in customers' own words what they want in goods and services in terms of product attributes and quality level. Customer satisfaction measurement should also provide insight into the price perspectives of customers. Current customers, lost customers, and potential customers should be included in measuring customer satisfaction.

A good example of a comprehensive customer satisfaction measurement program is that of the California Department of Parks and Recreation (DPR). Customer satisfaction surveys form a key component of DPR's quality improvement process. Data collected from 9,000 surveys per quarter at the 268 California state parks enable park management to continually fine-tune its service strategies. For instance, based on feedback from concerned visitors, park officials began collecting data on boating and jet-ski accidents at Lake Perris in southern California. Over a five-year period there were 480 accidents at Lake Perris, a majority of them involving drivers between 23 and 33 years old. Before the survey, rangers believed that the accidents were alcohol related and were ready to ban alcohol at the lake. However, the data revealed that the major cause of accidents was inexperienced operators. This insight led park officials to shift their focus to boating safety education. After monitoring the program's impact for one summer, they saw a 31 percent drop in vessel accidents.[33]

Like DPR, in order to begin improving customer satisfaction, a company needs to be able to clearly identify the attributes that convey value to the customer.[34] In order to identify these attributes, a company needs to measure customer expectations, perceptions of performance, and perceptions of importance for each value component—namely, product, service, and price. However, a good customer satisfaction measurement program generates more than just empirical data about customers' expectations and perceptions. It also captures qualitative inputs that do not typically result from traditional marketing research, making the customer an integral part of a firm's learning and decision processes. For example, a series of focus group interviews with small groups of customers could provide valuable input about how a company could improve delivery times or enhance customer service.

Customer Satisfaction or Customer Dissatisfaction?

When designing customer satisfaction measurement programs, businesses need to understand the *two-factor model of customer satisfaction*. This model suggests that the same factors that contribute to satisfaction *may not necessarily* contribute to dissatisfaction. One category of factors is called hygiene factors. **Hygiene factors** are factors *that contribute to customer dissatisfaction*. The second category is called satisfiers. **Satisfiers** are factors that *contribute to customer satisfaction*.

Customers can tell organizations why they are satisfied or dissatisfied with a product or a service. However, sometimes the factors that make customers dissatisfied are not the same as the factors that make them satisfied. The absence of, or low performance on, some attributes may quickly cause customer dissatisfaction. High performance on those same attributes may contribute very little to high levels of customer satisfaction. Conversely, the factors that cause customer satisfaction may not be identified as factors that cause customer dissatisfaction. Thus, low performance on attributes causing high satisfaction does not necessarily cause customer dissatisfaction. It is important to note that hygiene and satisfier factors may vary with different groups of customers. Customer satisfaction research can be designed to determine which factors customers perceive as belonging in the hygiene category and which factors they perceive as being satisfiers.

If a firm performs at a very high level in delivering the hygiene attributes, customers will perceive the product or service as being acceptable but not spectacular. Hygiene attributes collectively constitute some minimum level of satisfaction, and failure to meet that minimum will cause customers to become dissatisfied. Performing at a very high level on hygiene attributes might yield the customer response "So what? You're expected to do that."

For example, assume that customers expect a hotel room to be clean. If the room is not clean when they arrive, they will be dissatisfied. It will not matter if the bed is

9 Explain the two major determinants of customer satisfaction.

hygiene factors
Factors that contribute to customer dissatisfaction.

satisfiers
Factors that contribute to customer satisfaction.

comfortable, the colors of the room are pretty, or the bathroom is big and luxurious. Failure to deliver on the hygiene attribute of cleanliness will lead to customer dissatisfaction. If the room is clean, customers probably will not even notice, because cleanliness is, at minimum, what they expect. Thus, cleanliness does not have as strong an effect on satisfaction as it does on dissatisfaction.

The hygiene attributes must be delivered at an acceptable level of performance before the satisfiers become important. Once the customer's expectations on hygiene elements have been met, then the satisfiers have the potential to create higher levels of customer satisfaction. In the hotel example, if the room is clean, then the comfortable bed, pretty colors, and luxurious bathroom may each contribute to higher satisfaction levels.

When measuring customer satisfaction, both the hygiene factors and the satisfiers that are important to customers need to be identified and evaluated. Therefore, management needs to ask its customers the right questions. The experience of United Parcel Service, Inc. (UPS), is a good example of the importance of asking the right questions. UPS had always assumed that on-time delivery was the most important concern of customers, and all other activity came second. UPS's definition of quality centered almost exclusively on the results of time-and-motion studies. Knowing the average time it took elevator doors to open on a certain city block and calculating how long it took people to answer their doorbells were critical parts of the quality equation. The corners of delivery vans were shaved off so drivers could climb out of their trucks more easily. Customer satisfaction surveys asked clients whether they were pleased with UPS's delivery time and whether they

Ethics in Marketing

American Cancer Society Exchanges Endorsements for Donations

The American Cancer Society is selling its name to two corporate giants, offering exclusive endorsements to NicoDerm antismoking patches and Florida orange juice for at least $4 million.

Nicotine patches, worn on the arm, gradually ooze nicotine into the smoker's body, helping stave off the craving for cigarettes. SmithKline Beecham, the British-based drug manufacturer, will pay the cancer society at least $1 million per year in sales royalties for three years. In exchange, the society's logo will appear on NicoDerm CQ boxes and advertising, along with a reference to the two as partners in promoting smoking cessation.

In a similar deal, the Florida Citrus Marketers Association agreed to pay the American Cancer Society at least $1 million for one

year. Although there is no direct proof that drinking orange juice prevents cancer, the American Cancer Society says drinking it can be part of a healthy diet and "eating healthy is one of the major preventive measures against cancer."

Ethics watchdogs protested the deals, saying the society may seriously hurt its credibility. "If they want to endorse products, they should do it in the spirit of an educational agency, not as a paid shill," said Paul Root Wolpe of the Center for Bioethics at the University of Pennsylvania.

The deals—part of a rising trend of partnerships between nonprofit

groups and companies—will provide the society with needed cash to boost its cancer-fighting programs and to meet a $427 million annual budget at a time when donations are stagnant. They also give the marketers of these products instant credibility through their association with one of the nation's most respected health groups. But if the trend accelerates, Wolpe predicted, medical organizations will someday be endorsing everything from tires and chewing gum to sneakers.[36]

Do you think an endorsement from the American Cancer Society will influence consumers' satisfaction with NicoDerm and orange juice? If so, why? What ethical issues surround paid product endorsements?

thought the company could be faster. When UPS recently began asking broader questions about how it could improve service, it discovered that clients were not as obsessed with on-time delivery as previously thought. UPS management was surprised to learn that customers wanted more interaction with the drivers, which was the only face-to-face contact any of them had with the company. If drivers were less harried and more willing to talk, customers could get some practical advice on shipping.[35] Thus, for UPS customers, on-time delivery is a hygiene factor, whereas drivers who had time to interact is a satisfier.

Customer satisfaction is an important goal toward which companies should strive. However, as the "Ethics in Marketing" box indicates, striving for higher satisfaction levels may sometimes present ethical dilemmas.

Customer Loyalty

On average, American corporations lose half of their customers in five years.[37] Keeping customers satisfied by offering them superior value will increase the chances that they will become loyal customers, ensuring a company's long-time survival and growth. Loyal customers are more profitable to companies than those who are not loyal, as shown in Exhibit 13.4. The economic effects of customer loyalty include:

10 Name the economic effects of customer loyalty.

acquisition cost
The cost of bringing in new customers including advertising, sales calls, needs research, and data-entry costs.

1. *Lower acquisition cost:* **Acquisition cost** is the cost of bringing in new customers, including advertising, sales-calls, needs-research, and data-entry costs. While these costs may be the same per customer for loyal and nonloyal customers, overall acquisition costs will eventually be lower for companies with a large loyal cus-

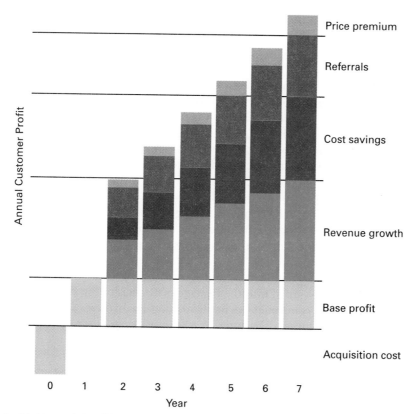

Exhibit 13.4
Why Loyal Customers Are More Profitable

The LX 450

Lexus gets more customers from referrals from satisfied customers than from any other source.
Courtesy of Lexus, A Division of Toyota Motor Sales, Inc. Photography: © Rick Rusing; © Kathleen Norris Cook.

base profit
The profit on basic purchases, unaffected by time, loyalty, efficiency, or other considerations.

tomer base because they need to generate fewer new customers on a regular basis.

2. *Base profit:* All customers buy some product or service and pay a price higher than the company's costs. This profit on basic purchases, unaffected by time, loyalty, efficiency, or other considerations, is called **base profit.** The longer a company keeps a customer, the longer it will earn this base profit.

3. *Revenue growth:* In most businesses, customer spending tends to accelerate over time. In retailing, for example, customers who buy clothing eventually notice that the store carries other products, like shoes or fine china, and begins to purchase these other products. Thus, per-customer revenues grow.

4. *Cost savings:* As customers get to know a business, they learn to be more efficient. They do not waste time requesting products or services the company does not provide, nor are they as dependent on employees for information and advice. In financial planning, for instance, planners spend about five times as many hours on a first-year client as they do on a repeat customer. Over time, collaborative learning between customer and company creates productivity advantages that directly translate into lower costs.

5. *Referrals:* Satisfied customers tend to recommend a business to others. For example, Lexus gets more new customers from referrals than any other source.

6. *Price premium:* Loyal customers who feel they are getting superior value will tend to be less price sensitive than nonloyal customers.

Along with customer loyalty, business loyalty has two other dimensions—employee loyalty and investor loyalty. U.S. corporations, on average, lose half of their employees in four years and half of their investors in less than one year. Companies with enduring records of success, however, have understood that they have to develop loyal customers and loyal employees so that investors can profit over the long haul.

One company that successfully practices loyalty-based management is USAA, a San Antonio, Texas, insurance and investment management firm that serves active and retired military officers and their families. USAA has grown from $207 million of assets under management 26 years ago to over $34 billion in 1996. With this growth, employee defection rates have shrunk from 43 percent to just over 5 percent. Customer retention is within one percentage point of zero defections. USAA has worked hard to understand the characteristics of loyalty, refined its ability to achieve continuous improvement in the creation of value, and incorporated what it has learned into the management decision-making process.

A number of companies are implementing ways of creating loyalty in customers and employees. The Internet is an effective tool for generating loyalty in customers, because of its ability to interact with the customer. With the Internet, companies can use e-mail for fast customer service, discussion groups for building a sense of community, and database tracking of buying habits for customizing products.[38] Cable and Wireless Communications, a long-distance carrier, has generated loyal business clients by providing the best customer support in the telecommunications industry. Cable and Wireless also provides direct sales consultation that gives salespeople intimate knowledge of what makes its customers successful, allowing prod-

uct customization.[39] To generate employee loyalty, Continental Airlines brings its workers into the decision-making process and rewards all employees every month the airline finishes in the top half of the Department of Transportation's rankings of on-time flights.[40] Kinko's attempts to remove barriers that hinder employees (called "coworkers") and give them good benefits.[41]

LOOKING BACK

The trends described in the story at the beginning of this chapter offer consumers greater value in terms of more convenience, less time and effort spent shopping, personal service, solid brands, packaging, and emotionally satisfying products. Most should agree that these benefits offer value. A number of companies, such as those discussed in this chapter, are currently providing these kinds of value to customers. You may also be able to identify companies in your area that offer superior value.

SUMMARY

1 *Define customer value.* Customer value is the ratio of benefits to the sacrifice necessary to obtain those benefits.

2 *Describe the customer value triad.* The customer value triad is based on three things: goods quality, service quality, and value-based prices. Customer value is created when customer expectations in each of the three areas are met or exceeded. If you fail to meet customer expectations in any one of the three areas, you have not delivered good customer value.

3 *Explain the techniques of quality improvement.* There are five important techniques of quality improvement. *Quality function deployment* (QFD) is a technique using a quality chart to relate the characteristics that customers want in goods to the

KEY TERMS

acquisition cost   *369*

base profit   *370*

benchmarking   *357*

continuous improvement   *357*

customer value triad   *353*

cycle time   *357*

gap model   *362*

hygiene factor   *367*

life cycle cost   *364*

way those goods will be designed and produced. *Benchmarking* is rating a company's product against the best in the world. *Continuous improvement* is a commitment to constantly do things better. Management adopts the perspective of preventing problems and systematically improving key processes instead of troubleshooting problems as they occur. *Reduced cycle time* means reducing the time from when production begins until the good is received by the customer. Companies with faster cycle times than their competitors can earn profits faster and can also dramatically increase growth. *Analysis of process problems* can be accomplished with such tools as statistical quality control, a method of analyzing deviations in manufactured materials, parts, and products; and Pareto analysis, which uses a bar chart to rank causes of variation in production and service in order to identify a company's biggest problems.

4 *Describe the roles of management, employees, and suppliers in quality improvement programs.* Quality improvement programs involve everyone in the organization. Top management must strongly and visibly commit to quality improvement, both with words and with actions. Employee empowerment (giving employees the authority to make decisions), teamwork, and training are critical to the success of quality improvement. Suppliers to companies involved in quality improvement must also adopt quality practices, because when a company is trying to produce defect-free output, it cannot tolerate defects in the materials and parts it buys from suppliers.

5 *Distinguish between the three categories of services.* The first category is presale services. Presale services usually furnish the customer with information and assistance in the decision-making process. The second category of services is transaction services. These are services that are directly associated with the exchange transaction between a firm and its customers. The third category of services consists of those that occur after the transaction, such as automobile maintenance and repair.

6 *Describe the components of service quality.* Customers evaluate service quality on five components. The first is reliability, which is the ability to perform the service dependably, accurately, and consistently. The second component is responsiveness, or the ability to provide prompt service to customers. The third component is assurance, which means the knowledge and courtesy of the employees and their ability to convey trust. Empathy is the fourth component, which involves caring, individualized attention to customers. The fifth component consists of tangibles, which are the physical evidence of the service (for example, facilities, equipment, and the appearance of personnel).

7 *Explain the gap model of service quality.* The gap model of service quality identifies five key discrepancies that can cause problems in service delivery and influence customer evaluations of service quality. When the gaps are large, service quality is low. As the gaps shrink, service quality improves. Gap 1 is the gap between customer expectations and management's perceptions of those expectations. Gap 2 is the gap between management's perception of what the customer wants and specifications for service quality. Gap 3 is the gap between service quality specifications and delivery of the service. Gap 4 is the gap between what service the company delivers and what the company promises to the customer through external communication. Gap 5 is the gap between customers' expectations of the service and their perceptions of how the service was performed.

8 *Describe the components of value-based pricing.* There are four components of value-based pricing. Transaction costs involve the immediate financial outlay or commitment a customer must make. Life cycle costs are the expected additional costs that a customer will incur over the life of the product. Risk involves uncertainty about life cycle costs. Nonmonetary sacrifice is the time and effort given up by consumers to purchase a product or service or to use postsale services.

9 *Explain the two major determinants of customer satisfaction.* The factors that contribute to satisfaction are not necessarily the ones that contribute to dissatisfaction. One category of factors, called hygiene factors, has been found to contribute to dissatisfaction. Hygiene factors collectively constitute a threshold level, and failure to meet that level will cause customers to become dissatisfied; however, performing at a high level will not contribute to satisfaction. The second category of factors, called satisfiers, has been found to contribute to satisfaction. Once the hygiene factors are delivered at an acceptable level, the satisfiers become important.

10 *Name the economic effects of customer loyalty.* The economic effects of customer loyalty are lower overall acquisition cost, more base profit over time, revenue growth, cost savings, more referrals from customers, and the ability to charge a price premium.

Discussion and Writing Questions

1. Using the definition and framework of value presented in the chapter, identify several firms in your town that you think are providing good customer value, and explain why you think they are. Identify firms that are not providing good value, and explain why you think they are not.

2. Go to the library and find information on a company that has recently won the Malcolm Baldrige National Quality Award. Write a short report on how this company won its award.

3. Pick a good or service that you have recently purchased, and identify the presale, transaction, and postsale services that are associated with it. In your opinion, which category of service could the firm most improve on?

4. Analyze a recent experience that you have had with a service business (for example, a hairdresser, movie theater, or restaurant) in terms of your expectations and perceptions about each of the five components of service quality.

5. Apply what you have learned about service quality to the U.S. Post Office or to your university food service, and make recommendations for change if needed.

6. What are the services likely to be associated with the following products?
   a. Television set
   b. Pair of jeans
   c. Newspaper
   d. Dishwasher (built-in)
   e. Automobile
   f. Furniture
   g. Telephone
   h. Pizza

7. For the products listed in Question 6, identify the transaction costs, life cycle costs, and risks that are involved.

8. Thinking in terms of the definition of customer satisfaction in the chapter, describe one situation in which you were satisfied with doing business with a company and one situation in which you were dissatisfied. What did you perceive to be the hygiene factors and satisfiers in these situations? Write a memo to the president of each company, explaining how the company performed on the two factors.

9. Create teams of four students. Two of the students in each group are to be "researchers" and two are to be "customers." Each group should choose a product or service to which the "customers" are loyal. (Examples would be carbonated beverages, a brand of blue jeans, doctors, and hairdressers.) The "researchers" should interview the "customers" about why they are loyal to the product or service.

10. Can an age group represent a culture? How could the culture of the baby boom generation influence marketers interested in providing greater value and satisfaction to those consumers?
http://www.enews.com/magazines/demographics/archive/120195.2.html

11. What is the Ethnic Heritage Council? How might local marketers be able to increase the value of their products and services from consulting with or sponsoring such an organization?
http://www.eskimo.com/~millerd/ehc/

Application for Small Business

Mary Smith has been in the accounting profession for eight years and has decided to open her own accounting firm. She will provide basic accounting services, as well as payroll services for her clients. Mary wants to open her firm in a suburban area adjacent to a large city. There are a number of large, well-established accounting firms in the city and several smaller ones in the suburban area, against which Mary will have to compete. Mary has five employees and an extensive, up-to-date computer system. She plans to design an Internet Web page for her business.

Questions

1. Explain how Mary could apply the customer value triad to develop a marketing strategy for her accounting firm.

2. How can Mary apply the five-component service quality framework (reliability, responsiveness, assurance, empathy, tangibles) to design a quality service? For example, what standards should she use for reliability? How can she be responsive to clients?

3. What could Mary do to develop loyal customers?

Video Case

Stew Leonard's

Stew Leonard's is featured in *Ripley's Believe It or Not* and the *Guinness Book of Records* as the world's largest dairy store. Over one million customers shop in Stew's Norwalk and Danbury, Connecticut, stores every month. With only 1,300 products (compared with the 20,000 to 25,000 products found in the average grocery store), the sales per square foot at Stew Leonard's is greater than those of any other food store in the world. Annually, this store moves $88 million in merchandise, compared to $14 million for leading grocery chains.

In 1921, Stew's father started the Clover Farms Dairy. By the 1950s, Stew was running the milk delivery business. As times changed, more people started buying milk from their local stores, and less milk was delivered. In the 1960s, Stew built a dairy store where customers could see the milk being processed and bottled fresh. In 1969, a petting farm was opened to entertain kids.

Four key elements make Stew Leonard's such a popular store. First, prices are good. Stew Leonard's buys direct from many suppliers, thereby eliminating the middleman. These savings are then passed on to the customers. For example, a gallon of low-fat milk at Stew Leonard's sells for $1.78, compared with $2.39 at competing stores.

Second, product quality is stressed. Stew Leonard's works as a team with its suppliers to ensure consistent quality food. Hot and cold prepared foods are made daily in Stew Leonard's sparkling kitchens. Fresh bakery goods are also prepared daily in the "world's largest store bakery," which sells $120,000 worth of breads, muffins, croissants, and cookies each week. The warehouse produce manager is instructed to reject a shipment if he is confident it does not meet quality standards.

Third, Stew Leonard had made his store a fun place to shop. For example, cartoon characters walk the store aisles, shaking hands with customers, posing for pictures, and handing out free samples. In-store robots serenade customers as they shop, and a mechanical cow moos whenever someone presses its nose. A toy train whizzes overhead in the dairy section, entrancing kids and adults alike.

Finally, satisfying the customer is an important part of the Stew Leonard philosophy. This philosophy is exemplified in the letters of Stew's name, which stand for Satisfy, Teamwork, Excellence, Wow, and Success. At Stew Leonard's, the customer is never wrong. Stew Leonard believes that everyone's job is to please customers because only happy customers come back. Key components in the company's customer service strategies include hiring from within, encouraging employees to wear name tags displaying only their first names, and offering customer service phones.

Stew also continually taps his customers for ideas. One idea generator is a suggestion box where customers place approximately 100 suggestions per day. These suggestions are typed every day and distributed to employees. Another way Stew finds out what his customers want is through frequent focus groups.

The company has also had a mail-order gift business for several years, focusing on major holidays such as Christmas, Valentine's Day, and Easter. In early 1995, Leonard began selling his private-label ketchup to a New York distributor, which placed it in Japanese supermarkets. Other private-label items being developed include mayonnaise, jellies, and bottled water. A third store location is planned for Connecticut or Westchester County, New York.

Questions

1. How does Stew Leonard's offer superior value to its customers?
2. Evaluate Stew Leonard's on the five components of service quality.
3. Explain what you think the satisfiers and dissatisfiers would be for customers of Stew Leonard's.

References

Phyllis Berman, "Like Father, Like Son," *Forbes*, 20 May 1996, p. 44.

Roseanne Harper, "Stew's Catalog for Valentine Gets Heartier," *Supermarket News*, 6 February 1995, p. 23.

Rosner, Hillary, "The Gospel According to Stew," *Brandweek*, 25 March 1996, p. 30.

"Stew Leonard's Eyes Site for Third Unit," *Supermarket News*, 1 January 1996, p. 6.

"Stew's Scores in Japan," *Progressive Grocer*, June 1995, p. 16.

Critical Thinking Case

SHAVING SYSTEMS BY GILLETTE

The Gillette Company has long dominated the shaving-systems market. From its humble beginnings in 1903, when it sold only 51 sets, it is now the world leader. But while it is best known for its shaving systems, it is in fact a diversified conglomerate with market leadership in writing instruments (Papermate and Waterman pens), household appliances (Braun), toothbrushes (Oral-B), and toiletries. Gillette sells its products in more than 200 countries and territories and manufactures them in 57 plants in 28 countries.

The safety razor exemplifies Gillette's skill in introducing new products. The Trac II and Atra systems were both introduced in the 1970s and were notable successes. But during the 1980s the market began to move toward disposable razors, at the expense of the more durable cartridge shaving systems. One study of the European shaving market revealed that most shavers under 45 years of age were regular users of disposable razors and were not particularly loyal to the Gillette brand name. In fact, the French company Bic had gained a strong foothold in the market for bulk-packaged, low-cost disposable shavers. Shaving implements were fast becoming a commodity, with most consumers shopping on the basis of price rather than quality or brand name.

The Gillette Sensor was introduced in the early 1990s in the U.S., Europe, and Japan, and was priced high compared to disposables. The Sensor sold for anywhere from $1.99 to $3.00 and enjoyed brisk sales in its initial months. The real profits, however, came from the sale of replacement blades. At $.75 each, they had a gross margin of almost 90 percent.

In the first year, the Sensor captured a 7 percent market for replacement blades in the U.S. and Europe, and 42 percent of the combined U.S. and European markets for nondisposable razors.

For customers, the Sensor provided tremendous functionality. It offered a twin-blade cartridge shaving system that was so flexible that it adjusted to the contours of the shaver's face. Moreover, the high-tech image of the sensor made it something more than a simple personal hygiene tool, and its affordable price provided excellent value.

In response to the Sensor's success, Schick introduced two new shaving systems. The Schick "Silk Effects" was exclusively designed for women. Its features included pivoting twin blades that self-adjust for a smooth, close shave, nonslip grooves on curved sides of the handle to ensure a firm grip, a holding tray for the razor, and a flip-top dispenser to house replacement cartridges. The men's version, Tracer, also had flexible blades that actually bend and flex to conform to the face, giving men with normal skin a closer, smoother shave. Both came with an unconditional guarantee.

Gillette did not relax after its early success with the Sensor. In 1994, it launched the SensorExcel, first in Europe and Japan, and later in the U.S. Using the latest technology available, the SensorExcel is considered to be the cream of the crop among razor systems. The new razor has tiny "fins" that stretch the skin

and allow the whiskers to stand up to meet the blades' share edges. As with previous systems, the replacement blades carry high margins so the introductory strategy was low prices, heavy couponing, and extensive sampling, particularly in supermarkets.

Early success with SensorExcel led to the introduction of SensorExcel for Women in early 1996, and by 1997 it ranked number one in U.S. razor sales among women. As a Gillette VP said, "SensorExcel changed basic perceptions about shaving among women, from an unappealing—but necessary—chore into an integral element of a woman's beauty routine."

When Gillette introduced its Atra razor systems in 1977, it cannibalized the Trac II system. Similarly, the Sensor and SensorExcel virtually eliminated Gillette's other brands of nondisposable shaving systems. With each new product, the company objective is not only to retain its loyal customer base, but also to gain additional market share from competitors and new users. New product development is, therefore, a continuous process of innovation.

The 1997 marketing effort for Gillette's SensorExcel incorporated a new, direct call to action for male disposable razor users, urging them to "Take the SensorExcel challenge— one shave and we bet you won't go back to disposables." This challenge was to be the brand's marketing platform in North America and western Europe, as well as being incorporated into advertising, consumer promotions, and retail display.

The resounding successes of the Sensor and SensorExcel reasserted Gillette's long-standing position as the market leader, leaving its major competitor Schick far behind. But more important, these successes led to the decline of the disposable, low-margin razors that had been so popular in the last decade. The high quality of the Sensor and SensorExcel blades and the manufacturing expertise of Gillette made it difficult for competitors to manufacture directly competitive products at a comparable price.

Questions

1. Why were the Sensor and SensorExcel a success, particularly against disposable razors?
2. Why was a separate SensorExel for Women introduced?
3. Continuous innovations in companies like Gillette have their risks. If a new product is successful, it cannibalizes the company's existing product line. How might a company judge innovative new products to decide when and how to introduce them?

References

"Taking a Bet on Gillette SensorExcel," *Chemist & Druggist,* 18 January 1997, p. 10.

"Gillette Excel for Women," *Business Wire,* 4 September 1996.

"New Gillette SensorExcel Advertising Takes Direct Aim at Disposable Razor Users," *Business Wire,* 18 December 1996.

Wall Street Journal, 22 April 1994, p. A8.

Additional information can be obtained from the following websites: www.shaving.com; www.gillette.com.br; and www.pbn.com.

Marketing Planning Activities

PRODUCT DECISIONS

The next part of the marketing plan is a description of the elements of the marketing mix, starting with the product or service offering. Be sure that your product plans match the needs and wants of the target market identified and described in the previous section. Also, refer to Exhibit 2.8 for additional marketing plan subjects.

1. What type(s) of consumer or business-to-business product is your chosen firm offering?

2. Place your company's offerings into a product portfolio. Consider the broader impact of marketing a product item within a line or mix. Factors to consider are those such as price, image, complementary products, distribution relationship, and so on.

3. Does your chosen company have a brand name and brand mark? If not, design both. If so, evaluate the ability of the brand name and mark to communicate effectively to the target market.

4. How is your firm's product packaged and labeled? Is the packaging strategy appropriate for the target market(s)? Does the package "fit" with distribution, promotion, and price elements?

5. Evaluate the warranties or guarantees offered by your firm, including product return policies.

Marketing*Builder* Exercise

- **Returns and Adjustments Policy** portion of the **Sales Plan** template

6. Place your company's product in the appropriate stage of the product life cycle. What are the implications of being in this stage? What should your firm prepare for in the future?

Marketing*Builder* Exercise

- **Product Life Cycles** portion of the **Market Analysis** template

7. What categories of adopters are likely to buy your company's products? Is the product diffusing slowly or quickly throughout the marketplace? Why?

8. What service aspects are provided with the product? How is customer service handled? What elements of service quality can your firm focus on?

Marketing*Builder* Exercise

- **Customer Service** portion of the **Sales Plan** template

9. With whom should your chosen company practice relationship marketing?

10. Does the product offer good customer value?

Marketing*Builder* Exercise

- **Product Launch Budget** in the **Marketing Budget** spreadsheet

Distribution Decisions

1 Explain what a marketing channel is and why intermediaries are needed.

2 Describe the functions and activities of marketing channel members.

3 Discuss the differences among marketing channels for consumer and industrial products.

4 Describe alternative channel arrangements.

5 Discuss the issues that influence channel strategy.

6 Discuss channel structure and decisions in global markets.

7 Explain the importance of physical distribution.

8 Discuss the concept of balancing physical distribution service and cost.

9 Describe the subsystems of the physical distribution system.

10 Identify the special problems and opportunities associated with physical distribution in service organizations.

11 Discuss new technology and emerging trends in physical distribution.

Chapter 14

Channels and Physical Distribution

Getting the attention of college students today is not easy. Just ask the large product manufacturers like Kellogg's and Calvin Klein who have attempted to introduce their products and services on campuses throughout the United States. These manufacturers have found that college students are not very receptive to marketing ploys. In fact, most college students maintain a general attitude of distrust toward marketing activities. In addition, most college students are very cautious about advertising and do not appreciate hard selling techniques.

In an effort to get the attention of college students and overcome their reluctance to marketing activities, manufacturers have contracted with marketing organizations who specialize in the college student market. Examples of such organizations include MarketSource, Collegiate Marketing Co., and American Collegiate Marketing who provide services such as distribution of college magazines and newspapers like *U* and *Link,* sponsorship of campus events like concerts and movies, local promotion of products by posters and flyers, and the distribution of sample products.

These specialty organizations have also experienced difficulty marketing to the college student market. Faulty distribution has plagued many of their efforts to distribute free samples and to promote products and services through campus activities. Some distribution problems for free samples include putting samples in areas students do not frequent, such as low-traffic areas of bookstores; making students show identification and sign in to receive samples; and losing samples to visitors, such as high school students or other noncollege students. In addition, there is often a lack of control over how many samples are taken by each person when the samples are distributed. For other promotional activities, such as magazine and newspaper advertisements, the placement of the advertisements may be untimely, with ads running the day after the activity, and posters may never be displayed.

To overcome these problems, organizations such as MarketSource have identified ways to distribute products and services to the college market with the least waste. First, they prefer not to use direct mail or bulk distribution. Oftentimes, the mail never leaves the large boxes in which it is delivered. If the bulk mail is removed from the box, it may never be placed into individual mail boxes. Instead, it is often placed in stacks for passersby. Second, bookstores are being monitored to ensure timely and efficient distribution of samples and promotional materials. Samples or flyers which are distributed through bookstores are coded so they can be tracked to determine which bookstores are following appropriate distribution procedures. For posters, companies are employing resident students to aid in distribution. Student employees are screened thoroughly and paid well to distribute posters and flyers on campuses. In order to monitor student employees, companies provide students with disposable cameras and ask that the students photograph their work. The students are then paid when the film is processed. All of these changes have managed to reduce, but not eliminate, waste in the channel from the product manufacturer to the intended recipients—college students.[1]

What other suggestions would you offer to help improve distribution of samples and promotional materials to college students? What would be the most efficient way to reach college students? Similar questions will be addressed throughout the chapter discussion on marketing channels and physical distribution.

MarketSource Corporation
How does MarketSource describe the college market? What advertising vehicles does it offer to reach college students?
http://www.marketsource.com/

MARKETING CHANNELS AND PHYSICAL DISTRIBUTION

1 Explain what a marketing channel is and why intermediaries are needed.

marketing channel (channel of distribution)
A business structure of interdependent organizations which reaches from the point of product origin to the consumer.

The term *channel* is derived from the Latin word *canalis*, which means canal. A marketing channel can be viewed as a large canal or pipeline through which products, their ownership, communication, financing and payment, and accompanying risk flow to the consumer. Formally, a **marketing channel** (also called a **channel of distribution**) is a business structure of interdependent organizations which reaches from the point of product origin to the consumer. Products move through marketing channels via physical distribution. Physical distribution has five distinct subsystems: warehousing, materials handling and packaging, inventory control, order processing, and transportation. Each of these subsystems, as well as future trends in physical distribution, will be discussed in greater detail later in the chapter. The chapter begins with a discussion of the three important needs fulfilled by marketing channels: providing specialization and division of labor, overcoming discrepancies, and providing contact efficiency.

Providing Specialization and Division of Labor

According to the concept of specialization and division of labor, breaking down a complex task into smaller, simpler ones and allocating them to specialists will create greater efficiency and lower average production costs. Manufacturers achieve economies of scale through the use of efficient equipment capable of producing large quantities of a single product.

Marketing channels can also attain economies of scale through specialization and division of labor by aiding producers who lack the motivation, financing, or expertise to market directly to end users or consumers. In some cases, as with most consumer convenience goods such as soft drinks, the cost of marketing directly to millions of consumers—taking and shipping individual orders—is prohibitive. For this reason, producers hire channel members to do what the producers are not equipped to do or what channel members are better prepared to do. Channel members can do some things more efficiently than producers because they have built good relationships with their customers. Therefore, their specialized expertise enhances the overall performance of the channel.

Overcoming Discrepancies

discrepancy of quantity
The difference between the amount of product produced and the amount an end user wants to buy.

Marketing channels also aid in overcoming discrepancies of quantity, assortment, time, and space created by economies of scale in production. For example, assume that Pillsbury can efficiently produce its Hungry Jack instant pancake mix only at a rate of 5,000 units in a typical day. Not even the most ardent pancake fan could consume that amount in a year, much less in a day. The quantity produced to achieve low unit costs has created a **discrepancy of quantity,** which is the difference between the amount of product produced and the amount an end user wants to buy. By storing the product and distributing it in the appropriate amounts, marketing channels overcome quantity discrepancies by making products available in the quantities that consumers desire.

Mass production creates not only discrepancies of quantity but also discrepancies of assortment. A **discrepancy of assortment** occurs when a consumer does not have all of the items needed to receive full satisfaction from a product. For pancakes to have maximum satisfaction, several other products are required to complete the assortment. At the very least, most people want a knife, fork, plate, butter, and syrup. Others might add orange juice, coffee, cream, sugar, eggs, and bacon or sausage. Even though Pillsbury is a large consumer products company, it does not come close to providing the optimal assortment to go with its Hungry Jack pancakes. To overcome discrepancies of assortment, marketing channels assemble in one place many of the products necessary to complete a consumer's needed assortment.

Pillsbury Company
How does Pillsbury use its Web site to increase demand for its products? Visit a related site, http://bakeoff.com/bakeoff/index.html, for additional clues.

http://www.pillsbury.com/

A **temporal discrepancy** is created when a product is produced but a consumer is not ready to buy it. Marketing channels overcome temporal discrepancies by maintaining inventories in anticipation of demand. For example, manufacturers of seasonal merchandise, such as Christmas decorations, are in operation all year even though consumer demand is concentrated during certain months of the year.

Furthermore, because mass production requires many potential buyers, markets are usually scattered over large geographic regions, creating a spatial discrepancy. Often global, or at least nationwide, markets are needed to absorb the outputs of mass producers. Marketing channels overcome spatial discrepancies by making products available in locations convenient to consumers. For example, automobile manufacturers overcome spatial discrepancies by franchising dealerships close to consumers.

discrepancy of assortment
Lack of all the items a consumer needs to receive full satisfaction from a product.

temporal discrepancy
Difference between when a product is produced and when a consumer is ready to buy it.

Providing Contact Efficiency

The third need fulfilled by marketing channels is a way to overcome contact inefficiency. Consider your extra costs if supermarkets, department stores, and shopping centers or malls did not exist. Suppose you had to buy your milk at a dairy and your meat at a stockyard. Imagine buying your eggs and chicken at a hatchery and your fruits and vegetables at various farms. You would spend a great deal of time, money, and energy just shopping for a few groceries. Channels simplify distribution by cut-

Supermarkets and warehouse stores, such as this Western-style store in Thailand, overcome inefficiency by enabling people to buy all of their household products and groceries in one location.
© Peter Charlesworth/SABA

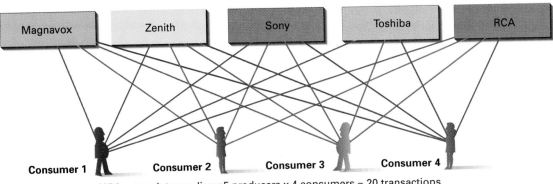

Without an intermediary: 5 producers x 4 consumers = 20 transactions

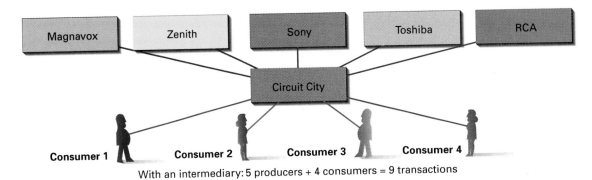

With an intermediary: 5 producers + 4 consumers = 9 transactions

Exhibit 14.1
*How Intermediaries
Reduce the Number of
Required Transactions*

ting the number of transactions required to get products from manufacturers to consumers and making an assortment of goods available in one location.

Consider another example, which is illustrated in Exhibit 14.1. Four students in your class each want to buy a television set. Without a retail intermediary like Circuit City, television manufacturers Magnavox, Zenith, Sony, Toshiba, and RCA would each have to make four contacts to reach the four buyers who are in the target market, totaling 20 transactions. However, each producer only has to make one contact when Circuit City acts as an intermediary between the producer and consumers, reducing the number of transactions to nine. Each producer sells to one retailer rather than to four consumers. In turn, your classmates buy from one retailer instead of from five producers.

This simple example illustrates the concept of contact efficiency. U.S. manufacturers sell to millions of individuals and families. Using channel intermediaries greatly reduces the number of required contacts. As a result, producers are able to offer their products cost effectively and efficiently to consumers all over the world.

CHANNEL FUNCTIONS

2 Describe the functions and activities of marketing channel members.

Intermediaries in marketing channels perform several essential functions that make the flow of goods between producer and buyer possible. The three basic functions that intermediaries perform are summarized in Exhibit 14.2. Transactional functions involve contacting and communicating with prospective buyers to make them aware of existing products and explain their features, advantages, and benefits. Logistical functions include sorting out, accumulating, allocating, and sorting products into either homogeneous or heterogeneous collections. For example, grading agricultural products typifies the sorting-out process while consolidation of many lots of grade A eggs from different sources into one lot illustrates the accumulation process. Supermarkets or other retailers perform the sorting function by assembling thousands of different items that match their customers' desires. The third basic channel function, facilitating, includes research and financing. Research provides information about channel members

Type of function	Description
Transactional functions	**Contacting and promoting:** Contacting potential customers, promoting products, and soliciting orders **Negotiating:** Determining how many goods or services to buy and sell, type of transportation to use, when to deliver, and method and timing of payment **Risk taking:** Assuming the risk of owning inventory
Logistical functions	**Physically distributing:** Transporting and storing goods to overcome temporal and spatial discrepancies **Sorting:** overcoming discrepancies of quantity and assortment by • *Sorting out:* Breaking down a heterogeneous supply into separate homogeneous stocks • *Accumulation:* Combining similar stocks into a larger homogeneous supply • *Allocation:* Breaking a homogeneous supply into smaller and smaller lots ("breaking bulk") • *Assortment:* Combining products into collections or assortments that buyers want available at one place
Facilitating functions	**Researching:** Gathering information about other channel members and consumers **Financing:** Extending credit and other financial services to facilitate the flow of goods through the channel to the final consumer

Exhibit 14.2

Marketing Channel Functions Performed by Intermediaries

and consumers by getting answers to questions such as: Who are the buyers? Where are they located? Why do they buy? Financing ensures that channel members have the money to keep products moving through the channel to the ultimate consumer.

A single company may provide one, two, or all three functions. Consider Kramer Beverage Company, a Coors beer distributor. As a beer distributor, it provides transactional, logistical, and facilitating channel functions. Kramer sales representatives contact local bars and restaurants to negotiate the terms of the sale, possibly giving the customer a discount for large purchases, and make arrangements for delivering the beer. At the same time, Kramer also provides a facilitating function by extending credit to the customer. Kramer merchandising representatives, meanwhile, assist in promoting the beer on a local level by hanging Coors beer signs and posters. Kramer also provides logistical functions by accumulating the many types of Coors beer from the Coors manufacturing plant in Golden, Colorado, and storing them in its refrigerated warehouse. When an order needs to be filled, Kramer then sorts the beer into heterogeneous collections for each particular customer. For example, the local Chili's Grill & Bar may need two kegs of Coors, three kegs of Coors Light, and two cases of Killian's Red in bottles. The beer will then be loaded onto a refrigerated truck and transported to the restaurant. Upon arrival, the Kramer delivery person will transport the kegs and cases of beer into the restaurant's refrigerator and may also restock the coolers behind the bar.

Although individual members can be added to or deleted from a channel, someone must still perform these essential functions. They can be performed by producers, end users or consumers, channel intermediaries such as wholesalers and retailers, and sometimes nonmember channel participants. For example, if a manufacturer decides to eliminate its private fleet of trucks, it must still have a way to move the goods to the wholesaler. This task may be accomplished by the wholesaler, which may have its own fleet of trucks, or by a nonmember channel participant, such as an independent trucking firm. Nonmembers also provide many other essential functions that may have at one time been provided by a channel member. For example, research firms may perform the research function; advertising agencies, the promotion function; transportation and storage firms, the physical distribution function; and banks, the financing function.

CHANNEL STRUCTURES

3 Discuss the differences among marketing channels for consumer and industrial products.

There are many routes a product can take to reach its final consumer. Marketers search for the most efficient channel from the many alternatives available. Marketing a consumer convenience good like gum or candy differs from marketing a specialty good like a Mercedes-Benz. The two products require much different distribution channels. Likewise, the appropriate channel for a major equipment supplier like Boeing Aircraft would be unsuitable for an accessory equipment producer like Black & Decker. In order to illustrate the differences in typical marketing channels for consumer and industrial products like these, the next sections discuss the structures of marketing channels for each product type.

Channels for Consumer Products

#34

direct channel
Manufacturers selling directly to consumers.

Exhibit 14.3 illustrates the four ways manufacturers can route products to consumers. Producers use the **direct channel** to sell directly to consumers. Direct marketing activities—including telemarketing, mail-order and catalog shopping, and forms of electronic retailing like online shopping and shop-at-home television networks—are a good example of this type of channel structure. For example, consumers can order Dell, Compaq, and Apple computers directly from a catalog, and Dell equipment can be purchased directly from Dell's Internet Web site. There are no intermediaries. Producer-owned stores and factory outlet stores—such as Sherwin-Williams, Ralph Lauren, Oneida, and West Point Pepperel—are other examples of direct channels. Farmers' markets are also direct channels. Direct marketing and factory outlets are discussed in more detail in Chapter 15.

Exhibit 14.3
Marketing Channels for Consumer Products

At the other end of the spectrum, an agent/broker channel involves a fairly complicated process. Agent/broker channels are typically used in markets with many small manufacturers and many retailers that lack the resources to find each other. Agents or brokers bring manufacturers and wholesalers together for negotiations, but do not take

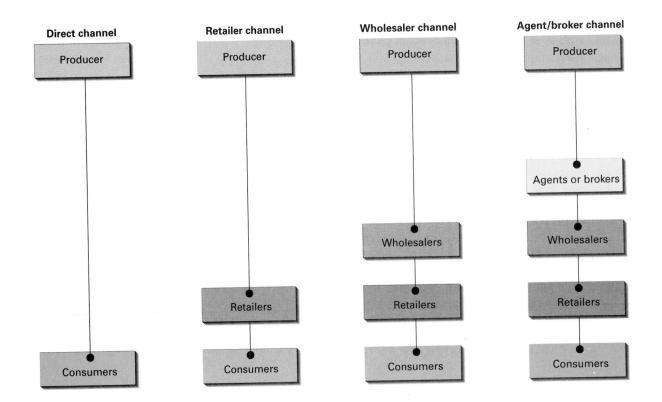

title to merchandise. Ownership passes directly to one or more wholesalers and then to retailers. Finally, retailers sell to the ultimate consumer of the product. For example, a food broker represents buyers and sellers of grocery products. The broker acts on behalf of many different producers and negotiates the sale of their products to wholesalers that specialize in foodstuffs. These wholesalers in turn sell to grocers and convenience stores.

Most consumer products are sold through distribution channels similar to the other two alternatives: the retailer channel and the wholesaler channel. A retailer channel is most common when the retailer is large and can buy in large quantities from the manufacturer. Wal-Mart, Sears, and car dealers are examples of retailers that often bypass a wholesaler. A wholesaler is frequently used for low-cost items that are frequently purchased, such as candy, cigarettes, and magazines. For example, Mars sells candies to wholesalers in large quantities. The wholesalers then break these quantities into smaller quantities to satisfy individual retailer orders.

Dell Computers
How does Dell use the Internet to establish a new channel for computer sales? What supporting services does Dell offer?

http://www.dell.com/

Channels for Industrial Products

As Exhibit 14.4 illustrates, five channel structures are common in industrial, or business-to-business, markets. First, direct channels are typical in industrial markets. For example, manufacturers buy large quantities of raw materials, major equipment, processed materials, and supplies directly from other manufacturers. Manufacturers

---

Marketing and Small Business

Crawfish to Your Doorstep Using the Internet

Cousins Brad and Carter Fourrier, both students at Louisiana State University, marked their first year of success in September 1997. Their new venture, "Crawfish To Your Doorstep," was made possible to a great extent by the Internet. Both had worked for a local seafood market for several years and wanted to have their own business. Their first idea was to start a catering service for boiled crawfish parties in the area surrounding Baton Rouge, Louisiana. After completing a business plan, however, they learned that the margins were higher and competition less with direct shipment of live and boiled crawfish throughout the United States.

In researching the idea, they used Internet search engines to look for information associated with keywords such as *food, home delivery, restaurants,* and so on. One of the first things they learned is that while a lot of firms were selling food over the Internet, few were selling seafood and even fewer were selling crawfish. By downloading information from other Web sites, they were able to develop effective procedures for taking, filling, packaging, and delivering orders and collecting money.

To make the market aware of their new venture, they hired a management information systems student from LSU to design and implement a homepage and Web site. The Web site included flashy graphics and a picture of a crawfish, and was hyperlinked to other relevant Web sites. Included on the Web site was a summary their product, experience, delivery options, pricing, and how to make purchases.

By using the Internet, the cousins were able to research their new venture, understand the opportunities and threats, and after deciding to move ahead, they were able to inform their potential market about how to purchase from them.

Should Brad and Carter begin selling other types of seafood? Would the use of a catalog or direct mail open up new markets for their venture? Why?

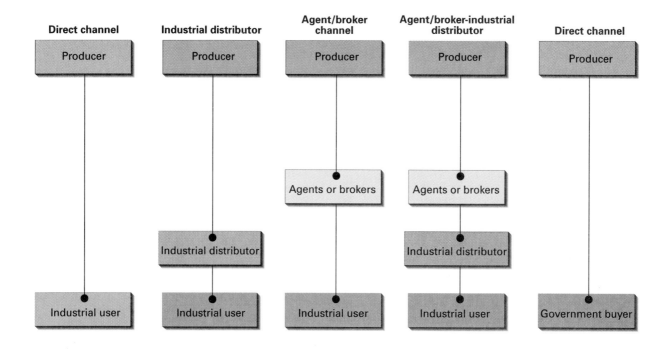

Exhibit 14.4
Channels for Industrial Products

that require suppliers to meet detailed technical specifications often prefer direct channels. The direct communication required between Chrysler and its suppliers, for example, along with the tremendous size of the orders, makes anything but a direct channel impractical. The channel from producer to government buyers is also a direct channel. As indicated in Chapter 7, much government buying is done through bidding. Thus, a direct channel is attractive.

Companies selling standardized items of moderate or low value often rely on industrial distributors. In many ways, an industrial distributor is like a supermarket for organizations. Industrial distributors are wholesalers and channel members that buy and take title to products. Moreover, they usually keep inventories of their products and sell and service them. Often small manufacturers cannot afford to employ their own sales force. Instead, they rely on manufacturers' representatives or selling agents to sell to either industrial distributors or users. For example, Alflex Corporation in Long Beach, California, relies on 34 independent manufacturers' representatives around the nation to sell its flexible conduit, a product used to protect copper wire and other products. The reps provide warehousing in their territories and ship the product to the distributor, which in turn sells to industrial users. However, manufacturers' reps and selling agents are not used solely by small manufacturers. Many large firms also use manufacturers' reps rather than funding an internal sales effort.

ALTERNATIVE CHANNEL ARRANGEMENTS

4 Describe alternative channel arrangements.

Rarely does a producer use just one type of channel to move its product. It usually employs several different or alternative channels, which include the following:

dual distribution (multiple distribution)
When a producer selects two or more channels to distribute the same product to target markets.

• *Multiple channels:* When a producer selects two or more channels to distribute the same product to target markets, this arrangement is called **dual distribution** (or **multiple distribution**). For example, Whirlpool sells its washers, dryers, and refrigerators directly to home and apartment builders and contractors, but it also sells these same appliances to retail stores that sell to consumers. Spiegel, which has traditionally used direct-mail channels, has now opened retail stores. Multiple channels may also be employed by producers with unique second brands. For example, Timex introduced its more expensive Nautica line of wristwatches to a new niche with a new level of distribution. To gain a foothold in the upscale market, Nautica watches are sold only in specialty stores, as opposed to the mass-merchandiser channels that Timex typically uses for its less expensive lines of watches. Goodyear Tire & Rubber Company is another company which is introducing a unique second brand. In addition to tires sold through distributors and discount outlets, Goodyear plans to introduce an exclusive line of tires to be sold only through its 3,000 independent dealers.[2]

- *Nontraditional channels:* Often nontraditional channel arrangements help differentiate a firm's product from the competition's. For example, manufacturers may decide to use nontraditional channels such as the Internet, mail order, or infomercials to sell their products instead of going through traditional retailer channels. Although nontraditional channels may limit a brand's coverage, they can give a producer serving a niche market a way to gain market access and customer attention without having to establish channel intermediaries. Nontraditional channels can also provide another avenue of sales for larger firms. For example, Taco Bell is testing sales of prepackaged Mexican-style food in grocery stores, airports, and schools. McDonald's is experimenting with selling burgers and fries through kiosks inside convenience stores, free-standing restaurants at Texaco stations, catering services, and home delivery. Kellogg's and General Mills are exploring vending machines as an option to expand the distribution of their snack-oriented brands.

- *Strategic channel alliances:* More recently, producers have formed **strategic channel alliances,** which use another manufacturer's already-established channel. Alliances are used most often when the creation of marketing channel relationships may be too expensive and time consuming. Ocean Spray formed a strategic channel alliance with Pepsi-Cola to help increase the market presence of Ocean Spray's brands. By sharing Pepsi's distribution channels, Ocean Spray can make cans and bottles of Ocean Spray cranberry juice cocktail, cranapple juice, and other juice drinks available in convenience stores, minimarts, and Pepsi-Cola vending machines. Similarly, Rubbermaid formed a close merchandising alliance with discounter Phar-Mor to supply most of the retailer's plastic housewares. Specially designed Everything Rubbermaid departments were created in Phar-Mor stores, which showcase as many as 560 Rubbermaid items. Strategic channel alliances are also developing in less traditional outlets such as electronic banking. Microsoft Corporation and Visa International are creating a system that will enable consumers to pay bills and utilize other banking functions through a computer network of Visa members banks.[3] Strategic channel alliances are also common for selling in global markets where cultural differences, distance, or other barriers can inhibit channel establishment. Anheuser-Busch struck an alliance with Kirin Brewing Company, which controls about half the Japanese beer market. Under the agreement, Budweiser Japan Company, as the alliance is called, will market and distribute Bud through Kirin's channels.[4]

strategic channel alliances
Producers' agreement to jointly use one producer's already established channel.

- *Reverse channels:* **Reverse channels** occur when products move in the opposite direction of traditional channels—from consumer back to producer. This type of channel is important for products that require repair or recycling. For example, automobile dealers generally have a service department to which consumers can bring their cars when they need repairs. A number of producers of high-tech products, like Sony, have established a national network of service centers that will repair the manufacturers' brands of electronic entertainment equipment. Soft-drink and beer manufacturers use reverse channels to collect and recycle glass bottles. They have also been big promoters of aluminum can recycling, mostly because it makes economic sense. Reverse channels for recycling have become more prevalent as producers realize the importance of limiting the solid waste that is normally dumped

reverse channels
When products move in the opposite direction of traditional channels—from consumer back to producer.

in landfills. Procter & Gamble is one producer that has redesigned its plastic bottles and containers to use recycled plastics instead of new plastics. To do so, P&G had to devise a reverse channel to get discarded plastic containers back for recycling. Now P&G works with channel intermediaries that collect, sort, shred, clean, and "pelletize" discarded plastic containers. The plastic pellets are then shipped back to P&G to become an ingredient in new plastic bottles and containers.

CHANNEL STRATEGY DECISIONS

5 Discuss the issues that influence channel strategy.

Devising a marketing channel strategy requires several critical decisions. Marketing managers must decide what role distribution will play in the overall marketing strategy. In addition, they must be sure that the channel strategy chosen is consistent with product, promotion, and pricing strategies. In making these decisions, marketing managers must analyze what factors will influence the choice of channel and what level of distribution intensity will be appropriate.

Factors Affecting Channel Choice

Marketers must answer many questions before choosing a marketing channel. The final choice depends on analysis of several factors, which often interact. These factors can be grouped as market factors, product factors, and producer factors.

Market Factors

Among the most important market factors affecting the choice of distribution channel are target customer considerations. Specifically, marketing managers should answer the following questions: Who are the potential customers? What do they buy? Where do they buy? When do they buy? How do they buy? Additionally, the choice of channel depends on whether the producer is selling to consumers or to industrial customers. Industrial customers' buying habits are very different from those of consumers. Industrial customers tend to buy in larger quantities and require more customer service. Consumers usually buy in very small quantities and sometimes do not mind if they get no service at all, as in a discount store.

Geographic location and size of the market are also important to channel selection. As a rule, if the target market is concentrated in one or more specific areas, then direct selling through a sales force is appropriate. When markets are more widely dispersed, intermediaries would be less expensive. The size of the market also influences channel choice. Generally, a very large market requires more intermediaries. For instance, Procter & Gamble has to reach millions of consumers with its many brands of household goods. It needs many intermediaries, including wholesalers and retailers.

Product Factors

Products that are more complex, customized, and expensive tend to benefit from shorter and more direct marketing channels. These types of products sell better through a direct sales force. Examples include pharmaceuticals, scientific instruments, airplanes, and mainframe computer systems. On the other hand, the more standardized a product is, the longer its distribution channel can be and the greater the number of intermediaries that can be involved. For example, the formula for chewing gum is about the same from producer to producer, with the exception of flavor and shape. Chewing gum is also very inexpensive. As a result, the distribution channel for gum tends to involve many wholesalers and retailers.

The product's life cycle is also an important factor in choosing a marketing channel. In fact, the choice of channel may change over the life of the product. For example, when photocopiers were first available, they were typically sold by a direct sales force. Now, however, photocopiers can be found in several places, including warehouse clubs, electronics superstores, and mail-order catalogs. As products become more common and less intimidating to potential users, producers tend to look for alternative channels. Gatorade was originally sold to sports teams, gyms, and fitness clubs. As the drink became more popular, mainstream supermarket channels were added, followed by convenience stores and drugstores. Now Gatorade can be found in vending machines and even in some fast-food restaurants.

Another factor is the delicacy of the product. Perishable products such as vegetables and milk have a relatively short life span. Fragile products like china and crystal require a minimum amount of handling. Therefore, both require fairly short marketing channels.

Producer Factors

Several factors pertaining to the producer itself are important to the selection of a marketing channel. In general, producers with large financial, managerial, and marketing resources are better able to use more direct channels. These producers have the ability to hire and train their own sales force, warehouse their own goods, and extend credit to their customers. Smaller or weaker firms, on the other hand, must rely on intermediaries to provide these services for them. Compared to producers with only one or two product lines, producers that sell several products in a related area are able to choose channels that are more direct. Sales expenses then can be spread over more products.

A producer's desire to control pricing, positioning, brand image, and customer support also tends to influence channel selection. For instance, firms that sell products with exclusive brand images, such as designer perfumes and clothing, usually avoid channels in which discount retailers are present. Manufacturers of upscale products, such as Gucci (handbags) and Godiva (chocolates), may sell their wares only in expensive stores in order to maintain an image of exclusivity. Many producers have opted to risk their image, however, and test sales in discount channels. Levi Strauss expanded its distribution to include JCPenney and Sears. JCPenney is now Levi Strauss's biggest customer.

Levels of Distribution Intensity #33

Organizations have three distribution options: intensive distribution, selective distribution, or exclusive distribution.

Intensive Distribution

Intensive distribution is distribution aimed at maximum market coverage. The manufacturer tries to have the product available in every outlet where potential customers might want to buy it. If buyers are unwilling to search for a product (as is true of

intensive distribution
Distribution aimed at maximum market coverage.

convenience goods and operating supplies), the product must be very accessible to buyers. A low-value product that is purchased frequently may require a lengthy channel. For example, candy is found in almost every type of retail store imaginable. It is typically sold to retailers in small quantities by a food or candy wholesaler. The Wrigley Company could not afford to sell its gum directly to every service station, drugstore, supermarket, and discount store. The cost would be too high.

Most manufacturers pursuing an intensive distribution strategy sell to a large percentage of the wholesalers willing to stock their products. Retailers' willingness (or unwillingness) to handle items tends to control the manufacturer's ability to achieve intensive distribution. For example, a retailer already carrying 10 brands of gum may show little enthusiasm for one more brand.

Selective Distribution

selective distribution
Distribution achieved by screening dealers to eliminate all but a few in any single area.

Selective distribution is achieved by screening dealers to eliminate all but a few in any single area. For example, Maytag uses a selective distribution system by choosing a select handful of appliance dealers in a geographic area to sell its line of washers and dryers and other appliances. Likewise, DKNY clothing is sold only in select retail outlets. Because only a few retailers are chosen, the consumer must seek out the product. Shopping goods and some specialty products are distributed selectively. Accessory equipment manufacturers in the business-to-business market also tend to follow a selective distribution strategy.

Several screening criteria are used to find the right dealers. An accessory equipment manufacturer like NEC may seek firms that are able to service its products properly. A television manufacturer like Zenith may look for service ability and a quality dealer image. If the manufacturer expects to move a large volume of merchandise through each dealer, it will choose only those dealers that seem able to handle such volume. As a result, many smaller retailers may not be considered.

Exclusive Distribution

exclusive distribution
The most restrictive form of market coverage entails only one or a few dealers within a given area.

The most restrictive form of market coverage is **exclusive distribution,** which entails only one or a few dealers within a given area. Because buyers may have to search or travel extensively to buy the product, exclusive distribution is usually confined to consumer specialty goods, a few shopping goods, and major industrial equipment. Products such as Rolls Royce automobiles, Chris-Craft power boats, and Pettibone tower cranes are distributed under exclusive arrangements. Sometimes exclusive territories are granted by new companies (such as franchisors) to obtain market coverage in a particular area. Limited distribution may also serve to project an exclusive image for the product.

Retailers and wholesalers may be unwilling to commit the time and money necessary to promote and service a product unless the manufacturer guarantees them an exclusive territory. This arrangement shields the dealer from direct competition and enables it to be the main beneficiary of the manufacturer's promotion efforts in that geographic area. With exclusive distribution, channels of communication are usually well established because the manufacturer works with a limited number of dealers rather than many accounts.

Although exclusivity has its advantages, it also can have its pitfalls. An exclusive network may not be large enough, for instance, if demand is brisk. In addition, the producer's insistence on exclusivity might put the channel in financial jeopardy during times of weak demand. Honda's Acura division, for example, uses an exclusive distribution strategy to create a distinctive image for its high-priced cars. Acura dealers struggled initially because of the car's small niche market, low resale demand, and iron-

Ethics in Marketing

Should Retailers Control Which Products We Buy?

The combination of powerful retailers and scanner technology collecting information on customer purchases has shifted the balance of power in marketing channels toward the large retailers. To reduce their risk in stocking new products, many large retailers charge slotting allowances—payments that manufacturers must make to buy space for new products on retailers' shelves. Retailers say they are justified given the uncertain impact on profit of the ever-growing number of new products. Some retailers even demand slotting allowances to keep established products on the shelves. Many manufacturers, particularly smaller ones, consider slotting allowances extortion.

Slotting fees have been common for years in Europe, Canada, and Australia, but are relatively recent in U.S. channels. They represent, however, over $1 billion of revenue annually to grocery retailers. One slot is the width of a single package on the shelf. In Los Angeles, the fee

associated with getting a new yogurt product into the market is $4,000 per grocery chain per slot. Thus, if 10 slots are required for adequate exposure and visibility of the new yogurt product, the fee is $40,000 for just one chain in one city. The fee for three chains would exceed $120,000. Clearly, only the larger and most profitable manufacturers can afford to introduce new products in Los Angeles, much less nationwide distribution.

Small manufacturers are vocal opponents of slotting fees because they prevent them from getting distribution in the large chain supermarkets. This means it is very difficult to get their products in front of most of their potential customers. Zapp's potato chips, a Cajun-flavored chip company in

south Louisiana, found it was impossible to get their new flavored chips in major supermarkets in their early years because they could not afford the slotting fees. They were forced to sell in independent stores until they were successful enough to pay slotting fees. Their story is similar to that of thousands of small manufacturers with new and innovative products. Some products are never introduced to the market while other good products fail because they are prevented from getting good distribution to potential customers.

Should retailers be permitted to charge slotting fees which prevent small manufacturers from using the best channels to reach their potential customers? Remember that supermarket margins typically are about 1 percent and some retailers insist that slotting fees are used just as a cost-covering device and not as a major source of profit.

ically, infrequent need for follow-up service and repair. But after several years, Acura dealerships have become very strong competitors by promoting quality and service.

GLOBAL MARKETING CHANNELS

Discuss channel structure and decisions in global markets.

Global marketing channels are important to U.S. corporations that export their products or manufacture abroad. Executives should recognize the unique cultural, economic, institutional, and legal aspects of each market before trying to design marketing channels in foreign countries. Manufacturers introducing products in global markets face a tough decision: what type of channel structure to use. Specifically, should the product be marketed directly, mostly by company salespeople, or through independent foreign intermediaries, such as agents and distributors? Using company salespeople generally provides more control and less risk than using foreign intermediaries. However, setting up a sales force in a foreign country also entails a greater commitment, both financially and organizationally.

Marketers should be aware that the channel structure abroad may not be very similar to channels in the United States. For instance, U.S. firms wishing to sell goods in Japan frequently must go through three layers of wholesalers and subwholesalers: the national or primary wholesalers, the secondary or regional wholesalers, and the local wholesalers. The channel types available in foreign countries usually differ as well. The more highly developed a nation is economically, the more specialized its channel types. Therefore, a marketer wishing to sell in Germany or Japan will have several channel types to choose from. Conversely, developing countries like India, Ethiopia, and Venezuela have limited channel types available; there are typically few mail-order channels, vending machines, or specialized retailers and wholesalers.

Now that you are familiar with the structure and strategy of marketing channels, it is important to also understand the physical means through which products move through a channel of distribution. The following sections discuss the role and scope of physical distribution.

THE IMPORTANCE OF PHYSICAL DISTRIBUTION

Explain the importance of physical distribution.

physical distribution
The ingredient in the marketing mix that describes how products are moved and stored.

logistics
A broader term that encompasses physical distribution includes the procurement and management of raw materials and component parts for production.

Physical distribution is the ingredient in the marketing mix that describes how products are moved and stored. Physical distribution consists of all business activities concerned with stocking and transporting materials and parts or finished inventory so they arrive at the right place when needed and in usable condition.

A broader term that encompasses physical distribution is **logistics,** which also includes the procurement and management of raw materials and component parts for production. Logistics and physical distribution management include these activities:

- Managing the movement and storage of raw materials and parts from their sources to the production site.
- Managing the movement of raw materials, semimanufactured products, and finished products within and among plants, warehouses, and distribution centers.
- Planning and coordinating the physical distribution of finished goods to intermediaries and final buyers.

In summary, logistics managers are responsible for directing raw materials and parts to the production department and the finished or semifinished product through warehouses and eventually to the intermediary or end user. Exhibit 14.5 depicts the logistics process.

Physical Distribution Service

physical distribution service
The package of activities performed by a supplier to ensure that the right product is in the right place at the right time.

Physical distribution service is the package of activities performed by a supplier to ensure that the right product is in the right place at the right time. Customers are

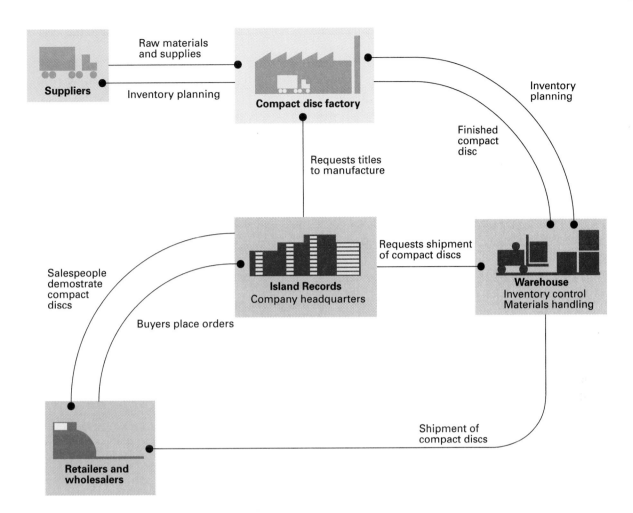

Exhibit 14.5
Logistics Process

rarely interested in the activities themselves; instead, they are interested in the results or the benefits they receive from those activities—namely, efficient distribution. Specifically, customers are concerned with how long it takes to receive an order and how consistent delivery is, how much effort it takes to place an order, and what condition the product is in when it is finally received. Order processing, order assembly, and delivery are of no consequence to the buyer. What matters most are the quality and timeliness of the supplier's performance.

When setting service levels, physical distribution managers must be sensitive to their customers' needs. At the most basic level, customers demand availability, timeliness, and quality. Availability is the proportion or percentage of orders that can be completely filled right away. Unavailable goods must be back ordered, causing time delays and extra costs, or the customer can simply cancel the order. Timeliness in physical distribution service is, for the buyer, minimal time elapsed between placing the order and receiving it. Quality is a low incidence of in-transit damage, shipment of incorrect items, and incorrect shipment quantity.

THE BALANCE BETWEEN SERVICE AND COST

Most distribution managers try to set their service level at a point that maximizes service yet minimizes cost. To do so, they must examine the total cost of all parts of the physical distribution system—warehousing, materials handling, inventory control, order processing, and transportation—using the total cost approach. The basic idea of the total cost approach is to examine the relationship of factors such as number of warehouses, size of finished-goods inventory, and transportation expenses. Of course,

Discuss the concept of balancing physical distribution service and cost.

the cost of any single element should also be examined in relation to the level of customer service. Thus, the physical distribution system is viewed as a whole, not as a series of unrelated activities.

Often the high cost of air transportation can be justified under the total cost approach. Rapid delivery may drastically reduce the number of warehouses required at distant locations. Therefore, the higher cost of using air freight may be more than justified by the savings in inventory and warehouse expenses, as shown in Exhibit 14.6. For example, by using air transport, Swedish carmaker Volvo is able to quickly get automobile parts to its North American Volvo dealers, thereby keeping customers happy and inventories down. Everything from nuts and bolts to parts as large as fenders is flown or trucked from Gothenburg to Oslo or Copenhagen in order to meet one of the shipper's daily U.S.-bound flights. The shipments are cleared through customs ahead of time so they can move quickly. Once in the United States, the shipment is transferred to a nearby Federal Express facility in time to make that evening's departure. With this system, Volvo can typically get parts to its U.S. dealers in as little as two days. This form of transportation is expensive, but Volvo's distribution system has become an integral part of its customer satisfaction program.

Volvo Cars of North America, Inc.
How does Volvo promote its retail channels via the Web? Which Volvo dealership is most convenient to you?

http://www.volvocars.com/

Implementing the total cost approach requires trade-offs. For example, a supplier that wants to provide next-day delivery to its customers and also to minimize transportation costs must make a trade-off between the desired level of service (expensive next-day delivery) and the transportation goal (minimal costs). Intel, for example, wanted to decrease variability in delivery times and to reduce customers' inventory levels. It turned to FedEx for distribution of its new Pentium microprocessor from a Manila plant to customers' receiving docks. Although the transportation method itself is more expensive, Intel increased on-time deliveries, cut the

Exhibit 14.6
How Using Air Freight Lowers Distribution Costs under the Total Cost Approach

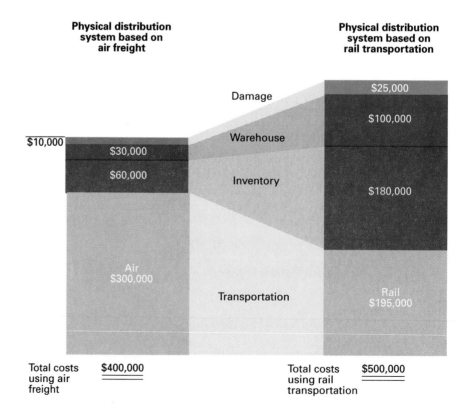

time it takes to process and deliver an order from 14 to 4 days, and reduced the costs of in-transit inventory.

Ideally, the distribution manager would like to optimize overall distribution performance—that is, to balance distribution activities so that overall distribution costs are minimized while the desired level of physical distribution service is maintained. If attempts to minimize costs and maximize service don't work, the result is suboptimization. The problem may be a conflict between physical distribution components. For instance, the transportation people may want to provide customers with same-day delivery, but the order-processing people may take two to three days to process an order.

Suboptimization often occurs in physical distribution because different managers oversee the distribution functions. For example, inventory handling may be a responsibility of the production department, and order processing may be assigned to accounting. More than likely, these managers have different goals for customer service and costs. The only cure is for top management to recognize the role of logistics and physical distribution in helping the firm reach its overall objectives and to build better coordination into the organizational structure. Sears has been very successful in implementing the concept of total distribution cost. In the past three years the company has cut overall costs by $45 million a year, with costs now representing only 21.6 percent of sales as compared to 23.8 percent for JCPenney, and merchandise is moving from suppliers to stores in half the time it took before. A related benefit of these cost savings and productivity increases has been a doubling in the value of the stock.[5]

PHYSICAL DISTRIBUTION SUBSYSTEMS

The **physical distribution system** consists of five distinct subsystems which serve several key functions of physical distribution managers: deciding on warehouse location, number, size, and type; setting up a materials-handling and packaging system; maintaining an inventory control system; setting procedures for processing orders; and selecting modes of transportation. These subsystems are shown in Exhibit 14.7. Although these subsystems are discussed here separately, they are, of course, highly interdependent.

Warehousing

Distribution managers oversee the constant flow of goods from the manufacturer to the ultimate consumer. However, the final user may not need or want the goods at the same time the manufacturer produces and wants to sell them. Products like grain

9 Describe the subsystems of the physical distribution system.

physical distribution system Consists of five distinct, interdependent subsystems which serve several key functions of physical distribution managers: warehousing, materials handling, inventory control, order-processing, and transportation.

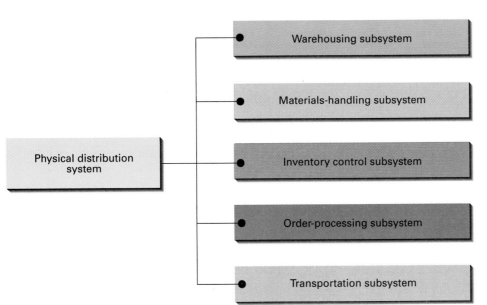

Exhibit 14.7
Subsystems of Physical Distribution

and corn are produced seasonally, but consumers demand them year-round. Other products, such as Christmas ornaments and turkeys, are produced year-round, but consumers do not want them until autumn or winter. Therefore, management must have a storage system to hold these products until they are shipped.

Storage is what helps manufacturers manage supply and demand, or production and consumption. It provides time utility to buyers and sellers, which means that the seller stores the product until the buyer wants or needs it. Even when products are used regularly, not seasonally, many manufacturers store excess products in case the demand surpasses the amount produced at a given time. Storing additional product does have disadvantages, however, including the costs of insurance on the stored product, taxes, obsolescence or spoilage, theft, and warehouse operating costs. Another drawback is opportunity costs—that is, the lost opportunities of using the money that is tied up in stored product for something else.

Materials Handling

materials-handling system
Moves inventory into, within, and out of the warehouse.

A **materials-handling system** moves inventory into, within, and out of the warehouse. Materials handling includes these functions:

- Receiving goods into the warehouse or distribution center.
- Identifying, sorting, and labeling the goods.
- Dispatching the goods to a temporary storage area.
- Recalling, selecting, or picking the goods for shipment (may include packaging the product in a protective container for shipping).

The goal of the materials-handling system is to move items quickly with minimal handling. With a manual, nonautomated materials-handling system, a product may be handled more than a dozen times. Each time it is handled, the cost and risk of damaging it increase; each lifting of a product stresses its package. With an automated system, many of these functions are combined and handled by a computerized system.

Baxter Health Care, a leading manufacturer and marketer of health care products, uses a sophisticated materials-handling system to reduce product handling and keep costs to a minimum. As goods are received into the warehouse, bar-coded labels are affixed to the pallets of incoming product, which are then placed on a fully automated conveyor to be sent to the storage area. There, truck operators scan the labels while an on-board, radio-controlled computer tells the operator exactly where to drop off the load. When the items to fill an order are picked off the shelves and placed in a carton, another bar-coded label is applied, and the carton is placed on the conveyor system. Automatic scanners posted throughout the intricate conveyor system read each bar code and divert each carton to the proper shipping lane. This automated system gives Baxter a high degree of control over how orders are handled, placed, picked, and sequenced for shipping.

With an automated materials-handling system, products are handled less frequently and thus are less likely to be damaged.
© David Joel/Tony Stone Images

Packaging

Packaging the product for shipment is a major concern of materials management. The packaging is what protects transported materials against breakage, spoilage, insects, and dirt.

Well-designed packaging restricts the material's movement. For instance, Waterford/Wedgwood, the distributor of Ireland's famed Waterford crystal, uses an adhesive-coated bubble wrap that sticks to the glass to cut down handling time and reduce product damage. Larger products, like furniture or computer equipment, may be shipped in vehicles that are themselves padded for protection.

Automatic Identification and Bar Coding

Materials handling, like many other subsystems in physical distribution, is being driven by the need for fast, accurate information. **Automatic identification,** or **auto ID,** is the use of identification technology to mark and read products as they enter and leave the warehouse or as they are received by a manufacturer or retailer. Auto ID may employ voice identification, radio frequencies, or magnetic strips, although bar coding is the most common method.

automatic identification (auto ID)
The use of identification technology to mark and read products as they enter and leave the warehouse or are received by a manufacturer or retailer.

Automatic Storage and Retrieval

Working side by side with auto ID are **automatic storage and retrieval systems (AS/RS).** AS/RS automatically store and pick goods in the warehouse or distribution center. These systems decrease product handling and ensure accurate placement of product. AS/RS also improve the accuracy of order picking and the rates of on-time shipment.

When a new shipment arrives at the warehouse, the product is generally bar coded and entered into the AS/RS. From there the product may be placed on an automated conveyor system. An automated guided vehicle can then pick it up and place it exactly where it belongs on the warehouse shelves. When an order is placed into the AS/RS, the automated guided vehicle scans the bar-coded products on the warehouse shelves, pulls the right ones, and places them on the automated conveyor system, which sends them to be packaged and shipped.

automatic storage and retrieval systems (AS/RS)
System that automatically stores and picks goods in the warehouse or distribution center.

Unitization and Containerization

Two important elements of modern materials handling are unitization and containerization. **Unitization,** or unitizing, is a technique for handling small packages more efficiently. It means grouping boxes on a pallet or skid, which is then moved mechanically, by a forklift, truck, or conveyor system.

Containerization is the process of putting large quantities of goods in sturdy containers that can be moved from ship to truck to airplane to train without repacking.

unitization
A technique for handling small packages by grouping boxes on a pallet or skid.

containerization
The process of putting large quantities of goods in sturdy containers that can be moved from ship to truck to airplane to train without repacking.

You're shipping food, corrosive chemicals, and raw animal hides to Japan. Can you load the ship properly and make sure it doesn't tip over en route? Try it at **Hot Link—Ship Loading.**

inventory control system
System that develops and maintains an adequate assortment of products to meet customers' demands.

just-in-time (JIT) inventory management
Redesigning and simplifying manufacturing by reducing inventory levels and delivering parts just when they are needed on the production line.

The containers are sealed until delivery, thereby reducing damage and theft. They are essentially miniature mobile warehouses that travel from manufacturing plant to receiving dock. A container, often a special form of truck trailer body, can be reused repeatedly. The average container lasts 10 years and can be repaired if damaged.

Inventory Control

Another important function of physical distribution is establishing an inventory control system. An **inventory control system** develops and maintains an adequate assortment of products to meet customers' demands.

Inventory decisions have a big impact on physical distribution costs and the level of physical distribution service provided. If too many products are kept in inventory, costs increase—as do risks of obsolescence, theft, and damage. If too few products are kept on hand, then the company risks product shortages and angry customers. The goal of inventory management, therefore, is to keep inventory levels as low as possible while maintaining an adequate supply of goods to meet customer demand.

Just-in-Time Inventory Management

Borrowed from the Japanese, **just-in-time (JIT) inventory management** is a way to redesign and simplify manufacturing. For the manufacturer, JIT means that raw materials arrive at the assembly line in guaranteed working order "just in time" to be installed, and finished products are generally shipped to the customer immediately after completion. For the supplier, JIT means supplying customers with products in just a few days, or even a few hours, rather than weeks. More and more U.S. manufacturing firms are using just-in-time inventory management systems, and almost 55 percent of all shipments in 1997 were sent just in time.

The basic assumption of JIT is that carrying excessive inventory is bad because it ties up capital. With JIT, the purchasing firm can reduce the amount of raw materials and parts it keeps on hand by ordering more often and in smaller amounts. General Motors and other carmakers, for example, generally maintain just an eight-hour supply of parts. Packard Electric consolidates and distributes automobile wiring harnesses to several carmakers. Because the wiring harnesses are scheduled to arrive on the assembly line as they are needed, shipment accuracy is crucial for Packard Electric.

Production facilities that adopt JIT techniques are usually redesigned to position all the machines involved in a process closer together, thus reducing work time. The JIT system transports parts to the point where they are needed, just when they are needed, on the production line. Hence, there are no piles of inventory waiting by each machine.

JIT benefits manufacturers most by reducing their inventories. For example, at Saturn's powertrain manufacturing and assembly plant in Spring Hill, Tennessee, the inventory of powertrains at any given time is barely two hours, in sharp contrast to the two weeks of inventory generally carried by other auto manufacturers. Additionally, JIT creates shorter lead times, or the time it takes to get parts from a supplier after an order has been placed. Manufacturers also enjoy better relationships with suppliers and can decrease their production and storeroom costs. Because there is little safety stock, and therefore no margin for error, the manufacturer cannot afford to make a mistake. As a result, a manufacturer using JIT must be sure it receives high-quality parts from all vendors and must be confident that the supplier will meet all delivery commitments. Finally, JIT tends to reduce the amount of paperwork. Exhibit 14.8 summarizes the benefits and risks of JIT.

Just-in-time inventory management is not without its risks, however. Implementation of JIT is a process of continuous improvement characterized by many small gains in efficiency over a long period. Many managers have tried to institute JIT too rapidly, only to be disappointed in the results. Shigeo Shingo, one of the initiators

Benefits of JIT:	Risks of JIT:

Reduced inventory levels
Shorter lead times
Improved supplier relations
Lower production and
   storeroom costs
Better-quality supplies
Less paperwork
	Implementing JIT principles too rapidly
	Cutting inventory without implementing
	   other JIT principles
	Increased delivery costs
	"Supplier shock"
	Employee stress
	Potential bottlenecks caused
	   by supplier delays

Exhibit 14.8

Benefits and Risks of Just-in-Time Inventory Management

of the JIT movement, acknowledges that it took Toyota Motors 20 years to develop JIT fully. He estimates that companies wanting to implement JIT now should expect that it will take at least 10 years to realize satisfactory results. In addition, many companies have incorrectly assumed that JIT means slashing inventory levels only, without paying attention to the other aspects of JIT, such as quality control, frequent communications, efficient plant layout, regularly scheduled maintenance, and simpler product design. Managers who ignore these related issues risk delivery delays, shortages of goods, and customer dissatisfaction.

Because of the lower inventory levels, JIT also demands smaller, more frequent, precisely timed deliveries from suppliers. At Saturn's plant, as many as 850 deliveries may be made by suppliers in a 24-hour period. Deliveries must be made within a five-minute window to be counted as "on time." Tardy suppliers that cause a production delay face being fined $500 a minute.[6]

JIT also has been known to create "supplier shock." Many suppliers have been strong-armed into cutting delivery times by manufacturers practicing JIT. In other instances, manufacturers' inventories have simply shifted from their warehouses to suppliers' warehouses. JIT can also create stress among workers. Experiences with a number of Japanese and U.S. companies show that sharp reductions in inventory may lead to a regimented work flow and increased levels of stress among production-line employees. Finally, JIT has the potential for causing disastrous bottlenecks in production due to even the slightest delays by suppliers. Consider the impact on General Motors' production if a labor strike should occur at its sole supplier of seat belts.

To combat the negative impact of JIT implementation on suppliers, many companies have adopted JIT II, an updated form of just-in-time inventory control. JIT II involves the sharing of up-to-the-minute internal, proprietary data such as sales forecasts with suppliers. In addition, agents of suppliers may be allowed to set up office in the manufacturer's facility and be asked to replace purchasing agents and place orders for themselves. However, like the original JIT, JIT II requires an adjustment period such that manufacturers and suppliers can develop trust in one another and overcome their fear of releasing too much confidential information. One solution to this problem is the utilization of detailed confidentiality agreements. JIT II has shown to be so successful in some areas that there is speculation on the development of JIT III.[7]

Federal Express and other overnight delivery companies are a critical component in the success of JIT channel strategies. These companies have made quick, efficient, and dependable distribution of many products possible. Benefits provided by overnight delivery include reduced inventory and carrying costs, lower capital investment in warehousing, and improved tracking of shipments. Many different types of products and companies have benefited from overnight delivery capability, including such diverse products as MK Diamond's saws and blades, National Semiconductor's chips, Daisytek computer and office automation supplies and accessories, and retailer Nieman Marcus. For more information, including case studies of distribution solutions, see the Federal Express Corporation Learning Lab on their Web site at www.fedex.com.

Order Processing

Another important activity of physical distribution is order processing. The role of proper order processing in providing good service cannot be overemphasized.

The Flow of Goods and Information

As an order enters the system, management must monitor two flows: the flow of goods and the flow of information. Often the best-laid plans of marketers can get entangled in the order-processing system. Obviously, good communication among sales representatives, office personnel, and warehouse and shipping personnel is essential to correct order processing. Shipping incorrect merchandise or partially filled orders can create just as much dissatisfaction as stockouts or slow deliveries. The flow of goods and information must be continually monitored so mistakes can be corrected before an invoice is prepared and the merchandise shipped.

Benefits of Automation

electronic data interchange (EDI)
Automated order processing through the use of computer technology.

Mode of transportation is chosen on the basis of cost, transit time, reliability, capability, accessibility, and traceability.
Courtesy Roadway Express

Like inventory management, order processing is becoming more automated through the use of computer technology known as EDI—**electronic data interchange.** The basic idea behind EDI is to replace the paper documents that usually accompany business transactions, such as purchase orders and invoices, with electronic transmission of the needed information. Companies that use EDI can reduce inventory levels, improve cash flow, streamline operations, and increase the speed and accuracy of information transmission. EDI is also believed to create a closer relationship between buyers and sellers. Approximately a third of all Fortune 1,000 firms—as well as their customers and suppliers—have adopted EDI. Purchase orders are the most common document electronically sent and received.[8]

It should not be surprising that retailers have become major users of EDI. For Wal-Mart, Target, Kmart, and the like, logistics speed and accuracy are crucial competitive tools in an overcrowded retail environment. Many big retailers are mandating that their suppliers acquire EDI technology. EDI works hand in hand with retailers' "efficient consumer response" programs, which are designed to have the right products on the shelf, in the right styles and colors, through improved inventory, ordering, and distribution techniques.[9] (See Chapter 15 for more discussion of retailers' use of EDI techniques.)

Transportation

Physical distribution managers must also decide which mode of transportation to use to move products from producer to buyer. This decision is, of course, related to all other physical distribution decisions. The five major modes of transportation are railroads, motor carriers, pipelines, water transportation, and airways. Distribution managers generally choose a mode of transportation on the basis of several criteria:

- *Cost:* total amount a specific carrier charges to move the product from the point of origin to the destination. Cost is usually figured in ton-miles. (A ton-mile is the movement of one ton, or 2,000 pounds, of freight a distance of one mile.)

- *Transit time:* total time a carrier has possession of goods, including the time required for pickup and delivery, handling, and movement between the point of origin and the destination.

FLASH!

Roadway's 24-Hour Voice Response System

Quick—where's that critical shipment? A call to 1-800-ROADWAY gets you the shipment information you need—fast. Track a shipment by freight bill, bill of lading, or P.O. number. Check routing and transit times. Make a cargo claim inquiry, ask for a proof of delivery fax, or catch up on the latest Roadway news. Easy as picking up a phone. Nothing in the industry comes close to the information-delivery power of Roadway's 24-hour Voice Response system. Reliable. Responsive. Roadway blends the most efficient network with the best work force in the industry to deliver exceptional customer service.

ROADWAY *Express*

For Voice Response Assistance Call...**1-800-ROADWAY (1-800-762-3929)** http://www.roadway.com e-mail: rexmail@roadway.com

Exceptional Service. . . *No Exceptions*

	Highest ●————————————————————————————● Lowest				
Relative cost	Air	Truck	Rail	Pipe	Water
Transit time	Water	Rail	Pipe	Truck	Air
Reliability	Pipe	Truck	Rail	Air	Water
Capability	Water	Rail	Truck	Air	Pipe
Accessibility	Truck	Rail	Air	Water	Pipe
Traceability	Air	Truck	Rail	Water	Pipe

Exhibit 14.9
Criteria for Ranking Modes of Transportation

- *Reliability:* consistency with which the carrier delivers goods on time and in acceptable condition.
- *Capability:* ability of the carrier to provide the appropriate equipment and conditions for moving specific kinds of goods, such as those that must be transported in a controlled environment (for example, under refrigeration).
- *Accessibility:* carrier's ability to move goods over a specific route or network.
- *Traceability:* relative ease with which a shipment can be located and transferred.

The mode of transportation used depends on the needs of the shipper as they relate to the six criteria described above. Exhibit 14.9 compares the advantages and problems of the basic modes of transportation on these criteria.

PHYSICAL DISTRIBUTION FOR SERVICES

The fastest-growing part of our economy is the service sector. Although distribution in the service sector is difficult to visualize, the same skills, techniques, and strategies used to manage inventory can also be used to manage service inventory—for instance, hospital beds, bank accounts, or airline seats. The quality of the planning and execution of distribution can have a major impact on costs and customer satisfaction.

10 Identify the special problems and opportunities associated with physical distribution in service organizations.

One thing that sets service distribution apart from traditional manufacturing distribution is that, in a service environment, production and consumption are simultaneous. In manufacturing, a production setback can often be remedied by using safety stock or a faster mode of transportation. Such substitution is not possible with a service. The benefits of a service are also relatively intangible—that is, you can't normally see the benefits of a service, such as a doctor's physical exam. But a consumer can normally see the benefits provided by a product—for example, a vacuum cleaner removing dirt from the carpet.

Because service industries are so customer oriented, customer service is a priority. Service distribution focuses on three main areas:

- *Minimizing wait times:* Minimizing the amount of time customers wait in line to deposit a check, wait for their food at a restaurant, or wait in a doctor's office for an appointment is a key factor in maintaining the quality of service.
- *Managing service capacity:* For a product manufacturer, inventory acts as a buffer, enabling it to provide the product during periods of peak demand without extraordinary efforts. Service firms don't have this luxury. If they don't have the capacity to meet demand, they must either turn down some prospective customers, let service levels slip, or expand capacity. For instance, at tax time a tax preparation firm may have so many customers desiring its services that it has to either turn business away or add temporary offices or preparers.

- *Improving delivery through new distribution channels:* Like manufacturers, service firms are now experimenting with different distribution channels for their services. These new channels can increase the time that services are available (like round-the-clock automated teller machines) or add to customer convenience (like pizza delivery or walk-in medical clinics). For example, alternatives to hospitals called *medical malls* have developed, offering one-stop shopping for all types of medical services. Like traditional malls, these shopping areas are equipped with fountains, food courts, and other amenities. The only difference lies in their product assortment, ranging from radiology and cardiac treatment to outpatient surgery.[10]

Another service where changes in distribution channels can be seen is banking. Banks are offering computer software which enables customers to manage their finances from remote locations. This paperless form of banking allows customers to do just about anything except get fast cash.[11] Customers soon will be able to use ATMs to cash checks, deposit checks without an envelope, print monthly statements, and purchase traveler's checks and plane and theater tickets.[12] In fact, this new form of banking will enable consumers to select from a number of banks nationwide. As a result, electronic banking will likely replace most traditional bank branch outlets.[13]

Although service organizations provide mostly intangible benefits, they still must have supplies, raw materials, and inventory systems. For example, a bank must have deposit forms, loan information packages, and computers to hold customer account information and produce monthly statements. Likewise, a restaurant keeps an inventory of plates, silverware, and glassware, along with a variety of foods and drinks, to be able to provide a dining experience for its customers.

FedEx and Domino's Pizza are two firms whose innovative distribution of services has influenced their industries. Both built significant market share by focusing on the time and location of the services delivered to the customer. FedEx satisfied an unmet need by offering guaranteed overnight delivery of packages and documents to commercial and residential customers. Domino's innovation was to concentrate on home delivery of pizza in 30 minutes or less. Now, however, the pizza giant has eliminated its delivery guarantee because of a lawsuit they lost when one of their pizza delivery drivers was in an automobile accident.

TRENDS IN PHYSICAL DISTRIBUTION

11 Discuss new technology and emerging trends in physical distribution.

Several technological advances and business trends affect the physical distribution industry today. These include automation, electronic distribution, environmental issues, third-party contract logistics and partnerships, quality issues in transportation, and global distribution.

Automation

Manual handling of distribution is now outdated. Computer technology has boosted the efficiency of physical distribution dramatically—for instance, in warehousing and materials management, inventory control, and transportation. This chapter has presented many examples of the use of computer technology and automation, ranging from satellite tracking for motor carriers to electronic data interchange, computerized inventory systems, and automatic identification techniques using bar codes.

One of the major goals of automation is to bring up-to-date information to the decision maker's desk. Shippers have long referred to the transportation system as the "black hole," where products and materials fall out of sight until they reappear some time later in a plant, store, or warehouse. Now carriers have systems that track freight, monitor the speed and location of carriers, and make routing decisions on the spur of the moment. The rapid exchange of information that automation brings to the distribution process helps each party plan more effectively. The links among suppliers, buyers, and carriers open up opportunities for joint decision making. And as more companies compete in global markets, timely information becomes even more important.

Electronic Distribution

Electronic distribution is the most recent development in the physical distribution arena. Broadly defined, this would include any kind of product or service that can be distributed electronically, whether over traditional forms such as fiber optic cable or through satellite transmission of electronic signals. As an example, the Internet Shopping Network (http://www.isn.com/), the largest online seller of computer hardware and software, just added a Downloadable Software division. Customers access the ISN over the Internet, select the software program they wish to purchase, transfer their credit card information, and the software is available for use immediately. In the near future, due to new technology that compresses data much more than in the past, movies and music CDs will be downloadable and playable on computerized home entertainment systems. This method will revolutionize physical distribution as we know it today for any product that can be transmitted through electronic means, including newspapers, books, magazines, audio and video entertainment, and so on.

electronic distribution
Any kind of product or service that can be distributed electronically, whether over traditional forms such as fiber optic cable or through satellite transmission of electronic signals.

Environmental Issues

Environmental laws and consumer concerns have a profound effect on how U.S. businesses operate, and logistics and distribution managers are becoming much more involved in the environmental matters that affect their firms. For example, the Department of Transportation now requires that all employees dealing with hazardous materials be trained and tested at least once every two years. This rule applies to all hazardous materials transportation, regardless of shipment size, frequency of shipment, degree of hazard of the products shipped, company size, or number of employees.

Concern over the environment has also made waste reduction a factor in the packaging process. Distribution managers are improving packaging design, eliminating overpackaging, reusing packages that were once discarded after a single use, and switching to less expensive packaging, materials with recycled content, or alternatives that take up less warehouse space. Ethan Allen, one of the largest U.S. furniture makers and retailers, has established an innovative recycling program for its packaging materials. The company contracted with United Parcel Service to retrieve Ethan Allen's foam-sheet shipping materials and return them to Ametek, the manufacturer of the foam sheeting. The program has reduced Ethan Allen's disposal costs and also earned the company additional dollars because Ametek pays the furniture maker for the returned material.

As distribution becomes more global, U.S. companies will also have to deal with the environmental laws of other countries. In the area of logistics and distribution, environmental standards in Europe alone vary enormously from country to country—for everything from packaging standards and truck sizes and weights to vehicle emissions and noise pollution control. Some European standards are far more stringent than those in the United States. In Germany, for instance, it is against the law to incinerate packaging or to dump it in a landfill. Also, manufacturers are responsible for taking back packaging after products have been purchased. To show compliance with the law, vendors must purchase "green dots" from government-approved third parties and apply them to all packaging. The money collected is used to subsidize package collection and recycling systems. Manufacturers incur penalties for green-dot packages that have been improperly disposed of. To meet the demands of the German market, Hewlett-Packard now ships its DeskJet printers without the usual cardboard packaging. Instead, the company devised a special tray that holds the printers securely wrapped in clear plastic. This method cuts down not only on packaging waste but also on damage. Handlers can now see they are handling a printer, not just a cardboard box.

Contract Logistics and Partnerships

contract logistics
Turning over the entire function of buying and managing transportation or another subsystem of physical distribution to an independent third party.

Contract logistics is a rapidly growing segment of the distribution industry. In **contract logistics,** a manufacturer or supplier turns over the entire function of buying and managing transportation or another subsystem of physical distribution, such as warehousing, to an independent third party. Contract logistics allows companies to cut inventories, locate stock at fewer plants and distribution centers, and still provide the same service level or even better. The companies then can refocus investment on their core business. General Motors, for example, is using Miami-based Ryder to boost Cadillac sales in Florida by shortening delivery times. GM has found that many luxury car buyers refuse to wait more than a couple of weeks for a custom model, so they have set up the experimental Cadillac Customer Rapid Delivery System that Ryder is managing, including a 1,400 Cadillac model distribution center in Orlando offering much greater variety than any single dealer could stock.[14]

Not surprisingly, contract logistics often leads a supplier, retailer, or manufacturer to form an exclusive partnership with a carrier, warehousing expert, or logistics management supplier. Many of the companies seeking partners are practicing just-in-time inventory management. Often sophisticated distribution systems are required to deliver component parts to assembly lines or fashions to the retail shelf within tight, predefined time windows. Contract logistics partnerships help companies meet delivery dates, speedily fill emergency orders, and achieve high accuracy in filling orders.

Coors Brewing uses contract logistics vendors to assist with the distribution of beer. After years of shipping its own product directly to more than 650 distributors, the brewer realized that this system could not keep up with demand. Coors set up alliances with 24 refrigerated public warehouses, all linked to Coors through a partnership with Burlington Northern Railroad. By using satellite warehouses and Burlington Northern, Coors was able to reduce costs and increase profitability.

Quality in Transportation

Companies that buy transportation know that quality transport is a critical part of their success. Many have developed formal quality measurement programs for the modes of transportation they use. The most important quality characteristics are on-time pickup and delivery, competitive rates and transit times, and dependable schedules. Most carriers have responded by developing systems for tracing and tracking shipments and cutting paperwork.

Buyers of transportation are also using fewer carriers and demanding more from them. It is not unusual to find as few as six or eight carriers handling as much as 90 percent of a shipper's transportation. Sears cut the number of motor carriers it deals with from 350 to fewer than 15. Schneider National, the largest U.S. truckload carrier, transports the bulk of Sears's merchandise through a partnership with the retailer. Sears promised enough freight so that Schneider National could dedicate certain equipment to Sears shipments alone. In return, Sears realizes substantial savings.[15] The advantages of forming partnerships with fewer carriers are many. Communication improves, and the carriers know they can rely on a certain level of business. Meanwhile, transportation buyers gain greater control over a central function in the distribution system.

Global Distribution

The world is indeed becoming a friendlier place for marketers. The surging popularity of free-market economics over the past decade or so has swept away many barriers. As a result, businesses are finding that the world market is more appealing than ever.

As global trade becomes a more decisive factor in success or failure for firms of all sizes, a well-thought-out global logistics strategy becomes more important. Uncertainty regarding shipping usually tops the list of reasons why companies, especially smaller ones, resist international markets. Even companies that have scored overseas successes often are vulnerable to logistical problems. Large companies have the capital to create global logistics systems, but smaller companies often must rely on the services of carriers and freight forwarders to get their products to overseas markets.

 One of the most critical global logistical issues for importers of any size is coping with the legalities of trade in other countries. Shippers and distributors must be aware of the permits, licenses, and registrations they may

Global Perspectives
Physical Distribution in China

China is the world's largest emerging economic powerhouse, with over 1.2 billion consumers. Estimates indicate annual economic growth in China of over 10 percent. But outdated port facilities, poor rail and road networks, overcrowded conditions, and the vastness of China make getting goods in and out a major problem.

Throughout China, urban roadways are usually clogged, and ports and rail stations generally lack the basic equipment, such as forklifts, to move cargo. Bandits are common along highways and roads, and in some areas village chiefs erect roadblocks and demand a toll in exchange for passage. Tariffs, as high as 200 percent on some products, stop many goods from even getting into China in the first place.

Consider, for example, a customer who orders a Volkswagen from VW's joint-venture plant in Shanghai. Delivery can be expected within six to eight weeks, but the customer should not count on a shiny new car with no scratches or dents and hardly any mileage on the odometer. The only way to get the VW to some customers is to drive it—in many cases, 2,000 miles or more over mountains, across

deserts, and down many unpaved dirt roads.

China's freight system also leaves a lot to be desired. Rail traffic is so unpredictable that 30 percent of all coal brought out of the country's mines each year still sits where it was dug, waiting for the trains to arrive. Moreover, rail shipments are different from those in more industrialized parts of the world where everything gets shipped in containers. As one IBM PC manager says, "Here, I've seen cargo handlers virtually throw our cartons into trains." But China is teaming with Russia, Iran, and Turkey to open up Central Asia to the outside.

China is only meeting a fraction of its aviation freight demand. One Hong Kong garment maker recalls watching his freight get loaded on a flight out of Shanghai and immediately unloaded to make way for some government goods.

A growing number of private trucking companies are emerging, but shipping is still a problem. De-

livery trucks are not allowed into Beijing in daylight, so companies like Compaq Computer and IBM must endure long delays and schedule midnight deliveries.

Perhaps the most significant distribution development in China has been along the Yangtze River. It is the world's third-longest river and one of its oldest commercial waterways. Improvements have brought auto makers such as General Motors, France's Citroen, and China's Dongfeng Motors to sites along the river, along with British safety-glass and Malaysian tire makers. International consumer-electronics giants Philips Electronics (Norelco), Samsung Electronics, and NEC, as well as Coca Cola, Glaxo, UpJohn, and Bristol-Myers Squibb, have also located along the river. But much still remains to be done as most of the river traffic is still primitive, consisting mainly of flat-bottomed ferries and small boats.

In what other areas of the world is the transportation infrastructure underdeveloped? What strategies can shippers use to help overcome poor roads, railroads, and port facilities?

Sources: Kyle Pope, "Rail-building Boom Begins to Open Doors to Central Asia Riches," *Wall Street Journal,* 11 July 1996, p. A1; David Hamilton, "PC Makers Find China Is a Chaotic Market Despite Its Potential," *Wall Street Journal,* 4 August 1996, p. A1; Marcus Brauchli, "The Mighty Yangtze Seizes a Major Role in China's Economy," *Wall Street Journal,* 13 December 1995, p. A1; Karen Thuermer, "To Maintain a Stronghold, Improve Service, Carriers Invest In China's Decayed Infrastructure," *Traffic World,* 4 April 1994, pp. 18–19.

need to acquire and, depending on the type of product they are importing, the tariffs, quotas, and other regulations that apply in each country. Another important factor to consider is the transportation infrastructure in a country. For example, the Commonwealth of Independent States (the former Soviet Union) has little transportation infrastructure outside the major cities, such as roads that can withstand heavy freight trucks, and few reliable transportation companies of any type. Pilferage and hijackings of freight are also common. Distributors have had similar experiences in China, as the "Global Perspectives" box relates.

LOOKING BACK

As you complete this chapter, you should be able to see how marketing channels operate and how physical distribution is necessary to move goods from the manufacturer to the final consumer. The structure of marketing channels often varies given the consumer target market. For example, as the opening story discussed, many product manufacturers are facing difficulty reaching the college student market. Since college students are cautious about marketers, many companies have employed fellow students to distribute their products on college campuses. In the future, these companies expect to utilize the Internet as a distribution channel for information about and purchase orders for their products and services.

KEY TERMS

automatic identification 399

automatic storage and retrieval systems (AS/RS) 399

containerization 399

contract logistics 406

discrepancy of assortment 383

discrepancy of quantity 382

direct channel 386

dual distribution (multiple distribution) 388

electronic data interchange (EDI) 402

electronic distribution 405

exclusive distribution 392

intensive distribution 391

inventory control system 400

just-in-time (JIT) inventory management 400

logistics 394

marketing channel (channel of distribution) 382

SUMMARY

1 *Explain what a marketing channel is and why intermediaries are needed.* Marketing channels are composed of members that perform negotiating functions. Some intermediaries buy and resell products; other intermediaries aid the exchange of ownership between buyers and sellers without taking title. Nonmember channel participants do not engage in negotiating activities and function as an auxiliary part of the marketing channel structure.

Intermediaries are often included in marketing channels for three important reasons. First, the specialized expertise of intermediaries may improve the overall efficiency of marketing channels. Second, intermediaries may help overcome discrepancies by making products available in quantities and assortments desired by consumers and business buyers and at locations convenient to them. Third, intermediaries reduce the number of transactions required to distribute goods from producers to consumers and end users.

2 *Describe the functions and activities of marketing channel members.* Marketing channel members perform three basic types of functions. Transactional functions include contacting and promoting, negotiating, and risk taking. Logistical functions performed by channel members include physical distribution and sorting functions. Finally, channel members may perform facilitating functions, such as researching and financing.

3 *Discuss the differences among marketing channels for consumer and industrial products.* Marketing channels for consumer and business products vary in degree of complexity. The simplest consumer product channel involves direct selling from producers to consumers. Businesses may sell directly to business or government buyers. Marketing channels grow more complex as intermediaries become involved. Consumer product channel intermediaries include agents, brokers, wholesalers, and retailers. Business product channel intermediaries include agents, brokers, and industrial distributors.

4 *Describe alternative channel arrangements.* Marketers often use alternative channel arrangements to move their products to the consumer. With dual distribution or multiple distribution, they choose two or more different channels to distribute the same product. Nontraditional channels help differentiate a firm's product from the competitor's or provide a manufacturer with another avenue for sales. Strategic channel alliances are arrangements that use another manufacturer's already-established channel. Finally, reverse channels exist when products move in the opposite direction of traditional channels—from consumer back to the producer. Reverse channels are often used for products that require repair or recycling.

5 *Discuss the issues that influence channel strategy.* When determining marketing channel strategy, the marketing manager must determine what market, product, and producer factors will influence the choice of channel. The manager must also determine the appropriate level of distribution intensity.

6 *Discuss channel structure and decisions in global markets.* Global marketing channels are becoming more important to U.S. companies seeking growth abroad. Manufacturers introducing products in foreign countries must decide what type of channel structure to use—in particular, whether the product should be marketed through direct channels or through foreign intermediaries. Marketers should be aware that channel structures in foreign markets may be very different from those they are accustomed to in the United States.

7 *Explain the importance of physical distribution.* In today's fiercely competitive environment, marketing managers are becoming aware of the importance of effective physical distribution. Rather than concentrating on product or price differentiation, many companies are developing more efficient methods of distributing goods and services to achieve a competitive advantage.

8 *Discuss the concept of balancing physical distribution service and cost.* Today, physical distribution service is recognized as an area in which a firm can distinguish itself from competitors. Therefore, many physical distribution managers strive to achieve an optimal balance of customer service and total distribution cost. Important aspects of service are availability of merchandise, timeliness of deliveries, and quality (condition and accuracy) of shipments. In evaluating costs, physical distribution managers examine all parts of the distribution system.

9 *Describe the subsystems of the physical distribution system.* The physical distribution system has five basic parts, or subsystems: warehousing, materials handling, inventory control, order processing, and transportation. When evaluating warehousing options, physical distribution managers must determine the number, size, and location of warehouses needed. Important elements of materials handling are packaging, bar coding, automatic storage and retrieval, and unitization and containerization. Inventory control systems regulate when and how much to buy (order timing and order quantity). Order processing monitors the flow of goods and information (order entry and order handling). Finally, the major modes of transportation include railroads, motor carriers, pipelines, waterways, and airways. Alternative methods of transporting goods are intermodal transportation and such supplementary carriers as freight forwarders.

10 *Identify the special problems and opportunities associated with physical distribution in service organizations.* Managers in service industries use the same skills, techniques, and strategies to manage physical distribution functions as managers in goods-producing industries. The physical distribution of services focuses on three main areas: minimizing wait times, managing service capacity, and improving delivery through new distribution channels.

11 *Discuss new technology and emerging trends in physical distribution.* Several trends are emerging in today's physical distribution industry. Technology and automation are bringing up-to-date distribution information to the decision maker's desk. Technology is also linking suppliers, buyers, and carriers for joint decision making and has created a new electronic distribution channel. As in many other industries today, concern for the environment is also making an impact on physical distribution. Companies are responding to government concern over the risks of hazardous shipments and developing programs to reduce packaging. Many companies are saving money and time by hiring third-party carriers to handle some or all aspects of the distribution process. Still another trend in distribution is the quest for quality in transportation. Carriers have improved on-time delivery and pickup, developed systems for tracking shipments, and implemented electronic communication with shippers.

Discussion and Writing Questions

1. Describe the most likely distribution channel for each of these consumer products: candy bars, Tupperware products, nonfiction books, new automobiles, farmer's market produce, and stereo equipment.

2. List three reasons for redesigning marketing channels. Illustrate your answer with specific examples.

3. Describe the distribution channel for a product you are familiar with. Explain why you think the channel is structured as you describe it.

4. You have been hired to design a distribution channel for a new firm specializing in the manufacturing and marketing of novelties for college student organizations. In a memo to the president of the firm, describe how the channel operates.

5. Is the goal of a physical distribution system to operate at the lowest possible cost? Why or why not?

6. Which physical distribution strategy do you think is optimal? Why?

7. Identify the most suitable method(s) of transporting these goods: lumber, fresh seafood, natural gas, fine china, and automobiles. Justify your choices.

8. Assume that you are the marketing manager of a hospital. Write a report indicating the physical distribution functions that concern you. Discuss the similarities and dissimilarities of physical distribution for services and for goods.

9. Choose one or two other students from your class and form a team. Identify two retailers from your community to interview. One should be a smaller, locally owned retailer and the other a larger chain or franchise operation. For example, select a local clothing retailer or restaurant and compare them to a regional or national chain. Interview the manager or assistant manager at each and determine what retailing mix factors the local retailer emphasizes to attract customers versus which ones the national chain uses. Prepare a report to present to your class which suggests how local retailers can compete with national retailers.

10. Quote three of the most interesting interview questions that GreenTree Associates is asking international distributors. (Include at least one marketing question.) Why did you select these three?

http://www.greentree.com/distbook.html

11. What is TradeNet World Service? How could such an organization affect established channels and distribution?

http://www.tradenet.org/

Application for Small Business

Francine and Bud had owned and operated a successful pest and rodent exterminating company for 14 years. One December, Francine bought Bud several custom-tailored dress shirts for Christmas. While at work one day, Bud accidently placed a ball point pen in one of the shirt's front pockets. Since it was a new gift and had cost almost $100, they both wanted to remove the spot. Quite by accident, they discovered that one of the chemicals they used in the pest spray also was an excellent spot remover. By testing it on several other items, they learned it was an excellent general-purpose spot remover.

Francine and Bud began making up, packaging, and selling the product through independent supermarkets and drug stores. The spot remover sold quite well, so they decided to try to sell it through national chains. When contacted, the national chains asked about product labeling, bar coding, production capabilities, slotting fees, and other similar questions. After almost two years they had had no success in convincing a national chain to distribute their spot cleaner, even though they had a long list of testimonials from satisfied customers.

One weekend they noticed several ads in the business section of the local newspaper. One was an attorney advertising his services for entrepreneurs, another was the Entrepreneurship Center at a local university, and the third was a local marketing consulting firm. They wondered if any of these organizations could help them obtain distribution for their spot cleaner.

Questions

1. What could Francine and Bud do to convince national chains to take on their spot cleaner?
2. Which of the three organizations should they contact and why?

Video Case
Ch. 14

United Parcel Service

UPS, the world's largest package distribution company, employs 335,000 people worldwide and provides services to more than 200 countries and territories. To compete with aggressive competitors such as FedEx, Roadway Package System, and Airborne Express, UPS has been changing the way it does business, introducing a new service every other month for the last six years. UPS used to think, and even tell customers, "We know what's best for you!" Today, UPS stresses customer satisfaction. This satisfaction is delivered using over $2 billion of the latest technology to keep up-to-the-minute tabs on shipments. Its system includes an integrated international shipping, tracking, and tracing system that interfaces with customs as well as customers' computers, and a portable electronic clipboard for signatures of package recipients. In fact, *Information Week* magazine recently ranked the company as the "best user of information technology" in the transportation industry. The system provides information to shippers on where their merchandise is prior to arrival, when it arrived, who signed for it, and how long it took to arrive. It also can show them how to save money on shipping by planning ahead.

Along with this technology, UPS is also offering upgraded services. Flexible pickup and delivery times, as well as customized shipment plans and discount prices to volume shippers, are all available to corporate clients. It is tough to fault the long-time success story of pioneer FedEx, but UPS is delivering what today's customers really want: choice and value, along with speed and reliability.

Attention to detail is another reason UPS has been able to deliver on customer satisfaction. The company has one of the largest fleets of aircraft in the world, has a massive computer network, processes over 11 million packages every day, and spends about $1.5 billion on capital improvements every year. But down-home managers boast that they measure costs in tenths of a cent and can predict within five or six minutes how long a driver will take on his or her 100-mile delivery and pickup round every day. Through such attention to detail as calibrating the depth of delivery drivers' pockets so that they don't have to dig too deeply for loose change, designating the right fingers to hold a key, or making truck seats easier to slide in and out of, UPS has acquired an enviable reputation for reliability. After 80 years, it delivers to more U.S. addresses than the U.S. Postal Service does, reaches over 80 percent of the people in the world, and picks up merchandise from all of the companies on the Fortune 500 list.

The company's Internet capabilities (http://www.ups.com/) have helped to maintain its competitive edge. Included online are the UPS drop-off locator to identify the nearest location to ship or pick up packages, an automated shipping solutions laboratory to process and manage UPS shipments and tracking, tracking software for Microsoft Windows, and much more. The company's homepage address gets an average of 200,000 hits per day, and features information and tracking capabilities in French, Italian, Spanish, German, and English. Moreover, the company's employees send package-tracking information continuously via almost 80,000 hand-held computers.

Questions

1. Why are air freight operators so important to businesses, both in the United States and abroad?
2. How have these carriers changed the distribution function?
3. Why is the information they provide as important as the actual shipment of merchandise?
4. What strategies could FedEx, Airborne, and Roadway use to compete with UPS?

1 Discuss the importance of retailing in the U.S. economy.

2 Explain the dimensions by which retailers can be classified.

3 Describe the major types of retail operations.

4 Discuss non-store retailing techniques.

5 Define franchising and describe its two basic forms.

6 List the major tasks involved in developing a retail marketing strategy.

7 Describe future trends in retailing.

8 Discuss present problems in retailing.

9 List the types of firms that perform wholesaling activities and describe their functions.

Chapter 15

Retailing and Wholesaling

In today's fiercely competitive world, retailers are struggling to find fresh ways to woo shoppers. Consumers who once considered shopping a recreational sport are increasingly thinking of shopping as a chore. Consumers' lack of interest has led to the untimely demise of many retailers including the department stores Edison Brothers Stores, Hastings Group, and Bradlees. As a result, consumers are opting for ways to purchase their goods more efficiently, requiring less time and less money. To address this problem, retailers are revisiting the golden rule to attract consumers: offer the right product, at the right time, at the right place, and at the right price. Put simply, today's consumers want more for less.

Retailers are responding in many ways. Target, for example, is jockeying to make sure to offer the right product. To do so, Target has implemented a strategy called *micromarketing,* whereby merchandise in each store is tailored to the specific preferences of its customers. Items such as greeting cards, home decor, music, and clothing can all be tailored to meet the preferences of local racial, ethnic, and age groups. As a result of its marked success, Target is aiming to contour 30 percent of its total store merchandise to reflect local preferences.

Targeting consumers' desire for the right product and the right price, Wal-Mart expanded its product selection while also dropping prices. Wal-Mart has cut costs at every stage, from manufacturer to wholesaler to the store shelf. Wal-Mart's expenses have decreased almost 4 percent in the past decade to just over 15 percent of sales.

Other retailers are attempting to make their product available at the right time and at the right place. For example, financial institutions are promoting their new "loans by phone." This program enables consumers to borrow funds for a variety of reasons by simply dialing the telephone. The inconvenience of having to make an appointment with a loan officer and having to visit the institution several times for paperwork has been removed from the loan process.

Eatzi's, a new restaurant owned by Brinker International, also hopes to capitalize on convenience. With a motto of "Meals for the Taking," it aims to capitalize on America's changing dining habits by combining the supermarket and restaurant concepts and providing home-meal replacement. By doing so, Eatzi's will address consumers' increasing desire for home-cooked meals without the added time needed for preparation. It will offer around 400 menu items prepared daily, in addition to hundreds of other items which consumers may want to buy in order to complete a meal at home, such as flowers, wine, and condiments.[1]

As demonstrated by these examples, attracting consumers is a major concern for today's retailers. In the future, what factors do you see as being important to a store's retailing mix? This chapter seeks to answer

this question and many more by discussing retailers and wholesalers as intermediaries in the channel of distribution. Each performs an important role in moving products and services to the ultimate consumer.

The chapter begins with a discussion of the role of retailing and the ways in which retail operations can be classified. Also included is a description of the decisions involved in developing a retail marketing strat-

egy. The chapter concludes with a summary of the types of wholesalers and the expected future trends in wholesaling.

THE ROLE OF RETAILING

1 Discuss the importance of retailing in the U.S. economy.

retailing

All the activities directly related to the sale of goods and services to the ultimate consumer for personal, nonbusiness use.

Retailing—all the activities directly related to the sale of goods and services to the ultimate consumer for personal, nonbusiness use—has enhanced the quality of our daily lives. When we shop for groceries, hair styling, clothes, books, and many other products and services, we are involved in retailing. The millions of goods and services provided by retailers mirror the needs and styles of U.S. society.

Retailing affects all of us directly or indirectly. The retailing industry is one of the largest employers; over 2 million U.S. retailers employ about 19 million people. Retailers ring up over $2 trillion in sales annually.[2] Small retailers, including small restaurateurs, account for more than half of that sales volume.

Although most retailers are quite small, a few giant organizations dominate the industry. Fewer than 10 percent of all retail establishments account for over half of total retail sales and employ about 40 percent of all retail workers. Who are these giants? Exhibit 15.1 lists the 10 largest U.S. retailers.

CLASSIFICATION OF RETAIL OPERATIONS

2 Explain the dimensions by which retailers can be classified.

A retail establishment can be classified according to its ownership, level of service, product assortment, and price. Specifically, retailers use the latter three variables to position themselves in the competitive marketplace. (As noted in Chapter 8, positioning is the strategy used to influence how consumers perceive one product in relation to all competing products.) These three variables can be combined in several ways to create distinctly different retail operations. Exhibit 15.2 lists the major types of retail stores discussed in this chapter and classifies them by level of service, product assortment, price, and gross margin.

Exhibit 15.1
Ten Largest U.S. Retailers

1995 Rank	Company	Retailing Formats	1995 Revenues ($ billions)	1995 Number of Stores
1	**Wal-Mart** Bentonville, AR	Discount stores, supercenters, and warehouse clubs	$89.1	2,943
2	**Sears, Roebuck and Company** Hoffman Estates, IL	Department stores and catalogs	34.9	2,306
3	**KMart** Troy, MI	Discount stores, supercenters, and home centers	34.4	2,477
4	**Kroger** Cincinnati, OH	Supermarkets and convenience stores	23.9	2,144
5	**Dayton Hudson Corporation** Minneapolis, MN	Discount stores and department stores	23.5	1,029
6	**JCPenney** Plano, TX	Department stores, catalogs, and drug stores	21.4	1,883
7	**American Stores Company** Salt Lake City, UT	Supermarkets and drug stores	18.3	1,650
8	**Price/Costco** Issaquah, WA	Warehouse clubs	18.2	240
9	**Safeway, Inc.** Pleasanton, CA	Supermarkets	16.4	1,059
10	**The Home Depot** Atlanta, GA	Home centers	15.5	423

Source: "The Chain Store 100," State of the Industry special report, *Chain Store Age*, August 1996, pp. 3A–4A.

Ownership

Retailers can be broadly classified by form of ownership: independent, part of a chain, or a franchise outlet. Retailers owned by a single person or partnership and not operated as part of a larger retail institution are **independent retailers.** Around the world, most retailers are independent, operating one or a few stores in their community. Local florists, shoe stores, and ethnic food markets typically fit this classification.

Chain stores are owned and operated as a group by a single organization. Under this form of ownership, many administrative tasks are handled by the home office for the entire chain. The home office also buys most of the merchandise sold in the stores.

Franchise outlets are owned and operated by individuals but are licensed by a larger supporting organization. Franchising combines the advantages of independent ownership with those of the chain store organization. Franchising is discussed in more detail later in the chapter.

independent retailers
Retailers owned by a single person or partnership and not operated as part of a larger retail institution.

chain stores
Stores owned and operated as a group by a single organization.

franchise outlets
Retail store owned and operated by individuals but licensed by a larger supporting organization.

Exhibit 15.2

Types of Stores and Their Characteristics

Type of Retailer	Level of Service	Product Assortment	Price	Gross Margin
Department store	Moderately high to high	Broad	Moderate to high	Moderately high
Specialty store	High	Narrow	Moderate to high	High
Supermarket	Low	Broad	Moderate	Low
Convenience store	Low	Medium to narrow	Moderately high	Moderately high
Full-line discount store	Moderate to low	Medium to broad	Moderately low	Moderately low
Discount specialty store	Moderate to low	Medium to broad	Moderately low to low	Moderately low
Warehouse club	Low	Broad	Low to very low	Low
Off-price retailer	Low	Medium to narrow	Low	Low

Level of Service

Factory outlet stores typically carry a broad assortment of merchandise with limited depth.

© 1996 PhotoDisk, Inc.

The level of service that retailers provide can be classified along a continuum from full service to self-service. Some retailers, such as exclusive clothing stores, offer high levels of service. They provide alterations, credit, delivery, consulting, liberal return policies, layaway, gift wrapping, and personal shopping. Discount stores usually offer fewer services. Retailers such as factory outlets and warehouse clubs offer virtually no services.

Product Assortment

The third basis for positioning or classifying stores is by the breadth and depth of their product line. Specialty stores—for example, Hallmark card stores, Lady Foot Locker, and TCBY yogurt shops—are the most concentrated in their product assortment, usually carrying single or narrow product lines but in considerable depth. On the other end of the spectrum, full-line discounters typically carry broad assortments of merchandise with limited depth. For example, Target carries automotive supplies, household cleaning products, and pet food. However, Target may carry only 4 or 5 brands of canned dog food; a supermarket may carry as many as 20.

Other retailers, such as factory outlet stores, may carry only part of a single line. Liz Claiborne, a major manufacturer of women's clothing, sells only certain items of its own brand in its many outlet stores. Discount specialty stores like Home Depot or Toys R Us carry a broad assortment in concentrated product lines, such as building and home supplies or toys.

Price

Price is a fourth way to position retail stores. Traditional department stores and specialty stores typically charge the full "suggested retail price." In contrast, discounters, factory outlets, and off-price retailers use low prices as a major lure for shoppers.

The last column in Exhibit 15.2 shows the typical gross margin for each type of store. **Gross margin** is how much the retailer makes as a percentage of sales after the cost of goods sold is subtracted. The level of gross margin and the price level generally match. For example, a traditional jewelry store has high prices and high gross margins. A factory outlet has low prices and low gross margins. Markdowns on merchandise during sales periods and price wars among competitors, in which stores lower prices on certain items in an effort to win customers, cause gross margins to decline. When Wal-Mart entered the grocery business in a small Arkansas community, for example, a fierce price war ensued. By the time the price war was in full swing, the price of a quart of milk had plummeted by more than 50 percent (below the price of a pint) and a loaf of bread sold for only 9¢, prices at which no retailer could make a profit.

gross margin
Amount of money the retailer makes as a percentage of sales after the cost of goods sold is subtracted.

MAJOR TYPES OF RETAIL OPERATIONS

There are several types of retail stores. Each offers a different product assortment, type of service, and price level according to its customers' shopping preferences.

3 Describe the major types of retail operations.

Department Stores

Housing several departments under one roof, a **department store** carries a wide variety of shopping and specialty goods, including apparel, cosmetics, housewares, electronics, and sometimes furniture. Purchases are generally made within each department rather than at one central checkout area. Each department is treated as a separate buying center to achieve economies in promotion, buying, service, and control. Each department is usually headed by a **buyer,** who not only selects the merchandise for his or her department but may also be responsible for promotion and personnel. For a consistent, uniform store image, central management sets broad policies about the types of merchandise carried and price ranges. Central management is also responsible for the overall advertising program, credit policies, store expansion, customer service, and so on.

department store
A store housing several departments under one roof.

buyer
Department head who selects the merchandise for his or her department and may also be responsible for promotion and personnel.

Large independent department stores are rare today. Most are owned by national chains. Among the largest U.S. department store chains are Sears, Dayton-Hudson, JCPenney, Federated Department Stores, and May Department Stores. All operate more than one chain of retail stores, from discount chains to upscale clothiers.[3] Two up-and-coming department store chains are Dillard's, based in Little Rock, Arkansas, and Nordstrom, with corporate headquarters in Seattle. Dillard's is known for its distribution expertise; Nordstrom offers innovative customer service. In the past few years, much attention has been centered on these two growing chains, and both have a very promising future.

Each year brings a dramatic new event to the department store sector of retailing. Consumers of the late 1980s witnessed the chaos of corporate takeovers, mergers, and acquisitions among the nation's largest and most widely recognized department store chains. Retail giants such as Bloomingdale's, Saks Fifth Avenue, and Marshall Field's were among the many put up for sale because of oversized debt and sluggish consumer demand. Many others were forced to cut expenses drastically to pay off debt. In the process, they became less innovative and in some cases were forced out of business.

JCPenney Company
Spiegel
Compare these cyberspace shopping alternatives. What benefits does online shopping offer customers? What disadvantages do you see?

http://www.jcpenney.com/
http://www.spiegel.com

In recent years, consumers have become more cost-conscious and value-oriented. Specialty retailers like The Gap, discounters, catalog outlets, and even online Internet shopping alternatives have capitalized on the department stores' plight by offering superior merchandise selection and presentation, sharper pricing, and greater convenience. They have also been quicker to adopt new technology and invest in labor-saving strategies. In addition, their leaner cost structure translates into lower prices for the customer. Meanwhile, manufacturers like Liz Claiborne, Bass, Calvin Klein, and Ralph Lauren have opened outlet stores of their own and more discount stores such as Wal-Mart and Target have upgraded their apparel assortments, taking more sales away from department stores.

Department store managers are using several strategies to preserve their market share. One is to reposition department stores as specialty outlets. They are dividing departments into miniboutiques, each featuring a distinct fashion taste, as specialty stores do. Department stores are also enhancing customer service to shift the focus away from price. Services include complementary alterations, longer store hours, personalized attention, after-sale follow-up, and personal wardrobe planning. Finally, department stores are expanding, remodeling, and revitalizing to show off new merchandising directions and to reflect the growth in their marketing areas.

Specialty Stores

specialty store
Retail store specializing in a given type of merchandise.

Specialty store formats allow retailers to refine their segmentation strategies and tailor their merchandise to specific target markets. A **specialty store** is not only a type of store but also a method of retail operation—namely, specializing in a given type of merchandise. Examples include children's clothing, men's clothing, candy, baked goods, gourmet coffee, sporting goods, and pet supplies. A typical specialty store carries a deeper but narrower assortment of specialty merchandise than does a department store. Generally, specialty stores' knowledgeable sales clerks offer more attentive customer service. The format has become very powerful in the apparel market and other areas. Benetton, Waldenbooks, Victoria's Secret, The Body Shop, Foot Locker, and Crate & Barrel are several successful specialty retailers. Read about Starbucks Coffee's experience in transporting their successful specialty format to Japan in the "Global Perspectives" box.

Specialty stores like Victoria's Secret tailor their merchandise to a specific target market.
© John Abbott

Global Perspectives

Japan Wakes Up and Smells Starbucks

Starbucks is giving Japanese coffee-bar chains the jitters. When a billboard proclaiming, "Opening Soon: Starbucks Coffee" appeared in Tokyo's fashionable Omotesando district in early 1996, local coffee bars went into a flurry of activity. One nearby coffee bar enlisted real estate agents to help determine where the new Starbucks might open shop. Other Japanese coffee bars began offering "Seattle Coffee" or remodeled their shops to look like those of Starbucks. Still others went on intelligence missions to the United States to study Starbucks' secrets.

Such anxiety may seem odd, given that Japan is already the world's number three coffee consumer, after the United States and Germany. With so many coffee shops and coffee vending machines already in place—Coca-Cola alone has more than 800,000 vending machines that sell canned coffee—Japan's market looks saturated. Meanwhile, the Japanese haven't developed a taste for espresso drinks like caffe latte and caffe mocha; instead, they drink a lot of instant coffee or ready-to-drink coffee in cans, as well as American-style hot coffee.

But Starbucks has a reputation for knowing how to create a thirst, and Japanese coffee purveyors fear that the new Starbucks' coffee bars, the first of which opened in August 1996 in Tokyo's swank Ginza shopping district, may be able to create new coffee markets in Japan where they have failed. "For the past few years, we've had this nightmare scenario that espresso drinks are going to swallow up Japan's coffee market," says Seiji Honna, president of Pronto Corporation, a big coffee-bar chain with 94 stores. "And we won't know how to make a good cup of espresso."

Starbucks' entrance in the Japanese market worries Japanese coffee executives like Mr. Honna because they don't know how to replicate its touch. The fact that the Japanese see big openings in Japan for a U.S. company like Starbucks suggests how far behind Japan is in fostering creative, consumer-oriented service companies.

Some Japanese coffee-chain operators admit they lack Starbucks' sophistication in what they call "packaging the store": meshing such elements as store design, package design, and other merchandising techniques into a compelling identity. And Starbucks's Japanese partner, Sazaby, Inc., is an expert at upscale retailing that should help Starbucks project a hip image in Japan.[4]

Japanese consumers might need a little hand-holding at first to guide them through the thicket of grandes and frappucinos. But Yuji Tsunoda, president of Starbucks Coffee Japan, thinks they'll catch on fast. "Four years ago, how many Americans knew what a latte, doppio espresso, or cappucino were?" he said. "It's up to us to help our customers understand coffee better."

Indeed, at Tokyo's new Starbucks outlet, the wall menu is posted in both English and Japanese. Starbucks is even providing Japanese-language versions of pamphlets like "Espresso—What You Need to Know." Employees and customers alike can refer to blueprintlike diagrams detailing the exact specifications of a caffe latte, down to the quarter-inch of foamed milk that goes on top. The Tokyo shop features the same colorful coffee paraphernalia featured in U.S. stores, including mugs, espresso makers, plunger coffee brewers, filters, and coasters.

While the coffee is cheaper at the Pronto coffee bar down the street—just 160 yen, or $1.50, versus 250 yen, about $2.30—the atmosphere at Pronto with its low ceiling, somber interior, and cafeteria-style trays hardly evokes the ambiance of a gourmet coffee house. Neither does the food. Coffee-accompanying snacks at Pronto include fried chicken with spaghetti on a hot dog bun and a salty fried noodle sandwich with seaweed on top. Starbucks, on the other hand, takes a more epicurean tack—cookies, muffins, croissants, and sandwiches made from pita bread and sesame-seed bagels.[5]

What other specialty retailers can you think of that could successfully export its format to a foreign country? What obstacles do you think they may face?

Consumers in specialty outlets usually consider price to be secondary. Instead, the distinctive merchandise, the store's physical appearance, and the caliber of the staff determine its popularity. Manufacturers often favor selling their goods in small specialty stores rather than in the larger retail and department stores. The manufacturer of the popular Thomas the Tank Engine toys, for example, withdrew its line of toys from big retailers like Toys R Us and offered it instead to mom-and-pop stores and other small specialty retailers. Selling through specialty toy stores creates an image of exclusivity for Thomas the Tank. Small specialty shops also provide a low-risk testing ground for new toy concepts.[6]

Supermarkets

U.S. consumers spend about 8 percent of their disposable income in supermarkets.[7] A **supermarket** is a large, departmentalized, self-service retailer that specializes in food and some nonfood items.

A decade ago, industry experts predicted the decline of the supermarket industry, whose slim profit margins of just 1 to 2 percent of sales left it vulnerable. These experts originally felt that supermarkets would merely need an ever-growing customer base to sustain volume and compensate for low margins. Although the annual population growth averaged less than 1 percent a year, supermarkets still experienced declining sales. As a result, experts were forced to examine not only population trends but also demographic and lifestyle changes of consumers. They have discovered several trends affecting the supermarket industry.

For example, consumers are eating out more. Of the more than $500 billion that consumers spend on food products annually, less than half is spent on food prepared at home, a decline from 70 percent in 1965. This trend is expected to continue, with spending on restaurants and takeout food overtaking the nation's grocery bill by early 1997. The growth in the away-from-home food market has been driven by the entry of more women into the work force and their need for convenience and time-saving products. Working couples need one-stop shopping, and the increasing number of affluent customers are willing to pay for specialty and prepared foods.

As stores seek to meet consumer demand for one-stop shopping, conventional supermarkets are being replaced by bigger superstores, which are usually twice the size of supermarkets. Superstores meet the needs of today's customers for convenience, variety, and service. Superstores offer one-stop shopping for many food and nonfood needs, as well as many services—including pharmacies, flower shops, salad bars, in-store bakeries, takeout food sections, sit-down restaurants, health food sections, video rentals, dry-cleaning services, shoe repair, photo processing, and banking. Some even offer family dentistry or optical shops. This tendency to offer a wide variety of non-traditional goods and services under one roof is called **scrambled merchandising**.

Another trend affecting supermarkets is consumers' focus on value. They have increasingly turned to warehouse clubs and discounters, which stock food staples at rock-bottom prices. Mass merchandise discounters like Wal-Mart and Kmart have added produce, meats, and bakeries; at the same time, supermarkets are now stocking more club-pack products, such as 12-roll bundles of toilet paper, 24-can cases of soft drinks, and cereal multipacks. As the distinction between these different types of retailers blurs, price usually becomes the focal point. Double and triple coupons, everyday low pricing, and price promotions have intensified the price wars.

Many supermarket chains are tailoring marketing strategies to appeal to specific consumer segments for an advantage over competitors that attempt to attract customers solely on the basis of low prices. By offering greater convenience and a broad variety of products, particularly in perishables and service departments, supermarkets are finding a way to stand out in an increasingly crowded marketplace.

Convenience Stores

A **convenience store** can be defined as a miniature supermarket, carrying only a limited line of high-turnover convenience goods. These self-service stores are typically located near residential areas and are open 24 hours a day, 7 days a week. Convenience stores offer exactly what their name implies: convenient location, long hours, fast service. However, prices are usually higher at a convenience store than at a supermarket. Thus, the customer pays for the convenience.

From the mid-1970s to the mid-1980s, hundreds of new convenience stores opened, many with self-service gas pumps. Full-service gas stations fought back by closing service bays and opening miniature stores of their own, selling convenience items like cigarettes, sodas, and snacks. Supermarkets and discount stores also wooed customers with one-stop shopping and quick checkout. To combat the gas stations' and supermarkets' competition, convenience store operators have changed their strategy. They have expanded their offerings of nonfood items with video rentals, health and beauty aids, upscale sandwich and salad lines, and more fresh produce. Some convenience stores are even selling Pizza Hut and Taco Bell products prepared in the store. Other retailers are experimenting with convenience stores offering fresh, prepared foods along with the traditional convenience store fare of salty snacks and beverages in an effort to attract more women. Circle K, for example, recently opened a larger experimental store called Emily's Meals & More which offers prepared meals, including desserts, hot entrees, and deli items.[8]

Discount Stores

A **discount store** is a retailer that competes on the basis of low prices, high turnover, and high volume. The discount industry has mushroomed into a major force in retailing, in part because of cautious spending by consumers brought about by the recession of the 1990s and changing demographics and priorities. The discounter of the 1960s focused solely on a full line of merchandise, but today discounters can be classified into four major categories: full-line discount retailers, discount specialty retailers, warehouse clubs, and off-price retailers.

discount store
A retailer that competes on the basis of low prices, high turnover, and high volume.

Full-Line Discounters

Compared to traditional department stores, **full-line discount stores** offer consumers very limited service and carry a much broader assortment of well-known, nationally branded "hard goods," including housewares, toys, automotive parts, hardware, sporting goods, and garden items, as well as clothing, bedding, and linens. Some even carry limited nonperishable food items, such as soft drinks, canned goods, and potato chips. As with department stores, national chains dominate the discounters. Full-line discounters are often called mass merchandisers. **Mass merchandising** is the retailing strategy whereby retailers use moderate to low prices on large quantities of merchandise and lower service to stimulate high turnover of products.

full-line discount store
Discount store that offers consumers very limited service and carries a broad assortment of well-known, nationally branded hard goods.

mass merchandising
Retailing strategy using moderate to low prices on large quantities of merchandise and lower service to stimulate high turnover products.

Wal-Mart is the largest full-line discount organization in terms of sales. With over 2,900 stores, Wal-Mart has expanded rapidly by locating on the outskirts of small towns and absorbing business for miles around. Much of Wal-Mart's success has been attributed to its merchandising foresight, cost-consciousness, efficient communication and distribution systems, and involved, motivated employees. The company expects to add over 100 new stores annually, increasing its revenues by 20 percent.[9]

Besides expanding throughout the United States, Wal-Mart has global expansion plans for Mexico, Canada, Puerto Rico, Brazil, Argentina, and China. Retailing abroad has proved to be quite a challenge for the giant discounter. In Mexico, for example, it has discovered differences in the ways that Mexicans and Americans shop. Its supercenters in Mexico operate on the notion that customers coming for general merchandise will also purchase groceries there. But Mexicans still shop at neighborhood butcher shops, bakeries, *tortillerias*, fruit stands, and egg shops, partly because items such as tortillas and *pan dulce* don't keep well overnight. Many Mexicans also favor neighborhood stores because they believe the meats and vegetables will be fresher.[10]

KMart, the number two discounter, has about 2,500 stores but has annual sales that are roughly a third of Wal-Mart's. KMart has been modernizing stores and boosting its merchandising and advertising to improve its image, but is still finding competition very stiff. In fact, KMart has had to close some stores and has experienced declining sales. Like Wal-Mart, KMart has also been expanding into Mexico, as well as into Eastern European countries. But penetration of these overseas markets has been tough, too.

A hybrid of the full-line discounter is the hypermarket, adapted from the Europeans. The flashy **hypermarket** format combines a supermarket and full-line discount store in a space ranging from 200,000 to 300,000 square feet. Although they have enjoyed widespread success in Europe, where consumers have fewer retailing choices, hypermarkets have been much less successful in the United States. Most Europeans, for example, still need to visit several small stores just for their food needs, which makes hypermarkets a good alternative. Americans, on the other hand, can easily pick among a host of stores that offer large selections of merchandise. According to retailing executives and analysts, American customers have found hypermarkets to be too big. Both Wal-Mart's Hypermart USA and KMart's American Fare hypermarket formats never got beyond the experimental stage.

Similar to a hypermarket, but only half the size, are **supercenters** which combine groceries and general merchandise goods with a wide range of services including pharmacy, dry cleaning, portrait studios, photo finishing, hair salons, and optical shops. These supercenters apply everyday low pricing to food shopping, which has made supermarkets across the nation take notice.[11] Wal-Mart now operates over 300 supercenters and plans to replace many older Wal-Marts with this format. Using supercenters as its primary growth vehicle, Wal-Mart officials note that general merchandise sales rise 20 to 30 percent after a Wal-Mart store is converted to a supercenter.[12] Along with KMart, which is opening similar Super KMart supercenters of its own, the two retailers pose a significant threat to traditional supermarkets. Target is also opening its first supercenter, which includes a more upscale general merchandise and apparel store combined with a grocery, bank branch, pharmacy, photo studio, and restaurant.[13]

Supercenters are also threatening to push Europe's traditional small and medium-sized food stores into extinction. Old-fashioned corner stores and family businesses are giving way to larger chains that offer food, drugs, services, and general merchandise all in one place. Many European countries are passing legislation to make it more difficult for supercenters to open. In France, for example, laws were passed that banned authorizations for new supercenters over 1,000 square meters (10,800 square feet). Belgium and Portugal have passed similar bans. In Britain and the Netherlands, areas outside towns and cities are off limits to superstores. By imposing planning and building restrictions for large stores, these countries are trying to accommodate environmental concerns, movements to revive city centers, and the worries of small shopkeepers.

Discount Specialty Stores

Another discount niche includes the single-line **specialty discount stores**—for example, sporting goods stores, electronics stores, auto parts stores, office supply stores, and toy stores. These stores offer a nearly complete selection of single-line merchandise and use self-service, discount prices, high volume, and high turnover to their advantage. Discount specialty stores are often termed **category killers** because they so heavily dominate their narrow merchandise segment. Examples include Toys R Us in toys, Circuit City in electronics, Staples/Office Depot in office supplies, Home Depot in home repair supplies, IKEA in furniture, and Lil' Things and Baby Superstore in baby supplies.

Toys R Us was the first category killer, offering a giant selection of toys, usually over 15,000 different items per store, at prices usually 10 to 15 percent less than competitors'. When Toys R Us came on the retail scene, department stores were generally limiting their toy assortments to the Christmas season. Toys R Us offered a broad assortment of inventory all year long. Additionally, the playing field was scattered with many small toy chains or mom-and-pop stores. With

---

hypermarket
Retail store which combines a supermarket and full-line discount store in a space ranging from 200,000 to 300,000 square feet.

supercenter
Retail store which combines groceries and general merchandise goods with a wide range of services.

specialty discount store
Retail store which offers a nearly complete selection of single-line merchandise and uses self-service, discount prices, high volume, and high turnover.

category killers
Term often used to describe specialty discount stores because they so heavily dominate their narrow merchandise segment.

its bright warehouse-style stores, Toys R Us gobbled up market share, and many small toy stores failed and department stores eliminated their toy departments. The Toys R Us chain—currently a $9 billion company with 1,200 stores worldwide—now commands some 25 percent of the U.S. retail toy business.[14] Toys R Us first went international in 1984—initially in Canada, then in Europe, Hong Kong, and Singapore. Since then, the company has opened over 200 stores in 11 foreign countries. International sales now account for 21 percent of the chain's total revenues, and Toys R Us plans to add 70 to 80 more stores around the world by the year 2000.[15]

Toys R Us
How does Toys R Us target parents through their Web site? How does Toys R Us target children?

http://www.toysrus.com/

A relatively new discount specialty store concept is the bridal superstore providing brides-to-be with a full selection of wedding products and services. The bridal superstore concept capitalizes on the fragmented U.S. bridal market—the average couple shops anywhere from 15 to 30 different places to put together their wedding. Additionally, bridal stores are consistently profitable and virtually recession-proof. The bridal superstore concept has been picking up steam since the late 1980s, fueled by changing lifestyles and shopping patterns, an influx of foreign manufacturers willing to do business with the discounters, and the departure of department stores from the service-intensive bridal business. Bridal superstores, such as David's Bridal and We Do—The Wedding Store, offer a broad assortment of bridal gowns, tuxedo rentals, dresses for attendants, accessories, wedding stationary, gifts for the bridal party, on-site alterations, and a broad selection of evening shoes and special occasion dresses. Wedding consultants are typically on hand to help couples plan the big event, offering information about local florists, photographers, caterers, musicians, limousine services, and reception sites.[16]

Warehouse Clubs

Warehouse membership clubs sell a limited selection of brand-name appliances, household items, and groceries. These are usually sold in bulk from warehouse outlets on a cash-and-carry basis to members only. Individual members of warehouse clubs are charged low or no membership fees.

warehouse membership clubs
Limited-service merchant wholesaler that sells a limited selection of brand-name appliances, household items, and groceries on a cash-and-carry basis to members, usually small businesses and groups.

Price-Costco is one of three warehouse chains that hold 80 percent of the market. Since groceries make up 60 percent of sales, warehouse clubs have had a major impact on supermarkets.
© David Strick

Warehouse clubs have had a major impact on supermarkets. Roughly 60 percent of warehouse club sales come from grocery-related items. Warehouse club members tend to be more educated, be more affluent, and have a larger household than regular supermarket shoppers. These core customers use warehouse clubs to stock up on staples; then they go to specialty outlets or food stores for perishables.

Fierce competition is commonplace in the warehouse club industry. Common practices include price slashing, selling below cost, locating outlets to compete directly with each other, and sometimes hiring away rivals' employees to get an edge in local markets. Currently, only three warehouse chains hold 80 percent of the market: Wal-Mart's Sam's Club, Price-Costco, and BJ's.[17]

Both Sam's Club and Price-Costco have been busy introducing Mexican consumers to the warehouse club concept. Club Aurrera, a joint venture between Wal-Mart and Cifra, Mexico's largest retailer, and Price Club Mexico have opened stores in Mexico City. Both have plans to blitz the country with warehouse stores.

Off-Price Discount Retailers

off-price retailer
Retailer that sells at prices 25% or more below traditional department store prices because it pays cash for its stock and usually doesn't ask for return privileges.

An **off-price retailer** sells at prices 25 percent or more below traditional department store prices because it pays cash for its stock and usually doesn't ask for return privileges. Off-price retailers buy manufacturers' overruns at cost or even less. They also absorb goods from bankrupt stores, irregular merchandise, and unsold end-of-season output. Nevertheless, much off-price retailer merchandise is first-quality, current goods. Because buyers for off-price retailers purchase only what is available or what they can get a good deal on, merchandise styles and brands often change monthly. Today there are hundreds of off-price retailers, the best known being T. J. Maxx, Ross Stores, Marshall's, and Tuesday Morning.

A couple of interesting variations on the off-price concept have emerged:

- *Single-price stores:* One new type of off-price retailer that has proliferated in the past few years is the single-price store. For a lump sum, usually $1 per item, consumers can buy anything in the store, from shoes to shampoo. Single-price stores generally offer no frills, and customers must search through piles of merchandise. Typically, single-price chains buy their merchandise in large quantities from many sources, including wholesalers and independent vendors. Most products they buy are close-out items and discontinued products. Although single-price stores experienced substantial growth in the early 1990s, major chains such as Value Merchants Inc. and All-for-a-Dollar are now faced with bankruptcy. Dollar stores are likely to gradually disappear due to widespread consumer perceptions that these stores have low-quality merchandise and an unpredictable product selection.

factory outlet
An off-price retailer that is owned and operated by a manufacturer.

- *Factory outlets:* A **factory outlet** is an off-price retailer that is owned and operated by a manufacturer. Thus, it carries one line of merchandise—its own. Each season, from 5 to 10 percent of a manufacturer's output does not sell through regular distribution channels because it consists of close-outs (merchandise being discontinued), factory seconds, and canceled orders. With factory outlets, manufacturers can regulate where their surplus is sold, and they can realize higher profit margins than they would by disposing of the goods through independent wholesalers and retailers. Factory outlet malls typically locate in out-of-the-way rural areas or near vacation destinations. Most are situated at least 30 miles from urban or suburban shopping areas so manufacturers don't alienate their department store accounts by selling the same goods virtually next door at a discount. Several manufacturers reaping the benefits of outlet mall popularity include Liz Claiborne, J. Crew, and Calvin Klein clothiers; West Point Pepperel textiles; Oneida silversmiths; and Dansk kitchenwares. Top-drawer department stores—including Saks Fifth Avenue and Neiman Marcus—have also opened outlet stores to sell hard-to-move merchandise. Dillard Department Stores has opened a series of clearance centers to make final attempts to move its merchandise which failed to sell in the department store. In order to move their clearance items, Nordstrom operates Nordstrom Rack and Boston's Filene's has Filene's Basement.

NONSTORE RETAILING

The retailing methods discussed so far have been in-store methods, in which customers must physically shop at stores. In contrast, **nonstore retailing** is shopping without visiting a store. Because consumers demand convenience, nonstore retailing is currently growing faster than in-store retailing. The major forms of nonstore retailing are automatic vending, direct retailing, and direct marketing.

4 Discuss nonstore retailing techniques.

nonstore retailing
Shopping without visiting a store.

Automatic Vending

A low-profile yet important form of retailing is automatic vending. **Automatic vending** is the use of machines to offer goods for sale—for example, the cola, candy, or snack vending machines found in college cafeterias and office buildings. Due to their convenience, consumers are willing to pay higher prices for products from a vending machine than for the same products in traditional retail settings.

automatic vending
The use of machines to offer goods for sale.

Retailers are constantly seeking new opportunities to sell via vending. For example, in an attempt to expand its distribution beyond supermarkets, convenience stores, and delicatessens, Snapple has developed a glass-front vending machine capable of offering 54 different flavors simultaneously. Another innovation is offering nontraditional kinds of merchandise, such as personal-size pizzas, french fries, cappuccino, quick dinners, and videos. Toy marketers are also using vending machines to sell toys in fast-food restaurants; about 20 Burger Kings in the South have installed machines to vend trading cards, and Pizza Hut units across the country are vending stickers and sports cards. Vending machines selling Kodak cameras and film can now be found in sports stadiums, on beaches, and on mountains. Another trend is a debit-card system for vending machines that have repeat customers.

Direct Retailing

In **direct retailing,** representatives sell products door to door, office to office or at home sales parties. Companies like Avon, Mary Kay Cosmetics, The Pampered Chef, Usbourne Books, and World Book Encyclopedia depend on these techniques. Most direct retailers seem to favor party plans these days in lieu of door-to-door canvassing. Party plans call for one person, the host, to gather as many prospective buyers as possible. Most parties are a combination social affair and sales demonstration.

direct retailing
Representatives selling products door-to-door, office-to-office, or at home parties.

The sales of direct retailers have suffered as women have entered the workforce. Working women are not at home during the day and have little time to attend selling parties. Tupperware, which still advocates the party plan method, is betting that working women have more money to spend but are just a little harder to reach. Its sales representatives now hold parties in offices, parks, and even parking lots. They hold "stop and shops" so women can just drop in, self-improvement classes, and "custom-kitchen" parties on cabinet organizing. Although most Avon sales are still made door to door, the company is now trying to pick up sales through a program called Avon Select, which offers products to customers via direct mail. The company has a toll-free number for telephone orders and will even take orders by fax.[18]

In response to the decline in U.S. sales, many direct retailers are exploring opportunities in other countries. Direct retailing is catching on in southern China, for instance, an area that has long been under communist rule. Avon began manufacturing and selling cosmetics in China in 1990. In the first year, sales were double the projections. Today, the company has more than 15,000 independent representatives selling Avon beauty products, many of whom earn more than $500 in monthly commissions, an amount most Chinese make in a year. More than 60 million people live within a 100-mile radius of Avon's Guangzhou factory, so the company has plenty of potential customers. In addition, Avon advertises on Hong Kong television, which broadcasts into China, so women in the area already are familiar with the Avon brand.

Direct Marketing

direct marketing (direct-response marketing)
Techniques used to get consumers to make a purchase from their home, office, or other nonretail setting.

Direct marketing, sometimes called **direct-response marketing,** refers to the techniques used to get consumers to make a purchase from their home, office, or other nonretail setting. Those techniques include direct mail, catalogs and mail order, telemarketing, and electronic retailing. Shoppers using these methods are less bound by traditional shopping situations. Time-strapped consumers and those who live in rural or suburban areas are most likely to be direct-response shoppers because they value the convenience and flexibility that direct marketing provides.

Privacy issues have become a major concern for many consumers and politicians in light of the advances in direct marketing techniques and the use of highly specialized database marketing. Many consumers today feel that direct marketing techniques invade their privacy. Consumers routinely receive mail from complete strangers with such highly personal information in it that they feel uncomfortable. Many consumers are raising questions about how much of the data collected and stored in databases is really necessary to making the sale. Addressing consumer concerns regarding privacy will be paramount for direct marketers as we approach the year 2000.

Direct Mail

Direct mail can be the most efficient or the least efficient retailing method, depending on the quality of the mailing list and the effectiveness of the mailing piece. With direct mail, marketers can precisely target their customers according to demographics, geographics, and even psychographics. Good mailing lists come from an internal database or are available from list brokers for about $35 to $150 per 1,000 names. For example, a Los Angeles computer software manufacturer selling programs for managing medical records may buy a list of all the physicians in the area. The software manufacturer may then design a direct-mail piece explaining the benefits of its system and send the piece to each physician. Today, direct mailers are even using videocassettes in place of letters and brochures to deliver their sales message to consumers.

Direct mailers are becoming more sophisticated in their targeting of the "right" customers. Using statistical methods to analyze census data, lifestyle, and financial information and past-purchase and credit history, direct mailers can pick out those most likely to buy their products. For example, a direct marketer like Dell Computers might use this technique to target 500,000 people with the right spending patterns, demographics, and preferences. Without it, Dell could easily mail millions of solicitations annually. Some solicitations could be targeted to only 10,000 of the best prospects, however, saving the company millions in postage while still preserving sales.

Rising postage and paper costs, increased competition, and possible government regulation threaten to cut into the profits of direct mailers. Direct-mail companies are now seeking alternative delivery methods—for instance, private delivery services.

Direct mailers have also suffered from the negative image of "junk mail." Consumers' mailboxes are filled daily with direct-mail solicitations, most of which are never read. An average consumer receives about a dozen pieces of direct mail each week, but typically opens and reads only about two-thirds of these mailings. The industry is also plagued by direct-mail scams. One common ploy is to notify consumers that they have won a fabulous prize or are a winner in a sweepstakes. When they try to collect their prize, they are informed that they must first make a purchase.

Catalogs and Mail Order

Consumers can now buy just about anything through the mail, from the mundane like books, music, and polo shirts, to the outlandish, such as a London taxi cab, an English country manor, or a diamond-studded bra.[19] Some 13 billion catalogs are mailed annually—51 for every man, woman, and child in the United States, with the typical household receiving a new mail-order catalog about every four or five days.[20] While women make up the bulk of catalog shoppers, the percentage of male catalog shoppers has soared in recent years. As changing demographics has shifted more of the shopping responsibility onto men, shopping via catalog or mail order is seen as a more sensible solution to men than a trek to a mall.[21]

Successful catalogs are usually created and designed for highly segmented markets. Sears, whose catalog sales had dropped off, replaced its "big book" with a collection of more successful specialty catalogs targeted to specific market segments. Certain types of retailers are also using mail order to good effect. For example, computer manufacturers have discovered that mail order is a lucrative way to sell computers to home and small-business users. Almost a fifth of all personal computers sold in the U.S. market are sold through the mail. Consumers can save up to 20 percent off traditional dealer prices by buying their computers from a mail-order house.[22] Some mail-order computer firms also offer free in-home repairs for a year, 30-day money-back guarantees, and toll-free phone lines for answers to questions.

Improved customer service and quick delivery policies have boosted consumer confidence in mail order. L.L. Bean and Lands' End are two catalog companies known for their excellent customer service. Shoppers may order 24 hours a day and can return any merchandise for any reason for a full refund. Other successful mail-order catalogs—including Spiegel, J. Crew, Victoria's Secret, and Lillian Vernon—target hard-working, home-oriented baby boomers who don't have time to visit or would rather not visit a retail store. To remain competitive and save time for customers, catalog companies are building computer databases containing customer information so they do not have to repeatedly give their addresses, credit card information, and so on. They also are working with overnight shippers such as UPS and FedEx to speed up deliveries. Indeed, some products can be ordered as late at 12:30 A.M. and still arrive the same day by 10:30 A.M.

Like their direct-mail counterparts, catalog retailers are suffering from rising postage rates and increased paper costs. To help cut down the costs of mailing, catalog producers are trying new delivery methods with rates as much as 5 to 15 percent below U.S. Postal Service rates. Alternate delivery, which typically involves hiring people to hang sales materials from doorknobs in plastic bags, provides several advantages over the mail: Arrival dates can be guaranteed, no laws restrict what can be delivered, and clutter is reduced.

U.S. catalog companies are also finding opportunities overseas, especially in Japan and Europe. Spiegel's Eddie Bauer division recently introduced its youthful leisurewear to Germany and has plans for a mailing in Japan. L.L. Bean already mails catalogs to over 150 countries. Nearly 70 percent of its foreign sales are from Japan, 20 percent from Canada, and 6 percent from Great Britain. Opportunities for selling by mail have increased overseas with the growth in two-worker families, quicker delivery service, and increased

L.L. Bean is known for its excellent customer service. Shoppers can order by phone 24 hours a day and return any item for any reason for a full refund.
Courtesy L.L. Bean

acceptance of shopping by mail. The fate of U.S. catalog companies in overseas markets will depend on how well they can reproduce their domestic marketing and distribution success. They must also adapt their operations to meet local competition. For instance, giant French cataloger La Redoute, wary of J. Crew's impending arrival, launched a book that offered clothing similar to J. Crew's and guaranteed free 48-hour delivery to some 800 points in France.[23]

Telemarketing

telemarketing
The use of the telephone to sell directly to consumers.

Telemarketing is the use of the telephone to sell directly to consumers. It consists of outbound sales calls, usually unsolicited, and inbound calls—that is, orders through toll-free 800 numbers or fee-based 900 numbers.

Outbound telemarketing is an attractive direct-marketing technique because of rising postage rates and decreasing long-distance phone rates. Skyrocketing field sales costs also have put pressure on marketing managers to use outbound telemarketing. Searching for ways to keep costs under control, marketing managers are discovering how to pinpoint prospects quickly, zero in on serious buyers, and keep in close touch with regular customers. Meanwhile, they are reserving expensive, time-consuming, in-person calls for closing sales.

Many consumers believe outbound telemarketing methods are intrusive. They resent persistent, obnoxious phone calls at inappropriate times by people selling everything from magazines to aluminum siding. When such calls are computerized, consumers' annoyance increases. Although the tarnished image lingers, outbound telemarketing has become a sophisticated, complex business. In particular, technological advances have enabled telemarketing firms to become more sophisticated in finding prospects and checking sales leads.

Inbound telemarketing programs, which use 800 and 900 numbers, are mainly used to take orders, generate leads, and provide customer service. Inbound 800 telemarketing has successfully supplemented direct-response TV, radio, and print advertising for more than 25 years. The more recently introduced 900 numbers, which customers pay to call, are gaining popularity as a cost-effective way for companies to target customers. One of the major benefits of 900 numbers is that they allow marketers to generate qualified responses. Although the charge may reduce the total volume of calls, the calls that do come through are from customers who have a true interest in the product.

Electronic Retailing

Electronic retailing includes the 24-hour shop-at-home television networks and on-line retailing.

Shop-at-Home Networks. The shop-at-home television networks are specialized forms of direct-response marketing. These shows display merchandise, with the retail price, to home viewers. Viewers can phone in their orders directly on a toll-free line and shop with a credit card. The shop-at-home industry has quickly grown into a billion-dollar business with a loyal customer following. Shop-at-home networks have the capability of reaching nearly every home that has a television set.

The best-known shop-at-home networks are the Home Shopping Network and the QVC (Quality, Value, Convenience) Network. Home shopping networks are now launching new services to appeal to more affluent audiences, and many traditional retailers, like Macy's, Nordstrom, and Spiegel, have experimented with their own networks. Home shopping networks have already reached the global market. Germany's first home shopping channel called H.O.T. (Home Order Television) aired in 1995 and home shopping via television is already in place in the United Kingdom, France, and 15 other European countries.[24]

Those in the industry foresee that home shopping networks will play a major role in interactive and multimedia services. Future home shopping services would essentially turn the consumer's television into a smart computer and cash register for buying pay-per-view movies, sports, shopping services, and the like. Already, subscribers in Florida can browse through a menu of over 20,000 products from a supermarket and 7,500 items from a drugstore. Using hand-held remote controls, they are able to rotate displayed products to read directions or identify ingredients.[25]

Online Retailing. Online retailing is a two-way, interactive service offered to people with personal computers. It provides customers with a variety of information, including news, weather, stock information, sports news, and shopping opportunities. Users "subscribe" to information and shopping services, usually by getting the required hardware and software and paying a monthly fee. They "log on" to online services through a modem. Or a retailer may develop and distribute CD-ROM catalogs for use with a personal computer. Spiegel, for instance, is hoping to change the face of electronic shopping and captivate women shoppers with its new CD-ROM catalog.[26]

Prodigy, CompuServe, GEnie, and America Online are the most popular electronic shopping and information services. Subscribers receive advertisements from marketers who might provide brochures, catalogs, and other information packets via the online service. Shoppers can then ask for more information or order the product directly from their computer screen. For example, a family in the market for a child's bicycle can view a picture of the model they want on the screen and find the retailer offering the best price. Once they decide, they use their computer to send a message to the retailer and electronically transfer the proper amount of money from their bank account to the retailer's. Then a delivery service can transport the bicycle to the home.

One of the most successful recent entries into online shopping is the Internet Shopping Network (ISN), a division of the billion-dollar television retailer Home Shopping Network, Inc. The Internet Shopping Network offers over 35,000 computer hardware and software products from over 600 manufacturers, and some of its software is immediately available through it Downloadable Store. The ISN includes product descriptions, specifications, and performance benefits, as well as real-time capabilities covering pricing, product changes, inventory updates, shipping, and billing. The ISN has been very successful because a large segment of the target market for computer products is computer literate.

Internet Shopping Network
What benefits does this online shopping source offer to members?
http://www.isn.com/

Despite its potential convenience, online shopping has had a slow start. The biggest problem is that relatively few people subscribe to online services, and those who do aren't typically shoppers. Users are overwhelmingly male, but most shopping dollars nationally are spent by women. Additionally, for most American consumers, shopping is fun; computing isn't. However, some online merchants are thriving. PC Flowers (http://www.pcflowers.com) has become one of the nation's biggest florists via Prodigy. Floral wire service is a perfect match to online demographics, because men buy the most flowers.

FRANCHISING

A **franchise** is a continuing relationship in which a franchiser grants to a franchisee the business rights to operate or to sell a product. The **franchiser** originates the trade name, product, methods of operation, and so on. The **franchisee**, in return, pays the franchiser for the right to use its name, product, or business methods. A franchise agreement between the two parties usually lasts for 10 to 20 years, at which time the franchisee can renew the agreement with the franchiser if both parties are agreeable.

5 Define franchising and describe its two basic forms.

franchise
The right to operate a business or to sell a product.

franchiser
Originator of a trade name, product, methods of operation, and so on, that grants operating rights to another party to sell its product.

franchisee
Individual or business that is granted the right to sell another party's product.

To be granted the rights to a franchise, a franchisee usually pays an initial, one-time franchise fee. The amount of this fee depends solely on the individual franchiser, but it generally ranges from $5,000 to $150,000. In addition to this initial franchise fee, the franchisee is expected to pay weekly, biweekly, or monthly royalty fees, usually in the range of 3 to 7 percent of gross revenues. The franchisee may also be expected to pay advertising fees, which usually cover the cost of promotional materials and, if the franchise organization is large enough, regional or national advertising. A Burger King franchise, for example, costs an initial $40,000 per store, with a 3.5 percent royalty fee and an annual advertising contribution of 4 percent of gross sales. Franchisee start-up costs, such as site location and purchasing initial supplies, are an additional $73,000 to $511,000. Fees such as this are typical for all major franchisers, including McDonald's, Wendy's, Appleby's, TGI Fridays, and so on.

Franchising offers many advantages to persons who want to own and manage a business:

- A chance to become an independent businessperson with relatively little capital.
- A product that has already been established in the marketplace.
- Technical training and managerial assistance.
- Quality-control standards enforced by the franchiser that help the franchisee succeed by ensuring product uniformity throughout the franchise system.

In turn, the franchiser gets company expansion with a limited capital investment, motivated store owners, and bulk purchasing of inventory. Franchisers also often rely on franchisees, who are much closer to the consumer than most officials at the chains' headquarters, to assist in new product development and help spot trends. For example, the Egg McMuffin, one of McDonald's best-selling items, was invented by a franchisee who spotted the opportunity to capitalize on fast-food breakfast.[27]

Franchising is not new. General Motors has used this approach since 1898, and Rexall drugstores, since 1901. Today there are over half a million franchised establishments in the United States with combined sales over $800 billion. Most franchises are retail operations. Of the $2 trillion in total retail sales, franchising accounts for over 42 percent.[28] Exhibit 15.3 provides some more facts about franchising. For more information, contact the franchising trade association, the International Franchising Association, in New York, or go to their Internet Web site at www.entremkt.com/ifa.

Exhibit 15.3
Franchising Facts

Sales	• Franchises had over $900 billion in sales in 1995. • Franchises accounted for over 42% of all retail sales. • Total franchise sales are expected to reach $1 trillion by the year 2000.
Jobs	• More than 9 million people are employed by franchise establishments. • In 1995, franchise establishments created more than 170,000 new jobs.
Growth	• A new franchise opens every 8 minutes of each business day. • The total number of franchises grew from about 550,000 in 1992 to almost 580,000 by 1997. • Less than 5% of franchises fail or are discontinued each year.
Franchisees	• 94% of franchise owners are successful. • 75% of franchise owners would repeat their franchise again; only 39% of U.S. citizens would repeat their job or business. • Average gross income of franchisees before taxes exceeds $150,000 annually. • Average total investment cost of a franchise is about $150,000 • There are more than 400 U.S. franchising companies with over 40,000 units in overseas markets.

Source: From "Franchising Facts," International Franchising Association @ www.entremkt.com/ifa. Reprinted by permission of the International Franchise Association, Washington, DC.

There are two basic forms of franchises today: product and trade name franchising and business format franchising. In *product and trade name franchising*, a dealer agrees to sell certain products provided by a manufacturer or a wholesaler. This approach has been used most widely in the auto and truck, soft-drink bottling, tire, and gasoline service industries. For example, a local tire retailer may hold a franchise to sell Michelin tires. Likewise, the Coca-Cola bottler in a particular area is a product and trade name franchisee licensed to bottle and sell Coca-Cola's soft drinks.

Business format franchising is an ongoing business relationship between a franchiser and a franchisee. Typically, a franchiser "sells" a franchisee the rights to use the franchiser's format or approach to doing business. This form of franchising has rapidly expanded since the 1950s through retailing, restaurant, food-service, hotel and motel, printing, and real estate franchises. Fast-food restaurants like McDonald's, Wendy's, and Burger King use this kind of franchising. Others who are offering similar types of franchises are Hyatt Corporation, Unocal Corporation, Mobil Corporation, and Dun and Bradstreet.[29]

 Like other retailers, franchisers are seeking new growth abroad. Australia is one of the more popular expansion countries for U.S. franchisers. Emerging nations such as Mexico, Turkey, Venezuela, and China also are appealing. In fact, the U.S. government is making it easier to open franchises in developing countries by guaranteeing 50 percent of loans obtained to open foreign franchise locations. Franchising is popular in Eastern European countries, too. Pizza Hut opened its first foreign franchise in Hungary and regularly has as many as 150 customers lined up outside. Fifteen more Pizza Huts will open in Hungary, as well as 22 KFC and 40 Dunkin' Donuts outlets.

Franchisers sometimes allow franchisees to alter their business format slightly in foreign markets. For example, McDonald's, with over 800 franchise locations in Japan, is testing food items with a Japanese touch, such as steamed dumplings, curry with rice, and roast pork-cutlet burgers with melted cheese. The McDonald's franchise in New Delhi, India, serves mutton instead of beef because some 80 percent of Indians are Hindu, a religion whose followers believe cows to be a sacred symbol of the source of life. The menu also features rice-based Vegetable Burgers made with peas, carrots, red pepper, beans, and Indian spices as well as Vegetable McNuggets.[30]

RETAIL MARKETING STRATEGY # 37

Retailers must develop marketing strategies based on overall goals and strategic plans. Retailing goals might include more traffic, higher sales of a specific item, a more upscale image, or heightened public awareness of the retail operation. The strategies that retailers use to obtain their goals might include a sale, an updated decor, or a new advertisement. The key tasks in strategic retailing are defining and selecting a target market and developing the retailing mix.

6 List the major tasks involved in developing a retail marketing strategy.

Defining a Target Market # 38

The first and foremost task in developing a retail strategy is to define the target market. This process begins with market segmentation, the topic of Chapter 8. Successful retailing has always been based on knowing the customer. Sometimes retailing chains have floundered because management loses sight of the customers the stores should be serving. For example, The Limited experienced phenomenal growth in the 1980s selling trendy apparel to young women. Today, however, many of the customers who made The Limited so successful have matured, and they now shop at stores that better reflect the sensibilities of an older consumer. Furthermore, The Limited moved into careerwear, an unsuccessful strategy that only confused its remaining customers. As a result, the company was forced to close some units.[31]

Determining a target market is a prerequisite to creating the retailing mix. For example, Target's merchandising approach for sporting goods is to match its product assortment to the demographics of the local store and region. The amount of space devoted to sporting goods, as well as in-store promotions, also varies according to each store's target market. Similarly, JCPenney's management redefined its target market to include more upscale consumers. The chain stopped selling hard goods like furniture, sporting goods, major appliances, and hardware and instead concentrated on the major profit makers of department stores: clothing, jewelry, and cosmetics. Stores were also remodeled to appeal to upscale consumers.

Target markets in retailing are often defined by demographics, geographics, and psychographics. A convenience store may define its main target as married men under 35 years old, in the lower income ranges, with two young children. A small local grocer might limit its target market to those living in the surrounding neighborhood. A department store may target fashion-conscious juniors, contemporaries who spend more money than other segments on quality clothing, and conservatives who want comfort and value.

Retailers must monitor and evaluate trends affecting their target market so the retailing mix can be adjusted if necessary. A surge in work-at-home employees and the expansion of small businesses, many launched by victims of corporate downsizing, has dramatically expanded the home-office market. These home-based workers account for roughly $6 billion in annual spending for personal computers, fax machines, and telephone products and services. Sears, one retailer tapping into the trend, has developed home-office centers specializing in equipment for home-based workers in some of its stores.

retailing mix
Combination of the six Ps—product, place, promotion, price, personnel, and presentation—to sell goods and services to the ultimate consumer.

Choosing the Retailing Mix

Retailers combine the elements of the retailing mix to come up with a single retailing method to attract the target market. The **retailing mix** consists of six Ps: the four Ps of the marketing mix (product, place, promotion, and price) plus personnel and presentation (see Exhibit 15.4).

Exhibit 15.4
Retailing Mix

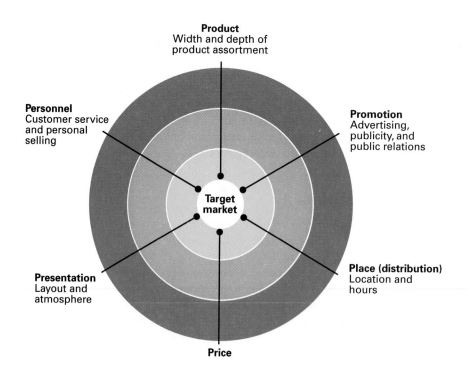

The combination of the six Ps projects a store's image, which influences consumers' perceptions. Using these impressions of stores, shoppers position one store against another. A retail marketing manager must make sure that the store's positioning is compatible with the target customers' expectations. As discussed at the beginning of the chapter, retail stores can be positioned on three broad dimensions: service provided by store personnel, product assortment, and price. Management should use everything else—place, presentation, and promotion—to fine-tune the basic positioning of the store.

The Product Offering

The first element in the retailing mix is the **product offering,** also called the *product assortment* or *merchandise mix.* Retailers decide what to sell on the basis of what their target market wants to buy. They can base their decision on market research, past sales, fashion trends, customer requests, and other sources. For example, after more companies began promoting office casual days, Brooks Brothers, the upscale retailer of men's and women's conservative business wear, updated its product line with khaki pants, casual skirts, and a selection of brightly colored shirts and ties.[32]

Developing a product offering is essentially a question of width and depth of the product assortment. *Width* refers to the assortment of products offered; *depth* refers to the number of different brands offered within each assortment. Price, store design, displays, and service are important to consumers in determining where to shop, but the most critical factor is merchandise selection. In an ambitious program to reposition itself into a competitive, moderate-priced department store, Sears, for example, has increased the amount of store space dedicated to clothes and home fashions and deemphasized tools and appliances. Sears's strategy has included a remodeling phase, as well as a push to bring women in the store to shop for apparel and cosmetics. This strategy has paid off for Sears, which has enjoyed sales gains significantly higher than rival stores.[33]

After determining what products will satisfy target customers' desires, retailers must find sources of supply and evaluate the products. When the right products are found, the retail buyer negotiates a purchase contract. The buying function can either be performed in-house or be delegated to an outside firm. The goods must then be moved from the seller to the retailer, which means shipping, storing, and stocking the inventory. The trick is to manage the inventory by cutting prices to move slow goods and by keeping adequate supplies of hot-selling items in stock. As in all good systems, the final step is to evaluate the entire process to seek more efficient methods and eliminate problems and bottlenecks.

One of the more efficient new methods of managing inventory and streamlining the way products are moved from supplier to distributor to retailer is called *efficient consumer response,* or ECR. At the heart of ECR is electronic data interchange, or EDI, the computer-to-computer exchange of information, including automatic shipping notifications, invoices, inventory data, and forecasts. In a full implementation of ECR, products are scanned at the retail store when purchased, which updates the store's inventory lists. Headquarters then polls the stores to retrieve the data needed to produce an order. The vendor confirms the order, shipping date, and delivery time, then ships the order and transmits the invoice electronically. The item is received at the warehouse, scanned into inventory, and then sent to the store. The invoice and receiving data are reconciled, and payment via an electronic transfer of funds completes the process.

Many retailers are experimenting with or have successfully implemented ECR and EDI. Dillard's, one of the fastest-growing regional department store chains, has one of the most technologically advanced ECR systems in the industry. Every item Dillard's sells has a bar code, so on any given day management knows how many pairs of 9 West slingback ladies' shoes, for instance, have been sold. If the shoes are sell-

product offering
The mix of products offered to the consumer by the retailer, also called the product assortment or merchandise mix.

ing fast, Dillard's ECR system automatically orders more from the company warehouse. The warehouse, in turn, reorders automatically from the vendor. Thus, Dillard's stores are less likely than competitors' to be out of popular items or loaded up with unfashionable ones that eventually have to be marked down.

Advances in computer technology have also helped retailers spot new opportunities, such as the latest fashions. These styles can be recreated on a computer, and the designs can be transmitted electronically to manufacturers for production. New merchandise can be produced and put on store shelves in weeks rather than months. This speed gives retailers like Dillard's a competitive advantage over other fashion retailers.

Promotion Strategy

Retail promotion strategy includes advertising, public relations and publicity, and sales promotion. The goal is to help position the store in consumers' minds. Retailers design intriguing ads, stage special events, and develop promotions aimed at their target markets. For example, today's grand openings are a carefully orchestrated blend of advertising, merchandising, goodwill, and glitter. All the elements of an opening—press coverage, special events, media advertising, and store displays—are carefully planned.

Retailers' advertising is carried out mostly at the local level, although retail giants like Sears and JCPenney can advertise nationally. Local advertising by retailers is more specific communication about their stores, such as location, merchandise, hours, prices, and special sales. On the other hand, national advertising by retailers generally focuses on image. The "Softer Side of Sears" national advertising campaign, for example, was used to help reposition Sears as a low-priced but fashion-conscious apparel retailer. An accompanying campaign, "Come See the Many Sides of Sears," was used to promote the retailer's nonapparel merchandise, such as tools, paint, and car parts.

Often large retailers and well-known clothing designers or manufacturers of exclusive specialty products share the spotlight in an advertisement. For example, ads linking Ralph Lauren and Foley's, a department store chain, let everyone know that Foley's sells the latest fashions. In turn, they enhance Ralph Lauren's prestige by associating it with a successful, distinguished fashion retailer. While this type of arrangement, called *cooperative advertising*, is prevalent in the apparel industry, it has only recently become more common between packaged goods companies and retailers. Traditionally, marketers would just pay retailers to feature products in store mailers or a marketer would develop a TV campaign and simply tack on several retailers' names at the end of a product commercial or at the bottom of a print ad. But now the spots have become more collaborative, with clear dual objectives. For example, Kool-Aid commercials in the Midwest invite viewers to "come on into Kroger" for 10 packs of their favorite thirst quencher at $1.29.[34]

Many retailers are forgoing media advertising these days in favor of direct mail or sales promotion. Restaurants have successfully used frequent diner programs for years. Now department store retailers like Macy's and Bloomingdale's are offering frequent shopper programs that shower top shoppers with perks ranging from advance warning on sales and free gift wrapping to store discounts based on spending. Other retailers are flocking to direct-mail and catalog programs in the hopes they will prove a cost-effective means of increasing brand loyalty and spending by core customers. Nordstrom mails catalogs featuring brand-name and private-brand clothing, shoes, and accessories to target the shop-at-home crowd. Home repair outlets such as Lowe's and Home Depot have also used direct mail, often around holidays when people have time off to complete needed repairs.

Sponsoring community events or supporting a good cause can also generate a lot of local publicity and goodwill for a retail establishment. Many large department stores still sponsor holiday parades; other retailers support community programs. Target, for example, donates 5 percent of its pretax profits to community service programs. The company is a large sponsor of Habitat for Humanity, an organization that builds homes for the poor. Target employees build 50 new homes each year, and Target contributes cash, supplies, and furnishings. Target also participates in the Good Neighbor Volunteer program, through which employees donate thousands of volunteer hours annually to various agencies; Child Care Aware, which helps parents identify and select quality child care; and Earth Day.

The Proper Location

Another element in the retailing mix is place, or site location. Selecting a proper site is a critical decision. First, it is a large, long-term commitment of resources that can reduce a retailer's future flexibility. Whether the retailer leases or purchases, the location decision implies some degree of permanence. Second, the location will affect future growth. The chosen area should be growing economically so it can sustain the original store and any future stores. Finally, the local environment may change over time. If the location's value deteriorates, the store may have to be relocated or closed.

Site location begins with choosing a community. This decision depends largely on economic growth potential and stability, the competition, political climate, and so on. Some of the savviest location experts in recent years have been T.J. Maxx and Toys R Us. Both retailers put the majority of their new locations in rapidly growing areas where the population closely matches their customer base.

Sometimes it is not the economic profile or political climate that makes a community a good location but its geographic location. One of Wal-Mart's most successful stores is located in Laredo, Texas, a city bordering Mexico. The store draws not only customers from Laredo but also Mexicans who cross the border to shop for U.S. goods. In Hawaii, KMart is a major attraction to Japanese shoppers. The Japanese come to Hawaii to buy products at reduced prices, making its geographic location a bonus for the discount retailers located there.[35]

At the mall, the local Taco Bell and Sears have a special retailing relationship. Try to name that relationship and figure out if Computerland has anything to do with it at **Hot Link—Sociobiology and Retailing**.

After settling on a geographic region or community, retailers must choose a specific site. In addition to growth potential, the important factors are neighborhood socioeconomic characteristics, traffic flows, land costs, zoning regulations, existing competition, and public transportation.

The undisputed winner in the locations race is Wal-Mart, whose strategy of being the first discounter to locate in small and rural markets made it the number-one retailer in the nation. Retailers like McDonald's, Target, and KMart now follow Wal-Mart's strategy, locating in small towns instead of large metropolitan areas, where the competition has grown fierce. However, many large retailers have not received the warm welcomes they expected, especially from small towns in the Northeast. Many merchants and citizens in small towns worry that a large national retailer will undermine local retailers, create traffic problems, and destroy the historic character of the town. For example, Home Depot experienced difficulty when it tried to open a store in Pequannock Township, New Jersey. A group called the Concerned Citizens for Community Preservation led a campaign against Home Depot which included fliers and signs documenting alleged crime and traffic and safety problems associated with the retailer.[36] Wal-Mart has experienced similar difficulties. Offering such services as hair salons, mail centers, optometrists, travel agencies, pharmacies, and food outlets, a discounter like Wal-Mart has every retail destination that the average small town has, translated to a single site.

One final decision about location faces retailers: whether to have a freestanding unit or to become a shopping mall tenant.

Freestanding Stores. An isolated, freestanding location can be used by large retailers like Wal-Mart, KMart, or Target and sellers of shopping goods like furniture and cars because they are "destination" stores, or those stores consumers will purposely plan to visit. In other words, customers will seek them out. An isolated store location may have the advantages of low site cost or rent and no nearby competitors. On the other hand, it may be hard to attract customers to a freestanding location, and no other retailers are around to share costs.

One store that thrives on its isolation is the Domino's outlet near Twenty-Nine Palms, California. The only pizza joint on a military base that is home to 11,000 Marines and their families, it sells close to 4,000 pizzas a week. Other fast-food outlets such as Burger King and McDonald's are locating on college campuses and even in high schools because of the captive market. Clothing retailers, including national chains like Talbots and The Gap, also are seeking freestanding facilities. These retailers have discovered that many consumers prefer to shop outside regional malls.[37]

Shopping Centers. The tremendous boom in shopping centers began after World War II, as the U.S. population started migrating to the suburbs. The first shopping centers were *strip centers*, typically located along a busy street. They usually included a supermarket, a variety store, and perhaps a few specialty stores. Essentially unplanned business districts, these strip centers remain popular.

Next, the small *community shopping centers* emerged, with one or two small department store branches, more specialty shops, one or two restaurants, and several apparel stores. These centers offer a broader variety of shopping, specialty, and convenience goods; provide large off-street parking lots; and usually span 75,000 to 300,000 square feet of retail space.

Finally, along came the huge *regional malls*. Regional malls are either entirely enclosed or roofed to allow shopping in any weather. Many are landscaped with trees, fountains, sculptures, and the like to enhance the shopping environment. They have acres of free parking. The "anchor stores" or "generator stores" (JCPenney, Sears, or major department stores) are usually located at opposite ends of the mall to create heavy foot traffic.

The largest mall in the United States opened in 1992 near St. Paul and Minneapolis, Minnesota. Covering 78 acres and 4.2 million square feet under one roof, The Mall of America boasts 400-plus stores, an 18-hole miniature golf course, 14 movie theaters, 13 restaurants, 2 food courts, and a 7-acre Camp Snoopy amusement park operated by Knott's Berry Farm. The mall promotes itself as a tourist attraction, and some 30 percent of its traffic comes from 150 miles away or more. It even publishes its own newspaper.

Locating in a community shopping center or regional mall offers several advantages. First, the facilities are designed to attract shoppers. Second, the shopping environment, anchor stores, and "village square" activities draw customers. Third, ample parking is available. Fourth, the center or mall projects a unified image. Fifth, tenants also share the expenses of the mall's common area and promotions for the whole mall. Finally, malls can target different demographic groups. For example, some malls are considered upscale; others are aimed at people shopping for bargains.

Locating in a shopping center or mall does have disadvantages. These include expensive leases, the chance that common promotion efforts will not attract customers to a particular store, lease restrictions on merchandise carried and

Many consumers prefer to shop outside regional malls so retailers, including national chain stores such as Talbots, are adding or increasing the numbers of free-standing sites in their location mixes.

Courtesy Talbots

WOMEN'S CLASSIC CLOTHING IN MISSES AND PETITE SIZES. FOR THE STORE NEAREST YOU OR OUR CATALOG, CALL **1-800-TALBOTS**.

hours of operation, the anchor stores' domination of the tenants' association, and the possibility of having direct competitors within the same facility.

Strip centers and small community shopping centers account for about 85 percent of all retail centers and only about 50 percent of total shopping center retail sales. Retail analysts expect that by the year 2000, U.S. consumers will do even more of their shopping at neighborhood strip shopping centers. With increasing demands on their time, they will choose speed and convenience instead of the elegance and variety offered by large regional malls. In fact, in anticipation of this trend, many of the nation's shopping malls are reinventing themselves to resemble open strip malls. This move to redevelop malls is being termed *demalling*, reflecting the move away from enclosed malls.[38]

Retail Prices

Another important element in the retailing mix is price. It is important to understand that retailing's ultimate goal is to sell products to consumers and that the right price is critical in ensuring sales. Because retail prices are usually based on the cost of the merchandise, an essential part of pricing is efficient and timely buying.

Price is also a key element in a retail store's positioning strategy and classification. Higher prices often indicate a level of quality and help reinforce the prestigious image of retailers, as they do for Lord & Taylor, Saks Fifth Avenue, Gucci, Cartier, and Neiman Marcus. On the other hand, discounters and off-price retailers, such as Target and T.J. Maxx, offer a good value for the money.

A pricing trend among U.S. retailers that seems to be here to stay is *everyday low pricing*, or EDLP. Introduced to the retail industry by Wal-Mart, EDLP offers consumers a low price all the time rather than holding periodic sales on merchandise. For example, retail giant Federated Department Stores, parent of Macy's and Bloomingdales, plans to phase out deep discounts and sales over the next several years in favor of everyday low pricing.[39] Similarly, The Gap reduced prices on denim jeans, denim shirts, socks, and other items to protect and broaden the company's share of the casual clothes market. Supermarkets such as Albertson's and Winn Dixie have also found success in EDLP.

In the British retailing market, a similar type of pricing is desired by consumers. A survey of British consumers found they wanted stores to offer everyday low pricing. In fact, consumers were willing to receive less service in exchange for better prices.[40]

Presentation of the Retail Store

The presentation of a retail store helps determine the store's image and positions the retail store in consumers' minds. For instance, a retailer that wants to position itself as an upscale store would use a lavish or sophisticated presentation.

The main element of a store's presentation is its **atmosphere,** the overall impression conveyed by a store's physical layout, decor, and surroundings. The atmosphere might create a relaxed or busy feeling, a sense of luxury or of efficiency, a friendly or cold attitude, a sense of organization or of clutter, or a fun or serious mood. For example, the look at Express stores is designed to make suburban shoppers feel as though they have just strolled into a Parisian boutique. Signage is often in French, and the background music has a European flair. Likewise, many supermarkets are transforming their stores to resemble old-fashioned European street markets complete with street-lamp lighting fixtures, sit-down cafes, and wooden kiosks with colorful awnings.[41]

More often these days, retailers are adding an element of entertainment to their store atmosphere. The Nike Town store in Chicago looks more like a museum than like a traditional retail store. The three-story space displays products amid life-size Michael Jordan statues and glassed-in relics such as baseball legend Nolan Ryan's shoes.

atmosphere
The overall impression conveyed by a store's physical layout, decor, and surroundings.

A History of Air exhibit explains the pockets of air on the bottom of some Nike shoes. A video theater plays Nike commercials and short films featuring Nike gear.

The layout of retail stores is a key factor in their success. Layout is planned so that all space in the store is used effectively, including aisles, fixtures, merchandise displays, and nonselling areas. Effective store layout ensures the customer's shopping ease and convenience, but it has a powerful influence on customer traffic patterns and purchasing behavior. Supermarkets have been among the most successful types of retailers in the design of store layouts. If you have ever wondered about why toothbrushes are often at eye level, or soup is not alphabetized, then read about it in the "Ethics in Marketing" box.

These are the most influential factors in creating a store's atmosphere:

- **Employee type and density:** Employee type refers to an employee's general characteristics—for instance, neat, friendly, knowledgeable, or service-oriented. Density is the number of employees per 1,000 square feet of selling space. A discounter like Kmart has a low employee density that creates a "do-it-yourself," casual at-

Ethics in Marketing
What Supermarkets Know About You

You may have thought that supermarket layout design mainly involved putting milk at one end and bread at the other to force the shopper to walk the length of the place, but that was years ago. Each inch of space is scientifically calibrated to hold only what you are most likely to buy at the highest profit margin, and it includes the effects of lighting, color, music, and odors. The more than 30,000 products are typically displayed to lure customers in, move them deliberately about, and send them out the door with bulging grocery bags.

Most supermarkets begin with produce or flowers in order to introduce the customer to an atmosphere of freshness and crispness, color and beauty. They then move on into what one expert refers to as "a chaotic opera of flattery, soothing you with a wealth of options, making you feel that you're a chef picking over the finest in meats, the most delicate in fresh greens, the best in imported condiments, even as your cart fills with familiar hamburger meat and iceberg lettuce, prepared cake mixes, and maybe

that new frozen popcorn shrimp you've heard about." This approach is quite effective because only 31 percent of customers arrive with a list, and an average of two-thirds of all items purchased are unplanned.

The layout is combined with research that reveals, for example, that the average "eye height" of women is 59 inches and of men is 64 inches; the best viewing angle is 15 degrees below the horizontal, and thus the choicest elevations on any aisle are between 51 and 53 inches off the floor; and customers like to stand about four feet away. Similarly, if background music is slowed from a lively 108 beats per minute to a slower 60 beats, then the speed of the average cart slows, more time is spent viewing merchandise, and purchases soar by as much as 38 percent. Finally, if you alphabetize soup, sales drop by 6 percent, and if toothbrushes

are placed at eye level, sales increase by 8 percent.

Scanner technology combined with the Universal Price Code (UPC) has enabled supermarkets to determine quickly and very precisely what customers are buying and at what price, and to change their merchandising strategies accordingly. In the near future, this data collection will become even more sophisticated, with shopping carts that feature "promotronics" that are computerized screens to alert shoppers about nearby deals or new products, and to keep track of each cart's journey through the store, collecting information about which displays yield the highest purchases, including how long was spent viewing each product, and so on. The days of the KMart "Blue Light Special" announcing special product sales will be short-lived.[42]

Should supermarkets be permitted to collect and use this information to influence customers' purchases? If yes, should it be controlled and how? If not, why?

mosphere. In contrast, Neiman Marcus's density is much higher, denoting readiness to serve the customer's every whim. Too many employees and not enough customers, however, can convey an air of desperation and intimidate customers.

- ***Merchandise type and density:*** The type of merchandise carried and how it is displayed add to the atmosphere the retailer is trying to create. A prestigious retailer like Saks or Marshall Field's carries the best brand names and displays them in a neat, uncluttered arrangement. Discounters and off-price retailers may sell some well-known brands, but many carry seconds or out-of-season goods. Their merchandise may be stacked so high that it falls into the aisles, helping create the impression that "We've got so much stuff, we're practically giving it away." IKEA, the Swedish home and furniture superstore, displays its merchandise in numerous showrooms and setups around the store. Each "room" is completely furnished and fully decorated with merchandise that can be found at IKEA, from the sofa or cabinetry to the candlesticks, pictures, and window treatments. The displays help shoppers visualize how a piece of furniture might look in a real-life setting as well as with complementary accessories. Shoppers then proceed to the sales floor where merchandise is stacked up in a "help-yourself"-type environment.

- ***Fixture type and density:*** Fixtures can be elegant (rich woods), trendy (chrome and smoked glass), or old, beat-up tables, such as in an antique store. The fixtures should be consistent with the general atmosphere the store is trying to create. Adding technology as a fixture is a recent successful trend in coffee shops and lounges. The most popular examples include adding PCs to provide Internet access to customers and ultimately get them to remain in the store longer. Retailers should beware of using too many fixtures because they may confuse the customers about what the store is selling. By displaying its merchandise on tables and shelves rather than on traditional pipe racks, the Gap creates a relaxed and uncluttered atmosphere. The display tables also allow customers to see and touch the merchandise more easily.

- ***Sound:*** Sound can be pleasant or unpleasant for a customer. Classical music at a nice Italian restaurant helps create ambience, just as country-and-western music does at a truck stop. Music can also entice customers to stay in the store longer and

The Gap displays merchandise on tables and shelves instead of on pipe racks, which creates a relaxed and uncluttered atmosphere.
© Elizabeth Heyert Studios, Inc.

buy more or eat quickly and leave a table for others. For instance, researchers have found that rapid music tends to make people eat more, chew less, and take bigger bites while slow music prompts people to dine more leisurely and eat less.[43] Music is likely to have its greatest effect when shoppers are involved in a highly emotional buying decision. For most consumers, that means buying jewelry, sportswear, and cosmetics. Retailers can tailor their musical atmosphere to their shoppers' demographics and the merchandise they're selling. Music can control the pace of the store traffic, create an image, and attract or direct the shopper's attention. For example, Harrods in London features music by live harpists, pianists, and marching bagpipers to create different atmospheres in different departments. Coffee shops are also getting into the music business as are theme restaurants like Hard Rock Cafe, Planet Hollywood, Harley Davidson Cafe, and Rainforest Cafe which turn eating a hamburger and fries into an experience. Au Bon Pain and Starbucks have both sold copies of their background music, hoping that the music will remind consumers of the feeling of being in their stores. Victoria's Secret also markets its own music which it believes to be integral to its atmosphere and store image.[44]

- *Odors:* Smell can either stimulate or detract from sales. The wonderful smell of pastries and breads entices bakery customers. Conversely, customers can be repulsed by bad odors, such as cigarette smoke, musty smells, antiseptic odors, and overly powerful room deodorizers. If a grocery store pumps in the smell of baked goods, sales in that department increase threefold. Department stores have pumped in fragrances that are pleasing to their target market, and the response has been favorable. Not surprisingly, good smells generally make customers happy while unpleasant smells can put them in a bad mood. A recent experiment by social psychologists found that the aroma of roasting coffee or the smell of baking cookies made shoppers twice as likely to provide a stranger with change for a dollar than if they were in unscented surroundings.[45]

- *Visual factors:* Colors can create a mood or focus attention and therefore are an important factor in atmosphere. Red, yellow, and orange are considered warm colors and are used when a feeling of warmth and closeness is desired. Cool colors like blue, green, and violet are used to open up closed-in places and create an air of elegance and cleanliness. Some colors are better for display. For instance, diamonds appear most striking against black or dark blue velvet. The lighting can also have an important effect on store atmosphere. Jewelry is best displayed under high-intensity spotlights and cosmetics under more natural lighting. Having found that natural lighting in certain departments led to increased sales, Wal-Mart is installing natural lighting in many of its facilities.[46] Outdoor lighting can also impact consumer patronage. Consumers have reported that they are afraid to shop after dark in many areas and prefer strong lighting for safety.[47] The outdoor facade of the store also adds to its ambience and helps create favorable first impressions by shoppers. For example, Harris Teeter supermarkets utilize rural forms, materials, and details to extend the store's interior farmers' market theme to the facade. The open, gabled roof and overall building silhouette are reminiscent of rural farming architecture. The facade conveys Harris Teeter's quality reputation and fresh food emphasis in a manner that makes shoppers feel comfortable.[48]

Personnel and Customer Service

People are a unique aspect of retailing. Most retail sales involve a customer-salesperson relationship, if only briefly. When customers shop at a grocery store, the cashiers check and bag their groceries. When customers shop at a prestigious clothier, the sales clerks may help select the styles, sizes, and colors. They may also assist in the fitting process, offer alteration services, wrap purchases, and even offer a glass of champagne. Sales personnel provide their customers with the amount of service prescribed in the retail strategy of the store.

Good service is even more important in a slow-growth economy, when companies survive by keeping the customers they have. Studies show that customer retention results in above-average profits and superior growth. Home Depot is one company that has embraced that philosophy and provides its customers with excellent service. Home Depot salespeople, often recruited from the ranks of carpenters and electricians, are encouraged to spend all the time needed with customers, even if it's hours. A similar strategy has been adopted by Lowe's.

Retail salespeople serve another important selling function: They persuade shoppers to buy. They must therefore be able to persuade customers that what they are selling is what the customer needs. Salespeople are trained in two common selling techniques: trading up and suggestion selling. Trading up means persuading customers

Marketing and Small Business

Expertise: A Critical Success Factor for Small Retailers

Sales expertise isn't dead in the large chain store environment, but it's rarely outstanding. This creates a perfect opportunity for small independent retailers who really know their product—and who, perhaps, are selling a product that's a bit off the beaten track.

An example is Record-Rama Sound Archives in Pittsburgh. The company operates a single 10,000-square-foot record store and also takes mail orders. It had estimated sales of $2.7 million in 1996. To the owner of Record-Rama, Paul C. Mawhinney, records aren't just a business. They're a passion. Turning a passion into a business is what made Mawhinney successful. Mawhinney started collecting records when he was a teenager in the 1950s. By 1968, he had amassed some 140,000 records. "I reached a point where I had to decide what to do with the rest of my life. Music was my first love, so I decided to devote myself full time to it," says Mawhinney, now in his 50s.

His small shop claims one of the largest record collections of sound recordings in the world, valued at some $50 million. It represents 99 percent of all hit records made from 1948 to the present and about three-quarters of the misses, too. A staggering total of 1.5 million singles,

85,000 CDs, and 750,000 LPs are categorically housed in library-like shelves that extend to the rafters. Research services are available.

Another example is Alcala's Western Wear in Chicago. The company operates a single 10,000-square-foot Western boots and apparel specialty store on the northwest side of the city. Its estimated 1996 revenues were $1.4 million. A family business founded in 1972, Alcala's began as a tiny storefront selling inexpensive clothing. It was business as usual until the mid-1980s, when Richard Alcala, the son of the founder, noticed that the few western items the shop carried were selling briskly. He urged his father to add more boots, hats, and shirts to the inventory.

Over the next several years, western apparel and boots took over the business. "None of it was really planned," Alcala says. "The more western items we brought in, the more we sold. So we just kept increasing the inventory."

Today, the store carries a full range of western apparel and ac-

cessories, from streetwear to saddles. But boots account for the bulk of its business. Shelves are jammed with more than 5,000 pairs in every size, width, and style imaginable, from ostrich to eel skin. By some estimates, Alcala's is responsible for 9 out of every 10 pairs of boots sold in Chicago.

Boot "expertise" is a big part of the company's success. Many of the boots are custom-designed by the store's staff. Employees go through several days of training on the fine art of boot fitting. "They have to love boots and wear them," says Alcala. "That's a requirement for the job." Wowing customers with selection, service, and expertise "is what sets us apart from the competition," he continues. "Merchandise alone won't do it. Expert boot and hat fitting, free on-premises tailoring, and a lifetime cleaning guarantee goes with each pair of boots we sell."[49]

Numerous small retailers have proven that expertise in and enthusiasm for their line of product can leverage their "smallness" as a competitive advantage over the "big guys." What other factors can you think of that might contribute to a small retailer's success?

to buy a higher-priced item than they originally intended to buy. However, to avoid selling customers something they do not need or want, salespeople should take care when practicing trading-up techniques. Suggestion selling, a common practice among most retailers, seeks to broaden customers' original purchases with related items. For example, McDonald's cashiers may ask customers whether they would like hot apple pie with their hamburger and fries. Suggestion selling and trading up should always help shoppers recognize true needs rather than selling them unwanted merchandise.

As noted at the beginning of the chapter, the level of service helps in classifying and positioning retail establishments. The level of service refers to the types of services offered (credit, delivery) and the quality of service. Examples of quality service include fast checkout versus slow checkout and knowledgeable, helpful salespeople versus uninformed, sloppy, and inaccessible clerks. Quality service can also be translated into expertise in, and enthusiasm for, the merchandise sold. Read about how several small retailers have used their knowledge and expertise to offer high-quality service in the "Marketing and Small Business" box.

TRENDS IN RETAILING

7 Describe future trends in retailing.

Predicting the future is always risky, but global retailing, retailers using entertainment to lure customers, and a shift toward providing greater convenience are three of the more important trends for retailing's future.

Global Retailing

It is no accident that U.S. retailers are now testing their store concepts on a global basis. With the battle for market share among domestic retailers showing no sign of abating and growth prospects dismal, mature retailers are looking for growth opportunities in the growing consumer economies of other countries.

Several events have made expansion across national borders more feasible. First, the spread of communication networks and mass media has homogenized tastes and product preferences around the world. As a result, the casual American lifestyle and the products that symbolize it, such as Levi's jeans and Nike sportswear, have become more appealing. Second, the lowering of trade barriers and tariffs, such as with the North American Free Trade Agreement (NAFTA) and the formation of the 15-member European Union (EU), has facilitated the expansion of U.S. retailers to Mexico, Canada, and Europe.[50] Finally, high growth potential in underserved markets is also luring U.S. retailers abroad into Latin America and Asia. China, for example, contains 25 percent of the world's population and only recently opened its markets to outside concerns. While the majority of China's population still lacks consumer spending power, projections call for the country's economy to eclipse all others in the next 50 years.[51]

Expansion to Canada and Mexico is simpler logistically for U.S. retailers than transporting their stores across oceans. Cultural similarities are also greater, particularly between the United States and Canada. Canadian consumers are just as cost-conscious as those in the United States—perhaps even more so because they are burdened with heavier taxes. Like their neighbors to the south, Canadians seek high quality and low prices. As a result, U.S. discount retailers like Home Depot and Winners Apparel stores have been quite successful.

Mexico has also been a magnet for some U.S. retailers because of its potential for a growing economy. With 38 percent of the population under age 14 and the ranks of the middle class growing, Mexico is an attractive market.[52] Additionally, Mexico is extremely "understored"; the country has 550 square feet of food and apparel stores per 1,000 people, compared to 19,000 square feet per 1,000 people in the United States.

Europe provides a different kind of opportunity for large U.S. retailers. Western Europe has 3.5 million shops (approximately 1 for every 100 people), most of which are small mom-and-pop operations. The highly fragmented European market appears ripe for well-capitalized U.S. retailers. When category killers—such as Woolworth's Foot Locker, with its large assortment of athletic footwear and casual clothing—enter these markets, they steamroll the competition. The worldwide homogenization of tastes has resulted in wide demand for U.S. sneakers and jeans. The low prices and broad array of merchandise that such retail outlets offer are a magnet for shoppers.

Sears and JCPenney are two retailers looking for growth in foreign markets to make up for stagnant growth at home. Sears has been quite successful in Mexico. Although the retailer has been present in Mexico since the late 1940s, it has boosted sales in the last several years by upgrading its stores to appeal to Mexico's affluent consumers. Sears de Mexico stores feature marble floors and subdued lighting and upscale fragrances, shoes, and fashions. JCPenney, meanwhile, is constructing stores in Mexico and adding nearly a million square feet of retail space in Japan by offering its private-label apparel in 300 department stores owned by Aoyama Trading Company, Japan's largest retailer of men's suits. JCPenney is also studying its prospects for retail locations in Chile, Greece, Taiwan, and Thailand.[53]

Entertainment

Adding entertainment to the retail environment is one of the most popular strategies in retailing in recent years. Small retailers as well as national chains are using entertainment to set themselves apart from the competition.

Entertainment is not limited to music, videos, fashion shows, or guest appearances by soap opera stars or book authors. Entertainment includes anything that makes shoppers have a good time, that stimulates their senses or emotions, and that gets them into a store, keeps them there, and encourages them to buy and to keep coming back. The quiet, comfortable couches and cafes of bookstores and combination book and music retailers such as Barnes & Noble, Books-a-Million, Borders, and Media Play are just as entertaining as the Gershwin tunes coming from the piano in a Nordstrom's atrium. But catching the attention of many younger consumers involves the flash and glitz of video screens on walls in clothing stores, hair salons, and theme restaurants. For example, The Daily Planet, a restaurant in LaGrangeville, New York, has a nostalgia theme with movie and cartoon posters, clips from old films on TV screens, and a juke box. Likewise, Larry's Shoes, a small chain of shoe stores in Colorado and Texas, has installed cappucino bars and gives free foot massages.

The increased focus on entertainment in retailing is due in part to the influence of MTV and the growth of entertainment in general as part of Americans' lives. This trend has proven to be a very effective way for retailers to differentiate their offering and to give potential customers a compelling reason for coming into their stores. "If they are happy, they may browse more, they may buy more—they won't go to the competition."[54]

Convenience and Efficiency

As discussed in this chapter's opening story, today's consumer is increasingly looking for ways to shop quicker and more efficiently. With 75 percent of women working full or part time, consumers no longer have the time to devote to shopping as they once did. Since 1980, shoppers have cut down from three mall visits a month to 1.6 visits. And instead of stopping by seven stores during one shopping trip, they're down to just three.[55] As a result, retailers must learn to better manage the patronage experience. Consumers are no longer satisfied because a store merely met their expectations. They desire delightful experiences brought about by retailers who anticipate consumers' expectations and go the extra mile to exceed them on a regular basis. Dimensions in which retailers can far exceed expectations include shopping assistance, the buying process, delivery and installation of the product, service after the sale, and disposal and renewal of the product.

In the future, consumers who need staples will be able to use home scanners to record bar codes and update electronic shopping lists.

© 1995 Chuck Savage/The Stock Market

Examples of ways this can be done include offering services such as pick-up for shoppers who do not want to fight traffic, baby-sitting services, free drinks and refreshments during shopping, and preferred-shopper parking spaces. For example, the Star Market in Boston offers parents a child-care center where they can leave their kids while buying groceries.[56] Some drugstores are adding conveniences such as drive-through windows to pick up prescriptions and offering additional services such as flu shots and cholesterol screenings.[57] In addition, retailers who maintain records of consumers' preferences in product features will be able to offer individualized attention to consumers during product selection. Sales associates can preselect items that are most likely to be preferred by the customer. For example, the store's records may indicate that a consumer prefers a particular style of suit, leading the sales associate to show the consumer the new suits for the season in that style.[58] Supermarket retailing experts predict that in the future, retailers, especially supermarkets, will become true marketers rather than marketers that act as distribution centers. For instance, packaged goods and staples won't be sold in supermarkets. Instead, they will be delivered directly to consumers at home, within 15 minutes of an order's placement, freeing shoppers to visit stores for things they enjoy buying—fresh produce, meats, and the fixings for a dinner party. Consumers who need staples would use hand scanners to record products' bar codes and update electronic shopping lists. Magazine ads would also carry bar codes so consumers could scan pages to put new products on their lists. Another new direction for supermarkets is to sell solutions rather than ingredients. For instance, the products for a spaghetti dinner would all be grouped in one part of the store. Other possible solutions would be the categories "kids' lunch," "diet," "bridge club," "tight budget," or "new and exciting." Several merchants in the Netherlands already follow this practice. A poultry shop, for instance, will sell all the ingredients needed to cook a complete meal. The explosion of warehouse clubs shows that consumers want a more convenient way to do the shopping they don't enjoy. Other industries have already taken steps to improve convenience. Automatic teller machines have made visiting the bank to get cash unnecessary. Pizza delivery service has made going to a pizzeria optional. Mail-order pharmacies have grown into a billion-dollar business, with the majority of all prescriptions now being refilled by mail. Home shopping channels and catalog shopping have boomed in the past several years. It's just a matter of time before supermarkets follow these trends.

CURRENT PROBLEMS AFFECTING RETAILING

8 Discuss present problems in retailing.

Although retailing is generally profitable, especially for the companies listed in Exhibit 15.1, the industry is not without its difficulties. Besides being in one of the most competitive industries, retailers today face several problems, including ineffective management, too many stores, category killers and alternative retailing formats, and a decrease in consumer shopping.

Proactive management, efficiency, and a thorough understanding of the market are requirements for success in this fiercely competitive arena. Small retail businesses run by people with a good idea but little experience, training, or capital rarely last even a year. As one seasoned executive put it, "Retailing is an industry that eats its young." Each year about 12,000 retailers go out of business.[59]

A problem plaguing retailing in general and department stores in particular is too many stores. This excess stems mainly from the overexpansion of chain retailers. The growth of retail space has consistently outstripped both population growth and consumer spending. Nationally, retail space has grown over 50 percent in the past decade, to 4.6 billion square feet—18 square feet for every citizen.[60] Meanwhile, retail sales per square foot, a key measure of productivity, have fallen by about 12 percent.[61] Thus, much more retail square footage is available than is needed to serve the population profitably.

Marketing to small, very specific segments (niche marketing) also has the potential to harm traditional department stores and specialty stores. The category killers offer an enormous selection in a single product category. Financial strength, marketing skill, and reasonably priced merchandise enable them to bully their way into almost any market, however saturated, and meet their profit objectives. This practice, of course, severely squeezes the smaller chains and the few remaining independent department stores.

Additionally, alternative retail formats such as catalogs, the Internet, and other online retailing alternatives pose a significant threat to traditional retail stores. The threat from online shopping will become even greater as appealing visual displays for products and interactive modes to attract customer attention are incorporated, and as the response speed increases and credit card security problems are resolved. Traditional retailers will have to give consumers a reason to leave their homes to purchase the same products they not only would be able to purchase without a trek to the shopping center, but also could have delivered to their doorsteps. Internet shoppers also have the advantage of comparison shopping online as well as finding product evaluations from online consumer advocate publications such as *Consumer Reports*.[62]

In spite of the strong economy during the 1990s, consumer spending in the United States has slowed compared to the 1980s. Consumers have accumulated many goods from the last decade's shopping spree and have curtailed spending and resumed saving. They now think twice about opening their wallets. Studies show that today's consumers are less interested in shopping than they were in the 1980s. Shopping is now considered a chore rather than a form of recreation. The attempt to limit the time spent shopping stands out markedly. In fact, it is so prevalent that this trend has been dubbed *precision shopping*. Many consumers have stopped going from store to store looking for bargains. Instead, they are choosing retailers that give them a good value every day, such as discounters and many forms of direct marketers.[63]

WHOLESALING INTERMEDIARIES   # 36

Another important member of the channel of distribution is the wholesaler. Wholesalers are organizations that facilitate the movement of products and services from the manufacturer to the retailer. Variations in channel structures are due in large part to variations in the numbers and types of wholesaling intermediaries. Overall, there are two main types of wholesalers: merchant wholesalers and agents and brokers. Typically, merchant wholesalers take title to the product (ownership rights); agents and brokers simply facilitate the sale of a product from producer to end user. Exhibit 15.5 shows these two main types of wholesaling intermediaries.

Generally, product characteristics, buyer considerations, and market conditions determine which type of wholesaling intermediary the manufacturer should use. Product characteristics that may dictate a certain type of wholesaler include whether the product is standardized or customized, the complexity of the product, and the gross margin of the product. Buyer considerations that affect wholesaler choice include how often the product is purchased and how long the buyer is willing to wait to receive the product. Market characteristics that determine wholesaler type include how many buyers are in the market and whether they are concentrated in a general location or are widely dispersed. Exhibit 15.6 shows these determining factors. For example, a manufacturer that produces only a few engines a year for space rockets will probably

9 List the types of firms that perform wholesaling activities and describe their functions.

Exhibit 15.5

Major Types of Wholesaling Intermediaries

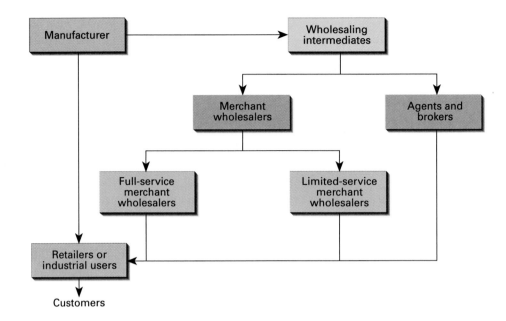

use an agent or broker to sell its product. In addition, the handful of customers that need the product are most likely concentrated near rocket-launching sites, again making an agent or broker more practical. On the other hand, a book publisher who prints thousands of books and has many widely dispersed customers with year-round demand for its product will probably use a merchant wholesaler.

Merchant Wholesalers

Slightly under 60 percent of all wholesale sales are conducted by merchant wholesalers, but they make up 80 percent of all wholesaling establishments.[64] A merchant wholesaler is an institution that buys goods from manufacturers and resells them to businesses, government agencies, other wholesalers, or retailers. All merchant wholesalers take title to the goods they sell. Most merchant wholesalers operate one or more warehouses in which they receive goods, store them, and later reship them. Customers are mostly small- or moderate-size retailers, but merchant wholesalers also market to manufacturers and institutional clients. Merchant wholesalers can be cat-

Exhibit 15.6

Factors Suggesting Type of Wholesaler to Use

Factor	Merchant wholesalers	Agents or brokers
Nature of product	Standard	Nonstandard, custom
Technicality of product	Complex	Simple
Product's gross margin	High	Low
Frequency of ordering	Frequent	Infrequent
Time between order and receipt of shipment	Buyer desires shorter lead time	Buyer satisfied with long lead time
Number of customers	Many	Few
Concentration of customers	Dispersed	Concentrated

Source: Reprinted by permission of the publisher from "Products and Markets Served by Distributors and Agents," by Donald M. Jackson and Michael F. D'Amico, pp. 27–33. In *Industrial Marketing Management,* February 1989. Copyright 1989 by Elsevier Science Inc.

egorized as either full service or limited service, depending on the number of channel functions they perform.

Full-Service Merchant Wholesalers

Full-service merchant wholesalers perform all channel functions. They assemble an assortment of products for their clients, provide credit, and offer promotional help and technical advice. In addition, they maintain a sales force to contact customers, store and deliver merchandise, and perhaps offer research and planning support. Depending on the product line, full-service merchant wholesalers sometimes provide installation and repair as well. Full service also means "going the extra mile" to meet special customer needs, such as offering fast delivery in emergencies.

Limited-Service Merchant Wholesalers

As the name implies, limited-service merchant wholesalers perform only a few of the full-service merchant wholesaler's activities. Generally, limited-service merchant wholesalers carry a limited line of fast-moving merchandise. They do not extend credit or supply market information. Limited-service wholesalers represent just a small part of the merchant wholesaling industry.

Agents and Brokers

Agents and brokers represent retailers, wholesalers, or manufacturers and do not take title to the merchandise. Title reflects ownership, and ownership usually implies control. Unlike wholesalers, agents or brokers only facilitate sales and generally have little input into the terms of the sale. They do, however, get a fee or commission based on sales volume. Many perform fewer functions than limited-service merchant wholesalers.

TRENDS IN WHOLESALING

Some large retailers find wholesaling intermediaries unnecessary. Although wholesalers were once vital links in the distribution pipeline, their value is now being questioned in such business segments as groceries, mass merchandising, pharmaceuticals, and industrial supplies. Manufacturers worry that wholesalers' markups will hinder their competitiveness. Retailers and end users feel their bargaining power is diminished when they cannot deal directly with vendors. Thus, pressure is coming from both ends of the marketing channel. For example, even in Japan, many retailing entrepreneurs are slashing prices by avoiding wholesalers altogether. By purchasing goods directly from the manufacturer, efficient new retailers are able to sell their goods for two-thirds of the department store price. Realizing that few of them will survive today on inventory alone, many savvy wholesalers are repositioning themselves as "value-added distributors" and playing more of a coordinating role between manufacturers and retailers. Wholesalers that can help identify and weigh distribution options, serve as the channel's information center, and at the same time reduce the delivered cost of product will be the winners in the future world of wholesaling. LCR, a multimillion-dollar plumbing supply wholesaler located in Baton Rouge, Louisiana, has been very successful doing just that. The company developed sophisticated telemarketing capabilities and added information collection and analysis as a value-added service to help customers make more informed decisions. But perhaps most innovative was a concept they labeled "Your-Other-Warehouse." They became a master wholesaler of plumbing supplies for small retail plumbing supply companies. By combining this with overnight delivery, they were able to take over the inventory function for their small retail customers and save them money. This innovative approach is now generating millions of dollars in sales annually that LCR did not have in the past and would not have otherwise gotten.

KEY TERMS

LOOKING BACK

Think back now to the opening story about changes in consumers' shopping patterns. Retailers are no longer just competing with other retailers such as discounters, specialty and department stores, and other forms of retailing such as direct-mail retailers; they are faced with having to identify ways to attract customer attention. Retailers are realizing that they must give consumers a good reason to shop in their stores. To do this, many stores are transforming their retailing strategies to reflect what the consumer wants: more for less.

SUMMARY

1 *Discuss the importance of retailing in the U.S. economy.* Retailing plays a vital role in the U.S. economy for two main reasons. First, retail businesses contribute to our high standard of living by providing a vast number and diversity of goods and services. Second, retailing employs a large part of the U.S. working population—over 19 million people.

2 *Explain the dimensions by which retailers can be classified.* Many different kinds of retailers exist. A retail establishment can be classified according to its ownership, level of service, product assortment, and price. On the basis of ownership, retailers can be broadly differentiated as independent retailers, chain stores, or franchise outlets. The level of service retailers provide can be classified along a continuum of high to low. Retailers also classify themselves by the breadth and depth of their product assortment; some retailers have concentrated product assortments while others have extensive product assortments. Last, general price levels also classify a store, from discounters offering low prices to exclusive specialty stores where high prices are the norm. Retailers use these latter three variables to position themselves in the marketplace.

3 *Describe the major types of retail operations.* The major types of retail stores are department stores, specialty retailers, supermarkets, convenience stores, and discount stores. Department stores carry a wide assortment of shopping and specialty goods, are organized into relatively independent departments, and offset higher prices by emphasizing customer service and decor. Specialty retailers typically carry a narrower but deeper assortment of merchandise and emphasize distinctive products and a high level of customer service. Supermarkets are large self-service retailers that offer a wide variety of food products and some nonfood items. Convenience stores carry a limited line of high-turnover convenience goods. Finally, discount stores offer low-priced general merchandise and consist of four types: full-line discounters, discount specialty retailers, warehouse clubs, and off-price retailers.

4 *Discuss nonstore retailing techniques.* Nonstore retailing, which is shopping outside a store setting, has three major categories. Automatic vending uses machines to offer products for sale. In direct retailing, the sales transaction occurs in a home setting, typically through door-to-door sales or party plan selling. Direct marketing refers to the techniques used to get consumers to buy from their homes. Those techniques include direct mail, catalogs and mail order, telemarketing, and electronic retailing, such as home shopping channels and online shopping over the Internet.

5 *Define franchising and describe its two basic forms.* Franchising is a continuing relationship in which a franchiser grants to a franchisee the business rights to operate or to sell a product. Modern franchising takes two basic forms. In product and trade-name franchising, a dealer agrees to buy or sell certain products or product lines from a particular manufacturer or wholesaler. Business format franchising is an ongoing business relationship in which a franchisee uses a franchiser's name, format, or method of business in return for several types of fees.

 # 38

6 *List the major tasks involved in developing a retail marketing strategy.* Retail management begins with defining the target market, typically on the basis of demographic, geographic, or psychographic characteristics. After determining the target market, retail managers must develop the six variables of the retailing mix: product, promotion, place, price, presentation, and personnel.

7 *Describe future trends in retailing.* With increased competition and slow domestic growth, mature retailers are looking for growth opportunities in the developing consumer economies of other countries. The homogenization of tastes and product preferences around the world, the lowering of trade barriers, and the emergence of underserved markets has made the prospects of expanding across national borders more feasible for many retailers. Additionally, adding entertainment to the retail environment is one of the most popular strategies in retailing in recent years. Small retailers as well as national chains are using entertainment to set themselves apart from the competition. Finally, retailers of the future will offer more convenience and efficiency to consumers. Staples won't be sold in stores but will instead be delivered directly to the consumer, freeing shoppers to visit stores for products they enjoy buying. Advances in technology will make it easier for consumers to obtain the products they want. Growing consumer demand for convenience will move retailers to be more solution oriented than product oriented.

8 *Discuss present problems in retailing.* Several problems plaguing the retailing industry include ineffective management, too many stores, category killers and alternative retailing formats, and a decrease in consumer shopping. First, retail managers often fail to be proactive and efficient or to gain a thorough understanding of the competitive market, leading to their stores' demise. Second, because of the overexpansion of chain retailers, the growth of retail space has consistently outstripped both population growth and consumer spending for the past several years. There are now too many stores for the number of shoppers. Third, by offering an enormous selection in a single product category at lower prices, category killers threaten traditional department stores and mass merchandisers and severely squeeze the smaller chains and the few remaining independent retailers. Additionally, alternative retail formats, such as home shopping and electronic retailing, also pose a significant threat to traditional retail stores. Finally, slow job growth and recession have caused consumer spending to slacken in the United States. As a result, today's consumers are less interested in shopping than they were in the 1980s.

9 *List the types of firms that perform wholesaling activities and describe their functions.* Wholesalers are classified into two basic categories: merchant wholesalers and agents and brokers. Merchant wholesalers are independent businesses that take title to goods and assume ownership risk. Full-service merchant wholesalers perform all channel functions. As their name suggests, limited-service merchant wholesalers perform only a few of the channel functions. Agents and brokers facilitate sales but do not take title to goods or set sales conditions. Brokers bring buyers and sellers together, whereas agents function as salespeople for one particular manufacturer or several manufacturers of complementary product lines.

Discussion and Writing Questions

1. Discuss the possible marketing implications of the recent trend toward supercenters, which combine a supermarket and a full-line discount store.

2. Explain the function of warehouse clubs. Why are they classified as both wholesalers and retailers?

3. Identify a successful retail business in your community. What marketing strategies have led to its success?

4. You want to convince your boss, the owner of a retail store, of the importance of store atmosphere. Write a memo citing specific examples of how store atmosphere affects your own shopping behavior.

5. Discuss the potential challenges of global retailing.

6. You have been asked to write a brief article about the way consumer demand for convenience and efficiency is influencing the future of retailing. Write the outline for your article.

7. Why is retailing said to be "an industry that eats its young"?

8. If you were to open a building products store, would you require the services of a wholesaler? If so, which type of wholesaler would you likely select and why?

9. Form a team with three classmates to identify the different retail stores in your city where VCRs, CD players, and TVs are sold. Team members should divide up and visit all the different stores and describe the products and brands that are sold in each. Prepare a report describing the differences in brands and products sold at each of the stores and the differences in store characteristics and service levels. For example, which brands are sold in Wal-Mart and KMart versus Campo and Silo versus independent, specialty outlets. Suggest why different products and brands are distributed through different types of stores.

10. Go to the Food Shop at the following Web site. How does the "Demonstration Kitchen" help retail sales of food and wine for this site?

   http://www.virtualvin.com/

11. How much does the most powerful computer with the fastest modem, most memory, largest monitor, biggest hard drive, and all the available peripherals cost at this Web site? Now configure a more affordable computer and compare the differences in features and prices.

   http://cmp.gateway2000.com/

12. Why should retailers market their printed catalogs online?

   http://www.catalogsite.com/

Application for Small Business

Ron Johnson is developing a strategy to open up his new athletic shoe and sports equipment store. He has decided to carry Nike and Converse as his two lines of athletic shoes. This will give him top-of-the-line merchandise (Nike) and a lower-priced, high-quality alternative (Converse). He obtained permission from one of his former professors to hold brainstorming sessions in a couple of his classes. From these sessions, he identified the following evaluative criteria customers might use in selecting a particular athletic shoe to purchase: (1) attractiveness/style/color, (2) brand name, (3) comfort, (4) price, (5) endorsement, and (6) quality. He also determined that location, a friend's recommendation, brands carried, and store atmosphere are important in selecting a place to purchase athletic shoes.

Questions

1. What type of retailing strategy should Ron use?

2. Which elements of the retailing mix are relatively more important?

Signature Series Video Case

Tandy Corporation

by John V. Roach
Chairman of the Board and Chief
Executive Officer, Tandy Corporation

Nineteen ninety-three was an "incredible" year. At the beginning of the year, we were ready to state unequivocally that Tandy Corporation could add more value to the consumer electronics and personal computer retailing world than we could to the consumer electronics and personal computer manufacturing world. Therefore, we announced on January 10, 1993, that we would spin off our manufacturing assets.

As our management energetically pursued the spin-off, the opportunity came to divest most of our manufacturing assets. Bill Bousquette, Bob McClure, and their team divested five multiplant entities essentially in parallel—an "incredible" task—and the result was about $615 million in cash and $100 million in notes receivable. As a result, Tandy strengthened its balance sheet for its planned retail growth in the 1990s.

Our retail growth strategy was simple: modest growth from the Radio Shack (http://www.radioshack.com) division; strong growth from Computer City, which opened 20 stores during the year; and the expansion of our newest concept, Incredible Universe, an electronics superstore offering a wide selection of home appliances, audio and video equipment, computers and computer software, as well as other electronic gadgets. The strategy was vigorously executed by our divisions.

In 1994, our retail growth strategy—basically the same simple strategy—had more ambitious goals:

- Radio Shack set its sights higher, with a commitment to increase its productivity, position itself even stronger in the marketplace, and introduce new programs to increase its top-of-mind awareness in the marketplace.

- Computer City planned to open even more stores—24 or more—and to continue testing its new smaller-market format, Computer City Express, a half-size store for markets of 100,000 to 400,000 population.

- Our Tandy Name Brand Retail Group planned to continue strengthening its formats for secondary markets and malls.

- The Incredible Universe opened its fourth store in February 1994 in Miami, Florida—our biggest opening yet—and planned up to five more openings.

Executing these ambitious plans would bring in an excess of $5 billion in revenue in 1994.

The heart of our strategy is to grow from strength. Radio Shack is unique as a consumer electronics service concept. Our geographic convenience; the availability of products in neighborhoods and remote areas not covered by competitors; our unique selection of products, parts, and accessories; our strong after-the-sale service; and our highly respected people in the store make it possible for us to say that Radio Shack has very little direct competition. Radio Shack's plan is to increase its services

this year with its new repair shop and "gift express" programs, further differentiating Radio Shack from others who sell electronic products.

Computer City's strategy is focused on providing the best brands, super selection, and great prices. The real focus is winning the battle for customer shopping experience. With only one national competitor, the competitive environment is better in the computer warehouse superstore business than in many other highly competitive retail industries.

Incredible Universe is a unique shopping experience, one we think is perfect for the future. Its real strength is that it caters to customers' intelligence. The customers—we call them "guests"—are offered incredible information about a great selection of products, a selection two to five times greater than competitors'. There is no pressure to buy specific products, service contracts, or other add-ons. Guests are encouraged to touch, use, understand, and have fun with the products and to enjoy a fun environment with everything from karaoke to food. As an Incredible Universe guest, you will receive incredible service, from speedy transactions and entertainment for your child while you shop, to help with loading your purchase in your car. Most important, with single locations per market and limited advertising, we offer "everyday low prices" so that our guests don't have to worry about the deal-driven mania of most competitors. Our strength is clearly our differentiation from other retailers.

Another of our strengths is a comprehensive infrastructure that is highly focused on customers' shopping experience. Our excellent financial position is also a major asset; when combined with our enviable market position, it permits us to deal from strength in this industry.

We will continue to develop ways of increasing the strengths of all of our formats. We currently have about half a dozen tests underway to enhance our retailing activities. We simply want to

be the market leader—the trusted market leader—in consumer electronics and personal computer retailing.

The Tandy team is made up of 42,000 people with a lot of pride in their achievements. Our management team is strong, with a deep sense of fairness for our customers and our employees. We thrive every day in a highly competitive arena, and I believe we've earned a high degree of trust from all those with whom we do business.

In our business, as in every business, selling is incredibly important. I end every company speech with the term "Sell, Sell, Sell." This is particularly important in facing what is perhaps the worst consumer electronics market in a decade, with profits not only at Tandy but also at rival retailers such as Best Buy and Circuit City slipping as shoppers show reluctance to take on debt to buy computers, big-screen TVs, or fancy stereos.

The Incredible Universe superstores and Computer City chain lost some $90 million in 1996. As a result, on December 30, 1996, Tandy decided to shut down its Incredible Universe electronics superstores and pare back the lackluster Computer City chain. We had attempted to create something totally new in the retail environment that was more high risk than anything we had ever done before, and it did not prove economically viable.

In 1997 Tandy will start getting things back on track again by adding 100 new Radio Shack stores annually for the next couple of years. It also will pursue other retail strategies that will maximize their existing retail formats and take advantage of Radio Shack's strength in hawking consumer-electronics parts.

Questions

1. Assess Tandy's decision to spin off its manufacturing assets and to focus on retailing in consumer electronics and personal computers.

2. Compare and contrast the retailing mixes (the six Ps) used to position Radio Shack, Computer City, and Incredible Universe. Why do you think Incredible Universe was unsuccessful?

3. Suggest appropriate annual growth strategies for Radio Shack.

4. Identify important environmental changes that you think will affect retailers of consumer electronics and personal computers in the next decade. What actions should Tandy take to benefit from these advancements, shifts, trends, and events?

References

Kathryn Hopper, *Tarrant Business*, October 7, 1996, pp. 15–18.

Stephanie Anderson Forest, "Promises, Promises at Tandy," *Business Week*, January 20, 1997, pp. 28–29.

Critical Thinking Case

WALGREEN COMPANY

"A pharmacy could be more than a place to buy drugs. It could be a comprehensive source of health information," according to Harvard Business School professors Richard Norman and Rafael Ramirez. Gone are the days when most drugstores were simply retail outlets with pharmacies in the back. Instead, most are evolving into vital providers in the health-care pipeline, thanks to the rise in managed health-care and increased competition from other retailers.

Since the mid-1980s, there has been a dramatic rise in the number of employers using managed care programs to lower the cost of their health-care benefits. In 1988, for example, less than a third of health-care insurance enrollees were in a managed care plan. By 1995, that figure had risen to well over 50 percent. Within a decade or so, that number is expected to increase to 90 percent of the insured U.S. population.

Managed care plans negotiate prescription costs with pharmacies, encourage the use of low-priced generics over branded prescriptions, and ask their physicians to prescribe only those drugs included in strictly defined "formulary" lists. In effect, these managed care plans have replaced individuals as the retail consumer. Oftentimes, negotiated reimbursement rates provided by managed care plans are so low that a drugstore's gross margins are reduced to the point that it becomes unprofitable.

On another front, the increased competition posed by supermarkets, discount chains and mail-order pharmacies is intensifying. Supermarkets in recent years have become more aggressive in marketing and pricing their nonfood merchandise, especially health and beauty aids which were long the mainstay of drugstore retailers. Discount chains, such as

Wal-Mart, Target, and KMart have also drastically increased their lines of health and beauty aids and over-the-counter medications. Almost all large supermarkets and discount chains today have their own pharmacy counters as well. Additionally, managed care plans encourage their subscribers to use mail-order pharmacies to fill prescriptions where costs are as much as 25 percent less than those filled at the local drugstore.

Walgreen Company is one drugstore chain that has responded remarkably well to the pressures of today's retail environment. As the nation's largest drug retailer in terms of sales, Walgreens has invested heavily in new technology, focused its merchandising and marketing on convenience, and positioned itself as a one-stop health-care center.

Information and technology have become more important to Walgreens in its efforts to lower costs and gain efficiency, especially as managed care grows as a vital element of the pharmacy business. Today, over two-thirds of all its prescriptions originate from third-party managed care providers. Walgreens was one of the first drugstore chains to install point-of-sale scanning and use this information to analyze sales, price, and performance data, as well as to manage inventory costs. Walgreens' Strategic Inventory Management System (SIMS) is totally integrated in all its distribution centers and is used by buyers in making purchasing decisions. Inventory reductions lead to savings since less work-

ing capital is tied up in inventory. By eliminating the need to price mark merchandise, scanning reduces labor costs. Labor scheduling has also been streamlined through better monitoring of sales fluctuations at various times of the day or week. As Walgreens' network advances to a just-in-time distribution environment including vendors, warehouses, and distribution centers, ordering and restocking will become increasingly efficient and increase store profits.

Increased customer information collected through computers and point-of-sale scanners also allows Walgreens to take a closer look at its customer base on a per store basis. If one store serves a larger number of diabetics, for instance, a chain can establish special services for diabetics at that location. Analysis of customer drug profiles also enables Walgreens to inform customers with specific ailments about new or superior medicines or therapies that may be available.

New, time-saving services also reflect Walgreens' attempts at catering to the convenience desires of its customers. Most new and many remodeled stores have single, double, or even triple drive-through pharmacy windows. Additionally, several hundred Walgreens stores now offer 24-hour service. Its 1-800-WALGREENS number offers emergency prescription delivery and, in some markets, phone systems permit customers needing a refill to call in, punch in their prescription number, and pick up the filled prescription at their convenience. Stores have also added more higher-margin convenience items, such as milk, one-hour photo finishing, and video rentals to promote convenience and increase profitability.

The quest for convenience has led Walgreens to spurn strip malls in favor of building new, freestanding stores in locations that have lots of parking and higher visibility to drive-by traffic. New stores are much bigger than the traditional Walgreens store, averaging 14,000 square feet. Store layouts are more organized to promote fast in-and-out shopping. Walgreens has also replaced the drab, narrow, and imposing shelves often found in today's drugstores with airier, lighter designs, colorful displays, staggered aisles, and bigger waiting areas at pharmacies. Additionally, a new format, called Rx-Press, is a smaller, pharmacy-only outlet with convenient drive-through service.

Recognizing that its strongest franchise is still the pharmacy business, Walgreens has positioned its stores as knowledgeable, service-oriented health-care centers. Pharmacists now offer professional counseling to help patients comply with their drug regimens and provide valuable information on health issues and fitness. To cultivate loyalty, its pharmacists study patient drug profiles to spot possible drug interactions, overuse of medications, or overly expensive use of medications. Walgreens pharmacies are also taking on routine medical tasks that many managed care organizations believe are too time consuming and costly to bother doctors with. Over 2,100 Walgreens stores now administer flu shots each fall. Additionally, Walgreens' Central Florida outlets recently offered women a screening program for osteoporosis.

Questions

1. Considering that managed care plans have replaced individuals as the retail consumer in the majority of prescription drug sales, what effect does this have on Walgreens' retail strategy? Specifically, with managed care plans as the target customer, how does this change Walgreens' traditional retailing strategy (i.e., product, place, price, promotion, presentation, and personnel)?
2. Do you feel that Walgreens will be successful at emphasizing convenience goods and services over their core pharmaceutical business? Why or why not?
3. What other convenience-oriented or health-oriented services might Walgreens offer customers?
4. What advantages does Walgreens realize by building free-standing locations and larger store designs? What advantages does it realize by building smaller, pharmacy-only outlets?
5. What other ways might Walgreens use its point-of-sale scanner information to build customer loyalty?

References

Walgreen Company 1995 Annual Report and various press releases found at Walgreens' Web site, *www.walgreens.com.*

Matt Murray, "Rx for Pharmacies: Bigger Line of Products and Services," *Wall Street Journal,* 12 September 1996, p. B4.

Marianne Wilson, "Drug Stores: Declining Margins Erode Profitability," State of the Industry Special Report, *Chain Store Age,* August 1996, pp. 29A–31A.

"Drugstores Evolve with the Times," *Standard & Poor's Industry Surveys,* 9 May 1996, pp. R95–R98.

"Drugstores Evolving into Healthcare Convenience Stores," *Standard & Poor's Industry Surveys,* 25 January 1996, pp. R64–R66.

"Adapting to a Competitive Environment," *Standard & Poor's Industry Surveys,* 15 June 1995, pp. R93–R96.

Richard Norman and Rafael Ramirez, "Value Chain to Value Constellation: Designing Interactive Strategy," *Harvard Business Review,* July-August, 1993, p. 51.

Marketing Planning Activities

DISTRIBUTION DECISIONS

The next part of the marketing mix to be described for the marketing plan is the "place" portion, or distribution. Be sure that your distribution plans match the needs and wants of the target market identified and described earlier and are compatible with the product and service issues discussed in the previous section. Also refer to Exhibit 2.8 for additional marketing plan subjects.

1. Discuss the implications of dual/multiple distribution. If your firm, for example, sells through a major department store and its own catalog, and then decides to have an online World Wide Web site and open its own store in a factory outlet, what will happen to channel relationships? To the final price offered to consumers? To promotional vehicles?

Marketing*Builder* Exercise

- **Distribution Channels** portion of the **Sales Plan** template

2. Decide what channel(s) your chosen company should be using. Describe the intermediaries involved and their likely behavior. What are the implications of these channels?

Marketing*Builder* Exercise

- **Alliances** portion of the **Sales Source Analysis** spreadsheet

3. Which distribution intensity level would be best for your company's product? Justify your decision.

4. What type of physical distribution facilities will be necessary to distribute the product? Where should they be located? How should the product be distributed? Justify your selection of transportation mode(s).

5. What types of retail establishments might be used for your firm's product? Are they in locations convenient to the target customers? What is the atmosphere of the facility?

Integrated Marketing Communications

1 Discuss the role of promotion in the marketing mix.

2 Discuss the elements of the promotional mix.

3 Describe the communication process.

4 Explain the goals and tasks of promotion.

5 Discuss the hierarchy of effects concept and its relationship to the promotional mix.

6 Describe the factors that affect the promotional mix.

7 Explain how to create a promotion plan.

8 Describe the ethical and legal aspects of promotion.

Promotion Strategy and Marketing Communication

On August 24, 1995, Microsoft Corporation debuted its long-awaited Windows 95 operating system and with it a promotional blitz that could make Revlon blush. The global marketing phenomenon used every medium and marketing scheme imaginable, ranging from television, print, and cooperative advertisements to massive in-store promotions, public relations, and publicity stunts. With a promotional budget of over $200 million for its first year alone and an additional $500 million from retailers and hardware and software companies, marketing historians were hard-pressed to come up with comparisons to the Windows 95 takeoff.

The software giant rested heavily on classic consumer marketing for the Windows 95 launch, focusing television and print advertising on the product and its benefits. To the tune of "Start Me Up" by the Rolling Stones, television ads showed the operating system's on-screen, mouse-click "start" button icon. This button symbolized Windows 95's ability to allow users to start doing computing tasks in new ways and to start doing more on a computer. The ads encouraged computer users to join the movement to Windows 95 and to participate in something that was changing the computing world. The television ads ran in some 23 countries around the world. Ads also appeared on World Wide Web sites that linked Internet surfers to Microsoft's own home page.

Sales promotions for the new operating system included a special run of 5,000 Cracker Jack boxes packing Windows 95 key chains and coupons for free personal computers to a few lucky winners. In Britain, Microsoft painted fields with giant Windows 95 logos for viewing by plane. In Toronto, it unfurled a 300-foot Windows 95 banner down the city's tallest building. In Australia, all babies born on August 24 received a free copy of the software, producing 700 new "early adopters" Down Under. The company also hosted launch events in 40 U.S. cities—from a shindig for 2,000 at the Las Vegas Luxor Hotel to an all-day "fun fest" for 4,000 at the Great America's theme park in Silicon Valley.

Computer retailers also took part in the hype surrounding the launch. Many retailers took part in "Midnight Madness," opening their stores at midnight on August 23 for 95 minutes to sell the first copies of Windows 95. Experts estimated that there were over 1.2 million in-store demonstrations of the Windows 95 operating system before the August 24 debut and over a quarter of a million in-store displays put up by computer retailers.

Despite the huge advertising and sales promotion budgets that surrounded the Windows 95 launch, perhaps the most effective promotion came at no or little cost at all to Microsoft. In a media circus rivaling a political convention, some 500 reporters and dozens of television crews descended on Microsoft's Redmond, Washington, headquarters for the launch event that took place on the campus. In print media alone, Windows 95 captured some 3,000 headlines and over 6,500 stories within the two months prior to the debut. On television, the Windows 95 launch rivaled other major television news coverage of the Bosnian war and Disney's takeover of Capital Cities/ABC.

Adding to all of this media hype was Bill Gates, Microsoft's founder and chairman, who lent his presence and fame to the Windows 95 campaign with an enthusiasm rivaled by few chief executives. Spreading his message on why Windows 95 will change the world of computing, Mr. Gates appeared on "Good Morning America" and "Larry King Live," participated in dozens of other television interviews, and attended dozens of parties. Mr. Gates also starred in a 30-minute, prime-time network infomercial focusing on the benefits of Windows 95 which aired over two days following the launch. Never press-shy, Mr. Gates even starred in a Coke commercial that appeared exclusively during his own infomercial.

All this promotional effort paid off for Microsoft: In the first 30 days on the market, Windows 95 sold more than 7 million copies worldwide. A year after its introduction, Windows 95 celebrated its first anniversary with sales of more than 40 million units.[1]

Microsoft used several forms of promotion to communicate its debut of the Windows 95 operating system. Advertisements promoted the benefits of the system; sales promotion activities by Microsoft and retailers created excitement and boosted sales; media publicity added to the hype; and public relations efforts featuring Microsoft's chairman spread Windows 95's message. Creating a promotional phenomenon around

the launch insured the success of the operating system and its adoption by millions of personal computer users.

As you can see, Microsoft places considerable emphasis on promotion in its marketing mix. What is the role of promotion in the marketing mix? What types of promotional tools are available to companies and what factors influence the choice of tool? How is the promotion plan created? The rest of the chapter answers these questions.

Microsoft Corporation
How does Microsoft promote Windows 95 via its Web page? What strategies does Microsoft use to influence potential customers?
http://www.microsoft.com/

THE ROLE OF PROMOTION IN THE MARKETING MIX

1 Discuss the role of promotion in the marketing mix.

promotion
Communication by marketers that informs, persuades, and reminds potential buyers of a product in order to influence an opinion or elicit a response.

promotional strategy
Plan for the optimal use of the elements of promotion: advertising, public relations, personal selling, and sales promotion.

Few goods or services, no matter how well developed, priced, or distributed, can survive in the marketplace without effective promotion. **Promotion** is communication by marketers that informs, persuades, and reminds potential buyers of a product in order to influence their opinion or elicit a response.

Promotional strategy is a plan for the optimal use of the elements of promotion: advertising, public relations, personal selling, and sales promotion. As Exhibit 16.1 shows, the marketing manager determines the goals of the company's promotional strategy in light of the firm's overall goals for the marketing mix—product, place (distribution), promotion, and price. Using these overall goals, marketers then combine the elements of the promotional strategy (the promotional mix) into a coordinated plan. The promotion plan then becomes an integral part of the marketing strategy for reaching the target market.

The main function of a marketer's promotional strategy is to convince target customers that the goods and services offered provide a differential advantage over the competition. A differential advantage is the set of unique features of a company and its products that are perceived by the target market as significant and superior to the competition. Such features can include high product quality, rapid delivery, low prices, excellent service, or a feature not offered by the competition. For example, Revlon's ColorStay Lipcolor promises unsmeared lipstick all day long. By effectively communicating this differential advantage through advertising featuring model Cindy Crawford, Revlon can stimulate demand for its smudge-free line of makeup. Promotion is therefore a vital part of the marketing mix, informing consumers of a product's benefits and thus positioning the product in the marketplace.

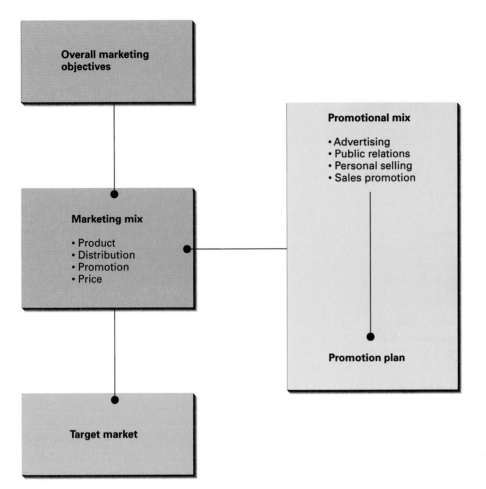

Exhibit 16.1
Role of Promotion in the Marketing Mix

THE PROMOTIONAL MIX

Most promotional strategies use several ingredients—which may include advertising, public relations, personal selling, and sales promotion—to reach the target market. That combination is called the **promotional mix**. The proper promotional mix is the one that management believes will meet the needs of the target market and fulfill the organization's overall goals. The more funds allocated to each promotional ingredient and the more managerial emphasis placed on each technique, the more important that element is thought to be in the overall mix.

Advertising

Almost all companies selling a good or a service use some form of advertising, whether it be in the form of a multimillion-dollar campaign or a simple classified ad in a newspaper. **Advertising** is any form of paid communication in which the sponsor or company is identified. Traditional media—such as television, radio, newspapers, magazines, books, direct mail, billboards, and transit cards (advertisements on buses and taxis and at bus stops)—are most commonly used to transmit advertisements to consumers. Marketers, however, are finding many new ways to send their advertisements, most notably through such electronic means as the Internet, computer modems, and fax machines.

One of the primary benefits of advertising is its ability to communicate to a large number of people at one time. Cost per contact, therefore, is typically very low. Ad-

2 Discuss the elements of the promotional mix.

promotional mix
Combination of promotion tools—including advertising, public relations, personal selling, and sales promotion—used to reach the target market and fulfill the organization's overall goals.

advertising
Impersonal, one-way mass communication about a product or organization that is paid for by a marketer.

"I'm getting a lot more car than what I'm writing a check for."
Steve Schlief
Former Acura Owner

"It's fun to drive."
Julia Maynard
Former Accord Owner

"It handles extremely well."
Kenneth Wilburn
Former Saturn Owner

EXCELLENT HANDLING.
GREAT RESPONSE.

STARTING AT
$18,545

FORD TAURUS
THE BEST-SELLING CAR IN AMERICA.

• 24-VALVE, DOHC DURATEC V-6 ENGINE™ • SPEED-SENSITIVE POWER STEERING • QUADRALINK
REAR SUSPENSION • STANDARD DUAL AIR BAGS (ALWAYS WEAR YOUR SAFETY BELT)
• SAFETY CELL CONSTRUCTION • AVAILABLE SIX-PASSENGER SEATING • www.ford.com
'97 Taurus G MSRP: LX shown w/PEP 210A MSRP $23,870. Tax, title extra. *LX model only.

      HAVE YOU DRIVEN A FORD LATELY?   *Ford*

Although the cost of advertising can be quite high, it has many benefits. For example, the millions of dollars Ford Motor Company spent advertising its redesigned Taurus resulted in sales that make it "the best-selling car in America."
Courtesy Ford Motor Company

public relations
Marketing function that evaluates public attitudes, identifies areas within the organization that the public may be interested in, and executes a program of action to earn public understanding and acceptance.

publicity
Public information about a company, good, or service appearing in the mass media as a news item.

vertising has the advantage of being able to reach the masses (for instance, through national television networks), but it can also be microtargeted to small groups of potential customers, such as with direct mail to a select group of customers or through print advertising in a trade magazine.

Although the cost per contact in advertising is very low, the total cost to advertise is typically very high. This hurdle tends to restrict advertising on a national basis to only those companies that are financially able to do so. For example, to introduce its redesigned 1996 Taurus, Ford spent approximately $55 million over three months on advertisements. Commercials for the new Taurus were placed on national TV and print ads appeared in consumer magazines. In one of its biggest launches ever, Ford even became the sole advertiser in key magazines, such as buying the entire *Sports Illustrated* special football issue, the fall *Elle* style and design issue, and the *Life* magazine issue featuring the Beatles.[2] Few small companies can match this level of spending for a national campaign.

Chapter 17 examines advertising in greater detail.

Public Relations

Concerned about how they are perceived by their target markets, organizations often spend large sums to build a positive public image. **Public relations** is the marketing function that evaluates public attitudes, identifies areas within the organization that the public may be interested in, and executes a program of action to earn public understanding and acceptance. Public relations helps an organization communicate with its customers, suppliers, stockholders, government officials, employees, and the community in which it operates. Marketers use public relations not only to maintain a positive image but also to educate the public about the company's goals and objectives, introduce new products, and help support the sales effort.

A solid public relations program can generate favorable publicity. **Publicity** is public information about a company, good, or service appearing in the mass media as a news item. The organization is not generally identified as the source of the information. For example, the wine industry received favorable publicity after several medical studies found a link between good health and the consumption of red wine. Sales of red wine jumped dramatically after the report.[3] This incident underscores a peculiar reality of marketing: No matter how many millions are spent on advertising, nothing sells a product better than free publicity.

Although an organization does not pay for this kind of mass media exposure, publicity should not be viewed as free. Preparing news releases and persuading media personnel to print or broadcast them costs money. Therefore, originating good publicity can be expensive. For example, winemakers wishing to capitalize on the results of the scientific studies (which they are not allowed to use in advertising) are sponsoring workshops and conferences that discuss the findings and their benefits to wine drinkers in the hopes that this information will be picked up by the media.[4]

Unfortunately, bad publicity can also cost a company millions. Through the mass media, the world learns when a firm pollutes a stream, produces a defective product, employs executives engaged in payoffs or bribes, or is accused of other undesirable acts. Negative consumer reactions may cost the firm plenty in lost sales. These negative reactions may also stretch to the industry as a whole. For instance, in the wake of the crash of a ValuJet airplane in the Florida Everglades, which was heavily covered by the media, many potential passengers feared that cost-cutting common with low-cost airlines comes at the expense of safety.[5]

Public relations and publicity are looked at further in Chapter 17.

Personal Selling

Personal selling is a situation in which two people communicate in an attempt to influence each other in a purchase situation. In this dyad, both the buyer and seller have specific objectives they wish to accomplish. The buyer may need to minimize cost or assure a quality product, for instance, while the salesperson may need to maximize revenue and profits.[6]

Traditional methods of personal selling include a planned presentation to one or more prospective buyers for the purpose of making a sale. Whether it takes place face to face or over the phone, personal selling attempts to persuade the buyer to accept a point of view or convince the buyer to take some action. For example, a car salesperson may try to persuade a car buyer that a particular model is superior to a competing model in certain features, such as gas mileage, roominess, and interior styling. Once the buyer is somewhat convinced, then the salesperson may attempt to elicit some action from the buyer, such as a test drive or a purchase. Frequently, in this traditional view of personal selling, the objectives of the salesperson are at the expense of the buyer, creating a win-lose outcome.

More current notions on the subject of personal selling emphasize the relationship that develops between a salesperson and a buyer. This is more typical with business- and industrial-type goods, such as heavy machinery or computer systems, than with consumer goods. Relationship selling emphasizes a win-win outcome and the accomplishment of mutual objectives that benefits both buyer and salesperson in the long term. Relationship selling does not seek either a quick sale or a temporary increase in sales; rather, it attempts to create involvement and loyalty by building a lasting bond with the customer.[7]

Personal selling and relationship selling are discussed in Chapter 18.

personal selling
Planned presentation to one or more prospective buyers for the purpose of making a sale.

Sales Promotion

Sales promotion consists of all marketing activities—other than personal selling, advertising, and public relations—that stimulate consumer purchasing and dealer effectiveness. Sales promotion is generally a short-run tool used to stimulate immediate increases in demand. Sales promotion can be aimed at end consumers, trade customers, or a company's employees. Sales promotions include free samples, contests, bonuses, trade shows, vacation giveaways, and coupons. A major promotional campaign might use several of these sales promotion tools. For example, Gillette sent free SensorExcel razors to 1.4 million 18-year-olds in the United States with a note, "For your eighteenth birthday . . . a gift from Gillette." The giveaway included a razor, shaving gel, and $2 in coupons for replacement razor blades. In 1996, Gillette gave away some 15 million more SensorExcels, hanging them on doors in Great Britain and distributing them to draftees in Sweden.[8]

Often marketers use sales promotion to improve the effectiveness of other ingredients in the promotional mix, especially advertising and personal selling. Research shows that sales promotion complements advertising by yielding faster sales responses. Gillette, for example, offered cents-off coupons during its promotional campaign to introduce the SensorExcel razor. Consumers who had seen the advertisements for the SensorExcel were prompted to try it at a lower introductory price through the coupon. Without the coupon, these consumers may have waited longer to purchase.

Sales promotion is discussed in more detail in Chapter 18.

sales promotion
Marketing activities—other than personal selling, advertising, and public relations—that stimulate consumer buying and dealer effectiveness.

MARKETING COMMUNICATION

communication
Process by which we exchange or share meanings through a common set of symbols.

Promotional strategy is closely related to the process of communication. As humans, we assign meaning to feelings, ideas, facts, attitudes, and emotions. **Communication** is the process by which we exchange or share meanings through a common set of symbols. When a company develops a new product, changes an old one, or simply tries to increase sales of an existing good or service, it must communicate its selling message to potential customers. Marketers communicate information about the firm and its products to the target market and various publics through its promotion programs. Pepsi commercials, for example, send messages to their target audience of kids through the use of sports figures such as basketball star Shaquille O'Neal. Read, in Shaq's own words, the power of Pepsi's communication efforts in the boxed article on page 466.

interpersonal communication
Direct, face-to-face communication between two or more people.

Communication can be divided into two major categories: interpersonal communication and mass communication. **Interpersonal communication** is direct, face-to-face communication between two or more people. When communicating face to face, people see the other person's reaction and can respond almost immediately. A salesperson speaking directly with a client is an example of marketing communication that is interpersonal.

mass communication
Communication to large audiences.

Mass communication refers to communicating to large audiences. A great deal of marketing communication is directed to consumers as a whole, usually through a mass medium such as television or newspapers. For example, when a company advertises, it generally does not personally know the people with whom it is trying to communicate. Furthermore, the company is unable to respond immediately to consumers' reactions to its message. Instead, the marketing manager must wait to see whether people are reacting positively or negatively to the mass-communicated promotion. And clutter from competitors' messages or other distractions in the environment can reduce the effectiveness of the mass communication effort.

3 Describe the communication process.

The Communication Process

Marketers are both senders and receivers of messages. As *senders*, marketers attempt to inform, persuade, and remind the target market to adopt courses of action compatible with the need to promote the purchase of goods and services. As *receivers*, marketers attune themselves to the target market in order to develop the appropriate messages, adapt existing messages, and spot new communication opportunities. In this way, marketing communication is a two-way, rather than one-way, process.[9] The two-way nature of the communication process is shown in Exhibit 16.2.

The Sender and Encoding

sender
Originator of the message in the communication process.

The **sender** is the originator of the message in the communication process. In an interpersonal conversation, the sender may be a parent, a friend, or a salesperson. For an advertisement or press release, the sender is the company itself. Microsoft Corporation, as discussed in the opening of the chapter, for example, would be the sender of a message introducing its Windows 95 operating system.

encoding
Conversion of the sender's ideas and thoughts into a message, usually in the form of words or signs.

Encoding is the conversion of the sender's ideas and thoughts into a message, usually in the form of words or signs. Microsoft might encode its message into an advertisement, or a Microsoft salesperson might encode the promotional message as a sales presentation.

A basic principle of encoding is that what matters is not what the source says but what the receiver hears. One way of conveying a message that the receiver will hear properly is to use concrete words and pictures. For example, copy for the new Windows 95 operating system reads "Start here. It's the Start button. It's not only a great way to launch applications, find specific files, get help, open the control panel, and generally start doing whatever it is you want to do. It's also a terrific metaphor." The

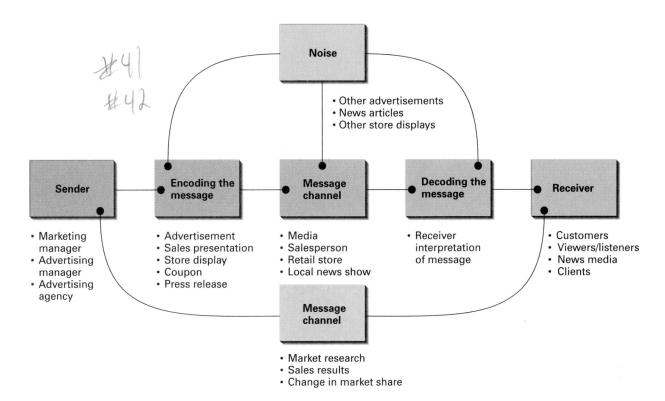

print advertisement shows a detailed photograph of the operating system's main screen and points out that one single click of the start button can simplify computing needs, making the average personal computer easy enough for the average person.

Exhibit 16.2
Communication Process

Message Transmission

Transmission of a message requires a **channel**—for example, a voice, radio, newspaper, or other communication medium. A facial expression or gesture can also serve as a channel.

channel
Medium of communication—such as a voice, radio, or newspaper—for transmitting a message.

In some advertising media, the noise level is very high, which prevents consumers from receiving the message.
© Jeff Greenberg

Dreamful Attraction

Shaquille O'Neal's Thoughts on Marketing and Advertising

What is marketing and why is it so important? I will try to answer these questions based on my experiences as an athlete and a marketer. Marketing is the process of planning and executing the concept, pricing, promotion, and distribution of ideas, goods, and services to create exchanges that satisfy individuals and organizational objectives. While on the outside looking in, I did not realize that marketing was so complicated. I never knew that a person, such as an athlete, could have such a powerful effect on peoples' thought processes and purchasing behavior. The use of a well-known athlete in marketing a product or service can have a great impact on the sales of that product or service. Look at Michael Jordan. Almost overnight most every kid either was wearing or wanted to wear Air Jordan shoes.

Why does this happen? Is it the appeal of a great athlete or is it great marketing? The answer is "none of the above." It's both. In my years as a professional basketball player, I have seen first hand the dramatic appeal that athletes have for the fans and public in general. Top-name athletes are like E.F. Hutton—when they talk, people listen. But why do they listen? I believe they listen to us, the athletes, because we have credibility. Companies sometimes use sports figures and other celebrities to

promote products hoping they are appropriate opinion leaders. The effectiveness of celebrity endorsements depends largely on how credible and attractive the spokesperson is and how familiar people are with him or her. The endorsement is most likely to succeed if an association between the spokesperson and the product can be established.

But marketers have to be careful when they select a celebrity to endorse a product. Bill Cosby failed as an endorser for E.F. Hutton but succeeded with such products as Kodak cameras and Jello. Consumers could not mentally link Bill Cosby with serious investment decisions but could associate him with leisure activities and everyday consumption. Bill Cosby. Investments? I don't think so. That may be why it is important to decide which product an athlete would en-

dorse. If the right product is chosen, then the athlete should have a very good chance at being successful in marketing the product. Because of an athlete's fame and fortune, or attraction, the athlete can often have the right credibility to be a successful spokesperson. The best definition of credibility that I could find was by James Gordon in his book, *Rhetoric of Western Thought.* He said that attraction "can come from a person's observable talents, achievements, occupational position or status, personality and appearance, and style."* That may be why a famous athlete's personality and position can help him or her communicate more effectively than a not-so-famous athlete. Persuasive promotion is designed to stimulate a purchase or an action—for example, to drink Coke (or even Pepsi). Often a firm is not trying to get an immediate response but rather to create a positive image to influence long-term buyer behavior. In the cola war, I can see that persuasion is very important for victory. The target audience has to be persuaded to buy a certain drink or to switch to a certain drink. That is a very clear goal that I see all the time when I am around the people at Pepsi. Persuasion can also be an important goal for very competitive mature product categories, such as many household items, soft drinks, beer, and banking ser-

Reception occurs when the message is detected by the receiver and enters his or her frame of reference. In a two-way conversation, such as a sales pitch given by a Microsoft sales representative to a computer retailer, reception is normally high. In contrast, the desired receivers may or may not detect Microsoft's message when it is mass-communicated, because most media are cluttered by "noise." **Noise** is anything that interferes with, distorts, or slows down the transmission of information. In some media overcrowded with advertisers, such as newspapers and television, the noise level

noise
Anything that interferes with, distorts, or slows down the transmission of information.

vices. The marketplace is now characterized by many competitors, and often the marketing manager must encourage brand switching. The manager hopes that a persuasive campaign will convert some buyers into loyal users.

Credibility is also a positive force because of what I like to call "dreamful attraction." For example, when I was young, I dreamed that I was like Dr. J., the famous basketball player for the Philadelphia 76ers. I would take his head off a poster and put my head on it. I wanted to be Dr. J. That is dreamful attraction. The youth of today are no different. Just the other day a kid stopped me and told me that he wanted to be like me. He had a dreamful attraction.

This dreamful attraction can help sell products. In my case, Pepsi, Spalding, Kenner, and Reebok are hoping that they are able to package properly and market whatever dreamful attraction I might have for their target audience—kids. But it is important that these companies do a good job researching market segments and determining the target market.

Marketing research plays a key role in marketing. It provides decision makers with data on the effectiveness of the current marketing mix and also insights for necessary changes. It also alerts managers to marketplace trends so they can respond to trends early rather than react to situations that have already occurred.

Marketing research can be used to learn what people think about marketing ideas. In this case, it could be used to get accurate information on the image of Shaq. It could help get accurate information on a new product. This information could be gathered through focus groups and surveys and be used to communicate positive impressions to the public. For example, look at the way in which Michael Jordan is able to communicate a positive impression for all the products that he endorses. Research gave the company the information they needed and Michael was able to successfully communicate the idea to the public. This information also can be used to overcome negative perceptions. For example, look at the negative image that professional basketball player Dennis Rodman has. With the proper research and information, Dennis' negative image could be corrected and he could try to communicate this new impression to the public. It seems that good marketing research would also be helpful in using my strategy of dreamful attraction because it would tell us the best way to appeal to the target audiences of the products and services I am endorsing.

There are many ways to communicate. I find that the most effective way for me is through television commercials. This avenue gives me a chance to express myself and show my real feelings about a message we are trying to communicate—either visually or vocally. I feel that I have what Clint Eastwood has—"Sudden Impaq." My impact is revealed through my sense of humor and my nonverbal communication. Take a look at the videos that come with this text and you will hear more about my role in developing TV commercials.

Why does Shaq sell? Communication. Although the verbal communication in many of my commercials is slim, the impact is still there. This makes me believe even more in the quote that who you are can almost be as important as what you say. But if you can blend the two together—who you are and what you have to say—then imagine how much more successful the communication message can be in the marketing process. Andre Agassi's favorite quote from his Canon commercial is "Image is everything." If it is not everything, it is almost everything. If you have the right image, match it with the right product and market it properly, then success should follow.

I have been involved in commercials and the marketing of products for only a short time, but I have learned a great deal. If there is one formula for success in selling products, it would be this: Marketing plus image plus effective communications equals increase in sales—hopefully.

Now, you can call me Dr. Shaq, M.E. (Marketing Expert).

Why has Shaq been such a success as an athlete-endorser?

*James Gordon, *Rhetoric of Western Thought*. Dubuque, Iowa: Kendall-Hunt Publishing Co., 1976, p. 207.

is high and the reception level is low. For example, reception of Windows 95 ads may be hampered by competing operating systems ads, such as Macintosh's or IBM's OS/2, hardware and software ads, or other computer-related stories in a magazine or newspaper. Transmission can also be hindered by situational factors, such as physical surroundings—light, sound, location, weather, and so on; the presence of other people; or the temporary moods consumers might bring to the situation. Mass communication may not even reach all the right consumers. Some members of the target audience may be watching television when the Windows 95 operating system is advertised, but others may not be.

The Receiver and Decoding

receiver
Person who decodes a message.

decoding
Interpretation of the language and symbols sent by the source through a channel.

Microsoft communicates its message through a channel to customers or **receivers,** who will decode the message. **Decoding** is the interpretation of the language and symbols sent by the source through a channel. Common understanding between two communicators, or a common frame of reference, is required for effective communication. Therefore, marketing managers must ensure a proper match between the message to be conveyed and the target market's attitudes and ideas.

Even though a message has been received, it will not necessarily be properly decoded—or even seen, viewed, or heard—because of selective exposure, distortion, and retention (refer back to Chapter 6).[10] Even when people receive a message, they tend to manipulate, alter, and modify it to reflect their own biases, needs, knowledge, and culture. Factors that can lead to miscommunication are differences in age, social class, education, culture, and ethnicity. A study of U.S. Army recruitment ads confirmed that the target audience, young men between the ages of 18 and 24, received both intended and unintended messages. One television commercial showed the firing of a cannon in order to symbolize teamwork. But the target market interpreted the image as representing a skill that would have little value in civilian life. In this particular study, message interpretation was largely influenced by differences in education, age, race, and prior army experience.[11]

Because people don't always listen or read carefully, they can easily misinterpret what is said or written. In fact, researchers have found that a large proportion of both printed and televised communications are misunderstood by consumers. Bright colors and bold graphics have been shown to increase consumers' comprehension of marketing communication. However, even these techniques are not foolproof. A classic example of miscommunication occurred when Lever Brothers mailed out samples of its new dishwashing liquid, Sunlight, which contains real lemon juice. The package clearly stated that Sunlight was a household cleaning product. However, many people saw the word sunlight, the large picture of lemons, and the phrase "with real lemon juice" and thought the product was lemon juice.

feedback
Receiver's response to a message.

U.S. marketers can use a single, customized promotional campaign or a standardized worldwide approach when entering global markets. Some companies have success using a combination of the two approaches.
© Jeff Greenberg

Feedback

In interpersonal communication, the receiver's response to a message is direct **feedback** to the source. Feedback may be verbal, as in saying "I agree," or nonverbal, as in nodding, smiling, frowning, or gesturing.

Because mass communicators like Microsoft are often cut off from direct feedback, they must rely on market research or analysis of sales trends for indirect feedback. Microsoft might use such measurements as the percentage of radio listeners or magazine readers who recognize, recall, or state that they have been exposed to the Windows 95 message. Indirect feedback enables mass communicators to decide whether to continue, modify, or drop a message.

In our increasingly global society, marketing managers must often create promotion messages for other countries. The "Global Perspectives" box discusses the challenges marketers face when selling on foreign soil.

Global Perspectives

Global Challenges in Marketing Communication

The most successful global marketing managers realize that a consumer's cultural environment plays a large role in the communication process and can significantly affect the way he or she decodes or perceives a promotional message. Thus a sender of a message who lives in a different cultural environment must know something about the intended receiver's culture in order to communicate effectively. Following this logic means developing promotional messages tailored to each country or region rather than one standardized message for all markets. For example, an American auto manufacturer selling its cars in Mexico, China, and India might research the cultures of each country, and possibly regions within a country, to develop tailored promotional messages.

Some would disagree, however, advocating a single promotional campaign for all countries. Following this standardized approach, the U.S. car manufacturer would develop one promotional message and deliver this same message, translated into the language of each country, to all target markets. Supporters of this approach insist that consumers everywhere have the same basic needs and desires and can therefore be persuaded by universal appeals. Furthermore, they say, standardized messages create unified brand images worldwide.

Possibly the best answer to this dilemma is to use a mixture of standardization and customization. That is, standardizing the message while paying attention to local differences in the message delivery. For example, Unilever uses a standardized message when promoting its Dove soap, but it uses models from Australia, France, Germany, and Italy to appeal to women in those places. Discovery Communications, parent company of the Discovery Channel and The Learning Channel, found success in global markets by keeping its message simple, consistent, and meaningful across countries. The message from Discovery is the same as here in the United States: give viewers a diversity of programming on nature, history, science and technology, world cultures, and human adventure with visually arresting images. However, they found that attention to dubbing and subtitles and using local translators to ensure proper dialects and accents were essential.

While this mixture of standardization and customization seems to be successful for many global marketers, it only works as long as the message truly plays to a worldwide audience. For example, because parents around the world are deeply concerned about the welfare of their children, advertising for childrens' products generally represents an area of universal concern or agreement. Fisher-Price, therefore, is effective using a standardized approach in their promotions since no matter what country, parents want the best for their kids.

Similarly, IBM successfully communicated a uniform, global message through its Subtitles campaign. Since people all over the world have similar information and computing needs, the overriding message of the Subtitles campaign is that IBM delivers solutions that are both simple and powerful enough to manage information anywhere, anytime, and for anyone. The global imagery is achieved through the use of the same footage in each country. The difference is the use of local subtitles to translate the "foreign" language of the commercial. Utilizing local subtitling allows each country to retain its home cultural accent and employ the country vernacular to enhance communication.

While efficiencies can be achieved by producing a single message for worldwide usage, the approach only makes sense if it does not run counter to social mores, ethnic issues, or religious taboos. For example, what could be wrong with a food commercial which shows hungry kids licking their lips in response to some tasty treat? Nothing, unless you air the ad in a country where exposing the tongue is considered obscene. Or, what could be offensive about a scene of a young couple running barefoot, hand-in-hand down a beautiful, sandy beach? Not a thing. Unless the commercial appears in a country in which naked feet are never to be seen by the public.[12]

While the marketers discussed here have been successful using a global approach to promotion, not every product or service is suited for a unified message. What types of products do you think would benefit from a standardized approach to promotion? What types would fare better using a tailored approach?

The Communication Process and the Promotional Mix

The four elements of the promotional mix differ in their ability to affect the target audience. For instance, promotional mix elements may communicate with the consumer directly or indirectly. The message may flow one way or two ways. Feedback may be fast or slow, a little or a lot. Likewise, the communicator may have varying degrees of control over message delivery, content, and flexibility. Exhibit 16.3 outlines differences among the promotional mix elements with respect to mode of communication, marketer's control over the communication process, amount and speed of feedback, direction of message flow, marketer's control over the message, identification of the sender, speed in reaching large audiences, and message flexibility.

From Exhibit 16.3, you can see that most elements of the promotional mix are indirect and impersonal when used to communicate with a target market, providing only one direction of message flow. For example, advertising, public relations, and sales promotion are generally impersonal, one-way means of mass communication. Because they provide no opportunity for direct feedback, they cannot adapt easily to consumers' changing preferences, individual differences, and personal goals.

Personal selling, on the other hand, is personal, two-way communication. The salesperson is able to receive immediate feedback from the consumer and adjust the message in response. Personal selling, however, is very slow in dispersing the marketer's message to large audiences. Because a salesperson can only communicate to one person or a small group of persons at one time, it is a poor choice if the marketer wants to send a message to many potential buyers.

Exhibit 16.3

Characteristics of the Elements in the Promotional Mix

	Advertising	Public relations	Personal selling	Sales promotion
Mode of communication	Indirect and impersonal	Usually indirect and nonpersonal	Direct and face-to-face	Usually indirect and nonpersonal
Communicator control over situation	Low	Moderate to low	High	Moderate to low
Amount of feedback	Little	Little	Much	Little to moderate
Speed of feedback	Delayed	Delayed	Immediate	Varies
Direction of message flow	One-way	One-way	Two-way	Mostly one-way
Control over message content	Yes	No	Yes	Yes
Identification of sponsor	Yes	No	Yes	Yes
Speed in reaching large audience	Fast	Usually fast	Slow	Fast
Message flexibility	Same message to all audiences	No direct control over message	Tailored to prospective buyer	Same message to varied target audiences

INTEGRATED MARKETING COMMUNICATIONS

So far, the chapter has discussed the communications process and four types of promotional mix elements marketers may use to communicate their message to consumers: advertising, public relations, personal selling, and sales promotion. Ideally, marketing communications from each marketing mix element should be integrated. That is, the message reaching the consumer should be the same regardless of whether it is from an advertisement, a salesperson in the field, a magazine article, or a coupon in a newspaper insert.

A company's communications, from the consumer's standpoint, are already integrated. The typical consumer does not think in terms of advertising, sales promotion, public relations, or personal selling. To them, everything is an "ad." The only people who can dis-integrate these communications elements are marketers themselves.[13] Unfortunately, many marketers neglect this fact when planning promotional messages and fail to integrate their communication efforts from one element to the next.

More often than not, the underlying reason for disparate messages is due to different departments and individuals having responsibility for advertising, public relations, personal selling, and sales promotion. Managers of these different functional areas may not communicate as a standard practice or they may disagree on promotional messages or objectives. The largest rift typically comes between the sales force and the advertising and sales promotion departments. All too often, messages delivered via advertising and sales promotion are in sync, yet the managers of these functional areas fail to keep the sales department abreast of the latest promotional campaign. The result is conflicting messages and, ultimately, confusion by the consumer. For example, banks have been notorious for departmentalizing their communications efforts. As a result, television ads look nothing like their direct-mail pieces and even less like in-branch signage.

This unintegrated, disjointed approach to promotion has propelled more companies to adopt the concept of **integrated marketing communications (IMC).** IMC is the method of carefully coordinating all promotional activities—media advertising, sales promotion, personal selling, public relations, as well as direct marketing, packaging, and other forms of promotion—to produce a consistent, unified message that is customer focused.[14] Following the concept of IMC, marketing managers carefully work out the roles the various promotional elements will play in the marketing mix. Timing of promotional activities are coordinated and the results of each campaign are carefully monitored to improve future use of the promotional mix tools. Typically, a marketing communications director is appointed who has overall responsibility for integrating the company's marketing communications.

One company which has successfully implemented IMC is Hewlett-Packard. With 100,000 employees, more than 2,000 different products, and hundreds of marketing managers within the company with different specialties and agendas, internal integration of marketing communications at Hewlett-Packard was an ambitious goal. The company began by integrating its advertising and media campaigns, and not long after found itself focusing on its entire marketing efforts. That meant integrating all of its field sales operations, product line teams, geographic marketing operations, and its corporate marketing division so that all elements were communicating together and sending out the same messages to consumers. To achieve its goal, Hewlett-Packard created "marketing councils" within the company to bring together representatives of all its marketing divisions. Through meetings and conferences, the marketing councils create a strategy by which all marketing messages flow for both current campaigns and new product launches. Once the councils outline strategies, various "marketing centers" within Hewlett-Packard implement those strategies using either more global messages that can be used broadly or very specific messages tailored to individual customer groups. Now, when Hewlett-Packard introduces a new computer

integrated marketing communications (IMC)
The method of carefully coordinating all promotional activities to produce a consistent, unified message that is customer-focused.

product, for instance, a coordinated plan helps insure that salespeople, product line teams, and the marketing communications people all work together.[15]

THE GOALS AND TASKS OF PROMOTION

4 Explain the goals and tasks of promotion.

People communicate with one another for many reasons. They seek amusement, ask for help, give assistance or instructions, provide information, and express ideas and thoughts. Promotion, on the other hand, seeks to modify behavior and thoughts in some way. For example, promoters may try to persuade consumers to eat at Burger King rather than at McDonald's. Promotion also strives to reinforce existing behavior—for instance, getting consumers to continue to dine at Burger King once they have switched. The source (the seller) hopes to project a favorable image or to motivate purchase of the company's goods and services.

Promotion can perform one or more of three tasks: *inform* the target audience, *persuade* the target audience, or *remind* the target audience. Often a marketer will try to accomplish two or more of these tasks at the same time. Exhibit 16.4 lists the three tasks of promotion and some examples of each.

Informing

Informative promotion may seek to convert an existing need into a want or to stimulate interest in a new product. It is generally more prevalent during the early stages of the product life cycle. People typically will not buy a product service or support a nonprofit organization until they know its purpose and its benefits to them. Informative messages are important for promoting complex and technical products, such as automobiles, computers, and investment services. Informative promotion is also important for a "new" brand being introduced into an "old" product class. For example, a new brand of detergent entering the well-established laundry detergent product category dominated by well-known brands such as Tide and Cheer. The new

Exhibit 16.4

Promotion Tasks and Examples

Informative promotion:

Increasing the awareness of a new brand or product class
Informing the market of new product attributes
Suggesting new uses for a product
Reducing consumers' anxieties
Telling the market of a price change
Describing available services
Correcting false impressions
Explaining how the product works
Building a company image

Persuasive promotion:

Building brand preference
Encouraging brand switching
Changing customers' perceptions of product attributes
Influencing customers to buy now
Persuading customers to receive a call

Reminder promotion:

Reminding consumers that the product may be needed in the near future
Reminding consumers where to buy the product
Keeping the product in consumers' minds during off times
Maintaining consumer awareness

product cannot establish itself against more mature products unless potential buyers are aware of it, understand its benefits, and understand its positioning in the marketplace.

Persuading

Persuasive promotion is designed to stimulate a purchase or an action—for example, to drink more Coca-Cola or to use H&R Block tax services. Persuasion normally becomes the main promotion goal when the product enters the growth stage of its life cycle. By this time, the target market should have general product awareness and some knowledge of how the product can fulfill their wants. Therefore, the promotional task switches from informing consumers about the product category to persuading them to buy the company's brand rather than the competitor's. At this time, the promotional message emphasizes the product's real and perceived differential advantages, often appealing to emotional needs such as love, belonging, self-esteem, and ego satisfaction.

Persuasion can also be an important goal for very competitive mature product categories, such as many household items, soft drinks, beer, and banking services. In a marketplace characterized by many competitors, the promotional message often encourages brand switching and aims to convert some buyers into loyal users. For example, to persuade new customers to switch their checking accounts, a bank's marketing manager may offer a year's worth of free checks with no fees.

Reminding

Reminder promotion is used to keep the product and brand name in the public's mind. This type of promotion prevails during the maturity stage of the life cycle. It

the ski instructor faded away 3 winters ago.
at least the sweater didn't.

when you care for something in **Woolite** it shows

Reminder promotion is used to
market established products or
brands like Woolite.

assumes that the target market has already been persuaded
of the good's or service's merits. Its purpose is simply to
trigger a memory. Crest toothpaste, Tide laundry detergent, Miller beer, and many other consumer products often use reminder promotion.

AIDA AND THE HIERARCHY OF EFFECTS

The ultimate goal of any promotion is to get someone to
buy a good or service or, in the case of nonprofit organizations, to take some action (for instance, donate blood).
A classic model for reaching promotional goals is called the
AIDA concept.[16] The acronym stands for Attention, Interest, Desire, and Action—the stages of consumer involvement with a promotional message.

This model proposes that consumers respond to marketing messages in a cognitive (thinking), affective (feeling), and conative (doing) sequence. First, the promotion
manager attracts a person's *attention* by (in personal selling) a greeting and approach or (in advertising and sales
promotion) loud volume, unusual contrasts, bold headlines,
movement, bright colors, and so on. Next, a good sales presentation, demonstration, or advertisement creates *interest*
in the product and then, by illustrating how the product's
features will satisfy the consumer's needs, *desire*. Finally, a
special offer or a strong closing sales pitch may be used to
obtain purchase *action*.

An expanded version of the AIDA concept is the **hierarchy of effects model** (see
Exhibit 16.5).[17] This advertising model also proposes that consumers follow a cogni-
tive-affective-conative sequence in responding to promotional messages. It assumes
that promotion propels consumers along the following six steps in the purchase-de-
cision process:

1. *Awareness:* The advertiser must first achieve awareness with the target market.
   A firm cannot sell something if the market does not know that the good or service exists. Imagine that Acme Company, a pet food manufacturer, is introducing a new brand of cat food called Stripes, specially formulated for finicky cats.
   To increase the general awareness of its new brand, Acme heavily publicizes the
   introduction and places several ads on TV and in consumer magazines.

2. *Knowledge:* Simple awareness of a brand seldom leads to a sale. The next step is
   to inform the target market about the product's characteristics. Print ads for
   Stripes cat food detail the ingredients that cats love—real tuna, chicken, or
   turkey—as well as the product's nutritional benefits.

3. *Liking:* After the target market learns about the product, the advertiser must generate a favorable attitude. A print ad or TV commercial can't actually tell pet
   owners whether their cats will like Stripes. Thus, Acme will compile a list of cat
   owners in several major metropolitan cities and send each a sample of the new
   cat food. Acme hopes to establish liking (by the cats as well as the owners) for
   the new brand.

4. *Preference:* Even though owners (and their cats) may like Stripes, they may not
   see any advantage over competing brands, especially if owners are brand loyal.
   Therefore, Acme must create brand preference by explaining the product's dif-

5 Discuss the hierarchy
of effects concept and
its relationship to the promotional mix.

AIDA concept
Model that outlines the
process for achieving promotional goals in terms of
stages of consumer in-
volvement with the mes-
sage; the acronym stands
for Attention, Interest,
Desire, and Action.

hierarchy of effects model
Model that outlines the six-
stage process by which
consumers make purchase
decisions: awareness,
knowledge, liking, preference, conviction, and purchase.

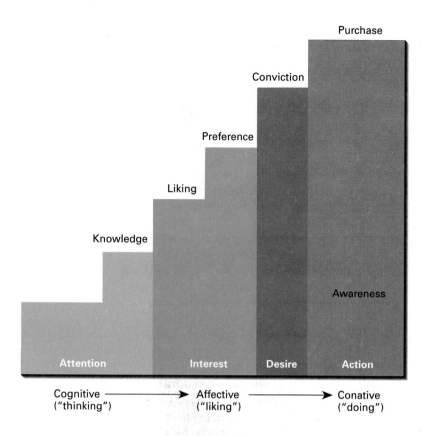

Exhibit 16.5
*AIDA and the Hierarchy
of Effects*

ferential advantage over the competition. Acme has to convince owners that Stripes is distinctly better than other cat foods in some respect. Specifically, Acme has to show that cats want to eat nothing else. Advertising at this stage claims that Stripes will satisfy "even the pickiest of the litter."

5. *Conviction:* Although pet owners may come to prefer Stripes to other brands, they still may not have developed the conviction (or an intention) to buy the new brand. At this stage Acme might offer the consumer additional reasons to buy Stripes, such as easy-to-open, zip-lock packaging that keeps the product fresh; additional vitamins and minerals that healthy cats need; or feline taste-test results.

6. *Purchase:* Some members of the target market may now be convinced to buy Stripes but have yet to make the purchase. Displays in grocery stores, coupons, premiums, and trial-size packages can often push the complacent shopper into purchase.

Most buyers involved in high involvement purchase situations pass through the six stages of the hierarchy of effects on the way to making a purchase. The promoter's task is to determine where on the purchase ladder most of the target consumers are located and design a promotion plan to meet their needs. For instance, if Acme has determined that about half its buyers are in the preference or conviction stage but have not bought Stripes cat food for some reason, the company may mail cents-off coupons to cat owners to prompt them to buy.

The hierarchy of effects model does not explain how all promotions influence purchase decisions. The model suggests that promotional effectiveness can be measured in terms of consumers progressing from one stage to the next. However, the order of stages in the model as well as whether consumers go through all steps has been much debated. For example, purchase can occur without liking or preference, perhaps when a low-involvement product is bought on impulse. Regardless of the order of the stages or consumers' progression through these stages, the hierarchy of effects model helps marketers by suggesting which promotional strategy will be most effective.[18]

The Hierarchy of Effects and the Promotional Mix

Exhibit 16.6 depicts the relationship between the promotional mix and the hierarchy of effects model. It shows that, although advertising does have an impact in the later stages, it is most useful in creating awareness and knowledge about goods or services. In contrast, personal selling reaches fewer people at first. Salespeople are more effective at developing customer preferences for merchandise or a service than at gaining conviction. For example, advertising may help a potential computer purchaser gain knowledge and information about competing brands, but the salesperson in an electronics store may be the one who actually encourages the buyer to decide a particular brand is the best choice. The salesperson also has the advantage of having the computer physically there to demonstrate its capabilities to the buyer.

Like advertising, a good sales promotion can build awareness of a new product. Sales promotion also can stir strong purchase intent. For example, coupons and other price-off promotions are techniques used to persuade customers to buy new products. Frequent-buyer sales promotion programs, which allow consumers to accumulate points or dollars that can later be redeemed for goods, tend to increase purchase intent as well as encourage repeat purchases. Frequent-customer cards for products and services are popular, especially among women, the affluent, and young people aged 25 to 34. Most of these consumers say that the availability of frequent-customer cards often influences their shopping decisions.[19] Retailers are increasingly using incentive programs to cultivate consumer loyalty and encourage repeat purchases. Shoppers who purchase $100 in baby merchandise from Abco supermarkets in Arizona, for example, receive a $10 gift certificate for baby food, formula, or diapers.[20] Similarly, Randall's food stores in Texas annually reward loyal shoppers with "turkey bucks" during the weeks prior to Thanksgiving. Turkey bucks can then be redeemed for free turkeys.

Public relations has its greatest impact in building awareness about a company, good, or service. Many companies can attract attention and build goodwill by sponsoring community events that benefit a worthy cause, such as antidrug and antigang programs. Such sponsorships project a positive image of the firm and its products into the minds of consumers and potential consumers. Good publicity can also help develop consumer preference for a product. Book publishers push to get their titles listed on the best-seller lists of major publications, such as *Publishers Weekly* or *The New York Times*. Authors also make appearances at book stores to personally sign books and speak to fans. First Lady Hillary Rodham Clinton, for example, embarked on an 11-city publicity tour to promote her book *It Takes a Village*.[21] Similarly, movie

Exhibit 16.6
When the Elements of Promotion Are Most Useful

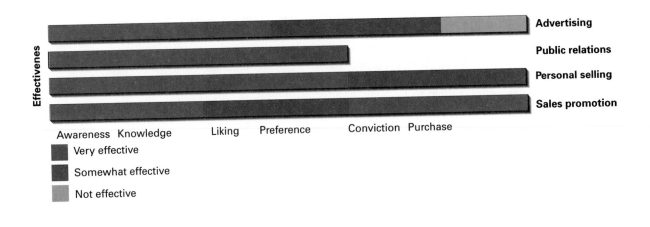

marketers use prerelease publicity to raise the profile of their movies and to increase initial box office sales. For example, many motion picture studios are creating pages on the World Wide Web to attract viewers to new movies. The pages typically include multimedia clips and publicity photos.[22] Furthermore, Academy Award-nominated motion pictures typically experience increased box-office earnings because of the publicity generated by the awards.[23]

Twentieth Century Fox Studios
How does Fox use the Internet to promote new releases and blockbusters?

http://www.fox.com/

FACTORS AFFECTING THE PROMOTIONAL MIX

Promotional mixes vary a great deal from one product and one industry to the next. Normally, advertising and personal selling are used to promote goods and services, supported and supplemented by sales promotion. Public relations helps develop a positive image for the organization and the product line. Yet, a firm may choose not to use all four promotional elements in its promotional mix, or it may choose to use them in varying degrees. The particular promotional mix chosen by a firm for a product or service depends on several factors: nature of the product, stage in the product life cycle, target market characteristics, type of buying decision, available funds for promotion, and use of either a push or a pull strategy.

6 Describe the factors that affect the promotional mix.

Nature of the Product

Characteristics of the product itself can influence the promotional mix. For instance, a product can be classified as either a business product or a consumer product (refer back to Chapter 10). As business products are often custom-tailored to the buyer's exact specifications, they are often not well suited to mass promotion. Therefore, producers of most business goods, such as computer systems or industrial machinery, rely more heavily on personal selling than on advertising. Informative personal selling is common for industrial installations, accessories, and component parts and materials. Advertising, however, still serves a purpose in promoting business goods. Advertisements in trade media may be used to create general buyer awareness and interest. Moreover, advertising can help locate potential customers for the sales force. For example, print media advertising often includes coupons soliciting the potential customer to "fill this out for more detailed information."

On the other hand, because consumer products generally are not custom-made, they do not require the selling efforts of a company representative who can tailor them to the user's needs. Thus, consumer goods are promoted mainly through advertising to create brand familiarity. Broadcast advertising, newspapers, and consumer-oriented magazines are used extensively to promote consumer goods, especially nondurables. Sales promotion, the brand name, and the product's packaging are about twice as important for consumer goods as for business products. Persuasive personal selling is important at the retail level for shopping goods, such as automobiles and appliances.

The costs and risks associated with a product also influence the promotional mix. As a general rule, when the costs or risks of using a product increase, personal selling becomes more important. Items that are a small part of a firm's budget (supply items) or of a consumer's budget (convenience products) do not require a salesperson to close the sale. In fact, inexpensive items cannot support the cost of a salesperson's time and effort unless the potential volume is high. On the other hand, expensive and complex machinery, new buildings, cars, and new homes represent a considerable investment. A salesperson must assure buyers that they are spending their money wisely and not taking an undue financial risk.

Buying specialty products such as jewelry and clothing involves a social risk. Consumers depend on salespeople to help them make the right choice.

© 1995 William Taufic/The Stock Market

Social risk is an issue as well. Many consumer goods are not products of great social importance because they do not reflect social position. People do not experience much social risk in buying a loaf of bread or a candy bar. However, buying some shopping products and many specialty products, such as jewelry and clothing, does involve a social risk. Many consumers depend on sales personnel for guidance and advice in making the "proper" choice.

Stage in the Product Life Cycle

Exhibit 16.7
Product Life Cycle and the Promotional Mix

The product's stage in its life cycle is a big factor in designing a promotional mix (see Exhibit 16.7). During the *introduction stage*, the basic goal of promotion is to inform the target audience that the product is available. Initially, the emphasis is on the gen-

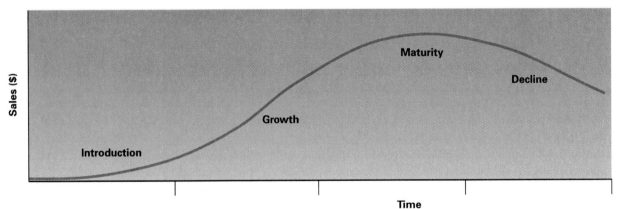

Preintroduction publicity; small amounts of advertising near introduction	Heavy advertising and public relations to build awareness; sales promotion to induce trial; personal selling to obtain distribution	Heavy advertising and public relations to build brand loyalty; decreasing use of sales promotion; personal selling to maintain distribution	Advertising slightly decreased—more persuasive and reminder in nature; increased use of sales promotion to build market share; personal selling to maintain distribution	Advertising and public relations drastically decreased; sales promotion and personal selling maintained at low levels

eral product class—for example, personal computer systems. This emphasis gradually changes to awareness of specific brands, such as IBM, Apple, and Compaq. Typically, both extensive advertising and public relations inform the target audience of the product class or brand and heighten awareness levels. Sales promotion encourages early trial of the product, and personal selling gets retailers to carry the product.

When the product reaches the *growth stage* of the life cycle, the promotion blend may shift. Often a change is necessary because different types of potential buyers are targeted. Although advertising and public relations continue to be major elements of the promotional mix, sales promotion can be reduced because consumers need fewer incentives to purchase. The promotional strategy is to emphasize the product's differential advantage over the competition. Persuasive promotion is used to build and maintain brand loyalty to support the product during the growth stage. By this stage, personal selling has usually succeeded in getting adequate distribution for the product.

As the product reaches the *maturity stage* of its life cycle, competition becomes fiercer, and thus persuasive and reminder advertising are more strongly emphasized. Sales promotion comes back into focus as product sellers try to increase their market share.

All promotion, especially advertising, is reduced as the product enters the *decline stage*. Nevertheless, personal selling and sales promotion efforts may be maintained, particularly at the retail level.

Target Market Characteristics

A target market characterized by widely scattered potential customers, highly informed buyers, and brand-loyal repeat purchasers generally requires a promotional mix with more advertising and sales promotion and less personal selling. Sometimes, however, personal selling is required even when buyers are well informed and geographically dispersed. Although industrial installations and component parts may be sold to extremely competent people with extensive education and work experience, salespeople must still be present to explain the product and work out the details of the purchase agreement.

Often firms sell goods and services in markets where potential customers are hard to locate. Print advertising can be used to find them. The reader is invited to call for more information or to mail in a reply card for a detailed brochure. As the calls or cards are received, salespeople are sent to visit the potential customers.

Type of Buying Decision

The promotional mix also depends on the type of buying decision—for example, a routine decision or a complex decision. For routine consumer decisions, like buying toothpaste or soft drinks, the most effective promotion calls attention to the brand or reminds the consumer about the brand. Advertising and, especially, sales promotion are the most productive promotion tools to use for routine decisions.

If the decision is neither routine nor complex, advertising and public relations help establish awareness for the good or service. For example, suppose a man is looking for a bottle of wine to serve to his dinner guests. Being a beer drinker, he is not familiar with wines. Yet he has seen advertising for Sutter Home wine and has also read an article in a popular magazine about the Sutter Home winery. He may be more likely to buy this brand because he is already aware of it.

In contrast, consumers making complex buying decisions are more extensively involved. They rely on large amounts of information to help them reach a purchase decision. Personal selling is most effective in helping these consumers decide. For example, consumers thinking about buying a car usually depend on a salesperson to provide the information they need to reach a decision. Print advertising may also be used for high involvement purchase decisions as they can often provide a large amount of information to the consumer.

Available Funds

push strategy
Marketing strategy that uses aggressive personal selling and trade advertising to convince a wholesaler or a retailer to carry and sell particular merchandise.

Chris Childers, owner of the Macon Christian Bookstore in Macon, Georgia, uses the customer data in his computer to generate customer-specific mailings about new items in his store.
© 1995 Nation's Business/T. Michael Keza

Money, or the lack of it, may easily be the most important factor in determining the promotional mix. A small, undercapitalized manufacturer may rely heavily on free publicity if its product is unique. If the situation warrants a sales force, a financially strained firm may turn to manufacturers' agents, who work on a commission basis with no advances or expense accounts. Even well-capitalized organizations may not be able to afford the advertising rates of publications like *Better Homes and Gardens*, *Reader's Digest*, and *The Wall Street Journal*. The price of a high-profile advertisement in these media could support a salesperson for a year.

When funds are available to permit a mix of promotional elements, a firm will generally try to optimize its return on promotion dollars while minimizing the *cost per contact*, or the cost of reaching one member of the target market. In general, the cost per contact is very high for personal selling, public relations, and sales promotions like sampling and demonstrations. On the other hand, for the number of people national advertising reaches, it has a very low cost per contact.

Usually there is a trade-off among the funds available, the number of people in the target market, the quality of communication needed, and the relative costs of the promotional elements. For instance, a company may have to forgo a full-page, color advertisement in *People* magazine in order to pay for a personal selling effort. Although the magazine ad will reach more people than personal selling, the high cost of the magazine space is a problem. Learn about how small businesses can make the most of their promotional dollars in the "Marketing and Small Business" box.

Push and Pull Strategies

The last factor that affects the promotional mix is whether a push or a pull promotional strategy will be used. Manufacturers may use aggressive personal selling and trade advertising to convince a wholesaler or a retailer to carry and sell their merchandise. This approach is known as a **push strategy** (see Exhibit 16.8). The wholesaler, in turn, must often push the merchandise forward by persuading the retailer to handle the goods. The retailer then uses advertising, displays, and other forms of promotion to convince the consumer to buy the "pushed" products. This concept also applies to services. For example, the Jamaican Tourism Board targets promotions to travel agencies, which in turn tell their customers about the benefits of vacationing in Jamaica.

At the other extreme is a **pull strategy,** which stimulates consumer demand to obtain product distribution. Rather than trying to sell to the wholesaler, the manufacturer using a pull strategy focuses its promotional efforts on end consumers. As they begin demanding the product, the retailer orders the merchandise from the wholesaler. The wholesaler, confronted with rising demand, then places an order for the "pulled" merchandise from the manufacturer. Consumer demand pulls the product through the channel of distribution (see Exhibit 16.8). Heavy sampling, introductory consumer advertis-

Marketing and Small Business

Guerrilla Promotions for Cash-Strapped Small Business Owners

Most small business owners will recognize this dilemma: You're short on cash and desperate to cut something. But suppliers and employees need to be paid and then there's rent and loan payments. What's left? Marketing costs. Slashing the ad budget and cutting a few promotions will put you back in the black. But then what? You still need to get the word out and growing by word of mouth alone is the slowest way to go.

Enter *guerrilla marketing,* a term that covers a range of inexpensive activities that small companies can use to promote their products and services. In guerrilla marketing, the entrepreneur's investment is typically time, energy, and imagination with little or no budget required. For example, such low-cost promotions as posting flyers on community bulletin boards or slipping notices under car windshield wipers can significantly increase awareness. Additionally, small business marketers can also chat with potential customers over computer online bulletin boards for a minimal cost to get the company's name out and announce any special offers to prospective clients. For a little more money, a professionally designed home page on the World Wide Web can also drum up business.

Need more ideas to stretch that marketing dollar? Focusing on a product or service's key target markets is sure to make a small business's promotional dollars work better. Placing ads in targeted publications and broadcast media, such as community papers, industry newsletters, and area radio and cable stations can save a lot of money while reaching those people who are sure to be interested in and ready to purchase their products and services.

A small business marketer doesn't necessarily have to use traditional media to reach his or her target customers. Attending trade meetings of local trade organizations and handing out business cards or brochures can increase awareness of a small company's name or products. Entrepreneurs can also contact various trade organizations and social groups about becoming a speaker.

Often a small company's best promotional tool is staring it right in the face. Instead of spending money on advertising, small business marketers can give away their products and services by inviting prospective clients in for free samples or free consultations. Or, small business marketers can find opportunities or high-profile events, such as marches to raise money to fight diseases, in which to give away their products or services as prizes.

Another relatively inexpensive promotional outlet is direct mail. Small business marketers can contact mailing-list brokers to determine if there are lists that match their target markets. For example, the ideal mailing list for a software development firm marketing software to travelers would include members of airlines' frequent-flier clubs who have also made mail-order purchases in the past.[24]

Can you think of some other low-cost methods for small business owners to use to promote their products and services? If you were opening a new business, such as selling computer software, what are some ways in which you would let potential customers know about your software titles? What types of public relations and publicity would you seek?

---

ing, cents-off campaigns, and couponing are part of a pull strategy. Using a pull strategy, the Jamaican Tourism Board may entice travelers to visit by advertising heavily in consumer magazines or offering discounts on hotels or airfare.

Rarely does a company use a pull or a push strategy exclusively. Instead, the mix will emphasize one of these strategies. For example, the pharmaceutical company Marion Merrell Dow uses a push strategy, through personal selling and trade advertising, to promote its Nicoderm patch nicotine-withdrawal therapy to physicians. Sales presentations and advertisements in medical journals give physicians the detailed information they need to prescribe the therapy to their patients who want to quit smoking. Marion Merrell Dow supplements its push promotional strategy with a pull strategy targeted directly to potential patients through advertisements in consumer

pull strategy
Marketing strategy that stimulates consumer demand to obtain product distribution.

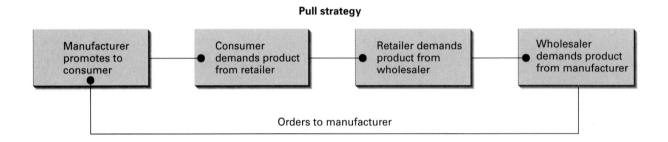

Exhibit 16.8
*Push Strategy versus
Pull Strategy*

magazines and on television. The advertisements illustrate the pull strategy in action: Marion Merrell Dow directs consumers to ask their doctors about the Nicoderm patch.

STEPS IN DEVELOPING THE PROMOTION PLAN

7 Explain how to create a promotion plan.

promotion plan
Carefully arranged sequence of promotional efforts designed around a common theme and geared to specific objectives.

A **promotion plan** is a carefully arranged sequence of promotions designed around a common theme and geared to specific objectives. Because promotion is something of an art, developing a promotion plan can be a challenging task. Despite many specific policies and guidelines, creativity still plays a key role. Effective planning can greatly stimulate sales; ineffective planning can waste millions of dollars and actually damage the image of the firm or its products.

The promotion plan consists of several distinct steps:

1. Analyze the marketplace.
2. Identify the target market.
3. Set promotional objectives.
4. Develop a promotion budget.
5. Choose the promotional mix.

Analyze the Marketplace

If firms truly accept the marketing concept of fulfilling consumer needs and wants, they must conduct research simply to find out what these needs and wants are. With the increasing complexity of the marketplace, proper research is necessary to ensure an effective promotion plan.

Research identifies the product's target market. Research also determines the plan's promotional objectives. As noted in Chapter 9, information can be obtained through either secondary research or primary research. Internal secondary research utilizes internal company data, such as sales data or data about the effectiveness of previous advertising efforts, to provide the marketing manager with valuable information for promoting a current brand. External secondary data are available through research firms that continually conduct research and sell the results to any company willing to pay. For example, national firms offer warehouse shipment volume, total sales volume, or market share data on consumer goods. They may also measure the flow of products into homes utilizing purchase diaries kept by consumer panels.

In other cases, primary research, or information collected exclusively for an immediate promotion problem, is necessary for proper planning. Yet market information is usually not available for a new product or a new product category. In that case, primary research might consist of an in-home use test, test marketing, or a focus group. These methods provide valuable insights into potential buyers' characteristics and help the marketer shape the promotion plan.

Identify the Target Market

Through market research, the market segment the firm wants to reach with a given promotion plan should be explicitly defined geographically, demographically, psychographically, or behaviorally. Naturally, the target market should be those most likely to buy the product within a defined period. For example, Honda has defined its target market for the Honda Civic as young married couples with young children. Similarly, McDonald's Arch Deluxe hamburger is aimed specifically at grownups. Advertisements for the Arch Deluxe feature Ronald McDonald in more adult settings, such as on a golf course.

Sometimes targeting specific groups with certain products, such as children, is determined to be unethical by consumer groups, as the "Ethics in Marketing" box reveals.

Set Promotional Objectives

Objectives have been discussed in previous chapters, but the need to be specific and realistic requires further explanation. Objectives are the starting point for any promotion plan. Indeed, marketing managers cannot possibly plan a promotion program

McDonald's features Ronald McDonald in more adult settings to advertise its Arch Deluxe hamburger.

© 1997 Todd Buchanan

Ethics in Marketing

Targeting School Kids

Marketers target some 30,000 commercial messages to kids every single day. And those are just the ads found on TV, radio, billboards, and the like. Product placement and advertising has also increasingly invaded the nation's schools. For instance, kids in Colorado Springs ride to class in school buses painted with ads for 7-Up. In some 400 schools nationwide, kids walk corridors filled with the sounds of pop music interspersed with commercials. Some schools even boast advertisements on bathroom walls. To make matters worse, once kids are in class, many of the study sheets, workbooks, audio-visuals, and other instructional materials come with a message from a sponsor—and it's often a highly biased or manipulative message. For example:

- Eating meat makes people taller, according to study materials from the National Live Stock and Meat Board.
- Clear-cut logging—stripping entire hillsides of trees—is good for the environment, said materials from Procter & Gamble.
- Rice Krispies Treats, snack bars made of Rice Krispies cereal and marshmallows, is a snack food to choose "more often," according to a Kellogg cereal guide that's supposed to help fourth- to sixth-graders learn "how to choose healthful foods."
- There are no endangered species, maintains the Council for Wildlife Conservation and Education, which turns out to be affiliated with the National Shooting Sports Foundation—an organization that has the same address as the National Rifle Association.
- Proving that Prego spaghetti sauce is thicker than Ragu, as a TV commercial did, is presented by Prego as a legitimate classroom experiment.

Teachers, facing declining budgets, are often eager to use the free materials handed out by businesses and trade associations. Many teachers obtain the materials directly or receive them unsolicited, often bypassing any formal review process by school administrators. But such materials may teach kids the wrong lessons. Further, commercially sponsored activities and materials may blur the line between education and propaganda. Many of the sponsored materials on political or social issues fail to present differing points of view, to reveal who financed the studies that support the sponsor's viewpoint, or to disclose information that reflects on the accuracy of the materials.

Businesses argue that their classroom materials and promotional programs augment tight school budgets, either by saving schools money or by giving them income from advertising. Proponents of corporate-sponsored materials argue that they can offer better-quality supplies or information not typically found in schools. Some suggest that in-school commercialism is a natural part of the movement to build closer partnerships between schools and the business community. But many parents and educators believe that this commercialism cheapens education. Even more serious is the potential to compromise the

teacher's ethics. When a teacher uses a commercially sponsored teaching aid, he or she is implicitly endorsing the sponsor or its product—and doing so before a captive audience of students who have been trained to trust what the teacher says.

Even more invasive than corporate-sponsored materials, is Channel One, a daily news program broadcast "free" to any school system that promises to make it a mandatory part of the classroom curriculum. The incentive to schools: free use of the satellite dish, VCRs, and classroom monitors needed to show the program to students. The catch: two minutes of each daily 12-minute program are devoted to paid commercials from such sponsors as Snickers, Rold Gold pretzels, CareFree bubblegum, Pepsi, and Reebok.

Channel One is now viewed five days a week in 350,000 classrooms across the country, reaching some 38 percent of students in grades 6 through 12—about 8 million kids. The program is disproportionately shown in schools located in poor communities, where money for educational programs and materials is most lacking. While Channel One focuses its existence on educating young people on news and current events, critics contend that students are forced to watch the mandatory programming and the commercials that go with it. Since teachers are no longer the driving force, they can't decide when to show the program and how to use it.

Direct advertising, in which the school itself becomes the medium, has mushroomed in recent years as well. For example, some school districts, hungry for funds, sell advertising space on the sides of school buses. By filling a school's hallways, lobby, and lunchroom with rock music and commercials, some school administrators bring in up to $20,000 a year in extra cash. Advertising panels, or wallboards, in hallways, lunchrooms, and even some restrooms are a commonplace sight for many students.

Sports scoreboards probably get more concentrated attention than any other school surface. A logo or ad on a scoreboard receives the equivalent of prime-time exposure throughout the sports season. Soft-drink bottlers and distributors are among the leading supporters of school sports activities.[25]

Should marketers be allowed to

promote their goods and services at school and in the classroom? Do you feel the government should regulate the promotional activities of marketers in the nation's schools? What steps could be taken to reduce commercialism to school kids?

unless they know what goals they are trying to reach. Some objectives a marketing manager may have include increasing awareness, improving or changing the consumer's attitude about the product or service, changing the consumer's buying behavior, reminding the consumer of the product, or increasing the consumer's recall of the product. Additionally, marketing managers must understand their current position in terms of each objective before a reasonable goal can be established. For an awareness objective, for example, the marketing manager should determine what awareness level the product currently enjoys. Later, the manager will be able to use this benchmark to determine how well the promotional effort affected awareness levels.

Promotional objectives should center on the consumer's stage in the hierarchy of effects, or the potential buyer's current stage in the purchasing process. The role of promotion is to change the receiver's attitudes and intentions toward the good or service, moving him or her through the hierarchy toward an action. At the same time, the consumer's response to the promotional message helps the marketer move to the next step in promoting the product.[26]

To be effective, promotional objectives should meet these four criteria:

- Objectives should be measurable and written in concrete terms.
- Objectives should be based on sound research and should identify a well-defined target audience.
- Objectives should be realistic.
- Objectives should reinforce the overall marketing plan and relate to specific marketing objectives.

Develop a Promotion Budget

After identifying the target market and specifying the promotion goals, the marketing manager can develop a concrete budget. This is no simple task, nor is there a cookbook approach that will create an ideal promotion budget.

Theoretically, the promotion budget should be set at a level that maximizes profitability and return on investment. This theory is not easy to apply, however, because it requires knowledge of the actual monetary benefits resulting from the promotion effort.[27] Easier techniques for setting budgets rely on the following approaches:

Advertisements aimed at children have made their way into the nation's schools. Companies provide free materials to teachers and school administrators sell advertising space to bring in needed funds.

© Mary Kate Denny/Tony Stone Images

arbitrary allocation
Method of setting a promotion budget that picks a dollar amount without reference to other factors.

all-you-can-afford approach
Method of setting a promotion budget that relies on determining how much the marketer can spend.

competitive parity
Method of setting a promotion budget that matches a competitor's spending.

percent of sales approach
Method of setting a promotion budget that allocates an amount equal to a certain percentage of total sales.

market share approach
Method of setting a promotion budget that allocates the amount needed to maintain or win a certain market share.

objective and task approach
Method of setting a promotion budget that begins with promotional objectives, defines the communication tools required to achieve those objectives, and then adds up the costs of the planned activities.

- *Arbitrary allocation and all-you-can-afford:* The easiest way to set a promotion budget is simply to pick a dollar amount; this method is called **arbitrary allocation.** Many companies use the arbitrary method for setting their promotion budgets, even though the budget allocated may or may not be enough to promote the product effectively. The **all-you-can-afford approach** is a form of arbitrary allocation because determining what is affordable can be based on many arbitrary criteria. Perhaps the reason for the popularity of these illogical approaches to budget setting is the difficulty of measuring the effectiveness of promotion or determining how much money is needed to meet promotional goals.

- *Competitive parity:* A second approach for setting a promotion budget is called **competitive parity.** The firm allocates enough money to meet the promotional expenditures of the competition. Perhaps the biggest problem with this technique is that it ignores creativity and media effectiveness. Marketers assume their competitor is spending the appropriate amount on promotions, disregarding its own unique situation, opportunities, strengths, and weaknesses. One advantage of the competitive parity method is that it does force the firm to examine competitors' actions.

- *Percent of sales:* Another method of setting a promotion budget is the **percent of sales approach** which typically uses a percentage of the previous year's total sales or a forecast of future sales to determine promotional expenditures. The percent of sales approach can also be based on sales by product, territory, or customer group. The inherent weakness of this approach is that the budget becomes a consequence of sales rather than a determinant of sales. As sales decline, the promotion budget also falls. Yet, research has shown that advertisers maintaining their promotion budgets during slow sales periods achieve better sales than those that do not. The percent of sales approach also bears little relationship, if any, to a firm's promotional objectives. However, the appeal of the percent of sales approach is its simplicity. It is easy for managers to use and understand because they often view costs in percentage terms.

- *Market share:* The **market share approach** to budgeting calculates how much promotion is needed to maintain or win a certain market share. If a firm is satisfied with its market share, it may decide to continue spending the dollar amount or percentage it spent in the past. If the organization plans to increase its market share, it can increase its budget to meet its goals. Like the percent of sales approach, however, this method ignores quality and creativity. Who is to say that spending $5 million this year will be more or less effective than spending $5 million last year? Moreover, the firm is letting its competition indirectly set its promotion budget. Aside from recognizing the importance of competition for market share, this approach does not greatly improve on the other methods.

- *Objective and task:* The determination of the promotional budget has evolved over the years toward more advanced and scientific techniques, the most popular of these being the **objective and task approach.** While this approach is not as simple as the methods already discussed, its underlying logic for budget setting is significantly more judicious. First, management sets objectives. Second, it defines the communication tools required to achieve those objectives. Then a budget is built by adding up the costs of the planned promotion activities.

    The objective and task approach requires that management understand the effectiveness of various promotion tools. The approach also assumes that achieving the objectives will be worth the costs. The major advantage of the objective and task method is that it explicitly incorporates planning into the budgeting process. Promotional objectives are defined, alternatives are analyzed, and the costs of each element in the promotion plan are determined. The objective and task approach has been more readily adopted in large companies and manufacturers of consumer products where promotional budgets are significant.[28]

Choose the Promotional Mix

Finally, marketing managers select the combination of elements—advertising, sales promotion, personal selling, and public relations—that will be included in the overall promotion plan. Recall that the promotional mix depends on such factors as the type of product, its stage in the product life cycle, target market characteristics, type of buying decision, available funds, and push versus pull strategies.

Managers may choose several different elements for one promotion campaign. Different elements are typically chosen to address consumers in different stages of the hierarchy of effects. For example, public relations might be used to create a positive corporate image among target customers. Advertising could focus on developing corporate and product awareness as a complement to personal selling. The function of personal selling might be to interact with customers, amplify and explain the advertising messages, and design the right product to meet customers' specific needs. Personal selling might also help secure proper distribution for the product. Sales promotion may enter the picture as a special discount to prospective buyers if they purchase right away.

LEGAL AND ETHICAL ASPECTS OF PROMOTION

Besides coordinating promotion plans, marketing managers must also understand and cope with the legal and ethical aspects of promoting their goods or services. Laws enacted by federal, state, and local governments may prohibit certain products from being advertised on television, give consumers the right to cancel an in-home sale for a specified period after an agreement is reached, or even require that a celebrity endorser actually use the product he or she promotes. While all advertising is required by law to be nondeceptive, many promotional activities, however, are not legally regulated. Consequently, the public must often rely on the ethics of the promoter.

8 Describe the ethical and legal aspects of promotion.

National Advertising Division (NAD)
Complaint bureau for consumers and advertisers, part of the Council of Better Business Bureaus.

Self-Regulation of Promotion

Although many laws regulating promotion activities have been enacted, marketers also practice self-regulation. The system they have established for policing promotion practices is the **National Advertising Division (NAD)** of the Council of Better Business Bureaus, which is a complaint bureau for consumers and advertisers. After receiving a complaint about a promotion, NAD starts investigating. It evaluates the information it collects and then decides whether the promotion's claims are substantiated. If the promotion is deemed unsatisfactory, NAD negotiates with the company for either changes or

Council of Better Business Bureaus, Inc.
How does the Better Business Bureau promote honest advertising? What specific issues does NAD address?

http://www.bbb.org/

discontinuation of the promotion. If the issue reaches a deadlock or the losing party wishes to appeal, the case is referred to the **National Advertising Review Board (NARB).**

Marketers want to avoid having to drop or modify promotional campaigns because of the potential costs: remaking an ad, overcoming bad publicity and ill will, destroying the timing of a campaign. For instance, Calvin Klein was recently forced to pull a series of ads that critics felt bordered on child pornography. The ads, featuring young men and women in suggestive poses in a cheap wood-paneled basement, ran in youth-oriented magazines such as *YM*, which has readers as young as 12 years old.[29] The controversial ads may have also created some ill will among potential buyers: A survey of consumers revealed that nearly one-fourth of adults and teens alike said the ads made them feel less favorable about buying Calvin Klein products.[30]

National Advertising Review Board (NARB)
Appeals board for cases in which the National Advertising Division rules in favor of the complaining party.

Deceptive advertising can be costly to companies in terms of lost consumer confidence, tarnished reputations, and squandered ad dollars—not to mention lawsuit settlements. But not all companies suffer the same way. Studies indicate that companies already held in low regard by consumers may suffer the most, while the public tends to believe that highly regarded companies deceive inadvertently. These consumers in turn tend to believe other claims made about the product.[31] In 1990, for example, Volvo ran an ad showing one its automobiles surviving a crash that destroyed the competition's car. What consumers found out later was that the Volvo had a notable advantage: it had been reinforced with steel for the commercial. While Volvo's overall reputation dipped as a result of media publicity of the scam, its product did not suffer considerably.

Federal Regulation of Promotion

corrective advertising
Advertisement that is run to amend the false impressions left by previous promotion.

When self-regulation doesn't work, the Federal Trade Commission (FTC) steps in. The FTC's main concern is with deception and misrepresentation in promotion. The FTC defines *deception* as "a representation, omission, or practice that is likely to mislead the consumer who is acting reasonably in the circumstances, to the consumer's detriment." The courts have ruled that deception can also cover what the consumer infers from the promotion, not only what is literally said. Critics of FTC regulations point out that any message, commercial or not, has the potential for deception. Moreover, even the most honest speaker cannot control the inferences the audience will make.

Often, the FTC will require the promoter to *substantiate* the claims made in its promotional messages. If the claims cannot be substantiated, the FTC's traditional remedy is the *cease-and-desist order*, otherwise known as the "go and sin no more" approach. This order bans use of claims found to be false or deceptive. In some cases, the FTC requires a corrective message. **Corrective advertising** is an advertisement or message run to amend the false impressions left by previous promotion. For example, Eggland's Best, a Pennsylvania company selling eggs, claimed in its advertising that "even a dozen Eggland's Best eggs a week caused no increase in serum cholesterol," in tests as part of a low-fat diet. The FTC charged the company with false and misleading advertising and forced the company to modify ads and halt nutrition claims. As part of the settlement, the FTC also ordered the company to label its egg cartons for a year with this message: "There are no studies showing that these eggs are different from other eggs in their effect on serum cholesterol."[32] *Fines* may also be levied against firms making false claims. For example, the FTC found that changes Eggland's Best made to subsequent advertisements weren't enough to alter its previous misleading claims on the health benefits of its eggs. As a result, the FTC fined the egg producer $100,000.[33]

Does corrective advertising work? The overall consensus is that corrective advertising seems to work, at best, moderately well—but not nearly well enough to correct the misrepresentations of deceptive advertising. For example, Warner-Lambert, the maker of Listerine, was required to use corrective promotion to amend advertising that led consumers to believe its product could prevent colds or sore throats. Nevertheless, after the corrective advertising was run, the majority of regular Listerine users still believed the misrepresented ads.

LOOKING BACK

Microsoft does not use just one element of the promotional mix to promote its operating system to personal computer users. Rather, it uses a mix of promotional elements: advertising, public relations and publicity, personal selling, and sales promotion. Promotion proved crucial to the software giant's successful launch of its

Windows 95 operating system. As you read the next two chapters, keep in mind that marketers try to choose the mix of promotional elements that will best promote their good or service. Rarely will a marketer rely on just one method of promotion.

SUMMARY

1 *Discuss the role of promotion in the marketing mix.* Promotion is communication by marketers that informs, persuades, and reminds potential buyers of a product in order to influence an opinion or elicit a response. Promotional strategy is the plan for using the elements of promotion—advertising, public relations, personal selling, and sales promotion—to meet the firm's overall objectives and marketing goals. Based on these objectives, the elements of the promotional strategy become a coordinated promotion plan. The promotion plan then becomes an integral part of the total marketing strategy for reaching the target market, along with product, distribution, and price.

2 *Discuss the elements of the promotional mix.* The elements of the promotional mix include advertising, public relations, personal selling, and sales promotion. Advertising is a form of impersonal, one-way mass communication paid for by the source. Public relations is the function of promotion concerned with a firm's public image. Firms can't buy good publicity, but they can take steps to create a positive company image. Personal selling typically involves direct communication, in person or by telephone; the seller tries to initiate a purchase by informing and persuading one or more potential buyers. More current notions of personal selling focus on the relationship developed between the seller and buyer. Finally, sales promotion is typically used to back up other components of the promotional mix by motivating employees and stimulating consumer and business-customer purchasing.

3 *Describe the communication process.* The communication process has several steps. When an individual or organization has a message it wishes to convey to a target audience, it encodes that message using language and symbols familiar to the intended receiver and sends the message through a channel of communication. Noise in the transmission channel distorts the source's intended message. Reception occurs if the message falls within the receiver's frame of reference. The receiver decodes the message and usually provides feedback to the source. Normally, feedback is direct for interpersonal communication and indirect for mass communication.

4 *Explain the goals and tasks of promotion.* The fundamental goals of promotion are to induce, modify, or reinforce behavior by informing, persuading, and reminding. Informative promotion explains a good or service's purpose and benefits. Promotion that informs the consumer is typically used to increase demand for a general product category or to introduce a new good or service. Persuasive promotion is designed to stimulate a purchase or an action. Promotion that persuades the consumer to buy is essential during the growth stage of the product life cycle, when competition becomes fierce. Reminder promotion is used to keep the product and brand name in the public's mind. Promotions that remind are generally used during the maturity stage of the product life cycle.

5 *Discuss the hierarchy of effects concept and its relationship to the promotional mix.* The hierarchy of effects model outlines the six basic stages in the purchase decision-making process, which are initiated and propelled by promotional activities: (1) awareness, (2) knowledge, (3) liking, (4) preference, (5) conviction, and (6) purchase. The components of the promotional mix have varying levels of influence at each stage of the hierarchy. Advertising is a good tool for increasing awareness and

KEY TERMS

advertising *461*

AIDA concept *474*

all-you-can-afford approach *486*

arbitrary allocation *486*

channel *465*

communication *464*

competitive parity *486*

corrective advertising *488*

decoding *468*

differential advantage *460*

encoding *464*

feedback *468*

hierarchy of effects model *474*

integrated marketing communications (IMC) *471*

interpersonal communication *464*

market share approach *486*

mass communication *464*

National Advertising Division (NAD) *487*

National Advertising Review Board (NARB) *487*

noise *466*

objective and task approach *486*

percent of sales approach *486*

personal selling *463*

promotion *460*

promotional mix *461*

promotional strategy *460*

promotion plan *482*

publicity *462*

public relations *462*

pull strategy *481*

push strategy *480*

receiver *468*

knowledge of a good or service. Sales promotion is effective when consumers are at the purchase stage of the decision-making process. Personal selling is most effective in developing customer preferences and gaining conviction.

6 *Describe the factors that affect the promotional mix.* Promotion managers consider many factors when creating promotional mixes. These factors include the nature of the product, product life cycle stage, target market characteristics, the type of buying decision involved, availability of funds, and feasibility of push or pull strategies. Since most business products tend to be custom-tailored to the buyer's exact specifications, the marketing manager may choose a promotional mix that relies more heavily on personal selling. On the other hand, consumer products are generally mass produced and lend themselves more to mass promotional efforts such as advertising and sales promotion. As products move through different stages of the product life cycle, marketers will choose to use different promotional elements. For example, advertising is emphasized more in the introductory stage of the product life cycle than in the decline stage. Characteristics of the target market, such as geographic location of potential buyers and brand loyalty, influence the promotional mix as does whether the buying decision is complex or routine. The amount of funds a firm has to allocate to promotion may also help determine the promotional mix. Small firms with limited funds may rely more heavily on public relations, while larger firms may be able to afford broadcast or print advertising. Finally, if a firm uses a push strategy to promote the product or service, the marketing manager may choose to use aggressive advertising and personal selling to wholesalers and retailers. If a pull strategy is chosen, then the manager often relies on aggressive mass promotion, such as advertising and sales promotion, to stimulate consumer demand.

7 *Explain how to create a promotion plan.* Effective promotion planning is crucial to a product's success. Promotion planning involves several distinct steps. First, promotion managers analyze the marketplace, usually by conducting research. Second, they define the target market in terms of demographic, geographic, psychographic, or behavioral variables. Third, promotion managers set specific promotional objectives. Fourth, promotion managers determine the promotion budget. Finally, they select the elements of the promotional mix.

8 *Describe the ethical and legal aspects of promotion.* Although many laws are in place to regulate promotional activities, much of the industry practices self-regulation. Promotional practices are monitored by industry and government. Industry regulation is overseen by the National Advertising Division of the Council of Better Business Bureaus and by the National Advertising Review Board. The Federal Trade Commission becomes involved in advertising regulation when industry regulation proves inadequate.

Discussion and Writing Questions

1. What is a promotional strategy? Explain the concept of a differential advantage in relation to promotional strategy.

2. Why is understanding the target market a crucial aspect of the communication process?

3. Discuss the importance of integrated marketing communications. Give some current examples of companies that are and are not practicing integrated marketing communications.

4. Why might a marketing manager choose to promote his or her product using persuasion? Give some current examples of persuasive promotion.

5. Discuss the role of personal selling and advertising in promoting industrial products. How does their role differ in promoting consumer products?

6. Assume that your firm's promotion efforts for a new product have failed to meet promotional objectives. Write a report suggesting the reasons.

7. Your company has just developed a complex electronic device that can automatically control all the appliances in a consumer's home. Write a brief promotion plan describing your market analysis efforts, target market, promotional objectives, and promotional mix.

8. Discuss why using the objective and task method to determine a product's promotion budget is superior to other budget-setting methods.

9. Your company would like to develop a promotional campaign for a brand of laundry detergent that will be sold in several different countries. Would you choose to use a localized promotional message or one that is more standardized? Explain your choice. What would your decision be if the product were perfume?

10. Choose a partner from class and go together to interview the owner or manager of several small businesses in your city. Ask them what their promotional objectives are and why. For example, are they trying to inform, persuade, or remind customers to do business with them? Also determine if they believe they have an awareness problem or do they need to persuade customers to come to them instead of competitors. Ask them to list the characteristics of their primary market, the strengths and weaknesses of their direct competitors, and how they are positioning their store to compete. Prepare a report to present in class summarizing your findings.

11. Take a look at the following Web site and list some of the technical difficulties you experience in accessing and understanding the information. Name other cultural groups that may face similar communication difficulties via Western-style Internet platforms.

http://www.chinatown-ny. com/

12. What statements does this Web site make about the buying power, size, and growth of the Hispanic market in the United States? Why are these statistics important for marketing communication and promotion strategy in the United States?

http://www.pm-a.com/

13. How does the "Inspiration" link at the following Web site influence your perception of this city? Describe the content in that link. What role might it have in the city's overall marketing communication strategy?

http://www.battlecreekmich. com/

Application for Small Business

The Varsity Shoppes comprise two retail stores selling men's and women's clothing. It is a family operation, and the third-generation son and daughter are currently co-owners. The store has two locations, one near the local college campus and another in a strip center near a major shopping mall developed about 20 years ago east of the downtown area.

Population trends indicate a southerly move by the stores' traditional target market, and so the owners have decided to open a third store in a relatively new strip center south of town. This new location will open in about three months. A promotion campaign is now being planned for the new store.

Questions

1. Which types of promotion should the campaign emphasize—informative, persuasive, or reminder?

2. Suggest a promotion plan that will make the target market aware of the new location. To what extent should the plan emphasize the new location versus the two existing locations?

Attracting Customers to Piccadilly Cafeterias

Piccadilly Cafeterias operates 129 cafeterias, mostly in the southern United States. With a check average of $5 to $6, Piccadilly Cafeterias serve a wide variety of home-style, ethnic, and regional dishes to a broad spectrum of diners in a traditional dining atmosphere. With restaurant competition increasing significantly in recent years, a top priority has been to maintain and/or increase customer counts. The strategy was to accomplish this through an intense focus on customer satisfaction. The results of this strategy have been very favorable: Same-store customer counts increased in 11 of the 12 months of the year. The only negative month was January which was impacted by bad weather in the first two weeks of the month.

Average unit sales volume of the 129 cafeterias was $2,058,000 for the year. This is the first time the unit volumes have exceeded the $2,000,000 level in several years, and it represents a 4.5 percent increase over the prior year.

Piccadilly's ability to serve a wide variety of high-quality wholesome foods for the entire family will continue to be the platform on which business is built. Highest quality food, liberal portions, and fair prices will remain the chain's motto.

Enhanced service is also a vital part of Piccadilly's business philosophy. To accomplish this, staff levels in each cafeteria have been increased. This is consistent with a long-term business-building strategy. While food may be delivered in a cafeteria format, dining room service will compete with any delivery format.

Just one look at the variety of dishes displayed on a Piccadilly Cafeterias serving line makes one thing abundantly clear. The difference at Piccadilly is the *food*. No one gets

Ronald A. LaBorde

bored with more than 80 items to choose from at every meal. Groups of coworkers, family members of all ages, baseball teams, youth groups, club members—*everybody* gets what they want at Piccadilly.

Variety has always been the greatest strength of cafeteria dining. But variety is valued only if the food is outstanding. And Piccadilly has worked hard to achieve that. As some dining customers work to reduce the fat and sugar in their diets, Piccadilly has begun offering items such as boneless, skinless grilled chicken breast and sugar-free pies. As always, the exceptional variety ensures that customers can choose items that suit both their diets and their palates.

Today, a hot trend in the restaurant business is "home-meal replacement"—for busy people who love to eat wholesome home cooking, but don't have time to cook. But this is nothing new at Piccadilly. As customers' lives have gotten busier, with their at-home cooking time reduced, Piccadilly has offered all of their fresh food to go. Full meals can be selected—á la carte—off the serving line. Whole cakes, pies, meats,

breads, and plus party trays are also available, as well as complete turkey dinners for Thanksgiving and Christmas. Moreover, while restaurateurs everywhere are talking about ethnic cuisine and regional specialties, both have been part of Piccadilly's menu for years.

To create awareness of its food offerings among new customer audiences and to remind current customers to return, Piccadilly uses television advertising as well as other promotional approaches. The promotional approaches are developed based on market research. Focus group findings conducted in 10 major metro markets where Piccadilly has cafeterias are summarized in Exhibits 16.A and 16.B.

The creative execution of television ads is designed to make viewers hungry for Piccadilly's food through its visual appeal and to motivate them to satisfy that hunger by coming to eat there often. Effective advertising campaigns are essential to maintain market share in an increasingly crowded food service marketplace.

Exhibit 16.A

What Are the Three Most Important Reasons for Selecting a Family Restaurant?

Reason	Importance Ranking, %
Quality of food	88%
Variety of menu items	50
Expected cost	38
Convenient location	33
Friendly service	33
Nutritious food	19
Fast service	16
Atmosphere	16
Special promotions and/or discounts	8

Note: Percentages indicate percent of participants indicating a particular reason. Multiple responses were permitted.

Exhibit 16.B *Summary of Focus Group Comments in Response to Questions*

Question: What comes to mind when you think of a cafeteria?

Vegetables; quick/fast; wholesome meals; freshly prepared foods; no tipping; informal; where you go when you don't want a hamburger; variety; get to see food beforehand; you can mix-and-match foods; time saving/don't have to wait; can eat there every day and eat something different; men and women can go there alone; wider selection; home-style cooking; well-balanced meals; each person gets what they want.

Question: What do you dislike about a cafeteria?

Teenage boys eat too much at cafeterias; too many old people; feel pushed to hurry in line; hard to decide what you want; atmosphere plain; they are like hospitals and schools; don't like to stand in line; suspicious about the quality of cafeteria food.

Question: How do you define quality when you think of food?

Fresh; not greasy; appetizing appearance; tastes good; not overcooked; nutritious; consistency in taste; vegetables not soggy; cooked the way you want; not out of a can; prepared from scratch; not frozen; not microwaved; freshly baked; like mother used to make; no preservatives.

Questions

1. What are the factors that motivate people to eat at family-style restaurants like Piccadilly? Why would people choose to go to a cafeteria instead of a restaurant that serves meals at the table?

2. Should Piccadilly's strategy for attracting customers emphasize creating awareness or persuading them to come to eat there?

3. How effective was the execution of the TV ads? Were the appeals consistent with market research findings? How could the ads be improved? Should the emphasis be on increasing frequency of dining at Piccadilly or spending more when they eat there (or perhaps both)?

LEARNING OBJECTIVES *After studying this chapter, you should be able to:*

1 Discuss the effect advertising has on market share, consumers, brand loyalty, and perception of product attributes.

2 Identify the major types of advertising.

3 Describe the advertising campaign process.

4 Describe media evaluation and selection techniques.

5 Discuss the role of public relations in the promotional mix.

Advertising and Public Relations

How do you design an effective and memorable advertising campaign, especially for one of the world's blandest, most boring of products?

That was just the quandary faced by Bozell Worldwide, the advertising agency hired to develop ads for the National Fluid Milk Processor Promotion Board. What the agency came up with was the "Milk, What a Surprise!" campaign, a surprisingly successful collection of advertisements that paired a simple, educational message with some titans of fashion and sports. The clincher: All the celebrities sported milk mustaches.

After three decades of declining milk sales, the National Fluid Milk Processor Promotion Board decided some action was needed to counter milk's image of being a drink only for kids. Nobody over 12 seemed to drink milk anymore. And, although low-fat, healthy diets were the rage, adults didn't view milk as a low-fat drink. The goal of the advertising campaign was to grab the attention of women aged 25 to 44 and tell them something educational, but not preachy, about the health benefits of milk, and change their beliefs that milk is fatty and unhip. Women were the largest segment of lapsed milk drinkers while also being the most at-risk for osteoporosis, a bone-deteriorating disease that can be prevented with the help of calcium found in milk.

With a $36 million ad budget, Bozell's first big decision was to sink the entire budget into magazine ads. By going only in magazines, the ads would get more exposure and dominate the medium. They chose not to compete in the world of television, where milk could get lost in the sea of Coke and Pepsi and the ad budget would be eaten up quickly.

Next, the agency settled on a style and execution of the ads that would make them stunning and catch people's attention. The finished ads were "simple, strong, intrusive" celebrity pictures designed to look more like a poster than a magazine ad. This same strategy had paid off for earlier campaigns for American Express and Blackglama furriers. The American Express "Portraits" campaign featured photojournalistic shots by famed photographer Annie Liebovitz of celebrity cardholders. Similarly, Blackglama's celebrity-chocked "What Becomes a Legend Most" ads featured more than 50 celebrities, such as Elizabeth Taylor, sporting custom-made fur coats. Both campaigns were huge successes.

The clincher for the poster-like milk ads was a screwball touch that Bozell gambled would make people chuckle, without taking away from their sex appeal: the milk mustache. As a universal symbol of people who drink milk, the agency was betting the mustache might push a lot of buttons. The milk mustache

was something the agency felt most people could identify with as well as conjure up memories of youth. And, it would look surprisingly funny on a celebrity's upper lip.

With the idea for the campaign developed, the Bozell team set about wooing celebrities who would appeal to their target audience of women aged 25 to 44. Celebrities the likes of Christie Brinkley, Iman, Kate Moss, and Isabella Rossellini were recruited to make milk seem hip and nonfattening. To reach older women, Bozell recruited Lauren Bacall and Joan Rivers. The agency also included some hunky jocks women could identify with, such as tennis star Pete Sampras and quarterback Steve Young.

The campaign began in February 1995 and ran through March 1996, with a total of 813 pages of ads running in 50 national and 6 regional magazines, such as *Family Circle, Working Woman, Parenting, Ebony, Time, Entertainment Weekly, People, Vogue,* and *Bon Appetit.* Each publication received between 7 and 30 ads on a continuous running schedule, creating one of the biggest print ad blitzes ever.

The results of the campaign were tremendous. While not only garnering wide praise from advertising critics, research found 22 percent more people saw milk as an adult beverage after the campaign, and 22 percent more thought of it as a good after-exercise drink. Additionally, there was a 17 percent increase in the perception of milk's health benefits and an 18 percent increase in people who thought skim milk was a good diet drink.

Phase two of the Fluid Milk Processor's campaign, which began in mid-1996, features 20 more celebrities and an expanded audience including men and teens. While phase one sought to change consumers' attitudes about milk, phase two of the campaign aims to start showing results at the cash register. The campaign slogan was changed to "Milk, Where's *Your* Mustache" in an effort to get consumers to take some action.[1] Visit the National Fluid Milk Processor Promotion Board's Internet site at http://www.whymilk. com for images from their latest campaign, customized diet and nutrition analysis, facts about milk, and links to magazines participating in the mustache ad campaign.

How can advertisers like the National Fluid Milk Processors Promotion Board change consumers' attitudes and beliefs and increase their product sales through advertising? How do advertisers decide what type of message should be conveyed? How do they create advertising campaigns and decide which media to use to reach consumers? Answers to these questions and many more will be found as you read through this chapter.

Bozell Worldwide
Review several campaigns from Bozell's portfolio. How do the message and media vary?
http://www.bozell.com/

EFFECTS OF ADVERTISING

1 Discuss the effect advertising has on market share, consumers, brand loyalty, and perception of product attributes.

Advertising is defined in Chapter 16 as any form of nonpersonal, paid communication in which the sponsor or company is identified. It is a popular form of promotion, especially for consumer packaged goods and services. Advertising spending increases annually, with estimated U.S. advertising expenditures now exceeding $150 billion per year.[2]

Although total advertising expenditures seem large, the industry itself is very small. Only about 272,000 people are employed in the advertising departments of manufacturers, wholesalers, and retailers and in the 5,000 or so U.S. advertising agencies.[3] This figure also includes people working in media services, such as radio and television, magazines and newspapers, and direct-mail firms.

Advertising Age
Visit the Ad Age DataPlace to find today's top advertisers. Which companies are top national advertisers? Which are top advertisers in global markets?

http://www.adage.com/

The amount of money budgeted for advertising by some U.S. firms is staggering (see Exhibit 17.1). Procter & Gamble, Philip Morris, and General Motors each spend over $2 billion annually on national advertising alone. That's over $5 million a day by each company. If sales promotion and public relations are included, this figure rises even higher. About 70 additional companies spend over $200 million each.

Spending on advertising varies by industry. For example, the game and toy industry has one of the highest ratios of advertising dollars to sales. For every dollar of merchandise sold in the toy industry, about 16¢ is spent on advertising the toy to consumers. Other consumer goods manufacturers that spend heavily on advertising in relation to total sales include book publishers, mail-order catalog companies, educational services, food manufacturers, and soap and detergent makers.[4]

Exhibit 17.1
*Top Ten U.S.
Advertisers: 1995*

Rank	Advertiser	Ad Spending Per Day (average)
1	Procter & Gamble	$7,608,400
2	Philip Morris	7,059,948
3	General Motors	5,607,975
4	Time Warner	3,581,013
5	Walt Disney	3,550,673
6	Sears, Roebuck	3,358,136
7	Chrysler	3,349,062
8	PepsiCo	3,279,568
9	Johnson & Johnson	3,214,444
10	Ford Motor	3,148,587

Source: Computed from data provided on "100 Leading National Advertisers," on the *Advertising Age* Web site at www.adage.com. Reprinted by permission of Crain Communications, Inc.

Advertising and Market Share

Today's most successful brands of consumer goods, like Ivory soap and Coca-Cola, were built by heavy advertising and marketing investments long ago. Today's advertising dollars are spent on maintaining brand awareness and market share.

New brands with a small market share tend to spend proportionately more for advertising and sales promotion than those with a large market share, typically for two reasons. First, beyond a certain level of spending for advertising and sales promotion, diminishing returns set in. That is, sales or market share begins to decrease no matter how much is spent on advertising and sales promotion. This phenomenon, called the **advertising response function,** is illustrated in Exhibit 17.2. Understanding of the advertising response function helps marketers use budgets wisely. For example, a market leader like Ruffles potato chips may spend proportionately less on advertising than a newcomer such as Frito-Lay's Baked Lay's brand. Frito-Lay spends more on its brand in an attempt to increase awareness and market share. Ruffles, on the other hand, spends only as much as needed to maintain market share; anything more would reap diminishing benefits. Because Ruffles has already captured the attention of the majority of the target market, it needs only to remind customers of its product.

The second reason that new brands tend to require higher spending for advertising and sales promotion is that a certain minimum level of exposure is needed to measurably affect purchase habits. For example, if Frito-Lay advertised Baked Lay's chips in only one or two publications and bought only one or two television spots, it certainly would not achieve the exposure needed to penetrate consumers' perceptual defenses, obtain awareness and comprehension, and ultimately affect their purchase intentions. Instead, Baked Lay's chips were introduced through advertising in many different media for a sustained period of time.

Advertising and the Consumer

Advertising affects everyone's daily life and influences many purchases. Consumers turn to advertising for its informativeness, as well as its entertainment value. The average U.S. citizen is exposed to hundreds of advertisements a day from all types of

advertising response function
Phenomenon in which spending for advertising and sales promotion increases sales or market share up to a certain level but then produces diminishing returns.

Exhibit 17.2
*Advertising Response
Function*

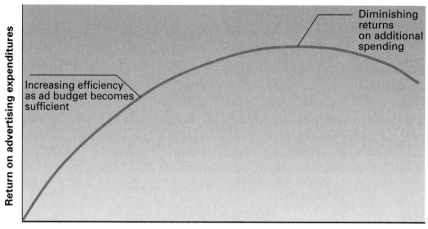

advertising media. In just the television media alone, researchers estimate that the average person spends over four hours a day watching TV. With network television airing an average of 18 minutes of commercials during each hour of daytime programming, consumers are surely affected in some way by advertising.[5] Advertising affects the TV programs people watch, the content of the newspapers they read, the politicians they elect, the medicines they take, and the toys their children play with. Consequently, the influence of advertising on the U.S. socioeconomic system has been the subject of extensive debate among economists, marketers, sociologists, psychologists, politicians, consumerists, and many others.

Advertising cannot manipulate society as much as some might fear because it cannot change strongly held values. Attitudes and values are deeply rooted within an individual's psychological makeup. Advertising seldom succeeds in changing an attitude that stems from a person's basic value system, or moral code, and that is strongly supported by his or her culture. Adolescents still in the process of forming their personal value systems, however, may be susceptible to the influences of advertising, as discussed in the "Ethics in Marketing" box.

However, advertising may succeed in transforming a person's negative attitude toward a product into a positive one. When prior evaluation of the brand is negative, serious or dramatic advertisements are more effective at changing consumers' attitudes. Humorous ads, on the other hand, have been shown to be more effective at shaping attitudes when consumers already have a positive image of the advertised brand.[6] Research has also shown that humor in advertising is more effective in generating a favorable attitude from persons whose need for information is low rather than high. That is, consumers specifically looking for information about a product or service don't find humorous ads humorous.[7]

Credibility is also a factor. Consumers' positive or negative attitudes toward an advertiser can also influence their attitudes toward the advertised product. Research has shown that when consumers believe an advertiser is trustworthy and credible, they are more likely to accept the advertised product's claim and more likely to change their attitudes and buying behavior.[8] For example, after 30 years of denying the hazardous effects of smoking, tobacco companies have lost considerable credibility with the consumer. As a result, consumers are reluctant to believe advertising by Philip Morris that the effects of second-hand smoke are not as serious as government reports suggest.[9]

Advertising and Brand Loyalty

Consumers with a high degree of brand loyalty are least susceptible to the influences of advertising for competing goods or services. For instance, new competitors found it hard to dislodge AT&T after deregulation of the long-distance telephone indus-

Ethics in Marketing

Are Kids Influenced by Joe Camel?

Are minors more susceptible to cigarette advertising than adults? One recent study suggests that marketing and advertising by tobacco companies plays a stronger role than peer pressure in influencing children to start smoking. The study, commissioned by the National Cancer Institute, counters the tobacco industry's longtime claim that kids start smoking because of peer pressure or the example of family members. The industry counters that its ads are pitched exclusively to adults who already smoke in an attempt to get them to switch brands.

A more recent study found that minors were three times more responsive to cigarette advertisements than adults. Of the nine major cigarette brands studied in the report, three—Marlboro, Camel, and Newport—showed the greatest disparity between advertising's impact on minors and its impact on adults. The study suggests the infamous Marlboro Man and Joe Camel ads have made an impression on teens, coupled with merchandising strategies and direct-mail campaigns. Marlboro, which represents about 13 percent of the cigarette advertising market—the greatest share of any brand in the study—had almost 60 percent market share among minors, compared with only about 22 percent of adults. Likewise, Camel, at about 5 percent of the advertising market, had roughly 9 percent market share among minors, while Camel's adult market share was about 4 percent. The Newport brand had similar, but smaller market share numbers among minors and adults.

Despite the industry's protests that it does not target minors with its advertising, these studies along with industry statistics show that tobacco campaigns have clearly in-

fluenced kids. Every day, it is estimated that some 3,000 American teenagers reach adulthood as confirmed smokers. That's roughly equal to the number of adults who give up smoking or die from the diseases it causes. Most teens started smoking before they were legally able to smoke. Kids under 18 smoke an estimated 17 billion of the 500 billion cigarettes sold each year in the United States. Teens are the primary source of new smokers; after they turn 20, almost none of them starts smoking. Indeed, a recent study funded by the National Institute of Drug Abuse found that cigarette smoking among high school students is on the rise, and the younger the smokers, the more dramatic the increase. The study found a particularly significant jump in smoking among eighth-graders, the youngest students surveyed.

Critics of the cigarette industry's advertising and marketing tactics portend that the images cigarette smoking emphasizes—in magazines popular with teenagers, on sporting event billboards, on the sides of buses, and in the doorways of convenience stores—resonate perfectly with the psychological and social needs of adolescents: social acceptance, personal independence, and weight control. Newport cigarette ads featuring confident-looking young couples having fun together, for example, play to the craving for popularity. Ads for Camel cigarettes feature the cartoon character Joe Camel in cool, trendy clothes and Ray-Bans that would appeal to teens. Further,

one of the main developmental tasks of adolescence is to assert independence from parents. Marlboro has exploited this need with its cowboy-alone-on-the-range images. Likewise, a recent Virginia Slims campaign touted the cigarette "as free-spirited as you." The weight control theme, often an obsession among teenage girls, is played out in ads by Misty ("slim and sassy") and Virginia Slims ("If I ran the world, calories wouldn't count"). The models in the ads are thin and fashionable. Even Misty and Virginia Slims cigarettes are themselves extra-slender.

The U.S. government is taking increasing action against the tobacco industry, as evidenced with President Clinton's approval in the summer of 1996 of the Food & Drug Administration's restrictions on tobacco marketing. The FDA's plan bans not only the cartoon camel and legendary cowboy, but all imagery on outdoor billboards, in many magazine ads, and at most points of sale. The restrictions would also bar tobacco companies from giving away merchandise with brand names and from sponsoring events and teams using brand names. Additionally, all outdoor ads would be barred within 1,000 feet of most schools. Advertising groups claim the restrictions will impact over $1 billion annually in tobacco marketing spending—an impact that will result in the loss of jobs, business opportunities, and creative freedom. Ad agencies as well as the cigarette industry plan to fight the restrictions.[10]

What is your opinion on the controversial issue of teen smoking? Do you believe tobacco advertisers' claims that they only promote to adults? Do you feel the tobacco industry should be restricted from promoting a product that is legal to sell?

institutional advertising
Form of advertising designed to enhance a company's image rather than promote a particular product.

product advertising
Form of advertising that touts the benefits of a specific good or service.

advocacy advertising
Form of advertising in which an organization expresses its views on controversial issues or responds to media attacks.

This ad for Amway Corporation is a good example of institutional advertising. Notice how the ad focuses on the corporation as a whole rather than on any specific products marketed by the corporation.
Courtesy Amway Corporation

try. After relying on "Ma Bell" for a lifetime of service, many loyal customers showed little response to advertising by competing companies.

Advertising also reinforces positive attitudes toward brands. When consumers have a neutral or favorable frame of reference toward a product or brand, they are often positively influenced by advertising for it. When consumers are already highly loyal to a brand, they may buy more of it when advertising and promotion for that brand increase.[11]

Advertising and Product Attributes

Advertising can affect the way consumers rank a brand's attributes, such as color, taste, smell, and texture. For example, in the past a shopper may have selected a brand of luncheon meat based on taste and variety of cuts available. But advertising may influence that consumer to choose luncheon meat on the basis of other attributes, such as calories and fat content. Luncheon meat marketers like Louis Rich, Oscar Mayer, and Healthy Choice now stress the amount of calories and fat when advertising their products.

Automobile advertisers also understand the influence of advertising on consumers' rankings of brand attributes. Car ads have traditionally emphasized such brand attributes as roominess, speed, and low maintenance. Today, however, car marketers have added safety to the list. Safety features such as antilock brakes, power door locks, and air bags are now a standard part of the message in many carmakers' ads.

MAJOR TYPES OF ADVERTISING

A firm's promotional objectives (refer back to Chapter 16) determine the type of advertising it uses. If the goal of the promotion plan is to build up the image of the company, or the industry, **institutional advertising** may be used. In contrast, if the advertiser wants to enhance the sales of a specific good or service, **product advertising** is used.

Institutional Advertising

Advertising in the United States has historically been product oriented. However, modern corporations market multiple products and need a different type of advertising. Institutional advertising, or corporate advertising, promotes the corporation as a whole and is designed to establish, change, or maintain the corporation's identity. It usually does not ask the audience to do anything but maintain a favorable attitude toward the advertiser and its goods and services. Nissan Motor Corporation, for example, recently embarked on a corporate campaign to promote the Nissan brand as a whole rather than one specific model. The campaign is designed to improve Nissan's image and increase credibility, while reminding customers of its Japanese heritage.[12]

A form of institutional advertising called **advocacy advertising** is typically used as a safeguard against negative consumer attitudes and to enhance the company's credibility among consumers who already favor its position.[13] Often, corporations use advocacy advertising to express their views on controversial issues. Other times, firms' advocacy campaigns react to criticism or blame, some in direct response to criticism by the media. Other advocacy campaigns may try to ward off increased regulation or damaging legislation. For example, R. J. Reynolds responded to proposed antismoking legislation by using advocacy advertising. In one ad, a nonsmoker declares: "The smell of cigarette smoke annoys me. But not nearly as much as the government telling me what to do."[14]

Product Advertising

Unlike institutional advertising, product advertising promotes the benefits of a specific good or service. The product's stage in its life cycle often determines which type of product advertising is used: pioneering advertising, competitive advertising, or comparative advertising.

Pioneering Advertising

Pioneering advertising is intended to stimulate primary demand for a new product or product category. Heavily used during the introductory stage of the product life cycle, pioneering advertising offers consumers in-depth information about the benefits of the product class. Pioneering advertising also seeks to create interest.

Food companies, which introduce many new products, often use pioneering advertising. For example, Frito-Lay used pioneering advertising to introduce Baked Lay's to American consumers. The company embarked on a glitzy ad campaign featuring supermodel Cindy Crawford greedily gobbling the low-fat potato chips. The pioneering ad campaign's goal was to attract women who had abandoned salty snacks because of diet concerns. The launch was considered one of Frito-Lay's biggest new product successes ever with some $35 million in Baked Lay's sold in less than two months.[15]

pioneering advertising
Form of advertising designed to stimulate primary demand for a new product or product category.

Competitive Advertising

Firms use competitive or brand advertising when a product enters the growth phase of the product life cycle and other companies begin to enter the marketplace. Instead of building demand for the product category, the goal of **competitive advertising** is to influence demand for a specific brand.

Often promotion becomes less informative and appeals more to emotions during this phase. Advertisements may begin to stress subtle differences between brands, with heavy emphasis on building recall of a brand name and creating a favorable attitude toward the brand. Automobile advertising has long used very competitive messages, drawing distinctions based on such factors as quality, performance, and image. For example, Ford stresses the theme "Quality is job one" in its advertising. Buick's "The new symbol for quality in America" and Mercury's "All this and the quality of a Mercury" slogans also emphasize superior workmanship. The beer, soft-drink, fast-food, and long-distance telephone service industries also wage advertising "wars."

competitive advertising
Form of advertising designed to influence demand for a specific brand.

Comparative Advertising

A controversial trend in product advertising is the use of comparative advertising. **Comparative advertising** directly or indirectly compares two or more competing brands on one or more specific attributes. Some advertisers even use comparative advertising against their own brands. Products experiencing sluggish growth or those entering the marketplace against strong competitors are more likely to employ comparative claims in their advertising. For instance, when the U.S. Food and Drug Administration approved three over-the-counter heartburn remedies—Pepcid AC, Tagamet HB and Zantac 75—the drugs' manufacturers waged an unprecedented advertising battle for market share. Comparative ads compared each remedy on safety, adverse interactions with other medications, frequency of physician recommendation, and the length of time the drug works. One Pepcid AC ad asserted: "My doctor told me that I didn't need Zantac for my occasional heartburn and acid indigestion."[16]

comparative advertising
Form of advertising that compares two or more specifically named or shown competing brands on one or more specific attributes.

Before the 1970s, comparative advertising was allowed only if the competing brand was veiled and unidentified. In 1971, however, the Federal Trade Commission (FTC) fostered the growth of comparative advertising by saying that it provided information to the consumer and that advertisers were more skillful than the government in communicating this information. Federal rulings prohibit advertisers from falsely describing competitors' products and allow competitors to sue if ads show their products or mention their brand names in an incorrect or false manner. These rules also apply to advertisers making false claims about their own products. In the over-the-counter heartburn market, for example, SmithKline Beecham, the maker of Tagamet HB, filed a false-advertising claim against ads for Johnson & Johnson/Merck's Pepcid AC heartburn remedy. SmithKline's suit alleged that television commercials for Pepcid AC exaggerated how long Pepcid remained effective. SmithKline also protested a Pepcid ad that claimed 8 out of 10 doctors and pharmacists chose Pepcid AC over Tagamet HB.[17]

Is comparative advertising worth the trouble? Much research suggests that comparative advertising is no more effective at increasing purchase intentions than noncomparative advertising. Marketers also risk brand misidentification and confusion when comparing different brands in advertising. Further, consumers often overgeneralize comparative price claims, jumping to the conclusion that since the advertised price for a company's particular product or service is lower than the competitor's, the company offers the lowest overall prices.[18] But on the positive side, research has produced these findings:[19]

- Direct comparisons in advertisements attract attention and may thereby enhance purchase intentions.

- Consumers perceive comparative messages as being more relevant than similar noncomparative ads and are able to recall more message points from the comparative ads.

- Comparative ads for relatively unknown brands can increase the association of those unknown brands with well-known brands to which they are compared.

- Comparative ads comparing "objective" brand attributes can generate more positive attitudes than comparative ads focusing on "subjective" brand attributes. For example, the claim that car A has eight more cubic inches of trunk space than car B (objective) is potentially more effective than the claim that soup X is tastier than soup Y (subjective).

- When comparative ads for a new brand are personally relevant and use a brand with high credibility for comparison, they have a more positive effect on purchase intentions than noncomparative ads have.

In some other nations, particularly newly capitalized countries in Eastern Europe, claims that seem exaggerated by U.S. standards are commonplace. More often, however, the hard-sell tactics found in comparative ads in the United States are taboo. Until the 1980s, Japanese regulations all but prohibited comparative ads; ads that failed to compare objectively were considered slanderous. Nevertheless, although the Japanese have traditionally favored a soft-sell advertising approach, consumers are witnessing a trend toward comparative ads. Germany, Italy, Belgium, and France, for example, do not permit advertisers to claim that their products are best or better than competitors' products, which are common claims in U.S. advertising. In fact, the French are so adamant toward comparative ads that a Paris court banned a Philip Morris ad campaign comparing second-hand smoke to eating cookies for violating comparative advertising laws, even though no specific brands of cookies were mentioned in the ad.[20]

3 Describe the advertising campaign process.

advertising campaign
Series of related advertisements focusing on a common theme, slogan, and set of advertising appeals.

STEPS IN CREATING AN ADVERTISING CAMPAIGN

An **advertising campaign** is a series of related advertisements focusing on a common theme, slogan, and set of advertising appeals. It is a specific advertising effort for a particular product that extends for a defined period of time. Management of advertising begins with understanding the steps in developing an advertising campaign and then making the important decisions relating to each step. Exhibit 17.3 traces the steps in this process.

The advertising campaign process is set in motion by the promotion plan (discussed in Chapter 16). As you will remember, the promotion planning process identifies the target market, determines the overall promotional objectives, sets the promotion budget, and selects the promotional mix. Advertising, which is usually part of the promotional mix, is used to encode a selling message to the target market. The advertisement is then conveyed to the target market, or receivers of the message, through such advertising vehicles as broadcast or print media.

Determine Campaign Objectives

The first step in the development of an advertising campaign is to determine the advertising objectives. An **advertising objective** identifies the specific communication task a campaign should accomplish for a specified target audience during a specified period of time. The objectives of a specific advertising campaign depend on the overall corporate objectives and the product being advertised.

The DAGMAR approach (Defining Advertising Goals for Measured Advertising Results) is one method of setting objectives. According to this method, all advertising objectives should precisely define the target audience, the desired percentage change in some specified measure of effectiveness, and the time frame in which that change is to occur. For example, the objectives of an advertising campaign for BMW's new, lower-priced models might be achieving a total of 50,000 consumer test drives within the first six months of introduction as a result of mailing video advertisements to a sample of the target audience.

advertising objective
Specific communication task a campaign should accomplish for a specified target audience during a specified period.

Make Creative Decisions

The next step in developing an advertising campaign is to make the necessary creative and media decisions. Note in Exhibit 17.3 that both creative and media decisions are made at the same time. Creative work cannot be completed without knowing which **medium,** or message channel, will be used to convey the message to the target market. However, in this chapter media decisions are addressed after creative decisions.

In many cases, the advertising objectives dictate the medium and the creative approach to be used. For example, if the objective is to demonstrate how fast a product

medium
Channel used to convey a message to a target market.

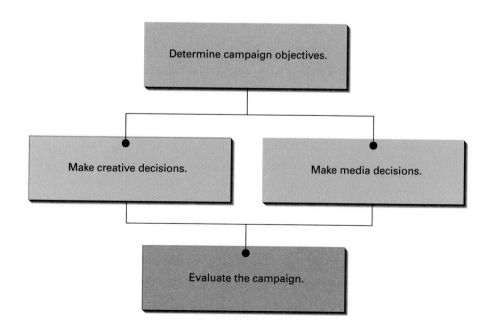

Exhibit 17.3
Advertising Campaign Decision Process

operates, then a TV commercial that shows this action may be the best choice. Creative decisions include identifying the product's benefits, developing possible advertising appeals, evaluating the advertising appeals and selecting one with a unique selling proposition, and executing the advertising message. An effective advertising campaign follows AIDA or other hierarchy of effects models, which were discussed in Chapter 16.

Identifying Product Benefits

A well-known rule of thumb in the advertising industry is "Sell the sizzle, not the steak." That is, in advertising the goal is to sell the benefits of the product, not its attributes. An attribute is simply a feature of the product, such as its easy-to-open package or special formulation. A benefit is what consumers will receive or achieve by using the product. A benefit should answer the consumer's question, "What's in it for me?" Benefits might be such things as convenience, pleasure, savings, or relief. A quick test to determine whether you are offering attributes or benefits in your advertising is to ask "So?" Consider this example:

> *Attribute:* "The Gillette SensorExcel razor has twin blades individually mounted on remarkably responsive springs to automatically adjust to the curves and contours of a man's face."
> "So . . . ?"
> *Benefit:* "So, you'll get a closer, smoother, and safer shave than ever before."

Marketing research and intuition are usually used to unearth the perceived benefits of a product and to rank consumers' preferences for these benefits.

Developing and Evaluating Advertising Appeals

An **advertising appeal** identifies a reason for a person to buy a product. Developing advertising appeals, a challenging task, is typically the responsibility of the creative people in the advertising agency. Advertising appeals typically play off of consumers' emotions, such as fear or love, or address some need or want the consumer has, such as a need for convenience or the desire to save money.

Advertising campaigns can focus on one or more advertising appeals. Often the appeals are quite general, thus allowing the firm to develop a number of subthemes or minicampaigns using both advertising and sales promotion. Several possible advertising appeals are listed in Exhibit 17.4.

Choosing the best appeal from those developed normally requires market research. Criteria for evaluation include desirability, exclusiveness, and believability. The appeal first must make a positive impression on and be desirable to the target market. It must also be exclusive or unique; consumers must be able to distinguish the advertiser's message from competitors' messages. Most important, the appeal should be believable. An appeal that makes extravagant claims not only wastes promotional dollars but also creates ill will for the advertiser.

The advertising appeal selected for the campaign becomes what advertisers call its **unique selling proposition.** The unique selling proposition usually becomes the campaign's slogan. Lever Brothers' Lever 2000 soap carries the slogan, "The deodorant soap that's better for your skin." This is also the soap's unique selling proposition.

Effective slogans often become so ingrained that consumers can immediately conjure up images of the prod-

advertising appeal
Reason for a person to buy a product.

unique selling proposition
Desirable, exclusive, and believable advertising appeal selected as the theme for a campaign.

This Revlon ad focuses on the product's benefits instead of its attributes. A benefit answers the question, "What's in it for me?"
Courtesy Revlon Products

uct just by hearing the slogan. For example, most consumers can easily name the companies and products behind these memorable slogans or even hum the jingle that goes along with some of them: "Have it your way"; "Tastes great, less filling"; "Ring around the collar"; and "Tum te Tum Tum."[21] Advertisers often revive old slogans or jingles in the hopes that the nostalgia will create good feelings with consumers. Kraft Foods, for instance, recently reintroduced advertising using Oscar Mayer's "B-o-l-o-g-n-a" and Maxwell House's "Perking Pot" jingles.[22] Similarly, after a 15-year absence, sunglasses manufacturer Foster Grant revived its famous "Who's that behind those Foster Grants?" slogan in a print advertising campaign.[23]

Getting appeals and slogans right can be a difficult task for advertisers in Islamic nations such as Iran, where the government generally censors all advertising. Read about the trials and tribulations of advertisers in Iran in the "Global Perspectives" box.

Executing the Message

Message execution is the way the advertisement portrays its information. In general, the AIDA plan is a good blueprint for executing an advertising message. Any ad should immediately draw the reader's, viewer's, or listener's attention. The advertiser must then use the message to hold consumers' interest, create desire for the good or service, and ultimately motivate action: a purchase.

This Healthy Choice ad appeals to consumers who are body-conscious or who want to be healthy.
Courtesy ConAgra Brands, Inc.

Profit	Lets consumers know whether the product will save them money, make them money, or keep them from losing money.
Health	Appeals to those who are body-conscious or who want to be healthy.
Love or romance	Is used often in selling cosmetics and perfumes.
Fear	Can center around social embarrassment, growing old, or losing one's health; because of its power, requires advertiser to exercise care in execution.
Admiration	Is the reason that celebrity spokespeople are used so often in advertising.
Convenience	Is often used for fast-food restaurants and microwave foods.
Fun and pleasure	Are the key to advertising vacations, beer, amusement parks, and more.
Vanity and egotism	Are used most often for expensive or conspicuous items, such as cars and clothing.
Environmental Considerate of others Consciousness	Centers around protecting the environment and being in the community.

Exhibit 17.4
Common Advertising Appeals

Global Perspectives

Iranian Censors Decide Many Topics Are Unmentionable in Ads

It seemed like a perfect pitch. To promote Damavand refrigerators in Iran, what better image than Mount Damavand, the 18,000-foot snow-covered peak that towers over Tehran? The slogan: "Only nature makes cold like Damavand." Then the Iranian Ministry of Islamic Guidance spoke: "You can't compare a refrigerator to nature," the censor said. "That's God's territory."

A few years ago, Iran's clerical rulers, giving up a revolutionary ghost, dumped socialism for capitalism and Iranian advertising was born. To guard against moral decay, however, advertisers were given some guidelines. Iranian ads can have no women, no English, no celebrities, no jokes, no product claims, and no hints, whatsoever, of sex, aristocracy, or America.

Moreover, many things not specifically prohibited are usually not allowed. Advertisers can't really give information about the product, only the name, making the task of advertising a delicate process. So delicate, in fact, that, to get through the censors, one billboard for an Iranian brand of women's lingerie displayed no women, no lingerie, and no mention of the unmentionable product at all. The ad's sole image was of the underwear's plain green box with the words "soft and delicate" written alongside. No one had a clue what it meant.

Similarly, ads for Iranian soaps and shampoos show bubbles and babbling brooks, never people. Promos for shoes stay strictly below the ankle. Dressmakers plug fashions on drawings of shapeless, even faceless models.

Billboards for Tehran's first Islamic Women's Games featured a stick figure racing over a high hurdle—an international symbol of athletics. Fine, except the gap between the runner's outstretched legs was filled in by an ankle-length robe. An ice-cream maker was reprimanded for using a silver spoon, a symbol of aristocracy. And a meat company had to redesign an ad after censors ruled that a candlelit table for two and the slogan "a memorable taste for a memorable moment" was considered too steamy.

To get around the censors, advertisers in Iran pay big fees to government agencies. They submit all ads for approval. Then the game of cat and mouse starts. After the underwear maker got its green box past the censors, workers hit the streets to affix little stickers to the bottoms of the billboards telling what was inside. To pitch tortilla chips, an entrepreneur told Health Ministry Officials the chips weren't North American but got the name from the Persian words *tord,* for crispy, and *diya,* meaning wild corn in an obscure Persian dialect. They believed him.

It took a little more wrangling, however, to allay the suspicions of the Ministry of Islamic Guidance official who scrutinized the motto for Piff Poff insect spray: "Whatever's bugging you, Piff Poff it!" Could it be the government, asked the official, that's bugging you?

Never, the company responded. The ad was cleared.

Aladdin vinegar got nothing right. Its mascot is a drawing of the barrel-chested character from "1,001 Nights," who, in the ads, holds a bottle of vinegar and says, "It's not magic. It's 25 years of experience." The Islamic Guidance official didn't like it because Aladdin was an Arab and Persians didn't necessarily like Arabs. Furthermore, there is no such thing as magic in Islam, he said, and Aladdin's unbuttoned vest and ponytail were sloppy. It took three days, but an ad executive cajoled the official into lightening up.

Foreign brands, however, get the most heat. Although a billboard with big red lips promoting South Korea's Goldstar television sets passed the censor, arsonists twice burned it down. Zealots also defaced ads for Japan's Sharp TV sets and General Electric refrigerators, scrawling the ubiquitous "Down with America" on GE's sign.

Most international campaigns are nonstarters in Iran. A European ad for France's Alcatel telephones had to be redesigned because it featured a man wearing a tie—highly unorthodox in postrevolution Iran. The local agency for the Parker Pen division of Gillette Company had to find a replacement for a European ad that was found to have a love letter printed in minuscule type.[24]

As Iran strives to continue its heritage as a conservative Islamic nation with a profound moral commitment to modesty and Islamic teachings, how will censorship of advertising affect the country's efforts to become part of the modern world?

Source: From ""Please Don't Show Your Lingerie in Iran, Even If It's for Sale" by Peter Waldman, *Wall Street Journal,* June 21, 1995. Reprinted by permission of *Wall Street Journal,* © 1995 Dow Jones & Company, Inc. All rights reserved.

The style in which the message is executed is one of the most creative elements of an advertisement. Exhibit 17.5 lists some examples of executional styles used by advertisers. Executional styles often dictate what type of media is to be employed to convey the message. Scientific executional styles, for example, lend themselves well to print advertising where more information can be conveyed. On the other hand, demonstration and musical styles are more likely found in broadcast advertising.

Injecting humor into an advertisement is a popular and effective executional style. Humorous executional styles are more often used in radio and television advertising than in print or magazine advertising where humor is less easily communicated. Humorous ads are typically used for lower risk, routine purchases, such as candy, cigarettes, and soft drinks, than for higher risk purchases or those that are expensive, durable or flamboyant.[25] M&M's, for example, recently used humor in its television advertising using animated M&M characters. The ads led to a 3 percent increase in sales and better "likability" for the brand.[26]

Executional styles for foreign advertising are often quite different from those we are accustomed to in the United States. Sometimes they are sexually oriented or aesthetically imaginative. For example, European advertising avoids the direct-sell ap-

Slice-of-life	Is popular when advertising household and personal products; depicts people in normal settings, such as at the dinner table. Taster's Choice ads with Tony and Sharon offer a soap opera twist to a slice of life.	
Lifestyle	Shows how well the product will fit in with the consumer's lifestyle. Levi's has made this concept popular with Dockers menswear ads.	
Spokesperson/ testimonial	Can feature a celebrity, company official, or typical consumer making a testimonial or endorsing a product. Tennis star and Olympic gold medalist Andre Agassi endorses Canon's EOS Rebel camera.	
Fantasy	Creates a fantasy for the viewer built around use of the product. Miller Light's "Can your beer do this" spots depict odd combinations of sports with everyday experiences.	
Humorous	Advertisers often use humor in their ads, such as Bud Light's popular "I Love You, Man" commercials and Little Caesar's wacky spots for pizza.	
Real/animated product symbols	Creates a character that represents the product in advertisements, such as the Energizer bunny or Coke's polar bears.	
Mood or image	Builds a mood or image around the product, such as peace, love, or beauty. Initial ads for the new-age drink Fruitopia featured kaleidoscope graphics with world peace messages.	
Demonstration	Shows consumers the expected benefit. Many consumer products use this technique. Laundry detergent spots are famous for demonstrating how their product will clean clothes whiter and brighter.	
Musical	Conveys the message of the advertisement through song. Timex ads for its Indiglo watch play off Frank Sinatra singing "Strangers in the Night."	
Scientific	Uses research or scientific evidence to give a brand superiority over competitors. Pain relievers like Advil, Bayer, and Excedrin use scientific evidence in their ads.	

Exhibit 17.5
Ten Common Executional Styles for Advertising

proaches common in U.S. ads and instead is more indirect, more symbolic, and above all more visual. Italian-based retailer Benetton is widely known for using symbolic images, often described as more art than advertising. Benetton's ads have featured such startling images as close-up photos of male and female genitalia, a black man's hand handcuffed to a white man's, and an AIDS patient and his family moments before his death.[27]

Benetton
Does Benetton's Web site reflect the company's usual visual style? How does Benetton respond to controversy generated by some of its more startling images?

http://www.benetton.com/

Japanese advertising is known for relying on fantasy and mood to sell products. Ads in Japan notoriously lack the emphatic selling demonstrations found in U.S. advertising, limit the exposure of unique product features, and avoid direct comparisons to competitors' products. Japanese ads often feature cartoon characters or place the actors in irrelevant situations. For example, one advertisement promotes an insect spray while showing the actor having teeth extracted at the dentist's office. One explanation of Japan's preference for soft-sell advertising is cultural: Japanese consumers are naturally suspicious of someone who needs to extol the virtues of a product. Additionally, unlike advertising agencies in the United States, which consider working for competing companies to be unethical, Japan's larger ad agencies customarily maintain business relationships with competing advertisers. Ads are less hard-hitting so as not to offend other clients.[28]

4 Describe media evaluation and selection techniques.

Advertising in Japan takes a soft-sell approach because Japanese consumers are naturally suspicious of companies that need to emphasize the virtues of a product.
© Tom Wagner/SABA

MAKE MEDIA DECISIONS

As mentioned at the beginning of the chapter, U.S. advertisers spend over $131 billion on media advertising annually. Where does all this money go? About 33 percent, or $43 billion, is spent in media monitored by national reporting services. The remaining 67 percent, or $85 billion, is spent in unmonitored media, such as direct mail, trade exhibits, cooperative advertising, brochures, couponing, catalogs, and special events. Exhibit 17.6 breaks down the dollar amount spent for monitored advertising by media type. As you can see, more than half of every dollar spent on monitored advertising is spent on TV advertising—including spot TV. Spot TV is lower-cost television advertising time that allows stations rather than advertisers to schedule the commercials.

Media Types

Advertising media are channels that advertisers use in mass communication. The five major advertising media are newspapers, magazines, radio, television, and outdoor media. Exhibit 17.7 summarizes the advantages and disadvantages of these traditional channels. In recent years, however, alternative media vehicles have emerged that give advertisers innovative ways to reach their target audience and avoid advertising clutter.

Newspapers

The advantages of newspaper advertising include geographic flexibility and timeliness. Because copywriters can usually prepare newspaper ads quickly and at a reasonable cost, local merchants can reach their target market almost daily. However, since newspapers are generally a mass-market medium, they may not be the best vehicle for marketers trying to reach a very narrow market. For example,

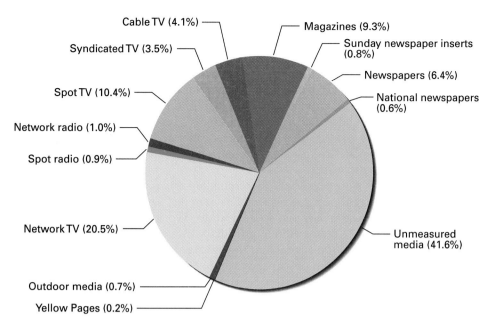

Cable TV (4.1%)
Magazines (9.3%)
Syndicated TV (3.5%)
Sunday newspaper inserts (0.8%)
Spot TV (10.4%)
Newspapers (6.4%)
National newspapers (0.6%)
Network radio (1.0%)
Spot radio (0.9%)
Network TV (20.5%)
Unmeasured media (41.6%)
Outdoor media (0.7%)
Yellow Pages (0.2%)

Exhibit 17.6
National Ad Spending by Media for 1995

Source: Figures obtained from *Advertising Age* Web site at www.adage.com. Repinted by permission of Crain Communications, Inc.

Exhibit 17.7
Advantages and Disadvantages of Traditional Advertising Media

Medium	Advantages	Disadvantages
Newspapers	Geographic selectivity and flexibility; short-term advertiser commitments; news value and immediacy; year-round readership; high individual market coverage; co-op and local tie-in availability; short lead time	Little demographic selectivity; limited color capabilities; low pass-along rate; may be expensive
Magazines	Good reproduction, especially for color; demographic selectivity; regional selectivity; local market selectivity; relatively long advertising life; high pass-along rate	Long-term advertiser commitments; slow audience buildup; limited demonstration capabilities; lack of urgency; long lead time
Radio	Low cost; immediacy of message; can be scheduled on short notice; relatively no seasonal change in audience; highly portable; short-term advertiser commitments; entertainment carryover	No visual treatment; short advertising life of message; high frequency required to generate comprehension and retention; distractions from background sound; commercial clutter
Television	Ability to reach a wide, diverse audience; low cost per thousand; creative opportunities for demonstration; immediacy of messages; entertainment carryover; demographic selectivity with cable stations	Short life of message; some consumer skepticism about claims; high campaign cost; little demographic selectivity with network stations; long-term advertiser commitments; long lead times required for production; commercial clutter
Outdoor media	Repetition; moderate cost; flexibility; geographic selectivity	Short message; lack of demographic selectivity; high "noise" level distracting audience

local newspapers are not the best media vehicles for reaching purchasers of specialty steel products or even tropical fish. These target consumers make up very small, specialized markets. Newspaper advertising also encounters a lot of distractions from competing ads and news stories; thus, one company's ad may not be particularly visible.

The largest source of newspaper ad revenue is local retailers, classified ads, and cooperative advertising. In **cooperative advertising,** the manufacturer and the retailer split the costs of advertising the manufacturer's brand. One reason manufacturers use cooperative advertising is the impracticality of listing all their dealers in national advertising. Also, co-op advertising encourages retailers to devote more effort to the manufacturer's lines.

Many newspaper publishers are responding to a new genre of readers with online versions of their newspapers. For example, *The Wall Street Journal* offers readers an Interactive Edition, located at its World Wide Web address at http://www.wsj.com. The online edition provides subscribers with up-to-the-minute news in business, technology, marketing, the law, sports, and weather. *USA Today* also features an online version of its paper at http://www.usatoday.com. Teaser advertisements appear on most editorial pages which readers can click to link to the advertiser's Web site for more detailed information about the product.

cooperative advertising
Arrangement in which the manufacturer and the retailer split the costs of advertising the manufacturer's brand.

Magazines

Compared to the cost of other media, the cost per contact in magazine advertising is usually high. However, the cost per potential customer may be much lower because magazines are often targeted to specialized audiences and thus reach more potential customers. The most frequent types of products advertised in magazines include automobiles, apparel, computers, and cigarettes.

One of the main advantages of magazine advertising is its market selectivity. Magazines are published for virtually every market segment. For instance, *PC Week* is a leading computer magazine; *Working Mother* targets one of the fastest-growing consumer segments; *Sports Illustrated* is a successful all-around sporting publication; and *Marketing News* is a trade magazine for the marketing professional.

Like newspapers, many magazines are also offering Internet versions of their publications complete with links to advertisers' Web sites. For example, a recent online version of *Time* magazine (http://www.time.com) featured ads for Sprint long-distance service and Merrill Lynch investment services. A special button on *Time's* front page also brings the online reader to an ad directory listing advertisers' home pages which provide product or service information. Electronic versions of magazines sometimes contain sound and video clips, offering something no print publication could possibly match.

Radio

Radio has several strengths as an advertising medium: selectivity and audience segmentation, a large out-of-home audience, low unit and production costs, timeliness, and geographic flexibility. Local advertisers are the most frequent users of radio advertising, contributing over three-quarters of all radio ad revenues. Like newspapers, radio also lends itself well to cooperative advertising. Radio is especially popular with small businesses as you will read in the "Marketing and Small Business" box.

Long merely an afterthought to many advertisers, radio advertising is enjoying a resurgence in popularity. As Americans become more mobile and pressed for time, other media, such as network television and newspapers, struggle to retain viewers and readers. But radio listening has grown in step with population increases mainly because its immediate, portable nature meshes so well with a fast-paced lifestyle. The ability to target specific demographic groups is also a major selling point for radio stations, attracting advertisers who are pursuing narrowly defined audiences that are more likely to respond to certain kinds of ads and products. Moreover, radio listen-

Marketing and Small Business

Radio: An Effective Advertising Medium for Small Marketers

Radio can be an effective medium for small firms to sell their products and services. Among its benefits to small marketers are its low cost, ability to target specific demographic audiences, the capability to change ads quickly, and its personal nature.

While radio spots are relatively cheaper than other media types, targeting power is one reason why many small marketers find radio to be much more cost effective than other media. When small business owner John Stewart began Audio Computer Information, Inc., he had an unusual concept—a series of audio tape tutorials for computer owners. Stewart used his skills as a former radio announcer to produce narrated audio tapes to provide more user-friendly instruction to computer novices than a 300-page jargon-filled user manual. Initially, advertising his tapes through national daily and weekly regional newspapers produced disappointing results. Finally, Stewart tried writing and narrating a series of radio ads that described his products. He placed the ads on two syndicated radio networks, Business Radio Network and Sun Radio Network, and calls began coming in from potential customers. Why did

the radio ads work? Because the spots were slated on business-related programs which attracted the customers Stewart was targeting.

Another benefit of radio to small marketers is that radio ads can be changed quickly. Steve Braunstein, president of SB Manufacturers Warehouse, a local clothing outlet in Farmingdale, New York, can change the scripts of his radio ads with only a day's notice. If the weather gets cold suddenly, for instance, he can have a new commercial promoting down coats recorded on a Tuesday and have it on the air Wednesday. Since producing radio ads only requires an announcer and a recording engineer, most stations can provide a studio and support staff for creating commercials.

Radio shows, especially talk radio, can also add personal endorsements to the message. Local talk shows or national talk shows, such as Rush Limbaugh and Howard Stern, urge listeners to call in with their opinions. Talk show

hosts typically plug products and services on the air, adding their own personal endorsements. The Vermont Teddy Bear Company, a small manufacturer of unique stuffed teddy bears, relied strictly on mail orders until it began advertising on national radio and urging calls to an 800 number. The company saw explosive growth in orders after being plugged on the air by Howard Stern. One Valentine's Day, Stern debated on air at length whether he should get his wife a Beargram, a message-bearing bear dressed in one of 150 different outfits. Callers offered various opinions about which outfit Stern should buy. As a result, the teddy bears got extra minutes of air time and free testimonials. The Vermont Teddy Bear Company's 800 number sales now account for 90 percent of its business, and its catalog mailing list includes more than 500,000 names. The company devotes 95 percent of its advertising budget to national radio, with most ads placed on major talk shows.[31]

What other media are beneficial and effective to small marketers? Are there any new, alternative types of media besides the traditional forms that could benefit small marketers?

ers tend to listen habitually and at predictable times, with the most popular radio listening hours during "drive time" when commuters form a vast captive audience.[29]

One advertiser who recently capitalized on the narrowly defined audience that radio offers is Warner-Lambert, the manufacturer of e.p.t. home pregnancy tests. Warner-Lambert chose to advertise its pregnancy test kits on a Milwaukee radio station known for its highest percentage of listenership among women in the peak childbearing age group of 18 to 34. The ad featured five women and one man asking, "Am I pregnant?" coupled with a promotion called the "Baby Derby," during which three couples competed for big prizes to be the first ones to conceive. During the two months it took for a couple to get pregnant, listenership and media coverage climbed. As the couples became Milwaukee's celebrities, e.p.t. received free publicity on local television shows and newspapers. When it was all over, e.p.t.'s local market share soared 20 percentage points.[30]

Television

Television broadcasters include network television, independent stations, cable television, and a relative newcomer, direct broadcast satellite television. ABC, CBS, NBC, and the Fox Network dominate network television. The networks rely on advertising income to support programming. In contrast, independent stations often rely on viewer contributions, as well as local advertising, for funds. Consumers pay to have cable television and direct broadcast satellite systems, such as DirecTV and Prime-Star, in their homes.

Television's largest growth market is cable television, with two-thirds of U.S. television homes with cable subscriptions.[32] Many major advertisers see cable as a way to segment the most desirable consumers in the mass television market. Today's cable subscribers can receive channels devoted exclusively to particular audiences—for example, women, children, African Americans, nature lovers, senior citizens, Christians, Hispanics, sports fans, and fitness enthusiasts. Other types of special programming feature news, rock and country music, cultural events, and health issues. Because of its targeted channels, cable television is often characterized as "narrowcasting" by media buyers.

Because television is an audiovisual medium, it provides advertisers with many creative opportunities. It also reaches a wide and diverse market. However, television has its disadvantages. Advertising time on television can be very expensive, especially for network stations, and even more so during prime time. Advertisers may spend anywhere from $100,000 to $500,000 or more for a 30-second spot during a network's prime-time programs. The average price for a 30-second prime-time spot during the Atlanta Summer Olympics telecast was $550,000, and a 30-second spot during Super Bowl XXX was a whopping $1.3 million.[33] Television advertising can also involve huge production costs. The budget for a professionally produced national commercial averages $222,000.[34]

infomercial
Thirty-minute or longer advertisement that looks more like a TV talk show than a sales pitch.

A relatively new form of television advertising is the **infomercial,** a 30-minute or longer advertisement. Infomercials bloomed in the mid-1980s, when deregulation freed television stations and cable networks to sell half-hour blocks of air time for advertising. The otherwise unprofitable late-night time slots have become the special domain of infomercials. Infomercials are an attractive advertising vehicle for many marketers because of the cheap air time and the relatively small production cost. Advertisers say the infomercial is an ideal way to present complicated information to potential customers, which other advertising vehicles typically don't allow time to do. For example, Sharper Image, the retailer and direct marketer of pricey new-age gadgets, recently turned to infomercials to boost catalog and store sales. Sharper Image's "gee-whiz" products lend themselves to demonstration on television, making an infomercial format an ideal way to advertise.[35]

Outdoor Media

Outdoor or out-of-home advertising is a flexible, low-cost medium that may take a variety of forms. Examples include billboards, skywriting, giant inflatables, minibillboards in malls and on bus stop shelters, signs in sports arenas, lighted moving signs in bus terminals and airports, and ads painted on the sides of cars, trucks, and buses. Outdoor advertising reaches a broad and diverse market. Therefore, it is normally limited to promoting convenience products and selected shopping products, such as cigarettes, business services, and automobiles.

The main advantage of outdoor advertising over other media is that its exposure frequency is very high, yet the amount of clutter from competing ads is very low. Outdoor advertising also has the ability to be customized to local marketing needs. For this reason, retail stores are the largest outdoor advertisers.

Outdoor advertising has been growing in recent years mainly due to the fragmentation of other media, more exposure as people spend more time commuting, and improved billboard quality through the use of computers.[36] Outdoor advertising

Outdoor advertising, including fully wrapped buses, reaches a broad and diverse market and so is used primarily to advertise products with wide appeal.
© Ed Quinn/SABA

is also becoming more innovative. For example, the Hoosier Lotto in Indiana uses LED readouts to display lottery jackpot amounts; Little Me children's wear manufacturer advertises on the rooftops of buses rolling through downtown New York City; and Universal Pictures used special-effects posters inside theaters with morphing, three-dimensional images of a skull to promote its movie *The Frighteners*.[37]

Alternative Media

To cut through the clutter of traditional advertising media, advertisers are now looking for new ways to promote their products. The alternative vehicles include fax machines, video shopping carts in grocery stores, computer screen savers, CD-ROMs, interactive kiosks in department stores, and advertisements run before movies at the cinema and on rented video cassettes. However, the most exciting alternative media today are undoubtably online computer services and the Internet and World Wide Web. Based on broadcast and publishing, online computer services and the Internet are unique in that they facilitate direct communication between individuals and organizations, regardless of distance and time. These new media vehicles allow marketers and advertisers to make available full-color virtual catalogs, provide on-screen order forms, and elicit customer feedback.[38]

Online computer service providers, such as America Online, CompuServe, and Prodigy, can transmit immediate, personalized advertisements through modems to consumers' computers. Viewers see teaser ads that instruct them to punch a key on their computer keyboard if they want more information. Viewers can then browse through advertisements for almost any product or service imaginable, order these products or services, conduct banking transactions, make airline reservations, and check the stock market from home. Advertisers pay online providers to have their products or services displayed.

The Internet and World Wide Web is essentially a free-for-all computer network of companies and organizations that have linked together into a "web" via modems and phone lines. Originally created by the government and educational institutions to share information among agencies and academicians, the Internet has in recent years become a commercial stomping ground for product manufacturers and service companies. Advertisers have flocked in record numbers to produce their own "home pages" or Web sites on the Internet in the hopes that the information superhighway will become the next mass medium. Additionally, popular Internet sites now sell advertising space or sponsorships to major consumer product and service companies to promote their goods and services. For example, Sprint and Gatorade sponsor the Web site for the National Football League (http://www.nfl.com). While Sprint is the official sponsor of the Cyber Showdown, which features a weekly real-time chat with two NFL opponents, Gatorade sponsors Coach's Corner, which plays off the coach's traditional dousing with Gatorade after big wins.[39] Both Web sites feature ads for their respective products.

Online and Internet media pose a daunting challenge for advertisers since consumers have more control over the marketing relationship than they have had with traditional advertising media. With traditional media, consumers passively view commercials during their favorite sitcom or avoid commercials by pushing a button on a remote-control device. Surfers on the Internet, however, generally have to find the marketer rather than vice versa. Some have likened the Internet to an electronic trade show and a virtual flea market—a trade show in that it can be thought of as a giant international exhibition hall where potential buyers can enter at will and visit prospective sellers; a flea market in the sense that it possesses the fundamental characteristics of openness, informality, and interactivity similar to a community marketplace.[40] One Web site actually pays consumers to view ads that have been automatically targeted to fit their interests. Consumers are paid in a form of digital currency which they can spend on anything from Internet access charges to subscriptions to online publications or for merchandise available over the Web.[41]

Another challenge for online and Internet advertisers is measuring the effectiveness of their electronic advertisement or site. While there are methods already in use that can count the number of visitors to an advertiser's Web site, what advertisers don't know is how their site ranks compared to the competition's. What is lacking as well are the kinds of in-depth demographic and psychographic information about Web page users that television, magazines, radio, and newspapers provide about their viewers and subscribers.[42]

In spite of these problems, Internet advertising topped $300 million in 1996 and is expected to rise to $5 billion a year by 2000.

Media Selection Considerations

Promotional objectives and the type of advertising a company plans to use strongly affect the selection of media. An important element in any advertising campaign is the **media mix,** the combination of media to be used. Media mix decisions are typically based on several factors, the most important being cost per contact, reach, and frequency. Less important factors include target audience considerations, flexibility to the medium, noise level, and the life span of the medium.

Cost per contact is the cost of reaching one member of the target market. Naturally, as the size of the audience increases, so does the total cost. The standard criterion for comparing media is **cost per thousand** (CPM, M being the Roman numeral for 1,000). Advertisers determine CPM by dividing the price of the media by the size of the audience, in thousands. For example, if the price of a television spot is $50,000 and the projected audience size is 24 million viewers, then the CPM is $2.08. CPM enables an advertiser to compare media vehicles, such as television versus radio or magazine versus newspaper, or more specifically *Newsweek* versus *Time*. An advertiser debating whether to spend local advertising dollars for TV spots or radio spots could consider the CPM of each. The advertiser might then pick the vehicle with the lowest CPM to maximize advertising punch for the money spent.

Reach is the number of different target consumers who are exposed to a commercial at least once during a specific period, usually four weeks. If 60,000 out of 100,000 radio listeners hear a commercial for the Ford Taurus in San Antonio, Texas at least once during a four-week period, the commercial's reach would be 60,000, or 60 percent of the total 100,000 listeners. The media plans for product introductions and attempts at increasing brand awareness usually emphasize reach. Yet high reach levels do not necessarily mean high degrees of brand awareness or advertising recall. It is not unusual to find that a campaign has achieved 90 percent reach but that only 25 percent of the target audience remembers the ad. Reach is a measurement of po-

media mix
Combination of media to be used for a promotional campaign.

cost per contact
Cost of reaching one member of the target market.

cost per thousand (CPM)
Standard criterion for comparing media, computed by dividing the price of a single ad by the audience size in thousands.

reach
Number of target consumers exposed to a commercial at least once during a specific period, usually four weeks.

tential. That is, a 90 percent reach means that 90 percent of an audience has an opportunity to see or hear a message. It does not measure retention.

Frequency is the number of times an individual is exposed to a message. Average frequency is used by advertisers to measure the intensity of a specific medium's coverage. For example, Ford might want an average exposure frequency of three for its Taurus radio ads; that is, among all the radio listeners who heard the ad, they each heard it an average of three times. Because the typical ad is short-lived and because often only a small portion of an ad may be perceived at one time, advertisers repeat their ads. They want consumers to remember the message. Retention tends to peak somewhere between the third and the fifth message perceived by the receiver. Additional exposures tend to be screened out and may create a negative reaction. The ad then loses its effectiveness.

Media selection is also a matter of matching the advertising medium with the product's target market. If marketers are trying to reach teenage females, they might select *Seventeen* magazine. If they are trying to reach consumers over 50 years old, they may choose *Modern Maturity*. A medium's ability to reach a precisely defined market is its **audience selectivity.** Some media vehicles, like general newspapers and network television, appeal to a wide cross-section of the population. Others—such as *Bride's, Popular Mechanics, Architectural Digest,* the Disney Channel, ESPN, and Christian radio stations—appeal to very specific groups.

The flexibility of a medium can be extremely important to an advertiser. In the past, because of printing timetables, pasteup requirements, and so on, some magazines required final ad copy several months before publication. Therefore, magazine advertising has not been able to adapt as rapidly to changing market conditions. While this is beginning to change as magazines move toward the creation of electronic ad images and layouts on PCs, the lead time on magazines is still considerably longer. Radio, on the other hand, provides maximum flexibility. Usually, the advertiser can change the ad on the day it is aired, if necessary.

Noise level is the level of distraction to the target audience in a medium. For example, to understand a televised promotional message, viewers must watch and listen carefully. But they often watch television with others, who may well provide distractions. Noise can also be created by competing ads, as when a street is lined with billboards or when a television program is cluttered with competing ads. During the 1996 Olympics, for example, viewers were barraged with advertising from some 50 advertisers during the 171 hours of televised coverage. Of the 80 hours of prime-time Olympics coverage, 12 hours were devoted to advertisers.[43] In contrast, direct mail is a private medium with a low noise level. No other advertising media or news stories compete for direct-mail readers' attention.

Media have either a short or long life span. Life span means that messages can either quickly fade or persist as tangible copy to be carefully studied. For example, a radio commercial may last less than a minute. Listeners can't replay the commercial unless they have recorded the program. One way advertisers overcome this problem is by repeating radio ads often. In contrast, a trade magazine has a relatively long life span. A person may read several articles, put the magazine down, and pick it up a week later to continue reading. In addition, magazines and catalogs often have a high pass-along rate. That is, one person will read the publication and then give it to someone else.

Media Scheduling

After choosing the media for the advertising campaign, advertisers must schedule the ads. A **media schedule** designates the medium or media to be used (such as magazines, televi-

frequency
Number of times an individual is exposed to a given message during a specific period.

audience selectivity
Ability of an advertising medium to reach a precisely defined market.

media schedule
Designation of the media, the specific publications or programs, and the insertion dates of advertising.

One aspect of media selection is matching the medium with the target market. Marketers who are trying to reach teenage girls might select *Seventeen* magazine.
© I. Burgum/P. Boorman/Tony Stone Images

sion, or radio), the specific vehicles (such as *People* magazine, the "Home Improvement" TV show, or the "Top 40 Countdown" radio show), and the insertion dates of the advertising.

There are three basic types of media schedules:

continuous media schedule
Media scheduling strategy, used for products in the latter stages of the product life cycle, in which advertising is run steadily throughout the advertising period.

flighted media schedule
Media scheduling strategy in which ads are run heavily every other month or every two weeks, to achieve a greater impact with an increased frequency and reach at those times.

pulsing media schedule
Media scheduling strategy that uses continuous scheduling throughout the year coupled with a flighted schedule during the best sales periods.

seasonal media schedule
Media scheduling strategy that runs advertising only during times of the year when the product is most likely to be used.

- Products in the latter stages of the product life cycle, which are advertised on a reminder basis, use a **continuous media schedule.** A continuous schedule allows the advertising to run steadily throughout the advertising period. Examples include Ivory soap, Coca-Cola, and Marlboro cigarettes.

- With a **flighted media schedule,** the advertiser may schedule the ads heavily every other month or every two weeks to achieve a greater impact with an increased frequency and reach at those times. For example, movie studios might schedule television advertising on Wednesday and Thursday nights, when moviegoers are deciding which films to see that weekend. A variation is the **pulsing media schedule** which combines continuous scheduling with flighting. Continuous advertising is simply heavier during the best sale periods. For instance, a retail department store may advertise on a year-round basis but place more advertising during holiday sale periods, such as Thanksgiving, Christmas, and back-to-school.

- Certain times of the year call for a **seasonal media schedule.** Products like Contac cold tablets and Coppertone suntan lotion, which are used more during certain times of the year, tend to follow a seasonal strategy.

Evaluate the Ad Campaign

Evaluating an advertising campaign can be the most demanding task facing advertisers. How do advertisers know whether the campaign led to an increase in sales or market share or elevated awareness of the product? Most advertising campaigns aim to create an image for the good or service instead of asking for action, so their real effect is unknown. So many variables shape the effectiveness of an ad that, in many cases, advertisers must guess whether their money has been well spent. Despite this gray area, marketers spend a considerable amount of time studying advertising effectiveness and its probable impact on sales, market share, or awareness. Testing ad effectiveness can be done either before or after the campaign.

Pretests

Before a campaign is released, marketing managers use pretests to determine the best advertising appeal, layout, and media vehicle. Common pretests include the following:

- *Consumer jury tests:* The consumer jury test, or focus group interview, uses a panel of consumers from the target market. They preview several advertisements and examine the unfinished ads or storyboards. Next, panel members rank the ads by perceived effectiveness and explain their rankings and their reactions to each ad. Focus groups may also play an important role in developing the advertising appeal and determining the appropriate slogan.

- *Portfolio or unfinished-rough tests:* The purpose of the portfolio test is to evaluate print advertising. Before marketing managers select a final advertising appeal and layout, they let a sample of consumers read several dummy magazines, complete with stories and different versions of the advertisement. Next, the consumers are asked what ads they remember (unaided recall). Then they respond to questions about specific ads (aided recall). Similarly, an unfinished-rough test measures the effectiveness of proposed television commercials. An unfinished rough, or a rough videotape of a TV commercial, is shown to consumers who are then asked to recall the message.

- *Physiological tests:* To avoid the bias sometimes encountered in other tests, some marketers have turned to physiological testing. Consumers have involuntary physical reactions to advertisements. Physiological tests measure these human responses, using galvanic skin response tests, eye movement experiments, and pupil dilation measurements as indicators of awareness of and interest in advertisements.

Posttests

After advertisers implement a campaign, they often conduct tests to measure its effectiveness. Several monitoring techniques can be used to determine whether the campaign has met its original goals. Even if a campaign has been highly successful, advertisers still typically do a postcampaign analysis. They assess how the campaign might have been more efficient and what factors contributed to its success.

The effectiveness of a campaign is usually tested through the following:

- *Recognition tests:* Readership or recognition tests are typically used to measure the effectiveness of magazine advertising. Consumers are asked about their ad readership and then grouped in three categories: those who noted the ad, those who can link the company name with the advertisement, and those who read at least 50 percent of the advertisement.

- *Recall tests:* A recall test can be used with ads presented through almost any medium, from television to billboards. Unlike recognition tests, recall tests do not show respondents the advertisement. Instead, to measure unaided recall, respondents are asked to remember the commercial or advertisement. This measure indicates how much information the target consumers learned. Aided recall provides cues about the advertisement to jog interviewees' memories. (Exhibit 17.8 lists the brands most often identified in television recall tests.) An implied assumption of recall tests is that consumers who can recall a specific product's advertisement are more likely to buy the product. An advertiser should not completely rely on this assumption, however. Consumers may recall an advertisement because of its style yet have no intention of ever using the product. Ad recall research has shown that many brands with the best-remembered commercials have had either flat or declining sales.[44]

- *Attitude measures:* Often attitude measures are incorporated into recall and recognition tests. Interviewers may ask interviewees whether a promotion seems be-

Rank	Brand	
1	Budweiser	www.budweiser.com
2	McDonald's	www.mcdonalds.com
3	Pepsi	www.pepsico.com
4	Little Caesar's	
5	Coca-Cola	www.cocacola.com
6	Pizza Hut	www.pizzahut.com
7	AT&T	www.att.com
8	Milk	www.whymilk.com
9	Bud Light	www.budweiser.com
10	Edy's/Dryer's	

Exhibit 17.8
Most Highly Recalled Brands Advertised in Television Campaigns

Source: Sally Goll Beatty, "Omnicom Menagerie Tops Poll of Most Popular TV Ads," *Wall Street Journal,* 11 March 1996, pp. B1, B6.

lievable, convincing, dull, imaginative, informative, phony, realistic, silly, and so on. They may also ask how much, if any, the ad affects the interviewee's desire to use or purchase the product.

- *Audience size measures:* Audience measures are generally made by the same research organizations that gauge advertising effectiveness. Organizations such as the Audit Bureau of Circulation, the American Research Bureau (Arbitron), Nielsen Media Research, and Statistical Research, Inc. (SRI) audit circulation figures of magazines and newspapers and measure radio and television audience sizes.

PUBLIC RELATIONS

5 Discuss the role of public relations in the promotional mix.

Public relations is the element in the promotional mix that evaluates public attitudes, identifies issues that may elicit public concern, and executes programs to gain public understanding and acceptance. Like advertising and sales promotion, public relations is a vital link in a progressive company's marketing communication mix. Marketing managers plan solid public relations campaigns that fit into overall marketing plans and focus on targeted audiences. These campaigns strive to maintain a positive image of the corporation in the eyes of the public. Before launching public relations programs, managers evaluate public attitudes and company actions. Then they create programs to capitalize on the factors that enhance the firm's image and minimize the factors that could generate a negative image.

Many people associate public relations with publicity. *Publicity* is the effort to capture media attention—for example, through articles or editorials in publications or through human-interest stories on radio or television programs. Corporations usually initiate publicity through a press release that furthers their public relations plans. For instance, a company about to introduce a new product or open a new store may send press releases to the media in hopes that the story will be published or broadcast. Savvy publicity can often create overnight product sensations. After publicists for Tyco Toys arranged the appearance of Tickle Me Elmo, a Sesame Street muppet doll, with talk show host Rosie O'Donnell and with Bryant Gumble on the "Today" show, retail sales of the doll quickly jumped. The doll subsequently became the most sought after toy during the 1996 Christmas shopping season.[45]

Public relations departments may perform any or all of the following functions:

- *Press relations:* Placing positive, newsworthy information in the news media to attract attention to a product, a service, or a person associated with the firm or institution.
- *Product publicity:* Publicizing specific products or services.
- *Corporate communication:* Creating internal and external messages to promote a positive image of the firm or institution.
- *Public affairs:* Building and maintaining national or local community relations.
- *Lobbying:* Influencing legislators and government officials to promote or defeat legislation and regulation.
- *Employee and investor relations:* Maintaining positive relationships with employees, shareholders, and others in the financial community.
- *Crisis management:* Responding to unfavorable publicity or a negative event.

Major Public Relations Tools

Several tools are commonly used by public relations professionals, including new product publicity, product placement, customer satisfaction phone lines, consumer education, event sponsorship, and issue sponsorship. A relatively new tool public relations professionals are using in increasing numbers is a Web site on the Internet. While many of these tools require an active role on the part of the public relations professional, for example, writing press releases and engaging in proactive media relations, many of these techniques, such as event and issue sponsorship, create their own publicity.

New Product Publicity

Publicity is instrumental in introducing new products and services. Publicity can help advertisers explain what's different about their new product by prompting free news stories or positive word-of-mouth about it. During the introductory period, an especially innovative new product often needs more exposure than conventional, paid advertising affords. Public relations professionals write press releases or develop videos in an effort to generate news about their new product. They also jockey for exposure of their product or service at major events or on popular television and news shows. In a massive public relations push for its new Arch Deluxe sandwich, for example, McDonald's public relations executives orchestrated the appearance of their spokesperson, Ronald McDonald, on the Academy Awards, the "Today" show, at the Kentucky Derby, and courtside with Dennis Rodman at a Chicago Bulls game. Similarly, in a publicity stunt for her new Elizabeth Arden Black Pearls fragrance, screen legend Elizabeth Taylor made cameo appearances on several CBS sitcoms that made references to a black pearl necklace lost by the actress. The unusual nature of the stunt, combined with the uncommon power of the star, generated a barrage of publicity for the new fragrance far greater than Arden-parent Unilever could have purchased with paid advertising.[46]

Product Placement

Marketers can also garner publicity by making sure their products appear at special events or in movies or television shows. On "Seinfeld," NBC's hit comedy, Jerry Seinfeld has sipped Snapple, and the distinctive neon sign of Colombo frozen yogurt has been shown. Jason Alexander, who plays George on the show, has snacked on Frito-Lay's Rold Gold pretzels. Compaq computers have shown up on the hit show "ER," and a Logo Athletic's Detroit Lions jacket has been modeled by Al on "Home Improvement."[47] Companies reap invaluable product exposure through product placement, usually at a fraction of the cost of paid-for advertising. Often, the fee for exposure is in merchandise. For example, Breyer's Ice Cream donated enough ice cream for a cast and crew party to get its product in the hands of Clint Eastwood in the 1993 movie *In the Line of Fire*. Movies and television shows are just two outlets for product placement; others include music videos, game shows, cable cooking shows, and even other companies' commercials. Mazda, for example, recently negotiated the placement of its Miata sports car in a Chevron ad.[48]

Customer Satisfaction Phone Lines

Organizations often set up systems to promote customer satisfaction and to answer consumers' questions about any matters regarding the organization or the product or services it promotes. Customer satisfaction programs are typically implemented through the use of toll-free 800 numbers. More often they are set up to minimize consumer dissatisfaction and properly handle complaints. Company representatives address the reason for the complaint and offer solutions to rectify the problem. Information gathered through customer satisfaction lines is used to make any necessary adjustments in the firm's policies, practices, or products.

Pillsbury is one company that makes an 800-number hot line available to consumers who have questions, complaints, or compliments. Company representatives answer an average of 2,000 calls a day from consumers complaining about product quality, needing reassurance that they have prepared the food properly, or wanting copies of the latest Pillsbury Bakeoff winning recipes. Other companies with active

800 lines include Kraft, General Foods, Mars, Nestlé, Duracell, Mattel, and Colgate-Palmolive. These companies generally offer consumers who call either a refund or a coupon to promote a positive image.[49]

Consumer Education

Some major firms believe that educated consumers are better, more loyal customers. Financial planning firms often sponsor free educational seminars on money management, retirement planning, and investing in the hopes the consumer will choose its organization for future financial needs. Likewise, computer hardware and software firms, realizing that many consumers feel intimidated by new technology and recognizing the strong relationship between learning and purchasing patterns, sponsor computer seminars and free in-store demonstrations. Microsoft, along with *Family PC* magazine and Gateway 2000 computer reseller, for example, sponsor Family Technology Nights at schools in major cities across the country. The free seminars, organized by schools' parent-teacher organizations and led by local technology experts, include an introduction to computer technology, information about current technology trends in schools, and tips for selecting hardware and software. The evenings also feature software demonstrations and hands-on learning opportunities. Microsoft software is offered for sale at discount prices with participating schools earning free software based on sales.[50]

Event Sponsorship

Public relations managers can sponsor events or community activities that are sufficiently newsworthy to achieve press coverage; at the same time, these events also reinforce brand identification. Coca-Cola, for example, was the sole sponsor of the 15,000 mile, 84-day journey of the Olympic torch to the Summer Olympic games in Atlanta. Called the Coca-Cola Torch Relay, staffers handed out millions of "I saw the torch" stickers and dispensed more than 300,000 bottles of Coca-Cola along the way. The event helped boost consumer awareness of Coke's international sponsorship of the Summer Olympics, outscoring all other Olympic sponsors.[51] Similarly, as the official time keeper of the Summer Games, Swatch scored big in consumer awareness when announcers repeatedly mentioned the "Swatch time" results during broadcast events.[52]

Sporting, music, and arts events remain the most popular choices of event sponsors, although many are now turning to more specialized events, such as tie-ins with schools, charities, and other community service organizations. Gin maker Tanqueray was hugely successful in an AIDS-related promotion that 200 other companies refused to consider. As sole sponsor of the Tanqueray American AIDS Rides, the gin maker garnered tremendous amounts of goodwill and publicity as five long-distance bicycle events rolled across the United States. More than 12,000 participants in the event raised $25 million for AIDS research, while the rides received live TV news updates and local and national press coverage.[53]

Issue Sponsorship

Corporations can also build public awareness and loyalty by supporting their customers' favorite issues. Education, health care, and social programs get the largest share of corporate funding. Firms often donate a percentage of sales or profits to a worthy cause that their target market is likely to favor. For example, pantyhose maker Hanes supports national breast cancer organizations and prints instructions for breast self-examinations on packages of pantyhose.

Swatch, the official time keeper of the Summer Olympic Games, gained a lot of consumer awareness when announcers repeatedly mentioned "Swatch time" results during broadcast events.

© 1996 Louis Psihoyos/Matrix

"Green marketing" has also become an important way for companies to build awareness and loyalty by promoting a popular issue. Large numbers of consumers, mostly older, female, and highly educated, profess a preference and are willing to pay more for products made by environmentally friendly companies.[54] By positioning their brands as ecologically sound, marketers can convey concern for the environment and society as a whole. For example, Burger King and McDonald's no longer use styrofoam cartons to package their burgers in an effort to decrease waste in landfills. In a similar effort, Wal-Mart has opened environmentally friendly stores to appeal to consumers' desire to save the environment. The stores' air conditioning systems use a non-ozone-depleting refrigerant, rainwater is collected from parking lots and roofs for watering the landscape, skylights allow natural light into the store, cart corrals are made of recycled plastic, and parking lots are recycled asphalt.

Internet Web Sites

Internet Web sites as public relations tools are a relatively new phenomenon in the marketing arena. While many marketers initially used their Web sites as a way to advertise their products or services, public relations professionals now feel these sites are an excellent vehicle to post news releases on products, product enhancements, strategic relationships, and financial earnings. Corporate press releases, technical papers and articles, and product news help inform the press, customers, prospects, industry analysts, stockholders, and others of the firm's products and services and their applications. The Web site can also be an open forum for new product ideas and product improvements and to obtain feedback on the Web site's usefulness to viewers. Additionally, a self-help desk at the Web site can also list the most common questions and answers to assist with customer support and satisfaction.[55]

Managing Unfavorable Publicity

Although the majority of marketers try to avoid unpleasant situations, crises do happen. Intel, for example, faced this reality after consumers became aware of an obscure flaw in its Pentium chip. In our free-press environment, publicity is not easily controlled, especially in a crisis. **Crisis management** is the coordinated effort to handle the effects of unfavorable publicity, ensuring fast and accurate communication in times of emergency.

A good public relations staff is perhaps more important in bad times than in good. For example, critics chastised Trans World Airlines after its plane crash off Long Island, saying the airline was slow and uncooperative with family members wanting information about survivors and calls from the media went unanswered. TWA's chief executive was also late in reassuring families and the public that his airline was doing all it could. All public relations professionals learned a valuable lesson from this blunder: Companies must have a communication policy firmly in hand before a disaster occurs, because timing is uncontrollable.

A rapid response to a crisis can generally minimize the damage to a company's image. For major image problems, marketers are urged not to waste critical time that could be spent addressing and ending the problem. Some general guidelines for handling a crisis situation follow:

- Start early. The worst damage to a company's or a product's reputation tends to occur immediately after the problem becomes public knowledge.
- To instill credibility with the public, the spokesperson during a crisis should be a senior executive, preferably the president or chief executive officer.
- Avoid the "no comment" response.
- Make a team effort. Rely on senior management, public relations professionals, attorneys, quality control experts, and manufacturing and marketing personnel.

crisis management
Coordinated effort to handle the effects of unfavorable publicity or of another unexpected, unfavorable event.

No single approach will work for every crisis, but sketching out some type of crisis management plan before problems arise will help minimize the damage. Many airline public relations departments, for example, make a point of preparing ahead for a crisis. United Airlines, for instance, has a network of five crisis centers that link up in an emergency. One of these centers is capable of dispatching 80 people to a disaster site in an hour—complete with 100 cellular phones. United executes drills of simulated crashes four times a year.[56]

A good public relations and crisis management plan helped steer Frito-Lay and Procter & Gamble during their test marketing of Frito-Lay's Max brand fat-free potato chips made with P&G's controversial fake fat olestra. The week before the rollout, P&G sent over 1,000 detailed brochures about the chips to health-care professionals in the test market cities. P&G's chairman as well as in-house scientists involved with olestra's development made personal pitches about the product's safety to local TV stations and newspapers. Meanwhile, Frito-Lay hired nutritionists from the test cities as consultants who received intensive training on olestra and handling the media. Frito-Lay also created a separate group to handle all consumer calls on Max chips, transferring any caller who complained about health problems to P&G. In an effort to help other employees feel comfortable with the product's controversial introduction, Frito-Lay's president also wrote to all company employees, assuring them that the company's safety and nutrition professionals had carefully reviewed P&G data on olestra's safety and would never risk its good name and trust with consumers.[57]

LOOKING BACK

As you finish reading this chapter, think back to the opening story about the advertising campaign for the National Fluid Milk Processors Promotion Board. The board's advertising agency goes through the same creative steps as other large marketers— from determining what appeal to use to choosing the appropriate executional style. Great effort is also expended in deciding which medium will best reach the desired target markets. The agency takes into account such things as audience and geographic selectivity of the medium, cost per contact, frequency, and reach.

KEY TERMS

advertising appeal   504

advertising campaign   502

advertising objective   503

advertising response function 497

advocacy advertising   500

audience selectivity   515

comparative advertising 501

competitive advertising   501

continuous media schedule 516

cooperative advertising   510

cost per contact   514

cost per thousand (CPM) 514

crisis management   521

SUMMARY

1 *Discuss the effect advertising has on market share, consumers, brand loyalty, and perception of product attributes.* First, advertising helps marketers increase or maintain brand awareness and, subsequently, market share. Typically, more is spent to advertise new brands with a small market share than to advertise older brands. Brands with a large market share use advertising mainly to maintain their share of the market. Second, advertising affects consumers' daily lives as well as their purchases. Although advertising can seldom change strongly held consumer values, it may transform a consumer's negative attitude toward a product into a positive one. Third, when consumers are highly loyal to a brand, they may buy more of that brand when advertising is increased. Finally, advertising can also change the importance of a brand's attributes to consumers. By emphasizing different brand attributes, advertisers can change their appeal in response to consumers' changing needs or try to achieve an advantage over competing brands.

2 *Identify the major types of advertising.* Advertising is any form of nonpersonal, paid communication in which the sponsor or company is identified. The two major types of advertising are institutional advertising and product advertising. Institutional advertising is not product-oriented; rather, its purpose is to foster a positive company image among the general public, investment community, customers, and employees. Product advertising is designed mainly to promote goods and services, and it is classified into three main categories: pioneering, competitive, and comparative. A product's place in the product life cycle is a major determinant of the type of advertising used to promote it.

3 *Describe the advertising campaign process.* An advertising campaign is a series of related advertisements focusing on a common theme and common goals. The advertising campaign process consists of several important steps. Promotion managers first set specific campaign objectives. They then make creative decisions, often with the aid of an advertising agency, centered on developing advertising appeals. Once creative decisions have been made, media are evaluated and selected. Finally, the overall campaign is assessed through various forms of testing.

4 *Describe media evaluation and selection techniques.* Media evaluation and selection make up a crucial step in the advertising campaign process. Major types of advertising media include newspapers, magazines, radio, television, and outdoor advertising such as billboards and bus panels. Recent trends in advertising media include fax, video shopping carts, computer screen savers, cinema and video advertising, online computer services, and the Internet and World Wide Web. Promotion managers choose the advertising media mix on the basis of the following variables: cost per thousand (CPM), reach, frequency, characteristics of the target market, audience selectivity, geographic selectivity, flexibility, noise level, and life span. After choosing the media mix, a media schedule designates when the advertisement will appear and the specific vehicles it will appear in.

5 *Discuss the role of public relations in the promotional mix.* Public relations is a vital part of a firm's promotional mix. A company fosters good publicity to enhance its image and promote its products. Popular public relations tools include new product publicity, product placement, customer satisfaction phone lines, consumer education, event sponsorship, issue sponsorship, and Internet Web sites. An equally important aspect of public relations is managing unfavorable publicity in a way that is least damaging to a firm's image.

flighted media schedule
516

frequency *515*

infomercial *512*

institutional advertising
500

media mix *514*

media schedule *515*

medium *503*

pioneering advertising *501*

product advertising *500*

pulsing media schedule
516

reach *514*

seasonal media schedule
516

unique selling proposition
504

Discussion and Writing Questions

1. How can advertising, sales promotion, and publicity work together? Give an example.

2. Discuss the reasons why new brands with a smaller market share spend proportionately more on advertising and sales promotion than brands with a larger market share.

3. At what stage in a product's life cycle are pioneering, competitive, and comparative advertising most likely to occur? Give a current example of each type of advertising.

4. What is an advertising appeal? Give some examples of advertising appeals you have observed recently in the media.

5. What are the advantages of radio advertising? Why is radio expanding as an advertising medium?

6. ✏ You are the advertising manager of a sailing magazine, and one of your biggest potential advertisers has questioned your rates. Write the firm a letter explaining why you believe your audience selectivity is worth the extra expense for advertisers.

7. ✏ As the new public relations director for a sportswear company, you have been asked to set public relations objectives for a new line of athletic shoes to be introduced to the teen market. Draft a memo outlining the objectives you propose for the shoe's introduction and your reasons for them.

8. Reports have just surfaced that your company, a fast-food chain, sold contaminated food products that have made several people seriously ill. As your company's public relations manager, devise a plan to handle the crisis.

9. Identify an appropriate media mix for the following products:
   a. chewing tobacco
   b. *Playboy* magazine
   c. Weed-eaters
   d. foot odor killers
   e. "drink responsibly" campaigns by beer brewers

10. ✏ Design a full-page magazine advertisement for a new brand of soft drink. The name of the new drink, as well as package design, is at the discretion of the student. On a separate sheet, specify the benefits stressed or appeals made in the advertisement.

11. Form a three-person team. Divide the responsibility for getting newspaper advertisements and menus for several local restaurants. While you are at the restaurants to obtain copies of their menus, observe the atmosphere and interview the manager to determine what he or she believes are the primary reasons people chose to dine there. Pool your information and develop a table comparing the restaurants in terms of convenience of location, value for the money, food variety and quality, atmosphere, and so on. Rank the restaurants in terms of their appeal to college students. Explain the basis of your rankings. What other market segments would be attracted to the restaurants and why? Do the newspaper advertisements emphasize the most effective appeal for a particular restaurant? Explain.

12. What associations and organizations are listed with the Black Information Net-work? How would you try to appeal to some of the diverse interests of these groups if you were an advertiser trying to reach these consumers?

http://www.bin.com

13. How may Nutrition University aid this corporation's public relations effort?

http://www.kelloggs.com/

Application for Small Business

Quality of service is increasingly the basis for deciding where to do business. Customers are five times more likely to return to a particular business if they perceive that it is providing higher quality service than the competition.

The Student Copy Center is a local business competing with Kinko's and a couple of other national franchise copy centers. Its owner, Mack Bayles, just attended a Small Business Administration workshop on customer service. He learned that when people say they expect good customer service, they most often mean they want prompt and accurate service from friendly, knowledgeable, and courteous employees. The presenter also emphasized that all market segments, even the most price conscious, expect good customer service. He wants to use this knowledge to develop an effective advertising campaign.

Mack had no idea what his customers thought about either his copy business or that of his competitors. He decided, therefore, to ask his customers to complete a brief survey while in his store. From his survey he learned that Student Copy Center is considered more friendly and courteous than the major competitors but is rated lower on speed of service.

Questions

1. What should Mack do before developing his advertising campaign?
2. Should Mack use comparative ads?
3. What advertising appeal would be most effective for Mack? Why?

Woman's Hospital Responds to Changing Market Opportunities

Teri Fontenot, President and CEO, Woman's Health Foundation

Woman's Hospital, a division of Woman's Health Foundation, is one of the largest women's and infants' specialty hospitals in the United States, delivering almost 7,000 infants annually. Its vision statement is: "By the 21st century, Woman's Health Foundation will be the regional resource of choice for a broad spectrum of services for women and children." The hospital provides care for women of all ages and in all stages of life. Services include obstetrics, gynecology, physical therapy, maternal-fetal medicine, gynecologic oncology, mammography, general surgery, pediatric

cardiology, fertility, genetics, radiology, and much more.

With birth rates declining and the aging of its primary target market of women of childbearing age, the hospital has been adapting its strategy for health care delivery. The emphasis has moved from primarily obstretrics—the delivery of babies—to a broader service offering. The focus now includes gynecology—the branch of medicine that deals with the treatment of diseases and hygiene of women of all ages—and neonatology—the branch of medicine concerned with the care, development, and diseases of newborn infants, particularly those that result from difficult pregnancies.

The promotional execution of this changing strategy includes a GYN (gynecology) surgery campaign. There are two objectives of this campaign, one for each of the target audiences. The consumer objective is to increase awareness of the GYN surgery procedures available at Woman's Hospital and the depth of experience Woman's Hospital offers in GYN surgery so that women will select the hospital as their provider for GYN surgery. The physician objective is to remind the GYN physicians that Woman's Hospital continues to provide the highest quality facilities and staff to serve women in the market, particularly for GYN surgery.

The budget for the campaign was $70,000 for television, $8,000 for radio, and $15,000 in print. Two flights of media were scheduled; the first flight lasted six weeks, then there was a one-month break, and the second flight lasted four weeks.

A recent survey revealed that Women's Hospital enjoys top-of-mind awareness of 91 percent among its target audience. Furthermore, it is the preferred alternative with 96 percent of the market. Finally, patient satisfaction with Women's has averaged 98 percent over the last five years.

The creative strategy of the promotional campaign was centered around: (1) the experience Woman's Hospital offers in serving the health-care needs of women of all ages; (2) the expertise Woman's Hospital offers in providing GYN surgery to thousands of women over the past 28 years; (3) the unique understanding that the physicians and nurses at Woman's Hospital have pertaining to the care and comfort of women before, during, and after GYN surgery; and (4) the delivery of the message clearly, directly, and in the strongest possible terms. Overall, the campaign was designed to encourage women to conclude, "Why would I go anywhere else other than Woman's Hospital for my GYN surgery?", and for physicians to conclude, "Why should I refer women patients to any other hospital for GYN surgery?"

Promotional execution includes television, radio, and print media. The television spots were developed around a series of black and white photos as visuals, rather than video. Employees were used as models in the photos to ensure realism and to meet budget constraints. A hand-tinted color effect was added to the photos to attract attention and assist in transitions between photos and the hospital logo presentation. Original music was produced for the campaign. The music is predominantly instrumental (piano chords) with a female vocalist providing limited accompaniment. The creative rationale for the TV spots was that still photos will add a unique sense of drama to this campaign and stand out among the unrelenting procession of fast-moving, loud, and often irritating commercials seen daily on local television. This visual approach matches the clear and direct copy approach the hospital typically utilizes. The production technique also enables a campaign of three commercials to be produced for the same budget allocated for one commercial using video.

The radio and print elements of the campaign reinforced and extended the television ads. Radio spots were executed by using professional female actors presenting their "testimonials" on why they or their friend or someone in their family chose or is choosing Woman's Hospital for GYN surgery, based on positive past experience with Woman's Hospital. The radio commercials also included the music track from the television spots.

The creative rationale of these spots was that they should reflect the mood of the television commercials and create the idea of the women seen in the TV spots actually telling their own, very personal stories.

The print execution involved using some of the same models photographed from the TV ads, but in different settings. The creative rationale was that consistency is vital to maintaining awareness as well as in attracting attention to this and other future resources for women available at Woman's Hospital.

Questions

1. Is the objective of this promotional campaign reasonable?
2. Are the media selection and mix appropriate for the campaign's objectives?
3. Could the budget achieve a frequency and reach that is adequate for the objective?
4. How effective was the execution of the promotional objectives? How could the execution be improved?

1 Define and state the objectives of sales promotion.

2 Discuss the most common forms of consumer sales promotion.

3 List the most common forms of trade sales promotion.

4 Describe personal selling.

5 Discuss the key differences between relationship selling and traditional selling.

6 Identify the different types of selling tasks.

7 List the steps in the selling process.

8 Describe the functions of sales management.

Sales Promotion and Personal Selling

The turning point in Sega of America's life as a marketer came when thousands of kids suddenly started doing "The Sega Scream." Everyone, from grade-schoolers to adults, was suddenly shrieking the word "Sega!" as it spontaneously took flight as a fad, baffling parents and teachers. Naturally, the fad turned out to be one more promotional phenomenon that helped the Sega Genesis game system maintain its number one brand position over Nintendo in the $6 billion videogame industry.

The Sega Scream was simply a TV commercial's voiceover tagline that caught on with kids, but Sega cleverly leveraged it into its sales promotion efforts to make it a marketing mantra. That kind of opportunism, plus a long list of deeply integrated promotions, special events, contests, tie-ins with other marketers, in-store point-of-purchase displays, on-pack premiums, and multimedia efforts, earned Sega *Advertising Age's* Promotional Marketer of the Year award.

There's no rule book at Sega on sales promotional strategy. Unlike most successful brand marketers, Sega has no promotional agency on record, no committee overseeing all promotions, and, until recently, no single executive responsible for coordinating each and every effort. The reason: "If you look too far ahead or start repeating ideas in this business,

you're dead," says Tom Abramson, Sega's VP-marketing of promotions. "You have to take risks constantly, relying on focus groups, feelers, and gut instinct. You can never get to feeling safe in this market, because it changes just about every six hours," he says.

Some of Sega's smartest moves involved getting closer to its quirky, hard-to-pin-down, mostly male audience on a street level. Its method was to infiltrate their environments by creating special events that put the Sega brand one on one with users in nontraditional settings. At recreational parks, at gyms, and on college campuses, Sega created a grassroots marketing army among its own users. At 50 college campuses nationwide, student marketers are paid to organize events and contests, while giving away substantial amounts of merchandise for sampling and testing.

Additionally, Sega lured hundreds of consumers into sampling its games at Dallas's All-Star FanFest, where many game titles for the mainstream 16-bit Genesis system were demonstrated. Sega also maintains a

heavy presence at Orlando's Universal Studios and Walt Disney World's Epcot Center, where thousands more play its games for free. "First-hand experience is what sells these games, and there's no better way to get word of mouth out there than to get kids face to face with the game," said Sega's director of marketing.

Equally important are the new frontiers Sega has developed: cable TV's Sega Channel, an exclusive relationship with CompuServ online service, and the establishment of its own site on the Internet. Another successful promotional coup was its online contest allowing users to try out their Sega Screams. Users uploaded recordings of their screams to Sega to compare against company president Tom Kalinske's version, which any user could download to hear on a home computer.

Perhaps Sega's biggest and most successful promotion was its worldwide videogame tournament for the launch of its "Sonic and Knuckles" game. The contest involved hundreds of thousands of videogame players nationwide from which final winners were flown to San Francisco's Alcatraz Prison for a last face-off. The event was televised live by MTV, which replayed the 30-minute program four times. In keeping with its constant pursuit of fresher promotions, Sega vows never to repeat the promotion.

With the launch of its new 64-bit Saturn game machine, Sega traveled along with the Lollapalooza concert tour, getting concertgoers to line up to play its new system for free, while 25 Sega vans criss-crossed the United States offering free Saturn experiences everywhere from parking lots to beaches.[1]

Sampling and contests have been two of Sega's most effective methods of gaining new users for its Genesis and Saturn game systems. If you were a loyal Nintendo game player, what promotions might entice you to switch to playing one of Sega's systems?

Sega
What online promotions, contests, and premiums do you find at the Sega site? How does this Web site target Sega's mostly male audience?
http://www.sega.com/

SALES PROMOTION

sales promotion
Offer of a short-term incentive in order to induce the purchase of a particular good or service.

In addition to using advertising, public relations, and personal selling, marketing managers can use sales promotion to increase the effectiveness of their promotional efforts. **Sales promotions** are those marketing communication activities, other than advertising, personal selling, and public relations, in which a short-term incentive, such as a lower price or added value, motivates consumers or members of the distribution channel to purchase a good or service immediately.

Advertising offers the consumer a reason to buy; sales promotion offers an incentive to buy. Both are important, but sales promotion is usually cheaper than advertising and easier to measure. A major national TV advertising campaign may cost over $2 million to create, produce, and place. In contrast, a newspaper coupon campaign or promotional contest may cost only about half as much. It is hard to figure exactly how many people buy a product as a result of seeing a TV ad. However, with sales promotion, marketers know the precise number of coupons redeemed or the number of contest entries processed.

consumer sales promotion
Sales promotion activities targeted to the ultimate consumer.

trade sales promotion
Sales promotion activities targeted to a channel member, such as a wholesaler or retailer.

Sales promotion is usually targeted toward either of two distinctly different markets. **Consumer sales promotion** is targeted to the ultimate consumer market. **Trade sales promotion** is directed to members of the marketing channel, such as wholesalers and retailers. Sales promotion has become an important element in a marketer's integrated marketing communications program. Sales promotion expenditures have been steadily increasing over the last several years as a result of increased competition, the ever-expanding array of available media choices, and consumers and retailers demanding more deals from manufacturers. Estimates of annual consumer sales promotion spending were in excess of $850 million for 1995, rising over 19 percent from the previous year. In contrast, advertising spending increased only about 9 percent in the same period.[2]

The Objectives of Sales Promotion

1 Define and state the objectives of sales promotion.

Sales promotion usually works best in affecting behavior, not attitudes. Immediate purchase is the goal of sales promotion, regardless of the form it takes. Therefore, it seems to make more sense when planning a sales promotion campaign to target customers according to their general behavior. For instance, is the consumer loyal to your product or to your competitor's? Does the consumer switch brands readily in

Exhibit 18.1
*Types of Consumers and
Sales Promotion Goals*

Type of buyer	Desired results	Sales promotion examples
Loyal customers People who buy your product most or all of the time	Reinforce behavior, increase consumption, change purchase timing	• Loyalty marketing programs, such as frequent-buyer cards or frequent-shopper clubs • Bonus packs that give loyal consumers an incentive to stock up or premiums offered in return for proofs of purchase
Competitor's customers People who buy a competitor's product most or all of the time	Break loyalty, persuade to switch to your brand	• Sampling to introduce your product's superior qualities compared to their brand • Sweepstakes, contests, or premiums that create interest in the product
Brand switchers People who buy a variety of products in the category	Persuade to buy your brand more often	• Any promotion that lowers the price of the product, such as coupons, price-off packages, and bonus packs • Trade deals that help make the product more readily available than competing products
Price buyers People who consistently buy the least expensive brand	Appeal with low prices or supply added value that makes price less important	• Coupons, price-off packages, refunds, or trade deals that reduce the price of brand to match that of the brand that would have been purchased

Source: From *Sales Promotion Essentials,* 2E by Don E. Schultz, William A. Robinson, and Lisa A. Petrison. Reprinted by permission of NTC Publishing Group, 4255 W. Touhy Ave., Lincolnwood, IL 60048.

favor of the best deal? Does the consumer buy only the least expensive product, no matter what? Does the consumer buy any products in your category at all?

The objectives of a promotion depend on the general behavior of target consumers (see Exhibit 18.1). For example, marketers who are targeting loyal users of their product actually don't want to change behavior. Instead, they need to reinforce existing behavior or increase product usage. An effective tool for strengthening brand loyalty is the frequent-buyer program that rewards consumers for repeat purchases. Other types of promotions are more effective with customers prone to brand switching or with those who are loyal to a competitor's product. The cents-off coupon, free sample, or eye-catching display in a store will often entice shoppers to try a different brand. Consumers who do not use the product may be enticed to try it through the distribution of free samples.

Once marketers understand the dynamics occurring within their product category and have determined the particular consumers and consumer behaviors they want to influence, they can then go about selecting promotional tools to achieve these goals.

TOOLS FOR CONSUMER SALES PROMOTION

Marketing managers must decide which consumer sales promotion devices to use in a specific campaign. The methods chosen must suit the objectives to ensure success of the overall promotion plan. Popular tools for consumer sales promotion are coupons, premiums, loyalty marketing programs, contests and sweepstakes, sampling, and point-of-purchase displays.

2 Discuss the most common forms of consumer sales promotion.

Coupons encourage product trial and repurchase and increase the amount of product bought.
© 1996 PhotoDisc, Inc.

coupon
Certificate that entitles consumers to an immediate price reduction when they buy the product.

Coupons

A **coupon** is a certificate that entitles consumers to an immediate price reduction when they buy the product. Consumers receive coupons by direct mail; through the media, as in a freestanding insert in Sunday newspapers; on the product's package; through cooperative advertising, which presents a manufacturer's coupon that can be redeemed only at the retailer's store; and through coupon-dispensing machines at retail stores. Coupons are a particularly good way to encourage product trial and repurchase. They are also likely to increase the amount of a product bought.

Coupon distribution has steadily increased over the years. Packaged-goods marketers distribute over 300 billion coupons a year through print media, saving consumers over $4 billion each year. But shoppers redeem only about 1 of these coupons in 50, or about 2 percent. Part of the problem is that coupons are often wasted on consumers who have no interest in the product—for example, dog food coupons that reach the petless. Another problem is that most coupons expire before the consumer has the opportunity to use them. Additionally, coupons are more likely to encourage repeat purchases by regular users of a product than to encourage nonusers to try the brand.[3] Thus, some marketers are reevaluating their use of coupons. Procter & Gamble, for example, has cut the number of coupons it gives to consumers in favor of a lower-price strategy. Kraft has opted to distribute "universal" coupons which offer money off on any of its 20 different Post and Nabisco brand cereals.[4] Other marketers are experimenting with online coupons over the Internet. Reebok, for example, distributed promotional online coupons for its products via its Web site (http://www.reebok.com) during the Atlanta Summer Olympic Games.[5]

In an effort to get a higher yield from promotions, many marketers are directing coupons to the place where they're most likely to affect customer buying decisions: in the aisles where consumers decide which product to buy. Coupon-dispensing machines, attached to the shelf below the featured product, have an 18 percent redemption rate (about one person uses the coupon out of every five who take one), nine times higher than for newspaper inserts. Marketers are also investigating the use of coupons dispensed at the checkout counter in response to a purchase the consumer has just made. Such machines dispense coupons for either the product purchased or a competing brand. Redemption rates for electronic checkout coupons are around 9 percent.[6]

Although the United States remains the world's leading coupon market, several other markets around the world are beginning to experience the same growth in couponing that occurred in the United States during the 1980s. In the European Community, political and economic changes have given marketers more opportunity to use creative promotional techniques. The United Kingdom and Belgium are the EC's most active coupon users; marketers distribute over 5 billion coupons annually in the United Kingdom alone. Couponing continues to grow in Italy, and couponing has just become legal in Denmark. Other European countries still have limited access to coupons, however. For example, in Holland and Switzerland, some major retailers refuse to accept coupons. Other regions are also slow to embrace couponing. In Russia, limited advertising media and the unavailability of many products make couponing difficult. In Japan, coupon redemption is still in its infancy. Although the print media are now allowed to carry coupons, Japanese retailers and consumers are still reluctant to use them. Many consumers feel that using coupons may make them look as though they do not have much money or are being "cheap."[7]

Premiums

A **premium** is an extra item offered to the consumer, usually in exchange for some proof that the promoted product has been purchased. Premiums reinforce the consumer's purchase decision, increase consumption, and persuade nonusers to switch brands. Premiums like telephones, tote bags, and umbrellas are available when consumers buy cosmetics, magazines, bank services, cars, and so on. Premiums can also include more product for the regular price, such as "two-for-the-price-of-one" bonus packs or packages that include more of the product. Kellogg's, for example, was hugely successful in its promotion of Pop Tarts that added two more pastries to the current six in a package without increasing the price. Kellogg's used the promotion to boost market share it had lost to private-label brands of pastries and new competitors.[8]

Marketers often require consumers to collect UPC symbols or some other proof of purchase that they later redeem for merchandise or more product. Pepsi's Pepsi Stuff promotion, for example, gave away merchandise with Pepsi logos, such as jackets, caps, and t-shirts, in exchange for Pepsi drinkers collecting award-points from Pepsi or Diet Pepsi bottles and packaging. The promotion invigorated Pepsi's core cola business while plastering the Pepsi logo on millions of loyal consumers. In fact, the Pepsi Stuff promotion was so popular among Pepsi drinkers that the company was forced to scale back its advertising for the promotion.[9]

The appropriateness of the premium is crucial to its success. Children's toys, for example, are a popular premium in boxes of sugary cereals. Fast-food companies often tie into movies or special events to give away souvenir cups and toys in kid's meal packages in an effort to attract kids to their establishments. For example, McDonald's gave away a record number of Teenie Beanie Babies as Happy Meal premiums in the Spring of 1997.[10]

> **premium**
> Extra item offered to the consumer, usually in exchange for some proof of purchase of the promoted product.

Loyalty Marketing Programs

The objective of **loyalty marketing programs** is to build long-term, mutually beneficial relationships between a company and its key customers. Popularized by the airline industry in the mid-1980s through frequent-flyer programs, loyalty marketing enables companies to strategically invest sales promotion dollars in activities designed to capture greater profits from customers already loyal to the product or company.[11] One study concluded that if a company retains an additional 5 percent of its customers each year, profits will increase by at least 25 percent. What's more, improving customer retention by a mere 2 percent can decrease costs by as much as 10 percent.[12]

Frequent-buyer programs are one of the fastest-growing forms of loyalty marketing. In a **frequent-buyer program**, loyal consumers are rewarded for making multiple purchases of a particular good or service. Retailers and small business and service marketers have become loyal followers of frequent-buyer programs (see the "Marketing and Small Business" box). Punch cards, where customers have their cards punched or stamped each time they make a purchase, are popular among small business retailers and service providers. For example, a golf driving range may punch golfers' cards each time they purchase a bucket of balls. After, say, the tenth bucket, the golfer receives a free bucket.

Larger companies use technology, such as scanners and computers, to build sophisticated databases designed to reward loyal customers. At the MegaMart supermarket in Milwaukee, for example, loyal customers swipe their frequent buyer card through a special kiosk at the front of the store. The computer prints out 24 items on special for the next three hours specifically for that shopper. The items are chosen based on the shopper's past purchases at the store which are stored in the supermarket's database. The computer is programmed to recognize that the shopper buys toothpaste, for example, every six weeks so the shopper receives a special on

> **loyalty marketing program**
> Promotional program designed to build long-term, mutually beneficial relationships between a company and its key customers.

> **frequent-buyer program**
> Loyalty program in which loyal consumers are rewarded for making multiple purchases of a particular good or service.

toothpaste on the fifth week after the last purchase. Other companies use their frequent-buyer programs to send their most loyal customers periodic newsletters filled with coupons or specials specifically tailored for each cardholder. If the customer has a cat, for example, he or she would receive offers on cat food but not dog food.[13]

Marketing and Small Business

Customer-Specific Marketing for Small Retailers

In 1993, the Coca-Cola Company published a report entitled "Measured Marketing" that has revolutionized supermarket and small retail marketing and promotion. The author, Brian Woolf, president of the Retail Strategy Center, Inc., spent six months visiting 83 supermarkets researching customer spending patterns.

During the course of his research, Woolf's biggest surprise was how few retailers collected and used information about their customers. Additionally, he found the best customers of a retail establishment not only shopped most frequently but also spent the most on each visit. Over the course of a year, the top 20 percent of a food retailer's customers spend 50 times the amount of its bottom 20 percent. Further, mass marketing, with its "one price fits all" approach, is obsolete because of the power available today for retailers to retrieve customer information.

From this research, Woolf developed the concept of *customer-specific marketing,* a practice he proposes to all retailers, large and small alike. This new concept in retail marketing concentrates on using a frequent-buyer card as a major marketing tool. Since loyalty marketing programs and frequent-buyer clubs are a relatively low-cost promotional tool, Woolf's concept is especially feasible for small retailers to implement.

Woolf believes that instead of retailers trying to get customers into their stores with sale periods where lower profits are made due to price reductions, they should focus on getting customers to shop with them when they can make the most profit. How? Through customer specific marketing programs designed to reward a retailer's best customers and thus boost sales. In customer-specific marketing, the most valuable customers are given frequent-buyer cards and are targeted with direct-mail efforts. In this way, store sales and marketing costs can be focused almost exclusively on the customers that do matter.

The two basic principles of customer-specific marketing are: (1) all customers are *not* equal and (2) behavior follows reward. First, Woolf's discovery that 20 percent of all customers spend the greatest amount of money in a business led him to question why these customers are treated the same as the ones who spend the least. Small business retailers should ask how valuable these customers are to their business. As an analogy, businesses don't pay all their employees the same wage. Their salary ties in with their job and how valuable they are to the business. The same principle works with customers. The more value, the greater the reward. Like employees, the reward should be varied in proportion to their contribution.

Second, Woolf purports that behavior follows reward. That is, if consumers perceive a reward for shopping at a certain store, they will patronize that store more frequently and spend more money. For example, a retailer might create a frequent-shopper club in which cardholders receive incremental rewards depending on the amount of money spent in the store. If card members spend up to $20 on merchandise, then they receive an additional 5 percent discount on "cardholder" identified items around the store. If card members spend between $20 and $50, they receive a 10 percent discount. If the purchase is more than $50, then a 20 percent discount is given. Does this encourage shoppers to buy more to save more? You bet!

Retailers know that the sale customer is important, but profits decline at sale time. With customer-specific marketing, the retailer can track its best customer and reward just them while increasing profits. And best of all, frequent-shopper clubs are relatively easy to implement and cost less with greater returns than some other forms of promotion. Woolf's advice to any retailer is that "the marketers who win in the long term will be those who understand and use their (customer) information most effectively."[14]

What valuable lessons can small retailers learn from Woolf? How might a small retailer use direct mail in conjunction with a frequent-shopper club to enhance the program? How might a frequent-shopper club affect the amount of dollars spent on other types of promotion, such as advertising?

Contests and Sweepstakes

Contests and sweepstakes are generally designed to create interest in the good or service, often to encourage brand switching. *Contests* are promotions in which participants use some skill or ability to compete for prizes. A consumer contest usually requires entrants to answer questions, complete sentences, or write a paragraph about the product and submit proof of purchase. Winning a *sweepstakes*, on the other hand, depends on chance or luck, and participation is free. Sweepstakes usually draw about 10 times more entries than contests do.

When setting up contests and sweepstakes, sales promotion managers must make certain that the award will appeal to the target market. For instance, a sweepstakes for an exotic honeymoon destination will definitely capture the attention of the many brides-to-be who read a bridal magazine. A contest sponsored by Guinness Import Company had contestants write a 50-word essay explaining what Guinness beer means to them. The writer of the best essay won a pub in Ireland. Response to the contest far exceeded any previous Guinness promotion and resulted in worldwide publicity.[15] Similarly, Philip Morris awarded winners of its sweepstakes a five-day trip aboard the luxury Marlboro Unlimited train through the "Marlboro Country" of Colorado, Wyoming, Idaho, and Montana.[16]

Online contests and sweepstakes on the Internet are gaining the attention of marketers as well. Internet surfers get the chance to win free merchandise while marketers create and strengthen ties with consumers by drawing Web site visitors and recording demographic data. Sendai, publisher of several electronic gaming magazines, recently launched an online contest in which participants searched for clues in several different puzzles, with a new puzzle appearing each week. The grand prize winner received a free laptop computer. As a result, Sendai's Web site Nuke Internetwork (http://www.nuke.com) received over one million hits by Internet surfers a week.[17]

Contests are used to create interest in goods and services and to encourage brand switching. Entrants answer questions, write essays, or submit proofs of purchase to win.
© 1996 Shawn Spence

Sampling

Consumers generally perceive a certain amount of risk in trying new products. Many are afraid of trying something they will not like (such as a new food item) or spending too much money and getting little reward. **Sampling** allows the customer to try

sampling
Promotional program that allows the consumer the opportunity to try the product or service for free.

Department stores often use sampling to entice shoppers to buy perfumes. Perfume samples also appear in magazines and direct-mail advertisements.
© 1996 PhotoDisc, Inc.

a product risk-free. However, sampling can be very expensive. As a general rule, then, free samples of a product should be offered only when two conditions exist. First, the benefits of the new product must be clearly superior to those of existing products. Second, the item must have a unique new attribute that the consumer must experience to believe in. Recent research on sampling effectiveness indicates that among those consumers who had never before purchased the product, 86 percent indicated that the free sample was an important element in their decision to buy the sampled product for the first time. Additionally, among those who had previously purchased the sampled product, one-half said that receiving the free sample had positively influenced their decision to buy it again.[18]

Sampling can be accomplished by directly mailing the sample to the customer, delivering the sample door to door, demonstrating or sampling the product at a retail store, or packaging the sample with another product. Sampling at special events is a popular, effective, and high-profile distribution method that permits marketers to piggyback onto fun-based consumer activities—including sporting events, college fests, fairs and festivals, beach events, chili cook-offs, and the like. Sampling at events garners greater publicity than might otherwise be received. The risk of event-related sampling is that awareness of the product may be overwhelmed by competing influences and distractions. Few people can be expected to pay close attention to a new beverage, for example, during an exciting or extremely tense sporting event. On the plus side, consumers at events are generally receptive to sampling because they are in a good mood and often share common demographic, ethnic, geographic, and psychographic profiles.[19]

Venue-based sampling, or distributing samples to specific location types where consumers regularly meet for a common objective or interest, is one of the most cost-efficient methods of sampling. Although too numerous to list, these venues could include hospitals, health clubs, churches, maternity wards, college bookstores, video and specialty retail outlets, and hotel rooms. The mechanics of the distribution, often the job of the staff at the location, reduce costs and add credibility to the offering. Another plus of venue-based sampling is the almost certain affinity the target consumers will have with the products being sampled. If someone visits a health club regularly, chances are he or she is a bona fide prospect, for example, for a health food product or vitamin supplement. Likewise, patients of doctors who specialize in diabetes management are excellent candidates for trial samples of sugar-free snacks, diagnostic kits, or other diabetes-related products. Additionally, the credibility of their being distributed at the doctor's office implies a powerful third-party endorsement.[20]

Point-of-Purchase Displays

point-of-purchase display
Promotional display set up at the retailer's location to build traffic, advertise the product, or induce impulse buying.

A **point-of-purchase** display is a promotional display set up at the retailer's location to build traffic, advertise the product, or induce impulse buying. One big advantage of point-of-purchase displays is that they offer manufacturers a captive audience in retail stores. Research by the Point-of-Purchase Advertising Institute indicates that over 70 percent of purchase decisions are made in-store.[21] Therefore, point-of-purchase displays work better for impulse products, those products bought without prior decision by the consumer, than for planned purchases.

Point-of-purchase displays include shelf "talkers" (signs attached to store shelves), shelf extenders (attachments that extend shelves so products stand out), ads on grocery carts and bags, end-aisle and floor-stand displays, television monitors at supermarket checkout counters, in-store audio messages, and audiovisual displays. An in-store display can be simple—for example, a shipping crate that converts to a floor stand—but to be effective, it should provide product information and be creative and entertaining.

Research shows the effectiveness of point-of-purchase displays. One study tested brands in six different product categories and in all instances found that point-of-purchase displays increased sales over stores where displays were not used. Sales of coffee in point-of-purchase displays, for instance, were over six times higher than sales of coffee displayed in its normal shelf position. Research conducted by Information Resources Inc., which uses scanner technology at cash registers to record the bar codes stamped on purchased items (discussed in Chapter 9), found that point-of-purchase displays could increase the sales of products such as frozen dinners, laundry detergent, soft drinks, snack foods, soup, and juice by more than 100 to 200 percent.[22]

Computers and interactive electronic devices are beginning to play an important role in point-of-purchase displays. High-tech displays, whether stand-alone kiosks or on-shelf units, grab attention. Warner-Lambert's Canadian division, for example, installed on-shelf computers in the cough-cold-allergy sections of more than 600 Canadian drugstores. The displays, which help shoppers choose a Warner-Lambert over-the-counter remedy that is appropriate for their symptoms, have increased sales significantly.[23] Similarly, PICS Previews installs interactive kiosks in music, video, and electronics departments of mass merchandise stores. The six-foot-high interactive kiosk includes a color TV and a touchpad with icons of music CDs, movies, or games sold in the store from which they can sample full-motion video or sound clips. The system has been proven to generate sales increases of featured items from 19 to 47 percent.[24]

TOOLS FOR TRADE SALES PROMOTION

Whereas consumer promotions *pull* a product through the channel by creating demand, trade promotions *push* a product through the distribution channel (see Chapter 14). When selling to members of the distribution channel, manufacturers use many of the same sales promotion tools used in consumer promotions—such as sales contests, premiums, and point-of-purchase displays. Several tools, however, are unique to manufacturers and intermediaries:

3 List the most common forms of trade sales promotion.

What does winning $100,000 have to do with selling smoked cooked ham? Does the chance of winning a pink automobile make sales representatives sell more cosmetics? To find out, check out **Hot Link—Sales Promotion.**

- *Trade allowances:* A **trade allowance** is a price reduction offered by manufacturers to intermediaries such as wholesalers and retailers. The price reduction or rebate is given in exchange for doing something specific, such as allocating space for a new product or buying something during special periods. For example, a local dealer could receive a special discount for running its own promotion on GE telephones.

- *Push money:* Intermediaries receive **push money** as a bonus for pushing the manufacturer's brand through the distribution channel. Often the push money is directed toward a retailer's salespeople. For example, the manufacturer may offer $50 to an electronics store's sales force for every television set of its brand sold. This practice, however, may foster more loyalty to the manufacturer than to the retailer.

- *Training:* Sometimes a manufacturer will train an intermediary's personnel if the product is rather complex—as frequently occurs in the computer and telecommunication industries. For example, if a large department store purchases an NCR computerized cash register system, NCR may provide free training so the salespeople can learn how to use the new system.

- *Free merchandise:* Often a manufacturer offers retailers free merchandise in lieu of quantity discounts. For example, a breakfast cereal manufacturer may throw in one case of free cereal for every 20 cases ordered by the retailer. Occasionally, free merchandise is used as payment for trade allowances normally provided through

trade allowance
Price reduction offered by manufacturers to intermediaries, such as wholesalers and retailers.

push money
Money offered to channel intermediaries to encourage them to "push" products—that is, to encourage other members of the channel to sell the products.

Trade promotions are designed to push a product through the distribution channel. For example, manufacturers offer trade allowances to wholesalers and retailers in return for space allocation or purchase of a product during special periods.
© William Taufic/The Stock Market

other sales promotions. For example, instead of giving a retailer a price reduction for buying a certain quantity of merchandise, the manufacturer may throw in extra merchandise "free" (that is, at a cost that would equal the price reduction).

- *Store demonstrations:* Manufacturers can also arrange with retailers to perform an in-store demonstration. For example, food manufacturers often send representatives to grocery stores and supermarkets to let customers sample a product while shopping. Cosmetic companies also send their representatives to department stores to promote their beauty aids by performing facials and makeovers for customers.

- *Business meetings, conventions, and trade shows:* Trade association meetings, conferences, and conventions are an important aspect of sales promotion and a growing, multibillion-dollar market. At these shows, manufacturers, distributors, and other vendors have the chance to display their goods or describe their services to customers and potential customers. The cost per potential customer contacted at a show is estimated to be only 25 to 35 percent that of a personal sales call. Trade shows have been uniquely effective in introducing new products; trade shows can

Cosmetic companies often promote their beauty aids by sending representatives to department stores to perform makeovers and facials for customers.
© 1996 PhotoDisc, Inc.

establish products in the marketplace more quickly than can advertising, direct marketing, or sales calls. Companies participate in trade shows to attract and identify new prospects, serve current customers, introduce new products, enhance corporate image, test the market response to new products, enhance corporate morale, and gather competitive product information.

Trade promotions are popular among manufacturers for many reasons. Trade sales promotion tools help manufacturers gain new distributors for their products, obtain wholesaler and retailer support for consumer sales promotions, build or reduce dealer inventories, and improve trade relations. Car manufacturers, for example, annually sponsor dozens of auto shows for consumers. Many of the displays feature interactive computer stations where consumers enter vehicle specifications and get a printout of prices and local dealer names. In return, the local car dealers get the names of good prospects. The shows attract millions of consumers, providing dealers with increased store traffic as well as good leads.

Sometimes trade deals are offered for competitive reasons—"because everyone else does it." Another source of pressure is retailers. Some big retailers have considerable channel power, and that power allows them to demand product discounts and payments for limited shelf space (called *slotting allowances*), especially for new-product introductions.

PERSONAL SELLING

Personal selling is direct communication between a sales representative and one or more prospective buyers in an attempt to influence each other in a purchase situation. In a sense, all businesspeople are salespeople. An individual may become a plant manager, a chemist, an engineer, or a member of any profession and yet still have to sell. During a job search, applicants must "sell" themselves to prospective employers in an interview. To reach the top in most organizations, individuals need to sell ideas to peers, superiors, and subordinates. Most important, people must sell themselves and their ideas to just about everyone with whom they have a continuing relationship and to many other people they see only once or twice. Chances are that students majoring in business or marketing will start their professional careers in sales. Even students in nonbusiness majors may pursue a sales career.

Personal selling offers several advantages over other forms of promotion:

- Personal selling provides a detailed explanation or demonstration of the product. This capability is especially needed for complex or new goods and services.

- The sales message can be varied according to the motivations and interests of each prospective customer. Moreover, when the prospect has questions or raises objections, the salesperson is there to provide explanations. In contrast, advertising and sales promotion can only respond to the objections the copywriter thinks are important to customers.

- Personal selling can be directed only to qualified prospects. Other forms of promotion include some unavoidable waste because many people in the audience are not prospective customers.

- Personal selling costs can be controlled by adjusting the size of the sales force (and resulting expenses) in one-person increments. On the other hand, advertising and sales promotion must often be purchased in fairly large amounts.

- Perhaps the most important advantage is that personal selling is considerably more effective than other forms of promotion in obtaining a sale and gaining a satisfied customer.

Personal selling might work better than other forms of promotion given certain customer and product characteristics. Generally speaking, personal selling becomes more important as the number of potential customers decreases, as the complexity of the product increases, and as the value of the product grows (see Exhibit 18.2). When there are relatively few potential customers, the time and travel costs of personally visiting each prospect are justifiable. Of course, the good or service must be of sufficient value to absorb the expense of a sales call—a mainframe computer, a management consulting project, or the construction of a new building, for instance. For highly complex goods, such as business jets or private communication systems, a salesperson is needed to determine the prospective customer's needs, to explain the product's basic advantages, and to propose the exact features and accessories that will meet the client's needs. Conversely, advertising and sales promotion more effectively and economically promote a product when the number of potential buyers is large, the product is less complex, the buyers are dispersed, and the product is low in value and high in standardization (for instance, toothpaste or cereal).

4 Describe personal selling.

personal selling
Direct communication between a sales representative and one or more prospective buyers in an attempt to influence each other in a purchase situation.

Exhibit 18.2
Comparison of Advertising/Sales Promotion and Personal Selling

Personal selling is more important if . . .	Advertising/sales promotion is more important if . . .
• The product has a high value. • It is a custom-made product. • There are few customers. • The product is technically complex. • Customers are concentrated.	• The product has a low value. • It is a standardized product. • There are many customers. • The product is simple to understand. • Customers are geographically dispersed.
Examples: insurance policies, custom windows, airplane engines	Examples: soap, magazine subscriptions, cotton T-shirts

Relationship Selling

5 Discuss the key differences between relationship selling and traditional selling.

Relationship selling emphasizes a win-win outcome.
Courtesy Acclivus

Until recently, marketing theory and practice concerning personal selling were focused solely on the transaction of the sale. That is, marketers were most concerned with making a one-time sale and then moving on to the next prospect. Traditional views of personal selling emphasized a planned presentation to prospective customers for the sole purpose of making the sale. Whether it took place face-to-face during a personal sales call or by selling over the telephone (telemarketing), traditional personal selling methods attempted to persuade the buyer to accept a point of view or convince the buyer to take some action. Once the customer was somewhat convinced, then the salesperson used a variety of techniques in an attempt to elicit a purchase. Frequently, the objectives of the salesperson were at the expense of the buyer, creating a win-lose outcome.[25] Although this type of sales approach has not disappeared entirely, it is being used less and less often by professional salespeople. Many people still associate traditional selling methods with the insincere, fast-talking, and slick salesperson, as you will read about in the "Ethics in Marketing" box.

In contrast, more conventional views of personal selling emphasize the relationship that develops between a salesperson and a buyer. This practice is an outgrowth of *relationship marketing*, which was discussed in Chapter 7. **Relationship selling,** or **consultative selling,** is the practice of building, maintaining, and enhancing interactions with customers in order to develop long-term satisfaction through mutually beneficial partnerships.[26] Relationship or consultative salespeople, therefore, become consultants, partners, and problem solvers for their customers. They strive to build long-term relationships with key accounts by developing trust over time. The focus shifts from a one-time sale to a long-term relationship in which the salesperson works with the customer to develop solutions for enhancing the customer's bottom line. Thus, relationship selling emphasizes a win-win outcome.[27]

Relationship selling's goal of creating long-term, repeat-purchase customers offers several advantages for a company. In general, the longer a customer stays with a company, the more that customer is worth. Long-term customers buy more, take less of a company's time, are less sensitive to price, and bring in new customers. Best of all, they have no acquisition or start-up cost. Good long-standing customers are worth so much that in some industries, reducing customer defections by as little as five points—from, say, 15 percent to 10 percent per year—can double profits.[28]

Traditional Personal Selling	Relationship Selling
Sell products (goods and services)	Sell advice, assistance, and counsel
Focus on closing sales	Focus on improving the customer's bottom line
Limited sales planning	Considers sales planning as top priority
Spend most contact time telling customers about product	Spend most contact time attempting to build a problem-solving environment with the customer
Conduct "product-specific" needs assessment	Conduct discovery in the full scope of the customer's operations
"Lone-wolf" approach to the account	Team approach to the account
Proposals and presentations based on pricing and product features	Proposals and presentations based on profit impact and strategic benefits to the customer
Sales follow-up is short term, focused on product delivery	Sales follow-up is long term, focused on long-term relationship enhancement

Exhibit 18.3
Key Differences Between Traditional Selling and Relationship Selling

Source: Robert M. Peterson, Patrick L. Schul, and George H. Lucas, Jr., "Consultative Selling: Walking the Walk in the New Selling Environment," National Conference on Sales Management, *Proceedings,* March 1996.

Relationship selling is more typical with selling situations for industrial-type goods, such as heavy machinery or computer systems, and services, such as airlines and insurance, than for consumer goods. Exhibit 18.3 lists the key differences between traditional personal selling and relationship or consultative selling. These differences will become more apparent as we explore the personal-selling process later in the chapter.

relationship selling (consultative selling)
Sales practice of building, maintaining, and enhancing interactions with customers in order to develop long-term satisfaction through mutually beneficial partnerships.

SELLING TASKS

The sales field provides many job opportunities, such as selling at the wholesale or retail level, telemarketing, selling a manufactured good, selling a service, or just strengthening sales of the good or service by performing a specific support function. In general, all sales positions can be classified into the three basic types of selling tasks: getting orders, taking orders, and supporting sales.

An **order getter** is someone who actively seeks buyers for a product. An order getter's main task is to convert both prospective and present customers into buyers of the firm's products. To obtain sales, an order getter must aggressively seek prospects and contact existing customers, determine their needs and if the product will meet their needs, propose a solution, and then persuade them to buy. An order getter can be either a member of a company's own sales force or an independent seller. Manufacturing firms often use manufacturers' representatives to sell to wholesalers, distributors, retailers, and sometimes consumers, as with Amway products and Avon cosmetics. Telemarketers also serve as order getters. Many companies set up telemarketing operations as a full-fledged selling arm for dealing with designated customer or product segments.

In contrast, order takers do not have to go out and seek new buyers for their goods or services because, in most cases, buyers come to them or accounts are assigned to them. Order takers can be either inside order takers or field order takers. **Inside or-**

Identify the different types of selling tasks.

order getter
Someone who actively seeks buyers for a product.

inside order taker
Someone who takes orders from customers over the counter, on the sales floor, over the telephone, or by mail.

Ethics in Marketing

Why the Bad Rap?

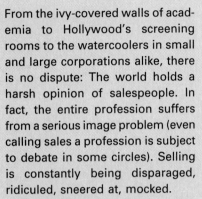

From the ivy-covered walls of academia to Hollywood's screening rooms to the watercoolers in small and large corporations alike, there is no dispute: The world holds a harsh opinion of salespeople. In fact, the entire profession suffers from a serious image problem (even calling sales a profession is subject to debate in some circles). Selling is constantly being disparaged, ridiculed, sneered at, mocked.

Our culture perpetuates, if not inflames, the despicable, greasy, slick, glad-handing image of salespeople. Try recalling a movie or novel in which a salesperson played the hero. Authors, playwrights, movie producers, and TV scriptwriters often stereotype salespeople: Arthur Miller's play *Death of a Salesman* featuring the tired, frustrated Willy Loman; David Mamet's play *Glengarry Glen Ross* portrays real-estate salesmen as slick, ruthless, conniving, cranky, and quota-crazy; and the popular 1970s sitcom "WKRP in Cincinnati" with sales rep Herb Tarlick schmoozing clients, promising plenty, and delivering rarely.

Clearly, the arts have done the sales profession few favors. But the stereotypes and downgrades are cultivated not just by our entertainment producers but by our everyday dialogues. We constantly hear of people "selling out" or being "sold a bill of goods." And you don't brag to mom about being compared to a "used car salesman" or a "traveling salesman." And how many of us want to be "hustled" or "pitched" or "closed?"

For people involved in sales—managers, sales instructors, corporate recruiters, purchasing managers, and, most important, salespeople—the stereotype is no laughing matter. Companies depend on the revenue reps generate to sustain them—and to bankroll the salaries of their nonsales employees. Consumers rely on reps for expertise on products they're thinking of buying and to funnel back their demands for new ones. The best salespeople spot trends before the competition, forecast growth opportunities, warn about downturns, and allow businesses to expand.

A 1995 Gallup poll found most people perceived car sales as the least ethical occupation among 26 careers considered. Insurance salesmen didn't fare much better; they were voted 23rd, ahead of congressmen but behind such folks as lawyers, labor union leaders, and even journalists.

And evidence exists that companies, consumers, and, yes, even salespeople themselves too frequently consider the job of selling in inferior terms. Recruiters admit that many college graduates reluctantly accept positions in sales only after they have been rejected by law schools, medical schools and their own marketing departments. And what's the insinuation when more and more companies no longer even call their salespeople "salespeople"? The trend is to use such euphemisms as *account executive, business manager, marketing rep,* or *customer advocate* in the place of *salesperson.*

Academia also seems to have a misconception of the importance of sales; only two universities in the United States offer an undergraduate major in sales and sales management: The University of Akron and the University of Memphis. Most university administrators view sales as a vocation, not a profession or field of study. And vocations rarely have a place in schools of higher education. Universities—which are in the game of selling and competing for customers like any other institution—would seem to be missing an opportunity to attract the job-conscientious undergrad by offering sales courses. Indications are that the demand for better-educated salespeople is growing. Companies such as Unilever fund salespeople's graduate studies, anticipating that an MBA will give them an edge in the more complex and global sales environment. Schools such as Columbia University, where sales courses have never been offered in its undergraduate and business schools, are filling the demand of sales executives with intense one- and two-week programs in sales and sales management.

Many business-to-business and industrial companies have made an effort to enhance their reps' image—their professionalism—with increased training and education, stricter codes of ethical conduct, and various forms of certification. People involved in sales insist the rep who perfected the wink to go with the "I'll see what I can do for you" died a decade ago with the introduction of strategic-, consultative-, and solution-based selling practices. And they may be right. Problem is, what will it take to convince Hollywood, the general public, academia, future salespeople, and many of today's salespeople that the image is buried?

Yep. A good sales job.

Source: From "Why the Bad Rap?" by Charles Butler, *Sales & Marketing Management,* June 1996. Reprinted by permission of Sales & Marketing Management.

der takers may take orders from customers over the counter, on the sales floor, over the telephone, or by mail. Examples include a cashier in a McDonald's restaurant, a sales clerk in a Macy's department store, and a salesperson for a retail mail-order catalog, such as Dell Computers or J. Crew. **Field order takers** focus on building repeat sales and accepting orders. These order takers visit their customers regularly, check inventory, write up new orders, and then deliver and stock the product for customers. They are normally found in the beer, food, and soft-drink industries. For example, Coca-Cola, Frito-Lay, and Miller Brewing Company all employ field order takers to service their retail customers.

Sales support personnel don't actually sell goods or services. Instead, they promote products through goodwill and after-the-sale customer service. Three important types of support personnel are missionary sales representatives, technical specialists, and selling teams. **Missionary sales representatives** work for manufacturers to stimulate goodwill within the channel of distribution and to support their company's sales efforts. Missionary sales reps are common in consumer packaged-goods industries such as food and drug products. At the retail level, missionary sales reps may set up displays, check the stock and shelf space, and explain new product offerings to retailers. For industrial goods they usually are a communication link between the manufacturer and key accounts. They relay any problems that arise to the manufacturer. Then new products or product applications are passed forward to the customer.

Technical specialists are salespeople with backgrounds in chemistry, engineering, physics, computers, or a similar field. They work out the details of custom-made products and communicate directly with the potential buyer's technical staff. A sales representative may make an initial presentation to a purchasing committee and then let the technical specialist take over during the question-and-answer phase. If the buyer develops an interest in the seller's product, the specialist plays a larger role, planning the product specifications and installation procedures and overseeing the installation. After making the sale, the sales rep usually relies on feedback from the technical specialist about installation dates, debugging time, and similar information.

Team selling has been growing in popularity in recent years as more and more companies embrace relationship selling practices and emphasize long-term relationships, after-the-sale service, and customer satisfaction. A **selling team** can be described as a combination of sales and nonsales people, under the direction of a leader whose primary objective is to establish and maintain strong customer relationships. The sales team may consist of one or more sales representatives, technical specialists, telemarketing reps, administrative assistants, account coordinators, and customer service workers. In fact, all people who in some way support the sales function have a critical impact on a sales force's success. A team approach is most profitable when a prospect represents 10 percent or more of a company's total sales and when a prospect that represents a small part of a company's total sales is actually large enough to buy more. Thus, most large customers are candidates for a selling team. Xerox, for example, uses a team approach for dealing with AT&T, one of its biggest customers. The sales team consists of over 200 salespeople, most at the district level. In addition, experts from other divisions—such as finance, administration, and service specialists—are also members of the team.[29]

A salesperson for a retail mail-order catalog such as J. Crew and Lands' End is an inside order taker.

© 1996 PhotoDisc, Inc.

J. Crew
Lands' End
How are these companies using the Internet in the order-taking process?

http://www.jcrew.com
http://www.landsend.com

field order taker
Someone who visits existing customers regularly, checks inventory, writes up new orders, and then delivers and stocks the product for the customers.

STEPS IN THE SELLING PROCESS

7 List the steps in the selling process.

missionary sales representative
Someone who works for a manufacturer to stimulate goodwill within the channel of distribution and to support the company's sales efforts.

technical specialist
Sales support person with a technical background who works out the details of custom-made products and communicates directly with the potential buyer's technical staff.

selling team
A group of sales and non-sales people, under the direction of a leader, whose primary objective is to establish and maintain a strong relationship with a particular customer or customers.

sales process (sales cycle)
The set of steps a salesperson goes through in a particular organization to sell a particular product or service.

Although personal selling may sound like a relatively simple task, completing a sale actually requires several steps. The **sales process,** or **sales cycle,** is simply the set of steps a salesperson goes through in a particular organization to sell a particular product or service. The sales process or cycle can be unique for each product or service, depending on the features of the product or service, characteristics of customer segments, and internal processes in place within the firm, such as how leads are gathered.

Some sales take only a few minutes, but others may take months or years to complete, especially when selling customized goods or services. Whether a salesperson spends a few minutes or a few years on a sale, these are the seven basic steps in the personal selling process:

1. Generating leads
2. Qualifying sales leads
3. Doing a needs assessment
4. Developing and proposing solutions
5. Handling objections
6. Closing the sale
7. Following up

Like other forms of promotion, these steps of selling follow the AIDA concept (see Chapter 16). Once a salesperson has located a prospect with the authority to buy, he or she tries to get the prospect's attention. A thorough needs assessment turned into an effective sales proposal and presentation should generate interest. After developing the customer's initial desire (preferably during the presentation of the sales proposal), the salesperson seeks action in the close by trying to get an agreement to buy. Follow-up after the sale, the final step in the selling process, not only lowers cognitive dissonance (refer back to Chapter 7) but also may open up opportunities to discuss future sales. Effective follow-up will also lead to repeat business in which the process may start all over again at the needs assessment step.

Traditional selling and relationship selling follow these same basic steps. What is different between the two selling methods is the relative importance placed on key steps in the process (see Exhibit 18.4). Traditional selling efforts focus on generat-

Exhibit 18.4
Relative Amount of Time Spent in Key Steps of the Selling Process

Key Selling Steps	Traditional Selling	Relationship/Consultative Selling
Generating leads	High	Low
Qualifying leads	Low	High
Doing a needs assessment	Low	High
Developing solutions	Low	High
Proposing solutions through a sales presentation	High	Low
Closing the sale	High	Low
Following up	Low	High

ing as many leads as possible, making presentations and closing sales; that is, getting the customer's signature on the order form. Minimal effort is placed on asking questions to identify customer needs and wants or matching these needs and wants to the benefits of the product or service. In contrast, the salesperson practicing relationship selling emphasizes an up-front investment in the time and effort needed to uncover each customer's specific needs and wants and matching them, as closely as possible, to the product or service offering. By doing their homework up front, the salesperson creates the conditions necessary for a relatively straightforward close.[30]

Let's look at each step of the selling process individually.

Generating Leads

Initial groundwork must precede communication between the potential buyer and the salesperson. **Lead generation,** or **prospecting,** is the identification of those firms and people most likely to buy the seller's offerings. These firms or people become "sales leads" or "prospects." Naturally, not everyone is a prospect for a firm's good or service, nor are all prospects equally likely to buy. It is important for the relationship salesperson to attract the right kind of customer for the relationship. Customers' accounts must be large enough to warrant the additional time and effort the relationship salesperson must invest.[31]

Sales leads are secured in several different ways:

- *Advertising and other media* are the foremost ways of securing leads. Advertisements are usually placed in trade publications or in some other highly targeted media vehicle, such as cable television. A coupon or a toll-free number is usually provided for the prospect who would like to request more information.

- Many sales professionals are also securing valuable leads from their firm's *Internet Web site.* Web surfers visiting a company site often have the opportunity to submit a request to have a salesperson follow up with more information concerning the firm's products or services. By knowing what other sites potential customers like to visit, a firm can gather more leads by setting up a hot link or ad in those areas, linking Internet surfers directly to the firm's site.[32]

- Favorable *publicity* also helps to create leads. Readers often call or write to publications and television stations inquiring about products of companies they have read about in recent articles or seen in the news.

- *Direct-mail and telemarketing programs* have become popular ways of generating sales leads. This type of lead generation usually starts with a list of potential clients with desirable characteristics, such as a particular occupation. For instance, if a medical equipment company is trying to sell a new piece of equipment used in heart surgery, it may start with a list of all cardiologists in the United States. With these sorts of programs, companies might send direct-mail letters or brochures, usually with a detachable coupon to be returned or an 800 number to be called for more information. Some companies employ telemarketing representatives who use client lists to contact potential customers by telephone.

- **Cold calling** is a form of lead generation in which the salesperson approaches potential buyers without any prior knowledge of the prospects' needs or financial status. This method is typically used with consumer-type goods, such as long-distance telephone service and encyclopedias.

- Another way to gather a lead is through a **referral**—a recommendation from a customer or business associate. **Networking** is the related method of using friends, business contacts, coworkers, acquaintances, and fellow members in professional and civic organizations to find out about potential clients. For example, an insurance agent may rely heavily on networking with neighbors, members of his or her church, or members of community organizations to locate new prospects. Sales

lead generation (prospecting)
Identification of those firms and people most likely to buy the seller's offerings.

cold calling
Form of lead generation in which the salesperson approaches potential buyers without any prior knowledge of the prospects' needs or financial status.

referral
Recommendation to a salesperson from a customer or business associate.

networking
Process of finding out about potential clients from friends, business contacts, coworkers, acquaintances, and fellow members in professional and civic organizations.

representatives selling noncompeting lines and company employees who are not in sales positions are also good sources of leads. For example, a company might encourage employees to look for sales leads when they're not at work. Employees who secure the most leads in a given time frame may then be eligible for a prize.

- *Trade shows and conventions* are yet another good source of leads. Because these events are designed around the interests of a specific product or industry, most of the leads generated are very likely prospects.

- *Company records* of past client purchases are another excellent source of leads.

Qualifying Sales Leads

When a prospect shows interest in learning more about a product, the salesperson has the opportunity to follow up, or qualify, the lead. Personally visiting unqualified prospects wastes valuable salesperson time and company resources. **Lead qualification** consists of determining whether the prospect has three things:[33]

- *A recognized need:* The most basic criterion for determining whether or not someone is a prospect for a product is a need that is not being satisfied. The salesperson should first consider prospects who are aware of a need but should not discount prospects who have not yet recognized that they have one. With a little more information about the product, they may decide they do have a need for it. Determining whether or not a prospect has a need for a product is not always an easy task. Preliminary interviews and questioning can often provide the salesperson with enough information to determine if there is a need. Some goods and services, however, are designed to meet intangible needs, such as prestige or status, which are hard to detect.

- *Buying power:* Buying power involves both authority to make the purchase decision and access to funds to pay for it. To avoid wasting time and money, the salesperson needs to identify the purchasing authority before making a presentation. An organization chart can provide valuable clues. Asking a switchboard operator or a secretary can also lead the salesperson in the right direction. If the salesperson is still uncertain, he or she can ask a simple, direct question to qualify a prospect—for example, "Can you sign the purchase order for this product?" In some cases, purchasing authority rests with a committee. The salesperson must then identify the most influential committee members. In other situations, buying authority may rest with a regional or headquarters officer located in a distant city. Determining ability to pay is often easier. Information about a firm's credit standing can be obtained from Dun & Bradstreet credit ratings or other financial reporting services. For smaller concerns, a local credit bureau can provide the needed information. A salesperson should heed this advice: It is better to qualify ability to pay now than to be left with an unpaid invoice months later.

- *Receptivity and accessibility:* The prospect must be willing to see and be accessible to the salesperson. Some prospects simply refuse to see salespeople. Others, because of their stature in their organization, will only see a salesperson or sales manager with similar stature.

Often the task of lead qualification is handled by a telemarketing group or a sales support person who *prequalifies* the lead for the salesperson. Prequalification systems free sales representatives from the time-consuming task of following up on leads to determine need, buying power, and receptiveness. Prequalification systems may even set up initial appointments with the prospect for the salesperson. The result is more time for the sales force to spend in front of customers. Robot Research, a San Diego–based manufacturer of closed-circuit video surveillance equipment, implemented a formal telemarketing program to prequalify leads for its sales force. Consequently, the sales force has jumped from following up on 8 to 9 percent to 80 percent of the leads handed over to them from the telemarketing staff.[34]

Doing a Needs Assessment

The salesperson's ultimate goal in a **needs assessment** is to find out as much as possible about the prospect's situation. This involves interviewing the customer to determine his or her specific needs and wants and the range of options the customer has for satisfying them. The salesperson should determine how to maximize the fit between what he or she can offer and what the prospective customer wants. As part of the needs assessment, the consultative salesperson must know everything there is to know about:[35]

- *The product or service:* Product knowledge is the cornerstone for conducting a successful needs analysis. That is, the consultative salesperson must be an expert on his or her product or service. How and where is it made? What are the technical specifications and do they meet the customer's requirements? What are the product's features and benefits, and what benefits can they provide the customer? What are the pricing and billing procedures? What kinds of warranty and service support are provided? How does the product's performance compare with the competition's? What experiences have other customers had with the product or service? What message is the company's current advertising and promotional campaigns delivering?

- *The customer and its needs:* When it comes to customers, the salespeople should know more about them than they know about themselves. That's the secret to relationship and consultative selling, where the salesperson acts not only as a supplier of products and services, but also as a trusted consultant and advisor. The professional salesperson doesn't just sell products. He or she brings to each client business-building ideas and solutions to problems. For the customer, consulting a professional salesperson is like having another vital person on the team at no cost. For example, one of the jobs of field representatives for SmithKline Beecham, a pharmaceutical company, is to gather information about their prospects, such as who is the decision maker, who influences him or her, and who are the front-desk contact people. The reps also record important information about the laboratories they call on, such as the size and the type of equipment available. Even though profiling customers requires some extra effort, most of SmithKline Beecham's reps like having the information when the time comes to plan the next sales call.[36]

- *The competition:* Who are the competitors and what is known about them? What are their products and services like and how do they compare? What are their advantages and disadvantages? What are their strengths and weaknesses? The salesperson must know as much about the competitor's company and products as he or she knows about his or her own company.

- *The industry:* Knowing the industry involves active research on the part of the salesperson. This means attending industry and trade association meetings, reading articles published in industry and trade journals, keeping track of legislation and regulation that affect the industry, being aware of product alternatives and innovations from domestic and foreign competition, and having a feel for economic and financial conditions that may impact the industry.

needs assessment
Determination of the customer's specific needs and wants and the range of options a customer has for satisfying them.

Developing and Proposing Solutions

Once the salesperson has gathered the appropriate information about the client's needs and wants, the next step is to determine whether his or her company's products or services match the needs of the prospective customer. The salesperson then develops a solution, or possibly several solutions, in which the salesperson's product or service solves the client's problems or meets a specific need.

These solutions are typically presented to the client in the form of a sales proposal presented at a sales presentation. A **sales proposal** is a written document or professional presentation that outlines how the company's product or service will meet or exceed the client's needs. The **sales presentation** is the formal meeting in which the salesperson has the opportunity to present the sales proposal. Because the salesperson often has only one opportunity to present a sales proposal, the quality of both the sales proposal and presentation can make or break the sale. The salesperson must be able to present the proposal and handle any customer objections confidently and professionally. If the salesperson doesn't have a convincing and confident manner, then the prospect will very often forget the information. Prospects take in body language, voice patterns, dress, and body type. In fact, they are more likely to remember how salespeople present themselves than what salespeople say.[37]

There are two basic approaches to making a presentation: stimulus-response and need-satisfaction. The second approach is most closely aligned with relationship selling.

The Stimulus-Response Approach

The **stimulus-response approach** recognizes that a given stimulus will produce a given response (see Chapter 6). When applied to a selling situation, this term means that the salesperson makes certain points (stimulus) about the good or service that ultimately lead to a sale (response). This approach is used most often in traditional personal-selling situations.

A memorized or **prepared sales presentation** lends itself to the stimulus-response approach. Many telephone sales pitches follow this structured or "canned" format. Advantages of the canned approach are that it ensures that the salesperson will tell a complete, accurate story about the product; that sales points will be arranged in a logical, systematic order; and that it addresses most or all potential objections.

However, the canned approach also has its drawbacks. Perhaps the biggest disadvantage is that it does not allow the salesperson to adapt the presentation to the prospect. Therefore, the salesperson and presentation may seem artificial and mechanical. The canned approach is rather inflexible and discourages the prospect's participation. A salesperson may even have trouble "resuming the pitch" if interrupted by the prospect.

The Need-Satisfaction Approach

In contrast, the **need-satisfaction approach** recognizes that people buy products to satisfy needs and solve problems. A salesperson employing this approach uses the prospect's particular needs as a springboard for the sales presentation. The salesperson begins by securing the prospect's agreement that a need exists and then offers a solution to satisfy the need. Altering the presentation to suit each prospect in response to the specific sales situation is called **adaptive selling.** This approach is most often used when the salesperson has a complex product line and is selling to a sophisticated audience.

The advantage of the need-satisfaction approach is its strong marketing and relationship orientation. It is designed to meet the needs of the marketplace and to build long-term relationships with the customer. Because of its relationship-marketing orientation, the need-satisfaction approach stresses solutions and how the product can provide solutions, not the physical aspects of the product.

The need-satisfaction approach requires salespeople to perform a needs assessment to understand customer needs, the competition, and the industry. The salesperson must be able to then match the product or service to the client's needs, present all

sales proposal
A formal written document or professional presentation that outlines how the salesperson's product or service will meet or exceed the prospect's needs.

sales presentation
Face-to-face explanation of the sales proposal to a prospective buyer.

stimulus-response approach
Sales pitch applying the concept that a given stimulus will produce a given response.

prepared sales presentation
Structured, or canned, sales pitch.

need-satisfaction approach
Sales pitch that focuses on satisfying a prospective buyer's particular needs.

adaptive selling
Sales technique using a pitch adapted for each prospect in response to the specific sales situation.

possible solutions, and then recommend the solution that is in the best interest of the customer. The need-satisfaction approach, therefore, requires much more time and considerably more skill than other approaches do. The skills needed for the need-satisfaction approach are focused toward listening and questioning rather than talking. The wise salesperson would not dare jeopardize the relationship by utilizing high-pressure sales techniques to force a premature sale. In contrast, the successful consultative salesperson uses the presentation time to advance the relationship with the client in concert with the buyer's preferences and time line for making a decision.[38] By building a personal and professional relationship with the client, the salesperson becomes more of a partner or a consultant than just another salesperson peddling some good or service.

 The need-satisfaction approach to sales presentations is very important in Japan, where long-term relationships between seller and customer are the norm. The Japanese traditionally do business only with those they know and trust. Toyota, for example, has more than 100,000 salespeople selling cars, primarily door to door. These salespeople maintain constant contact with customers. A sale typically requires a series of face-to-face meetings. Toyota salespeople call after a purchase to inquire how the car is running and send handwritten greeting cards and special invitations for low-cost oil changes and dealer events. Clients usually purchase cars from the same salesperson many times over many years.[39]

Handling Objections

Rarely does a prospect say "I'll buy it" right after a presentation. Often, there are objections raised or perhaps questions about the proposal and the product. For instance, the potential buyer may insist that the price is too high, that he or she does not have enough information to make a decision, or that the good or service will not satisfy the present need. The buyer may also lack confidence in the seller's organization or product.

One of the first lessons that every salesperson learns is that objections to the product should not be taken personally as confrontations or insults. Rather, a salesperson should view objections as requests for information. A good salesperson handles objections calmly and considers them a legitimate part of the purchase decision. Anticipating specific objections, such as concerns about price, is the best way to prepare for them.

Closing the Sale

At the end of the presentation, the salesperson should ask the customer how he or she would like to proceed. If the customer exhibits signs that he or she is ready to purchase and all questions have been answered and objections have been met, then the salesperson can try to close the sale. Customers often give signals during or after the presentation that they are ready to buy or are not interested. Examples include changes in facial expressions, gestures, and questions asked. The salesperson should look for these signals and respond appropriately.

Closing requires courage and skill. Naturally, the salesperson wants to avoid rejection, and asking for a sale carries with it the risk of a negative answer. A salesperson should keep an open mind when asking for the sale and be prepared for either a yes or a no. Rarely is a sale closed on the first call. In fact, a salesperson averages about four sales contacts before a sale can be made.[40] Some salespeople may negotiate with large accounts for several years before closing a sale. As you can see, building a good relationship with the customer is very important. Often, if the salesperson has developed a strong relationship with the customer, only minimal efforts are needed to close a sale.

negotiation
Process of both the salesperson and the prospect offering special concessions in an attempt to arrive at a sales agreement.

Often, negotiation plays a key role in the closing of the sale. **Negotiation** is the process of both the salesperson and the prospect offering special concessions in an attempt to arrive at a sales agreement. For example, the salesperson may offer a price cut, free installation, free service, or a trial order. Effective negotiators, however, avoid using price as a negotiation tool since cutting price directly affects the bottom line. Instead, effective salespeople emphasize the value of the product to the customer, rendering price a nonissue.[41]

More and more U.S. companies are expanding their marketing and selling efforts into global markets. Salespeople selling in foreign markets should tailor their presentation and closing styles to each market. For instance, in German-speaking countries—such as Germany, Austria, and parts of Switzerland—salespeople should expect a sober, rigid business climate and negotiations that lack flexibility and compromise. Negotiations with Central and South American customers typically include a great deal of bargaining. Personal relationships are also important in Central and South America, so salespeople should make face-to-face contact with their clients during meetings and presentations.[42] The Chinese tend to be extremely meticulous, looking to create long-term relationships with a supplier before agreeing to buy anything. Most deals in China are finalized in a social setting, either over drinks or dinner.[43] Read about other global dos and don't of selling in the "Global Perspectives" box.

Following Up

follow-up
Final step of the selling process, in which the salesperson ensures that delivery schedules are met, that the goods or services perform as promised, and that the buyers' employees are properly trained to use the products.

Unfortunately, many salespeople hold the attitude that making the sale is all that's important. Once the sale is made, they can forget about their customers. They are wrong. Salespeoples' responsibilities do not end with making the sales and placing the orders. One of the most important aspects of their jobs is **follow-up.** They must ensure that delivery schedules are met, that the goods or services perform as promised, and that the buyers' employees are properly trained to use the products.

While the traditional sales approach's extent of follow-up with the customer is generally limited to successful product delivery and performance, a basic goal of relationship selling is to motivate customers to come back, again and again, by developing and nurturing long-term relationships. Most businesses depend on repeat sales, and repeat sales depend on thorough and continued follow-up by the salesperson. Finding a new customer is far more expensive than retaining an existing customer. When customers feel abandoned, cognitive dissonance arises and repeat sales decline. Today, this issue is more pertinent than ever because customers are far less loyal to brands and vendors. Buyers are more inclined to look for the best deal, especially in the case of poor after-the-sale follow-up. More and more buyers favor building a relationship with sellers.

SALES MANAGEMENT

8 Describe the functions of sales management.

There is an old adage in business that nothing happens until a sale is made. Without sales there is no need for accountants, production workers, or even a company president. Sales provide the fuel that keeps the corporate engines humming. Companies like West Point Pepperel, Dow Corning, Alcoa, and several thousand other industrial manufacturers would cease to exist without successful salespeople or manufacturers' representatives. Even companies like Procter & Gamble and Kraft General Foods, which mainly sell consumer goods and use extensive advertising campaigns, still rely on salespeople to move products through the channel of distribution. Thus, sales management is one of marketing's most critical specialties. Effective sales management stems from a highly success-oriented sales force that accomplishes its mission economically and efficiently. Poor sales management can lead to unmet profit objectives or even to the downfall of the corporation.

Global Perspectives

Global Dos and Don'ts in Selling

Most large companies with operations on foreign soil are employing locals to sell their products; international buyers are often cold to Americans trying to peddle their wares. So the American who finds him- or herself trying to sell internationally had better be prepared.

Most selling skills that are successful in America also will work overseas. But knowing how to act in certain cultures can be the difference between closing the deal and losing a customer. There are certain things Americans take for granted that could easily cost them a deal overseas. A simple thumbs-up sign that we give every day could offend a customer in another country. Here are some things to watch out for in certain countries around the world.

Arab Countries: Don't use your left hand to hold, offer, or receive materials because Arabs use their left hand to touch toilet paper. If you must use your left hand to write, apologize for doing so.

China: Don't refuse tea during a business discussion. Always drink it, even if you're offered a dozen cups a day. Also, printed materials presented to Chinese business leaders should be in black and white, since colors have great significance for the Chinese. Never begin to eat or drink before your host does in China.

France: Don't schedule a breakfast meeting—the French tend not to meet until after 10 A.M.

Germany: Don't address a business associate by his or her first name, even if you've known each other for years. Always wait for an invitation to do so. Also, breakfast meetings are unheard of here, too.

Latin America: People here don't take the clock too seriously—scheduling more than two appointments in one day can prove disastrous.

Japan: Don't bring up business on the golf course—always wait for your host to take the initiative.

Don't cross your legs in Japan—showing the bottom of the foot is insulting.

Mexico: Don't send a bouquet of red or yellow flowers as a gift—Mexicans associate those colors with evil spirits and death. Instead, send a box of premium chocolates.

Vietnam: When meeting a Vietnamese woman, wait for her to extend a hand first—she may simply nod or bow slightly, the most common form of greeting in Vietnam. Vietnamese do not like to be touched or patted on the back or shoulders in social situations.

Miscellaneous: The thumbs-up gesture is considered offensive in the Middle East, rude in Australia, and a sign of "OK" in France. It's rude to cross your arms while facing someone in Turkey. In the Middle East don't ask, "How's the family?"—it's considered too personal. In most Asian countries, staring directly into a person's eyes is considered discourteous.[44]

Just as selling is a personal relationship, so is sales management. Although the sales manager's basic job is to maximize sales at a reasonable cost while also maximizing profits, he or she also has many other important responsibilities and decisions. The tasks of sales management are to:

1. Define sales objectives and the sales process
2. Design the sales organization
3. Develop the sales force
4. Direct the sales force
5. Evaluate the sales force

Let's look at each of these tasks.

Defining Sales Objectives and the Sales Process

Effective sales management begins with a determination of sales goals. Without goals to achieve, salesperson performance would be mediocre, at best, and the company would likely fail. Therefore, setting sales goals is one of the sales manager's most important jobs. Likewise, management is responsible for prescribing the process salespeople follow to most efficiently achieve the desired sales goals.

Setting Strategic Sales Objectives

Like any marketing objective, sales objectives should be stated in clear, precise, and measurable terms and should always specify a time frame for their fulfillment. Overall sales force objectives are usually stated in terms of desired dollar sales volume, market share, or profit level. For example, a life insurance company may have an objective to sell $50 million in life insurance policies annually, to attain a 12 percent market share, or to achieve $1 million in profits.

quota
Statement of the individual salesperson's sales objectives, usually based on sales volume alone but sometimes including key accounts (those with greatest potential), new accounts, and specific products.

Individual salespeople are also assigned objectives in the form of quotas. A **quota** is simply a statement of the salesperson's sales objectives, usually based on sales volume alone but sometimes including key accounts (those with greatest potential), new accounts, repeat sales, and specific products. In addition, quotas can be based on activity or on financial objectives. For example, a sales representative for a cellular phone company may have the sales quota of selling $1,000 worth of equipment or five new cellular systems per week. He or she may also have the objective of completing a certain number of sales calls per week. Many firms, especially those that are practicing relationship selling, place more emphasis on financial objectives that require the salespeople to take into account the profit contribution of the products they sell. Those products yielding higher profits for the company will thus receive more attention.

Defining the Sales Process

Great sales managers don't just focus on sales goals, but on the entire process that drives their sales organizations to reach those goals. Without a keen understanding of the sales process, a manager will never be successful—no matter how well defined the sales goals or how great the sales reps. Having talented and hard-working salespeople isn't enough. Managers must put systems in place to help them win. An important responsibility of the sales manager, therefore, is to determine the most effective and efficient sales process to follow in selling each different product and service.

While the basic steps of the sales process are the same as discussed earlier in the chapter (i.e., lead generation, needs assessment, proposal creation and presentation, closing and follow-up), a manager must formally define the specific procedures salespeople go through to do their jobs—what do they do to get from step to step in making a sale. Unfortunately, many managers find that reps follow no specific sales process at all. Often this is due to the fact that the company has never defined a sales process for its reps to follow. Other times, it is a result of little formal sales training. With no formal sales process to follow, sales reps are often reactionary rather than proactive to customer needs.

Determining the specific sales process needed involves knowing customers' buying processes (How do your customers want you to sell to them?) and interviewing sales reps to identify current sales cycle steps (What steps do your sales reps currently use to sell your product?). For example, after sales started to slip at Ralston Purina Company, sales management looked at the sales process its reps were following by surveying customers. What customers complained about most were that the sales reps didn't take time to understand their business, service calls were transferred too many times, and invoicing was atrocious. As a result, Ralston Purina's sales process was realigned to include all functions of the company's business. Representatives from marketing, logistics, sales, finance, and manufacturing were placed into sales teams to reduce the number of handoffs in the sales process. Having members on the team from all functional areas of the company also allows the company to present the whole Ralston package and uncover customer needs from all angles.[45]

Designing the Sales Organization

Because personal selling is so costly, no sales department can afford to be disorganized. Therefore, structuring the sales department or sales force and determining the size of the sales force are essential. Proper design helps the sales manager organize and delegate sales duties and provide direction for salespeople.

Determining Sales Force Structure

Sales departments are most commonly organized into the five types described and diagrammed below. Firms often combine these types.

- *Geographic organization:* A common method for organizing the sales force is assigning a salesperson to a particular geographic area called a **sales territory**—for instance, a region, state, city, or other trading area. A firm such as a consumer product organization with a small number of closely related, nontechnical products might use this method. Geographically structured sales departments are most appropriate when customers are widely dispersed or when there are large regional differences in customer buying behavior. For example, sales of snow tires in southern states would not warrant the creation of separate sales territories, but they would in northern states.

sales territory
Particular geographic area assigned to a salesperson.

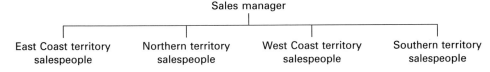

- *Product organization:* Another common method is structuring the sales organization by the product or brand that the salesperson sells. Structuring the sales force in this manner is most appropriate when products are complex, the differences between them are great, and the products or product groups are important enough to justify special attention. A sales force organized by product has greater knowledge of and expertise in specific product categories. Office equipment specialists are a good example of this structuring method.

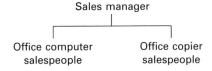

- *Functional organization:* A sales department organized by function focuses on needed sales activities, such as account development or account maintenance. This structure offers specialization and efficiency in performing selling activities and is best for companies selling only a few or very similar products to relatively few target markets. Because it requires more labor, this form of organization is difficult for very small firms to maintain. However, it can work well in medium-sized to large firms. These firms can afford the luxury of having their salespeople perform only one task or a small number of tasks. For example, many paper manufacturers employ representatives who work solely on selling to major clients. After the negotiations have been completed, service salespeople step in to take care of clients' postsale needs.

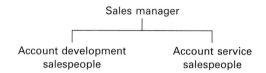

- *Market organization:* In this approach, the sales force is divided by customer groups, or target markets. A market orientation is most appropriate when customer needs and product purchases vary considerably from one target group to another. This method is also used when there is a great need to identify and solve different customer problems. For example, Eastman Kodak recently reorganized its sales force after realizing it was overextending its sales reps. Required to be familiar with more than 60 types of film for commercial labs, wedding and portrait labs, and professional resellers, Kodak reps were finding it difficult to call on such diverse groups of customers with such diverse needs. After careful analysis, Kodak realigned its sales force into nine distinct groups based on market segments: three for commercial services and six for portrait/wedding and photographers'/resellers' accounts. Salespeople were then assigned territories based upon the technical knowledge and marketing skills that would be required for different market segments. As a result of being able to focus on one type of customer, sales reps can pay more attention to market trends and help solve customer problems.[46]

- *Key account organization:* Many companies have taken the market-oriented structure one step further to an individual client or account level. This trend has occurred in conjunction with the increased emphasis on relationship selling. The organization typically assigns one salesperson or a team of salespeople to a client to provide better customer service. By reorganizing the sales force around customers, many companies hope to improve customer service, encourage collaboration with other arms of the company, and unite salespeople into customer-focused sales teams.

Determining Sales Force Size

Another task of designing the sales organization includes determining the ideal size of the sales force. Sales managers can use several methods to determine the number of salespeople needed. In the **workload approach,** the sales manager divides the total time required to cover a particular sales territory by the selling time provided by each salesperson. The major advantage of the workload approach is its simplicity. Successful application of the technique depends on the sales manager's ability to estimate the ideal frequency of calls and the number of potential customers. However, the workload approach fails to consider either the cost of increasing the workforce or the costs and profits associated with each sales call.

A second method for determining the optimal size of the sales force is the **incremental productivity approach.** According to this approach, a manager should increase the number of salespeople as long as the additional sales increase is greater than the additional increase in selling cost. Companies with good records know the

workload approach
Method of determining the optimal sales force size in which the total time required to cover the territory is divided by the selling time available to one salesperson.

incremental productivity approach
Method of determining the optimal sales force size in which salespeople are added as long as the total sales increase is greater than the increase in selling cost.

cost of training a salesperson. This cost, plus field expenses and the salary of a new person, can be compared with the revenue generated by sales activities. Unfortunately, many companies do not have these cost data available.

Sales managers rarely rely on a single method to determine sales force size. Instead, they combine their own opinions on other issues—such as economic factors, industry trends, growth of the market, and the needs of customers—with these formula methods to come up with the optimal size.

Developing the Sales Force

The sales manager has set goals, developed the sales process which salespeople will follow to achieve the goals, and designed the structure of the sales force in terms of territories and size. Now it is time to start setting this planning in motion by developing the individuals who will comprise an outstanding sales force. Developing the sales force involves recruiting and hiring the best salespeople to sell the firm's products. It also entails initial effective training of the sales force as well as ongoing training.

Recruiting the Sales Force

Sales force recruitment should be based on an accurate, detailed description of the sales task as defined by the company. The sales manager should then develop the job description to match the sales force objectives. From the job description, the sales manager should build a profile of the ideal candidate for the job. The profile may include such things as level of education, employment background and level of experience, stability of employment history, ability to work unsupervised and to travel, knowledge of sales techniques and previous sales training, level of oral and written communication skills and organization skills, and previous compensation.

Aside from the usual characteristics specified in the candidate profile, what traits should sales managers look for in applicants? What traits help ensure that a recruit will become an effective salesperson? The most important quality of top performers is that they are driven by their own goals. That is, they usually set personal goals higher than those management sets for them. Moreover, they are achievement-oriented, they talk about their sales accomplishments, and they are self-confident. Effective salespeople are also self-competitive; they keep close tabs on their own performance and compare it with their previous performance. They are optimistic, highly knowledgeable about the product, and assertive. They know how to listen to customers and are team players who support their coworkers. They are self-trainers who are continually engaged in upgrading their selling skills. The way sales candidates close the employment interview suggests how they will close a sale. Do they ask the manager how and when they are to follow up for the position or what the next step will be? Effective salespeople always plan the next step before they leave the client's office. Exhibit 18.5 also lists some basic qualities a manager might look for if focusing on relationship selling.

Training the Sales Force

After the sales recruit has been hired and given a brief orientation, training begins. A new salesperson generally receives instruction in five major areas: company policies and practices, selling techniques, product knowledge, industry and customer characteristics, and nonselling duties, such as filling out market information reports. A good training program boosts confidence, improves morale, increases sales, and builds better customer relations. Classroom instruction may last several days for company policies and several weeks or months for actual sales techniques. Trainees are taught everything from how to prospect to how to service the account after the sale.

Exhibit 18.5

Five Qualities of a Relationship Salesperson

Customer orientation (intent)	• Understands the buyer's needs and places them on par with his or her own needs (and the organization's) • Gives fair and balanced presentations (pros and cons) and clear statements of benefits • Advises rather than "sells"
Competence (ability)	• Displays technical command of products and applications • Possesses the skill, knowledge, time, and resources to do what is promised and what the buyer wants • Uses words and actions that are consistent with a professional "image"
Dependability (actions)	• Actions fulfill prior verbal promises • Actions fit a pattern of previously established dependable actions • Refuses to promise what he or she can't deliver
Candor (words)	• Presentations are balanced and fair such that the product limitations as well as the advantages are discussed • What the salesperson says agrees with what the buyer knows to be true • Uses credible proof to support words • Subsequent events prove statements to be true
Likeability	• Makes efficient use of the buyer's time • Is courteous and polite • Shares and talks with the buyer about areas of commonality, including goals and interests (extends to nonbusiness topics)

Source: Thomas N. Ingram, "Relationship Selling: Moving from Rhetoric to Reality," *Mid-American Journal of Business,* January 1997, p. 10.

Firms that sell complex products generally offer the most extensive training programs. New salespeople in Kodak's Health Science Division, which sells medical imaging equipment, receive a minimum six-month-long formal education. Trainees first come to Kodak's Marketing Education Center for six weeks of academics, where they

Constant training helps Dell Computer maintain its edge. Employees go through a five-week training program that includes coursework and exercises such as unpacking a computer.

© 1992 Robb Kendrick

learn Kodak's philosophy and basic selling skills. Then they are sent into the field with a mentor for a week. Because many of the new salespeople have no background in health care, exposure to the hospital environment is absolutely vital. Trainees then come back to the center for four weeks of intensive technical training and lessons in business and selling skills. After this, trainees are sent back into the field for eight weeks to put their new knowledge and skills to use. Once trainees graduate, they spend an additional six months in the field selling with their mentors. At the end of that six months, almost a full year after beginning the training program, the salesperson receives a territory.[47]

Most successful sales organizations have learned that training is not just for newly hired salespeople. Instead, training is offered to all salespeople in an ongoing effort to hone selling skills and relationship building. In pursuit of solid salesperson-client relationships, companies like Toshibia offer training programs to improve salespeople's consultative selling and listening skills and to broaden their product and customer knowledge. In addition, training programs stress the interpersonal skills needed to become the contact person for customers. Because negotiation is increasingly important in closing a sale, salespeople are also trained to negotiate effectively without risking profits. Finally, many companies are teaching basic selling techniques to employees who do not sell but who are part of the selling team—for example, engineers and customer-service personnel. Exposing these employees to the selling basics gives them a better understanding of how they can support the sales staff. Exhibit 18.6 lists the most popular ongoing training subjects.

Toshiba
What is the mission statement of the Toshiba National Sales Training Department? What sales training opportunities do they offer for their dealers?

http://www.toshiba.com/tacp

Training is becoming increasingly important to companies that manage sales forces in foreign countries. FedEx's sheer size and international reach, for example, dictate that it make training a top priority at strategic locations around the globe. All of the company's approximately 2,000 salespeople must be prepared to provide international transportation expertise to a variety of customers. Recruits in Asia and Europe, where the FedEx name is not as well known as it is here, are brought to Memphis headquarters to give them a better understanding of the

What Courses Sales Managers Think Their Salespeople Should Be Taking:	
Consultative selling	47%
Listening skills	29
Time management	24
Product knowledge	21
Negotiation	19
Closing	19
Presentation skills	14
Handling objections	13
Prospecting	5
Networking	4

Source: *Sales & Marketing Management*, April 1995, p. 39.

Exhibit 18.6
Popular Sales Training Courses

company. New salespeople are able to see how the superhub works and to get a sense of the size and scope of FedEx's service. They also hear from the company's founder, who talks to them about the company's strategies and the challenges of the global marketplace.[48]

Directing the Sales Force

Directing the sales force requires the unique skills of the sales manager. The ideal sales manager must possess analytical skills while also playing the role of motivator and cheerleader. While the sales manager's job in reality will include many more duties than discussed in this section, directing the sales force generally encompasses compensation planning, motivating salespeople to reach their goals, and effective leadership.

Compensation Planning

Compensation planning is one of the sales manager's toughest jobs. Only good planning will ensure that compensation attracts, motivates, and retains good salespeople. Generally, companies and industries with lower levels of compensation suffer higher turnover rates, which increases costs and decreases effectiveness. Therefore, compensation needs to be competitive enough to attract and motivate the best salespeople. Other firms tie compensation to their quarterly, yearly, or long-range sales and marketing plan. With this method, the firm can easily encourage its salespeople to carry out the company's overall objectives because it has created a compensation program that balances the interests of the company and those of the sales force.[49]

Many firms also take profit into account when developing their compensation plans. Instead of paying salespeople on overall volume, they pay according to the profitability achieved from selling each product. Still other companies tie a part of the salesperson's total compensation to customer satisfaction. A recent survey found that 26 percent of companies surveyed were specifically rewarding customer satisfaction in their sales compensation programs.[50] IBM, for example, ties sales bonuses to customer satisfaction (40 percent of the bonus) and the profitability of each sales transaction (60 percent). Local IBM managers survey customers frequently to measure satisfaction. They ask customers not just how happy they are with what they bought but also if the IBM salesperson is keeping up to date with what's going on at each customer's site. To help salespeople determine profit when negotiating a deal, IBM developed special computer software that gives each salesperson a complete profit picture at the point of sale.[51]

The three basic compensation methods for salespeople are commission, salary, and combination plans. A typical commission plan gives salespeople a specified percentage of their sales revenue. However, if the plan is a **straight commission** system, the salesperson receives no compensation at all until a sale is made. As a result, management often lacks control over straight commission paid to sales representatives. In addition, straight-commission salespeople normally have little loyalty to the company and are reluctant to perform nonselling activities that do not generate commissions. Firms with limited resources and those selling high-priced items typically use commission plans for at least part of the compensation package.

As its name suggests, a **straight salary** system compensates salespeople with a stated salary regardless of their productivity. While filling out information reports, servicing accounts, calling on smaller customers, and performing other nonselling tasks are undesirable to the commission salesperson, the salaried salesperson can tolerate these tasks. The straight-salary plan works effectively when customers require an extensive amount of postsale service or the sales organization is focused on relationship-selling techniques. In addition, in firms that use a team approach or that rely on missionary

straight commission
Method of compensation in which the salesperson is paid some percentage of sales.

straight salary
Method of compensation in which the salesperson receives a salary regardless of sales productivity.

sales representatives, it may be hard to tell who really closed a sale. Although it offers maximum control, one disadvantage of the straight-salary system is that it may give salespeople little incentive to produce new sales.

To achieve the best of both worlds, most companies offer a *combination system* that offers a salesperson a base salary plus an incentive—usually a commission or a bonus. Combination systems have benefits for both the sales manager and the salesperson. The salary portion of the plan helps the manager control the sales force; the incentive provides motivation. For the salesperson, a combination plan offers an incentive to excel while minimizing the extremely wide swings in earnings that may occur when the economy surges or contracts too much.[52]

Motivating the Sales Force

Goal setting and quotas give salespeople targets to strive for. Training equips salespeople with the tools they need for selling. The compensation plan motivates them to sell more. Yet, sometimes these things are not enough to produce the volume of sales or the profit margin required by sales management. Sales managers, therefore, often offer rewards or incentives to increase the sales of new products or of high-margin products that may require more effort. Sales incentives include various types of rewards, such as recognition at ceremonies, plaques, vacations, merchandise, and pay raises or bonuses.

Rewards may help increase overall sales volume, add new accounts, improve morale and goodwill, move slow items, and bolster slow sales. They can be used to achieve long-term or short-term objectives, such as unloading overstocked inventory and meeting a monthly or quarterly sales goal. Pay increases, promotions, improved working conditions, greater security, recognition, and opportunities for personal growth all help motivate salespeople.

Effective Sales Leadership

Perhaps the most critical, and often most difficult, component of the sales manager's job is to be an effective leader and teacher to his or her sales force. Successful sales reps aren't necessarily born; they're made—sculpted, molded, and shaped under the careful tutelage and direction of their sales manager.

An effective sales manager inspires his or her salespeople to achieve their goals through clear and enthusiastic communications. He or she has a clear vision and commitment to the mission of the organization and the ability to instill pride and earn the respect of his or her employees. Effective sales leaders continuously increase their knowledge and skill base while encouraging others to do the same. Devoting time to honing sales skills and learning new techniques is strongly advocated.

Building strong relationships not only with customers but with his or her salespeople as well is also a sign of an effective leader. Sales managers should spend considerable time with their salespeople, in the office as well as in the field, providing needed support and offering constructive criticism. This relationship building also extends to people working in other functional areas and those in lower or higher levels of management in the organization. This is essential in relationship selling, as the entire organization must commit to the customer. In sales organizations where service is an important part of the offering, this across and up-and-down commitment to the organization is even more important.[53]

Yet another important part of the sales manager's leadership job is to set an example for the rest of the sales force. Salespeople will imitate how a sales manager works. If a sales manager gives his or her salespeople a new automation tool, the sales manager should also use it. If a new prospecting system is put in place, the sales manager should endorse its use to the fullest.

Evaluating the Sales Force

The final task for sales managers is evaluating the effectiveness and performance of the sales force. To evaluate the sales force, the sales manager needs feedback—that is, regular information from salespeople. Call-record reports or real-time information fed into a central database from individual sales reps' automation software can give managers a relative idea of activities, such as number of sales proposals presented and the number of accounts closed.

Such information helps the sales manager monitor a salesperson's progress through the sales cycle and identify where breakdowns may be occurring. By knowing the number of prospects an individual salesperson has in each step of the sales cycle process and determining where prospects are falling out of the sales cycle, a manager can determine how effective a salesperson may be at lead generation, needs assessment, proposal generation, presenting, closing, and following up.

Knowledge of where a salesperson is losing prospects tells a manager what sales skills may need to be reassessed or retrained. For example, if a sales manager notices that a rep has many interested prospects at the beginning of the sales cycle, but seems to get few past the needs assessment stage, he or she may recommend that the salesperson brush up on listening or information-gathering skills. Likewise, if a sales rep seems to be letting too many prospects fall by the wayside after presenting proposals, he or she may need to help with developing proposals, handling objections, or closing sales.

Managers can also evaluate salespeople based on such performance measures as sales volume, contribution to profit, calls per order, sales or profits per call, or percentage of calls achieving specific goals (such as sales of products that the firm is heavily promoting). Qualitative, or subjective, methods may also be used to evaluate the sales force. Examples of subjective criteria include the salesperson's knowledge of the company; knowledge of its products, customers, and competitors; and knowledge of sales tasks.

LOOKING BACK

In this chapter, you learned about two very exciting and effective means of promotion: sales promotion and personal selling. In the opening vignette, you learned how Sega of America uses many sales promotion techniques, in particular sampling and contests, to target its young audience. Throughout the second half of the chapter, you learned how personal selling focuses on direct interaction with customers in an attempt to assess their needs and offer a product or service that meets those needs.

KEY TERMS

adaptive selling   *546*

cold calling   *543*

consumer sales promotion *528*

coupon   *530*

field order taker   *541*

follow-up   *548*

frequent-buyer program *531*

SUMMARY

1   *Define and state the objectives of sales promotion.* Sales promotions are those marketing communication activities, other than advertising, personal selling, and public relations, in which a short-term incentive, such as a lower price or added value, motivates consumers or members of the distribution channel to purchase a good or service immediately. The main objectives of sales promotion are to increase trial purchases, consumer inventories, and repeat purchases. Sales promotion is also used to encourage brand switching and to build brand loyalty. Sales promotion supports advertising activities.

2   *Discuss the most common forms of consumer sales promotion.* Consumer forms of sales promotion include coupons, premiums, loyalty marketing programs, contests and sweepstakes, sampling, and point-of-purchase displays. Coupons are certificates entitling consumers to an immediate price reduction when they purchase a product or service. Coupons are a particularly good way to encourage product trial and brand switching. Premiums offer an extra item or incentive to the consumer for buying a product or service. Premiums reinforce the consumer's purchase decision, increase consumption, and persuade nonusers to switch brands. Rewarding loyal customers is the basis of loyalty marketing programs. Loyalty programs are extremely effective at building long-term, mutually beneficial relationships between a company and its key customers. Frequent-buyer programs are the most common form of loyalty program. Contests and sweepstakes are generally designed to create interest, often to encourage brand switching. Because consumers perceive risk in trying new products, sampling is an effective method for gaining new customers. Finally, point-of-purchase displays set up at the retailer's location build traffic, advertise the product, and induce impulse buying.

3 *List the most common forms of trade sales promotion.* Manufacturers employ many of the same sales promotion tools used in consumer promotions, such as sales contests, premiums, and point-of-purchase displays. In addition, manufacturers and channel intermediaries use several unique promotional strategies: trade allowances, push money, training programs, free merchandise, store demonstrations, and meetings, conventions, and trade shows.

4 *Describe personal selling.* Personal selling is direct communication between a sales representative and one or more prospective buyers in an attempt to influence each other in a purchase situation. Broadly speaking, all businesspeople use personal selling to promote themselves and their ideas. Personal selling offers several advantages over other forms of promotion. Personal selling allows salespeople to thoroughly explain and demonstrate a product. Salespeople have the flexibility to tailor a sales proposal to the needs and preferences of individual customers. Personal selling is more efficient than other forms of promotion because salespeople target qualified prospects and avoid wasting efforts on unlikely buyers. Personal selling affords greater managerial control over promotion costs. Finally, personal selling is the most effective method of closing a sale and producing satisfied customers.

5 *Discuss the key differences between relationship selling and traditional selling.* Relationship selling is the practice of building, maintaining, and enhancing interactions with customers in order to develop long-term satisfaction through mutually beneficial partnerships. Traditional selling, on the other hand, is transaction-focused. That is, the salesperson is most concerned with making one-time sales and moving on to the next prospect. Salespeople practicing relationship selling spend more time understanding a prospect's needs and developing solutions to meet those needs.

6 *Identify the different types of selling tasks.* Sales tasks are generally classified into three basic categories: order getting, order taking, and sales support. Order getters, who actively seek prospective buyers and try to persuade them to buy, may be members of a firm's sales force or independent sellers. Order takers handle either inside ordering or field ordering. Inside order takers take orders over the counter, on the sales floor, over the telephone, or by mail. In contrast, field order takers visit clients to service accounts, check inventory, take new orders, and deliver and stock merchandise for customers. Sales support positions include the missionary sales representative, technical specialist, and selling teams. Missionary sales representatives provide a variety of promotional services to support company sales efforts. Technical specialists help the sales force by describing, designing, and installing products. Marketers practicing relationship selling have begun to form sales teams to meet their clients' needs. A selling team is a combination of sales and nonsales people whose primary objective is to establish and maintain strong customer relationships.

7 *List the steps in the selling process.* The selling process is composed of seven basic steps: (1) generating leads, (2) qualifying leads, (3) doing a needs assessment, (4) developing and proposing solutions, (5) handling objections, (6) closing the sale, and (7) following up.

8 *Describe the functions of sales management.* Sales management is a critical area of marketing that encompasses several important functions. Sales managers set overall company sales objectives and define the sales process most effective for achieving those goals. They design the sales force by establishing sales force structure based on geographic, product, functional, or customer variables and determine the size of the sales force. Managers develop the sales force through recruiting and training. Sales management directs the sales force through compensation planning, motivation, and effective sales leadership. Finally, sales managers evaluate the sales force through feedback from salespeople and other methods of determining their performance.

Discussion and Writing Questions

1. Why do consumers redeem only a small percentage of coupons printed annually? What measures are some firms taking to make coupons more effective as a promotional tool?

2. Discuss how different forms of sales promotion can erode or build brand loyalty. If a company's objective is to enhance customer loyalty to its products, what sales promotion techniques would be most appropriate?

3. Why is sampling an effective method of inducing new product trial?

4. What are the key differences between relationship selling and traditional methods of selling? What types of products or services do you think would be conducive to relationship selling?

5. You are a new salesperson for a well-known business computer system, and one of your customers is a large group of physicians. You have just arranged an initial meeting with the office manager. Develop a list of questions you will ask at this meeting to uncover the group's specific needs.

6. What does sales follow-up entail? Why is it an essential step in the selling process, particularly from the perspective of relationship selling? How does it relate to cognitive dissonance?

7. As the new sales manager for a firm, you have decided to adopt a compensation policy for the sales force that combines salary and commission. Write a memo to the president of the company explaining why you feel your plan will be successful.

8. Form a four-person team. Divide the responsibility for getting sales promotional materials among your team members. The Sunday newspaper should have some supermarket and other kinds of coupons. Look in magazines and perhaps go to some local businesses as well to obtain sales promotional materials. Prepare a table comparing the different types of sales promotional approaches used. Identify which market segment(s) would be most likely to respond to the sales promotions and why. Suggest ways to improve upon the sales promotion appeals utilized.

9. In what ways does this Web site generate a sense of personal selling?

   http://www.xerox.com/ soho.html

10. How is this restaurant generating sales via the World Wide Web?

    http://www.hww.com.au/ merronys

Application for Small Business

Harold's is a retail clothing store offering high-quality, reasonably priced merchandise. Its target markets include students at the local university and working individuals, primarily in the age range of 18 to 35.

The location is about three miles from the campus in an upscale strip center next to a small, local mall. For the past few years, the owner has been using several student interns as part-time salespersons and assistant managers. He has been able to find good workers, but turnover is high and training new employees takes a lot of time. Also, his sales training has consisted mostly of asking new stu- dent interns to review the internship reports of former student employees. To reduce this problem, he has con- sidered hiring a college graduate full time and using fewer part-time in- terns. The full-time employee should reduce turnover and the need for re- peated training and be able to help him develop a better sales training approach. He pays the interns be- tween $5.00 and $8.00 per hour, de- pending upon their experience. Col- lege graduates would have to be paid between $22,000 and $27,000 per year, plus benefits.

Questions

1. What factors must be considered in making this decision?
2. Should he hire a college graduate as a full-time employee? Why?

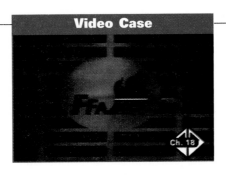

Ferrara Fire Apparatus (FFA) Pursues Relationship Selling

Ferrara Fire Apparatus (FFA) manu- factures a complete line of quality- built fire trucks and emergency vehi- cles that includes a wide range of custom and commercial pumpers/ tankers, aerial ladders, and platforms. FFA also manufactures command ve- hicles and special operation units as well as a complete line of light-, medium-, and heavy-duty "walk-in" and "non-walk-in" rescue, haz-mat, and air/light units.

All the vehicles FFA manufactures are custom built from the ground up. The starting point is the selection of any custom or commercially built two- or four-door chassis, typically purchased from chassis builders like International Harvester, GMC, Ford, or Freightliner. Customers specify the length, cab design, placement of storage areas and ladders, color com- binations, and even the size and lo- cation of the windows and doors. For example, one of the hazardous mate- rials vehicles recently manufactured included a specially designed com- mand module in the front cab with a table and seats around it so blueprints and other documents could be easily studied. As Chris Ferrara, president and CEO of FFA, says, "No other manufacturer in the world offers a greater variety of body styles, options or materials—from stainless and gal- vanized steel to Ferrara's specially designed, heavy-duty extruded alu- minum.

The Fire Apparatus Manufactur- ing Association estimates that the market for vehicles used for mitiga- tion purposes in North America is about 5,500 units annually. This in- cludes pumper and aerial fire trucks, rescue vehicles, crash trucks, haz-mat vehicles, and similar equipment. It does not include standard ambu- lances. Pierce Manufacturing, Emer- gency One, and KME are the three biggest manufacturers, accounting for about 2,100 vehicles a year, or about 40 percent. In terms of size, FFA is in the second tier with Cen- tral States, each selling about 200 units per year. This compares with sales of only about 85 units each year for FFA as recently as 1992. Indeed, FFA's annual revenues reached $45 million in 1997, more than twice what they sold in 1992. Over 90 percent of FFA's sales are in the North Amer- ica, but the export market is growing rapidly. FFA currently sells in Viet- nam and the Philippines, and expects to open up markets in China soon.

About 95 percent of FFA's cus- tomers are state and local govern- ments. The other 5 percent are from the private sector, including compa- nies like Exxon, Dow, and NASA, which use the equipment on their own sites. About 96 percent of the business is on a bid basis, while the rest is typically built to custom specs for a negotiated price. In general, customers are looking for affordable, high-quality, long-lasting equipment.

Jeff Bean, vice president of sales and marketing, identified the pri- mary features and benefits FFA of- fers customers. These are shown in Exhibit 18A with their importance rankings listed on the left side.

FFA generates sales leads primar- ily from advertisements in trade pub- lications. Its most effective trade pub- lication has been *Firehouse*, a monthly publication. Each ad in *Firehouse* costs $4,000, for total 1997 advertising ex- penditures in this publication of $48,000. This may sound high, but its most recent ad, shown on the next page, is generating about 200 sales leads a month. Moreover, the cost is offset by cooperative advertising arrangements with two suppliers— Spartan and UPF. FFA also has ad- vertised on the back cover of *Fire- fighter News* every issue for the last five years.

Exhibit 18A *FFA'S Evaluative Criteria*

Importance Rank	Features/Benefits
1	Guaranteed structural integrity (thick, durable materials; attention to detail in manufacturing process)
2	Performance through flexibility (numerous engine/transmission combinations)
3	Localized sales and service
4	Easy to service vehicles and components (standard parts/easily accessible)
5	Single-source warranty (FFA warrants all components, even if they outsource them)
6	Body design flexibility (modular body components)
7	Designed for firefighter safety
8	Cab versatility
9	Ergonomically designed cabs

To stretch its advertising dollars, FFA prepares sales literature with these same ads on the front and specs for vehicles on the back. The sales literature also is used in direct-mail campaigns and as handouts at trade shows.

FFA sells primarily through a network of 32 dealers in the United States and Canada. The dealers are organized around and report to three in-house sales representatives. Dealers are required to turn in monthly sales call reports summarizing the past month's activities and indicating their sales priorities for the next month. FFA makes no cold calls. Sales leads that come into the home office from trade publications and other sources are sent sales packets with the dealer's name in the area where the lead originated. If there is no dealer in the area, then the sales lead is followed up by the in-house sales team. The in-house sales team also takes sales calls that come directly into the home office over the phone.

Another major source of sales leads is an annual calendar. Each month of the calendar displays a picture of a recently sold piece of equipment, along with a description of the vehicle and the purchaser. The calendar generates almost 200 sales leads each year.

FFA also obtains sales leads by exhibiting at trade shows. The company usually does about 12 major national trade shows each year. Three national shows are done in the fall of each year in different locations at the International Association of Fire Chiefs show. Another three national shows are done in the spring at the Fire Department Instructor's Conference. The other six national shows are spread around other trade associations. In conjunction with dealers, they also do almost 50 other locally sponsored trade shows. At each of these shows, they display five or six demonstration vehicles; they also have a booth with sales literature, video presentations, and company representatives and a partially finished body section that enables customers to view the superstructure and its various cross-sections.

All qualified sales leads are shown a sales video. The sales video provides an overview of FFA's organization, line of products, and features and benefits. Dealers use the video for sales presentations, and all qualified sales leads in areas not represented by dealers are mailed one. For hot prospects, FFA pays their way to the home office for a plant tour and discussions. These plant tours have been so successful that FFA has closed almost 100 percent of the sales in which they have been used. To actually make the sale, FFA prepares proposals summarizing all the important information for the bids. The topics

No Ice. No Sweat. No Panic.

Introducing The Ferrara "Through-The-Tank" Ladder Storage

FERRARA
Leading The Way!

Dealer Inquiries Welcome

covered in the bid proposal are as follows:

- Cover letter/bid bond
- Sample contract
- FFA specifications
- Buyer specifications
- Warranties
- Insurance policies
- Overview of FFA
- Letters of reference
- Customer list
- Major component brochures
- Chassis literature
- Apparatus drawings

All of these sales and marketing activities help to make first-time sales. But repeat sales are the most profitable. As Jeff Bean says, "The intangible element is really what's important in developing long-term relationships. You must be seen as a resource to your customer, you must be responsive, timely and very service-oriented. For example, FFA works with customers to develop design and manufacturing specs, supplies engineering data, and provides all information and specs on component parts and equipment. In essence, we provide 'one-stop' shopping. Moreover, we are the only manufacturer to have a 24 hour/7 day service and warranty hotline. This service is very important because you do not typically have a back-up piece of equipment. If a pump on a fire engine breaks on Saturday night, you need immediate repair to put the truck back in service. You can't afford to wait till Monday to start the process. We believe that the intangible element has been a very strong factor in our more that 80 percent repeat business. As one example, Palm Beach County, Florida, has purchased over 20 vehicles from FFA in the last four years."

For more information on FFA, visit its Web site at www.ferrarafire.com.

Questions

1. What other methods could FFA use to generate sales leads?
2. How should FFA be using the evaluative criteria rankings identified by the vice president for sales? Do you agree with the rankings? Why or why not?
3. Can you think of any other items that should be included in the bid proposal?
4. What other activities could FFA offer to strengthen its relationship marketing efforts?

1 Understand the development and structure of the Internet and World Wide Web.

2 Describe the changing demographics of the Internet population.

3 Discuss the effects of the Internet on marketing strategy.

4 Explain how marketing research may be conducted online.

5 Describe the privacy and security issues surrounding Internet-based commerce.

6 Explain how the Internet impacts the traditional marketing mix.

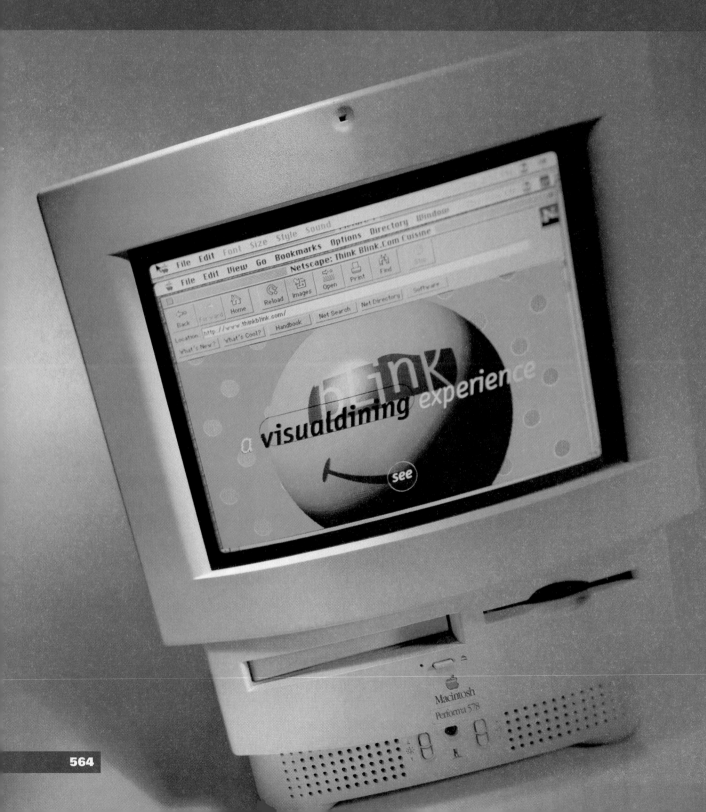

Chapter 19

Internet Marketing

*E*very major new communication medium has changed marketing. The telephone allowed managers in the 1890s to ship their products long distances, with much more elaborate control over distribution. When radio burst on the scene in the 1920s, it allowed a mass consumer market to be developed. Television in the 1950s furthered this process, with extensive advertising creating strong images and brands. The Internet has grown faster than any of these previous communication technologies. It may also change marketing more than any of these other technologies.

Using a New Set of Tools

The first way the Net changes marketing is by giving brand managers a new set of tools. There are several key features which are the foundations of the Internet. Each is important to understanding how it can be used:

1. The Internet is a digital technology. While this sounds like it refers to computers, what it really means is fast and cheap. Every 18 months for the last 30 years, the cost of digital technology has fallen by 50 percent. Nothing else in the economy has gotten so cheap for so long. One goal of marketing is to figure out how to harness this silicon resource.

2. The Internet allows everyone to talk to everyone. Like a telephone, the Net can be used to talk directly to a single consumer. But like TV, it can also talk to millions. This flexibility is powerful, and it means that everyone on the Net gains when more join the Net.

3. The Internet allows choice. Users of the Net can actively choose where they want to go simply with a click of the mouse. Consumers can find the smallest company located thousands of miles away. Companies can find isolated consumers with an interest in their product. Special interests can be served, very small market segments targeted, and a careful match between interests and products achieved.

Creating New Customer Value

Successful Net marketers realize this technology allows them to create new value for consumers. One of the most effective uses of the Net in marketing is to make existing "real-world" products better. Intuit makes the money-managing program Quicken better by adding online resources in insurance, financial planning, and college financing. The company also uses the Net to make its customer service department better and more responsive.

The next step in using the Net wisely is personalization. The speed of digital technology allows it, the network provides the necessary information, and individuals ask for it. Product really can match an individual's own tastes at a price very close to the standard mass-market offering.

Building Community

While user groups and customer relations have always been a part of marketing, the Net transforms this dramatically. Building community has become a critical way to use the technology to better serve consumers. Online bookstores have other readers post their reviews and comments, occasionally even directly to the author. This creates a real feeling of involvement, allowing virtual book clubs to emerge. Communities can develop around similar transactions, such as the purchase of a home or

the buying of baby products. And communities can develop due to shared adversity, allowing members to discuss their problems and solutions.

These communities can breed strong loyalty and commitment to whatever organization sponsors the online community. It also generates a predictable flow of consumers. These customer bases become very valuable assets of the Web site sponsors.

Impacting Advertising, Pricing, and Distribution

One of the greatest challenges of Internet marketing is getting noticed—sort of like being a single tree in the midst of a forest. This has led to the creation of an entirely new Web advertising industry, the placing of "www.something.com" in advertising, and other efforts to move traffic to Web sites.

A very important area of marketing which the Net is changing is pricing. Consumers can find much more information cheaply on products, dealers, and prices. This awareness is leading to higher price sensitivity. At the same time, companies are using the low-cost communication channels like e-mail to carry just-in-time prices for airplane seats, hotels, or bottles of wine.

An exciting part of Net marketing is the launching of thousands of new businesses, many of them hoping to save customers time and money by directly providing them goods and services. These new channels of distribution work best when they are Net savvy and use the powers of the Internet to better connect customers to products.

This is a great time to be studying marketing. Revolutions don't happen very often. And rarely do they create situations where products can be better, customers happier, and companies more profitable. But that is exactly what is happening right here, right now, online.

Ward Hanson
Stanford University
Graduate School of Business

Find this chapter at:

http://www.swcollege.com/lamb.html

Critical Thinking Case

COCA-COLA COMPANY

In its biggest soft-drink launch since Diet Coke in 1982, the Coca-Cola Company recently introduced a bright green, citrus-flavored, low carbonation soda called Surge to the U.S. soft-drink market. Surge is a direct challenge to PepsiCo's highly successful Mountain Dew, a citrus beverage spiked with caffeine aimed at the youth market. Surge also targets teens and young adults who are looking for a soda that has a kick. Along with a hefty dose of caffeine, Surge's ingredients also include maltodextrin, an energy-producing carbohydrate.

Coca-Cola has had limited success in the past with new product introductions. Over the past 25 years, Coca-Cola repeatedly has tried to build on the market leadership of its flagship brand by launching copycat brands in other flavors. But to date, Coca-Cola has had few successes with its copycat introductions. Mr. Pibb found little success against Dr. Pepper. Similarly, Mello Yello, the first Mountain Dew competitor launched in 1979, currently has sales about 10 times lower than Mountain Dew's.

More recently, the company's 1994 launch of Fruitopia was an attempt to cash in on the New Age beverage rage quickly snapped up by Snapple. But Coke was late getting into the market with its me-too product, and market share is only about one-third that of Snapple, the leader in the New Age juice-drink market. That same year, Coca-Cola introduced OK—an orange, peppery drink aimed at the MTV crowd—with less-than-okay results. The drink never rolled out nationwide.

In an attempt to appeal to young adults, and young males in particular, promotion for Surge leans toward the outrageous similar to Mountain Dew promotions. Mountain Dew has enjoyed tremendous success on the back of its "Dew Dudes" ad campaign, featuring a group of thrill-seeking teens. Introductory Surge slogans, "Feed the rush" and "Fully loaded citrus soda," suggest that drinkers will get a buzz from the soda. Innovative packaging, which shows the Surge trademark "bursting" off its bright red and green cans and bottles, includes a 12-ounce can with a larger-than-usual opening for "superior chuggability."

Surge was formally introduced to the U.S. soft-drink market with two television ads during 1997's Super Bowl XXXI followed by an aggressive advertising campaign. Within a month of its introduction, company executives estimate that 90 percent of households in Surge markets across the United States will have seen television ads for the new drink at least three times. In addition to television advertising, promotion of Surge also includes radio, point-of-sale advertising, and sampling to more than 5 million teens and young adults in the first month of the product's introduction.

Questions

1. Describe your perception of Surge's target market using specific demographic and psychographic descriptors.
2. Assume that you are the advertising manager for Surge. What would be the specific objectives of your campaign in light of the target market you described in Question 1?
3. Draft a statement of your creative decisions for the campaign. What will be the chief message or appeal? What will be your style of execution?
4. Given Coca-Cola's past track record with new product introductions and "me-too" products, how would you differentiate promotional messages and images for Surge from those already used by Mountain Dew?
5. What role would public relations play in your new product introduction of Surge? Give some specific examples.

References

Coca-Cola Company Web site, *www.cocacola.com.*

Mark Gleason, "Coca-Cola Faces Uphill Scramble with Surge Intro," *Advertising Age,* 23 December 1996.

Nikhil Deogun, "Coca-Cola Plans Splashy Rollout of Citrus Soda," *Wall Street Journal,* 16 December 1996, pp. B1, B11.

Nikhil Deogun, "Can Caffeine Give Soft-Drink Industry a Kick?" *Wall Street Journal,* 17 December 1996, pp. B1, B8.

Bob Garfield, "Super Bust," *Advertising Age,* 27 January 1997.

Marketing Planning Activities

INTEGRATED MARKETING COMMUNICATIONS

The next part of the marketing mix to be described for the marketing plan is the promotion element which covers areas such as advertising, public relations, sales promotion, personal selling, and Internet marketing. Be sure that your promotion plans match the needs and wants of the target market identified and described earlier and are compatible with the product, service, and distribution issues discussed in the previous sections. Also refer to Exhibit 2.8 for additional marketing plan subjects.

1. Evaluate your firm's promotion objectives. Remember that one cannot directly tie promotions with sales because there are too many other factors (competition, environment, price, distribution, product, customer service, company reputation, and so on) that affect sales. State specific objectives that can be tied directly to the result of promotional activities; for example, number of people redeeming a coupon, share of audience during a commercial, percent attitude change before and after a telemarketing campaign, number of people calling a toll-free information hotline, etc.

Marketing*Builder* Exercises

- **Marketing Strategy** portion of **Marketing Communications** template
- **Marketing Budget** spreadsheet
- **Operating Budget** spreadsheet
- **Source Code Master List** spreadsheet
- **Agency Selection Matrix** spreadsheet

2. What is your chosen company's promotional message? Does this message inform, remind, persuade, or educate the target market?

Marketing*Builder* Exercise

- **Advertising and Promotion** portion of the **Marketing Communications** template

3. Investigate different media placement rates (such as for a school newspaper, local newspaper, national newspaper, local radio station, local TV station, general or specialty interest magazine, local billboard, transit advertising, the Internet, and so on). You can either call local media or consult *Standard Rate and Data Services (SRDS)*. Which media should your firm use? Which media can your firm afford? When should media be used?

Marketing*Builder* Exercises

- **Advertising Schedule** template
- **Preliminary Media Schedule** portion of the **Marketing Communications** template

4. List the public relations activities that your chosen company should pursue. How should bad publicity be handled?

Marketing*Builder* Exercise

- **Public Relations** portion of the **Marketing Communications** template

5. Evaluate or create printed materials for your chosen company (such as data sheets, brochures, stationery, or rate cards). Does the literature sufficiently answer questions? Provide enough information for further contact? Effectively promote product features and customer service?

Note a differential or competitive advantage.

Marketing*Builder* Exercises

- **Collateral Planning Matrix** spreadsheet
- **Direct Mail Analysis** spreadsheet
- **Sales Support Collateral Materials** section of the **Marketing Communications** template
- **Corporate Capabilities Brochure** section of the **Marketing Communications** template

6. What trade shows could your firm attend? Search the *Eventline* database for trade shows appropriate to your firm. Order media kits and explore the feasibility and costs of attending that trade show.

Marketing*Builder* Exercises

- **Trade Show** portion of the **Marketing Communication** template
- **Trade Show Checklist and Schedule** template

7. What other sales promotion tools could your firm use? What are the costs? What is the impact of using these methods on pricing?

8. Identify and justify the best type (internal or external) and structure (product, customer, geographic, etc.) for your firm's sales force.

Marketing*Builder* Exercises

- **Current Selling Methods** portion of the **Sales Plan** template
- **Marketing Responsibilities** portion of the **Sales Plan** template
- **Sales Strategy** portion of the **Sales Plan** template
- **Sales Source Analysis** spreadsheet

9. How should your firm hire, motivate, and compensate its sales force?

- **Commission Sales Forecast & Tracker** spreadsheet

10. Design a sales approach for your company's sales force to use.

- **Next Steps** portion of the **Sales Plan** template

11. Explore the World Wide Web/Internet to research your company, its competition, and the industry in general. How is advertising and promotion being handled in this medium?

Pricing Decisions

LEARNING OBJECTIVES *After studying this chapter, you should be able to:*

1 Discuss the importance of pricing decisions to the economy and to the individual firm.

2 List and explain a variety of pricing objectives.

3 Explain the role of demand in price determination.

4 Describe cost-oriented pricing strategies.

5 Demonstrate how the product life cycle, competition, distribution and promotion strategies, and perceptions of quality can affect price.

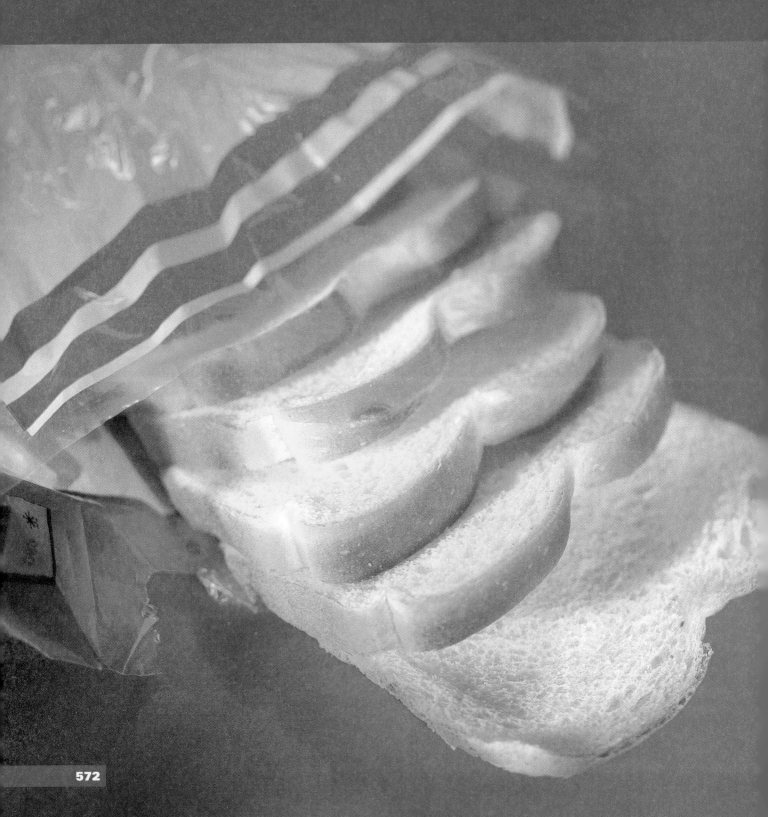

Pricing Concepts

*F*resh Fields, a natural-food store chain, has gone against the grain and cut prices sharply to attract more mainstream shoppers. Natural foods are usually more expensive than goods found in traditional supermarkets, and the cost tends to discourage all but the most devoted natural-food fans from shopping there. The company, based in Rockville, Maryland, has cut prices by up to 40 percent. The chain experimented with the policy at its four Chicago-area locations and has now expanded the effort to other stores in Connecticut, New Jersey, Virginia, and Washington, D.C.

The chain expanded its slogan for part of a promotional campaign from "good-for-you foods" to "good-for-you foods at good-for-you prices." Newspaper ads display the new prices next to the old prices. In the campaign, Fresh Fields underscores retaining quality with the slogan, "We've lowered our prices, but not our standards." Lowering prices has several major advantages, such as increasing the average transaction size and attracting noncore users, but the danger is that some con-

sumers will equate lower prices with lower quality. Dale Kamibayashi, purchasing director for Wild Oats Markets, Inc., a natural-food store chain based in Boulder, Colo., said natural-food consumers once had difficulty equating high-quality foods with high prices, but now they understand the correlation.

In appealing to noncore users, most of the reduced-price products at Fresh Fields are such base items as milk, bread, and produce. "Then they are not specifically going after natural-food shoppers," said Kamibayashi. "They would be focusing on the general public." He said price cuts cheapen the idea of natural-food stores and make them seem more like traditional supermarkets.

In appealing to noncore users, Fresh Fields is experimenting with the introduction of "nonnatural" products such as white, refined sugar and mainstream cere-

als. According to Fresh Fields, 0.3 percent of the $350 billion in sales from U.S. supermarkets and grocery stores is from "natural" products. By offering a wider variety, Fresh Fields is positioning itself as a "one-stop shop." With a wider variety of products and prices that more closely resemble prices at the traditional supermarkets, Fresh Fields feels it can compete with them.[1]

Does lowering the price always generate more revenue? How does cost fit into the pricing equation? Can price influence the perceived quality of a product? How does competition affect price?

THE IMPORTANCE OF PRICE

1 Discuss the importance of pricing decisions to the economy and to the individual firm.

Price means one thing to the consumer and something else to the seller. To the consumer, it is the cost of something. To the seller, price is revenue, the primary source of profits. In the broadest sense, price allocates resources in a free-market economy. With so many ways of looking at price, it's no wonder that marketing managers find the task of setting prices a challenge.

What Is Price?

price
That which is given up in an exchange to acquire a good or service.

revenue
The price charged to customers multiplied by the number of units sold.

profit
Revenue minus expenses.

Successful retailers like Target understand that "reasonable price" and "perceived reasonable value" are important to consumers.
Courtesy Target Stores

Price is that which is given up in an exchange to acquire a good or service. Price is typically the money exchanged for the good or service. It may also be time lost while waiting to acquire the good or service. For example, many people waited all day at Southwest Airlines's ticket counters during the company's 25th anniversary sale. Even then, some people didn't get the deep discounted tickets that they had been hoping for. Price also might include "lost dignity" for an individual who loses his job and must rely on charity to obtain food and clothing.

In a study of 2,000 consumers, 64 percent said that a "reasonable price" is the most important consideration in making a purchase.[2] "Reasonable price" really means "perceived reasonable value" at the time of the transaction. One of the authors of this textbook bought a fancy European-designed toaster for about $45. The toaster's wide mouth made it possible to toast a bagel, warm a muffin, and, with a special $15 attachment, make a grilled sandwich. The author felt that a toaster with all these features surely must be worth the total price of $60. But after three months of using the device, toast burned around the edges and raw in the middle lost its appeal. The disappointed buyer put the toaster in the attic. Why didn't he return it to the retailer? Because the boutique had gone out of business, and no other local retailer carried the brand. Also, there was no U.S. service center. Remember, the price paid is based on the satisfaction consumers *expect* to receive from a product and not necessarily the satisfaction they *actually* receive.

Price can relate to anything with perceived value, not just money. When goods and services are exchanged, the trade is called barter. For example, if you exchange this book for a chemistry book at the end of the term, you have engaged in barter. The price you paid for the chemistry book was this textbook.

$24⁹⁹

Stop and smell the bargains.

These delightful floral-patterned table linens and accessories are a great way to celebrate spring. The 52x70" tablecloth shown is just $24.99. The bargains are in full bloom at Target.

The Importance of Price to Marketing Managers

Prices are the key to revenues, which in turn are the key to profits for an organization. **Revenue** is the price charged to customers multiplied by the number of units sold. Revenue is what pays for every activity of the company: production, finance, sales, distribution, and so on. What's left over (if anything) is **profit**. Managers usually strive to charge a price that will earn a fair profit.

To earn a profit, managers must choose a price that is not too high or too low, a price that equals the perceived value to target consumers. If a price is set too high in consumers' minds, the perceived value will be less than the cost, and sales opportunities will be lost. Many mainstream purchasers of cars, sporting goods, CDs, tools, wedding gowns, and computers are buying "used or preowned" items to get a better deal. Pricing a new product too high may give an incentive to some shoppers to go to a "preowned" or consignment retailer.[3]

Lost sales mean lost revenue. Conversely, if a price is too low, it may be perceived as a great value for the consumer, but the firm loses revenue it could have earned. Setting prices too low may not even attract as many buyers as managers might think. One study surveyed over 2,000 shoppers at national chains around the country and found that over 60 percent intended to buy full-price items only.[4] Retailers that place too much emphasis on discounts may not be able to meet the expectations of full-price customers.

Trying to set the right price is one of the most stressful and pressure-filled tasks of the marketing manager, as trends in the consumer market attest:

- Confronting a flood of new products, potential buyers carefully evaluate the price of each one against the value of existing products.

- The increased availability of bargain-priced private and generic brands has put downward pressure on overall prices.

- A series of inflationary and recessionary periods has made many consumers more price sensitive.

- Many firms are trying to maintain their market share by cutting prices. For example, Ford Taurus became the best-selling passenger car in America in 1992, after taking the lead from the Honda Accord. The Accord has been catching up with the Taurus by offering large discounts on an old, but popular, car. Ford is matching the discounts in an attempt to maintain its market share.[5]

In the organizational market, where customers include both governments and businesses, buyers are also becoming more price sensitive and better informed. In the consumer market, consumers are using the Internet to make wiser purchasing decisions. Computerized information systems enable the organizational buyer to compare price and performance with great ease and accuracy. Improved communication and the increased use of telemarketing and computer-aided selling have also opened up many markets to new competitors. Finally, competition in general is increasing, so some installations, accessories, and component parts are being marketed like indistinguishable commodities.

A company must monitor its pricing objectives to determine their effectiveness.
© 1996 PhotoDisc, Inc.

PRICING OBJECTIVES

To survive in today's highly competitive marketplace, companies need pricing objectives that are specific, attainable, and measurable. Realistic pricing goals then require periodic monitoring to determine the effectiveness of the company's strategy. For convenience, pricing objectives can be divided into three categories: profit oriented, sales oriented, and status quo.

Profit-Oriented Pricing Objectives

Profit-oriented objectives include profit maximization, satisfactory profits, and target return on investment. A brief discussion of each of these objectives follows.

List and explain a variety of pricing objectives.

Profit Maximization

Profit maximization means setting prices so that total revenue is as large as possible relative to total costs. (A more theoretically precise definition and explanation of profit maximization appears later in the chapter.) Profit maximization does not always signify unreasonably high prices, however. Both price and profits depend on the type of competitive environment a firm faces, such as being in a monopoly position (being the only seller) or selling in a much more competitive situation. (See Chapter 3 for a description of the four types of competitive environments.) Also, remember that a firm cannot charge a price higher than the product's perceived value. Many firms do not have the accounting data they need for maximizing profits. It sounds simple to say that a company should keep producing and selling goods or services as long as revenues exceed costs. Yet it is often hard to set up an accurate accounting system to determine the point of profit maximization.

Sometimes managers say that their company is trying to maximize profits—in other words, trying to make as much money as possible. Although this goal may sound impressive to stockholders, it is not good enough for planning. The statement "We want to make all the money we can" is vague and lacks focus. It gives management license to do just about anything it wants to do.

Satisfactory Profits

Satisfactory profits are a reasonable level of profits. Rather than maximizing profits, many organizations strive for profits that are satisfactory to the stockholders and management—in other words, a level of profits consistent with the level of risk an organization faces. In a risky industry, a satisfactory profit may be 35 percent. In a low-risk industry, it might be 7 percent. To maximize profits, a small-business owner might have to keep his or her store open seven days a week. But the owner might not want to work that hard and might be satisfied with less profit.

Target Return on Investment

The most common profit objective is **target return on investment (ROI),** sometimes called the firm's return on total assets. ROI measures the overall effectiveness of management in generating profits with its available assets. The higher the firm's return on investment, the better off the firm is. Many companies—including DuPont, General Motors, Navistar, Exxon, and Union Carbide—use target return on investment as their main pricing goal.

Return on investment is calculated as follows:

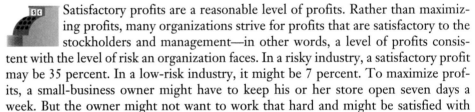

$$\text{Return on investment} = \frac{\text{Net profits after taxes}}{\text{Total assets}}$$

Assume that in 1996 Johnson Controls had assets of $4.5 million, net profits of $550,000, and a target ROI of 10 percent. This was the actual ROI:

$$\text{ROI} = \frac{550,000}{4,500,000}$$
$$= 12.2 \text{ percent}$$

As you can see, the ROI for Johnson Controls exceeded its target, which indicates that the company prospered in 1996.

Comparing the 12.2 percent ROI with the industry average provides a more meaningful picture, however. Any ROI needs to be evaluated in terms of the competitive environment, risks in the industry, and economic conditions. Generally speaking, firms seek ROIs in the 10 to 30 percent range. For example, General Electric seeks a 25 percent ROI, whereas Alcoa, Rubbermaid, and most major pharmaceutical companies strive for a 20 percent ROI. In some industries, however, such as the grocery industry, a return of under 5 percent is common and acceptable.

A company with a target ROI can predetermine its desired level of profitability. The marketing manager can use the standard, such as 10 percent ROI, to determine whether a particular price and marketing mix are feasible. In addition, however, the manager must weigh the risk of a given strategy even if the return is in the acceptable range.

Sales-Oriented Pricing Objectives

Sales-oriented pricing objectives are based either on market share or on dollar or unit sales. The effective marketing manager should be familiar with these pricing objectives.

Market Share

Market share is a company's product sales as a percentage of total sales for that industry. Sales can be reported in dollars or in units of product. It is very important to know whether market share is expressed in revenue or units, because the results may be different. Consider, for example, four companies competing in an industry with 2,000 total unit sales and total industry revenue of $4 million. (See Exhibit 20.1.) Company A has the largest unit market share at 50 percent, but it has only 25 percent of the revenue market share. In contrast, company D has only a 15 percent unit share but the largest revenue share: 30 percent. Usually, market share is expressed in terms of revenue and not units.

market share
A company's product sales as a percentage of total sales for that industry.

Many companies believe that maintaining or increasing market share is an indicator of the effectiveness of their marketing mix. Larger market shares have indeed often meant higher profits, thanks to greater economies of scale, market power, and ability to compensate top-quality management. Conventional wisdom also says that market share and return on investment are strongly related. For the most part they are; however, many companies with low market share survive and even prosper. To succeed with a low market share, companies need to compete in industries with slow growth and few product changes—for instance, industrial component parts and supplies. Otherwise, they must vie in an industry that makes frequently bought items, such as consumer convenience goods.

The 1990s have proven that the conventional wisdom about market share and profitability isn't always reliable. Because of extreme competition in some industries, many market share leaders either did not reach their target ROI or actually lost money. The airline, personal computer, and food industries had this problem. Procter & Gamble switched from market share to ROI objectives after realizing that profits

Company	Units sold	Unit price	Total revenue	Unit market share	Revenue market share
A	1,000	$1.00	$1,000,000	50%	25%
B	200	4.00	800,000	10	20
C	500	2.00	1,000,000	25	25
D	300	4.00	1,200,000	15	30
Total	2,000		$4,000,000		

Exhibit 20.1

Two Ways to Measure Market Share (Units and Revenue)

In the 1990s, many companies in the food industry failed to reach their target ROI or lost money because of too much competition. They realized that a large market share does not guarantee profits.
© John Lund/Tony Stone Images

don't automatically follow from a large market share. PepsiCo says its new Pepsi challenge is to be No. 1 in share of industry profit, not in share of sales volume.[6]

Still, the struggle for market share can be all-consuming for some companies. For over a decade, Maxwell House and Folgers, the biggest U.S. coffee brands, have been locked in a struggle to dominate the market. Their weapons have been advertising, perpetual rounds of price cutting, and millions upon millions of cents-off coupons. At this point, Maxwell House, a unit of Kraft General Foods, has regained a few drops of market share that it had lost to Folgers, a unit of Procter & Gamble, earlier in the war. Maxwell House's strategy has been to advertise heavily (spending over $100 million a year) and to introduce new products that lure consumers with taste rather than price. Examples include ready-made coffee in refrigerator cartons and coffee syrup, both designed for consumers to pour and microwave as needed. Nevertheless, Folgers is still the nation's best-selling coffee, although the Kraft General Foods brands, which include Yuban and Sanka, account for a 35 percent market share. P&G has 32 percent of the U.S. coffee market.

Research organizations like A. C. Nielsen and Ehrhart-Babic provide excellent market share reports for many different industries. These reports enable companies to track their performance in various product categories over time.

Sales Maximization

Rather than striving for market share, sometimes companies try to maximize sales. The objective of maximizing sales ignores profits, competition, and the marketing environment as long as sales are rising.

Kraft General Foods
Visit the Kraft pantry. Does Maxwell House emphasize taste in its Web advertising? If so, how?

http://www.kraftfoods.com/

If a company is strapped for funds or faces an uncertain future, it may try to generate a maximum amount of cash in the short run. Management's task when using this objective is to calculate which price–quantity relationship generates the greatest cash revenue. Sales maximization can also be effectively used on a temporary basis to sell off excess inventory. It is not uncommon, for example, to find Christmas cards, ornaments, and so on discounted at 50 to 70 percent off retail prices after the holiday season. In addition, management can use sales maximization for year-end sales to clear out old models before introducing the new ones.

Maximization of cash should never be a long-run objective, because cash maximization may mean little or no profitability. Without profits, a company cannot survive.

Status Quo Pricing Objectives

status quo pricing
Pricing objective that maintains existing prices or meets the competition's prices.

Status quo pricing seeks to maintain existing prices or to meet the competition's prices. This third category of pricing objectives has the major advantage of requiring little planning. It is essentially a passive policy.

Often, firms competing in an industry with an established price leader simply meet the competition's prices. These industries typically have fewer price wars than those with direct price competition. In other cases, managers regularly shop competitors' stores to ensure that their prices are comparable. Target's middle managers must visit competing Kmart stores weekly to compare prices and then make adjustments. In response to MCI's and Sprint's claims that its long-distance service is overpriced, AT&T struck back with advertisements showing that its rates are essentially equal to competitors'. AT&T was attempting to convince target consumers that it follows a status quo pricing strategy.

THE DEMAND DETERMINANT OF PRICE

After marketing managers establish pricing goals, they must set specific prices to reach those goals. The price they set for each product depends mostly on two factors: the demand for the good or service and the cost to the seller for that good or service. When pricing goals are mainly sales oriented, demand considerations usually dominate. Other factors, such as distribution and promotion strategies, perceived quality, and stage of the product life cycle, can also influence price.

The Nature of Demand

Demand is the quantity of a product that will be sold in the market at various prices for a specified period. The quantity of a product that people will buy depends on its price. The higher the price, the fewer goods or services consumers will demand. Conversely, the lower the price, the more goods or services they will demand.

This trend is illustrated in Exhibit 20.2(A), which graphs the demand per week for gourmet popcorn at a local retailer at various prices. This graph is called a *demand curve*. The vertical axis of the graph shows different prices of gourmet popcorn, measured in dollars per package. The horizontal axis measures the quantity of gourmet popcorn that will be demanded per week at each price. For example, at a price of $2.50, 50 packages will be sold per week; at $1.00, consumers will demand 120 packages—as the *demand schedule* in Exhibit 20.2(B) shows.

The demand curve in Exhibit 20.2 slopes downward and to the right, which indicates that more gourmet popcorn is demanded as the price is lowered. In other words, if popcorn manufacturers put a greater quantity on the market, then their hopes of selling all of it will be realized only by selling it at a lower price.

One reason why more is sold at lower prices than at higher prices is that lower prices bring in new buyers. This fact might not be so obvious with gourmet popcorn, but consider the example of steak. As the price of steak drops lower and lower, some people who have not been eating steak will probably start buying it rather than hamburger. And with each reduction in price, existing customers may buy extra amounts. Similarly, if the price of gourmet popcorn falls low enough, some people will buy more than they have bought in the past.

Supply is the quantity of a product that will be offered to the market by a supplier or suppliers at various prices for a specified period. Exhibit 20.3(A) illustrates the resulting *supply curve* for gourmet popcorn. Unlike the falling demand curve, the supply curve for gourmet popcorn slopes upward and to the right. At higher prices, gourmet popcorn manufacturers will obtain more re-

Exhibit 20.2

*Demand Curve and
Demand Schedule for
Gourmet Popcorn*

(A) Demand curve

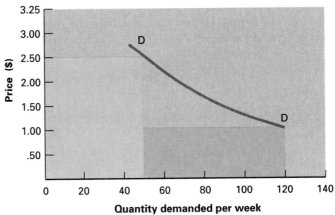

(B) Demand schedule

Price per package of gourmet popcorn	Packages of gourmet popcorn demanded per week
$3.00	35
2.50	50
2.00	65
1.50	85
1.00	120

sources (popcorn, flavorings, salt) and produce more gourmet popcorn. If the price consumers are willing to pay for gourmet popcorn increases, producers can afford to buy more ingredients.

Output tends to increase at higher prices because manufacturers can sell more packages of gourmet popcorn and earn greater profits. The *supply schedule* in Exhibit 20.3(B) shows that at $2 suppliers are willing to place 110 packages of gourmet popcorn on the market, but that they will offer 140 packages at a price of $3.

Exhibit 20.3

*Supply Curve and
Supply Schedule for
Gourmet Popcorn*

(A) Supply curve

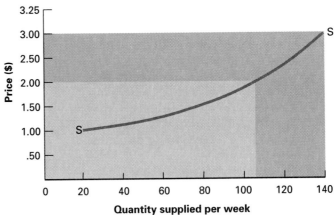

(B) Supply schedule

Price per package of gourmet popcorn	Packages of gourmet popcorn supplied per week
$3.00	140
2.50	130
2.00	110
1.50	85
1.00	25

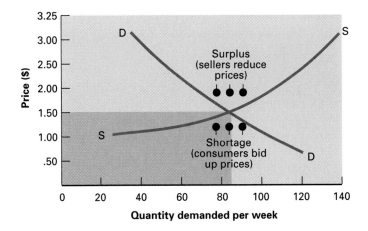

Exhibit 20.4
Equilibrium Price for Gourmet Popcorn

How Demand and Supply Establish Prices

At this point, let's combine the concepts of demand and supply to see how competitive market prices are determined. So far, the premise is that if the price is X, then consumers will purchase Y amount of gourmet popcorn. How high or low will prices actually go? How many packages of gourmet popcorn will be produced? How many packages will be consumed? The demand curve cannot predict consumption, nor can the supply curve alone forecast production. Instead, we need to look at what happens when supply and demand interact—as shown in Exhibit 20.4.

At a price of $3, the public would demand only 35 packages of gourmet popcorn. But suppliers stand ready to place 140 packages on the market at this price (data from the demand and supply schedules). If they do, they would create a surplus of 105 packages of gourmet popcorn. How does a merchant eliminate a surplus? It lowers the price.

At a price of $1, 120 packages would be demanded, but only 25 would be placed on the market. A shortage of 95 units would be created. If a product is in short supply and consumers want it, how do they entice the dealer to part with one unit? They offer more money—that is, pay a higher price.

Now let's examine a price of $1.50. At this price, 85 packages are demanded and 85 are supplied. When demand and supply are equal, a state called **price equilibrium** is achieved. A temporary price below equilibrium—say $1.00—results in a shortage, because at that price the demand for gourmet popcorn is greater than the available supply. Shortages put upward pressure on price. But as long as demand and supply remain the same, temporary price increases or decreases tend to return to equilibrium. At equilibrium, there is no inclination for prices to rise or fall.

An equilibrium price may not be reached all at once. Prices may fluctuate during a trial-and-error period as the market for a good or service moves toward equilibrium. But sooner or later, demand and supply will settle into proper balance.

price equilibrium
Price at which demand and supply are equal.

Elasticity of Demand

To appreciate demand analysis, you should understand the concept of elasticity. **Elasticity of demand** refers to consumers' responsiveness or sensitivity to changes in price. **Elastic demand** occurs when consumers buy more or less of a product when the price changes. Conversely, **inelastic demand** means that an increase or a decrease in price will not significantly affect demand for the product.

Elasticity over the range of a demand curve can be measured by using this formula:

$$\text{Elasticity } (E) = \frac{\text{Percentage change in quantity demanded of good A}}{\text{Percentage change in price of good A}}$$

elasticity of demand
Consumers' responsiveness or sensitivity to changes in price.

elastic demand
Situation in which consumer demand is sensitive to changes in price.

inelastic demand
Situation in which an increase or a decrease in price will not significantly affect demand for the product.

If E is greater than 1, demand is elastic.

If E is less than 1, demand is inelastic.

If E is equal to 1, demand is unitary.

unitary elasticity
Situation in which total revenue remains the same when prices change.

Unitary elasticity means that an increase in sales exactly offsets a decrease in prices so that total revenue remains the same.

Elasticity can be measured by observing these changes in total revenue:

If price goes down and revenue goes up, demand is elastic.

If price goes down and revenue goes down, demand is inelastic.

If price goes up and revenue goes up, demand is inelastic.

If price goes up and revenue goes down, demand is elastic.

If price goes up or down and revenue stays the same, elasticity is unitary.

Exhibit 20.5(A) shows a very elastic demand curve. Decreasing the price of a Sony VCR from $300 to $200 increases sales from 18,000 units to 59,000 units. Revenue increases from $5.4 million ($300 × 18,000) to $11.8 million ($200 × 59,000). The price decrease results in a large increase in sales and revenue.

Exhibit 20.5(B) shows a completely inelastic demand curve. The state of Nevada dropped its used-car vehicle inspection fee from $20 to $10. The state continued to inspect about 400,000 used cars annually. Decreasing the price (inspection fee) 50 percent did not cause people to buy more used cars. Demand is completely inelastic for inspection fees, which are required by law. Thus, it also follows that Nevada could double the original fee to $40 and double the state's inspection revenues. People won't quit buying used cars if the inspection fee increases—within a reasonable range.

Exhibit 20.6 presents the demand curve and demand schedule for three-ounce bottles of Spring Break suntan lotion. Let's follow the demand curve from the highest price to the lowest and examine what happens to elasticity as the price decreases.

Inelastic Demand

Exhibit 20.5
Elasticity of Demand for Sony VCRs and Auto Inspection Stickers

The initial decrease in the price of Spring Break suntan lotion, from $5.00 to $2.25, results in a decrease in total revenue of $969 ($5,075 − $4,106). When price and total revenue fall, demand is inelastic. The decrease in price is much greater than the increase in suntan lotion sales (810 bottles). Demand is therefore not very flexible in the price range $5.00 to $2.25.

When demand is inelastic, sellers can raise prices and increase total revenue. Often, items that are relatively inexpensive, but convenient, tend to have inelastic de-

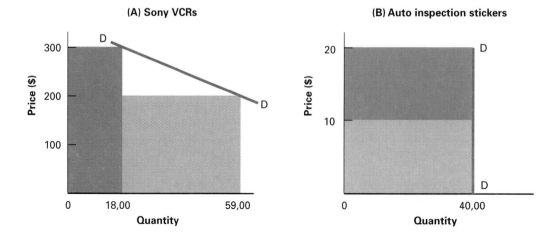

(A) Demand curve

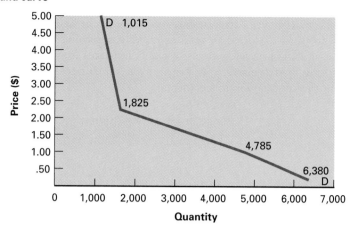

Exhibit 20.6
Demand for Three-Ounce Bottles of Spring Break Suntan Lotion

(B) Demand schedule

Price	Quantity demanded	Total revenue (price x quantity)	Elasticity
$5.00	1,015	$5,075	Inelastic
2.25	1,825	4,106	
1.00	4,785	4,785	Elastic
0.25	6,380	4,785	Unitary

mand. One such example is the fee you are charged for using an automated teller machine (ATM). Some people claim that bankers are aware of the associated inelasticity of demand and quickly raise prices. The following "Ethics in Marketing" box examines the ethics of this action.

Ethics in Marketing
Getting Ripped Off at the ATM

Many banks around the country are raising their fees for using an automated teller machine (ATM). Many bank customers don't seem to be especially concerned about the charges and feel that the convenience of an ATM is well worth the fee. Several consumer advocacy groups, however, are not pleased with the practice.

One woman nonchalantly accepted a $1.50 charge at a nearby ATM to withdraw $20 from her account, even though she could have avoided the charge by walking a block further to her own bank's automated teller. One consumer group did the arithmetic and pointed out that the woman paid 7.5 percent for the privilege of accessing her own money. They charge that the fees are unreasonable, unwarranted, and not understood by bank customers. The implication is that the banks are involved in a covert form of price gouging and that such practices are unethical.

It is no secret that it is far less expensive for a bank to handle a typical deposit or withdrawal transaction through an ATM than through a live teller. The differential is roughly four times: 27¢ for the ATM vs. $1.07 for the live teller. The reality, however, is that it is not as simple as merely replacing a manual transaction with an automated one. As ATM machines proliferate—a result of banks seeking an advantage over their competition—bank customers are making far more frequent transactions.

So banks find it necessary to establish even more of the machines, at a cost of $500,000 per machine. Much, if not all, of the savings are eaten up by the cost of additional machines. One industry expert is questioning whether the banks are making any money by their ATM charges.[7]

Do you think that banks are being unethical by raising ATM fees? Should they charge more for interacting with a live teller? Is this simply a case of taking advantage of inelastic demand?

Elastic Demand

In the example of Spring Break suntan lotion, shown in Exhibit 20.6, when the price is dropped from $2.25 to $1.00, total revenue increases by $679 ($4,785 − $4,106). An increase in total revenue when price falls indicates that demand is elastic. Let's measure Spring Break's elasticity of demand when the price drops from $2.25 to $1.00 by applying the earlier-mentioned formula:

$$E = \frac{\text{Change in quantity} \; / \; (\text{Sum of quantities} \; / \; 2)}{\text{Change in price} \; / \; (\text{Sum of prices} \; / \; 2)}$$

$$= \frac{(4,785 - 1,825) \; / \; [(1,825 + 4,785) \; / \; 2]}{(2.25) - 1 \; / \; [(2.25 + 1.00) \; / \; 2]}$$

$$= \frac{2,960 \; / \; 3,305}{1.25 \; / \; 1.63}$$

$$= \frac{.896}{.767}$$

$$= 1.17$$

Because E is greater than 1, demand is elastic.

Factors That Affect Elasticity

Several factors affect elasticity of demand, including the following:

- *Availability of substitutes:* When many substitute products are available, the consumer can easily switch from one product to another, making demand elastic. The same is true in reverse: A ticket on the *Concorde*, which flies twice the velocity of a bullet, is $4,509 one way from New York to London. British Airways can charge this price and fill the seats because there is no substitute.[8]

- *Price relative to purchasing power:* If a price is so low that it is an inconsequential part of an individual's budget, demand will be inelastic. For example, if the

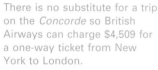

There is no substitute for a trip on the *Concorde* so British Airways can charge $4,509 for a one-way ticket from New York to London.
© Index Stock Photography

price of salt doubles, consumers will not stop putting salt and pepper on their eggs, because salt is cheap anyway.

- *Product durability:* Consumers often have the option of repairing durable products rather than replacing them, thus prolonging their useful life. For instance, if a person had planned to buy a new car and the prices suddenly began to rise, he or she might elect to fix the old car and drive it for another year. In other words, people are sensitive to the price increase, and demand is elastic.

- *A product's other uses:* The greater the number of different uses for a product, the more elastic demand tends to be. If a product has only one use, as may be true of a new medicine, the quantity purchased probably will not vary as price varies. A person will consume only the prescribed quantity, regardless of price. On the other hand, a product like steel has many possible applications. As its price falls, steel becomes more economically feasible in a wider variety of applications, thereby making demand relatively elastic.

variable costs
Costs that vary with changes in the level of output.

fixed cost
Cost that does not change as output is increased or decreased.

THE COST DETERMINANT OF PRICE

Sometimes companies minimize or ignore the importance of demand and decide to price their products largely or solely on the basis of costs. Prices determined strictly on the basis of costs may be too high for the target market, thereby reducing or eliminating sales. Or cost-based prices may be too low, causing the firm to earn a lower return than it should. However, costs should generally be part of any price determination, if only as a floor below which a good or service must not be priced in the long run.

4 Describe cost-oriented pricing strategies.

Why do people pay top dollar for perfume? How does Sony price a unique new product that will be quickly copied by its competitors? To learn how companies set their prices, check out **Hot Link—Pricing Concepts.**

Cost may seem simple, but it is actually a multifaceted concept, especially for producers of goods and services. **Variable costs** are those that deviate with changes in the level of output; an example of a variable cost is the cost of materials. In contrast, a **fixed cost** does not change as output is increased or decreased. Examples include rent and executives' salaries.

In order to compare the cost of production to the selling price of a product, it is helpful to calculate costs per unit, or average costs. **Average variable cost (AVC)** equals total variable costs divided by quantity of output. **Average total cost (ATC)**

average variable cost (AVC)
Total variable costs divided by quantity of output.

average total cost (ATC)
Total costs divided by quantity of output.

equals total costs divided by output. As plotted on the graph in Exhibit 20.7(A), AVC and ATC are basically U-shaped curves. In contrast, average fixed costs (AFC) decline continually as output increases, because total fixed costs are constant.

marginal cost (MC)
Change in total costs associated with a one-unit change in output.

Marginal cost (MC) is the change in total costs associated with a one-unit change in output. Exhibit 20.7(B) shows that, when output rises from seven to eight units, the change in total cost is from $640 to $750; therefore, marginal cost is $110.

All the curves illustrated in Exhibit 20.7(A) have definite relationships:

- AVC plus AFC equals ATC.
- MC falls for a while and then turns upward, in this case with the fourth unit. At that point diminishing returns set in, meaning that less output is produced for every additional dollar spent on variable input.

Exhibit 20.7
Hypothetical Set of Cost Curves and a Cost Schedule

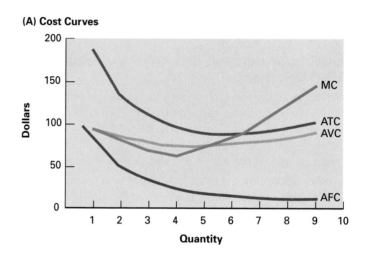

(A) Cost Curves

(B) Cost schedule

(1) Total product (Q)	(2) Total fixed cost (TFC)	(3) Total variable cost (TVC)	(4) Total cost (TC)	(5) Average fixed cost (AFC)	(6) Average variable cost (AVC)	(7) Average total cost (ATC)	(8) Marginal cost (MC)
			$TC = TFC + TVC$	$AFC = \dfrac{TFC}{Q}$	$AVC = \dfrac{TVC}{Q}$	$ATC = \dfrac{TC}{Q}$	$(MC) = \dfrac{\text{change in TC}}{\text{change in Q}}$
0	$100	$ 0	$ 100	—	—	—	—
1	100	90	190	$100.00	$90.00	$190.00	$ 90
2	100	170	270	50.00	85.00	135.00	80
3	100	240	340	33.33	80.00	113.33	70
4	100	300	400	25.00	75.00	100.00	60
5	100	370	470	20.00	74.00	94.00	70
6	100	450	550	16.67	75.00	91.67	80
7	100	540	640	14.29	77.14	91.43	90
8	100	650	750	12.50	81.25	93.75	110
9	100	780	880	11.11	86.67	97.78	130
10	100	930	1030	10.00	93.00	103.00	150

Total-cost data, per week — Average-cost data, per week

- MC intersects both AVC and ATC at their lowest possible points.
- When MC is less than AVC or ATC, the incremental cost will continue to pull the averages down. Conversely, when MC is greater than AVC or ATC, it pulls the averages up, and ATC and AVC begin to rise.
- The minimum point on the ATC curve is the least cost point for a fixed-capacity firm, although it is not necessarily the most profitable point.

Costs can be used to set prices in a variety of ways. The first two methods discussed here, markup pricing and formula pricing, are relatively simple. The other three—profit maximization pricing, break-even pricing, and target-return pricing—make use of the more complicated concepts of cost.

Markup Pricing

Markup pricing, the most popular method used by wholesalers and retailers to establish a selling price, does not directly analyze the costs of production. Instead, **markup pricing** is the cost of buying the product from the producer, plus amounts for profit and for expenses not otherwise accounted for. The total determines the selling price.

A retailer, for example, adds a certain percentage to the cost of the merchandise received to arrive at the retail price. An item that costs the retailer $1.80 and is sold for $2.20 carries a markup of 40¢, which is a markup of 22 percent of the cost (40¢ ÷ $1.80). Retailers tend to discuss markup in terms of its percentage of the retail price—in this example, 18 percent (40¢ ÷ $2.20). The difference between the retailer's cost and the selling price (40¢) is the gross margin, as Chapter 15 explained.

Markups are often based on experience. For example, many small retailers mark up merchandise 100 percent over cost. (In other words, they double the cost.) This tactic is called **keystoning.** Some other factors that influence markups are the merchandise's appeal to customers, past response to the markup (an implicit demand consideration), the item's promotional value, the seasonality of the goods, their fashion appeal, the product's traditional selling price, and competition. Most retailers avoid any set markup because of such considerations as promotional value and seasonality.

The biggest advantage of markup pricing is its simplicity. The primary disadvantage is that it ignores demand and may result in overpricing or underpricing the merchandise.

Profit Maximization Pricing

Producers tend to use more complicated methods of setting prices than distributors use. One is **profit maximization,** which occurs when marginal revenue equals marginal cost. You learned earlier that marginal cost is the change in total costs associated with a one-unit change in output. Similarly, **marginal revenue (MR)** is the extra revenue associated with selling an extra unit of output. As long as the revenue of the last unit produced and sold is greater than the cost of the last unit produced and sold, the firm should continue manufacturing and selling the product.

Exhibit 20.8 shows the marginal revenues and marginal costs for a hypothetical firm, using the cost data from Exhibit 20.7(B). The profit-maximizing quantity, where MR = MC, is six units. You might say, "If profit is zero, why produce the sixth unit? Why not stop at five?" In fact, you would be right. The firm, however, would not know that the fifth unit would produce zero profits until it determined that profits were no longer increasing. Economists suggest producing up to the point where MR = MC. If marginal revenue is just one penny greater than marginal costs, it will still increase total profits.

markup pricing
Cost of buying the product from the producer plus amounts for profit and for expenses not otherwise accounted for.

keystoning
Practice of marking up prices by 100 percent, or doubling the cost.

profit maximization
When marginal revenue equals marginal cost.

marginal revenue (MR)
The extra revenue associated with selling an extra unit of output or the change in total revenue with a one-unit change in output.

Exhibit 20.8
*Point of Profit
Maximization*

Quantity	Marginal revenue (MR)	Marginal cost (MC)	Cumulative total profit
0	—	—	—
1	140	90	50
2	130	80	100
3	105	70	135
4	95	60	170
5	85	70	185
*6	80	80	185
7	75	90	170
8	60	110	120
9	50	130	40
10	40	150	(70)

*Profit maximization

Break-Even Pricing

break-even analysis
Method of determining
what sales volume must be
reached before total rev-
enue equals total costs.

Now let's take a closer look at the relationship between sales and cost. **Break-even analysis** determines what sales volume must be reached before the company breaks even (its total costs equal total revenue) and no profits are earned.

The typical break-even model assumes a given fixed cost and a constant average variable cost. Suppose that Universal Sportswear, a hypothetical firm, has fixed costs of $2,000 and that the cost of labor and materials for each unit produced is 50¢. Assume that it can sell up to 6,000 units of its product at $1 without having to lower its price.

Exhibit 20.9(A) illustrates Universal Sportswear's break-even point. As Exhibit 20.9(B) indicates, Universal Sportswear's total variable costs increase by 50¢ every time a new unit is produced, and total fixed costs remain constant at $2,000 regardless of the level of output. Therefore, 4,000 units of output give Universal Sportswear $2,000 in fixed costs and $2,000 in total variable costs (4,000 units × 50¢), or $4,000 in total costs.

Revenue is also $4,000 (4,000 units × $1), giving a net profit of zero dollars at the break-even point of 4,000 units. Notice that once the firm gets past the break-even point, the gap between total revenue and total cost gets wider and wider, because both functions are assumed to be linear.

The formula for calculating break-even quantities is simple:

$$\text{Break-even quantity} = \frac{\text{Total fixed costs}}{\text{Fixed cost contribution}}$$

Fixed cost contribution is the price minus the average variable cost. Therefore, for Universal Sportswear,

$$\text{Break-even quantity} = \frac{\$2,000}{(\$1.00 - 50¢)} = \frac{\$2,000}{50¢}$$
$$= 4,000 \text{ units}$$

(A) Break-even point

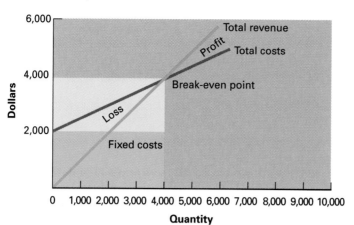

Exhibit 20.9

Costs, Revenues, and Break-Even Point for Universal Sportswear

(B) Costs and revenues

Output	Total fixed costs	Average variable costs	Total variable costs	Average total costs	Average revenue (price)	Total revenue	Total costs	Profit or loss
500	$2,000	$0.50	$ 250	$4.50	$1.00	$ 500	$2,250	($1,750)
1,000	2,000	0.50	500	2.50	1.00	1,000	2,500	(1,500)
1,500	2,000	0.50	750	1.83	1.00	1,500	2,750	(1,250)
2,000	2,000	0.50	1,000	1.50	1.00	2,000	3,000	(1,000)
2,500	2,000	0.50	1,250	1.30	1.00	2,500	3,250	(750)
3,000	2,000	0.50	1,500	1.17	1.00	3,000	3,500	(500)
3,500	2,000	0.50	1,750	1.07	1.00	3,500	3,750	(250)
*4,000	2,000	0.50	2,000	1.00	1.00	4,000	4,000	(0)
4,500	2,000	0.50	2,250	.94	1.00	4,500	4,250	250
5,000	2,000	0.50	2,500	.90	1.00	5,000	4,500	500
5,500	2,000	0.50	2,750	.86	1.00	5,500	4,750	750
6,000	2,000	0.50	3,000	.83	1.00	6,000	5,000	1,000

*Break-even point

The advantage of break-even analysis is that it provides a quick estimate of how much the firm must sell to break even and how much profit can be earned if a higher sales volume is obtained. If a firm is operating close to the break-even point, it may want to see what can be done to reduce costs or increase sales. Moreover, in a simple break-even analysis, it is not necessary to compute marginal costs and marginal revenues, because price and average cost per unit are assumed to be constant. Also, because accounting data for marginal cost and revenue are frequently unavailable, it is convenient not to have to depend on that information.

Break-even analysis is not without several important limitations. Sometimes it is hard to know whether a cost is fixed or variable. For example, if labor wins a tough guaranteed-employment contract, are the resulting expenses a fixed cost? Are middle-level executives' salaries fixed costs? More important than cost determination is the fact that simple break-even analysis ignores demand. For example, how does Universal Sportswear know it can sell 4,000 units at $1? Could it sell the same 4,000 units at $2 or even $5? Obviously, this information would profoundly affect the firm's pricing decisions.

OTHER DETERMINANTS OF PRICE

5 Demonstrate how the product life cycle, competition, distribution and promotion strategies, and perceptions of quality can affect price.

Other factors besides demand and costs can influence price. For example, the stage of the product's life cycle, the competition, and the product distribution strategy, promotion strategy, and perceived quality can all affect pricing.

Stage in the Product Life Cycle

As a product moves through its life cycle (see Chapter 11), the demand for the product and the competitive conditions tend to change:

- *Introductory stage:* Management usually sets prices high during the introductory stage. One reason is that it hopes to recover its development costs quickly. In addition, demand originates in the core of the market (the customers whose needs ideally match the product's attributes) and thus is relatively inelastic. On the other hand, if the target market is highly price sensitive, management often finds it better to price the product at the market level or lower. For example, when Kraft General Foods brought out Country Time lemonade, it was priced like similar products in the highly competitive beverage market because the market was price sensitive.

- *Growth stage:* Prices generally begin to stabilize as the product enters the growth stage. There are several reasons. First, competitors have entered the market, increasing the available supply. Second, the product has begun to appeal to a broader market, often lower income groups. Finally, economies of scale are lowering costs, and the savings can be passed on to the consumer in the form of lower prices.

- *Maturity stage:* Maturity usually brings further price decreases as competition increases and inefficient, high-cost firms are eliminated. Distribution channels become a significant cost factor, however, because of the need to offer wide product lines for highly segmented markets, extensive service requirements, and the sheer number of dealers necessary to absorb high-volume production. The manufacturers that remain in the market toward the end of the maturity stage typically offer similar prices. Usually only the most efficient remain, and they have comparable costs. At this stage, price increases are usually cost initiated, not demand initiated.

When hand-held calculators were first introduced, only a few companies made them and they were very expensive. Once consumer demand increased and there was greater competition, prices decreased.

Nor do price reductions in the late phase of maturity stimulate much demand. Because demand is limited and producers have similar cost structures, the remaining competitors will probably match price reductions.

- **Decline stage:** The final stage of the life cycle may see further price decreases as the few remaining competitors try to salvage the last vestiges of demand. When only one firm is left in the market, prices begin to stabilize. In fact, prices may eventually rise dramatically if the product survives and moves into the specialty good category, as horse-drawn carriages and vinyl records have.

The Competition

Competition varies during the product life cycle, of course, and so at times it may strongly affect pricing decisions. For example, although a firm may not have any competition at first, the high prices it charges may eventually induce another firm to enter the market.

The salty snack business provides a good example of how high prices entice competition. In the late 1980s, Borden noticed that the industry had only one big national competitor, Frito-Lay, which left room for a second. Also, yearly price increases by Frito-Lay kept profits rising about 20 percent annually. Borden made a full-scale commitment, and the strategy worked perfectly until Anheuser-Busch decided to expand its Eagle Snacks division. Eagle won shelf space in supermarkets by reportedly paying retailers as much as $500 a linear foot and by dropping prices. Competitors fought back. By the early 1990s, Eagle decided that it had to become more competitive to stay in the game, and it targeted Frito-Lay's Doritos tortilla chip business. Frito-Lay matched Eagle on every program. Eagle spent $15 million to $20 million in TV advertising and deep-cut price promotions. In 1995, Frito-Lay's market share jumped to 50 percent from 40, and Anheuser's Eagle brand never topped 6 percent. In the same year, Eagle lost $25 million, on sales of just $400 million. In 1996, Anheuser-Busch closed the Eagle snack business to concentrate on the "mother brands"—Bud and Bud Lite.[9]

When a firm enters a mature market without a "price umbrella" provided by a market leader, it has three options. It can price below the market, as Eagle Snacks did. Or, if the new competitor has a distinct competitive advantage, it can price above the market. Lifetime Automotive Products entered the windshield wiper market with wiper blades priced at $19.95, more than three times the average price. The firm's competitive advantage was a patented three-bladed wiper system that cleaned better than traditional wipers, plus a lifetime guarantee. Finally, companies can enter a market at the "going price," assuming that they can reach profit and market share objectives through nonprice competition. Entering at the existing price level helps avoid crippling price wars.

Price wars and intense competition are not limited to the United States. As the European Union moves toward greater economic unity, price is becoming more chaotic. Still, as the following "Global Perspectives" box explains, it is important to understand the market and then develop a pricing corridor.

Distribution Strategy

An effective distribution network can often overcome other minor flaws in the marketing mix. For example, although consumers may perceive a price as being slightly higher than normal, they may buy the product anyway if it is being sold at a convenient retail outlet.

Adequate distribution for a new product can often be attained by offering a larger-than-usual profit margin to distributors. A variation on this strategy is to give dealers a large trade allowance to help offset the costs of promotion and further stimulate demand at the retail level.

Global Perspectives

Chaotic Pricing Calls for Pricing Corridors

Gone are the days when markets were neatly separable, and gray imports were solely a concern of exotic high-price products such as French perfumes or Swiss watches. Today, almost every product is affected by the pressures for international price alignment.

A leading manufacturer of consumer products distributed through large local and pan-European retailers recently had its biggest retail customer request that all products be supplied at the lowest European price. The company had to comply, but the 20 percent price decline across Europe resulted in a profit disaster.

Some car models cost 30 percent to 40 percent less in Italy than in Germany because of the recent devaluation of the lira. The information systems of professional gray importers (see Chapter 14) who take advantage of international price differences, are close to perfect. Nothing is simpler than faxing a price list. The global-pricing time bomb is ticking, and many companies already have been hit while others are not yet fully aware of the threat.

Enormous price differentials exist between countries. For identical consumer products, prices typi-cally deviate 30 percent to 150 percent. In some markets, the differentials are even more extreme. A certain drug costs exactly five times more in Germany than in Italy. If you live in France but buy your car elsewhere, you can save 24.3 percent on a Citroen, 18.2 percent on a Peugeot, or 33 percent on a Volkswagen Jetta. These differentials are rooted in consumer behavior, distribution structures, varying market positions, and tax systems, and they are not going to disappear abruptly.

Pricing is typically intuition- or experience-driven and chaotically decentralized. Managers devote much more time and energy to costs than to prices, though both are equally important as profit drivers.

An international price corridor takes into account both the differences between countries and mounting alignment pressures. This corridor has to be determined by the company headquarters and its subsidiaries in the various coun-tries. No country is allowed to set its price outside the corridor. Countries with lower prices have to raise them, and countries with prices above the limit have to lower them. The corridor should consider market data for the individual countries, price elasticities in the countries, currency exchange rates, costs in countries, and data on competition and distribution. Corridors typically improve profits by 15 percent to 25 percent. Relative to this improvement, the costs of such a system are insignificant.[10]

With the many diverse cultures within the European Union, do you think that a coherent pricing strategy is possible? Sometimes multi-national firms grow through diversification. Thus, some countries are at the lower end of the price scale, while other countries are at the upper end. Some subsidiaries want to build market share and price aggressively, whereas others are market leaders, have high prices, and want no change. If the multinational operates with a decentralized strategy, will a pricing corridor work? If the system is working well without a pricing corridor, is "price discipline" necessary for the organization as a whole?

---

selling against the brand Stocking well-known branded items at high prices in order to sell store brands at discounted prices.

Manufacturers have gradually been losing control within the distribution channel to wholesalers and retailers, which often adopt pricing strategies that serve their own purposes. For instance, some distributors are **selling against the brand:** They place well-known brands on the shelves at high prices while offering other brands—typi-cally, their private-label brands, such as Craftsman tools, Kroger pears, or Cost Cut-ter paper towels—at lower prices. Of course, sales of the higher priced brands de-cline.

Wholesalers and retailers may also go outside traditional distribution channels to buy gray-market goods. As Chapter 15 explained, distributors obtain the goods through unauthorized channels for less than they would normally pay so they can sell the goods with a bigger-than-normal markup or at a reduced price. Imports seem to be particularly susceptible to gray marketing. Porsches, JVC stereos, and Seiko watches are among the brand-name products that have experienced this problem. Although consumers may pay less for gray-market goods, they often find that the manufacturer won't honor the warranty.

Manufacturers can regain some control over price by using an exclusive distribution system, by franchising, or by avoiding doing business with price-cutting discounters. Manufacturers can also package merchandise with the selling price marked on it or place goods on consignment. The best way for manufacturers to control prices, however, is to develop brand loyalty in consumers by delivering quality and value.

Promotion Strategy

Price is often used as a promotional tool to increase consumer interest. The weekly grocery section of the newspaper, for instance, advertises many products with special low prices. Crested Butte Ski Resort in Colorado tried a unique twist on price promotions. It made the unusual offer of free skiing between Thanksgiving and Christmas. Its only revenues were voluntary contributions from lodging and restaurant owners who benefited from the droves of skiers taking advantage of the promotion. Lodging during the slack period is now booked solid, and on the busiest days 9,000 skiers jam slopes designed for about 6,500. Crested Butte Resort no longer loses money during this time of the year.

Pricing can be a tool for trade promotions as well. For example, Levi's Dockers (casual men's slacks) are very popular with white-collar men ages 25 to 45, a growing and lucrative market. Sensing an opportunity, rival pantsmaker Bugle Boy began offering similar pants at cheaper wholesale prices, which gave retailers a bigger gross margin than they were getting with Dockers. Levi Strauss had to either lower prices or risk its $400 million annual Docker sales. Although Levi Strauss intended its cheapest Dockers to retail for $35, it started selling Dockers to retailers for $18 a pair. Retailers could then advertise Dockers at a very attractive retail price of $25.

Levi Strauss & Company
What are the FAQs (frequently asked questions) for Levi's? How does Levi's address the price issue?

http://www.levi.com/

The Relationship of Price to Quality

Consumers tend to rely on a high price as a predictor of good quality when there is great uncertainty involved in the purchase decision. Reliance on price as an indicator of quality seems to exist for all products, but it reveals itself more strongly for some items than for others.[11] Among the products that benefit from this phenomenon are coffee, stockings, aspirin, salt, floor wax, shampoo, clothing, furniture, perfume, whiskey, and many services. If the consumer obtains additional information—for instance, about the brand or the store—then reliance on price as an indicator of quality decreases.[12] In the absence of other information, people typically assume that prices are higher because the products contain better materials, because they are made more carefully, or, in the case of professional services, because the provider has more expertise. In other words, consumers assume that "You get what you pay for." One study has shown that some people believe "You get what you pay for" much more strongly than others. That is, some con-

Furniture is among the products that benefit from the fact that many consumers believe that a high price is an indicator of good quality.
© 1996 PhotoDisc, Inc.

sumers tend to rely much more heavily on price as a quality indicator than others do.[13] In general, consumers tend to be more accurate in their price–quality assessments for nondurable goods (such as ice cream, frozen pizza, or oven cleaner) than for durable goods (such as coffeemakers, gas grills, or 10-speed bikes).[14] Knowledgeable merchants take these consumer attitudes into account when devising their pricing strategies. **Prestige pricing** is charging a high price to help promote a high-quality image. A successful prestige pricing strategy requires a retail price that is reasonably consistent with consumers' expectations. For example, no one goes shopping at a Gucci's shop in New York and expects to pay $9.95 for a pair of loafers. In fact, demand would fall drastically at such a low price. Bayer aspirin would probably lose market share over the long run if it lowered its prices. A new mustard packaged in a crockery jar was not successful until its price was doubled.

Consumers also expect private or store brands to be cheaper than national brands. However, if the price difference between a private brand and a nationally distributed manufacturer's brand is *too* great, consumers tend to believe that the private brand is inferior. On the other hand, if the savings aren't big enough, there is little incentive to buy the private brand. One study of scanner data found that if the price difference between the national brand and the private brand was less than 10 percent, people tended not to buy the private brand. If the price difference was greater than 20 percent, consumers perceived the private brand to be inferior.[15]

In sum, the most recent research has shown that a well-known brand name is used by people in many countries as their primary indicator of quality. If the product does not have this feature, then price, followed by the physical appearance of the item, is used to judge quality. After a well-known brand name, price, and physical appearance, the reputation of the retailer is used by consumers as an indicator of quality.[16]

prestige pricing
Charging a high price to help promote a high-quality image.

LOOKING BACK

Look back at the story about Fresh Fields lowering its prices to attract more mainstream shoppers. Lowering prices does not always increase a firm's revenue. This will happen only if the demand is elastic. Cost determines the floor below which a price should not be set in the long run. A price set solely on cost may be too high and therefore not attract customers. Conversely, a price based on cost alone that is too low results in lost revenues and profits.

Price can have an impact on perceived quality. It depends on a number of issues, such as the type of product, advertising, and the consumer's personality. A well-known brand is usually more important than price in consumers' quality perceptions.

Competition can help hold down prices in the marketplace. A firm without competition that charges a high price will soon find competitors attracted to that market. As competitors enter the market, prices typically fall, since firms compete for market share by lowering prices.

KEY TERMS

average total cost (ATC) *585*

average variable cost (AVC) *585*

break-even analysis   *588*

demand   *579*

SUMMARY

1 *Discuss the importance of pricing decisions to the economy and to the individual firm.* Pricing plays an integral role in the U.S. economy by allocating goods and services among consumers, governments, and businesses. Pricing is essential in business because it creates revenue, which is the basis of all business activity. In setting prices, marketing managers strive to find a level high enough to produce a satisfactory profit.

2 *List and explain a variety of pricing objectives.* Establishing realistic and measurable pricing objectives is a critical part of any firm's marketing strategy. Pricing objectives are commonly classified into three categories: profit oriented, sales oriented, and status quo. Profit-oriented pricing is based on profit maximization, a satisfactory level of profit, or a target return on investment. The goal of profit maximization is to generate as much revenue as possible in relation to cost. Often, a more practical approach than profit maximization is setting prices to produce profits that will satisfy management and stockholders. The most common profit-oriented strategy is pricing for a specific return on investment relative to a firm's assets. The second type of pricing objective is sales oriented, and it focuses on either maintaining a percentage share of the market or maximizing dollar or unit sales. The third type of pricing objective aims to maintain the status quo by matching competitors' prices.

3 *Explain the role of demand in price determination.* Demand is a key determinant of price. When establishing prices, a firm must first determine demand for its product. A typical demand schedule shows an inverse relationship between quantity demanded and price. That is, when price is lowered, sales increase; and when price is increased, the quantity demanded falls. However, for prestige products, there may be a direct relationship between demand and price: The quantity demanded will increase as price increases.

Marketing managers must also consider demand elasticity when setting prices. Elasticity of demand is the degree to which the quantity demanded fluctuates with changes in price. If consumers are sensitive to changes in price, demand is elastic: If they are insensitive to price changes, demand is inelastic. Thus, an increase in price will result in lower sales for an elastic product and little or no change in sales for an inelastic product.

4 *Describe cost-oriented pricing strategies.* The other major determinant of price is cost. Marketers use several cost-oriented pricing strategies. To cover their own expenses and obtain a profit, wholesalers and retailers commonly use markup pricing: They tack an extra amount onto the manufacturer's original price. Another pricing technique is to maximize profits by setting price where marginal revenue equals marginal cost. Still another pricing strategy determines how much a firm must sell to break even and uses this amount as a reference point for adjusting price.

5 *Demonstrate how the product life cycle, competition, distribution and promotion strategies, and perceptions of quality can affect price.* The price of a product normally changes as it moves through the life cycle and as demand for the product and competitive conditions change. Management often sets a high price at the introductory stage, and the high price tends to attract competition. The competition usually drives prices down, because individual competitors lower prices to gain market share.

Adequate distribution for a new product can sometimes be obtained by offering a larger-than-usual profit margin to wholesalers and retailers. Price is also used as a promotional tool to attract customers. Special low prices often attract new customers and entice existing customers to buy more.

Perceptions of quality also can influence pricing strategies. A firm trying to project a prestigious image often charges a premium price for a product. Consumers tend to equate high prices with high quality.

Discussion and Writing Questions

1. Why is pricing so important to the marketing manager?

2. Explain the role of supply and demand in determining price.

3. If a firm can increase its total revenue by raising its price, shouldn't it do so?

4. Explain the concepts of elastic and inelastic demand. Why should managers understand these concepts?

5. Your firm has based its pricing strictly on cost in the past. As the newly hired marketing manager, you believe this policy should change. Write the president a memo explaining your reasons.

6. Why is it important for managers to understand the concept of break-even points? Are there any drawbacks?

7. Give an example of each major type of pricing objective.

8. Divide the class into teams of five. Each team will be assigned a different grocery store from a different chain. (An independent is fine.) Appoint a group leader. The group leaders should meet as a group and pick 15 nationally branded grocery items. Each item should be specifically described as to brand name and size of the package. Each team will then proceed to its assigned store and collect price data on the 15 items. The team should also gather price data on 15 similar store brands and 15 generics, if possible.

Each team should present its results to the class and discuss why there are price variations between stores, national brands, store brands, and generics.

As a next step, go back to your assigned store and share the overall results with the store manager. Bring back the manager's comments and share them with the class.

9. How does the stage of a product's life cycle affect price? Give some examples.

10. How should information on the Internet be priced? What are the pros and cons of the information-pricing models discussed at the following site?

   http://www-sloan.mit.edu/ 15.967/group17/home.html

11. If the Internet is accessible by people all over the world, how do marketers deal with consumers using different kinds of currency?

   http://www.burmex.com/ store/pricing.htm

 Application for Small Business

RoseAnn and Bob Peterson combined her children's theater experience and his business background to create The Kids' Bookstore in Nashville, Tennessee. Their goal was not to simply sell books, but to be a community resource as well. At its peak, the store held about 225 children-focused events per year. Events included readings, puppet shows, visits by authors, short plays, and dance recitals. Sales peaked in 1995 at $800,000, and the store carried 35,000 titles. The Kids' Bookstore featured a very knowledgeable staff, lots of special events, and free story hours. Today, Bob and RoseAnn are out of business: Four book superstores opened within a two-mile radius of the store. Bob and RoseAnn's story is not an isolated incident. In 1995 and 1996, over 200 independent booksellers succumbed to the giant chains.

Questions

1. Were Bob and RoseAnn selling a product with elastic or inelastic demand?

2. Why didn't the "special events" keep The Kid's Bookstore in business?

3. Do you think that Bob and RoseAnn faced a demand problem, cost problem, or both?

4. Look back at the "Other Determinants of Price." Explain how each one may have affected The Kids' Bookstore.

Fabulous Technology Offers Many New Features for Tomorrow's Automobiles— But Will the Consumer Buy It?

by Mary Klupp
Futures Research Manager,
Ford Motor Company

Technology has created dramatic changes in automobiles during the past few decades. Today's Ford is certainly not like your grandfather's. From fuel-efficient engines to numerous safety features, today's vehicles are a better value for the money because of technology. For example, many vehicles now offer a remote keyless entry system that enables you to open or lock your vehicle from outside with a push of a button.

Ford's engineers continue to be leaders in creating and designing new features for tomorrow's trucks, minivans, utility sports vehicles, and cars. A recent marketing research study conducted by Ford took a look at some of the new ideas generated by their engineers to determine: (a) if target customers were interested in a particular feature, and (b) if the concept has appeal, will consumers pay the suggested retail price. The research was conducted in both the United States and the United Kingdom.

Twenty-eight new technology features were evaluated using computer-aided multimedia personal interviewing on desk-top computers. Video descriptions were integrated with a computerized quantitative questionnaire for all feature evaluations. Focus groups were conducted (nine in the United States and ten in the United Kingdom) to clarify customer likes and dislikes on specific features.

Examples of the new technology and the proposed price are as follows:

Signature Series Video Case

Mary P. Klupp

Cargo Retention Device

Floor Mounted Cargo Net (US $50/UK £30)

Retractable Cargo Net (US $150/UK £100)

Liftgate Cargo Net (US $50/UK £30)

The *Cargo Retention Device* prevents objects in the cargo area of the vehicle from sliding forward in the event of a sudden stop. Three versions of the *Cargo Retention Device* are available: the Floor Mounted Cargo Net (secured with attachments at the ceiling and the load floor); the Retractable Cargo Net (similar to the Floor Mounted Cargo Net, but can be retracted into a roller shade on the back of the seat); and the Liftgate Cargo Net (automatically covers the cargo when liftgate is closed).

Cooled/Heated Seats (US $450, UK £160)

The Cooled and Heated Seat system controls the temperature of the driver's seat by pumping liquid through tubes inside the seat. This system is turned on by a switch on the dash board and can be adjusted to cool or heat. The System works on both cloth and leather seats.

Fingerprint Passive Entry (US $700, reg. power locks— $250/UK £360, central locks—£200)

Finger Print Passive Entry allows the driver to gain access to vehicles equipped with power locks, without the use of a key. The driver's own finger print is used as a unique identification to lock and unlock the vehicle. The vehicle recognizes the driver's finger print through the use of a touch pad. To lock the driver's door or all the vehicle's doors, simply touch the pad for half a second. (UK VERSION) Finger Print Passive Entry is also available for easy trunk or liftgate access. The vehicle can still be locked or unlocked with a key.

Fold Out Storage Container (US $150/UK £70)

The Fold Out Storage Container provides access to items stored in the forward part of the cargo area which is not easily accessible by shorter individuals. Items such as loose toys, or a stroller can be easily and conveniently stored.

Front Impact Warning

Indicator Light and Tone (US $300, UK £150)

Indicator Light and Voice (US $300/UK £150)

Indicator Light and Brake Tap (US $350/UK £180)

The Front Impact Warning System alerts drivers when approaching another vehicle or object. Sensors located in the bumper detect obstacles in front of the vehicle. The Front Impact Warning System combines an indicator light and audible tone to alert the driver. There are two alternative methods the system can use to alert the driver: A combined indicator light and voice warning, or a combined indicator light and automatic brake tap.

Infinite Door Check (US $25/UK £10)

The Infinite Door Check holds the door at any open position selected. When in a cramped parking space or on an inclined surface, the door can be stopped at any position without bumping the vehicle next to you.

Light Management System (US $150/UK £80)

The Light Management System automatically controls your headlamps to provide better illumination while driving. LMS adjusts the forward lighting system in response to changing environmental conditions. The system automatically turns on and adjusts the light for driving needs by altering the light as your vehicle gains or loses speed. Additional side lighting will allow a driver to see whatever obstacle may lie in the path of the vehicle before a turn is made. The LMS system allows the vehicle to switch the headlamps from high beams to low beams, and back again. The system can be manually changed at any time.

Night Vision System (US $1,500/UK £1,000)

The Night Vision System enhances driver visibility at night without causing glare to oncoming drivers. The system uses Infra Red headlamps to illuminate the road ahead. Sensors form an image of the road on a transparent display which lowers into the driver's view. An enhanced image of the road ahead is displayed on the screen, improving visibility.

Rear View Imaging System (US $1,000/UK £500)

The Rear View Imaging System replaces traditional rear view mirrors with miniature cameras which view the road behind the vehicle and relay this image onto an instrument panel display. There are three cameras: the first on the driver's side, the second at the center of the rear window, and the third on the passenger's side. Together, these three cameras create a panoramic view to the sides and rear of the vehicle.

Reversing Aid

Short Range (US $225/UK £120)

Long Range (US $300/UK £150)

The Reversing Aid alerts drivers to the distance between the rear of their vehicle and an obstacle. Sensors located on the rear bumper detect obstacles behind the vehicle. A series of tones will indicate when the vehicle is within six feet of an obstacle. As the vehicle moves closer, the tones become more frequent.

Skin Temperature Sensor (US $20, reg. ATC—$175/UK £10, reg. ATC—£300)

The Skin Temperature Sensor can be added to vehicles equipped with automatic temperature control to automatically cool the temperature inside the vehicle. The Skin Temperature Sensor uses an interior infra red sensor to measure a face's skin temperature. The sensor adjusts the fan and air conditioning to cool the vehicle's interior, until the skin temperature is within a normal range.

Sun Tracking Visor (US $30/UK £25)

The Sun Tracking Visor slides along a track from the inside rearview

mirror to the edge of both front side doors, providing more accurate coverage. This feature is easy to use and provides a wide range of coverage.

Voice Enhancement System (US $100/UK £50)

The Voice Enhancement System allows front and rear passengers to communicate, without having to turn around or speak loudly. The passengers' voices are picked up by overhead microphones located throughout the vehicle and can be heard through the vehicle's audio system. This system amplifies voices while minimizing the effect of other noises such as road and wind noise. If the vehicle has a hands-free cellular phone, a call can be routed through the microphones, allowing all passengers to participate in a conference call.

Vehicle Emergency Messaging System

VEMS With Integrated Cell Phone (US $550/UK £250)

VEMS With Docking Station (US $550/UK £250)

The Vehicle Emergency Messaging System obtains assistance in the event of an emergency. Through the use of a global positioning system, a vehicle's location is constantly updated. By pressing the emergency button on the overhead console, the control center can be contacted for assistance and a cellular signal is sent with the vehicle's current location. In an accident, when airbags deploy, the system automatically notifies the control center. This feature can also include a compatible cellular telephone docking station which allows you to connect your own portable telephone to the system.

Vehicle Tracking and Recovery System (US $300/UK £150)

The Vehicle Tracking and Recovery System enables police to locate and recover stolen vehicles. If a vehicle equipped with this system is stolen, the owner immediately calls the Police Network and provides them with a unique identification number. Once activated, the system emits a silent signal which is transmitted to police vehicles.

Electronic Memo Pad (US $40/UK £20)

The Electronic Memo Pad is an audio recorder built into the vehicle. A microphone located on the visor digitally records messages which can be played back at a later time. The Electronic Memo Pad also can record directly from the radio. (UK VERSION) The Electronic Memo Pad can be set automatically to record the last RDS traffic report. (UK VERSION) If your radio is equipped with a removable faceplate, the Electronic Memo Pad System can be removed so you may play back or record messages at another location. (US VERSION) With the removable faceplate option, the Electronic Memo Pad can be taken with you to play back messages at another location.

On-Board Navigation (US $1,000; CD ROM $50/UK £600, CD ROM £30)

Traffic Info (US $1,100/UK £600)

The On-Board Navigation System enables you to receive turn by turn route instructions while in your vehicle. This system uses route information stored on a CD-ROM to compute directions. Each disc covers up to a three-state area and can be updated periodically. Your vehicle's location is identified through the use of a global positioning system. In addition, you will receive automated voice directions through the radio speakers.

Key Findings

Given the geographic, climatic, and cultural differences between the United States and the United Kingdom, there were surprisingly few differences in consumers' reactions to the various features. Men viewed safety-related features as particularly desirable for their families. The most popular features addressed safety/driving concerns such as the night vision and light management systems. Most people would like to be able to see better at night, particularly middle-aged persons whose night vision is deteriorating.

Some concepts were perceived as a bit "gimmicky" or just "something else to break." For example, Fingerprint Passive Entry is not perceived as a benefit over current remote keyless entry systems. On the other hand, features that were inexpensive but offered high utility are desirable. Examples include the Sun Tracking Visor and the Infinite Door Check.

As might be expected, consumers overestimated the manufacturer's target retail price for some items and underestimated it for others. Correspondingly, consumers were willing to pay the manufacturer's suggested retail price for some features but not for others.

Questions

1. Why is this type of pricing research necessary?
2. What other techniques could Ford have used to access demand for this new technology?
3. Explain the general relationship between perceived value and the elasticity of demand.
4. Should Ford conduct any further pricing research on these new features? If so, what kind and why?

LEARNING OBJECTIVES *After studying this chapter, you should be able to:*

1 Describe the procedure for setting the right price.

2 Identify the legal and ethical constraints on pricing decisions.

3 Explain how discounts, geographic pricing, and other special pricing tactics can be used to fine tune the base price.

4 Discuss product line pricing.

5 Describe the role of pricing during periods of inflation and recession.

6 Discuss what the future might hold for pricing in the marketing mix.

Setting the Right Price

Designer Ralph Lauren, who built a fashion empire catering to the country-club set, is turning his sights to regular folks. During 1996, Mr. Lauren's 29-year-old Polo/Ralph Lauren Corp. signed up new licensees like Reebok International and Sara Lee Corp., in an effort to wring more growth from a $4 billion retail franchise that includes men's, women's, and children's apparel, fragrances, home furnishings, and even paint.

People familiar with the closely held Polo say the company's recent financial performance has been strong. Nonetheless, the patrician snob appeal that Polo epitomized in the 1980s isn't so coveted in the practical 1990s. Department stores have all but abandoned high-fashion collections for lack of demand, and design houses Adrienne Vittadini and Anne Klein & Co. have recently discontinued their top-tier collections to concentrate on lower priced lines.

Polo already has lowered the price of its signature logo knit shirts to $49 from $55. Polo jeans at $48 in the fall of 1996 and a moderately priced women's wear collection called Lauren compete with the likes of Liz Claiborne, Inc. In addition, new, less expensive Polo Sport menswear shops are being installed in some 300 department stores.

"As a designer, I can feel the pulse of the world," says the tanned Mr. Lauren, 56 years old, during an interview at his Madison Avenue headquarters. He's ready, he says, to court "consumers out there who like quality and taste, but can't afford Ralph Lauren." Jeans are a case in point: "We've never had a big jeans business," he says. "Why let that pass by?"

In fact, the Bronx, N.Y.-born designer has dabbled in down-market distribution before. His Chaps menswear division is lower priced, and Chaps fragrance is sold in drugstores, for example. Nor is he turning his back on the affluent market. Recently, a hand-ful of retailers quickly sold out of his new, limited-edition "purple label" $2,000 men's suits tailored in England.

But marketing to an array of price ranges and tastes carries risk. Calvin Klein, Inc., has managed to push jeans and underwear alongside $1,000 women's ensembles. But Italian designer Giorgio Armani flopped when he put his trademark on Armani A/X jeans.[1]

What are the advantages and disadvantages of setting a premium price on a product? What price strategy is Ralph Lauren following with his Polo line? What are some problems he may face as he lowers prices?

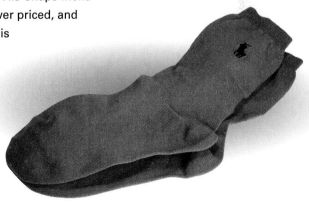

HOW TO SET A PRICE ON A PRODUCT

1 Describe the procedure for setting the right price.

Setting the right price on a product is a four-step process (see Exhibit 21.1):

1. Establish pricing goals.
2. Estimate demand, costs, and profits.
3. Choose a price strategy to help determine a base price.
4. Fine tune the base price with pricing tactics.

The first three steps are discussed below; the fourth step is discussed later in the chapter.

Establish Pricing Goals

The first step in setting the right price is to establish pricing goals. Recall from Chapter 20 that pricing objectives fall into three categories: profit oriented, sales oriented, and status quo. These goals are derived from the firm's overall objectives.

A good understanding of the marketplace and of the consumer can sometimes tell a manager very quickly whether a goal is realistic. For example, if firm A's objective of a 20 percent target return on investment (ROI), and its product development and implementation costs are $5 million, the market must be rather large or must support the price required to earn a 20 percent ROI. Assume that company B has a pricing objective that all new products must reach at least 15 percent market share within three years after their introduction. A thorough study of the environment may convince the marketing manager that the competition is too strong and the market share goal can't be met.

Exhibit 21.1

Steps in Setting the Right Price on a Product

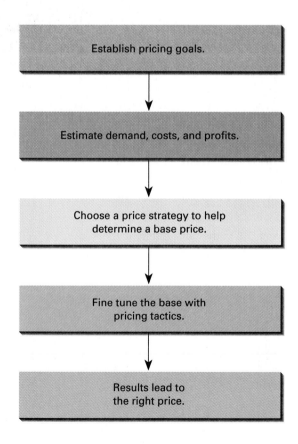

All pricing objectives have trade-offs that managers must weigh. A profit maximization objective may require a bigger initial investment than the firm can commit or wants to commit. Reaching the desired market share often means sacrificing short-term profit, because without careful management, long-term profit goals may not be met. Meeting the competition is the easiest pricing goal to implement. However, can managers really afford to ignore demand and costs, the life cycle stage, and other considerations? When creating pricing objectives, managers must consider these trade-offs in light of the target customer and the environment.

Estimate Demand, Costs, and Profits

Chapter 20 explained that total revenue is a function of price and quantity demanded and that quantity demanded depends on elasticity. After establishing pricing goals, managers should estimate total revenue at a variety of prices. Next, they should determine corresponding costs for each price. They are then ready to estimate how much profit, if any, and how much market share can be earned at each possible price. These data become the heart of the developing price policy. Managers can study the options in light of revenues, costs, and profits. In turn, this information can help determine which price can best meet the firm's pricing goals.

Choose a Price Strategy

The basic, long-term pricing framework for a good or service should be a logical extension of the pricing objectives. The marketing manager's chosen **price strategy** defines the initial price and gives direction for price movements over the product life cycle.

The price strategy sets a competitive price in a specific market segment, based on a well-defined positioning strategy. For example, a carmaker like Mercedes-Benz would set a base price at one of the six levels shown in Exhibit 21.2. The E-class models are in the premium range. Changing a price level from premium to superpremium may require a change in the product itself, the target customers served, the promotional strategy, or distribution channels. Thus, changing a price strategy can require dramatic alterations in the marketing mix. A carmaker cannot successfully compete in the superpremium category if the car looks and drives like an economy car.

A company's freedom in pricing a new product and devising a price strategy depends on the market conditions and the other elements of the marketing mix. For example, if a firm launches a new item resembling several others already on the market, its pricing freedom will be restricted. To succeed, the company will probably have to charge a price close to the average market price. In contrast, a firm that introduces a totally new product with no close substitutes will have considerable pricing freedom.

The three basic strategies for setting a price on a good or service are price skimming, penetration pricing, and status quo pricing. A discussion of each type follows.

Price Skimming

Price skimming is sometimes called a "market-plus" approach to pricing, because it denotes a high price relative to the prices of competing products. Radius Corporation produces unique oval-headed toothbrushes made of black neoprene that look like a scuba-diving accessory. Radius uses a skimming policy, pricing the toothbrushes at $9.95, compared to around $2.00 for a regular toothbrush.

The term **price skimming** is derived from the phrase "skimming the cream off the top." Companies often use this strategy for new products when the product is perceived by the target market as having unique advantages. For example, Caterpil-

price strategy
Basic, long-term pricing framework, which establishes the initial price for a product and the intended direction for price movements over the product life cycle.

price skimming
Pricing policy whereby a firm charges a high introductory price, often coupled with heavy promotion.

Exhibit 21.2 *Segmenting the Automobile Market by Price*

Price range	Model		
Ultra-premium *(over $100,000)*	Lamborghini Rolls Royce	 Lamborghini USA, Inc.	 By permission of Rolls-Royce Motor Cars, Inc.
Super-premium *($60,000–$100,000)*	BMW 850Ci Porsche 928 GTS	 BMW of North America, Inc.	 Porsche Cars North America
Premium *($40,000–$60,000)*	Mercedes E-Class Lexus LS 400	 Mercedes-Benz of North America, Inc.	 Lexus, A Division of Toyota Motor Sales, USA, Inc.
Moderate *($15,000–$40,000)*	Buick Regal GS Mazda Miata	 Buick Motor Division	 Mazda Motor of America
Economy *($10,000–$15,000)*	Saturn SL1 Honda Civic	 Saturn Corporation	 Honda Motor Company, Ltd.
Basic *(under $10,000)*	Geo Metro Ford Aspire	 Chevrolet Motor Division	 Ford Motor Company

lar sets premium prices on its construction equipment to support and capture its high perceived value. Genzyme Corporation introduced Ceredase as the first effective treatment for Gaucher's disease. The pill allows patients to avoid years of painful physical deterioration and lead normal lives. A year's supply for one patient can exceed $300,000.[2]

As a product progresses through its life cycle, the firm may lower its price to successfully reach larger market segments. Economists have described this type of pricing as "sliding down the demand curve." Not all companies slide down the curve. Genentech's TPA, a drug that clears blood clots, was still priced at $2,200 a dose four years after its introduction, despite competition from a much lower priced competitor.

Genentech, Incorporated
How does Genentech position and promote its products in light of the high prices often charged?

http://www.gene.com/

Price skimming works best when the market is willing to buy the product even though it carries an above-average price. If, for example, some purchasing agents feel that Caterpillar equipment is far superior to competitors' products, then Caterpillar can charge premium prices successfully. Firms can also effectively use price skimming when a product is well protected legally, when it represents a technological breakthrough, or when it has in some other way blocked entry to competitors. Managers may follow a skimming strategy when production cannot be expanded rapidly because of technological difficulties, shortages, or constraints imposed by the skill and time required to produce a product. As long as demand is greater than supply, skimming is an attainable strategy.

A successful skimming strategy enables management to recover its product development or "educational" costs quickly. (Often, consumers must be "taught" the advantages of a radically new item, such as high-definition TV.) Even if the market perceives an introductory price as too high, managers can easily correct the problem by lowering the price. Firms often feel it is better to test the market at a high price and then lower the price if sales are too slow. They are tacitly saying, "If there are any premium-price buyers in the market, let's reach them first and maximize our revenue per unit." Successful skimming strategies are not limited to products. Well-known athletes, entertainers, lawyers, and hairstylists are experts at price skimming. Naturally, a skimming strategy will encourage competitors to enter the market.

Penetration Pricing

Penetration pricing is at the end of the spectrum, opposite skimming. **Penetration pricing** means charging a relatively low price for a product as a way to reach the mass market. The low price is designed to capture a large share of a substantial market, resulting in lower production costs. If a marketing manager has made obtaining a large market share the firm's pricing objective, penetration pricing is a logical choice.

Penetration pricing does mean lower profit per unit, however. Therefore, to reach the break-even point, it requires higher volume sales than would a skimming policy. If reaching a high volume of sales takes a long time, then the recovery of product development costs will also be slow. As you might expect, penetration pricing tends to discourage competition.

A penetration strategy tends to be effective in a price-sensitive market. Price should decline more rapidly when demand is elastic, because the market can be expanded through a lower price. Also, price sensitivity and greater competitive pressure should lead to a lower initial price and a relatively slow decline in the price later. Southwest Airlines' success is based on penetration pricing. By flying only the Boeing 737, it realizes efficiencies in stocking parts and training pilots

penetration pricing
Pricing policy whereby a firm charges a relatively low price for a product initially as a way to reach the mass market.

Southwest Airlines Home Gate
How does Southwest promote its fare advantage on the Web?

http://www.iflyswa.com/

and mechanics. It also saves by avoiding a costly computer reservation system, such as Apollo or SABRE, and by not serving meals. Southwest has the lowest cost per seat mile in the industry. Costs per seat mile for the major carriers are USAir, 10.8¢; United, 9.6¢; Delta, 9.4¢; Northwest, 9.1¢; American, 8.9¢; and Southwest, 7.0¢. Around 800 people a week used to fly between Louisville, Kentucky, and Chicago; since Southwest entered the market, about 26,000 do. Southwest's move into the Florida market in 1995 produced revenues 40 percent higher than expected for the company. Competitors are nervously awaiting Southwest's new service to the northeast (New York and surroundings) in 1997.

The choice of pricing strategies depends on competitive conditions throughout the world. For example, Levi Strauss has cut into the foreign market while sustaining its U.S. sales. The company's success lies in its skill at wielding a double-edged price strategy: penetration pricing in the United States and price skimming abroad. Sometimes companies reverse this approach, using penetration pricing in the international market and skimming in the domestic market.

Consumers' perceptions of penetration pricing may not always hold true in the global marketplace. An American buying Levis in Germany quickly finds that the jeans aren't value priced. The same phenomenon applies to America's budget hotel chains abroad, as explained in the "Global Perspectives" box.
Global Perspectives

Status Quo Pricing

The third basic price strategy a firm may choose is status quo pricing, or meeting the competition. (See also Chapter 20.) It means charging a price identical to or very close to the competition's price. Montgomery Ward, for example, makes sure it is charging comparable prices by sending representatives to shop at Sears stores.

Although status quo pricing has the advantage of simplicity, its disadvantage is that the strategy may ignore demand or cost or both. But meeting the competition may be the safest route to long-term survival if the firm is comparatively small.

THE LEGALITY AND ETHICS OF PRICE STRATEGY

2 Identify the legal and ethical constraints on pricing decisions.

As we mentioned in Chapter 3, some pricing decisions are subject to government regulation. Before marketing managers establish any price strategy, they should know the laws that limit their decision making. Among the issues that fall into this category are unfair trade practices, price fixing, price discrimination, and predatory pricing.

Unfair Trade Practices

unfair trade practice acts
Law that prohibits wholesalers and retailers from selling below cost.

In over half the states, **unfair trade practice acts** put a floor under wholesale and retail prices. Selling below cost in these states is illegal. Wholesalers and retailers must usually take a certain minimum percentage markup on their combined merchandise cost and transportation cost. The most common markup figures are 6 percent at the retail level and 2 percent at the wholesale level. If a specific wholesaler or retailer can provide "conclusive proof" that operating costs are lower than the minimum required figure, lower prices may be allowed.

The intent of unfair trade practice acts is to protect small local firms from giants like Wal-Mart and Target, which operate very efficiently on razor-thin profit mar-

Global Perspectives

Budget Hotels Aren't Always a Bargain Abroad

Anne Auberjonois figured she'd save money if she stayed at a Best Western hotel in Paris. But the New York graphic designer ended up paying $180 a night for a room with chipped paint and no shower curtain. "Budget to me means clean, comfortable service for a good rate," she says. "But what I ended up getting was mediocre for a high price."

At a record pace, budget and midpriced hotels are popping up around the globe, now accounting for more than a third of all hotels. They're attracting everyone, from business travelers whose companies won't pay for luxury rooms anymore to pennywise vacationers. But there's a catch: Many of the budget hotels aren't cheap.

Part of the problem is expectations. When travelers reserve a room at a budget hotel, they figure they'll save money. But while bargains can still be found, Quality Inn, which typically charges $65 a night in the U.S., is getting as much as $160 a night in Rome. And the rates aren't much better in developing countries: The Holiday Inn in Beijing costs $160 a night, and a single night at a Best Western in New Delhi can cost $135.

It isn't necessarily the hotels' fault. The weak U.S. dollar is causing some of these loftier prices. Plus, overseas hotels are typically more expensive to operate. But consultants also say many hotel chains expanding abroad are capitalizing on limited lodging choices. In many undeveloped countries, the supply of hotels runs "somewhere between exclusive five-star properties and very shoddy youth hostels," says Rolfe Shellenberger of Runzheimer International, Inc., a management-consulting firm in Rochester, Wis. "The hotel chains know business travelers can and will pay more." "It comes under the heading of 'Let's take advantage of an opportunity,'" says Morris Lasky, president of Lodging Unlimited in West Chester, Pa., which manages hotels. "This is a simple matter of supply and demand."

Much of the growth in budget hotels is coming from vacationing Americans who are homesick for familiar and inexpensive accommodations. But business travelers are staying in a lot of these properties, too, because companies have cut back on upscale travel. A spokeswoman for Choice Hotels International, the franchiser of Quality Inns, Comfort Inns, and Sleep Inns, says roughly 65 percent of its overseas guests at big city locations are traveling on business. "These people are on budgets," says the spokeswoman. "They can't have some huge hotel bill on their expense account."

For their part, hotel officials blame higher overhead abroad for some of the prices. In Europe, overhead typically eats up more than half of a property's revenue, compared with just 30 percent at hotels in the U.S. That's partly because employers there are generally required to pay higher health and retirement benefits. Outside Europe, wages are lower, but hotels often have to hire larger staffs to compensate for unskilled labor forces.

"You might need two to three times more employees per room in developing countries than in the U.S., says Werner Braum, director of international development for Best Western. "The workers just don't have the same level of training." Start-up expenses are generally much higher outside the U.S. "Just the raw materials cost more," says the spokeswoman for Choice.[3]

Do you believe that the high prices charged overseas are justified? Is there anything wrong with charging more if you know the customer will pay more? How would you describe the price strategy of the budget chains?

gins. However, state enforcement of unfair trade practice laws has generally been lax, partly because low prices benefit local consumers.

Price Fixing

Price fixing is an agreement between two or more firms on the price they will charge for a product. For example, suppose two or more executives from competing firms meet to decide how much to charge for a product or to decide which of them will submit the lowest bid on a certain contract. Such practices are illegal under the Sher-

price fixing
An agreement between two or more firms on the price they will charge for a product.

man Act and the Federal Trade Commission Act. Offenders have received fines and sometimes prison terms. Price fixing is one area where the law is quite clear, and the Justice Department's enforcement is vigorous.

Currently, Archer Daniels Midland (ADM), the huge ($11 billion in sales) foodstuffs and chemicals company, has 11 class action price-fixing suits filed against it. Mark Whitacre, a former ADM executive now testifying for the prosecution, said the worldview of ADM is "the customer is our enemy; the competitor is our friend." ADM sells lysine, used primarily as an ingredient in hog and chicken feed. After an initial drop, the price of lysine has doubled in the 1990s. In the high-fructose corn syrup world, ADM is accused of price fixing. One plaintiff, Golden Eagle Foods of Alabama, says that ADM and rival Cargill played a friendly Ping-Pong game with prices, at his expense. One would raise the price of lysine, and then the other would. PepsiCo has joined a class action suit accusing ADM of conspiring with its competitors to set prices on liquid carbon dioxide.

Price Discrimination

The Robinson-Patman Act of 1936 prohibits any firm from selling to two or more different buyers, within a reasonably short time, commodities (not services) of like grade and quality at different prices where the result would be to substantially lessen competition. The act also makes it illegal for a seller to offer two buyers different supplementary services and for buyers to use their purchasing power to force sellers into granting discriminatory prices or services.

Six elements are therefore needed for a violation of the Robinson-Patman Act to occur:

- There must be price discrimination; that is, the seller must charge different prices to different customers for the same product.
- The transaction must occur in interstate commerce.
- The seller must discriminate by price among two or more purchasers; that is, the seller must make two or more actual sales within a reasonably short time.
- The products sold must be commodities or other tangible goods.

Price variations in perishable goods such as tomatoes are justified under the Robinson-Patman Act.
© Jeff Zaniba/Tony Stone Images

- The products sold must be of like grade and quality, not necessarily identical. If the goods are truly interchangeable and substitutable, then they are of like grade and quality.
- There must be significant competitive injury.

The Robinson-Patman Act provides three defenses for the seller charged with price discrimination (in each case the burden is on the defendant to prove the defense):

- *Cost:* A firm can charge different prices to different customers if the prices represent manufacturing or quantity discount savings.
- *Market conditions:* Price variations are justified if designed to meet fluid product or market conditions. Examples include the deterioration of perishable goods, the obsolescence of seasonal products, a distress sale under court order, and a legitimate going-out-of-business sale.
- *Competition:* A reduction in price may be necessary to stay even with the competition. Specifically, if a competitor undercuts the price quoted by a seller to a buyer, the law authorizes the seller to lower the price charged to the buyer for the product in question.

A proposed $409 million settlement of a lawsuit against major drug manufacturers was thrown out by a federal judge in late 1996 because it contained no provision for changes in manufacturers' pricing practices. Pharmacists, in a class action encompassing 40,000 independent retail pharmacies, had accused drugmakers of offering big discounts to some purchasers, such as mail-order pharmacies and large managed-care plans, while conspiring to charge the retail pharmacies and drugstore chains much higher prices. In his opinion, the judge wrote that "we believe that the evidence is sufficient to raise a reasonable inference of the existence of a conspiracy among all the manufacturer defendants."[6]

Predatory Pricing

Predatory pricing is the practice of charging a very low price for a product with the intent of driving competitors out of business or out of a market. Once competitors have been driven out, the firm raises its prices. This practice is illegal under the Sherman Act and the Federal Trade Commission Act. Proving the use of the practice is difficult and expensive, however. A defendant must show that the predator, the destructive company, explicitly tried to ruin a competitor and that the predatory price was below the defendant's average cost.

predatory pricing
The practice of charging a very low price for a product with the intent of driving competitors out of business or out of a market.

Despite the difficulty of proving predatory pricing, a state court in Arkansas ruled that Wal-Mart had engaged in predatory pricing by selling pharmacy products below cost. Three pharmacies in Conway, Arkansas, claimed that Wal-Mart was using predatory pricing to put them out of business. Wal-Mart admitted selling below cost, but denied that it was attempting to put anyone out of business. Wal-Mart noted that in 1987, when it started selling pharmaceuticals in Conway, there were 12 pharmacies and that the same 12 were still in business at the time of the court case. Also, the number of pharmacists had increased during that period from 38 to 58, because several food stores had also opened pharmacies. Nevertheless, Wal-Mart lost the case.[7] It has been appealed to the Arkansas Supreme Court.

TACTICS FOR FINE TUNING THE BASE PRICE

After managers understand both the legal and the marketing consequences of price strategies, they should set a **base price,** the general price level at which the company expects to sell the good or service. (Recall the car example in Exhibit 21.2.) The general price level is correlated with the pricing policy: above the market (price skimming), at the market (status quo pricing), or below the market (penetration pricing). The final step, then, is to fine tune the base price.

Fine-tuning techniques are short-run approaches that do not change the general price level. They do, however, result in changes within a general price level. These pricing tactics allow the firm to adjust for competition in certain markets, meet ever-changing government regulations, take advantage of unique demand situations, and meet promotional and positioning goals. Fine-tuning pricing tactics include various sorts of discounts, geographic pricing, and special pricing tactics.

3 Explain how discounts, geographic pricing, and other special pricing tactics can be used to fine tune the base price.

base price
The general price level at which the company expects to sell the good or service.

Discounts, Allowances, and Rebates

A base price can be lowered through the use of discounts and the related tactics of allowances and rebates. Managers use the various forms of discounts to encourage customers to do what they would not ordinarily do, such as paying cash rather than using credit, taking delivery out of season, or performing certain functions within a distribution channel. A summary of the most common tactics is as follows:

quantity discount
Price reduction offered to buyers buying in multiple units or above a specified dollar amount.

noncumulative quantity discount
A deduction from list price that applies to a single order rather than to the total volume of orders placed during a certain period.

cash discount
A price reduction offered to a consumer, an industrial user, or a marketing intermediary in return for prompt payment of a bill.

functional discount (trade discount)
Discount to wholesalers and retailers for performing channel functions.

Rebates help manufacturers stimulate demand and provide customers with real purchase incentives.
Courtesy of Canon U.S.A., Inc.

- *Quantity discounts.* When buyers get a lower price for buying in multiple units or above a specified dollar amount, they are receiving a **quantity discount.** A **cumulative quantity discount** is a deduction from list price that applies to the buyer's total purchases made during a specific period; it is intended to encourage customer loyalty. In contrast, a **noncumulative quantity discount** is a deduction from list price that applies to a single order rather than to the total volume of orders placed during a certain period. It is intended to encourage orders in large quantities.

- *Cash discounts.* A **cash discount** is a price reduction offered to a consumer, an industrial user, or a marketing intermediary in return for prompt payment of a bill. Prompt payment saves the seller carrying charges and billing expenses and allows the seller to avoid bad debt.

- *Functional discounts.* When distribution channel intermediaries, such as wholesalers or retailers, perform a service or function for the manufacturer, they must be compensated. This compensation, typically a percentage discount from the base price, is called a **functional discount** (or **trade discount**). Functional discounts vary greatly from channel to channel, depending on the tasks performed by the intermediary.

- *Seasonal discounts.* A **seasonal discount** is a price reduction for buying merchandise out of season. It shifts the storage function to the purchaser. Seasonal discounts also enable manufacturers to maintain a steady production schedule year-round.

- *Promotional allowances.* A **promotional allowance** (also known as a trade allowance) is a payment to a dealer for promoting the manufacturer's products. It is both a pricing tool and a promotional device. As a pricing tool, a promotional allowance is like a functional discount. If, for example, a retailer runs an ad for a manufacturer's product, the manufacturer may pay half the cost. If a retailer sets up a special display, the manufacturer may include a certain quantity of free goods in the retailer's next order.

- *Rebates.* A **rebate** is a cash refund given for the purchase of a product during a specific period. The advantage of a rebate over a simple price reduction for stimulating demand is that a rebate is a temporary inducement that can be taken away without altering the basic price structure. A manufacturer that uses a simple price reduction for a short time may meet resistance when trying to restore the price to its original, higher level.

Trade Loading and Everyday Low Prices

Trade loading occurs when a manufacturer temporarily lowers the price to induce wholesalers and retailers to buy more goods than can be sold in a reasonable time. Say that Procter & Gamble offers Super Valu an additional 30¢ off the normal price for a bottle of Prell. The Super Valu buyer jumps at the bargain and buys a three-month supply of Prell. Typically, Super Valu would pass along the discount to customers for about a month, but then return to the original price for the last two months, thereby reaping some extra profit.

Trade discounts like these have more than tripled in the past decade, to around $38 billion in 1996. The practice is most common in the consumer packaged-goods industry. An estimated $100 billion in grocery products, mostly nonperishables, sit at any one time on trucks and railcars or stacked inside distribution centers, caught in gridlock because of trade loading. This idle inventory is estimated to add about $20 billion a year to the nation's $400 billion grocery bill.[8]

However, it is estimated that such practices generate about 70 percent of wholesalers' profits and 40 percent of supermarkets' profits.[9] Wholesalers and retailers have understandably become addicted to trade-loading deals.

Unfortunately, trade loading ultimately costs consumers (and manufacturers) money, as shown in Exhibit 21.3. It "whipsaws" production and distribution and increases the manufacturer's costs. The largest U.S. packaged-goods manufacturer, Procter & Gamble, estimates that it has created over $1 billion worth of unproductive inventory which has sat in P&G's distribution pipeline. Moreover, P&G's former chairman, Edward Anzt, notes:

> Trade loading has caused the erosion of consumer loyalty. As retailers and wholesalers buy on deals and discounts, they pass wide price swings to consumers in an unpredictable pattern, and these shoppers, no dummies, increasingly "forward buy" themselves. People have reached the point where they won't buy unless a product is on sale. Shopping store to store for the best deal, they bulk up on whichever item—P&G's Crest or Colgate-Palmolive's Colgate, P&G's Tide or Lever Brothers' Wish—is on promotion that week.[10]

P&G has decided to attack the trade-loading problem with **everyday low prices** (EDLP), the tactic of offering lower prices (often 10 to 25 percent lower) and maintaining those prices while eliminating functional discounts that result in trade loading. Instead of selling, say, a case of cake mix for $10.00 most of the time and then for $7.00 to load the trade, P&G will sell the case for $8.50 all the time. Since 1994, P&G has reduced its list prices by 12 percent to 24 percent on all of its U.S. brands.[11] EDLP has worked, as profits are at a 21-year high for the company. By using EDLP on its liquid laundry detergents (i.e., Cheer, Tide), its market share has risen from 41 to 47 percent from 1993 to 1996.

Although Wal-Mart has been the EDLP leader for years, many companies are beginning to follow suit. In the summer of 1996, Phillip Morris cereals division decided to drop 20 percent off the price of Grape-Nuts and Raisin Bran and do away with trade loading and coupons. Other converts include Colgate-Palmolive, Ralston-Purina, Quaker Oats, and Kraft General Foods.[12] Ford, Chrysler, and GM are testing haggle-free EDLP. GM's successful EDLP in California are being expanded to other states. For example, GM prices a well-equipped Pontiac Grand Am for $14,995, versus a comparably equipped Honda Accord LX priced at $20,220 and a comparable Toyota Camry DX at $20,658.[13] It has been said that GM is "transforming itself into the Wal-Mart of the auto industry."[14]

Geographic Pricing

Because many sellers ship their wares to a nationwide or even a worldwide market, the cost of freight can greatly affect the total cost of a product. Sellers may use several different geographic pricing tactics to moderate the impact of freight costs on distant customers. Following are the most common methods of geographic pricing:

- *FOB origin pricing.* **FOB origin pricing,** also called FOB factory or FOB shipping point, is a price tactic that requires the buyer to absorb the freight costs from the shipping point. The farther buyers are from sellers, the more they pay, because transportation costs generally increase with the distance merchandise is shipped.

- *Uniform delivered pricing.* If the marketing manager wants total costs, including freight, to be equal for all purchasers of identical products, the firm will adopt uni-

seasonal discount
A price reduction for buying merchandise out of season.

promotional allowance (trade allowance)
Payment to a dealer for promoting the manufacturer's products.

rebate
Cash refund given for the purchase of a product during a specific period.

trade loading
Practice of temporarily lowering the price to induce wholesalers and retailers to buy more goods than can be sold in a reasonable time.

everyday low prices (EDLP)
Price tactic of permanently reducing prices 10 to 25 percent below the traditional levels while eliminating trade discounts that create trade loading.

FOB origin pricing
Price tactic that requires the buyer to absorb the freight costs from the shipping point ("free on board").

Exhibit 21.3
Costs of Trade Loading

With trade loading

The manufacturer stockpiles ingredients and packaging supplies to meet peak production levels.

Plants prepare huge runs. Scheduling is chaotic, with more overtime and temporary workers.

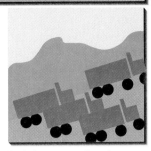

Freight companies charge premium rates for the manufacturer's periodic blow-out shipments.

Distributors overstock as they binge on short-term discounts. Cartons sit for weeks inside warehouses.

At distribution centers, the goods get overhandled. Damaged items go back to the manufacturer.

Twelve weeks after the items leave the production line, they may not be fresh for the consumer.

Without trade loading

No more panic purchases are necessary. The company cuts down on inventories, freeing up cash.

Factories run on normal shifts. The company cuts down on overtime pay and supplemental workers.

The manufacturer eliminates peak-and-valley distribution. That helps it save 5 percent in shipping costs.

Wholesalers' inventories get cut in half. That means storage and handling costs decline 17 percent.

Retailers receive undamaged products. The perception of the manufacturer's quality improves.

The consumer gets the goods 25 days earlier, and—even better news— at a 6 percent lower price.

Under FOB pricing, the buyer absorbs the freight costs from the shipping point. The greater the distance transported, the higher the costs.
© Greg Pease/Tony Stone Images

form delivered pricing, or "postage stamp" pricing. With **uniform delivered pricing,** the seller pays the actual freight charges and bills every purchaser an identical, flat freight charge.

- *Zone pricing.* A marketing manager who wants to equalize total costs among buyers within large geographic areas—but not necessarily all of the seller's market area—may modify the base price with a zone-pricing tactic. **Zone pricing** is a modification of uniform delivered pricing. Rather than placing the entire United States (or its total market) under a uniform freight rate, the firm divides it into segments or zones and charges a flat freight rate to all customers in a given zone. The U.S. Postal Service's parcel post rate structure is probably the best known zone pricing system in the country.

- *Freight absorption pricing.* In **freight absorption pricing,** the seller pays all or part of the actual freight charges and does not pass them on to the buyer. The manager may use this tactic in intensely competitive areas or as a way to break into new market areas.

- *Basing-point pricing.* With **basing-point pricing,** the seller designates a location as a basing point and charges all buyers the freight cost from that point, regardless of the city from which the goods are shipped. Thanks to several adverse court rulings, basing-point pricing has waned in popularity. Freight fees charged when none were actually incurred, called *phantom freight,* have been declared illegal.

uniform delivered pricing
Price tactic in which the seller pays the actual freight charges and bills every purchaser an identical, flat freight charge.

zone pricing
Modification of uniform delivered pricing that divides the United States (or the total market) into segments or zones and charges a flat freight rate to all customers in a given zone.

Special Pricing Tactics

Unlike geographic pricing, special pricing tactics are unique and defy neat categorization. Managers use these tactics for various reasons—for example, to stimulate demand for specific products, to increase store patronage, and to offer a wider variety of merchandise at a specific price point. Special pricing tactics include a single-price tactic, flexible pricing, professional services pricing, price lining, leader pricing, bait pricing, odd–even pricing, price bundling, and two-part pricing. A brief overview of each of these tactics

The U.S. Postal Service's parcel post rate structure is the best-known zone pricing system in the country.
© 1996 PhotoDisc, Inc.

freight absorption pricing
Price tactic in which the seller pays all or part of the actual freight charges and does not pass them on to the buyer.

basing-point pricing
Price tactic that charges freight from a given (basing) point, regardless of the city from which the goods are shipped.

single-price tactic
Policy of offering all goods and services at the same price.

flexible pricing (variable pricing)
Price tactic in which different customers pay different prices for essentially the same merchandise bought in equal quantities.

follows, along with a manager's reasons for using that tactic or a combination of tactics to change the base price.

Single-Price Tactic

A merchant using a **single-price tactic** offers all goods and services at the same price (or perhaps two or three prices). Retailers using this tactic include One Price Clothing Stores, Dre$$ to the Nine$, Your $10 Store, and Fashions $9.99. One Price Clothing Stores, for example, tend to be small, about 3,000 square feet. Their goal is to offer merchandise that would sell for at least $15 to $18 in other stores. The stores carry pants, shirts, blouses, sweaters, and shorts for juniors, misses, and large-sized women. The stores do not feature any seconds or irregular items, and everything is sold for $6.

Single-price selling removes price comparisons from the buyer's decision-making process. The consumer just looks for suitability and the highest perceived quality. The retailer enjoys the benefits of a simplified pricing system and minimal clerical errors. However, continually rising costs are a headache for retailers following this strategy. In times of inflation, they must frequently raise the selling price. The recession of the early 1990s resulted in the rapid growth of single-price chains.

Flexible Pricing

Flexible pricing (or **variable pricing**) means that different customers pay different prices for essentially the same merchandise bought in equal quantities. This tactic is often found in the sale of shopping goods, specialty merchandise, and most industrial goods except supply items. Car dealers, many appliance retailers, and manufacturers of industrial installations, accessories, and component parts commonly follow the practice. It allows the seller to adjust for competition by meeting another seller's price. Thus, a marketing manager with a status quo pricing objective might readily adopt the tactic. Flexible pricing also enables the seller to close a sale with price-conscious consumers. If buyers show promise of becoming large-volume shoppers, flexible pricing can be used to lure their business.

The obvious disadvantages of flexible pricing are the lack of consistent profit margins, the potential ill will of high-paying purchasers, the tendency for salespeople to automatically lower the price to make a sale, and the possibility of a price war among sellers. The disadvantages of flexible pricing have led the automobile industry to experiment with one price for all buyers. Ford started offering the Cougar at one price and has seen an 80 percent increase in sales. General Motors uses a one-price tactic for some of its models, including the Saturn and the Buick Regal.

Professional Services Pricing

Professional services pricing is used by people with lengthy experience, training, and often certification by a licensing board—for example, lawyers, physicians, and family counselors. Professionals sometimes charge customers at an hourly rate, but sometimes fees are based on the solution of a problem or performance of an act (such as an eye examination) rather than on the actual time involved. A surgeon may perform a heart operation and charge a flat fee of $5,000. The operation itself may require only four hours, resulting in a hefty $1,250 hourly rate. The physician justifies the fee because of the lengthy education and internship required to learn the complex procedures of a heart operation. Lawyers also sometimes use flat-rate pricing, such as $500 for completing a divorce and $50 for handling a traffic ticket.

Those who use professional pricing have an ethical responsibility not to overcharge a customer. Because demand is sometimes highly inelastic, such as when a person re-

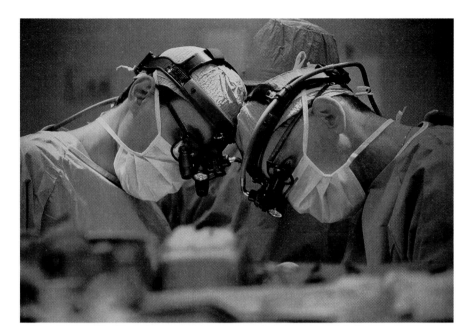

quires heart surgery or a daily insulin shot to survive, there may be a temptation to charge "all the traffic will bear." Although drug companies are often criticized for their high prices, they claim that their charges are ethical. They say prices for new drugs need to be high to recover the research costs incurred in developing the drugs. The "Ethics in Marketing" box takes a more detailed look at Crixivan, a promising new drug to fight AIDS.

Price Lining

When a seller establishes a series of prices for a type of merchandise, it creates a price line. **Price lining** is the practice of offering a product line with several items at specific price points. For example, Hon, an office furniture manufacturer, may offer its four-drawer file cabinets at $125, $250, and $400. The Limited may offer women's dresses at $40, $70, and $100, with no merchandise marked at prices between those figures. Instead of a normal demand curve running from $40 to $100, The Limited has three demand points (prices). Theoretically, the "curve" exists only because people would buy goods at the in-between prices if it were possible to do so. For example, a number of dresses could be sold at $60, but no sales will occur at that price because $60 is not part of the price line.

price lining
Practice of offering a product line with several items at specific price points.

Price lining reduces confusion for both the salesperson and the consumer. The buyer may be offered a wider variety of merchandise at each established price. Price lines may also enable a seller to reach several market segments. For buyers, the question of price may be quite simple: All they have to do is find a suitable product at the predetermined price. Moreover, price lining is a valuable tactic for the marketing manager, because the firm may be able to carry a smaller total inventory than it could without price lines. The results may include fewer markdowns, simplified purchasing, and lower inventory carrying charges.

Price lines also present drawbacks, especially if costs are continually rising. Sellers can offset rising costs in three ways. First, they can begin stocking lower quality merchandise at each price point. Second, sellers can change the prices, although frequent price line changes confuse buyers. Third, sellers can accept lower profit margins and hold quality and prices constant. This third alternative has short-run benefits, but its long-run handicaps may drive sellers out of business.

Ethics in Marketing

Are Drug Prices Based on "All the Traffic Will Bear?"

Merck & Co. expected a flood of praise for introducing a promising drug to fight AIDS. Instead, it has been the target of blistering attacks by AIDS activists and pharmacists who are upset by its distribution strategy. AIDS activists are angry that Merck is selling the new drug, Crixivan, in sharply limited quantities and primarily through a single mail-order distributor that is imposing a hefty 37 percent markup. Several AIDS organizations are calling for public protests against Merck and the distributor, a Pittsburgh company known as Stadtlanders Pharmacy.

Meanwhile, pharmacists are miffed that the distributor is selling the drug directly to patients, bypassing local pharmacies, which make big profits from supplying drugs to AIDS patients. A pharmacy trade group is waging a letter-writing campaign to federal regulators and is lobbying Congress to forbid drug companies to restrict distribution of their drugs. The reaction has caught Merck executives by surprise. The company has worked closely with AIDS activists in the past few years, keeping them informed of progress on new AIDS drugs. It spent 10 years and several hundred million dollars to produce Crixivan, pursuing the drug even after the costly failure of several earlier versions.

When the Food and Drug Administration approved the drug, Merck priced it far lower than the rest of the industry expected.

Worrying over how to fill the demand, Merck officials sought a distribution system that would allow them to control the number of patients who started on the drug and would guarantee those patients refills. A broader distribution, the company feared, might cause some patients to run out of the drug, a potentially disastrous outcome. "If therapy is discontinued, the virus will likely reemerge, perhaps in a form resistant to the drug," says Martin Markowitz, a researcher at the Aaron Diamond AIDS Research Center in New York. "Then the drug will be useless to the patient." Worse, that raises the risk that a drug-resistant strain could cross over into the general population.

The markup on a month's supply of an AIDS drug can mean a few hundred dollars to a pharmacy, far more than the $15 or so that drugstores get from a prescription for a more common drug. Stadtlanders pays Merck $365 for a month's supply of Crixivan for one patient and then charges a list price of $501.88 a month, a 37 percent markup. The markup for most drugs sold at pharmacies is 15 percent.

Stadtlanders says its actual profit is closer to 14 percent because most customers get discounts under various health plans. In addition, the company says, it had to hire 400 additional employees to monitor the drug's distribution. But AIDS activists still accuse the distributor of price gouging. "Stadtlanders has taken advantage of their virtual monopoly . . . by overcharging patients," says Gordon Nary, editor and publisher of the *Journal of the International Association of Physicians in AIDS Care.* Many AIDS patients "rely on their pharmacists as much as they rely on their doctors," he adds. "Merck wasn't sensitive to this at all."[15]

Is Merck being wrongly accused in this situation? Would you have handled the marketing of Crixivan differently? How? Are the pharmacists acting in an ethical manner with their letter-writing and lobbying campaign? Should new AIDS drugs simply be sold at cost?

Merck & Company, Incorporated How has Merck responded to the HIV/AIDS community via its Web site?
http://www.merck.com/

Leader Pricing

Leader pricing (or **loss-leader pricing**) is an attempt by the marketing manager to attract customers by selling a product near or even below cost, hoping that shoppers will buy other items once they are in the store. This type of pricing appears weekly in the newspaper advertising of supermarkets, specialty stores, and department stores. Leader pricing is normally used on well-known items that consumers can easily recognize as bargains at the special price. The goal is not necessarily to sell large quantities of leader items, but to try to appeal to customers who might shop elsewhere.

Bait Pricing

In contrast to leader pricing, which is a genuine attempt to give the consumer a reduced price, bait pricing is deceptive. **Bait pricing** tries to get the consumer into a store through false or misleading price advertising and then uses high-pressure selling to persuade the consumer to buy more expensive merchandise. You may have seen this ad or a similar one:

> REPOSSESSED ... Singer slant-needle sewing machine ... take over 8 payments of $5.10 per month ... ABC Sewing Center.

This is bait. When a customer goes in to see the machine, a salesperson says that it has just been sold or else shows the prospective buyer a piece of junk no one would buy. Then the salesperson says, "But I've got a really good deal on this fine new model." This is the switch that may cause a susceptible consumer to walk out with a $400 machine. The Federal Trade Commission considers bait pricing a deceptive act and has banned its use in interstate commerce. Most states also ban bait pricing, but sometimes enforcement is lax.

Odd–Even Pricing

Odd–even pricing (or **psychological pricing**) means pricing at odd-numbered prices to connote a bargain and pricing at even-numbered prices to imply quality. For years, many retailers have used this tactic to price their products in odd numbers—for example, $99.95 or $49.95—in order to make consumers feel that they are paying a lower price for the product.

Some retailers favor odd-numbered prices because they believe that $9.99 sounds much less imposing to customers than $10.00. Other retailers believe that the use of an odd-numbered price signals to consumers that the price is at the lowest level possible, thereby encouraging them to buy more units. Neither theory has ever been conclusively proved, although one study found that consumers perceive odd-priced products as being on sale.[16]

Even-numbered pricing is sometimes used to denote quality. Examples include a fine perfume at $100 a bottle, a good watch at $500, or a mink coat at $3,000. The demand curve for such items would also be sawtoothed, except that the outside edges would represent even-numbered prices and, therefore, elastic demand.

Price Bundling

Price bundling is marketing two or more products in a single package for a special price. Examples include the sale of maintenance contracts with computer hardware and other office equipment, packages of stereo equipment, packages of options on cars, weekend hotel packages that include a room and several meals, and airline vacation packages. Microsoft now offers "suites" of software that bundle spreadsheets, word processing, graphics, electronic mail, Internet access, and groupware for networks of microcomputers. Price bundling can stimulate demand for the bundled items if the target market perceives the price as a good value.

Services like hotels and airlines sell a perishable commodity (hotel rooms and airline seats) with relatively constant fixed costs. Bundling can be an important income stream for these

bait pricing
Price tactic that tries to get consumers into a store through false or misleading price advertising and then uses high-pressure selling to persuade consumers to buy more expensive merchandise.

odd-even pricing (psychological pricing)
Price tactic that uses odd-numbered prices to connote bargains and even-numbered prices to imply quality.

price bundling
Marketing two or more products in a single package for a special price.

Services, such as hotels, use price bundling to stimulate demand.

businesses because the variable cost tends to be low—for instance, the cost of cleaning a hotel room or putting one more passenger on an airplane.[17] Therefore, most of the revenue can help cover fixed costs and generate profits.

The automobile industry has a different motive for bundling. People buy cars only every three to five years. Thus, selling options is a somewhat rare opportunity for the car dealer. Price bundling can help the dealer sell a maximum number of options.

unbundling
Reducing the bundle of services that comes with the basic product.

A related price tactic is **unbundling,** or reducing the bundle of services that comes with the basic product. Rather than raise the price of hotel rooms, some hotel chains have started charging registered guests for parking. To help hold the line on costs, some department stores require customers to pay for gift wrapping.

Two-Part Pricing

two-part pricing
Price tactic that charges two separate amounts to consume a single good or service.

Two-part pricing means establishing two separate charges to consume a single good or service. Tennis clubs and health clubs, for example, charge a membership fee and a flat fee each time a person uses certain equipment or facilities. In other cases they charge a base rate for a certain level of usage, such as 10 racquetball games per month, and a surcharge for anything over that amount.

Consumers sometimes prefer two-part pricing because they are uncertain about the number and the types of activities they might use at places like an amusement park. Also, the people who use a service most often pay a higher total price. Two-part pricing can increase a seller's revenue by attracting consumers who would not pay a high fee even for unlimited use. For example, a health club might be able to sell only 100 memberships at $700 annually with unlimited use of facilities, for total revenue of $70,000. But perhaps it could sell 900 memberships at $200 with a guarantee of using the racquetball courts 10 times a month. Every usage over 10 would require the member to pay a $5 fee. Thus, membership revenue would provide a base of $180,000, with some additional usage fees coming in throughout the year.

PRODUCT LINE PRICING

4 Discuss product line pricing.

product line pricing
Setting prices for an entire line of products.

Product line pricing is setting prices for an entire line of products. Compared to setting the right price on a single product, product line pricing encompasses broader concerns. In product line pricing, the marketing manager tries to achieve maximum profits or other goals for the entire line rather than for a single component of the line.

Relationships Among Products

The manager must first determine the type of relationship that exists among the various products in the line:

- If items are *complementary,* an increase in the sale of one good causes an increase in demand for the complementary product, and vice versa. For example, the sale of ski poles depends on the demand for skis, making these two items complementary.

- Two products in a line can also be *substitutes* for each other. If buyers buy one item in the line, they are less likely to buy a second item in the line. For example, if someone goes to an automotive supply store and buys paste Turtle Wax for a car, it is very unlikely that he or she will buy liquid Turtle Wax in the near future.

- A *neutral* relationship can also exist between two products. In other words, demand for one of the products is unrelated to demand for the other. For instance, Ralston Purina sells chicken feed and Wheat Chex, but the sale of one of these products has no known impact on demand for the other.

Joint costs are used in oil refining to process fuel oil, gasoline, kerosene, naphtha, paraffin, and lubricating oils.
© Wayne Eastep/Tony Stone Images

Joint Costs

Joint costs are costs that are shared in the manufacturing and marketing of several products in a product line. These costs pose a unique problem in product pricing. In oil refining, for example, fuel oil, gasoline, kerosene, naphtha, paraffin, and lubricating oils are all derived from a common production process. Another example is the production of compact discs that combine photos and music.

Any assignment of joint costs must be somewhat subjective, because costs are actually shared. Suppose a company produces two products, X and Y, in a common production process, with joint costs allocated on a weight basis. Product X weighs 1,000 pounds, and product Y weighs 500 pounds. Thus, costs are allocated on the basis of $2 for X for every $1 for Y. Gross margins (sales less the cost of goods sold) might then be as follows:

joint costs
Costs that are shared in the manufacturing and marketing of several products in a product line.

	Product X	**Product Y**	**Total**
Sales	$20,000	$6,000	$26,000
Less: cost of goods sold	15,000	7,500	22,500
Gross margin	$ 5,000	($1,500)	$ 3,500

This statement reveals a loss of $1,500 on product Y. Is that important? Yes; any loss is important. However, the firm must realize that overall it earned a $3,500 profit on the two items in the line. Also, weight may not be the right way to allocate the joint costs. Instead, the firm might use other bases, including market value or quantity sold.

PRICING DURING DIFFICULT ECONOMIC TIMES

Pricing is always an important aspect of marketing, but it is especially crucial in times of inflation and recession. The firm that does not adjust to economic trends may lose ground that it can never make up.

5 Describe the role of pricing during periods of inflation and recession.

Inflation

When the economy is characterized by high inflation, special pricing tactics are often necessary. They can be subdivided into cost-oriented and demand-oriented tactics.

Cost-Oriented Tactics

One popular cost-oriented tactic is *culling products with a low profit margin* from the product line. However, this tactic may backfire for three reasons:

- A high volume of sales on an item with a low profit margin may still make the item highly profitable.
- Eliminating a product from a product line may reduce economies of scale, thereby lowering the margins on other items.
- Eliminating the product may affect the price–quality image of the entire line.

delayed-quotation pricing
Price tactic used for industrial installations and many accessory items, in which a firm price is not set until the item is either finished or delivered.

escalator pricing
Price tactic in which the final selling price reflects cost increases incurred between the times when the order is placed and when delivery is made.

Another popular cost-oriented tactic is **delayed-quotation pricing,** which is used for industrial installations and many accessory items. Price is not set on the product until the item is either finished or delivered. Long production lead times have forced this policy on many firms during periods of inflation. Builders of nuclear power plants, ships, airports, and office towers sometimes use delayed-quotation tactics.

Escalator pricing is similar to delayed-quotation pricing in that the final selling price reflects cost increases incurred between the times when an order is placed and when delivery is made. An escalator clause allows for price increases (usually across the board) based on the cost-of-living index or some other formula. As with any price increase, management's ability to implement such a policy is based on inelastic demand for the product. About a third of all industrial product manufacturers now use escalator clauses. However, many companies do not apply the clause in every sale. Often it is used only for extremely complex products that take a long time to produce or with new customers.

Any cost-oriented pricing policy that tries to maintain a fixed gross margin under all conditions can lead to a vicious circle. For example, a price increase will result in decreased demand, which in turn increases production costs (because of lost economies of scale). Increased production costs require a further price increase, leading to further diminished demand, and so on.

Demand-Oriented Tactics

Demand-oriented pricing tactics use price to reflect changing patterns of demand caused by inflation or high interest rates. Cost changes are considered, of course, but mostly in the context of how increased prices will affect demand.

Industrial builders use delayed-quotation pricing because long production times affect costs during inflation.
© Andy Sacks/Tony Stone Images

Price shading is the use of discounts by salespeople to increase demand for one or more products in a line. Often, shading becomes habitual and is done routinely without much forethought. Ducommun, a metals producer, is among the major companies that have succeeded in eliminating the practice. Ducommun has told its salespeople, "We want no deviation from book price" unless authorized by management.

price shading
Use of discounts by salespeople to increase demand for one or more products in a line.

To make the demand for a good or service more inelastic and to create buyer dependency, a company can use several strategies:

- *Cultivate selected demand:* Marketing managers can target prosperous customers that will pay extra for convenience or service. Neiman Marcus, for example, stresses quality. As a result, the luxury retailer is more lenient with suppliers and their price increases than is Alexander's Stores, a discounter. In cultivating close relationships with affluent organizational customers, marketing managers should avoid putting themselves at the mercy of a dominant firm. They can more easily raise prices when an account is readily replaceable. Finally, in companies where engineers exert more influence than purchasing departments do, performance is favored over price. Often a preferred vendor's pricing range expands if other suppliers prove technically unsatisfactory.

- *Create unique offerings:* Marketing managers should study buyers' needs. If the seller can design distinctive goods or services uniquely fitting buyers' activities, equipment, and procedures, a mutually beneficial relationship will evolve. Buyers would incur high changeover costs in switching to another supplier. By satisfying targeted buyers in a superior way, marketing managers can make them dependent. Cereal manufacturers have skirted around passing on costs by marketing unique value-added or multi-ingredient cereals, increasing the perceived quality of cereals and allowing companies to raise prices. These cereals include General Mills' Basic 4, Clusters, and Oatmeal Crisp; Post's Banana Nut Crunch and Blueberry Morning; and Kellogg's Mueslix, Nutri-Grain, and Temptations.

- *Change the package design:* Another way companies pass on higher costs is to shrink product sizes but keep prices the same. Scott Paper Co. reduced the number of sheets in the smallest roll of Scott Clean paper towels from 96 to 60 and actually lowered the price by 10¢ a roll. The increases in costs for paper towels are tied to a 50 percent to 60 percent increase in the cost of pulp paper in 1995. The company also changed the names of the sizes to deemphasize the magnitude of the rolls. "We used to have three sizes: big, extra large, and megaroll," said Pete Judice, spokesperson for Scott. "We changed the names to single, double, and triple because they're easier [for the consumers] to relate to."[18]

- *Heighten buyer dependence:* Owens-Corning Fiberglas supplies an integrated insulation service (from feasibility studies to installation) that includes commercial and scientific training for distributors and seminars for end users. This practice freezes out competition and supports higher prices.

Owens Corning
How does Owens Corning promote buyer dependence through its Web site?

http://www.owens-corning.com/

Recession

A recession is a period of reduced economic activity. Reduced demand for goods and services, along with higher rates of unemployment, is a common trait of a recession. Yet, astute marketers can often find opportunity during recessions. They are at an excellent time to build market share, because competitors are struggling to make ends meet.

Two effective pricing tactics to hold or build market share during a recession are value pricing and bundling. *Value pricing*, discussed earlier in the chapter, stresses to customers that they are getting a good value for their money. Revlon's Charles of the Ritz, usually known for its pricey products, introduced the Express Bar during the recession of the early 1990s. A collection of affordable cosmetics and skin treatment products, the Express Bar sold alongside regular Ritz products in department stores. Although lower priced products offer lower profit margins, Ritz found that increases in volume can offset slimmer margins. For example, the company found that consumers will buy two to three Express Bar lipsticks at a time. "The consumer is very conscious of how she spends her income and is looking for value and quality that she can find elsewhere in department stores," said Holly Mercer, vice president of marketing for Ritz.[19]

Bundling or *unbundling* can also stimulate demand during a recession. If features are added to a bundle, consumers may perceive the offering as having greater value. For example, suppose that Hyatt offers a "great escape" weekend for $119. The package includes two nights' lodging and a continental breakfast. Hyatt could add a massage and a dinner for two to create more value for this price. Conversely, companies can unbundle offerings and lower base prices to stimulate demand. A furniture store, for example, could start charging separately for design consultation, delivery, credit, setup, and hauling away old furniture.

Recessions are a good time for marketing managers to study the demand for individual items in a product line and the revenue they produce. Pruning unprofitable items can save resources to be better used elsewhere. Borden's, for example, found that it made about 3,200 sizes, brands, types, and flavors of snacks—but got 95 percent of its revenues from just half of them.[20]

Prices often fall during a recession as competitors try desperately to maintain demand for their wares. Even if demand remains constant, falling prices mean lower profits or no profits. Falling prices, therefore, are a natural incentive to lower costs. During the last recession, companies implemented new technology to improve efficiency and then slashed payrolls. They also discovered that suppliers can be an excellent source of cost savings; the cost of purchased materials accounts for slightly more than half of most U.S. manufacturers' expenses.[21] General Electric's appliance division told 300 key suppliers that they had to reduce prices 10 percent or risk losing GE's business. Allied Signal, Dow Chemical, United Airlines, General Motors, and DuPont have made similar demands of their suppliers. Specific strategies that companies are using with suppliers include the following:

- *Renegotiating contracts:* sending suppliers letters demanding price cuts of 5 percent or more; putting out for rebid the contracts of those that refuse to cut costs
- *Offering help:* dispatching teams of experts to suppliers' plants to help reorganize and suggest other productivity-boosting changes; working with suppliers to make parts simpler and cheaper to produce
- *Keeping the pressure on:* to make sure that improvements continue, setting annual, across-the-board cost-reduction targets, often of 5 percent or more a year
- *Paring down suppliers:* to improve economies of scale, slashing the overall number of suppliers, sometimes by up to 80 percent, and boosting purchases from those that remain[22]

Tough tactics like these help keep companies afloat during economic downturns.

PRICING: A LOOK AT THE FUTURE

6 Discuss what the future might hold for pricing in the marketing mix.

Predicting the future of anything is difficult. Nevertheless, a few changes in the area of pricing seem likely. One is related to the increase in direct-response marketing (mail-order, catalog, telephone, and computer electronic catalogs). Their popularity means that products will move more quickly from production lines to the consumer. Faster distribution means that fewer funds will be tied up in finished goods inventory, a cost savings to the seller that may or may not be passed on to the consumer.

A closely related phenomenon is the United States' rapid transformation to an information-based society. Consumers and purchasing agents will be able to use their terminals to compare product alternatives and prices from several suppliers. The popular America OnLine information system, for example, gives detailed reports from sources like *Consumer Reports* and lists "best buys." Consumers will become more "price aware," and therefore elasticity of demand will increase, particularly for relatively homogeneous items.

An offshoot of the information society is the "cashless society," brought forth by the electronic transfer of funds. Buyers may come to think of price as an accounting entry, a more abstract concept. Moreover, when consumers no longer have to write a check or count out the dollars, money management may change. Record keeping will be more accurate, thanks to the electronic recording of transactions. On the other hand, the concept of price will be less concrete, which could lead to overspending.

The information revolution is already aiding managers in price decisions, and it will provide more benefits in the future. Electronic data-capture techniques, such as bar codes, make data available on a real-time, on-line basis. A district manager for a supermarket like Kroger can vary prices on Kraft's mayonnaise at different stores in the district and quickly determine elasticity of demand. Similarly, a manager can analyze the impact of a 5¢-off coupon (or any other value) almost immediately. New research technologies, such as single-source marketing research (discussed in Chapter 9), accurately measure elasticity of demand. As this technology spreads, managers will become far more accurate in setting the "right price."

Car Buying Pain Relief

The newest, fastest, most hassle-free way ever invented to shop for a new car.

With the increase in direct-response marketing and the transformation of the U.S. into an information-based society, consumers are becoming more price-aware.

Courtesy Auto-By-Tel Corporation

LOOKING BACK

Look back at the story about Ralph Lauren that appeared at the beginning of this chapter. A premium price enables firms to maximize revenues if demand is inelastic. It also helps to recover product development or "educational costs" quickly. In addition, premium prices can enhance the perceived quality of a product. The primary disadvantage is that a premium price will attract competition.

Ralph Lauren has been practicing a skimming strategy. The company is now beginning to "slide down the demand curve" with the Polo line. As the prices fall, the company may lose its "exclusive image" and therefore lose purchasers that seek products with a selective image. Another danger is cannibalizing the sales of other premium-priced Ralph Lauren products.

SUMMARY

1 *Describe the procedure for setting the right price.* Setting the right price on a product is a process with four major steps: (1) establishing pricing goals; (2) estimating demand, costs, and profits; (3) choosing a price policy to help determine a base price; and (4) fine tuning the base price with pricing tactics.

KEY TERMS

bait pricing *617*

base price *609*

basing-point pricing *614*

A price strategy establishes a long-term pricing framework for a good or service. The three main types of price policies are price skimming, penetration pricing, and status quo pricing. A price-skimming policy charges a high introductory price, often followed by a gradual reduction. Penetration pricing offers a low introductory price to capture a large market share and attain economies of scale. Finally, status quo pricing strives to match competitors' prices.

2 *Identify the legal and ethical constraints on pricing decisions.* Government regulation helps monitor four major areas of pricing: unfair trade practices, price fixing, predatory pricing, and price discrimination. Enacted in many states, unfair trade practice acts protect small businesses from large firms that operate efficiently on extremely thin profit margins; the acts prohibit charging below-cost prices. The Sherman Act and the Federal Trade Commission Act prohibit both price fixing—an agreement between two or more firms on a particular price—and predatory pricing—undercutting competitors with extremely low prices to drive them out of business. Finally, the Robinson-Patman Act makes it illegal for firms to discriminate between two or more buyers in terms of price.

3 *Explain how discounts, geographic pricing, and other special pricing tactics can be used to fine tune the base price.* Several techniques enable marketing managers to adjust prices within a general range in response to changes in competition, government regulation, consumer demand, and promotional and positioning goals. Techniques for fine tuning a price can be divided into three main categories: discounts, allowances, and rebates; geographic pricing; and special pricing tactics.

The first type of tactic gives lower prices to those that pay promptly, order a large quantity, or perform some function for the manufacturer. Trade loading is a manufacturer's temporary functional discount to induce wholesalers and retailers to buy more goods than can be sold in a reasonable length of time. Trade loading increases inventory expenses and channel expenses and lowers the manufacturer's profits. A tactic meant to overcome these problems is "everyday low pricing," or maintaining low prices over time while eliminating the discounts that result in trade loading. Other tactics in this category include seasonal discounts, promotion allowances, and rebates (cash refunds).

Geographic pricing tactics—such as FOB origin pricing, uniform delivered pricing, zone pricing, freight absorption pricing, and basing-point pricing—are ways of moderating the impact of shipping costs on distant customers.

A variety of special pricing tactics stimulate demand for certain products, increase store patronage, and offer more merchandise at specific prices.

4 *Discuss product line pricing.* Product line pricing maximizes profits for an entire product line. When setting product line prices, marketing managers determine what type of relationship exists among the products in the line: complementary, substitute, or neutral. Managers also consider joint (shared) costs among products in the same line.

5 *Describe the role of pricing during periods of inflation and recession.* Marketing managers employ cost-oriented and demand-oriented tactics during periods of economic inflation. Cost-oriented tactics consist of dropping products with a low profit margin, delayed-quotation pricing, and escalator pricing. Demand-oriented pricing methods include price shading and increasing demand through the cultivation of selected customers, unique offerings, changing the package size, and systems selling.

To stimulate demand during a recession, marketers use value pricing, bundling, and unbundling. Recessions are also a good time to prune unprofitable items from product lines. Managers strive to cut costs during recessions in order to maintain profits as revenues decline. Implementing new technology, cutting payrolls, and pressuring suppliers for reduced prices are common techniques used to cut costs.

6 *Discuss what the future might hold for pricing in the marketing mix.* Several trends in marketing are likely to affect pricing in the future. First, an increase in direct-response marketing is simplifying distribution and creating savings for sellers that may be passed on to consumers. Second, better and more accessible information on products is likely to make consumers more price sensitive. Third, the electronic transfer of funds may create a "cashless society," in which record keeping is more accurate, but the concept of price is more abstract. Finally, marketers' manipulation and analysis of pricing strategies are likely to become more effective with the use of new technology.

Discussion and Writing Questions

1. A manufacturer of office furniture decides to produce antique-style rolltop desks, but formatted for personal computers. The desks will have built-in surge protectors, a platform for raising or lowering the monitor, and a number of other features. The quality, solid-oak desks will be priced far below comparable products. The marketing manager says, "We'll charge a low price and plan on a high volume to reduce our risks." Comment.

2. Janet Oliver, owner of a mid-priced dress shop notes, "My pricing objectives are simple: I just charge what my competitors' charge. I'm happy because I'm making money." React to Janet's statement.

3. Develop a price line strategy for each of these firms:
   a. a college bookstore
   b. a restaurant
   c. a video-rental firm.

4. You are contemplating a price change for an established product sold by your firm. Write a memo analyzing the factors you need to consider in your decision.

5. Do you see everyday low prices as a solution to trade loading? Why are many manufacturers resisting EDLP?

6. Columnist Dave Barry jokes that federal law requires this message under the sticker price of new cars: "Warning to stupid people: Do not pay this amount." Discuss why the sticker price is generally higher than the actual selling price of a car. Tell how you think car dealers set the actual prices of the cars they sell.

7. Explain the difference between freight absorption pricing and uniform delivered pricing. When would it be appropriate to use each?

8. What is the difference between a price policy and a price tactic. Give an example.

9. Divide into teams of four persons. Each team should choose one of the following topics: skimming, penetration pricing, status quo pricing, price fixing, EDLP, geographic pricing, adopting a single-price tactic, flexible pricing, or professional services pricing. Each team should then pick a retailer that it feels most closely follows the team's chosen pricing strategy. Go to the store and write down examples of the strategy. Interview the store manager, and get his or her views on the advantages and disadvantages of the strategy. Each team should then make an oral report in class.

10. How is the "information age" changing the nature of pricing?

11. During a recession, what pricing strategies would you consider using to gain or maintain product-market share? Explain your answer.

12. What pricing strategy does Microsoft seem to be using for the software offered via the following Web page?

    http://www.microsoft.com/ msdownload/

13. What pricing advantages does the Auto Connection™ seem to offer compared to traditional auto dealers?

    http://www.auto-connect. com/

14. Price a flight on Southwest Airlines, and price the same flight on American Airlines. Describe the kinds of price strategies used by each company.

    http://www.iflyswa.com/
    http://www.americanair.com/

15. What kind of pricing strategies are being offered by the following three telecommunication competitors?

    http://www.att.com/
    http://www.mci.com/
    http://www.sprint.com/
    http://www.gte.com/

Application for Small Business

Beth Hanks has come up with a new twist on an old idea: home delivery of consumer goods and services. Beth doesn't just deliver groceries; rather, she will pick up and deliver items like dry cleaning, videos, and gardening supplies. Her company, called Timesavers, delivers groceries once a week to a service box (consisting of a re-frigerator, a freezer, and a few open shelves) in each customer's basement or garage. Beth purchases groceries directly from wholesalers and manu-facturers, just as supermarkets do, and distributes them from her own 25,000-square-foot warehouse. Beth avoids supermarket costs but pockets the markups. As long as customers get their orders in by midnight the day before, the goods will arrive by 6 P.M. on the designated day. Beth hopes to ultimately sell many prod-ucts or services to homes—plane or theater tickets, lawn care, and uphol-stery cleaning, among others.

Questions

1. Advise Beth on a pricing strategy.
2. What are some ways that she can fine tune her base price?

Video Case

Ch. 21

Southwest Airlines

With over two decades of continued success, it is hard to believe that the plans for Southwest Airlines were first drawn on a cocktail napkin. At least this is the story that Herbert Kelleher, now chairman of the board, president, and chief executive officer of the company, likes to share with people about the inception of the air-line—an airline that is now one of the largest domestic carriers, as well as the most profitable in the United States.

Rollin King and Herb Kelleher conceived the idea for a Texas in-trastate airline in 1966. The plan was to provide low-cost air service to Houston and San Antonio from a Dallas base at Love Field. Imple-menting this plan was difficult in the regulated airline industry, and Southwest faced 34 judicial and ad-ministrative proceedings before its first flight took off in 1971.

While other airlines had agreed to leave Love Field and support the new Dallas-Fort Worth International Air-port, Southwest never wanted to abandon Love Field and favored the less congested and closer-to-down-town location. However, other air-lines believed that allowing a com-peting airline to fly from Love would jeopardize the financial future of the new airport. Ultimately, Congress passed the "Wright Amendment," which limits regularly scheduled Love Field air service only to points within Texas and its four contiguous states.

Early marketing campaigns cen-tered around a "Luv" theme. The air-line called itself "The somebody else up there who loves you." Its head-quarters has remained at Dallas Love Field despite the amendment, which has hindered its home-base growth.

Unlike most large air carriers who have suffered tremendous losses or even folded in bankruptcy, South-west has been profitable every year since 1973. This can be attributed to its no-frills service, which keeps its operating costs far below those of the competition:

- Only drinks and snacks (peanuts, pretzels, cookies) are served.
- Open seating and plastic reusable boarding passes are used.
- There is no baggage transfer to other airlines.
- Less congested airports, such as Love Field in Dallas and Midway in Chicago, are favored over larger, busier airports.
- Labor relations with its unions are characterized as "excellent."

- The time to "turn" an aircraft (i.e., the time spent at the gate between flights) is usually 15 to 20 minutes, compared to the industry average of 55 minutes.

In addition, the company operates a point-to-point flight system. After the industry was deregulated in 1978, most carriers rushed to build com-plex hub-and-spoke systems. South-west, on the other hand, stuck to its original short-haul strategy, with the average flight a mere 65 minutes. The airline has also maintained a fleet of only one type of aircraft, the 737, which leads to millions in sav-ings because flight training and main-tenance are greatly simplified.

The high frequency of flights and low fares attract business and leisure travelers alike, but the airline de-veloped other marketing tools to lure customers. A pricing promotion, "Friends Fly Free," enables passen-gers to purchase one ticket and re-ceive one free. Another marketing device, the airlines' frequent-flyer program, is very simple because it is based on actual trips, not mileage. Each time they travel, passengers re-ceive credit for each one-way trip. The program is also very convenient to join: Merely picking up a brochure at any Southwest counter.

As a short-haul niche carrier, the airline has differentiated itself with low fares and simple, but fun, service. The fun begins at the top with the wit and humor of Kelleher, who has been known to dress up as Elvis and even arm wrestle another airline executive over an advertising slogan. Kelleher serves as an example for over 16,000 employees who display the same enthusiasm about Southwest and their jobs. Even Southwest's advertisements contain humor, which has become symbolic of the airline.

In 1993, the airline acquired Morris Air, a Salt Lake City-based regional carrier that mirrored Southwest's operation in many ways. Morris flew only 737s and concentrated on short-haul, low-cost service. While the purchase increased Southwest's fleet by 22 planes, the primary advantage of the acquisition was that Morris did not compete with Southwest in any market. This gave Southwest instant service in several cities in the far Northwest.

Southwest plans to continue to expand in the Midwest, Florida, and the northeast and western United States, but will not name which cities it is considering. Commenting on the carrier's future, Kelleher explains:

I don't think anything will be different in the future. I'm talking about the philosophy of it, the foundation of it. I think that we will continue to emphasize that Southwest Airlines, in our opinion, is the best air transportation value in the industry. And that's a campaign that we launched several years ago. Basically, the core of it is "just plane smart": It's just plain smart to fly the carrier that has the best customer service record, one of the newest fleets in the industry, and the most hospitable people at the lowest price. It's really a value approach to marketing, and I think that the decade of the '90s throughout its entirety is going to be very receptive to that approach.

Questions

1. Discuss the role of price in Southwest Airlines' marketing mix.
2. Describe Southwest's pricing strategy.
3. Compare Southwest's pricing strategy to the strategies of other major airlines such as American Airlines, United Airlines, and Delta Airlines.
4. Discuss Southwest's approach to fine tuning its base price with pricing tactics.
5. Herbert Kelleher, chairman of the board, president, and chief executive officer of Southwest Airlines, says that the airline practices a "value approach to marketing." Explain this concept, and cite evidence to support Mr. Kelleher's claim.

Critical Thinking Case

GM'S MOVE TO "NO-HAGGLE" PRICING

General Motors Corporation plans to offer many more American consumers a simplified menu of vehicle prices, replacing the traditional and expensive a la carte system. The No. 1 automaker has been experimenting with such a consumer-friendly "value pricing" approach in California and now intends to extend the approach to several other states, individuals close to the situation say. This will be good news for car buyers because it signals an expansion of the biggest, most systematic effort by an automaker to take haggling and pricing mysteries out of the car-buying experience—something car buyers have been demanding for years.

GM's California experiment has a simple premise: Equip cars with the options most people want, and sell them for a price consumers are willing to pay. That is how most of American retailing works, and it has been talked about and tested endlessly in the auto industry. "No-haggle" pricing was one of the features that set GM's Saturn division apart in its early years.

Success in California

But in California, GM has applied the idea across all of its divisions, rather than leaving it up to individual dealers or marketing units to embrace it. The program has been so successful that GM has reversed a long-term slide in its share of the California vehicle market, taken sales away from Japanese automakers, and ousted rival Ford Motor Company as the California market leader. When it launched the program in 1993, GM applied the "value-pricing" scheme to a handful of cars it thought would appeal to import-car buyers. In 1996,

it included about 90 GM vehicles sold in California, which accounts for 10.7 percent of the U.S. vehicle market.

Here's how it works: GM has determined, for example, that California buyers most often want the Pontiac Grand Am SE sedan equipped with an AM/FM radio with cassette player, antilock brakes, dual air bags, air conditioning, a tilt steering wheel, and power door locks. So California Pontiac dealers are encouraged to offer that package for $14,995. Elsewhere in the U.S., customers can order the same car with the same equipment from dealers, but the sticker price could be substantially higher, and it is assumed that car buyers will try to negotiate a discount.

GM says the California program gives its dealers a competitive advantage. For example, in the case of the Grand Am, a comparably equipped Honda Accord LX is priced at $20,220, and a comparable Toyota Camry DX at $20,658, according to GM. Individuals close to the situation say GM plans to extend the California pricing strategy first to Washington and Oregon and, maybe soon, to Utah, Nevada, Colorado, and Florida.

In part, the GM program is an effort to address the auto industry's affordability crisis. With prices outpacing incomes, vehicle sales have been held below the peaks the industry had expected in the 1990s, based on historical trends. Over the past couple of years, GM has been trying to establish a reputation as the value-price leader.

GM officially introduced the program in Washington and Oregon when it rolled out the 1997-model vehicles. A GM spokeswoman would say only that "we are extremely encouraged by the results in California, and we are studying [the program's] expansion elsewhere." GM is evaluating a number of regional markets where its market share has eroded to determine whether simplified pricing would make a difference.

Cutting Down on Variations

Motivating the No. 1 automaker is a desire to win back market share lost to buyers of domestic as well as imported cars and light trucks. GM is particularly targeting buyers of imported vehicles, especially those made by Japanese companies. At the same time, the program helps GM to cut its manufacturing costs by reducing the number of vehicle variations its factories have to handle.

GM says it has found that consumers like simplified pricing because it's "more reliable and consistent throughout the model year," the GM spokeswoman said. She added that consumers find that the program makes it easier to shop for a car because they can focus on the vehicle rather than the bargaining process. "We can bring our prices pretty much in line with what the consumer is willing to pay and how they want the car equipped and thus minimize the use of incentives," a GM spokesman said.

GM already leads the Big Three domestic automakers in innovative pricing strategies. Its popular Saturn division has a one-price, no-haggle policy across all its models. Oldsmobile, meanwhile, has moved to a similar pricing policy, and other GM divisions are expected to follow. Elsewhere in the auto industry, it is mostly up to individual dealers to decide whether to adopt "no-haggle" pricing policies.

While the GM program is intended to be good for car buyers, it is unpopular with many dealers. They complain that the low "value-price" packages cut into their profit margins. Indeed, the trade-off for nonnegotiable sticker prices is that GM builds in less dealer profit. "It's just squeeze, squeeze, squeeze," complains Jim Weston, a dealer in Portland, Ore. "Yes, car prices have gone up, but not as much as dealer costs."

Moreover, dealers say, the haggling continues, even under the California program, as dealers compete to offer even lower prices, says Bob Longpre, a dealer in Southern California. Mr. Longpre says that any market-share gains GM has achieved the past few years have been a result of large-scale advertising, not the simplified pricing program. Meanwhile, he says that at his Pontiac dealership profit margins are down 35 percent from five years ago.

GM argues that by having more "credible" pricing, it has actually sta-bilized or increased dealer profit margins. Moreover, GM believes simplified pricing helps dealers sell more vehicles. Says a GM spokesman: "Dealers who understand how the pricing strategy really fits the needs of the consumer will recognize that in the long haul, both sides—GM and the dealer body—will prosper as partners."

Questions

1. Why do you think GM is moving toward a "no-haggle" pricing strategy? Do you think GM will expand the strategy nationwide?
2. Explain the role of the car dealer in GM's new pricing strategy.
3. Do you agree with the dealer's complaints cited in the case? If so, how would you rectify them?
4. Do you think that a "no-haggle" strategy is best for the consumer? What if a potential buyer is an excellent bargainer?
5. Would you say that "no-haggle" pricing is a price penetration strategy? Defend your answer.
6. What tactics could be used to fur-ther "fine tune" the final "no-haggle" price the customer pays for the car?

Suggested Readings

Gabriella Stern and Rebecca Blumestein, "GM Expected to Expand 'No Haggle' Pricing Plan," *Wall Street Journal,* 24 April 1996, pp. A3, A4.

Gabriella Stern and Rebecca Blumestein, "How Do You Sell a Slew of Stodgy Cars? Easily, If the Prices Are Right," *Wall Street Journal,* 15 January 1996, pp. A1, A5.

"Revolution In the Showroom," *Business Week,* 19 February 1996, pp. 70–76.

"High Technology, Low Aggravation," *Business Week,* 19 February 1996, p. 73.

Alex Taylor, "GM: Why They Might Break Up America's Biggest Company," *Fortune,* 29 April 1996, pp. 78–84.

Critical Thinking Case

LEVI STRAUSS AND COMPANY

Levi Strauss began his business venture in the late 1800s in San Francisco, stitching surplus tent canvas into work pants for gold prospectors. Today, the world's largest apparel maker has cornered a 22 percent share of the $6 billion jeans market. Trailing directly behind Levi Strauss are Wrangler (13 percent), Lee (11 percent), and Gitano (5 percent). These four jeans manufacturers control over 50 percent of the market. Another 20 to 25 percent of the market is composed of the private-label jeans (70 percent of market), followed by colored denims (20 percent). Acid-washed, stone-washed, oversized, and distressed-denim jeans are some of the most popular looks today.

Target Market for Blue Jeans

In 1989 the industry sold 350 million pairs of jeans, more than enough for every person in the United States to have a new pair. Still, the market for jeans has declined quite a bit since its peak in 1981, when the industry sold 520 million pairs. The main problem is the shrinking population of 14- to 24-year-olds, the key market segment for jeans. Baby boomers have always been one of the major market segments. However, as these consumers enter midlife, they buy fewer pairs of jeans and begin looking for different products. They continue to wear blue jeans, but mostly on weekends. They simply do not wear out their jeans as fast as they once did.

Each of the four major jeans manufacturers has taken a different approach to segmenting the market. In the past, Gitano used sultry models to promote its jeans. This sort of image advertising appealed to young women. The company then realized that many of its loyal customers were older and had children of their own. In an effort to expand its market, the company broadened its appeal. Gitano's Spirit of Family campaign is aimed at mom and her teenage daughters.

Lee competes in all market segments, but has directed its TV advertising at women. The company chose to focus on women for two reasons: Women constitute about 40 percent of the market, and they buy most of the children's clothes. The company emphasizes the benefits of its products—comfort and fit. Lee adopted the slogan "Nobody fits your body . . . or the way you live . . . better than Lee." The company targets the male market through the use of print advertising, trying to maintain a "family brand" image.

Wrangler, manufacturer of the official jeans of the Pro Rodeo Association, concentrates on the blue-collar male market. Long associated with its hard-core cowboy positioning, the company is broadening its market to include consumers who might imitate the cowboy look. To reach this new market, Wrangler hired Texas Rangers' pitcher Nolan Ryan as a spokesperson for its products.

Levi Strauss has segmented the market not only by age, but also by region and ethnic group. The company hired Spike Lee to direct a series of documentary-style ads for its 501 brand. Spike Lee has tremendous appeal with 14- to 24-year-olds. The company targets the market of 7- to 11-year-olds with the Wild Creatures campaign featured on Saturday morning television. In the West and Southwest, the company hits the Hispanic market with the appeal that jeans are appropriate for all occasions. This group wears jeans mostly for work only.

Product Line Adaptation

Levi Strauss produces a wide range of products. In addition to its denim jeans, the company makes a complete line of clothing.

The company has never lost sight of the changing marketplace. Levi Strauss was one of the first companies to adapt its product line to the changing lifestyle of aging consumers. In 1978, market research indicated that older men preferred dress slacks to jeans. Levi Strauss introduced Action Slacks—comfortable, easy-to-clean slacks with an expandable waistband. Levi Strauss made middle-aged adults feel good about their older bodies; no matter how much exercise people get as they age, their bodies just don't maintain youthful contours. By 1985, Action Slacks brought the company over $100 million in sales.

The company has another product hit with the Dockers line of clothing. Levi Strauss identified a new consumer who wanted something between jeans and Dad's pressed slacks. The Dockers line is not new to Levi Strauss. The company had marketed a line of loose-fitting chino pants under the name Dockers in both Japan and Argentina with little success. The key to the product's success in the United States is that the slacks are available in a multitude of colors. With a line of coordinated shirts and a massive promotional campaign, Dockers has become a major product category that did not previously exist. Even stores like Sears and JCPenney have created special Dockers departments. Without merchandising support from Levi Strauss, many of these stores would have missed this Dockers market segment.

LeviLink Computer Network

Making jeans is mostly a manual job. Workers hand-sew almost every seam and button on a pair of jeans.

In an industry with rapid changes in fashions and fads, retailers seldom stock large quantities of any specific size or style. Lower inventories reduce the risk to retailers when a specific style falls out of fashion, but increase the risk of lost sales due to stock outages. This problem is even more severe for large retail chain stores. These stores often handwrite all orders and then send them to a central purchasing department for processing. Restocking an item can take as long as three weeks. LeviLink, Levi Strauss's new computer system, is streamlining the procedures.

Each store is connected directly to Levi Strauss by computer terminal. After the orders are entered into the terminal, the store receives the shipment within six days. The faster turn-around time offers two key advantages. First, it eliminates a lot of lost sales due to stock outages. Second, the system helps reduce the risk of stocking huge inventories in a constantly changing fashion business. The company estimates that for the retailers using LeviLink, sales have increased 20 to 30 percent.

Levi Strauss CEO Bob Haas decided to put $500 million into the restructuring of Levi Strauss' manufacturing and distribution systems by the end of 1995. The ultimate goal is to bring the equivalent of just-in-time manufacturing to the apparel business. When an order for a pair of jeans is entered into the system, the system can request that another pair of jeans be made. The company is also using the system to adjust the quantities of materials it orders from suppliers. By tying the production system closer to product sales, Levi Strauss has eliminated the need for large inventories of fabrics in warehouses next to manufacturing facilities.

New Retail Outlets

In 1994, the Federal Trade Commission cleared the way for Levi Strauss to open its own retail stores, something the firm had been banned from doing since 1978. Although Levi Strauss does not intend to become a high-volume retailer, it does hope to open 200 stores nationwide by 1999, in downtown areas and upscale suburban malls. Each new store is expected to be one of three types: a joint venture with an existing retail chain, a Levi Strauss–owned Original Levi's Store, or a Levi Strauss–owned Dockers Shop.

Questions

1. Propose a business mission statement for Levi Strauss for now and the future.
2. Compare Levi Strauss to its competitors in today's market. Predict which competitors may challenge Levi Strauss' leadership in the jeans market.
3. Examine Levi Strauss' differential advantage. Propose a plan for Levi Strauss to maintain this advantage.
4. Prepare a situation analysis for Levi Strauss. Predict possible threats and weaknesses that might hamper growth at Levi Strauss.
5. Evaluate the corporate culture of Levi Strauss. Is this the type of company you would like to work for?

Suggested Readings

Bernie Knill, "Lesson from Levi's: Quick Response Too Slow for the '90s," *Industry Week,* 2 May 1994, pp. A16–A21.

Russell Mitchell and Michael Oneal, "Managing by Values," *Business Week,* 1 August 1994, pp. 46–52.

Nina Munk, "Designing Ambitions," *Forbes,* 28 February 1994, p. 136.

Bill Richards, "Levi Strauss Plans to Open 200 Stores in 5 Years, with Ending of FTC Ban," *The Wall Street Journal,* 22 December 1994, p. A2.

Laura Struebing, "Customer Loyalty: Playing for Keeps," *Quality Progress,* February 1996, pp. 25–30.

Steven Preece, Craig Fleisher, and James Toccacelli, "Building a Reputation Along the Value Chain at Levi Strauss," *Long Range Planning,* December 1995, pp. 88–98.

Marketing Planning Activities

PRICING DECISIONS

*T*he last part of the marketing mix to be described for the marketing plan is the price element. Be sure that your pricing plans match the needs and wants of the target market identified and described earlier and that they are compatible with the product, service, distribution, and promotion issues discussed in the previous sections. Also, refer to Exhibit 2.8 for additional marketing plan subjects.

1. List possible pricing objectives for your chosen firm. How might adopting different pricing objectives change the behavior of the firm and its marketing plans?

Marketing*Builder* Exercises

- **Return on Investment** portion of the **Market Analysis** template
- **Break-Even Analysis** spreadsheet
- **Margin Structure** portion of the **Sales Plan** template

2. Pricing is an integral component of marketing strategy. Discuss how your firm's pricing can affect or be affected by competition, the economic environment, political regulations, product features, extra customer service, changes in distribution, or changes in promotion.

Marketing*Builder* Exercises

- **Pricing** portion of the **Sales Plan** template

- **Pricing** portion of the **Market Analysis** template

3. Is demand elastic or inelastic for your company's product or service? Why?

4. What are the costs that have to be covered in your chosen company?

5. What price policy should your firm use? Are there any legal implications of this choice?

6. List and describe the specific pricing tactics that your chosen company should use, including discounts, geographic pricing, and special prices?

Appendix

Careers in Marketing

You can use many of the basic concepts of marketing introduced in this book to get the career you want by marketing yourself. The purpose of marketing is to create exchanges that satisfy individual as well as organizational objectives, and a career is certainly an exchange situation for both you and an organization. The purpose of this appendix is to help you market yourself to prospective employers by providing some helpful tools and information.

AVAILABLE CAREERS

Marketing careers have a bright outlook into the next century. The U.S. Bureau of Labor Statistics estimates that employment in marketing fields will grow 25 percent by the year 2010. Many of these increases will be in the areas of sales, public relations, retailing, advertising, marketing research, and product management.

Sales

There are more opportunities in sales than in any other area of marketing. Sales positions vary greatly among companies. Some selling positions focus more on providing information; others emphasize locating potential customers, making presentations to committees, and closing the sale. Compensation, often salary plus commission, sets few limits on the amount of money a person can make and therefore offers great potential. Sales positions can be found in many organizations, including manufacturing, wholesaling, retailing, insurance, real estate, financial services, and many other service businesses.

Public Relations

Public relations firms help create an image or a message for an individual or organization and communicate it effectively to a desired audience. All types of firms, profit and nonprofit organizations, individuals, and even countries employ public relations specialists. Communication skills, both written and oral, are critical for success in public relations.

Retailing

Retail careers require many skills. Retail personnel may manage a sales force or other personnel, select and order merchandise, and be responsible for promotional activities, inventory control, store security, and accounting. Large retail stores have a variety of positions, including store or department manager, buyer, display designer, and catalog manager.

Advertising

Many organizations employ advertising specialists. Advertising agencies are the largest employers; however, manufacturers, retailers, banks, radio and television stations, hospitals, and insurance agencies all have advertising departments. Creativity, artistic talent, and communication skills are a few of the attributes needed for a successful career in advertising. Account executives serve as a liaison between the advertising agency and the client. Account executives must have a good knowledge of business practices and possess excellent sales skills.

Marketing Research

The most rapid growth in marketing careers is in marketing research. Marketing research firms, advertising agencies, universities, private firms, nonprofit organizations, and governments provide growing opportunities in marketing research. Researchers conduct industry research, advertising research, pricing and packaging research, new-product testing, and test-marketing. Researchers are involved in one or more stages of the research process, depending on the size of the organization conducting the research. Marketing research requires knowledge of statistics, data processing and analysis, psychology, and communication.

Product Management

Product managers coordinate all or most of the activities required to market a product. Thus, they need a general knowledge of all the aspects of marketing. Product managers are responsible for the successes and failures of a product and are compensated well for this responsibility. Most product managers have previous sales experience and skills in communication. The position of product manager is a major step in the career path of top-level marketing executives.

WHERE TO LOOK

Not many people are fortunate enough to have a job fall into their lap when they graduate. It is your responsibility to find a career that satisfies both your needs and the needs of the employer.

So, where do you look? Several resources help narrow the search. Some of the obvious places to check are parents, friends, family members, career planning and placement centers, career counselors, and the companies themselves. A list of not-so-obvious resources is shown in Exhibit A.1.

The Internet can also be a useful tool for finding an employer. StudentCenter, a new, free on-line magazine and research tool based in New York, recently went on-line to help students with job searches. Its databases contain extensive industry profiles on more than 35,000 companies.

Step-by-step guidelines are included for writing resumes, cover letters, and thank-you notes. Definitions of key career terms and legal issues and employment rights are included.

Unlike other sources, the regularly updated material is written from a student's point of view, said Donna Grossman, StudentCenter's research and development director.[1]

The magazine includes a "virtual interview" that simulates the interview process. Users are asked multiple-choice questions and have their answers evaluated. An advice column, "Ask Donna," allows students to ask questions about jobs to be answered on-line.

You can expect to be entertained as well. "The Vegas Approach," for instance, allows students to randomly select silly fortunes and job selections. "Odd Jobs" lets one guess how celebrities got their start.

The online address is http://www.StudentCenter.com.

Advertising Career Directory
(Hawthorn, NJ: Career Press)

American Marketing Association, *Careers in Marketing*
(Chicago)

Business Week Careers

Changing Times Annual Survey: Jobs for New College Grads

Chemical Marketing Research Association, *Careers in Industrial Marketing Research*
(New York)

College Placement Council, *CPC Annual*

Dow Jones & Co., *Managing Your Career*
(published twice a year)

Lebhar-Friedman, Inc., *Careers in Retailing*
(published annually)

Magazine Publishers Association, *Guide to Business Careers in Magazine Publishing*
(New York)

National Employment Business Weekly

Peterson's Business & Management Jobs
(published annually)

COMPENSATION

Many college graduates want to know how much they will get paid in their new career. Although this is a topic that should be considered in your selection of a company, it should not be the only one. It is up to you to decide which criteria are most important in choosing a job.

Exhibit A.2 shows the average compensation range for various marketing positions. The range varies, depending on your education and preference for a certain geographic location. In addition to salary, marketing positions may include a company car, bonuses, or expense accounts, forms of compensation that are not common in other professions.

GETTING THE JOB

Before you begin to look for a job, you need to make a self-assessment and develop your resume and a cover letter.

Self-Assessment

When it is time to look for a job, it is important that you have a good idea of your personal needs, capabilities, characteristics, strengths, and weaknesses. The idea is to prepare, so you will be able to market yourself the best you can.

The following questions will help you analyze what is important to you in choosing the kind of work you will do and the kind of employer for whom you will work:

1. What do I do best? Are these activities related to people, things, or data?
2. Do I communicate better orally or in writing?

Exhibit A.2
Compensation for Selected Marketing Positions

Position	Compensation
Advertising	
Advertising media planner	$18,000–$45,000
Assistant account executive	22,000–$45,000
Account executive	28,000–$70,000
Account supervisor	45,000–$80,000
Marketing research	
Analyst	$ 23,000–$38,000
Project director	40,000–$70,000
Research director	75,000–$125,000
Product management	
Assistant product manager	$ 22,000–$38,000
Group manager	40,000–$85,000
Group product manager	55,000–$135,000
Retailing	
Trainee	$ 17,000–$25,000
Chain store manager	25,000–$95,000
Buyer	27,000–$65,000
Department store manager	35,000–$150,000
Sales	
Trainee	$ 17,000–$30,000
Real estate agent	15,000–$140,000
Insurance agent	19,000–$150,000
Manufacturer's representative	25,000–$100,000
Field salesperson	30,000–$80,000
Sales manager	40,000–$100,000
Securities salesperson	35,000–$400,000

3. Do I consider myself a leader of a team or a group?
   a. Do I see myself as an active participant in a team or group?
   b. Do I prefer to work by myself?
   c. Do I prefer working under supervision?
4. Do I work well under pressure?
5. Do I like taking responsibility? Or would I rather follow directions?
6. Do I enjoy new products and activities? Or would I rather follow a regular routine?
7. When I am working, which of the following things are most important?
   a. Working for a regular salary?
   b. Working for a commission?
   c. Working for a combination of both?
8. Do I prefer to work a regular 9 A.M.-to-5 P.M. schedule?
9. Will I be willing to travel more than half the time?
10. What kind of work environment do I prefer?
    a. Indoors or outdoors?
    b. Urban setting (population over a million)?
    c. Rural community?
11. Would I prefer to work for a large organization?
12. Am I willing to move?
13. Where do I want to be in three years? Five years? Ten years?

The FAB Student Model

The FAB matrix is a device adapted from personal selling that can help you market yourself to potential employers. FAB, which stands for Features-Advantages-Benefits, relates your skills to an employer's needs by citing the specific benefits you can bring to that company.[2] People want benefits, whether they are buying a car or hiring a marketing graduate to fill a job vacancy. An employer needs information that indicates how hiring you will specifically benefit the firm.

Exhibit A.3 is a model of FAB for students. The first step in FAB is as critical for you as it is for the salesperson: determining what the customer needs. In the case of the employer, the needs are what the job requires or the problems to be solved. These needs should be listed in order of priority, starting with the most important. Step 2 matches each need with a particular feature of the applicant (skill, ability, personality characteristic, educational attainment). In step 3, you arrange the needs and features in a FAB matrix, where they become information points that you can use to construct a cover letter, resume, or interview presentation.

You must approach a prospective employer with complete knowledge of that employer's features and job needs. Using the FAB matrix, you can match features with needs in a systematic, complete, and concise way.

Resume and Cover Letter

When developing a resume, you need to capture on paper your abilities, education, background, training, work experience, and personal qualifications. Many of these points can be developed from the FAB matrix or other self-assessment techniques. Your resume should also be brief, usually no more than one page. The goal is to communicate your qualifications in a way that will obtain a positive response: an interview from potential employers.

The cover letter is, in some ways, more important than the resume. It must be persuasive, professional, and interesting. Ideally, it should set you above and apart from the other candidates for the position. Each letter should look and sound origi-

Exhibit A.3 *The FAB Matrix*

Need of employer *"This job requires . . ."*	Feature of job applicant *"I have . . ."*	Advantage of feature *"This feature means that . . ."*	Benefit to employer *"You will . . ."*
Frequent sales presentations to individuals and groups	Taken 10 classes that required presentations	I require limited or no training in making presentations	Save on the cost of training and have an employee with the ability and confidence to be productive early
Knowledge of personal computers, software, and applications	Taken a personal computer course and used Lotus in most upper-level classes	I can already use Word 6.0, Lotus, dBase, SAS, SPSS, and other software	Save time and money on training
A person with management potential	Been president of a student marketing group and social fraternity president for 2 years	I have experience leading people	Save time because I am capable of stepping into a leadership position as needed

nal, tailored to the specific organization you are contacting. It should describe the position you are applying for and arouse interest, describe your qualifications, and indicate how you can be contacted. Whenever possible, cover letters should be addressed to the individual, not the title. Sample resumes and cover letters can be found in your local library or student placement center. Follow up the letter and resume with a telephone call.

THE INTERVIEW

The interview is the most important part of the job search process. An interview often decides whether or not you get the job. Here are some suggestions for before, during, and after an interview, as well as some questions interviewers frequently ask and some good questions you may want to ask them:

Before the Interview

- Interviewers have varied styles: to name a few, the "Let's get to know each other" style, the quasi-interrogation style (question after question), and the tough, probing "why, why, why" style. Be ready for anything.
- Practice being interviewed with a friend, and ask for a critique.
- Prepare at least five good questions whose answers are not readily available in company literature. (Obtain and read this literature, such as brochures, advertisements, catalogs, and annual reports, beforehand.)
- Anticipate possible interview questions, and frame suitable answers.
- Avoid back-to-back interviews, as they can be exhausting.
- Dress for the interview in a conservative style rather than in the height of fashion.
- Plan to arrive about 10 minutes early to collect your thoughts before being called.
- Review the main points you intend to cover.
- Try to relax.

During the Interview

- Give a firm handshake in greeting the interviewer. Introduce yourself using the same form the interviewer has used. (That is, use first names only if the interviewer does so first.) Make a good initial impression.
- Maintain enthusiasm throughout the interview.
- Good eye contact, good posture, and distinct speech are musts. Don't clasp your hands or fiddle with jewelry, your hair, or anything else. Sit comfortably in your chair. Do not smoke, even if given permission to do so. Bring extra copies of your resume with you.
- Know your "story" in detail. Present your selling points. Answer questions directly. Avoid one-word answers, but don't be wordy.
- Let the interviewer take the initiative often, but don't be passive. Find a way to direct the conversation to those things you want the interviewer to hear.
- The best time to make your most important points is toward the end of the interview, in order to leave on a high note.
- Don't be afraid to "close" the interview. You might say, "I'm very interested in the position, and I have enjoyed this interview."

After the Interview

- Upon leaving, make a note of any key points. Be sure you know who is to follow up on the interview and when a decision is to be made.
- Objectively analyze your performance during the interview.
- Send a thank-you letter that mentions any additional points of information you may have left out.

Questions Frequently Asked by Employers

- What are your long- and short-range goals and objectives, when and why did you establish them, and how are you preparing yourself to achieve them?
- What do you see yourself doing five years from now?
- What do you really want to do in life?
- How do you plan to achieve your career goals?
- What do you expect to be earning in five years?
- Why should I hire you?
- What do you think it takes to be successful in a company like ours?
- In what ways do you think you can make a contribution to our company?
- What qualities should a successful manager have?
- What do you know about our company?
- Do you think your grades are a good indicator of your academic achievement?
- What college subjects did you like most? Least? Why?
- What have you learned from your mistakes?
- How would you describe the ideal job for you following graduation?[3]

Questions to Ask Employers

- What are the opportunities for personal growth at this company?
- Identify typical career paths based on past records. What is a realistic time frame for advancement?
- How is an employee evaluated and promoted?
- Describe a typical first-year assignment.
- Tell me about your initial and advanced training programs.
- How would you describe your company's personality and management style?
- What are your expectations for new hires?
- What are the characteristics of a successful person at your company?
- What are the company's plans for future growth, and how will they affect me?[4]

FOLLOW-UP

The in-company interview can run from a few hours to a whole day. Your interest, maturity, enthusiasm, assertiveness, logic, and knowledge of the company and the position you seek will all be under scrutiny. But you also need to ask questions that are important to you. Find out about the environment, job role, responsibilities, opportunities, and any current issues that may be of interest. To avoid future embarrassment, try to remember the names of the people you have met. If all goes well, you may be working for this firm in the near future. Good luck!

Glossary

accessory equipment Goods, such as portable tools and office equipment, that are less expensive and shorter-lived than major equipment.

acquisition cost The cost of bringing in new customers including advertising, sales-calls, needs-research, and data-entry costs.

adaptive selling Sales technique using a pitch adapted for each prospect in response to the specific sales situation.

adopter A consumer who was happy enough with his or her trial experience with a product to use it again.

advertising Impersonal, one-way mass communication about a product or organization that is paid for by a marketer.

advertising appeal Reason for a person to buy a product.

advertising campaign Series of related advertisements focusing on a common theme, slogan, and set of advertising appeals.

advertising objective Specific communication task a campaign should accomplish for a specified target audience during a specified period.

advertising response function Phenomenon in which spending for advertising and sales promotion increases sales or market share up to a certain level but then produces diminishing returns.

advocacy advertising Form of advertising in which an organization expresses its views on controversial issues or responds to media attacks.

AIDA concept Model that outlines the process for achieving promotional goals in terms of stages of consumer involvement with the message; the acronym stands for Attention, Interest, Desire, and Action.

all-you-can-afford approach Method of setting a promotion budget that relies on determining how much the marketer can spend.

applied research Attempts to develop new or improved products.

arbitrary allocation Method of setting a promotion budget that picks a dollar amount without reference to other factors.

aspirational reference group Group that someone would like to join.

atmosphere The overall impression conveyed by a store's physical layout, decor, and surroundings.

attitude A learned tendency to respond consistently toward a given object, such as a brand.

audience selectivity Ability of an advertising medium to reach a precisely defined market.

audit Form of observation research that features people examining and verifying the sale of a product.

automatic identification (auto ID) The use of identification technology to mark and read products as they enter and leave the warehouse or are received by a manufacturer or retailer.

automatic storage and retrieval systems (AS/RS) System that automatically stores and picks goods in the warehouse or distribution center.

automatic vending The use of machines to offer goods for sale.

average total cost (ATC) Total costs divided by output.

average variable cost (AVC) Total variable costs divided by quantity of output.

baby boomers People born between 1946 and 1964.

bait pricing Price tactic that tries to get consumers into a store through false or misleading price advertising and then uses high-pressure selling to persuade consumers to buy more expensive merchandise.

base price The general price level at which the company expects to sell the good or service.

base profit The profit on basic purchases, unaffected by time, loyalty, efficiency, or other considerations.

basic research Pure research which aims to confirm an existing theory or to learn more about a concept or phenomenon.

basing-point pricing Price tactic that charges freight rates from a given (basing) point, regardless of the city from which the goods are shipped.

BehaviorScan Scanner-based research program that tracks the purchases of 3,000 households through store scanners.

belief An organized pattern of knowledge that an individual holds as true about his or her world.

benchmarking The process of rating a company's products against the best products in the world, including those in other industries.

benefit segmentation The process of grouping customers into market segments according to the benefits they seek from the product.

brainstorming Getting a group to think of unlimited ways to vary a product or solve a problem.

brand A name, term, symbol, design, or combination thereof that identifies a seller's products and differentiates them from competitors' products.

brand equity The value of company and brand names.

brand loyalty A consistent preference for one brand over all others.

brand mark The elements of a brand that cannot be spoken.

brand name That part of a brand that can be spoken, including letters, words, and numbers.

break-even analysis Method of determining what sales volume must be reached before total revenue equals total costs.

business analysis The second stage of the screening process where preliminary figures for demand, cost, sales, and profitability are calculated.

business product (industrial product) Products used to manufacture other goods or services, to facilitate an organization's operations, or to resell to other customers.

business services Expense items that do not become part of a final product.

business-to-business marketing The marketing of goods and services to individuals and organizations for purposes other than personal consumption.

buyer Department head who selects the merchandise for his or her department and may also be responsible for promotion and personnel.

buyer for export Intermediary in the global market that assumes all ownership risks and sells globally for its own account.

buying center All those persons who become involved in the purchase decision.

cannibalization Situation that occurs when sales of a new product cut into sales of a firm's existing products.

cash cow In the portfolio matrix, a business unit that usually generates more cash than it needs to maintain its market share.

cash discount A price reduction offered to a consumer, an industrial user, or a marketing intermediary in return for prompt payment of a bill.

category killers Term often used to describe specialty discount stores because they so heavily dominate their narrow merchandise segment.

central-location telephone (CLT) facility A specially designed phone room used to conduct telephone interviewing.

chain stores Stores owned and operated as a group by a single organization.

channel Medium of communication—such as a voice, radio, or newspaper—for transmitting a message.

closed-ended question Interview question that asks the respondent to make a selection from a limited list of responses.

cobranding Placing two or more brand names on a product or its package.

code of ethics A guideline to help marketing managers and other employees make better decisions.

cognitive dissonance Inner tension that a consumer experiences after recognizing an inconsistency between behavior and values or opinions.

cold calling Form of lead generation in which the salesperson approaches potential buyers without any prior knowledge of the prospects' needs or financial status.

commercialization The decision to market a product.

communication Process by which we exchange or share meanings through a common set of symbols.

comparative advertising Form of advertising that compares two or more specifically named or shown competing brands on one or more specific attributes.

competitive advertising Form of advertising designed to influence demand for a specific brand.

competitive parity Method of setting a promotion budget that matches a competitor's spending.

component lifestyles Practice of choosing goods and services that meet one's diverse needs and interests rather than conforming to a single, traditional lifestyle.

component parts Either finished items ready for assembly or products that need very little processing before becoming part of some other product.

computer-assisted personal interviewing Interviewing method in which the interviewer reads the questions from a computer screen and enters the respondent's data directly into the computer.

computer-assisted self-interviewing Interviewing method in which a mall interviewer intercepts and directs willing respondents to nearby computers where the respondent reads questions off a computer screen and directly keys his or her answers into a computer.

computer disk by mail survey Like a typical mail survey only the respondents receive and answer questions on a disk.

concentrated targeting strategy A strategy used to select one segment of a market for targeting marketing efforts.

concept of exchange Idea that people give up something to receive something they would rather have.

concept test Test to evaluate a new product idea, usually before any prototype has been created.

consumer behavior How consumers make purchase decisions and how they use and dispose of the purchased goods or services.

consumer decision-making process Step-by-step process used by consumers when buying goods or services.

consumer product Product bought to satisfy an individual's personal wants.

Consumer Product Safety Commission (CPSC) Federal agency established to protect the health and safety of consumers in and around their homes.

consumer sales promotion Sales promotion activities to the ultimate consumer.

containerization The process of putting large quantities of goods in sturdy containers that can be moved from ship to truck to airplane to train without repacking.

continuous improvement A commitment to constantly seek ways of doing things better in order to maintain and improve quality.

continuous media schedule Media scheduling strategy, used for products in the latter stages of the product life cycle, in which advertising is run steadily throughout the advertising period.

contract logistics Turning over the entire function of buying and managing transportation or another subsystem of physical distribution to an independent third party.

contract manufacturing Private label manufacturing by a foreign company.

control Provides the mechanisms for evaluating marketing results in light of the plan's goals and for correcting actions that do not help the organization reach those goals within budget guidelines.

convenience product A relatively inexpensive item that merits little shopping effort.

convenience sample A form of nonprobability sample using respondents who are convenient or readily accessible to the researcher, for example, employees, friends, or relatives.

convenience store A miniature supermarket, carrying only a limited line of high-turnover convenience goods.

cookies Computer codes that were originally developed to customize Web sites for individual visitors.

cooperative advertising Arrangement in which the manufacturer and the retailer split the costs of advertising the manufacturer's brand.

core service The most basic benefit the consumer is buying.

corporate social responsibility Business's concern for society's welfare.

corrective advertising Advertising that is run to amend the false impressions left by previous promotion.

cost per contact Cost of reaching one member of the target market.

cost per thousand (CPM) Standard criterion for comparing media, computed by dividing the price of a single ad by the audience size in thousands.

countertrade Form of trade in which all or part of the payment for goods or services is in the form of other goods or services.

coupon Certificate that entitles consumers to an immediate price reduction when they buy the product.

credence quality A characteristic that consumers may have difficulty assessing even after purchase because they do not have the necessary knowledge or experience.

crisis management Coordinated effort to handle the effects of unfavorable publicity or of another unexpected, unfavorable event.

cross-tabulation A method of analyzing data that lets the analyst look at the responses to one question in relation to the responses to one or more other questions.

culture The set of values, norms, attitudes, and other meaningful symbols that shape human behavior, as well as the artifacts, or products, of that behavior as they are transmitted from one generation to the next.

customer satisfaction The feeling that a product has met or exceeded the customer's expectations.

customer value The ratio of benefits to the sacrifice necessary to obtain those benefits.

customer value triad Goods quality, service quality, and value-based prices—the components of customer value.

cycle time Time from when production begins until the good is received by the customer.

database marketing The creation of a large computerized file of customers' and potential customers' profiles and purchase patterns.

decision support system (DSS) An interactive, flexible computerized information system that enables managers to obtain and manipulate information as they are making decisions.

decline stage A long-run drop in sales.

decoding Interpretation of the language and symbols sent by the source through a channel.

delayed-quotation pricing Price tactic used for industrial installations and many accessory items, in which a firm price is not set until the item is either finished or delivered.

demand The quantity of a product that will be sold in the market at various prices for a specified period.

demographic segmentation Segmenting markets by age, gender, income, ethnic background, and family life cycle.

demography The study of people's vital statistics, such as their age, race and ethnicity, and location.

department store A store housing several departments under one roof.

derived demand The demand for business-to-business products.

development Stage in the product development process in which a prototype is developed and a marketing strategy is outlined.

differential advantage One or more unique aspects of an organization that cause target consumers to patronize that firm rather than competitors.

diffusion The process by which the adoption of an innovation spreads.

direct channel Manufacturers selling directly to consumers.

direct foreign investment Active ownership of a foreign company or of overseas manufacturing or marketing facilities.

direct marketing (direct-response marketing) Techniques used to get consumers to make a purchase from their home, office, or other nonretail setting.

direct retailing Representatives selling products door-to-door, office-to-office, or at home parties.

discount store A retailer that competes on the basis of low prices, high turnover, and high volume.

discrepancy of assortment Lack of all the items a consumer needs to receive full satisfaction from a product.

discrepancy of quantity The difference between the amount of product produced and the amount an end user wants to buy.

discretionary income Money beyond necessities and taxes.

diversification A strategy of increasing sales by introducing new products into new markets.

dog In the portfolio matrix, a business unit that has low growth potential and a small market share.

download Intentional storage of information from a Web site.

dual distribution (multiple distribution) When a producer selects two or more channels to distribute the same product to target markets.

dumping The sale of an exported product at a price lower than that charged for the same or a like product in the "home" market of the exporter.

80/20 principle Principle that holds that 20 percent of all customers generate 80 percent of the demand.

elastic demand Situation in which consumer demand is sensitive to changes in price.

elasticity of demand Consumers' responsiveness or sensitivity to changes in price.

electronic cash Method used to transfer payment online.

electronic data interchange (EDI) Automated order processing through the use of computer technology.

electronic distribution Any kind of product or service that can be distributed electronically, whether over traditional forms such as fiber optic cable or through satellite transmission of electronic signals.

e-mail surveys Interviewing technique in which researchers use batch-type electronic mail to send surveys, and respondents send reply via e-mail.

empowerment Delegation of authority to solve customer's problems quickly—usually by the first person that the customer notifies regarding a problem.

encoding Conversion of the sender's ideas and thoughts into a message, usually in the form of words or signs.

environmental management When a company implements strategies that attempt to shape the external environment within which it operates.

environmental scanning Collection and interpretation of information about forces, events, and relationships in the external environment that may affect the future of the organization or the implementation of the marketing plan.

escalator pricing Price tactic in which the final selling price reflects cost increases incurred between the times when the order is placed and when delivery is made.

ethics The moral principles or values that generally govern the conduct of an individual or a group.

evaluation Gauging the extent to which marketing objectives have been achieved during the specified time period.

everyday low prices (EDLP) Price tactic of permanently reducing prices 10 to 15 percent below the traditional levels while eliminating trade discounts that create trade loading.

evoked set (consideration set) Group of brands, resulting from an information search, from which a buyer can choose.

exclusive distribution The most restrictive form of market coverage entails only one or a few dealers within a given area.

experience quality A characteristic that can be assessed only after use.

experiment Method a researcher uses to gather primary data.

export agent Intermediary that acts like a manufacturer's agent for the exporter. The export agent lives in the foreign market.

export broker Intermediary who plays the traditional broker's role by bringing buyer and seller together.

exporting Selling domestically produced products to buyers in another country.

express warranty A written guarantee.

extensive decision making Most complex type of decision making exhibited by consumers buying unfamiliar, expensive or infrequently bought items; requires use of several criteria for evaluating options and much time for seeking information.

external information search Seeking information in the outside environment.

factory outlet An off-price retailer that is owned and operated by a manufacturer.

family brand Marketing several different products under the same brand name.

family life cycle (FLC) A series of stages determined by a combination of age, marital status, and the presence or absence of children.

Federal Trade Commission (FTC) Federal agency empowered to prevent persons or corporations from using unfair methods of competition in commerce.

feedback Receiver's response to a message.

field order takers Someone who visits existing customers regularly, checks inventory, writes up new orders, and then delivers and stocks the product for the customers.

field service firm Firm that specializes in interviewing respondents on a subcontracted basis.

firewall Special computer programs that check all incoming and outgoing information streams for proper identification and authorization.

fixed cost Cost that does not change as output is increased or decreased.

flexible pricing (variable pricing) Price tactic in which different customers pay different prices for essentially the same merchandise bought in equal quantities.

flighted media schedule Media scheduling strategy in which ads are run heavily every other month or every two weeks, to achieve a greater impact with an increased frequency and reach at those times.

FOB origin pricing Price tactic that requires the buyer to absorb the freight costs from the shipping point ("free on board").

focus group Seven to ten people who participate in a group discussion led by a moderator.

follow-up Final step of the selling process, in which the salesperson ensures that delivery schedules are met, that the goods or services perform as promised, and that the buyers' employees are properly trained to use the products.

Food and Drug Administration (FDA) Federal agency charged with enforcing regulations against selling and distributing adulterated, misbranded, or hazardous food and drug products.

Foreign Corrupt Practices Act Prohibits U.S. corporations from making illegal payments to public officials of foreign governments to obtain business rights or to enhance their business dealings in that country.

four Ps Product, place, promotion, and price, which together make up the marketing mix.

frame error Error that occurs when a sample drawn from a population differs from the target population.

franchise The right to operate a business or to sell a product.

franchise outlets Retail store owned and operated by individuals but licensed by a larger supporting organization.

franchisee Individual or business that is granted the right to sell another party's product.

franchisor Originator of a trade name, product, methods of operation, and so on, that grants operating rights to another party to sell its product.

freight absorption pricing Price tactic in which the seller pays all or part of the actual freight charges and does not pass them on to the buyer.

frequency Number of times an individual is exposed to a given message during a specific period.

frequent-buyer program Loyalty program in which loyal consumers are rewarded for making multiple purchases of a particular good or service.

full-line discount store Discount store that offers consumers very limited service and carries a broad assortment of well-known, nationally branded hard goods.

fully industrialized society The fifth stage of economic development, a society that is an exporter of manufactured products, many of which are based on advanced technology.

functional discount (trade discount) Discount to wholesalers and retailers for performing channel functions.

gap model A model of service quality that identifies five gaps that can cause problems in service delivery and influence customer evaluations of service quality.

General Agreements on Tariffs and Trade (GATT) Provided loopholes that enabled countries to avoid trade-barrier reduction agreements.

generation X People who are currently between the ages of 18 and 29 years of age.

generic product A no-frills, no-brand name, low-cost product that is simply identified by its product category.

generic product name Identifies a product by class or type and cannot be trademarked.

geodemographic segmentation Segmenting potential customers into neighborhood lifestyle categories.

geographic segmentation Segmenting markets by region of the country or world, market size, market density, or climate.

global marketing Marketing to target markets throughout the world.

global marketing standardization Production of uniform products that can be sold the same way all over the world.

global vision Recognizing and reacting to international marketing opportunities, being aware of threats from foreign competitors in all markets, and effectively using international distribution networks.

green marketing The marketing of products and packages that are less toxic than normal, are more durable, contain reusable materials, or are made of recyclable materials.

gross margin Amount of money the retailer makes as a percentage of sales after the cost of goods sold is subtracted.

group dynamics Interaction essential to the success of focus group research.

growth stage The second stage of the product life cycle when sales typically grow at an increasing rate, many competitors enter the market, large companies may start acquiring small pioneering firms, and profits are healthy.

heterogeneity Characteristic of services that makes them less standardized and uniform than goods.

hierarchy of effects model Model that outlines the six-stage process by which consumers make purchase decisions: awareness, knowledge, liking, preference, conviction, and purchase.

hygiene factors Factors that contribute to customer dissatisfaction.

hypermarket Retail store which combines a supermarket and full-line discount store in a space ranging from 200,000 to 300,000 square feet.

hypertext Text-based communication links among documents; when a linked word or phrase in one document is selected, another related document is displayed.

ideal self-image The way an individual would like to be.

implementation The process that turns marketing plans into action assignments and ensures that these assignments are executed in a way that accomplishes the plans' objectives.

implied warranty An unwritten guarantee that the good or service is fit for the purpose for which it was sold.

in-bound telephone surveys A new trend in telephone interviewing in which an information packet is sent to consumers who are then asked to call a toll-free, interactive voice-mail system, and answer questions.

incremental productivity approach Method of determining the optimal sales force size, in which salespeople are added as long as the total sales increase is greater than the increase in selling cost.

independent retailers Retailers owned by a single person or partnership and not operated as part of a larger retail institution.

individual branding Using different brand names for different products.

industrializing society The fourth stage of economic development when technology spreads from sectors of the economy that powered the takeoff to the rest of the nation.

inelastic demand Situation in which an increase or a decrease in price will not significantly affect demand for the product.

inflation A general rise in prices without a corresponding increase in wages, which results in decreased purchasing power.

infomercial Thirty-minute or longer advertisement that looks more like a TV talk show than a sales pitch.

informational labeling Designed to help consumers make proper product selections and lower their cognitive dissonance after the purchase.

InfoScan A scanner-based sales-tracking service for the consumer packaged-goods industry.

innovation A product perceived as new by a potential adopter.

inseparability Characteristic of services that allows them to be produced and consumed simultaneously.

inside order takers Someone who takes orders from customers over the counter, on the sales floor, over the telephone, or by mail.

institutional advertising Form of advertising designed to enhance a company's image rather than promote a particular product.

intangibility Services that cannot be touched, seen, tasted, heard, or felt in the same manner in which goods can be sensed.

integrated interviewing A new interviewing method in which a respondent is interviewed on the Internet.

integrated marketing communications (IMC) The method of carefully coordinating all promotional activities to produce a consistent, unified message that is customer-focused.

intelligent agents Software tools that automatically comparison-shop for the lowest prices on internationally available brand-name merchandise.

intensive distribution Distribution aimed at maximum market coverage.

internal information search The process of recalling information stored in the memory.

internal marketing Treating employees as customers and developing systems and benefits that satisfy their needs.

Internet A network of computers.

interpersonal communication Direct, face-to-face communication between two or more people.

introductory stage The full-scale launch of a new product into the marketplace.

inventory control system System that develops and maintains an adequate assortment of products to meet customers' demands.

involvement The amount of time and effort a buyer invests in the search, evaluation, and decision processes of consumer behavior.

ISO 9000 A standard of quality management, hugely popular in Europe, that is rapidly taking hold in the United States and around the globe.

joint costs Costs that are shared in the manufacturing and marketing of several products in a product line.

joint demand The demand for two or more items used together in a final product.

joint venture When a domestic firm buys part of a foreign company or joins with a foreign company to create a new entity.

just-in-time (JIT) inventory management Redesigning and simplifying manufacturing by reducing inventory levels and delivering parts just when they are needed on the production line.

keiretsu Japanese society of business, which takes one of two main forms: a bank-centered keiretsu, or a massive industrial combine centered around a bank; and a supply keiretsu, or a group of companies dominated by the major manufacturer they provide with supplies.

keystoning Practice of marking up prices by 100 percent, or doubling the cost.

lead generation (prospecting) Identification of those firms and people most likely to buy the seller's offerings.

lead qualification Determining of a sales prospect's authority to buy and ability to pay for the good or service.

leader pricing (loss-leader pricing) Price tactic in which a product is sold near or even below cost in the hope that shoppers will buy other items once they are in the store.

learning The process that creates changes in behavior through experience and practice.

licensing The legal process whereby a licensor agrees to let another firm use its manufacturing process, trademarks, patents, trade secrets, or other proprietary knowledge.

life cycle cost The expected additional cost that a customer will incur over the life of the product.

lifestyle A mode of living, identified by a person's activities, interests, and opinions.

limited decision making Type of decision making exhibited by consumers buying regularly purchased, inexpensive goods and services; requires moderate search and decision time.

logistics A broader term that encompasses physical distribution and includes the procurement and management of raw materials and component parts for production.

loyalty marketing programs Promotional program designed to build long-term, mutually beneficial relationships between a company and its key customers.

Maastricht Treaty Agreement among all twelve countries of the European Community to pursue economic, monetary, and political union.

macrosegmentation Method of dividing business markets into segments based on general characteristics such as geographic location, customer type, customer size, and product use.

major equipment (installations) Capital goods such as large or expensive machines, mainframe computer, blast furnaces, generators, airplanes, and buildings.

mall intercept interview Survey research method that involves interviewing people in the common areas of shopping malls.

manufacturer's brand A brand name owned by a manufacturer.

marginal cost (MC) Change in total costs associated with a one-unit change in output.

marginal revenue (MR) The extra revenue associated with selling an extra unit of output or the change in total revenue with a one-unit change in output.

market People or organizations with needs or wants and the ability and willingness to buy.

market attractiveness/company strength matrix Tool for allocating resources among strategic business units on the basis of how attractive a market is and how well the firm is positioned to take advantage of opportunities in that market.

market development Attracting new customers to existing products.

market opportunity analysis The description and estimation of the size and sales potential of market segments that are of interest to the firm and the assessment of key competitors in these market segments.

market penetration A marketing strategy that tries to increase market share among existing customers.

market segment A subgroup of people or organizations sharing one or more characteristics that cause them to have similar product needs.

market segmentation The process of dividing a market into meaningful, relatively similar, and identifiable segments or groups.

market share A company's product sales as a percentage of total sales for that industry.

market share approach Method of setting a promotion budget that allocates the amount needed to maintain or win a certain market share.

marketing The process of planning and executing the conception, pricing, promotion, and distribution of ideas, goods, and services to create exchanges that satisfy individual and organizational goals.

marketing audit A thorough, systematic, periodic evaluation of the goals, strategies, structure, and performance of the marketing organization.

marketing channel (channel of distribution) A business structure of interdependent organizations which reaches from the point of product origin to the consumer.

marketing concept Idea that the social and economic justification for an organization's existence is the satisfaction of customer wants and needs while meeting organizational objectives.

marketing-controlled information source Product information source that originates with marketers promoting the product.

marketing intelligence Everyday information about developments in the marketing environment that managers use to prepare and adjust marketing plans.

marketing mix A unique blend of product, distribution, promotion, and pricing strategies designed to produce mutually satisfying exchanges with a target market.

marketing myopia Business defined in terms of goods and services rather than in terms of the benefits that customers seek.

marketing objective A statement of what is to be accomplished through marketing activities.

marketing orientation Philosophy that assumes that a sale does not depend on an aggressive sales force but rather on a customer's decision to purchase a product.

marketing plan A written document that acts as a guidebook of marketing activities for the marketing manager.

marketing planning Designing activities relating to marketing objectives and the changing marketing environment.

marketing research The process of planning, collecting, and analyzing data relevant to a marketing decision.

marketing strategy The activity of selecting and describing one or more target markets, and developing and maintaining a marketing mix that will produce mutually satisfying exchanges with target markets.

markup pricing Cost of buying the product from the producer plus amounts for profit and for expenses not otherwise accounted for.

Maslow's hierarchy of needs Popular theory which arranges needs in ascending order of importance: physiological, safety, social, esteem, and self-actualization.

mass communication Communication to large audiences.

mass customization A strategy that uses technology to deliver customized services on a mass basis.

mass merchandising Retailing strategy using moderate to low prices on large quantities of merchandise and lower service to stimulate high turnover products.

master brand A brand so dominant in consumers' minds that they think of it immediately when a product category, use situation, product attribute, or customer benefit is mentioned.

materials-handling system Moves inventory into, within, and out of the warehouse.

maturity stage A period during which sales increase at a decreasing rate.

measurement error Error that occurs when there is a difference between the information desired by the researcher and the information provided by the measurement process.

media mix Combination of media to be used for a promotional campaign.

media schedule Designation of the media, the specific publications or programs, and the insertion dates of advertising.

medium Channel used to convey a message to a target market.

Mercosur The largest new trade agreement which includes Brazil, Argentina, Uruguay, and Paraguay.

micromarketing The development of marketing programs tailored to prospective buyers who live in small geographic regions, such as neighborhoods, or who have very specific lifestyle and demographic characteristics.

microsegmentation The process of dividing business markets into segments based on the characteristics of decision-making units within a macrosegment.

mission statement The firm's long-term vision based on a careful analysis of benefits sought by present and potential customers and analysis of existing and anticipated environmental conditions.

missionary sales representatives Someone who works for a manufacturer to stimulate goodwill within the channel of distribution and to support the company's sales efforts.

modified rebuy Situation where the purchaser wants some change in the original good or service.

monopolistic competition A situation in which a relatively large number of suppliers offer similar but not identical products.

monopoly When one firm controls the output and price of a product for which there are no close substitutes.

morals The rules people develop as a result of cultural values and norms.

motive The driving force that causes a person to take action to satisfy specific needs.

multiculturalism When all major ethnic groups in an area—such as a city, county, or census tract—are roughly equally represented.

multimedia Any combination of text, graphics, sound, or other data formats in a single document.

multinational corporation A company that is heavily engaged in international trade, beyond exporting and importing.

multiplier effect (accelerator principle) Phenomenon in which a small increase or decrease in consumer demand can produce a much larger change in demand for the facilities and equipment needed to make the consumer product.

multisegment targeting strategy A strategy that chooses two or more well-defined market segments and develops a distinct marketing mix for each.

National Advertising Division (NAD) Complaint bureau for consumers and advertisers, part of the Council of Better Business Bureaus.

National Advertising Review Board (NARB) Appeals board for cases in which the National Advertising Division rules in favor of the complaining party.

need-satisfaction approach Sales pitch that focuses on satisfying a prospective buyer's particular needs.

needs assessment Determination of the customer's specific needs and wants, and the range of options a customer has for satisfying them.

negotiation Process of both the salesperson and the prospect offering special concessions in an attempt to arrive at a sales agreement.

networking Process of finding out about potential clients from friends, business contacts, coworkers, acquaintances, and fellow members in professional and civic organizations.

new buy A situation requiring the purchase of a product for the first time.

new product Product new to the world, the market, the producer, the seller, or some combination of these.

new-product committee An ad hoc group whose members manage the new product development process.

new-product department Performs the same functions as a new product committee but on a full-time basis.

new-product strategy Linking the new product development process with the objectives of the marketing department, the business unit, and the corporation.

niche One segment of a market.

noise Anything that interferes with, distorts, or slows down the transmission of information.

nonaspirational reference groups Groups that influence our behavior when we try to maintain distance from them. Also known as dissociative groups.

noncumulative quantity discount A deduction from list price that applies to a single order rather than to the total volume of orders placed during a certain period.

non-marketing-controlled information source Product information source that is not associated with advertising or promotion.

nonmonetary sacrifice The time and effort customers invest when making a purchase or receiving postsale services.

nonprobability sample Any sample in which little or no attempt is made to get a representative cross section of the population.

nonprofit organization An organization that exists to achieve some goal other than the usual business goals of profit, market share, or return on investment.

nonprofit organization marketing The effort by nonprofit organizations to bring about mutually satisfying exchanges with target markets.

nonstore retailing Shopping without visiting a store.

norms The values and attitudes deemed acceptable by the group.

North American Free Trade Agreement (NAFTA) An agreement between Canada, the United States, and Mexico that created the world's largest free-trade zone.

objective and task approach Method of setting a promotion budget that begins with promotional objectives, defines the communication tools required to achieve those objectives, and then adds up the costs of the planned activities.

observation research Research method that relies on three types of observation: people watching people, people watching activity, and machines watching people.

odd-even pricing (psychological pricing) Price tactic that uses odd-numbered prices to connote bargains and even-numbered prices to imply quality.

off-price retailer Retailer that sells at prices 25% or more below traditional department store prices because it pays cash for its stock and usually doesn't ask for return privileges.

oligopoly An industry where a relatively small number of firms dominate the market for a good or service.

online database A collection of public information accessible to anyone with the proper computer facilities.

online database vendor An intermediary that acquires databases from database creators.

open-ended question Interview question that encourages an answer phrased in the respondent's own words.

opinion leaders Group leaders who influence others.

optimizers Type of business customer that considers numerous suppliers, both familiar and unfamiliar, solicits bids, and studies all proposals carefully before selecting one.

order getter Someone who actively seeks buyers for a product.

Pareto analysis A method for identifying a company's biggest problems using a bar chart that ranks problems in descending order, usually based on the events' frequency of occurrence.

penetration pricing Pricing policy whereby a firm charges a relatively low price for a product initially as a way to reach the mass market.

percent of sales approach Method of setting a promotion budget that allocates an amount equal to a certain percentage of total sales.

perception The process by which we select, organize, and interpret stimuli into a meaningful and coherent picture.

perceptual mapping A means of displaying or graphing, in two or more dimensions, the location of products, brands, or groups of products in customers' minds.

perishability Characteristic of services that prevents them from being stored, warehoused, or inventoried.

personal selling Planned presentation to one or more prospective buyers for the purpose of making a sale.

personality Ways of organizing and grouping the consistencies of an individual's reactions to situations.

personalized economy Delivering goods and services at a good value on demand.

persuasive labeling Focuses on a promotional theme or logo and consumer information is secondary.

physical distribution The ingredient in the marketing mix that describes how products are moved and stored.

physical distribution service The package of activities performed by a supplier to ensure that the right product is in the right place at the right time.

physical distribution system Consists of five distinct, interdependent subsystems which serve several key functions of physical distribution managers: warehousing, materials handling, inventory control, order-processing, and transportation.

pioneering advertising Form of advertising designed to stimulate primary demand for a new product or product category.

planned obsolescence The practice of modifying products so those that have already been sold become obsolete before they actually need replacement.

planning The process of anticipating future events and determining strategies to achieve organizational objectives in the future.

point-of-purchase display Promotional display set up at the retailer's location to build traffic, advertise the product, or induce impulse buying.

portfolio matrix Tool for allocating resources among products or strategic business units on the basis of relative market share and market growth rate.

position The place a product, brand, or group of products occupies in consumers' minds relative to competing offerings.

positioning Developing a specific marketing mix to influence potential customers' overall perception of a brand, product line, or organization in general.

poverty of time Lack of time to do anything but work, commute to work, handle family situations, do housework, shop, sleep, and eat.

predatory pricing The practice of charging a very low price for a product with the intent of driving competitors out of business or out of a market.

preindustrial society A society in the second stage of economic development, involving economic and social change and the emergence of a middle class with an entrepreneurial spirit.

premium Extra item offered to the consumer, usually in exchange for some proof of purchase of the promoted product.

prepared sales presentation Structured, or canned, sales pitch.

prestige pricing Charging a high price to help promote a high-quality image.

price That which is given up in an exchange to acquire a good or service.

price bundling Marketing two or more products in a single package for a special price.

price equilibrium Price at which demand and supply are equal.

price fixing An agreement between two or more firms on the price they will charge for a product.

price lining Practice of offering a product line with several items at specific price points.

price shading Use of discounts by salespeople to increase demand for one or more products in a line.

price skimming Pricing policy whereby a firm charges a high introductory price, often coupled with heavy promotion.

price strategy Basic, long-term pricing framework, which establishes the initial price for a product and the intended direction for price movements over the product life cycle.

primary data Information collected for the first time. Can be used for solving the particular problem under investigation.

primary membership groups All groups with which people interact regularly in an informal, face-to-face manner, such as family, friends, and coworkers.

private brand A brand name owned by a wholesaler or a retailer.

probability sample A sample in which every element in the population has a known statistical likelihood of being selected.

problem child (question mark) In the portfolio matrix, a business unit that shows rapid growth but poor profit margins.

problem recognition Result of an imbalance between actual and desired states.

processed materials Products used directly in manufacturing other products.

product Everything, both favorable and unfavorable, that a person receives in an exchange.

product advertising Form of advertising that touts the benefits of a specific good or service.

product category All brands that satisfy a particular type of need.

product development Marketing strategy that entails the creation of new products for present markets; process of converting applications for new technologies into marketable products.

product differentiation A positioning strategy that some firms use to distinguish their products from those of competitors.

production orientation A philosophy that focuses on the internal capabilities of the firm rather than on the desires and needs of the marketplace.

product item A specific version of a product that can be designated as a distinct offering among an organization's products.

product line A group of closely related product items.

product line depth The number of product items in a product line.

product line extension Adding additional products to an existing product line in order to compete more broadly in the industry.

product line pricing Setting prices for an entire line of products.

product mix All products an organization sells.

product mix width The number of product lines an organization offers.

product modification Changing one or more of a product's characteristics.

product offering The mix of products offered to the consumer by the retailer, also called the product assortment or merchandise mix.

profit Revenue minus expenses.

profit maximization When marginal revenue equals marginal cost.

promotion Communication by marketers that informs, persuades, and reminds potential buyers of a product in order to influence an opinion or elicit a response.

promotion plan Carefully arranged sequence of promotional efforts designed around a common theme and geared to specific objectives.

promotional allowance (trade allowance) Payment to a dealer for promoting the manufacturer's products.

promotional mix Combination of promotion tools—including advertising, public relations, personal selling, and sales promotion—used to reach the target market and fulfill the organization's overall goals.

promotional strategy Plan for the optimal use of the elements of promotion: advertising, public relations, personal selling, and sales promotion.

psychographic segmentation Market segmentation on the basis of personality, motives, lifestyles, and geodemographics.

public relations Marketing function that evaluates public attitudes, identifies areas within the organization that the public may be interested in, and executes a program of action to earn public understanding and acceptance.

public service advertisement (PSA) Announcement that promotes a program of a federal, state, or local government or of a nonprofit organization.

publicity Public information about a company, good, or service appearing in the mass media as a news item.

pull strategy Marketing strategy that stimulates consumer demand to obtain product distribution.

pulsing media schedule Media scheduling strategy that uses continuous scheduling throughout the year coupled with a flighted schedule during the best sales periods.

purely competitive market A large number of sellers marketing a standardized product to a group of buyers who are well informed about the marketplace.

push money Money offered to channel intermediaries to encourage them to "push" products—that is, to encourage other members of the channel to sell the products.

push strategy Marketing strategy that uses aggressive personal selling and trade advertising to convince a wholesaler or a retailer to carry and sell particular merchandise.

pyramid of corporate social responsibility Model that suggests corporate social responsibility is composed of economic, legal, ethical, and philanthropic responsibilities and that the firm's economic performance supports the entire structure.

quality function deployment (QFD) A technique that helps companies translate customer design requirements into product specifications.

quantity discount Price reduction offered to buyers buying in multiple units or above a specified dollar amount.

quota Statement of the individual salesperson's sales objectives, usually based on sales volume alone but sometimes including key accounts (those with greatest potential), new accounts, and specific products.

random error Error that occurs because the selected sample is an imperfect representation of the overall population.

random sample Sample arranged in such a way that every element of the population has an equal chance of being selected as part of the sample.

raw materials Unprocessed extractive or agricultural products, such as mineral ore, lumber, wheat, corn, fruits, vegetables, and fish.

reach Number of target consumers exposed to a commercial at least once during a specific period, usually four weeks.

real self-image How an individual actually perceives himself or herself.

rebate Cash refund given for the purchase of a product during a specific period.

receiver Person who decodes a message.

recession A period of economic activity when income, production, and employment tend to fall—all of which reduce demand for goods and services.

reciprocity A practice where business purchasers choose to buy from their own customers.

reference groups All formal and informal groups that influence the buying behavior of an individual.

referral Recommendation to a salesperson from a customer or business associate.

relationship marketing The name of a strategy that entails forging long-term partnerships with customers.

relationship selling (consultative selling) Sales practice of building, maintaining, and enhancing interactions with customers in order to develop long-term satisfaction through mutually beneficial partnerships.

repositioning Changing consumers' perceptions of a brand in relation to competing brands.

research design Specifies which research questions must be answered, how and when the data will be gathered, and how the data will be analyzed.

retailing All the activities directly related to the sale of goods and services to the ultimate consumer for personal, nonbusiness use.

retailing mix Combination of the six Ps—product, place, promotion, price, personnel, and presentation—to sell goods and services to the ultimate consumer.

revenue The price charged to customers multiplied by the number of units sold.

reverse channels When products move in the opposite direction of traditional channels—from consumer back to producer.

risk The uncertainty about long-term costs.

routine response behavior Type of decision making exhibited by consumers buying frequently purchased, low-cost goods and services; requires little search and decision time.

sales orientation Idea that people will buy more goods and services if aggressive sales techniques are used and that high sales result in high profits.

sales presentation Face-to-face explanation of the sales proposal to a prospective buyer.

sales process (sales cycle) The set of steps a salesperson goes through in a particular organization to sell a particular product or service.

sales promotion Marketing activities—other than personal selling, advertising, and public relations—that stimulate consumer buying and dealer effectiveness.

sales proposal A formal written document or professional presentation that outlines how the salesperson's product or service will meet or exceed the prospect's needs.

sales territory Particular geographic area assigned to a salesperson.

sample A subset of a larger population.

sampling Promotional program which allows the consumer the opportunity to try the product or service for free.

sampling error Error that occurs when a sample somehow does not represent the target population.

satisficer Type of business customer that places an order with the first familiar supplier to satisfy product and delivery requirements.

satisfiers Factors that contribute to customer satisfaction.

scaled-response question A closed-ended question designed to measure the intensity of a respondent's answer.

scanner-based research A system for gathering information from a single group of respondents by continuously monitoring the advertising, promotion, and pricing they are exposed to and the things they buy.

scrambled merchandising The tendency to offer a wide variety of nontraditional goods and services under one roof.

screening The first filter in the product development process which eliminates ideas that are inconsistent with the organization's new product strategy or are obviously inappropriate for some other reason.

search quality A characteristic that can be easily assessed before purchase.

seasonal discount A price reduction for buying merchandise out of season.

seasonal media schedule Media scheduling strategy that runs advertising only during times of the year when the product is most likely to be used.

secondary data Data previously collected for any purpose other than the one at hand.

secondary membership groups Groups people associate with less consistently and more formally, such as clubs, professional groups, and religious groups.

segmentation bases (variables) Characteristics of individuals, groups, or organizations.

selective distortion Occurs when consumers change or distort information that conflicts with their feelings or beliefs.

selective distribution Distribution achieved by screening dealers to eliminate all but a few in any single area.

selective exposure Process whereby a consumer notices certain stimuli and ignores other stimuli.

selective retention Remembering only information that supports personal feelings or beliefs.

self-concept How consumers perceive themselves; self-perception.

selling against the brand Stocking well-known branded items at high prices in order to sell store brands at discounted prices.

selling team Combination of sales and nonsales people, under the direction of a leader, whose primary objective is to establish and maintain a strong relationship with a particular customer or customers.

sender Originator of the message in the communication process.

servers Computers that host Web sites.

service The result of applying human or mechanical efforts to people or objects.

service mark Trademark for a service.

shopping product Product that requires comparison shopping, because it is usually more expensive than a convenience product and found in fewer stores.

simulated (laboratory) market testing Presentation of advertising and other promotion materials for several products, including a test product, to members of the product's target market.

simultaneous product development A new team-oriented approach to new product development.

single-price tactic Policy of offering all goods and services at the same price.

situation analysis Extensive background investigation into a particular marketing problem.

social class A group of people who are considered nearly equal in status or community esteem, who regularly socialize among themselves both formally and informally, and who share behavioral norms.

socialization process Passing down cultural values and norms to children.

societal marketing concept The idea that an organization exists not only to satisfy customer wants and needs and to meet organizational objectives but also to preserve or enhance individuals' and society's long-term best interests.

spamming Broadcasting unsolicited commercial e-mail across the Internet.

specialty discount store Retail store which offers a nearly complete selection of single-line merchandise and uses self-service, discount prices, high volume, and high turnover.

specialty product A particular item that consumers search extensively for and are very reluctant to accept substitutes.

specialty store Retail store specializing in a given type of merchandise.

standard industrial classification system (SIC) A detailed numbering system developed by the U.S. government to classify business and government organizations by their main economic activity.

star In the portfolio matrix, a business unit that is a fast-growing market leader.

statistical quality control (SQC) A method of analyzing deviations in manufactured materials, parts, and goods.

status quo pricing Pricing objective that maintains existing prices or meets the competition's prices.

stimulus Any unit of input affecting the five senses.

stimulus discrimination Learning to differentiate among similar products.

stimulus generalization A learning process that occurs when one response is extended to a second stimulus similar to the first.

stimulus-response approach Sales pitch applying the concept that a given stimulus will produce a given response.

stitching niches Strategy for multicultural marketing which combines ethnic, age, income, and lifestyle markets, on some common basis, to form a large market.

straight commission Method of compensation in which the salesperson is paid some percentage of sales.

straight rebuy Buying situation in which the purchaser reorders the same goods or services without looking for new information or investigating other suppliers.

straight salary Method of compensation in which the salesperson receives a salary regardless of sales productivity.

strategic alliance (strategic partnership) A cooperative agreement between business firms.

strategic business unit (SBU) A subgroup of a single business or collection of related businesses within the larger organization.

strategic channel alliances Producers' agreement to jointly use one producer's already established channel.

strategic planning The managerial process of creating and maintaining a fit between the organization's objectives and resources and evolving market opportunities.

strategic window The limited period during which the "fit" between the key requirements of a market and the particular competencies of a firm are at an optimum.

subculture A homogeneous group of people who share elements of the overall culture as well as cultural elements unique to their own group.

supercenter Retail store which combines groceries and general merchandise goods with a wide range of services.

supermarket A large, departmentalized, self-service retailer that specializes in food and some nonfood items.

supplementary services A group of services that support or enhance the core service.

supplies Consumable items that do not become part of the final product.

supply The quantity of a product that will be offered to the market by a supplier at various prices for a specified period.

surfer Person who explores the Internet/World Wide Web from a computer.

survey research The most popular technique for gathering primary data in which a researcher interacts with people to obtain facts, opinions, and attitudes.

sustainable competitive advantage A differential advantage that cannot be copied by the competition.

SWOT analysis Identifying internal strengths (S) and weaknesses (W) and also examining external opportunities (O) and threats (T).

takeoff economy The third stage of economic development involves a period of transition from a developing to a developed nation.

target market A group of people or organizations for which an organization designs, implements, and maintains a marketing mix intended to meet the needs of that group, resulting in mutually satisfying exchanges.

target return on investment (ROI) Measures the overall effectiveness of management in generating profits with its available assets.

teamwork Collaborative efforts of people to accomplish common objectives.

technical specialists Sales support person with a technical background who works out the details of custom-made products and communicates directly with the potential buyer's technical staff.

telemarketing The use of the telephone to sell directly to consumers.

temporal discrepancy Difference between when a product is produced and when a consumer is ready to buy it.

test marketing The limited introduction of a product and a marketing program to determine the reactions of potential customers in a market situation.

total quality management (TQM) Coordination, throughout the entire organization, of efforts to provide high-quality goods, processes, and services in order to ensure customer satisfaction.

trade allowance Price reduction offered by manufacturers to intermediaries, such as wholesalers and retailers.

trade loading Practice of temporarily lowering the price to induce wholesalers and retailers to buy more goods than can be sold in a reasonable time.

trade sales promotion Sales promotion activities targeted to a channel member, such as a wholesaler or retailer.

trademark The exclusive right to use a brand or part of a brand.

traditional society A society in the earliest stages of economic development, largely agricultural, with a social structure and value system that provide little opportunity for upward mobility.

transaction cost The immediate financial outlay or commitment that a customer must make, the purchase price.

two-part pricing Price tactic that charges two separate amounts to consume a single good or service.

unbundling Reducing the bundle of services that comes with the basic product.

undifferentiated targeting strategy Marketing approach that views the market as one big market with no individual segments and thus requires a single marketing mix.

unfair trade practice act Law that prohibits wholesalers and retailers from selling below cost.

uniform delivered pricing Price tactic in which the seller pays the actual freight charges and bills every purchaser an identical, flat freight charge.

unique selling proposition Desirable, exclusive, and believable advertising appeal selected as the theme for a campaign.

unitary elasticity Situation in which total revenue remains the same when prices change.

unitization A technique for handling small packages by grouping boxes on a pallet or skid.

universal product codes (UPC) Series of thick and thin vertical lines (bar codes), readable by computerized optical scanners, that represent numbers used to track products.

universe The population from which a sample will be drawn.

unsought product A product unknown to ``the potential buyer or a known product that the buyer does not actively seek.

Uruguay Round An agreement to dramatically lower trade barriers worldwide.

usage rate segmentation Dividing a market by the amount of product bought or consumed.

value An enduring belief that a specific mode of conduct is personally or socially preferable to another mode of conduct.

value-based pricing A pricing strategy that has grown out of the quality movement.

value engineering (value analysis) The systematic search for less expensive substitutes.

variable costs Costs that vary with changes in the level of output.

vendor analysis Vendor rating systems used to compare suppliers on attributes the buying center views as important.

venture team A market-oriented group staffed by a small number of representatives from different disciplines.

want When someone has an unfulfilled need and has determined that a particular good or service will satisfy it.

warehouse membership clubs Limited-service merchant wholesaler that sells a limited selection of brand-name appliances, household items, and groceries on a cash-and-carry basis to members, usually small businesses and groups.

warranty Confirms the quality or performance of a good or service.

workload approach Method of determining the optimal sales force size, in which the total time required to cover the territory is divided by the selling time available to one salesperson.

World Trade Organization (WTO) A new trade organization that replaces the old General Agreement on Trade and Tariffs (GATT).

World Wide Web A subset of the Internet that has multimedia and hypertext capability.

zone pricing Modification of uniform delivered pricing that divides the United States (or the total market) into segments or zones and charges a flat freight rate to all customers in a given zone.

Endnotes

Chapter 1

1. Barbara Maddux, "How One Red Hot Retailer Wins Customer Loyalty," *Fortune*, 10 July 1995, pp. 72–79. Reprinted by permission of *Fortune*, © 1995 *Fortune*. All rights reserved worldwide.
2. Peter D. Bennett, *Dictionary of Marketing Terms*, 2d ed. (Chicago: American Marketing Association, 1995), p. 115.
3. Philip Kotler, *Marketing Management*, 9th ed. (Englewood Cliffs, NJ: Prentice-Hall, 1996), p. 11.
4. Stephen Baker, "A New Paint Job at PPG," *Business Week*, 13 November 1995, pp. 74, 78.
5. John A. Byrne, "Strategic Planning," *Business Week*, 26 August 1996, pp. 46–52.
6. Valarie A. Zeithaml and Mary Jo Bitner, *Services Marketing* (New York: McGraw-Hill, 1996), p. 31.
7. Tara Parker-Pope, "Spiked Sodas, an Illicit Hit With Kids in U.K., Head for U.S.," *Wall Street Journal*, 12 February 1996, p. B1. Reprinted with permission of the *Wall Street Journal*, © 1996 Dow Jones & Company, Inc. All Rights Reserved Worldwide.
8. Ken Zino, "We Want to Keep You Satisfied," *Parade Magazine*, 1 October 1995, p. 8.
9. Robert L. Crandall, "AA-BA: A Great Combination," *American Way*, 15 July 1996, p. 14.
10. Rahul Jacob, "Why Some Customers Are More Equal Than Others," *Fortune*, 19 September 1994, p. 216.
11. Kevin J. Clancy and Robert S. Shulman, "Marketing—Ten Fatal Flaws," *The Retailing Issues Letter*, November, 1995, p. 4.
12. Roland T. Rust, Anthony J. Zahorik, and Timothy L. Keiningham, *Service Marketing* (New York: HarperCollins, 1996), p. 375.
13. Zeithaml and Bitner, p. 173.
14. Leonard L. Berry, "Relationship Marketing of Services," *Journal of the Academy of Marketing Science*, Fall 1995, pp. 236–245.
15. Berry, p. 240.
16. Berry, p. 241.
17. Malcolm Fleschner with Gerhard Gschwandtner, "The Marriott Miracle," *Personal Selling Power*, September 1994, p. 25.
18. Leonard L. Berry and A. Parasuraman, *Marketing Services* (New York: Free Press, 1991), p. 49.
19. Berry and Parasuraman, p. 49.
20. Greg Bounds and Charles W. Lamb, Jr., *Introduction to Business* (Cincinnati, OH: South-Western Publishing Co., 1997).
21. Gary Samuels, "CD-ROM's First Big Victim," *Forbes*, 28 February 1994, pp. 42–44.
22. Samuels, p. 42.
23. "King Consumer," *Business Week*, 12 March 1990, p. 90.
24. Cyndee Miller, "Nordstrom Is Tops in Survey," *Marketing News*, 15 February 1993, p. 12.
25. "The Rebirthing of Xerox," *Marketing Insights*, Summer 1992, pp. 73–80.
26. "King Customer," p. 91.
27. Fleschner, p. 26.
28. Joseph Kahn, "P&G Viewed China As a National Market and Is Conquering It," *Wall Street Journal*, 12 September 1995, p. A1. Reprinted by permission of the *Wall Street Journal*, © 1995 Dow Jones & Company, Inc., All Rights Reserved Worldwide.
29. Philip Kotler, *Marketing Management*, 9th ed. (Englewood Cliffs, NJ: Prentice-Hall, Inc., 1997), p. 22.
30. Laura Koss-Feder, "Franchising: A Recipe For Your Second Career," *Business Week*, 4 March 1996, pp. 128–129.

Chapter 2

1. William M. Bulkeley, "The Fastest Jet May Not Win the Race," *Wall Street Journal*, 1 August 1996, pp. B1, B5.
2. Peter Coy, "Is it an Airplane or a Helicopter? Well, Both," *Business Week*, 27 May, 1996, p. 97.
3. Tary Knight, "The Relationship Between Entrepreneurial Orientation, Strategy, and Performance: An Empirical Investigation," in Barbara Stern, George Zinkhan, Peter Gordon, and Bert Kellerman, eds., *1995 AMA Marketing Educators' Conference Proceedings* (Chicago: American Marketing Association, 1995), pp. 272–273.
4. Theodore Levitt, "Marketing Myopia," *Harvard Business Review*, July–August 1960, pp. 45–56.
5. Saturn Corporation, *Face to Face with the Future* (Detroit: Saturn Corporation, 1994).
6. Kathy Rebello, "Inside MicroSoft," *Business Week*, 15 July 1996, pp. 56–67.
7. Manjeet Kripalani, "A Traffic Jam of Auto Makers," *Business Week*, 5 August 1996, pp. 46–47.
8. Rebello, pp. 56–67.
9. Elisabeth Malkin, "On Your Mark, Get Set—Phone!" *Business Week*, 6 May 1996, p. 54.
10. Carlos Tejada, "Pickle Queen Turns Farm Fare Into a Fancy City Treat," *Wall Street Journal*, 31 January 1996, pp. B1–B2.
11. Who Really Makes That Cute Little Beer?" *Wall Street Journal*, 15 April 1996, pp. A1, A8.
12. Stanley Slater and John Narver, "Improving Performance in the Market Oriented Business," in Barbara Stern, et al., ed., 1995 *American Marketing Association Educators' Conference Proceedings*, p. 367.
13. Jennifer Merritt, "The Belle of the Golf Balls," *Business Week*, 29 July 1996, p. 6.
14. "How Three CEOs Achieved Fast Turnarounds," *Wall Street Journal*, 21 July 1995, pp. B1, B2.
15. Karen Axelton and Stephanie Osowski, "Not Just Child's Play," *Entrepreneur Magazine On-Line*, August 1996.

Chapter 3

1. Joseph Pereira, "Toy Business Focuses More on Marketing and Less on New Ideas," *Wall Street Journal*, 29 February 1996, pp. A1, A4.
2. "Tracking Study Looks at Perceptions of Multimedia/Interactive Technologies," *Quirks Marketing Research Review*, January 1996, pp. 27, 29.
3. "A Caddy That's Not for Daddy," *Business Week*, 18 December 1995, pp. 87–88.
4. "Levi's vs. The Dress Code," *Business Week*, 1 April 1996, p. 57.
5. "Welcome to the Age of 'Unpositioning,'" *Marketing News*, 16 April 1990, p. 11.
6. "Federal Express's Lobbyists, Led by Chairmen, Are Proving to be Major Force in Washington," *Wall Street Journal*, 8 August 1995, p. A14.
7. Susan Caminiti, "The New Champs of Retailing," *Fortune*, 24 September 1990, p. 98.
8. Leonard L. Berry, A. Parasuraman, and Valarie A. Zeithaml, "Improving Service Quality in America: Lessons Learned," *Academy of Management Executive*, 8, no. 2, 1994, p. 36.
9. "Smart Selling: How Companies are Winning Over Today's Tougher Customer," *Business Week*, 3 August 1992, pp. 46–48.
10. "The Overloaded American," *Wall Street Journal*, 8 March 1996, pp. R1, R4.
11. "Sorry, Boys—Donna Reed Is Still Dead," *American Demographics*, September 1995, pp. 13–14.
12. Gerry Myers, "Selling To Women," *American Demographics*, April 1996, pp. 36–42.
13. Ibid.
14. Ibid.
15. Ibid.
16. James McNeal and Chyon-Hwa Yeh, "Born to Shop," *American Demographics*, June 1992, pp. 34–39. Copyright © 1992 *American Demographics*. Reprinted with permission.
17. Ibid.
18. "Photography Companies Try to Click with Children," *Wall Street Journal*, 31 January 1994, pp. B1, B8.
19. The material on teenagers is taken from Peter Zollo, "Talking to Teens," *American Demographics*, November 1995, pp. 23–28.
20. "Marketing to Generation X," *Advertising Age*, 6 February 1995, p. 27.

21. Susan Mitchell, "How to Talk to Young Adults," *American Demographics*, April 1993, pp. 50–54.
22. "Understanding Generation X," *Marketing Research*, Spring 1993, pp. 54–55.
23. "Xers Know They're a Target Market, and They Hate That," *Marketing News*, 6 December 1993, pp. 2, 15.
24. "Easy Pickup Line? Try Gen Xers," *Advertising Age*, 3 April 1995, pp. 5–22.
25. "The Baby Boom Turns 50," *American Demographics*, December 1995, pp. 22–27.
26. "Survey Sheds Light on Typical Boomer," *Marketing News*, 31 January 1994, p. 2.
27. Cheryl Russell, "The Master Trend," *American Demographics*, October 1993, pp. 28–37.
28. Nikhil Deogun, "O Say Can You See: Proliferation of Flags Is Blinding Richmond," *Wall Street Journal* 21 December 1995, pp. A1, A9.
29. Russell, pp. 28–37.
30. "The Baby Boom at Mid-Decade," *American Demographics*, April 1995, pp. 40–45.
31. Russell, pp. 28–37.
32. Ruth Hamel, "Raging against Aging," *American Demographics*, March 1990, pp. 42–45.
33. "American Maturity," *American Demographics*, March 1993, pp. 31–42.
34. "Boomers Come of Old Age," *Marketing News*, 15 January 1996, pp. 1, 6.
35. "Mature Market Often Misunderstood," *Marketing News*, 28 August 1995, p. 28.
36. Michael Major, "Promoting to the Mature Market," *Promo*, November 1990, p. 7.
37. "Bond Stronger with Age," *Advertising Age*, 28 March 1994, pp. 5–6.
38. "Baby-Boomers May Seek Age-Friendly Stores," *Wall Street Journal*, 1 July 1992, p. B1.
39. Charles Schewe and Geoffrey Meredith, "Digging Deep to Delight the Mature Adult Customer," *Marketing Management*, Winter 1995, pp. 21–34.
40. "Americans on the Move," *American Demographics*, June 1990, pp. 46–48.
41. "The Hottest Metros," *American Demographics*, April 1995, pp. 4–5.
42. Willian Frey, "The New White Flight," *American Demographics*, April 1994, pp. 40–47.
43. "Work Slowdown," *American Demographics*, March 1996, pp. 4–7.

44. Martha Farnsworth Riche, "We're All Minorities Now," *American Demographics*, October 1991, pp. 26–33.
45. William Dunn, "The Move toward Ethnic Marketing," *Nation's Business*, July 1992, pp. 39–44; "The Numbers Bear Out Our Diversity," *Wall Street Journal*, 24 April 1994, p. B1.
46. Dunn, p. 40; "How to Sell across Cultures," *American Demographics*, March 1994, pp. 56–58.
47. Jon Berry, "An Empire of Niches," *Superbrands: A Special Supplement to Adweek's Marketing Week*, Fall 1991, pp. 17–22.
48. Ibid.
49. "Is America Becoming More of a Class Society?" *Business Week*, 26 February 1996, pp. 86–92.
50. "Rethinking Work," *Business Week*, 17 October 1994, p. 80.
51. "Motorola's Prospects Are Linked to New Technologies," *Wall Street Journal*, 11 April 1996, p. B4.
52. "Could America Afford the Transistor Today?" *Business Week*, 7 March 1994, pp. 80–84.
53. "Frito-Lay Devours Snack-Food Business," *Wall Street Journal*, 27 October 1995, pp. B1, B4.

Chapter 4

1. "Did Whirlpool Spin Too Far Too Fast?" *Business Week*, 24 June 1996, pp. 136–138.
2. "Potato Chips—To Go Global—Or So Pepsi Bets," *Wall Street Journal*, 30 November 1995, pp. B1, B10.
3. Edmund Faltermayer, "Is 'Made in the U.S.A.' Fading Away?" *Fortune*, 24 September 1990, pp. 62–73.
4. "Riding High: Corporate America Now Has an Edge Over Its Global Rivals," *Business Week*, 9 October 1995, pp. 134–146.
5. Ibid.
6. Paul Krugman, "Competitiveness: Does It Matter," *Fortune*, 7 March 1994, pp. 109–116; and "New Lift for the U.S. Export Boom," *Fortune*, 13 November 1995, pp. 73–75.
7. U.S. Central Intelligence Agency, *The World Fact Book* (Washington, DC: Government Printing Office, 1993), p. 334; U.S. Department of Commerce, Bureau of the Census, *Statistical Abstract of the United States* (Washington, DC: Government Printing Office, 1993), p. 722.

8. *The World Almanac* (Mahwah, NJ: World Almanac Books), 1996, p. 426.

9. "Economists Predict Strength in Exports," *Wall Street Journal*, 29 December 1995, p. A2.

10. U.S. Central Intelligence Agency, p. 334; U.S. Department of Commerce, p. 722.

11. "U.S. Trade Deficit Fell $9.18 Billion in Quarter," *Wall Street Journal*, 13 March 1996, p. A2.

12. Neil Jacoby, "The Multinational Corporation," *Center Magazine*, May 1970, p. 37.

13. Robert Reich, "Who Is Them?" *Harvard Business Review*, March–April 1991, pp. 77–89.

14. "The Stateless Corporation," *Business Week*, 14 May 1990, pp. 98–105.

15. "A World of Greased Palms," *Business Week*, 6 November 1995, pp. 36–38.

16. Theodore Levitt, "The Globalization of Markets," *Harvard Business Review*, May–June 1983, pp. 92–102.

17. Saeed Samiee and Kendall Roth, "The Influence of Global Marketing Standardization on Performance," *Journal of Marketing*, April 1992, pp. 1–17; see also James Willis, Coskun Samli, and Laurence Jacobs, "Developing Global Products and Marketing Strategies: A Construct and a Research Agenda," *Journal of the Academy of Marketing Science*, Winter 1991, pp. 1–10.

18. "For Peruvians, Fizzy Yellow Drink Is the Real Thing," *International Herald Tribune*, 27 December 1995, p. 3.

19. "Global Products Require Name-Finders," *Wall Street Journal*, 11 April 1996, p. B5.

20. "Don't Be An Ugly-American Manager," *Fortune*, 16 October 1995, p. 225.

21. "Trainers Help Expatriate Employers Build Bridges to Different Cultures," *Wall Street Journal*, 14 June 1993, pp. B1, B6.

22. "Portrait of the World," *Marketing News*, 28 August 1995, pp. 20–21.

23. "In the New Vietnam, Baby Boomers Strive for Fun and Money," *Wall Street Journal*, 7 January 1994, pp. A1, A5.

24. Vladimir Kvint, "Don't Give Up on Russia," *Harvard Business Review*, March–April 1994, pp. 4–12.

25. Thomas Kamm, "Brazil Swiftly Becomes Major Auto Producer As Trade Policy Shifts," *Wall Street Journal*, 18 April 1994, pp. A1, A4.

26. "India Opening Up to Western Marketers, But Challenges Abound," *Marketing News*, 6 November 1995, pp. 1–2.

27. "Pop Radio In France Goes French," *International Herald Tribune*, 2 January 1996, p. 2.

28. Ibid.

29. "This Is One the White House Can't Duck," *Business Week*, 8 April 1996, p. 52.

30. Ibid.; also see Moshe Givon, Vijay Mahajan, and Eitan Muller, "Software Piracy: Estimation of Lost Sales and the Impact on Software Diffusion," *Journal of Marketing*, January 1995, pp. 29–37.

31. Marie Anchordoguy, "A Brief History of Japan's Keiretsu," *Harvard Business Review*, July–August 1990, pp. 58–59.

32. Robert Cutts, "Capitalism in Japan: Cartels and Keiretsu," *Harvard Business Review*, July–August 1992, pp. 48–50.

33. "U.S. Sees Progress in Talks with Japan, but Seeks More Action on Trade Gap," *Wall Street Journal*, 31 July 1992, p. B2.

34. "How NAFTA Will Help America," *Fortune*, 19 April 1993, pp. 95–102.

35. Karl Zinsmeister, "Swallowed Up at Work," *American Enterprise*, January 1996, pp. 16–19.

36. "How NAFTA Will Help," pp. 95–102.

37. "NAFTA Rivals Debate Impact on Jobs," *Dallas Morning News*, 26 February 1996, p. 1D.

38. "Latin Nations, Unsure of U.S. Motives, Make Their Own Trade Pacts," *Wall Street Journal*, 9 January 1996, pp. A1, A4.

39. "Road to Unification," *Sky*, June 1993, pp. 32–41.

40. Tony Horwitz, "Europe's Borders Fade, and People and Goods Can Move More Freely," *Wall Street Journal*, 18 May 1993, pp. A1, A10. Reprinted by permission of the *Wall Street Journal*, © 1993 Dow Jones & Company, Inc. All Rights Reserved Worldwide.

41. Rahul Jacob, "The Big Rise," *Fortune*, 30 May 1994, pp. 74–90.

42. Ibid.

43. "Plan Helps Exporters Fish Abroad From Docks at Home," *Wall Street Journal*, 5 March 1996, p. B2.

44. "Making Global Alliances Work," *Fortune*, 17 December 1990, pp. 121–123.

45. "For Whirlpool, Asia Is the New Frontier," *Wall Street Journal*, 25 April 1996, pp. B1, B4.

46. Joel Bleeke and David Ernst, "The Way to Win in Cross-Border Alliances," *Harvard Business Review*, November–December 1991, p. 130; also see P. Rajan Varadarajan and Margret Cunningham, "Strategic Alliances: A Synthesis of Conceptual Foundations," *Journal of the Academy of Marketing Science*, Fall 1995, pp. 282–296; George Day, "Advantageous Alliances," *Journal of the Academy of Marketing Science*, Fall 1995, pp. 297–300; and Johny Johansson, "International Alliances: Why Now?" *Journal of the Academy of Marketing Science*, Fall 1995, pp. 301–304.

47. "Major U.S. Companies Expand Efforts to Sell to Consumers Abroad," *Wall Street Journal*, 13 June 1996, pp. A1, A6.

48. "FedEx: Europe Nearly Killed the Messenger," *Business Week*, 25 May 1992, p. 124.

49. "The New U.S. Push into Europe," *Fortune*, 10 January 1994, pp. 73–74.

50. "TI Teams Up In Asia," *Dallas Morning News*, 4 February 1996, p. H1.

51. David Szymanski, Sundar Bharadwaj, and P. Rajan Varadarajan, "Standardization versus Adaptation of International Marketing Strategy: An Empirical Investigation," *Journal of Marketing*, October 1993, pp. 1–17.

52. "P&G Viewed China As a National Market And Is Conquering It," *Wall Street Journal*, 12 September 1995, pp. A1, A6.

53. "'Made in America' Isn't the Kiss of Death Anymore," *Business Week*, 13 November 1995, p. 62.

54. "Global Ad Campaigns, after Many Missteps, Finally Pay Dividends," *Wall Street Journal*, 27 August 1992, pp. A1, A8.

55. "Can TV Save the Planet," *American Demographics*, May 1996, pp. 43–47.

56. "Machine Dreams," *Brandweek*, 26 April 1993, pp. 17–24.

57. "Ewing Shoots to Shoe Planet," *Brandweek*, 7 March 1994, p. 10.

58. "Marketing Board Games Is No Trivial Pursuit," *Dallas Morning News*, 14 January 1996, pp. 1F, 4F.

59. "Ford's Global Gladiator," *Business Week*, 11 December 1995, pp. 116–118.

60. "Hmm. Could Use a Little More Snake," *Business Week*, 15 March 1993, p. 53.

61. "Europe's Unity Undoes a U.S. Exporter," *Wall Street Journal*, 1 April 1996, p. B1.

62. "Can Rubbermaid Crack Foreign Markets?" *Wall Street Journal*, 20 June 1996, p. B1.

63. "The Rumble Heard Round the World: Harleys," *Business Week*, 24 May 1993, pp. 58–59.

64. "Unknown Fruit Takes On Unfamiliar Markets," *Wall Street Journal*, 9 November 1995, pp. B1, B5.

65. "Greeks Protest Coke's Use of Parthenon," *Dallas Morning News*, 17 August 1992, p. 4D.

66. "Kiddi Just Fine in the U.K., But Here It's Binky," *Marketing News*, 28 August 1995, p. 8.

67. Cyndee Miller, "U.S. Firms Lag in Meeting Global Quality Standards," *Marketing News*, 15 February 1993, pp. 1, 6, reprinted with permission of American Marketing Association; Ronald Henkoff, "The Hot New Seal of Quality," *Fortune*, 28 June 1993, pp. 116–120; "Competition At Home Pushes More Companies to Seek an International Rating," *Wall Street Journal*, 1 September 1995, p. A1.

68. Ibid.

69. "PC Makers Find China Is a Chaotic Market Despite Its Potential," *Wall Street Journal*, 8 April 1996, pp. A1, A9.

70. "Why Countertrade Is Hot," *Fortune*, 29 June 1992, p. 25; Nathaniel Gilbert, "The Case for Countertrade," *Across the Board*, May 1992, pp. 43–45.

71. "Revolution in Japanese Retailing," *Fortune*, 7 February 1994, pp. 143–146.

72. "Flouting Rules Sells GE Fridges In Japan," *Wall Street Journal*, 31 October 1995, pp. B1, B2.

73. "To All U.S. Managers Upset By Regulations: Try Germany or Japan," *Wall Street Journal*, 14 December 1995, p. A1.

74. "PC Makers Find China. . . .," p. A9.

75. Ibid., p. A1.

Chapter 5

1. Adapted from Alix M. Freedman, "Tinier, Deadlier Pocket Pistols Are in Vogue," *Wall Street Journal*, 12 September 1996, pp. B1, B14; "Wal-Mart Bans Sheryl Crow Album Over Lyric," *U.S.A. Today*, 11 September 1996, p. D1; and Alix M. Freedman, "A Single Family Makes Many of the Cheap Pistols That Saturate Cities," *Wall Street Journal*, 28 September 1992, pp. A1, A6–A7; Andrea Gerlin, "Wal-Mart Stops Handgun Sales Inside Its Stores," *Wall Street Journal*, 23 December 1993, pp. B1, B8; Kevin Goldman, "NRA Calls Ads for Women Educational," *Wall Street Journal*, 28 September 1993, p. B6; Joseph Pereira and Barbara Carton, "Toys 'R' Us to Banish Some 'Realistic' Toy Guns," *Wall Street Journal*, 14 October 1994, pp. B1, B12.

2. Hank Walshak, "Let's Hear It For Ethics In Marketing," obtained from www.stellar.org, September 1996, pp. 1–2.

3. Elyse Tanouye and Michael Waldholz, "Merck's Marketing of AIDS Drug Draws Fire," *Wall Street Journal*, 7 May 1996, pp. B1, B6.

4. Andrea Gerlin, "How a Penney Buyer Made Up to $1.5 Million On Vendor Kickbacks," *Wall Street Journal*, 7 February 1995, pp. A1, A12.

5. Jerry E. Bishop, "TV Advertising Aimed at Kids Is Filled with Fat," *Wall Street Journal*, 9 November 1993, p. B1.

6. Helene Cooper, "CPC Advocates Use of Condoms in Blunt AIDS-Prevention Spots," *Wall Street Journal*, 5 January 1994, p. B1.

7. Wendy Bounds, "Active Seniors Do Laps of the Mall—Then Cool Down by Eating Fast Food," *Wall Street Journal*, 9 January 1993, p. B1.

8. Sharon Harris, "The Advertising of Nature's Substitutes: Societal Issues and Implications," *Proceedings of the American Marketing Association*, Summer 1996, pp. 404–405; Thomas M. Burton, "Methods of Marketing Infant Formula Land Abbott in Hot Water," *Wall Street Journal*, 25 May 1993, pp. A1, A5.

9. Mary L. Carnevalle, "Parents Say PBS Station Exploits Barney in Fund Drives," *Wall Street Journal*, 19 March 1993, pp. B1, B8.

10. Based on Edward Stevens, *Business Ethics* (New York: Paulist Press, 1979).

11. Anusorn Singhapakdi, Skott Vitell, and Kenneth Kraft, "Moral Intensity and Ethical Decisionmaking of Marketing Professionals," *Journal of Business Research*, 36 (1996), pp. 245–255; Ishmael Akaah and Edward Riordan, "Judgments of Marketing Professionals about Ethical Issues in Marketing Research: A Replication and Extension," *Journal of Marketing Research*, February 1989, pp. 112–120; see also Shelby Junt, Lawrence Chonko, and James Wilcox, "Ethical Problems of Marketing Researchers," *Journal of Marketing Research*, August 1984, pp. 309–324; and Kenneth Andrews, "Ethics in Practice," *Harvard Business Review*, September–October 1989, pp. 99–104.

12. O.C. Ferrell, Debbie Thorne, and Linda Ferrell, "Legal Pressure for Ethical Compliance in Marketing," *Proceedings of the American Marketing Association*, Summer 1995, pp. 412–3.

13. Paul Nowell, "Critics Fuming over Joe Camel's Female Friends," *Houston Chronicle*, 19 February 1994, p. 1D.

14. "Teens' Favorite Cigarettes Are Also Most Advertised," *Wall Street Journal*, 19 August 1994, p. B1; Joanne Lipman, "Surgeon General Says It's Time Joe Camel Quit," *Wall Street Journal*, 10 March 1992, pp. B1, B7; see also John P. Pierce et al., "Does Tobacco Advertising Target Young People to Start Smoking? Evidence from California," *Journal of the American Medical Association*, 11 December 1993, p. 3154; and Michael B. Mazis et al., "Perceived Age and Attractiveness of Models in Cigarette Advertisements," *Journal of Marketing*, January 1992, pp. 22–37.

15. Eben Shapiro, "FTC Confronts 'Healthier' Cigarette Ads," *Wall Street Journal*, 21 March 1994, p. B7; Larry Dietz, "Who Enjoys the Right of Free Speech? Jane Fonda, Joe Camel, You, and Me," *Adweek Western Advertising News*, 20 April 1992, p. 44.

16. Eben Shapiro, "California Plans More Antismoking Ads," *Wall Street Journal*, 26 January 1993, p. B7.

17. Suein L. Hwang and Alix M. Freedman, "Smokers May Mistake 'Clean' Cigarette for Safe," *Wall Street Journal*, 30 April 1996, pp. B1, B2.

18. Sharon Harris, pp. 404–405.

19. Laura Bird, "Critics Shoot at New Colt 45 Campaign," *Wall Street Journal*, 17 February 1993, p. B1.

20. Joanne Lipman, "Foes Claim Ad Bans Are Bad Business," *Wall Street Journal*, 27 February 1990, p. B1.

21. Deborah Schroeder, "Life, Liberty, and the Pursuit of Privacy," *American Demographics*, June 1992, p. 20.

22. Jonathan Berry, "A Potent New Tool for Selling," *Business Week*, 5 September 1994, pp. 56–62.

23. James A. Roberts, "Green Consumers in the 1990s: Profile and Implications for Advertising," *Journal of Business Research*, 36 (1996), pp. 217–231.

24. Schwartz and Miller, p. 28; Terry Lefton, "Disposing of the Green Myth," *Adweek's Marketing Week*, 13 April 1992, pp. 20–21.

25. Doug Vorhies, C.P. Rao, and John Ozment, "Marketing Capabilities and Marketing Effectiveness as Antecedents to Financial Performance," *Proceedings of the American Marketing Association,* Summer 1996, pp. 39–40.

26. Terry Lefton, "Beating the Green Rap," *Adweek's Marketing Week,* 27 January 1992, p. 6; Joe Schwartz, "Turtle Wax Shines Water, Too," *American Demographics,* April 1992, p. 14.

27. See "Green Marketing," located at www.aa.net/garage/scrape1/ green.html, October 1996; and "Research Group Says Some Green Marketers Are Only Pretending," *Marketing News,* 20 January 1992, p. 3.

28. See "The Green Business Conference," located at www.ecoexpo.com/Eco-Expo/noframe/show/gbc.html, October 1996; and "It Ain't Easy Being a Green Retailer," *Wall Street Journal,* 20 December 1993, p. B1.

29. Adapted from Robert W. Armstrong, "An Empirical Investigation of International Marketing Ethics: Problems Encountered by Australian Firms," *Journal of Business Ethics,* March 1992, pp. 161–171.

30. This section adapted from Archie B. Carroll, "The Pyramid of Corporate Social Responsibility: Toward the Moral Management of Organizational Stakeholders," *Business Horizons,* July–August 1991, pp. 39–48.

31. Stephanie N. Mehta, "Black Entrepreneurs Benefit From Social Responsibility," *Wall Street Journal,* 19 September 1995, p. B1.

32. Barbara Clark O'Hare, "Good Deeds Are Good Business," *American Demographics,* September 1991, pp. 38–42.

33. Suzanne Alexander, "Life's Just a Bowl of Cherry Garcia for Ben & Jerry's," *Wall Street Journal,* 15 July 1992, p. B3.

34. Cara Appelbaum, "Jantzen to Pitch In for Clean Waters," *Adweek's Marketing Week,* 6 April 1992, p. 6.

35. Elyse Tanouye, "Drug Firms Start 'Compliance' Programs Reminding Patients to Take Their Pills," *Wall Street Journal,* 25 March 1992, pp. B1, B5.

36. Andrew Pollack, "Un-Writing a New Page in the Annals of Recycling," *New York Times,* 21 August 1993, p. 17.

37. Rebecca Goodell, "National Business Ethics Survey Findings," *Ethics Journal,* Fall–Winter 1994, pp. 1–3.

38. O. C. Ferrell and John Fraedrich, *Business Ethics,* 3d ed. (Boston: Houghton Mifflin, 1997), p. 173.

Chapter 6

1. Kevin Goldman, "Coke Contours New Ads to Fit 'Cultural Icon' of Shapely Bottle," *Wall Street Journal,* 14 February 1995, p. B6; Stephen Kindel, "Anatomy of a Bottle: How Coca-Cola Has Cashed In on Its Curvaceous New Packaging's Cultural Currency," *I.D.,* September–October 1995, p. 68(6); Ellen Ruppel Shell, "Package Design: The Art of Selling, All Wrapped Up," *Smithsonian,* April 1996, p. 54(9); Maria Mallory and Kevin Whitelaw, "The Power Brands," *U.S. News & World Report,* 13 May 1996, pp. 58–59; Charles Siler, "The Shape of Patents to Come in the U.K.: Coke's Contour Bottle Protected by New Rules," *Advertising Age,* 18 September 1995, p. 54.

2. Angelo Henderson, "Coming in Tomorrow's Car Seat: Storage, Built-In Safety Belts and Surround Sound," *Wall Street Journal,* 22 January 1996, pp. B1, B8.

3. Valerie Reitman and Gabriella Stern, "Adapting a U.S. Car to Japanese Tastes," *Wall Street Journal,* 26 June 1995, pp. B1, B6.

4. D. S. Sundaram and Michael D. Richard, "Perceived Risk and the Information Acquisition Process of Computer Mail-Order Shoppers," in *1995 Southern Marketing Association Proceedings,* eds. Brian T. Engelland and Denise T. Smart (Houston: Southern Marketing Association, 1995), pp. 322–326.

5. Eric D. Bruce and Sam Fullerton, "Discount Pricing as a Mediator of the Consumer's Evoked Set," in *1995 Atlantic Marketing Association Proceedings,* eds. Donald L. Thompson and Cathy Owens Swift (Orlando: Atlantic Marketing Association), pp. 32–36.

6. F. Kelly Shruptrine, "Warranty Coverage: How Important in Purchasing an Automobile," in *1995 Southern Marketing Association Proceedings,* eds. Brian T. Engelland and Denise T. Smart (Houston: Southern Marketing Association, 1995), pp. 300–303.

7. Don Umphrey, "Consumer Costs: A Determinant of Upgrading or Downgrading of Cable Service," *Journalism Quarterly,* Winter 1991, pp. 698–708.

8. Robert L. Simison, "Infiniti Adopts New Sales Strategy to Polish Its Brand," 10 June 1996, pp. B1, B7.

9. Stephen L. Vargo, "Consumer Involvement: An Historical Perspective and Partial Synthesis," in *1995 AMA Educa-tors' Proceedings,* eds. Barbara B. Stern and George M. Zinkhan (Chicago: American Marketing Association, 1995), pp. 139–145.

10. See Gail Tom, "Cueing the Consumer: The Role of Salient Cues in Consumer Perception," *Journal of Consumer Marketing,* Spring 1987, pp. 23–27; and Joan Meyers-Levy and Laura A. Peracchio, "Understanding the Effects of Color: How the Correspondence between Available and Required Resources Affects Attitudes," *Journal of Consumer Research,* Volume 22, Number 2, September 1995, pp. 121–138.

11. Richard Gibson, "Anheuser-Busch Makes Price Moves in Bid to Boost Sales of Flagship Brand," *Wall Street Journal,* 28 February 1994, p. A7A.

12. William Boulding and Amna Kirmani, "A Consumer-Side Experimental Examination of Signaling Theory: Do Consumers Perceive Warranties as Signs of Quality?" *Journal of Consumer Research,* June 1993, pp. 111–123.

13. Teresa M. Pavia and Janeen Arnold Costa, "The Winning Number: Consumer Perceptions of Alpha-Numeric Brand Names," *Journal of Marketing,* July 1993, pp. 85–98.

14. Sean Mehegan, "A Picture of Quality: Kodak Leads EquiTrend Survey of Brand Quality for the Second Consecutive Year," *Brandweek,* 8 April 1996, p. 38.

15. Kathleen Deveny, "What's in a Name? A Lot If It's 'Texas,'" *Wall Street Journal,* 24 November 1993, pp. T1, T4.

16. Elizabeth J. Wilson, "Using the Dollarmetric Scale to Establish the Just Meaningful Difference in Price," in *1987 AMA Educators' Proceedings,* ed. Susan Douglas et al. (Chicago: American Marketing Association, 1987), p. 107.

17. Sunil Gupta and Lee G. Cooper, "The Discounting of Discounts and Promotion Thresholds," *Journal of Consumer Research,* December 1992, pp. 401–411.

18. Dana Milbank, "Made in America Becomes a Boast of Europe," *Wall Street Journal,* 19 January 1994, p. B1.

19. Matt Murray, "Americans Eat Up Vitamin E Supplies," *Wall Street Journal,* 13 June 1996, pp. B1, B8.

20. Maria Mallory and Kevin Whitelaw, "The Power Brands," *U.S. News & World Report,* 13 May 1996, p. 58.

21. Cynthia Crossen, "Fright by the Numbers: Alarming Disease Data Are Frequently Flawed," *Wall Street Journal,* 11 April 1996, pp. B1, B5.

22. Richard Gibson, "Can Betty Crocker Heat Up General Mills' Cereal Sales?" *Wall Street Journal*, 19 July 1996, pp. B1, B6.

23. Patricia Braus, "The Baby Boom at Mid-Decade," *American Demographics*, April 1995, pp. 40–45; "In the Wake of the Baby Boom," *Sales & Marketing Management*, May 1993, p. 48.

24. Karen Ritchie, "Marketing to Generation X," *American Demographics*, April 1995, pp. 34–38; Nicholas Zill and John Robinson, "The Generation X Difference," *American Demographics*, April 1995, pp. 24–33. Also see Susan Mitchell, "How to Talk to Young Adults," *American Demographics*, April 1993, pp. 50–54.

25. Steven Lipin, Brian Coleman, and Jeremy Mark, "Pick a Card: Visa, American Express, and MasterCard Vie in Overseas Strategies," *Wall Street Journal*, 15 February 1994, pp. A1, A5.

26. Kevin Goldman, "BMW Banks on Affordability and Safety," *Wall Street Journal*, 17 January 1994, p. B3; Kevin Goldman, "BMW Shifts Gears in New Ads by Mullen," *Wall Street Journal*, 21 May 1993, p. B10.

27. Tara Parker-Pope, "New Agency Says It's No Baloney: Spam's Good Enough to Eat Alone," *Wall Street Journal*, 26 December 1995, p. B3.

28. Norihiko Shirouzu, "Flouting 'Rules' Sells GE Fridges in Japan," *Wall Street Journal*, 31 October 1995, pp. B1, B2.

29. Yumiko Ono, "Broadening War against Smoking Proves a Blessing to Gum Makers," *Wall Street Journal*, 29 March 1994, p. B9.

30. Oscar Suris, "Will Extra Doors Lure More Drivers into Trucks, Vans?" *Wall Street Journal*, 21 November 1996, pp. B1, B10.

31. Miriam Jordan, "In Rural India, Video Vans Sell Toothpaste and Shampoo," *Wall Street Journal*, 10 January 1996, pp. B1, B3.

32. Maxine Wilkie, "Names That Smell," *American Demographics*, August 1995, pp. 48–49.

33. Nora J. Rifon and Molly Catherine Ziske, "Using Weight Loss Products: The Roles of Involvement, Self-Efficacy and Body Image," in *1995 AMA Educators' Proceedings*, eds. Barbara B. Stern and George M. Zinkhan (Chicago: American Marketing Association, 1995), pp. 90–98.

34. Yumiko Ono, "Home Hair-Color Sales Get Boost as Baby Boomers Battle Aging," *Wall Street Journal*, 3 February 1994, p. B6; Suein L. Hwang, "To Brush Away Middle-Age Malaise, Male Baby Boomers Color Graying Hair," *Wall Street Journal*, 2 March 1993, pp. B1, B10.

35. Elyse Tanouye, "Pitching Wrinkles as Medical Malady, J&J Launches Rx Cream for Aging Skin," *Wall Street Journal*, 13 February 1996, p. B1, B9.

36. Matt Murray, "GNC Makes Ginseng, Shark Pills Its Potion for Growth," *Wall Street Journal*, 15 March 1996, pp. B1, B3.

37. Allanna Sullivan, "Mobil Bets Drivers Pick Cappuccino Over Low Prices," *Wall Street Journal*, 30 January 1995, pp. B1, B4.

38. Cyndee Miller, "Not Quite Global," *Marketing News*, 3 July 1995, pp. 1, 7–9; G. Pascal Zachary, "Major U.S. Companies Expand Efforts to Sell to Consumers Abroad," *Wall Street Journal*, 13 June 1996, pp. A1, A6; "Coke's Lunar New Year Ad," *Wall Street Journal*, 15 February 1996, p. B5; Kevin Goldman, "U.S. Brands Trail Japanese in China Study," *Wall Street Journal*, 16 February 1995, p. B10; and Raju Narisetti, "Can Rubbermaid Crack Foreign Markets?" *Wall Street Journal*, 20 June 1996, pp. B1, B4.

39. John W. Schouten and James H. McAlexander, "Subcultures of Consumption: An Ethnography of the New Bikers," *Journal of Consumer Research*, June 1995, pp. 43–61.

40. Yumiko Ono, "Kraft Hopes Hispanic Market Says Cheese," *Wall Street Journal*, 13 December 1995, p. B7.

41. Patrick M. Reilly, "How Do You Say 'Bestseller' in Spanish?" *Wall Street Journal*, 4 January 1995, pp. B1, B6.

42. Susan Warren, "New Beer Pins Its Appeal on State Pride," *Wall Street Journal*, 5 April 1995, pp. T1, T3.

43. Chip Walker, "Word of Mouth," *American Demographics*, July 1995, pp. 38–44.

44. "Maximizing the Market with Influentials," *American Demographics*, July 1995, pp. 42–43.

45. Ibid.

46. Kevin Goldman, "Women Endorsers More Credible Than Men, a Survey Suggests," *Wall Street Journal*, 12 October 1995, B1.

47. "Chrysler, Johnson & Johnson Are New Product Marketers of the Year," *Marketing News*, 8 May 1995, pp. E2, E11.

48. Robert Boutilier, "Pulling the Family's Strings," *American Demographics*, August 1993, pp. 44–48.

49. Diane Crispell, "The Very Rich Are Sort of Different," *American Demographics*, March 1994, pp. 11–13.

50. Diane Crispell, "Middle Americans," *American Demographics*, October 1994, pp. 28–35.

51. Kenneth Labich, "Class in America," *Fortune*, 7 February 1994, pp. 114–126.

52. Steve Liesman, "Rising Prosperity: More Russians Work Harder, Boost Income, Enter the Middle Class," *Wall Street Journal*, 7 June 1995, pp. A1, A6.

53. Adapted from Steve Rabin, "How to Sell Across Cultures," *American Demographics*, March 1994, pp. 56–57.

Chapter 7

1. Adapted from Robert W. Haas, *Business Marketing*, 6th ed. (Cincinnati, OH: South-Western College Publishing, 1995), p. 232.

2. Alan M. Patterson, "Customers Can Be Partners," *Marketing News*, 9 September 1996, p. 10.

3. Frank G. Bingham, Jr. and Barney T. Raffield III, *Business Marketing Management* (Cincinnati, OH: South-Western College Publishing, 1995) pp. 47–48.

4. Bingham and Raffield, p. 48.

5. Haas, pp. 213–220.

6. Michael D. Hutt and Thomas W. Speh, *Business Marketing*, 4th ed. (Fort Worth, TX: Dryden Press, 1992), p. 265.

7. James B. Treece, Karen Lowry Miller, and Richard A. Melcher, "The Partners," *Business Week*, 10 February 1992, pp. 103–104.

8. Adapted from Robert L. Rose, "For Whirlpool, Asia Is the New Frontier," *Wall Street Journal*, 25 April 1996, pp. B1, B4.

9. Hutt and Speh, p. 3.

10. Bingham and Raffield, pp. 18–19.

11. Gary McWilliams, "Small Fry Go Online," *Business Week*, 20 November 1995, pp. 158–164.

12. For a comprehensive review of the SIC system and its uses, see Haas, pp. 231–263.

13. Haas, p. 248.

14. Kelly Shermach, "Steel Industry Hopes to Raise Awareness for Food Products," *Marketing News*, 22 May 1995, pp. 1, 13.

15. Jonah Gitlitz, "Direct Marketing in the B-to-B Future," *Business Marketing*, July/August 1996, pp. A2, A5.

16. Haas, p. 190.

17. "Johnson & Johnson, Voluntary Hospitals Reach Supplies Pact," *Wall*

Street Journal, 10 November 1992, p. B5.

18. Bingham and Raffield, p. 608.

19. Tom Hayes, "Using Customer Satisfaction Research to Get Closer to the Customers," *Marketing News*, 4 January 1993, p. 22.

20. Harris Gordon, "B-to-B Marketing in the Interactive Age," *Business Marketing*, July/August 1996, p. A2.

21. Amy Cortese, "Here Comes the Intranet," *Business Week*, 26 February 1996, p. 76.

Chapter 8

1. Richard Gibson, "McDonald's Plays Catch-Up with BLT Burger," *Wall Street Journal*, 2 May 1996, p. B1.

2. "Coke Targets Young Men with OK Soda," *Marketing News*, 23 May 1994, p. 8.

3. Faye Rice, "Making Generational Marketing Come of Age," *Fortune*, 26 June 1995, pp. 110–114.

4. "IBM, 15 Banks Introduce Online Service Company," *Arlington Star Telegram*, 10 September 1996, p. C4.

5. J. L. Hazelton, "Hey, Little Spenders," *Fort Worth Star Telegram*, 24 April 1996, p. B1.

6. Faye Rice, "Making Generational Marketing Come of Age," *Fortune*, 26 June 1995, pp. 110–114.

7. "How Spending Changes During Middle Age," *Wall Street Journal*, 14 January 1992, p. B1.

8. Jane Perley, "Poland Starting to See the Emergence of 'Puppies'," *Fort Worth Star Telegram*, 16 May 1996, p. C4.

9. Pam Weisz, "The New Boom Is Colored Gray," *Brandweek*, 22 January 1996, pp. 28–29.

10. Marc Spiegler, "Betting on Web Sports," *American Demographics*, May 1996, p. 24.

11. "New Ford Mustang Designed to Attract More Female Buyers," *Marketing News*, 3 January 1994, p. 27; Fara Warner, "New Cadillac Reconnaissance: Women and African Americans," *Brandweek*, 28 February 1994, pp. 1, 6; Fara Warner, "Midas Increases Bid to Attract Women," *Brandweek*, 14 March 1994, p. 5; Pam Weisz, "There's a Whole New Target Market Out There: It's Men," *Brandweek*, 21 February 1994, p. 21; Adrienne Ward Fawcett, "Ads Awaken to Fathers' New Role in Family Life," *Advertising Age*, 10 January 1994, pp. 5–8.

12. Faye Rice, "Making Generational Marketing Come of Age," *Fortune*, 26 June 1995, pp. 110–114.

13. Valerie Reitman, "Will Americans Go for Tiny Sport-Utility Cars?" *Wall Street Journal*, 31 January 1996, pp. B1, 2.

14. Louise Lee, "Discounter Wal-Mart Is Catering to Affluent to Maintain Growth," *Wall Street Journal*, 7 February 1996, pp. 1, 6.

15. "Blacks' Family Incomes Grew During 1980s, Census Says," *Fort Worth Star-Telegram*, 25 July 1992, p. A3.

16. Eugene Morris, "The Difference in Black and White," *American Demographics*, January 1993, pp. 44–46.

17. "Marketers Pay Attention! Ethnics Comprise 25 Percent of the U.S. Market," *Brandweek*, 18 July 1994, p. 26.

18. "Coors Courts Blacks with Research, Events," *Advertising Age*, 17 April 1996, p. 46.

19. "Spiegel, Ebony Aim to Dress Black Women," *Wall Street Journal*, 18 September 1991, pp. B1, B7.

20. "The Largest Minority," *American Demographics*, February 1993, p. 59; "Profile: Hispanics," *Advertising Age*, 3 April 1995, p. S–18.

21. Stuart Livingston, "Marketing to the Hispanic Community," *Journal of Business Strategy*, March–April 1992, pp. 54–57.

22. "Specific Hispanics," *American Demographics*, February 1994, pp. 44–53.

23. "To Reach Minorities, Try Busting Myths," *American Demographics*, April 1992, pp. 14–15; "Poll: Hispanics Stick to Brands," *Advertising Age*, 15 February 1993, p. 6.

24. "Advertising in Hispanic Media Rises Sharply," *Marketing News*, 18 January 1993, p. 9.

25. Elizabeth Roberts, "Different Strokes," *Adweek's Marketing Week*, 9 July 1990, p. 41; also see "What Does Hispanic Mean?" *American Demographics*, June 1993, pp. 46–56.

26. Sydney Roslow and J. A. F. Nicholls, "Hispanic Mall Customers Outshop Non-Hispanics," *Marketing News*, 6 May 1996, p. 14.

27. "Asian Americans," *CQ Researcher*, 13 December 1991, pp. 947–964.

28. Adapted from William O'Hare, "A New Look at Asian Americans," *American Demographics*, October 1990, pp. 26–31. Reprinted with permission © *American Demographics*, October 1990. For subscription information, please call (800) 828-1131.

29. "Asian Ads Shuffled Behind Curtain," *Advertising Age*, 3 April 1995, p. S-26.

30. Jerry Goodbody, "Taking the Pulse of Asian Americans," *Adweek's Marketing Week*, 12 August 1991, p. 32. Used by permission of A/S/M Communications, Inc.

31. Alex Taylor III, "Porsche Slices Up Its Buyers," *Fortune*, 16 January 1995, p. 24.

32. Gregory A. Patterson, "Target 'Micromarkets' Its Way to Success; No 2 Stores are Alike," *Wall Street Journal*, 31 May 1995, pp. 1, 9.

33. Kate Fitzgerald, "Happy Birthday (Name Here)," *Advertising Age*, 21 February 1994, p. 17.

34. "x $ = ?" *Brandweek*, 31 January 1994, pp. 18–24.

35. Stan Rapp and Thomas Collins, *The New Maxi Marketing*, exerpted in *Success*, April 1996, pp. 39–45.

36. "IBM Realizes Marketing," *Marketing News*, 6 June 1994, p. 1.

37. Much of the material in this section is based on Michael D. Hutt and Thomas W. Speh, *Business Marketing Management*, 4th ed. (Hinsdale, IL: Dryden Press, 1992), pp. 170–180.

38. Kelly Shermach, "Niche Malls: Innovation for an Industry in Decline," *Marketing News*, 26 February 1996, pp. 1–2.

39. Tim Triplett, "Game Stores Find a Niche among the Competitive," *Marketing News*, 23 May 1994, p. 14.

40. Susan Chandler, "Kids' Wear Is Not Childs' Play," *Business Week*, 19 June 1995, p. 118.

41. Leon Jaroff, "Fire in the Belly, Money in the Bank," *Time*, 6 November 1995, pp. 56–58.

42. Chad Rubel, "Less Privacy Seen as Trade-Off for Better Target Marketing," *Marketing News*, 3 July 1995, p. 2.

43. Tim Triplett, "Consumers Show Little Taste for Clear Beverages," *Marketing News*, 23 May 1994, pp. 1, 11.

44. Tim Triplett, "Marketers Eager to Fill Demand for Gambling," *Marketing News*, 6 June 1994, pp. 1, 2.

45. These examples were provided by David W. Cravens, Texas Christian University.

46. Steve Gelsi, "Staying True to the Sole," *Brandweek*, 8 April 1996, pp. 24, 26.

47. Elaine Underwood, "Sea Change," *Brandweek*, 22 April 1996, pp. 33–36.

48. Kathryn Hopper, "Polished and Profitable," *Fort Worth Star Telegram*, 22 March 1996, pp. B1, 3.

49. Cyndee Miller, "Firm Touts Milk Product as Hip Alternative to Soda," *Marketing News*, 23 May 1994, p. 6.

Chapter 9

1. Adapted from Chad Rubel, "Boston Market Also Likes to Serve Up Fast Research," *Marketing News*, 26 February 1996, p. 12.
2. "A Potent New Tool for Selling—Database Marketing," *Business Week*, 5 September 1994, pp. 56–62.
3. Jagdish Sheth and Rajendra Sisodia, "Feeling the Heat–Part 2," *Marketing Management*, Winter 1995, pp. 19–33.
4. Ibid.
5. Ibid.
6. "Coupon Clippers, Save Your Scissors," *Business Week*, 20 June 1994, pp. 164–166.
7. Jim Costelli, "How to Handle Personal Information," *American Demographics*, March 1996, pp. 50–58.
8. "Keebler Learns to Pay Attention to Research Right from the Start," *Marketing News*, 11 March 1996, p. 10.
9. "Pizza Hut Explores Customer Satisfaction," *Marketing News*, 25 March 1996, p. 16.
10. Andrew Bean and Michael Roszkowski, "The Long and Short of It," *Marketing Research*, Winter 1995, pp. 21–26.
11. Scott Dacko, "Data Collection Should Not be Manual Labor," *Marketing News*, 28 August 1995, p. 31.
12. John Vidmar, "Just Another Metamorphosis," *Marketing Research*, Spring 1996, pp. 16–18; Sharon Munger, "Premium Medium," *Marketing Research*, Spring 1996, pp. 10–12; and William Nicholls, "Highest Response," *Marketing Research*, Spring 1996, pp. 5–8.
13. Diane Pyle, "How to Interview Your Customers," *American Demographics*, December 1990, pp. 44–45.
14. "New Product Survey Uses Voice Mail," *Dallas Morning News*, 14 October 1995, p. 2F.
15. Trish Shukers, "Integrated Interviewing," *Marketing Research*, Spring 1996, pp. 20–21.
16. "E-Mail Surveys–Potentials and Pitfalls," *Marketing Research*, Summer 1995, pp. 29–33.
17. Ibid.; see also "Net? Not Yet," *Marketing Research*, Spring 1996, pp. 26–29.
18. "Stay Plugged In to New Opportunities," *Marketing Research*, Spring 1996, pp. 13–16.
19. "More, Better, Faster," *Quirk's Marketing Research Review*, March 1996, pp. 10–11, 50.
20. Tibbett Speer, "Nickelodeon Puts Kids Online," *American Demographics: 1994 Directory of Marketing Information Companies*, pp. 16–17.
21. Chris Van Derveer, "Demystifying International Industrial Marketing Research," *Quirk's Marketing Research Review*, April 1996, pp. 28, 35.
22. "Refining Service," *Quirk's Marketing Research Review*, January 1996, pp. 10–11, 35.
23. Michael McCarthy, "James Bond Hits the Supermarket: Stores Snoop on Shoppers' Habits to Boost Sales," *Wall Street Journal*, 25 August 1993, pp. B1, B8.
24. "Do Not Adjust Your Set," *American Demographics*, March 1993, p. 6; "Nielsen Rival to Unveil New Peoplemeter," *Wall Street Journal*, 4 December 1992, p. B8.
25. "Nielsen Schmielsen," *Business Week*, 12 February 1996, pp. 38–39.

Chapter 10

1. Pam Weisz, "Avon Broadens Mix with Housewares," *Brandweek*, 2 October 1995, p. 4.
2. Ibid.
3. Chris Roush, "At Times, They're Positively Glowing," *Business Week*, 12 July 1993, p. 141.
4. Terry Lefton, "Still Battling the Ozone Stigma," *Adweek's Marketing Week*, 16 March 1992, pp. 18–19.
5. Matthew Grimm, "Kentucky Fried (Not) Chicken Set to Turn Rotisseries on Full Blast," *Brandweek*, 12 July 1993, pp. 1, 6.
6. Noreen O'Leary, "The Old Bunny Trick," *Brandweek*, 18 March 1996, pp. 26–30.
7. Ibid., p. 29.
8. Brandon Mitchener, "Mercedes Adds Down-Market Niche Cars," *Wall Street Journal*, 21 February 1996, p. A10.
9. "Miller Launches New Flagship Beer Brand," *Marketing News*, 8 March 1996, p. 9.
10. "Make it Simple," *Business Week*, 9 September 1996, p. 96.
11. Ibid.
12. Jim Carlton, "Apple CEO Outlines Survival Strategy," *Wall Street Journal*, 14 May 1996, pp. A2, A4.
13. "Teens Name Coolest Brands," *Marketing News*, 12 February 1996, p. 6.
14. Keith J. Kelly, "Coca-Cola Shows That Top-Brand Fizz," *Advertising Age*, 11 July 1994, p. 3.
15. Cited in Alexandra Ourusoff, "Who Said Brands Are Dead?" *Brandweek*, 9 August 1993, pp. 20–33.
16. Peter H. Farquhar, et al., "Strategies for Leveraging Master Brands," *Marketing Research*, September 1992, pp. 32–43.
17. Rahul Jacob, "Asia, Where the Big Brands Are Blooming, *Fortune*, 23 August 1993, p. 55.
18. Holly Heline, "Brand Loyalty Isn't Dead—But You're Not off the Hook," *Brandweek*, 7 June 1993, pp. 14–15.
19. Diane Crispell and Kathleen Brandenburg, "What's in a Brand?" *American Demographics*, May 1993, pp. 26–32.
20. Based on Jeannine Aversa, "Group Wants Young Web Users Protected," *Fort Worth Star-Telegram*, 29 March 1996, pp. B1, B3.
21. Sandra Baker, "Savvy Shoppers," *Fort Worth Star Telegram*, 31 March 1996, p. D1.
22. Chad Rubel, "Price, Quality Important for Private Label Goods," *Marketing News*, 2 January 1995, p. 24.
23. "Kmart Accelerates Private Label Push," *Brandweek*, 29 January 1996, p. 6.
24. Bruce Orwall, "Multiplying Hotel Brands Puzzle Travelers," *Wall Street Journal*, 17 April 1996, p. B1.
25. Kelly Shermach, "Cobranded Credit Cards Inspire Consumer Loyalty," *Marketing News*, 9 September 1996, p. 12.
26. Karen Benezra, "New Tabasco Product a Chip Shot For Frito," *Brandweek*, 22 April 1996, p. 8.
27. "Food Fax," *Fort Worth Star-Telegram*, 22 May 1996, Section E, p. 4.
28. "Cobranding Just Starting in Europe," *Marketing News*, 13 February 1995, p. 5.
29. "Register The Rumble," Harley-Davidson Motor Company, 20 November 1995.
30. Steven C. Bahls and Jane Easter Bahls, "Fighting Fakes," *Entrepreneur*, February 1996, pp. 73–76.
31. Carrie Dolan, "Levi Tries to Round Up Counterfeiters," *Wall Street Journal*, 19 February 1992, pp. B1, B8; Damon Dorlin, "Coca-Cola's Sprite Enters South Korea; Local Sprint Follows," *Wall Street Journal*, 21 February 1992, p. B5.
32. Maxine Lans Retsky, "Who Needs the New Community Trademark," *Marketing News*, 3 June 1996, p. 11.
33. "Motorola Bets Big On China," *Fortune*, 27 May 1996, p. 116.
34. Marcus Brauchli, "Chinese Flagrantly Copy Trademarks of Foreign-

ers," *Wall Street Journal*, 20 June 1994, pp. B1, B5.

35. Robert Greenberger, "U.S. Sharply Attacks China Over Intellectual Property," *Wall Street Journal*, 1 May 1996, pp. A3, A14.

36. Ibid.

37. Raju Narisetti, "Plotting to Get Tissues Into Living Rooms," *Wall Street Journal*, 3 May 1996, pp. B1, B12.

38. Judith J. Riddle, "J&J Ready to Flip Lid on Tylenol," *Brandweek*, 3 May 1993, p. 3.

39. Ibid.

40. "Just Enough Packaging," *Wall Street Journal*, 7 September 1995, p. A1.

41. "A Biodegradable Plastic Gains Notice," *Wall Street Journal*, 4 February 1993, p. A1; Robert McMath, "It's All in the Trigger," *Adweek's Marketing Week*, 6 January 1992, pp. 25–28.

42. Pam Weisz, "Price Tools for Pfixer-Uppers," *Brandweek*, 18 April 1994, p. 8.

43. Beverly Bundy, "What's in It for You?" *Fort Worth Star-Telegram*, 4 May 1994, p. D1.

44. Jacqueline Simmins, "Using Labeling Rules to Pitch a Product," *Wall Street Journal*, 25 March 1994, p. B1.

45. Steve Rivkin, "The Name Game Heats Up," *Marketing News*, 22 April 1996, p. 8.

46. Hugh Filman, "A Brand New World: Packaged Goods Companies Go Global with Their Wares," *Marketing Executive Report*, June 1992, pp. 22–23.

47. "Make it Simple," p. 102.

Chapter 11

1. Karen Benezra, "Frito Max-es Out With Olestra Line," *Brandweek*, 29 April 1996, p. 4.

2. Marian Burros, "No One Can Eat One Bag," *Star-Fort Worth Telegram*, 23 May 1996, p. E8.

3. Ibid.

4. *New Product Management in the 1980s* (New York: Booz, Allen and Hamilton, 1982), p. 8.

5. Sam Bradley, "Hallmark Enters $20B Pet Category," *Brandweek*, 1 January 1996, p. 4.

6. Greg Erickson, "New Package Makes a New Product Complete," *Marketing News*, 8 May 1995, p. 10.

7. Yumiko Ono, "Nonsmearing Lipstick Makes a Vivid Imprint on Revlon," *Wall Street Journal*, 16 November 1995, pp. B1, B3.

8. Betsy Spethmann, "Tang Blastoff," *Brandweek*, 11 March 1996, pp. 1, 6.

9. Don Clark, "H-P Unveils Lower-Priced Color Copier," *Wall Street Journal*, 2 October 1995, p. B3.

10. *New Product Management*, p. 3.

11. Ibid., pp. 10–11.

12. Suein L. Hwang, "Critics Say 'Smokeless' Cigarettes Are Aimed at Women," *Wall Street Journal*, 31 May 1996, pp. B1, B5.

13. Brian Dumaine, "Payoff from the New Management," *Fortune*, 13 December 1993, pp. 103–110.

14. "Search and Employ," *Forbes*, 3 June 1996, p. 88.

15. George Gruenwald, "Some New Products Spring From Unsystematic Process," *Marketing News*, 8 May 1995, p. 4.

16. David W. Cravens, *Strategic Management*, 5th ed. (Homewood, IL: Richard D. Irwin, Inc., 1997), p. 255.

17. Kathleen Kerwin, "The Shape of the New Machine," *Business Week*, 24 July 1995, pp. 60–66.

18. Tom Lynch, "Internet: A Strategic Product Introduction Tool," *Marketing News*, 22 April 1996, p. 15.

19. "Procter & Gamble Co. To Test a New Spray For Removing Odors," *Wall Street Journal*, 8 May 1996, p. A5.

20. Christopher Power, "Will It Sell in Podunk? Hard to Say," *Business Week*, 10 August 1992, pp. 46–47.

21. Ibid., p. 46.

22. Ibid.

23. John Bissell, "What's in a Brand Name? Nothing Inherent to Start," *Brandweek*, 7 February 1994, p. 16.

24. Lynch, p. 15.

25. Bissell, p. 16.

26. Joel Baumwoll, "Why Didn't You Think of That?" *Marketing News*, 22 April 1996, p. 6.

27. David W. Cravens, *Strategic Marketing*, 5th ed. (Chicago: Irwin, 1997), pp. 244–245.

28. "Chrysler Considering Building a Small Car For Markets in Asia," *Wall Street Journal*, 16 October 1995, p. A2.

29. Timothy D. Schellhardt, "David in Goliath," *Wall Street Journal*, 23 May 1996, p. R14.

30. "Blue-Sky Research Comes Down to Earth," *Business Week*, 3 July 1995, pp. 78–80.

31. Benezra, p. 4.

Chapter 12

1. Keith H. Hammonds, "Oxford's Education," *Business Week*, 8 April 1996, pp. 108, 110.

2. Shannon Dortch, "Metros At Your Service," *American Demographics*, May 1996, pp. 4–5.

3. Ronald Henkoff, "Service Is Everybody's Business," *Fortune*, 27 June 1994, pp. 48–49. © 1994 Time, Inc. All rights reserved.

4. Ibid.

5. "The Manufacturing Myth," *Economist*, 19 March 1994.

6. "That's Entertainment," *Services Marketing Today* [Services Marketing Division newsletter, American Marketing Association], May–June 1994, p. 4.

7. Lynn Beresford, "Visual Aid," *Entrepreneur*, March 1996, p. 38.

8. "UPS Studies Adding Passenger Flights," *Fort Worth Star-Telegram*, 9 May 1996, p. B1.

9. "Saturn, Luxury Car Brands Score Big," *Fort Worth Star-Telegram*, 17 June 1994, p. B4; Stephanie Anderson Forest, "Radio Shack Goes Back to the Gizmos," *Business Week*, 28 February 1994, p. 102.

10. "Inside Job," *Entrepreneur*, June 1996, p. 32.

11. Much of the material in this section is based on Christopher H. Lovelock, *Services Marketing* (Englewood Cliffs, NJ: Prentice-Hall, 1996), pp. 39–40.

12. "Baby Pictures Just a Phone Call Today," *Services Marketing Today* [Services Marketing Division newsletter, American Marketing Association], March–April 1994, p. 4.

13. Steve McLinden, "Microtel Selects Site in Arlington," *Fort Worth Star-Telegram*, 24 May 1996, p. B1.

14. Joseph B. Pine II, *Mass Customization: The New Frontier in Business Competition* (Boston, MA: Harvard Business School Press, 1993).

15. Hammonds, pp. 108, 110.

16. "American Express Plans New Financial Services," *Fort Worth Star-Telegram*, 16 May 1996, p. C2.

17. Dan Reed, "Airlines Go On Line to Cut Costs," *Fort Worth Star-Telegram*, 13 April 1996, p. B1.

18. Mark S. Leach, "A Blockbuster Opens in Wal-Mart," *Fort Worth Star-Telegram*, 23 May 1996, p. C2.

19. Henkoff, pp. 52, 56.

20. Laurie Freeman, "Samaritan Applies Business-to-Business Approach to Revise

Image, Lure Patients," *Business Marketing*, December 1995, p. 25.

21. Patricia Seelers, "Yes, Brands Can Still Work Magic," *Fortune*, 7 February 1994, pp. 133–134.

22. Much of the material in this section based on Lovelock, pp. 238–240.

23. Leslie Gornstein, "MCI Introduces Bundled Services on Single Billing," *Fort Worth Star-Telegram*, 30 April 1996, pp. B1–2.

24. Much of the material in this section is based on Leonard L. Berry and A. Parasuraman, *Marketing Services* (New York: Free Press, 1991), pp. 132–150.

25. Joshua Levine, "Relationship Marketing," *Forbes*, 20 December 1993, pp. 232–234.

26. "Car Rental: Hertz—#1," *Services Marketing* [Services Marketing Division newsletter, American Marketing Association], July–August 1993, p. 4.

27. Berry and Parasuraman, pp. 151–152.

28. "Business Giants to Plow $100 Million Into Child and Elder Care," *Fort Worth Star-Telegram*, 14 September 1995, p. B1.

29. Aaron Bernstein, "United We Own," *Business Week*, 18 March 1996, pp. 96–102.

30. Sam Bradley, "One World, One UPS," *Brandweek*, 5 February 1996, p. 20.

31. Edward Felsenthal, "How a Tiny Charity Transformed Itself into a Used-Car Giant," *Wall Street Journal*, 23 April 1996, p. 1.

32. Andrea Petersen, "Charities Bet Young Will Come for the Music, Stay for the Pitch," *Wall Street Journal*, 7 September 1995, p. B1.

33. Nevin J. "Dusty" Rodes, "Marketing a Community Symphony Orchestra," *Marketing News*, 29 January 1996, p. 2.

34. Silvia Sansoni, "Gucci, Armani and . . . John Paul II?" *Business Week*, 15 April 1996, p. 108.

35. Louise Nameth, "A Safety Net for Net Surfers," *Business Week*, 15 April 1996, p. 108.

Chapter 13

1. Robert Posten, "Consumers Will Be Picky About Packaged Goods," *Marketing News*, 2 December 1996, pp. 7, 18.

2. Kenneth Labich, "Is Herb Kelleher America's Best CEO?" *Fortune*, 2 May 1994, pp. 45–52.

3. David Greisling, "Quality: How to Make It Pay," *Business Week*, 8 August 1994, pp. 54–59.

4. Much of the material in this chapter regarding the customer value triad is based on Earl Naumann, *Creating Customer Value* (Cincinnati, OH: Thomson Executive Press, 1995).

5. Michael Treacy and Fred Wiersema, "How Market Leaders Keep Their Edge," *Fortune*, 6 February 1995, pp. 88–98.

6. Mari Yamaguchi, "Japanese Consumers Shown Local Catalogs to Buy American," *Marketing News*, 2 December 1996, p. 12.

7. Otis Port and John Carey, "Questing for the Best," *Business Week*, 25 October 1991, p. 10.

8. Keith H. Hammonds and Gail De-George, "Where Did They Go Wrong?" *Business Week*, 25 October 1991, p. 35.

9. Mark Henricks, "Step By Step," *Entrepreneur*, March 1996, pp. 70, 72, 74.

10. Port and Carey, p. 14.

11. Michael E. Milakovich, *Improving Service Quality* (Delray Beach, FL: St. Cecil Press), pp. 31–33.

12. Peter Wendel, "Supplier Quality in the Automobile Industry," *The Quality Observer*, March 1996, pp. 9–10.

13. Michael Barrier, "Small Firms Put Quality First," *Nation's Business*, May 1992, p. 30.

14. "The Quality Accomplishments of Five Automotive Aftermarket Companies," *The Quality Observer*, March 1996, pp. 17–19, 20.

15. Jordan D. Lewis, "Western Companies Improve Upon the Japanese 'Keiretsu'," *Wall Street Journal*, 12 December 1995, p. A21.

16. Mike Vasilakes, "Wilson Oxygen Teams Up with Employees and Suppliers to Improve Quality," *Welding Distributor*, March–April 1993, pp. 65–70.

17. Dan Reed, "Class Consciousness," *Fort Worth Star Telegram*, 7 February 1996, pp. B1–2.

18. Helen Manley, "Great Expectations," *Australian Hotelier*, July 1995, pp. 45–47.

19. Paul Magnusson and Keith H. Hammonds, "Health Care: The Quest for Quality," *Business Week*, 8 April 1996, pp. 104–106.

20. Naumann, pp. 81–84.

21. Mary Kuatz, Lori Bongiorno, Keith Naughton, Gail DeGeorge, and Stephanie Anderson, "Reinventing the Store," *Business Week*, 27 November 1995, pp. 84–96; and Keith Naughton, Kathleen Kerwin, Bill Vlasic, Lori Bongiorno, and David Leonharat, "Revolution in the Showroom," *Business Week*, 19 February 1996, pp. 70–76.

22. Valarie A. Zeithaml and Mary Jo Bitner, *Services Marketing* (New York: The McGraw-Hill Companies, Inc., 1996).

23. Larry Light, ed., "Up Front," *Business Week*, 12 August 1996, p. 4.

24. Heather Page, "Equal Access," *Entrepreneur*, July 1996, p. 28.

25. Zeithaml and Bitner.

26. Chad Rubel, "Managers Buy into Quality When They See It Works," *Marketing News*, 25 March 1996, p. 14.

27. John E. Martin, "Unleashing the Power in Your People," *Arthur Andersen Retailing Issues Letter* [Texas A&M University, Center for Retailing Studies], September 1994, p. 1.

28. Much of the material in this section is based on Naumann, pp. 101–121.

29. Bill Saporito, "Behind the Tumult at P&G," *Fortune*, 7 March 1994, p. 75.

30. Brian S. Moskal, "Consumer Age Begets Value Pricing," *Industry Week*, 21 February 1994, p. 36.

31. Elaine Underwood, "Hilton, Hyatt, Clarion Eye 'Smart' Check Tech," *Brandweek*, 27 November 1995, p. 21.

32. Jim Fuquay, "Fast-Track Treatment," *Fort Worth Star Telegram*, 9 May 1996, pp. B1, B5.

33. "California State Parks Listen to Customers," *Quality Digest*, May 1996, p. 9.

34. Much of the material in this section is from Earl Naumann and Kathleen Giel, *Customer Satisfaction Measurement and Management* (Cincinnati, OH: Thomson Executive Press, 1995).

35. Greisling, p. 56.

36. Steve Sakson, "Anti-cancer Group Selling Right to Name," *Fort Worth Star Telegram*, 17 August 1996, p. C1.

37. Much of the material in this section is based on Frederick F. Reichheld, *The Loyalty Effect* (Boston, MA: Harvard Business School Press, 1996).

38. Jonathan B. Levine, "Customer, Sell Thyself," *Fast Company*, June–July 1996, p. 148.

39. Treacy and Wiersema, pp. 94–95.

40. Scott McCartney, "Taking Wing," *Fort Worth Star Telegram*, 16 May 1995, p. C1.

41. Chad Rubel, "Treating Coworkers Right is the Key to Kinko's Success," *Marketing News*, 29 January 1996, p. 2.

Chapter 14

1. Cyndee Miller, "College Campaigns Get Low Scores," *Marketing News*, 8 May 1995, pp. 1, 8.

2. Faju Narisetti, "Goodyear Plans to Offer Tire Models Available Only for Independent Dealers, *Wall Street Journal*, 23 January 1996, p. A5.

3. "Microsoft Teams Up with Visa on System of Electronic Banking," *Wall Street Journal*, 15 February 1996, p. B6.

4. Yumiko Ono, " 'King of Beers' Wants to Rule More of Japan" *Wall Street Journal*, 28 October 1993, pp. B1, B8.

5. Robert Berner, "Retired General Speeds Deliveries, Cuts Costs, Helps Sears Rebound," *Wall Street Journal*, 16 July 1996, p A1.

6. Ernest Raia, "Saturn: Rising Star," *Purchasing*, 9 September 1993, pp. 44–47.

7. Fred R. Bleakley, "Strange Bedfellows: Some Companies Let Suppliers Work on Site and Even Place Orders," *Wall Street Journal*, 13 January 1995, pp. A1, A6.

8. Kate Evans-Correia, "Purchasing Now Biggest EDI User," *Purchasing*, 21 October 1993, pp. 47, 59.

9. E. J. Muler, "Faster, Faster, I Need It Now!" *Distribution*, February 1994, pp. 30–36.

10. Robert Tomsho, "At Medical Malls, Shoppers Are Patients," *Wall Street Journal*, 29 December 1995, pp. B1, B6.

11. Vanessa O'Connell, "PC Banking Puts Accounts at Your Fingertips," *Wall Street Journal*, 25 October 1995, pp. C1, C17.

12. Nikhil Deogun, "Newest ATMs Dispense More Than Cash," *Wall Street Journal*, 5 June 1996, p B1.

13. Timothy L. O'Brien, "The Home War: On-Line Banking Has Bankers Fretting PCs May Replace Branches," *Wall Street Journal*, 25 October 1995, pp. A1, A13.

14. Jon Bigness, "In Today's Economy, There Is Big Money to Be Made in Logistics," *Wall Street Journal*, 6 September 1995, p A1.

15. Robert Berner, "Retired General Speeds Deliveries, Cuts Costs, Helps Sears Rebound," *Wall Street Journal*, 16 July 1996, p A1.

Chapter 15

1. Gregory A. Patterson, "Different Strokes—Target 'Micromarkets' Its Way to Success; No 2 Stores Are Alike," *Wall Street Journal*, 31 May 1995, pp. A1, A9; Mary Kuntz, Lori Bongiorno, Keith Naughton, Gail DeGeorge, and Stephanie Anderson Forest, "Reinventing the Store," *Business Week*, 27 November 1995, pp. 84–96; Jeff D. Opdyke, "Dallas Eatery Aims to Cash in on Taking Out," *Wall Street Journal*, 22 November 1995, pp. T1, T4.

2. U.S. Department of Commerce, Bureau of the Census, *Statistical Abstract of the United States* (Washington, DC: Government Printing Office, 1995).

3. "The Chain Store Age 100," State of the Industry Special Report, *Chain Store Age*, August 1996, pp. 3A–4A.

4. Norihiko Shirouzu, "Japan's Staid Coffee Bars Wake Up and Smell Starbucks," *Wall Street Journal*, 25 July 1996, pp. B1, B8.

5. Seth Sutel, "Japan Wakes Up and Smells the Latte—Starbucks Is Here," *The San Diego Daily Transcript*, Internet address: /96wireheadlines/08_96/DN96_ 08_02/DN96_08_02_fa.html, 2 August 1996.

6. Joseph Pereira, "Toys 'R' Them: Mom-and-Pop Stores Put Playthings Like Thomas on Fast Track," *Wall Street Journal*, 14 January 1993, pp. B1, B5.

7. Karen J. Sack, "Supermarkets: Sales and Earnings Begin to Rebound, But . . . ," *Standard & Poor's Industry Surveys*, 5 May 1994, p. R87.

8. Matt Nannery, "Convenience Stores Get Fresh," *State of the Industry* special issue, *Chain Store Age*, August 1996, pp. 18A–19A; Louise Lee, "Circle K Pushes for a New Look at Convenience Stores," *Wall Street Journal*, 6 November 1995, p. B4.

9. Bill Saporito, "And the Winner Is Still . . . Wal-Mart," *Fortune*, 2 May 1994, pp. 62–70.

10. Bob Ortega, "Tough Sale: Wal-Mart Is Slowed by Problems of Price and Culture in Mexico," *Wall Street Journal*, 29 July 1994, pp. A1, A5.

11. "Supercenters Providing Super Opportunity," *Chain Store Age*, August 1995, pp. 4B–5B.

12. Louise Lee and Kevin Helliker, "Humbled Wal-Mart Plans More Stores," *Wall Street Journal*, 23 February 1996, pp. B1, B4.

13. Laura Liebeck, "Supercenters Have Upscale, Trendier Look," *Discount Store News*, 18 April 1994, p. 33.

14. "Superstores as Industry Leaders," *Standard & Poor's Industry Surveys*, 9 May 1996, p. R85; "State of the Industry," *Chain Store Age*, August 1996, p. 4A.

15. Gale Eisenstodt, "Bull in the Japan Shop," *Forbes*, 31 January 1994, pp. 41–42; Susan Caminiti, "After You Win the Fun Begins: Toys 'R' Us," *Fortune*, 2 May 1994, p. 76.

16. Marianne Wilson, "Wedding Stores Go Big," *Chain Store Age*, October 1995, pp. 31–35; Stephanie N. Mehta, "Bridal Superstores Woo Couples with Miles of Gowns and Tuxes," *Wall Street Journal*, 14 February 1996, pp. B1, B2.

17. Bob Ortega, "Retail Combat: Warehouse-Club War Leaves Few Standing, and They Are Bruised," *Wall Street Journal*, 18 November 1993, pp. A1, A6; "Competition from Warehouse Clubs Hits Peak," *Standard & Poor's Industry Surveys*, 5 May 1994, p. R88.

18. Laurie M. Grossman, "Families Have Changed but Tupperware Keeps Holding Its Parties," *Wall Street Journal*, 21 July 1992, pp. A1, A13; Suein L. Hwang, "Ding-Dong: Updating Avon Means Respecting History Without Repeating It," *Wall Street Journal*, 4 April 1994, pp. A1, A4.

19. Laura Bird, "Forget Ties; Catalogs Now Sell Mansions," *Wall Street Journal*, 7 November 1996, pp. B1, B4.

20. Karen J. Sack, "Challenges Continue in the Coming Year," *Standard & Poor's Industry Surveys*, 15 June 1996, p. R75.

21. Calmetta Y. Coleman, "Mail Order Is Turning into Male Order," *Wall Street Journal*, 25 March 1996, p. B9A.

22. Neal Templin, "Veteran PC Customers Spur Mail-Order Boom," *Wall Street Journal*, 17 July 1996, pp. B1, B5.

23. Gregory A. Patterson, "U.S. Catalogers Test International Waters," *Wall Street Journal*, 19 April 1994, pp. B1, B2.

24. Irene Bejenke, "Home-Shopping Comes to German TV Amid Concern From Rivals, Regulators," *Wall Street Journal*, 20 October 1995, p. B11; Michelle Pentz, "Teleshopping Gets a Tryout in Europe," *Wall Street Journal*, 9 September 1996, p. B10A.

25. Patrick M. Reilly, "Home Shopping: The Next Generation," *Wall Street Journal*, 21 March 1994, p. R11.

26. Calmetta Y. Coleman, "Spiegel Catalog to Publish CD-ROM Version . . . Again," *Wall Street Journal*, 15 February 1996, p. B4.

27. Jeffrey A. Tannenbaum, "Role Model," *Wall Street Journal*, 23 May 1996, p. R22.

28. International Franchise Association, *Franchise Fact Sheet*, November 1995.

29. Jeffrey A. Tannenbaum, "Big Companies Bearing Famous Names Turn to Franchising to Get Even Bigger," *Wall Street Journal*, 18 October 1995, pp. B1, B2.

30. Donna Bryson, "McDonald's Opens Eatery in New Delhi," *The Advocate*, Baton Rouge, Louisiana, 14 October 1996, p. 11A.

31. Sack, "Challenges to Continue in the Coming Year," p. R75.

32. Tara Parker-Pope, "Brooks Brothers Gets a Boost From New Look," *Wall Street Journal*, 22 May 1996, pp. B1, B4.

33. Robert Berner, "Sears's Softer Side Paid Off in Hard Cash This Christmas," *Wall Street Journal*, 29 December 1995, p. B4.

34. Raju Narisetti, "Joint Marketing With Retailers Spreads," *Wall Street Journal*, 24 October 1996, p. B6.

35. Jim Carlton, "Japanese Skip Waikiki, Head for Kmart," *Wall Street Journal*, 29 June 1995, p. B1.

36. Eleena de Lisser and Anita Sharpe, "Stealth Warfare—Home Depot Charges a Rival Drummed Up Opposition to Stores," *Wall Street Journal*, 18 August 1995, pp. A1, A5.

37. Mitchell Pacelle, "More Stores Spurn Malls for the Village Square," *Wall Street Journal*, 16 February 1996, pp. B1, B10.

38. Mitchell Pacelle, "The Aging Shopping Mall Must Either Adapt or Die," *Wall Street Journal*, 16 April 1996, pp. B1, B13.

39. Laura Bird, "Back to Full Price?: Apparel Stores Seek to Curb Shoppers Addicted to Deep Discounts," *Wall Street Journal*, 29 May 1996, pp. A1, A10.

40. Barbara Coe, "Preferences of British Consumers as Related to Desired Changes in British Retailing: A Pilot Study," *The Cutting Edge IV, Proceedings of the 1995 Symposium on Patronage Behavior and Retail Strategy*, ed. William R. Darden, American Marketing Assoc., May 1995, pp. 95–126.

41. Marianne Wilson, "Market Design Transforms Pick'n Save," *Chain Store Age*, September 1996, pp. 120–121.

42. Jack Hitt, "What Supermarkets Know About You," *New York Times Magazine*, 10 March 1996.

43. Diane Welland, "Rhythm and Chews," *Cooking Light*, January/February 1997, p. 22.

44. Louise Lee, "Background Music Becomes Hoity-Toity," *Wall Street Journal*, 22 December 1995, p. B1.

45. "Mall Study Reveals Aromas Boost Kindness Tendencies," *The Advocate*, Baton Rouge, Louisiana, 14 October 1996, p. 3A.

46. John Pierson, "If Sun Shines In, Workers Work Better, Buyers Buy More," *Wall Street Journal*, 20 November 1995, pp. B1, B7.

47. Carol F. Kaufman and Paul M. Lane, "Who's Afraid of the Dark: Shoppers and Their Safety Concerns," *Marketing: Foundations for a Changing World*, ed. by Brian T. Engelland and Denise T. Smart. Proceedings of the Annual Meeting of the Southern Marketing Association, November 1995, pp. 207–211.

48. "Storefronts Show Advantage of Curb Appeal," *Chain Store Age*, November 1996, pp. 102–103.

49. "Success, Technology and the Small Retailer: Critical Success Factors for Small Retailers," *Chain Store Age*, October 1995, pp. 5A–7A.

50. Karen J. Sack, "Mergers, Rivalry, and Price Sensitivity Will Continue," *Standard & Poor's Industry Surveys*, 9 May 1996, pp. R75–R78.

51. "China: Poised for Retail Explosion," *Global Retailing: Assignment Asia*, Coopers & Lybrand special report for *Chain Store Age Executive*, January 1995, pp. 10–16.

52. "Mexico: Regrouping After the Fall," *Global Retailing: Assignment Latin America*, Coopers & Lybrand special report for *Chain Store Age*, April 1996, pp. 6–7.

53. Bob Ortega, "Penney Pushes Abroad in Unusually Big Way as It Pursues Growth," *Wall Street Journal*, 1 February 1994, pp. A1, A7.

54. Joyce M. Rosenberg, "That's Entertainment—And Retail," *The Advocate*, Baton Rouge, Louisiana, 28 August 1996, pp. 8A, 9A.

55. Kuntz, Bongiorno, Naughton, DeGeorge, and Forest, "Reinventing the Store," p. 85.

56. Steve Stecklow, "Some Supermarkets Get Kid-Friendly in an Effort To Build Customer Loyalty," *Wall Street Journal*, 18 June 1996, p. B13A.

57. Matt Murray, "Rx for Pharmacies: Bigger Line of Products and Services," *Wall Street Journal*, 12 September 1996, p. B4.

58. Ahmed Taher, Thomas W. Leigh, and Warren A. French, "The Retail Patronage Experience and Customer Affection," *The Cutting Edge IV, Proceedings of the 1995 Symposium on Patronage Behavior and Retail Strategy*, ed. William R. Darden, American Marketing Assoc., May 1995, pp. 35–51.

59. Sack, "Mergers, Rivalry, and Price Sensitivity Will Continue," p. R75.

60. Sack, "Challenges to Continue in the Coming Year," p. R75.

61. U.S. Department of Commerce, Bureau of the Census, *Statistical Abstract of the United States* (Washington, DC: Government Printing Office, 1995).

62. Bruce Fox, "Gates and Panel Debate the Future of Retailing," *Chain Store Age*, June 1996, pp. 57–58.

63. "The Key to Retailing: Understanding the Consumer," *Standard & Poor's Industry Surveys*, 15 June 1995, pp. R78–R80.

64. U.S. Department of Commerce, Bureau of the Census, *Statistical Abstract of the United States* (Washington, DC: Government Printing Office, 1995).

Chapter 16

1. Bradley Johnson, "Windows 95 Opens with Omnimedia Blast," *Advertising Age*, 28 August 1995, pp. 1, 32; Kathy Rebello and Mary Kuntz, "Feel the Buzz: Win95's Marketing Blitz Will Be Loud—And Costly," *Business Week*, 28 August 1995, p. 31; "For Microsoft, Nothing Succeeds Like Excess," *Wall Street Journal*, 25 August 1995, pp. B1, B4; Bradley Johnson, "Windows 95 Ads Built on 'Nuts and Bolts,'" *Advertising Age*, 21 August 1995, p. 8; Laurianne McLaughlin, "Windows 95: The First 30 Days," *PC World*, December 1995, p. 70(2); Deborah DeVoe and Ed Scannell, "Windows 95: One Year Later; 40 Million Candles on the Cake," *InfoWorld*, 29 July 1996, p. 1(2).

2. Steve Gelsi, ""Bull Market: Taurus $55M Reintro Blankets the Networks' Schedules," *Brandweek*, 17 July 1995, p. 1(2); Steve Gelsi, "1996 Ford Taurus," *Mediaweek*, 17 July 1995, p. 26.

3. Kevin Goldman, "Winemakers Look for More Free Publicity," *Wall Street Journal*, 29 September 1994, p. B4.

4. Ibid.

5. Eleena de Lisser, "Low-Fare Airlines Mute Their Bargain Message," *Wall Street Journal*, 22 May 1996, pp. B1, B8; Susan Carey and Jonathan Dahl, "Flying

Scared: Travelers Feel Psychic Impact of Flight 800," *Wall Street Journal*, 22 July 1996, pp. B1, B8.

6. Frank G. Bingham, Jr., Charles J. Quigley, Jr., and Elaine M. Notarantonio, "The Use of Communication Style in a Buyer-Seller Dyad: Improving Buyer-Seller Relationships," *Proceedings: Association of Marketing Theory and Practice*, 1996 Annual Meeting, Hilton Head, South Carolina, March 1996, pp. 188–195.

7. Ibid.

8. Suzanne Oliver, "Happy Birthday, from Gillette," *Forbes*, 22 April 1996, p. 37(2).

9. Philip J. Kitchen, "Marketing Communications Renaissance," *International Journal of Advertising*, 12 (1993), pp. 367–386.

10. Ibid., p. 372.

11. Major Gary Lee Keck and Barbara Meuller, "Observations: Intended vs. Unintended Messages: Viewer Perceptions of United States Army Television Commercials," *Journal of Advertising Research*, March–April 1994, pp. 70–77.

12. James Caporimo, "Worldwide Advertising Has Benefits, But One Size Doesn't Always Fit All," *Brandweek*, 17 July 1995, p. 16; Ali Kanso, "International Advertising Strategies: Global Commitment to Local Vision," *Journal of Advertising Research*, January–February 1992, pp. 10–14; Wayne Walley, "Programming Globally—With Care: Cultural Research Ensures Discovery's Success Abroad," *Advertising Age*, 18 September 1995, p. I14; Wayne M. McCullough, "Global Advertising Which Acts Locally: The IBM Subtitles Campaign," *Journal of Advertising Research*, May–June 1996, pp. 11–15; Martin S. Roth, "Effects of Global Market Conditions on Brand Image Customization and Brand Performance," *Journal of Advertising*, Winter 1995, p. 55(21). Also see Carolyn A. Lin, "Cultural Differences in Message Strategies: A Comparison Between American and Japanese Television Commercials," *Journal of Advertising Research*, July–August, 1993, pp. 40–47; and Fred Zandpour et al., "Global Reach and Local Touch: Achieving Cultural Fitness in TV Advertising," *Journal of Advertising Research*, September–October 1994, pp. 35–63.

13. James R. Rosenfield, "Integrate, Don't Dis-integrate," *Sales & Marketing Management*, April 1995, pp. 30–31.

14. See Don E. Schultz, Stanley I. Tannenbaum, and Robert F. Lauterborn, *Integrated Marketing Communications* (Lincolnwood, IL.: NTC Business Books, 1993).

15. John F. Yarbrough, "Putting the Pieces Together," *Sales & Marketing Management*, September 1996, pp. 69–77.

16. AIDA concept based on the classic research of E. K. Strong, Jr., as theorized in *The Psychology of Selling and Advertising* (New York: McGraw-Hill, 1925) and "Theories of Selling," *Journal of Applied Psychology*, 9 (1925), pp. 75–86.

17. Hierarchy of effects model is based on the classic research of R. C. Lavidge and G. A. Steiner, "A Model for Predictive Measurements of Advertising Effectiveness," *Journal of Marketing*, 25 (1961), pp. 59–62. For an excellent review of the AIDA and hierarchy of effects models, see Thomas E. Barry and Daniel J. Howard, "A Review and Critique of the Hierarchy of Effects in Advertising," *International Journal of Advertising*, 9 (1990), pp. 121–135.

18. Barry and Howard, p. 131.

19. Jennifer Fulkerson, "It's in the Consumer Cards," *American Demographics*, July 1996, p. 44(3).

20. Murray Raphel, "Frequent Shopper Clubs: Supermarkets' Newest Weapon," *Direct Marketing*, May 1995, p. 18(3).

21. Daisy Maryles, "Behind the Bestsellers," *Publisher's Weekly*, 29 January 1996, p. 18.

22. Leonard Wiener, "Going to the Movies Online," *U.S. News & World Report*, 20 November 1995, p. 110.

23. Leonard Klady, "To Cash in on Oscar, Timing Is Everything," *Variety*, 19 February 1996, p. 9(2).

24. Jeffrey A. Tannenbaum, "Priceless Promotions," *Wall Street Journal*, 22 May 1995, p. R20; Ann Brown, "High Profile—Low Price; Keep Advertising Costs from Busting Your Budget," *Black Enterprise*, June 1995, p. 46; Laura M. Litvan, "Taking Your Best Shots," *Nation's Business*, August 1996, p. 73.

25. "Selling to School Kids," *Consumer Reports*, May 1995, pp. 327–329. Adapted from the *Consumer's Union* report "Captive Kids: Commercial Pressures on Kids at School."

26. David B. Jones, "Setting Promotional Goals: A Communications' Relationship Model," *Journal of Consumer Marketing*, 11 (1994), pp. 38–49.

27. Peter J. Danaher and Roland T. Rust, "Determining the Optimal Level of Media Spending," *Journal of Advertising Research*, January–February 1994, pp. 28–34; see also Barbara Jizba and Mary M. K. Fleming, "Promotion Budgeting and Control in the Fast Food Industry," *International Journal of Advertising*, 12 (1993), pp. 13–23.

28. J. Enrique Bigne, "Advertising Budgeting Practices: A Review," *Journal of Current Issues and Research in Advertising*, Fall 1995, pp. 17–31.

29. Kevin Goldman, "Calvin Klein Halts Jeans Ad Campaign," *Wall Street Journal*, 29 August 1995, p. B7.

30. "Klein Sheds Ads, Not Appeal," *Advertising Age*, 18 September 1995, p. 52.

31. Anne G. Perkins, "Advertising: The Costs of Deception," *Harvard Business Review*, May–June 1994, p. 10(2).

32. "A New Shell for an Old Ad Claim," *Consumer Reports*, March 1995, p. 134.

33. "Fine for Egg Producer," *Wall Street Journal*, 14 March 1996, p. B8.

Chapter 17

1. Sally Goll Beatty, "Milk-Mustache Ads: Cream of the Crop," *Wall Street Journal*, 20 May 1996, p. B6; T. L. Stanley, "The Gods of the Milk," *MediaWeek*, 20 May 1996, p. 44(2); Melanie Wells, "Milk Group Ads Unveil New Celebrity Mustaches," *USA Today*, 10 July 1996, p. 2B; Mark Gleason, "Men Are Newest Target for 'Milk Mustache' Ads," *Advertising Age*, 1 July 1996, p. 10.

2. *Standard & Poor's Industry Surveys*, 20 July 1995, p. M17.

3. U.S. Department of Commerce, Bureau of the Census, *Statistical Abstract of the United States* (Washington, DC: Government Printing Office, September 1995), p. 416.

4. "1996 Advertising-to-Sales Ratios for the 200 Largest Ad Spending Industries," *Advertising Age*, 1 July 1996, p. 11.

5. "Time Spent with Media," *Standard & Poor's Industry Surveys*, 14 March 1996, p. M1. "Radio & TV Broadcasting: Commercials Clog the Airways," *Standard & Poor's Industry Surveys*, 12 May 1994, p. M35.

6. Amitava Chattaopadhyay and Kunal Basu, "Humor in Advertising: The Moderating Role of Prior Brand Evaluation," *Journal of Marketing Research*, November 1990, pp. 466–476.

7. Yong Zhang, "Responses to Humorous Advertising: The Moderating Effect of Need for Cognition," *Journal of Advertising*, Spring 1996, pp. 15–34.

8. Marvin E. Goldberg and Jon Hartwick, "The Effects of Advertiser Reputation and Extremity of Advertising Claims on Advertising Effectiveness," *Journal of Consumer Research*, September 1990, pp. 172–179.

9. Rick Stoff, "AD/PR Notes: Developments in Advertising and Public Relations of Tobacco Firms, *St. Louis Journalism Review*, September 1994, p. 17.

10. Yumiko Ono, "Ads Do Push Kids to Smoke, Study Suggests," *Wall Street Journal*, 18 October 1995, pp. B1, B7; Timothy Noah, "Study Says Minors Respond More to Cigarette Ads Than Do Adults," *Wall Street Journal*, 4 April 1996, p. B2; Richard W. Pollay, S. Siddarth, Michael Siegel, Anne Haddix, Robert K. Merritt, Gary A. Giovino, and Michael P. Eriksen, "The Last Straw? Cigarette Advertising and Realized Market Shares Among Youths and Adults, 1979–1993," *Journal of Marketing*, April 1996, pp. 1–16; "Hooked on Tobacco: The Teen Epidemic," *Consumer Reports*, March 1995, pp. 142–147; "Should Ads Like This Be in Your Kid's Face?" *Consumer Reports*, June 1996, p. 6; Suein L. Hwang, "Teenage Smoking on Rise, Particularly Among the Youngest, U.S. Study Finds," *Wall Street Journal*, 20 July 1995, p. B7; Ira Teinowitz, "'Historic' Attack on Cig Marketing," *Advertising Age*, 26 August 1996, pp. 1, 28; and "Nicotine Attack: Cigarette Regulation is Formally Proposed; Industry Sues to Halt It," *Wall Street Journal*, 11 August 1995, pp. A1, A10.

11. Rajiv Grover and V. Srinivasan, "Evaluating the Multiple Effects of Retail Promotions on Brand Loyalty and Brand Switching Segments," *Journal of Marketing Research*, February 1992, pp. 76–89; see also S. P. Raj, "The Effects of Advertising on High and Low Loyalty Consumer Segments," *Journal of Consumer Research*, June 1982, pp. 77–89.

12. Bradley Johnson and Mark Rechtin, "Nissan Packs $200 Mil into Yearlong Drive for Brand," *Advertising Age*, 5 August 1996, p. 3.

13. Michael Burgoon, Michael Pfau and Thomas S. Birk, "An Inoculation Theory Explanation for the Effects of Corporate Issue/Advocacy Advertising Campaigns, *Communication Research*, August 1995, p. 485(21).

14. Eben Shapiro, "R. J. Reynolds Ads Spotlight Nonsmokers," *Wall Street Journal*, 25 July 1994, p. B4.

15. Judann Pollack, "Marketing 100: Baked Lay's Rebecca Johnson," *Advertising Age*, 24 June 1996, p. S2.

16. Elyse Tanouye, "Battle Brews in the Heartburn Business as Two Old Drugs Go Over the Counter," *Wall Street Journal*, 22 May 1995, p. B1; Jonathan Welsh, "More Heartburn Relief Unsettles Market," *Wall Street Journal*, 7 February 1996, p. B8.

17. Robert Langreth, "SmithKline Claims It Can't Stomach Ads on Heartburn," *Wall Street Journal*, 30 August 1995, p. B2; Elyse Tanouye, "Heartburn Drug Makers Feel Judge's Heat," *Wall Street Journal*, 16 October 1995, p. B8.

18. Cornelia Pechmann, "Do Consumers Overgeneralize One-Sided Comparative Price Claims, and Are More Stringent Regulations Needed?" *Journal of Marketing Research*, May 1996, pp. 150–162.

19. For a comprehensive review of academic research on the effectiveness of comparative advertising, see Thomas E. Berry, "Comparative Advertising: What Have We Learned in Two Decades?" *Journal of Advertising Research*, March–April 1993, pp. 19–29. See also Cornelia Pechmann and David W. Stewart, "The Effects of Comparative Advertising on Attention, Memory, and Purchase Intentions," *Journal of Consumer Research*, September 1990, pp. 180–191; Darrel D. Muehling, Jeffrey J. Stoltman, and Sanford Grossbart, "The Impact of Comparative Advertising on Levels of Message Involvement," *Journal of Advertising*, 4 (1990), pp. 41–50; Jerry B. Gotleib and Dan Sarel, "Comparative Advertising Effectiveness: The Role of Involvement and Source Credibility," *Journal of Advertising*, 1 (1991), pp. 38–45.

20. Martin DuBois and Tara Parker-Pope, "Philip Morris Campaign Stirs Uproar in Europe," *Wall Street Journal*, 1 July 1996, pp. B1, B5; "French Block Philip Morris Ad," *New York Times*, 26 June 1996, p. C5.

21. Joanne Lipman, "It's It and That's a Shame: Why Are Some Slogans Losers?" *Wall Street Journal*, 16 July 1993, pp. A1, A4.

22. Sally Goll Beatty, "Staid Brands Put New Spin on Old Jingles," *Wall Street Journal*, 19 January 1996, p. B11.

23. Kevin Goldman, "Foster Grant Slogan Makes a Comeback," *Wall Street Journal*, 29 March 1995, p. B12.

24. Peter Waldman, "Please Don't Show Your Lingerie in Iran, Even if It's For Sale," *Wall Street Journal*, 21 June 1995, pp. A1, A8.

25. Marc G. Weinberger, Harlan Spotts, Leland Campbell, and Amy L. Parsons, "The Use and Effect of Humor in Different Advertising Media," *Journal of Advertising Research*, May–June 1995, pp. 44–56.

26. Noreen O'Leary, "New Life on Mars," *Brandweek*, 6 May 1996, p. 44(3).

27. Debra Goldman, "The French Style of Advertising," *Adweek*, 16 December 1991, p. 21; Lisa Bannon and Margaret Studer, "For 2 Revealing European Ads, Overexposure Can Have Benefits," *Wall Street Journal*, 17 June 1994, p. B8.

28. Johnny K. Johansson, "The Sense of 'Nonsense': Japanese TV Advertising," *Journal of Advertising*, March 1994, pp. 17–26.

29. "Radio: No Longer an Advertising Afterthought," *Standard & Poor's Industry Surveys*, 20 July 1995, p. M36; Rebecca Piirto, "Why Radio Thrives," *American Demographics*, May 1994, pp. 40–46.

30. Piirto, pp. 43–44.

31. Phil Hall, "Make Listeners Your Customers," *Nation's Business*, June 1994, p. 53R; Rebecca Piirto, pp. 40–46.

32. Rebecca Piirto, "New Markets for Cable TV," *American Demographics*, June 1995, pp. 40–46.

33. Jensen and Ross, p. 27; Sally Goll Beatty, "Super Bowl Ad Play: 'Hut, Hut, Value!'," *Wall Street Journal*, 16 January 1996, p. B5.

34. Joe Mandese, "Cost to Make TV Ad Nears Quarter-Million," *Advertising Age*, 4 July 1994, p. 3.

35. Laura Bird, "Sharper Image's New Gadget: Infomercials," *Wall Street Journal*, 19 September 1995, p. B6.

36. Rhonda L. Rundle, "Outdoor Plans Billboard-Sized Purchase," *Wall Street Journal*, 11 July 1996, p. B6; Cyndee Miller, "Outdoor Gets a Makeover," *Marketing News*, 10 April 1995, pp. 1, 26.

37. Miller, p. 1; Michael Wilke, "Outdoor Ads Entering Whole New Dimension," *Advertising Age*, 29 July 1996, p. 20.

38. Pierre Berthon, Leyland F. Pitt, and Richard T. Watson, "The World Wide Web as an Advertising Medium: Toward an Understanding of Conversion Efficiency," *Journal of Advertising Research*, January/February 1996, pp. 43–54.

39. Kim Cleland, "NFL, ESPN, Starwave Take Web Strategy to New Level," *Advertising Age*, 5 August 1996, p. 24.

40. Berthon, Pitt and Watson, pp. 44–45.

41. "Web Start-Up Pays People to Read Ads," *Yahoo! Headlines*, 25 June 1996.

42. Laurie Freeman, "Internet Visitors' Traffic Jam Makes Buyers Web Wary," *Advertising Age*, 22 July 1996, pp. S14–15.

43. Jeff Jensen and Chuck Ross, "Centennial Olympics Open as $5 Bil Event of Century," *Advertising Age*, 15 July 1996, pp. 1, 27; Emory Thomas, Jr., "Crush of Olympic Sponsors Inspires Efforts to Break Out From the Pack," *Wall Street Journal*, 15 July 1996, pp. B1, B10.

44. Laura Bird, "Loved the Ad. May (or May Not) Buy the Product," *Wall Street Journal*, 7 April 1994, p. B1.

45. Joseph Pereira, "Toy Story: How Shrewd Marketing Made Elmo a Hit," *Wall Street Journal*, 16 December 1996, pp. B1, B7.

46. Judann Pollack, "New Marketing Spin: The PR 'Experience,'" *Advertising Age*, 5 August 1996, p. 33.

47. Fara Warner, "Why It's Getting Harder to Tell the Shows from the Ads," *Wall Street Journal*, 15 June 1995, pp. B1, B8.

48. Damon Darlin, "Junior Mints, I'm Gonna Make You a Star," *Forbes*, 6 November 1995, p. 90(4).

49. Richard Gibson, "Pillsbury's Telephones Ring With Peeves, Praise," *Wall Street Journal*, 20 April 1994, pp. B1, B4; Carl Quintanilla and Richard Gibson, "'Do Call Us': More Companies Install 1-800 Phone Lines," *Wall Street Journal*, 20 April 1994, pp. B1, B4.

50. Mary Anne Mather, "Family Computing Workshops Are the Latest Rage," *Technology & Learning*, September 1995, p. 60.

51. Aminda Heckman and Kate Fitzgerald, "Fired Up Over Torch," *Advertising Age*, 1 July 1996, p. 20.

52. Emory Thomas, Jr., "Handicapping the Corporate Games," *Wall Street Journal*, 19 July 1996, p. R14.

53. Kate Fitzgerald, "Cycle of Success," *Advertising Age*, 10 June 1996, pp. 40–41.

54. James A. Roberts, "Green Consumers in the 1990s: Profile and Implications for Advertising," *Journal of Business Research*, 36 (1996), pp. 217–231.

55. G. A. Marken, "Getting the Most From Your Presence in Cyberspace," *Public Relations Quarterly*, Fall 1995, p. 36(2).

56. Carl Quintanilla, "TWA's Reponse to Crash Is Viewed as Lesson in How Not to Handle Crisis," *Wall Street Journal*, 22 July 1996, p. A4.

57. Raju Narisetti, "Anatomy of a Food Fight: The Olestra Debate," *Wall Street Journal*, 31 July 1996, pp. B1, B6.

Chapter 18

1. Kate Fitzgerald, "Sega 'Screams' Its Way to the Top," *Advertising Age*, 20 March 1995, pp. S-2, S-9; Kate Fitzgerald, "Just Playing Along," *Advertising Age*, 17 July 1995, p. 24.

2. Kenneth Wylie, "Marketing Services: With Growth in High Teens, Direct Response and Promotion Prove Cross-Fertilization a Hit," *Advertising Age*, 5 August 1996, pp. S1–S4.

3. Laura Reina, "Manufacturers Still Believe in Coupons," *Editor & Publisher*, 28 October 1995, p. 24; Betsy Spethmann, "Coupons Shed Low-Tech Image; Sophisticated Tracking Yields Valuable Consumer Profile," *Brandweek*, 24 October 1994, p. 30(2); Scott Hume, "Coupons Set Record, But Pace Slows," *Advertising Age*, 1 February 1993, p. 25; and Scott Hume, "Coupons: Are They Too Popular?" *Advertising Age*, 15 February 1993, p. 32.

4. Kate Fitzgerald, "Kraft Goes 'Universal' as Others Rejigger Couponing," *Advertising Age*, 24 June 1996, p. 9.

5. Jeff Jensen, "Reebok Offers Online Coupons," *Advertising Age*, 24 June 1996, p. 37.

6. Kathleen Deveny and Richard Gibson, "Awash in Coupons? Some Firms Try to Stem the Tide," *Wall Street Journal*, 10 May 1994, pp. B1, B6; Matt Walsh, "Point-of-Sale Persuaders," *Forbes*, 24 October 1994, p. 232(2).

7. "International Coupon Trends," *Direct Marketing*, August 1993, pp. 47–49; "Global Coupon Use Up; U.K., Belgium Tops in Europe," *Marketing News*, 5 August 1991, p. 5; Kamran Kashani and John A. Quelch, "Can Sales Promotion Go Global?" *Business Horizons*, May–June 1990, pp. 37–43.

8. Judann Pollack, "Pop Tarts Packs More Pastry for Same Price," *Advertising Age*, 5 August 1996, p. 6.

9. Robert Frank, "Pepsi Cancels an Ad Campaign as Customers Clamor for Stuff," *Wall Street Journal*, 27 June 1996, pp. B1, B8.

10. Karen Benezra and Marla Matzer, "Marketing 101," *Brandweek*, 5 August 1996, p. 1(2).

11. Mark Lacek, "Loyalty Marketing No Ad Budget Threat," *Advertising Age*, 23 October 1995, p. 20.

12. Ginger Conlon, "True Romance," *Sales & Marketing Management*, May 1996, pp. 85–90.

13. Murray Raphel, "Customer Specific Marketing," *Direct Marketing*, June 1996, p. 22(6).

14. Murray Raphel, "Customer Specific Marketing," *Direct Marketing*, June 1996, p. 22(6); Murray Raphel, "Measured Marketing," *Direct Marketing*, December 1995, p. 30(3); Murray Raphel, "Frequent Shopper Clubs: Supermarkets' Newest Weapon," *Direct Marketing*, May 1995, p. 18(3).

15. Kate Fitzgerald, "Ale-ing Essayists Vie for Guinness Pub," *Advertising Age*, 16 May 1994, p. 38.

16. Richard Corliss, "Chuff Chuff, Puff Puff,", *Time*, 8 January 1996, p. 51; Ann Marsh, "Red Thunder: Philip Morris' Latest Promotion Campaign," *Forbes*, 1 January 1996, p. 238.

17. Amanda Plotkin, "Online Gold Mine Awaits Exploitation," *Advertising Age*, 4 March 1996, p. S4.

18. Thomas O. Mooney, "The Proving Ground: Research Used to Be Hit or Miss; Now It's Dead-On," *Brandweek*, 13 March 1995, p. S15(2).

19. "Free for All; There Are a Lot of Good Ways to Get the Word—and Your Products—Out There," *Brandweek*, 13 March 1995, p. S5(4)

20. "Free for All . . . ," p. S5(4); Kate Fitzgerald, "Venue Sampling Hot," *Advertising Age*, 12 August 1996, p. 19.

21. Adrienne Ward Fawcett, "Listening to the In-Store Ad Song," *Advertising Age*, 23 October 1995, p. 34.

22. Kmart/Procter & Gamble Study, Point-of-Purchase Advertising Institute, as reported in Lisa Z. Eccles, "P-O-P Scores with Marketers," *Advertising Age*, 26 September 1994, pp. P1–P4. Also see Kathleen Deveny, "Displays Pay Off for Grocery Marketers," *Wall Street Journal*, 15 October 1992, pp. B1, B5.

23. "Technology Gives P-O-P a New Look," *Advertising Age*, 26 September 1994, p. P6.

24. Leah Haran, "Kiosks' Mass Appeal," *Advertising Age*, 6 November 1995, p. 35.

25. Frank G. Bingham, Jr., Charles J. Quigley, Jr., and Elaine M. Notarantonio, "The Use of Communication Style in a Buyer-Seller Dyad: Improving Buyer-Seller Relationships," Association of Marketing Theory and Practice, *Proceedings*, 1996 Annual Meeting, March 1996, Hilton Head, South Carolina, pp. 188–195.

26. Donald W. Jackson, Jr., "Relationship Selling: The Personalization of Relationship Marketing," *Asia-Australia Marketing Journal*, August 1994, pp. 45–54.

27. Bingham, Quigley, and Notarantonio, pp. 188–195.

28. Frederick F. Reichheld, "Learning from Customer Defections," *Harvard Business Review*, March–April 1996, pp. 56–69.

29. Mark A. Moon and Gary M. Armstrong, "Selling Teams: A Conceptual Framework and Research Agenda," *Journal of Personal Selling & Sales Management*, Winter 1994, pp. 17–30; Henry Canaday, "Team Selling Works," *Personal Selling Power*, September 1994, pp. 52–58.

30. Roger Brooksbank, "The New Model of Personal Selling: Micromarketing," *Journal of Personal Selling & Sales Management*, Spring 1995, pp. 61–66; Donald W. Jackson, Jr., "Relationship Selling: The Personalization of Relationship Marketing," *Asia-Australia Marketing Journal*, August 1994, pp. 45–54.

31. Jackson, p. 47.

32. "Generating Electronic Sales Leads," *Sales & Marketing Management*, August 1996, p. 93.

33. Marvin A. Jolson and Thomas R. Wotruba, "Selling and Sales Management in Action: Prospecting: A New Look at This Old Challenge," *Journal of Personal Selling & Sales Management*, Fall 1992, pp. 59–66.

34. Robyn Griggs, "Taking the Leads," *Sales & Marketing Management*, September 1995, pp. 46–48.

35. Adapted from Bob Kimball, *Successful Selling*, American Marketing Association, 1994.

36. Nancy Arnott, "Break Out of the Grid!" *Sales & Marketing Management*, July 1994, p. 68–75.

37. Andy Cohen, "Delivering the Right Pitch," *Sales & Marketing Management*, September 1994, p. 44; Sondra Brewer, "How to Present So Prospects Listen," *Personal Selling Power*, April 1994, p. 75.

38. Thomas N. Ingram, "Relationship Selling: Moving from Rhetoric to Reality," *Mid-American Journal of Business*, January 1997, pp. 5–13.

39. Valerie Reitman, "Toyota Calling: In Japan's Car Market, Big Three Face Rivals Who Go Door-to-Door," *Wall Street Journal*, 28 September 1994, pp. A1, A6.

40. Perri Capell, "Are Good Salespeople Born or Made?" *American Demographics*, July 1993, pp. 12–13.

41. Joseph Conlin, "Negotiating Their Way to the Top," *Sales & Marketing Management*, April 1996, pp. 57–62; Gregg Crawford, "Let's Negotiate," *Sales & Marketing Management*, November 1995, pp. 28–29.

42. Sergey Frank, "Global Negotiating: Vive Les Differences!" *Sales & Marketing Management*, May 1992, pp. 64–69.

43. "Negotiating: Getting to Yes, Chinese-Style," *Sales & Marketing Management*, July 1996, pp. 44–45.

44. Andy Cohen, "Global Do's and Don'ts," *Sales & Marketing Management*, June 1996, p. 72; Esmond D. Smith, Jr., and Cuong Pham, "Doing Business in Vietnam: A Cultural Guide," *Business Horizons*, May–June 1996, pp. 47–51.

45. Andy Cohen, "Designing the Process: Starting Over," *Sales & Marketing Management*, September 1995, pp. 40–44.

46. Melissa Campanelli, "Managing Territories: A New Focus," *Sales & Marketing Management*, September 1995, pp. 56–58.

47. Bob Alexander, "Picture Perfect: How Kodak Trains for Sales Success," *Personal Selling Power*, March 1994, pp. 19–23.

48. Malcolm Fleschner, "100% Success at Federal Express," *Personal Selling Power*, March 1994, pp. 44–52.

49. Robert G. Head, "Restoring Balance to Sales Compensation," *Sales & Marketing Management*, August 1992, pp. 48–53.

50. "Compensation: More Sales Pay Linked to Satisfied Customers," *Sales & Marketing Management*, June 1995, p. 37.

51. Henry Canaday, "Creative Compensation," *Personal Selling Power*, April 1994, pp. 24–28.

52. Head, pp. 48–53.

53. Ingram, p. 11.

Chapter 20

1. Chad Rubel, "Natural-Food Chain Targets Unnatural Shoppers," *Marketing News*, 8 April 1996, p. 2.

2. "Price Rises As a Factor for Consumers," *Advertising Age*, 8 November 1993, p. 37.

3. "Cost-Conscious Shoppers Seek Secondhand," *USA Today*, 14 March 1996, p. B1.

4. "Retailers Are Giving Profits Away, *American Demographics*, June 1994, p. 14.

5. "Honda Accord Pulls Up Alongside Ford Taurus," *Wall Street Journal*, 11 April 1996, p. B1.

6. "The Big Squeeze," *Adweek's Marketing Week*, 12 November 1990, p. 22.

7. Kirk Davidson, "The Ethics of Increasing Fees for Bank Services," *Marketing News*, 20 May 1996, p. 25.

8. "Unsold Seats Sully Concord's Snooty Image," *Wall Street Journal*, 23 February 1996, p. B1.

9. "How Eagle Became Extinct," *Business Week*, 4 March 1996, pp. 66–69.

10. Hermann Simon, "Pricing Problems in a Global Setting," *Marketing News*, 9 October 1995, pp. 4, 8.

11. Praveen Kopalle and Donald Lehmann, "The Effects of Advertised and Observed Quality on Expectations About New Product Quality," *Journal of Marketing Research*, August 1995, pp. 280–290; Akshay Rao and Kent Monroe, "The Effect of Price, Brand Name, and Store Name on Buyers' Perceptions of Product Quality: An Integrative Review," *Journal of Marketing Research*, August 1989, pp. 351–357; Gerard Tellis and Gary Gaeth, "Best Value, Price-Seeking, and Price Aversion: The Impact of Information and Learning on Consumer Choices," *Journal of Marketing*, April 1990, pp. 34–35.

12. William Dodds, Kent Monroe, and Dhruv Grewal, "Effects of Price, Brand, and Store Information on Buyers' Product Evaluations," *Journal of Marketing Research*, August 1991, pp. 307–319; see also Akshay Rao and Wanda Sieben, "The Effect of Prior Knowledge on Price Acceptability and the Type of Information Examined," *Journal of Consumer Research*, September 1992, pp. 256–270.

13. Phillip Parker, "Sweet Lemons: Illusory Quality, Self-Deceivers, Advertising, and Price," *Journal of Marketing Research*, August 1995, pp. 291–307; Michael Etgar and Naresh Malhotra, "Determinants of Price Dependency: Personal and Perceptual Factors," *Journal of Consumer Research*, September 1981, pp. 217–222; Jeen-Su Lim and Richard Olshavsky,

"Impacts of Consumers' Familiarity and Product Class on Price–Quality Inference and Product Evaluations," *Quarterly Journal of Business and Economics*, Summer 1988, pp. 130–141.

14. Donald Lichtenstein and Scott Burton, "The Relationship between Perceived and Objective Price-Quality," *Journal of Marketing Research*, November 1989, pp. 429–443.

15. "Store-Brand Pricing Has to Be Just Right," *Wall Street Journal*, 14 February 1992, p. B1.

16. Dawar Niraj and Phillip Parker, "Marketing Universals: Consumers' Use of Brand Name, Price, Physical Appearance, and Retailer Reputation as Signals of Product Quality," *Journal of Marketing*, April 1994, pp. 81–95.

Chapter 21

1. Teri Agins, "Ralph Lauren Tries to Bring Polo to the Masses," *Wall Street Journal*, 24 April 1996, pp. B1, B8.

2. "What's Fair," *Wall Street Journal*, 20 May 1994, p. R11.

3. Jacqueline Simmons, "Budget Hotels Aren't Bargains Abroad," *Wall Street Journal*, 17 November 1995, pp. B1, B8.

4. *United States v. Sacony-Vacuum Oil Co.*, 310 U.S. 150 (1940).

5. "ADM Watch: Price Fixing Lawsuits Are Piling Up," *Fortune*, 18 September 1995, p. 20.

6. "Judge Rejects Settlement of Drug Suit," *Wall Street Journal*, 6 March 1996, p. A4.

7. "Wal-Mart Admits Selling Below Cost, but Denies Predatory Pricing Charge," *Wall Street Journal*, 24 August 1993, p. A9; "Wal-Mart Loses a Case on Pricing," *Wall Street Journal*, 13 October 1993, p. A3.

8. Patricia Sellers, "The Dumbest Marketing Ploy," *Fortune*, 3 October 1992, pp. 88–94. © 1992 Time, Inc. All rights reserved.

9. "Eliminated Discounts on P&G Goods Annoy Many Who Sell Them," *Wall Street Journal*, 11 August 1992, pp. A1, A6.

10. Sellers, pp. 88–89.

11. "Ed Artzt's Elbow Grease Has P&G Shining," *Business Week*, 10 October 1994, pp. 84–86. For an excellent study on EDLP and its impact on retailers and manufacturers, see Stephen J. Hoch, Xavier Dreze, and Mary E. Purk, "EDLP, Hi-Lo, and Margin Arithmetic," *Journal of Marketing*, October 1994, pp. 16–27.

12. "Brand Managers Get Old-Time Religion," *Wall Street Journal*, 23 April 1996, p. A19.

13. "GM Expected to Expand 'No Haggle' Pricing Plan," *Wall Street Journal*, 24 April 1996, p. A3.

14. "The Frills Are Gone In GM's Showrooms, But Profits Are Back," *Wall Street Journal*, 15 January 1996, pp. A1, A5.

15. Elyse Tanouye and Michael Waldholz, "Merck's Marketing of an AIDS Drug Draws Fire," 7 May 1996, pp. B1, B6.

16. Charles Quigley and Elaine Notarantonio, "An Exploratory Investigation of Perceptions of Odd and Even Pricing," in *Developments in Marketing Science*, ed. Victoria Crittenden (Miami: Academy of Marketing Science, 1992), pp. 306–309.

17. Francis Mulhern and Robert Leone, "Implicit Price Bundling of Retail Products: A Multiproduct Approach to Maximizing Store Profitability," *Journal of Marketing*, October 1991, pp. 63–76;

Dorothy Paun, "Product Bundling: A Normative Model Based on an Orientation Perspective," in *Developments in Marketing Science*, ed. Victoria Crittenden (Miami: Academy of Marketing Science, 1992), pp. 301–305; Manjit Yadav and Kent Monroe, "How Buyers Perceive Savings in a Bundle Price: An Examination of a Bundle's Transaction Value," *Journal of Marketing Research*, August 1993, pp. 350–358; R. Venkatesh and Vijay Mahajan, "A Probabilistic Approach to Pricing A Bundle of Services," *Journal of Marketing Research*, November 1993, pp. 509–521; and Asim Ansari, S. Siddarth, and Charles Weinberg, "Pricing a Bundle of Products or Services: The Case of Nonprofits," *Journal of Marketing Research*, February 1996, pp. 86–93.

18. "Marketers Try to Ease Sting of Price Increases," *Marketing News*, 9 October 1995, p. 5.

19. "Value Strategy to Battle Recession," *Advertising Age*, 7 January 1991, pp. 1, 44.

20. "How to Prosper in the Value Decade," *Fortune*, 30 November 1992, pp. 89–103.

21. "Cut Costs or Else," *Business Week*, 22 March 1993, pp. 28–29.

22. Ibid.

Appendix

1. Ryan Slight, "Graduates Can Find Employment Online," *University of Texas at Arlington Shorthorn-Career Special*, April 3, 1996, p. 6.

2. C. F. Siegel and R. Powers, "FAB: A Useful Tool for the Job-Seeking Marketing Student," *Marketing Education Review*, Winter 1991, pp. 60–65.

3. Ibid.

4. Ibid.

Company and Organization Index

Fuji Xerox, 89
Fuld & Company, 305

G. D. Searle, 138
G. Heileman Brewing Company, 33
Gamesa, 219
Gap, The, 60, 286, 417, 436, 437, 439
Gateway 2000, 520
Genentech, 605
General Electric Company, 24, 36, 88, 103, 114, 116, 168, 315, 506, 535, 622
General Mills, 36, 158, 165, 246, 311, 389, 621
General Motors Corporation, 13, 28, 29, 54, 71, 86, 88, 89, 103, 104, 106, 109, 153, 162, 171, 189, 196, 234, 243, 248, 258, 262, 282, 283, 315, 331, 364, 400, 401, 406, 407, 430, 496, 497, 576, 611, 614, 622, 628
General Tire Company, 116
GEnie, 429
Genzyme Corporation, 605
Gerber Products Company, 244
Gillette, 86, 104, 282, 283, 287, 296, 312, 376, 463, 504, 506
Gitano, 630
Glaxo, 407
Glock, 121–122
GMC, 561
GNC, 169
Godiva, 20, 40, 391
Gold Medal Footwear, 95
Golden Eagle Foods, 608
Goodyear Tire & Rubber Company, 112, 389
Green Business Conference, 134
Green Tree Associates, 410
GTE Directories, 355
GTE, 31, 127
Gucci, 295, 391, 437, 594
Guess?, 60, 160, 286, 297
Guinness Import Company, 533
Gulf Oil, 239
Gulfstream Aircraft, 23

H&R Block, 17, 30, 252, 291
H.O.T., 428
Habitat for Humanity, 435
Hallmark Greeting Cards, 161, 256, 286, 302, 416
Hanes, 520
Hard Rock Cafe, 440
Harley-Davidson Cafe, 440
Harley-Davidson Motor Company, 98, 113, 116, 172, 291
Harris Corporation, 21
Harris Methodist Hospital, 366
Harris Teeter, 440

Harrods, 440
Hasbro, 51, 52, 79
Hastings Group, 413
Head Golf, 299
Head Sports, 299
Healthy Choice, 500, 505
Heinz, 35, 159
Henkel KGAA, 15
Hershey, 229, 231, 291
Hertz Corporation, 336, 337
Hewlett-Packard, 16, 37, 89, 127, 303, 365, 405, 471
Hilton Hotels and Resorts, 244, 366
Hitachi, 88
Holiday Inn, 261, 290, 607
Home Depot, 9, 415, 416, 422, 434, 435, 441, 442
Home Shopping Network, 428, 429
Honda, 89, 483, 575, 604, 611, 628
Hooters, 145–146
Hoover, 251
House of Good Samaritan Hospital, 334
Hyatt Hotels, 13, 292, 366, 431, 622
Hyatt Legal Services, 292, 332
Hyundai, 29

IBM, 24, 34, 37, 88, 103, 117, 154, 188, 189, 200, 214, 226, 227, 290, 292, 354, 356, 407, 467, 469, 479, 556
Ice House, 141
IDS Financial Services, 248
IKEA, 422, 439
IMS International, 251
Independent Grocers' Association (IGA), 289
Infiniti, 157
Information Resources, Inc. (IRI), 268, 269, 272, 311, 535
Integrion Financial Network, 214
Intel, 37, 38, 290, 396, 521
International Franchising Association, 17, 430
International Harvester, 561
International Organization for Standardization, 114
Internet Shopping Network, 405, 429
Intuit, 565
IRI. *See* Information Resources, Inc.
Itochu, 88

J

J. Crew, 424, 427, 428, 541
J.D. Powers, 356
Jaguar, 159, 221
Jamaican Tourism Board, 480, 481
Jamie's World Class Bicycles, 181
Jantzen, 138
Japan Fair Trade Commission, 101
JCPenney, 64, 289, 391, 397, 415, 417, 432, 434, 436, 443

Jewish Educational Center (JEC), 341
Jewish Introductions International, 245
Jiazhou Hotel, 92
Johnson & Johnson, 15, 127, 169, 203, 287, 294, 497, 502

K

Kao Corporation, 15
Keebler, 246, 247
Kellogg Company, 103, 157, 158, 168, 195, 287, 288, 293, 352, 381, 389, 484, 531, 621
Kenner, 51, 79, 467
Kentucky Fried Chicken, 98, 284, 330, 362, 431
Kids' Bookstore, The, 596
Kimberly Clark, 243, 293
Kinko's, 371, 524
Kirin Brewing Company, 389
Kmart, 37, 51, 55, 162, 235, 289, 402, 415, 420, 421, 422, 435, 436, 438, 579
KME, 561
Knight-Ridder, 252
Kodak. *See* Eastman Kodak
Kojima, 116
Kraft General Foods, 28, 32, 33, 78, 172, 189, 243, 244, 302, 311, 505, 520, 530, 548, 578, 590, 611, 623
Kramer Beverage Company, 385
Kroger, 231, 415, 434, 592, 623

L

La Redoute, 428
Labatt Brewing Company, 108
Lady Foot Locker, 416
Lamborghini, 604
Lands' End, 159, 427, 541
Lanier Worldwide, 21
Larry's Shoes, 443
Lazy Boy, 63, 289
LCR, 447
Leadership Council on Advertising Issues, 131
Lee, 630
L'eggs, 133
Lever Brothers, 36, 468, 504
Levi Strauss and Company, 20, 53–54, 60, 69, 138, 165, 291, 292, 295, 299, 391, 442, 507, 593, 606, 630
Lewis Woolf Griptight, 114
Lexus, 9, 70, 78, 206, 352, 370, 604
Lifestyle Matrix Marketing, 217
Lifetime Automotive Products, 591
Lifetime Security Plan, 217
Lil' Things, 422
Lillian Vernon, 427
Limited, The, 431, 615
Lincoln, 64
Little Caesar's, 123, 517
Little Me, 513

Subject Index

Internet Index